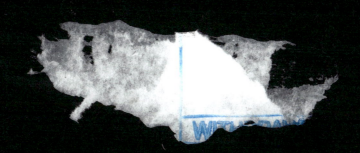

Modern Architect
The Life and Times of Robert Matthew

Modern Architect
The Life and Times of
Robert Matthew

MILES GLENDINNING

RIBA ⬛ **Publishing**

© Miles Glendinning, 2008

Published by RIBA Publishing,
15 Bonhill Street, London EC2P 2EA

ISBN 978 1 85946 283 6

Stock Code 61865

British Library Cataloguing in Publications Data
A catalogue record for this book is available from the British Library.

Author: Miles Glendinning
Publisher: Steven Cross
Commissioning Editor: Matthew Thompson
Project Editor: Susan George
Copy Editor: Lionel Browne
Designed and typeset in Swift Light by Geoff Green Book Design, Cambridge
Printed and bound by Cambridge University Press

RIBA Publishing is part of RIBA Enterprises Ltd.
www.ribaenterprises.com

Front cover: © Colin Westwood / RIBA Library Photographs Collection.

Every effort has been made to contact copyright holders. Queries should be addressed to RIBA Publishing, 15 Bonhill Street, London EC2P 2EA

Contents

Foreword

This is a big book about a big but neglected man. Current forgetfulness about Robert Matthew is easy to understand. In recent years, the culture of developed countries has lurched sharply towards the visual. Fixtures on our retinas like actors, sports stars and mere celebrities have become our points of reference, relegating second-rank politicians and almost all professionals to obscurity. History has followed the pattern. Much of the present book is devoted to the post-war years in Britain, the so-called age of austerity. In interpreting that period, equal authority is now attached to the styling of the 2CV or the hemline preoccupations of *Vogue* as to the feeding, housing, schooling and employing of populations – the great cause of the era.

Architecture, always a schizophrenic subject, has gained and lost from this shift in emphasis. The art side – the aspect of architecture that can be well presented by imagery – has profited immeasurably. That has helped the subject recover a public prestige which collapsed, at least in Britain, around the time that Matthew died. At the same time the sense of architecture as a complex yet powerful social and political pursuit has withered away, sometimes it seems to the verge of extinction. If it still attracts social idealists, they seem mostly to believe that a strong design idea diffused through the magic of imagery will be enough to transform lives, without the hard grind of process.

Robert Matthew's career offers a corrective to any such reading. It shows that getting things done in architecture transcends design. Matthew's is probably *the* representative architectural career in post-war Britain. Not that he was a better artist than, say, Denys Lasdun or Peter Smithson or even his friend and rival Basil Spence; Miles Glendinning carefully avoids that claim. What he could do supremely well was to answer the great call of his time to make architecture effective, as John Summerson put it. He did so in many places and at an astonishing variety of levels, in his native Edinburgh, in London, in Ulster, through planning, teaching, politicking and international diplomacy, once through helping set up a shop, most consistently through the activities of the Edinburgh arm of his firm, Robert Matthew, Johnson-Marshall and Partners. In time he became British architecture's supreme diplomat and first great globetrotter.

It is usually held these days that such activity is uncreative and debases the primacy to which architectural design is entitled. The author offers two answers to that. Firstly, he shows that Matthew did design a lot, and kept doing so after he had perfected the arts of delegation. On the evidence presented a creative role must now be reascribed to him, for instance, in the design of the Royal Festival Hall, during the years when he was architect to the London County Council.

But the better answer is that being effective is also, in broader terms, a form of creativity. To understand what that means, the reader must follow the twists and turns of the projects presented in this book and view them in all their social and political ramifications – en gros. Miles Glendinning has the rare ability to turn such matter into clear and compelling narrative. In so doing, he explains much about modern architecture but more about the wider histories of modern Scotland, Northern Ireland, Britain and indeed beyond. The life-story of Robert Matthew is not just about his personal career but about how things happened during the special and perhaps, to many, now rather puzzling period in which he lived.

This then is a book for those who like to see their architecture whole, or as part of a larger whole, not as some art-bound, intellectual or rarefied pursuit. But it is also about an attractive, charismatic, energetic, resilient man: one who engendered deep personal loyalties; who could bully, charm or hold his peace as occasion demanded; and who could handle the Queen, Fidel Castro and the difficult Johnson-Marshall brothers with equal adeptness. It is also pre-eminently about Matthew's native Scotland and native Edinburgh, and the unique and continuing status that country and that city have long enjoyed within the wider context of British architectural achievement.

One of the strengths of these pages is their detail. The author has gathered the testimony of a wide range of people who knew Matthew personally, and skilfully weighed and deployed it. That is peculiarly valuable for a period when architecture was understood to be a collective art and the complex process of making it was esteemed as just as important as the product. On the value of the British architectural products of the post-war period the jury may still be out. But without studies in such imposing detail as this, we would lack the evidence to come, in due course, to judgement.

ANDREW SAINT

Modern Architect

Acknowledgements

A wide range of people have helped over the past twelve years in the research and publication of this book. Thanks are due firstly to Alison, Kitty, Sali and Amy-Felicity for tolerating an additional 'member of the family' for this extended period, and also to the Matthew family (particularly Aidan and Jessie Matthew, Janet O'Neill, and the late Lorna and Stuart Matthew) for their generosity and tolerance in making available to me Sir Robert Matthew's diverse personal papers, along with their own recollections.

Among the institutions and individuals that assisted the project, those that helped through financial sponsorship, or through research interviews, are listed separately below. Institutions that gave more general help included the Edinburgh University Library Special Collections (including the 'rescue' of papers following the death of Lady Matthew and sale of Keith Marischal in 2003); RMJM Scotland; the Royal Commission on the Ancient and Historical Monuments of Scotland (especially the Photographic Section); Edinburgh College of Art School of Architecture (including the MSc students of the Scottish Centre for Conservation Studies); and the Royal Festival Hall. Thanks are also due to other people who helped in various ways, including: Ian Arnott; Ian Campbell; Louise Campbell; June, Kitty and Brendan Douglas-Hamilton; Sir James Dunbar-Nasmith; Clive Fenton; Ian Gow; Elain Harwood; Tim Jilani; Tony Kettle; Maurice Lindsay; Aonghus MacKechnie; Kasia Murawska-Muthesius; Stefan Muthesius; David Page; Sylvia Platt; John and Margaret Richards; Ted Ruddock; Andrew Saint; Moira Seftor; Fiona Sinclair; Geoffrey Stell; Jane Thomas; Ben and Mary Tindall; Ola Uduku; David M Walker; David W Walker; Ian Wall; Diane Watters; David Whitham; Iain Boyd Whyte; Sue Wilson.

LIST OF INTERVIEWEES

See endnotes for specific contexts. Asterisked interviews were carried out during a previous phase of research, *c*.1990, for the book *Tower Block* (with Stefan Muthesius)

Bill Allen
Dennis Ashmead
* George Atkinson
* A W Cleeve Barr
* Duncan Black

Anthony and Gillian Blee
* Walter Bor
Chris Butler-Cole
Bill Campbell
* Kenneth Campbell

* Ronald Cant
Ralph Cowan
* Oliver Cox
Zena Daysh
* Lady Evelyn Denington
Sir Andrew Derbyshire
Ken Feakes
Laurie Fricker
Kenneth Graham
* Andrew Gilmour
* Sir Robert Grieve
Elspeth Hardie
Patrick Harrison
Arnold and Elsa Hendry
* Ted Hollamby
Flora Isserlis
April Johnson-Marshall
* Percy Johnson-Marshall
* Lord Joseph
Jim Latimer
Maurice Lee
* Arthur Ling
* Berthold Lubetkin
Hugh McIlveen
Sir Leslie Martin
Aidan Matthew

Jessie Matthew
Lady Lorna Matthew
Stuart Matthew
Peter Moro
Eleanor and James Morris
Robert Scott-Morton
Sir James Dunbar-Nasmith
Patrick Nuttgens
* J A Oliver
Janet O'Neill
* John Partridge
* J L Paterson
Sylvia Platt
* Sir Philip Powell
Charles Robertson
* Ian Samuels
Christine Somerville
Tom Spaven
* Rose Stjernstedt
Dorothy Taylor
Frank and Mary Tindall
Sir Anthony Wheeler
* H J Whitfield-Lewis
Alan Wightman
Peter Winchester

Publishing Partners

The publication of this book has been generously supported by:

The Carnegie Trust for the Universities of Scotland

A **Dorothy Stroud Bursary** awarded by the Society of Architectural Historians of Great Britain

Edinburgh College of Art

Edinburgh World Heritage

EDINBURGH WORLD HERITAGE

Historic Scotland

Ian Wall FRICS Hon FRIAS

LDN Architects and **Sir James Dunbar-Nasmith**
The founding partners of our practice, Graham Law and James Dunbar-Nasmith, were amongst the first to be employed when Robert Matthew began his Edinburgh practice. The current chairman of LDN Architects, Colin Ross, studied under Matthew at the University of Edinburgh and worked in his officeafter graduation. Robert Matthew's attitude and approach are a continuing influence on our architecture.

Marc Fitch Fund

Page \ Park
As architects working throughout Scotland and further afield,
Page \ Park work in the wake of Robert Matthew - one of the major influences
of his time - and are pleased to support this publication

The Paul Mellon Centre for Studies in British Art

The Saltire Society's Robert Hurd Memorial Trust

The Scouloudi Foundation in association with the **Institute of Historical
Research**

Financial support was received from **The Strathmartine Trust**, a Scottish
Charity set up to promote education and research in relation to Scottish
History

Thanks to **RMJM** for their support

Supported by the **Royal Incorporation of Architects in Scotland**

Introduction

ἀνδρῶν γὰρ ἐπιφανῶν πᾶσα γῆ τάφος καὶ οὐ στηλῶν
μόνον ἐν τῇ οἰκείᾳ σημαίνει ἐπιγραφή, ἀλλὰ καὶ ἐν τῇ
μὴ προσκούσῃ ἄγραφος μνήμη παρ᾽ ἑκάστῳ τῆς γνώμης
μᾶλλον ἢ τοῦ ἔργου ἐνδιαιτᾶται.

For the whole earth is the memorial of the famous. They are marked out not so much by the inscriptions on their gravestones at home, as by the way their memory endures and grows abroad – not in any visible form, but lodged in people's hearts.

Thucydides[1]

Of all the branches of history, biography derives a special appeal from its intrinsic tension between the experience, passions and emotions of real people, and the context provided by institutions and wider historical movements – forces that shape individuals, and are often shaped by them. As Robert Skidelsky, the recent biographer of J M Keynes, puts it, individuals and their personalities '*do* make a difference to history', yet one also needs to 'enfold [the subject's] private life in his public achievements', analysing the subject as an exemplar of an epoch – without, of course, being drawn into excessive hero-worship, or into viewing the period through the lens of the subject's own value system.[2]

Architecture is an especially suitable target for this approach. It is characterised by a strong institutional tension between its intrinsic links to the ruling power – given the huge sums involved in building projects – and its high esteem of individual leaders and innovator-figures. Architecture's diverse networks of cultural and institutional connections ensure that the activity of any individual is inherently 'theorised' and contextualised from the beginning.

This book skirts between the extremes of biographical history: between, on the one hand, the somewhat depersonalised character of a practice history or art-historical monograph, or an issue-based biography in which an edifying theme takes over the person; and, on the other hand, the extreme personalisation of novelistic biography, autobiography or collected diaries. It is neither a history of the period in the guise of a biography, nor the opposite. Echoing, to some extent, the Marxist concept of the economic 'base' and the cultural or personal 'superstructure', it interweaves the individual and contextual, the personal and the public, throughout the life of a key figure in 20th-century British architecture, showing how they reinforced one another, or, more occasionally, came into conflict.

As emphasised in its title, the book is

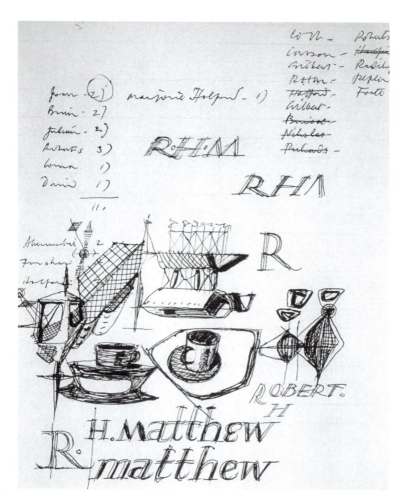

0.1 Doodle by Robert Matthew, c.1957. (EULMC)

above all about Modern architecture – a movement of vast ambition and achievement. The original motive for researching and writing it was a feeling that this achievement had been obscured, distorted and even misappropriated by the architecture that followed it, a process that spanned several decades and phases. The blanket hostility and active 'forgetting' during the Postmodernist 1980s and early 1990s had been followed, from the late 1990s, by a more complex pattern: now, a new visual fashion for Modernist forms was tied to an economic and cultural foundation of uncompromising, laissez-faire capitalism. Arguably, this new 'Iconic Modernism' had a particularly distorting effect on historical understanding of the post-war Modernist legacy, anachronistically foregrounding values of competitive individualism, and emphasising the primacy of the 'heroic' or 'signature' designer.[3]

The reality of the Modern Movement

in post-war Britain was very different, and the individuals who shaped its governing ethos were quite different too. They were concerned mainly with collective, public tasks and ideals rather than self-promoting commercialism. And so this account is emphatically not just another showcase book on the work of one of the 'heroic masters' – Aalto, Le Corbusier, Foster, Gehry or whoever. Instead, it is concerned with one of the foremost of the great 'public architects' of the post-war years in Britain. Although Robert Matthew was the principal designer of buildings as well known as the Royal Festival Hall and New Zealand House, he was at no stage an 'iconic' figure. Rather, he was one of the most illustrious exemplars of that central grouping within Modern architecture, the 'organisation architects', who spent their time as much in negotiations with people as in sitting at the drawing board, and depended for work and activity especially on the interactive, controlling role of the state. However, in contrast to some architects, who tied themselves firmly to one particular doctrinaire position or field of patronage, Matthew's career choices and values also reflected several phases in the dramatic story of the Modern Movement, including the fall as well as the rise of 'public architecture'. Hence his biography does not illuminate just one episode of Modern architecture in Britain; in some ways it spans the entire epoch of its ascendancy. But that dramatic trajectory of 'rise' and 'fall' was not purely a matter of Modern architecture; it pervaded contemporary society, too.

In this book, the story of that context, of the background *mentalités* of Robert Matthew's life and career, are traced at several levels. The broadest and most overarching is no less than the general social, political and economic evolution of society in the developed industrial world. The late 19th and early 20th centuries saw the questioning and overthrow of laissez-faire 'liberal Modernity' by a new disciplined, ordered approach bound up with an era of mass warfare and ideological confrontation, and based around collectivising, standardising structures and practices. This ethos of discipline and dynamism began, however, to fade and disintegrate almost as soon as it was established, and started after the 1960s and 1970s to slide back into a global capitalism similar in some respects to that of the 19th century.

Narrowing the contextual focus slightly, our story also highlights the particular form this process took within Britain – evolutionary rather than revolutionary. Overall, the late 19th and 20th centuries saw a progressive reconfiguration of the Victorian ethos of the gentleman, whose moral leadership role was clothed in a self-controlled, easy-going exterior of good manners. This package of social norms, originally associated with assertive, self-improving imperialism and muscular Christianity, was subtly adapted to serve the new ethical framework of state-led welfarism and managerial/professional leadership. The result was a hybrid generation of gentlemanly social professionals, dubbed 'Our Age' by one of its leading figures, academic administrator Noel Annan.[4] In his considered judgement, the achievements of Our Age were essentially elaborations and modifications of the values of the original age of revolutionary ferment and modernity, the 19th century: 'Our Age played their tunes in a minor key … we played variations on our predecessors' tunes', exploiting the 'protean' malleability of the 'Establishment'. In particular, the ferocious, crusading dynamism of Victorian evangelical reform remained at the core of things: 'The liver and lungs were torn out of the old theology, leaving the heart still beating.'[5] Robert Matthew's life and career, as we shall see, exemplified this ethos of the social-democratic gentleman-leader.

What had changed drastically, though, was the politico-economic balance of the system within which individual leaders operated: by the 1940s, when Matthew first attained positions of national influence, it had swung from open individualism to a far more collective formula. As the coordinating role of the state became stronger, so the Victorian values of laissez-faire enterprise were ever more universally condemned for their chaotic wastefulness. But condemnation of the 19th century for its authoritarian pomposity did not mean a total rejection of individuality. In fact, there was a new ideal of modern, private freedom, linked to the liberating, society-wide democratic egalitarianism of the period, in contrast to the class-bound straitjackets of the 19th century. Annan recalled that 'our belief in giving the greatest possible freedom to people in their private lives … [for example] conflicted with our belief in the duty of the state intervening to prohibit factories being built in the best of the countryside.'[6] This contrast between outward conformity and inner freedom had also, of course, been true of the Victorian gentleman – another of whose characteristics, the commitment to empire-building, proved remarkably resilient right up until the 1950s.[7]

Another key cultural 'context' for Matthew's life story concerned the country (Scotland) and city (Edinburgh) of his birth – the two geographical affiliations that remained, arguably, the most important to him throughout his life. Internationally, and in the overall UK context, the role and image of Scotland throughout the whole period of Matthew's life tended to be bound up especially with values of a cultural-geographic kind, especially about 'national character' and natural landscape. Such concepts, transposed into individual relationships, helped shape, for example, the at times tense relationship between Matthew and his English post-1956 private-practice partner, Stirrat Johnson-Marshall. But what was more significant for our story than these 'timeless' national stereotypes was the radical and very real decline of Scotland's position within the UK for several decades in the early and mid 20th century, from a spearhead of British imperialism to a relatively dependent status, reliant in many ways on power sources in London and southern England, even as the first stirrings of administrative 'devolution' were under way.[8] Ever since the Union of the Crowns in 1603, influential Scots had been well used to the road to and from London, but in Matthew's time the relationship became even more important: it was for good reason that during the late 1950s and the 1960s he spent, on average, two nights a week on the Edinburgh–London sleeper train.

The story of Matthew's career also illustrates more directly the specifically *architectural* themes of the 20th century. For example, in the organisation and the socio-economic structure of architecture and the architectural profession, his career reflected accurately the radical shift from laissez-faire values towards social models of organisation. Where in 1889 Scotland's foremost late-Victorian architect, R Rowand Anderson, could champion 'free trade in art, as in everything else', the more collectivist ethos of the mid 20th century was exemplified by Matthew's own 1958 definition of the profession's key task as 'solving, architecturally, the most difficult of social problems'.[9] Partly, this was a reflection of the wider 20th-century trends towards professionalisation and standardisation, as well as the slightly contrary effects of the ever-increasing division of labour, aimed not just at creating new markets but also at shaping new and more interesting specialised professional fields – such as that connected with the analysis of, and design for, user needs. But architecture reflected these trends in its own specialised way. Although pre-Modernist private-practice designers in the Lutyens mould were widely accepted to be a dying breed, the role of the individual designer-leader did not disappear after 1945, as shown both by 'Establishment' figures such as Spence, and the new, more radical generation of innovators such as Lasdun or the Smithsons. Perhaps more significant still, Matthew's own post-1953 private practice, from 1956 in partnership with Stirrat Johnson-Marshall, showed how the private sector could successfully cooperate with the new patrons of the welfare state, and adopt many of the rational, interdisciplinary work practices of public architectural offices.[10] At any rate, the old type of aristocratic architect-dilettante all but disappeared from the scene, with occasional important exceptions such as Lionel Brett, Lord Esher – leaving the competition between private and public systems largely contained within the same broad middle-class grouping.

The story of Matthew's career also gives us many insights into the more esoteric landscape of architectural theory and debate. This was a world that sometimes closely reflected contemporary political and social developments and at other times determinedly maintained its autonomy, especially through architecture's ingrained tradition that any new movement should establish its credentials by extreme polemical condemnations of its predecessors as utilitarian and alienating – a tradition ingrained in architectural debate since A W N Pugin's *Contrasts* of 1836.

Overall, the dominant force within architectural discourse during this time was the rise and ascendancy of the Modern Movement, with its strong emphasis on rational, scientific progress. It reflected the demands of a materialist, secular age, and integrated the scientific pursuit of precise, research-based solutions rather than the old ad hoc building efforts.[11] The drive for scientific progress also had a collective social aspect, with government research organisations such as the Building Research Station (founded in 1921) playing a prominent role, and the dynamic creed of socialism providing a general ethical framework. Analogies used to characterise the new pattern of rational-scientific public architectural organisation varied from the peaceful (an orchestra) to the more militant (an army or revolutionary cadre). Some of Modernism's new breed of public architects, especially those converted to socialist or communist radicalism during the 1930s, spent most or all of their careers in the 'public service', as in the case of A W Cleeve Barr, Kenneth Campbell or Donald Gibson. Many others, such as Matthew and Stirrat Johnson-Marshall, shifted from public offices in the collectivist 1940s to socially orientated private practice in the more affluent 1950s and 1960s, without, however, losing their respect for the state. Stirrat Marshall, on his knighthood in 1971, typically let slip that his great unfulfilled ambition was to become architectural adviser to the Treasury, to help discourage false economies in the design of public buildings. A key role was also played by 'enlightened', *dirigiste* civil servants such as Dame Evelyn Sharp, administrative head of the English government housing and planning ministry from 1955 to 1966.[12]

But the rational and scientific aspects of the Modern Movement were not the whole story. It was equally bound up with the moral and spiritual values of its times, and exemplified the post-religious search for a new, secular wholeness in an alienated age, within the formal framework dramatised and polarised in Ferdinand Tönnies's famous 1887 book, *Gemeinschaft und Gesellschaft* (Community and Society). The word 'community' was used, invariably positively, as the focus for a succession of urban visions that drew inspiration either from what already existed or from what might be created.[13] The Modernist pursuit of the universal future was often mixed with strong hankerings for the past and the particular, in movements such as the 'vernacular'. And the 'sacred' language often associated with Modernist rhetoric was also bound up with a somewhat contrary variation of the visionary poet-leader, a pattern linked to the 18th century's search for 'originality' in architecture. Within Britain, the first generation of Modern Movement individualists, such as Spence and Gibberd, were closely bound up with Arts and Crafts ideals, but the 1950s and 1960s saw the work of a younger generation, such as the Smithsons, Lasdun and Stirling, who responded to the gradual retreat of wartime discipline and the return to a more commercial climate – although all were still united in rhetorical condemnation of the 'chaos' of Victorian capital-

ism. But finally, from the mid and late 1960s onwards, all of these contextual frameworks were swept aside by the beginnings of a completely new set of relationships and *mentalités* – the start of a new phase of 'disembedding' that would tear apart and discard the painfully constructed structures of collective cohesion, including the dominance of the state, the pursuit of the new, and the insistence on 'planning'.[14]

Within the world of architecture, that final shift was expressed through yet another phase in the 'Puginian' tradition of extreme moral condemnations by each new movement of its predecessor – a tradition that the Modern Movement had exploited to establish itself vis-à-vis the Victorian age, and which was now turned against it.[15] But that culture of polemically expressed development of ideas obscured the substantial continuities at either end of the period – continuities that would very largely dominate the early and final phases of Robert Matthew's career. For, as we shall see in the next chapter, Matthew's architectural upbringing was dominated by Arts and Crafts traditions of contextual, morally infused Modernity that would very largely shape the way in which he initially embraced the Modern Movement around 1930; and the last five or so years of his career, in the early 1970s, were dominated by his equally strenuous efforts to achieve an orderly transition from Modernism to the environmentalism and conservationism that replaced it. Other establishment figures, too, managed to straddle the rhetorical gulf of those years: for example, housing minister Richard Crossman, who presided over the crash system-building programme of the mid 1960s, equally felt able to condemn Dame Evelyn Sharp (his chief civil servant) for her 'utterly contemptuous and arrogant' attitude to local communities and her 'illiterate' belief in a 'false dichotomy' of progressive Modernism and reactionary conservation.[16]

As we shall see in the concluding chapter of this book, all these subtle nuances were obscured in the decades of anti-Modern reaction from 1970 to the late 1980s, and during the neo-capitalist 'Modernist revival' of the late 1990s onwards. For now, however, we need to begin our story by returning to the previous age of capitalist ascendancy – to turn-of-century imperialist, Presbyterian Scotland, a society from which, in 1906, sprang the young Robert Matthew. The main chapters that follow are arranged roughly chronologically – to correspond with Matthew's own experience – but are grouped into subordinate themes, to allow the reader to trace the interaction of his own career and the external constraints that helped shape it. Finally, a concluding chapter briefly draws together and synthesises the disparate threads of 'life' and 'times'. For while the contextual factors of culture, politics and society are complex enough to define and disentangle, what is more challenging still, and can emerge only gradually over the course of these chapters, is the task of trying to correlate them with the equally diverse and conflicting nuances of Matthew's own personality.

Robert Matthew's character, as we shall see, reflected most of the wider cultural forces of the age, but always with an individual twist. He typified the 20th century professional-cum-gentleman, in his combination of a sense of natural leadership and personal mission with a strong commitment to collective ideals and a hatred of commercial competition. In many ways, he exemplified, too, the sharp mid-20th-century division between 'public' and 'private' life. His highly compartmentalised lifestyle combined a highly developed, affable public persona and dense network of issue-based friendships with a more restless 'private' side to his character, compulsively addicted to change and attracted to unconventional characters and situations. In the concluding chapter we shall try to draw together, and make some sense of, this plethora of contextual and personal threads – bearing constantly in mind the fact that the resulting synthesis would probably have seemed somewhat artificial to the subject of the biography himself!

From Traditionalism to Modernism

Lorimer, the Matthew Family and the Edinburgh Crafts Heritage, 1906–24

In my young days in Edinburgh, nothing changed, and the streets and buildings seemed to bear an immortal stamp.

Robert Matthew, 1964

Novus Homo: John F Matthew and the founding of an architectural dynasty

The story of Robert Matthew, the man, is contained entirely within the 20th century, from his birth on 12 December 1906 to his death on 21 June 1975. But for an *architectural* biography the wider context is arguably as important as the individual personality itself. Thus the story of Robert Matthew, the architect, begins somewhat earlier, in May 1893, when a newly established Edinburgh architect, Robert S Lorimer, went in search of his first assistant and apprentice, and lighted on a 17-year-old youth, John F Matthew – Robert Matthew's father. Lorimer (1864–1929), who became Edinburgh's most important early-20th-century architect, sprang from the heart of the capital's late-19th-century cultural and architectural establishment, which, by the late 19th century, had fused the rationalism of the Edinburgh Enlightenment and New Town with the Old-Edinburgh romanticism of Walter Scott and R L Stevenson. The son of James Lorimer (1818–90), Professor of Public Law at Edinburgh University – one of the founders of modern international law and an early advocate of a federal Europe (*The Institutes of the Law of Nations*, published 1884) – Lorimer was brought up in

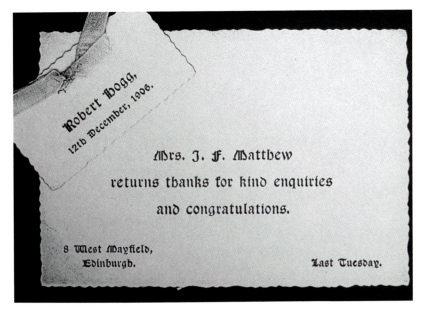

1.1 Birth announcement card for Robert Matthew, December 1906. (Stuart Matthew)

an atmosphere of artistic intellectualism. In 1878 the family took out a long lease on the picturesque Fife castle of Kellie, establishing early in his mind the contrast between 19th-century Baronial architecture and 'genuine' castellated houses – and a penchant for bohemian life in a heritage context. From 1884 the young Lorimer embarked on an architectural career. Like all intellectually ambitious architects in Edinburgh, he fell under the spell of the burgeoning late-19th-century Edinburgh branch of the Arts and Crafts Movement – 'Traditionalism' – led by Robert Rowand Anderson (1834–1921).[1] Lorimer was a drivingly ambitious young architect with a strong eye to social advancement. Returning to Edinburgh in 1892, Lorimer began his first major job – not a new building but a restoration of a small Renaissance castle, Earlshall, Fife, for an artistically minded industrialist and friend of his parents, R W R Mackenzie; and in May 1893 he set up his first office at 49 Queen Street, beginning a steady growth in activity and fame.

During early/mid 1893, working under pressure, Lorimer initially got help from friends – with Begg, for example, drawing his most celebrated perspective of Earlshall – but soon he decided a young assistant/apprentice was an urgent necessity, and almost immediately his sister Louise stumbled on a possibility. Visiting a flat she owned, to collect rent, she noticed on the mantelpiece a small wooden scale model of Holyrood Palace, made with remarkable skill and precision. This, she learned, had been made by a friend of the tenant's son – the young John F Matthew, a trainee of the Edinburgh School of Applied Art, established the previous year by Anderson, and now working in the Old Town bookshop of Andrew Stevenson at 9 North Bank Street, on the Mound. She showed the model to her architect brother Robert, who, seizing the moment, immediately called on Matthew at the bookshop – short-cutting the normal procedures of paid indenture – and offered him £5 (a month's salary) as a transfer fee to leave Stevenson's and become his first assistant and sole employee at 49 Queen Street.

In some ways, John Matthew was ideally suited to become the apprentice to the aspiring traditionalist architect, as he shared much of Lorimer's romantic leanings and his aspirant Edinburgh professional-cum-commercial background, with an additional dash of military-ceremonial colour; he was bright and eager, but, with his more emollient personality, would be unlikely to challenge or threaten his mentor. His family stemmed ultimately from Kettle in Fife, where draper David Matthew and Rachel Red [sic] were married in 1738 – names that might suggest a Jewish ancestry. Their grandson soon moved to Edinburgh and set up a family shoemaking business in George Street, and his son Thomas (John's father), a Baptist by religion, established himself as a military tailor, running his own business from a shop in Queen Street and supplying ceremonial cords and braid for state events at Holyrood Palace and Edinburgh Castle. John, born in 1875, as the oldest of a large family, grew up steeped in this Edinburgh establishment culture of military ceremony and ephemera. While at James Gillespie's School in his early teens, John's love of decoration, uniforms and gadgets spawned a growing skill at drawing and model-making, and a love of old books – all activities that potentially impinged on the world of architecture.[2] Twice, in the 1880s, John served as a page to the Lord High Commissioner to the General Assembly of the Church of Scotland, at the formal procession at Holyrood Palace – a duty that involved wearing a smart red tail coat and with hair curled and powdered – and in 1888, when he served as page to the Earl of Hopetoun, he made the model of Holyrood Palace later seen by Lorimer.

In the early 1890s, on leaving school, John developed his drawing activity further by attending classes at the School of Applied Art, established in 1892 by Rowand Anderson – in the wake of the city's 1889 Art Congress – as part of a revolt against the allegedly utilitarian rigidity of the South Kensington art education system at the city's official art school, the Trustees' Academy. The SAA's classes, orientated towards direct education for artists and craftsmen, and emphasising direct sketching of the Scottish heritage, were held in the same building – the Doric-columned Royal Institution building at the foot of the Mound. Eventually, in 1903, the two institutions amalgamated, and in 1907 became Edinburgh College of Art.[3]

John Matthew had picked up strong elements of this ethos, especially those aspects (such as Anderson's love of ceremony and heraldry) that chimed in with his own hobbies. However, he had already begun to make influential contacts in the Arts and Crafts world, and in 1893 had acted as an assistant to artist Phoebe

Traquair when she commenced her vast fresco paintings in Anderson's Catholic Apostolic Church. John's role in Lorimer's office was a strictly subordinate one: subordinate in character, with his emollient manner constantly overshadowed by Lorimer's overweening ambition; and subordinate in his role, which was not that of a fully participating artist-designer, but, rather, first that of an apprentice and then that of an office manager, helping to mollify junior staff members enraged by Lorimer's overbearing manner, or defusing tension through his jokes and self-deprecating sense of the ridiculous. The relationship was a two-edged one: Lorimer's talent and connections provided John and his family with the opportunities to advance in his wake, but Lorimer's dictatorial self-righteousness ensured that that advancement was bought at the price of constant humiliation. It is unclear whether this sharp polarisation between dominant and weak personalities, and the tension between the positive and negative aspects of dominance, was something that also began to shape John's own character and, in due course, family life, or whether it was a latent tendency brought into life by the relationship with Lorimer, but at any rate this complex of attitudes and relationships was one that would perpetuate itself to a striking degree during the ensuing life of the Matthew family – including the work and relationships of John's son, Robert.

As charted in Savage's account, the growth of Lorimer's practice was comprehensively structured by the interlocking values of Scottish traditionalism – values ultimately derived from the English Gothic Revival via the Arts and Crafts and Aesthetic Movements, which included social-reformist repugnance to mass commercialism, and architectural dislike of the conventional classical hierarchy of building types in favour of the 'ordinary home'.[4] He maintained a small, economical practice, emphasising one-to-one relations with favoured craftsmen, such as the Clow brothers, while relying on astute self-publicity and the use of architectural periodicals to 'ensnare' rich clients: for example, Lorimer wrote offering his services whenever a country house burned down in Scotland.[5]

John and Annie Hogg: from the Transvaal to the Grange

For the first six years of his time with Lorimer, John Matthew worked humbly away in his subordinate office-manager role, uncomplainingly tolerating the parsimony of Lorimer's office regime, with its unheated rooms and constant penny-pinching. In 1897, for example, the £15 due at the end of his apprenticeship had to be deferred owing to shortage of money. But his love of military ceremony and discipline would ultimately help shift this balance. In the 1890s John became a volunteer and territorial, joining the Queen's Edinburgh Rifle Volunteer Brigade, and through a social network of rifle clubs he met and became attached to the girl who would ultimately become his wife: Annie Broadfoot Hogg, fifth daughter of Robert Hogg and Margaret Douglas Russell. A remote descendant of the poet-farmer and friend of Walter Scott, James Hogg (the 'Ettrick Shepherd'), Annie (or Dolly) was born in 1878 in Broomieknowe in the parish of Cockpen, but her paternal family were essentially upwardly mobile urban dwellers, resident in Abbeyhill in Edinburgh.[6] Although, in the opinion of her youngest son Stuart, Annie 'had only little intellectual development', like Lorimer she had a domineering character streak, and this would ultimately drive John to emancipate himself from his servitude to Lorimer.

For the moment, however, no permanent liaison was possible – especially as Lorimer himself was now actively seeking a wife – and in 1899 the outbreak of the South African War abruptly shifted John's attention to his military career. Now aged 24, he was called up to serve in the 1st Battalion Royal Scots. The unit, comprising just over 1,000 men, travelled in October from Queenstown (Ireland), and reached South Africa on 3 December. Immediately, they began participating in the strategy of pursuing Kruger's Boer forces around the country, occupying themselves mainly with protection of lines of communication, and travelling by train or on foot, at first in the Orange Free State and later in the Transvaal, in the advance on Pretoria. John served in H Company, which first saw action in January 1900 at the Loperberg, and later in 1900 and 1901 at the battles of Paardeplatz (in the Drakensberg) and Zwaggershoek at the entrance to Dullstroem Pass. Over the year of John's absence, during 1900–1, however mountainous the seas or vexatious the locusts or shrapnel, he sent regular and enormously detailed letters to his family and to Annie, including small plans of encampments and diagrams of the pursuit of the Boers, and sketches of local architecture, such as a 1900 sketch of Piet Cronje's House, Pretoria.[7]

In May 1901 this interlude in John's career finally ended, when the troop ship *Kildonan* docked at Southampton, and a telegram from there confirmed to Annie that John would be passing through Edinburgh at 10.00 the next morning en route to Glencorse Barracks. During Matthew's absence, Lorimer had been helped out by Begg. He agreed to give Matthew half pay on his return. But when his assistant came back, there was a subtle change in their relationship. Lorimer wrote to a friend that Matthew was

> twice the man physically he was when he left. He had a fortnight's holiday, I handed him £40, being the half pay for the year, and he started work on Monday, as if he's only been away for a week in place of fifteen months' hard campaigning. He's a rare useful sort of man and I'm glad to have an office boss again.

Matthew's status had risen markedly, and henceforth he was always known in the office as 'the military man'. For his future family, this background of pride in Scottish militaria would remain a strong influence, whether positive or negative. In 1902 Lorimer increased his salary to three guineas a week, on the understanding that 'the word screw was not to be mentioned for two years', but within months he was confounded when John announced his impending marriage to Annie Hogg – a year in advance of his own marriage to the 39-year-old heiress Violet Wyld. Lorimer complained, 'Think that a how d'ye do, the blooming clerk getting married when his blooming boss can't afford it!'[8]

John and Annie were married on 3 April 1902 at Annie's family home, 48 Mayfield Road, by her local minister, from Fountainhall United Free Church – which thereafter became their family's own regular church. In contrast to the Episcopalian Lorimer, the Matthews' own church – the product of the 1900 merger of the Free and United Presbyterian Churches – was the preferred denomination of Edinburgh's liberal intellectual and professional classes. But within this framework their family, like many other middle-class households, was beginning to move beyond Presbyterian religiosity towards a more sceptical, agnostic position.[9] Annie's family was relatively well off, and she continued to maintain a somewhat free-spending middle-class lifestyle, despite John's modest means.

Immediately seeking a rural setting for family life, the Matthews moved into one of the vernacular-style harled 'rustic cottages' under construction to Lorimer's designs in Colinton, just outside Edinburgh on the edge of the Pentlands. Within a year the Matthews' first child, John, was born, but he died within months. In 1905, dispirited, Annie and John left 5 Rustic Cottages, with its now melancholy associations, and returned to the South Side, renting a 'delightful, trim little terraced house', single-storey, classical and of *c*.1830, at 8 West Mayfield. In these compact, but elegant, suburban surroundings their second child, Robert Hogg Matthew, was born on Tuesday 12 December 1906.[10] Robert was seen, quite explicitly, as a 'replacement' for the lost John – a position that may explain the fierce pride and ambition that Annie later invested in him.

1.2 The seven-year old Robert Matthew and his brothers Douglas and Stuart, 1913. (James C H Balnain, 69 Shandwick Place, Edinburgh)

1.3 Robert seen with Douglas, c.1913. (Stuart Matthew)

Certainly, their relationship was a complex one, and sharply divided between Robert's infant years, when Annie devoted her most forceful efforts to nurturing and propelling him forward, and the years from his teens onwards, when he largely withdrew from that intense influence and, in turn, developed his own patterns of dominance and control over others. Robert's wife, Lorna, speculated that 'having been so frightened of his mother when he was little, nothing could frighten him after that – he was never scared of anything or anyone!'[11]

Soon another baby was expected, and with 8 West Mayfield obviously too cramped for the growing family, the pattern became established of moving immediately before the arrival of each new child. John's own father had moved house many times, and John inherited the same *Wanderlust*. In any case, the normal pattern (for almost all social classes) was not to buy but to rent their homes, on an annual basis, which encouraged a degree of local mobility. In 1909 the Matthews moved to a larger house at 22 Glenorchy Terrace – part of a large, flatted 19th-century corner block – and there, on 27 July, another boy, (George) Douglas, was born. The following year,

1.4 Robert's first 'architectural drawing', c.1914. (Stuart Matthew)

1910, saw the next South Side move, to a semi-detached 19th-century villa, 30 Mayfield Terrace, where on 27 June 1912 the youngest son, Stuart Russell, was born. This succession of births and moves was crowned by the birth of a girl, Margaret A G M (Nannie) on 31 March 1915, which immediately followed a move to 31 Dick Place, a house in a quiet street in the Grange. This turn-of-century single-storey stone villa, heightened in black-and-white timber framing, was rented in 1914 by the family on a longer,

13

1.5 8 West Mayfield, Edinburgh:
Robert Matthew's birthplace.
(RCAHMS, 2003)

1.6 31 Dick Place, Edinburgh.
(RCAHMS, 2003)

five-year lease from a Miss Anderson, who
had moved out of Edinburgh during the
Great War: 'a delightful little villa – one
of the prettiest in the Grange'.[12]

Wartime idyll: 31 Dick Place and the Edinburgh Institution

It was in the six years that they occupied
the sylvan cottage setting of Dick Place,
until 1920, that the complex social mosaic
of the Matthew family began to coalesce
fully. The first element in this mosaic was
the fact that both parents were fully
preoccupied with war-related activities.
Stuart recalled that

the years in Dick Place were packed
with events. Young lives were encountering their first experiences. My
father was not much in evidence.
Although he lived at home for most of
the time, he was largely away on army
duty, and my mother managed the
household, attended to her brood, and
was always busy organising fund-
raising events for the troops.

John Matthew's career entered another
period of relative uncertainty. In 1916 he
rejoined the army as a major in the Royal
Queen's Signals. Although some restoration and extension work, such as
Balmanno (from 1916), continued
through the war, by 1917 work was so
short that Lorimer closed the office altogether for a year, and privately considered sacking Matthew or putting him on
half pay. Needless to say, with Lorimer's
unerring social-climbing instincts, there
was no social contact between the
Lorimers and the Matthews, and Annie
became more and more vociferous in
pointing to the 'unfairness' of the relationship, and in pressing John to assert
and emancipate himself.

The children, of course, knew nothing
of these troubles. What was obvious was
the effort devoted by Annie to Red Cross
work, including the organisation of con-
certs and other fund-raising events, and
using the house as a collection point for
the sphagnum moss used for bandaging
wounded soldiers. For the children these
events, with their constant crowds of
friends and relatives in the drawing
room, provided some opportunity for collective participation and inventiveness.
Robert, in particular, began to develop a
talent for meticulously planned show-
manship – usually setting this egotism
within a strongly collaborative framework. Stuart described how, on one typical occasion in 1916, the ten-year-old
Robert

did a little show in the 'L' wing, or
recess, of the dining room, along with

a friend, John Moffat, one of a large and active family who lived just round the corner in Lauder Road. They rigged up a little stage and curtaining, leaving a proscenium opening about 2 to 3 feet wide, up about 3′ 6″ or so from the floor, with a table on either side, and together they formed a dwarf figure, one in front and the other behind, with his arms pushed through, with shoes on the hands as 'feet'; in this guise they danced about on the table, and twisted and kicked – all dressed up as if they were a single 'performer'! The audience sat about on chairs. And later, between musical items, my brother did all kinds of magical tricks with cards, which, I'd say now, most of them saw through.[13]

Robert and John Moffat did numerous other performances of card tricks and palmistry, with Robert – in a foretaste of his methodical approach to career matters later – devoting much time to poring over instruction books of magic tricks and puppetry.

For much of the time, as so often during wartime, the children were left to their own devices, to improvise their own friendships and entertainment. Although the family was not wealthy enough to afford a car, even in wartime the children were plentifully supplied with toys, including Meccano, tricycles, a grey stuffed elephant on wheels, rabbit nine-pins and various dolls, including 'a black doll, Bumps, which did much to make us all fond of coloured children and their parents'. John Matthew's experience of colonial travel also indirectly helped establish a streak of cosmopolitanism, and aversion to racial prejudice, within the family – a trait that, as we shall see, would re-emerge strongly in Robert's later years. There were frequent trips to the shops in Princes Street, carefully supervised by Annie: 'My mother would say to hold her hand if a tipsy man was approaching!' And there were frequent excursions and holidays, whether merely to Blackford Hill for walking and studying, or to seaside towns such as Gullane.

In these activities, key aspects of Robert's character began to emerge into stronger focus. Most prominent was a compulsive seeking for dominance, especially in relation to other forceful boys – a trait seen especially sharply in his childhood conflicts with Douglas, another strong personality, but disadvantaged vis-à-vis Robert in both size and intellect. Their clashes were observed unsympathetically from the sidelines by the infant Stuart:

> Robert certainly could be a horrible bully at that time, and had Douglas crying many times, when we were at Dick Place, and even after we moved in 1920 – in fact, we nicknamed Douglas the 'water tap' because he was forever crying. What all the fights between the two of them were about, I don't know!

But in reality, Stuart conceded readily, Robert *was* indeed an exceedingly complex character, torn between the nervous anxieties that afflicted the whole Matthew family. On the one hand, in reaction to his mother's doting ambition for him, there developed an almost obsessive self-containment and control, coloured with an increasing sense of confidence and even self-importance: by the age of about ten, he spent much of his time shut away in his room, avoiding family parties and meals and pursuing solitary hobbies such as model-making and drawing – carefully signing even his earliest efforts in the latter field with the initials 'RHM', as if already documenting for posterity the seeds of future greatness. On the other hand, always present below the surface – visible as a child, but sealed away from view by adulthood – was the nervous, neurotic, argumentative energy, and even the self-doubting instability, of his father, whose own domination by Lorimer served as a constant warning, and spur, to Robert. Stuart argued that

> in his innermost heart, Robert was actually one of those nervous, unsure individuals who had to erect a barrier of ruthlessness and coldness to protect himself. In childhood, he smiled only

occasionally, and never said much, except when the depths of emotion were stirred – for example, by the frequent illnesses in our family. But at heart, he was so utterly emotional that he had to hold back – at what long-term cost to himself I can hardly imagine. He seemed so impenetrable, because he daren't let his emotions loose.[14]

Perhaps Robert's 'strong' character and Stuart's 'neurotic' or 'weak' character partly represented the contrasting reactions of the oldest and youngest son to a dominant mother – the one breaking away by force, the other subdued and fragmented. Increasingly, that pattern of self-repression and restless, external energy became entrenched, and the mask of control slipped only in times of crisis. One such cathartic event happened in 1916. Stuart recalled that when the family's living-in housemaid

managed to set the house on fire by adding to the fuel in her bedroom fire a fair helping of petrol poured from a can. The stuff flowed over the floor, carrying flames with it and spreading from the bedroom through several store cupboards into my father's workroom and, from there, down through the drawing-room ceiling, where it left a charred hole. After it had been put out, I stood eagerly watching as my father went up a step ladder to examine the dark hole – at the very moment that a helpful neighbour, Mr Findlay, emptied a bucket of water from above, right on to his head. But Robert's reaction to the fire was very different from mine. The violation of the house by the fire simply shattered him: he just went to pieces, and couldn't bear to stay in the house or anywhere near it. He just ran off – to an aunt's house, as we later found – and vanished until the next day. He was last seen disappearing into the distance, rather like Charlie Chaplin at the end of one of his films.

Other unusual traits already perceptible were Robert's 'prodigious, computer-like' memory, which would later allow him to recall verbatim the proceedings of lengthy committee meetings, and his ambidextrousness in writing and drawing: originally left-handed, he had been forced by his mother to write with his right hand also.[15]

The family was not directly affected much by the war – although one Zeppelin raid in April 1916 forced them to take refuge under the parlour table. Only later would the dissolution of the pre-war ethos of imperialist pride help shape Robert's character as an adult.[16] All in all, the Dick Place days imprinted themselves on the Matthew children's memories as a sunlit idyll. Although the world of poverty – children with bare feet and torn clothes, and staggering drunks – was always close at hand, it was the leafy Grange, with its profusion of walls and tall, bizarrely spiky 'monkey puzzle' (*Araucaria araucana*) trees peeping over, that imprinted itself on the memory. Robert recalled 50 years later that

I have a warm regard for suburbia, as my own childhood was spent in such an 'Arcadia' – and its quality still remains. High rubble walls fringed with trees; narrow, quiet streets; and the rocky outcrop of Blackford Hill – a wild mountain for the young,

And, in 1964, he contrasted the then 'revolutionary' stage of architecture with the unchanging Edinburgh of his childhood: 'In my young days in Edinburgh, nothing changed, and the streets and buildings seemed to bear an immortal stamp.'[17]

The external world of Edinburgh professional culture impinged on Robert's consciousness chiefly through his education. At first this was broadly based: up to the age of eight he attended the nursery department at St Margaret's School, Craigmillar Park. But from 1914 its focus shifted radically, from suburban villadom to the grand classical axes of the New Town, when he started in the junior department of the Edinburgh Institution – one of the New Town's three major boys' day schools, and part of the capital's elaborate and wide-ranging system of private schools. In contrast to the purpose-built Royal High School and Edinburgh Academy, the ''Stution' had been housed since its foundation in 1832 in converted houses – first in Hill Street, and then in the grand mansion designed by Robert Adam in 1770–1 for Lord Chief Baron Orde at 8 Queen Street. Stuart, who joined the school directly as a four-year-old in 1917, recalled it as 'a small, interesting school, full not only of professional people but brewers and boozy people, every kind of people, people from all over the world'. The building itself was 'all very gloomy on the winter mornings, with a memorable damp smell off a row of coats hanging in a narrow entrance corridor'. But, despite the squalor, the grand classical architecture began inexorably to exert its influence on Robert and Stuart, offsetting the 'Gothic' romantic leanings of their Lorimer Arts and Crafts roots: 'The house was full of the most lovely detail and proportion, not that we understood it, but something that we took to be simply part of our life.' In 1920 the school moved to the austerer setting of Melville Street: 'Just like the office, except stripped of even the office's few comforts!' Even by the time of the 1920 move, Robert's drive and ambition were already having results at school, in a series of exceptional results in almost all subjects.[18]

43 Minto Street: family life, sports and pastimes

In the wake of the war, Lorimer's architectural practice revived dramatically – but in a strikingly different direction, towards projects of a public, even state-financed, character. Partly through the recommendation of Lutyens, Lorimer was appointed as one of the six permanent architects of the Imperial War Graves Commission, and began an intense burst of foreign travel, followed by a succession of domestic war memorial commissions, culminating in the vastly complex and contentious Scottish National War Memorial of 1924–7. Although the firm's last office, at 17 Great Stuart Street, was grandiose in scale, Lorimer had kept his

1.7 The Scottish National War Memorial, Edinburgh Castle (1924–7), view of 'Shrine' c.1928. (Stuart Matthew)

own staff small, ignoring Matthew's entreaties for expansion; his secretary from 1916, Miss Margaret Brown, recalled that the staff worked like slaves in the unheated office, without tea breaks and well into the evenings. Matthew's role was still that of conciliator and organiser, the 'great talker', dealing with estimates and smoothing over feathers ruffled by Lorimer's outbursts.[19]

The wholesome Arts and Crafts intensity of the traditionalist ethos permeated office and house. Stuart recalled that

my earliest recollection was in my father's room, at home, filled with drawings for Balmanno – the whole atmosphere seemed to be suffused with architecture – it seemed to be just part of the air you were breathing. In our family, we never discussed the whys and the wherefores of architecture – it was all just inborn, a sort of tacit understanding. There was also, in the house, a trunk full of all his various uniforms, and after the Great War he would appear every now and then in his major's uniform. For me, as for Robert, it was fascinating to be told of the refinements in the detail of uniforms and the significance of accessories, and it was a special thrill to try on jackets, top hats, busbies, pillbox hats and even to have a look at a sword or badges.

Even more significantly, beyond the house there were weekend visits to the office and trips around 'Old' and 'New' Edinburgh. Robert's most fundamental attitudes to architecture were shaped by this stimulus. Stuart recollected these outings in some detail:

As a special treat, my father would take us down to Great Stuart Street, where we'd see all these incredible things just lying around: heraldic things, plaster casts, drawings. The office was a bare and cold place except the little room used by Lorimer, who was never to be seen – it was pretty posh, with a rug and bits of polished furniture. In the main office, there was a mean-sized coal fire, a kiosk with the main telephone, with some knights' crests made for the Thistle Chapel perched on top. Upstairs, John Sutherland, the great heraldic artist, would be working. Usually, after my father had answered my questions about the things lying about, we'd leave on one of our many trips by tram, so he could show me old buildings with bits of stones about them, usually in the High Street closes, as well as newer buildings, including, often, the buildings that were just then being built from office drawings and the drawings at home. It was on these Edinburgh trips that I, and Robert before me, met a lot of my father's associates, lots of the craftsmen and site workers. Those visits were vitally important to both of us. They left me, and, I think, Robert too, both traditionalists at heart.[20]

The five-year lease for Dick Place came to an end in 1920. Fuelled by the firm's post-war boom in work, and bolstered by a £650 loan from Lorimer – a considerable gesture, which should be set against the criticisms of Lorimer's 'parsimony' – the Matthews decided to jump off the now sinking ship of rented tenure and buy their own, larger house. They settled on a semi-detached, porticoed classical villa of two storeys and basement at 43 Minto Street, the main street in Newington, and stayed there, with only short intervals, until ill health forced them to move away in the 1950s. There was some delay in moving in, as workmen were making a number of customised alterations designed by John – notably the construction of an additional bedroom in the roof space for the now 14-year-old and increasingly independent Robert. It was here that the Matthew children developed their own autonomous social lives – an informal 'coming and going' somewhat different from the more stratified social circles in which the Lorimers moved. Stuart recalled that

the drawing and dining rooms were used a lot for parties – from children's gatherings to grown-up affairs. There was always a noisy adult party on New Year's night. Relatives and friends came in and shed some of their years dancing about, playing wild games and chattering away; Irish songs almost always brought tears.

John kept up his interest in military-style recreation through helping with Boy Scout activities. This activity was shot through with a degree of social competitiveness on the part of Annie, and free spending on consumer goods beyond John's means.[21]

Robert would shape into a more forceful and calculating personality than his more openly emotional father, or, for that matter, his younger brother. But, by now, he had begun to cut himself off from this everyday childhood hubbub, and joined the family mainly for meals, church and holidays. Even here, he pushed against the limits, and 'once or twice dared bring a book to the table, because he was bored with the family chat: he was rather severely ticked off for it!' Robert's relations with Douglas became more mature and normalised, as the latter himself grew into bumptious adolescence. At first, Douglas showed none of his elder brother's driving ambition, concentrating instead on obsessive pursuit of rugby, as well as compulsive gambling at the Powderhall dog races (requiring visits by the 12-year-old Stuart to the pawn shop to retrieve wireless sets, cameras and other gadgets); later, having broken free from the 'family profession', he became an eminent obstetrician. Robert remained on good, although distant, terms with Stuart, who would eventually follow him into architecture, but who had by now embarked on a lifelong succession of illnesses, including, in the early 1920s alone, pneumonia, diphtheria and a skull fracture inadvertently inflicted by Douglas in a 1923 golfing accident. The family continued to holiday en bloc, and 1920 saw the first of several lengthy seaside stays at the sedate Fife resort of Elie. Architectural interest was not altogether neglected, as Elie was surrounded by historic burghs, and Robert also joined a rare social visit led by his father to Lorimer at Kellie, but outdoor exercise was the predominant activity, including hazardous swimming in the open sea, with 'my mother gasping, always horrified, as Robert, to annoy her, remained under water until the last second, until it looked as if he had disappeared for ever'.[22]

Church-going, at Fountainhall United Free Church, a neo-Gothic design of 1896–7 by Graham Fairley, was another collective activity from which Robert was now gradually detaching himself. Within this setting of restrained social mixture, typical of the declining evangelical intensity of early-20th-century urban Presbyterian culture, Robert himself initially played the role of young do-gooder, diligently attending Sunday school and helping with the transfer of wheelchair-bound patients from the nearby Longmore Hospital. But Scots Presbyterianism's emphasis on the individual pursuit of salvation always had the potential to slide into humanistic scepticism, and Robert soon followed this well-trodden path, scornfully dismissing such central Calvinistic doctrines as the predestination of the soul. One Sunday evening, indeed, a visiting minister, the Revd Geoffrey Bellhouse, was so shocked after discussing this subject with Robert at Minto Street that he angrily stormed out of the house: 'Robert's argument was "If it's all already worked out divinely, then I don't need to make much effort: if life is predetermined, why choose, decide – or make any effort at all?"'[23] Of course, with the discrediting of Christian militarism in World War I, society as a whole was witnessing a rise in rebellious 'free-thinking'.[24] Within Scotland, the target for rebellion was evangelical Presbyterianism's special recipe of authoritarian individualism, and the characteristics of that rebellion helped to shape Robert's character, provoking him into a lifelong quest for alternative, humanistic value systems, including an enduring infatuation with the ideals of international goodwill and social justice. The Presbyterian tradition of charismatic minister-leaders also found an echo in Robert's personality, and contributed to his skill in organising others. Although he ridiculed the literal religious doctrine of predestination, nevertheless his life and career could be interpreted partly in terms of the strivings of a self-conscious child of destiny, pre-ordained to help construct a 'godly society'. For Matthew's generation in Britain, individualism now became a subordinate theme, to be played out in an increasingly dominant climate of collectivism. An overtly competitive, self-promoting approach to personal ambition would be largely alien to Robert; for him, the quest for fame and destiny was an inherently social activity.[25]

More central to Robert's late teenage life than any of these family-based activities, however, were his own pastimes and social activities. His driving ambition was still unfocused, and his socialising was still confined to all-male camaraderie. For the moment, he was above all an assiduous follower of boys' practical hobbies, still almost all in the categories of gadgetry, drawing and sport laid down by his father long ago; these now, in Robert's life, increasingly played the role

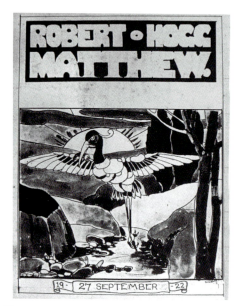

1.9 'Architectural' drawings from 1922 sketchbook by Robert Matthew. (Stuart Matthew)

Moffat, in the early 1920s. Robert assiduously cultivated the companionship of Moffat's versatile children, especially Teddy, and his older brother Pelham, who had lost an arm in the war. Teddy was a fanatical constructor of wireless sets, and his 20-valve set inspired Robert to a succession of imitations, including a small blue crystal set:

> When the cat's whisker touched the rough wee bit of crystal, a voice from London miraculously came through the earphones. To let us all hear at once, the set was put on the mahogany dining room table. A pudding basin was beside it and the two earpieces separately put, with some skilled placing, in the bowl. Then we all leaned over the contraption to get a share of the magic result. In that way, we had moved into the world of Progress!

Significantly, Robert also faithfully reflected his father's leanings towards drawing, both serious and humorous. For example, a series of surviving albums of 1922–3 is filled with animal and human sketches in a pawky style, with one drawing of cheeky, chatty parrots grandiloquently signed 'This is done by RHM'. There were also romantic 'architectural' scenes, including towered cathedrals and a farm building with street sign marked 'Stobo', probably drawn on a Scottish Schoolboys' Club expedition to the Borders village of that name in 1922.[26]

In the early 1920s, however, Robert reserved his greatest passion not for hobbies as such, but for the activities bound up with his school, where he now emerged as the Edinburgh Institution's most outstanding all-rounder of the decade; the school was, in effect, the first of his several successive 'careers'. It should be remembered that the Institution was a city day school, not a 'public school' in the traditional British or English mould, with its dominant Tory landed values; the end-of-term prize-giving was held in the Queen's Hall or Freemasons' Hall and presided over by the Lord Provost. The 'Stution ethos

of intellectually relaxing distractions or escape mechanisms from his own inner driving force. Robert's personality was a somewhat compulsive one, whether in his career pursuit or in his escape mechanisms; but his growing desire for self-control, a compulsion in its own right, would lead him to disguise these urges and tensions beneath an ever-harder shell of imperturbability.

In most of his hobbies, Robert relied heavily on the mentor role of older boys – although, in due course, as his career and confidence progressed, these were all, in turn, sloughed off and left behind. One important set of relationships stemmed from his father's close friendship with painter and philosopher John

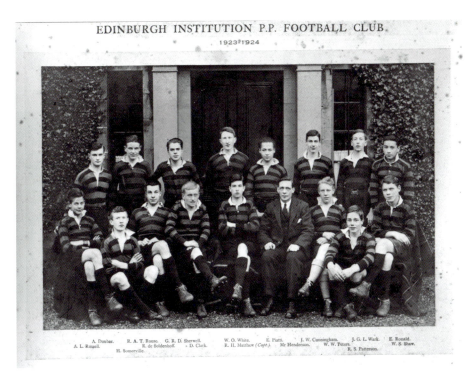

1.10 Edinburgh Institution (rugby) 1st XV, 1923–4. (R Swan Watson)

1.11 Robert seen in 1923 in his 'Stution head prefect's uniform, in the back garden of 43 Minto Street. (Stuart Matthew)

combined a somewhat meritocratic, intellectual openness with a tinge of forceful elitism – late-Victorian Scottish values that left their mark on Robert's adult character. His academic prowess culminated in his becoming dux of the Institution in 1923, and at the prize-giving following his Higher Leaving Certificate in that year he had such a load of prize books (including the complete works of Sir Walter Scott) that the family had to take them home in a taxi from the Queen's Hall. Of this episode Stuart commented ruefully that

then, as for much of my life, he was held up to me as an example. Of course, his great achievements were something to enjoy and admire. But of course, like Douglas and his gambling successes, we never heard of the failures. Mine were all too obvious!

Robert's successes by 1923 put him in a quandary. He had now decided to follow his father into the architectural profession, but was a year too young to begin studying at ECA's Edinburgh School of Architecture. He decided, therefore, to stay an extra year at school, devoting himself to sports activities as well as part-time study at Edinburgh University (see Chapter 2): he became head prefect and captain of the cricket and rugby teams. Stuart recalled Robert's carefree final school year, when he and his friends would go in an open charabanc to the cricket matches around Edinburgh, or at the school pitches at Ferryfield. But there was driving ambition at work here too. In contrast to the English public-school ethos of 'fair play' and gentlemanly self-restraint, for Robert and the 'Stution, sporting and academic success was more of an aim in itself. His cousin Ian Hogg, a top rugby player at rival day school George Watson's, recalled that 'in matches against us, Robert always used to follow his own rules!'[27]

Ironically, Robert's rugby career came to a sudden end during the course of 1924, in an accident that also, arguably, had more far-reaching effects on the subsequent course of his career. A kick in the head in a school game at Ferryfield left him severely concussed. A young boy, Stewart Kaye, was sent home in a taxi

1.12 Group photograph of Scottish Schoolboys' Club camp, Stobo, April 1922. Robert Matthew is 17th from left in the front row. (Stuart Matthew)

1.13 Photograph by Robert Matthew of visit by Edinburgh Institution pupils to the Wembley Empire Exhibition, 1924. (Stuart Matthew)

with him, and, to his distress, several times had to restrain the befuddled Robert from trying to leap from the moving taxi. On his return to Minto Street he was put in bed and tested with a candle by the next-door neighbour, Dr Scott. Stuart recollected that

> Robert asked for his rugby and cricket caps to be put in the posts at the end of the bed, so he could see them. He stared at them with a strange, distant look on his face, as the candle went from side to side, insisting in an odd, vague voice that he was perfectly well.

It took Robert a long time to recover, and he never fully returned to his previous

state. Although his photographic memory was unaffected, his short-term concentration was severely impaired, and he was able to focus on only one significant task at a time. Partly in response, he developed a highly compartmented way of working, which was to stay with him all of his life, and was to develop into a reliance on delegation. There were other radical and unexpected effects. For instance, Robert, previously a keen piano player, now found himself, for several years, unable to play the instrument: 'It was a strange sight to see someone who had sat at the piano so often, so suddenly cut off from it.' By the late 1930s, however, he had completely recovered his playing skills.[28]

In compensation for this setback, Robert could fall back on a well-developed range of alternative sporting and outdoor activities. Boxing had already been tried, and rapidly dropped, in 1921, when, to his mother's horror, he returned from a session at Charlie Cotter's boxing school at Leith with blood plastered over his nose and neck. Increasingly, he gravitated towards less aggressive sports, such as golf or swimming. His father's fascination for collective camp life also, at first, had a considerable hold on Robert, who became an enthusiastic member of the Edinburgh Institution cadet force, and attended the annual camps at Archerfield, smartly blancoing his belt and spats. Rapidly, however, he turned away from openly military gatherings towards camps associated with the Christian philanthropic wing of the burgeoning

outdoor youth movement, catering especially for disadvantaged children. Here, Robert could begin developing his leadership techniques: he became a mainstay of the Scottish Schoolboys Club, a YMCA offshoot founded in 1912 by Stanley Nairne, and in April 1922, for example, attended a camp spanning several days at Stobo, Peeblesshire, with 400 boys from 12 to 18. Robert continued to help organise SSC camp meetings until at least 1926.[29]

The YMCA movement provided Robert with his first glimpse of internationalism and foreign travel – later to become one of his life's chief preoccupations. In August 1923 the SSC opened a small summer camp in France at Chateau Mouchac, Grezillac, Gironde – a small, romantic castle with round corner towers. This was Robert's first foreign trip, in which he experienced for the first time the exotic savour of foreign countries, and befriended Bernard de Serech, son of the chateau's owner. Further travel ensued the following year, including a family tour of France and Central Europe (perhaps in connection with war cemetery work), taking in Northern Italy, Switzerland and Vienna. In August 1925, again through the SSC, he took part in a far more ambitious international goodwill exercise, a week-long YMCA-sponsored 'First

International Older Boys Conference' at the 'Camp unioniste Romand de Vaumarcus', held in a rural chalet setting by the shores of Lake Neuchatel in Switzerland. This expedition involved a complex railway journey over several days via London and Paris, and five days in the camp as part of a group of 85 boys from 19, mostly European, countries. Matthew's meticulous diary recorded a routine of 6.30 a.m. starts, and days filled by physical jerks, forest rambling, singing, and – the essence of the camp – themed discussions on religion, war, international and 'inter-racial' differences, patriotism, and relations between boys and girls. The report on the camp in the YMCA magazine recorded the passion of these discussions, in which the boys 'shared with each other their deepest thoughts' ... 'few will forget the morning when the boys of one nation [presumably Germany] compared war with the suffering of the past seven years and felt war was more acceptable.' But, overall, the consensus was that there existed a 'higher loyalty than to the State', namely, to 'humanity as a great brotherhood'. The boys

discovered for themselves a mighty truth that, in the realm of thought

(left) **1.14** Robert seen with local friends on his 1923 trip to Chateau de Mouzac, Gironde. (EULMC)

(right) **1.15** Family picture of c.1926 in the back garden at 43 Minto Street. (From left: Stuart, Annie, Robert, John, Nannie) (Stuart Matthew)

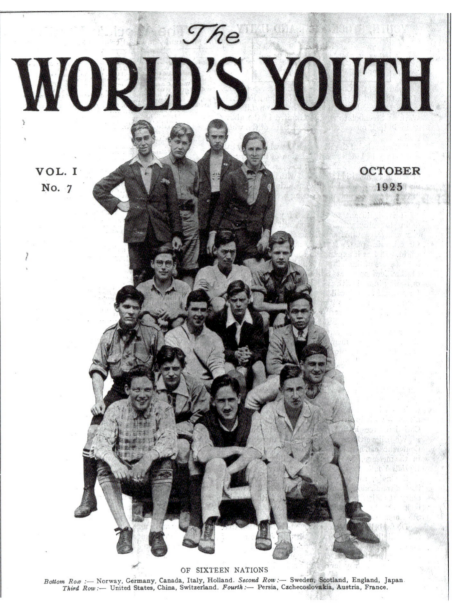

The **WORLD'S YOUTH**

VOL. I
No. 7

OCTOBER
1925

OF SIXTEEN NATIONS

Bottom Row :— Norway, Germany, Canada, Italy, Holland. *Second Row* :— Sweden, Scotland, England, Japan. *Third Row* :— United States, China, Switzerland. *Fourth* :— Persia, Czchecoslovakia, Austria, France.

and spirit, true international understanding can be found … Each saw his country in a truer light, not as a lone conqueror but as a member … of the great family of nations.[30]

Robert's enjoyment of these camps showed a steady trend away from his father's militarism towards a pacific internationalism, which would ultimately dominate his thinking. In a sense, this minor struggle, early in his life, was a microcosm of the fundamental contest, throughout his life, between restless ambition and deeper impulses of humanistic sympathy. At the same time, it also reflected the qualified post-World War I shift in Britain away from the values of the Victorian age, while retaining its fundamental ethical assumption that the privileged had a responsibility of service to society, and a corresponding right to exercise power and influence in pursuit of those ends. Those ends were now increasingly assumed to be concerned with social redistribution – to be guaranteed by an interventionist state.[31]

Education and re-orientation: Geddes, Mears and the Modern planning ethos, 1924–35

welding the work of the Engineer, Surveyor, Architect and Local Government Officer with that of the Economist, Sociologist and the Politician into that of the Planner.

E A A Rowse, 1935

Classicist, Goth – or Modernist? Robert Matthew, architecture student

So far, Robert Matthew's career had faithfully shadowed that of his father, while at each stage starting from a more privileged social position, and applying throughout a more unremitting determination. Now, in his choice of an adult career, the same pattern continued: having decided to become an architect, Robert determined to study at the School of Architecture in Edinburgh College of Art (ECA) – successor institution to the School of Applied Art, housed in a purpose-built classical building since 1909, and owned and administered by Edinburgh Town Council. Architecture was one of four constituent sections of the college, and headed since 1922 by Lorimer's long-time friend and collaborator John Begg, newly returned from a spell as consulting government architect in India. Although Robert was too young to begin at ECA in 1923, he was determined to do more than just play rugby over the following year, and so he enrolled on a part-time course at the Geology Department of Edinburgh University, one of the first buildings in the new West Mains (King's Buildings) science campus on the southern edge of the city. John and Annie had

also promised him a motor-bike if he became head prefect at school, but, fearful of the danger of accidents, they managed to defer fulfilment of the promise for another couple of years, before eventually yielding in 1926 and buying him a 'Matchless'.[1]

At the Geology Department Robert was able to augment the Arts and Crafts' intuitive feel for regionally diverse stonework, with which he had been imbued within the family, with a more scientific appreciation of the chemical and constructional qualities of Scotland's variegated building stones – a love that remained with him for the rest of his life. Ironically, the first buildings of the new West Mains campus – although later

25

augmented by a stone-fronted departmental building designed by Lorimer and John Matthew – seemed to contrast sharply with any kind of stone sobriety. Robert recalled 40 years later this stark environment, with the 'raw new chemistry buildings, built in brick – a material that at that time was associated in Edinburgh with working men's cottages and brewery warehouses – standing in a great open windy field'.[2]

In October 1924 Robert finally began his full-time (Day School Stage I) studies at ECA; unlike many students, who worked part time in an architectural practice, he followed from the start the new, more professional path of full-time study. This was a time when the governing framework of architectural education in Britain had begun to change radically. Despite the enduring prestige of Arts and Crafts values, in these years architectural education in Britain was dominated by the Beaux Arts movement, a francophile systematic ethos of building programming, construction and design, popularised in Britain by Glasgow-based architects such as (Sir) J J Burnet.[3] Beaux Arts teaching depended on the organisation of students into atelier-like year groupings, and on the tradition of grand architectural competitions involving working-up of entries from sketches '*en loge*' to fully finished schemes. The pinnacle of this competition system was the Grand Prix de Rome d'Architecture, and other countries set up competitions in imitation of this, including the RIBA's Rome Prize, established in 1912 at the height of pre-1914 Beaux Arts fervour in England.[4]

Although national influences were also important – for example, the establishment of an RIBA-endorsed Board of Architectural Education in 1904 as the cornerstone of a system of recognition of architecture schools and exemption from the RIBA Intermediate and Final examinations – the decisive shift towards a higher education-based Beaux Arts institutionalisation of architectural teaching was above all the achievement of the Liverpool School of Architecture under Charles Reilly, Professor of Architecture from 1904. Reilly's course spawned two generations of able, logical students, such as Lionel Budden, who eventually succeeded him as professor.[5] Liverpool, along with the Architectural Association, was one of the first schools to gain Intermediate exemption, but by 1931 they had been joined by 29 more. The 1930s saw more systematic state intervention in architectural education, culminating in the establishment of the Architects' Registration Council of the UK in 1938. The Beaux Arts ethos of Reilly and Liverpool also exerted a key influence on the move towards a more systematised education in town planning, with the country's first town planning university department and first chair, Stanley Adshead (1868–1946, appointed 1912). This process would enhance the role of the combined architect-planner, with feet firmly rooted in the world of architectural design, as the prime mover within town and regional planning for the next two decades.[6] Aside from Liverpool, other architectural schools maintained a more eclectic position. The Edinburgh School at ECA was torn between the two extremes of Arts and Crafts romanticism and Beaux Arts Modernity. Its multidisciplinarity was also accentuated by its artistic organisation, which made it possible to study drawing and painting: all students did a one-year basic course in sculpture. In 1924, following sharp criticism of the quality of teaching at the school in an RIBA report, several new appointments were made, including one of Lorimer's assistants, Henry (Harry) Hubbard, who became an assistant instructor in 1925. Matthew's eyes were now opened to the qualities of classical architecture. He later recalled that at ECA 'I came suddenly to realise that I had been educated [at the 'Stution] in a building designed by Robert Adam – [whereas previously] our juvenile eyes might as well have been closed from the day we entered the school to the day we left it'.[7]

But there was also an additional factor specific to ECA's curriculum – the influence of the humanistic philosophy of urban regeneration advocated by the biologist and pioneering planner Patrick Geddes. His optimistic ethos of reform, founded in 19th-century post-Christian ideas like those of the St-Simoniens, or Ferdinand Tönnies's concepts of *Gemeinschaft und Gesellschaft* (1887), fused scientific faith in evolutionary progress with a romantic ideal of the unity of past, present and future and of the importance of the old culture-city, as an acropolis-like spiritual beacon and inspiration for solutions to modern urban degradation.[8] To Geddes, the historic city of Edinburgh was like a living textbook of social and spiritual evolution, good and bad. He argued that it was vital to enhance 'the spirit and individuality of our city, its personality and character'; to provide a framework for human self-fulfilment. This concept built on a history of local efforts of civic amenity pressure and fierce resistance to commercial desecration of romantic Edinburgh.[9] By the late 1920s Geddes's philosophy was being transmitted to ECA students by his son-in-law, Frank Mears, who was Robert's teacher of architectural history and city planning at the college, following the establishment of planning studies in 1925. Mears was the foremost Scottish example of the 'private consultant' town planners who were burgeoning throughout Britain, as the framework of local-authority-dominated planning gradually gained strength. Although Mears's lectures rarely made direct reference to Geddes, the latter's spirit of historically based renewal, and his concept of Edinburgh as an exemplary or micro-cosmic city, suffused his teaching as a whole.[10]

Despite his own individualism, Geddes's philosophy of 'civics', with its mixture of rationalism and post-religious spirituality, proved very influential in the 20th-century development of a more collective ethos of 'scientific humanism' in architecture and planning. It was translated into large-scale practice by educators such as the architect-planner Raymond Unwin, who was a key international propagandist for state intervention in the built environment, as well as a central establishment figure in the professionalisation of town planning in Britain from 1914. And Geddes's emphasis on diagnostic survey as an essential precursor to planning action, and on the planning of the city in its regional hinterland ('Valley Section'), entered the mainstream of interwar British planning thought, especially through the work of Patrick Abercrombie.[11] For younger architect-planners of Robert Matthew's generation all this was already in the bloodstream from the start. Like the traditionalist ideals of Lorimer, earlier, this *Weltanschauung* would become so pervasive in Matthew's student years and later career that it would virtually slip from his conscious awareness.

Yet alongside all this idealistic speculation, at heart the Edinburgh School – in the years Robert Matthew studied there – was still 'a school where buildings were studied, drawn and designed'. The students worked in two large studios, at the southeast corner of the building, by the sculpture court, with a locker each, and a largely hierarchical arrangement with little contact between the year groups. John Begg steered a practical middle course, and was popular among the students for his tolerant and easy-going attitude towards the incessant pranks.[12]

In keeping with this practical Arts and Crafts ethos, much of Robert's time in his first two years was devoted to practical drawing – including countless thumbnail sketches, drawn from textbooks, of famous foreign buildings. In his Stage I studies in 1924–5 he filled his notebooks with systematic lecture notes, covering building construction, services, drainage and ventilation, as well as the antiquarian sketches long familiar to the Arts and Crafts architect, and the detailed study of the Greek and Roman orders. During Stages II and IIIa, in the 1925/6 academic year, he passed in History and Building Construction, and was awarded a £10 minor bursary. There were also the first modest drawing projects, including a surviving detailed classical elevation of a small 'provincial bank', and the drawing

27

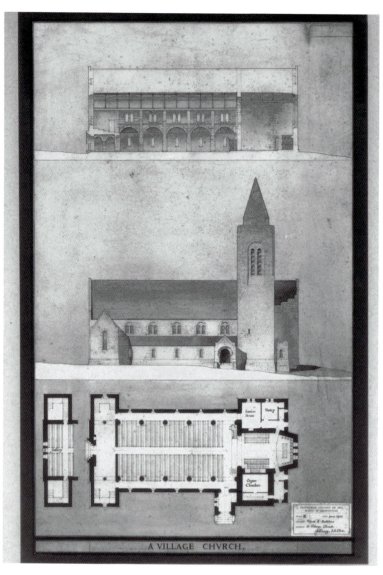

A VILLAGE CHVRCH.

of lettering and balusters for senior students under the college's fagging system:
ECA still stood four-square in the hybrid
Beaux Arts–traditionalist tradition of
restrained stylistic eclecticism.[13]

The year 1926 brought renewed
sketchbook touring opportunities – in
the Easter holidays to castellated and
medieval buildings around Edinburgh
and Aberdeen, and in the summer to
France, on a 16-day trip to Brittany, taking in St Malo, Dinan and Mont St
Michel. These solo travels were still a
tremendous excitement to Robert, and
were recorded with obsessive detail in a
series of hour-by-hour diaries – an intense
focus that would fade away later in his
life, as he became more blasé about travel, and changed his working methods to

a reliance on delegation.

The trip to Brittany cost him £12, of
which £1 was a subsidy from his parents
and 10s came from his aunt Aggie, while
the remainder was earned himself, in a
somewhat unusual fashion – as we shall
see later. The parsimonious lifestyle this
necessitated was duly set out in his diary,
including a confession of the 'awful
extravagance' of 36 francs for a replacement razor; his holiday reading was a
textbook on electricity. The diary also
revealed all the prejudices of an all-male-
educated Presbyterian youth, to whom
both France and England seemed somewhat alien societies: in Brittany he
remarked on 'the pop-eyed Frenchies …
eating with great noise and gusto', and in
England he remarked disparagingly on

'the twit-twit-twitter of gibbering church females and artist persons' on a train journey, and reacted with shock on encountering 'what they call porridge – I don't know what it is made with – certainly *not* oatmeal, and they put no salt whatever into it!' At Dinan he simply recorded, 'Englishman at hotel, looks like a cad!' London was still a foreign city to Robert: although there was the reassurance of a test match at the Oval, he also remarked in surprise that 'I went to the South Kensington Museum, but found it was only natural history, and was directed round the corner to the Victoria and Albert Museum'.[14]

Robert's third academic year, October 1926–June 1927, saw a widening range of tasks, including compositions of classical and Gothic details, specific projects such as a Norman Shaw-like 'Village Church', and 24-hour *esquisses*. His June 1927 exams saw him pass Design and Colour with especially high marks, and Measured Work, Freehand, History of Architecture and Applied Construction with only slightly lesser grades. These exams also qualified him for his first external milestone: his 1927 certificate of exemption from the RIBA Intermediate examination. While spring 1927 saw a short sketching tour in Italy, during that summer his main tour was restricted to England, exploiting the greater mobility afforded by his smart new yellow Matchless motor-bike, and his folding Kodak camera. The Matchless rapidly became an object of family envy, with Stuart and his friends vying to borrow it for recklessly fast runs in the Lothian hinterland. Robert's summer tour focused on East Anglia, with copious sketches of parish churches; two of his Norfolk drawings were published in the RIAS *Quarterly* in 1928. Again, a spartan lifestyle was required, with 'digs' at the back of a café. But this was combined with a still naively elitist Edinburgh world view, which, even when Robert was writing tongue in cheek, reflected the popular Darwinian language of the day: 'The low level of the great mass of the population is our fault ... our task should be, either to educate them up to a proper standard of culture, to "ensure the progress of the race", or to extinguish them altogether.'[15]

'Merciless times': the breakdown of John Matthew

Soon, this somewhat callow world view would be rubbed down and matured under the competitive influence of other talented College students of that era. In the meanwhile, however, a far more unsettling challenge to Robert's equilibrium – knocking away the last childhood props to his identity – emerged at home, in the form of the almost complete nervous breakdown of his father from 1926 onwards, and the collapse of his family as a cohesive or morally authoritative unit. Already, since the end of the war, John had suffered from blinding migraines, brought on by the intolerable demands stemming from the firm's booming postwar workload. In Stuart's view, 'Lorimer was utterly selfish, and once he'd got his link with a client, he'd just buzz off and leave the rest to Papa.' Stuart recalled of the years around 1924–5 that 'although we were never without sounds of music – instrument and voice – we were all well disciplined in keeping complete silence when my father had one of his excruciating migraines.' But the controversial Scottish National War Memorial project ratcheted the stresses of the office up to a new level.[16]

Under these pressures, the relationship between Lorimer and Matthew grew tense, and in 1926 Matthew persuaded Lorimer to make him a partner, in recognition of the immense stresses falling on them both (the partnership was formalised in 1927). But things only got worse, and finally, at the end of 1926, it was not Lorimer but Matthew who gave way. Doubtless, existing family tensions had also contributed: 'My mother was weighed down by her sense of responsibility, which must in turn have undermined my father's sense of personal adequacy.' Stuart recalled:

Merciless times they were for him, and for my mother, who could discern his

2.3 Picture of c.1928 by Robert showing the family in their Pentland Hills rented cottage at Waterloo. (Stuart Matthew)

feeling from his look and voice. Their social life was nil. For as long as he could stand it, my father continued to examine annual groups of boy scouts, in our back garden, for their signalling badges, causing noise and flapping of semaphores. But his illness just went on and on, and he never really recovered. He never complained, but it was very plain to see when he was tense and reduced to tears, or silent in a room on his own. It was very sad that their silver wedding party was held while he was so ill. About seventy relatives and friends were there in McVities on 4 April 1927. A little party was held at Minto Street, but my father left the dining room and I ran down and found him holding a jar of Sanatogen and breathing with difficulty. All I could think to do was to hit him hard in the middle of his back; it worked but he was in a poor state and only really recovered much later.

Various remedies were tried during 1927, including a September tour of Norfolk churches that ended abruptly when 'he was found there on a railway station without any idea of where he was; after the police had phoned to Minto Street, Robert rushed down to bring him home.'[17]

In 1927, through a supreme effort, John forced himself to attend, with his party of six family members, the opening of the War Memorial, and then to host, along with Lorimer, a supper for 200 guests (in Crawford's, Princes Street), to celebrate completion of the work. Finally, in 1928, the family decided that a move away from the stresses of Edinburgh was necessary, and rented a house in the countryside southwest of Edinburgh, at Waterloo, on the old drove road from West Linton to Carlops.

Then, on 13 September 1929, Lorimer, too, was suddenly struck down, by a fatal attack of appendicitis, leaving John as sole partner, but in a state of complete collapse. Stuart recalled that 'in a way, this made matters even more dreadful for my father, but there must have been some relief to have been rid of a man so self-seeking and so lacking in professional principles.' Arguably, however, Lorimer had shown forbearance in maintaining the partnership during Matthew's breakdown, especially as the latter, unlike himself, had never developed the vital skill of attracting new business. At any rate, in this year of the Wall Street Crash, the office's prospects suddenly began to look bleak. The demand for large churches and mansions suddenly dried up, and one of the firm's former assistants, Leslie Grahame Thomson, began to attract commissions they themselves had expected, such as the Reid Memorial Church, Edinburgh – whose rubbly design was very close to that of the War Memorial.[18]

Modern Architect

In this darkening climate, radical staff cuts were made at Lorimer & Matthew: for example, assistant Harry Hubbard was paid off, eventually setting up his own firm. And a tussle began between John Matthew and Lorimer's son, Hew. A year younger than Robert, Hew had expected in due course to enter the practice as an heir apparent. He had already shown a character very different from the single-minded Robert when, in 1925, he left Loretto School in Musselburgh to spend an abortive year at Magdalen College, Oxford, abandoning his studies there after failing his exams.[19] Hew then took up part-time study of architecture at ECA, but in 1929 John, citing the firm's parlous finances, refused to take him on as an associate or partner. Faced with this rebuff, Hew then shifted to the ECA school of sculpture, with the encouragement of Alexander Carrick, the head of sculpture, and under the strong influence of Eric Gill. Hew later argued that John 'got going by a rotten trick – insisting on being made a temporary partner, then, after Lorimer's death, getting Hew out of the way.' He believed that he had been excluded to keep a place free for Stuart to join the practice, and subsequently blamed John and Stuart for the final collapse of the firm around 1960. But Hew, a romantic and unworldly Catholic convert in the spirit of the 3rd Marquess of Bute, was ill attuned to the demands of 20th-century architecture, being opposed by temperament to its bureaucracy and state interventionism. And more importantly, from John's perspective, with work drying up, the practice could not afford a second associate – as was underlined in 1930, when Robert had to help out on token pay. John had only just had to pay Lady Lorimer, in 1929, the (then) vast sum of £4,000 for Lorimer's share in the practice (including fees due and office effects), and doubtless felt that after 30 years he 'had had enough of Lorimers and didn't want any more of them'.[20]

However, John's own state of collapse rendered any such speculation beside the point. He saw it as enough of a burden and source of resentment that he felt obliged to continue to employ the young secretary, Margaret Brown (later Swan), who had recently joined Lorimer. In late 1929, to try to raise the family's spirits and allow Stuart rest to prepare for his entrance examinations for the Edinburgh School of Architecture the following year, John, Annie, Stuart and Nannie went for an extended holiday in Bournemouth, and ordered new upholstery for all the drawing-room furniture for when they returned. But even here, misfortune struck, for when they stopped off in London,

> my father had a very bad turn just after we arrived – somewhere beside the river. We just sat in a shelter for a long time, with my mother wondering how we could ever get back to the hotel in Southampton Row – to continue by tram was totally out of the question! In the end, we had to take a boat along the river – a frightful journey, but we got back eventually.[21]

Leaving the nest: college friendships and romances

This mounting chaos at home, in effect, gave Robert a final substantial push out of the family nest – rather as he had fled in the face of the literal conflagration at Dick Place. For him, the inexorable collapse of his once authoritative parental unit into a state of abject incapacity provided a powerful impulse to harden his own personality, reinforcing his existing tendency to project to the world, above all else, an image of calm and self-controlled dignity. From the late 1920s Robert intervened only occasionally and somewhat commandingly in Minto Street family matters. In 1929, for instance, returning to Minto Street from a grand bazaar in the Queen's Hall to raise funds for an extension of the Edinburgh Institution's Ferryfield Sports Ground, as Stuart recalled:

> I and three others, including Nancy Sutherland – quite a girlfriend of Robert's at that time – packed into a horse cab, and Robert sat up in the

cabman's seat. We cantered along through the dark, past the glowing wire-covered globes of the street lights, until, on the North Bridge, Robert asked to take over the reins and the whip. He lashed the air with loud cracks, and the nag suddenly doubled its speed – we felt the difference very noticeably! That was Robert – wanting to control rather than be controlled.[22]

In the mid and late 1920s Robert's social life was also subtly in transition. His old 'Stution male-cameraderie friendships were fading in significance, and rugby acquaintances were 'dropped' in favour of a new college circle of architectural friends; as part of his growing desire to control his own 'image', his pre-college life was gradually edited out of his life story. All in all, Robert was developing a more fluid pattern of social relationships, linked strictly to his career, and based ultimately on power. Among his fellow students, Robert made few friends in his own year, but instead accumulated satellites in the younger years, such as the mild-mannered David Carr and Johnny Paterson, in the year below him. Others in that year were kept somewhat at a distance, notably Basil Spence, whose brilliant draughtsmanship marked him out from his entry to the college in 1925 as a potential rival; his scenographic talents were recognised as early as 1926, when a drawing of Edinburgh Old Town was published in the *RIAS Quarterly*.[23] Although Spence had been educated at George Watson's College, his colonial Indian birth and family roots, and his Anglican rather than Presbyterian religious background, gave him an enigmatic character, less strongly anchored in Edinburgh society than Matthew; characteristically, after four years' study at the college, he began his first work experience with Lutyens and others in London. One younger contemporary at the college recalled that 'he and Robert were utterly different. Basil was one year behind, very much the artist, temperamental, brilliant, a bit of a show-off, whereas

Matthew never appeared to be nervous about anything; they weren't particularly friends.'[24]

At this stage Matthew seemed very much the more dominant of the two, being not only older but physically much more charismatic, in contrast to Spence's diminutive, somewhat shy image. But, architecturally, they soon became rivals. Matthew recalled 30 years later his 'slim figure at the desk in front of me – and the breathtaking sketches which came so easily from his pencil and brush – the envy of us all!'[25] Spence was influenced especially strongly by the Beaux Arts/classical *esquisse* tradition of the initial sketch solution carried through into detailed realisation, whereas Matthew preferred to evolve buildings by a more protracted process of testing numerous alternative designs. But, thus far, there was nothing to distinguish the two in their work as opposed to their character. In 1965, at an Edinburgh Architectural Association dinner held at ECA in their joint honour, Matthew recalled that, in contrast to the Liverpool School classical tradition, he and Spence had both been brought up as 'Gothic men'; he also recalled that he had 'once embodied the rear half of a horse in a student rag', the front half being Spence.[26]

The most significant of Matthew's 'subordinate' friends, the only one to whom he became truly attached, was Alan Reiach. In stark contrast to Matthew's intense roots in his home city, Reiach's upbringing, like Spence's, was more peripatetic, and left him with a legacy of instability throughout his youth. Born in 1910 to unmarried parents, his father being a print-works owner and amateur boat designer, Alan was brought up between the ages of two and six by a foster-mother in Acton and thereafter by an aunt and grandmother in Mill Hill, becoming a prep-school boarder in Eastbourne until 1921. In that year his aunt moved to Edinburgh, and Alan attended Edinburgh Academy from 1922 to 1928. Always interested in art and design, he decided to become an architect, and in 1928 entered Lorimer's office as an apprentice, transferring to ECA in 1932 for two finishing years of full-time study. After qualifying with distinction in 1934 and winning several RIBA student prizes, Reiach took the college's new one-year postgraduate town planning course in 1935 and then travelled for nine months in Europe, the United States (where he called on Wright at Taliesin) and the USSR. Thereafter, in 1937, he spent a year in London in the progressive-Modernist office of Robert Atkinson, before returning to Edinburgh to take up a two-year ECA fellowship; his research focused both on design of modern social community centres and on study of Scottish vernacular buildings.[27]

With his highly strung character and dandy-like manner, Reiach was in some ways similar to Robert's own father, but was more pliable and, of course, was four years younger than Robert himself, who felt quite at ease in his company. As Matthew's son, Aidan, recalled,

Robert enjoyed Alan's wit, while Alan regarded Robert as an authority figure, and started imitating his mannerisms, going about without a watch and never knowing the time, or never having any money on him. Robert thought it was funny that Alan wore a beret, bow ties, and affected painterly ways. He was very amusing but also very moody as a young man; my father was much more high-powered.

On Robert's part, there was not yet any clue of firm Modernist or traditionalist affiliations – hardly surprising, as in Britain it was only during the 1930s that the battle lines for or against began to harden around International Modernism. But Robert kept something of a distance from traditionalist colleagues, such as Esme Gordon or William Kininmonth, 'a somewhat self-opinionated chap who was always overshadowed by someone – especially, at this stage, by Basil'.[28]

With the exception of Reiach, these architectural and planning acquaintances, from the mid or late 1920s, were not casual or 'real' friends: Robert 'would never allow himself the enjoyment of relaxing, even in friendship – as an adult, he didn't do things like just going to the theatre or to a concert "with" other chaps.' Whereas in his schoolboy days he depended on a circle of male friends for his genuine friendships, now, for emotional support, Robert tended to look increasingly to female companionship, armed with the confidence and reassuring sense of control that stemmed from the growing realisation of his charismatic attractiveness to the opposite sex, as early as the mid 1920s. For example, Christine Somerville, an older friend of his sister Nannie at St Trinneans School, recalled that 'when Robert was dux I had a bit of a crush on him, as he was captain of everything and rather handsome.'[29]

It was not just Robert's own individual circumstances – the combination of his dominant character and increasingly fragmented family background – that influenced the course of his relationships, but also the wider context of social mores in 1920s Edinburgh. Across early-20th-century Britain, pioneered by avant-garde circles such as the Bloomsbury Group, old-fashioned stuffy convention and morally authoritative dogmas were on the wane.[30] During the years when Robert Matthew was emerging into adulthood, the liberal lifestyle, sexual freedom and aesthetic Modernism championed by the Edwardian avant-gardists was spreading throughout the upper middle class, penetrating places and societies, such as Presbyterian Edinburgh, that had previously been firmly closed to them.[31]

These wider cultural trends interacted powerfully with the maturing of Robert's own character and circumstances. Robert's varied relationships with girlfriends developed, initially in the early 1920s, out of the circle of family neighbourhood connections: girls like Nancy Sutherland, a member of the Fountainhall Road Church, who would go to rugby matches with him. Robert rapidly developed a strong predilection for combative or feisty rather than docile girlfriends, although his own methods of courtship, rooted in the male hobby ethos, avoided any romantic sentimentality. For example, in pursuing the daughter of a Dr Alison, a near-neighbour in Minto Street, he 'made a model of a bomb, six or seven inches long, from which the tail could be removed. Rolled up inside was a little sheet, not worded in flowing declarations of love, but, typically of him, set out as a record of fact.'[32]

By the mid and late 1920s Robert was becoming drawn towards more serious relationships, within which, characteristically, he was as much the object of pursuit and competition as the other way round. The two most determined contestants were Anita Gallie, daughter of one of Nannie's friends, who lived nearby in Mayfield Gardens, and Lorna Louise Pilcher, daughter of R Stuart Pilcher (the Liverpool-born manager of the Edinburgh Corporation Tramways) and Louisa Niven (an Aberdonian by birth), whose house was also nearby, at 24 Craigmillar Park. Lorna had been born in Aberdeen in October 1910, and first met Robert in 1926 at a party, when she was 16 and he was 19. Stuart and Nannie began to notice that 'Lorna always seemed to be passing our house in Minto Street, en route to or from St Trinneans School in Dalkeith Road', and the relationship developed rapidly. At first there was a fierce struggle between Anita and Lorna: 'Anita would try to get hold of Robert for a date, and Lorna, with her red hair, would get fizzy about that – but meanwhile Robert was just getting on with his studying – nothing would put him off that!'[33] Eventually, Lorna decisively saw off her rival, and she and Robert began to see each other almost daily – in the short periods between his work commitments – and became unofficially engaged.

In contrast to Robert's obsessive study, Lorna gave up her initial ambition to become a doctor at the end of the 1920s, after a year's abortive study of medicine – probably in anticipation of marriage to Robert. But Lorna was far from being a submissive, housewifely cipher. She was a determined and astute individual, whose strong character was effectively concealed in a vivacious yet unworldly outward manner, combining a striking facial and physical beauty, a strong sense of style in dress and domestic decoration (relying especially on a collage-type crafts aestheticism), and an animated manner, which could swing from merriment to fiery temper as the occasion demanded. This manner was distilled – no doubt unconsciously – from the mildly bohemian elements of the aesthetic Bloomsbury lifestyle. For example, Lorna always showed an aversion to conventional domesticity or household management, and followed an ad hoc approach to housework and childcare, exploiting the help of older relatives and others.

In the mid 1920s the Pilcher household was, like that of the Matthews, fertile breeding ground for the new and relatively free-living ethos among children emerging into adulthood, owing to its already rather open and inclusive character: 'You never knew who you'd find at the table for supper!' Initially, the link with Lorna brought Robert some unexpected study benefits. To begin with, during the General Strike of 3–11 May 1926, he and Douglas were able to get highly paid temporary strike-breaking jobs in the transport department, Robert as a bus driver and the 16-year-old Douglas as a tram conductor. The General Strike in Scotland was characterised by a high degree of violence and sabotage. In an early indication of lack of sympathy with the left-wing radicalism later favoured by 1930s architectural contemporaries, the two brothers, with some relish, negotiated streets lined with jeering and stone-throwing strikers, and on one occasion Robert returned home in great excitement with the news that his bus had been ambushed in the High Street, that bricks had been thrown through his cab windows, but that he had driven on determinedly through the baying mob. For this week-long adventure Robert and Douglas earned the substantial sum of £21 between them, and Robert's share of £10 10s paid precisely for the balance of the expenses of his trip to Brittany in August of that year.[34]

His sketching trips on the Matchless continued apace, including a cathedral tour in mid 1928, which produced a humorous drawing of 'Mr Kinnimonth [sic] hard at work' sketching Gloucester Cathedral, with William's 'Big Feet' prominently noted. July 1929 saw another meticulously logged tour, to Yorkshire and (later) the Midlands and East Anglia, with the usual spartan regime (total expense £2 5s 2d): putting up a tent in a field outside York, then finding it torn up by a pony; pigs squealing deafeningly in the next field after dark; cadging some dirty water from a nearby cottage; washing the following morning in a partitioned-off corner of the local post-office. The notebooks combined the usual profusion of skilful drawings of parish churches and cathedrals with typical Arts and Crafts remarks and judgements: thus, at Cherry Burton, 'I saw a tower, and the name seemed to call up visions of something very picturesque, but it proved to be a mere modern erection.' The trip culminated in a day at Easingwold getting the Matchless repaired: 'What an afternoon, stewing, boiling in the garage, to

35

Education and re-orientation

Note the 3 days' beard

BIG FELLA

MR KINNIMONTH
HARD AT WORK

Gloucester
Cathedral
in the
distance

Robt AMatthew.
July 1928.

2.5 July 1928 drawing by Robert Matthew of 'Mr Kinnimonth [*sic*] hard at work' sketching Gloucester Cathedral. (EULMC)

the merry sound of biffs, bangs, crashes, and the oily smells so typical of anything to do with cars or bikes!' Nothing here seemed to suggest revolutionary discontent on Robert's part: to jolt him out of all this required a new mentor, and in 1928 one duly arrived, in the form of lecturer E A A Rowse.[35]

Prizes, competitions and privations

During his final two academic years, from October 1927 to June 1929, Robert's career at the College blossomed into full maturity, with his 1928 and 1929 project work producing, for example, striking drawings for a Greek Doric order, and a range of building types and styles, including a Romanesque spired village church and a grand domed exhibition hall with tall Art Deco windows and a small hall and garage underneath. In 1928 the 'fierce and awe-inspiring' C D Carus-Wilson retired as lecturer (to enter practice with Mears), and was replaced at the end of that year by two Assistant Instructor appointments: John Summerson, a London architectural writer and historian, and E A A Rowse. This change immediately began to swing the orientation of

the school towards a subtly Modernist ethos, reviving it (in the students' opinion) from 'a long, long winter's lethargy'. Of the two, it was Rowse who struck an immediate chord with Robert. In due course, his advocacy of a scientific research-based architectural philosophy, merging Taylorist efficiency and Geddesian humanism, would exert a very strong and specific influence on him. But, for now, Rowse's impact was more straightforward, in persuading Matthew to project himself for the first time outside the now claustrophobic world of Edinburgh traditionalism, through the medium of the pan-British student competitions: 'Rowse said: "You ought to be doing these competitions!" – which Robert had hardly even heard of!'[36]

And there now ensued a succession of prize triumphs that outdid any other contemporary Scottish student, even including Spence. Robert began by winning the RIBA Pugin Travelling Studentship (for study of medieval architecture) in January 1929, with richly detailed measured drawings of the structure of Bath Abbey and Wells Cathedral, with much of the detail being 'devilled' by friends such as Johnny Paterson, David Carr and others. Lorna accompanied him on many of his sketching trips and 'helped hold the other end of the tape!' The work of Pugin preparation coincided with the start of one of Lorimer & Matthew's last major projects, for classical department buildings at West Mains, which replaced the prefabricated wooden hutting of the Geology Department. Robert's father acquired a section of the hutting and had it erected in the back garden of Minto Street for the use of Robert and his friends in the Pugin work. In Robert's final exams, for his diploma, he gained full marks for Design and hardly less for the other subjects, and won an honourable mention in the RIAS Rowand Anderson Competition.

Following completion of his course, in June 1929 (followed the next year by his diploma award), the emphasis shifted from the Gothic of the Pugin to the 'classic'. 1930 saw the first of two attempts, in

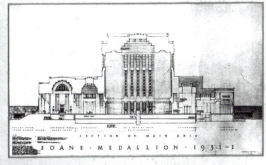

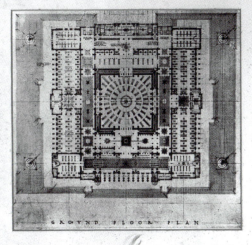

THE SOANE MEDALLION
1931-2

DESIGN FOR A NATIONAL LIBRARY

ROBERT · H · MATTHEW
EDINBURGH COLLEGE OF ART

1930 and 1931, at the summit of the interwar national competition pyramid, the Rome Scholarship, which carried a prize of a two-year residence in the British School at Rome. Organised by the Rome School's highly conservative faculty of architecture with RIBA assistance, the annual competition took four stages: preliminary examination of portfolios by the Rome faculty; interview of selected candidates in London; *en loge* preparation of an *esquisse* (sketch) design for a set subject during two days' incarceration in March at the RIBA; and finally the working-up of the full design over two and a half months. It was understood by all entrants that an essay in mainstream symmetrical, axial, Beaux Arts classicism was required; the competition would be won chiefly on the basis of nuances of logical planning. For the 1930 competition the subject was 'A Museum of Archaeology in an Important Mediterranean City' – a subject redolent of the Rome School's

traditions of 'north versus south Europe' cultural interaction. Matthew made it through to the final stage, and proposed a rather grand solution, with a three-storey hall in the centre, proudly inscribed with the names of Roman emperors above the cornice, and a monumental front with three-bay centrepiece and thermal windows to give an overtly 'Roman' touch. The winning design, by William Holford, a South African starlet from Charles Reilly's Liverpool stable, was rather different in character, arguably more subtle and neoclassical with its several axes and avoidance of any dominant facade – an approach that also anticipated the anti-monumental Modernist ethos rather more than Matthew's.[37] In 1931 Matthew had another try at the Rome Scholarship and again made it to the finals, with a towered, dumb-bell-planned design for a town hall and courthouse, reminiscent of the Art Deco monumentality of Bertram Goodhue's Nebraska

2.6 Robert Matthew's Soane Medallion-winning design (subject: 'A National Library in a Capital'), 1932. (EULMC)

ENGLISH INN FOR EDINBURGH SUBURB

A sketch of the English type of inn, for which a licence was granted by Edinburgh Licensing Court yesterday and which will be erected at Balgreen Road. The architect is Mr John F. Matthew, F.R.I.B.A.

State Capitol (1920–32).

These 'near misses' were frustrating, but by the 1930s the prestige of the Rome Scholarship was strongly on the wane, and with it the entire hierarchical system of competitions that it symbolised. Indeed, in the post-1933 political polarisation it was coming to be 'regarded as highly reactionary', and thus ECA's three successive wins in 1937–9, by William Walker, Alexander Wylie and Ralph Cowan, were less prestigious than they might have seemed. Matthew continued with his competition efforts for a while, and with some success. In 1932 he won the RIBA Soane Medallion (another *en-loge*-based competition involving extended trips to London), and £150 cash, for his design for a 'National Library in a Capital' – a vast, stepped, cubic block – and details of a Lutyensesque brick classical 'Sports Club'. The same year saw him competing with Basil Spence, and winning jointly with him, the Arthur Cates Prize for 'Promotion of Architecture in Relation to Town Planning' – Raymond Unwin being chairman of the board of adjudicators for that year.[38]

Up to and beyond his eventual graduation in 1930, Robert continued to take a very full part in the social life of the college. This included episodes of early environmental activism, as for instance when he, Spence and Paterson, objecting

to the 'eyesore' of a new public toilet adjacent to the classical Royal Scottish Academy, daubed humorous slogans on it one night (including the prominent words 'New City Chambers'). More important, however, were the set-piece ceremonies and events, including the annual 'Revel'. College capping (graduation) ceremonies were also 'shocking affairs – when Robert was processing down the aisle to get his mortar board, someone took the lid off a Roman plaster urn in the gallery, and threw a large number of hens down into the audience and platform party'.[39] On his graduation in 1930, Robert joined Lorimer & Matthew for work experience, initially working for a year without pay. He helped out at first with detailing and supervision of the few current schemes, such as the Walpole Memorial Hall for St Mary's Episcopal Cathedral (1931–3), a Dutch-gabled, steep-roofed Lorimerian design with pointed concrete roof inside. He also produced drawings for the bungalow-like Douglas Haig Memorial Homes, Stenhouse (1931). To supplement his meagre income, after his election as ARIBA in June 1931 he also began teaching part time as an ECA instructor. Within Lorimer & Matthew, Robert started to make neat drawings of typical details of work by the office – roof drainage, damp proofing and so on – which almost became an office book of

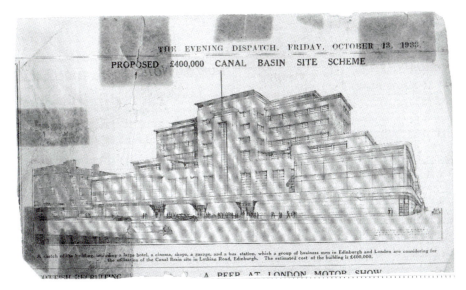

rules. His contribution was in no way stylistically 'Modern', but was still poised between classicism and steep-roofed 'vernacular simplicity'.[40]

With the extreme precariousness of the firm's workload, Robert struggled on intermittently at Lorimer & Matthew until 1934, combining this with bursts of postgraduate research work or other projects, and doing perspectives and drawings for other architects – an activity in which he and Spence continued to be great rivals, with Spence's sweeping, painterly verve matched by Robert's tendency towards a more aggressively dynamic Art Deco treatment. Working for Lorimer & Matthew in late 1933, Robert produced the detailed drawings for a new public house commissioned by his uncle Bobby (Robert Hogg) in Balgreen Road: the concept of a playfully Lorimerian, steep-gabled block stemmed from his father, but the detailed realisation, stylised and geometrised in a slightly Art Deco manner, was Robert's own work. The climax of Robert's 'dynamic Art Deco' phase came at the same time as this (in October 1933), when he prepared some strikingly stylish drawings as his contribution towards a £400,000 scheme for redevelopment of the Port Hopetoun canal basin in Lothian Road then being hatched by his father. Robert 'knocked together' John's sketch layout into a striking, unified scheme, rakishly monumental: the main street block was stepped up pyramidally at the centre and banded with Art Deco windows, and would contain modern service flats with shops, hotel, a garage and bus station below. But, eventually, there was bitter disappointment for John, as the scheme was 'poached' and simplified by a commercial Edinburgh architect, Stewart Kaye. In the years 1933–4 Robert also worked on the Loretto School Memorial Hall (1933–5, a similar rubbly design to the Walpole Memorial Hall), and a small shop conversion for T B Campbell, faced in travertine, at 8 Picardy Place (1934–5).[41] Fired up by the grandeur of the Port Hopetoun scheme, John Matthew had gone on another spending spree, buying a big family-size car – a Crossley saloon: it was obtained at a reduced price through Lorna's father, who by then had moved (from 1930) to become head of Corporation Transport in Manchester.[42]

Robert and Lorna: marriage and independence

In late 1931 Robert took the final step away from the family when he and Lorna, to whom he had been engaged for some time, decided to get married. Although the Matthews were not a morally censorious family by the standards of the day, nonetheless pressure from Annie concerning the relationship had been building up – motivated, probably, more by maternal jealousy than by moral disapproval. When Robert

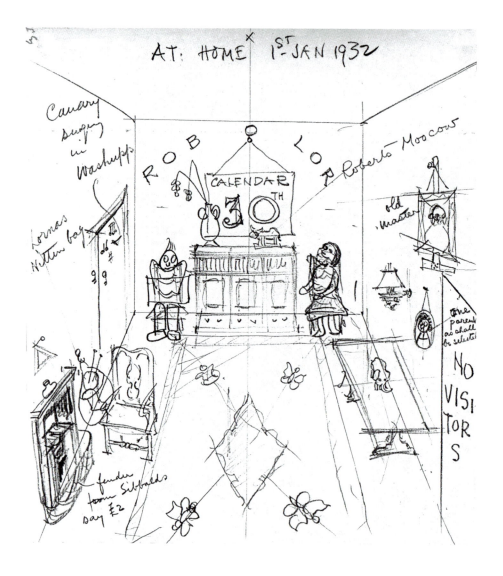

and Lorna signalled their intention to go off on a sketching holiday in France, 'my mother-in-law made a bit of a scene, and my father-in-law, backing her up as he had to, said, "If you do that, you'll have to leave the office!"' There was also a suggestion that Annie regarded Lorna as 'scatty' and 'wilful', and, indeed, had another more 'practical' girl (now no longer identifiable) lined up for Robert. Fortified by the guarantee of at least another year for Robert in the office – even if on virtually no pay – he and Lorna reluctantly agreed to get married, but, to minimise the number of guests, and the cost, insisted on holding the wedding on Christmas Day – at Fountainhall Road Church, with a reception at the Roxburghe Hotel.[43]

Initially, Robert and Lorna's married life was spartan in the extreme, and they even had to pawn their wedding presents after a year to raise some money. Their first accommodation was a rented room in a house belonging to one of Robert's aunts at 5 Maclaren Road, the cramped dimensions of which were offset by Robert's frequent trips to London in pursuit of competition success and prize money: Lorna recalled that 'it was all organised by Robert's mother – I always loathed it!' In Aidan's view, 'My father had lived in the greatest luxury in his mother's house, with servants, and all his clothes hand-made for him. Lorna felt she could not, and would not, go down that route herself – which must have been a bit of a culture shock for him.' Frustrated by this shoebox environment, and by the continuing instability of Robert's parents, they decided to opt instead for a rural existence, and managed (with financial help from Lorna's father) to find a delightful small gatehouse lodge – single-storey, early 19th-century, classical – at a country estate at Lamancha, 15 miles southwest of Edinburgh. Conditions there were primitive: it had two rooms, kitchenette and bathroom, with cooking on an oil stove. Lorna had never cooked or done any kind of 'housework' before, and her mother used to send them large food parcels. But Robert had no intention of spending much time there. Stuart recollected that

he worked hard and never knew when to stop, and he travelled into Edinburgh every morning: he wasn't a 'club' person or a social-climber, it was all done by sheer hard work. He always had something to 'do first': 'Let's push Lorna out of the way and get on with the job!' – that was rather the attitude.[44]

To give them independent mobility, Robert and Lorna acquired for £30 a small Austin 7 car, which had to be pushed out every day, even at times of deep snow. She recalled that 'on one winter occasion, I remember pushing it down the main street of Carlops after it broke down in the cold.' The Austin was eventually replaced by another, marginally less antique car, a Morris light tourer. In this lonely setting, on the many days when she stayed at home, Lorna felt bored and isolated, both from her friends and from Robert. To keep her company, they bought a Great Dane, 'Dougal', but the experiment proved a disaster, as 'it had something that affected its brain, and the huge beast went wild in the tiny cottage: they had to get rid of it.'[45] Eventually, after about three years at Lamancha, Lorna became so fed up with the privations of rural existence that they decided to rent a flat in Edinburgh, keeping Lamancha until 1938 for weekend trips. In 1934 they found a flat at 12 Darnaway Street, occupying a stately 'outlook tower' position at the top of an

1820s New Town classical tenement. With this dual base they were able for two or three years to enjoy a free social life, both together and separately: they each kept up a wide circle of friends, male and female, with frequent expeditions and parties, and a continuing degree of freedom in relationships. Particular friends at this time included Alan Reiach and his future wife Julie, the painter John Cook, Robert Scott Morton, and his sisters Elspeth and Beatrice.

One surviving member of this social group recalled the strong residual 19th-century values implicit in Matthew's assumptions of social 'leadership', and in his differing relations with men and women:

Those walks and picnics and other events were all such fun – in the Pentlands, or around Lamancha. Robert was always the host – but, just like a Victorian or Edwardian gentleman, he never carried or organised anything – the work had to be done by someone else. And whereas in the Victorian era, all the work was done by the servants, now we women had to be the 'servants'. Robert was fond of the countryside and of gardens, so long as someone else did all the work! Yet it was done in the most warm, charming way – he'd tell stories, crack

2.10 Adaptation by J F Matthew of newspaper cartoon, c.1932. (Stuart Matthew)

2.11 Robert and Lorna seen at the wedding of a friend in the early 1930s. (EULMC)

Education and re-orientation

2.12 Photograph by Robert of Lorna standing in the door of the Lamancha cottage, mid 1930s. (EULMC)

jokes. Robert was dominant but not domineering, and certainly wasn't in any way an unattractive character – quite the reverse – for that was exactly why so many people worshipped him. In particular, we women all fell in love with him, of course! With women he could unwind a bit, he could be a very warm and emotional character, highly strung – if you're living on your nerves you can never really relax – but the tension was more on the male side. Men had to be his equal to be respected at all: people like Alan, and his brother Stuart, were certainly in awe of him. With women it was a little different, but still, to be sure, you had to stand up to him, you had to have a sense of humour to get on with him. In general, you either had to be his minion or strong enough to resist – there was no middle way.[46]

Research and travel in an age of revolution

Robert's own change in circumstances, and his breakaway from his unstable family, coincided with a period of flux and instability on the international stage, as the economic slump of 1929–31 encouraged a widespread disillusionment across the Western world with conventional parliamentary government – and the turmoil and political polarisation that followed would irrevocably shape the consciousness of young, newly qualified

architects. At the one extreme was the mushrooming popularity of communism. Among leftist architects and commentators, concentrated especially in London, a Marxist-style rhetoric of industrial mass efficiency became commonplace. For example, J M Richards in 1935 cited Le Corbusier on 'the aesthetic value of regimentation', and hailed the military parade ground as an exemplar of 'modern organisation ... with its tendency to turn the individual into an impersonal unit'.[47] The more extreme positions of those years, both left-wing and (more infrequently) right-wing, amounted in their fervour to secular religions, and were often led by continental émigrés with a strong respect for the power of the state. But among the British intelligentsia a more important place was occupied by older liberal traditions that balanced acceptance of state leadership with a continued tolerance of private individualism: Keynes, for example, wrote in 1937 that the state held its power 'in trust'.[48] The same applied to many of the young: Annan wrote that the 'vaguely Liberal, vaguely Labour, the non-political yet opposed to Hitler, have been forgotten'.[49] For architects of this persuasion a growing fascination was exerted by countries that seemed to be tackling the crisis without abandoning the democratic system. There was, for example, Roosevelt's USA, with its New Deal Public Works Administration (PWA) programme from 1933.[50] And there was the gentler model of social-democratic Sweden, which had seemed, in the wake of the 1930 Stockholm Exhibition, to have managed effortlessly the transition from national-romanticism to humane social functionalism.[51] Robert Matthew was in many ways typical of this unsung grouping. They were tied to the more radical intelligentsia by a faith in the 'humanist' ethos of modern progress and planning, epitomised most popularly by the books of H G Wells, but by the 1930s propagated especially by figures such as the communist scientist Desmond Bernal. In the built environment the advocacy of 'modern research' fused the spiritual resources of Geddesian survey and analysis and of Arts and Crafts utopianism with the more radical rhetoric of continental Modernists such as Lubetkin, and new scientific influences such as the foundation of the Building Research Station (from 1920).[52]

Many of the tenets of this 'scientific humanist' movement – such as its stress on justice and world peace – would help shape the post-1945 world order in institutions such as the UN and UNESCO. They also had long roots, stretching back to the 18th-century French Revolution, and the teleological salvation and damnation rhetoric of Christianity.[53] But it was above all the ideal of 'planning' that united a wide variety of architectural and planning interest groups, 'progressive' or 'reactionary'.[54] In Britain, following the passing of the 1932 Town Planning Act, with its call for local planning schemes, planning diploma courses began to spring up in a range of higher-education institutions. And 1933, the revolutionary year, saw two academic appointments in England that would greatly bolster this movement. The first was the appointment of Matthew's old planning tutor, Rowse, as Assistant Director of the AA School of Architecture in London. Within ECA, Rowse had in 1932 founded Scotland's first department of civic design, with Matthew one of the first students to follow its one-year diploma course as a follow-up to his architecture diploma. Following this, Rowse turned down an offer of the headship of the Edinburgh school and instead moved to the AA, where he unleashed a multifaceted revolution, embracing socialism, collective 'group working' of students, and a Geddesian, research-based diagnostic method of working – the germ of the development-group method of working that would become typical of institutional Modernism.[55] At ECA, the day-to-day running of the planning course was taken over by Mears's partner, H A Rendel Govan. After his promotion to AA Principal in 1935, Rowse reorganised the five years into 15 'units' and reorientated the workload towards social projects, including redevelopments of slum areas by students such as Max Lock. Some of these became converted, in effect, into communist cells, by students such as Richard Llewelyn Davies. In January 1935 Rowse further enhanced the profile of planning in the AA by founding the postgraduate School of Planning and Research for National Development (SPRND); housed at 7 Bedford Square, it was renamed in 1940 the School of Planning and Research for Regional Development. The SPRND was intended as a multidisciplinary centre for promotion of modern regional planning, with influential correspondence courses organised by CIAM stalwart Jaqueline Tyrwhitt. It rapidly expanded to a two-year course, and in a brochure of 1935 Rowse gushed that its work, rooted in social 'reality' rather than 'academic isolation', had 'little or no precedent', in 'welding the work of the Engineer, Surveyor, Architect and Local Government Officer together with that of the Economist, Sociologist and the Politician into that of the Planner'.[56]

Rowse's initiatives left a tangle of leads that would permeate the post-war world of public architecture. But Matthew became connected to the planning movement far more directly and fruitfully through the second key academic appointment of 1933: that of Lionel Budden, in succession to Reilly, as director of the Liverpool School of Architecture. Ironically, this connection stemmed not from Matthew's own efforts but from his marriage to Lorna, whose mother was a close friend of Budden's wife Maud. Budden had already been de facto head of the school during and since the war, and had helped Reilly design its new building in 1933. Like J F Matthew with Lorimer, Budden had played the role of office manager for the flamboyant Reilly, whose boastful biography he dismissed as 'an amusing work of light fiction'. Budden steered the school towards Modernism in a far quieter, more incremental manner than Rowse at the AA, introducing group-working and social projects alongside continued drilling in

2.13 Double photograph of the Matthews' summer 1933 visit to Liverpool. *Top view*: Abercrombie, Budden and Robert Matthew; *bottom view*: Lorna Matthew and Maud Budden. (EULMC)

2.14 1933 photograph by Robert Matthew of the brand-new Slussen transport interchange in Stockholm (seen from the south, with the old town in background). (EULMC)

holder of the Lever chair of town planning at Liverpool. He was also able to renew his acquaintance with Holford, who had now acquired socialistic world views and an associate professorship, and was fast building up research-based group working in the department.[58]

During the early 1930s, while his Lorimer & Matthew and college work brought him a meagre income, Robert's career hopes were pinned mostly on postgraduate research, spanning the two years following his Cates Prize win in 1932. Where Spence had made relatively little of his Cates win, Robert, under the influence of Rowse, had plunged voraciously into a variegated research programme, orientated towards the reformist agenda of research-driven housing and planning that formed the core of the Modern Movement in Britain. As appropriate for one inclined towards a compartmentalised, detached stance, Robert's location in Edinburgh allowed him to soak up unobtrusively all the information and propaganda produced by the London architectural intelligentsia, and to keep in touch with the steady progress in the Liverpool School.

To be sure, in the face of the mounting economic and political crisis, Robert Matthew, like many of his architectural contemporaries, felt frustration and alienation from the traditional parliamentary parties, and alarm at the violent expansion of fascism: visiting the Bauhaus in Dessau, he was dismayed to find that it had been converted into a domestic science school. In uneasy parallel with the continuing measured individualism of his own private life, Robert eagerly engaged in his career with the collectivist, galvanising spirit of the times. But this entanglement was not filtered through politics as such, and Robert's political views shifted, at most, from the Liberalism of his family towards a moderate Fabian socialism. He had no time for communist zealotry, but instead passionately engaged with the collectivist ideologies and concerns of architecture itself – above all, with the linked issues of housing and planning. Partly under

the Orders, and training a range of influential younger Modernists such as Max Fry, Donald Gibson and, in the early 1930s, the young Anglo-Indian brothers Stirrat and Percy Johnson-Marshall.[57] At a town planning summer school in Liverpool in summer 1933 Robert met not only the newly appointed Budden, but also a range of colleagues, including above all Patrick Abercrombie, doyen of interwar town planning in Britain, and

Rowse's influence, he had come to believe fervently in the need to address the housing of the ordinary people, and that this was *the* key architectural challenge of the age. For him, it was the disinterested experts, including architects, who could best guarantee social justice and solve the spreading problem of the slums. In the 1950s Matthew put this straightforwardly to a group of his students in Edinburgh: 'The job of an architect, quite simply, is to solve other people's problems.'[59]

Although the focus of Robert's research would, inevitably, eventually be the innovative housing design movements of the Continent, he meticulously began with a vast, somewhat Geddesian (or Rowse-like) trawl of environment-related aspects of current affairs. For example, a Low cartoon, cut out from the Manchester *Guardian* in May 1934, showed an inefficient Parliament, swathed in overcoats, sweltering under the intense sun of the dictatorships. For many an aspiring Modern architect Germany was the clear focus of architectural and political concern, and with typical catholicity Robert showed some attraction to all the different varieties of rationalist German architecture, traditionalist as well as Modern.[60] In 1933 and 1934 Robert augmented this reading with the essential supplement of foreign touring – now not just to sketch old buildings, but mainly to take photographs, with his folding Kodak camera. In both cases the focus of the trip was Germany, with add-on trips to Denmark, Sweden and the Netherlands: in all these he photographed and sketched a mixture of urban vernacular houses, churches and modern housing and public buildings. During both visits the atmosphere was highly charged, and the 1933 trip coincided with the Reichstag fire, which ushered in Hitler's consolidation of power: 'We saw the brownshirts and blackshirts careering round Berlin on motorcycles, and were there when Hitler drove from the Wilhelmstrasse to the Reichstag to deliver his speech following the fire.'

First projects: the Mercia Memorial

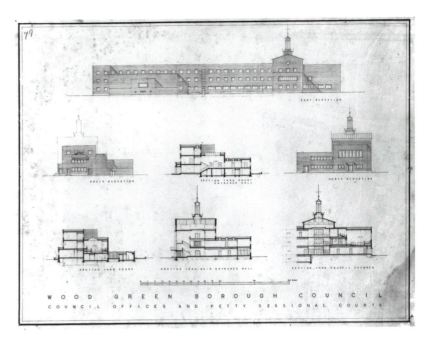

and the Bossom Studentship

Part of the luck of Matthew's career stemmed from the way in which advances and opportunities emerged at seemingly exactly the right time. As Stuart put it, 'It all seemed almost to be "timed": one thing seemed to go into another like a sort of jigsaw.' And sure enough, while Lorna and Robert were in Berlin, in July 1934 news came through that Robert had won an Andrew Grant Bequest Fellowship – a further ECA scholarship that would pay (at £250 p.a.) for two postgraduate years of further research on housing and planning, up until 1936. The Andrew Grant research, as we shall see shortly, would lead directly to further opportunities. At the same time, to supplement his otherwise still meagre income, Robert had already embarked on a series of entries for public architectural competitions. Mostly, these were for municipal headquarters complexes, and were approached in a pragmatic, somewhat staid way, making no attempt at Modernist innovation. Drawings survive for eight separate competitions of this kind between 1933 and 1937, showing a gradual evolution in style from Beaux Arts classicism to a Dudok-like asymmetrical Modernity, with spindly, Stockholm-like towers. The first, for Prestwick Burgh Chambers and Public

2.15 Competition entry of c.1937 by Matthew and Reiach for Wood Green Borough Council headquarters, Middlesex. (EULMC)

Education and re-orientation

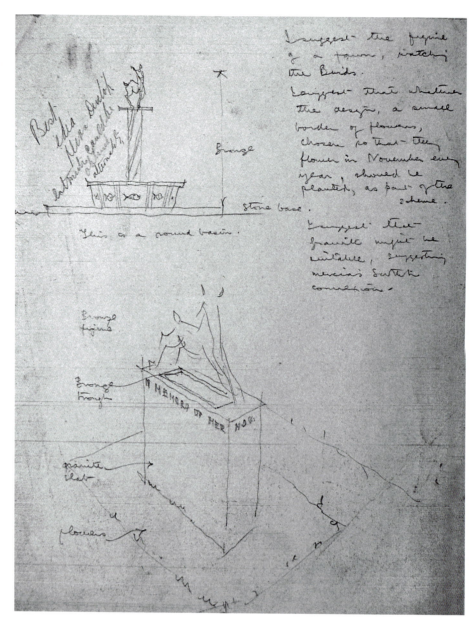

Baths, in April 1933, was done with Reiach's help, under the aegis of Lorimer & Matthew, but by 1935 Robert was entering competitions jointly with Reiach and Robert Scott Morton, using his private address: the general approach of all these was classical, axial and neo-Georgian.

None of these competition entries came to fruition – but in November 1934 an unexpected family tragedy brought Robert his first, small-scale executed commission, in a somewhat different classical manner from the monumental Beaux Arts, after Lorna's 12-year-old sister Mercia died from diabetes-related complications at the Pilchers' home in the

Manchester suburb of Sale. Born in Craigmillar Park and initially raised in Edinburgh, with Lorna devotedly involved in her upbringing, Mercia had moved to Sale with her parents when Stuart Pilcher took up his Manchester Corporation job in 1930. There she developed an intense love of nature and animals, as well as the beginnings of the nostalgia of the expatriate Scot: her head teacher at Culcheth Hall School, Altrincham, recalled in a memorial album that 'as a true daughter of Edinburgh, her eyes shone when the city or its famous men came under discussion.' Although Mercia's body was brought back to Edinburgh for burial, at Liberton Cemetery, the distraught Stuart and Louisa Pilcher decided also to commission a small monument to her in the grounds of their home in Sale, and, as Mercia had been a frequent and happy visitor to Robert and Lorna's Lamancha cottage during her holidays, it seemed only natural that Robert should be asked to design the memorial. He suggested two alternative designs, a rectangular granite slab and a slender bronze column in a round basin, in either case to be surmounted by 'the figure of a faun, watching the birds': the figure would be commissioned from sculptor Phyllis Bone (1894–1972), who had worked extensively on the Scottish National War Memorial. A small floral border would also be planted, so as to flower in November each year. The Pilchers chose the second, columnar alternative: the finished monument, largely in stone rather than bronze, echoed in a modest way the classical delicacy and humanity of the Scandinavian examples Robert had recently seen and sketched – such as Carl Milles's 1928 fountain in the courtyard of Ivar Tengbom's Swedish Match Company headquarters, with its column set in a pool and topped by a figure of Diana awakening the woodland animals.[61] The shock of Mercia's death triggered the virtual collapse of her mother, with a series of strokes in the following years, which soon left her chair-bound. For Lorna, too, the death of her little sister was a devastating blow, and may well have prompted her and Robert to begin immediately trying to start their own family.

By early 1935, however, Robert was hard at work on his Andrew Grant studies, which rapidly led him away from any of the interwar variants of stately classicism. In a report written in collaboration with W T Sutherland, he listed two main areas of research, 'Scottish Traditional Architecture' and 'Housing and Town-Planning', whose juxtaposition reflected the traditionalist and Geddesian insistence on the old as a context for the new. In the standard rhetoric of the 1930s, he contrasted the supposedly corrupt

2.17 Memorial to Mercia Pilcher, 1934: photograph of the completed sculpture. (photographer unknown)

2.18 Photograph by Robert Matthew of slums in the St Leonards area of Edinburgh South Side. (EULMC)

fussiness of 19th-century eclectic Scotch Baronial with the wholesome inspiration of the 'fine, simple work which has remained through a hundred years of decadence', echoing proto-preservationists such as the Marquess of Bute and Ian Lindsay by stressing the urgent need to survey old Scots burgh houses 'before all traces are obliterated by the rush of mediocre contemporary work'. But this recording of the old, he insisted, should be paralleled by confident modern 'Planning for the Social Body', focusing on slum redevelopment with mass housing.[62]

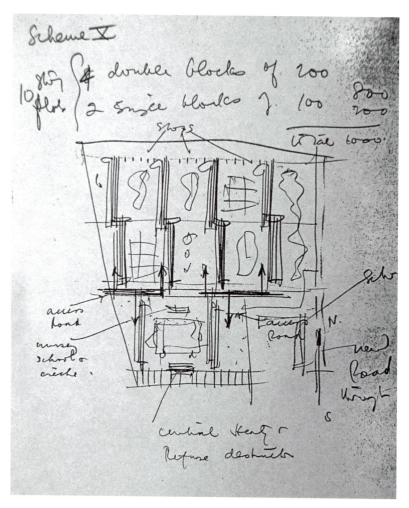

2.19 1935 layout sketch by Robert Matthew for Bossom Studentship redevelopment proposal. (EULMC)

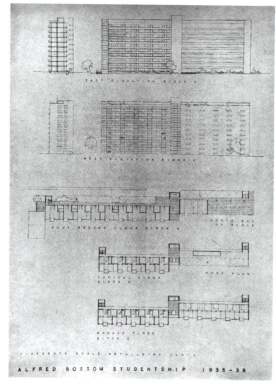

2.20 Drawings of *Zeilenbau* slab blocks from Matthew's Bossom Studentship entry, 1935/6. (published in *JRIBA*, 22 February 1936, 397) (EULMC)

Robert Matthew began his own redevelopment study by undertaking a Geddes-style survey of a slum area of Edinburgh, St Leonards – an area of working-class tenements overlooking Holyrood Park. Here he now had another, more specific purpose in mind. He had decided to enter for the Alfred Bossom Travelling Studentship, another RIBA-based competition, instituted in 1925 by the renowned skyscraper enthusiast, which provided for a study tour of 'commercial architecture' in the United States, and whose 1935/6 subject was slum clearance. Clearly a research- and survey-based programme of Modernist replanning was called for, and Matthew's entry, which won the first prize, was completed on the basis of an exceptionally detailed investigation (with Lorna's help) of St Leonards, social and economic as much as spatial, including a survey of 1,500 files of individual slum families in collaboration with the Corporation Public Health Department. The survey analysis was dramatised with rhetoric in the time-honoured tradition of Medical Officer of Health slum exposés. Alongside these colourful descriptions were presented complex analyses of wages, grocery costs and household budgets, as a basis for extrapolating possible rentals, building heights and constructional/contractual costs of a redevelopment scheme. He and Lorna had been profoundly shocked by the degraded conditions they had discovered – an aspect of their own city of which they had previously been unaware. Matthew also canvassed background information from other sources, including Leeds's Modernist-leaning City Architect, R A H Livett, who sent him confidential information, including accommodation schedules, on the Quarry Hill flats project in November 1935.[63]

Matthew's approach here reflected the most up-to-date ideas of Geddesian planning based on social survey, then being taught in London by Rowse at the AA, and, slightly earlier, proselytised in a rhetorical 1934 exhibition by the Modernist architecture research group 'MARS'. Many other exhibitions and articles on slum development during the mid/late 1930s followed a similar course, proceeding from research-led, inductive aspirations to deductive, slogan-led reality.[64] Also largely standard was the architectural formula for what should replace the slums: layouts of slab blocks of flats, both low-rise (up to five storeys) without lifts, and on the ten-storey high-rise model established by Brinkman and van der Vlugt's newly completed Bergpolder slab in Rotterdam, and by Lubetkin & Tecton's Highpoint 1 in Highgate. These should be laid out in the strictly parallel *Zeilenbau* layout, optimised for daylight and sunlight, popularised in the publications of Ludwig Hilberseimer and Le Corbusier, and the early 1930s housing projects of Gropius.[65] The years from 1933 saw a Niagara of research initiatives into such blocks. From April 1934 onwards, for example, the *AJ* published a series of supplements on London and foreign 'housing achievements', all of which were collected methodically by Robert Matthew as part of his Bossom research. Generally, steel-framing and balcony access on the Bergpolder model or, less frequently, reinforced concrete construction were assumed.[66] Very often, the results were presented polemically, linking Modern flats and the greenery of the garden city as a joint remedy for the chaos of laissez-faire. For Matthew, Reiach and others at ECA, a special stimulus stemmed from a visit to Edinburgh in 1934 by Gropius, who argued that 12-storey slab blocks assured an optimum level of light, air and building economy.[67]

Robert Matthew's Bossom proposal for the replacement housing of 'his' redevelopment area followed this by now standard manifesto formula of tall *Zeilenbau* slabs, arguing that the advocacy of integrated, multidisciplinary research would allow social architecture to progress beyond mere simple functionalism and 'at last to receive the breath of imagination'.[68] For the moment, all this still seemed, like most other CIAM-type exercises, to lie mainly in the realms of propaganda; but the very next year, as we shall shortly see, Matthew would take the first essential step towards putting his ideas into practice – by moving himself out of the private practice world into the newly central arena of official government architecture and planning.

The Foundations of Social Reconstruction

Chapter 3

Public architect and regional planner, 1935–46

The gradual decay of the Humanitarian
  way
Was a thing I contemplated with anxiety.
Yet all I could suggest, in a world that's
  headed west
Was to turn again to Presbyterian piety.
But the fathers of the Church had rather
  left us in the lurch
By concentrating on the problems of sobri-
  ety.
Now unless we're fairly slick, with a trump
  to turn the trick
There simply won't be any more Society!

Robert Matthew, 'double clerihew'

dated 8 May 1940

Abercrombie was absolutely decisive, in
teaching him to go for the people that
mattered – to go for power – to go for the
grand design.

Aidan Matthew, 1997

Public servant, private life: Robert Matthew in the late 1930s

If the 20th-century period of state control of the built environment now seems an aberration, for the young architects emerging into the system in the mid 1930s this context constituted an ever-more overwhelming reality. Just as Robert Matthew's careful collections of news cuttings and articles recorded the apparent bankruptcy of conventional liberal bourgeois politics, so in architecture, too, the conventional system of pupillage, private practice and elite building projects – the world that had buoyed Lorimer (and John Matthew) to success –

3.1 Late 1930s self-portrait photo by Matthew at his flat, 12 Darnaway Street, Edinburgh. (EULMC)

now seemed threadbare and discredited. 'Social building' and planning for the people were what was demanded, and the state seemed the obvious architectural patron and, increasingly, employer.

Within the civil service, these years saw a correspondingly radical shift away from the self-contained, non-specialist 'administrative' tradition towards the wholesale co-opting of academics – a convergence between government and academia that began in World War I, in the careers of men such as J M Keynes, who felt an increasingly visceral respect for state managerial initiative and contempt for private enterprise.[1] In Scotland, the collapse of the old, imperialist military-industrial structure produced a vehement reaction, even in Edinburgh, shielded from the worst of the slump.

Under the system of gradually deepening Scottish administrative devolution since 1885, all aspects of social building had by the 1930s come under the oversight of the Scottish Office, a Whitehall ministry itself divided into four subordinate departments. Most aspects of social welfare, including housing and planning, were the responsibility of the largest of these, the Department of Health for Scotland (DHS), which by 1939 contained 800 staff, and was pursuing a methodical agenda of planned interventionism.[2] The DHS had its own architectural section, which involved itself in the national programme of council housing through its vetting of housing and slum-clearance schemes put forward for government loan sanction by local authorities. The section also advised on the architectural work of the other Scottish Office departments, and prepared reports or circulars on exemplary practice. Later, during World War II, this advisory role would also be extended to the field of strategic town and country planning; by 1944 the section would contain nearly 40 people, including nearly twice as many young planners as architects.

In 1935, however, all this potential lay in the future, and the section consisted of four elderly architects, all inherited from the former Board of Health, led by John Wilson and his deputy G D Macniven. Wilson had had a distinguished career, having followed private practice from 1892 until 1910 (latterly as lead designer in J M Dick Peddie's large office); thereafter, as Architectural Inspector to the Local Government Board, he drew up an important report in 1917 advocating the large-scale, government-backed building of working-class garden suburbs. By 1935, sensing he had been left behind by the march forward of the interventionist state, and the mounting demand for 'comprehensive' solutions based on scientific research into 'needs' and 'standards',[3] Wilson was beginning to articulate pressure for a modest expansion in his section. This pressure was built up from two specific sources. First, he faced a likely rise in casework stem-ming from new 1935 housing legislation, which set more exacting standards for overcrowding. Second, there had been a gradual build-up of pressure from the architectural establishment against the utilitarian planning and architecture of typical council housing schemes: these, Wilson suggested in early 1935, were conceived not in terms of 'community planning' but 'merely as units of accommodation unrelated to their environment'. Like Matthew, Wilson felt that Scotland should take inspiration from modern continental housing, and in 1935 a deputation, led by DHS Secretary John Highton, toured a number of West/Central European countries (e.g. Germany, Austria and the Netherlands) and published a report that praised the more unified, open-planned European schemes.[4]

By late 1935 Wilson had secured authorisation for a new junior post of Assistant Architect, which was duly advertised in October. Continuing their friendly rivalry, both Matthew and Spence applied for this DHS post – in Matthew's case, on the strong advice of Lionel Budden.[5] Spence was also now married, and living in a cottage outside Edinburgh, at Milton Bridge. He was actually the more experienced in council housing design, as his private-practice work with William Kininmonth (in the Rowand Anderson & Paul & Partners practice) had included no less than four public housing schemes in East Lothian and Berwickshire, and a small town-planning scheme at Dunbar. But Matthew seemed subtly the more intellectually heavyweight of the two, and the more attuned to the modern era of research and programme building, with his already-established interest in continental housing, and the sophistication and methodical industry of his Bossom report. Provoked by the shock of his slum fieldwork, he had also acquired an emotional passion over the 'housing question' that was to motivate him for the rest of his life – a driving social idealism that was entirely absent from Spence's world outlook. Accordingly Matthew, rather than Spence, was awarded the job – in itself a humble post, but one that was to form the springboard for his entire subsequent career, as well as, arguably, to shut Spence off from participation in the state sector. Thereafter, their divergent orientations became self-reinforcing, as Matthew gravitated towards social architectural practice and Spence towards a more traditional, private-practice model. In later life they would occasionally compete or collaborate on particular projects, but never again would they compete head to head over something that could change the course of their careers. For Robert, the move to government architecture also had the benefit of distancing him from the possibility of ever having to work under a 'big boss' in private practice, as had his father before him with Lorimer.

Robert began his new job, based at the DHS branch office at 125 George Street, in early May 1936, forgoing the American trip that his Bossom win had earned; galling though this must have been, the cosmopolitan travels of his later career would compensate for this sacrifice a hundredfold. The security of a civil service post seemed particularly irresistible as Lorna was now at last (after the distress of at least one miscarriage) expecting their first child: a boy, born at Darnaway Street in July and named Robert Aidan (known as Aidan); their second child, Janet Frances Catriona, was born over two years later in March 1939, also in Darnaway Street. The three years prior to the beginning of World War II were dominated by an ad hoc juggling of the demands of Robert's new job with a continuing variety of behind-the-scenes private initiatives to supplement his limited salary and further his career.

This somewhat schizophrenic existence accentuated Robert's already compartmentalised approach to his life. He finished off, in the evenings and weekends, a new private house in the Grange, at 14 Kilgraston Road, that he had begun designing under Lorimer & Matthew auspices for Dr Kemp-Smith: white-painted, steep-gabled, somewhat Lorimerian but more simplified and with modernistic

3.2 Alan Reiach seen c.1938 in the drawing room of his flat at 14 Randolph Place, Edinburgh. (EULMC)

interiors. His competition entry work continued, almost all for towns in England, but he still had to be careful of criticisms by local Edinburgh architects of the propriety of a salaried architect competing with private practice. Income was supplemented by taking in a succession of lodgers in Darnaway Street, beginning with Alan Reiach. Although Alan was present in the house at the time of Aidan's birth, he left straight afterwards, and took a nearby flat at 14 Randolph Place. These were the years when Robert and Alan were at their closest, with the constant collaboration on competitions, usually at nights or on unofficial days off: 'Alan always thought it was fearfully funny, when Robert was exhausted from working through the night on something, the way that he'd say to Wilson, "I have to be at home today for a family gathering!", or that he'd had an attack of lumbago!' Reiach was intensely influenced both by contemporary Scandinavia and by the growing concern with 'vernacular' Scottish architecture, and fed those elements in Robert's outlook.[6]

Robert and Lorna subsequently took a succession of other lodgers in Darnaway Street, not least to provide childcare for Aidan. First came a Miss Inez Arnold, Swiss co-founder of the Edinburgh Rudolf Steiner School (see below), who acted also

(above left) **3.3** Sketch by Robert Matthew of eastward view (along Heriot Row) from his flat at 12 Darnaway Street. (EULMC)

(below right) **3.4** Family gathering at Longside, Aberdeenshire, 1936. From left to right: William Scott (cousin of Lorna's mother); Lorna; Aidan (six weeks old); Aunt 'Nelly' Scott; Robert. (EULMC)

as a Waldorf-style 'governess' for the infant Aidan, and then a paid German au pair named Francisca, who was interned at the outbreak of war. Constant travel now, for the first time in Robert's life, became the norm, and another car, a Morris tourer, was bought – and soon nearly wrecked in an accident with a tram, when under tow one day with Stuart at the wheel, at the junction of Palmerston Place and West Maitland Street. Inevitably – as so often following the birth of a first child – there was now something of a deterioration in Robert and Lorna's relationship. Robert's absences, coupled with the stresses of the new baby, left Lorna feeling even more isolated, fluctuating between emotional dependence and resentment at the curtailment of their old, carefree existence. The Edinburgh grouping to which Robert and Lorna belonged continued to emphasise an artistic sensitivity, displaying an aversion to any simple authoritarian morals, and a leaning towards a certain elitist fluidity in personal relationships. All this existed in a strange, almost schizophrenic tension with the new emphasis on scientific rationalism, and the friendships that stemmed from that. For example, Robert in 1938 met for the first time someone who was soon to be a great ally: Bill Allen, a Canadian architect and acoustician working at BRS, who visited Edinburgh on official business and was

introduced to Robert, then 'living on scholarships', by Bobby Carter, the influential socialist RIBA librarian and editor of the *Architects' Journal*.[7]

Robert and Lorna also channelled their strong personalities towards various shared goals, to considerable effect. For example, this was a time, partly under Lorna's influence, of a final and decisive separation from the authority of Robert's mother. Annie's exasperation with Robert and Lorna bubbled up impotently, for example, when they decided against a conventional nursery-school education for the infant Aidan, and instead became involved in the setting up in 1939, in Edinburgh, of Scotland's first Rudolf Steiner School. The school had been co-founded by Robert's old friend Dr Pelham S Moffat, along with English-born teacher Helen St John and the Matthews' Darnaway Street lodger, Inez Arnold, who impressed on them the anthroposophical educational ethos of hostility to modern materialism and 'premature intellectualisation'. Initially the school was confined to 3–8-year-olds, with Helen St John the first kindergarten teacher; Miss Arnold provided the equivalent of a Steiner kindergarten for Aidan at the Darnaway Street flat. Predictably, Robert soon rose to become chairman of the school committee, and original organiser, along with Pelham, of the school's initial accommodation. Although Rudolf Steiner

Modern Architect

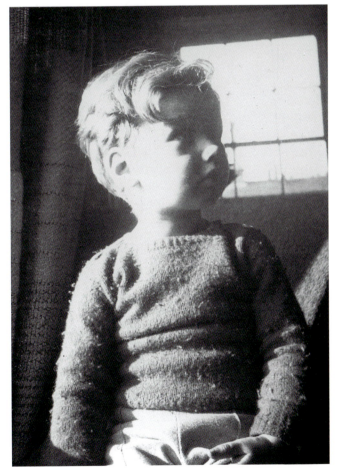

subconscious, as suggested also by his fascination, in later life, with synthesising architectural philosophies.[8]

Partly in reaction to the estrangement from Annie, correspondingly relations with Stuart became very close for a while: in the late 1930s, for example, Robert helped Stuart design some furniture for Loretto School Chapel, originally enlarged by Lorimer & Matthew. Stuart would often borrow Robert's car – for example, for an icy winter trip to London to see a celebrated Chinese art exhibition in the same years. Shortly after Reiach's departure from Darnaway Street,

(above left) **3.5** Photograph taken by Reiach at an unidentified railway station on an excursion, *c.*1939. From left: Julie Dittmar, Robert Scott Morton, Aidan Matthew, Lorna Matthew, Elspeth Morton, Robert Matthew. (EULMC)

(above right) **3.6** Photograph by Robert Matthew of interior of 12 Darnaway Street, 1940. (EULMC)

(left) **3.7** Photograph by Robert Matthew of Aidan at 12 Darnaway Street, *c.*1938. (EULMC)

himself attached great importance to architecture as a potential synthesis of the arts, it seems unlikely that Robert was specifically interested in the architectural aspects of anthroposophy. The attraction may instead have been when Stuart fell ill with impetigo – a disfiguring facial rash – Robert and Lorna invited him to stay at Darnaway Street for several months.[9]

As the threat of war and the fear of mass bombing grew in 1938/9, at a time

57

Public architect

3.8 View of c.1939 of Hamilton House, Prestonpans, showing the large walled garden. (EULMC)

when Lorna was expecting their second child, they began to think of moving the main family base out of Edinburgh. Robert became aware, through his slum clearance work in DHS (on which see below), that a dilapidated 16th-century town house, Hamilton House, in the small coastal town of Prestonpans, ten miles east of Edinburgh, was scheduled for demolition as a slum: it had been divided into six working class single-ends with outside WC on the wooden stairs. Prestonpans was a small historic town that now stood in a mining area, swamped by industrial development and population. Its Labour town councillors, some of communist sympathies, were, like many others across Scotland, now set on complete demolition of the historic High Street, and redevelopment with council housing under the powers of the 1935 Housing Act. By the late 1930s, with the tacit support of DHS Secretary John Highton, the most egregious excesses of municipal slum clearance were being moderated by the pioneering lists of historic burgh houses being drawn up under NTS auspices by architect Ian Lindsay, with finance by the 4th Marquess of Bute. Lorna went to look at Hamilton House, and immediately enthused Frank Mears and Robert Hurd, a conservationist architect much involved in the Saltire Society (founded 1936) and the slightly older National Trust for Scotland (1931). Mears and Hurd persuaded NTS to take it on and restore it, with East Lothian County Council overcoming the demolition plans of the town councillors, and in early 1939 Lorna, Robert, Aidan and baby Janet moved in, as the Trust's first tenants.

Lamancha was now given up, but 12 Darnaway Street was kept on, however, until around 1940 as a town base, beginning a pattern – New Town flat and country 'castle' – reminiscent (perhaps unconsciously) of the Lorimers, and which would re-emerge on a more grandiose scale in the mid 1950s.[10]

In the short time before war began to disperse Robert's Edinburgh circle, Hamilton House became the centre of a lively social life – an existence within which the schizophrenic tendencies of the late 1930s, between public collectivist conformity and private individualism, were expressed to the full. Friends would come round to help gather potatoes from the garden, and then, in the evening, come into the house and make merry.[11] Elspeth Morton (later Hardie) recalled that

we often went down for the wonderful parties at Hamilton House, hosted of course by Robert. Lorna was organiser-in-chief, helped by various people, as her children were small. Robert was great fun, but he couldn't have done these events without Lorna – for example, if there was someone he didn't specially like, Lorna was rather good at keeping them occupied and happy. Although he must have been formidable if crossed, I never once saw Robert losing his temper.

Elspeth's architect brother Robert, who was by then (as we shall see) a close colleague of Robert at DHS, recalled that

Hamilton House was such a delightful building – white harled, two storeys – and although 'conservation' was a word I never heard from Robert in those days, he certainly loved that house at Prestonpans – more than any other he lived in, I think. It was full of 'Old Scottish' character, with a long room through which Robert would stride, at parties, reciting clerihews he'd made up. He'd compose them completely on the spur of the moment, with a high-class, rapier-sharp wit. But Robert would only unwind like this with a few friends.[12]

Robert's Hamilton House circle also showed increasing leanings towards a more cosmopolitan lifestyle. For example, he and Lorna befriended a young German émigré, Hildegard Luft, who had settled in Edinburgh after her Scottish mother had become estranged from her father, largely on account of his Nazi sympathies; her two brothers remained in Berlin during the war. She was a frequent visitor to Hamilton House, coming down especially at the weekends to play the piano, and after the war she became involved in refugee resettlement, based in Vienna, and occasionally kept in touch with Robert and Lorna.[13]

Foundation-building: life as a junior government architect, 1936–9

Set alongside the ambition and confidence already evident in his private persona, Robert Matthew's official duties at first seemed disappointingly humble in character. Twenty-five years later he recalled that within DHS in the 1930s, unlike local-authority executive architects such as Livett, the architect-cum-expert was a mere 'second-class citizen', kept on the fringes of authority, well

below 'the stratosphere of policy makers'.[14] The role of the architects formed part of a strictly regulated procedure in which plans of proposed public housing schemes, whether by in-house or private consultant architects, were vetted, from a strictly 'architectural' point of view, without reference either to the wider town-planning context or even to the relation of one housing project to another. Robert Scott Morton recalled that

all there was in the office was four old men and Robert. John Wilson was quite elderly, very dignified, white haired, but not terribly progressive. He certainly didn't have much interest in town planning. His deputy, Macniven, was also getting on, and they must have felt rather embarrassed privately about being so unaware of the Modern Movement. You can imagine that he breathed a new spirit into the office, and began to persuade Wilson to take in younger people – including myself![15]

Matthew later claimed, of his early casework, that

The only results I was able to achieve were, first, continually to annoy the administrative machine by querying the wisdom of allowing small groups

3.9 Photograph by Robert Matthew of East Saltoun council housing scheme, East Lothian, 1937. (EULMC)

of houses to be planted everywhere and anywhere regardless of convenience, topography, community facilities or further development, [and, second,] to boost up in a very minor way the deplorable designs continually submitted for office approval by surveyors and others (there was even one case where the house was designed by the local undertaker) and to try to make those buildings very slightly resemble the traditional buildings they were fondly imagined by their designers to be.[16]

One of Matthew's most regular activities stemmed from the frequent requests from local authorities to the department to produce a revised layout or elevation design for a contentious scheme. Hitherto these adjustments had been dominated by utilitarian considerations of economy – for example, in avoiding excessive road frontages, or in adjusting the proportions of different house sizes. Matthew, however, emphasised the need to encourage more unified designs, generally in a traditionalist manner similar to Lorimer & Matthew schemes of the early 1930s such as the Douglas Haig Memorial Homes. For example, in the late 1930s, in the village of East Saltoun, a group of East Lothian County Council houses with a shop at a focal point in the village centre, was designed in the form of two single-storey terraces flanking a higher block, the shop picked out by a columned entrance recess, all roofs pantiled in vernacular fashion, and the group fronted by a low, wavy rubble screen wall.[17]

By 1937 and 1938 Matthew was beginning to spread his wings by working on special proj-

ects for the Department. For example, in December 1937 a Kincardineshire councillor and rural housing reformist, G Herbert Russell, instigated a DHS/RIAS competition for a new range of rural housing types, to replace a now out-of-date range designed by Frank Mears and Leslie Grahame Thomson in 1932 for the Association for the Preservation of Rural Scotland. Wilson, with DHS colleague E A Hogan, organised the competition, and Matthew secured Mears's support. A range of drawings was submitted, including some (for a pair of cottages) drawn by Matthew in a private capacity. Following the competition, Matthew then prepared for DHS a range of standard workers' cottage types, all of one and two storeys, and of a simplified Lorimerian vernacular character with steep gables, shutters and water butts.[18]

In 1938 Matthew began to enjoy success in his attempts to expand the work of the architectural staff, which at that stage was still only six strong.[19] Another growing activity was that of advising on the designs of hospitals, and encouraging

3.10 1936 competition design by Matthew for 'A Pair of Cottages near Edinburgh'. (EULMC)

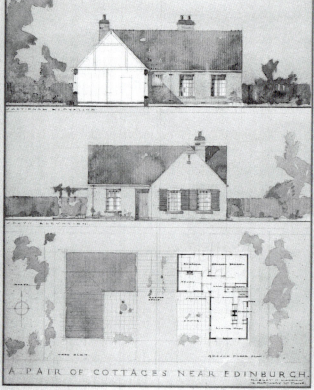

the building of health centres on the Finsbury and Peckham model as part of slum clearance schemes. For this purpose he secured the appointment of his friend Robert Morton, whom he also envisaged as a 'helper' in another, more important area of expansion – town planning.[20] Already, Matthew had persuaded Wilson to employ Mears as an occasional consultant, but from 1938 he got approval to begin building up a planning section within the department. Throughout 1937 he had assiduously prepared for this expansion by developing the work he had already carried out for his Andrew Grant and Bossom research – in particular, the project of an EAA-led civic survey of Edinburgh, and a propaganda exhibition designed to show local authorities 'how community planning fits into the whole framework of social life'. In all this, he drew heavily on the work of Geddes, Rowse and Abercrombie, with their emphasis on positive rather than negative planning, the need for regional solutions, and the scientific-humanist demand to fuse sociological expertise with 'the imagination of the Technician-Artist'.[21]

On the basis of this philosophy – essentially, a fusion of Geddesian culture-city utopianism with a more technocratic, mid-20th-century outlook – Matthew proceeded in 1937 with his plan of an EAA-led civic survey and town planning exhibition at the Royal Scottish Academy, organised by a group of Bossom students. The concept of the polemical town-planning exhibition, for the purpose of propaganda against laissez-faire chaos, grew steadily in popularity before and during World War II.[22] Matthew's planning exhibition was more modest in scale, but typical of the Geddesian propaganda genre. Edinburgh was seen as a Greek *polis*-style culture city, harmoniously embracing both the medieval Old Town and the classical New Town, whose integrity had been violated by the late 19th and early 20th centuries' materialistic unplanned development – whether harsh industry, jostling commercial affluence (as in Princes Street), or bungaloid

3.11 Edinburgh Architectural Association town-planning exhibition at Royal Scottish Academy, 1937.

suburban sprawl: 'The development of Edinburgh is the degeneration of a noble city into mediocrity.' The neotechnic remedy was clear: 'Planning is now a practical necessity: other British cities are planning – why not Edinburgh?' First there should be a 'complete survey' – material, scientific and cultural. Then, after that, 'a comprehensive plan is vitally necessary', including not just new building and rebuilding but 'conservation of the good remains'. It was typical of Matthew's Geddes-influenced approach, in contrast to the working-class materialism and communism of London contemporaries, that he should have focused exclusively on his native Edinburgh rather than on the industrial heartland around Glasgow. And however far he travelled, and however cosmopolitan he became later in his career, that east-coast rather than west-coast perspective on Scotland remained with him all of his life.[23]

By the late 1930s, however, Matthew recognised that, never having studied for any formal planning qualifications, he at least had to expand his planning work to a Scotland-wide scale, including Clydeside, as soon as possible. A first opportunity to do this came with the 1938 Empire Exhibition – a morale-boosting expo in a Glasgow park, sponsored by Clydeside industrialists and designed on

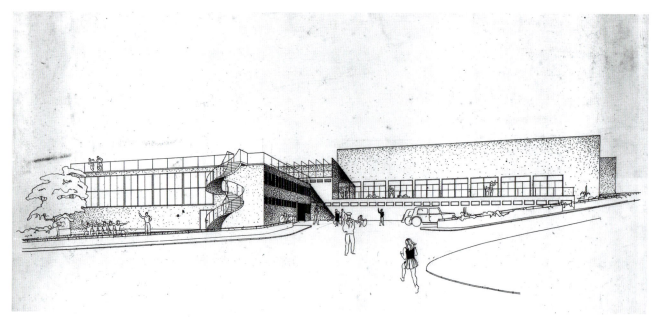

3.12 November 1938 perspective by Matthew of his and Reiach's competition-winning design for Ilkeston Community Centre and Fire Station. (EULMC)

a Modernistic Beaux Arts layout by Thomas Tait. Matthew acted as official government adviser to the town planning exhibition in the Scottish pavilion, and in February 1939 wrote thanking the conference secretary, and declaring that the exhibition work 'was good fun, which I thoroughly enjoyed', as a welcome respite from everyday officialdom.

Although war clouds were by now overshadowing the architectural and planning scene, Matthew's own unobtrusive private architectural activity continued up to the last moment, in the form of a notable competition success, whose built realisation was frustrated by the outbreak of war. In December 1938 he and Alan Reiach finally won one of their series of municipal office competitions, but now for a more openly Modern, social-orientated programme: a community centre and fire station to be built on two adjacent sites for the borough council of the East Midlands industrial town of Ilkeston. Their design, entered solely under Reiach's name (to avoid compromising Matthew's official post) was, actually, largely the work of Matthew, who prepared it, as usual, at night in between his DHS day work. Matthew's taste was clear in the severely rectilinear, flat-roofed profile of the buildings, somewhat in the style of the Bonatz school with its gridded lines of windows set in heavy

expanses of brick walling. The layout envisaged the placing of the two buildings in a *Zeilenbau* parallel relationship. Their project, won following a personal interview with the town clerk, finance committee chairman and borough treasurer, and with some advice from Lionel Budden, was unexecuted owing to the war's outbreak, but they both received £590 in fees in 1940.[24]

Wartime years of wandering

For Matthew, the outbreak of war at first brought a sudden reining-in of these growing opportunities, until new and far wider vistas eventually began to open up before him. For middle-class professionals like him the polarisation between public conformity and private individualism became stretched to the limits. On the one hand, within architecture as elsewhere there was the harsh rhetoric of disciplined national struggle. On the other hand, there was the reality of the disintegrative effect of wartime destruction on conventional family life, civic morality, social restraints and so forth. In the gap between rhetoric and reality, many ambitious younger men, like Matthew, found themselves presented with unexpected opportunities to exploit the disruptions of war, and begin forming the *mentalités* that would carry them on into post-war eminence.[25]

Most public architects, including the apolitical as well as the communistic, were stirred up by wartime rhetoric into a zeal to enlist in the armed forces, but mostly were prevented from doing so by being declared 'reserved'. This brought frustration to those of a patriotic or bellicose disposition, who were denied the glamour of a uniform and the well-nourished as well as often dangerous existence of the forces, but at the same time, with the mushrooming of public architecture and planning in the wartime context, put them all 'at an enormous advantage' compared with the private-practice architects who found themselves conscripted. Both Robert Matthew and Bill Allen (of BRS) found themselves 'reserved', and although Robert, with his family heritage of military service, then attempted to join the merchant navy, this too was turned down. He was finally reduced to serving in the Home Guard in Prestonpans, which had now become a restricted coastal defence zone, spending freezing nights standing around on muddy fields and beaches. In this role he was nearly shot one night, when on guard duty in 1941, by a fellow soldier who accidentally discharged his rifle while cleaning it: Matthew was asleep on a nearby bed, and a bullet thudded into the mattress an inch away from him.

For Robert's own family, the outbreak of war now largely negated the usefulness of the move to Hamilton House, although with rationing the garden now found an enhanced usefulness. In the first months of the war, following the attempted bombing of Rosyth and the Forth Bridge, Lorna evacuated herself and the children for several months to a cottage (belonging to a Mrs Bremner) in the rural northeast, near Rothiemurchus, and organised some local girls to help her with the household work. The Darnaway Street flat, being now redundant, was given up altogether. Within months the family were back in Prestonpans, and attempted to resuscitate the congenial atmosphere that had prevailed prior to the war – but gradually

3.13 1939 view of Briar Corner, Alderley Edge. (photographer unknown)

the existence there, too, became intolerable, as travel to and from Edinburgh now required constant showing of identity cards and traversing of barbed wire checkpoints.[26]

So, in 1941–2, a new plan was devised, more secure but leaving the family in a state of greater fragmentation. In anticipation of the family's evacuation, the Pilchers in 1940 had bought a spacious, half-timbered interwar bungalow, 'Briar Corner', in the elite Cheshire suburb of Alderley Edge. The entire Pilcher household now moved there, as an extended family that comprised not only Lorna's father (as Manchester Transport Manager a figure of consequence, picked up by chauffeur each morning) and chair-bound mother, but also her two aunts, Attie (Isabella Helen Niven) and Maimie (Mary Ingram Niven) – both retired nurses. At Alderley Edge, in 1942, Aidan started at a small local prep school, the Rileys School, but Lorna began to worry that he was being 'spoilt' by his doting grandparents, and so after another Hamilton House interlude he was moved two years later (1944), unwillingly, to Winstone's, a Steiner boarding school just outside Stroud in Gloucestershire. Janet stayed at Prestonpans and Alderley Edge with Lorna, and eventually started at the nearby nursery department of St Hilda's preparatory school. After VE Day finally lifted the bombing threat, Lorna and the children moved straight back to Prestonpans, and both Aidan and Janet embarked on almost two years at the Edinburgh Steiner School.[27]

During the wartime years Robert

followed a peripatetic existence, based largely in Hamilton House and travelling down to Manchester during holidays. Across Scottish and British society in general, the war was a time of maximum disruption to conventional family life and, indeed, of estrangement of husbands and wives.[28] Ironically, although Robert and Lorna's relatively bohemian pre-war life had avoided any staid nuclear-family stereotype, their own wartime existence, although mired in austerity, was far less disrupted than that of many. Over two and a half million women in Britain were almost completely deprived of the presence of their husbands for several years, whereas Robert was able to keep in far more frequent touch with the family, even after Lorna's move to Alderley Edge. Lorna travelled often up to Hamilton House, leaving the children in the care of Attie, Maimie and her father and mother (who, out of dislike of conventional grandparent titles, had dubbed themselves 'Jolly' and 'Loosie' for the benefit of Aidan and Janet). Of necessity, Robert's visits to Cheshire were irregular, and the separate pressures of his own work, and Lorna's childcare duties, made for a high level of stress. Lorna recalled that

On one occasion, he arrived for the weekend, exhausted. Aidan and Janet were dashing around making a commotion, and Robert said simply, 'I'm not sitting in the same room as those children!' – he just didn't have time for small children in those years! – so I had to get everyone to help me hump everything upstairs. Then, as I was pushing Aidan upstairs – he was only six – he turned round and said 'I'll report you to the SPCC!' It sounds funny in retrospect, but at the time it was all quite difficult!

In the more depopulated circumstances that now prevailed at Hamilton House, Robert and Lorna took in a succession of lodgers, to help especially with upkeep during their absences. First, in the middle of the war, there was Helen Lenman, a trainee doctor and cousin; her brother Andrew later became a professor at Ninewells Hospital. Then, around 1944, there came Paddy and Helen Mulgrew: a war-wounded, Prestonpans-born Royal Scots soldier and his California-born wife, a nurse who had tended him at the Edinburgh Royal Infirmary.

He had only one eye, half his face was shot off, and he was in a terrible way, with awful headaches – but he was able to stoke the fires and the boilers, and she helped with the housework. My parents gave them accommodation to make sure there was a constant presence in the house.

Matthew's official DHS workload immediately changed radically on the outbreak of war, and the number of architects in the office shrank gradually, from 13 in 1939 to eight in 1943. Matthew's main work between 1939 and 1943 was the design of base and auxiliary hospitals throughout Scotland for the Emergency Hospitals Service. This included, in Scotland, the construction of seven new standard hutted hospitals with 7,038 beds, and the conversion of other institutions, including 60 country houses, with a total of 3,426 beds, and two hotels (Gleneagles and Turnberry) with 910 beds. Immediately following the outbreak of war, his workload also included inspections of housing schemes to be finished off, and conversions of schools for ARP and shelter use. Following the heavy bombing of Clydebank in 1941, Matthew and two colleagues set off immediately to drive through the icy darkness to assess the still-burning ruins.

The construction of Scottish national planning

In June 1942 Budden sounded out Matthew about the possibility of taking up the directorship of Glasgow School of Art, shortly to become vacant: he wrote to Matthew that he had mentioned it to Holford, who had said 'you wouldn't look at it'.[29] In an echo of Holford's own wartime career trajectory (see below), Matthew's loyalty to DHS, and his growing status within the department, stemmed above all from his growing involvement, from 1941, in the town and regional planning side of its work – an involvement that became full time from the beginning of 1943. With his unerring eye for the exploitation of opportunity, he sensed that the wartime years had brought planning to a peak of confidence and prestige, and that the field was now wide open to the ambitious architect-planner.[30] This boost to his work would leave him, by the end of 1944, occupying the Chief Architect's post, as a successor to Wilson and Macniven. In only eight years Matthew had shot from the bottom to the top of the office, leaving him with the reputation, among English public architect colleagues, as 'the uncrowned king of Scotland', and providing him with the springboard for an even more daring career move in 1946.[31]

Across the architectural and planning world the gradual growth of confidence of eventual victory, after the Soviet and US entry into the war, stimulated the beginnings of preparation for post-war reconstruction in the built environment. This increasingly feverish activity, initially directed within government by the evangelical energy of BBC founder Lord Reith, appointed Minister of Works in October 1940, was all now grounded in the scientific humanist principles of research-based planning: at last, in the heat of the war, the 'boffin' could realise his destiny of transforming society and inaugurating the Neotechnic Age. The first strand of these efforts was that of the scientific transformation of the building process, especially through standardisation and industrialisation of mass housing, the proliferation of building studies, and the radical expansion of the BRS, founded in 1920.[32]

The second strand of the new, post-1941 reconstruction preoccupations was concerned with 'strategic' city and regional planning. This cause had been proselytised energetically before the war by private agencies such as Rowse's planning school and the TCPA, which called in 1939 for a 'National Planning Front', while writers such as Metropolitan Police Assistant Commissioner Alker Tripp advocated modernised, grade-separated roads.[33] In some occupied countries it continued 'underground', as in Poland or in France, with Le Corbusier's 'ASCORAL' planning-research collective. In Britain, however, it was now fully co-opted into central government by Reith, who moved, following his appointment as Minister of Works, to set up a Britain-wide national planning ministry to build on the Barlow, Uthwatt etc. reports – an initiative that spawned a plethora of working and research groups or boosted those already existing.[34] Encouraged by Reith, the RIBA set up a reconstruction committee in spring 1941, with a membership including influential younger Modern architects, such as Jane Drew and Leslie Martin; it produced two major London exhibitions in 1943 ('Rebuilding Britain' and 'London Master Plan') and a housing report in 1944. And Rowse's SPRND, revitalised with CIAM activist Jaqueline Tyrwhitt (1905–83) as head of its planning school in 1941–8, helped train a generation of British post-war planners in the Modern Movement's confidently scientific reconstruction philosophy.[35]

In 1942 Reith's departure from his Ministry of Works and Planning removed some of this evangelical crusading force, but the subsequent splitting-off of a dedicated Ministry of Town and Country Planning allowed a vast, multifaceted planning apparatus to emerge, and to generate a copious output of planning research and advocacy, all under the oversight of Bill Holford (with George Pepler as chief administrator).[36] In Scotland these debates were seen somewhat at second hand, filtered through the thick lens of the national identity question, as ably exploited by Tom Johnston, Churchill's newly appointed (February 1941) Labour Secretary of State. Johnston used the bogeyman of possible Scottish nationalist opposition to the war effort to block most Westminster attempts to construct new Britain-wide planned social welfare frameworks on the back of the wartime emergency. He later recalled that 'every now and then, some ingenious gentleman in London would exude a plan for a centralised planning of our industries or our housing'; he insisted, for example, on an equal role alongside Bevin in drafting the original National Health Service plan in 1944. Johnston set up a 'Council of State' of former Secretaries of State, soon renamed the 'Scottish Council on Post-war Problems' (SCPP), as a peg around which to hang autonomous policy developments, aimed at matching or blocking Westminster initiatives; it met for a total of 16 times between 1941 and 1945. In the field of planning, in July 1941, Johnston's first act was to ensure that Reith would not set up research groups working for him in Scotland, but would leave this to the SCPP – in other words, to DHS staff.[37]

In the same month, Reith conceded that Johnston should have oversight over strategic planning in Scotland. Motivated by these political concerns, rather than by any idealistic zeal for reconstruction, Johnston arranged for Matthew to be brought into the planning field straight away – initially part time, and then, from late 1942, full time – to begin overseeing the work of building up a research-based planning organisation within DHS, followed by the establishment of a separate strategic planning system based around separate east and west central Scottish planning authorities – all with the aim of drawing a 'chalk line at the Cheviots' that Reith could not ignore'.[38] Matthew began in 1941 by compiling a dossier, marked 'secret', on all the various aspects of planning research being covered by Reith's efforts, with the extent of Scottish coverage in each case. He scanned other publications, too: his copy of the 1941 *Ground Plan of Britain*, for instance, was firmly annotated in several places 'NOT in Scotland'. And his background reading extended into the social and political developments of the years of wartime alliance. In September 1941 senior planning administrator James McGuinness explained that while various groups were doing research for Reith on forward planning, and 'his mandate extends *de jure*, if not *de facto*, to Scotland', up to now no research groups were specifically work-

ing for him in Scotland, and 'it has been assumed that the Secretary of State for Scotland will deal with this.'[39] Thus, he advocated, the SCPP should 'set up an expert committee' to investigate equivalent forward planning questions to England and Wales. With Matthew's help he had drawn up a list of possible subjects: for example, a wartime social survey of popular attitudes to location of dwellings in towns was commissioned by DHS in 1943, to help in 'the planning of new urban communities'.[40]

At the end of 1942 Matthew's growing planning responsibility was reinforced by a rapid advance in his career. The years of waiting in the slightly uncomfortable position of 'a youngster surrounded by old men' now suddenly bore fruit, when the retirements were fixed first of Wilson (in March 1943) and then Macniven (in December 1944).[41] With the intention of grooming Matthew for the succession, there was a temporary split between architecture and planning: Macniven was appointed only acting Chief Architect, with oversight confined to the architects, whereas Matthew was appointed Deputy Chief Architect in sole charge of planning, with a £100 responsibility allowance on top of his £831 basic salary. By 1943 the department was left with an 'acute' shortage of architects – nearly 40 per cent down on 1939 – with which to cope with a multitude of new tasks, including preparation of plans for the new Scottish Housing Advisory Council, in addition to the established tasks of civil defence, work on a new programme of converting emergency hospitals for general civilian use, and rural housing improvement work.[42]

Of the two main strands of the DHS's post-war reconstruction preparations, one – that of industrialised housing – was increasingly delegated to J Austen Bent, while Matthew himself focused on the second element, that of planning. Negotiations with the Treasury came to a head in October 1944, with the DHS arguing that, with Macniven now in his 67th year, it was a matter of urgency to re-unify the Chief Architect post, and appoint Matthew to it: he was 'not holding a pistol to our heads', and had not used outside offers as a 'lever' in negotiation, but had expressed 'strong views about the salary of the Chief Architect's post', on the grounds that 'he will be letting the profession down by accepting less than the Chief Engineer'. The Treasury was warned that Matthew had had 'at least one tempting offer from outside', and 'could develop a lucrative practice as a planning consultant'. Eventually, Matthew was appointed to the Chief Architect post, with effect from 1 January 1945, at a pay rate of £1,400, the same as the Chief Engineer: his salary had risen meteorically in parallel with his promotion, doubling since 1941 (from £706 gross).[43]

How did Matthew set about his expansion of the Department's planning arm? Even prior to 1943, he had begun building up his corps of planners, beginning, unsurprisingly, with Alan Reiach. His family background had imbued him deeply with the Traditionalist ethos of loyalty to subordinate collaborators, but his own helpers were not craftsmen and women like the Clow brothers or Phyllis Bone, but Modernist researcher-architects and planners who could help him with particular aspects of his wider strategic initiatives. Among those helpers, Reiach was the one, at this stage, to whom he returned most repeatedly and loyally. Reiach had provided him with 'cover' for his competition activities, and Matthew returned the compliment, on the outbreak of war, and before his own move to a specifically planning-orientated role, by securing his appointment in late 1940 as a junior architect-planner, and as a planning researcher from September 1941. Reiach's short-lived marriage to Julie Dittmar followed immediately on his return to Scotland; he stayed at DHS until 1946, and, after Matthew's return from London to private practice in 1953, would for a time harbour vain hopes of being taken into partnership. In 1941, in a private capacity, Reiach and the architect-conservationist Robert Hurd published their polemical blast *Building*

Scotland – a short picture-book structured into the good–bad oppositions traditional in architectural polemic since Pugin's *Contrasts* a century before. Like Matthew's parallel 1935 research proposals on vernacular architecture and housing/planning, *Building Scotland* made a damning comparison between the 'harmony' of pre-industrial Scottish architecture and the supposed chaos of 19th-century commercial eclecticism, and called instead for a vigorous Functionalist planning, but one that was equally able to adopt a more harmonious, tradition-attuned face in the country and in historic towns. Robert Scott Morton, a younger sympathiser with the nascent Modernist world outlook, recalled of *Building Scotland* that 'Hurd did most of the writing while Alan did the photos – but over all this loomed Robert Matthew. He had an overwhelming presence, as an intellectual and a person.'[44]

From the beginning of his Deputy Chief responsibility in April 1943 Matthew began recruiting planning staff at a furious rate, in an attempt to match the research and survey teams already established in London by Holford, who headed the English reconstruction secretariat from 1942 and became MTCP Chief Technical Officer from 1943. Matthew's tasks included building up an entirely new organisation, comprising central and regional planning officers, a central mapping and information bureau, and a research staff working on general planning standards and new town planning techniques. Despite the previous political tension between the departments over overall planning responsibility, Matthew had established excellent working relations with Holford – whom he, of course, already knew well through his Budden links.[45] By June 1944 he was in charge of a planning team of 14, including some familiar names. Three regional planning officers, including T Arnold Jeffryes (formerly of Edinburgh School of Architecture, and Rowse's School of Planning and Research for Regional Development), and two supporting researchers, including Arthur Geddes, covered the country on a geographical basis. And a central team of researchers included Reiach along with David Spreull (seconded from Holford's staff in London) and Robert Littler. Matthew's policy was to take on a mixture of trusty personal acquaintances and talented young people, such as Mary Miller (later Tindall), a young AA architectural student, taken on in spring 1944 by Matthew to spend just over a year in the research team. She later recalled at length the mushrooming department's ad hoc atmosphere and wildly disparate workload, with many of the tasks allocated to her (such as walking round derelict industrial land in West Lothian mapping old pit heaps and quarries) being arguably more appropriate to a geographer than an architect.[46]

Regional planning in action: researching and writing the Clyde Plan, 1943–6

In addition to the building-up of its own staff, Matthew's new planning organisation also had a politically much more immediate and important task: to provide the support for three major regional plans authorised by Johnston – in the Clyde Valley, Southeast Scotland (i.e. Forth Valley and hinterlands), and East Central Scotland (i.e. Tayside) – again with the political aim of further shutting out the MTCP from Scottish affairs.[47] In the cases of the Clyde Valley and the Southeast, an eminent private consultant was appointed to prepare the report – Mears for the Forth and Patrick Abercrombie for the Clyde – but in both cases with a DHS planner as his deputy: Jeffryes for Mears, and Matthew himself for Abercrombie.[48] In the negotiations that preceded the start of work on the Clyde and Forth reports Matthew maintained a somewhat neutral public stance, while unobtrusively transferring his immediate planning allegiance from his old teacher, Mears, to the more influential and cosmopolitan Abercrombie. The negotiations were structured by the assumed primacy within Scottish planning issues of the 'Glasgow [or Clydeside] problem' – the conjunction of industrial

obsolescence, slum housing and 'outmoded' local authority boundaries. Nothing else – even the ongoing crisis of the Highlands, and certainly not the situation of Edinburgh and Eastern Scotland – could compare in infamy to this multifaceted, ever-ongoing crisis, especially in the way its definition was bound up with Labour Party political power. But the pre-war assumption that Glasgow Corporation could deal with its problems autonomously, especially by extending its boundaries and building peripheral housing schemes, was thrown into doubt by the Barlow Committee's wartime report of 1940, with its calls for strategic redistribution of population and industry overriding municipal boundaries.[49]

Despite his own past history as a left-wing firebrand, Johnston had no love of the entrenched Labour municipal barons of Glasgow Corporation, and these same radical Labour credentials gave him the authority to do something about it. He lost no time in trying to import the Barlow framework from early 1942 onwards. By March 1943, despite the growing protests of Glasgow Corporation, he had secured the agreement of all 28 of the Clydeside planning authorities to the reconstitution of the Clyde Valley Regional Planning Advisory Committee, and the appointment of a consultant to prepare an integrated regional plan. Johnston himself, for nationalistic reasons, favoured Mears as a Scot, but Sir William Whyte, secretary of CVRPAC and a senior Lanarkshire official who had served on Barlow with Abercrombie, strongly pressed for the latter, insisting that whereas Mears was 'just a planner', Abercrombie, as an 'architect, planner and humanist', would carry more weight with the Board of Trade in any negotiations on strategic relocation, especially in view of the prestige of his County of London and Greater London plans.[50] Abercrombie, who had been at the centre of national UK planning debates and garden city initiatives since 1914/15 – when he had won an influential planning competition for Dublin and, at the age of 36, had succeeded Adshead as civic design professor at Liverpool – was an obvious choice to front any attempt to confront the Glasgow city-engineering juggernaut. A product of the same cultured Liberal tradition as Keynes and Beveridge, Abercrombie shied away from extreme state-dominated solutions to the planning question, such as land nationalisation. His own personal interpretation of scientific humanism was characterised by a Geddesian fondness for socio-spiritual catchphrases, and a liking for Beaux Arts stately layouts: he argued that 'to the concepts of the sociologist and the discourses of the scientist must be added the imagination of the technician-artist, if we are to construct the environment in which the human organism may rightly function.'[51] In September 1943 Johnston reluctantly agreed to the appointment of Abercrombie as CVRP consultant, protesting that he would be too remote to do an effective job, but offsetting that by adding Matthew to the project team as a 'Scottish' deputy consultant. A West End house off Great Western Road at 3 Redlands Terrace was rented by Whyte to serve as the headquarters of the CVRPAC, and copies of Abercrombie's planning research material were brought up as a starting point.[52]

Thus far, Matthew himself had been too junior to play a significant role in the Clyde Plan negotiations. Now, however, with his extended planning brief and his CVRP deputy post, he was able to begin directly influencing the emerging regional planning system at all levels. With Abercrombie and Matthew settled as Clyde consultants, the next step was to give Mears the Forth as a consolation prize: by early October 1943 Matthew was in discussion with Mears and his 'parent' committee about staffing, and agreed to a total budget of £17,000, including 13 staff for a two-year period (cost £13,000), Mears's own fees (£3,000), and the publication costs (£1,000).[53] Matthew, with his Geddesian background, was intuitively sympathetic to the approach that Mears adopted, with its somewhat anti-urban focus, and its strong concerns about rural depopulation and the regeneration of smaller towns: the plan eventually advocated a 'return' of ten per cent of the urban population to the countryside – a formula of population overspill to expanded old towns arranged in 'constellations', rather than large new towns. Here, the industrial context was one of expansion rather than contraction, with the regionally specialised teams working on 'exciting' possibilities for new coalfield communities in Fife or Midlothian. Mears drew heavily on his Edinburgh and ECA contacts to staff the project, which was headquartered in Glencairn Crescent, Edinburgh, and then in the Outlook Tower itself, including conservation-orientated architects such as Robert Hurd and the Berlin-born, ECA-based refugee Anthony Curtis Wolffe.[54]

The Clyde planners, such as the Glaswegian Robert Grieve, were scornful about Mears's team. Grieve recalled that

> Our approach was just as much influenced by Geddes as theirs: we took a great industrial conurbation, and set about rescuing it from Palaeolithic chaos, by tracing its life-force from the shepherd right down to the river. But Mears's approach was much more romantic. He was stirred by the Highlands and the Borders, the ballads, the pipes, the Gaelic, and Uncle Tom Cobleigh and all!

To try and restrain Mears's more florid tendencies, Matthew seconded Jeffryes as his deputy, but the latter was increasingly ineffective: he pleaded to Matthew that an attack of jaundice had forced him to 'drop out on the last lap' – allowing Mears to 'finish up the report any old way he likes' – without inserting planned appendices on railways and industry.[55] Mary Tindall recalled that 'Tom was brilliant but lazy beyond belief, but Robert liked him – he was always so loyal to people he'd known earlier in life!'[56]

However, despite his fondness for Mears's more old-fashioned interpretation of Geddes, Matthew's own destiny lay with the Clyde Plan itself, with its more Modern *dirigiste* ethos – made very plain by Abercrombie on his arrival in

THE CLYDE VALLEY
REGIONAL PLAN 1946

A REPORT PREPARED FOR
THE CLYDE VALLEY REGIONAL PLANNING
COMMITTEE

Consisting of Representatives from the Corporation of the City of
Glasgow, the large Burghs of Airdrie, Ayr, Clydebank, Coat-
bridge, Dumbarton, Greenock, Hamilton, Kilmarnock,
Motherwell and Wishaw, Paisley, Port Glasgow,
Rutherglen and the County Councils of
the Counties of Ayr, Dumbar-
ton, Lanark, Renfrew,
Stirling

BY

SIR PATRICK ABERCROMBIE
MA, F.R.I.B.A., P.P.T.P.I. Planning Consultant
AND
ROBERT H. MATTHEW, A.R.I.B.A.
Deputy Planning Consultant

EDINBURGH: HIS MAJESTY'S STATIONERY OFFICE
1949

3.14 Title page and frontispiece of Clyde Plan, showing Geddes-style 'valley section' panorama of the conurbation (CVRPAC).

Glasgow in January 1944, when he talked of imposing a 'new order' on Clydeside and discarding the old municipal boundaries in favour of conurbation-level or regional-level government.[57] To allow him to give the project the close attention Johnston required, Matthew immediately moved through to Glasgow and lived 'on the job' in an upstairs flat at 3 Redlands Terrace for nearly two years – adding further to the complexities of his domestic arrangements, as he continued to spend nearly half his time in St Andrew's House and London on mainstream DHS business, and now became a relatively occasional visitor to Hamilton House – now largely tended by the Mulgrews – while Lorna commuted between Cheshire, Prestonpans and Glasgow. The complications were increased by the fact that Matthew now, for the first time, began to experience serious trouble with the family 'bad back', with recurrent periods confined to bed: one of the CVRP staff recalled that several progress meetings were actually held in Matthew's bedroom at Redlands Terrace.

The full-time CVRP staff totalled ten, and comprised five senior technical officers (architects Alan Reiach and John S Baillie; planners Robert Grieve and Peter Macfarlane – the latter ex-Greater London

Plan – and engineer Ronald Walker); a physiologist, Vishna Prasad; a sociologist, Sarah Gillespie; and two draughtswomen and a clerical officer. Thirty-two other people were involved part time at critical junctures. Matthew's initial role was largely organisational, acting as a go-between between Abercrombie, the DHS, and the senior researchers charged with writing the texts: Macfarlane on industry; Grieve on population, open space and recreation; Walker on transport and railways; Baillie on housing. However, to deal with two more specific, smaller-scale architectural aspects – study of the region's vernacular architecture, and preparation of a pilot plan for a specimen new neighbourhood unit and town centre, with the Vale of Leven selected as a context – Matthew imported Reiach on secondment from DHS; he moved through to live with him at Redlands Terrace.[58]

Matthew learnt a lot from the Clyde Plan experience, not only from his own work in organising collaborators and subordinates but, even more, from working closely with Abercrombie. The most important lessons from Abercrombie were not about the specifics of planning theory – since Matthew had already been imbued at ECA with all aspects of the Geddesian humanistic approach – but about how to compose and project himself as an 'important person', at a time when such a status lay just around the corner for him. In 1966 he recalled simply that 'Abercrombie was *the* great influence on my life'; and Aidan later argued that 'Abercrombie was absolutely decisive, in teaching him to go for the people that mattered – to go for power – to go for the grand design.'[59] This was the last major building block in Matthew's character formation. He had always had an overdrive coupled with a sense of his own potential importance – he had always been *capax imperii* – but previously much of that drive had been dissipated into detail.[60] Abercrombie showed him how it was possible to achieve much more, within a limited time, by establishing and exerting a natural authority over others,

Modern Architect

allowing delegation across the board, and using a more detached attitude, including devices such as constant cat-naps, to help offset the inevitable stresses and tensions of such a lifestyle. Grieve recalled Abercrombie as

a benign but harried man – never quite sure where he was – he'd be up and down on the sleeper to London, staying in the Automobile Club in Glasgow, and having odd little naps all the time between his constant succession of meetings and site inspections. We'd take him on trips in the car to places where we wanted him to make a decision, and on one occasion, after going to sleep after a long discussion in the car, he jolted awake at traffic lights in Greenock, looked up at the Town Hall and said, 'Oh, yes – Birmingham!' – for a moment he hadn't the slightest idea where he was![61]

Restless as ever for new stimuli, Matthew voraciously soaked up from Abercrombie's example the techniques of cultivating *auctoritas*. On starting work on the Clyde Plan, he immediately set about imitating Abercrombie's delegation technique, and concentrated at first on selecting the best staff and allowing them to stretch themselves. One of the researchers, Kirsteen Borland, recalled that Matthew

interviewed me and very much supervised my work – for most of the project, his role was the overview one, persuading people to do things, getting Alan and his staff – Esme Cousin and Krzysztof Munnich – to spend a year working out a plan for the Vale of Leven. When things went wrong and some people's text had to be re-done – for example the useless stuff by Baillie on housing, or by Colonel Walker on roads – he at first got Bob [Grieve] to do some new text. But eventually, at the end, he himself had to write the whole introduction.

He acted as an intermediary between Abercrombie and chief DHS planning administrator J H McGuinness on the one hand, and individual project members

such as Reiach and Grieve on the other. The latter recalled that whereas Matthew was 'what the Chinese would call "a superior person"' – a mind of some magnitude, well-read philosophically, but too busy, and not always well', Reiach

was an artist, a quintessential architect, with his drawings of fishing villages, but he never lost sight of detail. He and I were great friends – I remember one day we were walking to lunch down Great Western Road, and ended up laughing uproariously, pushing each other up against the aristocratic railings – laughing, really, at the inability of our ossified society to rise to the demands of a plan like the Clyde Valley.[62]

Reiach's eventual contribution to the report included most of Chapter 9 (on architectural 'character'), some of the drawings of colour-washed vernacular buildings, and all of the aerial perspective drawings of imaginary urban developments and recreation centres near Loch Lomond.

As the radical implications of Abercrombie's planning strategy began to emerge, inevitably a major confrontation with Glasgow Corporation arose – especially as Bailie Hugh T McCalman, chairman of the CVRPAC, was a Glasgow councillor. In mid October 1944 Abercrombie reported to Matthew that a 'row' had already developed over the Glasgow section of the report – a dispute that intensified after publication of its first instalment, the Interim Report on Housing Sites, which emphasised that local authority boundaries should not dictate distribution of houses. By mid 1945 a counter-plan by Glasgow City Engineer Robert Bruce had been tabled, proposing a replanning programme entirely within the extended pre-war city limits. In mid 1945, with the deepening controversy, and following Matthew's partial diversion back to mainstream DHS activities (see below), Abercrombie became increasingly disillusioned with the Clyde Plan. He wrote to Matthew, after receiving a tempting offer from

Edinburgh's Lord Provost to undertake a plan for the capital:

> I wonder what McCalman would say if I were to drop the Clyde and take on Edinburgh? The Clyde – on the unsatisfactory terms it has taken – 1) the partial loss of you; 2) the Whyte complex; 3) The Bruce revolt (chiefly important because our Chairman is also his) 4) the lightness of finance 5) the Awkwardness of the local authorities. On the other hand there is that fine staff which has become a real instrument (could they not carry on without their conductor?) Anyhow I shall wait to see a) what becomes of Whyte's Memo and b) the preface to Bruce's Report.[63]

In the event, however, Abercrombie decided to take on Edinburgh in a more restricted form, with the city's consultant town planner Derek Plumstead working as his deputy, and to stay with the Clyde Report. As the work of synthesising the Clyde research and map data proceeded in late 1945, and Abercrombie's disengagement from the project became more and more marked, Matthew's role became correspondingly more central, and he intervened decisively where necessary, sometimes over the phone from Edinburgh or London, to resolve contentious issues.[64]

Matthew's most intense commitments in connection with the Clyde Plan came at the end of the main preparation period, in early 1946. DHS had set out a daunting programme of completion by February, submission to CVRPAC, and printing in May, and Matthew set to work writing the introduction. In March, without prior warning, Abercrombie agreed to take on a planning consultancy in Addis Ababa, and abruptly vanished from the scene, writing to Matthew in April that

> I feel I have left you completely in the lurch, running off so suddenly, but when I agreed to go to Ethiopia towards the end of March, and we had arranged to complete the Clyde Report by the end of February, I never

dreamed that there would be (1) so unholy a rush to get the report printed; (2) so much unwritten at the actual date of submission. Those two last chapters of Walker's Railways and Transport plan, I am afraid, will have to be completely rewritten, and if Maclehose's programme is adhered to, the whole Report in his hands before I get back. This will be throwing a fearful weight upon you, as Cruickshank can't do much more than edit!

Abercrombie promised to contact Matthew immediately he returned at the end of April 1946, adding (somewhat disingenuously, as we shall see) that 'perhaps by then you will be installed at the [London] County Hall!'[65]

The 'partial loss' of Matthew to which Abercrombie referred in his 1945 letter was a consequence of Matthew's final step up the DHS architectural ladder, to the post of Acting Chief Architect and Planning Officer, confirmed on 20 December 1944. Immediately, Matthew was plunged back into the mainstream of the Department's architectural work, working with Bent, Jeffryes and others, and his planning responsibilities inevitably faded a little from view. The light damage from bombing in Scotland following the 1941 Clydebank attacks allowed attention to move soon to active replanning initiatives. Two streams of architectural work were most prominent. First, having beaten off Ministry of Works claims to become a centralised housing authority for Scotland, England and Wales, there was the preparation or oversight of new advisory housing type plans and guidelines for the use of local authorities or the Scottish Special Housing Association (SSHA) – a government-funded and controlled national house-building trust set up in 1937. Second, there was research and advisory design work on hospital planning in anticipation of the introduction of a Scottish branch of the National Health Service. In the housing area, several DHS designers, including Reiach and Bent, had already been at work drawing up standard house types under the supervision of senior administrator Craig Mitchell, mostly for 'non-traditional' prefabricated construction using timber framing or concrete, but some in 'vernacular' style for rural locations. This was part of the preparation for the Scottish Housing Advisory Committee's 1944 report *Planning our New Homes* (the Westwood Report), the 1944–7 'prefab' building drive, and the introduction of higher space standards and subsidies for local authority housing. Matthew made only occasional interventions in the prefab housing drive (otherwise overseen by administrators), for example in advising 'from an architectural point of view' that 'AIROH' aluminium bungalows could be built in semi-detached pairs.[66]

Matthew also became increasingly involved, either personally or *ex officio* as a DHS representative, on various committees with a pan-British remit – a role that allowed him to make frequent visits to London, and begin developing a professional and personal social life there, staying at first in the Reform Club and basing himself in the Scottish Office's temporary wartime home: Fielden House, an interwar classical office block at 10 Great College Street. From 1943 to 1945 Matthew was a member of various committees of the Ministry of Works Postwar Building Directorate, including the original inter-departmental committee on housing construction (the Burt Committee), and represented DHS on the Building Research Board and BRS postwar programme committee. From 1944 he was a member of a government committee on design and layout of roads in built-up areas (report published 1946); and he became a member of the RIBA's Official Architects and Town & Country Planning committees.[67] The V1 and V2 bombing period was a very trying time, with one or two near-misses. Stuart, who was in Southeast England for most of that period, recalled that

> Robert used to chide us before he started going to London, 'What are you making all the fuss about those bombs for?' But one day, I remember meeting him outside Fielden House, just as a flying bomb landed nearby. It

was just like the fire at Dick Place all over again: he was absolutely shattered. That was the first bomb he'd actually heard at reasonably close range, ever since the Zeppelin raid on Edinburgh back in World War I.[68]

But once the bombing stopped, in early 1945, Robert was able to begin to enjoy the social possibilities of London, albeit at this stage in the intermittent style of a visitor.[69]

From Stockholm to East Kilbride: initiatives of 1945–6

In March 1945 Matthew diced with mild danger once again when, after vigorously arguing the case for Scottish representation, he secured a place in a small British official delegation to Sweden and Finland, tasked with attempting to organise the large-scale export of prefabricated timber houses to Scotland and England. This trip, which was unexpectedly prolonged to over two months' length, was a significant milestone in Matthew's career, as, on it, he was able to begin developing for the first time a fully fledged international social circle of architects, planners and others. Along with a smaller study trip to the USA in 1949, this was one of the last trips that Matthew documented in his traditional detailed diary style.[70]

The Swedish–Finnish trip began on 4 March, in a blacked-out night flight from Leuchars in Fife to Stockholm Bromma, tucked in with rugs, oxygen and parachutes, and 'little to do except doze … like travelling in the guard's van but in a comfortable seat'. Matthew might have been less relaxed had he known – as he later discovered in Sweden – that the German air force in Norway had full information from Bromma on the timing of all flights to and from Britain. In Stockholm he met the other three members of the party: C C W Goodall, Ministry of Works Director of Contracts, and the delegation leader; Arthur Kenyon, eminent establishment architect and housing specialist, currently working as consultant to MoW; and Herbert Setchell, commercial councillor at the

Trähusdelegationen i arbete.

British Embassy in Stockholm since 1944. Their main Swedish liaison officer, Vinell, was also an ex-diplomat and chairman of a delegation set up by Svenska Trähus, a consortium of prefabricated timber exporters. It was immediately agreed to engage a Swedish architect independent of the timber trade to represent the delegation, and Dr Anders Tengbom, son of the eminent architect Ivar Tengbom, was engaged. The delegation enjoyed their visits to the Tengbom family house, an old timber log house near the royal palace in an 18th-century neoclassical style.[71]

Expecting their stay to be a short one, the visitors flung themselves furiously into a programme of touring timber houses and existing 19th-century housing, and meetings with ministers and officials to discuss shipping, costs and government subsidies. They also found time to visit the more recent Modern architectural set pieces, completed since Matthew's last visit in 1934. He hailed Asplund's Woodland Cemetery, for example, as 'exceptionally impressive', not least for its workmanship and materials. Conversely – in an interesting insight into the limits of Matthew's tolerance of the mid-20th-century ethos of rationalist planning – he reacted very negatively to the new Södersjukhus (Southern Infirmary), a monumental slab block

complex of 1938–44 on the outer edge of Stockholm, designed by the engineer Hjalmar Cederström on stringently Functionalist lines, with rigidly parallel blocks of clinics and wards. The hospital, despite its 'high standard of equipment and planning', was 'a warning what NOT to do – grim and polished outside and in, but little of the human side to cheer up the patient'. The project formed part of a wider 'social plan' of 'functional research' drawn up and published as a book by Cederström in 1944, envisaging the rational treatment of the sick human being as an element in an all-embracing scheme of social security, including compulsory work. Matthew described Cederström as 'a queer bird, elderly, with knots on his face, and rather a fanatic ... who thinks that Sweden has a mission to improve the world after the war, as she has had the opportunity through 140 years of peace to develop in a way denied to more warlike countries!' By contrast, Matthew was 'much taken' with the more informally planned, new groups of cooperative housing, including the new building type of the tall 'point block' – for example at Danviksklippan (1943). More appealing still, to one trained in the Edinburgh Arts and Crafts tradition, was the Skansen open-air museum (opened in 1891 by Artur Hazelius), with its assemblage of relocated timber vernacular buildings.

At the end of March the group flew across for a weekend visit to Finland to inspect houses produced by the Warkaus group – the rather naive underlying hope on MoW's part being to 'play off the Swedes and Finns' against each other to reduce the cost. Alvar Aalto, in his capacity as consultant architect to Warkaus, coordinated the visit, which was calculated to outbid the Swedes in lavish hospitality – and indeed, this trip was important less for its housing outcome, which was minimal, than as a forerunner of the post-war international-goodwill architectural exchanges, to which Matthew himself would become so wedded. He recorded that 'Aalto was in good form, very glad to see us – small, about 50, fat, good-humoured but tough; his eyes close when he grins.'[72] After a formal dinner at the Finnish Architecture School on the first night, on the second day the party motored out to Aalto's house at Munkaniemi, outside Helsinki, for a welcome party attended by prominent Finnish architects. Matthew found himself sitting next to the eminent classical designer Sigurd Frosterus, who revealed that he was an avid reader of Scottish and English authors, and especially of the books of Eric Linklater. In his speech of welcome, Aalto explained that the Finnish architects 'feel strongly that this visit is the first sign of a linking-up again with Western civilisation, which they need desperately as a counterbalance to the Russians, who hang over them like a menace.'[73]

Ultimately, however, the negotiations with the Finnish authorities proved abortive, owing partly to the lack of firm MoW commitments. The departing party was given 'forget-me-nots and a page of cartoons drawn by two girls in Aalto's office', but, following an abrupt change of plan by the Soviet military (who controlled Helsinki airport), the party found themselves unexpectedly back for another night's stay, and another dinner with Aalto, lasting until 2.30 a.m. Matthew recorded that he was 'as usual poetical, [and] soon had his jacket off, looking like a prize fighter with one eye tending to close'. On their return to Sweden, the delegation began to run into the growing frustration of constant changes of plan and an evasiveness on the part both of MoW in London and of the Swedish government. Negotiations were thrown into disarray when the Ministry cabled Goodall on 7 April, without warning, that the maximum unit price per house must be £300. On this basis, negotiations fluctuated around a potential total of 8,000–10,000 houses of three or four bedrooms. Matthew commented that the possibility of 'hundreds of one type of

3.16 The UK delegation seen visiting Fogelfors Bruk, Sweden, 9 March 1945: Matthew third from left. (Bruksagare Thorsten Ekstromer, Fogelfors)

house on one site … will be ghastly if not watched very carefully and leavened with other types'. By 18 April a total consignment of 10,800 was being discussed.

Eventually, however, after a further two weeks, with numerous cables to the Ministry, some directly to Sir Hugh Beaver, it became clear that no conclusive decision could be reached, and Goodall decided to use some of his 'superabundant leisure' to set out in a cable to MoW a blow-by-blow critique of the Ministry's inefficiencies and 'cavalier treatment of us all'. He argued that it had been a waste of time to send the Director of Contracts and then instruct him merely to get the cheapest houses, and useless to try to play off the Swedes and Finns, as 'it was clear to me at a very early stage that the Swedes and Finns were in contact'. He concluded that 'we have been here for so long without accomplishing anything that our presence is becoming a matter for humorous comment – I resent being a joke.'[74] The team's seemingly never-ending stay presented Matthew with the problem of rendering him inaccessible at a critical time in preparation of the Clyde Plan. Although not normally a conventional family man, he also found himself increasingly missing the children: 'Telegram from home to say all well. Aidan back at school. Hope I'll be back in time for the summer holidays – sorry I have missed him – he will be growing up a lot.'

Increasingly, the team used their time

in leisure rather than work activities. They spent much time 'hanging about the office' waiting for phone calls from London, or studying the war maps in the newspapers. Eventually, Kenyon became fed up with waiting, and began to spend most of his time shopping. Matthew noted that 'Kenyon has worn a hole in his trousers and has had to buy a new pair. He suggests (a) setting up a business for teaching English or (b) setting up a small hotel.' The party became friendly with an Edinburgh expatriate architect, F R (Eric) Stevenson, a 'bald, pink and healthy' young man of 'pretty good judgement – a very bright lad' with Scandinavian and American contacts, married to a Dane and (unbeknown to them) engaged in intelligence work. Matthew suggested he should come to Scotland for a year rather than go to the USA; during the 1950s, as we shall see in Chapter 8, Stevenson would become a close academic associate of Matthew's. Most evenings in Stockholm were spent eating as a group in their hotel, or unwillingly going to events such as the 'hearty gatherings' of the Swedish-British Society; so the occasional informal evening in a private house came as a relief.[75] There was much discussion of a possible early departure for home, and Stevenson suggested returning overland via Moscow and Cairo to avoid the risk of being shot down. Eventually, Kenyon managed to get a seat on a flight back at the beginning of May, but Matthew and Goodall were still stranded in Stockholm on VE Day. Matthew set out his impressions of the day: 'A magnificent day – sunny and warm. Swedish, Danish and Norwegian flags blossoming everywhere – ONLY Scandinavian flags. Relief – through intact – not dragged into war by Germans – terrified they'd be pulled in at last minute.'

At last, Matthew was able to fly back directly to Scotland, and made an unannounced reappearance at St Andrew's House. As a farewell present, Vinell, Goodall, Kenyon and the others gave him a commemorative book on Skansen. Mary Tindall recalled that

while Robert was stuck in Sweden, the office got out of hand. Nobody knew what to do, and everyone was squabbling; Tom Jeffryes was deputising, after a fashion. So someone suggested the office should take the initiative and do a prototype plan for a neighbourhood – the notional site was Dunfermline. All the alternative schemes for the neighbourhoods were pinned up in Tom's room. Then Robert came back unexpectedly, and called everyone to account. He came into the presentation of the Dunfermline schemes, and sat at the back while I did my little talk. I'd done a total Radburn, which nobody liked – except Robert. He said – 'That's the one!'[76]

It required a further one-week visit by Matthew in mid-June to finally set out all the details for the Swedish Timber House programme, involving complex discussions with Tengbom and Svenska Trähus officials, and an MoW contract was placed for 5,000 houses in four types.[77] Matthew had rapidly prepared a revised set of plans of all four types since his return, and Tengbom was now to prepare final plans, incorporating Matthew's alterations, and the Svenska Trähus engineers' drawing office would produce detailed working drawings. Specimen houses erected by a variety of companies would be built under the aegis of Tore Munthe, UK representative of the Swedish Timber House Export Association, and would be inspected by Stockholm City Council Inspectors on MoW's behalf.[78]

On his second return from Sweden, Matthew threw himself back into his mainstream DHS work with vigour – although he still found the time for some private behind-the-scenes activity. In particular, he lent a hand to Stuart in late spring 1945, to help him exploit an unexpected opportunity to break into the field of social architecture, in a competition for a complex of family housing for severely disabled ex-servicemen: the Thistle Foundation, on the southeast edge of Edinburgh. Envisaged in 1944 by its founder, Sir Francis Tudsbery, as a visionary project to integrate the disabled into the wider community, the Thistle Foundation was later overtaken by the onset of the National Health Service. In April 1944 Sir Francis had stipulated a 'garden court' layout for the scheme, to avoid 'uniformity' or 'any suggestion of an institutional character', and hoped that the project could contribute to 'raising the standard of housing in Scotland'; and in spring 1945 a limited competition was announced – amended in May, after the death of Tudsbery's son, Robin, to include a small non-denominational chapel and meeting room.[79]

As with the pre-war competition entries done with Reiach, Matthew, with his official housing responsibilities, could under no circumstances openly enter the competition himself. So instead he submitted a collaborative entry with Stuart, who was looking for an excuse to return to Edinburgh to help his father, having turned down a partnership with C H James & Pierce. To provide specific background on design for disabled people, Stuart embarked on a whirlwind tour of hospitals in Scotland and the South of England, including Erskine and the Ministry of Pensions hospital at Stoke Mandeville, and sketched out some initial ideas, but went no further. As with some later jobs, such as Loretto Chapel, it then required the intervention of Robert to pull the project together and prepare plans. Robert consulted Douglas, to provide the necessary medical contextual background, and then, in the time-honoured manner, set to work on the competition entry at home, after a full day's work at DHS. Aidan recalled seeing him 'sitting up all night, producing reams of drawings for the Thistle Foundation'. Potentially, the Thistle Foundation project seemed to hold out a potentially exciting alternative approach to new community design on suburban sites, compared either with the established utilitarian patterns of cottages or tenements, or with the more thoroughgoing Modernist formula of tall blocks in

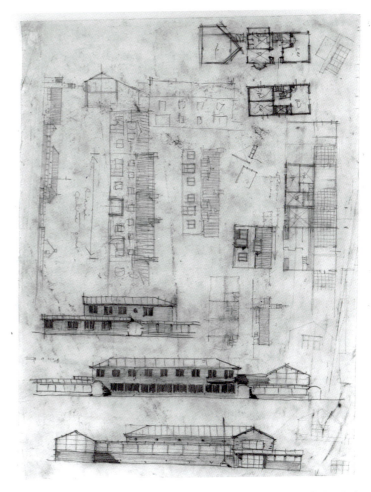

rectilinear patterns, with a health or social centre at the core. Robert's original drawings envisaged an open courtyard plan interspersed with short terraces to give a *Zeilenbau* impression. A long entrance avenue led up to a focal square, with the Robin Chapel at its centre, flanked by clinic, gym, pool and community facilities, and ringed at the back by a rather formal semicircular terrace, a little reminiscent of Lorimer's first proposal of 1919 for the Scottish National War Memorial, in the form of a cloister with projecting, taller 'shrine'. The style of the chapel and the one-and-a-half-storey terraces would be a harled, steeply pitched-roof vernacular reminiscent of the more rural drawings in the Westwood Report, as well as semi-collective housing groups of folk character built in various countries.[80] Thirty-five other entries were submitted to the competition, with A G Henderson as architectural adviser, and when Stuart's entry was selected as the

3.17 Thistle Foundation, Robert Matthew's sketch drawings of May/June1945 for houses and (unbuilt) community centre. (EULMC)

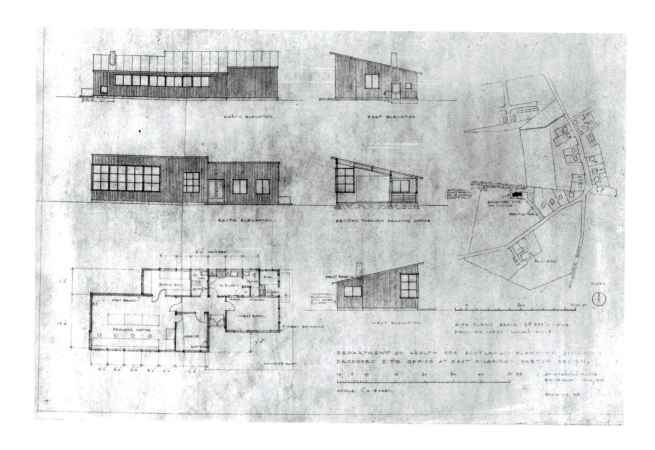

3.18 July 1946 drawing by Robert Matthew for DHS site office and 'outlook platform' to north of future East Kilbride New Town centre. (EULMC)

winner in November 1945, Tudsbery expressed concerns about his limited portfolio. Accordingly, on 1 January 1946 Stuart went into formal partnership with his father, while working separately from 6 Melville Place; the scheme was built in slightly cut-down form in 1947–50.[81]

A further planning opportunity bound up with Edinburgh came in January 1946, when Abercrombie recommended that Matthew or Mears should be appointed town planning consultant to Edinburgh University, then contemplating a radical programme of post-war expansion. Mears, too, emphatically suggested Matthew to the university, arguing that he might give up his Scottish Office job to take it on; but Robert was not, for the moment, to be shifted, and Charles Holden was appointed consultant instead in February 1946.[82] Robert's main concern in the months after his return from Sweden remained the completion of the Clyde Plan and its appendices. Gradually, from February 1946 onwards, the focus shifted from finishing and printing of the report itself to the Department's role

in the active strategic decentralisation process that would follow up the report. Following the Labour victory in the spring general election, Johnston was replaced as Secretary of State by Joseph Westwood, who agreed in May 1946 to designate the first of the Clydeside New Towns at East Kilbride (despite furious objections by Glasgow), followed immediately by the first of the smaller new towns proposed as part of the Mears regeneration strategy, at Markinch in Fife (later named Glenrothes). Matthew's team was charged with preparing the first town and neighbourhood plans for East Kilbride and Glenrothes. With the urgency of the 'Glasgow problem', East Kilbride was obviously the more pressing of the two, and by July 1946 Matthew had personally designed a site office for DHS staff at East Kilbride, modestly 'vernacular' and timber-clad, yet clearly Modernist in its triangular, monopitch-roof section; it was located on a low ridge overlooking the future town centre, on a site now occupied by the Dollan Baths. From this base, the energetic surveying of the

10,000 acre site of East Kilbride, planned ultimately to house a 45,000 population, could begin. Robert took Lorna for an initial inspection, and she recalled 'tramping over the fields where the town was to be built'. Now the planners and architects, such as Grieve or Robert Scott Morton, could be set to work on the site.[83]

The 1945 war triumph and Labour election victory were seen by many as having expunged the shame of the pre-war appeasement era, and consigned the Victorian laissez-faire era to oblivion.[84] For the moment, it seemed obvious that the ongoing mass struggle called for a radical widening of state provision under the new welfare state, itself 'an essay in utilitarianism'.[85] As part of the parallel expansion of the British cultural establishment, new or revitalised national and regional institutions began to proliferate, many steered by ambitious younger people of Matthew's generation, who had exploited the wartime flux to emerge on top. In the immediate post-war months Matthew's biggest career opportunity of all lay just around the corner – a leap in fortune that would distance him temporarily from the Scottish scene, and would establish him, within a handful of years, as the most influential public architect-planner in Britain.

Chapter 4

The Grand Design: London architecture and the Royal Festival Hall, 1946–53

[Under Matthew] the LCC, more than any other office, attracted the best of the young architects, who were prepared to sink their individuality in pursuing a social as well as an architectural ideal. It grew and flourished, becoming one of the most powerful forces in English architecture: a great empire in which the concrete never set.

J M Richards[1]

A state within a state: the crisis of LCC architecture

Matthew's rise as a public authority architect-planner had been rapid in the last three wartime years, both through his own efforts and through the good luck of his early connections and pre-war career choices. But his reputation was still confined largely to Scotland, and he had not benefited from the sudden wartime opportunities to realise ideals of planning and production as much as some of his contemporaries, such as Holford, based nearer the centre of gravity of the British war machine. As 1945 drew to an end, with work on the Clyde Valley Plan reaching a climax, Matthew had good reason to be satisfied, but none to suspect that he was just about to be presented with his most decisive career opportunity of all, 400 miles away from home, as Architect to the London County Council.

The LCC was one of the most important public authorities in Britain, but it was also, and above all, an elected municipal council. It was a 'state within a state ... as central as the sun in the solar system of British local government'. The reliance of the Welfare State on direct municipal control of many services, and the resultant strong local politicisation of social building campaigns, above all that of mass housing, was largely unique to Britain. In London, the LCC formed the upper, strategic level of a special two-tier government system, half a century old by the time of World War II. Its tasks included planning and most housing, but it regarded itself in many ways as the equal of central government, and its elected members saw themselves as an 'enlightened' elite, a cut above the supposedly myopic norm of municipal councillors. The Labour-controlled LCC had maintained its overall power during the war, coordinating local emergency services. After Herbert Morrison's departure in 1940, Charles Latham maintained the centralist Labour regime he had set up; in 1947, Latham in his turn was succeeded by his deputy, Isaac (Ike) Hayward.[2]

Within this apparatus, however, the position of architecture was uncertain, to say the least, and suffered a major symbolic defeat in 1945 – stemming from the tension over the 'numbers game' in housing, which would ultimately open the way to Matthew's unexpected accession to the Architect post. The vast interwar output of inner-city 'block dwellings' flats and 'out-county' cottage estates had remained faithful to traditional Unwinian or neo-Georgian patterns. During the war, the department, headed since 1941 by J H Forshaw, had energetically modernised itself. Before the war, when Forshaw was architect to the Miners' Welfare Commission (1926–39), his programme of pithead baths had been the first large-scale programme of Modernist social building in Britain, including Scotland, and Matthew regarded his work with respect, above all for its social implication 'that "architecture" could be applied to the mundane process of cleaning up miners before they went home'. Like Matthew at DHS, Forshaw had exploited the boom in city and regional planning as a vehicle for expansion. His predecessors, E P Wheeler (1935–9) and F R Hiorns (1939–41), had absorbed the town-planning function in 1937 from the department of the Valuer and expanded the department's staff to around 2,000. Forshaw became Deputy LCC Architect in 1939 and Architect in 1941, with special responsibilities for damage clearance and heavy rescue, but his special passion was the drive for grand city and regional planning, where he worked as Abercrombie's collaborator on the County of London Plan (1943).[3]

The council's 'progressive' elements had also, during the war, enthusiastically backed the sweeping replanning proposals of Abercrombie's 1944 Greater London Plan, which would see London give up much of its potential growth, and even existing population, to overspill: within that framework would fit the equally ambitious internal reconstruction proposals of Abercrombie and Forshaw's 1943 County of London Plan. Forshaw had acted, in relation to this advisory plan, as a helper and facilitator to Abercrombie, like Matthew on the Clyde Plan. Immediately after the war, however, he overreached himself in attempting to use this theoretical framework to obstruct post-war housing output, which had been entrusted largely to the utilitarian department of the Valuer, Cyril Walker (recruited during the war from Croydon Borough Council), to boost output. In 1945, as the war neared its end, Forshaw began to argue that the old pre-war classical housing types should be phased out altogether: 'He'd hoped that

planning could take over London, leaving Walker with the out-county sites.'[4] This attempt to block, or take over, the post-war emergency housing drive was a rash move, and it misfired badly. The Valuer and his key allies, Housing Committee Chairman Charles W Gibson and Deputy Clerk T G Randall, protested that this 'clean start' would cripple housing production, and Latham came down decisively on their side. In October 1945 it was decided that, to protect output, from January 1946 responsibility for all new housing, including design, was to be passed to the Valuer. Despite public protests from the RIBA and a deputation to the LCC led by Abercrombie and Reilly, the proposal was approved by the council – albeit by a mere six votes, the lowest margin since the start of Labour rule in 1935. Faced with this rebuff, including even the loss of his housing architects, Forshaw grasped at a dignified way out, when the Chief Architect post at the Ministry of Health came up. In output terms, Latham's move paid handsomely: within four years, by using the pre-war designs and avoiding 'flights of fancy', Walker's 'military operation' had directly completed over 19,000 dwellings.[5] But this result had been achieved at the cost of a direct affront to the national architectural and planning establishment, leaving people such as Reilly anxious to settle the score.

In early November 1945 Matthew wrote to Forshaw congratulating him on his new job (which commenced on 1 January 1946). In December the latter's old LCC post was advertised, with its new, reduced responsibilities. It included the design of all council buildings except housing, and all town planning matters, including development control and historic building preservation. Under the title 'Superintending Architect of Metropolitan Buildings' it also oversaw all building regulation in the capital. Much of its building control and planning work, as we shall see, was taken up by routine bomb damage duties. Matthew at first did not consider applying, as he was hardly settled in his DHS job. Some external prompting was required, and it came, appropriately enough, from Charles Reilly, now a born-again advocate of Modernism and (since 1944) a member of MARS (the Modern Architecture Research Group), and an outspoken critic of the 1942 Lutyens-inspired classical Royal Academy plan for the rebuilding of Central London.[6] In November 1945 Reilly sent a copy of Isaac Wolfe's new book, *The Reilly Plan* (an outline of his own community planning concepts), to LCC Clerk Sir Eric Salmon, inscribed with 'best wishes for a happy solution to the present difficulty – and any others'. Reilly began urgently to canvass potential candidates for the LCC job. One of these was Matthew, who was appointed in late October 1945 alongside Reilly, Ling, Kenyon and others to an ad hoc RIBA committee tasked with organising a 'Re-Planning of Britain' exhibition in Stockholm in May 1946. At its first meeting, in November, Matthew later recalled, 'A Liverpool professor passed me a note which read, "Are you thinking about the LCC?" I hardly knew him and I didn't know what he was talking about, but I thought I had better do something about it.'[7]

Prompted by this reminder, Matthew applied for the LCC job in January – a decision that perhaps accounted for his failure to take up the Edinburgh University planning offer in January. Out of the 37 applicants (including 12 LCC staff), the Clerk and General Purposes Chairman selected a shortlist of eight, of whom Matthew, at 39 years old, was the second youngest. For his referees, Matthew relied on his regional planning contacts: Whyte wrote that the Clyde Valley Plan had been 'largely planned and directed' by him, and Mears stressed his ability to collaborate positively with local authorities. Abercrombie wrote that 'hardly any English or Scottish younger architects have greater experience in housing and town planning'. This qualified endorsement contrasted with Abercrombie's glowing reference for one of the 'inside candidates', Edwin Williams. Williams, a former Liverpool

student, was ten years older than Matthew, and had helped Abercrombie on the Sheffield Plan in 1923; since 1935, he had spent a decade in the LCC working in methodical Beaux Arts style on a range of relatively mundane tasks: cottage estates, civil defence and development control. Abercrombie wrote that

I believe you would be a worthy successor to Hiorns and Forshaw ... There is an immense task before you, requiring not only vision but continual vigilance. I deplore the fact that Housing has been taken out of the Architect's hands ... You will carry on with the work, courageously and successfully.

From Abercrombie's perspective, Matthew clearly seemed an outside candidate. But Abercrombie's own aura of influence had emboldened Matthew to set his sights higher, and now he was about to confound his mentor, and move beyond him into new territory.[8]

At his LCC interview on 6 May 1946, Matthew had in his favour the fact that, despite his early training by Rowse and his housing and regional planning work for DHS, he stood outside the various factions of English public architecture and planning, yet his youth and Modernist planning ethos clearly put him a cut above the relatively old-fashioned salarymen candidates such as Williams. At his interview he was asked whether, if he were appointed, he would 'consider this just another step in the invasion of England by the Scots' – and replied that he 'would be a willing hostage'.[9] After making it through to a final shortlist of three, along with Bristol City Architect J Nelson Meredith and LCC Principal Architect Cecil Kennard, Matthew was eventually unanimously chosen, at a maximum salary of £3,000 (later raised to £3,500), starting on 2 September. Immediately, as the congratulations started flooding in, he began to experience for the first time the standing of a national public figure, with instant entry to almost all architectural circles in Britain – other than the most traditional, conservative ones, who would henceforth associate Matthew with suspect socialism. Although it was not until mid 1949 that he and Abercrombie were on first-name terms, the latter immediately showed him a new respect, for example by arranging an informal dinner with Forshaw. And the lobbying began: private architect and housing specialist Anthony Chitty wrote that 'We look to you to reverse the scales which have been swinging too far back since Forshaw left.' From Scotland, on the other hand, came laments at his early departure: senior DHS administrator Henderson grudgingly admitted that 'we realise you felt impelled to move to bigger things', whereas Elspeth Morton, working as a physiotherapist with the occupation army in Germany, wrote that 'Robert [Morton] is so worried as to what will happen to the Department of Health and planning in Scotland – Oh Robert ... I hope it doesn't mean you have deserted Scotland!'[10]

Despite the imposing trappings of his new job, including a vast staff, grand office and secretariat, and chauffeur-driven transport, at first Matthew's London existence was dominated by more prosaic necessities. The first was to find somewhere to live. Abercrombie stepped in initially, by effecting an introduction to Clough Williams-Ellis, a gentlemanly fighter since the 1920s against planning chaos and sprawl. Williams-Ellis later recalled that

> one of my very oldest and dearest friends, Pat Abercrombie, said, 'A great friend of mine – a large Scot – is just coming to London to be chief architect to the LCC and has nowhere particular to stay. Could you take him in until he fixes himself up? I know you would like him'. How right he was![11]

Although the 'bedsit' provided by Ellis in Carlton Terrace Mews was cosy and agreeable, Matthew immediately set about finding more permanent family accommodation. Cyril Walker, perhaps mischievously, suggested he could rent a semi-detached house on the LCC Woodberry Down estate, warning that it

was not the 'best residential part of London', while a firm of architects hoping for LCC schools work offered him part of the subdivided Manor House at Blackheath.[12] By November 1946 Matthew had decided to rent (from the council) a much more conveniently located bomb-damaged Georgian town house at 36 Kensington Square, then being converted into two maisonettes by the LCC.[13] While the work proceeded in fits and starts, Lorna came down intermittently to help direct the conversion, but otherwise she and the children stayed on in Prestonpans, along with all the family goods and chattels, with the Mulgrews continuing to provide intermittent help. Matthew spent the weekends and evenings driving round London, map in hand, to get to know the city, and sketching

(top) **4.1** Matthew being received by Vienna's Burgermeister, Dr Koerner, at the opening of the 'England in Aufbau' exhibition. (Pressestelle der Stadt Wien)

(bottom) **4.2** 36 Kensington Square, seen in 2005. (M Glendinning)

bombed historic buildings. Only in July 1947 could the family finally fully move to London, while Liberal MP Jo Grimond took over the tenancy of Hamilton House. Aidan and Janet began at London day schools until 1949, with Aidan thereafter moving to Michael Hall, a Steiner school at Forest Row, Sussex, followed two years later by Janet.

This move allowed a return, with a vengeance, to the lifestyle that Robert and Lorna had enjoyed in the mid/late 1930s at Darnaway Street and Hamilton House – now in a far more cosmopolitan and prestigious manner. Lorna reverted to the role of family coordinator and hostess. Now, however, the Edinburgh architects' circle was in turn virtually dropped and a new London and overseas social life was put in its place. Although, nationally, the late 1940s and 1950s saw a further bolstering of public collectivism and of the ethos of family domesticity, for a figure of Matthew's new standing, firmly entrenched in a fashionable London setting, these rules did not apply so strictly. Indeed, the colourful atmosphere of Kensington Square contrasted forcibly with Matthew's life of outward bureaucratic sobriety at County Hall.

One young friend of Aidan's, who first visited the family there around 1949–50, recalled that

> my first impression was of a most eccentric household, full of odd lodgers and visitors. You might arrive and hear Julian Budden playing the bassoon upstairs, or there might be Clough Williams-Ellis striding about in breeches, yellow stockings, purple waistcoat and monocle. And Lorna would be presiding over everything, with her good looks and stylish clothes. She was extravagant, generous, vivacious, full of life and hospitality – and manipulative, too! She was no shrinking violet: she wouldn't have survived with Robert otherwise. However many visitors or guests there were, however much partying or merriment, Lorna always coped, partly because she had help in the house, often of an eccentric kind. And you

could usually reckon on dramas of one sort or another happening in or around the Matthew family.[14]

As recollected by Aidan:

> The first lodgers were an engaged Polish couple: he was a nice man, studying to be a doctor, very educated, with lots of degrees in Poland – he did all the cooking and cleaning, whereas she was useless in the house, and lay about in a sickly manner, with members of the Polish community bringing her flowers. Eventually he got an ulcer and collapsed, and my mother had to get rid of them. Immediately after that, there was a group of three young students, who called themselves the 'Pan-Slav Washing-Up Movement': they were Vilma Worth, a Czech refugee, who was put in touch with my mother by Tom Jeffryes's wife; Brian Bonfield, a newly graduated Oxford law student; and Julian Budden, son of Maud and Lionel, who was studying to be a conductor at the Royal College of Music, and later had a very distinguished career, becoming director of Opera at the BBC. They helped my mother generally around the house, when my father was away. Then, after the Pan-Slavs left, her main stalwart was a well-organised Irish housekeeper from County Cork, called Kathleen O'Callaghan; she had epilepsy, but wouldn't take the proper pills, with occasionally embarrassing results – she'd sometimes drop things with a tremendous smash! Alongside these, there was also a succession of various au pairs, who were also lodgers in a sense, but whose role was chiefly to keep an eye on us![15]

Matthew relaxed at home when his work pressures allowed: Janet recalled that 'to me, he was a reassuring background presence at Kensington Square: he loved to play the piano often, and I grew up with the sound of Chopin, Mozart, Bach and Beethoven.' In 1950 the president of the Royal Australian Institute of Architects, Adrian Ashton, following a visit to London during a round-the-world trip, recalled the furnishings and decoration of the 'charming Georgian house in Kensington Square', which he had visited for a farewell lunch: the party was held in Matthew's

> delightful living-room studio, which runs the full width of the house, and is a real artist's environment: cheerful fire, grand piano covered with plans, drafting table behind a Chinese screen, Persian rugs on the floor, fumed oak panelling with colourful pictures and Japanese prints, the whole commanding a view of the square with its old trees and Georgian buildings.[16]

Although the family was now fully reunified for the first time since the wartime disruption, new stresses now emerged, especially during Robert's periods of intense engagement on key LCC projects, such as the Festival Hall project. Lorna had a job for two years in the publishing firm of Faber's, and also took a growing interest in the London branch of the Saltire Society (an influential cultural-nationalist grouping with an interest in Modern art and architecture as well as traditional Scottish culture), as well as in the 'artistic' shops of Kensington High Street. Number 36 Kensington Square became a focus for many gatherings of London Scots – including fortnightly Scottish country dancing classes held in the house. Through the Saltire Society, and through Robert's contacts with the Council of Industrial Design, the family made one particularly flamboyant contact, in the form of William Francis, 19th Baron Sempill (1893–1965), laird of Craigievar and Fintray houses in the northeast, pioneer aviator, papal nuncio and member of the proto-fascist 'Right Club', who had helped set up the Japanese air force in the 1920s and was later awarded the 3rd Order of the Rising Sun for his work; Sempill was also an honorary colonel in the Venezuelan air force. Some three years after his accession to his title and the death of his first wife, Sempill had just remarried, to Cecilia Dunbar-Kilburn, a high-powered

'art in industry' organiser and COID member. Although there was no question of sympathy with Sempill's political views, he was a charismatic figure, and the Craigievar link appealed to Lorna's hankering for her northeastern roots. Lorna and Sempill attended various social events together, and she and Robert became frequent visitors to Craigievar: Cecilia and William spent the summer there, and the rest of the year in Kensington.[17]

During those years, Robert's primary focus was, inevitably, the task of climbing the sharp learning curve of architectural leadership, learning a new set of skills appropriate to a great public figure, and experiencing the sharp change from the somewhat marginal position of the DHS architects to the strong executive power of the local authority architect: he hailed the pioneering interwar role of Keay in Liverpool and Livett in Leeds, in bringing the architect 'from the fringes of society right into the centre'. Administration should be a merely enabling function, 'to provide the conditions under which the technologist can make his maximum contribution at all levels'. Now, in the wake of the war, the architect for the first time had been 'asked to put as his first problem that of production', embracing not just elite monuments but 'the wide area of general building'. The only precondition for taking this allotted place was that the architect should take to heart the politicians' concern with quantity of production, and balance that alongside their own concerns of design quality.[18]

It was Forshaw's failure to respect that balance between political production needs and design values that had opened the job to Matthew in the first place. Now he was faced with the task of rebuilding the department from the low base bequeathed by Forshaw, and of exploiting the widespread resentment within the architectural establishment at the disregarding of their protests. He later recalled that in 1946

> the Department was still largely on a war footing. It was divided into two:

planning and civil defence (war damage) and was in the charge of a triumvirate: Jones, Chief Administrative Officer; Cecil Kennard, District Surveyor; and Ralph Wilson, a fine man of the old pre-war department, now nearing his retirement. This division of the department into planning and civil defence gave it a kind of schizophrenic atmosphere. The aura of Abercrombie was strong down the corridors, and enthusiasm for post-war planning was tremendous. Men like Ling, Lane and Craig were up and coming and the reputation of this part of the department was high. The remainder, in civil defence, were dispirited, knowing there was still a vast amount of mess to be cleared up. Little or no normal building was in progress.[19]

On both the planning and civil defence sides much of the workload was of a very mundane, regulatory kind, dominated by vast quantities of development control casework. A four-inch-thick file of some 500 cases, handled routinely without any reference to Matthew other than the use of his Roneoed signature, was submitted every fortnight to the Town Planning Committee for rubber-stamping. The building regulation casework dealt with under his 'Superintending Architect' aegis through his formidable corps of district surveyors, and in the terms of the 1930 and 1939 London Building Acts, was of the same everyday character: there was much discussion of numbering and naming of streets, the condition of bomb-damaged roofs, and the demolition of Anderson shelters. To sustain this burgeoning bureaucracy the workload of the several hundred surveyors and engineers had more than doubled between 1946 and 1948.[20]

A substantial amount of Matthew's time was spent at first on emergency building-control cases. He recalled later that

weekends constantly brought inspections of dangerous buildings and a winkling out of magistrates to sign eviction orders. ... Going into a tall

terrace house, one summer's day, to persuade an elderly man and his wife to leave, it visibly trembled as the trains passed by in an open cutting. He stood on his independence, and would not be shifted. There were no tiles on the roof, and the rain all too evidently came straight down to the ground floor. On top was their bedroom, open to the sky, but with an outsize umbrella over a large double bed, ingeniously hoisted and balanced by a system of strings. 'But,' I asked, 'what about winter?' 'No problems at all', he replied briskly. 'Seven hot water bottles and we're fine.'

Some of these cases concerned damaged or decaying historic buildings, and here Matthew's latent conservationist tendencies began to emerge: soon after his arrival, 'I found myself persuading the LCC to put in reverse a demolition order already issued on Holland's Mount Clare in Roehampton. (I can still see the dry rot sprouting fearsomely from the walls.)'[21]

Matthew's challenge was to convert this vast apparatus of municipal regulation into a powerhouse of modern architecture and planning, but during his first year the difficulties seemed almost insuperable, as the entire weight of the Department seemed separate from, even opposed to, the main values of design. In July 1947 he wrote in frustration to Budden in Liverpool of 'the difficulty of getting the right kind of man here on design. I am very anxious to build up a first class team, particularly on schools.' He asked whether Budden had 'any good men who are looking to London at present (not very likely, I am afraid, in view of the housing position)', and complained that he had 'to overcome a considerable "anti-official" feeling', something Keay had broken down in Liverpool and so 'naturally gets first choice!' As late as June 1948, Birmingham's influential City Engineer, Herbert Manzoni, could not even spare a few minutes to call on Matthew when visiting County Hall to discuss housing; he was interested only in talking to the Valuer.[22]

At this stage, the fortunes of classical and Modernist architecture still seemed fairly evenly balanced.[23] Methodically and quietly, therefore, Matthew set about building a range of new alliances. His own planners were influenced both by SPRND-style scientific humanism, with its mixture of Taylorist research-based efficiency and leftish radicalism, and by a persistent strain of the older teamwork humanism of the Arts and Crafts. Arthur Ling, the senior planner in Matthew's department, stemmed from the more down-to-earth Liverpool School variant of this world view.[24] But it soon became clear that the planners could not turn matters around for Matthew on their own – not only because of their Soviet communist sympathies, which became extremely awkward for Matthew around 1949–50, during the short-lived anti-Soviet purges in Britain, but also because of the relatively lesser importance accorded to the visual aspects of architecture in their overarching planning concepts. Indeed, when Ling turned his attention to architecture at all, he showed a typically Liverpool fondness for residually classical axes and socialist realism – not altogether dissimilar to the Beaux Arts classicism of Matthew's own architects, such as Williams, or the planning schemes of some other prominent architect-planners, such as Gibson's Broadgate project at Coventry.[25]

For Matthew's fightback in London, by contrast, 'proper' Modern architects were needed, and here the most obvious potential supporters were other Modern architects in London, to whom Matthew could offer some work on school design. In November 1946, for example, he met F R S Yorke and C S Mardall for dinner at the Danish Club. Other potential allies included Philip Powell (1921–2003) and Hidalgo Moya (1920–94), whose winning *Zeilenbau* scheme in the nationally prominent Pimlico redevelopment competition (1946) coincided almost exactly with his own LCC appointment.[26] He soon began to win friends even among Walker's allies within the council. More important was the 'progressive' outlook of many influential councillors, including women chairs such as Mrs Dalton, Mrs Bethune (Education), Mrs Patricia Strauss (Parks, sculpture), Mrs Bolton (Town Planning), Evelyn Denington (vice chair of housing from 1950), and also including Lord Latham, the council leader, and Ike Hayward, his deputy. Matthew's Achilles heel at first was a grumbling continuation of his lumbago and sciatica, which confined him to bed for spells of several weeks at a time; he continued to be troubled by the 'family back' for many years, and only later, in the 1970s, did he more or less resolve the problem by adopting the Alexander technique, which advocated keeping up and moving rather than staying in bed.

The post-Forshaw retrenchment of the department, which forced Matthew effectively to mark time for the first year or so of his appointment, also had the important incidental benefit of allowing him to continue informally his work on the Clyde Valley Plan, and more generally to maintain his contacts with Scottish affairs. Following publication of the draft report in June 1946, the next task was to press ahead with editing and publishing the full book version. But, with Matthew's departure, the Clyde Valley team had been left somewhat in limbo, with Ronald Walker the only senior member still involved. Grieve complained to Matthew in November 1946 that the Plan had been lost in the 'vast anonymity' of DHS – 'The Plan is nobody's baby north of the Border' – and that the department was now sorely short-staffed in relation to its vastly expanded responsibilities.[27] In late 1946 and early 1947 Matthew continued, with the close help of Reiach and Grieve, to organise the detailed editing, printing and financing work for the book form of the report, against the background of continual deferrals and cost cuts: in 1947 Reiach joked that 'by the time the book does come out, we shall have quite forgotten what was in it!' In August 1947 the Clyde Plan Advisory Committee was disbanded, and Walker wrote to Matthew of his 'deep depression' over the government 'failure' to implement the plan. The work on illustrations and publication continued into mid 1948, and the book was eventually published on 20 August 1949, projecting back into public debate the argument for decentralisation of Glasgow on a large scale.[28]

By early 1947 Matthew's long-distance efforts to reinvigorate Scottish regional planning were focused on the need to fill his old post with a forceful organiser and ally – especially given Glasgow Corporation's bitter opposition to East Kilbride at the public inquiry, and the lack of interest of the new Labour ministers in the planning cause. The department was deeply involved with the first two new towns: all the plans were drawn up directly by DHS, as the development corporations were only in embryonic form. But divisions were emerging between an 'architectural' faction led by Robert Scott Morton, working on the layout for the first neighbourhood unit at East Kilbride, and a planning team, led by A B Wylie, developing the first unit at Markinch (Glenrothes). As an interim expedient, Matthew secured the promotion of Frank Connell as senior planning officer, with a remit to coordinate a unified policy of traffic-free 'precinct' planning. But, behind the scenes, he was working hard at a more permanent solution, by positioning one of his Liverpool School contacts, Robert Gardner-Medwin – since 1944 the government chief architect for the British West Indies – to assume the succession. Offered the job in March 1947, by August Medwin was consulting Matthew and Abercrombie on ways of strengthening the Clyde Valley Plan framework, and in September he arranged for Matthew, Holford, Mears and Abercrombie to evaluate the provisional outline plan for East Kilbride prepared by Connell's staff: the planned population had been cut from 60,000 to 40,000 and the area of development confined south of the main railway line, with a total of 11 'primary school neighbourhood sub-units'.[29]

Cultural centre to concert hall: the Royal Festival Hall, early 1947 to mid 1948

Something big, something sensational was needed to allow Matthew to break out of this initial impasse at the LCC. Paradoxically, although the department's reputation would ultimately stand or fall on its social building and planning work, if he was, in the short term, to escape the vicious circle of low architectural expectations within his department, and circumvent the political and ideological difficulties associated with the planners, such a *deus ex machina* would preferably have to come from the more traditionally prestigious areas of architecture. And by mid 1947 just such an opportunity was beginning to show itself, in the form of an ambitious project for an LCC-designed 'cultural centre' on the decayed, industrial south bank of the Thames, opposite central London. This idea had first been adumbrated by Abercrombie and Forshaw in the County of London Plan, in a proposal for a comprehensive redevelopment of the river front from County Hall to Southwark Cathedral in a grand Beaux Arts monumental style of repetitive, ponderous pavilions. It was to be carried out in three stages from west to east, beginning with a cultural quarter between County Hall and Waterloo Bridge, with theatres, assembly hall and concert hall; the need for the latter had been sharpened, after the bombing of the Queens Hall in Langham Place, by the emergence of the huge popular wartime audience for classical music. The LCC began clearing the site for the first phase, which was now also to accommodate government offices and a new National Theatre, and in March 1947 appointed Charles Holden to coordinate these disparate elements. His plan, still essentially in the grand classical manner, envisaged later contruction of a substantial concert hall on a somewhat unpromising site just to the east of the noisy Hungerford railway bridge.[30]

During mid 1947 Matthew moved quickly to make sure that his staff, rather than Holden, would design this project. But why was it that the saviour of Matthew's ambitions in social construction should be a grand public building? In fact, during the period of the general establishment of modern architecture in Britain in the 1940s and early 1950s, much of the work of proselytising was done by emblematic buildings that fused traditional and Modern elements. For example, Matthew's former classmate, Basil Spence, went rather further towards the older, stately, 'artistic' approach at Coventry Cathedral (1951–62).[31] More generally, one of the key international strands of the Modern Movement in the late 1940s was the pressure to invent a Modern monumentality to celebrate the new social conditions of the post-war age, without falling back on the old, grandiose classicism. Lewis Mumford's wartime and early post-war writings had called for a civic ritual-based, Geddesian re-embedding of the city, to help combat 'the catastrophe that has been steadily engulfing our whole civilisation'.[32] This new monumentality was above all a social ideal: nothing could better symbolise it than a grand, new, democratic cultural centre designed within a public office, by modern architectural teams.[33] Britain, because of its victor status and limited war damage, had the opportunity to test out these ideas rather sooner than most other countries. In the specific context of post-war Britain the movement towards monumentality chimed in most closely with the neo-Romantic movement, a 1940s attempt, led by John Piper, Graeme Sutherland and others, to found a romantic, Picturesque school of British landscape art.[34] But the search for a more spiritual, monumental Modern architecture remained far more closely bound up with contemporary international developments and with the practical building world.

The South Bank Cultural Centre concept, it soon became clear, offered a substantial opportunity for the new public architectural patronage and practice. But there was a substantial obstacle to this, in the character of Matthew's own archi-

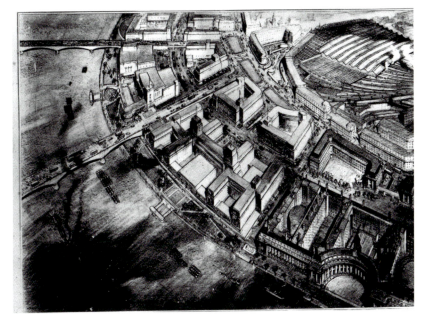

tectural staff. In contrast to the artistic and crafts-influenced ethos of Edinburgh, the LCC staff architects were, on the whole, representatives of the Modern Beaux Arts ethos of the Liverpool School: as exemplified in Williams's work. This was immensely systematic, rationalist, tied into city planning by the teaching and plans of Abercrombie, but also quite old fashioned in its loyalty to a pre-Modernist hierarchy of decorum. What none of Matthew's existing LCC staff – whether Beaux Arts worthies or planner-radicals – seemed capable of doing was to devise a concept for a large public building that would be both respectably Modernist and also able to win the support of the LCC's various political ruling factions. Matthew himself, however, brought to London a distinctive world outlook that made him uniquely fitted to shape the proposed Cultural Centre into a showpiece of the 'new monumentality'. A key element in this was the Geddesian stress on Edinburgh's exceptionally cohesive sense of place and cultural identity – as an inspiration for any strategy of reforming the chaos and injustice of Victorian laissez-faire 'palaeotechnic' settlement. The focus of Geddes's Greek city-state conception of a culture city was the acropolis, which would serve as an 'outlook tower', a spiritual and metaphysical centre to house dramatic and

4.3 South Bank redevelopment, perspective of scheme by consulting architect (Charles Holden), showing the 'Holden Line' that enforced a uniform set-back of all new buildings from the river. The National Theatre is visible above (to the east of) the concert hall. (London County Council)

theatrical rituals and generally condense the cultural essence of a city. This *Weltanschauung* remained with Matthew even after he evolved a more Modernist position in the mid 1930s. His evening and weekend drives round London, for example, during 1946–7, constituted a kind of informal Geddesian diagnostic survey of the capital's *genius loci*.[35]

What Matthew brought to London, in fact, was a modified vision of a 'valley section', for which the external framework and context would be provided by Abercrombie's (and Forshaw's) plans, as well as Steen Eiler Rasmussen's slightly earlier overview of the city, *London, The Unique City*.[36] Matthew's own role would be to give substance to that framework, through specific planning initiatives and through housing, if he could get the latter back. But the renewed London would require not just an Attica – a well-planned hinterland – but also a spiritual acropolis, of fitting character for the social age. In the proposal for a cultural centre, just such an acropolis had potentially dropped into Matthew's lap. Its cultural character would have to be quite different from the quiet ideal of anonymous serial-production teamwork emphasised by the English scientific-humanist tradition, which was in those years developing its influence within building programmes such as the Hertfordshire Schools. To stand a chance of success in the 1940s' age of austerity, this project would have to be led from the front with a dose of Geddesian propaganda and an eye for a gesture, while of course avoiding excessive flamboyance. From the start, the LCC would need to arm itself with a concept that could shape both the eventual building and its reception, as a set piece of the new Modern architecture.

To ensure that this would be a Modern multipurpose building rather than an old-style concert hall, he invited all the other chief officers and some members to 'have a whack at suggestions for the "Cultural Centre"'. Suggested elements, in addition to concert halls and theatres, included swimming baths, gymnasia, arenas and stadia, a youth centre, a funfair and even a planetarium. From the start, Matthew was determined that this should not be a mere introverted concert hall like the circular Usher Hall in Edinburgh (1910–14 by J Stockdale Harrison), its horseshoe auditorium ringed by utilitarian corridors. It must be 'a centre for musical activities of all kinds ... with ample space round the Hall for walking and talking, eating and drinking, and sitting about quietly', and plenty of opportunity to look outwards across the Thames while doing all those things.[37] This concept of a broader, more inclusive Cultural Centre, an outlook tower over the reshaped London, was the first of the key elements that formed the Festival Hall of today. Its promotion and acceptance were almost entirely Matthew's achievement.

Matthew's vision of the Cultural Centre was also shaped specifically by modern trends in concert hall design. Internationally, the grand tradition of concert hall planning, with its hierarchical tiers of private boxes in the tradition of La Scala, had been democratised over the previous century, first in the admission of the working classes in Garnier's 1861–75 Paris Opera, and then in the adoption of more unified, 'democratic' plans and simple, monumental styles. The idea of a symbolic Cultural Centre had been elaborated since the days of Geddes, and the welfare state ethos, with its demands for greater social integration, led to demands for integration of concert halls with other cultural functions. For example, in 1934–41 Sven Markelius's unbuilt plan for a Folkets Hus (cultural centre) in Stockholm proposed a vertically stacked, 2,000-seat upper congress hall and a 1,065-seat lower concert hall, encased by a flowing pattern of foyers and rooms. The Palazzo dei Congressi at the E'42 World's Fair (EUR) in Rome (by Adalberto Libera, 1937–54) also featured a vast meeting hall with foyers and service areas around and below.

So far, none of the South Bank proposals was seriously intended for construction within the next five years, but already, in January, a possible acceleration of the timetable had come into view. In that month, the government finally abandoned its idea of holding a great international exhibition on the centenary of the Great Exhibition in 1951 – an idea originally suggested by Gerald Barry, editor of the *News Chronicle*, and by the 1946 Ramsden Committee – and began to consider instead a 'more modest British exhibition', possibly on the South Bank site. As conceived by Barry and other key supporters, such as J B Priestley, the exhibition was one of the last flourishes of nationalistic neo-Romanticism. As early as 1946 Barry called for 'a new national style', embodying 'moral and spiritual values' as well as technical standards.[38] At a meeting with Max Nicholson of the Cabinet Office, Matthew was told that 'the LCC Cultural Centre might be given some priority in this connection'. By June 1949, he was in discussions with the Arts Council about possible financial support to make sure one first-class concert hall was ready for the 1951 Festival of Britain exhibition; to bolster the LCC's claims to build it, he was now asked to draw up a schedule of accommodation for the cultural centre, and some conceptual sketches. Clough Williams-Ellis recalled that already, in early 1947, 'there was Robert in his bed-sitter or by the living-room fire with a board balanced across his knees, working away at his draft for the Royal Festival Hall, all in our cherished little Carlton Terrace Mews house.' In mid June 1947 the LCC General Purposes Committee issued Matthew with a general accommodation brief, which would continue generally in force until the project was finally commenced, in a truncated form, in May 1949.[39] The brief stipulated that the centre should contain a large concert hall, seating 3,500–5,000, a small theatre seating 1,000, a restaurant overlooking the river, an exhibition gallery, and meeting rooms. Matthew recalled that 'this bare list of primary elements was handed to me and I was asked to say what area of ground would be required.' Matters were looking optimistic, and in his July 1947 letter to Budden about his difficulty in attracting

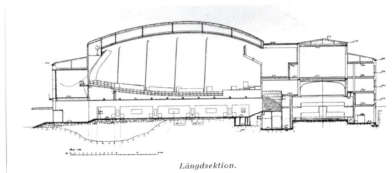

Längdsektion.

designers Matthew added that 'in the near future I am hoping our "Cultural Centre" on the South Bank will come along'.[40]

Immediately, Matthew identified a double acoustics problem as the core of the design challenge of the cultural centre: first, how to insulate the concert hall from the deafening rumble of the trains only 40 feet away; and, second, how to arrive at an optimum shape for the auditorium itself, to give the best quality of sound transmission. The first response, in Geddesian and Modernist terms, was survey and scientific data-gathering. During the summer 1947 Council recess he threw himself into a crash tour of concert halls in England, France, Denmark and Sweden, including the Liverpool Philharmonic, Salle Pleyel, Copenhagen Broadcasting House, the State Theatre at Malmö, and the concert halls at Stockholm and Göteborg.[41] Scandinavia was still a prime focus of his overseas friendships, and he was able to visit a

(top) **4.4** Front facade of recently completed Göteborgs Konserthus, c.1940. (C A Traeff, Göteborg)

(bottom) **4.5** Long-section of Göteborgs Konserthus, 1939. (published in A Romdahl, *Göteborgs Konserthus*, Goteborgs Litografen)

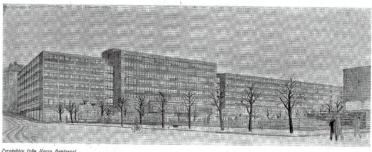

Perspektiv från Norra Bantorget

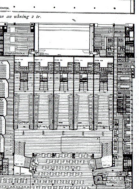

Plan av våning 2 tr.

Plan av våning 1 tr.

SVEN MARKELIUS: *Folkets Hus, Stockholm.* Projekte-
rat 1934–41 för Folkets hus förening, Stockholm. Ej ut-
fört. Betong och tegel.

Sektion

Bottenplan 1 : 800

111

4.6 Perspective, section, plans of Sven
Markelius's unbuilt Folkets Hus,
Stockholm, 1934–41, showing
multi-level sectional arrangement.
(*Undervisning*, 1934, 111)

large number of old and new acquaintances in Sweden and Denmark, such as
Anders Tengbom in Stockholm or Steen
Eiler Rasmussen in Copenhagen. Sweden,
especially, seemed to be a key influence
on his early ideas for the Cultural Centre.
He was particularly impressed by Nils
Einar Eriksson's Göteborgs Konserthus,
opened in 1935. It contained a main hall
with 1,370 seats, plus choir and orchestra, and a small 450-seat hall behind,
both with rectangular plans. What was
specially important was that the main
hall, internally clad in 20 mm thick timber sheets in flowing acoustic profiles,
was entirely ringed by sweeping public
promenades and refreshment areas,
including a huge, fully glazed front foyer
to Götaplatsen, and was raised up above a

ground floor of cloakrooms. The
Göteborgs Konserthus was less than half
the size of the proposed London centre,
and somewhat classical and monumental
in character, with fairly sharp segregation of floors and spaces. At a similar
scale, Hellden, Lallerstedt and
Lewerentz's newly completed City
Theatre in Malmö, praised for its 'fine
combination of boldness, elegance and
efficiency' in a 1946 *Builder* article on
contemporary Swedish architecture, featured a foyer flowing under the auditorium; the building mass was polarised
between a low, front foyer block and a
tall fly-tower.[42]

With these Scandinavian precedents,
the second of the two main conceptual
elements of the project began to fall into
place. Matthew had already ensured that
it would be envisaged as a 'Cultural Centre'
and social focus. Now it was becoming
clear that this aim could be partly secured,
even without the planetarium and funfair, by linking the large and small halls
and the catering space through an
enveloping, three-dimensionally planned
social foyer. Matthew's next stage of
Geddesian survey, on his return to London
in late summer 1947, was to immerse
himself in the technical aspects of the
project, and consult the experts. Eriksson
had advised Matthew to read a number of
acoustics texts by American-based
researchers Professor V O Knudsen and
Professor Cyril M Harris. He later recalled
that 'I was very glad he did, as I was able
subsequently to understand our consultants!' He also contacted his closest friend
in the world of architectural research,
Bill Allen, who was by now BRS Deputy
Head of Physics (1937–53; later, BRS Chief
Architect 1953–61), and who had developed a particular interest in acoustics.
Matthew now reported to Allen that he
had

met Mattson, the general adviser on
acoustics and studio planning to the
Swedish broadcasting people, and Dr
Jordan, a similar consultant to Danish
broadcasting. The concert halls at
Gothenburg and Copenhagen are

very fine, and very good acoustically – once the holidays are over, I would like to have a chat with you on this subject.'[43]

By December 1947 it had been decided that the 1951 national display was to comprise a single large exhibition of industrial and technological progress, called the 'Festival of Britain', along with a variety of provincial themed exhibitions, all to open in May 1951. On 21 July 1948 the newly appointed Festival Council settled on the South Bank site, and endorsed the LCC Cultural Centre plan. The government approved the proposal on condition that the LCC build a new river wall along the entire frontage of the exhibition by 1950. Late in July Herbert Morrison, as Lord President, contacted the new and ambitious LCC leader, Isaac Hayward, to ask whether it would be possible to complete the hall strictly in time for the opening of the festival; if so, top priority on materials would be guaranteed. Hayward, anxious to keep the project in-house for prestige reasons, approached Matthew, ignoring RIBA objections that the job should go to competition among private practices. Matthew later recalled that to accept was 'not a very difficult decision to make', as he knew the project would attract the best architects, builders and craftsmen – instantly solving his recruitment problem! He demanded a short-cut administrative procedure, with a special subcommittee chaired by Hayward with full powers in all matters. The General Purposes Committee authorised £10,000 for action during the summer recess, including preliminary drawing and boring work.[44]

By July 1948 Matthew was already busy producing initial drawings of the hall – but under rather unusual conditions. After a visit to Sweden in April to study prestressed concrete construction, he had been struck down by his back pains once more, and was confined to bed for over two months. To allow him to continue working on the Cultural Centre, a special drawing board was constructed for him in his bedroom at Kensington Square. Stuart and Joan Matthew, en route back from a trip to Switzerland to study hospitals and housing, visited 36 Kensington Square in July, and found an unexpected sight:

Robert was lying flat, with a great contraption of tubular steel above him, over the bed; on to that was fixed, upside down, a double-elephant drawing board – he could tilt it one way or another. From a rail above that, his instruments, such as his pencils and knife, were dangling, suspended on elastic. He would pull them down, and draw a bit, then rest – he was in great pain with his back, and pumped full of morphia, but he was determined to keep working on the concert hall.[45]

We shall shortly look in more detail at the various design solutions proposed at this early stage, during mid 1948. But, at the same time, Matthew equally had to push on with the staffing of the project. Here, although never explicitly discussed, it was vital to secure architectural design staff of standing who were committed to the Modern Movement, however broadly defined. For the moment, Matthew had to rely on the help of Edwin Williams, but his elevation sketches were unacceptable, being 'in the Dudok manner, brick, with overflowing flowerboxes'.[46] Nor was Arthur Ling, despite his planning skills, any use. To sideline Williams and the other old-timers, Matthew decided on a strategy comprising three linked elements. The first was to appoint a dozen young, temporary 'school-trained architects of distinguished ability ... hand-picked with the help of the art schools and associations', to do the donkey work of detail design. The second was to appoint a personal architectural assistant to help him on the project. The third was to attract a high-calibre figure to fill the post of Deputy Architect, unsuccessfully advertised since August 1947 (in itself, an indication of the LCC's still low architectural standing). The 12 temporary architects would be formed into a new Concert Hall Section, formally administered by Williams, but directed architecturally by

Matthew, his assistant and the Deputy, in whichever permutation seemed most expedient; Williams could then be left with the more humdrum tasks, assisted by Principal Assistant Architect Stanley H Smith.[47]

In yet another demonstration of his loyalty to friends and helpers, Matthew had Alan Reiach specifically in mind for the personal assistant post. This, although he was not to know it at the time, would in the event have been a decisive breakthrough in Reiach's career, to a British and even international status. But the mid 1940s saw him in a highly strung frame of mind, after the failure of his marriage to Julie Dittmar in 1946. In the end, he was not prepared to move to London at Matthew's bidding, and after several frustrating months of discussion he finally failed to turn up to an interview at County Hall in November 1948, ruling himself out of any participation in the project. Matthew, in frustration and exasperation, wrote him a rare angry letter, and thereafter distanced himself markedly from Reiach. Robert Scott Morton recalled in his memoir that Matthew

had him [Reiach] in mind for developing and detailing the design of the Hall. Alan was offered the post; but back in Edinburgh he changed his mind. He had had enough of London [where he had spent a year, in 1937, as an assistant in Robert Atkinson's office]; he had a charming new house in Edinburgh; and, above all, the idea of being one among a huge staff was highly unattractive to him. He wrote turning it down. Matthew wrote a stinging letter back. But late in life he told Alan he had been right! There is no doubt that on the score of his whole character and sensibilities he *was* right.[48]

As a result of this protracted negotiation, Matthew had lost valuable time, and so the quasi-autonomous role of the 'Reiach' post, it was now clear, would have to be sacrificed; all would now have to be overseen by the new Deputy. Here

there was already far better progress to report, with the appointment of Leslie Martin from 11 October 1948. In the spring of 1948, beginning to despair, after nearly a year of trying, that he would ever find anyone suitable, Matthew had phoned Bill Allen at BRS, and the latter had suggested Martin's name (the BRS and LMS technical offices being near one another, in Watford). At 39, Martin was two years younger than Matthew. He had been a prominent inter-war Modernist teacher and designer, as well as an editor of the avant-garde magazine *Circle*, in 1937. In 1939 – the same year as he and his wife Sadie Speight published *The Flat Book*, an influential manual of Modernist domestic design intended to 'set out certain standards of contemporary design' – he had become deputy architect to the LMS Railway's engineering and planning division (under C H Hamlyn), where he set up the first architectural 'development group' specifically to use that term, dedicated to the pursuit of research, standardisation and dimensional coordination. He was joined there in 1942 by Richard Llewelyn-Davies, the Communist former mentor of the politicised students at the AA.[49] In 1945, for example, the unit had designed an experimental steel-framed prefabricated station. During the war, Martin had maintained a high profile in Modernist architectural circles, serving (for instance) on the RIBA's Recons-truction Committee from 1941, and in the same year taking part in a series of Home Service radio discussions on post-war planning. During his session on house planning, with Elizabeth Denby and Llewelyn-Davies, he asked:

Do we want to live as we do now, all in the same kind of home with our personality splashed across the facade of the house in Tudor gables and stained glass windows? Or, are we prepared to have a house which suits ourselves and our families as individuals, and yet externally forms part of a well-ordered plan? It's for the people to decide.[50]

Now, in 1948, Martin was increasingly anxious to leave his LMS railway job, owing to a personality clash with Field-Marshal William Slim, the newly created deputy head of the nationalised British Railways Executive. Allen recalled that

> Robert rang me up one day at BRS, and asked if I knew anyone who could take the role of developing the Concert Hall design. I said, 'Well, what about Leslie? – he's looking for an appointment.' Robert said, 'My good-ness – I never thought of him! I've read his book [i.e., *The Flat Book*] but never met him. Could you effect an introduction?' I phoned Leslie, and got him to phone Robert, who said, 'Come and meet me at the LCC.

In competition with Ling and Williams in a July 1948 interview, Martin was the easy winner, and was appointed at a salary of £2,000–2,500.[51]

Shaping a modern masterpiece: the Royal Festival Hall, August –November 1948

Final Cabinet approval of the South Bank scheme, including the Hall, came in August, when Matthew was on holiday in Shetland, and Morrison telegraphed him and phoned him directly with the news. During a week spent in Edinburgh en route back to London, in late August and early September, he had a number of long phone discussions with Hayward, to finalise the staffing arrangements of the new Concert Hall Section, and begin site investigations, so that a comprehensive proposal (drawn up largely by Matthew in Shetland) for the project, costed at £1.25 million, could be put to the General Purposes Committee on 4 October. Martin would start work on 11 October, and immediately begin recruiting his team of temporary architects; the team would be installed in the former members' dining room, a bomb-damaged room along the corridor from his and Martin's rooms. A range of specialist consultants was to be engaged, including Bill Allen and Peter Parkin's acoustics group at BRS (starting four days after Martin), the eminent acoustician Hope Bagenal, and engineers Scott & Wilson.[52] Slightly later, Ralph Downes, organist at the

4.7 Comparative sections of Royal Festival Hall and five other auditoria. (*Royal Festival Hall: The Official Record,* London, 1951, 84–5) (Royal Festival Hall)

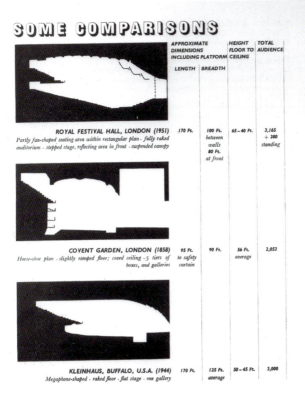

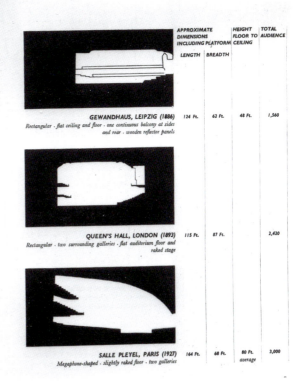

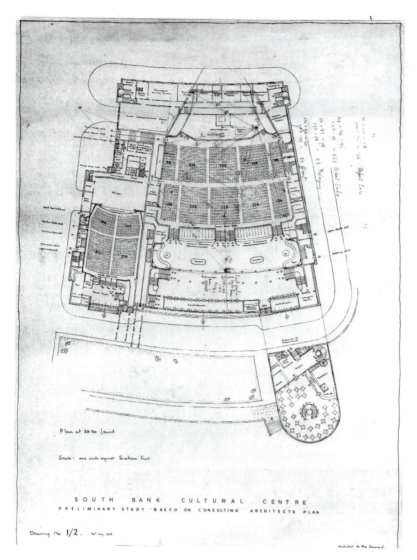

SOUTH   BANK   CULTURAL   CENTRE
PRELIMINARY STUDY · BASED ON CONSULTING ARCHITECTS PLAN

Drawing No 1/2.

4.8 Concert Hall 'Scheme 1', 30 August 1948, street-level plan with annotations by Matthew and with river-front building line dictated by the Holden plan. (EULMC)

Brompton Oratory, was appointed design and specification consultant for the organ, and the composers Ralph Vaughan Williams and Benjamin Britten and conductor Malcolm Sargent were also consulted. All remaining services would be provided by a joint group drawn from the LCC architect's and engineer's departments. Throughout his early career Matthew had aspired to lead a Lorimer-like circle of helpers and co-workers, reshaped in the scientific-humanist terms of Modernism. Now, suddenly, he had succeeded beyond his wildest dreams. Underlying his Geddesian concept of a monumental Modern acropolis that would assist the neotechnic evolution of the capital, and indicating his determination to shape the 'reception' of the Festival Hall as a set piece work, he

promised the council confidently, in an August 1948 report, that he and his deputy would design what 'will, in fact, be one of the historical buildings of London'.[53]

The key design issue for the Centre as a whole, given the June 1947 brief, was how to arrange the required accommodation on the site: should the various elements be spaced out horizontally alongside one another, or should they in some way be compressed? Here, the South Bank masterplan prepared by consulting architect Holden, between his March 1947 appointment and his July 1948 presentation of a finished scheme to the LCC, provided a significant constraint, if not influence, on the evolution of the design, through the form of its overall 'footprint' and its set-back river-front building line. It provided for a wedge-shaped main block (containing a large auditorium at the southwest and a small hall at the northeast, both fan-shaped) and a curved, somewhat Art Deco restaurant spur projecting forward to the river front, the two halls being raised up above a continuous ground floor of car parking. Equally important alongside these layout issues was the question of how the main hall itself should be shaped on plan. Modern acoustic requirements stressed the need to reduce the length of reverberation time to obtain a more precise, highly defined sound, rather than the more fuzzy, echoing effect of older halls. For this, the consensus was that the only two Modern alternatives were a rectangular ('shoebox') or a fan-shaped plan; horseshoe or circular plans were thought to be obsolete. The fan shape was thought to give the better definition, but at the risk of 'long-path echoes' or 'slap back' from curved surfaces, whereas the former was thought by some to favour a 'singing tone', at the cost of excessive width at the orchestra end. As Matthew worked on his initial sketches, he debated this issue on an ad hoc basis with outside advisers, including Allen, Dr Richard H Bolt of MIT and Danish acoustician F Ingerslev. During the summer, trial measurements continued, including a performance of Vaughan Williams's E minor Symphony in Edinburgh's Usher Hall.[54]

At first, up until early October 1948, all the sketch plans featured a fan-shaped auditorium, but were highly diverse otherwise. In late 2003 a large, carefully wrapped roll of drawings of these early schemes was discovered at Matthew's family house, Keith Marischal, East Lothian (now passed to Edinburgh University Library (Special Collections)). The newly discovered plans are all either partly or wholly in Matthew's hand; none has any apparent handwriting input by Martin; most are undated. They show three main alternative solutions to the June 1947 General Purposes Committee brief for a Cultural Centre, including large and small hall, restaurants, exhibition space and meeting rooms. These are listed here as 'Schemes 1, 2 and 3'. In a continuation of that sequence (see below), Scheme 4 is that approved by the Council in November 1948, and Scheme 5 the truncated project actually built. Three other undated sketch layouts of mid 1948 in Matthew's hand show variant side-by-side permutations of the large and small hall arrangement.[55]

Scheme 1, presented in a fully inked-up, stencil-lettered form, with handwritten captioning by Matthew, is dated 30 August 1948. It uses, quite literally, the footprint indicated in Holden's July masterplan, with its large (southwest) and small (northeast) halls and curved restaurant spur, the halls all being raised above the ground-floor parking level.[56] Scheme 2 – a group of sparsely captioned, undated sketch plans and section – is entirely in Matthew's own hand. It occupies the same footprint as the Holden scheme, including the restaurant spur, and halls raised above ground-level car park, but arranges the accommodation differently, with the fan-shaped large hall at the northeast and the small hall in a rectilinear block along the southwest side. Although sketchy in character, it seems lighter and more Modernist in general treatment.

Scheme 3, drawn and lettered almost entirely in Matthew's own hand, takes us dramatically nearer the finished hall. It is similar to the approved (November 1948) Scheme 4, but shows both halls as fan-shaped. In response to growing pressure to reduce the area of site used, the most obvious response, on the Göteborg and Stockholm precedent, was to lift the main auditorium up above the small hall, extending the foyer space below as well as around the main hall. Accordingly, the main auditorium is raised up in a fully fledged 'egg-in-a-box' fashion, above the same arrangement of flowing foyers and staircases, with the small hall/theatre pushed in behind, and the restaurant/exhibition areas nestling below on the river-front side. Probably in association with Scheme 3, a new and more detailed schedule of accommodation, dated 4 October 1948, was prepared. The large hall was now to have a maximum of 3,500 seats, with rear balconies, raked or stepped sightlines and stepped reflecting ceiling; it would be entered from double cut-off lobbies from continuous circulation areas arranged around the perimeter of the auditorium, with enough foyer space to accommodate 70 per cent of the audience in the intervals.[57]

A possible chronology of Schemes 1–4 is as follows. Schemes 1 and 2, together with the 'minor variant' sketches, probably date from the July–August 1948 period, with Scheme 1 prepared officially with the help of Williams and the staff,

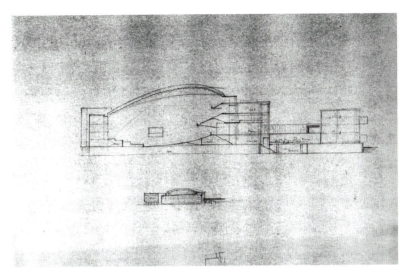

4.9 Concert Hall 'Scheme 2' (probably July–August 1948), long section drawn by Matthew. (EULMC)

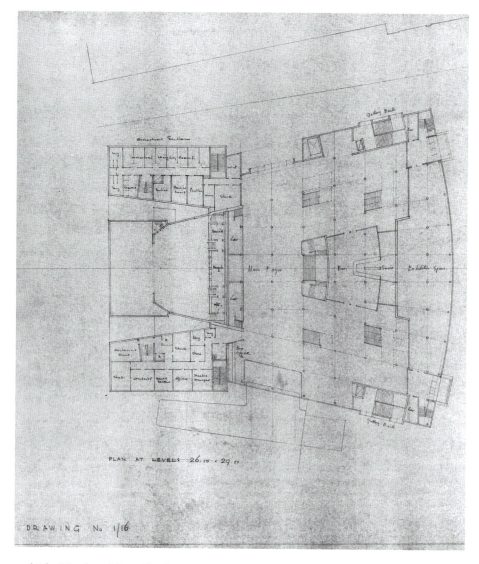

and 2 by Matthew himself at home, during his lumbago incapacitation, as a more up-to-date alternative. Scheme 3 can perhaps be identified as the fan-shaped sketch design worked up in September and early October, following the restriction of the site but before the arrival of Martin and the acoustics consultants – who inspired the rectangularised and slightly more compact Scheme 4.

This sequence reinforces the impression of a design process dominated not by a single masterly conceptual gesture, but by a rather messy stage-by-stage compression and paring away of the ancillary Cultural Centre elements, culminating, as we shall see, in the drastically truncated scheme of February 1949. But how could it be that, as the drawings suggest, Matthew could have substantially

originated three such different potential solutions within such a short time, and even in parallel – one of them being stodgily conservative and the other two more 'Modern'? A significant clue was given by Sir James Dunbar-Nasmith, one of Matthew's first assistants in his post-1953 private practice (on which see Chapter 6). He recalled that Matthew's initial response to a brief was to produce a vast range of alternative sketch designs, and focus in on one in particular only after extended consideration, and discussion within the office – a somewhat even-handed, low-key and collegiate approach, rather appropriate to a collectivist 'cultural centre'.

From mid October, Scheme 3 (the fan-shaped egg-in-a-box) was fundamentally challenged by the new team. First, the

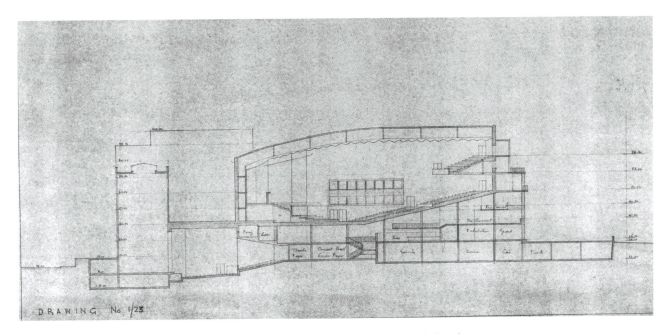

DRAWING No 1/23

requirement to cut down the amount of ground used at the sides (which had led to the stacked arrangement in Scheme 3) was reinforced further. More serious, Bagenal and the BRS team trenchantly objected to the fan-shaped auditorium, believing that it risked echoes. They insisted on immediate substitution of a shoebox plan, trying to overcome its restriction on seating by giving it a slightly tapering end.[58] From this point, having apparently set out the key conceptual solutions, the project became a strict team effort. Shifting decisively from his 'detail' to 'delegated' mode, Matthew was happy to leave almost the entire detailed working-through of the design to his deputy and team, as he had already spent time enough on the project, and needed to begin focusing on other developing aspects of his work. This did not mean that the design work now transformed itself into a unified process of realisation. The project was organised in far too loose and decentralised a manner for that, and would face – within months, as we shall see – a further unexpected and fundamental redesign.[59]

During October, Martin himself worked on conceptual sketches, using an apartment in the nearby Artillery Mansions as a retreat. At the same time, he urgently set about building the team of designers. His most important choice was

Peter Moro, an émigré German Modernist who had been a MARS group participant and member of the Tecton practice in 1937–9, a partner (briefly) of Richard Llewelyn-Davies in 1938, and an influential teacher at Regent Street Polytechnic since 1941. Moro was initially engaged in October simply as a specialist in interior design and fittings, working on a quarter-time basis only, as Alan Reiach was still (until November) potentially in the frame as a special assistant to Matthew. With the growing realisation that Reiach was not likely to materialise in London, and that he himself could not afford to spend more time on design work, Matthew gave up his own architectural assistant post altogether, and allowed Martin to use the funds to build up Moro's part-time involvement instead, rising to half time from November, so that he rapidly became Martin's right-hand man. On the advice of his friend (and, from 1956, future architectural partner) Stirrat Johnson-Marshall, Matthew organised the Concert Hall Section on the same decentralised lines as the Hertfordshire County Council schools architects (and Rowse's student units in the pre-war AA), allowing even quite junior designers great freedom in their aspects of the job.[60]

Within this loose hierarchy Moro – as a kind of part-time consultant, entitled 'Associated Architect' – had an especially

4.12 Front cover of *Weekly Scotsman*, 13 October 1949, showing Matthew at his desk in County Hall, along with the concert hall model and South Bank site views. (Scotsman Publications)

privileged position, not least in the fact that Martin delegated to him the selection of most of the assistant designers, something that arguably reinforced Moro's own individual design contribution. The latter recalled in 1995 that

the egg-in-a-box concept existed in a very diagrammatic form when I arrived. Whether it was Matthew or Martin's idea I don't know for sure – probably it was a bit of both – but I wasn't there at the time! My job was

to realise it and turn it into a building. I had all sorts of privileges, which was very nice. I didn't have to sign on, and I could recruit my own staff. I'd been teaching for seven years at Regent Street, and Leslie and Robert let me pick eight of my best students – I'd brainwashed them all for seven years, so there would be no arguments over aesthetics! Another group of in-house architects dealt with unglamorous things like lavatories and boiler houses. I started at 9.30 or 10, and

Modern Architect

stayed until 7 or 8 with one or two of my chaps, then went on to the pub.

The LCC establishment officer reported to Matthew and Martin in astonishment one morning: 'Do you know, I went round your office at eight last night and all your chaps were still working there!'[61]

To reinforce the egg-in-a-box concept, Parkin and Allen also became convinced that the 'egg' itself needed further insulation, with double concrete walls and specially muffled double entrance doors to the auditorium. To prove the point, in late October a special hut, or block-house, was built by BRS in the corner of the site, right by the railway viaduct, with full-scale walls and roof; to convince Hayward's doubting committee, they were locked in the hut while loud explosions were set off outside it. By the end of November a revised scheme, Scheme 4, now officially titled 'Concert Hall' rather than 'Cultural Centre', was ready for approval.[62] The 3,100-seat auditorium, weighing 22,000 tons with its 'acoustic box' of double thickness concrete walls and arched double-shell concrete roof, together with its side boxes and sloping floor, was surrounded by an envelope of access stairs, galleries and foyers, with the fan-shaped small theatre hall below and behind. The main entrance was on the east (side) facade on the ground floor, with the main ascent route at right

angles – adding to the spatial complexity. Emphasising the hall's affinity with the light, temporary architecture of the surrounding Festival of Britain, the entire structure around the auditorium was to be of steel framing, built by Redpath Brown.[63] The first drawings for Scheme 4 by Martin's team showed the small hall squeezed in part of the way beneath the main auditorium, but still with an ungainly block projecting from the rear. If the building had actually been

(top) **4.13** 1951 group photograph of post-October 1948 Concert Hall design team. From left, Peter Moro, Leslie Martin, Robert Matthew, Edwin Williams. (Royal Festival Hall)

(bottom) **4.14** Concert Hall, section, northeast side elevation and plan of unexecuted Scheme 4, including projecting small hall on left. (Royal Festival Hall)

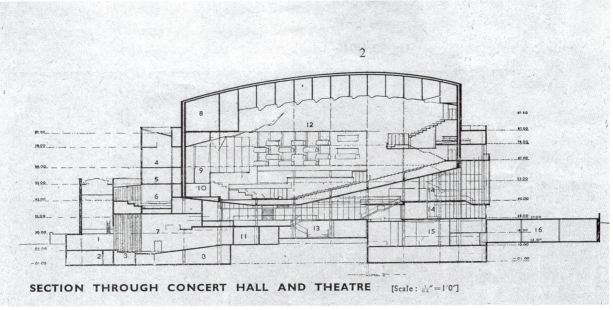

SECTION THROUGH CONCERT HALL AND THEATRE [Scale : $\frac{1}{64}$" = 1'0"]

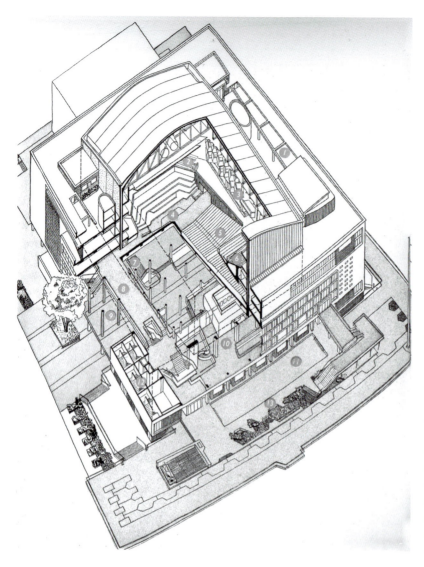

4.15 Concert Hall, cutaway perspective of Scheme 4 (seen from north), showing egg-in-a-box section and small hall. (*Royal Festival Hall, The Official Record*) (Royal Festival Hall)

constructed in this form, it would not have been the Festival Hall we know today.[64] Externally, the effect would have been more abruptly boxy than the hall as built, and somewhat more like a conventional town hall, with its heraldic ornament. In short, it would have seemed less harmoniously unified and monumental.

Monument to austerity: the Royal Festival Hall, late 1948 to early 1949

Even this fresh version of the design was not, in the event, destined to be built. Almost immediately there were further radical changes of plan, stemming not from the designers but from external pressures. The report accompanying the November 1948 plan had warned that, as

the site could not be cleared until February 1949, the small hall might have to be omitted until after the Festival of Britain. By January 1949 this cut was made unavoidable by an even worse problem – a sudden shortage of steel, with only 1,600 tons now to be allowed for the hall. This would make it necessary to construct the entire building in reinforced concrete, costing 50 per cent more than the £1.25 million estimate and taking far longer. This was a strategic crisis tailor-made for the unflappable Matthew. He had to decide whether to scrap the now functionally superfluous egg-in-a-box concept and revert to the previous concepts of a cheaper, one-level layout. Further design delays would be fatal to the overriding deadline, so Matthew decided against this, and instead elected to defer the rear third of the building, including the small hall and the stage and administrative areas, finishing the rear (south) wall with temporary cladding and providing temporary changing rooms in the bar areas. He was helped in his decision by the discovery that the Tube tunnels below the building were ten feet higher than had been thought, which would have complicated the insulation of the small hall. The influence of Morrison allowed the release of Portland stone for the external cladding and timber for the huge front window.[65] No longer linking two halls, the foyer now took on an autonomous importance. The project had assumed its final conceptual form not through one masterly design decision, but rather through a series of accidental, reactive developments. The result, with its temporary asbestos-cement rear facade screen, was actually somewhat neater on plan, as it omitted the untidy rear projections, but it would be very obviously unfinished on the day of formal opening. This state of affairs would be successfully disguised by the triumphal, propagandist presentation of the building, orchestrated largely by Matthew over the following two years.

At last, in late February 1949, tenders for the reduced Scheme 5 could be invited. Six major contractors submitted a priced schedule, time chart and organisation scheme for the 21-month contract, to stretch from May 1949 to the end of 1950. Although the lowest tender, by Gee, Walker & Slater, was £20,000 cheaper, the £1,628,000 tender by Holland, Hannen & Cubitt was accepted, on the advice of the quantity surveyors; the £50,000 organ was to be built by Harrison & Harrison. The London *Evening Standard* hailed the decision to commence the 'great palace of culture', and Matthew's old DHS chief, the now ailing John Wilson, wrote his congratulations, adding lugubriously that 'I shall not be able to see it!'[66]

Over the following two years, with detailed design and construction running almost in parallel, the teamwork principle was safeguarded and developed by Matthew. He and Martin had arrived, by stages, at the overall spatial concept of the egg-in-a-box, however redundant the latter now was in practical terms. It was now chiefly the task of Moro and his team to bring a richness and warmth to this design, drawing on the rich seam of 1930s Tecton precedent.[67] The results were highly diverse, to the point of potential incoherence, especially once the furnishings, fittings and decoration were being installed. Matthew kept a general eye on the process, and intervened occasionally with Moro and Martin to rein in any confusing detail. For example, the splayed auditorium side walls, clad in Australian walnut, had been conceived by Moro in the form of bent, curving veneered panels, with concealed light fittings of a decorative triangular shape. He recalled that

> when Robert saw all this, he said it was too fussy, and substituted a much plainer design. I was cross at the time, but now I think he was right. There was no practical need for lights there: the acoustic people had said the surface should be broken up, but they soon changed their minds!

Matthew could exploit his building-control oversight role within the LCC, and his persuasive powers with councillors, to 'give himself waivers' that would

allow some design details to be modified. For instance, considering one balustrade obtrusively high, 'Robert told the committee that the location would normally be too crowded to allow anyone to be pushed over, and that in any case there was a tube station right below the building, with crowded platforms unprotected by any railing!' Martin maintained a closer, day-to-day oversight over consistency of detail. He recalled that

> with individuals working as a team, you could take each particular area, say the area round the cloakrooms, or the restaurants, and develop them consistently, yet in an individual way: there were so many things that needed special design, like the chairs in the auditorium and the restaurant, all designed by Robin Day, or the spotted carpets and mobile music stands by Peter Moro's team, or Trevor Dannatt's temporary back wall.[68]

The heady, nationalistic rhetoric of teamwork and urgency discouraged negative interpretations of this somewhat hybrid,

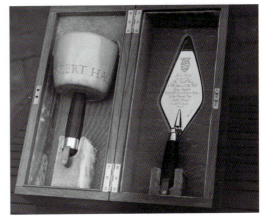

(top) **4.16** Matthew assisting at the laying of the Concert Hall foundation stone by Prime Minister Clement Attlee on 12 October 1949. (Fox Photos Ltd)

(bottom) **4.17** The ceremonial mallet and trowel used by Attlee at the foundation-stone ceremony. (Festival of Britain)

individual-collective design process. Moro argued that 'we were so turned on and inspired that we worked like mad to achieve this within time and within cost. Neither Martin nor I have ever done anything as good ever again!'[69]

From construction to reception: the Royal Festival Hall, May 1949 to May 1951 – and beyond

From early May 1949 building work at the Concert Hall was under way, as the contractors 'attacked the site with a frenzy of energy'. The project was now a traditional, heavy *in situ* concrete job, designed as one unit with expansion joints and complex reinforcement, with London's largest-ever mechanical excavators ploughing their way into the saturated subsoil. In the matter of contract supervision, Martin's chief job now was to keep up the production of detailed drawings and supervise the day-to-day work of the contractors and consultants, while Matthew's was to coordinate overall strategic and contract progress.[70] At this point, having overcome the key hurdle of getting construction of a finalised design started, Matthew's tendency towards mental compartmentalisation came once more to the fore, and he began to turn his mind to other things. First, however, he decided to switch off completely for two months, by accepting an invitation to join an Anglo-American building productivity tour of the East Coast and Midwest US in July and August 1949, as part of a large party of builders, engineers and architects.[71] During this expedition, which we shall return to in detail in Chapter 5, Matthew left Martin completely 'in charge of the shop'. Without Matthew's steadying hand, Martin had an anxious time with the myriad practical demands of the job. A senior LCC administrator colleague wrote to Matthew that 'I believe the Deputy Architect is having a somewhat harassing time with the Concert Hall, as the contractors are treading on the tails of the draughtsmen, but, of course, we knew from the start that the supply of drawings would be a hand to mouth business.'[72] The August 1949 *JRIBA* wrote that 'Britain's first post-war non-austerity and non-essential building' was under way.[73]

On his return, Matthew began the process of diversifying his attention to other tasks, including, as we shall see in Chapter 5, the supreme challenge of recovering housing from the Valuer. Following the setback of an attack of his recurrent lumbago in December 1949, Matthew had to return over the winter to a spell of day-to-day supervision of the Festival Hall contract in order to keep up

(top) **4.18** 1950 sketches by Matthew for armorial panels on the Royal Festival Hall. (Royal Festival Hall)

(bottom) **4.19** May 1950 visit by the King and Queen to the construction site. (Fox Photos)

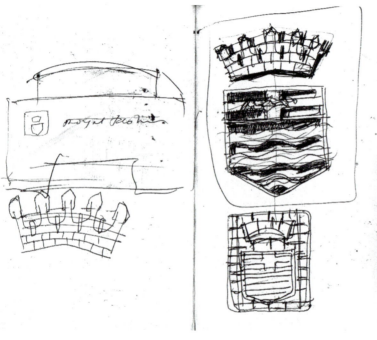

4.20 Perspective by Bryan de Grimeau of the Royal Festival Hall/Festival of Britain construction site. (*Illustrated London News*, 23 December 1950) (Illustrated London News Group)

progress. He turned down one Scottish lecturing invitation by explaining that 'the concert hall is at a very critical constructional stage, and takes up all my energies just now, and I really find no time to think about outside affairs.' By now he was also beginning to turn his mind from the creation of the Festival Hall to its reception, to begin the fostering of a legend. A crescendo of ceremony and acclaim began, both in the wider world and in architectural circles. In October 1949, with the superstructure now appearing, and the 40 m bowstring trusses of the auditorium roof being delivered to the site, Matthew assisted Prime Minister Clement Attlee in the foundation stone ceremony, attended also by Morrison and councillors; a casket of documents and relics was duly buried. In May 1950 he escorted the King and Queen on an inspection of the site.[74]

By mid and late 1949 key administrative decisions that would shape the profile and standing of the future hall were also having to be made, and Matthew made it his business to participate fully in these, while avoiding entering into the more polarised political issues, such as the allegedly communist character of the London Philharmonic Orchestra. By March 1950 the question of the hall's name was being debated. Matthew argued forcefully, in somewhat

Geddesian terms, that the word 'Hall' was 'non-descriptive', even misleading, as the complete project would be 'much more than a "Hall" – indeed it started life in my department as a "Cultural Centre" – a not unsuitable description, if rather ponderous.' He felt 'very strongly' that the name should be 'comprehensive of the whole building, as a meeting place, concert hall, restaurant, theatre and social concourse' and suggested 'Royal Belvedere', to emphasise the 'beauty of the London scene which may be viewed from its terraces, galleries and roof gardens'. In the end, a completely different name was adopted in March 1950, owing to a bizarre administrative bungle, when the Clerk to the Council accidentally failed to send for royal approval the preferred name, 'Queen Elizabeth Hall', and King George instead put forward a new suggestion of his own, 'Royal Festival Hall'.[75]

Matthew could exert a more precise and authoritative influence over the reception of the Hall in the professional, architectural media. Especially after the royal visit in May, the project suddenly assumed an overarching symbolic prominence in the wider British architectural world, including the architectural press. The *Architects' Journal*, for instance, ran regular progress reports on the construction, and its complex spatial

Their Majesties The King and Queen have graciously signified their intention of being present

The Chairman of The London County Council and Mrs J. W. Bowen request the honour of the company of Mr and Mrs Robert H. Matthew at the Dedication and Opening of The Royal Festival Hall at 7 p.m. on Thursday 3rd May 1951

Carriages 9.30 p.m.

Please reply on the enclosed card by 31st March so that admission tickets may be sent

This card does not admit

Evening Dress, Decorations, Dinner Jacket, Lounge Suit

4.21 Robert and Lorna's invitation to the Royal Festival Hall dedication ceremony and inaugural concert, 3 May 1951. (EULMC)

concept was analysed in elevated, even reverent terms.[76]

By the end of September 1950 the structural roof was successfully complete – albeit allegedly cast to the wrong thickness by the contractors – and the application of the Portland stone wall cladding and copper auditorium roof cladding was under way; in October the total number of men on site reached its maximum of 935, and in late November the roof was complete.[77] Where an old-style provincial municipal engineer such as Herbert Manzoni could not spare so much as a few minutes to chat to Matthew in 1948, only two years later a succession of international architectural celebrities was regularly passing through the department, attracted by its youth and dynamism. In early 1951 the visiting Le Corbusier hailed the 'exhilarating youthfulness' of the design team, while Frank Lloyd Wright, on entering Matthew's office in July 1950 and catching sight of him and Martin, exclaimed, 'Why, you're just a coupla boys!'[78]

Even by early 1951, with the basic fitting-out largely complete, the practical difficulties were not yet over. For when the main attention turned to the testing and refining of the auditorium acoustics, yet another disagreeable surprise lay in wait

for Matthew's team. The design had aimed at a middling reverberation time of 2.2 seconds, homogenised as far as possible over the entire hall, to give every seat a 'democratic' equality of sound clarity. But in acoustic test with a full orchestra in February, the actual reverberation proved to be only 1.5 seconds – rather too clear and clinical for comfort, although Sargent quipped that 'English orchestras should simply learn to play better!'[79] The main reason was the unexpected absorbency of the auditorium materials, and a frenzy of minor adjustments began: Parkin devised a system of 'assisted resonance' using hundreds of tiny built-in microphones in the ceiling, but this could only be installed later. A host of other small difficulties emerged, but in view of the prestige of the royal opening ceremony, matters could not simply be left to a later snagging stage, every detail having to be corrected beforehand. Matthew's response was to revive his old, youthful Arts and Crafts passion for minutely detailed study: he decided that he, Martin and the entire design team should spend one week in April personally scouring the building, 'looking at every detail to make sure it's absolutely right before we open in three weeks'. For evening relaxation during this stressful period Matthew devoted much time to making two puppet theatres out of Meccano, clad in red velvet curtains from Festival Hall scraps, all for Janet's 12th birthday.[80]

The arrangements for the opening concert and dedication ceremony for the Royal Festival Hall, on 3 May 1951, proved to be fraught with difficulty. For example, the originally envisaged grand symphonic programme, conducted by Arturo Toscanini, had to be displaced to 4 May when the King insisted on an 'all-British' programme as a precondition for his attendance. There would now be a miscellany of items 'on the theme of Music and of England', including Handel and Elgar's 'Land of Hope and Glory', with Malcolm Sargent, Sir Adrian Boult and Sir Thomas Beecham all invited to conduct. The entire evening's events, officiated by the

Archbishop of Canterbury, would cost the LCC some £2,800.[81] Despite the somewhat overwrought atmosphere, as the opening night loomed Matthew once again showed his powers of mental compartmentalisation by switching abruptly back from 'detail' to 'delegation' mode. In the event, the inaugural night of the Royal Festival Hall passed off without disaster, as the crowds outside 'grew and swelled to VE Day size' in anticipation of the arrival of the royal party and other grandees. Clough Williams-Ellis recalled that

> on the opening night, Robert had invited us and others to dine with him at the hall before the ceremonies and concert began. Though the catering department was clearly as yet unready for action, Robert displayed not the slightest anxiety about the crucial test to which his great work was about to be submitted, but continued to play the part of the entirely relaxed and genial host without a care in the world – when he must, inside, have been secretly just as anxious as Wellington on the eve of Waterloo – yet equally and outwardly as completely unflappable.

In the wake of the opening night, Matthew was inundated with hundreds of congratulatory letters and telegrams: for example, Robert Gardner-Medwin wrote from DHS that the hall was 'the talk of Edinburgh as well as London'.[82]

The days immediately after the inauguration saw an outpouring of journalistic and architectural evaluations of the exhibition and the hall, mostly in a somewhat exalted language interlaced with assertions about national identity. Concerning the Festival of Britain as a whole, the King proclaimed, in his inaugural speech outside St Paul's Cathedral, that it was 'a record of our national character and its history', and government minister and former LCC chief Herbert Morrison more openly evoked the spirit of national rivalry: 'The richness of the Festival programmes will give us a new kind of prestige, such as France and certain other countries have held for many generations'; modern architecture could help 'our success as an exporting nation'. The communist *Daily Worker*, on the other hand, argued that it was no more than an attempt 'to present ruling-class ideas as the ideas of Britain, and carefully to edit Britain's turbulent history to conform with the theme of the preservation of capitalism and imperialism'. Architectural evaluations also focused on national identity, often in terms of complementary opposites: Lionel Brett wrote that the festival was 'overwhelming' because of the absence of 'pomposity': it was 'engineering touched with magic'; the nationalistic Lion and Unicorn pavilion exuded a creative tension between 'fanciful irresponsibility and ponderous sententiousness'.[83]

While the slender, metallic exhibition pavilions could be seen as directly opposed to traditional, hierarchical monumentality, the Festival Hall was in a more ambiguous position. In its stone-faced, near-symmetrical massiveness, however much offset by large windows and flowing internal spaces, and in its stand-alone situation, it clearly still had at least one foot in the world of stately grandeur. But in the exalted atmosphere that prevailed around its opening, that twin-headed character, even more than in the case of Coventry Cathedral, ensured the hall would at first attract almost universal praise. Its prestige stemmed, at the most general level, not from its architecture but from its role as a 'soft' nationalistic symbol of post-war revival, as the centrepiece of the Festival, and as 'Britain's first post-war non-austerity and non-essential building'. It was acclaimed by non-architects in inclusive, overarching terms, as a synthesis of modern national 'democratic' pride with the mass veneration of classical music: Malcolm Sargent, for instance, hailed it as 'the temple of those spiritual joys which are so mystic but so very real'. Only the more conservative conductor Sir Thomas Beecham doggedly stood aside from the chorus of praise, and asked 'whether in 350 years there has ever been erected on the soil of this grand old country a more repellent, a more unattractive, a more ugly and a more monstrous structure'.[84] The Festival Hall's specifically architectural reception was in turn shaped by this heady, consensual praise.

Although it was hailed above all as a standard bearer for modern architecture – with the visiting Le Corbusier, for example, assuring the LCC design team in 1951 that 'the whole world will admire your concert hall' – it also attracted the approval of Traditionalist designers, the sole exception being Sir Albert Richardson, who attacked it in similar terms to Beecham.[85]

Although the hall was the only substantial structure left after the Festival of Britain was dismantled, it was left for many years as an only partly realised concept. In early 1952, hearing Matthew's plans to leave the LCC in mid 1953, Moro wrote to tell him 'how much I enjoyed working with you and Leslie on the Concert Hall,' and to hope that 'we can finish the work together'. That was a vain hope: despite various abortive proposals for the missing service accommodation, it was only in 1963–4 that the LCC Architect secured the required enlargement, albeit with a new main upper entrance from the river walkway, which cut the lower parts of the foyer out of the main circulation route; an alternative proposal by Martin would have relocated the entrance to the rear street level.[86] Over the following years, the Festival Hall's mixture of Modern design with a traditional grand building type ensured it was one of the few large Modern Movement buildings to escape the vilifications of the 1970s and 1980s. With the increasing prevalence of 'signature architecture', there were attempts to single out Martin as the 'real' designer, at the expense of the teamwork tradition.[87] Acoustically, however, its dry, non-reflective reverberation characteristics remained unpopular with musicians and conductors, who felt fewer inhibitions about speaking out as the years went on. Thus, in contrast to the success of the hall's social and aesthetic ambitions, including its general popularity with audiences, arguably the elaborately researched scientific aspects of its Modernism would ultimately prove a failure.

In May 1951, however, all that lay far

in the future. Those involved in the Festival Hall project had been catapulted into the public eye, and now had to make what they could of the experience. But, even for Matthew, the next step also seemed uncertain: he recalled later of the inaugural concert that 'as we came out, a distinguished lady said to me, "This is surely the apex of your career".'[88] Matthew's task now was to prove that prediction wrong, by building on this triumph to advance his wider career, and further promote the cause of Modern architecture and planning in London.[89]

Chapter 5

Planning and housing the new London, 1946–53

To be head of a great organisation and also an artist is the hardest of all tasks. Outside the Cabinet, there is no job that affects the lives and happiness of so many people as that of Architect to the London County Council.

R Furneaux Jordan, 1956

[Matthew was] the most conspicuous of the new kind of architect that emerged in Britain after 1945, who believed that if one could get the system right, the rest would follow.

Lord Esher, 1986[1]

Communities and neighbourhoods

Even as the Royal Festival Hall was still under construction, Matthew had begun capitalising on its prestige to implement more far-reaching reforms within the LCC, which would help shape the wider course of the social building programme across Britain. His overarching aim was to recover responsibility for housing design and, more generally, to reclaim the overall field of London social building for his department, reversing the humiliation suffered at the Valuer's hands.

At first, his main effort necessarily had to be concentrated in the school-building drive, the only major programme under his design control. The chief task was to repair war-damaged existing schools, but with the post-war expansion of education the new-building programme grew from £640,000 in 1946 to £3.5 million in 1953. The Korean re-armament crisis of 1950, however, caused

a major cutback. Many of the projects were dealt with by private architects under Matthew's oversight, but the County Schools Section of his Schools Division designed a substantial number. In 1949, replacing a retiring senior architect, Matthew drafted in the young and energetic Kenneth Campbell, trained at Regent Street Polytechnic, formerly of Forshaw's pithead baths team at the Miners' Welfare Commission, and from 1943 enlisted by Forshaw in his County of London Plan team: by August of that year, Campbell was already 'doing an excellent job on the organisational side' of the new schools programme.[2] The reorganisation, along with the formation of the Concert Hall Section, did much to undermine the LCC's old pyramidal hierarchy in favour of a decentralised network of semi-autonomous groups, on the model popularised especially in the contemporary Hertfordshire school programme: the new Ministry of Education Chief Architect (from 1948) and former Herts Deputy County Architect, Stirrat Johnson-Marshall, helped back Matthew in this change.

During Matthew's time at the LCC, the main focus of school-building in the County of London was still primary schools. A small number of Uni-Seco schools had been built immediately after the war, but with a big backlog of jobs, the Schools Division under Campbell's leadership decided to borrow the Hills 8 ft 3 inches lightweight system for building primary schools as used in Hertfordshire,

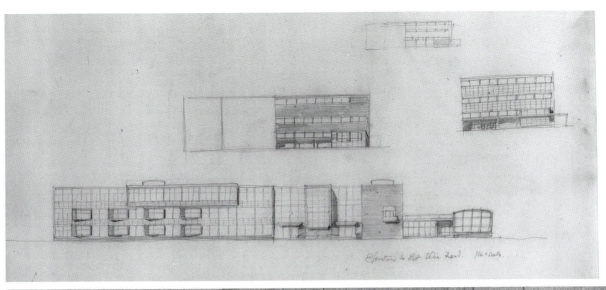

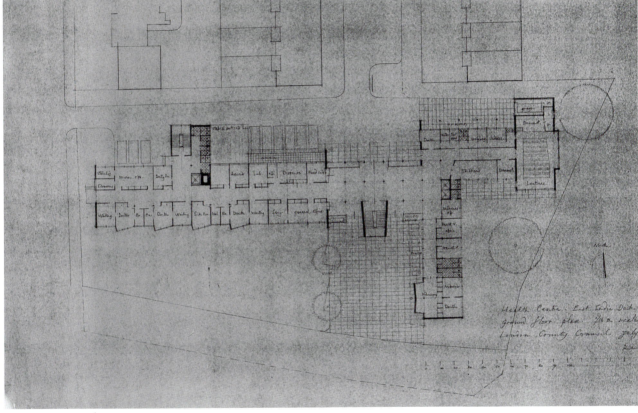

and modify it for two-storey use on the tighter sites available in London. Seventeen such schools were built between 1950 and 1954. The most original of the LCC primary schools built during Matthew's time, however, were farmed out to private architects, like the two designed in Hammersmith and Putney by Ernö Goldfinger, and the Susan Lawrence School at Lansbury by Yorke, Rosenberg and Mardell, who adapted the Hills sys-tem to their own ends. While this was going on, the Schools Division was start-ing to think about secondary schools in the light of the LCC decision to build comprehensives, which no one had attempted before. It was soon decided to follow the Ministry of Education's advice and design these schools to a 3 ft 4 inches module, generally again using the Hills light-steel frame and patent cladding. But there was much uncertainty as to

5.1 Elevation and plan of July 1949 scheme by Matthew for an LCC Health Centre, East India Dock Road, Poplar – like Woodberry Down, a fully fledged modernist design, in a similar style to Ilkeston. The project was also eventually shelved, as an austerity measure. (EULMC)

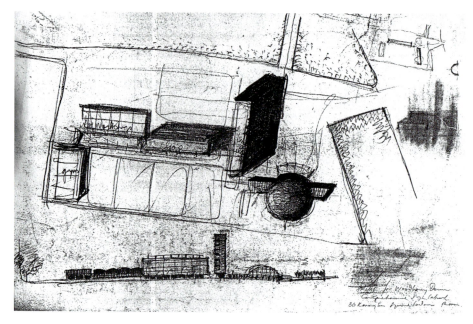

whether to build high and densely, as in an early sketch of 1948 by Matthew for Woodbury Down School (the first school on the drawing boards though not the first built), or to favour a looser style of planning as preferred by the Ministry. Matthew appears to have favoured the high, dense pattern, but had left the LCC before it found its extreme expression in the nine-storey curtain-walled classroom block at Tulse Hill (1953–6).

But the schools programme, however large, was not going to change the entire face of the capital. The only way to do that was to properly exploit the link between town planning and mass housing, as Forshaw had tried to do prior to his departure. Matthew set out to revisit that territory and, by a slower and more patient approach, to succeed where Forshaw had been rebuffed. His task resembled the Festival Hall project in its reliance on teamwork rather than individualism, but in all other ways it was different: it was diffuse, rather than concentrated, and was concerned as much with reports and statistics as with drawings and buildings. The groundwork had been laid in the wartime era of vast strategic planning aspirations, fuelled by Lord Reith's transformation of the Ministry of Works into a ministry of active reconstruction planning (1940–2) – whose intrusion into Scotland Matthew

had played a major part in helping repel. Even these official efforts seemed tame alongside the radical utopianist wartime proposals of private groups such as MARS, envisaging sweeping redevelopment of London with arrays of towers and lines of *Zeilenbau* blocks.[3]

In 1941 Reith imposed on the LCC the County of London Plan project, to be masterminded by Abercrombie, with Forshaw as right-hand man.[4] Forshaw was allowed to build up his Statutory and Town Planning Division, under H B Mackenzie, to support the CLP work with a corps of several dozen planners, especially in the 'New Plan Research' section of the Planning Group; Edwin Williams was in charge of administering the existing limited statutory planning scheme under the 1932 Act. The most ambitious and talented of the 'New Plan' researchers was Arthur Ling. Both he and Kenneth Campbell were not only committed to radical planning reconstruction, they were also card-carrying members of the Communist Party. When the CLP team was formally incorporated into the Planning Division after the formal LCC approval of the CLP in 1945, Ling became Senior Planning Officer, at the age of only 32. Abercrombie and Forshaw's analysis of the capital's planning problems focused on the mixed-together yet sprawling environments that resulted from the centripetal attraction of London, combined with the centrifugal movement to the suburbs within London. The aim was to impose a structure on this chaos, by strategic road-building and a system of three concentric rings of zoned densities for housing (dropping from 200 persons per acre at the centre to 136 in the middle suburbs and 70 on the edge), in tandem with large-scale population dispersal to planned new towns. Within this more orderly, thinned-out structure, it was hoped to reassert the capital's socio-spatial essence – a 'highly organised and inter-related system of communities' or areas 'with a special local feeling or tradition', represented most memorably in the amoeba-like coloured blobs of Ling's 'social and functional analysis' map.[5]

The basic planning tool for structuring these communities was the neighbourhood unit, a concept of an urban community subdivision, ringed by greenery and planned on largely traffic-free, Modernist lines, with a mixture of different types and sizes of housing, including as much as one-third in the form of houses with gardens, and with the possibility of multi-storey towers, set in open space and greenery, as one element. Originally devised in the United States in the 1920s by Clarence Perry and others, propagated by the International Federation for Housing and Town Planning, and further elaborated in an influential development plan for Amsterdam just before World War II, the neighbourhood unit idea was rapidly developed in a variety of wartime reconstruction proposals in both Britain and other countries, including Nazi Germany (*Ortsgruppe als Siedlungszelle*).[6] Abercrombie set the CLP in a regional framework a year later in the Greater London Plan, researched and produced in 1942–4 under the aegis of the Standing Conference on London Regional Planning, at the ultimate instigation of the chief government planner, George Pepler. Although publication was delayed by air raid damage to the Ministry in February 1944, it duly recommended   the dispersal of 800,000 people from 'congested'

London, and the restructuring of the 2,600 square mile region on 'community' lines by a 'Regional Planning Board': architect-landscapist Peter Shepheard worked up the neighbourhood-unit concept in greater detail in 1945, in a theoretical project for an Essex new town at Ongar.

In 1945, after two years of consultations, the LCC duly approved the CLP. Its concept of the neighbourhood community structure of London, to be clarified by strategic roads and the three density rings, with a mixture of houses and flats in each, had become Council policy by the time of Matthew's arrival. Matthew was well qualified to take on that task, given his equivalent role in the Clyde Plan, as Abercrombie's deputy, to Forshaw's in the CLP. In addition, Matthew had experienced the Geddesian world outlook of survey-based planning earlier and more comprehensively than his English equivalents; the AA graduates had received it only at second hand, through Rowse.[7] Matthew was faced immediately with the challenge of the ambitious new Town and Country Planning Bill (later the 1947 Act), with its framework of compulsory, statutory three-year plans based on extensive survey; he would be able to use its powers to work up the council's CLP-based development principles into a formal development plan. In a January 1947 lecture Matthew argued that Geddes's insistence on methodical study of 'the city as a living organism' was the foundation of the Bill's methodology. It had replaced 'static' planning with 'much more flexible' regional-based planning in 'broad outlines'.[8]

Perhaps the most important advantage of Matthew's Geddes-influenced outlook was the way it chimed in with the growing climate of realism and moderation, moving away from the wartime explosion of radical reconstruction plans. Matthew's view of London was that, while Reith's 'first fine frenzy of reconstruction' had been essential, to make sure there was 'a plan ready, before the great tide of reconstruction and expansion again began to flow', realistically one was 'dealing with a living and working city where we cannot wipe clean the slate and start all over again'.[9] It was just as important to safeguard the existing character of the city: 'The amenities of London should be safeguarded by harmonious architectural development, by the preservation of buildings of historical and architectural importance' – and by the teasing out of the *genius loci* of the 350 neighbourhood areas.[10] Redevelopment would now inevitably be a piece-meal affair. This localised formula had already been set in motion by Holford, whose MTCP team in 1944–7 had developed the plot-ratio concept – to allow mixed-height commercial redevelopment at high density – and then, in the City of London, opened the way to tower-and-podium developments, beginning with Fountain House, 1954–8. Among the second-tier metropolitan borough councils, the most powerful, Westminster, took the initiative in 1946 in its influential Pimlico redevelopment competition, won by the young Powell & Moya with a *Zeilenbau* layout.[11] For the LCC itself, the chief focus, of course, was the great Geddesian 'belvedere' of the Cultural Centre/Concert Hall in its South Bank setting. The South Bank was one of three initial redevelopment projects, all recommended in the CLP, which were picked out in March 1947 by Matthew's planners for immediate commencement.[12]

Following the passing of the 1947 Act, the number of planners in Matthew's department was raised to roughly 250 (compared with around 140 in 1939). At his instigation, Ling reorganised the Planning Division into four groups: Applications, Information & Research, Development Plan and Reconstruction.[13] The most potentially innovative was the Reconstruction group, tasked with drawing up and overseeing plans to rebuild bombed areas. Its work overlapped significantly with housing design, and thus was a potential bridgehead in the campaign to claw back the Valuer's advances. To head the group, Matthew signed up Stirrat Johnson-Marshall's brother Percy

(1915–93). He, after graduating from Liverpool, had worked for the MTCP and various local authorities, including Coventry. There he had become a protégé of Donald Gibson, as had Stirrat before him in the 1930s. In the late 1950s and 1960s this elder-brother relationship with Gibson was replaced by a similar relationship with Robert Matthew, for whom they filled the helper role previously occupied in the 1930s and 1940s by Alan Reiach. Percy, like Arthur Ling (but unlike Stirrat and Gibson), had strong communist convictions, and both of them opposed the grand wartime Modernist *tabula rasa* plans from a Socialist Realist perspective, which combined grand boulevards and landmark buildings with elements of 'people's vernacular'. Although Matthew, with his Fabian-Liberal leanings, had no particular sympathy for their political views, they were natural allies for his Geddesian concern for *genius loci*, combined with faith in the rule of government experts.[14]

But the new concern to infuse Modern architecture with vernacular or organic informality had far wider architectural support than this restricted grouping of communist zealots. Across the whole spectrum of Modern architecture the years since the mid 1930s had seen successive attempts at a more natural or spiritual approach. In the work of Le Corbusier, Aalto and others, ideas of *genius loci* and natural vernacular were ever more explicitly foregrounded, in the use of 'primitive' materials and forms: within Britain, Marcel Breuer's Gane Pavilion, Bristol (1936; with F R S Yorke), inspired ultimately by Le Corbusier's Pavillon Suisse (1930–2), combined Modernist open planning and flat roofs with rubble and timber materials; and in the late 1930s the magazine *Focus* made strenuous efforts to bring together regionalism and the avant-garde.[15] The same concerns were further elaborated after 1945: for example, at CIAM 7, held in 1949 in the historic Italian city of Bergamo on the theme of the search for an organic urbanism, Polish socialist-realist architect Helena Syrkus argued

Modern Architect

that 'The Bauhaus is as far behind us as Scamozzi'; and at CIAM 8 in Hoddesdon (1951) the zoned formula of the Charter of Athens was widely criticised amid calls for 'human scale' and 'spontaneity'. Amid the post-war accelerations of scientific progress and of ideological confrontation, the old certainties of 'socialist' International Modernism were dissolving into myriad new interpretations.[16] In Britain, the New Romantic movement in Modern art chimed in with a contemporary town-planning drive to revitalise the Picturesque as a 'national English style', under the name 'Townscape' – an adaptation of Sitte's ideas propagated especially by planner Thomas Sharp, whose 1940s/1950s books invoked medieval towns as the main precedent. The key common ground with New Romanticism was a fondness for collaging of forms and materials.[17]

This broad movement of place-sensitive planning and architecture chimed in strongly with Matthew's own Edinburgh Arts and Crafts and Geddesian background. But what were its implications for the specific challenges of replanning and reconstruction in 1940s London? At a June 1948 RIBA conference on 'Neighbourhood Planning in Urban Areas', Matthew argued that 'It is the first task of the planner to attempt to disentangle this [inherent] structure ... to separate these old communities – rather like unscrambling some hundreds of eggs – and give them a new life, with all the things that people need today.' What was vital was to avoid wholesale clearance: 'The significance of that cosy, if untidy, backwater, with the noise of traffic just within earshot, between the pub at the corner and the fish and chip shop, in the daily round of Bill Shadwell and his friends will be overlooked at the peril of losing the soul of community life.' Today, the task of the architect was to create or preserve 'that sense of comfortable local atmosphere, that *genius loci*, which people living there will be glad to identify as their own'. Where high-quality historic buildings were affected by redevelopments, these should if at all possible be

safeguarded: for example, in 1951 Matthew stepped in to serve a buildings preservation notice on the Georgian St Peter's Square, Hammersmith, to stop uncontrolled repairs, citing the square's 'exceptional charm and beauty'. But that did not mean imitating old buildings: 'It would be as stupid to do that as to design a motor car to look like a Roman chariot ... All really good modern buildings will have a common character – common also to aeroplanes, ships, cars and telephones.'[18]

Lansbury: resurrecting the East End

The focus of the efforts of the

(top) **5.3** 1950 model of Lansbury district, seen from south. (Barratts Photo Press Ltd)

(bottom) **5.4** Matthew escorts the King and Queen on a visit to Lansbury in November 1950. (International News Photo)

5.5 Matthew shows King George a model of Lansbury, November 1950. (photographer unknown)

ideal of socially variegated community? The bogeyman was the 'deadly monotony' of Walker's massive block dwellings, yet the CLP zoned density of 136 ppa (despite requiring nearly 60 per cent overspill of the pre-war population) would dictate that 'the scene will have to be frankly urban'. The solution seemed to lie in a picturesquely disposed combination of terrace houses and low-rise flats – a 'three dimensional planning' concept already pioneered in Frederick Gibberd's Somerford Street development in Hackney (1946–7), and in the first plans for some of the New Towns.[20] Additional social and visual variety could be obtained by selective use of multi-storey blocks. The bewildering pace with which rival utopianist visions of 'good housing' in England succeeded one another ensured that this pattern would enjoy only a short-lived popularity.[21] But in 1949 an opportunity arrived to put it into practice on a relatively large scale within the Stepney–Poplar Reconstruction Area. As in the case of the concert hall, the spur was the Festival of Britain, which threw up, in late 1948, a proposal for a 'live' architectural exhibition focused on a new housing project, with the aim of 'putting on show part of a replanned, living community'.[22] The LCC was asked to mount the exhibition in the 30-acre first phase of Stepney–Poplar 'Neighbourhood 9', a 124-acre area to be renamed 'Lansbury' after the Labour Party pioneer.

The exhibition area of Lansbury was conceived as a section of a neighbourhood unit, laid out by Ling's team on CLP lines to accommodate mixed houses and flats, but designed entirely by private architects; the Valuer's involvement was confined to one slab block. To further the Geddesian cause of social survey, Matthew allowed Johnson-Marshall to engage a sociologist, Margaret Willis, to canvass the residents. The plan was conditioned by the combination of the 136 ppa zoning with a variety of dwelling types and a 2:1 ratio of flats and houses. Matthew was able to persuade the Town Planning Committee in June 1949 to appoint Gibberd to develop a 'market

Reconstruction Group was the heart of the bombed East End, where the LCC in April 1946, following Abercrombie's recommendation, identified a 2,000 acre area in Stepney and Poplar boroughs for comprehensive treatment, and in 1947 began large-scale compulsory purchase. Even working under the wide powers of the 1947 Act, Ling's division could only shape this project indirectly, through masterplanning and development control. In 1948 Matthew evoked the Georgian age as a precedent: the LCC, as landlord, 'may do as the great landlords of the 18th century did in west London – plan on comprehensive, spacious and dignified lines a new East End'. Matthew's Scottish perspective sharpened his appreciation of the area's character, which seemed strange and even alien in its combination of an intense, heavy industrial character with a lack of urban monumentality: 'a homely, domestic scale, worthy of preservation'. The key to achieving this was to safeguard 'the small house, with its small but all-important garden'.[19]

Out of this outlook, and the English socialist realism of Ling's team, a formula of London vernacular urbanism began to emerge. The area was subdivided into 11 neighbourhoods. How should those be structured internally, to emphasise the

place free of traffic', with clock tower, at Chrisp Street: Gibberd's design for this was based on 'the traditional form of English market place'. The construction of Lansbury, like the Festival Hall, was closely followed in the popular and architectural press: the King and Queen visited the site in November 1950.[23] Lansbury was also celebrated in a range of popular and specialised commentaries. In his text for a visitors' leaflet Matthew claimed that Lansbury was 'not an exhibition neighbourhood but a neighbourhood on exhibition'; it was 'meant for people ... not just for architects!' The plan for the covered market, underpinned by Willis's sociological survey work, had 'started with the people'. In a June broadcast to schools Matthew stressed the link between Picturesque planning, *genius loci* and the encouragement of a self-contained community: the aim was 'how to make Lansbury something more than a name on a map – a real place – a part of London, yet with a character of its own that its people will make and recognise ... The very fact that we are planning a real neighbourhood with its many blocks of buildings gives us just that variety you saw in [medieval] Durham.' The plan tried to 'make the community look inwards towards itself – to be really neighbourly in fact'. At a conference on redevelopment at the Housing Centre he explained that Lansbury would be 'a living neighbourhood ... not just a vast housing scheme', with 'a tight urban pattern of terraces and squares', its 'intimacy of scale dovetailing easily into the traditional pattern of London's East End houses and streets'.[24]

The 'return' of housing

Even before Lansbury was under construction, it had begun to become clear that it would not provide Matthew with a way back into large-scale housing and community design. Architecturally, its semi-traditional layout of rather heavy brick terraces was clearly behind the march of fashion, which was increasingly tending towards more highly contrasted patterns, including multi-storey blocks:

in 1951 J M Richards attacked Lansbury as 'architecturally negative and dull'.[25] And it did nothing to dislodge the Valuer from the general housing programme. For example, in April 1948 Matthew and Walker went on separate fact-finding tours of concrete precasting factories, in Sweden and France respectively: Matthew actually visited a large number of housing sites, although his report had to emphasise the potential relevance to the schools programme. And in July 1948, despite his protests, it was decided to extend the Valuer's controls for another year, as, in the Clerk's opinion, they were just 'getting into their stride'.[26]

Faced with this rebuff, Matthew decided that the Valuer's camp would have to be softened up with outside criticism from the wider architectural world. The chance for a decisive counter-attack came in March 1949, with the Concert Hall safely out to tender. The attack was orchestrated by Matthew with J M Richards and Colin Boyne, respectively editors of the *AR* and *AJ*, both familiar with the now standard formula of orchestrated journal campaigns in support of controversial Modernist buildings.[27] The opening shot was a withering radio critique of LCC housing design in early 1949 by Richards, in his capacity as regular panellist on the BBC arts programme *The Critics*: 'I chose for discussion that week some of the very boring and clumsy LCC estates that were going up ... the [other panellists] all declared themselves appalled by them, whereupon the LCC protested and demanded the right to a reply.' Following inept attempts at defence by the LCC housing chairman, Charles Gibson, and an LCC exhibition of 'block dwellings' in County Hall and at Charing Cross Station, which 'met with equally fierce criticism', there then followed a three-month torrent of critical letters in the architectural journals and national newspapers, which amounted to a roll-call of Modernists in Britain, including a generation of up-and-coming AA students. The attacks steered away from the real grievance – the lack of Modern style – and instead concentrated

on generalised social-ethical complaints. For example, letters to the *AJ* branded the blocks as 'inhuman'. They reduced people to 'units' or 'digits', with their 'quite terrifying density' and 'crude and insensitive' design: 'Housing is the most human of all building activities, and therefore has to be the most various; for human beings are of infinite variety.' The blocks' 'grim, soulless', 'deadening' appearance symbolised 'Man's inhumanity to man'. And Robert Gardner-Medwin generalised the issue of the public architect's status, asking: 'How can one expect good architecture from a regiment of architects commanded by a Valuer or, for that matter, by a city engineer or a burgh surveyor?' The only dissident voice against this torrent of invective was that of A E Richardson, grand old man of the diehard classicists, who wrote in praise of the Valuer's 'fine work' – ensuring that he would for ever be the laughing stock of all Modernists, of whatever hue.[28]

Despite Richardson's lonely support, Walker, Gibson and their supporters, such as Deputy Clerk T G Randall, were stunned by the onslaught – not least because of the uncannily accurate way it was targeted. Ling recalled that

Robert and I were in the heart of the conspiracy! For example, I drafted a letter for Professor Charles Reilly to write to the *The Times*. It amused me, because the next day in the LCC luncheon room, there was Randall, the Deputy Clerk, saying in consternation, 'Just look at this letter in *The Times* – they certainly seem well informed!'

Walker and Gibson defended their position lamely, arguing that the blocks contained 'comfortable homes' inside, and promising 'greater variety of elevational treatment' in future.[29] But the main damage was in the criticisms' effect on councillors, who traditionally saw the LCC as a beacon of cultural enlightenment, standing above normal municipal myopia, and were thus sensitive to any claims of philistinism. The Planning Committee, under Bill Fiske, was already squarely behind the architects, and even in the Housing Committee the balance of power was already shifting away from Gibson to younger modernisers: in a bid to strengthen the latter, Hayward installed the reformist Evelyn Denington as Gibson's deputy. Now, in the wake of this public embarrassment, the council leader engineered a decisive change of policy, carefully prepared beforehand with Matthew: 'The criticisms of the exhibition really shook the council, and they had to make a fresh start. Robert was a driving force in that change, as he badly wanted the housing back.'[30]

With Martin largely preoccupied with the day-to-day Festival Hall matters, Matthew mostly dealt with this propaganda campaign and its consequences himself. There was, however, one significant exception to this rule. In late July 1949 Hayward convened a meeting of the chairs and vice chairs of the housing and planning committees to discuss a proposal that housing design should revert to Matthew at the end of 1949. With Denington in place, the voting was heavily weighted against the Valuer: 'Ike was a very acute politician, and I'm sure I was put there for the purpose of splitting the "housing" vote – he engineered it.'[31]

5.7 Cartoon sketch by Matthew (under nom de plume 'J F McCosh'), captioned: 'I may be old, but there's a lot to be said for the jolly old traditional prefab'. (EULMC)

Although Matthew was away on a study tour to America, he carefully briefed Martin to stand in for him. Unlike Matthew, the fastidious Martin detested the rough world of councillors and committees, but on this occasion the meeting went well: Martin reported to Matthew that 'Walker is naturally very cut up about the whole thing. I tried to be scrupulously fair but have not avoided getting myself into a rather unpleasant correspondence with Walker – all arising from the fact that when I was asked if the architects' office could improve the housing design, I said "Yes"!'[32]

After further negotiations, in December the Council finally decided to end 'the present temporary arrangements', and reassign to Matthew design responsibility for all completely new projects within the county (out county work remained with the Valuer); Gibson was replaced as housing chairman by the reformist Reginald Stamp. At first, Matthew had to fend off attempts by Walker to continue an involvement in new projects within London, complaining to Hayward that 'new types submitted by Walker don't seem to comply with the terms of the order; design is an individual matter, and cannot be a joint matter between architects.' But by mid 1950 Walker gave up the struggle, and the two men gradually returned to cordial relations. Now Matthew was faced with the challenge of balancing design quality with the pressure to maintain numbers and hold down costs – at a time when, it should be remembered, the Festival Hall construction work was at its height. This juggling act had to be accomplished in a highly diverse institutional setting, with 'instructions' received from the LCC Housing Department, the LCC Housing and Town Planning Committees, and the ministries covering housing and planning: Matthew quipped in 1951 that 'I have three clients, and sometimes they don't all speak with one voice!'[33]

The new responsibilities meant an immediate expansion of Matthew's department. A new Housing Division was set up, with a nucleus staff of 20, including a principal housing architect and an assistant housing architect as his deputy. In both cases Matthew looked to innovative private practices specialising in multi-storey flats, as he was aware that the department needed to move on beyond the vernacular socialist realism of Ling's team. The assistant post was filled first, in April 1950, by Michael Powell, one of the partners (along with his brother Philip) of Powell & Moya, designers of the path-breaking Pimlico redevelopment – which was at that stage, owing to building licensing curbs, in a fallow period, leaving the firm in danger of breaking up. On his arrival Powell, ignoring warnings from Walker that it would take five years to win council acceptance of innovations such as high blocks or new type plans, immediately began investigating those very ideas. In May, on Denington's recommendation, Matthew appointed J Whitfield Lewis, of Norman & Dawbarn, to the principal post – after a controversy concerning Kenneth Campbell (see below). Beneath them, the decentralised group organisation adopted on Stirrat Johnson-

Marshall's recommendation for the Concert Hall was applied on a far larger scale: eventually, by the beginning of 1956, Lewis and Powell, and four assistant senior architects, were overseeing 22 groups of up to 15 staff each, dealing with a £64 million programme.[34]

Now that the council's centralist regime was fully behind the architects, and the triumph over the Valuer was added to the 'Festival Hall effect', Matthew, Martin, Lewis and Powell were able to begin attracting a host of the most able architects and architect-planners, consigning to oblivion the frustrations about his department's lack of prestige, expressed in his 1947 lament to Budden, and establishing the LCC as the newest and brightest star in the firmament of modern public architecture, alongside Herts, Coventry, the New Towns and the Ministry of Education.[35] Some, like Oliver Cox (and Percy Johnson-Marshall in planning), came straight from the Herts schools programme, and most also belonged to the architectural trade union, the AASTA/ABT. Others came straight out of the armed forces. The transition was helped by the fact that many of the architectural design staff had been transferred to Walker, under the housing reorganisation, and were anxious to get back again. One of the three first group leaders, Rosemary Stjernstedt, had met Matthew before the war, and now joined the Housing Division in May 1950 to escape factional intrigue within Stevenage Development Corporation. Another, Colin Lucas, represented a link to the pre-war world of Modernist and MARS Group 'pioneers'. Matthew put him and Oliver Cox in charge of a research and development group, to develop new 'standard type plans', and allowed them to poach sociologist Margaret Willis from Ling's planners.[36] Once the main Housing Division had been set up, new groups were also formed for historic buildings and for furniture and equipment, and the reorganisation of the powerful District Surveyors was pressed through – a potentially tricky operation, owing to their virtually autonomous status under the London Building Acts.

The architects' new prestige provoked resentment from Ling's planners. Lewis recalled that

the planners had had the run of the aesthetics for a while, and they didn't like this new architectural organisation being set up, with lots of young architects. They'd been doing layouts themselves, but in Ling's rather Haussmann-like way. They wanted to go on doing it after the new Housing Division was formed. But we were quite capable of designing a housing scheme without any help from the planners! At first, Arthur Ling and Percy didn't see it that way, which was quite understandable: they'd seen all this rubbish being churned out for year after year by Cyril Walker, but they didn't realise that they themselves were now a bit old-fashioned. But the problems were short-lived, and in Stepney–Poplar we were soon working extremely closely with Percy's team, which included a lot of progressive people.

Ling's team also had some very different, politically driven reasons for welcoming the new and lusty Housing Division. With the rapid increase in the staff of the Housing Division, Matthew had generalised the principle of delegated diversity and creativity pioneered in the Concert Hall Section: henceforth, it would be his preferred principle for all organisations that he set up. This diversity, coupled with the LCC's freedom from Ministry loan-sanction vetting of council housing, meant that, despite the talk of 'type plans' and functionalist standardisation, each new scheme could really be treated as a one-off. But this variety was not a matter of complete individual freedom. Rather, it was channelled into the emergence and growth of two rival ideological factions, even dynasties, of designers, within the department: on the one hand, the 'Softs' (or 'humanists', 'organicists' and 'empiricists'); on the other, the 'Hards' (or 'formalists' and 'rationalists').

Both groups reacted against not only the residual classicism of Richardson but also the pre-war 'pioneering' Modernism, with its combination of socialist utopianism and clinical rectilinearity; their positions perpetuated and exaggerated a wider debate that had already been under way in English architecture during the late 1940s.[37] The Softs came first, and despite their name they actually stood for a more disciplined, politicised position on housing. They were descended mostly from the pre-war socialist radicals of the ABT/AASTA, including some former students of Arthur Ling and Maxwell Fry. Already, in 1948–9, a Communist Party cell had coalesced in the Planning Division around Ling and Percy Johnson-Marshall. Ling's own position was one of straightforward socialist realism and, even, Stalinism.[38] Now, the cause was bolstered as more young communists poured into both divisions, including Ted Hollamby, Oliver Cox, Graeme Shankland and A W Cleeve Barr.[39]

As late as 1948, communist architects could still agitate in relative freedom.[40] But, as the Iron Curtain clanged down, a growing anti-communist reaction set in, with accusations of disloyalty and, even, espionage being bandied about by right-wingers. Especially outspoken was Kent's County Architect, Sidney Loweth, previously a rival for Matthew's LCC job, and later a trenchant upholder of the rights of the private as opposed to the public architect: he demanded a purge of leftists in public architectural jobs and trade unions, arguing that many posts had access to sensitive security information, and denouncing the 'communist menace' as 'utterly disgusting and thoroughly un-English'.[41] However, the intransigence of the communists' rhetoric also alienated many architects who were neutral or even favourably disposed to socialism. For example, a December 1949 Third Programme radio debate between Percy Johnson-Marshall and Frederick Gibberd degenerated into a slanging match, with Marshall branding the big private office 'a great menace to good architecture' and Gibberd countering that, according to

Percy, 'here am I, some sort of sinister capitalist, grinding the faces of my staff, and you, Marshall, burning with desire to do a social service, with not a thought of your salary or your increments or your pension. What absolute nonsense!'[42]

The anti-communist invective of other architects was soon bolstered by official establishment machinations, as the Whitehall machine geared up for its own diluted version of McCarthyism. With the political polarisation that followed the outbreak of the Korean war and rearmament in 1950, and an attack on the left in the *Builder*, Matthew found his department targeted by MI6 investigations, especially after Ling began a high-profile, Soviet-orchestrated 'British Peace Campaign' in mid 1950: 'The Communist people had shot themselves in the foot, by mouthing Stalin's slogans, and so there were a lot of sweaty palms, especially in Planning Division.'[43] Although Matthew's own views were no further left than Fabianism or even social Liberalism, he defended his communist staff fiercely – perhaps the most striking instance of his dogged loyalty to protégés and friends throughout his career. In particular, he fought unsuccessfully to ensure that Kenneth Campbell was given an opportunity to bid for the Principal Housing Architect post, eventually filled by Lewis; Campbell recalled 35 years later that

> I saw him really angry only once ... when I was refused not only promotion but even an interview. He walked up and down his office using most un-Robert like language about politicians and council members. I hardly knew him then, and he certainly did not share my politics, but all his instincts of justice and fair play were outraged.[44]

The new Soft recruits accepted the necessity of Modern architecture, but insisted it should be softened by picturesque planning and vernacular 'people's detailing', including pitched roofs, coloured brickwork and timber or tiled cladding. Under Stjernstedt's influence, there was above all a fascination with the empiricist pragmatism and 'spontaneity' of 1940s Swedish and Danish social building, which seemed to combine elements of daring Modernity, such as slim 'point blocks', with a more restrained and tasteful background context of landscaping and low-rise houses.[45]

The Hards were generally a younger generation: post-war graduates alienated by the Softs' communist politicisation and advocating a more intensely formal approach, influenced especially by Le Corbusier's recent work, but also by the geometrical *Zeilenbau* slab layouts of the Lubetkin school. They included young designers such as Sandy Wilson, Alan Colquhoun, and the foursome of Howell, Killick, Partridge and Stan Amis. The Softs, for their part, dismissed the Hards as politically unprincipled aesthetes and prima donnas. The resulting tensions, however creative, required complex diplomatic management skills. Martin, although similar in design approach to the Hards, had no stomach for these conflicts or for rough negotiations with councillors, and stood well back, leaving Matthew and Lewis (both with empiricist design leanings) and Powell (who was completely neutral) to hold the ring. Their most acute flash of inspiration was to put some of the young Hards as an autonomous group under the wing of pre-war Modernist Colin Lucas, who had joined in 1950 but was now newly displaced from the development group by the thrustingly ambitious communist Cleeve Barr. Whitfield Lewis recalled that

> Bill Howell, Killick, Stan Amis and Gill Sarson came for interview all together in a group. I can remember the scene, even today, with Robert Matthew in the chair. They said, 'We either all come in a group, or we don't come at all.' Matthew said after they went out, 'We have to have them!'[46]

As the two factions became more entrenched, debate became more intense and rarefied. Partridge recalled that in 1951, for example,

> there was a meeting [of the Hards] in a pub chaired by Sandy Wilson, with

about eighty people there, to discuss whether the housing programme should go the way the 'Swedes' [i.e., the communist faction] thought it should go: it's difficult to conceive now that people could feel so passionately about this, that they'd stay for a meeting in the evening. But at the same time, we shared 98% of our beliefs with the Cox/Cleeve Barr grouping.[47]

Roehampton: point-block pioneer

In contrast to the only partial success of gritty, urban Lansbury, the multi-phase Roehampton project, in the parkland setting of London's southwest edge, became an internationally acclaimed set piece of the creativity, and factional diversity, nurtured by Matthew.[48] It was clear from the beginning that Roehampton offered a golden opportunity for the division to show its spurs with a really Modern combination of high blocks, space and greenery, and in spring 1950 Powell and his research and development colleagues began working on ways to exploit it, in the hope that it would legitimise the more general use of high flats. Already, in June 1949, Matthew had used his Superintending Architect role to argue for a relaxation in the 100 ft London building height limit, for sites on high ground near open space. Now, for Roehampton, rather than pre-war-style *Zeilenbau* slabs, Stjernstedt advocated the slimmer, pencil-like Swedish 'punkthus' (anglicised as 'point block'); and by autumn 1950 the LCC's first point block type, with T plan and three flats per floor, and up to 11 storeys high, had been designed by Lucas, Powell and Partridge for use on the first available Roehampton site, at Princes Way.[49] Princes Way was almost tailor made for high blocks, as it consisted of several separate gardens of demolished villas, which would be impossible to develop with low blocks without crowding. Using slim point blocks it would also be possible to fit in low-rise flats and even cottages, suitable for larger families with children. This formula of varied building types specifically for var-

ied social groups, explicitly opposed to the massive uniformity of Walker's block dwellings, was now referred to as 'mixed development'.[50] Matthew argued persuasively for it with the Housing Committee: Lewis recalled that 'he had a way with committees, whereas Martin didn't come to the Housing Committee – he didn't give a lot away, he wasn't a terribly communicative type.' Faced with arguments from Walker that the new point block type might be unpopular with tenants, Matthew countered that the 'exceptional site' justified a 'new type of building', and a 'very high standard of open planning', responding to *genius loci* and contrasting with the 'urban intricacy' of Lansbury; the mixed development formula

(top) **5.8** Matthew and Whitfield Lewis inspect a model of the Princes Way (Ackroydon) project – the first of the Roehampton mixed developments – in County Hall, December 1950. (London Metropolitan Archives)

(bottom) **5.9** 1951 model of the LCC's Portsmouth Road (Alton East) development – designed by Rose Stjernstedt and others, and the most celebrated of the early mixed developments. (*AJ*, 8 November 1951, 548)

5.10 Frank Yerbury, Lorna Matthew, Rose Stjernstedt and Robert Matthew at the Architectural Association Annual Reception, 1951. (Sam Lambert)

would house small households in the point blocks to free the rest of the site for lower density development. Roehampton also witnessed one of Matthew's first significant conservation initiatives, when he persuaded the council to refurbish, rather than demolish, a derelict Georgian villa, 'Mount Clare'.[51]

Princes Way was rather too small to make a major national impact, and the complicated T-shaped point block proved to be very costly in relation to the number of flats. The second site, at Portsmouth Road, was much larger and more prominent. Now began the leapfrog process of the various stages of Roehampton, with Princes Way commencing construction in December 1951, but a more important successor already in view. At Portsmouth Road the team was dominated by the Softs, with Stjernstedt supported by Cox, Cleeve Barr and others. By March 1951, with help from Ove Arup, Matthew presented a new and more compact 11-storey square plan with four flats on each floor.[52] These were interwoven with four-storey maisonettes and two-storey cottages in a brick-clad vernacular style, in picturesque landscape planting. In 1953 Matthew argued, in a discussion on naming, that 'the description "Point" is suggested for the 11-storey blocks, as being more appropriate than the usual "Court" or "House",

and to distinguish this new conception of buildings in English housing, which occupy a small area in open landscape.'[53] Meanwhile, Lucas and his new team of zealots was at work, with Powell's backing, on the third and most famous part of the project, at Roehampton Lane. This combined the 11-storey square point blocks with a proudly angled array of Corbusier-style maisonette slab blocks, all unified with concrete panel cladding. Once the building of maisonettes in multi-storey rather than four-storey form was established, a succession of other large projects followed: for example, arguing for approval of a new narrow-fronted maisonette type for the Lough-borough Road site in 1952, Matthew claimed that 'it is reasonable to assume that tenants have a liking for maisonettes ... as they have more the feeling of a private house'. The Softs, too, continued to develop their ideas, including a small but important programme of housing reha-bilitation, included at Matthew's insis-tence. It began with a group of almshouses restored as part of a project by Stjernstedt for point blocks at Trinity Road, Wandsworth (from 1953), and pro-ceeded to the far more ambitious 19th-century terrace rehab element of the Brandon Estate project (from 1956, by Ted Hollamby).[54]

From late 1951 the department's repu-tation in housing began its rapid growth, building on the established achievement of the Concert Hall earlier in the year.[55] And although financial constraints continued to limit the overall expansion of the housing drive, as the schemes left with the Valuer worked their way through the system the pro-portion dealt with by the division steadi-ly grew, from three per cent in 1950 (compared with 38 per cent by the Valuer and 59 per cent by private archi-tects), to 31 per cent in 1952 (compared with 39 per cent and 29 per cent), and further still after that.[56] By 1956, fuelled largely by the housing expansion, the architect's department had grown to nearly 3,000 staff, and Furneaux Jordan could proclaim that 'once again, after forty years, there was an ideology, an architectural target'.[57]

From County of London Plan to Development Plan

With housing returned to the architectural fold, the prospects for the planning of London now suddenly brightened. The great task set by the 1947 Act, of preparing a development plan to give statutory effect to the CLP, could now be completed in the expectation that it might actually be implemented on the ground. In the first draft, put to the council in 1949, Matthew's planners tried to tighten up the Abercrombie proposals a little, for example (against Walker's opposition) by enforcing the density rings and open space provisions more rigorously: the areas just south of the Thames were now to be planned at 136 rather than 200 ppa. In the two years until June 1951 the plan was worked out in detail, including town and programme maps that defined the 'traditional, functional and architectural character' of individual neighbourhoods across London, chiefly by primary use zoning of new developments. Eventually, in December, the council approved the completed plan. Matthew's report commented that 'it is our aim to preserve what is best in London, to respect and develop its character and to remedy its manifest defects.' Dame Evelyn Sharp, the top civil servant at MHLG (the housing and planning ministry), wrote to Matthew in January 1952 that his real achievement of 1951 was not building the Concert Hall but getting the Development Plan 'through so quickly – and in the Festival year'.

Matthew also began the complex task of neutralising outside opposition in advance of the public local inquiry into the plan, scheduled to start in Central Hall, Westminster, in September 1952: in May, for example, he turned down a lecturing invitation as he was 'immersed in vast preparations for the Public Inquiry into the Development Plan'. He established cordial relations with the potential reception authorities for LCC overspill: for example in a major meeting with Kent at

Maidstone in June 1952, where the county expressed worries about the LCC's role of absentee landlord. Objections from the Valuer – mostly about cuts in the zoned density of his housing sites – were also parried.[58] And the department started working through the countless individual objections to the plan, satisfying the objectors usually through minor map changes or corrections of drafting errors; 500 of the more than 6,000 objections were immediately withdrawn.[59] Matthew was on hand to provide patient rebuttals of the most dogged and nit-picking objections, mostly from Central London owners objecting to the rescinding of temporary permission for office use and restoration of residential zoning.

Overseas links in the late 1940s and early 1950s

Alongside Matthew's architectural and planning tasks in London, the LCC also gave him the opportunity to develop his taste for cultural diplomacy – that combination of *Wanderlust*, gregariousness and sensitivity to cultural differences and 'causes' that had stayed with him ever since his Vaumarcus days, and had been reignited by his Scandinavian trips in 1945. Here, too, Abercrombie remained his mentor and intermediary, involving him immediately in a range of exhibitions and meetings under the aegis of the RIBA and the International Federation for

5.11 Public Local Inquiry into the LCC Development Plan seen in progress in Central Hall, Westminster, October 1952. Matthew and Ling are visible two rows behind the 'Counsel for the LCC'. (Sport and General Press Agency)

5.12 August 1949 view of the UK Building Trades Productivity Team, en route back from the USA on the *Queen Elizabeth*. Matthew is second from left. (photographer unknown)

Housing and Town Planning. Alongside the wave of British patriotism epitomised in the New Romantic movement and the Festival of Britain, the immediate post-war years had also witnessed an enthusiastic British participation in a renewed climate of internationalism, as seen in the work of figures such as Jaqueline Tyrwhitt. Now, in reflection of the founding of the United Nations, the most important initiative of architectural internationalism was the fledgling Union Internationale des Architectes/ International Union of Architects (hereafter IUA). This was founded in 1946/8 as a reconstructed and enlarged version of the pre-war International Reunion of Architects (RIA), a Paris-based society headed by architect Pierre Vago, Hungarian-born Modernist and former editor of *L'Architecture d'Aujourd'hui*.[60]

Earlier in the century, Britain had played an enthusiastic role in hosting pioneering attempts at architectural internationalism. Now, in 1946, basking in the wartime victory, the British section of the RIA (prompted by RIBA and MARS) took the initiative in setting up an architectural body able to negotiate and collaborate with the fledgling UN and UNESCO. With the founding of the IUA in mind, Britain convened the first post-war RIA meeting at the RIBA in September 1946, with observers from CIAM and IFHTP. Representing the British section, Holford argued that 'a new international-ism' was dawning, within which an

architect could aspire to be 'a World Citizen in the same way as members of other professional communities'; what was needed was information services and exchanges relating to technical planning issues, while avoiding more emotive issues of 'culture'. On this basis, a small IUA secretariat headed by Vago was set up in Paris, and an inaugural IUA congress was organised at Lausanne in 1948, with Abercrombie as first president. The initial congress declaration emphasised the paramount aim as being international-ism largely for its own sake: 'In the wake of a tragedy which spread ruin and mourning throughout the world, the architects of all countries deemed it more than ever necessary to unite.' A British IUA committee was set up, with Matthew as a member. Immediately, it had to deal with the growing tensions of the Cold War, coupled with the suspicious attitude of more traditionalist factions within the RIBA.[61] During the mid and late 1940s there had still been a close cooperation between the Western IUA groups and the enthusiastic Polish committee, headed by CIAM vice-president Helena Syrkus.[62] Now, from 1950, this cooperation was sharply undermined by the Korean war and the growth of socialist realism. RIBA Secretary Cyril (Bill) Spragg, an old-style ex-military and colonial man who, like Loweth, disliked the collectivist influence of public architects, began to foment opposition within the British IUA committee: Abercrombie wrote to Matthew in exasperation that 'the way of anyone trying to keep an even balance between extremist political groups is not easy today!'[63]

If his IUA work brought him into contact with more socialistic Europeans, the even-handed Matthew was also careful to develop corresponding contacts within the United States. His golden opportunity to do so came in July 1949, when he was sent on an eight-week tour to the USA, as one of four architect members of a Building Trades Productivity study team, led by builder R O Lloyd. The visit took the form of a return journey by sea from Southampton to New York (going out on

16 July via Le Havre and Cobh, travelling cabin class on the Cunard White Star *Mauretania*, and returning on the *Queen Elizabeth*), and a rail trip from New York to Washington, Detroit, Cleveland, Buffalo and Boston. For Matthew the trip was effectively an official 'holiday' after the Festival Hall design negotiations, and his notes reverted to his old detailed approach, even as his daily routine reverted to the sporting preoccupations of 'Stution days. On the outward voyage he noted incredulously that his cabin-mate, RIBA President (1948–50) Michael T Waterhouse, was spending most of the time 'actually doing serious reading of official documents!' Matthew, by contrast, spent the entire crossing in energetic leisure. The daytimes were spent in deck games: two days into the voyage, he was 'somewhat stiff after thirty games of tennis' with an Australian sheep farmer and an LCC councillor he had bumped into. Every night he won several pounds at bingo (significantly augmenting his spending allowance), while sweating off pounds on the dance floor – a pursuit in which he was rivalled only by the 'indefatigable' Dundee builder, Robert S (Bob) Gray.[64] The tour combined visits to important projects, such as the United Nations Secretariat construction site in New York, with organisational inspections of practices, companies and public corporations, and discussion meetings, although Matthew and the other British visitors were also much preoccupied ferreting out luxury goods and preserved foods (tinned ham, boiled sweets, etc.) unobtainable under rationing at home.[65]

The aim of the tour was to study how it was that the American industry could build faster and more efficiently than the British. The overall conclusion was a somewhat negative one: that the greater wealth of the USA allowed a combination of competition and lavish organisational back-up that would be impossible in impoverished post-war Britain, and probably undesirable in a planned, social-democratic economy. Matthew argued that

no one expects the American way of life to be transplanted and to flourish here, but I would go one step further, and say that out of our necessity to plan at high level, can come our greatest hope of substantial advances in building technique and reductions in cost.[66]

Matthew's distrust of the US as an exemplar was sharpened by the effects of laissez-faire society on the general environment, and by the increasingly shrill anti-communist climate in America, which offended his preference for political neutrality. On his return he wrote to Dennis Winston, an Australian friend: 'What a field there is for planning in the US! (but I imagine the heartbreaks to a conscientious planner would be pretty killing). The political atmosphere is all-pervading and so a long-term view is almost impossible.'[67] The US tour was the last foreign trip where Matthew's role was anything less than a leading one, but it was of great use to him in establishing a wide range of US contacts, both architectural and planning. For example, Ralph Walker, AIA President, who officially welcomed the party to New York on 5 August, became a firm friend, as did architectural journalist Fritz Gutheim and pioneering community planner Clarence Stein. These links were then cemented by a policy of open-door hospitality back in London, using his own LCC and public architectural connections to provide UK contacts for visiting Americans.[68]

Matthew in London, 1951–3: the long farewell

By mid 1951, largely through his own patient work and planning, Matthew had more than recovered the lost status of the LCC Architect's Department, in the process securing himself an unchallengeable position as one of the chief inspirers and brokers of 'Modern Public Architecture' in Britain. In that respect, he found himself in the vanguard of a nationwide revolution in architectural patronage. The wartime years, as in

1914–18, had seen a further dramatic jump in the level of public spending, which had soared to 74 per cent of GDP in 1943 (from a pre-war minimum of 29 per cent). Colin Lucas's decision to join the LCC in 1950 only confirmed the growing prestige of public architecture. Alongside the county councils, whose schools programmes were redoubts of architect control, government ministries began to adopt Modernist group working and R&D practices too: 1948 saw the setting up within the Ministry of Education of an Architects and Buildings Branch under Stirrat Johnson-Marshall and administrator Anthony Part. The reaction of the architectural establishment to this change was equivocal, to say the least. Within the RIBA, although the elected leadership was still monopolised by traditional private practitioners such as A G Henderson (president 1950–2), salaried members' and official architects' committees had been formed in 1928 and 1937 respectively, and in 1946 a negotiating officer was appointed to champion their case on pay and conditions. Seven out of ten members elected to the RIBA council in 1950 were Modernists, but only two (including Matthew) were publicly employed. Up to the mid 1940s the advocacy of public architectural practice within the RIBA was led by ABT communists, but after that group's loss of influence in the 1949–50 anti-communist reaction it began to fall to less politicised people to take the lead in furthering the cause.[69]

Within this grouping Matthew now suddenly found himself one of the foremost figures. The effect of his sudden advance, in professional terms, was the equivalent of becoming a film star overnight – ignored by the likes of Herbert Manzoni in 1948, but now fêted across the British and, even, international architectural and planning world. That astonishing transformation in status, however carefully prepared for, had happened more or less overnight, since late 1949. There was widespread recognition of the symbolic victory in housing in achieving this status: George Pepler told one young architect that 'In the LCC, the Valuer had been everything and the Architect nothing – yet this chap Matthew comes from Scotland, and within a couple of years or so the whole situation was reversed!'[70] Matthew was now securely lodged at the centre of an increasingly dense and international web of contacts and ideas, supported chiefly by the post-war Labour drive to build the planned welfare state, but stretching in a great many other directions. Moreover, this had been done in a way that satisfied the long-standing demand within English architecture to balance the professional and the artistic. Indeed, he had now almost caught up in status with his near-contemporary William Holford, another non-Englishman (South African) who had exploited the drive for publicly led reconstruction in England.[71]

For the moment, the public reception of Matthew's work was balanced between Modernist collectivism and traditional elite values: the congratulations on his CBE in 1952 focused chiefly on the Festival Hall.[72] Matthew now took the opportunity, in a succession of lectures and articles, to explore his collective role as a public architect – one of 'the servants of the new Patrons of Architecture – the 20th Century local authorities'. Although, for the moment, he paid considerable lip service to the prevalent language of rationalist efficiency, he was not wedded to any individual aspect of Modernist dogma, and he freely acknowledged the problems as well as the opportunities stemming from the emergence of the state as chief building patron, coupled with 'Britain's unique lay councillor and committee system of local government'. 'For the first time since the fifth century BC, public architecture has become popular architecture – in the strict sense, by the people, for the people.' Yet there was the often depressing reality, deadened by 'complicated administration and Bumbledom': 'To mention in the same breath the Periclean Age and the 20th century is at once to give the measure of failure: a failure to match up to opportunity, truly abysmal in its entirety.'[73] In Matthew's view, the main

5.13 Extract from the last 'guest-edited' *AJ* article of 1952. From left: Stirrat Marshall, Robert Matthew, Robert Gardner-Medwin, Donald Gibson. (*AJ*, 18 December 1952, 72)

THE ARCHITECTS' JOURNAL for December 18, 1952 [727

The last major article* by this year's Guest Editors is on the vitally important issue of Town Planning, a subject now often unjustly maligned. This series of articles will be concluded in two subsequent issues by comments which the Guest Editors have received over the year from readers and by a final article summarizing the Guest Editors' view points on the fundamental problems they have discussed during the year. In the following article the Guest Editors describe and refute some of the criticisms of town planning made today, and point out how essential it is that the architect should equip himself to be an architect-planner and the co-ordinator of the planning team.

The Guest Editors

THE PUBLIC ARCHITECT AND TOWN PLANNING

IN our first article on the scope of the work we referred to Town and Country Planning as follows:—" In spite of its zealous advocates, the need for town and country planning dawned slowly on the country as a whole. A new and complex planning service has recently been established. It began as an extension of housing, and hence became an advisory duty of the Ministry of Health, who followed existing procedure by producing a set of model clauses, rather like model building by-laws, and by demanding that plans should be submitted to them for examination.

" The whole system was comparatively ineffective for a number of reasons, which need not be mentioned here, but the impact on our cities of wartime bombing hastened overdue legislation. The new Ministry of Town and Country Planning was established in 1943. It was given both advisory and executive powers from the outset. Its recent legislation (principally the Town and Country Planning Act, 1947) created a completely new planning system, backed by much larger financial and legal powers.

"The Act enables local planning authorities to deal comprehensively with large urban areas. This is an opportunity which has been denied to the urban designer since the 18th century. It would take too long to describe all the responsibilities either of the Ministry or of the local planning authorities, but as their activities impinge so much on public architecture, it is inevitable that we shall refer to some of them in due course."

In our second article, when describing the scope of the work in different types of local authorities, we said:—" The architectural department of a county borough council may be in charge of the overall planning, of the housing, schools, and of all other building work which the council is obliged or wishes to undertake. The chief architect may also be the technical officer responsible for briefing private architects on work which is given out to them. This type of office is most favourably placed for developing the architect as a town designer—since he can be responsible for, or can have a say in, nearly all the design elements which go to make the urban environment, from the overall planning to the smallest details of townscaping. The work is helped by the fact that the average county borough area is reasonably compact, and, while not being too large and unwieldy, is yet large enough to maintain a fair-sized and varied building programme."

Elsewhere we argued that the local authorities were now effectively taking the place of the great building owners and developers of the past, whose 18th century activities left us some of the finest achievements of British Town Planning.

MAJOR CONTRIBUTION FROM ARCHITECT-PLANNERS

Looking back, it is possible to see some of the reasons for the collapse of our Town Planning tradition in the 19th century. The noble art of town or civic design, in which the whole added up to something so much greater than the sum of the parts, decayed and was forgotten by the profession which created it, chiefly because it was out of tune with the philosophy of industrial capitalism. " Where there's muck there's money " was a typical slogan which might almost be on the coat-of-arms of many of our industrial cities. But the resulting evil went far deeper than visual ugliness—it affected the whole life of the inhabitants of the new and expanded cities of the 19th century.

As we pointed out in previous articles, the local authority technical services largely grew out of the repeated attempts to deal with the worst aspect of the industrial city—its menace to health.

And so town planning was reborn, a new and almost unrecognizable offspring of the municipal health services. It has now grown into a complex synthesis of science and art, presenting a new challenge to the Public Architect as a team leader rather than as a solo designer. For modern town planning has to solve a hundred problems before it can approach the final problem of civic design—yet civic design is inherent in every one of the others. It would be possible to develop a town with the correct zoning, with well laid out communications and services, with every health requirement met, even with good individual buildings, and yet it could fail as civic design, and remain an ignoble and inert mass.

For these reasons, if for no other, it is essential that the officer in charge of *town* planning should be an architect-planner, and that the major (but by no

* During the preparation of this article one of the Guest Editors, S. A. W. Johnson-Marshall, chief architect to the MOE, was absent.

---

problem of local-authority-sponsored architecture was how to deal with repetition, with programmes of similar buildings. For this, the attitudes of the old pre-war chief architect, the 'Great Man' concerned with detailed design, were completely inapplicable: their absurdities were exemplified by the thunderings of Sir Albert Richardson, 'the great panjandrum of taste, that sensitive interpreter of the latent aesthetic aspirations of the Common Man'. The new-style chief architect must be skilled in controlling the 'multiple-bodied creature' of public architecture, a 'technologist' adept at 'programming', 'allotment of work', 'general quality of staff', 'general direction of design and planning policy', and 'coordination with other departments'.[74]

By 1952, with the new Conservative government beginning to take tentative steps to lift the most interventionist state controls, there was a subtle change in climate, initially towards a less *dirigiste* public-authority architecture, but soon (as we shall see) even towards a restrained element of private practice – which could, of course, further ease the advance

129

Planning and housing

of Modern architects within the RIBA. While the younger public architects continued to meet and agitate as before, with designers from Herts, Coventry, the LCC, Notts and the MoE meeting as a self-styled 'Chain Gang' in the basement of the Architectural Press, an informal 'Upper House' now also emerged, comprising Matthew, Stirrat Marshall, Robert Gardner-Medwin and Donald Gibson, and took the lead in campaigns such as that for increased public-architectural representation in the RIBA.[75] Other apolitical public architects such as Bill Allen also helped. Allen recalled that

> Stirrat was the best schemer in the profession. He was active in the RIBA from 1951 onwards, where he had a big reputation and popularity from his Herts and Education Ministry programmes. The city, county and Ministry architects were trying to build themselves up in opposition to the private architects, who'd always run the RIBA. Stirrat helped get people like Peter Shepheard and Cleeve Barr on the council – I was already on – and then in no time, Robert was elected – in about 1954. We used to met at Stirrat's office before council meetings to decide how we wanted the council to vote – although Robert, with his aura of exceptional integrity, never really involved himself closely in Stirrat's more devious schemes! Of course, to the RIBA traditionalists, to people like Cyril Spragg, even Robert Matthew was himself scarcely respectable, being the leader of a socialist hotbed![76]

All in all, the prestige of public architecture was now beginning to diminish slightly, and the newly established unity of Modern architects and planners, symbolised above all by Matthew's own department, started to fragment, with the architects moving towards more individualistic visual-social conceptions, and the planners towards a more technocratic, regulatory ethos. Already, in 1946, Powell & Moya's famous competition win for the Pimlico redevelopment had spot-lighted a potential role for innovative private practice within the public social building programme. Matthew played a key role in the fevered debates that accompanied this shift in attitudes. Appropriately, during 1952, the *Architects' Journal* ran a series of special articles on the theme of 'Public Architecture', prepared by a team of guest editors, comprising Matthew and his Upper House allies – Donald Gibson, Stirrat Johnson-Marshall and Gardner-Medwin. In fact, most of the organisation of the series was carried out behind the scenes (for a fee of £300) by Percy Marshall, 'under the advice and guidance of Robert Matthew and Leslie Martin at the LCC'. In January, the scope of the series was defined: 'architecture as an essential public service', embracing 'all aspects of urban design', including the entire building industry, as 'Building is the acknowledged province of the architect'. Predictably, the team endorsed the Herts/LCC/MoE 'group' system as the best model of office organisation. But the term 'group' was ambiguous, as it was also used in architecture schools to denote a completely democratic system. What was meant here was a flattish, non-pyramidal hierarchy, but a hierarchy all the same, tied together by the semi-autonomous figures of the group leaders, and by the chief architect, who had to be both an 'able designer' and a 'team leader ... not an autocrat'.[77]

The most impassioned of the debates between the 1952 *AJ* guest editors concerned the growing tension between architects and planners – perhaps the most telling harbinger of the break-up of the grand disciplined reconstruction consensus that had swept Matthew to power. For this debate, chaired by Matthew, the architects were bolstered by Herts chief C H Aslin and private practitioner Raglan Squire. The discussion rapidly became polarised between exaggerated advocacy of individual designer freedom and intransigent defence of context, scale and civic cohesion. The planners, represented by Gibson and Percy Marshall, blasted their opponents as a throwback to Victorian liberalism, just as Percy had done in the 1949 radio debate with Gibberd.[78] Stirrat Marshall retorted that the average planner was a mediocre bureaucrat, not a designer:

Donald's being utterly, dreadfully selfish ... the type of machinery he demands, to enable him to get what he wants in Coventry, will give those chaps powers which they're not fit to exercise ... for the beauties of Coventry, it's not worth hamstringing the rest of England!

Matthew backed the planning side, but mainly from a perspective of respect for historic context:

Suppose there was a bomb on one of the terraces of Bath – would you allow someone to put up a tall block there? The key is control of 'scale'. But you're saying that there is no merit in the relation of one building to another – you're saying, 'To hell with them!' – I just wonder what your principle is!

In response, Squire intransigently rejected 'context':

If someone wants to put up the Empire State Building in front of St Paul's, I would let them. I think one cannot be that sentimental about the past ... there's a terrible danger that Frank Lloyd Wright or someone else would be unable to put up their buildings in this country.[79]

And Aslin flatly declared, 'We don't want the planner. He is going to be "out" very shortly!'[80] Arguably, that was just what happened over the following decade: in 1959, Matthew would complain that regional and urban planning had slipped into the 'slough of despond'.[81] Advanced architects lost any interest in zoning maps, coalfield surveys and 'strategic population decanting'. However, Matthew's own planning ethos was rooted not in technocratic Functionalism but in the Geddesian concept of cultural and historic context, and thus it would eventually come into its own again, after the Modern Movement as a whole was called into question in the 1970s.

5.14 Drawing by Robert Matthew to mark the move to Bill Holford's house, 5 Cambridge Terrace. (EULMC)

But, by the time of these collaborations, Matthew had already decided that his long-term future lay not in the LCC, but back home in Edinburgh. Still only 45 years old, temperamentally opposed to long-term encumbrances and commitments, and addicted to change and diversity, Matthew doubted he could sustain his motivation and enthusiasm at the LCC in the face of a gradual decline in the status and cohesion of public architecture-planning. Unlike Basil Spence, the footloose Indian colonial, who was preparing to move permanently from Edinburgh to London in the wake of his 1951 Coventry Cathedral competition win, Matthew was bound to Scotland by the closest family and emotional ties, and had no intention of settling permanently anywhere else. He only exaggerated slightly when he declared in 1962 that 'I am an Edinburgh man myself, born, bred and working – I have only been out of Edinburgh for seven years of my life.' Throughout Matthew's time at the LCC he had continued to maintain his professional links

5.15 Drawing by Robert of the newly born Jessie Ann, June 1952. (EULMC)

with Edinburgh, including his EAA and RIAS memberships, and joined the Melville College London branch. The five-year lease of Kensington Square ended in early 1952, but Matthew could easily have stayed at the LCC a few more years, to see though key developments such as Roehampton. In precipitating the precise timing of his return, career considerations proved decisive: by the end of 1951 Matthew was, as we shall see below, already engaged in secret negotiations with Edinburgh University to secure his return in an academic capacity, and so, on leaving Kensington Square, to tide over the intervening months the family moved along with Kathleen into temporary accommodation in the top floor of Bill and Marjorie Holford's house at 5 Cambridge Terrace. With Rose Stjernstedt lodging in the attic above, Bill and Marjorie occupying the main floor below, and Kathleen in the basement, this was clearly a temporary arrangement. Janet recalled that 'my mother hated leaving Kensington Square – we all did – and it

was a very tricky arrangement at the Holfords' house. Marjorie was a charming lady, but she was very sensitive to noise!' Ironically, in view of the transience of this accommodation, the Regent's Park area would thereafter become a focus for the Matthew family in London.[82]

Aidan summarised his father's thinking in embarking on this radical change of direction:

> My father always argued that success-ful men should only stay in one job for about five years; any longer than that, and they would be going over old ground, and not moving on. Now, at the LCC, with the 1951 exhibition over, he felt it was time to go, and that all that was left was loose ends. He also wanted, I think, to have a go at private practice, which he'd never done before, apart from the brief spell in his father's office. And he was beginning to become extremely inter-ested in education, and was looking for a professorship – and Edinburgh seemed a natural choice. Unlike Basil, he wanted to come back home: he felt he was young and vigorous enough to start out again, and get involved in private practice and in education.[83]

Another significant factor that may have had a bearing on Robert's return home was the fact that Lorna had become pregnant with their third child at the beginning of September 1951, less than a month before a new academic career opening for him back home in Edinburgh began to emerge. After a diffi-cult pregnancy, dogged by high blood pressure, Jessie Ann was eventually born at Cambridge Terrace on 1 June 1952. This unexpected family enlargement may have been prompted by the fact that, with Aidan and Janet away at boarding school (from 1949 and 1951 respectively), 36 Kensington Square may have begun to seem a little empty, and perhaps Lorna also hoped that the appearance of a new baby, at a time when Robert's major LCC challenges were behind him, might inspire him to spend more time with her. Other family pressures were also important in motivating the move back to Scotland. In particular, the demands of the relatives back home were becoming more urgent and disruptive.[84] Both his father and Stuart had effectively suffered nervous breakdowns in 1950, the one following and feeding on the other. His father, who had never recovered from his crises of the late 1920s, had been catastrophically demoralised by the war, and subsequently (following Stuart's entry into partnership with him in 1946) all the pressure of maintaining the Lorimer & Matthew office fell on the latter.[85] In 1949–50, in the wake of a stressful project for a hotel at Bridge of Lochay, Stuart, in his turn, had a 'collapse', leaving Robert (at 400 miles' distance) and Douglas (without any architectural training) to try to help their father to keep the firm afloat.

The Thistle Foundation project, already hit by a post-war austerity cut in numbers from 140 to 100 dwellings, was now caught up in this crisis, with the design of the housing and the clinic complete, but the Robin Chapel still on the drawing board. John F Matthew took over, and, against Stuart's wishes, changed it to become more heavy, with Lorimerian rough rubble, 'strongly Scottish in character'. Protesting bitterly, Stuart resigned his commission and dissociated himself from the Foundation in 1950.[86] Eventually, after two months, Robert and Douglas had to abandon the attempt to help with Lorimer & Matthew – not least because Robert's Royal Festival Hall and housing reorganisation work was at its height – and Stuart instead established a partnership with David Carr. In mid 1951 Lorimer & Matthew was wound up in all but name, J F Matthew retired, and Stuart moved from the Great Stuart Street office to a separate house at Lynedoch Place. There he eventually became incapacitated, some years later, by bouts of agoraphobia and other illnesses – although he continued to maintain a thriving office until around 1960. Unsurprisingly, Robert began to feel that he should keep a closer eye on this increasingly convoluted and distressing situation, while at the same

time insulating himself from its most overwrought excesses.[87]

Any possible return was eased by the fact that since 1949, although the completion of the Clyde Plan had somewhat curbed his Scottish contacts, Robert had maintained a continuing interest in architectural affairs north of the border. Having helped secure Robert Gardner-Medwin his DHS chief architect post, he now relied on him as a kind of viceroy in Scottish public architecture. Medwin kept Matthew and Abercrombie posted on progress, or the lack of it, in the major civic and regional planning projects. For example, in October 1951 Abercrombie lamented to Matthew that Edinburgh Corporation were cold-shouldering his plan, and that Plumstead had now left – but, he added, 'I don't think the Lord Provost quite realises the steel under Gardner-Medwin's smile.' Medwin also chaired the 'SPAR' group, a Scottish public-architecture branch of CIAM, with members including Egon Riss, Anthony Wheeler and Justin Blanco-White, and Matthew an occasional guest visitor. Eventually, in late 1951, Medwin became disillusioned by the lack of political support for regional planning, and began looking for another job; in 1952 he secured a chair that would take him back home to Liverpool University.[88] Even after that, Matthew continued to keep apace with the progress of East Kilbride, and by early 1953, with his own Development Plan at the LCC almost complete, he began to turn a critical eye to the first draft of Glasgow's plan, declaring himself 'horrified' by its continuing self-contained approach and distrust of overspill.[89]

5.16 View of Aidan Matthew (on right) with his friend (and, later, wife) Sylvia Cassidy and her father, at Brier Corner, Alderley Edge, 1952. (photographer unknown)

133

Planning and housing

Perhaps in reaction to the difficulties in establishing Modernist regional planning in Scotland, Matthew's interventions there were concerned as much with the past as with the future; it was as if his latent traditionalist roots were bound up nostalgically with 'home'. For example, in February 1949 Lorna arranged for him to lecture to the Saltire Society London branch on the future of Scottish architecture, mingling stock denunciations of Victorian facade styles and haphazard modern bungalows with praise of the 'more truly Scottish ... simple, often almost standardised elements' of the 'vernacular'. He argued that there was no future in an Arts and Crafts response: Lorimer could 'build spectacularly in the vernacular' but, unlike the Danes, was unable to bring the 'tradition right through to modern work'. It was vital, instead, to reconnect Scotland with a wider international context: he had been chagrined to discover, when meeting Östberg in the 1930s and Aalto and Rasmussen in 1945, that none of the Scandinavians had even heard of Lorimer or the Scottish National War Memorial. The 'vernacular', suitably used, could be the 'stepping-off point for some future architecture that could 'put Scotland on the architectural map'.[90]

His most forceful interventions were in the field of conservation. In October 1949, following a tip-off from Lorna, he sent Robert Medwin 'another plea for a Scottish building': a request that DHS should spot-list or otherwise safeguard Mackintosh's threatened Ingram Street Tearooms.[91] His overarching conservation concern, with the fate of the Edinburgh New Town, now began to emerge. In September 1950, after returning from a visit in connection with the 'Lorimer & Matthew problem', he reported to Medwin with alarm that many 'Adams' [sic] interiors were now being ripped out, and urged him to take 'special action', beginning with a survey of the New Town.[92]

By the time Gardner-Medwin left public architecture for academia and home in 1952, Matthew had already deter-

mined on a similar course for himself. Town and country planning education was still striding forward, with the first five-year course established in 1945 at King's College Newcastle. But Matthew focused above all on architectural education, in the belief that the new ethos of public practice and group working was not being adequately supported by the schools and the RIBA: 'the Schools have not caught up with the post-war situation'. By 1951 Budden had secured an external examiner appointment for him at Liverpool, and he was appointed a member of the RIBA Board of Education.[93] But the more important aim was to return home, and, with the wartime head-hunting approach from Glasgow doubtless still in his mind, he kept a watchful eye on developments back in the Edinburgh College of Art. Here a new degree course, linked with the existing diploma, was being developed in conjunction with Edinburgh University. In 1946 it was decided to establish a joint chair, vested in the university but also acting as ECA head of school, to administer this degree, with a salary of £1,500. Matthew was apprised of all this in mid 1947, when his old mentor E A A Rowse, perhaps sensing the likely demise of his School of Planning and Research for Regional Development in London (a threat implemented in 1952/3), unsuccessfully applied, with his support, for an architecture lectureship at the college; by September, Medwin was briefing him that a new chair would probably be created. Then, a year later, the new joint chair was indeed established: the university hopefully sent a copy of the prospectus to Matthew, but as the Concert Hall challenge was at its height, he unsurprisingly did nothing about it. Instead, the university and ECA in effect kept the post 'warm' for him by appointing in 1948, as Architecture School head, R Gordon Brown, principal of the AA since 1945 (and, prior to that, a Parachute Regiment major). Eased out of the AA to make way for Furneaux Jordan, within two years Brown was already on his way out from Edinburgh as well, after claims of financial improprieties. During the ensuing two-year interregnum the ECA architecture school was administered by Ralph Cowan, a former ECA graduate and Rome Prize winner, who by that stage was also Alan Reiach's partner.[94]

In the meantime, the university once more began to sound out Matthew, in an elaborately genteel manner – and in late 1951, with his third baby on the way, they found him in an increasingly receptive mood. In October his brother Douglas, at that time a lecturer in the Department of Obstetrics and Gynaecology at 60 George Square, passed on a message that a 'high official of the university' had 'unofficially' asked him whether Robert would be interested in the Edinburgh chair, at a salary of £2,000 (one-third paid by the university and two-thirds by the college), supplemented by 'unrestricted private practice' to make up the £1,000 difference from his LCC salary. When Douglas responded with Robert's key precondition – in recognition of his new status after the completion of the Festival Hall – that he would under no circumstances 'compete for the chair', the 'high official' had indicated that this would probably be acceptable to the 'influential circles' charged with finding a new professor. By May 1952 the Principal, Sir Edward Appleton, was able to write openly to him, and in June Matthew further cemented his university links by inviting Professor David Talbot Rice, the eminent Byzantine art historian, to lunch at the Reform Club; the selection committee to confirm his appointment was convened to coincide with an RIBA conference in Edinburgh at the end of June. William Kininmonth, as a member of the ECA staffing committee, was a member of the corresponding appointment board in the college.[95]

Now, without giving any hint yet in London of the negotiations under way in Edinburgh, Matthew was able to begin working out the organisational and financial aspects of the move, focusing especially on two aims: first, the need to delay the start date until the Development Plan Inquiry was effectively over;

and, second, the inevitable shortfall in income until he could build up his private practice. Matthew might be ready to throw over the prestige and power of his LCC post in pursuit of change, but he was reluctant to subject himself and his (expanding) family to a radical curtailment of lifestyle. Nor was he minded to enter into any kind of collaboration or partnership with his more stay-at-home Edinburgh contemporaries. The most potentially awkward relationship was with Kininmonth, precariously established as the university's preferred consultant architect: he had not only helped with Matthew's appointment within ECA, but had also assisted in sounding out University secretary Charles Stewart on the possibility of a short-term loan of £900. As Stuart Matthew had agreed to help organise his move, this three-year loan was actually advanced to Stuart, in instalments from February 1953. But Robert, although grateful for Kininmonth's help, tactfully evaded suggestions of a partnership with his waspish ex-classmate by pleading family opposition to any link other than with Lorimer & Matthew – although any association with the disintegrated family firm was actually the last thing he would have contemplated! Kininmonth replied that

It's a pity that family commitments prevent you from going into partnership with a firm which could make up the difference ... we need people like you in Edinburgh – although I'm most apprehensive of you as a ravening wolf snatching the mutton from the rest of us ... PS: the whole world seems to know you have been offered the chair and it's common gossip you will take it.[96]

Once the formal letter of appointment was received, in mid September, Matthew officially notified the LCC of his resignation, which would be delayed until the end of April 1953.[97] Just as in London in 1946, the congratulations and the lobbying began immediately. His London-based Scots friend Jimmy (C H) James, who had vainly pressed a partnership on Stuart on

5.17 Sketch by Matthew of his unsuccessful 1953 entry (with Peter Moro) for the Märzpark competition, Vienna. From left: ice-hockey stadium, open-air assembly area, covered circular main hall. (EULMC)

completion of the Norwich Plan at the war's end, wrote that 'I feel you all will be happier north of the Border – and perhaps you'll be able to look after Stuart, who seems incapable of looking after himself!'[98] The university immediately inducted Matthew onto the works committee and began to consult him on major and minor projects: in December 1952 he advised on the positioning of a small war memorial. Immediately, potential tensions with Kininmonth began to surface, with the latter initially trying to play Matthew off against Spence, by lobbying him in March 1953 against Spence's appointment to design a university staff club in Chambers Street: he complained that fine-art professor David Talbot Rice was

> pushing Basil Spence on the grounds that he will design beautiful furniture (and also that they are 'buddies'). Personally, I feel just as competent as Basil both as an architect and an 'interior decorator', and in any case feel I have a prior claim. I hope you feel you can agree.[99]

At the same time, Matthew began making his preparations to begin private practice. His first 'dry run', in late 1952/early 1953, was an unsuccessful competition entry for a 25,000 seat municipal assembly and Olympic sports hall at Vogelweidplatz, in the Märzpark, Vienna. He entered jointly with Moro, commissioning perspectives from Gordon Cullen, but the design was ruled out as it built over too much of the site, with

massive stairs and terraces. It included a huge circular hall, 12,000 square metres in size, and open air assembly space. By November, more productive negotiations were also under way with the Scottish Aerodromes Board, for what would ultimately become his first private job, a new Edinburgh airport terminal at Turnhouse: the first sketches were hastily done in the flat at Cambridge Terrace. Matthew would immediately need an assistant on starting his practice, but he weighed up a number of approaches before making his selection. In January 1953, for example, he was approached by Ian Melville, an architect-planner at East Kilbride and former Liverpool School lecturer. Misjudging the reason for Matthew's move, Melville argued that public-authority architecture was completely discredited and that 'private practice must now take the lead': 'What Scotland so sorely needs is something physical, not political, to be patriotic about ... your future practice could have great influence here.' Matthew tactfully replied that he intended to set up a 'small private office ... I would hope to make it a good one', and suggested a chat at Easter.[100] But by then he had already found the assistant he wanted: Tom Spaven, a former assistant of Reiach's on the East Kilbride flats, who wrote to Matthew in March at Reiach's suggestion.[101]

In March and April 1953, after showing off the department and the new tower block designs to one final VIP visitor (Marshal Tito of Yugoslavia, on 17

March), all that remained at the LCC was the ceremonial leave-takings.[102] Now Matthew was able to sum up what he felt had been achieved, and what had not been possible – emphasising general programmes and planning frameworks rather than the showpiece of the Festival Hall. Speaking to the staff, he regretted that he would not be able to see through to completion any of the 'great schemes' of housing, or even the Development Plan. To the council, he listed his four main aims: reorganisation, to allow big programmes to be tackled; the setting of a general architectural standard; preservation of 'architectural gems of the past' such as Mount Clare; and making sure the CLP's 'relatively undefined scope and sweep' were transformed into the 'harder realities' of the Development Plan. In response, Victor Mishcon, chairman of the General Purposes Committee, spoke of the 'humble folk in his department ... who think in terms almost of adoration of the man who, together with Dr Martin, has put London architecture on the map.'[103]

Matthew's LCC legacy

To succeed Matthew, Martin was appointed as Architect – a decision that was almost a foregone conclusion. Medwin wrote to Matthew that he had been very interested in the job and almost applied, but in the face of the 'strong competition', decided against it.[104] But the more reticent, cerebral Martin proved to be far less adept than Matthew at balancing the demands of production and design, raising both in parallel with each other. The department continued to grow, and to produce award-winning projects that would attract further talented young architects – especially those of a more 'hard', Corbusian persuasion. Indeed, by the mid 1950s it had become 'the ultimate finishing school for aspiring postwar architects'.[105] But Martin, like Forshaw in the 1940s, proved unable to maintain the level of output that would satisfy the capital's urgent pressures for new houses. This was partly the result of external constraints, such as the government-

encouraged shift away from large-scale greenfield sites to more complex, brownfield redevelopments. All this was exacerbated, however, by the increasingly self-contained design ethos of the department: one new recruit to Colin Lucas's group recalled that 'under Martin ... the whole of the Housing Division seemed like a giant nursery school, whose main object was the happiness of architects.'[106] The crucial change came in the conception of design teamwork, which was in the process of evolving from a collective, almost intentionally diverse response to urgent political pressure into a relatively self-contained, intellectualised dialogue among architectural factions. Without Matthew's firm but unobtrusive grip on reality, decadence set in. Three years later, under mounting political pressure over the 'breakdown' in output, Martin, too, had departed for academia and private practice, leaving the department in the more humdrum hands of Hubert Bennett, the Yorkshire county architect (criticised harshly by Matthew in the 1952 *AJ* debates). And the 1964 London local government reorganisation, replacing the LCC by a larger but feebler regional authority, the Greater London Council, would still further dilute Matthew's legacy.[107]

From all this one might reasonably conclude that the post-war welfare state architectural world that produced the Festival Hall was, by 1951, already invisibly fractured by the reviving forces of worldly individualism. Certainly, Matthew's departure for private practice in 1953 seemed to many at the time an important symbolic gesture that brought these latent trends into the open, by setting

5.18 Matthew shows models of the Princes Way (Ackroydon) housing project to the Yugoslav leader, Marshal Tito, on a visit to County Hall, on 17 March 1953. (NPA Rota Photograph)

in train the inexorable atrophying of the life and prestige of public architecture, and the diversion of welfare state building patronage towards large, multidisciplinary private practices.[108] By the time he was joined in partnership in 1956 (see Chapter 7) by Stirrat Johnson-Marshall, mastermind of the 'Herts Schools' and the Ministry of Education 'CLASP' system, the pattern seemed to have been established of the 'leaders' of symbolic, heroic-era welfare state 1940s–early 1950s projects, whether individual or serial in nature, fanning out across the architectural landscape into private practice, where they were able to develop highly individual approaches.

Yet this diversity must be balanced by an equal acknowledgement of the cultural fundamentals shared by all these people and their supporting factions. These diverse emigrants from the public service – such as Matthew, Martin and the two Johnson-Marshalls (Stirrat and Percy) – would in turn transform private practice

through the values that united them. These included an unshakeable commitment to architecture as an integrated element of social betterment, and a distrust of the effects of competitive 'free enterprise', whether in the built environment or within the architectural profession. In their wake, assisted by the academic reforms in architectural training masterminded by Leslie Martin in the late 1950s, there would develop an entire generation of hybrid 'public-private' architects of the welfare state.[109] As we shall see in the next few chapters, far from dissolving or springing apart in the 1950s, the diverse recipes of individual and collective initiative represented and legitimised by buildings such as the Festival Hall and the Roehampton housing developments continued to thrive well into the 1960s, with the political and social demands of the welfare state providing a firm counterweight to the imaginative efforts of the most innovative individuals.

Consolidating the Modern Revolution

Chapter 6

The returning hero: teaching and private practice, 1953–6

The task of effectively inserting a design-based discipline, involved in contemporary problems, into a Scottish university was a little like trying to bore an underground freeway into the Great Pyramid. When one eventually got a glimpse of the inner chamber, it was all too clear that a formidable gap in communication still lay ahead, and the language on the walls was unfamiliar!

Robert Matthew, 1968

'Broad sunlit uplands'? The Laird of Keith Marischal

During his 'brief incursion into English affairs', Matthew had been suddenly catapulted up onto a high plateau of national and international status.[1] The story of this rise, and of the chance or opportunistic developments that contributed to it, was now over. The rest of his career, and indeed of his life, saw his restless energy redirected to the exploitation of that status: in the short term, through the pursuit of variety, change, excitement; and in the long term through a gradually increasing commitment to a world outlook of global environmental regeneration. The linear, teleological, disciplined sequence he had hitherto followed, with one activity relentlessly built on the shoulders of the last, now shattered; after 1953 the restless, nervous idealism latent in Matthew's character began to reassert itself alongside, and sometimes in conflict with, any simple quest for power. He embarked on a succession of overlapping activities, each one

commenced in a flurry of zeal, only to be impatiently discarded once it became bogged down in prosaic and discordant reality. From this point, too, Matthew's talent for delegation was increasingly used to slough off each ossified shell, as his restless spirit drove him on to fresh adventures. This change of life created a sharply divergent career trajectory from some of his close contemporaries or rivals. Alongside Basil Spence, for example, Matthew had always seemed more rigorously focused and career-orientated, whereas from now on, paradoxically, it was Basil Spence who became more rigidly preoccupied with one activity – the creation of architectural projects – while Matthew continued to develop eclectically in many different directions.

Matthew began this new phase of life, appropriately, by throwing himself into a position of comprehensive flux, personal and professional – giving up a well-paid official post for an uncertain future of teaching and private practice, and moving 400 miles into the bargain. The first and foremost task was to find somewhere to live in the Edinburgh neighbourhood, as both Hamilton House and Darnaway Street had now long been given up. With the new baby, another city centre flat seemed impracticable, and so Lorna and Robert began to look further out. An out-of-town location was also suggested by Robert's determination to start home absolutely afresh, although he willingly accepted help from Stuart in house-hunting. The initial front-runner was

Christmas Greetings from KEITH MARISCHAL
·1953·

Lorna
Robert.   Aidan.   Janet
Humbie. East Lothian.   Jessie Ann Matthew

6.1 Christmas card from Keith Marischal, December 1953: earlier that year, Matthew wrote that Keith 'now houses our family, Lorna's two elderly aunts and her parents, also elderly, all in various parts of the building – plus the Mulgrew family (who were with us for a time in Hamilton House) in the kitchen wing. The planning of the house is such that four family units can live an independent existence without impinging on each other.' (EULMC)

Nairne House, Willowbrae Road, a neo-classical villa of *c*.1805, whose name stemmed from the fact that it had been owned between 1806 and 1830 by the famous composer and collector of Scots songs, Carolina Oliphant, Lady Nairne (1766–1845). Doubtless the romantic attraction of Nairne House was enhanced by Matthew's own family link to James Hogg – but the architectural reality was that it was just a large, plain, bow-windowed villa on a noisy suburban arterial road. It was soon discarded and forgotten when something of far more explicitly romantic architectural character was unearthed by Stuart: Keith Marischal, a dilapidated late-16th-century tower-house situated at Humbie, in rolling East Lothian countryside some 15 miles southeast of Edinburgh.

Put up for sale by neighbouring farmer Denis Cadzow, who wanted to be rid of the bother of maintaining it, Keith included 15 acres of rough woodland and rhododendron planting. The house itself comprised an original castellated tower of 1589 at the east end, and elongated 19th-century western extensions, some by Kinnear & Peddie, with a low kitchen wing at the extreme west end; there was also a small gate lodge. They sent for details, and 'Robert said, "That certainly looks a rather stupid and impracticable place!"' But then one day, in Janet's

words, 'Alan Reiach took my mother to visit it, arriving by the scenic garden entrance. She fell in love with it then and there, and won my father round to moving there.' Perhaps, too, the traditionalist in Robert was attracted by Keith's castellated 'Scottishness'.[2] But the house was in a very run-down state, without heating and with rampant woodworm in the roof and dry rot in the floors. It might have seemed a wildly impractical solution, had it not chimed in with the needs of Lorna's own family. Her mother had never recovered her equilibrium since Mercia's death, and Lorna felt increasingly strongly that she should keep a closer eye on her parents and aunts. When Stuart Pilcher eventually retired on reaching 70 in January 1952, Lorna suggested that all four of them should move to Keith, and help with the cost of buying and running it.[3] Robert's own move back home had also been partly motivated by the desire to keep a closer eye on his own parents and younger brother. But here the tables were briefly turned on him at this juncture. Robert, wrapped up in the closing stages of his LCC work, found these family negotiations so difficult that eventually it was left to Stuart to take the initiative and make all the arrangements. He recalled:

This was one of those personal matters where Robert, who was so decisive normally, simply couldn't cope. He simply couldn't get to the point, and eventually I had to get him and Denis Cadzow to meet at the house, one freezing winter's day. They stood there humming and hawing in the cold – it was awful! – and at the end I had to break in and say, 'We want to get in, and get it fixed up – so how much do you want for it?' Robert just couldn't get to the point! So Cadzow agreed a price of £2,600, with the drive and lodge to be extra. Then we came to the question of how to pay for it, and, it was left to me to arrange a loan from the Abbey National and to fix with Stuart Pilcher and Lorna's aunts how much they would contribute – and

collect the money from them, to pay the Abbey National. Then there was the structural condition of the place: as a precondition of the loan, I had to go up and look around in the roof, especially above the tower, and make arrangements to deal with the woodworm! But finally, there came the enjoyable bit: buying furniture, where I was given a completely free hand![4]

Keith Marischal was bought in February 1953, and in early May the family moved up from London. Lorna recalled that 'Keith was in a state of chaos, freezing cold – Jessie was four months old and in her carry-cot, and I had next to no help at first: my helper Vanessa only came up on our first reconnaissance visit.' Robert and Lorna had reached adulthood during the years when middle-class professionals still expected some sort of domestic help, and at first her existence with the infant Jessie was a hard and lonely one, cut off from her London circle of friends in a largely unheated house, and ferrying the children around in the car. Somehow, though, Lorna continued to muddle along effectively, as much of the house was in fact occupied by her relatives:

Loosie and Jolly occupied a self-contained group of rooms at the west end of the first floor, and Maimie and Attie largely used the second floor and the eastern tower-house section. Furniture was a mixture of pieces from London and Alderley Edge with those bought by Stuart. All three households had their own kitchens, and made their own cooking provision – in the case of Attie, including the keeping of hens and constant cooking of smelly hens' meal. The area of the house occupied by Robert, Lorna and the children was mainly at the eastern end: as a kitchen, they used the vaulted laundry room (complete with 'jawbox' sink) at the foot of the tower section. Lorna and helpers would 'trot up and down' the turnpike staircase to and from this room: only after six months, in November 1953, could the luxury of an Aga cooker be afforded.[5] To provide assistance, the Mulgrew family agreed to move back 'into residence' for a time, providing over the first couple of years a 'constant presence' in the ground-floor Victorian kitchen wing and the flat above: she helped with the cooking while he (in as much as his war injury permitted) gave limited help in stoking the fires and looking after the boilers.[6]

(above left) **6.2** 1956 visit to Keith by W W Wurster, Dean of Architecture at Berkeley; Matthew's Morris is visible on the right. (EULMC)

(above right) **6.3** Drawing by Robert Matthew of Jessie at Keith, September 1955. (EULMC)

The returning hero

Initially, Matthew had the idea of developing Keith into a combined home/atelier 'Frank Lloyd Wright type of establishment'.[7] When his own private practice did begin to develop, he found, as we shall see, that the Taliesin ideal was impracticable – owing to Keith's inaccessibility by public transport – and that a city-centre location was essential.[8] Instead, Keith began to develop as a focus for architectural entertainment and hospitality, for which, with its romantic chateau air, it was well suited.[9] Architecturally and environmentally, the shift from the south of England was a shock for all the children, and not always for the better. In a late 1953 lecture to the Council for Industrial Design Scottish Committee Matthew revealed that

> my own children, who happened to spend most of their formative years among the rather gay and colourful villages of Sussex, found it difficult recently, coming back to Scotland, to accept the drabness of the average East Lothian village. When I pointed out that these are riots of colour compared to those of the real industrial belt, they were unbelieving – but not for long.[10]

For Aidan (by now in his late teens, and still boarding at Michael Hall in Sussex), Keith seemed to be in a constant state of flux and chaos:

> My grandparents and great-aunts had their own flats in the house, with their own kitchens – and from one visit to the next, you'd never know what was where. We had no money, so our own quarters were jolly uncomfortable for a long time. We couldn't even redecorate, let alone alter it – and our own kitchen was just disastrous! The old folks would be around a lot, but my father wouldn't see them, often, for two months at a time, as he and my mother and Jessie and Janet would be away in London or elsewhere.[11]

On turning 17 and completing his O-levels at Michael Hall, Aidan spent his last school year back at the Steiner School in Edinburgh, taking an A-level in French and moving on to Basil Paterson's to cram part time for another A-level, while working in the evenings at the Art College to work up a portfolio. For he had by now decided to follow the family tradition, and duly enrolled at the Architectural Association in London in 1955.

Keith Marischal, having been bought with a mortgage from Abbey National, was duly insured for £15,000. Under the terms of the mortgage Matthew undertook to treat the roof timbers, eradicate woodworm and dry rot, and overhaul the slates and pipework within six months of acquisition. Transport was kept modest too, in the form of a crumbling pre-war Morris 8: Lorna recalled the 'big change from the LCC days, where he had two people working for him as full-time secretaries, to his return home as a penury-stricken professor, driving an ancient car with dry rot'. Of course, new cars were almost unobtainable during the first post-war decade.[12] On top of these expenditures, Matthew began his new life outside the comforts of the public service with a high level of tax liability – nearly £400 for the tax year 1953/4 – inherited, in arrears, from his last LCC salary. Aidan recalled that the change in financial circumstances

> really hit him hard when he came north – he had to exist on a professor's salary, paying his LCC tax, and surtax, a year in arrears. In some ways, he never really recovered from that – and it began to challenge his Labour principles. For the rest of his life, for example, he distrusted dealing in cheques – instead, he'd carry wodges of £5 notes around in his pockets.[13]

Ultimately, as we shall see later, the development of Matthew's architectural private practice provided a way to plug this gap. But that practice would take time to build up, and would have to be carefully offset against tax bills. A useful 'bridging' facility was provided in early 1954 by a £2,500 staged advance of fees from Musselburgh building contractor

Harry Cruden – the most venturesome of a number of Scottish engineer- or builder-entrepreneurs who emerged into prominence during the first 'systems' boom of the 1940s. In anticipation of both council housing and school building contracts and a lifting of licensing restrictions on private housebuilding, Cruden engaged Matthew as a consultant architect for a range of villa types of speculative building, low-rise council housing and several standard designs for schools, as well as plan types suitable for a prototype scheme of point blocks to be built at Spey Street (off Leith Walk) by Edinburgh Corporation.[14] By 1955 Matthew was able to write to the manager of his branch that 'I have now secured a number of commissions, bringing in estimated fees of over £30,000 for 1956 ... [but] it is most unfortunate that I should embark on private practice when the Treasury is doing its best to knock everyone out of business.'

The older Pilchers eventually began to disappear from the Keith Marischal scene in the early and mid 1960s: Maimie died in 1960, Jolly and Loosie in 1962–3 and Attie in 1966. From then on the house gradually passed more fully into Robert and Lorna's occupation, but with concomitant difficulties in running the household. The Mulgrews had long since moved on back into Edinburgh, and were followed by a succession of couples staying in the lodge, with the husband generally looking after the garden and the wife doing the housekeeping: these were essentially lodgers, who helped out in exchange for accommodation. Both John and Annie Matthew had already died, in 1955 – Robert's father at Nannie's South Queensferry home in February, and his mother in an Edinburgh nursing home in July; the executors were Robert, Douglas and Stuart. John's death finally ended the period of nearly 30 years' intermittent incapacitation and decline since his breakdown in 1926/7. Now the mantle of infirmity began to pass decisively to Stuart, who had been authorised by John to conduct the business of Lorimer & Matthew on his behalf since 1952, but

now himself became increasingly beleaguered by agoraphobia and nervous breakdowns.[15] Now Robert was finally and irrevocably cut off, or emancipated, from the family influence of his upbringing.

Between two stools: Robert Matthew, Professor

But at first it was not his private practice that absorbed much of Matthew's attention, but his academic post – or rather posts, since he combined in his person two different titles: Professor of Architecture at Edinburgh University, and head of his alma mater, the School of Architecture at Edinburgh College of Art. The wider context of Matthew's move from the LCC was the growing pressure for professionalised, university-based training for architects – itself, to some extent, just a specific manifestation of a more general move towards the university education that had been under way across the professions since the mid 19th century, and especially after the creation of the University Grants Committee in 1919 as a conduit for massive state funding. The drive towards university-based architectural education was also powered by specifically built-environment factors, above all the early post-war conviction of a new centrality and power of architectural and planning professions within society: 'the belief that education had not kept pace with the vast power for good or evil that the architect and planner now wielded'.[16] A post-war RIBA committee of investigation had demanded a university training system inspired by that of medicine – a national strategy that would reach fruition after the 1958 'Oxford Conference', at which Matthew, as a member of the RIBA Education Committee, would play a key role.[17]

In his new double post, Matthew was catapulted into a situation of makeshift, transitional character. Instituted in 1948, the Forbes Chair of Architecture was an attempt to give a quasi-university standing to the school, while leaving the existing courses largely unchanged. Most students carried on doing the same diploma as before, but a new joint honours degree in architecture was instituted, which required students to do the full diploma course, supplemented by an extra-curricular range of university options, and leaving graduates with both a college diploma and a university MA (Hons) degree. Five students began the new course in 1948, but only one of them, Pat Nuttgens, eventually completed this 'lunatic degree' (with first-class honours).[18] Nuttgens, a brilliant and passionate young architect/historian, was to form the mainstay of Matthew's new academic structure, and in 1954 it could accurately be said that he was the only person with an Edinburgh University degree in architecture![19]

Matthew's arrival in the College, in May 1953, made a strong contrast with the flamboyance of his erratic predecessor, Gordon Brown. Nuttgens recalled that

he came toot-tootling through the college gates in a dilapidated Morris, decorated with an L plate [for Aidan's use] – an extraordinary, informal guy in a poky car ... It occurred to me that only somebody with a massive self-confidence and the certainty of achievement could afford to arrive in so unpretentious a manner. But he was professor without experience of teaching or the management of education.[20]

Matthew's understated self-confidence doubtless stemmed partly from a feeling that he was returning home to his old school. But he also had an agenda for reform of the school, to turn it into a respectably Modernist institution with an integrated component of academic research, rather than the Scottish traditionalist and design-based institution it had remained. What he had not appreciated as a student was that the municipal governing structure of the College – with councillors constituting half the management board, the Lord Provost in the chair, and the Town Council physically owning the ECA building – was profoundly inimical to change, owing to the lack of any equivalent to faculty or senate.

The sobering realities of the situation at ECA soon dawned on Matthew after his arrival in May 1953. In an Aberdeen lecture in March the following year he lamented that

Edinburgh College of Art is run by Edinburgh Corporation like a department. Its governors are the Finance Committee of the Corporation, but most of the finance comes from the Scottish Education Department ... My own view is that the school must become a university department in the hands of academic staff ... enjoying academic freedom.

The key to this, he argued, was – just as with his Bossom prize – 'to integrate postgraduate research with the new public building programmes and the potential of industrial production': architecture had now ceased to be a 'precious' activity of an elite, and had 'moved from the fringe of society almost to the centre.'[21] Of the 13 teaching assistants, only Alan Reiach (then fifth-year studio master) and, to a lesser extent, Ralph Cowan were unqualified Modernist allies; Cowan recalled that 'Alan was a devotee of Robert Matthew – he worshipped him.'

The most important obstacle to Matthew's plans was the fact that the Principal of the College had general executive authority over the School of Architecture, including the right to vet staff applications, and even outgoing correspondence. Departmental heads within the College also had 'no administrative staff of any kind! Compared to the elaborate organisation in County Hall, where everything was immediately to hand at the push of a button, [this was] a salutary experience!'[22] If there had been goodwill on both sides, none of this might have been an insuperable problem, but in this case the relationship was doomed from the start. The Principal between 1942 and 1960, Robert Lyon (MA (Dunelm) ARCA FRSE and Rome Scholar), was a mural and portrait painter of a traditional mould, and a faculty member of the British School of Rome. To such a figure, Matthew must have seemed a dangerous,

Modern Architect

probably communist, interloper, while Matthew for his part made little effort to conceal his contempt for Edinburgh's 'provincial' artistic and architectural elite, which blackballed his membership of the Royal Scottish Academy several times.[23] But more important than any ideological difference was the bad chemistry between two dominant men. Nuttgens recollected that 'Lyon, whom we all despised, couldn't get on with Matthew, and insisted on seeing all his correspondence. Matthew, for his part, had been head of the LCC architects, and wasn't going to do anything that Lyon said!' Ralph Cowan, in charge of teaching, was caught in the middle of this conflict: he recalled that Matthew, from the moment of his arrival, 'emanated power', while 'Lyon could be extremely charming, but like all powerful men when their power is threatened, he could turn extremely nasty!'[24] Matthew's relationship with the mild-mannered Cowan was a less extreme version of that with his brother Stuart, and although Cowan was eventually left exhausted by the Matthew-Lyon conflict, he and Matthew nevertheless remained on friendly terms throughout. By contrast with the tension at the College, the University seemed very welcoming: Matthew wrote to John Patterson on his arrival in Edinburgh that 'I find the university atmosphere congenial – I was introduced to the Senate yesterday – profs seem friendly ... [and] I was put on the Works Committee.'[25] From the very beginning, he enjoyed excellent relations with both the new, forceful University Secretary (from 1948), Charles Stewart, and the new Principal (from 1949), physicist Sir Edward Appleton.

At first, Matthew tried to draw on his London connections to help enhance and modernise the ECA course, engaging Stirrat Johnson-Marshall as an external lecturer on schools development work, and retaining Donald Gibson as an external examiner. He recalled in 1964 that 'Donald was my first external examiner – the sharp impact of that confrontation echoed down the academic corridors for

many days.' By the end of 1953 and the beginning of 1954 a string of petty harassments, including interference with his outgoing mail, as well as clashes with the other (non-university) schools of architecture on external assessment procedures, and the evident impossibility of reforming the creaking Art School framework within a reasonable timescale, began to prompt Matthew to begin plotting an escape route, with some urgency, drawing on his connections to provide precedents:[26] in January 1954, for example, he procured details of MIT's postgraduate research courses via Bill Allen. In mid 1954 he was presented with a *casus belli*, when Lyon took advantage of an extended round-the-world trip by Matthew (see below) to overrule his shortlist for two architectural and construction instructor posts. Matthew checked informally with Stewart that the university professorship was not formally bound up with the College headship; in August he wrote to Bill Holford that the degree course 'is not a good course' but that, with the university's blessing, 'I am altering it fundamentally'. In early September he offered his resignation as ECA Architectural School head, protesting 'most strongly' about the selection of staff without reference to him. He was persuaded to stay on *pro tem*, but confirmed his preference for a separation of the two positions, and wrote three months later to Appleton that the present degree course was 'unworkable', and should be modified, if possible, to the 'ideal' of a course completely within the university.[27]

To maintain his university chair – hitherto just a nominal element in his job – Matthew would clearly have to set up a department. In behind-the-scenes discussions Appleton, a strong ally, backed this, but made it clear that a new course would have to be established, replacing the old MA degree, and to this end he, Stewart and Matthew set about 'engineering' the transfer of architecture to the University. Matthew would set up a new BArch course, for which students would do their first three years at ECA to 'ordinary' level, then proceed on to the university for the fourth and fifth years. The aspiration was to set up after that a postgraduate and research structure, which would allow greater attention to be given to the cause of planning.[28] Matthew's intention seems to have been either that the ECA school should wither away altogether after his succession, or that Cowan should take over the school headship as a professor in his own right, ensuring that he would have a fairly compliant ally in his old ECA post. Meantime the students who had started already would complete the existing course, with all its problems. Hugh McIlveen (from 1954) recalled that there were only two others following the course in his year, and over the eight or nine years that it was operating, only around four people actually completed it; in the case of him and his contemporaries, studio work continued to be done at ECA, under tutors such as Andrew Wylie, Andrew Carnegie, Peter Whiston and Michael Laird.[29]

Matthew faced difficulties on both sides in forcing this change through. Among university traditionalists architecture was seen as a primarily vocational, insufficiently intellectual subject: when the proposal was debated in the Senate, Arthur Beattie (Professor of Ancient Greek) protested, 'Good God – the next thing we'll be asked for is a chair of plumbing!' Over a decade later, Matthew recalled that

the task of effectively inserting a design-based discipline, involved in contemporary problems, into a Scottish university was a little like trying to bore an underground freeway into the Great Pyramid. When one eventually got a glimpse of the inner chamber, it was all too clear that a formidable gap in communication still lay ahead, and the language on the walls was unfamiliar![30]

More serious was the opposition from the College side, from traditionalists such as Leslie Grahame Thomson, who saw the change as potentially eviscerating a great Edinburgh institution, and driven into the bargain by someone they resented and feared, with the collaboration of Ralph Cowan. These resentments burst dramatically into the open in early 1955 in a bizarre dispute between Matthew and William Kininmonth, concerning a new multi-storey examination building in Chambers Street designed by the latter. In deference to Robert Adam's university quadrangle opposite, the building was called 'Adam House', and Kininmonth designed it with a vaguely Robert Adam-style front facade, compressed and neoclassical in arrangement with a low-relief arch, but with a more utilitarian, but modern, back facade on the steeply falling site. Stuart Matthew recalled that 'Kinnie was always a self-opinionated chap, but was always overshadowed by someone – especially by Basil.' Now, he began to refocus his resentment on Matthew as the more significant threat to his position as semi-official university architect.[31] In January 1955 the classical frontage of Adam House was attacked by

(below and opposite) **6.4** Two-page extract from article in *The Student*, 10 Febuary 1955, attacking Kininmonth's Adam House – here caricatured with wildly exaggerated pedimented 'top hamper'. (*The Student*)

30

Adam Hovse -- Debate Continues

THE ARCHITECTURE OF COMPROMISE

HORACE Walpole, floating in enthusiasm for the architecture of Wyatt and in a corresponding abhorrence to the work of Adam, grumbled about the latter's excursions at the Adelphi, and pronounced upon them: "What are the Adelphi Buildings? Warehouses laced-down the seams, like a soldier's trull in a regimental old coat."

Adam's reputation has ignored such bludgeonings. We are inclined to ignore Walpole; Adam deserved a finer memory. He has (unless the reference is to Genesis) had a building sculpted to his fame.

Adam House shows already many successful and attractive features; and no doubt the general layout and provision of rooms fulfill adequately the requirements set by the University. Basically, it is two buildings. The front building, entered from Chambers Street, contains the entrance hall, two staircases to the lobbies on the other floors, and lavatories and other odds and ends in the basement. We might call this circulation building neo-Georgian, especially on the outside. Joined to it, but separated from it also by a clear break in both structure and architectural idiom, is the back building, containing (in ascending order) the theatre, examination halls and art gallery. We might call this part 20th century, not only on the outside.

Suppose we make a little inspection of each of these two buildings, as if they were quite separate; suppose we then walk a long way off, and peer at the whole. It will be a useful operation; for Adam House raises a number of questions important in architectural theory.

In the front building, the plan has to a certain extent been modified to allow scope for the treatment of the façade. Thus one landing is punctured by a large circular well, to admit light to the floor beneath, which has no windows to the street. The resulting severe reduction of useful lobby space must therefore be justified by reference to the enhanced beauty of the exterior façade clamped to the concrete structural frame.

Does the clearly incised name of Adam imply, one wonders, that this façade is in some way an essay in the style of Adam? Surely not. Perhaps in that of Kent or the Palladians in general? In the firm, bold massing of Vanbrugh? Less likely still. The massing is both cramped and ill-proportioned, cramped inwards from the sides to shoot at the top in a top-heavy pediment. The relation of window to wall, the spacing of these windows, appears to follow no known rule or model of proportion. A handful of windows has been thrown at the building, and they have stuck in strange places. Is he not deeply sad, that poor little depressed fellow in the middle, a babe in the wood? The central feature is indeed unhappy. Are these windows beneath their relieving arch some hint of the University itself, or some surreptitious illegitimate of that basic Palladian motif from which Adam and his predecessors developed so successful a feature? Surely not again; for the grouping has lost

The reaction of Adam on seeing his Hovse

(continued on page 32)

6.5 Cartoon of Matthew by Jimmy Allen. (*The Scotsman*, 5 January 1956)

two articles in the university *Student* magazine, the second being initialled by Nuttgens.[32] Nuttgens attacked not only the 'schizophrenic' contrast of facade and interior, but also the design of the facade itself, as 'cramped and ill-proportioned', and 'only one of many dismal decorated boxes rising in Edinburgh'; the design, he thundered, was 'makeshift building, timid building, fit-in, hope-for-the-best, keep-the-council-happy building. Dead building.' Ironically, in view of Matthew's own struggles over University redevelopment in Edinburgh during the late 1950s and 1960s, he asked rhetorically whether the university would 'know good building from bad when it bulldozes George Square'.[33] Kininmonth complained to the RIAS about Nuttgens's 'virulent' and 'shocking' attitude, which threatened 'the disruption of the profession in Edinburgh'. Worse still, he alleged that a draft copy of the article had been seen in the college room shared by Matthew and Cowan – implying that Matthew had put Nuttgens up to this attack. Matthew counter-attacked vigorously, flatly denying Kininmonth's allegations, accusing him of advocating 'censorship' of student magazines, and lamenting 'the unfortunate impression created at the University end, at a time when I am anxious to get all the support I can to achieve full university status for Architectural Education.'[34]

Whether or not Matthew did actually instigate the articles in the first place is unclear, although the episode certainly bore an uncanny resemblance to the 1949 LCC housing furore, orchestrated by Matthew behind the scenes; it also arguably anticipated the more flamboyant student 'Anti-Ugly' campaign of 1958–9 in London against 'reactionary' architecture, including the Cambridge work of Robert Hurd.[35] Like the 1949 LCC row, this dispute did seem, if anything, to accelerate the reform Matthew sought. In May 1955 Stewart wrote to ECA confirming agreement to separate the two posts while maintaining collaboration: a Joint Committee would be set up. And in October, Matthew just having turned

down the offer of a part-time chair of architecture at Leeds University,[36] the establishment of a Department of Architecture within the university was finally agreed, along with new BArch and research MArch degrees, beginning in October 1956. The university agreed to give the new department accommodation in two or three rooms on the ground floor of an 18th-century house, 16 George Square, and authorise the appointment of one senior lecturer, one secretary, and one lab technician by the end of 1956. Also in October 1955 Cowan was formally appointed Head of School and Professor at ECA with effect from 1 January 1956. From that date the joint appointment of university chair and head of school would terminate: Matthew vacated the room he had shared with Cowan, and seldom came back. At first, it seemed as if the next development would be the closure of the ECA school of architecture: Cowan recalled that he now found himself in

> a state of siege, a sink-or-swim position – either I'd manage to rescue the school or it would collapse, and I took it as my job to keep it going. After Robert Matthew left, being the chap he was, the RIBA did what he wanted, and set up an inspection board with the obvious intention of closing us down – but when these 'big guns' arrived, they found they couldn't do it, as we were obviously in quite good fettle.

Under Cowan, the college's course was restructured as a 'sandwich' programme with full-time years flanking part-time study.[37]

What sort of new department would be built up on these modest foundations? Matthew was determined, above all, that it would be a cosmopolitan one, free of what he saw as the parochial jealousies of the old-style ECA regime. In late April and May 1954 he embarked on an ambitious overseas trip, partly to reinforce this internationalist orientation. Invited on an expenses-paid trip to give two papers at the Fourth Australian

Architectural Convention in Sydney, Matthew decided to add on a ten-day research visit to the USA at the beginning, paid for by the university (a £100 subsidy).[38] This was Matthew's first round-the-world air trip, and, indeed, his first major overseas expedition since his 1949 US building delegation trip, another world away, in the now fading era of leisurely sea travel. For Matthew the rule from now on was first class travel by air, even though, for the moment, transcontinental flying was still very much an elite affair, and his entire round-the-world fare totalled £560 – over one-fifth of the price Matthew and his family had paid for Keith Marischal! Later, his air fares would be paid for mainly by his private practice, but for now more ad hoc arrangements were needed.

During late 1954 and 1955 Matthew began to put together his BArch and post-graduate proposals, drawing very largely on the experience and help of Nuttgens. The latter, after his graduation in 1954, had begun research for a PhD, within the School of Scottish Studies but still under Matthew's effective tutelage. Nuttgens's thesis subject – a methodical survey of the 18th- and 19th-century planned villages of the northeast of Scotland – reflected Matthew's own 1950s search for a vernacular modernism, while acknowledging the difficulty of reconciling that concept, with all its romantic Arts and Crafts connotations of pre-Modern organicism, with the two-centuries legacy of radical 'Improvement' that pervaded the built environment of rural Scotland.[39] To supplement this research Matthew offered Nuttgens a part-time job as Departmental Registrar in his new department, at a salary of £490. Using the tiny initial accommodation of 16 George Square, Nuttgens put together a course of induction lectures for the students in years 1–3, organised the new 4th and 5th years, and suggested an onward five-year plan, including the establishment of a Nuffield-supported postgraduate research project. Inspired by Richard Llewelyn-Davies's renowned hospital research unit, it could work on 'live' projects such as a neighbourhood unit for the next new town, a central area redevelopment scheme for the LCC, and rural housing:

Matthew came to Edinburgh just as everyone was going mad about research. I said to him, 'Every other department in the University is doing research, so we must too!' For him, that meant research on housing: he saw housing as the key to modern social architecture.[40]

Meanwhile, Matthew was canvassing other contacts for advice or support, including a recent visitor from California, William W Wurster, and Dame Evelyn Sharp of the Ministry of Housing in London (lobbying for support for a Nuffield funding application).[41] However, when the new department eventually began its work, as we shall see, Matthew confined his active input almost entirely to its further expansion. The university, and his chair, was above all useful to him as an independent address for projects and correspondence of a personal or intellectual character – a kind of psychological bolt-hole as his private practice developed into a vast, impersonal empire. To keep his finger on its pulse, he prioritised attending the regular Wednesday morning departmental staff meeting, answering correspondence on the same visit.

But Matthew had little interest in the main pedagogic aspects of the job – the interaction with students – as Nuttgens later recalled in some detail:

His teaching involvement was, really, shockingly low. During my whole eight years under him at the university, he only gave four lectures, two of which I wrote for him and one of which, on the vernacular architecture of the world, I actually gave on his behalf, because he had a sore throat. I didn't mind doing that, even though I'd no idea what the slides showed, but what I did slightly object to was his coming and listening to the lecture! Now all this wasn't lost on the

(over) **6.6** Double-page spread from *AJ*, 19 June 1952, pp.762–3 (RIBA Conference number: articles on Cowan, Reiach, David Carr and Stuart Matthew). (AJ)

151

The returning hero

Ralph Cowan

Head of the school of architecture at the Edinburgh College of Art, Mr. Cowan has 12 full-time staff and 180 full-time and 55 part-time students. The latter are apprenticed to architects and attend school two days a week. Mr. Cowan lives in an unusual Georgian house (see above, and living room interior) in South Edinburgh. In partnership with Alan Reiach, his design for a house in Greendykes Road, Edinburgh (below) hangs in the RSA.

Alan Reiach

Apprenticed to Robert Lorimer and studying at the school, he won Tite Prize in 1933. Today, in partnership with Ralph Cowan, he has designed a college of agriculture for Edinburgh and the East of Scotland, shown below. The building is in three elements : the teaching and research wing, the administrative

block and the recreation section. Construction : part concrete, part calculated brickwork. This is sited south of the city. This design will be illustrated more fully in a future issue of the JOURNAL. *Above is the living room of a house which he has converted from a studio.*

ing to music. The BBC has not yet unearthed them and the Saltire Society, founded comparatively recently to encourage Scottish culture, does not include many among its members. And as already indicated they are not normally to be found at their headquarters in Rutland Square.

One thing *is* known and that is they all work within the New Town area. Some live there, also, and one or two combine office and home in the same building. Basil Spence does, and Leslie Grahame-Thomson. It is therefore all the more extraordinary that there is not more intercourse, or perhaps that is one of the reasons for it. We do not wish to give the impression that the architects are unfriendly; it is only that there is a curious lack of contact and of interest in each other's work. It is quite possible that this is due to outside causes and it is fair to say it is less true of the younger generation. We have said

that the architects as a whole do not mix in the cultural life of Edinburgh, and, in trying to describe this side of the city's life, we come up against the same difficulty because the artists also do not lead a very corporate existence.

Musically Edinburgh is dying, if not dead, except in summer time when she wakes and feasts gluttonously for the three weeks of the Festival. When, at the start of the war, the BBC evacuated most of its personnel and all of its orchestra with Ian Whyte, its distinguished conductor, it did musical Edinburgh a great disservice. The uprooting of all their families was an undertaking not to be repeated except in a state of emergency and the Orchestra and Ian Whyte remain in Glasgow. Musicians, therefore, are in short supply and the city has lost a composer and a very vital personality. For the phenomenon of the Festival, citizens have to thank not themselves but the Glynde-

Site plan

David Carr and Stuart Matthew

These two architects are in partnership, Stuart Matthew is also associated with his father's firm of Lorimer and Matthew, and with this firm is responsible for the design illustrated below for a clinic, housing estate, church, gymnasium, etc., for disabled ex-service men at Craigmillar. David Carr, Edinburg h trained conducts a separate practice with W. F. Howard in London. In association with Matthew, he is concerned mostly with work outside Edinburgh. He spent one and a half years in an ECA research fellowship studying prefabrication. He came to the conclusion that the smaller the component the better. Stuart Matthew (his brother, Robert, is also an architect —to the LCC) started in private practice in 1945. The design for the ex-service men's home —known as the Thistle Foundation—was the winning entry in an open competition. The design will be further illustrated in a future issue of the JOURNAL.

bourne Opera Company and a cultured Lord Provost (Sir John Falconer, lawyer), for discovering in the city an almost perfect setting.

Artistically Edinburgh is still alive, as is evidenced by the work exhibited by William Gillies, John Maxwell in landscape and still-life, and by R. H. Westwater in portraiture and William Wilson in stained glass. Even the lesser known and lesser painters generally show more individuality and exuberance than the practitioners of the other arts, though these two qualities can scarcely be denied to the poet Sydney Goodsir Smith, and work of some worth is being done in drama by Robert Kemp and in various categories of prose writing by Moray McLaren. The Arts Club where we should expect to find most of these people is now largely frequented by business men and both the Pen Club and the Saltire Society, which made promising

starts, rapidly attracted too large a proportion of amateurs of the wrong kind. The community is perhaps too small to produce enough first rate artists to form a group at our present stage of civilization, and there is something in the Scottish character which drives the individual artist to the country places and remote islands.

Bohemian Edinburgh scarcely exists; in the Café Royal some years ago artists, writers and musicians would be found almost any day, and very occasionally an architect might be seen. Now they tend to foregather in different places and generally at the weekends only. Parties are more spontaneous and smaller, though the quality of conversation and the stamina remain the same. The last-named quality is an essential during the Festival when private parties are continually being given, often on the spur of the moment, in honour of visiting artistes. The Festival Club,

students, of course, and they eventually got their revenge when we canvassed suggestions for an external examiner – and someone wrote up 'Professor Matthew'. He was absolutely furious about that! To the traditional academic minds, he was quite a puzzle, with his capacity for analysis, his almost computer-like brain, able to recall verbatim almost everything that had been said at a three-hour meeting – and his massive common sense. One senior academic asked me 'whether Professor Matthew was as stupid as he seemed'. I said, 'Don't count on it!'[42]

Teaching contact with undergraduates was confined largely to 'crit' sessions.[43] One early student recalled that 'he was on the one hand very nice, but on the other very distant: he could focus on you or through you, as he smoked his little cheroots. He could be very personable, and then something remote came into his eye – but his influence on me was a very deep one.'[44] Day-to-day teaching was at first left largely to Nuttgens:

> I said to him, one day, 'I really haven't got enough money to live on!' He said to me, 'Look, you run the place – why don't you just get on with it, and sort it out?' He didn't dominate, but would delegate, and would just trust you to get on with it. On one occasion, he delegated me to give a lecture to some medical students, but I completely forgot, and there was a row. I went to see him and apologised. Matthew said, 'Have you not got a decent diary?' He gave me some money and sent me out to buy one, so it wouldn't happen again. He wrote a letter to the Vice-Chancellor taking the total blame for it, and showed it to me, saying 'It *won't* happen again, will it?' Although he'd never praise people to their face, he was incredibly loyal to them – which was why I, and many others, were so devoted to him![45]

Matthew's status within architectural education was as much external as internal to the university: in mid 1955 he was appointed to the University Grants Committee as its first architect member, and devoted much attention to the introduction of costing techniques and briefs for new projects.[46]

8 Palmerston Place: into private practice

In reality, however, Matthew was not just an administrator but also someone who still remained fascinated by the designing and putting up of buildings. And the same restless principle of energetic proselytising and setting up, followed by delegation and benign neglect as his interest moved on to new subjects, also applied in Matthew's new private practice. As we noted in Chapter 5, Matthew had already begun laying the foundations for a modest practice in October 1952, when the possibility of a project at Turnhouse Airport was broached with him at an Architecture Club dinner by Sir Alfred le Maitre, Minister of Aviation. We shall look at that project in more detail in a moment, but we first need to briefly review the way in which Matthew set about organising his practice. Most importantly, it was completely unconnected with Lorimer & Matthew or with any of the existing Edinburgh architectural establishment.

As in his dealings with the ECA traditionalists, Matthew's relations with both the EAA and the RIAS were distant from the beginning. They resented him as a cosmopolitan interloper, and he reciprocated, by making sure that up-and-coming young designers were steered away from old-fashioned practices like Leslie Grahame MacDougall or J R MacKay. Conversely, he ceaselessly tried to advance the cause of Alan Reiach: for example, he wrote to one enquirer that his was the only Scottish practice he could recommend: 'a very small office concentrating on one job – an outstanding architect who has had comparatively little work, but only recently has had the go-ahead for his magnum opus (a large agricultural college in Edinburgh)'.[47] Although, as we shall see shortly, Matthew was a strong supporter of an outward-looking 'cultural nationalism', he vehemently opposed any restrictive practices that might benefit traditional Scottish architectural firms. In August 1954, for instance, he noticed with surprise that Montrose Town Council had announced a competition for a new Town Hall with himself as assessor – having forgotten to approach him! In correspondence with the Town Clerk and Bill Spragg of the RIBA, Matthew explained that the competition must be fully open, rather than a 'small Nationalist affair'; 15 years later his political views on the latter front would have changed markedly, as we shall see in a later chapter.[48]

By 1952 the rump of Lorimer & Matthew was in a state of some confusion, with the effective breakdown of John coinciding with the decline of Stuart. From now on, a diminishing minority of jobs, such as the Robin Chapel or Warriston Crematorium (1956), was assigned to Lorimer & Matthew. A much greater workload, including large projects such as the Meadowfield housing scheme, Edinburgh (1952–7), was carried on under the aegis of David Carr and Stuart Matthew's joint practice, which remained a considerable one throughout the 1950s. Robert, however, was determined to start afresh, by building up a small practice unconnected to his squabbling relatives, or to the mercurial Reiach:

He'd clearly come back north to start a completely new phase of his life, and didn't want anything to do with the past. Alan gave the strong impression that he thought he and Robert would go into partnership when Robert came back north, but Robert had no intention of doing any such thing!

Initially, with his focus on his academic work, Matthew needed just a single architectural assistant to deal with the drawings for Turnhouse, and eventually settled, for safety, on someone recommended by Reiach – his former chief draughtsman during the College of Agriculture job (between 1950 and early 1952), Tom Spaven. He, for the previous

six months, had been working in the National Coal Board architects' department, which at that time, under Egon Riss, was something of a nursery for young Modern architects in Scotland: Spaven recalled that 'Reiach himself was going through a despondent patch at the time, lying in bed in the mornings', but he was as reliable a contact for Matthew as ever. By early December 1952 it had been fixed that Spaven would start on the working drawings for Matthew in his spare time, and would leave the NCB to work full time for him as the job progressed.[49]

Spaven recalled:

I lived at Fountainhall Road in the Grange, and at that time was a disgruntled member of the NCB production department. I remember reading the *Evening News*, and spotting a tiny snippet which said that Robert Matthew was being appointed to do Turnhouse. I wondered, 'Who's going to do his working drawings?' And I contacted Alan, who arranged an interview with Robert at the beginning of December 1952 – the first time I ever met him. He said, 'Once the Ministry of Aviation get approvals, they'll want everything to begin tomorrow.' I took up with him full time in June 1953. The first 'office' was a small dressing room in my house at 26 Fountainhall Road, measuring 5 by 7 feet, just about big enough for a drawing board. Robert's priority was establishing himself at the college, so he left things to me. Looking back, it was a strange interlude. If anything extra was needed, I had to say. He could not afford more staff, so I worked in my room, doing everything – as assistant, office-boy,

6.7 1971 portrait of Tom Spaven. (John Dewar Studios)

The returning hero

charlady and typist. He'd heard from Alan that I could type, keep the books and petty cash, and all that sort of thing. The typewriter was an Oliver – I was no typist, using one finger only, and it would jump every odd time you hit the keys. Then we got an office at 8 Palmerston Place, next to the church, with two ground-floor rooms, front and back; my main priority was getting a drawing board and desk. We got that from David Carr and Stuart Matthew – an old-fashioned kind of desk that they wanted to get rid of, a high table with legs. The board had a chunk of wood propping it up. Some of my secretarial work was for the university – it seemed to be taken for granted I'd cope with that, too – unlike later, when Robert's various 'lives' were kept much more segregated from each other.[50]

Rapidly, however, the staff began to grow, although the office was run quite parsimoniously: until at least 1960, for example, there was no car, and most staff walked or used bicycles and public transport. Matthew made all the appointments himself without reference to Spaven, giving preference to younger people with outside experience, preferably in London. By the end of 1954 there were seven staff: Margaret Little (appointed December 1953), James Dunbar-Nasmith (April 1954), Ron Thurgarland (September 1954), Margaret Brown (later Richards; October 1954), secretary (October 1954), and Graham Law (November 1954). Dunbar-Nasmith was in his final term at ECA when Matthew arrived, and initially approached him in mid 1953: 'He said, "Oh! I can't afford to pay you just now, I'm afraid – and I don't know what you can do" – so I went back the next day with my whole portfolio, and left it with him.' Finally, after a six-month interlude working with Leslie Grahame Thomson, Matthew agreed to take him on to help Spaven with Turnhouse, when the latter went on site.[51] Compared with the grandeur of Thomson's well-established practice, Palmerston Place seemed

makeshift in the extreme. Dunbar-Nasmith recalled that

There was no secretary; we had to do the letters ourselves, using his father's old typewriter. Margaret Little said: 'How old are you? When she found out I was two weeks younger than her, she said, 'So *you* can make the tea!' I thought, 'What have I got myself into?' – yet at the same time, it was all immediately fascinating, and stayed that way. I was there for three years, and learnt more about architecture in those years than I had in five years' full-time education. Matthew would arrive in the office at 9.00, leave at 9.25 to go up to the College of Art, only returning at 5.30 – he was never in the office during the day, except for meetings.

But then, on his return to Palmerston Place in the afternoon,

after spending half an hour or so in the office, Robert would take away home to Humbie in the evening a roll of drawings with everything there was on a project – notes, site plans, initial sketch ideas – and then on Monday morning, or even the next day, he'd come back with umpteen fully worked-up designs – say, twelve alternatives, maybe even twenty! Some were usually just awful, but one or two would be brilliant – and he'd bring them *all* back to us, without giving any hint he saw any difference between them! He'd discuss with us, as an equal, the good and bad points of each – and then eventually, somehow, the best one would emerge. He'd say, 'Let's go ahead with that one, then!' – and he'd head off to the university, and we'd begin doing the working drawings.[52]

Thurgarland – a specialist in industrial architecture, and ex-NCB like Spaven – was taken on in anticipation of a series of hydroelectric power station commissions. Both Margaret Little and Margaret Brown, who were friends, came from elite circles within the London housing-architecture world: Little from the LCC, and Brown from Powell & Moya. The Kingussie-born daughter of an engineer, Brown had had a peripatetic childhood, and began at Kingston School of Architecture at the age of 16, starting with Powell & Moya in 1952 straight after graduation. Her two years with the firm plunged her straight into the Pimlico project in Westminster, probably the most renowned housing development of the day, where she became job architect for one of the long slab blocks.[53] Her interview had followed an initial phone call to Matthew at Craigievar:

> When I then got through to Lord Sempill, he said, 'I'll summon him from the battlements.' Robert said to me, 'I can see you next week at Holford's office.' I went there, was offered the job, and started straight away, arriving in Edinburgh on 4 October 1954. The office was very squalid, with dreadful old T squares. But Robert was very much the leader – 'I want it like this!' We didn't have many jobs, but we did various competitions, with Robert coming in on Friday evenings and saying, 'We've got to have X or Y finished by Monday morning' – and everyone would get down and do it. Some of the jobs were very tiny – memorial plaques, shops and so on.

Dunbar-Nasmith recalled, 'Robert always got what he wanted – he could be absolutely impossible!'[54]

Matthew's private practice was, in pragmatic terms, concerned chiefly with supporting him and his family after the loss of his LCC salary and public-sector benefits. But, like all his other post-1953 activities, it also at first had a strong motivating ideal – the typical 1940s /1950s quest for a more 'organic' Modern architecture, rooted in place. This concern, in effect, displaced Matthew's passion for regional planning, during the period when the latter movement seemed discredited among architects as a bumbling, bureaucratic machine – especially at the time of the 'Crichel Down'

scandal.[55] Some post-war adherents of a vernacular-inspired Modernism, like Matthew, combined a somewhat Arts and Crafts concept of a pre-industrial golden age with a continued allegiance to the utopian rationalism of the interwar years.[56] What the 'modern vernacular' and the Arts and Crafts movement had fundamentally in common was a rejection of the 19th-century era of industrial mass-produced ornament. But the difficulty faced by the advocates of more localised Modernisms was that any move away from strictly universal Modernity would inevitably reintroduce an element of style or eclecticism. Almost inevitably, one would start to design industrial buildings or blocks of flats differently from rural cottages or churches. Two pointers towards such an approach came from Italy: the early 1950s' 'neo-realist' movement of vernacular-inspired architecture, and the slightly later 'neo-Liberty' movement, with its introduction of overt historical references (in buildings such as BBPR's Torre Velasca, Milan, 1950–7, or F Albini and F Helg's Rinascente store in Rome, 1961).[57]

As already hinted above, Matthew set out his views on the current state of Modern architecture in a series of lectures and papers in 1953–6. On the one hand, Modern architecture had brought a 'new universal expression' in architecture, based on integration of the work of the architect with 'great blocks of building ... coordinating big production programmes'.[58] Yet, on the other hand, a 'consistent' architectural culture, a 'thread of organic building', had existed before, in the Middle Ages, and 'in the "vernacular", it has always been with us.' If one learnt from vernacular buildings, one could free oneself from 'the tyranny of the flat roof' and from the rhetorical excesses of le Corbusier, including the excessive use of exposed concrete, 'grey, blotched ... unattractive'. Some Modern architects, especially in Scandinavia, had begun to learn these lessons, resulting in everyday buildings of 'breathtaking beauty'. The inspiration of the vernacular would hopefully provide a way to reconcile all the conflicting demands on the Modern Movement.[59] Throughout the late 1940s and 1950s Matthew assiduously collected books about vernacular buildings in other countries: for example, on the back of a 1958 book on Polish vernacular architecture, he had jotted lists of similar books on Romania, Hungary and Czechoslovakia.

Matthew's return to Scotland had coincided with a short-lived surge in nationalist sentiment, although he himself was hostile to political nationalism at this stage. Certainly, however, his attempt to devise a new organic Modernism in Scotland chimed in with the wider cultural climate. Behind his controlled exterior, national identity was, and remained, one of his irrational passions – to a point that it almost constituted one of his substitutes for religion. In Nuttgens's view, 'Matthew was very romantic about Scotland, about his childhood in the Grange. He saw God, on the one hand, in Rational Analysis, but also, on the other, in Scotland.'[60] And his own architectural values stayed close to the 'modern traditionalism' of the late 1930s in Scotland – perhaps unsurprisingly, for an interwar admirer of architects such as Bonatz and Asplund. When Matthew found himself in opposition to Hurd on the George Square demolition furore around 1960, he was actually forced to distance himself publicly from some of his core values. But for Matthew, unlike Hurd and other continuing traditionalist proselytisers such as George Scott-Moncrieff (convener of the Saltire Housing Award), it was equally vital that the new post-war Scottish architecture must clearly signal itself as part of the Modern Movement.[61] Anything smacking of the historicist ornamentation and facadism of 'socialist realism' was ruled out on principle: in 1954, he openly questioned 'the architecture of social realism ... "the people's architecture": is this the free expression of architectural as opposed to *political* thought?'[62] What was needed, rather, was something 'clean and straightforward, all false sentiment shed away'. This would be made 'Scottish' largely by its

use of materials. In 1954 he wrote to a Greek critic, Vasilides, that Scotland and Greece shared an 'informal and romantic' architecture of 'human scale', in contrast to Rome and the Renaissance. And in Scandinavia he felt the Modern Movement was virtually identical with 'vernacular', and 'simply means contemporary building'.[63]

Although 'overwhelmed with committees' in Scotland since returning home, Matthew found time for a range of national cultural activities, including membership of the Royal Fine Art Commission for Scotland and the Scottish National Buildings Record (which, in 1953, his representations prevented from being completely swallowed up by the Ministry of Works).[64] His followers continued to control the DHS architects' department – headed from 1953 by Jeffryes with Morton and Woodcock as assistants, and F J Evans and Grieve as regional planners. From 1956 F R Stevenson was promoted, along with Grieve, to become Deputy Chief Architect and Planning Officer.[65] Conservation was a continuing concern: in July 1953 he agreed to a plea from traditionalist architect James Shearer, on behalf of the National Trust for Scotland, to look over a draft development plan for Arbroath, to help resist demolition of listed buildings in High Street and the Shore. But he was more cautious, by 1956, about an approach from the Georgian Group (London) about possible help in setting up an Edinburgh Georgian Group to resist proposed development of George Square, as pointed to in Basil Spence's masterplan of 1955; he added ominously that, as university professor, he was 'very much involved in the George Square issue'.[66] Matthew's most important 'nationalist' connection of all was with Cecilia and William Sempill, who provided his family with an open house retreat at Craigievar, any time he wished to throw himself into a project without distraction. It was largely at Cecilia's instigation that Matthew, in 1953, joined the Scottish Committee of the Council of Industrial Design, and the Scottish Craft

Centre, based in the 17th-century Old Town setting of Acheson House, Canongate (restored by Hurd in 1935–7), and dedicated to promoting 'a Scottish style' in contemporary crafts work.[67]

What did Matthew's advocacy of a Scottish Modernism actually mean, in architectural terms? The key was to build in Scottish materials, above all stone, in a way that he thought appropriate to those materials: 'Scotland has a great inheritance of fine building – a range of building stones [that make up] simple, almost standardised elements, unconsciously in the right places ... rich in texture, vernacular building.' His October 1953 Edinburgh University inaugural lecture made a strong call for the Modernist application of scientific method to the use of stone in building. Partly, Matthew's obsession with stone went back to his pre-ECA geology course, which left him with a comprehensive familiarity with the building stones of Scotland. This influence was coupled with a Lorimerian Arts and Crafts love of rubble construction, modified by a strong reaction against the recessed pointing that had been common at the turn of century and in the inter-war work of his father and Lorimer, and an insistence on flush pointing, or 'slaistering'.[68] Occasionally he used ashlar stonework, but rubble was far more frequent.

Other vernacular materials could be used in combination with stone – timber cladding, low-pitched pantiled roofs, and smooth render or rough harling. But then, these elements could also be freely combined with the trademarks of Modernism – large areas of glass, flat roofs, openings or structures clearly dependent on steel or reinforced concrete construction, and even multi-storey blocks. The result was a distinctive personal style with a thread of 'common affinity' through the use of stone, but which took a slightly different form on each job, often using a centrifugally planned or agglomerative disposition of contrasting masses. Eventually, around 1960, Matthew became largely disengaged from active design, and the ideal of vernacular Modernism had in any case fallen from fashion.[69] In the perspective of John Richards, one of the younger post-war generation of designers, contemptuous of all vernacular or folk approaches, who flocked to Matthew's practice in the late 1950s, Matthew seemed

schizoid about all Arts and Crafts things and attitudes. His houses were full of chunky furniture he'd designed, and folksy objects he'd picked up from all over the world – just like a jackdaw. Architecturally, his approach was the same. He saw buildings as picturesque collages of objects, assemblages of forms rather than as complete realisations derived from some ideal or Platonic form. He regarded buildings as objects you saw in perspective rather than as abstractions or ideas. Things which bothered me, like cladding the whole of a tower block in random rubble, didn't bother him at all – just like post-Cubist painters introduced scraps of familiar material into their paintings.[70]

How did Matthew's strong but amorphous ideas of 'rooted' Modernism inform the beginnings of his private practice? His first commission, for the 'tiny but delightful job' at Turnhouse Airport, required a single, relatively small terminal building, with concourse, buffet, administration and customs accommodation. The initial target cost for the project, which had been in gestation since 1952, was £40,000, but this was increased as the project evolved, in response to a fourfold traffic increase (to 70,000 passengers a year) from 1951 to 1955. A year previously, faced with a similar commission for the new Clydeside airport at Renfrew, Kininmonth had devised a flamboyant design fronted by a paraboloid concrete arch, which might have looked at home as a pavilion at the 1938 Glasgow Empire Exhibition. Matthew's conception could not have been more different from Kininmonth's attempt at a monumental gesture. His first sketches, produced in Holford's Cambridge Terrace

The returning hero

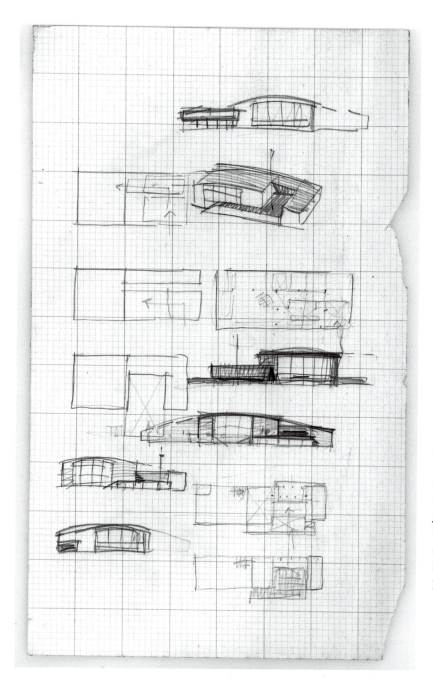

6.8 1952 concept sketches for Turnhouse airport by Robert Matthew. (EULMC)

with a curved, wavy roof over the central block, Matthew settled on a solution of the utmost sobriety, all flat-roofed and rectangular, with a higher central block and lower wings in a near-symmetrical arrangement.[71]

On a three-day flying trip (29 November–1 December 1952) Matthew inspected the existing Turnhouse facilities, discussed his new plans with the users, and visited Reiach's office to meet Spaven. In what would become Matthew's favourite internal design formula, a large central space, flowing into the side blocks, was entered by a low door, and interpenetrated by smaller spaces around it.[72] The interpenetration of the spaces was reflected in the external play of rectangles. The construction was lightweight steel with welded portal frames, which allowed big rectangular windows to the south, but the walls were clad largely in stone and timber. The structure, hailed as the largest 'external wooden building in the UK', was designed by structural engineer T Harley Haddow in late 1953/early 1954; its construction, which cost £72,000, spanned from September 1954 to April 1956, under the supervision of James Dunbar-Nasmith and Margaret Brown.[73] A relentless attention to detail, as in the Festival Hall, was applied by Matthew throughout the building process. For example:

Turnhouse had a boiler room, with an RC column in it. I had to go to site meetings with Nathaniel Grieve, the main contractor, and Russell, the concrete subcontractor, and had to supervise and brief them – I'd never been on to a building site. When the contractors cast this column and struck the shuttering, it had bowed on one side, by about half an inch. Matthew made them take down the whole column and do it again – both to make sure they didn't make silly mistakes where it really did matter, and to show us that you had to be firm. And, boy, did he know about stonework! I had thought Lorimer's stonework was best, but Robert didn't like it. He want-

flat during the two and a half weeks after accepting the commission on 8 November 1952, quickly arrived at the basic solution of a central public circulation block, with ground floor concourse and buffet above – and offices and kitchen in the west wing, and customs and baggage handling in the east wing. The flow of traffic was from front to back, and the building was designed to be capable of lengthways extension at either end. After toying with a variety of treatments, including a symmetrical arrangement

ed the pointing to be absolutely flush – like the wall at Turnhouse – 'slaistered' to make it absolutely smooth, like Scottish stone should be built![74]

The same attention to detail applied to the process of fitting out, with the most meticulous focus on architect control of the minutiae of equipment and fittings. Dunbar-Nasmith recalled that

The main entrance on the airside had a great plane of a timber ceiling – it acted as a rainshield on the outside, and was decorative inside, with little spotlight lamps recessed into it. Robert looked up and said, 'But the names on the bulbs are going to show – couldn't we get one with names on the sides rather than the bottom?' And I then had to spend most of the day phoning Osram and the other firms to try and get this. There was a great 'do' about the main clock – it had to have special Roman numerals, a traditional touch which did surprise me. Perhaps even more extreme was the case of one of the bar tops, which was to be done in glass mosaic: I said to him, 'Do you want it done in repeated or random patterns?' He said, 'Give me a grid, and the colours.' I gave him twenty prints of the drawing to take back to Humbie, and he came back with twenty different designs, all done in coloured crayons – just for the mosaic top of a bar. Now, however astonishing that might have been, you could say it was a total waste of his talents – but maybe the reason was that we were new staff, and he saw it as part of our training, as Lorimer would doubtless have done, to take us through some things in great detail.

All in all, Dunbar-Nasmith recalls, 'I learnt from Turnhouse, never to accept anything you are told at face value.'[75]

The Turnhouse terminal was opened, on 12 April 1956, by Harold Watkinson, Minister of Transport.[76] Although its scale was modest, its impact in Scotland would be difficult to overstate. In Nuttgens's opinion, 'it was *the* early symbolic building of the Modern Movement

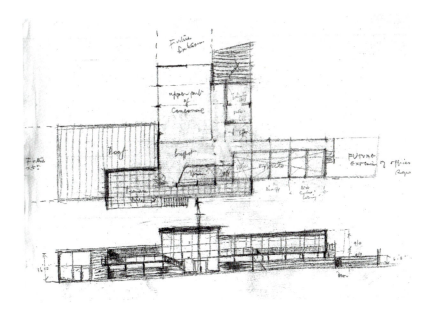

in Scotland – what could be more symptomatic of its age than an air terminal, what could have been more expressive of that age and that function than the way in which Matthew handled it?' And another young Scottish Modernist, Michael Laird, hailed it as 'a building of elegance and distinction which may fair-

(above) **6.9** 1953 concept sketches for Turnhouse airport by Matthew: the wings are the opposite way round as built. (EULMC)

(below) **6.10** 1954 drawing of Turnhouse (annotated by M Brown). (RMJM)

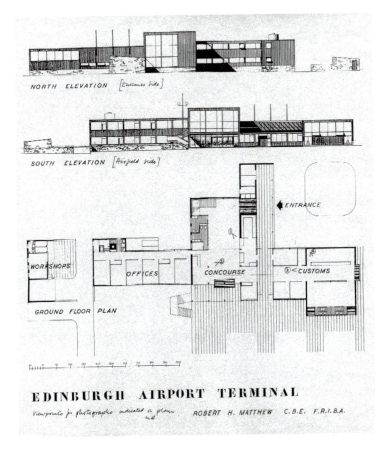

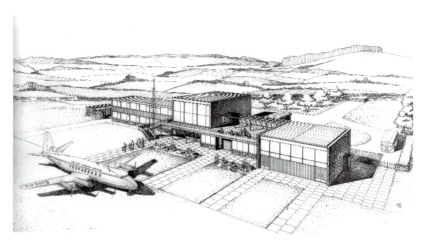

6.11 1954 perspective of Turnhouse. (RMJM)

ly be the matrix of a new Scottish vernacular in the Modern Movement'; in the 'international' style, the design was 'a natural agglomeration of architectural qualities arising from a clear analysis of the primary and diverse requirements of a building'. Its 'sharply cut rectangular shapes' exemplified 'vigour and restraint', and a 'chaste quality which permeates the building to the smallest detail'. Even the Edinburgh Architectural Association was forced grudgingly to acknowledge its success, awarding Matthew its newly instituted Centenary Bronze Award for art and architecture, designed by its Traditionalist president, Esme Gordon; the assessor was John Summerson, who argued that

> the extreme simplicity is deceptive. A fairly busy schedule of administrative and circulation requirements has been completely mastered, and one has that impression of stability and harmony which is the right answer for a building which is the first one entered after descending from a possibly bumpy sky.

Spaven recalled that the EAA's award stemmed from their

> guilt complex about Turnhouse: it irked them that, at the same time as their stalwarts like Leslie Grahame MacDougall were putting up, or proposing, great monumental stumps, Turnhouse was bringing a breath of fresh air and hope to younger architects. It simply made a lot of people sit up.

Indeed, however much the Edinburgh establishment may have resented Matthew's lack of interest in their institutions, 'it is a tribute to the man that whenever Edinburgh architects got together, you'd be certain that the name Robert Matthew would rapidly come into the conversation.'[77]

But the EAA award was a verdict of 1957, when Matthew's practice had really taken off. Initially, its existence was very hand-to-mouth, and dependent on a range of uncertain competitions and small jobs. He was soon at work, for example, on his Cruden commission to design standard speculative house types, producing drawings showing (for the time) somewhat luxurious detached houses in linked interlocking groups, massed in a manner reminiscent of Turnhouse. At the same time, Dunbar-Nasmith also got to work on drawings for a competition between package-deal developers to build a block of multi-storey flats for Edinburgh Corporation on a small redevelopment site at Spey Street, off Leith Walk. Matthew's design envisaged a slender, T-shaped block, not unlike the pioneering towers his LCC housing team had produced for Princes Way at Roehampton, 1950; however, a rival design, by Scotcon Ltd (Orlit), was chosen instead, in 1955. In February 1954 Matthew also produced drawings of standardised two-stream Cruden primary schools, in a relatively conservative corridored style. Eventually, in the absence of sufficient work to offset against it, Matthew repaid most of Cruden's loan.[78]

Despite Matthew's avoidance of family ties in architecture, a few of his early jobs were inherited from Lorimer & Matthew – exposing some unexpected emotional links with his own heritage, such as his love of armorial decoration. Robert retained a special interest in the works of Lorimer & Matthew: for instance, in February 1954 he was called in by Pilkington Jackson, as a representative of his father, to help protest against lighting changes and cleaning work in the Scottish National War Memorial. The first instance of a family-derived job came in

September 1953, when Robert's father asked him to deal with a request from the Society of Friends of Dunblane Cathedral to design a commemorative panel listing all the recorded clergy of diocese and parish. Matthew quickly produced a rough sketch for the society, and suggested a collaboration with Maxwell Allan (the sculptor he later used almost invariably for such work). The panel was large (8 ft long by 3 ft high), surrounded by a residually Lorimerian edge-roll moulding and containing blocks of plain classical text.[79]

A range of small-scale 'private' building opportunities was also opened up through James Dunbar-Nasmith's good connections, including an abortive £32,000 scheme in June 1954 for Leopold de Rothschild, for conversion of a historic barn at Cublington as a house for his sister, including the gutting of the ground floor; Law & Dunbar-Nasmith's first job, subsequently, would be a pair of farm cottages at Cublington.[80] Dunbar-Nasmith, with his Morayshire family origins, was also the source of what was probably Matthew's most bizarre project – an experimental energy-saving house at Gogarbank, near Edinburgh, anticipating by several decades the recent drive for 'sustainable design'.

This remarkable project was commis-sioned by a Lossiemouth-based philanthropist, Boyd Anderson, a friend of Dunbar-Nasmith's family, who proved to be fully Matthew's match in doggedly getting his own way. Anderson was a wealthy and relentlessly cheerful engineer who had made his money in tea plantations in Burma, and was preoccupied to the point of obsession with experimental methods of heating and energy conservation, combined with a keen amateur love of gardening. Nasmith recalled that 'Boyd was a kindly, altruistic but somewhat difficult personality – I brought the job to the office and Robert lived to regret it.' Margaret Brown put it more bluntly: 'Boyd was actually an utter madman, an amiable madman, who kept changing everything the whole time: his house as built had double if not triple glazing, and gadgets in every nook and cranny!'[81] Anderson's world outlook, in its architectural expression, was a *reductio ad absurdum* of the Functionalist preoccupation with precisely researched and measured mod. cons. He lived in Lossiemouth, on one of the coldest and most exposed stretches of the northeast coast, and, after an initial project to build highly insulated hen-batteries, then proceeded to the idea of commissioning an experimental group of houses – beginning with one for his own occupation –

6.13 1954 sketch drawings by Matthew of proposed detached houses for Crudens. (EULMC)

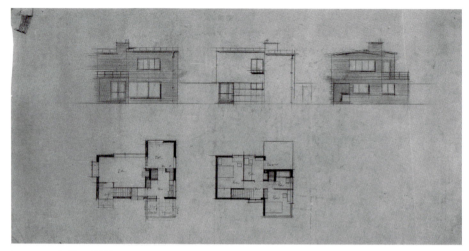

6.14 1954 sketch drawings by Matthew of proposed standard primary school for Crudens. (EULMC)

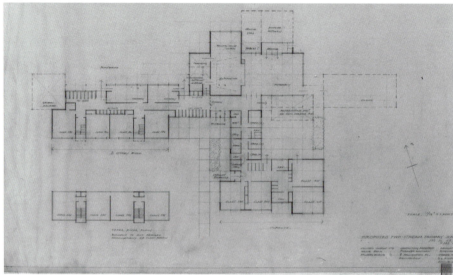

to try out different permutations of equipment, rather like the government's 1944 terrace of demonstration houses built in Northolt, London, to test different heating methods.

Having found a suitable site, by a quarry on the south side of Lossiemouth, Anderson began by designing, himself, a wildly impractical project for a six-storey tower-like structure set in the quarry, with one room on each floor and a rooftop garage, onto which one would drive from the quarry edge; there would be no staircase, but only a lift, which would double as a telephone kiosk. Having become convinced of the impracticability of this, in early 1954 Anderson commissioned Matthew (with Dunbar-Nasmith as project architect) to design a 'sensible house' at the same general location (but outside the quarry); the project

was initially seen by Matthew as 'a bit of light relief'.[82] Anderson's ideal was 'a house that is to help others' by using the sun and shielding the wind, through insulation, economic heating, forced air ventilation, radiator panels, floor-warming heat piping, solar heat storage, wind generator, and double glazing – as well as architectural aspirations such as combined living/dining room planning, and an up-to-date kitchen. Anderson was partly inspired by American concepts of free planning, 'bringing the outside indoors', although economy was also an aim, and 'the American idea of the whole house being 70°F' was sternly ruled out. Rather, the house was to perpetuate the Scottish walled-garden tradition, being set in sheltered and enclosed landscaping. From June 1954 Dunbar-Nasmith began to do sketch plans for a one-and-a-half-storey house, based on a flat-roofed courtyard plan. Rapidly, it became clear that Anderson expected to participate as a co-designer, and saw the philanthropic rationale of the project as justifying an endless succession of meetings, changes of plan, and general jovial contentiousness. He began to bombard Matthew and his colleagues with alternative plans of his own, including a bizarre 'diamond plan' incorporating a courtyard.[83]

Matthew, throughout the commission, treated Anderson with unfailing courtesy, recognising his essentially well-intentioned motives, his main refuge being the passive one of shielding behind Dunbar-Nasmith and Spaven: 'in the office, he said to James, "You brought him here – so you sort him out!"'[84] But even this approach failed Matthew when confronted with the 'diamond plan', and he had to protest more bluntly that he was 'at a loss what to do next', and unable to visualise how such 'awkward' shapes could be used to produce anything which 'I could feel some confidence in as an architect'. But no sooner had Anderson given in to Matthew on this point than he suddenly abandoned the Lossiemouth site, owing to a dispute with Moray County Council over the construction of a road across his land.[85] Refocusing his attention on the Edinburgh hinterland, Anderson found a new and more convenient location, at Gogarbank, only three miles from Turnhouse. By February 1956 the slightly larger (3,274 sq ft) revised design for this new location was finished, and in July work began – resulting in a remarkably coherent, geometrically sharp essay in timber and brick, considering the plethora of gadgets with which it was stuffed: 'In many ways it was a mad house, but very interesting too.'[86] The Gogarbank house retained the courtyard plan conception, orientated so that sunshine was focused on the bedroom wing, living room and a greenhouse. In addition to double-glazed windows to the living room, part of the roof was glazed; in a small concession to tradition one coal fire was provided in the living room, but otherwise the house was heated by

'Cadidec' electric cables in the floors, in an early example of underfloor heating.[87] By early 1957 Dunbar-Nasmith could report that although Anderson was 'still swithering about thermostats, simmerstats and rheostats, light is beginning to dawn!' From 1957 onwards Anderson focused instead on developing the complex, sheltered garden to the south and southwest of the house, complete with Matthew-designed rubble gazebos in a somewhat Portmeirionesque style.[88]

In retrospect, the Gogarbank project can be seen as an internationally pioneering essay in environmental design. But to Matthew and his colleagues it seemed at times no more than a freakish aberration. For example, the house, as completed, had 48 power points – a huge number for the time: 'He must have needed a power station to keep the place going!' – and the insulation caused great condensation problems. All in all, 'that experience firmly warned us off the idea of private clients.'[89]

Towards a 'vernacular' Modernism

From the end of 1954 the pace of work began to quicken in Matthew's small office, and the number of staff rose from seven to nine by December 1955 and 14 a year later – exceeding already the size of Carr & Matthew. Most of the additional

6.15 Gogarbank House under construction, 1956. (RMJM)

The living-room corner and terrace from the garden

Upper: *Greenhouse and sun room on the west side have double-glazed roof windows with insulated sliding shutters to keep out excessive sun. Bed-sitting room on the near corner is for a resident servant or additional guest accommodation. Lower: double garage for family cars, and carport large enough for two cars to be under cover by the front door*

Looking from living-room towards sun room. *Above log store on right is a hatch to bar*

Decorated glazed screen partitions greenhouse and allows sunshine to flood the living area. Most of the furnishings are traditional and came from the Andersons' previous home

The house that laughs at the weather

WITH THE SAME precise approach to fitness for purpose that he applied as a leader of the team which designed London's Festival Hall, Professor Robert H. Matthew, C.B.E., F.R.I.B.A., has designed a "weather-perfect" house at Gogarbank on the outskirts of Edinburgh. "Millbuies," the home of Mr. and Mrs. G. B. Anderson, is indifferent to changing weather conditions—hot, cold, wet or stormy.

To prove that it is possible to live in complete comfort however fickle Scottish weather may be, Professor Matthew, with partner S. Johnson-Marshall, A.R.I.B.A., chose a courtyard plan orientated so that the bedroom wing, living-room and

greenhouse receive maximum sunshine.

In addition to double-glazed windows in the living-room, part of the roof is also glazed. Too-brilliant summer sunlight is kept in check by a sliding insulated roof shutter and Venetian blinds.

Except for a coal fire in the living-room, "Millbuies" is heated by Cadidec electric cables in the floors. Overall heating is controlled by an outdoor McLaren thermostat, and there are individual room controls.

Ventilation, too, is not left to chance. To prevent open-window draughts upsetting the delicate thermal balance, an air-conditioning fan draws in filtered air and ducts it to living and bedroom wings.

Continued on page 153

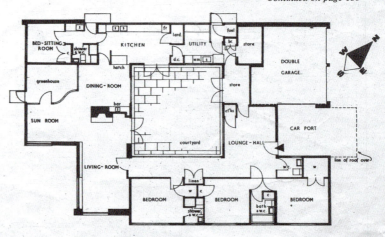

scale of feet

staff were architects, but there were two secretaries, including Christine Somerville, a childhood friend of Nannie's. A tough clerk of works, Arnot Waugh, was taken on in May 1956: he became 'absolutely devoted' to Matthew, and doubled as a general handyman for him and for the firm – making furniture for Keith, for example.[90] The overwhelmingly dominant element in the firm's work in this period was the 'vernacular' strain. In some cases the projects were still quite small, a typical example being a Burtons high street branch shop in the Borders textile burgh of Hawick, a 'little job' costing a mere £8,600, which was authorised in April 1955. Given a free hand by the firm's London property department, Matthew personally 'designed the shop front in harmony with the Scottish tradition, namely, using local stone with pantiles on the roof in order to get as much local colour as possible.' In a contradiction typical of vernacular Modernism, rubble and pantiles could not have been further from the actual local colour of Hawick, dominated as it was by grey ashlar and slate roofs![91] Building in small

burghs, with their strong associations of traditional civic pride and autonomy, held a particular symbolic significance for the Geddes- Mears-Hurd tradition of 'conservative surgery', and Matthew would, a few years later, carry this preoccupation to an extreme in an ambitious building programme for the small Ayrshire town of Cumnock.[92]

The only building context of even greater emotional resonance for Scottish Modernism than the tight-knit historic burgh was its opposite – the wildernesses of the Highlands. And from 1954 onwards an opportunity began to open up for Matthew to design a type of building that, more than any other, symbolised the 20th century's attempt to bring planned modernity to the Highlands: a hydroelectric power station. The North of Scotland Hydro-Electric Board (NSHEB) had been founded in 1943 by Tom Johnston to promote social and economic regeneration through rural electrification. By the early 1950s Johnston was out of political power, but installed as head of the NSHEB board, and set in train an architectural modernisation initiative

(opposite) **6.16** Article about Gogarbank House in *Ideal Home*, March 1959. (*Ideal Home*)

6.17 Burtons' Store, High Street, Hawick (1955). Spaven recalled that 'despite the small size of this job, Robert was very much involved in the initial design, and handed it over to me for detailing, and for me to search for sources of suitable local whinstone for the rubble'. The job architect was Andrew Grindall: Dunbar-Nasmith recalled that 'Andrew did a drawing of the pantiled roof without being very careful, and Robert looked at him and said, "Hmm – I've seen slates that diminish towards the top, but never pantiles that diminish towards the right!' (RCAHMS)

167

The returning hero

that opened the door to the potential involvement of Matthew. In hydro stations the problems of balancing architecture and engineering took a different form from conventional thermal stations, with the stations relatively much smaller, and overshadowed in size not only by the vast and entirely engineer-determined structures of the dams, but also by the grandeur of the landscape itself. The first stations, designed in the late 1940s by architects Tarbolton and Shearer, adopted a conventional heavy stone or concrete monumental classicism. As Nuttgens pithily put it, these projects 'looked as if some authority had, in a moment of madness, erected a bank or a public library in a remote glen.' But for Matthew what was needed was not to abandon stone but to use it in a non-monumental way, in combination with other vernacular materials.[93]

The hydro-station commission, predictably, came to Matthew in a rather oblique way. From the beginning of 1952 he had begun to gear himself up for a possible return to Scottish public life, and in January he had accepted Johnston's offer of a place on the non-executive NSHEB 'Artistic Advisers' Panel' of architects, alongside Shearer and Hurd. But when, in February 1953, Johnston also offered him the chair of the Board's executive Amenity Committee, and added a caveat that this would preclude any paid architectural work for the Board in his own right, Matthew met Johnston for lunch at the Reform Club to seek clarification. On learning that he would otherwise be 'likely to get a share' of the forthcoming Breadalbane scheme in Perthshire, he declined the Amenity chair, as he would be 'sorry to miss the opportunity' of this work.[94]

From mid 1954 the outlines of Matthew's likely hydro commission became firmer: three generating stations at Lochay, Lubreoch and Cashlie, with Lochay being started first, and Cashlie and Lubreoch each forming part of an ensemble with a huge dam: the board merely asked him to 'review' the Lubreoch and Stronuich dams to provide 'that

artistic touch which might otherwise be lacking'.[95] Matthew was lucky that the consultant civil engineers assigned by the board, James Williamson & Partners of Glasgow, were 'an enlightened firm, genuinely interested in architecture', whereas the electrical engineers (Merz & MacLellan) and the NSHEB officials (including chief engineer A A Fulton and general manager T Lawrie) were all of a more conservative disposition. From the beginning, Matthew took personal charge of the project, and conceived the stations initially as vernacular, Turnhouse-style enclosures, largely in timber and glass, on a stone base. Almost immediately, opposition sprang up, stemming largely from the Board's policy that it should determine all constructional materials: 'Robert didn't take kindly to that!'[96] In February 1955 Fulton warned Matthew that the Board had reviewed his initial Lochay drawings and had shown 'apprehensions' about the use of a 'large extent of glass' in a setting so far north, and expressed a 'strong preference' for a design in 'traditional' stone.[97] Matthew eventually gave way, and designed the station with a low-pitched copper roof. Gradually, however, Matthew was able to win the Board round, and wean them off the 'slightly "fascist" pattern they were used to, and get them to agree even to buildings with curves in them'.[98]

From mid 1955 the hydro project had begun to take on Matthew's more conventional delegated pattern, with ex-NCB assistant architect Ron Thurgarland drafted in to do detailed design and, eventually, site supervision. With stone construction now agreed, the key concern was with the selection of the 'correct' local stone – for Lochay, from Ben Lawers, and for Cashlie and Lubreoch, from Miller's quarry at Moar in Glen Lyon. All detailed questions of materials were vetted closely by Matthew: by August 1956, he was turning his attention to the degree of batter and the stone finish on the transformer house walls, and in October Thurgarland gave NSHEB preliminary notice that sample walls for Lubreoch and Lochay would be needed in both Moar and Ben Lawers

Modern Architect

stone, and the mason would need to discuss 'the finishing and pointing required by Mr Matthew' in detail before any work started.[99] The realisation of these stations, after 1957, will be dealt with in Chapter 8. But already they had begun to make their mark: Nuttgens argued that

> what gave it a Scottish character was not, in short, anything traditional in its features or familiar in its form, but the materials used in a traditional Scottish vernacular, rural way, and an uncompromising functionalism (including a pitched roof) that is typical of Scottish rural buildings. He had added a new dimension to the vernacular.[100]

Kincardine: from cathedral to casing

While a vernacular treatment seemed only appropriate for Matthew's hydro station commissions, a very different approach was obviously called for by another, far larger-scale generating-station commission that began to materialise in 1953, that of acting as architectural consultant for the largest power station yet planned in the UK: a 720 MW coal-fired station at Kincardine, on the north bank of the Forth. Seen in purely visual terms, his solution for this vast project was a design of far more mainstream International Modern kind, which seemed unremarkably in character with the work of the practice when it was eventually completed, in late 1958, but in its initial context, alongside Matthew's overtly 'Scottish' designs, highlighted the eclectic character of his early private practice.

But power stations, in general, were a very unusual kind of architectural commission, because so much of the expense – usually around seven-eighths for thermal stations – was accounted for by plant, and only around 10 per cent by buildings. The architectural design of a thermal power station was not a task easily reconcilable with the tripartite Vitruvian 'beauty–usefulness–structure' definition of architecture, let alone the form-follows-function tenets of CIAM Modernism. It

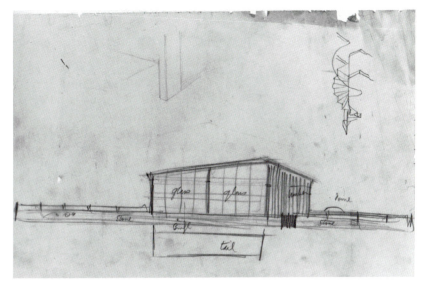

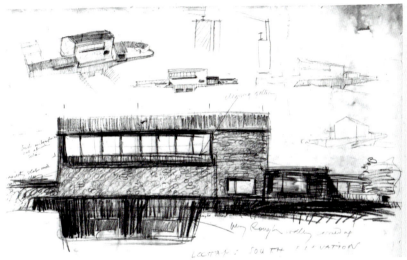

was essentially a styling job, concerned with providing a seemly casing that would somehow ennoble a miscellany of large and expensive objects that had already been designed by the all-important consultant electrical engineers. Up until the 1950s the response to this quandary had been, in Matthew's words, 'to cover this mass of complicated machinery and plant with a vast and ponderous shell and pretend that it is a cathedral'. While there existed some interwar precedents for Modernist industrial design, a greater impetus in the power station field stemmed from post-war initatives – for example, by the firm of Farmer & Dark, a long-established practice that had decided around 1953 that 'its reputation for "brick cathedrals" had to change', and had brought in a raft of young AA

(above) **6.18** Lochay power station, initial sketch drawing by Matthew, 1954. (EULMC)

(below) **6.19** Lochay power station, revised sketch drawing by Matthew, April 1955, showing more 'massive' construction. (EULMC)

6.20 Kincardine Power Station, 1955, charcoal drawing by Matthew. (EULMC)

graduates to work on the influential March-wood project, creating an LCC-style R&D group that developed a new approach based on lightweight steel framing.[101] Matthew's approach, in contrast to the agglomerative picturesqueness of his 'Scottish' style, tried to balance the now orthodox Modern Movement concept of the 'ordinary' as a potentially ennobling factor with an acute awareness of the inherently cosmetic essence of the task: 'The most utilitarian modern human artefacts, namely industrial plant, can have a positive effect in a cultural sense', but 'it still remains true that everything created is either good to look at or it isn't – if it isn't, it is a social evil, and not to be tolerated.'[102]

Matthew's Kincardine commission stemmed from an initiative by the eminent engineer and former wartime MoW Director, Sir Hugh Beaver, in his capacity as chairman of the 1952–3 government Committee on Power Station Construction. In early 1953, following Royal Fine Art Commission criticisms of recently built 'cathedrals of power', Beaver called on the British Electricity Authority (BEA) to embrace more Modernist types of lightweight-clad structure and to involve architects from the beginning – in effect, a Britain-wide equivalent to Johnston's design initiative at NSHEB. The Kincardine

project had already been commissioned by BEA in 1952, and the London firm of Kennedy & Donkin had been appointed electrical consultants. In early May 1953, at their suggestion, BEA tentatively approached Matthew.[103] He had, of course, no direct experience in this field, and immediately sought advice from Bill Holford, who sent him a simple list of architecturally 'good' and 'bad' recent power stations in England. At a September 1953 meeting with Kennedy & Donkin, Matthew surprised them by asking questions about the plant itself, and responded to their surprised queries by saying 'that if I had been asked to design a new Elephant House for the Zoo, I would expect to be given some basic facts about the animal and its habits without being accused of zoological aspirations!'[104] Matthew's basic brief of moving from a massive structural shell to a lightweight enclosure was already set in 1953. His main contribution, initially, was focused on broad matters of materials, where he and Spaven unsuccessfully fought for a large expanse of glazing to allow all the machinery to be floodlit externally – 'a purely architectural lighting scheme!' – but eventually a maximum of 18 per cent glazed external area was imposed.[105] Thereafter the main concern became the external walling material, where Matthew energetically lobbied against any significant element of exposed concrete: 'I, personally, would not readily use in-situ concrete as an exposed building material surface on any important building that can be seen from close quarters.' Although he acknowledged that Le Corbusier and some architectural students might like it, his view was that in practice 'the result is abysmally dismal.' Instead, he lobbied for the use of industrial brickwork for the lower walls and lightweight 'Kynalok' aluminium cladding above, giving a sharp, bold section.[106] Eventually, two 400-ft chimneys, rather than one large chimney, were decided on, and in early 1955 Matthew produced a strikingly atmospheric charcoal perspective of the sketch design, rather in his theatrical

1930s Art Deco manner, to promote the project to the BEA.[107]

In 1955, as the start of construction approached, discussion focused on Matthew's unsuccessful advocacy of a tidy screen wall in front of the external precipitators, 'a conglomeration of various sizes and shapes'; from November 1954 onwards all this detail work was largely the responsibility of a newly arrived assistant, Graham Law, Clydeside-born but Cambridge-trained. Dunbar-Nasmith recalls that

Graham, after long efforts, finally got into Robert's firm – as assistant number five, just after Margaret Brown. There wasn't enough space for him in the back room, so he had to go on his own in the front. Tom said, 'We can't have this poor chap working on his own – James, you'd better move in with him.' I was really cross at first, and we were both quite shy of each other on the first day. He was a dark Highlander, and when he said he came from Rhu, I at first thought he'd said 'Peru'! After that misunderstanding was cleared up, conversation ceased for a while, and we both started humming and whistling. He was whistling a Mozart opera, and I took up the refrain – and by lunchtime, we realised we had a lot in common. Graham immediately took over Kincardine, and from then on he was the only person who worked for Robert on it.[108]

The construction phase of Kincardine, in 1956–8, would be dealt with in a completely different way, following the reconstitution of the firm as a joint London-Edinburgh venture – as we shall see below. Already, with his strong London connections, Matthew's practice had begun to attract a trickle of potential commissions in England. His links with Stirrat brought him two school commissions: Swinton (from October 1953) and Ruddington (from December 1955). Matthew's first, abortive commercial design also stemmed from his LCC connections. In 1955 the Lavington Street,

Southwark, paper merchants Spicers approached four practices, including Matthew's, to produce proposals for a new and dramatic multi-storey garage, stacked on four floors on a very tight site. The company asked for something 'modern without being garish', and conveying a 'house style', and Matthew responded with plans for a reinforced concrete stack of parking floors connected by lifts, with the vertical feature of a full-height glass lift shaft supporting a neon sign; however, the job was eventually, in September 1955, awarded to Graham Henderson.[109]

University pathfinders: Aberdeen and Edinburgh

As in the case of power stations, where Kincardine led to a lengthy series of subsequent commissions of the same building type, another project originating in 1953, for Aberdeen University, paved Matthew's way into the wider field of education building. The Aberdeen project established a pattern that was to become very prominent in his private practice – an institutional commission of modest character, that 'grew and grew', sometimes in unexpected ways, over a number of years. In spring 1953, with his town planning rather than architectural hat on, Matthew was asked by the formidable but lugubrious University Secretary, William Angus, to prepare an overview report on student accommodation on the Old Aberdeen campus – which at that time was focused around the quadrangular Kings College group, facing onto the Old High Street, with its traditional burgage plots and backlands on either side. In early September, following a detailed walk around the area, Matthew prepared an outline development plan of impeccably Geddesian conservative-surgery character. This proposed extensive rehabilitation of the High Street to 'maintain its character', and concentration of new buildings around a series of 'courts' formed in the backlands. To the west of High Street, Matthew suggested that the library could be placed south of Meston Walk, with one 'hostel' (hall of residence) to its north and another at the far north

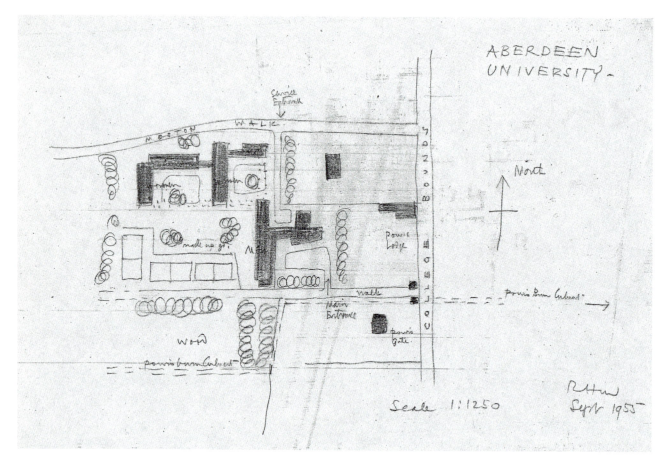

6.21 Aberdeen University, Meston Walk residences (Crombie Hall), initial 1955 sketch layout by Matthew. (EULMC)

end of Old Aberdeen. Matthew's initial sketches of October and November 1953 indicated the Meston Walk hostel as a compact, three-dimensional rectangular grouping, with a residential tower of around six storeys at the centre, a lower slab block along one side, and a wide refectory hall at one end – all with low pitched roofs. The overall effect was more abruptly picturesque and 'traditional' than Turnhouse – not unlike some 1930s/1940s Scandinavian social complexes such as Århus University (1935–47, by Kay Fisker, C F Møller and Povl Stegmann).[110]

Over the following two years this Aberdeen hostel project gradually matured. An initial scheme for piecemeal rehabilitation around High Street was prepared by Spaven and Brown, but was eventually carried out by Robert Hurd's firm. Increasingly Matthew focused on two aspects of the project: the design of Crombie Hall, first major post-war hall of residence; and, later, the preparation of an Old Aberdeen masterplan. Cost

restraints forced deferral of the building of Crombie Hall until 1957–60, but Brown's main design effort was finally under way by June 1955 – by which time the site had been shifted south of Meston Walk. Brown's final working drawings showed the women's blocks brought into a tight courtyard grouping with the central block, their timber facing and two-storey height contrasting effectively with the more muscular forms of the men's block, with its harling and rubble, and jutting external service stair; the refectory was more free-flowing again, with its wedge shape, swept-up roof and dramatic timber internal roof cladding. Travelling to Aberdeen to present the scheme to the University Court on 13 March 1956, Matthew's schedule obliged him to travel up by overnight train from London. Nuttgens recalled that

Tom Spaven and I had to meet Matthew while the London–Aberdeen train was stopped at Waverley for a few minutes changing engines – we

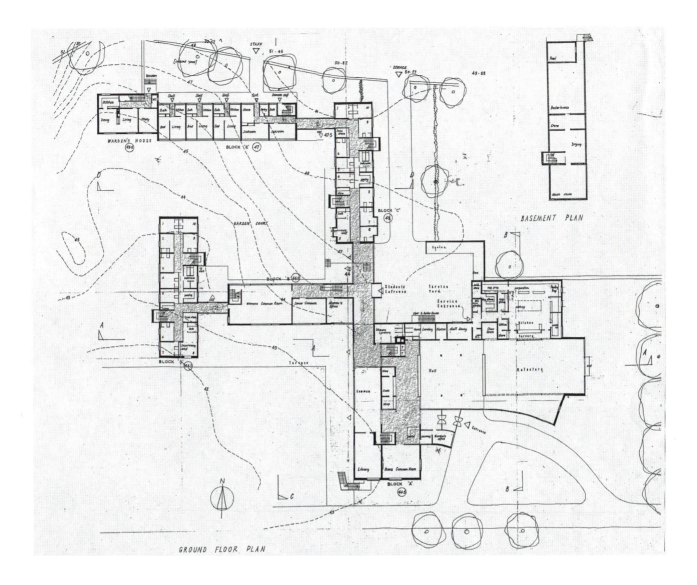

GROUND FLOOR PLAN

BASEMENT PLAN

handed the Crombie Hall plans in through the window, briefed him quickly, and by the time he arrived in Aberdeen he'd completely mastered the brief. He was a phenomenon!

Matthew's covering note for the scheme explained that it had avoided any 'monumental character' out of respect for the 'generally small-scale, intimate' townscape of Old Aberdeen.[111]

While Matthew's initial Aberdeen planning commission led fairly straightforwardly to a succession of building projects, in Edinburgh his position as professor of architecture was much more complex. We saw in Chapter 3 that in 1946 Matthew had turned down the possibility of a planning consultancy to

carry through the University's planned south-side area redevelopment around George Square, a development that, despite the avalanche of protest generated by initial proposals of 1946, had by 1954 proceeded as far as the granting of planning permission for change of zoning to a university campus. Edinburgh was unusual among universities in beginning its post-war building programme as early as 1950, at the instigation of Stewart and Appleton – some four years before the start of general government funding for university development.[112] With Matthew's appointment as professor in 1953, he was faced with the predicament of whether to try to follow the principle vehemently argued by Reilly in 1906, and claim a place as chief

6.22 Aberdeen University, Meston Walk residences, October 1956 layout plan as built (drawing by Margaret Brown). (RMJM)

The returning hero

6.23 McEwan Hall, Edinburgh University, detail of staircase light fitting; 1954 drawing. (EULMC)

designer of any new university buildings. Unwilling to alienate the now well-established Kininmonth, Matthew at first did nothing of the sort, accepting only one tiny university commission in 1953, to design a brass lamp fitting for a niche on the top stair landing of the McEwan Hall. This became Dunbar-Nasmith's first job on his arrival in 1954, and was drawn out in a floridly classical style appropriate to its 1890s neo-Renaissance setting.[113]

Rather than plunge into large building projects, Matthew at first chose a much subtler, more oblique way to extend his influence, through an extended collaboration with Basil Spence. In April 1954 Matthew secured Spence's appointment as planning consultant for the entire redevelopment, and the two of them began to formulate a six-stage plan for survey and design of individual new buildings. In November 1954 they met various professors, and Spence, sensitive to the likely resurgence of public opposition to any redevelopment, suggested preserving the west side of the square.[114] By March 1955 Spence's redevelopment plan was ready, envisaging a network of courtyards, with landmark tower blocks along the east side and a main library at the southwest. Its 'seductive sketches' and persuasive advocacy, including the westside retention, won the approval of the University Court and Corporation planners. Spence spoke of his plan as 'a vision ... comparable with Cambridge'; an Oxford association, conversely, was evoked by the suggested renaming of

George Square as 'the Great Quad'.[115] By 1956 Matthew would be ready to claim openly a key role in the George Square programme – that of designer of a new Arts faculty group – but until then he continued to keep a low architectural profile within the university, confining his involvements to very small-scale jobs, including a 1955 commission, handled by Dunbar-Nasmith, to design metal light fittings for a student common room in Old College.[116]

Tower of learning: Queen's College, Dundee

The climax of Matthew's 'vernacular' style, paradoxically, was not in the Highlands or a small burgh, but a university tower block in the centre of a large city – a new and very prominent main building complex facing Perth Road, for Queen's College Dundee (later Dundee University). The driving force behind the job was the principal of St Andrews University, Dr Thomas Knox, a leading authority on Marx and Hegel, who had in October 1954 secured university approval in principle for a complex including a library, administration, ceremonial rooms and 'Great Hall'. Although the traditionalist architect Reginald Fairlie had been planning consultant to the college, and had conceived the idea of giving it a more 'handsome and dignified ... frontage', it was now intended to go for a more forceful Modern approach, including a tower as a landmark feature – as shown in a sketch drawn by St Andrews historian and conservationist Ronald Cant. It was just at this time that Spence was working out his multi-storey landmark proposal for Edinburgh's George Square, and in February 1955 (after informal consultations with Spence, in which the George Square commission was foregrounded) he, Matthew and Joseph Gleave of Glasgow were invited to meet the works committee on 3 March to discuss a two- or three-stage development programme.[117]

Matthew was accompanied on the trip to Dundee by Dunbar-Nasmith, whose recollection of the day gives a flavour of

NEW FRONTAGE BUILDING   QUEENS COLLEGE DUNDEE

Job 14

Matthew's now multi-stranded existence, reliant on delegation in sometimes quirkish ways:

Robert and Basil, of course, were fully aware they were both in for the job, as they had discussed it beforehand – they were both on the RIBA Council. Now, Robert still had at that time his dreadful old wreck of a Morris tourer, whereas I'd just persuaded my father to let me have a brand new Austin A4 – so Tom said, 'You've got to take him in the new car – we can't allow him to turn up in the Morris.' His interview was at 3 pm, and once we'd arrived in Dundee, after detouring via an antique shop in Perth, Robert said, 'Basil's coming in after me – his interview's at 3.30 – why don't you go down to the station and meet him?' After Robert had been ushered into the interview room, Principal Knox came out and said, 'Where should Mr Spence be put so that they don't meet?' I then left and went down to the station – I hadn't met Basil before, but I easily picked him out – his train was five minutes or so late – and we went back up. I dropped Basil off outside the university building and went back in, to find Robert, just emerged from his interview, with the Principal desperately trying to get rid of him: 'Would you like a taxi, Professor?' – to

which Robert said drily, 'Oh, no thank you, I've got a car here, but it's gone down to the station to meet Basil Spence.'[118]

Subsequently, Knox wrote that Matthew had been unanimously selected to design this 'unusual' group of buildings, and sent him a copy of Cant's sketch. The university secretary later told Spaven that 'whereas Basil came in brandishing lavish drawings, Robert just sat there and said virtually nothing, other than asking a few penetrating questions: he would never "sell his wares" – that was typical of him.'[119]

Phase 1 of the Dundee complex was to be a laboratory, and Phase 2 would be the 'Tower', containing offices, teaching rooms and college hall. Within a month it became clear that, in the absence of UGC cost guidelines, the wealth of St Andrews University would allow considerable cost flexibility: Knox wrote that while the whole group should cost no more than £600,000, the Phase 1 element might cost twice the original estimate. The height of the tower would offset the cost, but 'the important thing was to provide a dignified range of buildings.'[120] The university's original concept was for a monumental group with a low tower of perhaps six storeys. Matthew immediately set about loosening up the group in a more modern fashion, while the practical

175

The returning hero

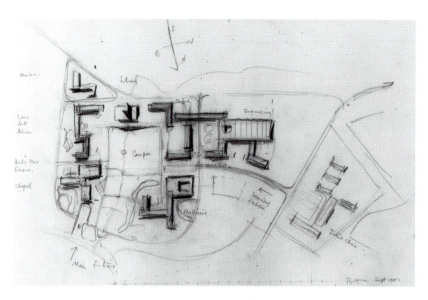

6.25 University College, Dublin: sketch layout of September 1955 by Matthew at new site at Stillorgan Road. (EULMC)

accommodation requirements steadily expanded. Eventually, in spring 1956, with deadlines looming, a plan including a much taller tower, 145 ft high, with three lifts, was settled: the tower had very little usable floor space on each floor, and was essentially a glorified podium for a high-level council chamber, enjoying a Geddesian outlook-tower view across to the 'mother university' in St Andrews. The library had now become three storeys high, with reading room and gallery. Partly at the instigation of Matthew, and partly of Spaven, the full range of 'vernacular' materials was applied even at this much more urban scale, including Auchinlea stone facing to the full height of the RC-framed tower, and cedar infill panels between the large strip windows on each floor. John Richards, later of Matthew's Edinburgh staff, argued that

> to the structural purists of the generation which followed Robert – my generation – his idea of sticking thick and extremely heavy stone walls on an 11-storey tower seemed absurd. The nature of rubble masonry is to carry loads in compression, and for this purpose it should be thick in relation to its height. Robert used it here like wallpaper!

Detailed design – including 'the challenge of making those facing blocks of stone stay up!' – was entrusted to a newly

appointed, 25-year-old Ulsterman, Jim Latimer.[121]

In November 1956, just prior to the start of Stage 1, Matthew and university librarian Dickie went on a study tour to Stockholm and Helsinki, visiting especially the Helsinki University Student Library (1953–5) by Einari Terasvirta, a modestly scaled, L-planned building. By the time the tower building, costing an estimated £400,000, was started in 1958, the UGC was intervening more closely in the project, insisting on a three-stage contract, with Stage 1 starting in 1957. An increasing number of assistants were working on the project with Latimer, but Knox insisted on continuing involvement by Matthew: Bill Campbell recalled one protracted meeting in St Andrews in 1957 when 'Matthew said, at length, "Well, I shall have to go, I've got another appointment" – whereupon Knox said, "You won't go until we've finished the business." That was the only time I've ever seen anyone publicly quell Robert Matthew!'[122]

Infirmary initiatives at Ninewells and Edinburgh Royal

By 1955 Matthew was increasingly having to deal with a whole array of major commissions for the design, rather than merely restyling (as with Kincardine) of large building complexes – all pointing forward to the need to develop a large, multidisciplinary staff. For example, in 1955 he became involved with the beginnings of two protracted projects to design an entire modern teaching hospital, one at Ninewells, Dundee, on a completely new greenfield site, and the other for the *in situ* city-centre redevelopment of the Edinburgh Royal Infirmary. In both cases the projects had been under discussion for several years.

At Ninewells, an initial proposal by the Eastern Regional Hospital Board and the University of St Andrews for a new teaching hospital and medical school was approved by the Secretary of State in 1945, and in mid 1955 a shortlist of only two architects, the other being J L Gleave (architect of Scotland's first post-war

Modern hospital, Vale of Leven, from 1952), was interviewed. Hospital administrator J K Johnston was on the interview board, and recalled that whereas

> Gleave had been very smartly dressed, in a sharp, dark suit, and talked eloquently and flamboyantly about his recent hospital work, Matthew conveyed a very different impression. He was wearing an old duffle-coat, teddy-bear fawn in colour, a shabby pair of trousers and no hat – he never wore one. It was all terribly informal, and when asked, 'Have you any hospital experience?' he said, 'Oh no, none whatever, just as I've no experience designing a church, but I've no doubt whatever that, if I'm furnished with all the appropriate information, it'll be well within my capabilities to do a good job.' We were so impressed at this impression of casual authority that he won hands down.[123]

Owing to cost restraints, however, the Ninewells project seriously got under way only in the late 1950s (see Chapters 8 and 9).

At Edinburgh, Matthew's involvement stemmed directly from his university connections, and from his brother Douglas's senior teaching post; but here also there had been a decade's debate and planning beforehand, focusing on the issue of whether to redevelop on the existing site or to relocate on a Ninewells-like site on the outskirts: in the Edinburgh City Development Plan, published by the Town Council in 1953, a site of 30 acres at Fairmilehead was zoned for hospital buildings between 1959 and 1973.[124] But in the mid 1950s, with the growing impetus towards redevelopment of the university in the George Square area, culminating in Basil Spence's 1955 development plan, the greenfield idea rapidly fell from favour with both the university and the hospital authorities.

In June 1955 the chairman of the Edinburgh board of management, Sir George Henderson, convened a meeting to consider a four-stage redevelopment plan, prepared by Dr Francis, Medical Superintendent, and the hospital architect/engineer, Thomas W Turnbull. The plan envisaged a piecemeal rebuilding process, with further massive Art Deco blocks of the type already built by Turnbull in the 1930s. On the advice of the Regional Hospital Board, the Board of Management engaged Matthew in September 1955 as a consultant to report on the project and 'produce a master-plan for the coordination of the proposed developments'. He began with 'interim development control' assessments, advising Francis that any infills should be 'very temporary', with 'no prejudice to future development'.[125] There then followed three months of further discussion with infirmary staff, preparation of four designs of 'main traffic streams', focusing on the impossibility of extending the site, and the building problems of poor lighting, sound insulation, circulation and amenity. Matthew eventually submitted a report in March 1956 that activated the multi-phase concept, including the possibility of adapting and infilling existing buildings, but avoided Turnbull's massive U-shaped block concept in favour of an overtly Modernist free-standing slab block eight to ten storeys high, to circumvent the 'poor lighting' problem. He hinted at a multi-storey solution for stages 3 and 4 as well.[126]

Only after a further three years of investigation of the requirements of a rebuilt Edinburgh infirmary did the focus return to Matthew. By now, in a pattern that would repeat itself several times subsequently, his role had changed and expanded from that of consultant to consultant architect for the rebuilding itself. But the framework set by Matthew's 1956 report remained unaltered, with its rejection of dense, packed insertions, and its insistence on Modern standards of light and air – which would necessitate blocks of a height liable to excite controversy in Edinburgh's heritage-laden planning world. Ultimately, this would prove a self-defeating strategy, which would eventually open the way again to the revival of the greenfield new-building option.

Home and abroad in the mid 1950s

Overall, as shown by projects such as these, the balance of Matthew's work was inexorably shifting away from a relatively small-scale, personal, east-coast Scottish affair to something bigger and more diffuse. Increasingly it became clear to him, from the views of younger architects in his practice and within the university department, that his crusade for a Scottish Modernism was no longer feasible, and the basis of his personal interest began to shift to the other extreme, towards overseas contacts emphasising international goodwill and social regeneration. The spirit of Vaumarcus had lodged deeply within him, and now began working its way back to the surface; from this point onwards 'his eyes were never off the far horizon'.[127]

This extroverted impulse was if anything strengthened by the passing worry, on his arrival back in Edinburgh, that he now risked isolating himself not only from international contacts but more generally from the cosmopolitanism of his London life: for example, a June 1953 letter from former Festival Hall assistant Trevor Dannatt (by now editor of the *Architects' Year Book*) promised that he would 'certainly let you know as and when I hear of foreign lecturers visiting the country'.[128] So far as Matthew's London profile was concerned, the years 1953–5 were, indeed, a temporarily low-key phase. His difficulty was that his network of contacts hitherto had almost all been concerned with public architecture/planning, but that he himself was now an architect-academic in private practice – and his own lack of natural affinity with both the communist/socialist Softs and the Corbusian Hards denied him even a more general ideological connection to his former colleagues. Up to 1953 he had formed an integrated part of the London socialist public-architecture world, and could exert his influence through collective agencies such as the Salaried and Official Architects Committee of the RIBA. Now, he was more dependent on long-distance

contacts, especially with the two Johnson-Marshalls, to keep in touch: Percy wrote to him in October 1953 and February 1954, for example, to update him on 'our campaign' to get public architects onto RIBA committees, and another letter of March 1955 (doubtless one of many) set out a detailed update on restructuring negotiations in the Planning Division consequent on Ling's move to Coventry, and urged Matthew to stand for election as an RIBA Fellow – duly achieved in October 1955.[129]

Like many who had risen to prominence in the 1940s, Matthew's connections with the guardian organisations of orthodox pre-war Modernism were relatively slight. Although a passive and uninterested member of the MARS group, he did not attend any of the post-war CIAM meetings, even those in England. Instead, he focused on a more diffuse range of connections within the UK – as, for example, with his appointment to the UGC in 1955 – and beyond, as his international contacts steadily grew and diversified, even without the reinforcement of his official post. For example, in March 1954 Professor M Hogan of the engineering school at University College, Dublin, formally approached him to serve as chairman of an Architectural Advisory Board to the university, and to help draw up a masterplan for a new campus at Stillorgan Road. Little material survives from this responsibility, but eventually, in late 1955, Matthew produced an outline layout plan, laid out on rectilinear campus lines, with the main buildings grouped around a large landscaped court.[130]

It was above all through the more ideologically neutral IUA, rather than the increasingly crisis-ridden CIAM, that Matthew's internationalising impulse, at this stage, found its chief expression. Abercrombie's status as Honorary President of the Union facilitated Matthew's transition from membership of the British committee to international committee posts (in which capacity he was able to begin establishing friendships with key IUA figures, including above all

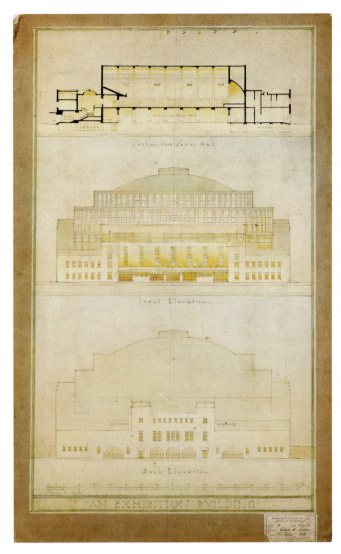

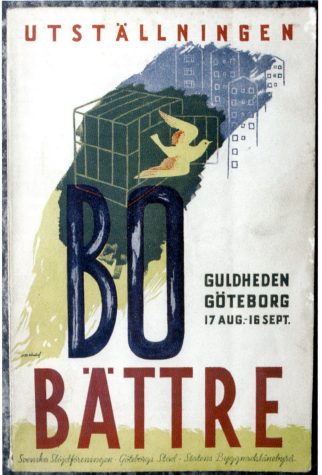

C1. Edinburgh College of Art, Stage V, project by Robert Matthew for 'Exhibition Hall'. (EULMC)

C2. Front cover of catalogue for Bo Bättre (Build Better) exhibition, Göteborg (including the pioneering Guldheden housing project by Gunnar Wejke and K Ödeen), collected by Matthew on his second visit to Sweden, in summer 1945. (*Elanders Boktrycken Aktiebolag*, 1945)

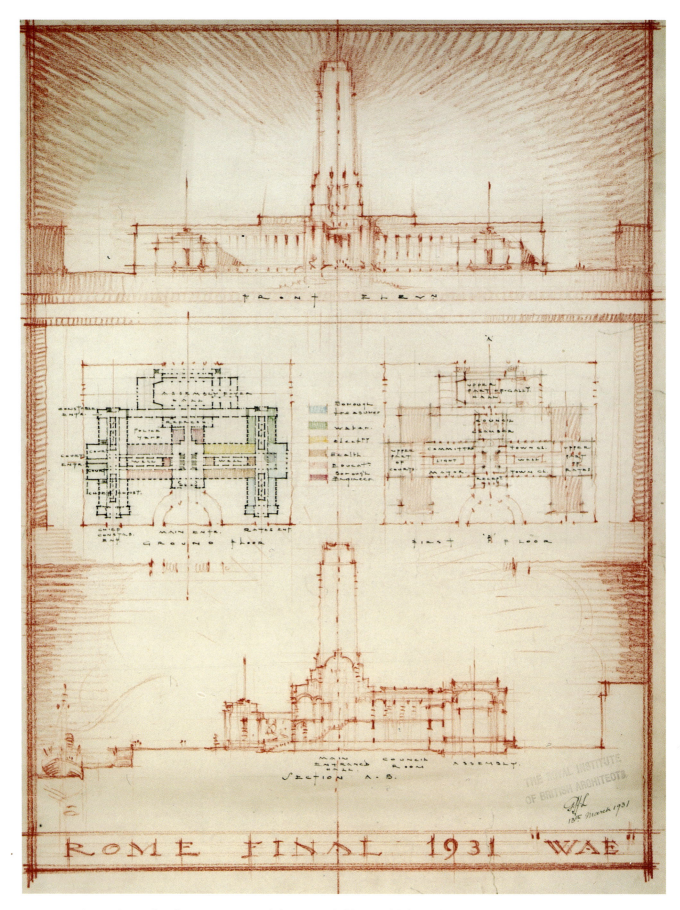

C3. Esquisse drawing by Matthew for 1931 Rome Prize (subject: town hall by seaside). (EULMC)

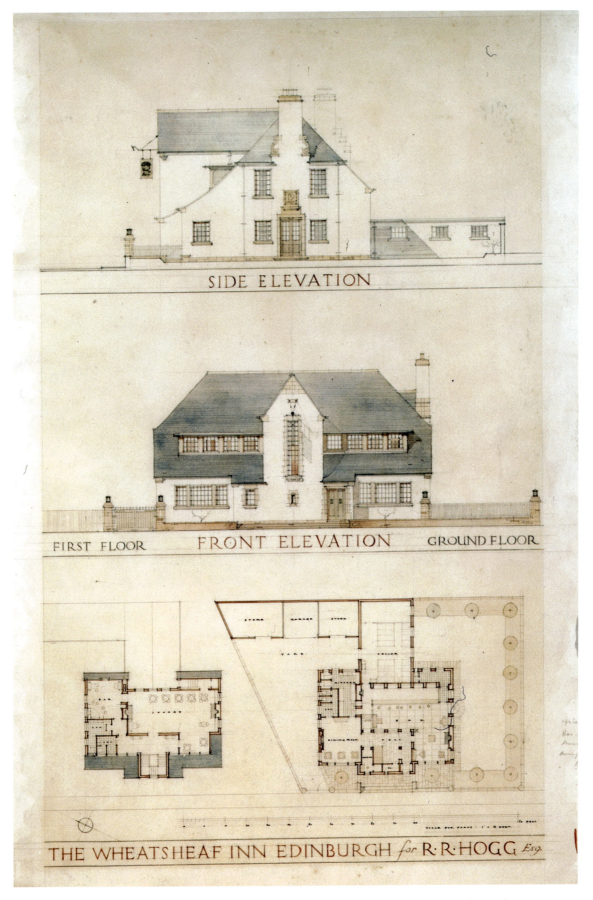

SIDE ELEVATION

FIRST FLOOR   FRONT ELEVATION   GROUND FLOOR

THE WHEATSHEAF INN EDINBURGH *for* R·R·HOGG *Esq.*

C4. Plan and elevations of 'Wheatsheaf', Balgreen Road, Edinburgh, drawn by Robert Matthew, 1933. (EULMC)

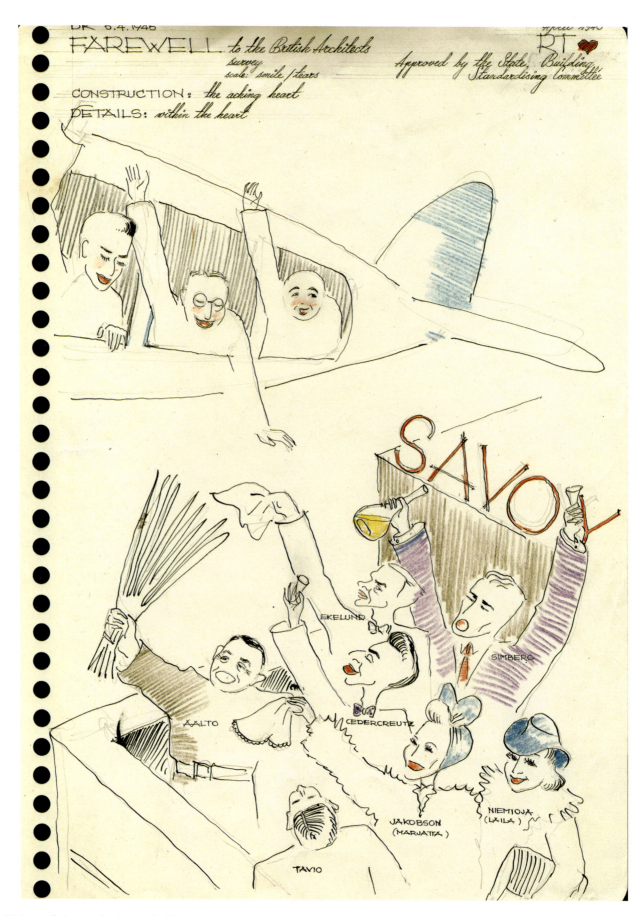

C5. Farewell drawing for the British delegation's April 1945 trip to Helsinki, prepared by Alvar Aalto's staff (on plane, from left: Matthew, Kenyon, Goodall). (EULMC)

C6. Colour photo of Royal Festival Hall by Percy Johnson-Marshall, April 1954, showing 'temporary' south wall. (EULMC)

C7. The ground-floor kitchen originally used by Robert and Lorna in the tower-house section of Keith Marischal (latterly occupied by Aidan Matthew; note William Gordon tiles on floor.) (RCAHMS)

C8. Colour view of the newly completed Queen's College Dundee project, c.1962. (RMJM)

C9. Slide taken by Matthew from flying boat en route back from Wellington to Australia in 1954 or 1956.

C10. 1957 revised 'squared-off' model of New Zealand House, on display at 24 Park Square East. (RMJM)

C11. 1963 photo of High Commissioner's office, New Zealand House. (RMJM)

C14. View of the newly completed Crombie Hall, Aberdeen University, in 1960. (RMJM)

C15. Lochay Power Station under construction in 1958. (RMJM)

Modern Architect

C16. 1960 layout model by RMJM of Hutchesontown/Gorbals Area B development, Glasgow (RMJM)

C17. 1963 picture of the completed Barshare Phase 1 housing development, Cumnock. (RMJM)

C18. The Hutchesontown Area B towers seen under construction in 1962. (RMJM)

Modern Architect

C19. 1963 view of the Hutchesontown Area B towers, showing John Paterson's 'Hieronymus Bosch' floodlighting. (RMJM)

C20. The Edinburgh University Arts Tower (David Hume Tower) from south-east, 1996. (RCAHMS)

C21. Lorna and Jessie seen outside the south (garden) facade of Keith, c.1958–9. (EULMC)

C22. Photograph by Matthew (taken at the IUA 1958 Moscow congress) of a prototype eight-storey prefabricated tower block at Noviye Chery-omushki. (EULMC)

C23. Matthew welcomes Prince Philip on an 'informal' visit to the IUA London Congress, 6 July 1961. (EULMC)

C24. Buckminster Fuller in discussion with Spanish students at the 1961 IUA Congress. (EULMC)

C25. Model of 1966 proposal by Jim Latimer for RMJM's new headquarters at Miller Row, in Edinburgh's Dean Village: the 'bottle store' is the plain, grey-roofed building along the top of the site. (RMJM)

C26. Loretto School Chapel enlargement: October 1964 view of building work in progress. (RMJM)

the permanent Secretary-General, Pierre Vago). In November 1953 Abercrombie and Godfrey Samuel invited him to become UK representative on the Executive Committee, as well as various housing- and teaching-related committees, and thereafter he held one office or another virtually continuously for over a decade, becoming Vice-President in 1957 and President in 1961–5.[131] Initially, the activities of the IUA were concentrated in two main areas: harmonisation of professional standards, education qualifications and competition regulations; and housing and town planning research. In the first area, the emphasis was on trying to get UNESCO to adopt and enforce the IUA's rules on international architectural competitions, something that finally happened in 1955.[132] In the field of housing and town planning, the IUA pursued its aims chiefly through collaboration with the already well-established International Federation for Housing and Town Planning (IFHTP), with which Matthew had become closely involved, again through the agency of Abercrombie, during his LCC days. Matthew and Abercrombie tried to ensure that the IUA and IFHTP kept on positive and constructive terms, helped by Holford, who was also on the executive council of the Federation at that time. At the 1954 IFHTP Congress held at Edinburgh, Matthew organised and chaired a session dealing with town planning, and helped organise an exhibition on Geddes to coincide with the Congress. In those years, architects opposed to 'narrow' Functionalism were increasingly using the term 'habitat' – borrowed from anthropology and geography – to describe housing in its wider spatial, social and economic environment. The word had been adopted by CIAM at Bridgwater in 1947 (at the instigation of the French delegation) and expanded at Bergamo in 1948 into a proposal for a 'Charter of Habitat' to replace the Charter of Athens, and a 'UNESCO-like' UN organisation focused on housing.[133]

But Matthew equally recognised that there were practical time limits on the proliferation of collaborative initiatives and societies. In 1955, when Robert Gardner-Medwin warned that the regional planning movement was 'in decay', with planning retrenching to an exclusively urban concern, and began to take steps to set up an international society on regional planning and development, Abercrombie and Matthew tactfully strove to head off the formation of 'yet another international federation'. Abercrombie complained to him, 'Can the world support one more international union?', with the concomitant requirement for 'headquarters, secretary general, bulletin, congresses, international representation etc. etc.'.[134] On the whole, however, the chief focus of the IUA's activities continued, as in its formative years of the 1940s, to be the pursuit of international cultural goodwill, and the counteracting of any cold-war tendencies within architecture. During 1954–5 the continuing presence of Helena Syrkus on the Executive Committee, organising a well-attended June 1954 meeting in Warsaw to tour post-war reconstruction, especially helped counteract division from the 'east'. Matthew contributed from the start to the maintaining of relations, encouraging for example the admission of North Korea in June 1955. He led the UK delegation at the 1955 IUA congress at The Hague, with its vastly ambitious exhibition devoted to social housing progress, and, immediately afterwards, kept up a vigorous information exchange on housing neighbourhood-unit layouts with East German academics at the Technische Hochschule in Dresden. The Hungarian crisis severely challenged this balance, with the Hungarian-born Vago initially proposing an interventionist line, attempting to send a delegation to contact the Hungarian section. Paradoxically, however, it was the relative American lack of interest in the IUA that was of the greatest help in preventing any sharp east–west split. In the early 1960s all that would change; but at the April 1956 Executive Committee meeting at Capri no one could have expected that the innocuous invitation by the Cuban delegation to hold the 1961 conference in Havana – the first in the Americas – would ultimately be the cause of the most serious east–west dispute in the IUA's history.[135]

Increasingly, Matthew was beginning to focus on another IUA-related issue, concerned essentially with decolonisation. As one who had risen to prominence through internal social reconstruction within the UK, Matthew was not, even after his departure for private practice, one of those architects who immersed themselves in architectural or planning consultancy work throughout the former empire, as did Max Fry, Jane Drew, Max Lock or Otto Koenigsberger, or more 'commercially adept' Modernists such as Raglan Squire. Rather, his internationalism was focused from the beginning on architectural diplomacy and, in particular, on addressing the anomalous position of the countries of the former British Empire within the IUA.[136] In 1956 Matthew, as the only anglophone member of the executive, was challenged by Vago on the 'conspicuous absence' of Commonwealth countries in the IUA, which was becoming 'unbalanced' by the full representation of 'the Soviet Union and its satellites'; Bill Allen wrote to him that 'although the RIBA sets itself up as a kind of father to Commonwealth architects, it does not, in fact, enjoy very wide support in this function, and that somehow we might do better by them.'[137]

Increasingly, a division began to open up between his domestic and international activities and collaborators, with the internationals treated by Matthew as equals in status, and the former treated as subtly lower in standing. Alan Reiach, for example, now belonged firmly to the second category: Matthew valued him for his 'irrepressible buoyancy ... which made him an ideal receptacle: there was no fear of competition where Alan was concerned!'[138] Nuttgens recalled that Matthew by the late 1950s had changed his old Morris to

a nice Triumph Mayflower roadster, a boxy, stylised shape, and he quite

often got me to run him to Turnhouse in it to catch a plane. As a seasoned traveller, of course, he always made sure to get to the airport with just minutes to spare. On one occasion, we were racing down the road to the airport, and I said to him, 'I suppose, to you, catching a plane is like catching a bus to us!' He replied, 'I don't think I've ever caught a bus!'

Little did Nuttgens suspect that Matthew had not only travelled in buses, but had even driven one through a hail of strikers' stones in 1926! At meetings, he was able to hone to perfection the air of quiet authority he had developed at the LCC:

He would only occasionally put in a word, but always at a decisive point in the meeting. ... He'd discover who were the people in power before going to a committee, and would only look at or address them. Matthew never wasted his charm on people of no consequence. ... He'd break down any resistance with that famous fixed stare over his spectacles. Were it not for his lack of vanity, I'd swear he wore them for effect: Robert's secret weapon![139]

The single-mindedness of Matthew's public persona was, however, offset by a streak of mischievous or sardonic humour, which occasionally cut across his everyday dealings. For instance, at a Turnhouse site meeting in late 1955, a subcontractor

came up to Robert and said brightly, 'Ah, Mr Spaven, I didn't recognise you.' Robert replied, 'I'm not Mr Spaven – that's perhaps why you didn't recognise me.' Then, 'Ah, it's Mr Matthew. How nice to see you! How's your father?' 'He's dead.' 'Oh, I'm so sorry – how's your mother?' 'She's dead.' All this with an absolutely straight face. Then, from the flustered builder, by now backing away, 'Oh, dear, dear – they were such lifetime companions!' He certainly never dared come to another site meeting![140]

With Matthew's polycentric lifestyle, his family in some respects formed part of the 'domestic' category, following in his wake. One of Matthew's university secretaries recalled that Lorna sometimes conveyed a 'high, querulous, plaintive impression, a "What's Robert up to now?" tone in her voice, trying to keep track of him – yet, I always thought, she was very tough underneath.' Janet recalled that 'in domestic affairs, my father was really quite dependent on her. He'd wander around Keith after her, saying, "Lorrie, Lorrie, where are my slippers?"'[141] With Matthew's growing standing as an international cultural ambassador, the family remained in many ways just as decentralised as before in its structure. And when his different 'worlds' met, sparks inevitably flew between them. Nuttgens recalled one occasion at 16 George Square around 1957 when

> our secretary, Dorothy Taylor, showed me a letter she'd just opened, postmarked the Raffles Hotel, Singapore, and apparently from a lady friend. I got a bit of cow gum and sealed it up. But Dorothy couldn't resist a dig at him, and said brightly when he came in, 'Ah, Professor Matthew, here's a letter from Singapore for you!' Without a word, he just grabbed it and stuffed it into his pocket!

With the passing of the years, he was also increasingly aware of the effects of ageing and, in particular, the inexorable and irreversible toll imposed on his waistline and formerly athletic physique by his lifestyle, alternating as it did between frenzied activity and sedentary repose. Occasional lapses in memory also now had to be allowed for: office secretary Christine Somerville recalled that in 1958, for example, he returned from an excursion to Sochi following the IUA Moscow congress (see Chapter 8),

> saying he'd need to get another passport as his own one had been stolen. I got him a form for a new passport, and went in with it, and said, 'Here's your form!' – and he said, 'What form?

I haven't lost my passport!' He flatly denied all knowledge of it! I phoned his University secretary, Dorothy, and said, 'Do you know anything about this – what on earth's going on?' She said, 'Oh no! It wasn't stolen at all – he'd left it in Sochi and it was returned to us in the Department!' He just didn't want to admit he'd lost it![142]

The mid/late 1950s also saw a subtle but significant change in his pattern of family relationships, a shift that became more prominent after the birth of Jessie in 1952. When Aidan and Janet were small, Robert had spent as much time with them as he could, even during the stressful LCC years, and Janet recalled him as a warm and affectionate parent: 'He was a shy man, as so many Scots are, not extravagant with his words, as some Englishmen might have been – yet the affection was always clear!' In 1952, for example, anticipating that the birth of the new baby might cause Janet resentment, Lorna astutely suggested Robert should take her on a holiday trip round the Highlands: 'It was a great success, as I had him to myself for a while!' Jessie's childhood, however, coincided with a more 'hands-on' approach by Robert from the 1950s, and she proved especially able to penetrate his emotional armour and establish a more direct rapport. Nuttgens's wife Biddy recalled that

> Robert was absolutely devoted to Jessie as an infant and child – he made time to play games and read to her, he would send her things from all over the world, and would take her with him and Lorna to meetings and conferences. His face, normally so controlled, simply lit up when he saw her. On one occasion, I had to fetch him at home to take him to the station to get the sleeper, and I found him reading Jessie a bedtime story. The two of them were sitting quietly in a circle of lamplight, and Jessie looked up and glared possessively at me. I can still remember that image as if it was yesterday – the two heads set in the circle of light, with shadow all around.

Jessie recalled that 'I always dreaded Daddy going away – not knowing when he'd come back – but every time he did come back from his foreign trips, right up to my teens, he always brought me a doll in national costume, from wherever he'd been!'[143] And however long his absences, the entire family also benefited more generally from Robert's ever-more diverse circle of acquaintances, which constantly threw up new and interesting social links, and provided a growing opportunity for exotic foreign travel, at a time when that was still the preserve of an elite.

All in all, by late 1955 and early 1956 Matthew could justifiably feel that the calculated gamble of his move back home, and out of the cocooning security of the public service, was beginning to pay off. It was just at this point, as we shall see in the next chapter, that – typically of his restless spirit – he decided to throw up some of his career cards in the air again, and, 'like a bolt out of the blue', to embark on a major restructuring of his new private practice so as to anchor his lifestyle more firmly back in the cosmopolitan diversity of London.[144]

Modern Architect

Chapter 7

A beacon of modernity: planning and building New Zealand House, 1954–62

unmistakeably modern ... in the belief that the best compliment that can be paid to the older buildings surrounding the site is to design the best possible building for its day and age.

Robert Matthew, 1956[1]

harsh and overpowering in scale ... a conspicuous and aggressive interrupter of what is now a reasonably calm and settled skyline ... a powerful and dynamic mass symbolic of an intention to dominate at all costs its architectural environment.

Report by Sir Howard Robertson, Sir Edward Gillett and Anthony Minoprio, April 1956[2]

Embassy of hope: representing social-democratic New Zealand

During its first three years Matthew's private practice career, in contrast to that of Spence, seemed to have generated no 'monumental', representational projects that could compare in standing or stately grandeur to the Festival Hall or Coventry Cathedral. But appearances proved in this case highly deceptive, as Matthew had already, since May 1954, been hard at work on a dramatic and controversial new project of a potentially high-profile nature. For the real highlight of Matthew's round-the-world trip in that month was not his Australian convention or his American tour, but an unobtrusive additional excursion fitted at short notice in the middle of his stay in Sydney. On 15 May, after delivering his conference lecture, Matthew set off, with minimum publicity, on an unscheduled overnight journey by flying boat to Wellington, the capital of New Zealand, for discussion with the Prime Minister, the Rt Hon (later Sir) Sidney George Holland, along with his Minister of Works and the chief government architect, F Gordon Wilson. The subject of their meeting was an ambitious project to build a new High Commission (the Commonwealth equivalent to an embassy) for New Zealand in London, a project that had been under active development since 1949. Although Matthew was ostensibly in New Zealand to advise the government on the project, within a month he had been officially confirmed as architect of 'New Zealand House' – the building that, as the first free-standing 'skyscraper' in the ceremonial district of central London, was to become not only the most important individual project of his private practice, but also the stimulus that provoked a fresh restructuring of his career. Later, Matthew rhetorically painted his flight to Wellington as a bolt from the blue, heralded dramatically by a piece of paper passed to his lecturer's rostrum by a New Zealand representative. In fact, however, it was preceded by over a month of informal contacts, in which a crucial role was played, significantly, by his future partner, Stirrat Johnson-Marshall.[3]

As in the case of the Festival Hall and Coventry, the design of an embassy was one of the areas in which the traditional expectations of the hierarchy of decorum were at their highest, and the potential disjunction with the free-flowing spatial conventions of CIAM Modernism was at its sharpest. In some cases, such as Spence's later British Embassy in Rome (1960–71), that challenge was answered through a relatively traditional stately design, whereas in many of the post-war embassies of the USA, as well as other institutions of equally high status, such as the United States Air Force Academy at Colorado Springs, there was an attempt to achieve a nationally symbolic grandeur within the rectilinear forms and free spaces of the international Modern Movement.[4] The architectural demands of an embassy were also further complicated by the need for it to face both inwards and outwards – to communicate the values of its country to the world, and vice versa. Within New Zealand itself New Zealand House was one of the architectural set pieces of the four-decades-long ascendancy of social-democratic government, in a country that was still closely allied to Britain, and whose colonial culture was especially intimately linked to Scotland. In 1936 the accession to power of the Labour Party had inaugurated a wave of public-works campaigns intended to 'modernise' the former colony, including widespread public housing and urban renewal efforts. This campaign began to take on Modernist architectural overtones with an influx of European refugee architects between 1933 and 1939, such as Ernst Plischke or Frederick H Newman, who acted as influential proselytisers of social Modernism in New Zealand. The new social-democratic ethos in New Zealand rejected the old-style conservative values of British colonial architecture, as well as the more individualistic patterns of inter-war New Zealand architecture, influenced by the US West Coast, in favour of an emphatic pursuit of social values – which led to a re-convergence with 1940s British trends.[5]

After the war, the public services, including the government architect's office (headed from the mid to the late 1950s by Gordon Wilson), played a key role in the introduction and spread of modern architecture across New Zealand. The replacement of the Labour government (following a wartime coalition) by the anti-socialist National Party in December 1949, with Holland as Prime Minister, made little appreciable difference to this new 'social' orientation of government architecture, despite Holland's populist right-wing stance as a fighter against state *dirigisme* and trade union power.[6] It was in this modernising context that the previous Labour government, earlier in 1949, had acquired a 99-year lease from the Crown Estates Commission (the UK government land-holding agency) on a very prominent London site for a new building to rehouse its High Commission, hitherto scattered in five separate locations.[7] For New Zealand, cautiously advancing as the British Empire retreated, the London project was also of high ideological significance. The country was culturally still the closest to Britain of all the former 'dominions', and the London High Commission was still its most important diplomatic post. The new site was at the foot of Haymarket, overlooking the north-west corner of Trafalgar Square, and occupied, in two plots, by a dilapidated hotel and a commercial arcade, with possession not until 1958, when it would be vacated by the Ministry of Works. The lease required New Zealand to erect, by 1970, a building approved by the Crown Estates Commissioners and, if possible, by the LCC, the Royal Fine Art Commission, the MTCP and (as the site overlooked a royal park) the Ministry of Works. There was assumed to be scope for a later extension to the north, on a site occupied by the massive Franco-Renaissance bulk of C J Phipps's Her Majesty's Theatre (1896–7); to the rear (west) of the site ran Nash's Royal Opera Arcade of 1816–18.[8]

Although LCC planning consent was not legally required for this embassy building, consultations for outline permission were set in train in 1949–50 as a courtesy – something that would have given Matthew, as LCC architect, a degree

Modern Architect

of advance warning that the project was at least in the offing. But the formal process that would lead to his appointment was set in train in June 1953, when Holland, leaving London after the Coronation festivities, confirmed publicly that the government would be going ahead with a new High Commission, which was to be a 'good modern building'. The then High Commissioner, Sir Frederick Doidge, enthusiastically hailed the Prime Minister's decision, and immediately established close contact with the UK Minister of Works, Sir David Eccles, to press for an earlier start than 1958, and stress that what New Zealand required was a 'modern building of the highest quality … the best of modern creative architecture', hopefully not unduly impeded by the need to 'make concessions' to the historic environment. As to the choice of designer, the original intention to employ a panel of New Zealand architects resident in the UK was quietly dropped, as likely to produce dry committee architecture. At a Guildhall dinner the Deputy High Commissioner, Dick Campbell, had already informally canvassed Eccles about a possible single UK designer, and had been startled at his enthusiasm for a modern solution to symbolise New Zealand's youthful society: 'David Eccles was as keen on the new NZ building as could be – almost as if it was his own main interest: "London's best site, a really fine, modern building, NZ showing London what should be done, etc."' During the following three months Campbell and colleagues looked round recent London office buildings, in case any 'would inspire one to discover its architect. Result: Nil.'[9]

It was only in April and May of 1954 – through a series of personal contacts within government – that the final choice of architect was made. At the suggestion of senior civil servant John Maud, Campbell arranged to call on Stirrat Johnson-Marshall, on the pretext of discussing a proposed fact-finding visit to English schools from New Zealand.[10] Then, as he later recalled in a manuscript account of 'The Battle' to build the new

embassy, 'my "afterthought" query' about New Zealand House drew a 'cautious, genial Johnson-Marshall pause, "Ah hah!" says he, "that's a question one would like notice of!"', and suggested lunch at Simpson's the following week, on 15 April. There:

> Johnson-Marshall was un-English enough, not just to broach the shop topic before coffee, but before lunch began! He said, 'I've been thinking about your question, and I'm sure I have the ideal architect. BUT I've been a civil servant long enough to know that the ideal thing is never done – we put up with compromises. So I won't be disappointed when you don't get the man I name. He has FOUR qualifications: (i) knows London and all its snags and byelaws; (ii) will give you a really good, modern building; (iii) won't lie down, or get discouraged by frustrations, of which there'll be plenty; and (iv) he's a Scotsman – and I gather New Zealanders and Scots get along' – which nomination bracketed with something like final firmness the right, inevitable, providential choice.

Immediately on returning to his office, Campbell phoned Matthew at Palmerston Place (their first contact in what would become a long friendship) and asked

> if he might be informally consulted on the problem of how to go about a new building. 'Alas,' came the reply, 'next week I'm off to Sydney for a congress of architects, and won't be in London before going.' Impasse – but only for an hour or so. A ring back from Robert Matthew (subconscious, or Scots second sight, etc., scenting something mutually acceptable) to say that on further thought he could be in London next Thursday.

Perhaps Matthew had been tipped off by Stirrat Johnson-Marshall, but he was also strongly recommended in the meanwhile by Eric Bedford, MoW Chief Architect – possibly at Eccles's instigation – and on 21 April he met Campbell and Doidge,

A beacon of modernity

and indicated his willingness to 'give some advice about the new building'.[11]

A week later, Matthew was airborne on his round-the-world trip. Holland authorised New Zealand's Senior Trade Commissioner in Australia to contact him at his Sydney hotel, to ask him to

> call at Wellington on his homeward journey, ostensibly for general consultation on the new London building, but in fact for possible offer of the task to himself. Then, Robert Matthew being in Wellington, PM Holland and others (inevitably) impressed, and details of the engagement easily settled.

In fact, a final agreement was delayed by a fresh obstacle, in the form of the energetic lobbying of (in Campbell's diplomatic words) an 'outstanding New Zealand-born architect working in London': namely Basil Ward, now Professor of Architecture at the Royal College of Art. After a fresh intervention by Bedford, Matthew's appointment was finally confirmed, to Ward's forthright 'disappointment'. But Matthew's eventual success in forcing through a forthright symbol of New Zealand's modernity, in the teeth of British establishment opposition, would in the end more than compensate for his Scottish, rather than New Zealand, national origin.

The formal offer of the commission was sent by Campbell on 8 June 1954. Taking up a suggestion made by Matthew in Wellington, he was asked, if possible, to seek out young London-based New Zealand architects who could be employed as assistants in his team. This was an aspiration that, owing to the circumstances and location of his practice, eventually proved impracticable. But what it did, crucially, imply was that he would at least have to open a London office. The June letter of appointment laid out a departmental requirement for a building of 44,000 sq ft of offices, plus accommodation for the High Commissioner, foyers, ground-floor shops and service spaces, totalling 180,000 sq ft. Fees were to taper from five per cent on expenses up to £750,000 to four per cent on those over £1 million: 0.5 per cent would be paid in advance and a further one per cent on approval of sketch plans. Matthew replied that 'I look forward to working with you and your colleagues on this very important building: I trust we can make it an outstanding one.'

Owing to the difficulties in early release of the site, this was not a job that needed to be rushed. Accordingly, during mid 1954 Matthew occupied himself with leisurely preliminary research: for example, in three days in early July he visited all the existing New Zealand offices in London. Only in August did he receive a rough schedule of accommodation, and even then there was doubt about the phasing of the two parts of the site; the theatre site might not be released until around 1970. In August 1954 he visited the new American embassies in Copenhagen and Stockholm with government architect Wilson and Frank Corner, secretary for External Affairs, and had preliminary discussions with LCC planners. The first task was to incorporate the lessons of the most recent post-war Modernist developments in the planning of office buildings. Under the influence of CIAM Modernism, and pioneering US projects such as SOM's Lever House (1951–2), with its 22-storey slab block and two- to three-storey podium set back

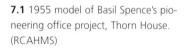

7.1 1955 model of Basil Spence's pioneering office project, Thorn House. (RCAHMS)

Modern Architect

behind a public plaza, the old pattern of massive, dense blocks filling the entire plot – exemplified by the government office buildings erected in London under the 'Lessor Scheme' of the late 1940s – began to be rejected in favour of the freer plot ratio formula, allowing for more variegated combinations of high and low blocks. In a January 1954 speech at the Mansion House Eccles had publicly attacked the Lessor Scheme, and warned that 'unless swift and effective action is taken, we shall see fat and familiar, mediocre and characterless neo-Georgian architecture rising from Hitler's ruins to betray the confident spirit of the new reign.'[12] Only with designs such as Spence's Thorn House, in Upper St Martin's Lane (completed 1959), did the free-standing tower-and-podium Modernist formula reach the heart of London.

At any rate, on the plane back from Copenhagen in August 1954, Matthew drew out the first sketch of a solution for the New Zealand project, including a tower block, and using a high (5:1) plot ratio. In early September he visited other 'Dominion' high commissions in London – massive classical office blocks that served as warnings of what *not* to do. An August draft of the 1954 agreement with the New Zealand Government Property Corporation stipulated that Matthew was to supply sketch plans within a year, followed, within two years, by detailed drawings suitable for QS costing. By August 1955 he was ready to begin plunging into the process of producing an initial design, by closeting himself away in the high attic of Craigievar: 'There is no more congenial place in the world – where the Sempills had thoughtfully provided a four poster bed to which I retired every few hours during a couple of weeks of sheer delight.'[13]

We shall return later to that design, which would prove a highly controversial one in the context of mid 1950s London. But first – alongside these architectural matters – Matthew now had to confront the equally important issue of the overall structure of his practice.

7.2 Drawing by Matthew of Craigievar woodland, August 1955. (EULMC)

Organisationally, the early 1950s had seen the beginnings of the loosening of the strict public-architectural dominance of the immediate post-war years, a trend that gathered pace with the 1954 easing of government building controls. Where John Summerson in the 1940s had written confidently of a permanent, open-ended dominance of the public sector patron and designer, now these structures were rapidly dissolving, as 'the public sector was overwhelmed by the actual building demands of the 1950s.'[14]

Throughout the years of austerity a strong strand of private practice had continued, maintaining at least implicitly the old distinction between commercial and artistic approaches; now, in the late 1950s office boom, a new raft of commercial practices such as Seifert and Fitzroy Robinson would duly emerge. The private practices most obviously well placed to exploit the new climate were those that had remained private, yet established a strong public-sector patronage base, such as Frederick Gibberd, who had shifted from his wartime AA principal job to become architect-planner of Harlow New Town in 1946; or Lionel Brett, 4th Viscount Esher, who, despite his image as 'the quintessential English gentleman', had established himself as architect-planner to Hatfield New Town in 1949 and member of the Royal Fine Art Commission from 1951 to 1969.

An arguably even more effective response to the challenge of the changing

A beacon of modernity

7.3 24 Park Square East, 2007 view. (M Glendinning)

social and economic circumstances was to establish hybrid private practices perpetuating some of the multidisciplinary characteristics of the new public offices, and able to compete for the large serial social building commissions of the welfare state. One way of doing this was for a Modernist 'pioneer' to take on more partners, as did F R S Yorke (author of *The Modern House*, 1934) with E Rosenberg and C S Mardall.[15] Matthew followed this precedent, in a slightly different form. We traced in Chapter 6 the growth of his firm from the engagement of Spaven in June 1953 to a total of seven staff at the end of the following year, and nine in December 1955. That was adequate to service his growing Scottish practice, but not to cope with a major building project of international standing in the heart of London. To begin with, he no longer had even a temporary London house. For example, on a visit to London in May 1953 he stayed on successive nights with – significantly – Percy and Stirrat Johnson-Marshall. At other times, he stayed back at Bill Holford's house, or in his club (the Reform); more often, his accommodation was simply a berth on the overnight sleeper to or from Edinburgh.[16]

And if he had no London base, he also had no London staff. The initially leisurely pace of the New Zealand House job, however, allowed him to begin preparations to establish a London office in a slow and careful manner. In July 1954,

for example, he wrote gratefully accepting an offer from a quantity surveyor acquaintance, Monty Thackray of Franklin & Andrews, to act on his behalf while he established his office. Matthew asked Thackray, without success, whether he could recommend any New Zealand-born quantity surveyors that he could employ.[17] Franklin & Andrews acted for Matthew throughout the whole New Zealand House commission. Among the Edinburgh staff, Margaret Brown's employment was in fact initially envisaged as part of the New Zealand House project, but once the mid 1955 deadline for preliminary sketch designs was established, Matthew diverted Brown immediately to his Scottish projects.

Some improvement in Matthew's own financial resources was also necessary before he could establish a London office. The fees paid for New Zealand House were a vital lubricant of this. In April 1956, for instance, Matthew wrote to the New Zealand Ministry of Works for a further advance payment of fees 'to assist me in the full establishment and maintenance of my London office, which is undertaking this work'.[18] The first substantial instalment of fees had followed completion of his first set of sketch plans in August 1955. By then, Matthew had identified a suitably imposing potential London base, very near to his previous quarters in Holford's house, and within easy walking distance of the RIBA: 24 Park Square East, part of a Greek Ionic terrace of 1823–5 just north of Marylebone Road that (with its matching twin) formed part of the Nash Regent's Park development. Owned by the Crown Commissioners, the house was at that stage in a slightly down-at-heel condition, and used as a doctor's surgery and house. Inside, it was a typical large London town house, with two big rooms on each floor, one front and one back. Having negotiated about it for several months, in August he successfully applied to the LCC for change of use to architect's office and house, and in January 1956 he took on a 17-year lease for it. In Edinburgh, too, his expanding workload required more imposing quarters than the poky flat in Palmerston Place, and so in March 1956 the practice purchased 31 Regent Terrace, a neo-Grecian house of 1825–33 in one of the terraces ringing Calton Hill. The house was of three bays and two storeys, attic and basement, ashlar fronted, and with two main rooms on each floor.[19] Finally abandoning the idea that Keith Marischal could be made into a Taliesin and, effectively, reviving the role once filled by Darnaway Street, as a town house in tandem with a country base, Robert decided number 31 would have an office on the lower floors and a private flat above – the same arrangement that Basil Spence would follow in his Canonbury house. To carry out conversion work, and to help fill this larger space with elegant furniture, Stuart Matthew was again called in, as at Keith.

Unlikely partners? Robert Matthew and Stirrat Johnson-Marshall

The key issue, in the context of New Zealand House, was how Matthew should set about creating, and organising the staffing of, a London office. Within the compressed timescale now required, the easiest solution – rather than setting up an organisation from scratch – would be to take on a London-based partner with good connections. For this, the ideal would be someone who was prominent (preferably in public rather than private architecture) and reliable, yet not so forceful in character as to challenge his own position. In earlier years, his choice would automatically have fallen upon Alan Reiach, but by the early 1950s Reiach had begun to fade subtly from view in Matthew's professional life, and was replaced chiefly by the two Johnson-Marshall brothers. As we shall see in Chapter 8, Percy would become the mainstay of Robert's expanding university department in Edinburgh from 1958. But, as an architectural partner, Matthew's choice fell on Stirrat, whom he perhaps saw as a potential private-sector equivalent of Leslie Martin in the LCC – a talented and reliable deputy. Of course, as we have seen, Stirrat Marshall,

alongside Eccles and Bedford, had played a key role in the recommendation of Matthew to New Zealand in the first place. And Stirrat stipulated that he should be able to bring with him into the partnership his two closest deputies at the Ministry of Education: Maurice Lee and Peter Newnham. Lee, who lived almost next door to Stirrat in Welwyn Garden City – both, in contrast to Matthew, in modestly sized modern bungalows – recalled that

> one evening in November 1955, Stirrat came down here, stood around in front of our fireplace and said that Robert had just suggested to him that they form a partnership – but that he had told Robert he'd only consider it if he could take Peter and myself in with him.

Stirrat also tried to persuade Percy to join him in the practice, but Percy's communist principles forbade any such entanglement with private practice.[20]

Just as important, however, was Stirrat's own character and world outlook, which in many ways, despite all that happened later, made him an ideal partner in a decentralised, two-centre architectural practice focusing on projects of public, social architecture. Born in 1912, Stirrat was the same age as Stuart Matthew and two years younger than Reiach. Like Spence, he and Percy were born (the latter in 1915) in colonial India, as sons of a colonial civil servant, and initially inherited much of the imperial-destiny ethos, and manners of gentlemanly restraint, of the age. In the 1930s, however, those atavistic views were overlaid by the organisation-orientated, semi-Modernist semi-socialism of a Liverpool School architecture course (in 1930–5), followed by a succession of local authority architectural jobs, in the course of which he became a close ally of Donald Gibson, a Liverpool predecessor and (from 1938) city architect at Coventry. But whereas Percy became a declared communist, Stirrat's political views, like Robert's, always remained ambiguous – somewhere between 'Young Liberal'

A beacon of modernity

imperialism and Fabian socialism. In the opinion of Lee, one of his closest collaborators:

No one knew where Stirrat's cross would be put on the voting paper. He was an enigma. On the one hand, he seemed to be a very strong socialist. Yet he was also a very strong 'Little Englander'. He paid enormous attention to titled people, people who had an inheritance – and he was very illiberal on race. He and Percy had developed in opposite ways from their colonial upbringing. Percy was liberal, and adored India, whereas Stirrat was an Indophobic, and was worried about having coloured students in the office. In that respect, Percy was much more like Robert – they both had an unadulteratedly universal outlook, prepared to be friends with anybody, with no exclusion of race, colour or politics. For Percy, you didn't have to be a communist to be his friend.[21]

Stirrat joined the army in World War II, but after experiencing at first hand, and narrowly escaping, the trauma of the capture of Singapore, he turned inwards towards social reform 'at home'. In his 1945–8 work at Herts County Council he dedicated himself to an astringent ideal, mingling Taylorist efficiency and Arts and Crafts 'stylelessness', of a reformed public sector architecture, perfectly integrated within society. Sir Andrew Derbyshire (one of Stirrat's later partners in the firm) recalled that, after his Singapore ordeal, 'he never wanted to venture out again – he was passionately loyal to his country, Britain, and sick of all things foreign.' In Lee's opinion:

Stirrat was highly analytical. You got to know as much as possible of the client's needs, kept him in the planning picture the whole time, and the architecture would look after itself. You must grind the function down to the sullen grain, reduce it to a 'system', and let it express itself fully – a strongly mechanistic idea, an ideal I felt great sympathy with, but ultimately couldn't accept, because you just can't treat schools or housing as you could the motor industry! Stirrat wrote, or designed, virtually nothing. He'd always say, 'I draw through other people's pencils – I speak through other people!' But although he was a shy man in some ways, he also had a lot to say!

Stirrat's ascetic world outlook, and the persistent unwillingness of society to reform as he wished, led naturally to periodic bouts of discontent and alienation, and he had reached just such a stage in 1955; indeed, he had nearly applied for the LCC Architect post in 1953.[22] In Andrew Derbyshire's opinion,

Stirrat realised he'd done all he could at the Ministry and was looking round for something new to do. He was greatly wedded to the ideal of building becoming systematised, industrialised, and now began to think that, to make any real impact, you had to move that ideal into private architecture.

It can also be speculated that, like Percy, Stirrat had avoided conspicuous wealth-accumulation and might therefore, by this stage, have been short of money: 'He had never saved, the Ministry at that time paid poorly, and he had considerable financial commitments, having growing children and a new house he and his wife had just built for their family.'[23]

In many ways, then, Stirrat Marshall seemed the ideal partner for Matthew. With his stay-at-home, retiring preoccupations he could never threaten Matthew's burgeoning pre-eminence as an outgoing internationalist – yet the two shared fundamental architectural and ethical values, in their common insistence on a socially rooted, collaborative approach to architecture as a public service, strongly integrated with interventionist government activity. Both were committed to entering private practice in order to transform it, infusing it with the ideals, tasks and patrons of public architecture. And they had cooperated closely throughout the preceding eight years in a range of conspiratorial schemes, aimed chiefly at raising the status of public sector architects in the RIBA and elsewhere.[24] Derbyshire recalled that Stirrat 'had admired Robert's administrative efficiency and skill as a politician, and they became, not friends, but people who had a lot of respect for one another. Robert also declared himself to be a socialist, and Stirrat was that way inclined too.'[25]

What was a little anomalous, in fact, was not so much Robert and Stirrat's partnership itself, as the building project that sparked it off: that most un-Modern building type, an embassy. At any rate, on 25 May 1956 Robert and Stirrat signed a partnership heads of agreement, drawn up in Robert's hand. This specified 1 July – the date of first payment of rent on Park Square East – as the date of commencement of the partnership. There would be a 60:40 split of profits for the first two years, and thereafter 50:50, and it was specified that 'the name of the firm [is] to be Robert Matthew and Johnson-Marshall.' When the agreement was formally drawn up, it was made clear that Robert was the senior partner, with a casting vote in the event of any future partnership deadlock.

Chapter 8 of this book traces in detail the way in which the combined practice's general workload began to develop, organisationally and architecturally, in the late 1950s, to the point where it emerged as a diverse, multidisciplinary organisation dealing with huge building projects. Here, by contrast, we are concerned solely with the initial core of the enterprise: the personal chemistry between the two individuals, Robert and Stirrat. For in the asymmetrical aspects of the partnership, which preserved in perpetuity Matthew's right to a say in the London partnership, without a reciprocal role for Stirrat in Edinburgh, the seeds were sown of a growing disharmony between the two men and 'their' offices. In Derbyshire's opinion, the two 'discovered that they'd made a horrible mistake about each other' in assuming that they shared 'a fundamental affinity' stemming from their public service back-

ground. In a sense, the problem was simply a case of too much of a good thing – of a productive alliance poisoned by too much contact – and in that respect, their deteriorating relationship was a striking case of the autonomy of individual, willed agency and personality as against

7.4 Copy of 25 May 1956 heads of agreement on partnership between Matthew and Stirrat Marshall. (EULMC)

the power of socio-economic systems. The effect, at any rate, was that Stirrat soon began to resent what he saw as Robert's dominance, and sought by quiet devices to separate off and insulate his operations: the partnership was arguably 'an error of judgement for Johnson-Marshall professionally'.[26]

On Robert's side, the behaviour patterns were familiar ones – reflecting his own childhood relations with his younger brothers, and perhaps also Lorimer's relations with John F Matthew – although now almost completely disguised, other than to those most closely involved. Lee recalled that

Robert was a great interactor, a great and attractive personality, a great listener, yet also a bully in an indirect way. He wasn't what you might call a 'dominant Scot', in the sense that he ever became angry or lost his temper. But he always got his own way, though, in a way that made almost everyone feel happy. Stirrat felt differently, though; he felt bullied by Robert.

He claimed to younger colleagues that even during the negotiations in 1956 to form the partnership, 'at one meeting, when he put in front of Robert a paper proposing an equal share of the profits, Robert simply tore it up and left the room. At that point, Stirrat said, the scales fell from his eyes!'[27] April Johnson-Marshall, sister-in-law of Stirrat, took an even-handed view of the relationship:

I got on very well with Robert myself, and fundamentally his relationship with my husband [Percy] was a good one, too. With Stirrat it was a different matter. He liked Robert less and less as time went on – but he wouldn't fight back directly, he'd withdraw and try to get round another way. For example, there'd be a narrowly averted clash in London during the day, and then ten phone calls that night. He thought Robert was crass and bluff, thought that his overpoweringness was vulgar and unnecessary. In fact he scorned Robert, wrongly thinking he

was not as bright as himself. And he bottled this all up, and would never be rude to Robert's face. Instead, he'd make quiet but passionate statements of his views, and would sometimes come round to Percy to get it off his chest and say, 'Oh – that man...!' His wife Joan, of course, got most of it – that may partly have been why Stirrat took to drink in the end.

Stirrat's resentment was accentuated by the 'schism' that developed within his own team after 1956, as Maurice Lee began to emancipate himself from his former mentor and to work more closely with Matthew on projects such as Kincardine Power Station – and New Zealand House. With Stirrat's colonial background, personal dislike also became unconsciously sharpened by nationalistic stereotyping: 'He thought Matthew's pride in all things Scottish was outlandish, and thought Scotland itself was the edge of barbarism – whereas Percy, like Matthew, adored Geddes, and became quite "Scottish" himself.'[28] Interpreting the relationship through a 17th-century historical metaphor, Stirrat also saw himself as something of a 'puritan', responding to the dominance of a Stuart-style absolute monarch with self-denying asceticism.[29]

But there was an equal and opposite perspective. Arguably, it was precisely Matthew's 'Presbyterian' insistence on blunt directness that made him impatient with what he increasingly saw as Stirrat's deceitful manner. One Edinburgh partner tactfully recalled that Stirrat 'conveyed the impression of a true "English gentleman" – quiet, and sometimes speaking in riddles for fear of being too specific.'[30] More directly, Maurice Lee argued that

Robert was invariably straightforward, whereas Stirrat was temperamentally addicted to duplicity. Once, for instance, when we were coming back in a taxi from a meeting to Park Square East, Stirrat was taking a duplicitous line on something or another, and Robert got incensed and said, 'Look, come clean, Stirrat, come clean!'

Those suspicions of Stirrat's sincerity percolated down to Robert's junior colleagues:

> Robert hated pretence and humbug, and we, too, thought Stirrat pretended to be more democratic than he was: in fact it was Robert who delegated more widely, whereas Stirrat liked to see exactly what was going on at his end, and kept a tight hand, via all his little devices.[31]

Weathering the storm: the New Zealand House approvals controversy, March 1956 to February 1957

By the time the partnership of Robert Matthew and Johnson-Marshall was established in July 1956, the New Zealand House project was dominated by a completely different set of concerns from those of architectural organisation and personality: namely, a head-on clash with powerful forces in the British Establishment over the design prepared by Matthew – a crisis that would be resolved only at the end of the year, by the unexpected intervention of a geo-political *deus ex machina*, in the form of the Suez crisis. This prolonged trial of nerves was, as Stirrat had uncannily predicted in his initial reaction to Campbell, tailor-made for Matthew's coolly controlled negotiating manner – so much so that he eventually succeeded in turning the forceful arguments of his opponents back against them, so as to further accentuate the scale and prominence of the building. The great struggle over New Zealand House was of significance not only for Modern architecture but also for modern city planning, whose proud and self-conscious 'advances' over the 40 years from the 1930s to the 1970s were driven forward largely by a succession of causes célèbres.[32]

The furore burst out at the end of March 1956, when Matthew had completed a refined version of his August 1955 sketch plans together with a model of the scheme, which it was planned he should take directly to New Zealand at the end of the month to show to the Prime Minister and cabinet. This initial scheme, arrived at after the drawing-out of innumerable permutations in Craigievar, was in some respects a high-rise, reinforced-concrete-framed variant of the Turnhouse concept, with a two/three-storey low podium, interpenetrated by a taller tower, containing the office accommodation,

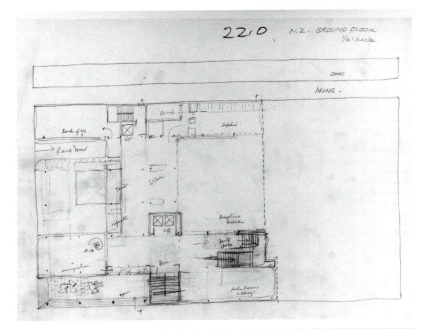

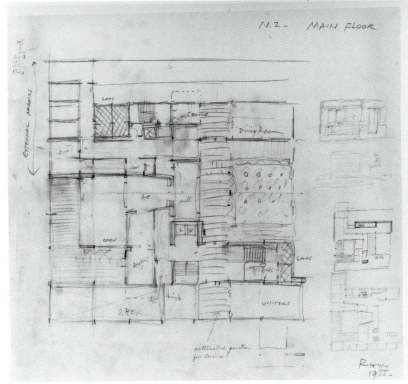

(top) **7.5** New Zealand House, 1955 sketch plans, ground floor. (EULMC)

(bottom) **7.6** New Zealand House, 1955 sketch plans, main upper floor. (EULMC)

A beacon of modernity

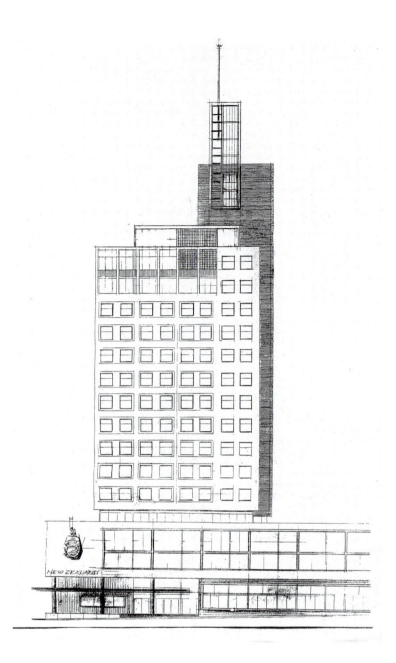

a courtyard, enclosed except to the south, facing Pall Mall, where there would be a slender screen visually pierced to allow views straight up from the street to the L-planned tower. This would contain repetitive, potentially lettable office floors crowned, in Geddesian outlook tower fashion, by a balconied penthouse, including the High Commissioner's flat. The design would allow for construction in two phases, with eventual demolition of the theatre allowing a northern extension of the podium.[33]

But the internal planning, of course, was not the controversial thing about this design. To express these varied internal spaces, Matthew proposed a startlingly modelled external form. Unlike the slender LCC point blocks, dominated by window bands, this tower was quite massive, totalling 5,400 sq ft gross area on each floor, and rising to a total height of 237 ft above ground level. It would be punctuated with separate window openings, set in polished granite-clad walls, in a gesture to the traditional Georgian streetscape and, perhaps also, to the 'New Monumentality'. At the top, it broke silhouette and sprouted a smaller, ornamental tower, finally terminating in a flagpole, with a total height of 315 ft. One wonders whether this hint of a turret might have been inspired partly by the place in which it was conceived: Craigievar Castle. Although there were strong suggestions of Dudok or Thomas Tait – an affinity that 'horrified' some younger assistants in the Edinburgh office – there were also more up-to-date Modernist parallels for an 'ornate tower' solution, including BBPR's Torre Velasca, or the 'Venetian Gothic' patterning of Paul Rudolph's initial design for the Jewett Arts Center at Wellesley College (1956); the decorative Modernism of Wright also provided an alternative reference point for architects sick of orthodox Functionalism. And, with its emphasis on a dynamic play of sliding verticals, Matthew's initial design also anticipated the more strongly modelled 1960s interpretations of the tower block, as seen for example in Chamberlin, Powell & Bon's

standing 12 floors and penthouse high – a similar arrangement to Queen's College, Dundee. The scheme took full advantage of the flexibility of the modern plot ratio system, but, owing to the cramped site, made no attempt to create a Lever House-style plaza. The essence of the plan of the podium was a central, multi-floor circulation space, spanned by various bridges and staircases, and from which sprang a variety of mutually interpenetrating public spaces for cultural or ceremonial use, stretching right up to the third-floor High Commissioner's suite. At the top of the podium would be

43/45-storey Barbican towers (built from 1963).[34]

Interestingly, however, Matthew, perhaps sensing controversy, and even maybe envisaging the 'ornamental' version mainly as an initial negotiating ploy, had the model made so that the upper tower could be removed, leaving a much plainer, squared-off tower, 207 ft in total height, as an alternative: these variants would later be referred to as Scheme A (with ornamental tower) and B (without). But neither alternative was, in the event, destined to be built in precisely that form. For as soon as the design started to emerge into the public realm, a diverse but powerful grouping of establishment figures launched vigorously into the attack. The centre of opposition lay in the landlords of the site, the Commissioners of Crown Lands, a department that had just been severely chastened by the 1950–4 Crichel Downs scandal, focused on the issue of the government retention of wartime-requisitioned land. Following a damning inquiry and follow-up review, the chairman of that review, Sir Malcolm Trustram Eve, then became chairman of the reformed department, to be renamed the Crown Estate Commissioners. As a result, Eve and the CCL had an obsession with the need for caution and avoidance of controversy, as well as a grandiose pretension to act on behalf of 'the Crown' rather than the 'mere ministers' of the government. Eve never actually had to come out in open public opposition, as he was able to

call on a whole network of allies, spanning most branches of the (Tory) Anthony Eden government – not least because most government members were deeply suspicious politically of Matthew, chief designer of the detested South Bank socialist palace of culture. It was a mark of the patronising ineptitude of this oligarchy in decolonisation matters that their conduct of the New Zealand House affair would – as we shall see shortly – succeed in making an intransigent enemy of Sidney Holland, himself hardly a supporter of state socialism!

The 'proper channel' for communication of Establishment views to the New Zealand Government was Lord Home, a Scottish laird who was minister in charge of the Commonwealth Relations Office, and his permanent secretary, Sir Gilbert Laithwaite, both implacable opponents of Matthew's scheme. The Ministry of Works, previously headed (until 1955) by Eccles, was responsible for the thorny question of the overlooking of the royal parks, and the new minister, Patrick Buchan-Hepburn (another Scottish aristocrat), was so vehemently hostile that his chief architect, Eric Bedford, also duly began to 'wobble', and warned Campbell that the plan would have a 'rough passage'.[35] Almost all UK ministers, with the important but unreliable exception of Duncan Sandys (as Minister of Housing and Local Government, responsible for the planning system), and his permanent secretary, Evelyn Sharp, were equally opposed, as was the Prime Minister

211

A beacon of modernity

7.9 Perspective of original proposal by Matthew. (EULMC)

himself.[36] And the advisory, but influential, Royal Fine Art Commission (with the sole exception of Holford) was intransigently opposed, from beginning to end, and provided Eve's first public line of defence against the proposal. It is vital to appreciate that, almost until the point of final success and approval at the end of 1956, the designs were not openly published, and so the entire debate took place out of public view. Nor were they ever actually refused by any executive authority; the only body to rule formally on them was the RFAC. Thus, right up to the last minute, the whole battle was actually a case of shadow-boxing![37] Importantly, the RFAC opposition also stemmed from Modern as well as Traditionalist architects. Lionel Esher, who 'always saw Robert as a Scots romantic in the Lorimer tradition', recalled that 'the view I took, and I think most of us took, at the RFAC was that it was a good building in the wrong place (one of the few classically planned and scaled areas

of Central London).' But the opposition of the RFAC was not as fatal as it might have been. Founded in 1924, the Commission was not only advisory in function, but also conducted its representations in private, something that one long-standing member, J M Richards, objected to, as 'the first duty of a watchdog is to bark'.[38]

In New Zealand Matthew also faced an uphill task, as Holland, although keen on the idea of a new building, was at first worried about the tower block, owing to the likely UK opposition, and was won round only by Matthew's 'exposition' at a prolonged meeting on 4 April. Holland was eventually pacified by the insertion of a grander visiting prime ministerial suite, and government architect Gordon Wilson suggested some other detailed adjustments, including more basement space and the elimination of proposed coloured cladding on the tower. From that point on Holland became an unshakeable supporter, and throughout the rest of the saga he repeatedly hardened his position when faced with any displays of what he saw as 'English self-righteousness' – to the point where the issue ultimately became a government-to-government one.[39]

But by that stage the tide of battle was flowing strongly in the other direction.[40] In early April Eve swung what he hoped would be a knock-out blow: a damning report prepared for the CCL by establishment architects Sir Howard Robertson, Sir Edward Gillett and Anthony Minoprio. Evaluating Matthew's design by the standards of 'civic obligations ... neighbourliness and civic dignity', they accused it of a deliberate attempt to disrupt the historic townscape: 'a conspicuous and aggressive interrupter of what is now a reasonably calm and settled skyline ... a powerful and dynamic mass symbolic of an intention to dominate at all costs its architectural environment'. The intemperate language of the report riled the New Zealanders, and made them all the more determined to dig in their heels: Campbell, briefing the High Commissioner, branded the report 'a piece of professional malice ... As a judgement of the work of one of Britain's greatest architects, [it] is so lacking in understanding as to be beneath contempt.'[41] Matthew also weighed in with a vigorous defence, contesting that the 50 ft high 'plinth' of the building actually tried 'to reduce, not to enlarge, the scale of the street architecture of the area' from a Victorian back to a Georgian scale; and argued, contrary to the 'negative "preservationist" view', that the area's skyline was not 'calm' but dull, and much in need of 'new and adventurous building' at 'focal points'.[42]

During an official visit to London by Holland for a Commonwealth prime ministers' conference in late June and early July, Eve, puffed up with confidence in his own Machiavellian skills, misguidedly made what he believed was his final push to cement victory. He learnt that Holland, accompanied by Matthew, had met Sandys and the Minister of Agriculture, Derek Heathcoat-Amory, at the House of Commons, again with model, to bolster ministerial support following the 29 June meeting, and that Holland had been promised that Matthew and Sandys would meet again to thrash out a final agreed design, retaining the high tower. Eve stepped in to block that meeting, boasting to his staff that 'I put my foot down.' This was a fatal error, as it left Holland incandescent with rage at the 'double-cross' and determined, as a point of principle, that New Zealand should ultimately inflict a humiliating defeat on Eve, Home and the other establishment figures: in this context, 'Tory' political affinities between the two governments counted for nothing![43]

Unaware of his fatal blunder, Eve then gaily began issuing his own orders to the New Zealanders, while at the same time protesting that specific instructions were outside his remit. He began with an instruction that Matthew should design an alternative, lower-scaled block, with a slimmer, lower tower ('Scheme C'), and with 4,400 rather than 5,400 sq ft on each upper floor; to maintain the overall level of accommodation, the podium should be increased in height by a storey. Then, in October, he suggested that this scheme should be submitted to the RFAC. Adding insult to injury, they then, doubtless as part of a hands-off campaign of attrition orchestrated by Eve, proceeded to reject that scheme, too, and insisted on yet another height reduction.[44] Scenting triumph, Eve began to press for further cuts in the area of the tower and to speculate that, if this made the project unviable, he would welcome the surrender of the site by New Zealand – in effect, suggesting a total capitulation.[45] At a late 1956 dinner with New Zealand diplomats, Prince Philip, a clandestine supporter of the project despite Eve's stance as 'defender of the Palace', let it be known unofficially to the High Commission that 'if it was blocked, they cannot lay it at my door – it's time we saw some buildings from Buckingham Palace!' The Queen also privately expressed her support for the project.[46] By late October 1956, with £14,000 architect's fees already paid to Matthew, it became clear that the deadlock was about to be broken in one way or another. Finally losing his patience with Eve's elaborate, circular obstacle course, Holland cabled the High Commissioner that, because of the 'obstructive attitude in all quarters' in London, he was about to authorise the Government to make a strong public protest. It seemed that the matter was now at last to be decided through a public confrontation.[47]

But little did any of the likely protagonists suspect that all this would suddenly be avoided, through a dramatic and unexpected reversal of fortune due to geopolitical developments thousands of miles away. In early November British, French and Israeli forces invaded the Suez Canal territory in Egypt, against the background of widespread international condemnation that would eventually, in early December, force their withdrawal, followed by the downfall of the Eden government. The only two other countries to back the British position were New Zealand and Australia, which made public statements of solidarity on 1 November. New Zealand, having been deceived about the extent of collusion

A beacon of modernity

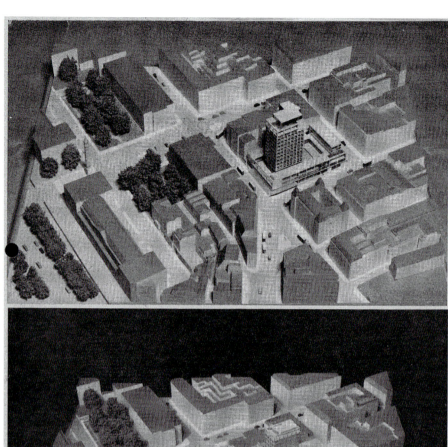

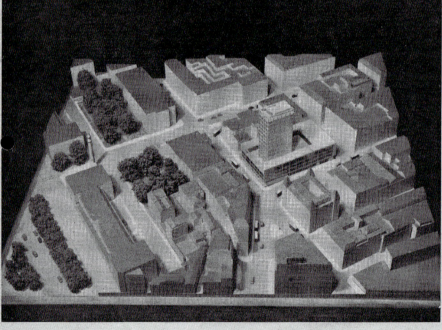

DESIGNS FOR NEW ZEALAND HOUSE

The top picture shows Professor Robert Matthew's design for the new building, favoured by the New Zealand Government but which met with objection from the Royal Fine Art Commission. Below is the second design prepared by the architect. This design also has failed to receive the Commission's blessing. The site is where the Carlton Hotel now stands at the corner of Haymarket and Pall Mall. The view is from Trafalgar Square looking down Cockspur Street. See Abner's comment and news note. Further details next week

between Britain, France and Israel, even allowed an RNZN cruiser, HMNZS *Royalist*, to be attached for several days to the invasion force of the Mediterranean Fleet.

The sudden unfolding of this external crisis was matched by a sudden collapse in the 'enemy' position over New Zealand House, allowing Holland to claim victory while avoiding an open confrontation

with his London adversaries. Immediately following the 1 November New Zealand declaration of support for Britain, Eve unexpectedly phoned the High Commission and offered to come in person, with Crawford, for a meeting on 9 November. Like some allied field-marshal hurrying to Compiègne in November 1918, Matthew cancelled all appointments and flew specially down for this meeting; a New Zealand government car was waiting to pick him up at London Airport.[48] In the follow-up negotiations Matthew, quietly rubbing salt in the wound sustained by the Edenites, stressed that the tower would form 'a bold climax to one of the longest street vistas in central London': namely, the vista stretching towards the socialist Royal Festival Hall![49]

The *coup de grâce* was administered on 1 December when, 'in the aura of reasonableness induced by the Suez crisis', Eve and the government finally agreed to a press release of the projected plans – including both the original (Scheme B) and revised (C) versions.[50] The public reaction was almost uniformly positive: for example, *The Times* urged, 'We hope that the New Zealand government will stick to its guns about New Zealand House ... the continued resistance to tall buildings in London is ridiculous.' In Campbell's words,

> So helpful was the response in the press, lay and professional, once the plans had been published – and so grateful all in authority in UK government must inevitably have been for New Zealand's stand in Suez affairs just then – that opposition crumpled. Only details remained. The plans for a tall and contemporary building were agreed to early in 1957.[51]

It was now guaranteed that some sort of Matthew skyscraper would be built; the only question was: would it be Scheme B or C, or some further variant? Exploiting the weakness of the opposition, Matthew now moved to follow through his decisive victory with a number of opportunistic revisions that would leave the tower even taller and more dominant than in his original proposal.

The ground for these changes was softened up, during January, February and the beginning of March 1957, by an increasingly acrimonious barrage of demands directed by Holland at the CCL (now renamed the Crown Estates Commissioners, or CEC).[52] Despite the positive rhetoric, behind the scenes the Prime Minister was 'still hopping mad at the way he was fobbed off while he was in London, and is really not prepared to consider the merits of an alternative scheme.'[53] At this point an unlikely saviour of the remnants of Eve's dignity stepped forward: Robert Matthew. Realising that Eve, in his overriding anxiety to save face, might well accept an even larger building, perhaps approaching the size of Scheme B, so long as it was formally identified as a modification to Scheme C, Matthew proposed, as a 'compromise' solution, that the proportional relationship between podium and tower could be restored if between one and three extra storeys were added to the tower, and if the tower was enlarged in area again. Where Scheme B had envisaged a two-storey podium, and a 12-storey and penthouse tower 207 ft in total height, now, in March 1957, a total height of 225 ft (three-storey podium plus tower of 13 storeys and penthouse) was agreed. Matthew had exploited Eve's discomfiture to add two more floors to the building, along with a fatter tower (54 ft by 90 ft).[54]

The consolidation of victory: refining and building New Zealand House, 1957–62

Up until this stage in the New Zealand House project the task had been solely one of negotiation, involving Matthew alone. Now, from the beginning of 1957, Stirrat Johnson-Marshall and his colleagues could be brought fully into the planning and implementation process, and after the March agreement they were passed Matthew's existing set of 1/16 in pencil drawings and took over all further detailed work for development into a detailed design, with Maurice Lee as project architect. Lee recalled:

> Robert and Stirrat Marshall had a short morning meeting at Park Square East once a fortnight, and went over every development we were jointly involved in. I was left largely in charge of the project, with Ken Feakes as my team leader. But Robert still kept his

(next page) **7.11** Elevation and section of New Zealand House as built. (*Architectural Design*, July 1963, 315) (RMJM)

215

A beacon of modernity

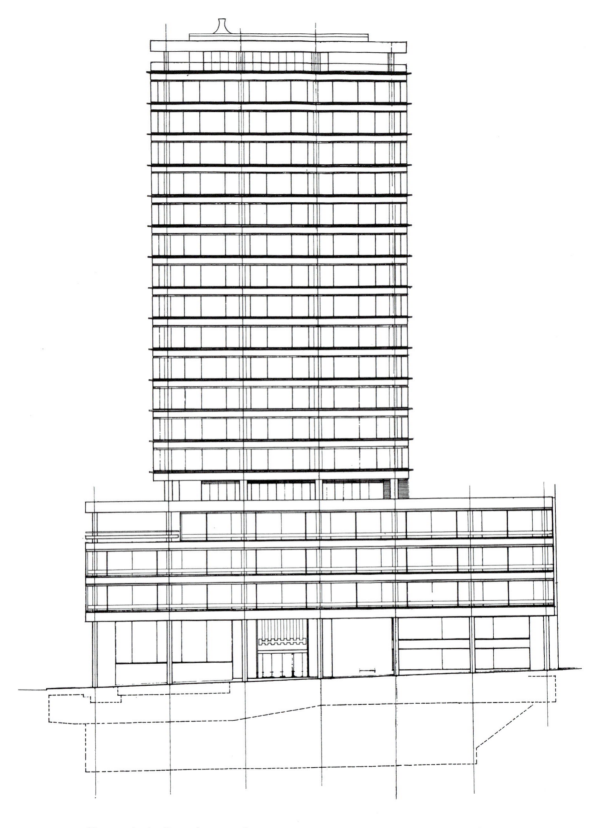

Above: main elevation and cross-section
Right: photo of the tower from the south-east

Haymarket elevation

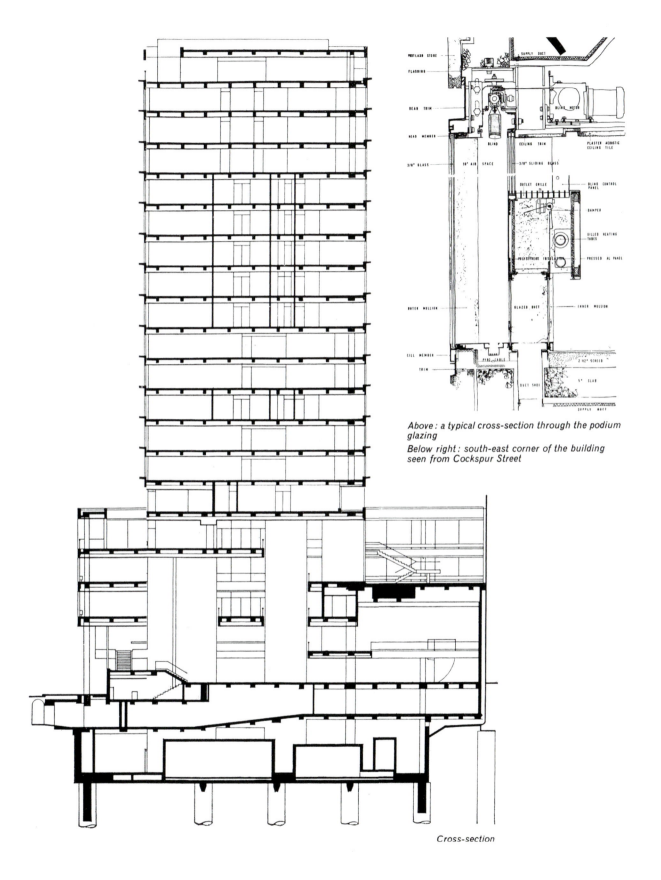

PORTLAND STONE

FLASHING

HEAD TRIM

HEAD MEMBER

3/8" GLASS

3/8" GLASS   10" AIR SPACE   3/8" SLIDING GLASS

SUPPLY DUCT

BLIND

BLIND MOTOR

CEILING TRIM

PLASTER ACOUSTIC
CEILING TILE

OUTLET GRILLE

BLIND CONTROL
PANEL

DAMPER

GILLED HEATING
TUBES

POLYSTYRENE INSULATION   PRESSED AL PANEL

OUTER MULLION   GLAZED DUCT   INNER MULLION

CILL MEMBER

TRIM

PYRO-CABLE

DUCT SHOE

2 1/2" SCREED

5" SLAB

SUPPLY DUCT

Above: a typical cross-section through the podium glazing

Below right: south-east corner of the building seen from Cockspur Street

Cross-section

New Zealand House

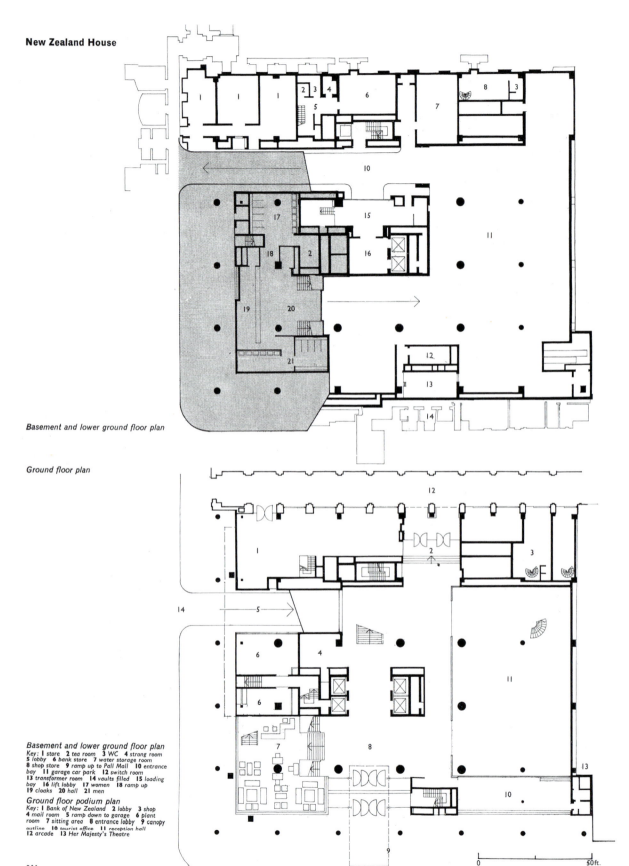

Basement and lower ground floor plan

Ground floor plan

Basement and lower ground floor plan
Key: 1 store 2 tea room 3 WC 4 strong room
5 lobby 6 bank store 7 water storage room
8 shop store 9 ramp up to Pall Mall 10 entrance
bay 11 garage car park 12 switch room
13 transformer room 14 vaults filled 15 loading
bay 16 lift lobby 17 women 18 ramp up
19 cloaks 20 hall 21 men

Ground floor podium plan
Key: 1 Bank of New Zealand 2 lobby 3 shop
4 mail room 5 ramp down to garage 6 plant
room 7 sitting area 8 entrance lobby 9 canopy
outline 10 tourist office 11 reception hall
12 arcade 13 Her Majesty's Theatre

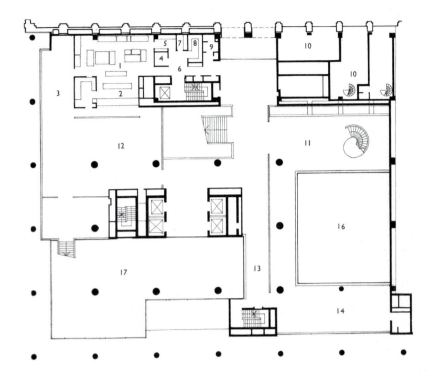

Mezzanine plan

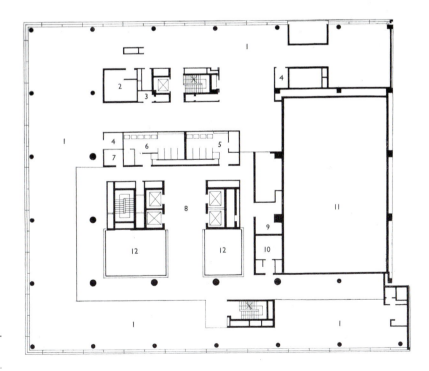

First floor plan

7.13 Ceramic sculpture by William Gordon, New Zealand House (in courtyard of High Commissioner's penthouse). 1963 photograph by Henk Snoek. (Snoek: RIBA Library)

eye on the detail, and never became totally detached. As in everything, Robert would always come in at the crucial moment, and he'd give a very strong sense of direction.

The process of squaring off the design continued, with Matthew's full involvement, and all traces of the original dynamic conception of verticals sliding against one another, and 'Midway Gardens-like' clustering, were expunged. The first significant fruit of the collaboration was a final, two-stage enlargement of the tower area, steamrollering over the now impotent protests of the CEC. Remarkably, the tower's floor area was now larger than in Scheme B: 5,670 rather than 5,400 sq ft.[55]

Now the definitive planning of the complex had to begin – especially as payment was by now running ahead of production of drawings. Here, in contrast to the penny-pinching, cramped social-building projects Robert and Stirrat were used to, the problem was rather the opposite – one of too much space! Although Matthew's original idea of a processional staircase from ground-floor reception right up to the High Commissioner's department on the third floor had now gone, the design still included a two-storey double-height reception hall

(previous page) **7.12** Floor plans of New Zealand House as built. (*Architectural Design*, July 1963, 311–2) (RMJM)

Modern Architect

with a mezzanine gallery, a mezzanine-level visitors' lounge, and an upper-level cinema and library. Segregated private zones within the podium included the High Commissioner's suite (with its own Pall Mall terrace, giving another outlook-tower opportunity in addition to the observation terrace in the tower penthouse) and the offices of the External Affairs, Finance and Immigration departments, as well as a branch of the Bank of New Zealand and tourist offices, and a ramp-accessed basement car park; it would still be possible to look from Pall Mall right up into the podium-top courtyard.[56]

Externally, the new team focused above all on how best to deal with the new, more squared-off profile, and the higher podium, which they heartily disliked: 'We thought it was like St Peter's in Rome, with no sense from below of where the dome is!'[57] During July 1957 Matthew worked intensively alongside Stirrat, Lee and junior colleagues on a substantially reordered concept, with a calmer, more horizontal emphasis. The tower now became an absolutely regular rectangle on plan, and the idea of stone walls studded with individual windows was dropped, and an almost totally glazed solution for the tower was substituted. But this would be glazing with a difference, as

we felt very strongly at the London end that there were a great number of high-rise buildings which were merely curtain-walling, leading inevitably to the vertigo factor. So we devised a section which had a very low sill with a projection which cut off the angle of view, and avoided vertigo despite floor-to-ceiling glazing: the elevation studies began to look more and more like Spence's Thorn House, but what we didn't want was a building with banded glass!

Derbyshire recalled that Matthew's 'main concern was to achieve what he called the "metropolitan scale" and preserve the views up from Haymarket through the inside of the podium – on the model of the flowing Festival Hall foyer.'[58]

At this stage Matthew was still firmly in charge of all design work, while Stirrat was acting rather in a Martin-like deputy role: the surviving correspondence casts an interesting light not only on Matthew's general practice of developing a design through innumerable alternative feasibility drawings, but also, retrospectively, on the equivalent relationships that may have obtained on the Festival Hall project. In August 1957, for instance, junior architect Peter Collymore of the London office sent Matthew 'two alternative elevations of the New Zealand House facade – we are drawing out the other alternative which you sketched while you were here.'[59] Sending Gordon Wilson the final sketch plans in late August, Matthew argued that, while the tower design had become more bland, the higher podium had allowed 'a more interesting – even exciting – interpenetration of levels within the building.'[60]

One should bear in mind that, with the political and cultural closeness between Britain and New Zealand, this was not felt to be an 'embassy' in a conventional, distanced sense, with attendant problems of security. The lack of precision in the brief left the architects of New Zealand House very free to rearrange the design as they wanted: 'Basically, they just wanted to fill the whole of the podium, and most of the tower, with the High Commission departments and cultural spaces, and let out a few tower floors commercially.' The entire building, it was now decided, was to be air-conditioned – a scientific enhancement influenced by Stirrat's rationalist ethos.[61] Ken Feakes recalled the experience of the younger London designers in working with Matthew on the project:

Sometimes, we in the New Zealand House team would get rather pissed off: Robert would walk round the boards at the weekend with his pen, shifting this bit there or marking 'Do this'. I'd come in on Saturday morn-

7.14 View of the newly completed New Zealand House from southwest. 1963 photograph by Henk Snoek. (Snoek: RIBA Library)

ings to sort things out, and talk through some feature of the design with him. He could be a pretty hard nut, almost autocratic, and he had some terrible design quirks – rubble cladding and so on! But there would also be plenty of debate about problems. For example, after a lot of discussion it had been agreed that structural concrete was to be to be clad in grey Marathon marble, and then Robert came along one day and said, 'Actually, I'd like to see it all in grey Purbeck marble, over everything' – which would have made it look like marzipan. We, who'd been bred – unlike Robert – to differentiate between structure and cladding, were horrified, but luckily the quarry hadn't got enough supply, which let us off the hook.[62]

It was also left largely to Lee and his London colleagues to deal with the last

On 9 May the Queen opened New Zealand House designed by the President RIBA. The photograph was taken while Her Majesty was being shown by Sir Robert the splendid view from the penthouse terrace

7.15 Illustration from *RIBA Journal* showing Matthew and Queen Elizabeth at the official opening of New Zealand House on 9 May 1963. (*JRIBA*, September 1963, 219)

major obstacle that reared up its head – a complex wrangle with the LCC, including a somewhat unsympathetic Edwin Williams, over provision of fire escape routes, ultimately settled by the insertion into the plan of a fireman's lift.[63] Eventually, in April 1959, the lowest tender for Phases 1 and 2 together, by Holland Hannen & Cubitts (previously the contractors for the Festival Hall), for £1,728,000, was accepted, and foundation work began on 25 May of that year.[64]

As the project neared its final stages, Lee's project team, long accustomed to the austerity of school-building programmes, and hitherto constrained even here at New Zealand House under the firm discipline of Thackray's construction costings, now had a pleasant surprise:

The finishing brief was marvellous, one of the best experiences of my life. New Zealand House was seen as a building of such symbolic importance,

that if we could find what we felt was appropriate, it was left up to us. Perhaps in compensation for the failure to use New Zealand architects on the project, New Zealand materials were sought out where at all possible – even if that sometimes involved a little sleight-of-hand. We had total design responsibility, right down to the door knobs, and were allowed to use really high quality materials – Pentelic marble on the floor, lots of glass, imported antique New Zealand timber (Rimu and Kauri), high quality aluminium. For the flooring, we discovered there was a New Zealand offshoot of Kidderminster Carpets – the New Zealand Carpet Manufacturing Company – and so the carpet was eventually made of New Zealand wool but woven in Kidderminster. Then, finally, for the main staircase hall, we had the idea of commissioning a piece of sculpture to go up through that space, and Inia Te Wiata, a sculptor working in London, undertook to do the 'totem pole' that's there today.

This final burst of lavishness was followed by an inevitable last-minute overspending crisis, which Matthew was asked to resolve:

> The contractors, Holland Hannen & Cubitt, were jumping up and down and demanding to see the High Commissioner, and we could see years of arguing ahead, but Robert just took the High Commissioner out to lunch so that the two of them could sort it all out there and then, and he just came back and told the contractors, 'That's it sorted!' Eventually, although the building cost was 25% more than anticipated, a subsequent High Commissioner freely admitted that if Robert hadn't insisted on high quality materials, they'd have been shelling out vast amounts for maintenance by then – whereas in fact over ten years it hadn't so far cost them a cent.[65]

The final process of artistic enhancement also brought Matthew for the first time into close contact with the artist William Gordon, a gifted ceramics designer who had worked on a range of Modernist projects, including some of Spence's 1950s churches. At New Zealand House he collaborated closely with Feakes and Lee on design of a great glass chandelier for the lobby, and designed a ceramic totem pole for the High Commissioner's private garden in the penthouse. Over the following years Gordon gradually became integrated with the Matthew family, spending increasing amounts of time at Keith, as well as in his sister's London house: ultimately, around 1990, he moved permanently to Keith. Sylvia Matthew recalled that he was 'a most original, eccentric and endearing person, and I always thought his position in the family resembled one of those peripheral characters in a Russian play or novel, a relative or acquaintance who gradually becomes a permanent feature with no assigned role.'[66]

New Zealand House: a social 'icon'?

The official opening of New Zealand House by Queen Elizabeth took place on 9 May 1963, and the following year American historian Henry-Russell Hitchcock summed up the building's controversial architectural and urbanistic impact:

> The objection to New Zealand House is doubtless to its location among buildings of conventional six-storey height at the corner of the Haymarket and Pall Mall in a highly representational area of London; for certainly this glazed tower, in the elegance of its proportions, the fineness of its materials, and the quality of its finish, is intrinsically one of the best post-war buildings in London, rivalled in these respects only by Denys Lasdun's relatively modest block of luxury flats in St James's Place. Indeed it was the decision, surely made for urbanistic reasons if not because of actual London County Council insistence, to provide a thicker podium, of the same height as the neighboring structures, brought out to the existing pavement line, that somewhat vitiates the virtues above-mentioned. As a result the building is best appreciated, as is true of most skyscrapers, from a certain distance: in this case from Trafalgar Square looking along Pall Mall East or Cockspur Street.[67]

The project had begun as a highly individualistic, personal design by Matthew, but, in the hands of the London team, it had been modified so as to conform more closely to the international norm of curtain-walled Modernist office blocks.[68] And although the subsequent expansion of his private practice was something that brought enhanced material prosperity to Matthew and his colleagues, as well as helping keep them in the public eye, that process would coincide with a gradual decline in his personal involvement in the practice, and in designing buildings under its aegis. Rather, Matthew, like a Victorian gentleman, saw his fame

and relative affluence as the underpin-
ning for a social obligation to spend ever
more time helping better the world. In
many ways, the socialist age of the mid
20th century perpetuated many of the
social structures and values put in place
by the 19th century to help offset the
excesses of extreme capitalism. Arguably,
the entire workload and ethos of Robert's
and Stirrat's partnership, with its almost
exclusive concentration on public programmes, was an example of this process.
As we shall see in the next chapter,
Matthew, however forcible his own will
and his own sense of status as a Great
Man, saw that status as inseparable from
a world of collective groupings and activities – and these groupings, from 1957
onwards, were becoming steadily more
diverse.

Chapter 8

Teamwork architecture: Matthew and the Johnson-Marshalls, 1957–61

We have the means to build to new stan-
dards of beauty and utility ... Insistence on
'conformity' with the past can only be
interpreted as fear of the present and of
the future. It is one of the deadly sins at
this key moment in our history.

Robert Matthew, 1959[1]

'Stamp collecting': Matthew's multi-strand life in the late 1950s

In the late 1950s Matthew's restless search for new stimuli reached a climax, and a turning point. Since 1952 he had been, in effect, stamp collecting – building up a range of different potential 'careers' to follow up his LCC success. All of them were based around an organising principle reminiscent of the Victorian ideal of gentlemanly philanthropy, as filtered via the modern 20th-century civic-social ideal of public architecture. Despite the ideal of integration within public architecture, each of these areas of activity was structured and compartmentalised with its own support system, shaped like a mini-LCC, with its hierarchy of chief helpers, delegated executants and everyday secretary-organisers. In due course some of these initiatives would succeed, and some would wither away. The late 1950s saw them at their most diverse and prolific: this was the last period when everything within Matthew's career still seemed to hold together. From now on there would be a gradual weeding-out of the stamp collection, a process of focusing that became dominant only in the later 1960s.[2] But amongst all this

network of delegated struggles Matthew still retained his capacity for intense personal application, and in January 1959 the *Architects' Journal* named him a 'Man of the Year' – 'one of the few really dynamic, powerful and progressive personalities in the profession'. What was not yet clear was the direction in which that concentration would ultimately be focused. Until then, compartmentalisation and delegation remained the rule, leaving his ancillary helpers to sort out things as best they could.[3]

In all his areas of activity Matthew projected a liberal, humanistic world outlook in the 19th-century tradition: that is, not excessively concerned with money or detailed organisational matters, but always ready with financial generosity and concern when appropriate. In 1960–1, for example, he took under his wing an impoverished engineering student from Northern Rhodesia (later Zambia), Willie Musonda, who was faced with eviction and legal action for rent arrears at a time when his daughter had just died from measles. Matthew negotiated the deferral or cancellation of some of his debts, and Musonda thanked him as 'like a father to me in more ways than one ... I shall never fear being so far from home in a strange country.'[4] It proved, however, increasingly challenging to support this expansive lifestyle. Although there were other sources, such as Robert's university salary or competition fees, following the successive deaths of Lorna's parents and aunts (for whom

Robert acted as sole executor) the main support derived increasingly from his and Stirrat's private practice, Robert Matthew and Johnson-Marshall (RMJM). For example, in April–September 1958 Matthew drew £2,587 net from the firm, including £150 paid direct each month into his own account; equally significant were in-kind expenses, which totalled £890 during the same period. Like Basil Spence's practice, Matthew now had three bases: Keith Marischal, Regent Terrace and Park Square East – but unlike Spence, whose personal involvement was confined to his home-cum-atelier in Canonbury, Matthew kept a looser involvement in all three: both Keith Marischal and Park Square were kept as fully functioning homes, and a bed was always kept made up in the large first-floor back bedroom at Regent Terrace. Of course, the subsequent further expansion of the practice led to a further proliferation of everyday offices, especially in London, which Matthew rarely if ever visited.

Oxford and Edinburgh: the mushrooming of Matthew's university department

We shall return later to the expansion of RMJM; but in many ways the most rapid growth during this period was in Matthew's new university department, which began truly to mushroom in size as his strategy of creating a rival to his old school at ECA reached fruition. John Richards, one of his later partners at RMJM, recalled that 'he had withdrawn from the headship at ECA to an environment where he could think out the future for a new kind of architectural education, based on a broad university curriculum and what he saw as an improved scale of architectural practice.' But although, in 1956, Matthew secured funding of a lecturer post for Nuttgens, the wider expansion proved a more protracted process, with a BA Hons course instituted in 1958, and success the following year in gaining RIBA recognition (after one failed attempt) of the course up to Intermediate exam level; final-level

exam recognition would come only in 1961.[5]

Matthew's strategy at Edinburgh also formed part of a wider national movement to shift architectural training into a university degree setting – a struggle in which he was a prime mover. Conventionally, the revolutionary transformation in architectural training in Britain from the late 1950s has been associated with a single, formal event: the conference on architectural education at Magdalen College, Oxford, in April 1958, organised by Leslie Martin and others, including Matthew. Its conclusions called for a blanket raising of entry standards to the profession, stipulating that all architectural courses should be full time or 'sandwich', and based in architecture schools within universities and colleges, with A-level or Higher entry. The old (post-1892) system of pupillage and night-school study, leading to RIBA exams, would be abandoned, and courses would become more intellectual in character, informed by theory and research. At the conference, Martin and others stressed repeatedly that the ultimate purpose was to improve the profession's 'standards of competence at all levels'. In response, the RIBA comprehensively overhauled its Board of Architectural Education and (in 1964–70) its exam system.[6]

In reality, however, the Oxford conference was merely a symbolic point of transition within a wider, incremental shift in climate across Britain from the fixed, orderly Beaux Arts ethos to a Modernist system of education, whose expanded definition of design would be better attuned to the new post-war era of social and technological revolution, and would hopefully allow architects to retain leadership of the building process. In Noel Annan's opinion, 'perhaps no profession faced the future with such confidence as did the [Modern Movement] architects of Our Age.'[7] And that confidence drove them forward to 'capture' one architectural school after another, a process that had begun in the mid and late 1930s with Rowse at the AA and Martin at Hull, and continued into the 1940s and 1950s with the full conversion of Manchester and Liverpool. During the 1940s and early/mid 1950s a series of RIBA reports on education partly maintained a liberal balance between Beaux Arts and Modernist values, but with the balance always shifting gradually to the latter: a 1955 report, for example, abolished *en-loge* exercises, one of the last Beaux Arts vestiges. The real *coup de grâce* to the old educational system was actually delivered just prior to the Oxford conference, when the Beaux-Arts-dominated Bartlett School received a damning RIBA visitor report, and after the Institute threatened to withdraw its examination exemption, the ex-communist Modernist Richard Llewelyn-Davies was installed in 1960 as professor.[8] But the Oxford conference provided an arresting symbol of this change, led as it was by Martin, whose department, since his appointment in 1956, had led the way in striving for a rational philosophy of integrated modernist education – for instance, by working towards establishment of a graduate research unit.[9]

Although Matthew's new university department, located in Scotland, would not be able to compete fully with the Oxbridge prestige Martin now commanded, he set out to make it a model of the Oxford conference formula, spiced with evocations of the Geddes spirit. Matthew argued that at the time when

> the university was (somewhat unwillingly) persuaded to give the Forbes Professor of Architecture the solid substance of a department ... in spite of the almost solitary light held by Frank Mears, a blanket of darkness had dropped over the city of Patrick Geddes: the Outlook Tower stood on the Castle Hill, a curiosity unregarded either by Town or by Gown.

In January 1959 the *AJ* 'Man of the Year' article could still describe the department, with its ten undergraduates and one lecturer, as the 'smallest and newest' of the university architecture departments in Britain – one of seven with a chair; by 1960 Matthew had seven

8.1 Matthew and Professor Pier Luigi Nervi (second from right) in Chambers Street, Edinburgh, on graduation day, 1960. (EULMC)

architectural students in the fifth year and four in the fourth year.[10] But a year later there was a fully fledged department with planning and landscape architecture arms, and a postgraduate research unit, itself with eight staff as the 'nucleus of a larger group', and intended to pursue live research projects in new housing areas in a new town and a rural area. Matthew's prestige attracted a stream of international-calibre visiting lecturers, including (within the first two years) Nervi, Kahn, Pevsner, McGrath, Max Fry and Mumford. From 1957 Martin became the department's first external examiner, an appointment extended in 1959 and 1962.[11]

The key to the expansion was Matthew's success in securing the appointment of two full-time university senior lecturer posts, together with a five-year, £60,000 research funding package from Nuffield, topped up by Carnegie and DSIR, to finance the establishment of his long-desired housing research unit, complete with director and several junior research posts. The new senior lecturers would develop two postgraduate specialisms: planning and landscape. Matthew justified this choice of subjects as 'above all, a widening of horizons: science, urban planning, landscape design, and management, hitherto marginal to normal architectural courses, all had to be integrated with the basic discipline of design.' Nuttgens, re-designated

Depart-mental Registrar, was made responsible especially for the administration of the department, but Matthew was unable to secure a salary rise for him, and had to supplement his pay out of his own pocket. He was academically somewhat sidelined by the changes – a little like Spaven in the practice – as Matthew brought in more senior figures to head the new, devolved teams: Percy Johnson-Marshall and Frank Clark as senior lecturers for planning and landscape architecture, and F R (Eric) Stevenson as director of the housing research unit. All three appointments, typically for Matthew, balanced a slightly eccentric professional competence with a degree of malleability and subordination to himself.[12]

Of the three, Percy Johnson-Marshall would prove by far the most important and valuable to Matthew. After Matthew's departure from the LCC, Percy had remained within the Planning Division, eventually rising, under Walter Bor, to take charge of the programme of planning-led Comprehensive Development Areas adumbrated in the 1951 Development Plan. In the wider context of the 'public architecture' movement, he and Stirrat continued to collaborate closely with Matthew as part of 'our campaign' to extend public-architecture representation on RIBA committees – to the point where, in 1961, Hugh Casson unsuccessfully protested to Matthew about 'inexcusable' lobbying for Percy in open council, and expressed resentment at being 'bounced to accept him'.[13] Of course, there were ideological differences between them, such as Percy's fervent, idealistic communism, and his tendency to carry his planning affiliation into an overtly 'anti-architectural' stance. But here, as in other aspects of his character, such as his internationalism, Percy was equally motivated by sibling rivalry with Stirrat, which was exacerbated by mounting difficulties over the treatment of their elderly mother, who had had to live for 15 years in Percy's house – despite their large family and relative poverty: 'They had a tremendous grudge against Stirrat over that.' Now, to complicate things further, Robert Matthew had lodged himself in the midst of this tense extended family, like a new 'brother-in-law' twice over.[14]

But, for Percy, the relationship with Matthew had a far more positive balance sheet, despite the stresses of close coexistence.[15] Even in the mid 1950s Percy had shown signs of eagerness to move to Scotland; perhaps his anti-Soviet revulsion after Hungary had sparked off a desire for a clean start somewhere remote from the LCC, or perhaps, as with Stirrat, shortage of money was a simpler motive. In 1957 Matthew had supported an unsuccessful application by Percy to become chief architect-planner of Cumbernauld (a post eventually won by Hugh Wilson).[16] Increasingly, however, Percy was becoming fascinated by the challenge of revitalising the ideal of the humanistic architect-planner in the context of the regeneration of historic cities.[17] This emerging Geddes-cum-Sitte world outlook clearly pointed the way to Edinburgh, and Matthew continued to woo him, promising that 'he'd be able to run a three-legged stool in Edinburgh: teaching, research and practice'. The latter would take the form of work as a consultant planner operating in tandem with RMJM; although an initial idea of including him in the firm as a third partner was not proceeded with, Matthew promised Percy informally that he and Stirrat would not themselves set up a planning arm, and that an existing modest planning section would actually be disbanded.[18]

In 1958 Percy, then living in North Square, Hampstead Garden Suburb, agreed in principle to move to Edinburgh the following year, but before he would send April, his Argentinian wife, and their seven children up, Matthew had to find him accommodation. Eventually, through the initiative of Nuttgens and the finance of RMJM, Matthew provided Percy with a substantial tied house: Bella Vista, a villa in the picturesque suburb of Duddingston. Nuttgens saw it advertised for sale, dashed out to see it and told Matthew, 'I think I've found you the ideal place for Percy'! Matthew bought it straight away – it cost £7,500, which he arranged through Tom Spaven: He turned to Tom and said, 'It doesn't matter how much it costs – we must have it!'

Matthew's solicitor, Maurice Kidd, also advised him to buy it as an investment. After some pressure from Stirrat, the firm agreed to lease it to Percy.

> The problem was that Percy, as a good socialist, hadn't any money. I said to Robert, 'I expect Percy will have his own furniture to go in there?' and Matthew replied, 'Percy! He's got no bloody furniture at all! We'll have to buy that, too!' Matthew originally thought he himself might move to Bella Vista when he retired – but of course he never *did* retire![19]

On Percy's arrival in Edinburgh in 1959 it soon became clear that he had little experience of teaching. His lectures, for instance, largely took the form of extended slide-shows:

> There would be thousands upon thousands of them: he'd start in the aeroplane, with twenty slides before he'd even landed. And in his enthusiasm and excitement, he'd never stop talking and talking. He'd say, 'Now this is Bogota,' – but all you could actually see would be the wing of the aeroplane and a smudgy horizon.[20]

Yet although planning was only a small part of the undergraduate course, Percy soon began to expand his activity, in 1960 establishing a diploma course in civic design, orientated openly towards urban comprehensive redevelopment, and the task of getting a 'civilised environment' in contexts likely to be dominated by 'urban motorways, pedestrian segregation, helicopters and multipurpose buildings'.[21] And ideas were already moving on further still: in 1960, to help teach the new university- and Nuffield-funded diploma planning course, Matthew brought in from the

LCC an American part-time lecturer, Eleanor Morris, who saw the term 'civic design' as somewhat old-fashioned – redolent of a kind of Beaux Arts stateliness: 'People like Robert and Percy had one foot in the previous generation.'[22] Indeed, once Percy was settled in Edinburgh, his revolutionary fervour began to abate: imitating Matthew's Triumph car, he bought a Rolls-Royce, and, as his courses and responsibilities proliferated (especially after establishment of a Planning Research Unit in 1962, with a 'Lothians Regional Plan' for the Livingston New Town area as its first task), he rapidly embedded himself in the Edinburgh scene, proud (unlike Stirrat) of his grandfather's Scottish origins.[23]

A postgraduate diploma course was also the favoured option for the expansion of landscape architecture teaching.[24] To direct the course, Matthew made another inspired but slightly quirkish choice: H Frank Clark, a 57-year-old lecturer at Reading University, one of the most distinguished Modernist landscapists active in Britain, and President of the Institute of Landscape Architects. Like Percy, Clark had first met Matthew during the LCC years – in his case, when working as chief landscape consultant to the Festival of Britain team in 1949–50, with Maria Shephard as his assistant. His background was also expatriate, but of a far more eclectic kind: after World War II he had become a teacher and authority on the 18th-century English landscape garden, and in 1948 had authored an influential book, *The English Landscape Garden*. During the late 1950s Clark was experiencing difficulties at Reading and looking for a change, and, after a chat

8.2 Percy Johnson-Marshall, seen in 1957 in Watney Street Market, Stepney, as Group Planning Officer. (*AJ*, 16 January 1958, 86)

229

Teamwork architecture

with Matthew at the Reform Club, agreed in July 1959 to join the Edinburgh department immediately. He was, in effect, offered the same research–teaching–practice package as Percy, and began teaching, at first mainly in Years 4 and 5; in 1962 his diploma course was set up, with the help of new lecturer Laurie Fricker.[25] On his move to Edinburgh Clark also began work with RMJM on a series of landscape commissions, including, in due course, York and Stirling new universities. Clark, unlike Percy, was an experienced teacher, and began to build up a small cadre of dedicated students, such as John Byrom. He was also a considerable eccentric. Nuttgens recalled that

> Frank was one of the most irrepressible stumblers in the world – he'd go to the wrong town, arrive the wrong week, give the wrong lecture, attend the wrong class, and leave stations, trains, buses and the houses of friends littered with coats, scarves, hats, cases and papers. Nor was it ever clear, in his lectures, what he was lecturing about, for his notes got out of order, his spectacles fell off, and in the middle of one lecture he rattled a box of matches in his pocket so violently that he set himself on fire.[26]

Despite his brilliance as a landscapist, Clark's inoffensive and disorganised manner allowed Matthew to exert a quiet but effective dominance, but Matthew's attempt to apply the same principle to the higher-profile work of the new Housing Research Unit (HRU) – in many ways, the centrepiece of his drive to establish a research-driven Modernist teaching ethos – turned out less successfully. Whereas, within pre-Modern architecture, buildings were designed without any distinct evaluation of the way they might be used, for Modernists, reflecting the key role they attributed to social science, the 'user' was of central importance – the linchpin of a circular process of research, design and feedback that appeared so obvious to them as to seem virtually self-implementing.[27] It was, above all, in public housing that the

post-war Modern Movement sought to apply this circular process: and thus, within Matthew's new department, the Housing Research Unit was by definition of central importance, and was started off on a substantial scale, with its five-year Nuffield funding package, supplemented by free university accommodation and secretarial staff. It was envisaged as, in effect, a housing equivalent of the long-standing Nuffield hospitals research unit, directed during the early 1950s by Llewelyn-Davies.[28]

It was all the more regrettable, then, that the staff of the new Housing Research Unit descended almost immediately into three years of destructive in-fighting, which arguably sapped much of the initial vitality of the department as a whole. After lengthy and unsuccessful negotiations with an (unidentified) ex-LCC colleague, in 1959 Matthew turned to Eric Stevenson to fill the position of director. Stevenson, who had since 1953 been working under Jeffryes as one of the three senior DHS Regional Planning Officers, seemed to be another potentially competent but malleable subordinate drawn from Matthew's past acquaintances. But this case was different, and provoked strong differences of opinion. Some, as we shall see, felt that Stevenson was ultimately the victim of a persecution campaign. Nuttgens, on the other hand, was among the critics, and recalled that while

> all Matthew's appointments were a bit dotty, this one was by far the dottiest: he was, entirely personally, responsible for bringing Stevenson in. Eric was a kindly man, well-motivated, not in the least bit nasty – somewhat comic, perspiring, always late, and with a pompous manner that was caricatured by the students. But everything he did always seemed to be followed by dissension and conflict.[29]

Arguably, the underlying difficulty was that Matthew's increasingly polycentric lifestyle, restlessly skimming from one cause to another, was beginning to tempt him to take greater risks in delegation.

The Housing Research Unit was formed in April 1959, with no less than eight staff appointments, including three research assistants (H Roland Wedgwood, a BRS lighting specialist who had just worked for a spell with Doxiadis in Greece; M J Calthrop; and J A Gray), a Maltese research student (A Zammit), a sociologist (N Dunhill), a quantity surveyor and a technical assistant. They and the planners and landscapists were given a separate office, elsewhere in George Square, which caused resentment on the part of Nuttgens: 'The research unit people were stand-offish, and would have nothing to do with the department.'[30] At first, in 1959, Matthew tried unsuccessfully to define the HRU's work so as to embrace his vernacular preoccupations.[31] But it soon became clear that the HRU's researches, given its lavish, multidisciplinary staffing, must of necessity concentrate on the socio-scientific user-study concerns more typical of the technocratic early 1960s: its advisory committee included, for example, sociology professor David Donnison and the 'rigid, disciplined' communist government architect Cleeve Barr.[32]

The HRU began by embarking on an ambitious programme of two major research-led housing development projects, both brokered by Matthew, and including desk studies and post-completion user studies: a supposedly rural 90-dwelling development at Cuthill, Prestonpans, for East Lothian County Council, followed by a larger urban residential grouping at Cumbernauld New Town. Both projects, however, rapidly got into significant organisational difficulty. The Cuthill project, laid out on an innovative low-rise, high-density pattern of courtyard houses, ran into unexpected difficulties when it became obvious that the County Council was expecting the University to pay for the building work, but by late 1960 some substantial research results were emerging, especially as a result of Dunhill's investigations of tenant reaction to various layouts of dwellings and furniture and 'other aspects of home-making'.[33] The

Cumbernauld project, which originally envisaged construction of three low-rise, high-density enclaves in contrasting tenurial patterns, for social-economic comparative purposes, was eventually built in the early 1960s as an exclusively New Town Development Corporation rental development, in the Park 3 area.[34]

More serious, however, were the growing personal tensions within the Unit, which rapidly became embroiled in dissension, with a growing polarisation between Stevenson and some other staff, who in 1961 (backed by Nuttgens) went to Matthew, asking for Stevenson's resignation. The demands of conflicting loyalties provoked in Matthew a mixture of indecisiveness and stubbornness. His initial response was to stand by his own choice, Stevenson, and acquiesce in the subsequent departure of Nuttgens and another colleague.[35] But, after that, the situation hardly improved:

In the end, the rows got worse – for example, Eric and Percy were hardly on speaking terms – and eventually, late in 1961, it was Frank who had the brainwave of moving Eric sideways to teach architectural history. To make this possible, Robert had to persuade the university to approve an additional senior-lecturer post for Eric – who readily accepted it – and also persuade Percy to take temporary charge of the Unit.

In this way, Percy now began to emerge as a clear deputy to Matthew himself within the department. He recalled in 1975 that when the HRU 'was threatened with imminent disaster in 1961, I agreed to become its Director and to find a successor.' As we shall see in Chapter 9, Percy also had to stand in for Matthew as head of department in 1962–4, during the latter's RIBA presidency.[36]

Throughout the expansionist period of the late 1950s the departmental secretariat stayed at 16 George Square, still with chickens roaming the back yard. Nuttgens's de facto burden of running the department was eased by the

231

8.3 Stuart Matthew, seen in the late 1950s. (Stuart Matthew)

appointment of another lecturer, Tony Forward, who was brought in to organise the courses. Matthew's direct involvement was still confined largely to presiding over the monthly departmental meetings, and, in between, visiting the department frequently to deal with a wide range of academic and personal correspondence: here, he devoted most attention to brokering international connections and lecturers for the department.[37] Dorothy Taylor recalled that:

> He relaxed a bit in the department, and used it as a place where there was less pressure than in the RMJM office – less pressure by his unusual standards, of course. He'd arrive for a couple of hours, then reel off a long list of instructions about various things and just leave us to it. He was very trusting, and would just sign lots of sheets of departmental headed paper in the middle or the bottom of the sheet, as he wouldn't be there when they were eventually typed out. What was special about the department was its informality. You didn't get paid any extra if you worked long hours or came back in the evening to get things finished. For example, Pat and I spent the whole of one Saturday bundling up papers for one of our RIBA course acceptance applications. Matthew simply inspired a general loyalty.

Nuttgens recollected that 'he unintentionally treated Dorothy rather badly by conventional standards, as he'd arrive about 5.30 or 6 pm on a Friday, dictate fifteen letters and assume she'd just cope with it, rubbing salt in by saying things like, "It's all right, I don't need them till first thing Monday morning!"'[38]

The *esprit de corps* within the department extended to a generally defensive attitude towards the possibility of closer organisational integration with ECA: in 1961, when a possible reorganisation was mooted, under which all undergraduate teaching would be concentrated at ECA and all postgraduate and research work at George Square, a staff meeting raised strong objections to any sort of negotiations with Cowan, as, in Eleanor Morris's words, 'our course was terribly new, only a few years old, and the College of Art seemed an obvious predator.'[39]

Multi-polar practice: the first years of 'RMJM'

Although some outside diehards, such as Matthew's old adversary Sydney Loweth, were still stirring against the supposedly unfair ability of university professors to pursue private practice at the same time, there was now no question of a conflict between Matthew's Edinburgh University and RMJM work at the expense of the former – not least because, by around 1960, he had begun subtly to lose interest in both of them.[40] Both, in combination, were similar to his LCC workload after 1951, when both the Festival Hall and the housing reforms had been achieved. Within his private practice, the impetus of his drive to establish a Scottish Modernism had now begun to dissipate in the face of the wider architectural trend towards more technocratic, universalising urban visions.

Alongside his RMJM work, Matthew kept going a succession of smaller-scale commissions designed to provide a stream of modest work for Stuart. He, by around 1959–60, was becoming incapacitated with a range of physical and mental illnesses, and his own joint practice with David Carr was rapidly contracting. 'Robert was actually very good, after my breakdown, in trying to provide me with opportunities to do things. He'd say, "Could you do this … or that", always in an indirect way.' Initially, Stuart was offered projects, both architectural and planning, with RMJM or Percy Johnson-Marshall as a back-up or working in association with him. Matthew's first idea was to involve Stuart in university

Modern Architect

development-plan work, where deadlines were less urgent: for example, in the somewhat Geddesian development plans for Dundee University and Glasgow Royal College (later Strathclyde University) campuses, where he worked with Robert's own architect-planners. In neither of these two commissions did Stuart make an effective contribution. At Dundee, the original plan of May 1959 and revised plan of 1962 defined a 50-acre site north of his tower building as a coherent precinct, within which various new buildings could be inserted – including RMJM's botany and zoology building, conceived by Robert in 1958–9 as a rectangular steel-framed structure on a sloping site with stone and cedar cladding – not unlike Gogarbank and Turnhouse; an extension zone to the north, facing Hawkhill, was planned in the form of loosely arranged courtyards, similar to Robert's Old Aberdeen development plan.[41]

At Glasgow, the outcome was more negative still. The revised development plan (submitted 1962), produced by Stuart with Kris Buczynski and Spaven, planned to cater for a proposed doubling of student numbers by 1970 through an extension planned on two steeply sloping sites, bounded by Cathedral and Richmond Streets. It, too, envisaged a series of loose courtyards, but with more dramatic urban gestures, such as a 19-storey tower for Biological Sciences and projecting platforms with parking below. But progress was still slow, and eventually in August 1962 the university proposed a renegotiation of the commission, and Matthew resigned in exasperation.[42] By 1960, as we shall see later, the issue of the replacement of Basil Spence, in the far more sensitive role of consultant planner for Edinburgh University, was coming up, and here Matthew made no attempt to involve Stuart; instead, Percy was appointed planning consultant to the university in January 1961.[43]

Generally, architectural jobs assigned to Stuart tended to be less urgent or one-off in character. For example, he designed much of the conversion work to 31

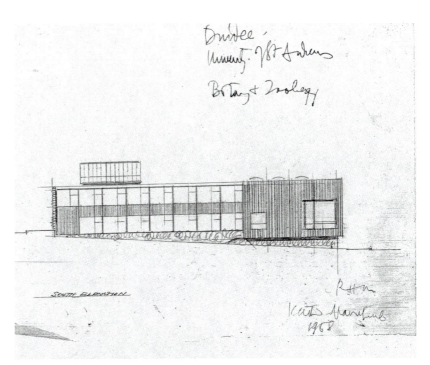

Regent Terrace, adapting it as Robert's office and flat by inserting, among other things, a shower and drinks area. One potential scheme steered Stuart's way was a modest job at the Army and Navy Club, St James Square, Westminster, where Robert was asked in 1960 by the rather old-fashioned architects, T P Bennett & Son, to provide a more modern front elevation for a proposed rebuilding scheme, in the wake of a Royal Fine Art Commission refusal. The drawings had to be prepared while Matthew was away on holiday with Lorna, Janet, Aidan, his wife Sylvia and William Gordon in a villa (Rosa d'Abril) at Castelldefels, near Barcelona. This was a typical example of the family's Mediterranean holidays, invariably organised by Lorna either in rented accommodation or with friends. Here the stay was arranged through Lorna's Spanish au pair, Josephine, and the party was joined by Percy Johnson-Marshall's daughter and a gaggle of friends, and also, incongruously, by contractor Harry Cruden and his sister Ruby, who came to stay for a fortnight, complete with Spanish maid and chauffeur-driven car. Sylvia recalled that 'this was very much one of Lorna's set-ups, complete with snags, such as the lack of pillows or a cooker when Aidan and I

8.4 Robert Matthew's initial sketch design of 1958 for the Queen's College, Dundee Botany and Zoology Department. (EULMC)

Teamwork architecture

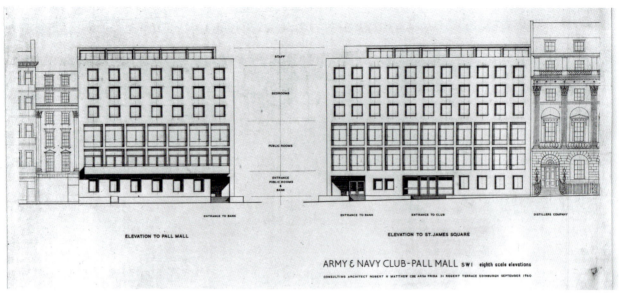

ARMY & NAVY CLUB - PALL MALL SW1 eighth scale elevations

CONSULTING ARCHITECT ROBERT H MATTHEW CBE ARSA FRIBA 31 REGENT TERRACE EDINBURGH SEPTEMBER 1960

8.5 Robert and Stuart Matthew's alternative elevation for the Army and Navy Club, London, September 1960. (Stuart Matthew)

arrived as the advance party!' On this occasion, after informal consultations in London between Robert and Basil Spence (in his RFAC capacity), Stuart was left with detailed instructions for the Army and Navy Club: in contrast to Bennett's plain, classical scheme, the drawing would have to be 'bold and decisive – to convince the client, LCC and RFAC – with interesting fenestration' – a sign of how radically the thinking within RFAC had evolved in the few years since the New Zealand House confrontation. As Robert was scheduled to travel direct from Spain to Copenhagen a week later, Stuart arranged to phone him in a local shop in Castelldefels to discuss final details, while Robert spread the drawings out on the counter. All, however, was to no avail, as the RFAC rejected even the revised design, and the project was eventually abandoned altogether.[44]

During the late 1950s the RMJM office went into a period of increasingly rapid expansion, becoming closely attuned to the increasing boom in public sector construction. Between December 1956 and December 1958, for example, the Edinburgh office increased from 14 to 26 staff. Prior to April 1961 Matthew and Marshall were the only two partners, following which Spaven, Newnham and Lee were taken into partnership and the firm became known as Robert Matthew, Johnson-Marshall & Partners (RM & JMP,

shortened in this account to RMJM). Spaven argued that, with his longer service, he should have a higher share of the profits, but Matthew, anxious to avoid discriminating against the London staff, insisted, to Spaven's resentment, on equal treatment. As the practice expanded, Spaven felt himself more and more sidelined into an administrative-helper role. One colleague remarked that 'Twenty-four hours a day of Tom's time wasn't enough – but, of course, that's partly what "greatness" is about – driving people.'[45] Spaven recalled that 'my wife would say, "Robert's taking advantage of you." But I'd reply, "I saw the chance back in 1953, and took it."'[46] In some respects Matthew's relation to Spaven resembled Lorimer's to his own father: highly asymmetrical, yet mutually beneficial.

Initially, the London office remained quite small, with fewer than ten staff for the first couple of years, and Park Square East (re-leased in 1956 until 1973) remained under Matthew's sole control.[47] At the same time, Stirrat's staff gradually spread into offices in other nearby locations, focusing eventually on 42–46 Weymouth Street. In Edinburgh the office was at first, in 1956, concentrated in the two downstairs rooms at Regent Terrace, but the mushrooming of the practice gradually led to the acquisition of branch offices, beginning with Alva Street (in 1957), South Charlotte Street and then Hill Street. Regent Terrace gradually took on an elite character, rather like Spence's Canonbury house: 'People would bring things to him. He was never "in" any of the other Edinburgh offices.'[48]

Matthew held together the two branches, Edinburgh and London, by his obsessive travelling: Lee recalled that

New Zealand House gave us the great break, and we'd got the promise of the Commonwealth Institute. Then started the great period of RM and JM – building as much social architecture as possible, for as little money as possible. Robert spent three, sometimes four nights a week on the Edinburgh–London sleeper and worked by day, or went by air.

Ken Feakes, who joined the London office in April 1957, recalled that 'he'd often take the night sleeper down on Friday night, come to the office in the weekend, then go back on Sunday night: we didn't see a lot of him.' His peripatetic lifestyle could cause confusion for his subordinates. At meetings at Park Square East:

You never knew how long Robert would stay there. We always had a tin of cigars ready in the front room at Park Square East for any meeting. Then, during the meeting, you had to stay alert, for the little flashes – 'Do you *really* think that's good enough?' – looking over his glasses – and you watched for the moment when he'd reach for a cigar, start puffing away and making little whistling noises, and you knew the meeting was coming to its end – sometimes, whether the business was finished or not.

Matthew's photographic memory allowed him to combine delegation with intervention at will: Jim Latimer recalled that

what impressed me was that he'd come in for a project review, look quickly at the proposals, pick out a detail for correction, and then go. Then, several months later, he'd come

8.6 Firhill Secondary School, Edinburgh, seen newly completed in 1960; photograph by John L Paterson. (RMJM)

back and say, 'Now, that detail ...' And he'd lift up the plans and papers and find it straight away![49]

The difficulties of joint Edinburgh–London working had been underlined by the experience of a number of the schools projects from Matthew's own workload, following the 1956 agreement. These included two smaller projects in England – Ruddington and Swinton – as well as a major secondary school in Edinburgh, Firhill, which materialised in July 1956 in a brief to Matthew from City Architect Steele, as a 1,050-pupil complex with 'house'-blocks and central accommodation, on a steep south-facing site. Initially, the project was dealt with like New Zealand House, with Matthew preparing concept sketches and Stirrat and Peter Newnham following up, with Matthew prodding and tweaking them. The sketch plans, prepared between October 1956 and February 1957, envisaged a layout of terraces with stone- and hardwood-faced *in situ* concrete buildings grouped around the social centre of a quadrangle; the house blocks would be treated as 'bases, to which the children will feel they belong'.[50] But by mid 1957, as more staff were required, a note of confusion had crept in, with Edinburgh-based Spaven and Gaston Gottier acting as intermediaries between Steele and Newnham, and Matthew feeding in suggested alterations directly.[51] Finally, it was decided that decisions would be taken by 'Mr Matthew in London, where

Teamwork architecture

the whole story can be given him', with design work also concentrated in London, and responsibility for dealing with the client shared between London and Edinburgh.[52] The essence of Matthew's and Stirrat's concept was retained, with its terraced, linear arrangement: at the centre were a four-storey slab block of classrooms, an assembly hall, library and main entrance, linked by corridors to three main house blocks. In January 1960 it was formally opened, but by then the lesson of its slightly 'shambolic' organisation had been learnt. Increasingly, as the schools 'shipped down by Robert' were completed, the 'colossal track record' of Stirrat's team in education building began to dominate: for example, 'when Swinton wanted an extension, they came back direct to us.'[53]

Other jobs, such as Kincardine Power Station, were also shaped partly by this climate of flux. Ken Feakes recalled that:

I was based in London, but all the work I did at first, from around 1957, was for Robert Matthew, especially on Kincardine, where his right-hand man, Graham Law, had just left to go into practice with James Dunbar-Nasmith. As the engineers, Kennedy & Donkin, had their offices down in Weybridge, Robert shipped the work down to London, having discussed it with Maurice Lee. I rarely ever got close to Stirrat: you felt you were working in a split office, working in London, but for Robert – who greatly inspired me. You were given the boldness to take decisions on big projects by the example of someone like Robert – but he kept an eye on the detail, too. For example, I was doing the drawings for the turbine house control room windows, with great chunky bits of teak, and Robert took one look at them and said, 'They're not big enough – double the scale.' I thought, 'Christ, they're going to look absolutely massive!' But when they were eventually installed, I thought, 'He was quite right – in that huge environment, the original details would have looked very thin.' From

that, I learnt something new about scale.[54]

In the years around 1960 the work of the two offices increasingly separated out into distinctive streams, as Stirrat sought to carve out a distinct area of activity free of Robert's dominance – something that John F Matthew had also tried to do, with less success, in the last years of Lorimer's life.

Stirrat had become bitter about Robert and felt he'd been virtually abandoned in London, unsupported except for the firm's name, while Robert had his professorship, his wonderful house in Park Square East, furnished to perfection inside. Robert did exactly what he wanted and went where he wanted, and Stirrat couldn't compete – not that he would have wanted to![55]

Another Edinburgh assistant recalled of these visits that

Robert often seemed to treat Stirrat a little like a schoolchild. I remember on one occasion, when they were out for lunch, seeing him 'directing' Stirrat's efforts to reverse a car out of Rose Street Lane, standing there with poor Stirrat flustering away inside. The scene was rather like a cameo of their relationship.[56]

The two associates Stirrat had brought into the firm with him, Maurice Lee and Peter Newnham, also began to carve out distinctive trajectories. While Lee, with his overseas colonial experience, became closer to Matthew, Newnham stayed closely allied to Stirrat and the ethos of 'system' design. In this context, Stirrat's antipathy began to take on overtones of paranoia:

His suspicion also extended to people from 'our' side who got on well with Robert; he used to say unkind, waspish things about Maurice [Lee], for example, like, 'He's an elephant that takes a long time to make up its mind before it walks on the plank!'

Indeed, some London staff did secretly harbour ideologically disloyal thoughts in relation to Stirrat's passion for system-building: 'Robert thought CLASP was a complete load of rubbish – and a lot of us in the South did too!'[57]

The separate development of the London office was driven forward by the award of another prestigious Common-wealth-related commission – the project to replace the massive, eclectic Renaissance pile of the old Imperial Institute in South Kensington (by Thomas Collcutt, 1886–93) with a permanent, modern exhibition of the history, products and culture of the Commonwealth countries.[58] Completed in 1962, the Commonwealth Institute was dominated by geometrical drama: a hyperbolic paraboloid roof for the main, square exhibition hall, jarringly interpenetrated by a lower, plainer linear block of offices and gallery. Derbyshire recalled that

> Roger Cunliffe had been commissioned by the *AR* to do an article on curved shells, and came into the office one day with a model of a hyperbolic paraboloid. Stirrat, who'd been grappling with the problem of getting a roof over James Gardner's design for the new Institute, saw Roger's model and said, 'That's it!' – and so it was!

Internally, the 93 sq ft vaulted space was theatrically spanned by bridges and a platform, in a combination of structural panache and metallic boldness reminiscent of an 'expo' pavilion, or some of the monumental Modernist public buildings of Soviet bloc countries in the Khrushchev and Brezhnev years.[59]

Ironically, the London office now, despite Stirrat's own personal antipathy towards overseas travel, also began to acquire a substantial programme of overseas Commonwealth work, all of a public sector character. The jobs were handed straight to Lee and others to deal with, and thus fell into a transitional territory between Robert and Stirrat. Lee recalled that:

> in 1957, Donald Gibson, by now chief architect at the War Office, came to Stirrat and said, 'I've got two big boarding schools to build for expat

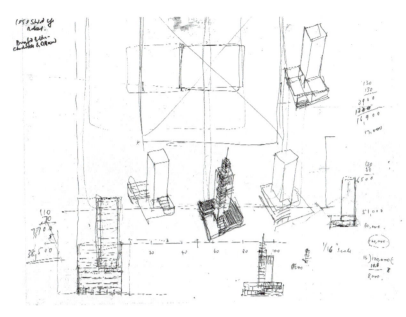

families in Singapore and Malaya.' These would be top-class grammar schools, and although with independence, the Malaya one was cancelled, the Singapore one, St John's, went ahead, with the strong support of Lee Kwan Yew. But although these jobs originally came to us in London, the link with Robert was still useful: our architectural associates in Singapore, who we used to run the job on site, were all Scots – Swan, MacLaren and others. They couldn't bear Stirrat, and adored the fact they'd have a contact with Robert. That was typical of the way we in London benefited from Robert, even though he wasn't involved himself in our jobs: he could act as a general ambassador for the firm, as he was always ready to jump on a plane, whistle around and turn up anywhere, whereas Stirrat had a claustrophobic fear of flying![60]

This substantial overlap between the two partnership arms underlined how well, in reality, the two partners were matched, despite their increasing personal tension:

> What you had was two completely different, but equally effective, ways of getting work: on the one hand, it was Robert's connections and reputation round the world that got us the

8.7 1959 sketches by Robert Matthew for a proposed Standard Life Assurance office development in Montreal, in conjunction with Canadian architects Durnford Bolton-Chadwick & Ellwood. Although Matthew's overseas commitments were now increasingly orientated towards architectural politics rather than building projects, he also kept up a limited succession of personal projects such as this unbuilt office proposal: Matthew's sketch envisaged a slightly taller version of his New Zealand House concept, complete with small upper tower and finial. (EULMC)

Architects on and off duty : top, the Dean of Guild Court. This court, peculiar to Scotland, sits every Friday and all building proposals over a certain sum have to be submitted to it. It ensures that byelaws are observed and allows a hearing to the possible grievances of property owners adjoining a proposed alteration or development of property. The present president, James Fulton Ford, is an architect. Bottom : an example, for Puritan Scotland, of emancipation—Linda Westwater, one of the few women architects practising in Scotland, having a drink in a pub with her husband, Robert Westwater, an eminent portrait painter and well-known broadcaster.

THE ARCHITECT
IN
EDINBURGH

8.8 Linda Westwater and her painter husband Robert in 1952. (*AJ* 19 June 1952, 760) (*AJ*)

overseas work – which we and Stirrat would never have got by ourselves, as Stirrat was so hostile to working overseas. But Stirrat was an equally effective operator, in his own very different way. I don't think he ever had an expensive lunch with anyone, but he'd come into the office, then up goes the phone at 10 am, down it goes at 6 pm, and the jobs were still dropping off the end of the phone.[61]

That was probably one of the things that drew Robert to take on Stirrat in the first place, his dexterity in manipulating the corridors of power: where Robert had the gift of overseas work in his hand, Stirrat knew everyone who either was a Permanent Secretary already, or who was going to become one.[62]

As a two-centre practice, it was highly successful because of this tension, with both poles straining against each other.[63]

This creative organisational tension was achieved at the cost of deteriorating personal relations between Stirrat and Robert, ultimately resulting in a relationship based on avoidance and non-communication: 'Other people would say, "That was a very shrewd get-together of

two people: they've stitched up the market!" But that wasn't how the two of them saw it, though.'[64]

How, then, did Matthew organise his own, initially predominant 'half' of the partnership?[65] At first, the essence of the Edinburgh office was its informality, combined with trust.[66] Bill Campbell recollected that

Young people were flocking into the office because of its growing reputation, and were finding themselves, within five or six years of leaving college, handling huge jobs. You had a ridiculous amount of liberty so long as Robert approved of you – you were given frighteningly too big jobs to do – far too big – which made people very loyal, and made the office a training ground for many practices of the next generation.

Jim Latimer recalled of Queen's College, Dundee, that 'it was an amazing thing for someone of my age to arrive and find yourself immediately dealing with a job that size!' Although some of the original assistants, such as Graham Law and James Dunbar-Nasmith (in 1957), were beginning to leave to set up their own practices, many more were now join-

238

Modern Architect

ing.[67] Just as in the LCC, the hot-bed atmosphere of the office began to attract a growing variety of (mostly) young architects, although any differences were far more diluted – architectural rather than political.

Some younger assistants, like the LCC 'Hards' before them, rejected the 'humanist' ethos associated with Matthew's older followers. For example, John Richards, who came to the firm from the AA in November 1957, after a rigorous training at the hands of socially committed tutors such as Robert Furneaux Jordan, the communist Arthur Korn, and Peter Smithson, was a devotee of a more 'Cartesian', ascetic-minimalist Modernism, and at first regarded Matthew's Arts and Crafts-influenced approach to design with some scorn. Sent up by Korn, with his classmate David Whitham, to work in the NCB office of Egon Riss, Richards arrived in Edinburgh

seeing our people as the SAS of the Modern Movement – we were all very big-headed. ... I was pretty obnoxious about people like Alan Reiach, for what I saw as their unprincipled folksiness – whereas I saw myself as more forward-looking and concerned with programme and purity.'

Richards moved to RMJM in November 1957, after an interview at Park Square East: Margaret Brown recalled being 'fed up when John arrived and started saying how much he disliked all our vernacular materials.[68] However, Brown and Richards soon overcame their architectural differences in RMJM's 'first office romance', followed by marriage in May 1958 and a six-month expedition round Europe, taking part in an archaeological excavation in Crete and spending three months at the British School at Rome. After their return to Edinburgh, Margaret came back part time to the firm, with Bill Campbell taking over the lead role at Crombie Hall.[69]

John Paterson, who began a month before Richards, cut a mildly iconoclastic air, reflecting the post-Smithson fascination with 'everyday', 'consumer' culture:

'We used to tease him as "Hot Dog Paterson" – he wore grey suede shoes and was a zealot for de Stijl, and you sat on chairs made of parallel planks in his flat.' Alongside these more intellectually engaged figures, the office also spawned 'characters' of no ideological pretension. In the back room at Regent Terrace worked housing specialist Rachel Wilson, along with Linda Westwater, a contemporary of Matthew's at ECA, who joined in March 1957 and worked on a succession of self-contained projects, notably the Edinburgh University Department of Animal Genetics at King's Buildings (1957–60), a modestly scaled single-storey block of animal houses with brick and cedar cladding. Margaret Richards recalled Westwater as

a very neat, competent, older character – the wife of an artist who lived in Thistle Street. Linda would get a job and basically do all of it: she was rather a worrier and one morning said she'd had a nightmare that she was titling the Animal Genetics drawings 'Rabbit Matthew and Johnson-Mousehole'![70]

In the front room, working perched on high stools along with Richards, Brown, Campbell and others, were Gaston Gottier, an 'elegant' French schools specialist who joined in August 1957 and 'had the privilege of his own drawing-board in the window', but died relatively young – and Crispin Worthington, son of the neo-Georgian interwar Manchester architect Hubert Worthington, whom Matthew took on in November 1956 at Leslie Martin's suggestion after Crispin failed his Cambridge exams. And there were the occasional visiting assistants from abroad, such as Anders Tengbom's son, Jonas, who worked in the office for six months: 'a tall, handsome Swede, who broke the hearts of all the girls in Edinburgh!'[71]

One RMJM colleague felt in retrospect that that was one of the greatest things Robert did for Edinburgh:

the office and department were international meeting places, with exotic

people popping in and out all the
time. The Edinburgh architects would
grumble about him, but they didn't
appreciate this, and even the more
broad-minded people like Alan Reiach
couldn't have afforded the often prodigious level of hospitality that was
needed to keep it all going![72]

And one of his university assistants
highlighted the role of Keith as an elite
social condenser, so remote from the
usual stereotype of the country house:

Matthew used Keith Marischal as a
place where we'd all meet casually –
where you could bump into people
right up through the strata of power,
helping architecture to percolate
through to national development. He
was trying to raise a whole generation
accustomed to working together in
bettering the built environment.

Matthew was not completely oblivious
to the demands of financial economy, but
his mother's insistence on maintaining a
lavish lifestyle had inculcated in him an
instinctive no-expenses-spared attitude
where show was concerned: 'Things
would just "happen", like impromptu
parties for a couple of dozen Russian
architects, or going for lunch at Prestonfield House and finding yourself next to
people like Nervi or Doxiadis.'[73]

This was still a time balanced between
wartime austerity and affluence, and the

office was initially still run on economical lines: 'There was no car – most people
walked, went by bike or public transport.'[74] Thus Matthew's parties made all
the more impact. Paid for by RMJM and
often organised by Lorna, they fused
together the firm's interests with his university and international connections,
with the aim also of keeping Scotland
and Edinburgh on a wider architectural
world stage. In 1957 Matthew pleaded
that '[as] small countries are outstandingly the leaders in architectural thought
today, let us take heart from our own
past – a small group of young men in the
18th century made Edinburgh for a time
the focus of the world.' And he continued
to proclaim – now echoed by Percy – a
passionate admiration for Geddes as a
'sadly neglected great Scot'.[75] Nuttgens
recalled that:

Some of the parties were really something. For example, in July 1959, a
party of Soviet architects, from the
USSR Union of Architects, came for an
official visit. Matthew discovered nothing had been done to entertain them,
and so, in his capacity as president of
the UK committee of the IUA, he took
it on himself to arrange hospitality for
them in London and Edinburgh. I was
sent out to order the drink – General
Grant whisky, nothing else, literally
boxes and boxes of bottles. None of the
Russians spoke any English, but they
all made it quite clear by one means
or another that it was the best party
they'd ever been to! I first met Frank
Clark outside that party: I was sitting
up on the crossbar of a street light,
Frank was standing on the pavement
below, and we duly introduced
ourselves.[76]

But the increasing cost of this expansive
activity began to put a growing strain on
the firm's finances, and underlined the
need to maximise income.

From vernacular Modernism to historic-burgh regeneration

The workload overseen by this diverse
and growing band of 'followers' at Regent

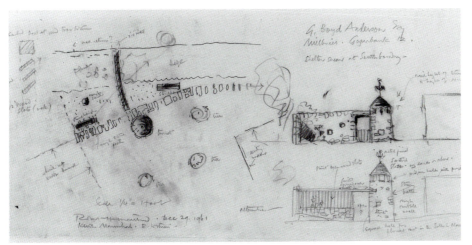

Terrace and its branches was drifting slowly, but inexorably, away from Matthew's 'vernacular' preoccupations – a trend that began to leave Matthew slightly alienated from the firm. Of course, with the long lead-time of major projects, the vernacular projects still continued to appear predominant during this period, and received some reinforcement in May 1958 with the arrival of Kenneth Graham, a Newcastle-trained schools and housing specialist, who had previously worked in Buckingham County Council, Peterlee and Norwich, under the eminent, Townscape-orientated city architect David Percival. Although Matthew's own interest in vernacular architecture was shifting into the field of research, the construction still continued of previous vernacular RMJM projects, large and small. At Gogarbank, for example, Matthew added a succession of rubbly garden features in a somewhat Portmeirion-like vein – such as a stone shelter screen and circular gazebo in 1961: 'probably the last building that came from his own hand'.[77]

At the Aberdeen University project, construction of Crombie Hall – now with 129 student bedrooms – began in 1957, largely under Spaven and Campbell's oversight, but with Matthew maintaining his exacting standards of vernacular roughness to the last. For example, in May 1958 one of the women's two-storey hostel ranges, with a big rubble-clad gable wall facing north to Meston Walk, was under construction. When the gable had reached a height of 10 ft, Spaven suddenly spotted to his horror that the walling, intended by him as slaistered, rock-faced, snecked rubble, was being built by local contractor Halls in recessed-pointed, smooth-faced snecked rubble.

I knew Robert would have a blue fit and indeed he did: 'It'll have to come down, Tom!' By that time it had gone even higher and the cost of remedying it was going to be £800. The question was, who was going to pay? To Robert, the only thing that mattered was that it was a nasty piece of walling, which would just have to come down, whatever the cost.'[78]

Almost immediately after the completion of Crombie Hall in 1960, Matthew and Spaven set Campbell to work on a follow-up hall of residence (Johnston Hall) immediately to the south, also laid out around courtyards, but in a more homogeneous, four-storeyed manner. Campbell recalled that

I'd spent the whole weekend doing a freehand perspective of the new hall, with a deadline of Monday morning. Matthew just stood behind me with Tom Spaven and said, 'You know, Tom, we'll have to get someone in this office who can draw.' You might have been a potato for all he seemed to notice, and it wasn't said in a humorous way – or if it was, the humour was well suppressed.[79]

In parallel with the Crombie project,

Matthew continued to pursue his master-planner role at Old Aberdeen, persevering with his Geddesian conservative-surgery concept of renewal of the High Street area through courtyard-plan backland infills. For example, it was at his express suggestion that George Bennett Mitchell & Son designed the new Arts Building (Taylor Building, built from 1961 onwards) in the form of two somewhat classical blocks linked by a colonnaded arcade, and Matthew defended the extra cost of the colonnade with characteristic forcefulness when challenged by a visiting delegation of UGC architects, led by Guy Oddie – a vetting system that, with its cost constraints, he had, ironically, helped set up himself during his recently finished term on the UGC.[80] In the early 1960s Matthew's Geddesian vision for Aberdeen University came under increasing threat from the dramatic rise in the projected student population, with the target envisaged for 1962 rising by 80 per cent to 4,500, and consequent demands for a 300 per cent increase in building for arts and sciences. Although he began to suggest building of higher blocks on the periphery of the campus, and RMJM retained a limited architectural involvement, Matthew gradually lost interest, his attendance at meetings tailed off, and there was a brief and unsuccessful attempt to involve Stuart in the development plan work. Eventually, in 1964, Matthew gave up the architecture/planning consultancy to London-based Douglas Jefferriss Matthews.[81]

The hydro schemes, too, remained a redoubt of Matthew's vernacular style for the remainder of the 1950s. At the first to be started, Lochay (begun in January 1957) – again with Alexander Hall as main contractor – progress was relatively straightforward, albeit complicated by the special demands of the vernacular ethos. The job architect, industrial specialist Ron Thurgarland, took up residence in a local hotel and began the arduous combined job of site supervision to ensure the correct slaistered feel, and a searching of local quarries for suitable stone. By March 1957 Thurgarland was

writing with trepidation to Spaven that the stone being produced by the local Moar quarry was now pink, rather than grey, and Spaven replied that, although Matthew was on holiday, 'I can think of no colour he would like less than pink.'[82] April 1957 brought a start on the superstructure of Lochay, a satisfactory local source of quarry stone having been found, and an attempt by the contractor's mason to infiltrate 'rather nasty' recessed pointing having been rebuffed.[83] Greater controversy lay ahead over Cashlie station, adjoining Stronuich dam – and Matthew's way of resolving it, as with the cases of LCC housing, Adam House, New Zealand House and the ECA dispute with Lyon, was to precipitate a cathartic conflict in order to quell conservative opposition to his own plans and conceptions. During the second half of 1957 the board of NSHEB began to show increasing discontent about the proposed design, which envisaged a tall turbine house and lower control-room annexe, ranged round a compound, and clad partly in stone, and partly in rubble, with large windows and a split main gable. The NSHEB board and amenity committee blasted this as inappropriate for a Highland setting, and insisted on a 'simple traditional building in local stone'.[84]

At this point, in January 1958, Matthew exploded in frustration, and penned a broadside back to Fulton, expressing incredulity that the Amenity Committee could have disapproved his design, as 'I think I know, to a fair degree, a good building from a bad one, even allowing for a bias in favour of my own work!' He continued:

Special pleading for the Highlands as an area where new buildings should be 'traditional' is to my mind wholly mistaken. Any restriction of this kind, placed on the architect, must result in weak compromise as against firm conviction and clarity of expression ... I do believe that this backward looking view is largely responsible for the very small contribution that Scotland has made to the sum total of the highest quality architecture of the time. NSHEB has a unique opportunity to put Scotland firmly in the forefront.

The word 'traditional', Matthew argued, should be avoided altogether: 'To me, the greatest lesson to be learnt from tradition is that of adaptability to changing conditions – surely the whole function of making electricity from water power does give just this opportunity for the use of traditional materials, especially stone, in a fresh way.'[85] Faced with this determination, resistance crumbled: in March 1958 the Board 'reluctantly approved' the stone, but 'reserved the right to dissociate' itself should there be criticism. And eventually, despite problems caused by shortages of suitable local stone, the Cashlie station was finished in late 1963.[86]

As the technocratic 1960s dawned, the impetus gradually began to ebb from Matthew's stone vernacular movement. But vernacular design did not disappear altogether from the firm's output. Instead, its force began to divert into a different direction – towards the design of modern, but picturesquely laid out, housing projects, often in historic burgh contexts. This approach, pioneered by Basil Spence in his Dunbar infill fishermen's housing of 1949–53, was enthusiastically taken up by the 'engaging, self-deprecating' Kenneth Graham, who soon established a separate central Edinburgh branch office for group 'B' – specialising in housing – at 13 South Charlotte Street, and would eventually (with John Richards) become a full partner in 1964.[87]

The opportunity to begin this programme, however, had come slightly earlier than Graham's arrival. The key date was 1956, which had seen the beginning of a remarkable commission to Matthew to replan and reshape a small but forward-looking Ayrshire burgh, Cumnock. The impetus for this entire regeneration project, which would stretch over nearly 20 years, came from Cumnock's part-time town clerk, Bobby Hunter:

8.11 1958 model of Barshare housing development, Cumnock. (RMJM)

Bobby 'was' Cumnock, and was determined to make Cumnock something. He was the local solicitor, a paraplegic, who used crutches, but was a big man in every way – a big thinker, and a dynamic personality, who felt his council should have the best architect for their town, and persuaded the councillors to appoint Robert.[88]

In November 1956, out of the blue, Hunter wrote to Matthew, broaching the subject of a proposed 550-dwelling housing scheme at Barshare, on a prominent hillside on the edge of the town, and explaining that although the council had until then used the Burgh Surveyor's services, it was anxious to employ a good architect, and that Matthew's name had been recommended by Peter Rendle, an influential, design-minded Scottish Office administrator.[89]

Matthew's initial concept drawing for Barshare, followed up in detail by Rachel Wilson, envisaged a low-density neighbourhood unit at 12 houses per acre (36 persons per acre), with local services and low-rise flats grouped around a small square as the focus, combining picturesque planning with elements of *Zeilenbau* parallel layout, and Radburn planning including some culs-de-sac. By September 1957 a range of assistants was working alongside Matthew, Spaven and Wilson, developing the house types for Barshare, using terraced layouts of one- and two-storey dwellings and a few four-storey maisonettes, in a variegated

243

(top) **8.12** 1961 view of completed first phase at Barshare: photograph by Henk Snoek. (RIBA)

(bottom) **8.13** 1962 view of completed first phase of Barshare (EULMC)

vernacular style, freely using timber and local red sandstone walling. The layout was a modified Radburn plan, making use of courtyards and narrow lanes, yet ultimately based on a rectangular gridiron layout – a dense inner-urban solution adapted for a suburban site. At a meeting that month Matthew and Spaven met the entire town council, and showed them a 1:500 model.[90] In a setting such as this, proselytising to a large and socially varied gathering, Matthew was in his element, and his close relationship with the town was now cemented. The entire situation, combining community egalitarian action with a degree of small-burgh Scots tradition, appealed greatly to him, and from now on he made every effort to attend Cumnock events. Graham recalled that

> Hunter and the town councillors had a great affection for Matthew, and he reciprocated: he even went to their official Burns supper there one year! For all his international fame, if Cumnock's mining councillors asked him to go to something, he'd bend every effort to fit it in: they seemed to enjoy his company, and he was with people that he thought mattered.[91]

Arguably, for Matthew, this kind of community fellowship or issue-friendship with independent-minded people, such as the Cumnock councillors or his later international environmental-reformist allies, largely took the place of more conventional close personal relationships.

Matthew's chief challenge at Barshare was to overcome the conservatism of the councillors. At the September 1957 meeting there was lengthy discussion of the traditional mining-village preference for single-storey rows and the suspicion of flats, and the proportion of single-storey

houses in Stage 1 was duly raised to 20 per cent. In October 1957, however, the *Cumnock Chronicle* proudly trumpeted the modernity of 'Cumnock's Million-Pound Housing Scheme'. By mid 1959, with work under way on construction of the 84-dwelling Stage 1, the second phase was being designed, along with another, separate neighbourhood, Barrhill, on a sloping site, including four-storey maisonettes. Cumnock work was now generally overseen by Graham, who took over in October 1958. Graham tried to make further inroads among the more conservative elements in the burgh, pressing for inclusion of further four-storey maisonettes, and Hunter also took every opportunity to encourage a more 'progressive' line, emphasising to councillors the need to press on with completion of the full project, to accelerate 'appreciation of Barshare as a new kind of place to live in'.[92] As we shall see later, in the successive stages of Barshare and Barrhill, and in subsequent projects elsewhere, Graham was able to develop in a consistent manner a judicious balance between modernity and tradition. By 1959, too, the County Council had engaged Matthew to prepare a development plan for the burgh, including a comprehensive redevelopment concept for the central area, with pedestrian precinct in the main square, shopping centre and blocks of flats.[93]

The return to 'urbanism': renewal visions for Glasgow's Gorbals

By the late 1950s, reflecting wider architectural trends, Matthew's practice and, to a certain extent, his personal thinking were shifting inexorably from a humanistic vernacular orientation towards a more assertively urbanistic approach. Recovering fast from the tension of the Suez debacle, decolonising Britain was now embarked on a decade of growing national prosperity, balanced between social democracy and capitalism.[94] Architecturally, the old, disciplined public-service architectural ethos of the early post-war years, and its built expression in tower blocks or garden suburbs, suddenly seemed comprehensively out of date, and a whole kaleidoscope of new positions took its place, ranging from a more expressly poetic individualism of key architects, to new, complex theories of human association. Among younger London housing architects in the late 1950s there was a move towards advocacy of a more dense, mixed-together urbanity, rejecting free-standing tall blocks in open space.[95] The CIAM principles of separated, airy *Zeilenbau* development were now debased into a run-of-the-mill, engineer-dominated formula, often combined with industrial prefabricated systems or urban motorway infrastructure.[96] The gradual decline of old-style Functionalism was symbolised, in Britain, by the final dissolution of the MARS group in mid 1957, with Matthew remaining a passive member up until the end. He had initially in 1953 shown some enthusiasm about revitalising the Scottish planning and architecture research offshoot of CIAM ('SPAR'), but by mid 1956 SPAR was declared 'completely moribund'.[97]

Matthew's attitude to the new urbanism was ambiguous, to say the least. In principle, he backed a liberal concept of diversity, inveighing in 1958 against the repetitiveness of 'mass housing' and arguing that 'my own inclination is towards the greatest possible degree of individual freedom'.[98] And he participated enthusiastically in the growing debates on 'urban renewal', from 1959, in collaboration with figures such as Lionel Brett (Lord Esher) and the new and design-conscious junior minister at the Ministry of Housing and Local Government, Keith Joseph.[99] In the national debate of 1959–62 about high buildings policy, especially in London, it was naturally and correctly assumed that Matthew, as the designer of New Zealand House, would be on the side of more tall buildings. But although Matthew fulsomely praised Chamberlin, Powell and Bon's 'exhilarating' multi-decked plans for the Barbican, his own ideal of the urban tall block was a somewhat older one, a Gibberd-like or even Beaux Arts concept of the slender tower as landmark. He called for the breaking-down of large urban developments into 'smaller and contrasting masses': only through 'comprehensive development' could a properly variegated city townscape be secured, which 'inevitably brings tall buildings into the picture'. For him, the leading exemplar of redevelopment was still Coventry, where Ling was methodically planning out a network of axes and slender towers. In 1962 Matthew argued it was the first city in England to which 'people are being drawn in their thousands – to see contemporary architecture'; he praised the 'cheerful, almost gay' effect of the centre, whose 'human scale ... has successfully avoided pomp and monotony'.[100] To be sure, buildings much in excess of 20 or 30 storeys would prove uneconomic, and 'indiscriminate' building of skyscrapers as in the USA would be 'disastrous', as would the 'shortsighted but vastly expensive schemes for urban motorways' in city centres.[101] But, all in all, the years around 1960 saw a high point of Matthew's confidence in the viability and necessity of large-scale redevelopment. 'If the city is to live and thrive,' then people would have to accept the 'dynamic disruptive process' of large-scale rolling redevelopment, to expunge 'that Dickensian drabness and squalor that the Communist part of the world so loves to caricature'.[102]

The qualified nature of Matthew's engagement with the new thinking was underlined in his unsuccessful entry for the April 1957–February 1958 *Hauptstadt Berlin* competition, promoted by the West Berlin Senate as a symbolic reunification gesture. Matthew entered in his own right, assembling a supporting team that included Michael Laird and Patrick Nuttgens, as well as the young John Paterson, newly qualified from Edinburgh College of Art, and greatly sympathetic to the new, harder urbanism. Their entry, prepared after three months' work, envisaged multilevel podium planning at particularly dense points, such as Friedrichstrasse, linking east and west, with a cluster of tower blocks (including cross-circulation ele-

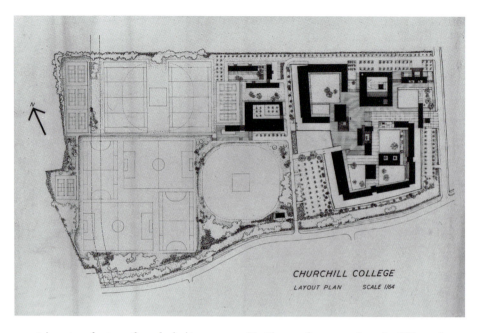

CHURCHILL COLLEGE
LAYOUT PLAN   SCALE 1/64

ments) on top; but on the whole it remained faithful to Matthew's LCC ideals of mixed development, open space and variegated townscape profile. The text, by Nuttgens, stressed the principle of maximum concentration in the economic zone and maximum free ground space elsewhere. In Geddesian fashion, the 'humanistic' aspirations of the project were emphasised by placing a university quarter at the junction of east and west, as the kernel of a future unified Berlin. The 151 entries included 11 from Britain, and were judged in June 1958 by Aalto, Vago, Bartning, van Eesteren and no less than 17 German advisers and politicians: Matthew's entry was eliminated in the second round (along with Stam's and Utzon's). An entry by Percy Johnson-Marshall with Boissevain and Osmond made it as far as the third round (at which stage Le Corbusier's was also eliminated). The winning scheme, by German architects Sprengelin, Eggelin and Pempelfort, was a more straightforwardly rectilinear Modernist conception of big slab blocks at right angles.[103]

The shift in Matthew's work towards an emphasis on urban renewal was highlighted in his contribution, from the late 1950s onwards, to the planned regeneration of Glasgow – a sharp contrast with his more cautious approach to university redevelopment in Edinburgh. For

Matthew, of course, the rebuilding of Glasgow was strictly to be seen as part of the Clyde Valley Plan's twin-track approach to Glasgow's overcrowding and slum problems, with population overspill running alongside inner-area redevelopment. Here, the early 1950s had seen little progress on either front, but in 1955 the designation of Cumbernauld presaged more hopeful times. By 1959 he was able to adopt a more confident tone, arguing of the Clyde Plan that while at first 'both the analysis and the solution were received almost with incredulity', now Scotland may be 'taking a lead in making town planning theory a practical proposition'.[104] Now, at last, it began to seem feasible to pursue in tandem both the complementary aspects of the Clyde Plan framework – overspill and inner redevelopment.[105] Matthew well knew that the original New Town formula was now roundly condemned for its low density. But in the emerging plan for Cumbernauld by Hugh Wilson's team, with its avant-garde multilevel centre and its tight 'cluster' planning avoiding separate neighbourhood units, Matthew saw a potential remedy for all these challenges: in 1960 he boasted that 'in a very short time, the New Town of Cumbernauld will, in its planning and architecture, have stepped ahead of every New Town in the country, England included.'[106]

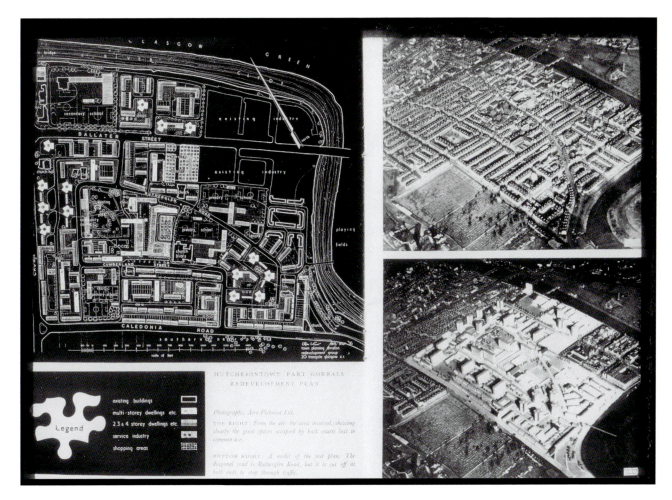

8.15 1956 aerial view and aerial perspective of the City Architect's masterplan for the Hutchesontown/Gorbals area, Glasgow. (Planair)

Within Glasgow itself, the architect-planners within the Corporation architecture department worked with Scottish Office planners to devise a workable formula of comprehensive redevelopment, relying pragmatically on the tried and tested CIAM formula of towers and slabs in open space, at a moderately high density (150 habitable rooms/acre). But to design the main sections of the Corporation's first and most prestigious redevelopment area, Hutchesontown/Gorbals, Glasgow's City Architect, Archibald Jury, instead approached Matthew and Spence at the beginning of 1957. The two areas were next to one another – Matthew's (Area 'B') overlooking the Clyde opposite Glasgow Green, Spence's ('C') immediately to the south of it in the heart of the Gorbals. By now, the friendly personal collaboration between Matthew and Spence had become increasingly overlaid by a contrast of ethos between the two practices: on the 'Matthew' side, for example, Richards and Spaven claimed that 'Spence's approach was essentially scenographic, like an artist standing in a smock in front of an easel, and sometimes even doing a perspective of a building before handing it out to someone else to work out the plans!'[107] In Area C, Spence, helped by assistants in his Canonbury atelier office such as Michael Blee and Charles Robertson, gathered his housing into two monumental slab blocks, 20 storeys high, with complex split-level maisonette flats and inset communal balconies, which he fancifully advocated to the Housing Committee as 'hanging gardens'. The scheme proved awkward to design and problematic to manage, culminating in its premature demolition in 1993. Matthew lavishly praised it as 'a tremendous block ... incorporating [Spence's] famous "hanging gardens", and one of the few "world standard" new buildings of Scotland'. But, beyond two initial liai-

Teamwork architecture

8.16 RMJM 1958 perspective of pedestrian zone of Hutchesontown/Gorbals Area B development. (RMJM)

son meetings in 1957, the schemes were developed in total isolation from one another. Matthew's project architect, Ian Arnott, recalled that 'there wasn't *any* suggestion that the two great men should get together, and of course the two schemes were totally unrelated. The only consultation was when Charlie Robertson and I met in a pub – infrequently!'[108]

For his own area of the Gorbals Matthew chose a very different approach, less flamboyant and more methodical in character. At the first liaison meeting in May 1957 'Basil was already rhapsodising about his hanging gardens, but Robert just sat there with nothing, and asked for the brief.' His first tentative sketches, in June 1957, showed a right-angled pattern of 15-storey towers and 11-storey slabs, but during the summer investigations revealed the very poor bearing capacity of the riverside site: 55 ft piles would be needed for anything higher than four storeys, and thus a far more polarised solution of low-rise rows and slender towers was indicated.[109] At this point, in late 1957, the focus of Gorbals-related design activity unexpectedly shifted to Edinburgh – showing that the two cities were not completely separated in Matthew's mind. Here the Corporation, stung by criticism of recent package-deal multi-storey projects, had announced an

open architectural competition for Leith Fort, the first of a series of redevelopment instalments in the decayed port area of Leith, and occupied by a redundant 18th-century barracks complex. Matthew took the opportunity afforded by this competition to work up a new scheme that could also be used, slightly modified, for the Gorbals. It comprised a mixture of 18-storey towers and four- and three-storey terraces planned in a rectilinear alignment around a central focus of pedestrian spaces, with the high blocks set diagonally to maximise daylighting and sunlighting; all existing buildings would be swept away. Owing to the urgency, a variety of staff were pulled into the project, under Spaven's overall direction – including chiefly Ian Arnott, and Margaret Brown, who was sent to the Berlin Interbau housing demonstration project to look in detail at a tower block by Dutch designers J H van den Broek and J B Bakema, whose 'cross-over' plan and split-level section, with central corridor (in turn, inspired by Le Corbusier's duplex flats), seemed to offer a way of fitting a large number of dwellings into a tower block while obtaining lighting from both sides.[110] Brown was also working, at the same time, on the firm's unsuccessful entry for the 1959 competition for Churchill College, Cambridge: a quadrangular design with deep section

blocks, inspired by Powell & Moya's St John's College residences. Leslie Martin was the assessor for Leith Fort, and his January 1958 judgement put RMJM in second place; the winner was a more adventurous scheme of contrasting tower blocks, deck block spine and low-rise high-density patio housing by three young architects – Ian Baikie, Shaw-Stewart and Frank Perry. The failure to win Leith Fort hardly bothered Matthew, who clearly saw it chiefly as a dry run for the Gorbals. Bill Campbell recalled that

> when we got the result, Stirrat Johnson-Marshall, 'over the top' and eager to be loved as ever, sent a bubbly, ingratiating telegram, which ended, 'We bathe in your reflected glory!' Matthew, who was reading it over my shoulder, just snapped curtly, 'What does the man mean, 'glory'? We were beaten, weren't we?'[111]

But by January 1958 planning of the Gorbals project, using all the Leith Fort experience, was well under way. Matthew began to talk of the Gorbals with increasing expansiveness, using a rhetoric of aggressive newness that represented a startling swing from his earlier 'vernacular' and 'contextual' language – which would before long begin reappearing in his growing embrace of conservation. But, for now, the aim was unfettered

dynamic Progress. As he would write in a 1959 newspaper article, the task in Glasgow was now a 50-year programme of urban renewal. There was no question of conservative surgery. Boldness was imperative both in the redevelopment areas and in 'Operation Overspill': 'insisting on conformity' with the past would be a betrayal of the present and future, and thus 'one of the deadly sins at this key moment in our history'.[112] At the end of January 1958 Matthew presented the council with two alternative layouts, one designed to follow the existing street pattern, and the other, orientated optimally for daylight and sunlight, which would require a diagonal relationship to existing streets and to the Spence blocks. The diagonal plan was accepted, coupled with an inward-looking layout with glimpses across to Glasgow Green and 'continuous free space' at ground level. The central pedestrian zone, sunk four feet below the surrounding area to mark it off, was envisaged by Matthew as a social and visual 'hub': the pedestrian would be 'allowed to dominate'.[113]

Immediately, the deep planning envisaged by Matthew for the towers unearthed a formidable opponent within the Corporation: William Horne, the Medical Officer of Health, who doggedly resisted the introduction of internal mechanically ventilated bathrooms and internal kitchens. Horne was steeped in the traditions of late 19th/early 20th century public-health medicine, with his declamatory condemnations of slum conditions and demands for maximum ventilation and openness. Ironically, Matthew's Functionalist ethos of 'scientifically determined' standards was also indebted to this discourse, but here the two were pitted in opposition, with Horne thundering that the 'Glasgow housewife' would find internal bathrooms 'repugnant ... from a practical, hygienic and social point of view'. Horne's opposition was overcome only after 'he was incautious enough to remark that "the reason why Professor Matthew doesn't want outside bathrooms is that bathrooms would spoil his pretty elevations" – whereupon Matthew replied acerbically that "I can design bathroom windows just as well as any other windows!"'[114] Detailed design work on the blocks during late 1958 involved both Spaven and a succession of project architects, but Matthew continued to be extremely closely involved, making all significant design decisions. The design was generally inspired by current LCC work, and Matthew accordingly organised a visit to Roehampton, Brandon and other relevant London estates; but, in detail, the project was worked out afresh. Ove Arup devised a completely new, semi-traditional construction system, combining *in situ* concrete and load-bearing brick. The plan and section were equally innovative. The Berlin 'original' had been a relatively simple conception, combining a crossover section with a symmetrical plan of only four flats per upper floor. The Gorbals block had to have five, forcing the corridor to kink from side to side, with a central service core served by two lifts.[115]

Much of the detailed design was the work of John Paterson, who was taken on by Matthew in October 1957 as assistant in the preparation of the *Hauptstadt Berlin* entry, followed immediately by Hutchesontown B. For the 26-year-old Paterson this was a tremendous opportunity to put his 'urbanist' ideals into practice: 'I learnt architecture on the job for

five years!' He enjoyed relatively far more freedom than Charles Robertson at Area C, who, he thought, 'had to conform strictly to Basil's office aesthetic and Basil's sketches – I used to tease him that Basil had pinched the idea from Kunio Maekawa's enormous block in Tokyo, with its huge legs.' After vainly advocating more 'hard, regular, even brutal' finishes, including broken bottles in the gable wall facing aggregate, Paterson finally made his mark in the lighting of the development, where he opposed ordinary lamp standards as too confusing and fussy, and advocated floodlights mounted on top of the tower blocks – inspired by Hieronymus Bosch and William Blake. Initially, Glasgow Corporation 'fell about laughing, but, the thing about Glasgow is, they will give everything a whirl'. So, eventually, the floodlights were duly installed, and proved so effective that they were used for all subsequent tower blocks in the city! The low-rise blocks were designed by a different team, but Paterson dealt with the local shops integrated with the precinct:

a Miesian concept of a circular drum with a box above – timber-clad, with no windows. It was all, of course, an imposed aesthetic, but we did succeed in creating an urban environment – whether Miesian or Corbusian – that didn't look suburban or rural, with rubble walls or pantiles – although that, in turn, meant that any 'Scottish' element was lacking.[116]

Construction of Hutchesontown B proved difficult and slow. Perhaps surprisingly, these troubles stemmed not from the main contractor – the Corporation's direct labour organisation – but from the *in situ* contractor, A A Stuart: a 1960 report argued that 'apathy pervades the site', with constant turnover of workforce, rubbish tipped off the uncompleted tall blocks, and incessant breakdowns of the crane hoists. Where the original January 1960 programme showed all four multi-storey blocks scheduled for completion by April 1961, in fact the last one was finished only in January 1963. In that year, the delays and mounting costs of this project prompted a 'devastating show of sharp claws' from the chief housing engineer, Lewis Cross – an equivalent of the LCC Valuer – who exploited it to advance his agenda of maximising output in the city's multi-storey housing drive.[117] In reality, of course, much of the disruption stemmed from the 'multifaceted, hydra headed' character of Glasgow Corporation, whose own grossly inefficient and divisive contractual arrangements were dictated solely by the demands of local political patronage. But Matthew's own insistence on comprehensive rather than piecemeal planning inevitably raised Glasgow hackles. Two follow-on projects were allocated to Matthew by Jury in redevelopment areas north of the Clyde – Royston B and Springburn A – with the intention of reusing the 18-storey and low-rise types.[118] In both cases small gap sites were immediately available, but Matthew pressed hard for delay until a more substantial site could be built up, rather than simply building 18-storey blocks on the gap sites. Resentment built up among the councillors at 'one of these prima-donna Edinburgh architects trying to grab a bit more of Glasgow', and eventually the sites were reallocated by Cross to commercial package deals – an outcome that Matthew, who had by now lost interest in the Glasgow housing projects, did not bother to contest.[119]

The regeneration of the Gorbals, however, continued to generate a succession of other opportunities for the firm – all handled with only initial input from Matthew. In 1959 a project was proposed for a 270 ft high, 20-storey air terminal hotel for Grampian Holdings Ltd, overlooking the Clyde just northwest of Hutchesontown. Sketch designs were produced, inspired especially by Arne Jacobsen's contemporary SAS hotel in Copenhagen (1958–60), but economic conditions led to its cancellation. On the river-front site next door July 1960 saw the beginning of work on a College of Nautical Studies for the Corporation: here, project architect David Sturrock designed a multi-storey complex, with the teaching rooms concentrated in a nine-storey street-frontage block, and low-rise decked accommodation stretching north towards the river boathouse. At a sharply contrasting scale, from 1961 Paterson began work on a nursery school for the area – the first new post-war nursery school in Scotland – serving separate Protestant and Catholic groups of 40 infants. The low-rise design, echoing the surrounding housing in its rectilinear formality, expressed this duality with two blocks accessed by a common axis, and sharing an enclosed courtyard.[120]

8.18 1960 sketch by Matthew of alternative (unbuilt) proposal for Standard Life's George Street office development, Edinburgh. (EULMC)

Modernist renewal in Georgian Edinburgh: the 'Battle of George Square'

Matthew's increasingly ambitious Edinburgh projects, for university and infirmary, presented a curious mixture of parallels and contrasts with the Glasgow situation. His Edinburgh RMJM work also increasingly emphasised boldly scaled, multi-storey design solutions, but in a far more challenging context of consensually supported historical townscape; here, other than in areas such as Leith Fort, Glasgow's slum-driven, political pressure for radical surgery was lacking. In general, Matthew was a defender of the cultural-historical prestige of Edinburgh, but in these years – the climax of 'Progress'-driven redevelopment boldness in his thinking – he struck out in a different direction in his Edinburgh schemes. When working

in the classical context of the New Town, Matthew remained generally faithful to a conservative-surgery approach of traditional street scale – for example in a succession of office extensions to the Standard Life Insurance Company, George Street, planned from 1960 onwards in conjunction with Michael Laird, with stone-faced facade to George Street and curtain walling and columns to the rear. But in his enduringly contentious proposals for the extensive university redevelopment in the 18th-century George Square Matthew adopted a different and more assertive tone, with the result that all the Edinburgh tensions about scale and historic context came to a head in a cause célèbre, which would eventually rival New Zealand House in complexity and passion.

In general, Matthew enthusiastically advocated selective landmark tower blocks in Edinburgh, to accentuate what he saw as its exciting contrasts of scale, but opposed 'indiscriminate' high building. As with other contemporaries, such as Nikolaus Pevsner, who were becoming more unambiguously associated with the conservation cause, the stress was still on extreme selectivity: in 1960 Matthew argued that, while he would 'personally die in the last ditch for the Scott Monument', only a few buildings 'qualify for immortality'. And this restricted definition of heritage, it was clear from the start, did not include the mid-18th-century vernacular classicism of George Square.[121] Here as in the Gorbals, but less overtly, Matthew worked in alliance with Basil Spence. We saw in Chapter 6 how the university had already taken in 1954 the unusual step of securing planning permission for change of use, and that Spence's 1955 university replanning report had set out, and received outline permission for, the principle of a redevelopment of all but the west side of George Square, with traditionally scaled modern buildings punctuated by tall blocks, and laid out around an array of Oxbridge-style quadrangles stepping up to the McEwan Hall. In 1959 Spence helped further soften up architectural opinion in Edinburgh for change, with a terrific attack against the 'mediocrity' of new Edinburgh architecture.[122]

Throughout the mid 1950s Robert Matthew, sensing an emerging opportunity, but well aware of the furore that would be stirred up by even partial redevelopment of George Square, continued to bide his time and refrain from any public intervention. In March 1956 he politely declined requests by Angus Acworth, Secretary of the (London) Georgian Group, to help start an Edinburgh group dedicated to opposing George Square redevelopment, arguing that, as a university professor of architecture, he was 'very much involved in the George Square issue', and drawing attention to Spence's plan.[123] From the perspective of the outside world, this involvement continued to seem very much one of an advisor and assessor – for example in December 1956, when the job of designing the new university library in George Square was provisionally assigned to Spence.[124] Throughout the late 1950s Matthew continued his established succession of modest projects for the university, including a conversion of 8 George Square for the Housing Research Unit in 1958–9, supervised by Nuttgens with input from Linda Westwater. In 1957–8 Matthew helped Spence and the university address the problems of George Square's first major redevelopment parcel, the massive medical building by traditionalist W N W Ramsay; he advised on cuts in the scale of the building, and on the issue of stone facing.[125] In 1958 Matthew's advisory role was amplified further, when the university, with a 50 per cent increase in student population forecast, set up a new Major Buildings Committee, with Matthew as convener and Stewart as a member, to oversee the necessary building programme, instead of the existing Works Committee. Matthew was thus in a key position to nominate other architects for individual components of the redevelopment, and began to do so immediately: in 1960, for example, he recommended Morris & Steedman for the new Student Centre.[126]

8.19 September 1958 sketch by Matthew for the Edinburgh University Arts Faculty development, showing the Arts Tower in an alternative position slightly further south, abutting Buccleuch Place. (EULMC)

8.20 Matthew seen in 1960 explaining his George Square model at a public meeting, with Hardie Glover (Spence's partner) on the left. (source unknown)

In 1959 the UGC approved a shift in the balance of the George Square 'Central Development Area' towards arts accommodation, and Spence and Matthew collaborated on a revised masterplan. What was less publicly obvious was that, ever since 1956, Matthew had been deeply involved in discussions with the university on his own potential direct involvement as designer of a new Arts Building, for which a site at the southeast corner of the square was available. As in the case of Dundee, Matthew took it as his first task to draw out the full accommodation implications of the university's require-ments, and to argue that a much bigger building was needed. 16,000 sq ft could potentially be fitted on the site at 47–51, and £350,000 had provisionally been earmarked for the project by the university; but in his first estimates of accom-modation, in October 1956, Matthew argued that 120,000 sq ft, with a likely cost of £720,000, would in fact be needed. As a result, he contested, 'one thing stands out – the south half frontage of the east side of George Square by itself cannot provide a site for a worthy faculty building'; it would either have to be planned eastwards in depth, or be

PRINCIPAL ANSWERS THE GEORGE SQUARE CRITICS
PLAN IS MINIMUM DISLOCATION OF HUMAN LIVES

To the EDITOR of "THE SCOTSMAN"

From Sir Edward Appleton
The Old College, South Bridge,
Edinburgh,
September 7, 1959

Sir,—The Dean of the Faculty of Arts has aptly called attention to the University's duty to make the future of young people of talent a matter of primary concern. The number of such young people who flock to our doors is increasing.

suggest themselves: (1) "Several millions" is an astonishing figure, even at compulsory purchase prices; substantiation seems called for. (2) In the intervening 12 years most of the property could have been acquired at relatively low cost. (3) The University of Oxford is spending several millions to repair the ravages of atmosphere and traffic on its old buildings; George Square requires no such repairs. Is one to assume that the Edinburgh University authorities would regard the Oxford expenditure as misguided, better spent on substituting new buildings?

8.21 September 1959 cutting from the *Scotsman* letters column, showing both sides of the George Square redevelopment controversy. (*Scotsman*)

extended along the south side of the square, creating a dog-leg site.[127]

With a minimum of publicity, Matthew began working quietly on a variety of solutions, involving permutations of either of these solutions or both together. Innumerable sketches of 1958 and 1959 survive, showing that from the beginning, as in Dundee, a modern open-planned development was envisaged, with a tall tower as the centrepiece – rupturing the corner of George Square with a fragment of Modernist space while still respecting the general framework of Spence's plan. All the variants showed a high block at the centre, lower ranges along the square's facade lines, and substantial lecture theatres adjacent. The starting point of this sequence was a tracing of part of Spence's 1955 masterplan, made in July 1957 by Matthew, who shaded in proposed buildings to the southeast of the square – a square tower and four long rows – straddling Buccleuch Place. By September 1958 the layout had begun to assume roughly its present form, with three phases and a total of seven blocks identified: Phase 1, at the southeast, with a tall north–south slab block to maximise immediate accommodation gain, and a lecture theatre to its east; phase 2 to the north of that, with two low-rise slabs; and phase 3, to the west, with an east–west low-rise slab and two square, low blocks. The 'grand plan' would be decked and on two levels.[128]

In August 1958 Matthew was formally appointed architect for the Arts Faculty project, and wider consultations (still in private) began within the university. Basil Spence was kept in touch, rather belatedly, through his Edinburgh partners: Hardie Glover reported to him, following a meeting with Matthew in December 1958, that 'the issue of point blocks within the area of the Square itself has been cunningly avoided by placing the high block of his scheme outwith the immediate square precinct.'[129] In the same month Matthew showed the model to the UGC, stressing the 'national character' conveyed by the rubble-clad basement walls, and the strong modelling of the tower facades, with recesses to denote the position of departmental libraries. Spence was at that stage working on his preliminary scheme for the library, and completed a perspective of the view of it from the Meadows in January 1959. But by November 1959 he and Matthew had fallen somewhat out of touch on the project, and Spence testily asked Glover, 'Can you get hold of Robert Matthew's scheme for the Arts Building? Everyone seems to have seen it except me.'[130]

Among some progressive-minded younger staff Matthew's appointment was greeted with fervent excitement: for example, in June 1959 Richard Sillitto, a natural philosophy lecturer (and 'patron' of a small Modernist house then being built by Matthew's ex-students, Morris & Steedman, at Charterhall Road, Edinburgh), bubbled that 'we are fortunate indeed to have him as our architect – he has already given Scotland its finest modern building, and the Edinburgh architects' grapevine is already humming with excited rumours of the design he is producing for us.'[131] But elsewhere, as the details of Matthew's concept slowly filtered out, reactions were more mixed – even within his own department. Nuttgens recalled that 'while Basil Spence did the overall design for wrecking George Square, I well remember the first occasion when Matthew came back with a sketch design for the Arts building: my reaction was "That's exactly what

I don't want!"' The 'Georgian Group of Edinburgh', formed in embryo in March 1956, was formally inaugurated in March 1957, with 25 members, and Eleanor Robertson as its secretary and the Earl of Haddington as first president; in 1961 it became the Scottish Georgian Society.[132]

But the fundamental reality of the scheme was that outline planning permission for zoning change had already been granted in 1954, and in mid 1958 the Secretary of State duly refused the Cockburn Association's request for a public inquiry into the plans. In June 1959 Edinburgh Corporation gave approval to the general layout, mass, density and height of Matthew's scheme, which the university now presented as the first major realisation of Spence's precinct vision.[133] From that point, with Matthew's project now firmly in the public domain, a public campaign of opposition against it got firmly under way, bringing together a wide coalition in the time-honoured Edinburgh tradition of cultural-environmental outrage campaigns. Protest letters to the *Scotsman* lambasted the 'arrogant indifference of Edinburgh University to the opinion of its own graduates and of the citizens of Edinburgh', in planning this 'rape of George Square', while counter-arguments stressed the social progressiveness of the project, and the urgent practical need to relieve overcrowded university accommodation: the Dean of the University wrote on 4 September 1959 that, while George Square was undeniably attractive, 'young people come before old buildings'.[134]

In parallel with this debate, Robert Hurd set to work with more practical opposition, focusing on whether a review in the phasing of the project, with the tall block retained, but built closer to the backs of the houses on the eastern side of the square, might allow the latter to be retained. However, his own position was potentially compromised by his acceptance in 1959 from the University, on Spence's recommendation, of a commission to report on rehabilitation of the west side; he was also now generally identified as a 'reactionary' designer following the protests in the same year by the 'Anti-Ugly Action' group against his new building at Emmanuel College, Cambridge. In June 1959 a further plea for a public inquiry was again refused, but by December the vehemence of opposition had forced a re-evaluation, and the Secretary of State announced in the House of Commons that a working group (including Matthew, Hurd, Town Planning Officer Hewitson and individual conservationists) would evaluate whether the planning of Phase 1 could be adjusted to allow construction to go ahead without demolition of the old buildings. Hurd worked out a plan under which the existing 18th-century houses, still used residentially, would be converted to teaching rooms in place of the two new low blocks, while building the 14-storey tower block just behind them, at a cost £200,000 less than Matthew's plan. Piling on the pressure, Ian Lindsay, traditionalist architect and head of the DHS historic buildings branch, listed the George Square 18th-century ranges at Category A.[135]

Unlike Spence, who was notably thin-skinned about criticism of his designs, Matthew now imperturbably set about circumventing these opponents, in much the same way as he had done at New Zealand House – and despite the fact that, in this case, his own views were ambiguous. In 1957, for example, he had assisted the beginnings of statutory listing in Scotland by sourcing English data through the RIBA, and he praised Lindsay's own work for its 'timeless quality of the vernacular'; yet in 1960 he warned sternly that it would be 'fatal' if preservation absorbed all the energies of the post-war upsurge in interest in the environment. John Richards, who would become Matthew's project architect for the Arts development, felt that:

Matthew was schizoid about George Square. He loved the buildings there and was very friendly with some of the key conservationists, such as Robert Hurd and Colin McWilliam. He was neither firmly in the conservationist

8.22 1989 aerial photograph of George Square from east (cf. C27) showing Matthew's Arts development (at lower left corner of square) flanked by the Spence library (upper left) and Alan Reiach's First-Year Science block (lower right). (RCAHMS)

camp nor in the anti-conservationist camp. Personally and intellectually, he was in favour of conservation as a matter of general principle. But another side of him saw the need for change and felt he should have a hand in shaping it – and that was the side that prevailed at that juncture!¹³⁶

The die was now cast, and although the project was not such an important one in his career as New Zealand House, and he was faced with weaker opposition, he now focused the same negotiating tactics on them, mingling confrontation and collaboration, to bring about the same outcome: a voluntary surrender by his opponents. At New Zealand House Matthew had done this by exploiting the differences between the various versions of the tower. In the George Square working group – which met six times in January and early February 1960 – his strategy was to discredit the plan worked out by Hurd, by making it appear unworldly and impractical. Then the choice could be polarised between full implementation of his own plan and a return to first

principles – something he knew would be completely unacceptable to the university, with the constant increase in student numbers and the risk of jeopardising UGC support by any programme slippage. One key Edinburgh conservationist recalled that 'to watch [Matthew] operating on a committee was to observe someone who always knew the outcome that he sought; a man who had mastered the issues in any brief, and who had manipulated the group dynamic to achieve the required end'.

The fifth meeting of the group, on 4 February, was the crucial one. Matthew would undoubtedly have worked hard on the telephone beforehand, to ensure the result he wanted. Now, pressing home his cause, he attacked uncompromisingly both the new-build and reuse aspects of Hurd's plan, portraying them as attacks against his own competence. The suggestion that the tall block could be moved slightly was intolerable in planning terms, as it 'would put the Faculty of Arts on back land', complicate the planning of a lecture theatre ... and make impossible the principle of covered communication between all departments. Worse still, it was 'quite ridiculous to suggest that he had not suggested the best site', and thus 'he was not prepared to reconsider the siting unless he was actually instructed to do so' by the university. The existing houses were 'uneconomic', inflexible, and 'substandard in relation to modern concepts of planning', by comparison with the 'standard size of unit' that the modern low-rise blocks would provide.¹³⁷ The tactic of converting the George Square debate into an issue of confidence paid off handsomely. Matthew's opponents had already hemmed in their own position by expressing 'admiration' for Matthew's planning solution, and pledging 'minimum' interference with his plans in view of the 'urgency' of extending the faculty accommodation. Nor could the opponents' plan be truly presented as a conservationist solution, as its partial preservation of George Square depended on massive compensatory demolitions elsewhere, including the whole of Buccleuch Place. Now, finally, the working group concluded that the building of a tower block on its present site was incompatible with retaining the George Square frontages, and the choice was thus between Matthew's plan and 'lengthy reconsideration of the whole development' – which, the university representatives made clear, was 'totally unacceptable', as Scottish universities would have to create 5,000 more places by 1965 to accommodate 'the rising generation'.[138]

Matthew could hardly have scripted the outcome better, and he later conveyed a slightly sophistic impression in an off-the-cuff remark to postgraduate Laurie Fricker (whom he knew to be neutral on the issue): 'Of course, if I'd been on the other side, I'd have succeeded too – using the opposing arguments!'[139] Despite further protests, by early March 1960 it was clear that the 'Battle of George Square' was effectively over. The emphasis moved firmly to the field of practical planning, with the efforts of the UGC, the Major Buildings Committee, the Project Sub-Committee and the Tower Users Committee to define the internal planning of the tower reaching fever pitch. By July 1960 the £600,000 Phase 1 Arts Tower (David Hume Tower) scheme was finalised as a 14-storey block of small rooms and a low block of lecture rooms, adjoined by a cast coffered slab deck, with all the central Arts Faculty services underneath; Phase 1 would contain 82,000 sq ft of accommodation. In the later phases a further expansion in planned student numbers would be met by adding an extra floor to the low blocks. John Richards succeeded Steedman as Matthew's chief assistant (later, as project architect) for the project, helped by Euan Colam and, eventually, seven others.[140] Gradually, with all the controversy over, Matthew began to try to reinterpret his plan along Geddesian conservative-surgery lines: at the opening of the tower in 1963 he claimed that he was 'following a great tradition' of university-led enhancement of the city.[141]

Towards the 'embedded' hospital

The complex challenges of dense urban development or redevelopment were echoed and intensified in the design of new teaching hospitals, with their multi-layering of function and patronage, their requirement for a hyper-developed scientific infrastructure of planning and services, and their highly demanding, expert user-group. Hospitals were a building type not favoured by the London arm of RMJM, as the more highly strung Stirrat 'found the attitudes of doctors inconsistent, uncomprehending and intransigent'.[142] To Robert Matthew, however, such a client group posed a challenge rather than a threat. Architecturally, too, the task was a stimulating one: in 1965, indeed, Matthew told the Royal Society of Medicine that the building of new hospitals can and should make an important contribution towards providing a much needed sense of purpose in the bewildered society of the angry young man. More, perhaps, than any other type of architecture, the modern hospital should express the value of science to the physical and mental well-being of man, and the ideals of service to society.[143]

In the architectural context of the late 1950s, with its growing emphasis on dense urbanity, the programme of an 'embedded' teaching hospital, requiring complex interpenetration of two different building types, medical and educational, seemed to point almost by definition to a highly integrated, multi-layered megastructural solution. Matthew was closely involved with two major projects of this kind – the abortive inner-city Edinburgh Royal Infirmary redevelopment and the outer-suburban Ninewells project.

We saw in Chapter 6 that the nascent Edinburgh Royal Infirmary redevelopment was a university as much as a health-board project – sitting literally alongside the George Square project as the other key element in a swathe of redevelopment along the north side of the Meadows. Here, too, a dense multi-storey solution – something Matthew had

257

Teamwork architecture

ARCHITECT EXPLAINS HOSPITAL'S REDEVELOPMENT

Professor Robert Matthew demonstrates to Mr John S. Maclay, the Secretary of State for Scotland, with models, how a helicopter can land on the roof of the proposed new Royal Infirmary buildings.

(top) **8.23** Matthew shows his first RIE scheme (with multi-storey slab) to the Secretary of State for Scotland in January 1961. (*Scotsman*, 14 January 1961)

(bottom) **8.24** August 1960 model of the first RIE scheme, seen from south. (RMJM)

been familiar with since his 1945 visit to Stockholm – seemed from the beginning inevitable. But under the far more acute pressures of planning an embedded hospital on a highly restricted site, these tendencies were developed at Edinburgh in a more densely assertive way, beginning in December 1959, when Matthew's feasibility study appointment was enhanced by the Regional Health Board into a formal appointment as architect for redevelopment.[144]

In his initial 1956 report Matthew had advocated staged redevelopment, provided that buildings of suitable height were allowed. The fact that a sufficient decanting momentum could be achieved only by an unacceptably tall development on the highest part of the site was the fatal contradiction of this *in situ* redevelopment

concept, and a problem that would eventually undermine the entire programme, as it fluctuated between proposals that were too bulky or too complex. That fact would, in the end, be grasped only after 15 years of proposal and counter-proposal. After three years of inconclusive debate between the health and university authorities, chiefly over the optimum number of beds, in January 1959 the South-Eastern Regional Hospital Board formally endorsed the concept of staged, *in situ* redevelopment, beginning with a new block of outpatient and casualty accommodation, and in December Matthew was formally appointed architect, with Llewelyn Davies as supporting consultant (with the one per cent fee divided half-and-half between them).[145] In June 1961, after a year of preparation overseen in RMJM from mid 1960 largely by Gwent Forestier-Walker (a hospital specialist), Matthew was able to present a large-scale feasibility model to the Secretary of State, Lord Provost, Principal Appleton and chairman of the Regional Board. This made clear that, at this juncture, he had thrown all his weight behind the front-loaded approach. The entire northwest and centre of the site would be cleared – avoiding not only the 1930s Simpson Maternity Pavilion and Nurses Home, but also the late-19th-century complex of medical and surgical Nightingale wards, which would function normally until completion of the new block, and would thereafter be demolished and left largely as open space. The new main building, an 800-bed general hospital and embedded medical school, would be a massive 17-storey block, shaped on a T plan and rising from a podium; the main ward block (the 'top' of the T) would face south, for maximum sunlight, and the northern leg of the T would contain academic and laboratory accommodation.[146]

This proposal not only shifted the bulk of the accommodation up to the top of the site, but also more than doubled the building's height – towering 170 ft above Lauriston Place and intruding on the Edinburgh skyline from several angles. It is unclear whether Matthew viewed this concept as a serious building proposal or, rather, as a polemical device to draw the fire of any potential opposition and allow a 'compromise' to be subsequently accepted. Perhaps he felt emboldened by his own victory over Trustram Eve at New Zealand House, and by the numerous other high buildings, such as Spence's Hyde Park Cavalry Barracks, that were subsequently negotiating the planning system in those years – all, however, very slender towers rather than massive slabs. As we shall see in Chapter 9, during the early 1960s Matthew's proposals for the Edinburgh project did begin to swing back towards a more contextual approach, similar in scale to the surrounding 18th- and 19th-century buildings. But this medium-rise alternative, incorporating elements of decked and megastructural planning in a manner familiar from countless medium-rise high-density housing designs of the early 1960s, did not appear in a vacuum. Rather, it was the organic outgrowth of a formula already in course of development within the firm itself, in the very different, anti-urban setting of the Ninewells project in Dundee.

We saw in Chapter 6 the seemingly casual way in which Matthew was appointed architect in 1955 for the Ninewells project – a joint commission by the Eastern Regional Hospital Board and the University of St Andrews. As it had been decided from the very beginning that the hospital should be sited at the extreme western tip of the city, the phasing-derived tension between concentrated and dispersed architectural alternatives never arose, and the architects enjoyed fairly wide freedom of action in proceeding to approved sketch design stage. Architecturally, the overall emphasis was towards deep, compressed layouts, suitable for the embedded layouts dictated by the UGC, under the influence of Matthew himself and of the 1955 report of Llewelyn-Davies's influential, multidisciplinary Nuffield Provincial Hospitals Trust research team.[147] The main obstructing factor at this stage was financial:

the lack of funds within the Scottish government hospital building allowance – a delay that allowed the brief for the scheme to be considered and debated exhaustively between 1956 and 1961.

Matthew's principal client body here was the Joint Planning Committee of the hospital and university, supplemented by a smaller 'Planning Group' whose most active members were the Hospital Board Secretary, J K Johnston, bacteriology lecturer Dr T Sommerville, and Donald Douglas, Professor of Surgery. Although Tom Spaven was always present in the background in meetings on Ninewells, before long the role of Matthew's main assistant in the project was filled by a newcomer to RMJM, Alan Wightman, who joined in late 1957 from Farmer & Dark, and was immediately catapulted, from early 1958, into an ever-intensifying round of trips to Dundee, initially twice weekly. Eventually, in late 1959, a decision was taken to set up a separate design office in Dundee for the project – initially in a room in a flat in Windsor Street, and then in a classical villa at 10 Hawkhill Place ('Hawkhill House').[148]

In April 1959, after much debate between Wightman, Matthew and client representatives, and after a study trip to America suggested by Matthew, Wightman produced a paper suggesting a radically innovative solution for the planning of Ninewells. It rejected any kind of multistorey formula and instead proposed an all-low-rise complex, to give 'a loose knitting of the various parts in a way that meets the needs of compactness, adaptability, and organic growth'.[149] Typically of the Modern Movement, innovation was here driven not by a general abstract ideal but by specific experimental data about practical use – namely, a large body of evidence from US studies of new 1,000-bed hospitals, suggesting that multi-storey stacked plans were both more expensive and less efficient.[150] Wightman's conclusion was that the sloping site of Ninewells could be exploited through a stepped courtyard plan, to allow a 'domestic scale' to be achieved with segregated multilevel planning;

Teamwork architecture

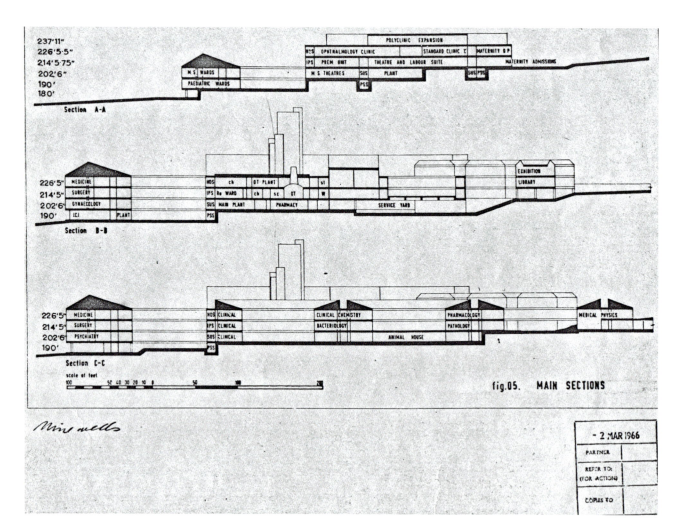

Section A-A

Section B-B

Section C-C

scale of feet

fig.05. MAIN SECTIONS

- 2 MAR 1966

PARTNER

REFER TO:
(FOR ACTION)

COPIES TO

8.25 Schematic sectional concept drawing of Ninewells Hospital, 1960, showing the contoured, low-rise formula. The closest parallels to Ninewells were other densely planned medium-rise collective ensembles of the mid 1960s, especially in England, such as Lancaster University (from 1963) or Southwark Borough Council's Bonamy-Delaford housing scheme in London (1963–5). (RMJM)

internally, the buildings could use deep plans and artificial ventilation, but with six-bed open rooms rather than small individualised ones. He recalled that while Matthew's initial, instinctive reaction to this proposal was 'to ask, "Why not a multi-storey solution, to exploit this magnificent site?" – when he was presented with the logical case for a low-rise solution, he readily accepted it.'[151] His hand was, in any case, forced in the late summer of 1959 when Wightman's report was accidentally passed by RMJM secretarial staff to Douglas and Sommerville – who recalled that the 'seminal paper ... caused something of a stir [by making] a persuasive case' for a low-rise solution – and a 'high-level meeting' was convened by Principal Knox to discuss the proposal.[152] Wightman recalled Matthew's typically unruffled response to what followed:

Knox opened the meeting by saying, 'We've read this paper with interest, but we gather you haven't had an opportunity to see it and make observations, Professor Matthew.' Matthew said, 'No, in fact I have read it.' Knox replied, 'Can you tell us whether you agree with its observations and conclusions?' I thought, 'Matthew's on the spot – so I'm in hot water!' But he just said, 'Yes, we agree.' The meeting went on from there – but from that moment, the general planning principle was settled, that Ninewells was to be a low-rise building.[153]

By May 1960 an overall plan, based on this principle, was adopted by the Joint Planning Committee, and in May 1961 a detailed design report was presented by Matthew, accompanied by a scale model.[154] The executed design was planned, essentially, in the form of three-storey spurs flanking a three-tiered east–west internal 'street', with wards facing south on one side, and departments on the other. The 'racetrack' wards to the south were arranged in T-shaped pairs, and the corresponding clinical department to each ward was, if possible, always at the same level. The potential for conflicting movements in such a compact layout was tackled by providing for complex patterns of segregation, both vertically and horizontally. The slope of the site was used to create three main decks, each with direct external access: the main public access was at the top level, the ambulance access was at mid level, and the bulk stores entrance was at the bottom.[155] At the centre of the main hospital complex a north–south transverse concourse block of five/seven storeys, with a big boiler chimney immediately to the east – all distinctly higher than the rest of the building (as at Bath University) – formed 'the "hinge" of the whole layout', with the main public and ambulance entrances at its north end: the public pedestrian entrance gave access directly into a hall-like space of both warmth and grandeur, which provided visitors with a comprehensible yet dignified focus from which to access the whole complex.'[156] Construction was to comprise traditional reinforced concrete, with some precast concrete cladding, and low pitched roofs.

All in all, the Ninewells concept developed by Wightman and Matthew (helped by junior designers such as Michael Calthrop) represented an exceptionally complete, unified solution to the demands of a large, multi-element social building institution, all the more impressive for its consistent avoidance of ostentation or monumental vertical accentuation – as might have been tempting on such a large, open greenfield site. Its consistency and coherence were, arguably, greater even than those of RMJM's other new university complexes. And, as realised, it was certainly more coherent, as we shall see, than Matthew's own other main personal design achievement of the 1960s, the New University of

Ulster, Coleraine, although in some ways the overall planning principle of Coleraine – with its linear layout of courtyards flanking a spine, offset by an emphatic transverse pedestrian concourse at the centre – was actually very similar.[157]

The main complex was designed to be extensible at either end, but there were also two separate groups of associated buildings: an engineering complex to the east, and nurses' residences to the west. Wightman recalled that, following extensive consultation with nurses, which suggested that their accommodation should be planned around four-person flats rather than study-bedrooms, Matthew took charge of the design process that followed, deciding the building's site and overall layout.[158] More generally, Matthew concentrated most of his contribution to the Ninewells project into a burst of feverish activity during the first three months of 1961, a time of intense sketch-plan preparation leading up to the May publication of the design report: during this time, his diary records twice-weekly visits to Dundee for meetings with the design team and clients. This was essentially the same pattern that he had pioneered in the Festival Hall

8.26 February 1958 drawing by Robert Matthew of a 'House for Jessie Ann to copy': cf. the Barshare and Hawick schemes. (EULMC)

project: drawing threads together, resolving crises and difficulties, and ensuring that all details were right.

Birth of a statesman: private and public life in the late 1950s and early 1960s

The five years covered by this chapter were a time of gradual transition away from Matthew's initial enthusiasm and commitment to reformed architectural training and private practice within Britain, and towards a new and more enduring 'mission' of global architectural statesmanship. Throughout the period his representational commitments steadily increased, as he laid the ground for the period of primacy that was to follow, in the early/mid 1960s. As with a Victorian gentleman, his domestic lifestyle was still moulded largely around his emerging public persona. In the opinion of April Johnson-Marshall, for instance:

> Robert was a marvellous, but paternalistic chap – fierce, not very understanding – and absolutely determined that what he wanted to do was the right thing. That inevitably affected his family. Lorna used to be dragged off to places like Russia or Mexico, complaining, 'I'd rather stay here and have a new pair of shoes!' It wasn't so nice for her and the older two children: Aidan and Janet were in some ways overpowered by him, whereas Jessie Ann got under his skin – she was rather stronger, and you had to be pretty strong to stand up to his will!

Jessie recalled that 'Mummy found the constant trips up and down on the sleeper quite trying – she suffered from bad nosebleeds and often spent much of the journey in the ladies' room.'[159]

By the late 1950s both Keith Marischal and Park Square East were maintained as immaculate stage-sets for Matthew's public life: 'like a new pin – spotless, with polished floors – he made the ladies take their shoes off, to avoid damaging the wood!' Park Square East was divided fluidly between work and family. Matthew's own office always occupied the large front downstairs room, with RMJM rooms behind and (contrary to the lease) in the basement; the family used the first floor and Aberdonian housekeeper Margaret Hemslie the attic. On Aidan's marriage in July 1958 to Sylvia Cassidy, whom he had met at Michael Hall, the basement of Park Square East was converted to become their first married home, while Aidan completed his training, keeping him within the family orbit; Robert and Sylvia also established a good rapport: 'they'd share crosswords!'[160] Aidan had begun at the AA in 1955, with tutors including James Gowan, John Killick and John Summerson, and married after his third year. On graduating in 1960 he did his year out with Arup Associates, but already the long architectural shadow of his father was falling over him. Sylvia recalled that:

> One aspect of Robert's inability to cope with the family was that he gave little real support to Aidan in his training – although he was very keen that he should succeed ... We lived there for four years, until 1962, in a basement partly shared with the office – and, because this was London in the 1950s, with all the smogs, it was really filthy: you could dust the place, and ten minutes later, enormous lumps of soot would be floating in.

The newlyweds also, on occasion, experienced Robert's quirkish humour, as for example when 'a group of Jehovah's Witnesses knocked on the door upstairs at Park Square East, and my father sent them down to us, saying later, "I thought they'd be interested in you!" That was his idea of a joke – he'd say anything, if he felt like it.'[161] Jessie, in the meantime, attended junior day-schools in St John's Wood and Paddington, and lived more or less full time in London.

But the obligations of a *patronus* also included loyalty to *clientes*, and Matthew was unstinting in his efforts on behalf of old friends, both publicly and behind the scenes. For instance, the late 1950s were a very depressing time for Alan Reiach, with the continuing stagnation of his private practice.[162] Matthew subsequently never lost an opportunity to help Reiach's cause – in 1957, for example, by helping expedite his project for an Edinburgh University Veterinary Field Station (at the Bush) through the University Works Committee.[163] Nor were lesser contacts overlooked either: in March 1957, for example, he endorsed a former Festival Hall assistant's successful town planning appeal against refusal of a vernacular Modernist-style house at Haslemere, Surrey.[164]

This was, however, still a time of transition for Matthew to full establishment status, and in his overall *auctoritas* he still lagged slightly behind some of his contemporaries. Spence, benefiting from his Coventry aura and untainted by the stigma of presumed socialist convictions, had surged forward, becoming RIBA president in 1958–60, and was knighted in 1960. Leslie Martin had also for the moment 'overtaken' Matthew, having been knighted in 1957; he had been able to exploit the prestige of Oxbridge without embroiling himself in the petty financial intricacies of private practice. Matthew could hardly expect such a smooth ride, as public architecture was now sliding in its reputation, and his chosen power base as an architectural statesman was the more diffuse international arena of the IUA.[165]

In pursuing his strategic aims through advances within the Establishment, one of the most vital areas for networking and persuading was the RIBA itself. As one of the key members of Council, Matthew played a central role in facilitating the final victory of the public-architecture-led revolt against gentlemanly private practice hegemony, which had been gathering force during the 1950s. 1950 had witnessed an AGM membership rebellion against the RIBA's learned-society status, and the 1958 AGM saw an unprecedented motion, moved predictably by Cleeve Barr, to censure the council – a 'great revolt', overwhelmingly backed in the subsequent vote, that led to

the replacement of Spragg as Secretary by the 'progressive' Gordon Ricketts, and the establishment of a Constitutional Committee under Barr – all in the same year that saw the Modernist educational triumph of the Oxford conference.[166] Organisationally, the Spence and Holford years seamlessly carried forward this wave of reform, with a growing move towards Civil Service-style departmental organisation of the Institute. By 1960 five Assistant Secretaries had been appointed, heading a range of departments that included a new Information Services Department. In 1959 the old, unwieldy Executive Committee had been replaced by a smaller Policy Committee, and the following year research was started for a far-reaching study of professional organisation, *The Architect and his Office*. In the wake of Ricketts's arrival, 1960 witnessed another adventurous appointment, to the new post of Chief Information Officer – that of Malcolm MacEwen, a public-school-educated, communist journalist, whose wife worked in the LCC Architect's Department. MacEwen was just the kind of individualistic firebrand character that Matthew was well used to dealing with, and the two got on well, as MacEwen began to bring a new verve, and radical socialist slant, to the RIBA's external projection.[167]

Ultimately, the presidencies of both the RIBA and IUA were firmly in Matthew's sights, and although some commitment of time and effort would be required to finally secure them, there was considerable scope for manoeuvre as to how to set about this. Sometimes, those moving towards the RIBA presidency had served a period of apprenticeship in one of the lesser ceremonial posts, as did Spence, for example, as Honorary Secretary from 1956 to 1958; eventually, in the mid 1960s, the vice-presidency would be regularly used in this way. In other cases, such as that of Holford, the individual was of such obviously high Establishment standing that nothing of this kind was needed. Matthew's approach was a pragmatic compromise, reflecting his preference for the reality

Teamwork architecture

rather than the symbols of power.[168] From 1959 he was one of the founding members of the RIBA's new 'cabinet', the nine-strong Policy Committee, four of whose members were *ex officio* and the remaining five – Matthew, Cleeve Barr, Gibson, Gibberd and Denis Clarke Hall – fairly evenly balanced between 'public' and 'private': here, he could directly influence, and accelerate, reformist initiatives such as the 'Office Study'.

Matthew's other main contribution to the RIBA in those years was equally shrewd, as it also advanced his cause within the IUA at the same time. During the late 1950s he took on a major organisational challenge rivalling the Oxford conference in complexity – the coordination of the sixth biennial IUA International Congress, held in London in 1961. Little

could Matthew have suspected, in July 1956, when he was appointed to the UK organising committee for the Congress, that he was in fact embarking on a completely new and increasingly dominant phase of his life – as diplomat, conciliator and bringer of calm reason to tempestuous disputes. Previously, all Matthew's activities had shown some overt sign of forceful personal ambition, but now he was about to launch into a more mature kind of activity that would require him to work with equals on a truly collective basis – while ensuring he would be protected from excessive intimacy by the distancing effect of 'foreignness' and diplomatic courtesy. His Congress commitment would require him to work in close collaboration with the foreign-relations staff of the RIBA, as the host institution.

Originally, in 1956, it had been envisaged that the London Congress would take place in 1959, following the Fifth Congress in Moscow, scheduled for 1957. In late 1956, however, the IUA had been thrown into turmoil by the successive blows of the Soviet invasion of Hungary and the Anglo-French invasion of Suez. Outrage at the first triggered off a forceful move, led by Hungarian-born IUA Secretary Pierre Vago, for an overt condemnation of the USSR by the IUA, on grounds of the 'persecution' of Hungarian architects, and the embarrassment of the second deterred the RIBA from entering the fray: in the words of Bill Ellis to Matthew, 'as the English have equally been censured by UNO as aggressors, we are in no position to take a moral line!'[169] To Matthew, the politicisation of 'professional' debate was a matter of visceral revulsion, and he worked closely with Abercrombie to divert the IUA into the safer ground of humanitarian assistance for endangered architects.[170] Eventually, in August 1957, as a token gesture, it was agreed to defer the Moscow Congress by a year, to 1958, and consequently to defer London also, but by two years, to 1961, in order to return the Congress to odd-numbered years.[171]

In March 1957 Abercrombie suddenly

and unexpectedly died at the age of 77, at his home at Aston Tirrold, Berkshire, shortly after completing a masterplan for Addis Ababa: Matthew wrote to Vago that he had met Abercrombie a week previously, and he had 'seemed to be his usual self'.[172] Matthew had made it clear the previous year that he was not (yet) a potential candidate for the IUA presidency, but he now gave in to pressure from Vago and agreed to become a vice-president, to represent 'the great family of English-speaking countries'. He had already intervened in 1956 within IUA, on behalf of the powerful British architectural journals, to block attempts by Le Corbusier to levy royalties on photographs of his buildings reproduced in Britain.[173] Initially, with the London Congress now pushed slightly back over the horizon, and with the benevolent shadow of Abercrombie removed, Matthew concentrated on widening his own involvements in IUA affairs. In late 1957, however, his main effort was devoted to bolstering RIBA support for the Union. Matthew vigorously and successfully counter-attacked against proposals for drastic cuts in RIBA funding to the IUA, deploying the somewhat nationalistic argument that

> we do not always appreciate the prestige we still enjoy among other countries in cultural and intellectual fields, and I am certain that a perceptible slackening of our interest ... might well have an unfortunate effect in many quarters that hitherto have looked to this country for a lead.

In the lead-up to the Moscow Congress, Matthew, as an *ex officio* member of the Congress steering committee, fought hard to maintain his ideal of political abstinence – for example by dismissing a propaganda brochure sent by the Polish Section about an 'International Institute of Peace' in Vienna. Arthur Ling, still steadfast in his pro-Soviet beliefs, was invited to the conference as a guest of the Soviet section; Matthew (as delegation leader) and Holford accompanied him to Moscow on the RIBA's behalf – perhaps partly acting as chaperones.[174] Aidan and

Sylvia's selection of 16 July for their wedding obliged Matthew, to his annoyance, to interrupt his stay in Moscow in the lead-up to the Congress – which opened with a formal inaugural session, addressed by Construction Minister V Kocherenko, in the Great Hall of the Kremlin on the morning of 21 July – and fly briefly to London and back. The theme of the Congress was an implicitly Euro-centric one of post-war reconstruction (1945–57) – an evaluation of how far the rebuilding efforts had succeeded or not – and Matthew stressed, in his formal message of greeting to Soviet architects, that the post-war pursuit of international goodwill had been the paramount aim of Abercrombie and the other IUA founders. However, a wider global vision was set out in the closing resolution, which demanded creation of a UN commission on habitat – a vital marker for the future trajectory of Matthew's own internationalist efforts.[175]

As it turned out, Moscow was a general turning point in Matthew's emerging ideal of global architectural fellowship. This was not so much because of the formal proceedings, which were dominated by grand sessions in the Assembly Hall of the Socialist Realist skyscraper of Moscow University, receptions in the Kremlin and elsewhere, and papers focusing on Soviet-style expositions of state control of land and building production. Nor was it because of the post-war architecture of Moscow, although Matthew praised the new, Modernist housing schemes such as Noviye Cheryomushki, and even conceded that the Stalin-era skyscrapers were 'dramatic ... elements in the townscape', despite their 'crude and curious' appearance to Western eyes.[176] More important was the scale and cosmopolitanism of the Congress: compared with the 700 at The Hague in 1955, there were 1,500 delegates from 51 countries at Moscow. This rekindled the spirit of Vaumarcus in Matthew with a vengeance, as he emphasised by quoting Burns's 'A man's a man for a' that' in his conference speech of 23 July, which hailed the 'exhilarating' experience of establishing personal friend-

8.29 Exhibition of Soviet town planning at the 1958 IUA Congress. (USSR IUA Section/Gosstroiizdat 1960)

8.30 IUA executive dinner, Lisbon, September 1959: Jessie and Lorna in foreground; Ralph Walker and Henry Churchill (USA) are second and third right of Matthew. (Jacques Blomet Lda., Lisboa)

ships across a stark ideological-cum-military divide. In his report to the RIBA on his return, Matthew lavishly praised Pavel Abrossimov, president of the Soviet organising committee and secretary-general of the USSR Union of Architects, as a 'most genial and indefatigable host' to the UK party, and enthused that 'at a time of extreme international tension' it had been possible for

> capitalist, communist and uncommitted alike, to study and discuss, with a minimum of political bias, and with great friendliness, architectural problems of great importance to mankind ... to learn and make friends, meet personally architects from many countries, whose outlook may be different from our own. This kind of meeting is one of the few bridges over which a flow of understanding is still possible'.[177]

The climax to the Moscow Congress for Matthew, however, came quite unexpectedly, when the 20 members of the executive were invited to a 90-minute meeting with CPSU general secretary Nikita Khrushchev himself – a crucial sign of the Congress's importance within the USSR in legitimising the dethronement of Stalinist monumentalism in favour of a more technocratic ethos, as well as the adoption of Western Modernist planning devices such as the neighbourhood unit. Earlier in the proceedings, leading Soviet architect K Alabyan had repudiated the

'errors' of 'false classicism and schematism', and Khrushchev had already, in 1954, urged the All-Union Conference of Builders and Architects towards an 'all-out drive' for standardised mass production.[178] To someone such as Matthew, by now well accustomed to exercising power in a professional sphere, and mingling easily with the national political-administrative elite within Britain, only a personal encounter with a foreign political or cultural leader of global stature could now count as truly intoxicating. His report on the conference emphasised that this meeting was 'not simply a courtesy call but a detailed give and take on building and reconstruction problems. In spite of the international situation at this time, Khrushchev seemed not in any hurry to get rid of his guests.' The 'relaxed and cheerful' discussion ranged from building prefabrication methods, through the heights of multi-storey blocks, to the general development of Soviet architecture, with Khrushchev vigorous in his denunciation of the 'mistakes' of Moscow University and the old monumental socialist realist set pieces.[179] To Matthew, ever vigorous in defence of professional solidarity, Khrushchev's political criticism of the Soviet architectural profession required some rejoinder, and at a IUA meeting some 12 years later he recalled proudly the little episode that followed, as evidence of the potential symbolic importance of 'architectural diplomacy':

> At the end of the meeting, we rose and shook hands one by one. I wondered, should I say something or not, and I did, as follows: 'Mr Khrushchev, you know as well as we do, that your architectural profession has a great responsibility for the development of your country. It's no good blaming your architects for what they did in the past – they did exactly as they were told.' He looked for a moment – I wondered whether I'd be put up against a wall – and then he broke into a typical Khrushchev chuckle, and we passed on. Afterwards, I asked the Russian architects if I had made an appalling

gaffe – but, as it turned out, that meeting, and possibly my intervention, did in fact strengthen their hand.[180]

Ever since his LCC days Matthew had enjoyed the status of an honest broker between communist architects and planners in Britain, and the Establishment as broadly defined. After his return from Moscow that status was further enhanced, especially given his wide range of new friends among Soviet architects. These links, of course, only further alienated traditionally minded people in the architectural establishment, which in turn provoked Matthew – with his instinctive intransigence in the face of opposition, and despite his lack of political sympathy for communism – to make even more explicit gestures of conciliation. In 1958 he attended several post-Congress reunions of pro-communist architects in London, and acted as prime mover behind a 'Moscow evening' at the RIBA in January 1959; Percy Johnson-Marshall, still at the LCC, wrote excitedly to him asking for 'news of your old Moskwa days'. Yet behind the scenes Matthew was cautious, and confidentially warned one of his RMJM assistants to avoid becoming caught up in Percy's political 'schemes'.[181] He established himself and Lorna as fall-back hosts for visiting parties of Soviet architects, including not only the major 1959 delegation but a further group of 40 in March 1961, and yet more (including his friend Professor Nikolai Kolli – Le Corbusier's assistant on the Tsentrosoyuz building) during the IUA Congress in July 1961. In late 1959, just after the successful Soviet visit to Edinburgh, Matthew worked closely with Pavel Abrossimov to secure the accession of both Germanies simultaneously to the IUA – a double membership almost unparalleled among international cultural organisations. And in May 1961, on hearing of Pavel's unexpected death, he wrote both to the USSR Union of Architects and to his widow Valentina, hailing the late president as 'a tower of strength to the international union'. Yet almost in the same breath he emphasised

his political neutrality by writing to the South African Institute of Architects of his 'delight' at South Africa's impending accession to the IUA.[182]

Like Bobby Hunter of Cumnock, people such as Abrossimov, Kolli and Vago were Matthew's substitute for close personal friends – people he could respect for their achievements and ideals, but who were sufficiently 'other' from his day-to-day life to pose no threat of trespassing on his emotional privacy. Some years later he spoke with affection of the IUA executive in those days:

8.31 IUA executive meeting, Lisbon, 1958: from right to left: Robert Matthew; Henry Churchill (of the USA); Prof. Jan Zachwatowicz (the renowned Polish conservationist, and mastermind of the post-war reconstruction of Warsaw). (Jacques Blomet Lda., Lisboa)

The impression given by the group was a powerful one. In Pierre Vago, I saw we had a dedicated man, with whom I for one could easily work, and did work closely for more than 20 years. The members of the executive, representing their own countries, had considerable individuality ... and yet all seemed to have a resolve to stick together whatever difficulties might arise.[183]

But, fellowship and pleasantries aside, from September 1958 Matthew became preoccupied with the far more specific and challenging task of chairing the organising committee for the Sixth Congress, which was to be held in London from 3 to 7 July 1961, with preceding Executive and General Assembly meetings from 28 June to 2 July at the RIBA. The conference secretariat was directed by Building Centre director Gontran Goulden, who was vice chairman of the organising committee, supported by Malcolm MacEwen as publicity coordinator and Diana Mead as 'social secretary'. Between September 1958 and May 1961 Matthew attended no less than 17 full meetings of the main organising

Teamwork architecture

(top) **8.32** Robert Matthew escorts Anthony Armstrong-Jones to the opening ceremony of the IUA congress in the Royal Festival Hall, 3 July 1963. (Barratts Photo Press)

(middle) **8.34** General view from south of the 1961 IUA Congress buildings on London's South Bank: the exhibition building is on the left, the Congress HQ on the right. (Organizing Committee of 6th IUA Congress)

(bottom) **8.33** Prince Philip talking to Sir William Holford, Pierre Vago (behind Holford) and Matthew in the IUA Congress Exhibition Pavilion, 6 July 1961. (Organizing Committee of 6th IUA Congress)

committee, and – just as with the post-October 1948 organisation of the Festival Hall project – oversaw a complex range of delegated activities, beginning with the selection of the venue, which rapidly headed in a very familiar direction.[184]

Already, in July 1957, Matthew had impressed on Vago that the London conference, unlike Moscow, should concentrate on 'discussion' rather than 'solemn receptions', and he now pushed for a maximum of plenary sessions to increase opportunities for debate – with the result that the Royal Festival Hall itself, as London's only modern hall of over 2,000 capacity, was selected as the plenary conference venue. It would be supported by two large, prefabricated, temporary buildings adjacent to each other: an exhibition hall, and an administrative building on the site of the 1951 Dome of Discovery, constructed of aluminium, steel framing, asbestos sheeting, and roof formed of pyramids on a space deck.[185] The theme of the Congress, as appropriate to the prefabricated construction of these buildings, was 'The Architecture of Technology'.[186] Matthew secured the appointment of architect Theo Crosby as designer of the integral exhibition, but soon a difference of opinion emerged over its implementation. Crosby, determined to avoid 'the sheer boredom of the standard IUA show', with its miscellany of displays by individual countries, proposed a largely unified design, around the time-honoured theme of the synthesis of art with technology and manufacturing: the main sub-groups were 'Materials' and 'Possibilities'. Eventually, a combination of national contributions and UK coordination was agreed, with supporting students' exhibition: Dennis Sharp recalled that 'as students we had not seen anything like it since the "This is Tomorrow" exhibition at the Whitechapel Gallery in 1956.'[187]

The RIBA helped organise a full-time conference staff of 10, and co-organised a parallel exhibition at the Arts Council on 1956–61 building achievements, 'Architecture Today'.[188] Lewis Mumford was also to receive the RIBA Gold Medal in person from Matthew at the conference. There were difficulties, too, over speakers, with Mumford and Pevsner declining invitations to speak: eventually, US historian Henry-Russell Hitchcock and the Polish architect Jerzy Hryniewiecki (editor of *Project* magazine) were secured instead, with J M Richards acting as rapporteur-general, summing up the proceedings in a final session at the Festival Hall. Social events included: an 'ice-breaking' visit by each foreign delegate to a British architect; an array of evening receptions, including a 'huge and boisterous party' hosted by Spence at the Building Centre, with 'English cheeses served in great variety'; and an afternoon party for 3,000 (requiring a fleet of coaches) at the Cement and Concrete Association research establishment at Wexham Springs. Requests for participation in the conference by an 'International Institute for Peace' were politely rebuffed by Matthew, who had been tipped off by Gordon Ricketts that 'the Foreign Office tell me this is a thorough-going copper-bottomed communist-controlled organisation on the best Russian lines.'[189]

At first, there were severe resource problems, stemming largely from the financial difficulties of the RIBA, which had a mortgage of over £40,000 and a reserve of £5,000 in its development fund, while the cost of the Congress was £10,000; it had been determined that financial 'break-even' could be attained at the Moscow figure of 1,500 delegates.[190] Eventually, however, although the Moscow delegate total was substantially exceeded, with 1,811 delegates from 65 countries attending, the RIBA still had to make up a £4,000 deficit. The anticipated debates on technology (and its synthesis with art) were to be channelled through a fiendishly complex hierarchy of meetings, with plenary sessions followed by debates in separate working groups and comment sessions for national groups: Richards's overview speech as rapporteur-general mischievously noted, in Thucydidean fashion, that 'it is difficult to resist the temptation to include, in my summary, contributions that ought to have been made, even if they were not, since no one listening to me knew what had been said at the meetings of other groups than their own.'[191] Of the three main speakers, Hitchcock offered a his-

torical survey of modern construction, Nervi an overview of the future, and Hryniewicki an analysis of industrialisation. The tone of the sessions varied, with Nervi, for example, talking in exalted terms of the 'sublime serenity' of the 'ideal forms' derived from technological advance, and arguing that this offered 'an efficacious method of promoting universal brotherhood', but architect David Rock scorning this 'grand talk' as 'a lot of rubbish ... a waste of time for the British architect'.[192] Summing up, Richards claimed that the conference had achieved a 'higher intellectual standard' than its predecessors, owing to the opportunity it gave for utopian debate about 'the technological potential of modern architecture'.[193] But, in the end, the attempt to distance the London conference from Moscow and the others by generating a more intellectually stimulating atmosphere, within the convoluted organisational framework needed for IUA events, seemed to have succeeded only imperfectly: in his official concluding message as RIBA president, Holford conceded that 'our discussions did lack the cut and thrust of continuous debate', and that the Congress would be 'inevitably remembered more for the social and personal contacts ... than for the formal discussions'.[194]

With the 1961 Congress successfully under way, Matthew was able to relax. Nearly ten years later, at his RIBA Gold Medal presentation, he recalled fondly the final evening conference party on 7 July, at the RIBA – organised by E D Jefferiss Matthews – as the time that

brought the fullest life to this building in which I have spent so many hours, with so many people ... from top to bottom, the RIBA was transformed: tents on the roof, bands playing, a multitude of tongues, gaiety and lights everywhere – the building full to capacity and more. During the course of the evening, I slipped up the street, brought my small daughter out of her bed, and took her to the top landing of the side staircase, and we stood watching the colourful throngs. Maybe she has already forgotten this – but many of us have not.

The party, with a bar or buffet in virtually every room, continued until 3 a.m., presided over by the Matthews and the Holfords: in his letter of thanks to Matthew a month after the Congress, Nic Kolli of the USSR singled out for thanks Lorna and his family, and 'particularly the nice little dancing girl'.[195]

With this substantial achievement under his belt, Matthew now began to reap the rewards. He was duly elected as IUA President, with effect from the Executive Committee meeting the day after the conference ended. The question of the RIBA presidency also began to surface. At the June 1959 RIBA Executive Committee meeting Cleeve Barr, Brett and Ling had proposed Matthew for the vice-presidency, followed two years later by the presidency itself, but Matthew turned down this plan, citing the huge time commitment involved in the presidency. Barr reported that, after the executive meeting, 'in a brief and friendly chat with Basil ... I let fall the thought, no doubt in a stupid and unguarded manner – that I understood that you had agreed to stand for President the following year'. That rumour, Barr explained, had originated with Stirrat Marshall, who had now retracted it, so that 'now I feel I have rather made a goose of myself'. But nonetheless 'a number of us, including the chaps mentioned above, and Percy, feel that you really owe it to the profession, and that you could make a tremendous contribution to the office.'[196] To appear to push himself forwards for any position, however, was anathema to Matthew; he would have to be asked, and for the moment his support base within the RIBA was still slightly too narrow and too left-wing in character for that. In preference to taking on the vice-presidency, he continued working on a range of key committees – the IUA UK and 1961 conference committees, and the RIBA Policy, Education, Royal Gold Medal and Commonwealth committees. Eventually, in February 1962, the anticipated summons

came, and Ricketts wrote asking, 'Would you think it too early to have a word about the Presidency over lunch? It is a two-year sentence, and hard work at that.'[197]

We shall trace in Chapters 9 and 11 the outcome of Matthew's influential presidencies of the two organisations. Already, however, he was trying to pursue the two linked causes that would dominate his work as an elder statesman in the 1960s – the quest for an architectural contribution to the global causes of better low-cost housing and settlement planning, and the drive to bring the countries of the former British Empire – many, themselves, with the severest problems of housing – into full participation in international architectural affairs. In the first area, low-cost housing (increasingly, since CIAM 1947, referred to by architects as 'habitat'), it was recognised by the IUA from the very beginning that the UN would be an essential collaborator, and in September 1959 Henry S Churchill, the IUA's permanent delegate to the UN, informed the IUA General Assembly in Lisbon of a 'UN Long Term Programme for Concerted International Action in the Field of Low Cost Housing and Related Community Facilities' – a convoluted name that hinted at the bureaucratic tangle in which the initiative would remain stifled, after a decade and a half's effort. At first, a working party was set up to liaise with the UN Bureau of Social Affairs, including Matthew, Vouga, Abrossimov, Steen Eiler Rasmussen of Denmark and Jean Dubuisson of France, and a range of demonstration projects and regional studies was proposed. By October 1961 Churchill was already disillusioned, and wrote to Matthew that 'this whole pursuit of the UN makes little sense'; the following month Vago wrote advising Matthew not to 'waste your time' with the meetings of experts and government bureaucrats: 'true architects like you and me cannot afford the luxury of spending 25 days in vain discussion'.[198]

Matthew's other main international 'cause', his drive to embrace the

Commonwealth countries, met with far more immediate success. Partly, it stemmed from his own family background, steeped since childhood in a combination of post-imperialism and pacifist internationalism, including Geddes's strand of cultural cosmopolitanism – all of which left Matthew with that characteristic post-war combination of residual paternalism and emancipatory idealism. And, partly, it stemmed from Vago's discontent, in the mid 1950s, with those countries' non-representation in IUA. In 1957 Matthew suggested that the Commonwealth countries' abstention might stem from a feeling that the IUA was too Eurocentric, and that they instead 'look very much to the RIBA for a lead in many matters'.[199]

In general, the 1950s were a time of gradual, rather than revolutionary, transformation in architectural attitudes across the Commonwealth, with developments still dominated by Britain and the white dominions. Part of the impetus for change came from the rationalistic ethos of the Modern Movement: in planning, the old race-based imperial expansionism had, by the 1940s, been replaced in countries such as Australia and New Zealand by a professional planning movement committed to a Geddes-like survey/plan framework, and in building construction the BRS in 1948 took the lead, through George Atkinson, in setting up a colonial liaison service and publishing *Tropical Building Studies*.[200] The design of 1950s tropical architecture in the Commonwealth was dominated by British-based forms such as Architects' Co-Partnership or Max Fry and Jane Drew, whose 1956 book, *Tropical Architecture in the Humid Zones*, argued in the language of 1930s–1950s Modernist regionalism that a vernacular Modernism, 'reflecting the society and climate of tropical countries', had been successfully achieved, and now needed only to be generally proselytised. In Africa, where European domination of architecture was at its strongest, the beginnings of a shift away came with the 1957 independence of Ghana, whose first leader, Kwame Nkrumah, had already (as

government head since 1951) initiated an ambitious modernisation programme enthused by humanist socialism, including construction of a new, Modernist, College of Technology at Kumasi – designed by James Cubitt & Partners.[201] There would be a decisive shift in attitude only with the emergence of a new generation of African architects, such as Nigeria's Oluwole Olumuyiwa (1929– 2000), who, following training in Manchester (1949–54) and work with ACP, returned home in 1958 to open the first ethnic Nigerian private practice at the same time as co-founding the NIA – initially closed to expatriates.

As a private individual working under his Edinburgh University academic affiliation, Matthew assiduously fostered links with the former imperial territories. In 1959, for instance, he encouraged the Scottish-born architect of the Hong Kong Housing Authority, J R Firth, to coordinate the 97-strong Hong Kong Society of Architects' affiliation to the IUA: Firth wrote that the colony's housing problem was so acute that he might have to cease being an architect and 'become a sausage manufacturer instead!' In fact, the Housing Authority went on, over the following 40 years, to orchestrate the most remarkable and vigorous multi-storey housing drive in the world, and Matthew continued his long-standing work as external examiner for Professor W G Gregory's course at Hong Kong University, and delivered a repeat of his 1960 RICS paper on tall buildings at a golden jubilee conference of the university in September 1961.[202]

One of the most high-profile routes for international architectural outreach was provided by international architectural competitions, a field in which the IUA increasingly sought to intervene and foster a regulatory role for itself. Here, Matthew's IUA connections gave him a head start, but the results could prove frustrating in practice. For example, in 1960, in a former British-dominated territory beyond the strict Commonwealth, Matthew was nominated as IUA representative (and only non-Arab member) on a

Teamwork architecture

8.35 Matthew seen at work on the competition jury for the National Museum of Kuwait, 1960. (EULMC)

competition jury for a new national museum of Kuwait. After a four-day judging session in Kuwait, the 'brilliant and original' scheme by Michel Ecochard of Paris – which envisaged a vast, parasol-like shelter structure – was selected: Ecochard's credentials as a Western–Arab mediator were strengthened by his early 1950s Moroccan work on vernacular-based housing typologies with 'ATBAT-Afrique'. The competition, however, ended in acrimony when Ecochard's fees were not paid.[203] There could also be compensations for competition involvement, as Matthew found especially in 1957 when, on IUA recommendation, he was appointed a member of the jury for the international monument for the Qaid-e-Azam Monument at Karachi, a highly symbolic structure to house the mausoleum of Mohamed Ali Jinnah, founder of the Pakistani state. Within Pakistan, the IUA was guided chiefly by the newly formed (1957) Institute of Architects, Pakistan, and especially by its enthusiastic young Secretary, Zahir-ud-Din Khwaja, a Bombay- and Liverpool-trained senior architect in the government's central Public Works Department. Working with advice from member Pier Luigi Nervi, whose ability to instantly assess the structural viability of any proposal greatly impressed Matthew, the high-powered jury eventually selected in February 1958,

out of the 57 entries, a daring design by London architect Raglan Squire. This avoided any suggestion of solid monumentality by proposing an ethereal cluster of hyperbolic paraboloid canopies, based on an earlier unrealised project for a cathedral portico in Bangalore, and here clad in gold mosaic, with pale blue undersides, with 'traditional Moghul' marble tiled flooring and terraced landscaping around. The Karachi story ended in debacle, however, when Jinnah's elderly sister, who controlled the funds for the project, intervened to insist on a more traditional architectural expression, and Squire withdrew from the commission. Eventually, a more traditionally monumental structure was built by another architect, Yahya Merchant of Bombay.[204] Despite the frustrating outcome of the competition itself, the contacts made by Matthew in Pakistan would eventually lead to a major personal commission to plan part of the country's new capital, Islamabad – whose first chief architect-planner would be none other than Zahir-ud-Din himself (see Chapters 11 and 13).

At this stage, architects such as Fry and Drew, Raglan Squire and Leo de Syllas (1917–64) of Architects' Co-partnership (an ex-editor of *Focus*) still had a far longer track record of involvement than Matthew in overseas building projects. But for many Commonwealth architects Matthew was nevertheless now becoming a key initial point of 'networking' contact in the UK.[205] And increasingly, as we shall see in the following chapters, he was beginning to focus on the possibility of a more concerted institutional reform to bring the Commonwealth countries into the global architectural field.

Section IV

Modernism Ascendant

Chapter 9

Architect to the Welfare State, 1962–8

Architecture today is more than an art, ... it is a service to the client and to the community. Our task now is to do everything possible to ensure that this service achieves the highest possible levels in design, teaching and management.

Robert Matthew, November 1962[1]

Public and family life in the 1960s

From the early 1960s Matthew decisively entered a new phase in his life, largely casting off day-to-day involvement in RMJM work in the UK and the Edinburgh University department, and throwing himself into a new, intense concentration on architectural 'diplomatic' tasks, as well as some completely new challenges – including the start of a commission to mastermind the replanning of the devolved statelet of Northern Ireland. He explained to his family that 'you don't want to go on with any one thing for ages – for more than about ten years – so, for example, he eased himself gradually out of the university.'[2]

The start of this new phase was signalled formally by the award of a knighthood: Lorna and Jessie accompanied Robert to the investiture ceremony at 10.15 on 13 February 1962 at Buckingham Palace. Donald Gibson, now chief architect to the War Office, was knighted on the same day, and the two exchanged congratulatory notes: both of them, with their former 'socialist' associations, had clearly been somewhat overtaken in the honours stakes by private or academic

practitioners. Among the avalanche of congratulations, some acknowledged the implicit snub: Bill Allen wrote that the award was 'very belated, of course, but thank goodness it came at last'.[3] But, in any case, Matthew was not greatly interested in 'domestic' honours. Aidan recalled that

he did appreciate the awards by foreign architectural societies, but the knighthood, although it had a nice ring, concerned him less: it was my mother who was *very* keen on it. What he liked was not the trappings and titles, but power itself, the power to change things![4]

Despite these slight tensions and differences of emphasis, the 'public architectural' elite to which Matthew belonged

9.1 Jessie, Robert and Lorna Matthew seen outside Buckingham Palace following Robert's knighthood ceremony on 13 February 1963. (EULMC)

JESSIE ANN MATTHEW
19. FEB. 1962
24 PARK SQ. E. LONDON

PAPA AT THE PALACE
(KT) 13 FEB 1962
(from a photo.)

PRINTED IN GREAT BRITAIN

Jo   daddy
from - Jessie Ann
Feb 1962

9.2 February 1962 drawing by Jessie, inscribed on back by Robert Matthew. (EULMC)

individual establishment events, such as the royal opening of New Zealand House in May 1963, where Matthew escorted the Queen up to the panoramic penthouse terrace to inspect the view over the royal park. Matthew's RIBA presidency, in particular, fuelled his return to a position of comfortably supported power in London, for the first time since his LCC days – complete with a fully fledged personal secretary. To allow him to run his IUA and RIBA presidencies in parallel with his other work, and use 24 Park Square East as an extension of Portland Place, the RIBA paid for the employment of a retired Indian army officer and noted polo player, Lt Col Patrick Massey, MC, to serve from mid 1962 as his 'personal assistant'. Working from Park Square East, the 'tall, distinguished' Massey, with his 'smart coat and upper-crust accent', helped with a range of tasks, ranging from the strictly architectural to taking Jessie to school. Massey's London-based employment ended in mid 1965, but by then, during 1964, with the shift in his family life towards Edinburgh, Matthew had himself engaged a private secretary, Cicely Naismith, to work for him at Regent Terrace: she remained continuously in this role until December 1975 (including several months helping put his papers in order after his death). During Massey's time with Matthew a system of 'VIP support' was developed for him, including, for example, standardised forms to provide background information in compiling lecture texts or concerning the personalities and activities of host institutions.[6] The process was carried much further with the 'amazingly efficient' Naismith, who 'organised his entire life', allowing Matthew to subtly distance himself from both practice and university. Cicely was 'like a nanny, really – he was constantly ringing her, especially when he was on holiday, to find out what he was doing.'[7]

At first glance, the six or seven years from 1962 might have seemed to represent the peak of Matthew's commitment to meetings and committees, to 'talking' rather than 'doing' or 'designing'. It also

had now passed into a period of general ascendancy, and mutual reinforcement in facing the outside world.[5] This camaraderie – with its overtones, for Matthew, of an extended family – also had interdisciplinary tentacles, for example to include engineer Ove Arup, who wrote to Matthew in May 1965 to thank him for the 'heroic' gesture of flying down for his 70th birthday party in London, and catching the sleeper back up immediately afterwards.[6] Having cleared this hurdle of establishment respectability, however, honours and presidencies rained down on Matthew thick and fast: alongside his IUA presidency of 1961–5, he became RIBA president for the two years from July 1962, and then, in immediate succession, founder president of a new post-imperial body, the Commonwealth Association of Architects, serving for two terms in 1965–9.[7] There were also

represented, like his LCC years, a time when he became relatively less engaged with Scottish affairs, and more focused again on London activity. Had he, then, become bored with university politics and routine private practice, only to plunge still further into mundane organisational work? In reality, the reverse was true. First, in the targeting of his 'works', the committee work of the 1960s was a logical intermediate step in his evolution from someone concerned with specific projects, in the 1950s, to someone concerned mainly with an idealistic and even utopian sense of 'mission', in the 1970s. Second, in the development of his own character: just as, in the late 1930s, Matthew's official persona as government official had concealed a private world of merriment and eccentricity, so now his travels and cosmopolitan contacts allowed him to cultivate the acquaintance of more individualistic, flamboyant figures, such as Constantinos Doxiadis or Buckminster Fuller. His role as an analytical, drily humorous foil to more fiery characters was now a well-established one: as Guy Oddie, his successor as Edinburgh professor, put it, 'His penetrating mind liked to have a strange situation to bite on.'[8]

But not everything stood still: somewhat to his regret, perhaps, there was an imperceptible shift in Matthew's social profile, towards the standing of a 'very distinguished-looking' elder statesman; he spoke with regret in 1963, for example, of 'my lamentable girth'.[9] In some ways, his life now was more nomadic than ever. And certainly, during the RIBA presidency, he was almost permanently in London or abroad, travelling all the time and snatching odd moments of sleep where he could. Aidan argued that 'he *didn't* exist on four hours' sleep, contrary to appearances – he needed his eight hours, and got it, but in little bits.'[10] However prodigious Matthew's capacity for self-discipline, his lifestyle was highly stressful, with periods of intense exertion coupled with sedentary phases and irregular eating habits, varying from official banquets to spartan

snacking on the move; whether or not it contributed to his premature death in 1975 is unclear. Mentally, too, behind the calm, controlled front, stresses were constantly at work. For instance, Aidan recalled that

although he projected himself as a decisive man of action, in fact he was always putting things off, tasks like writing speeches or getting a grip on a problematic project. In those kinds of things, he was incredibly indecisive and unsure. He used his abstract mind-games, above all, as escape devices to allow him to put things off. He would sometimes spend hours putting on the lawn at Keith, with twenty or so golf balls. And where you or I could just break off if we needed, he would have to carry on to the bitter end, sometimes for four hours or more!

Other pastimes included 'playing the piano endlessly, painting, sketching, reading, doing crosswords, and, of course, watching the Test matches – he'd call the offices, say he was at a meeting, draw the curtains and stay inside all day.' Only on holidays could he really relax, 'spending long periods floating on his back in a swimming pool'.[11]

The apparent shift away from Scotland in Matthew's own professional activities was counterbalanced, from the early 1960s, by a significant and permanent shift in the family's residential patterns towards the Edinburgh area. In 1962, coinciding with the establishment of Matthew's RIBA 'secretariat' in Park Square East, Aidan left Arup and signed up for a one-year civic design course at Edinburgh. He and Sylvia vacated the basement flat and moved to Edinburgh,

9.3 Charcoal abstract drawing of 1962 by Robert Matthew. (EULMC)

where they initially stayed in the attic flat at 31 Regent Terrace, and at the end of the year Aidan decided to join RMJM – despite attempts at dissuasion by Sylvia, who attributed the decision to Robert's 'overpowering' personality. After a year's travel in the USA, researching American work practices for the firm (see below), Aidan and Sylvia settled permanently in Edinburgh.[12] Equally important was the fact that after Jessie had spent several years at day school in London, in 1964 Lorna decided to send her to Oxenfoord Castle School, and accordingly began to base herself far more at Keith – with Margaret Hemslie keeping matters in order at Park Square East, always in readiness to receive unexpected guests to stay or to a meal. However far away Robert travelled, Jessie's welfare and progress were never far from his thoughts: as early as 1968, for example, he began making preliminary enquiries at Sadler's Wells Theatre in London about possible courses in stage design.[13] Increasingly, although the family maintained their peripatetic lifestyle in general, Keith Marischal and Park Square East became somewhat polarised in character. Especially after Jessie's move to Oxenfoord, no. 24 became more clearly Robert's domain, and 'perpetually full of architects, from all over the world, staying for a night, coming for a meal'. It was now fully fitted out in a somewhat stately and 'masculine' style, with strongly coloured carpets, antique or modern Danish furniture, and 'folk' pieces collected from abroad – a relatively conventional 'Modern Movement' juxtaposition of the modern and the vernacular.[14]

The same 'masculine' character applied, to a lesser extent, at Regent Terrace, whereas Keith was dominated by more informal, collage-type juxtapositions of unusual 'junk furniture'. Needless to say, all these interiors were largely the work of Lorna, who chose most of the furniture: 'She had, if anything, a rather better eye than Robert, and, of the two of them, was the one who "created" the houses.' The two front rooms in the east, tower-house part of

Keith were fitted out as Robert's 'territory'.[15] They were reached by a door off a separate turnpike stair, whereas Lorna occupied and used the main sequence of first-floor rooms as her territory, all facing south over the garden, including the main drawing room, and the room to its east, with an iron staircase down to the garden. It was at this stage that Lorna came into her element as a coordinator of an at times chaotic and unpredictable social life.[16] By the early 1960s, whereas Regent Terrace and Park Square East, with their public representational function, had considerable modernising efforts lavished on them, Keith Marischal was still in a state of some dilapidation, including primitive kitchen facilities.[17] When staying at Keith, Matthew in effect followed the well-trodden pattern of intellectual urban bohemianism, shunning 'county' or landed social activity, but instead continuing to focus on his established professional extended community. During the 1960s William Gordon became an increasing fixture at Keith, as well as designing tiles for the kitchen at Park Square East.[18]

Perhaps more emotionally important to Matthew was the mosaic of friendships built up cumulatively over the now nearly two decades of life as a public figure in the world of architecture. In a testimony to the continuing battle between self-control and emotion, he displayed a dogged loyalty, without regard for practical career advantage, to a range of often maverick people from his past. In 1965–7, for example, he devoted immense effort to masterminding a campaign to win a public honour for the 82-year-old Clough Williams-Ellis – by that stage, a wildly unfashionable and eccentric figure. Undeterred by Harold Wilson's opposition to knighting someone so elderly and ill, Matthew bombarded housing minister Richard Crossman with forcefully worded letters, hailing Ellis as 'one of the major influences in educating public opinion on ... the creation and preservation of quality of environment'; but it was only under the post-1970 Tory administration, in 1972, that Ellis was finally knighted – at the age of nearly 90![19]

With the exception of Matthew's special bond with Jessie Ann, he continued to feel more comfortable in such friendships than with the more insistently immediate relationships of close family. His relationship with Stuart, for example, remained a strained one: the latter had, with apparently fateful inevitability, by around 1962 followed his father's precedent, by becoming mired in a succession of nervous breakdowns and disabling illnesses, which culminated in 1963 in a period of voluntary confinement and electric-shock treatment in the Crichton Royal Hospital, Dumfries.[20] Eventually, Stuart's relations with Robert began to resemble, in more benign form, their father's relationship to Lorimer: a slightly resentful dependence on the one hand, and, on the other, an impatient but not unkind dominance. As we shall see later, Robert after 1963 in effect took over Stuart's office and most of his staff, and thereafter kept Stuart supplied with a succession of small jobs, including virtually all design work for personal or family projects. He was more cautious with external commissions, after embarrassments with jobs abandoned half done by Stuart made it necessary for RMJM to step in and save the day. Alongside these architectural odd-jobs, Stuart's eclectic and fitfully active character led him into a range of other activities, including starting an antiques business, helping in the establishment of St Mary's Music School and, in the late 1960s, more bizarrely, setting up his own pop group.[21] Some of the family work passed to Stuart concerned minor alterations at Keith or Regent Terrace, a category of work attended by frustrations for the dependent Stuart. He recalled that:

I did up various bits of Keith for Robert, and once, in the early 1960s, I put a fireplace into one very fine room, for burning logs – the kind of fireplace used by Lorimer & Matthew, and also exactly the kind we had in our own cottage, at Vorlich, Loch Earn. You had to put in the logs at 45

degrees, which was slightly unusual. Robert said, 'It's no good, it doesn't work!' I told him how to do it, but he was so pig-headed, he wouldn't even try. He wanted it to remain that it wouldn't work, as he'd said, and he didn't want to see it working![22]

Keith Ingram

The most important 'family' initiative of the 1960s – in whose beginnings Stuart played a central role – was the decision to set up an Edinburgh-based company and shop specialising in interior design, furnishing and crafts. Named Keith Ingram (the 'Ingram' being one of Lorna's forebears), it was founded in 1963, initially at the instigation of Robert and Stuart, in order to provide Stuart, following his recent breakdown, with an easily manageable occupation, but very soon passed mainly into the sphere of influence of the female members of the Matthew family; indeed, from the start, one aim was also to provide an outlet for Lorna's collecting of exotic crafts objects on foreign trips. Stuart recalled that 'I went out to Keith one day and said "I'd like to start a shop," and Robert said he'd been thinking the same way.' For Robert, the idea would potentially help compensate for the failure of Keith Marischal to develop into a Taliesin-style atelier.[23] Although there was never any formal 'business plan', the initial aim, anticipating the Habitat fashion, was to establish 'the first real boutiquey shop in Edinburgh', with a dual focus of activity: sale of commissioned or imported objects, including furniture, ceramics, carpets, clothes and toys; and design and supply of new furniture and fittings for architectural clients, especially (but not exclusively) RMJM – who provided the initial finance for the venture, along with personal loans from Robert himself totalling some £11,000.[24]

In early 1963 Stuart set about looking for premises, and found two shops at 124–6 Rose Street, one being an old bottle store. After a 'small fortune' had been spent clearing out the bottles, Stuart designed the shop, with RMJM help in

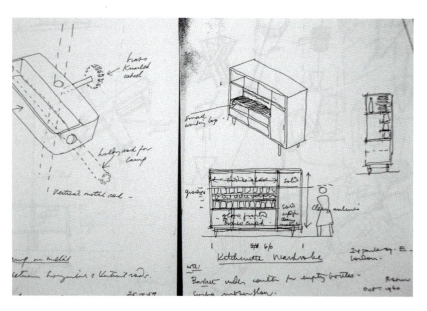

9.4 Sketches of 1959–60 by Matthew for furniture and fittings. (EULMC)

preparing drawings (June 1963), and found a part-time actress, Betty Davies, to help run it. Alan Wightman recalled that 'in the Edinburgh office one day in 1963, someone said, "Do you know, I've just passed the place where Keith Ingram is going to open next week, and there was Robert Matthew on his knees, setting up the window dressing!"' Although financed by RMJM, Robert and Stuart, as architects, could not be involved as directors; instead Lorna and the family solicitor, Maurice Kidd, were named. Initially, Robert and Stuart themselves designed ranges of prototype objects: some sketches by Robert date from as early as 1959–60, but the bulk of his surviving sketches are dated August 1963 (many done in the Royal Station Hotel, York). They show numerous permutations of objects such as lamp stands, bookshelves, chairs and glass jugs – the furniture all in a Modernist variant of the time-honoured Puginian/Arts and Crafts approach, with exaggeratedly articulated or 'honest' construction in contrasting materials.[25] These designs, as with Matthew's later efforts at tensegrity structures, were a three-dimensional offshoot of his fascination with doodling and other abstract mental-recuperation activities, exploiting his still phenomenal memory. The latter ranged from charcoal drawings, in which he made no claim to anything other than derivative status, to

magazine puzzles, such as that of the *Scientific American*, and newspaper crosswords, usually done in his head without filling them in.[26]

Eventually, the serious business of designing furniture for large-scale production was entrusted largely to a newly formed furniture section within RMJM with RCA-trained industrial designers Harold Medd and Edward Willcock. Some of the RMJM contracts were quite big – for example, including much of the furniture for the Royal Commonwealth Pool (1967–70) and for student residences at York and Stirling universities. Unlike Matthew's own idiosyncratic efforts, these more corporately designed products stood four-square in the mainstream design of Modernist workplace furniture and office systems, exemplified since the late 1930s by firms such as Herman Miller and designers such as Charles and Ray Eames, George Nelson and others.[27] By 1965 direction of the Keith Ingram business had effectively passed into the hands of Sylvia Matthew, who, 'looking for something to do' in Scotland following her and Aidan's return from their USA–China tour, from which they sent back crates of rugs and other objects (see Chapter 11), first became involved with buying, and then became managing director of the firm. Helped by a talented young assistant, Dorothy MacAlister, 'who had a natural sense of design and kept the displays constantly varied', Sylvia steadily expanded the shop business until, following redevelopment of the original Rose Street shop in the late 1960s, Keith Ingram moved to a larger shop at 39 Frederick Street. But the financing was precarious and the firm always ran on overdrafts, and by the early 1970s, as we shall see, with competition from Habitat and declining interest on Sylvia's part, it was decided to wind up the company.[28]

Generally speaking, the mid and late 1960s were a time of relative affluence for Matthew and his family, and thoughts began to turn gradually to the tax implications of that position. Mary Tindall recalled that, as early as 1957, she had

Modern Architect

'bumped into Robert in Princes Street one day, and he invited me to join him and Max Fry for a drink at the Café Royal, where they sat and discussed income tax, and the way you had to "throw money at the Exchequer".' The position grew more complicated during the early 1960s, with a host of overlapping benefits and liabilities. On the one hand, the lifestyle of Matthew and his family was still substantially supported by RMJM. Even after John Richards and Kenneth Graham became partners (paying Matthew £8,000 each for the privilege, partly in the form of five-year overdrafts guaranteed by him), he still received a substantial gross annual income from the firm. This rose to a freak maximum of £32,000 in 1963, owing to overpayment of fees for a hospital project in Newcastle, but settled at around £13,000 a year in the later 1960s. This was supplemented until 1968 by his £6,000 gross university salary, but punitive taxation slashed his net (spendable) income to around £8,000. This was offset, however, by numerous RMJM 'perks'. In a typical month, such as May 1967, Matthew drew his regular £400 from the firm to transfer to his personal bank account, supplemented with about £100 of other expenses – house insurances, car repairs, telephone bills, milk, theatre tickets, parking fines, valet services, flowers and housekeeping.[29] This picture was not wildly out of keeping with Matthew's contemporaries: for example, in correspondence with Hugh Casson in 1966, it emerged that Casson's net annual income from his practice was £5,000, with university teaching income in addition.[30] On the other hand, there were also massive potential liabilities, as Matthew was the legal part-owner of several of the properties owned by the practice. A detailed evaluation in February 1965 by the company accountant valued his total aggregate estate at £80,000, including Keith Marischal (£13,200 plus £3,000 contents) and Regent Terrace (£9,300 plus £2,500 contents), the contents of Park Square East (£4,000), £10,000 of life assurances, a £27,000 share in RMJM properties, and a £19,300

share in the firm's financial assets; against the assets were counted a £6,500 mortgage on Keith Marischal and £2,150 in overdrafts.[31]

Thus, while Matthew's predominant contribution to building up and sustaining the firm's reputation was reflected in its support for his lifestyle, equally he fed back a proportion of 'his' share of the firm's current account to help support the property acquisition drive that would support the firm's expanded operations in the 1960s. This, it only began to become obvious in 1965, posed a latent danger to the practice, owing to his own estate duty liability – estimated at 45 per cent of his entire estate in 1965. This might, if he were to die unexpectedly, force the sale of the company's main working offices. Moreover, he was still the sole guarantor of the firm with its bank. A number of counter-strategies were suggested by the company accountant in the late 1960s, including transfer of assets to Lorna, and the drawing of lump sums out of Robert's share in the firm's assets, but all this coincided with a time of growing financial problems for the firm, and pressure by its bank for reduction of its large overdraft.[32] To help alleviate the firm's financial problems, some of the properties were now sold, including Hawkhill House for £5,000, and Bella Vista (to Percy) for £5,020, in mid 1967; Matthew had held a half share in both of these properties. The expenses of Park Square East were dealt with by the London office, including £410 annual rent, and expensive dry rot remedial work in mid 1967.[33] Eventually, as we shall see below, rather than retiring from RMJM, Matthew chose to go part-time in the university in 1968, resulting in a cut of more than £200 per month in his income.

Matthew's architectural thinking in the age of Modernist triumph

In a way, the balance of Matthew's financial affairs in the 1960s – confident, expansive, but with a background of concern about the long-term future – reflected his wider outlook on architecture.

Here, too, there was a mixture of sweeping assertiveness and unease about key aspects of the Modern architectural 'revolution'.

It was when he was speaking with his hortatory RIBA presidential hat on in 1963 that Matthew's language of heady optimism was at its boldest. Now, 'architects are held in high and growing esteem', and there was 'a general realisation that the temper of the country is behind us'. All in all, 'the architect and his work rank higher than at any time I can remember', and today 'we feel we are wanted'. This was, above all, due to the wider social involvement of the modern architect. No longer did architects merely 'embellish the fringes of the environment'. Now, they were 'near the centre of the social arena ... concerned with about every phase of life'.[34] That achievement was the result partly of improved training, research and management, but also partly of the strong strain of utopian social idealism in architecture, especially Modern architecture: in July 1965, for example, he told the IUA Congress in Paris that 'we, as Architects, are dedicated not to self interest, but to the urgent improvement of Man's physical estate ... we all have our own vision of the good society.'[35]

These were the years when the vision of Modern architecture *as* social betterment – in Matthew's own 1958 words, 'solving, architecturally, the most difficult of social problems' – began to seem well on the way to actual realisation – for example in the expansion of the number of universities from 17 in 1951 to 42 in 1968, and the effective trebling of the university population since 1945. In the opinion of some this was now also the age of realisation of the 1940s' worship of science as a modern doctrine of salvation: C P Snow argued in 1960 that 'scientists have it within them to know what a future-directed society feels like, for science itself, in its human aspects, is ... like that.'[36] And the rise of men such as Richard Llewelyn-Davies to senior teaching posts (heading the Bartlett from 1961) ensured that the banner of scientific-

cum-social betterment would stay raised high. It was in these years that Matthew's own acceptance of the Modernist drive for the New, and especially the need for radical surgery and rebuilding of the built environment, became strongest. In a 1964 lecture, 'Where have we got to in Architecture?', he argued that architecture was now in a 'revolutionary, not evolutionary phase', and derided the 'vision of a new medieval England' in Morris's *News from Nowhere* – a vision that 'came from nowhere and went nowhere'. The presumption was now for change rather than stability: jokingly, he recalled that Jessie, the previous year, had pleaded, 'Daddy, take me to see the Ritz before it's pulled down!' And in a November 1965 letter to the BBC General Advisory Council he argued that the greatest single task 'facing the British people for the next 30–40 years [is] the reconstruction of large parts of our cities and towns to provide an environment for a better life: we shall have to replace half of all existing buildings.'[37]

But despite all these confident assertions of faith in Progress, there were also, by the mid 1960s, growing doubts, both in the world of architecture and in the wider political context. For example, the new Minister of Housing, Richard Crossman, combined a continuing political support for mass-housing production with increasingly trenchant criticisms of the simplistic pursuit of material progress by his senior civil servants: he wrote in his diaries of Dame Evelyn Sharp's 'patrician ... utterly contemptuous and arrogant' paternalism towards local authorities, and remarked of her opposition to conservation that 'she who counted herself a modern iconoclast took the – yes, I will say it – illiterate view that there was a clear-cut conflict between "modern" planning and "reactionary" preservation.'[38] Some of the new criticisms, of course, were simply matters of nuance. There was a growing consensus that Modernism's totalising approach should no longer be conceived of in the crude mass production terms of 1920s Fordism or Taylorism. Instead, with the accentuation of 'technological change', the need was now for 'flexibility' and even 'indeterminate' design in institutions such as hospitals and universities: 'there is no such thing as an ultimate form'. Nor, indeed, was there any such thing as 'a natural law affecting the development of societies'.[39]

We can best recover Matthew's mid-1960s thinking on architecture under two broad headings: the social place of architecture, and the physical forms of the built environment. In the former area, unlike the former communists such as Percy Marshall, Matthew broadly accepted the status quo of the middle way between socialism and capitalism. For example, what was clear from the private commentary he wrote on his 1964 China trip (see Chapter 11) was the surprising depth of his personal animosity towards communism: he expressed an utter contempt for the 'childlike outlook' of a populace indoctrinated by propaganda. His own values, even at this climactic stage of government intervention in Britain, remained much closer to the Liberal personal ethos of J M Keynes, with its visceral aversion to state *dirigisme*. In Britain, Matthew argued in 1965, 'our unique form of welfare state is still based on the competitive commercial ethic, however much the line between state and private enterprise may be blurred'; he conceded that 'I am not one of those who automatically shudders at the thought of buildings being created and sold as a commodity.' But there were disadvantages, too. There was the risk of 'anarchy'; and 'one of the least endearing features of private enterprise is its discouragement of the free flow and exchange of ideas'.[40] The shifting balance of debate and status between public and private was especially contentious in housing, as public housing steadily lost its prestige, politically and architecturally – challenging Matthew's assumption that the years since his victory over the Valuer had been a time of continuous progress.[41]

In such a context of flux, Matthew's instinctive reaction, in the early 1960s, was to stress the vital role of the professions, as 'a public safeguard against the crudities of commercial exploitation, [as] the "amateurs" game is played out'. 'The fact is that hard-won professional status (and the principle of public protection that goes with it) just does not go with the commercial principle of *caveat emptor*.' He was well aware of the growing polarisation within the architectural profession between public authority architecture and the new, thrusting model of overtly commercial architect, riding on the back of the office- and system-building booms and covertly flouting the RIBA Code of Professional Conduct's strict ban on overlap of professional and business interests – a trend that would culminate in the John Poulson scandal of 1972–4.[42] But he insisted that any assimilation of the professions with capitalist marketing should be treated with utmost suspicion: in 1963 he unenthusiastically advocated the use of radio- and television-based public relations 'to put over the image (much as I dislike the term) of the architect ... but I will never believe that any publicity is better than none'.[43] In a 1962 interview for *Scottish Field*, Matthew projected an image of academic 'vagueness', and when asked about his 'commercial interests', ... 'annoyance pitches his voice higher when he says, "No, no, I am a professional man."' Confronted at a lunch in 1965 with the aggressively free-market views of Alistair Burnet, editor of *The Economist*, Matthew wrote of his 'shock to find some of our fundamentals treated with scorn if not derision ... How widespread is this view? We naively assume most people agree with us.'[44] With the continuing liberal-cum-Fabian slant of his world view, it was assumed by relations and close colleagues that, at least during the 1950s and 1960s, Matthew continued his consistent support for Labour, not from passionate socialist conviction but out of the greater force of his aversion to the competition ethos.[45] Increasingly, Matthew saw the high-tax welfare state regime as a lesser of two evils: he 'grumbled about the high taxes during the 1960s – but voted Labour all the same!' Aidan recalled that 'although he still voted Labour, by the 1960s he had become quite a dyed-in-the-wool private-practice man, and was beginning to get very cross over the way so much was being taken away in taxes: eventually he might even have considered voting Conservative!'[46]

Throughout the mid 1960s Matthew continued generally to place trust in the elite professional and intellectual institutions as both an education conduit and a safety valve for criticisms. For example, in 1965 he unsuccessfully pleaded with the BBC to give more specific attention to architecture and the built environment, arguing that the great reconstruction campaign in prospect required an 'informed and critical public opinion' to support it, and 'to criticise us intelligently'. The BBC must 'lead a cultural revolution ... helping to make our cities, towns and landscape both the concern and the pride of the British people'. There was not, as yet, any acceptance of the ideals of 'direct participation': 'He wasn't interested in laymen getting involved in the design process. What he wanted to do was to find out what they needed and then go away and do it.'[47] What *was* possible was internal reform in the architectural profession – for example, by advocating the advancement of women in architecture, a preoccupation of his since the 1958 Oxford conference, and the 1962 RIBA Office Survey Team report, *The Architect and his Office*, which had broadened the social scope of the profession without resolving the 'curious and unsatisfactory situation' that only 1,165 out of the 25,788 RIBA members were female.[48]

Matthew's attitudes to the changing built environment *itself* were also permeated with subtle ambiguities. His acceptance of the need for massive redevelopment was tempered by strong, and growing, reservations about its most egregious technocratic excesses – notably, the anarchic effects of the aggressive use of multi-storey blocks, large-scale road engineering and system building. In this, he stood squarely in the polemical tradition of Clough Williams-Ellis, a tradition that was powerfully reinvigorated in the 1950s

and 1960s by Ian Nairn, Britain's first popular architectural journalist.[49] As early as his RIBA inaugural address of October 1962, Matthew was beginning to argue that the mechanical achievement of Modern standards might even be counterproductive. He recalled that, in his 1952 *AJ* series, he and his fellow guest-editors had pointed out how a town built with all the correct zoning provisions could 'remain an ignoble and inert mass, devoid of character', and that large-scale redevelopment 'could even, in a sense, be a disaster if, because the skill and imagination of the architect are lacking, it led to the monotonous repetition of standard mass-produced units.'[50] By 1968 the alarm was more explicit: in a BBC television programme he pleaded that 'high building has been disastrously ... indiscriminately ... applied to existing centres. Tall blocks are planted into the old, tight pattern like a miniature flower bed. Used in this way, tall buildings can be utterly destructive to the environment.' Equally culpable were the civic leaders wedded to the car as a 'sacred cow' ... 'tearing their towns to bits in a desperate effort to cope with traffic'. But the remedies still lay within the Modern Movement: what was needed was a more compact, integrated, flexible, less sprawling formula, as provided from the beginning at Cumbernauld, 'the first to step right out of the Garden City era'.[51] For existing towns, what was needed was some way of integrating modern engineered roads within protected zones, as was then being argued most articulately by planner Colin Buchanan.[52] And on the 'systems' front, he argued vehemently against the application of highly prefabricated, mass-produced approaches to housing, which above all required flexibility.[53]

Significantly, Matthew recognised from the start that there was much force in Jane Jacobs's 'terrific frontal attack on the planners' from 1961 onwards: he conceded that many planned urban redevelopments 'conceived in optimism' had indeed destroyed the 'character, community life and diversity' of the 'older, so-called unplanned and blighted areas', through their rigid and 'uniform' segregation of land uses, creating 'arid wastes in place of teeming vitality'.[54] The destructiveness of Modernist redevelopment, Matthew now agreed, stemmed both from its insistence on rigid zoning and from its violation of 'our architectural heritage'. Calls for ever-expanding redevelopment, as in Wilfred Burns's influential 1963 book *New Towns from Old*, now suddenly seemed out of date.[55] Yet preservation of buildings 'merely' because they were old was dismissed. 'Total immersion' in either the Old or the New ('for the antiquarian or the astrologer') was unacceptable as a practical solution. What was needed was an outlook that faced both ways, towards 'life and the progression of life', an outlook based explicitly on Geddes's approach as well as in the new, post-CIAM discourse of 'urban design', its future aspirations grounded firmly in the existing heritage.[56] In reaction to the decline in prestige of ideas of 'regional', 'national' or 'vernacular' Modernism, Matthew now began to focus on global environmental issues: he argued in 1964 that all efforts should be channelled towards 'the relatively simple matter of providing for the elementary shelter of mankind on the surface of the earth', and the following year proclaimed at a US conference on President Johnson's 'Great Society' that, 'as architects, we also recognise we are members of an even wider society. We are One World, and our responsibilities are world wide!'[57]

Matthew's precise ideological position at the time is most clearly displayed in a direct comparison with contemporaries: in an *Illustrated London News* article of October 1967 he was able to sketch out his overall architectural world outlook in immediate juxtaposition to those of Basil Spence and Peter Smithson.[58] Even in their 'preferred photographs' that headed the pieces, the three men struck somewhat stereotypical poses: Matthew evenly lit, and impassively serene; Spence more dramatic and backlit, with the hint of a smile; and Smithson seemingly caught informally in the middle of some debate,

his mouth combatively open in mid-disputation. Their pieces uncannily reflected these portraits. Matthew's seemed to be the most straightforwardly confident example of mainstream Modernist rhetoric, hailing the British achievement in mixed-economy social architectural programmes as a comprehensive achievement of Progress, requiring only the fine-tuning of greater flexibility and 'feedback' on the effects of different environments on 'people's lives'.[59] Smithson, for all his assertively avant-garde presentation, also offered a broadly optimistic picture of Modern rationalism, arguing that architecture was shifting decisively away from mass production and collective state control towards a new, flexible individualism, to reflect the diversity of modern life.[60] Spence, more presciently, wrote of a gathering crisis, caused by Modernism's excessive reliance on abstract scientific values such as prefabrication and traffic-led planning, that might soon seem outmoded and 'archaic': 'In the future, I think there will be a swing towards more human thinking, more human buildings. People will look for and demand a more intimate background for their family lives as technology gets more elaborate and more abstract.' Of the three, it seemed to be Spence's analysis that most accurately, and Matthew's that least, predicted the late 1960s and 1970s revulsion against public authority architecture and technocratic Modernism.[61] But, in the event, as we shall see in Chapters 12 and 13, the only one of the three who would succeed in making the transition to the new humanism of conservation and environmentalism would in fact be Robert Matthew.

Overall, a general pattern can be discerned in Matthew's own activities during the 1960s as a whole: a rapid decline in the amount of time devoted to his private practice, at least within Britain, and his university work – both of which were losing their novelty and appeal to him – and a rapid increase in a variety of other, more diverse contacts, especially emphasising international and environmentalist links. The three chapters cover-ing those years, 1960–9 (Chapters 9, 10 and 11), are arranged, in effect, in ascend-ing order of interest and personal motiva-tion from Matthew's perspective. Let us first look in detail at the 'declining' activ-ities – his private practice and university work – before passing on to the 'rising' ones – beginning, in this chapter, with his architectural-political involvements 'at home' in Britain, and then passing in Chapters 10 and 11 to challenges overseas.

RMJM in the 1960s: diversity and detachment

From the mid 1960s Matthew's day-to-day involvement with RMJM went into grad-ual decline: within a few years, it was reduced to a combination of attendance at partners' meetings, and a substantial contribution to design of a select few projects and occasional 'call-in' monitor-ing of other major jobs. Most 'progres-sive' Modernist private practices were undergoing a similar process of institu-tionalised expansion at the time – for example, Yorke, Rosenberg & Mardall in December 1961 took on three more part-ners, and opened a new office, immedi-ately followed in 1962 by the death of Yorke; and even Gibberd reluctantly con-ceded that 'the prima-donna architect ... is becoming extinct', replaced by multi-disciplinary group-working.[62]

With the continued huge expansion in RMJM's workload, the London office had now developed into an almost com-pletely autonomous operation, united at least superficially by Stirrat's 'ideological' emphasis on the use of systems: 'They were brought up with CLASP as their mother's milk!'[63] While continuing to assert seigneurial dominance over affairs in Edinburgh, Matthew pragmatically allowed his earlier authority over the London office to diminish and disappear almost altogether, with the result that tensions with Stirrat gradually eased. Although Matthew was, in general, high-ly suspicious of the early 1960s systems mania, he never directly criticised Stirrat's overriding preoccupation with

systems, allowing instead 'his opinion to be seen more in the neglect. Edinburgh built some quite enormous buildings, like hospitals and universities, but each one was approached differently and on its own merits; it was an entirely differ-ent frame of mind.'[64] Equally, Stirrat kept his criticisms of the Edinburgh office largely private, seeking out kindred spir-its (usually ex-AA people) when visiting, and 'speaking very quietly to us, in case anyone else could hear'.[65]

Rapidly, the London office began to attract talented new adherents to Stirrat's cause, such as the gifted, AA-trained com-munist Hugh Morris, who imported to the Bath University project from his work for the LCC on the abortive Hook New Town a new stress on 'cluster' urbanism. Some of the newcomers adopted a more assertive attitude towards Matthew than did their chief. In 1961, for example, Stirrat invited Sheffield's Deputy City Architect, Andrew Derbyshire, who then was working on the RIBA Office Survey, to join the practice to oversee the York project. From the beginning, he took Stirrat's side vis-à-vis Matthew, and even-tually, during one partners' meeting around 1965, became

so fed up at Robert's autocratic behav-iour at these meetings that I said bluntly to him, 'Robert, stop bullying me, for God's sake!' He'd previously treated me as Stirrat's lackey – and Stirrat himself was afraid of Robert and didn't stand up to him in these meetings. Now, he just stopped in his tracks, and looked at me silently over his glasses for a few moments. And from then on, I've got a dim memory that he treated me with noticeably more respect![66]

Of course, with separation, there came the assumption among some London staff that they were the senior branch or even the headquarters. John Richards recalled that 'it was a constant battle in the sixties to get London to realise that they weren't the "head office"!'[67]

Within Edinburgh, Matthew remained unambiguously in charge of affairs, but even here the mushrooming of the firm's work, with the 1960s welfare state boom, encouraged a much more decentralised system to emerge, including a polarisation between 'elite' and 'everyday' offices. Alan Wightman recalled that 'the office became a collection of teams, with RHM always at least a background influence, and sometimes an important player in a crisis.'[68] Regent Terrace was kept as Matthew's personal redoubt in Edinburgh, with the upstairs flat for family or guests. It was used for partners' meetings and Matthew's own selective project call-ins, which he used as a way of keeping his finger on the pulse of the office's workload. Andrew Gilmour, a young ex-LCC architect entrusted from 1962 with the planning and building of a complex multi-storey redevelopment in the Tyneside borough of Jarrow, recalled that

> Matthew's way of keeping in touch with each job was to have a meeting with the job architect at a crucial stage. Mine was at 8 am, over his breakfast! He would ask two or three leading questions, which might not make immediate sense and could seem offputting, but if you answered them OK, he obviously decided you were competent enough to be trusted; if he decided against you, that was the death-knell![69]

The 'routine' Edinburgh offices soon spread to include 13 South Charlotte Street, 8 Melville Street and then (after a woodworm crisis forced temporary closure of South Charlotte Street) 15 Hill Street. Initially, these handled a mixture of work, but from 1964 the increasing workload made possible a greater functional segregation, linked to the appointment of Graham and Richards as partners to join Matthew and Spaven.[70] Where Spaven had largely filled the role of executant and helper to Matthew, now he 'settled contentedly' into a more general role of office manager, while large projects and programmes were totally delegated to Graham and Richards, but in quite differing ways. Both had risen to

partner status within six years of joining. Graham, who headed Group 'B' at South Charlotte Street, handled a mixture of jobs, with a distinct emphasis on social housing, whereas Richards gravitated towards large public complexes, including Stirling University and the Royal Commonwealth Pool.

Although both were committed to the general RMJM ethos of social building, Graham's rather bluff and folksy approach contrasted strongly with Richards's quieter and more precise manner, which tended towards 'perfectionism'.[71] Whereas Matthew had been content to allow previous assistants to percolate away to form their own practices, now he made sure that Graham and Richards were encouraged to stay. He had orchestrated the staffing of the office, and of his university department, in a way that ensured that there was no one so efficient or talented as to risk challenging his dominance. Now, that 'rule of iron' was slightly relaxed, and 'the stronger ones were given their head, but still he made sure that his successors weren't anywhere near him – he didn't want to have them breathing down his neck!' One of the practice secretaries, Flora Isserlis, recalled that 'although Kenneth was strictly speaking next in seniority to Tom Spaven, by the late 1960s John Richards had caught up with him in the pecking order; Sir Robert had spotted in him a quiet ambition and an ability to manage large projects.'[72] Yet at the same time Matthew, in his characteristic compartmented way, tended to turn to Graham rather than Richards in matters of per-

9.5 1971 picture of Kenneth Graham. (John Dewar Studios)

Architect to the welfare state

9.6 Matthew saw little of some small projects organised from Regent Terrace, such as this temporary stand at the 1961 Royal Highland Show at Ingliston for animal feed manufacturer A & R Scott Ltd; job architect John McNeil developed a boldly trabeated, glazed and corrugated-clad timber-framed design, with balconied directors' room perched above a wider ground-floor showroom. (Photo Illustrations Scotland)

sonal and even emotional judgement, as opposed to technical organisation: 'I travelled a lot with Robert, and we talked a lot, but I'm not a very technical sort of chap, and so it was hardly ever "shop" talk about building design. Instead, he'd tell me extraordinary things about people, and ask my advice, using me as a kind of sounding-board.' Once in the late 1960s, 'during the Pilgrim Street job in Newcastle, when I was down south looking at a precasting works, staying at a hotel in Stamford, one night, very late, Robert unexpectedly rang me up in my room, asking me about one of the other people in the office – what was my instinct about them, did I trust them, and so forth? I found it rather extraordinary!'[73]

Architecturally, the two different characters of Richards and Graham were expressed in contrasting approaches – Graham emphasising pitched-roof housing and perpetuating Matthew's 1950s 'vernacular' preferences, and Richards, with his AA training and admiration for the 1950s Californian 'Case Study' houses of architects such as Pierre Koenig, tending towards a slender, post-and-lintel architecture of metal and glass. Although Richards was sceptical of the 'anti-style' extremes of Stirrat's systems ethos, he emphatically advocated a greater use of prefabricated construction, claiming that

'in a scientific age' architecture was 'increasingly influenced by aesthetic and ethical preferences for precision and logic'.[74]

Other Edinburgh partners created during the 1960s included Chris Carter, operating at 98 George Street and focusing on design of a succession of three large thermal power stations to follow Kincardine (Cockenzie, Longannet, Inverkip); hospitals work was kept at Regent Terrace with the exception of Ninewells, Dundee, whose huge size initially demanded a separate Dundee office. Some of the largest jobs, such as Richards's Royal Commonwealth Pool and Stirling University, were developed with only token reference to Matthew. All in all, the 1960s organisation of the firm in Edinburgh was, as Aidan Matthew recalled, 'a very clumsy arrangement, with messengers rushing back and forth between all these little fiefdoms'. Spaven argued that 'it was just like a cluster of small practices working loosely together. Ideally, Robert would have liked to control everything, but pragmatically accepted he couldn't. Stirrat, who did things very differently, thought this was all very strange.'[75] By the mid 1960s, therefore, there were moves to try to reunify this scattered patchwork of offices, and help diminish the danger posed to the firm by Matthew's estate duty liability, by developing a centralised headquarters on the land owned by the firm at Bells Brae, Dean Village – the upper half being occupied by a derelict bottle store, and the lower half by the fire-damaged ruins of a fancy dress warehouse. Early concepts of 1966–9, prepared by Jim Latimer, proposed a low-rise, high-density, stepped design, tiered down the steep slope to the river, including flats to attract high-quality architectural staff from London, but this ambitious project remained unrealised.

In addition to the strictly 'architectural' practice, as part of the agreement with Percy for the latter's move north, Matthew had undertaken to shut down the small planning arm of RMJM's Edinburgh office, and to transfer the staff to Percy, to allow him to set up his own planning consultancy. Percy Johnson-Marshall & Associates was duly launched in 1960 with a dowry of existing projects, largely university based and including the Edinburgh University masterplan (transferred in early 1961 from Spence). Percy's new practice was based in temporary hutted accommodation ('The Studio') in the Bella Vista garden. For a time, in the early 1960s, he was involved at the planning stage of almost all RMJM urban projects, and the Edinburgh RMJM office's small planning team was transferred to his payroll: it included Richard Bigwood, George Duncan and J Kris Buczynski (a former LCC colleague of Percy's).[76] By 1964, although the close integration with RMJM was fading, with Percy's growing academic interests in Edinburgh University the Bella Vista team were engaged in a number of even more ambitious new projects on their own account, including the planning of a multilevel complex for Halifax, Nova Scotia, to give the city centre 'new identity', and a vastly ambitious, £22m redevelopment of an 87 acre site in the decayed Lancashire city of Salford, where they charted out a masterplan for decked development and a multilevel centre ringed by tower blocks. Here, in preference to any direct architectural involvement by RMJM, the Edinburgh University ARU took on one of the housing redevelopment units, including five 17-storey tower blocks, as an experimental live project.[77]

Initially, relations between Percy and RMJM were harmonious, and that position was maintained in relation to the RMJM Edinburgh office. But relations with RMJM London turned sour when, in February 1966, the government commissioned RMJM to undertake a planning study for the Central Lancashire (Preston/Leyland) New Town, and George Duncan without prior warning moved from Percy's staff to join Derbyshire's team in London, taking the job with him – although Matthew and Percy had been involved in negotiations since late 1965 to handle the project as an Edinburgh

job. This whipped up to fever pitch Percy's already strong paranoid suspicion that his brother was attempting to choke off his development of private consultancy work, not least by encouraging confusion over the name 'Johnson-Marshall'. Matthew, although feeling angry and somewhat humiliated at the London office's coup, reined in his annoyance with characteristic self-restraint. He continued to attend Central Lancashire-related meetings during 1966, but otherwise refused to intervene on Percy's behalf, insisting that his formal commitment to Percy had been confined to the university lecturership. Equally characteristically, Stirrat was too afraid to confront Matthew himself, and instead persuaded Derbyshire to 'go up to Edinburgh and have a breakfast meeting with Robert, to explain to him why he wasn't getting the job. I've never had a more uncomfortable meeting!' Then, matters only got worse. Derbyshire recalled that

after that, I completely upset the applecart again between Stirrat and Percy, by attracting George Duncan and Roy Stewart down to work on the Central Lancashire Plan. Percy never forgave me for this – but the two of them had been very unhappy – he'd paid them next to nothing, and took all the credit for things, so they'd have gone somewhere else otherwise![78]

There were also still a number of architectural and planning projects that Matthew 'liked to keep for himself', reserving the right to vary the level of involvement by RMJM and Percy as appropriate. Some of these – notably the New University of Ulster at Coleraine, which involved architectural work by Robert and regional planning by Percy (see Chapter 10) – were major projects where

9.7 July 1961 concept model of Percy Johnson-Marshall's Salford redevelopment plan (perspective: from southeast). (RMJM)

Architect to the welfare state

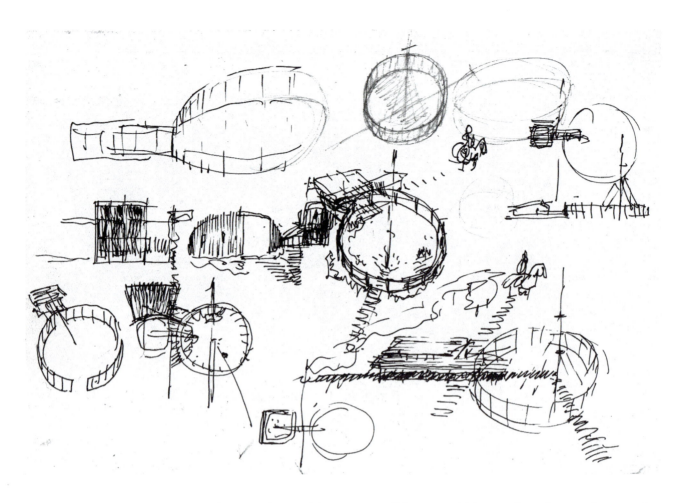

9.8 Bannockburn NTS site, 1962 concept sketches by Matthew of potential development and landscaping schemes, showing visitor centre attached to rotunda. His Bannockburn project also parallelled the circular 'Cyclorama Center' (1961) at the site of the US Civil War battle of Gettysburg, an ambitious 'cultural interchange' complex designed by Richard Neutra as part of the US National Parks Service's 'Mission 66' programme. (EULMC)

his personal supervision was a condition of appointment, but in these cases, as we shall see, he almost always eventually divested himself of day-to-day responsibility, once the project had been effectively launched.[79] Others, almost always in the Edinburgh neighbourhood, were of a more personal, 'family' character, and were dealt with by Matthew himself or with help from Stuart. Some of these came to nothing: for example, a joint entry with Stuart in 1962 for the competition for a new choir school behind St Paul's Cathedral in London; or, in 1966, a proposed 'tremendous redevelopment' of St Mary's Catholic Cathedral, in Edinburgh, which fell through after preliminary meetings between Robert, Stuart and church officials – including Cardinal Gray himself.[80]

Also initially delegated to Stuart, owing to the long-standing association of Lorimer & Matthew with additions to Loretto School, in Musselburgh, was an ambitious project of 1962–5 for a massive reconstruction of the school chapel, financed anonymously to the tune of £50,000 (later doubled) by a wealthy old boy, Mungo Campbell, of Morpeth. In August 1962 Campbell initially wrote to Robert Matthew, suggesting the possibility of enlarging the middle of the existing neo-Gothic chapel, in order 'to preserve some continuity'. Matthew replied that the proposal interested him 'in a particularly personal way', owing to his Lorimer & Matthew connection, and as 'both my brother (who works with me) and I have worked from time to time' at the school for Loretto.[81] By March 1963 Stuart, with Robert's help, had arrived at the fundamental concept of the project: to make a monumental enlargement of the east end, with a huge east window of contemporary glass, while keeping the existing roofline and retaining several western bays of the nave. After consultation with headmaster R B Bruce Lockhart, who produced his own sketch suggestion for a slightly larger extension (for 480 rather than 370 worshippers), in August 1963 disaster struck, when Stuart suffered his most devastating nervous breakdown, and design progress ground to a halt. Spurred by reminders from Campbell, who fretted that he 'would like the job to be completed in my lifetime', Robert took a crisis decision to absorb the job fully within RMJM, and allow Kenneth Graham – who got on well with Stuart – to work up the latter's concept into a detailed design.[82] Most important would be the internal structure of this new, broad eastern space, a matter that Stuart had not yet tackled, and Graham set to work with Arup to develop a bold roof design of laminated timber trusses, resting on a perimeter wall of stone-clad reinforced concrete, spanning 30 ft at the centre, with huge dormers to east, south and north, framed by Y-shaped laminated timber and glass-fibre trusses. The project was completed in July 1965 at a cost of £67,500 – well within the scope of Campbell's gift.[83]

A slightly different private commission, unconnected with RMJM and working not with Stuart but through a university-based team, with Eric Stevenson as 'executant' architect and Frank Clark as landscapist, was carried out in 1960–4 for the National Trust for Scotland (NTS) at the site of the Battle of Bannockburn, as part of the preparations for the 1964 celebrations of the battle's 650th anniversary. The 1940s and 1950s had seen a succession of proposals by different societies and committees for the 'Borestone' site, which was then an open field crowned by a tall flagpole of 1870 and a rubble cairn. Since 1954, sculptor C d'O Pilkington Jackson had been working on a project for an appeal-funded equestrian statue of Bruce, initially in conjunction with William Kininmonth as architect for the whole setting, under the aegis of a private Appeals Committee headed by General Sir Philip Christison. In 1955, after Pilkington Jackson had visited the Waterloo battle site in Belgium, the pair had proposed a more grandiose

scheme, including a memorial hall, circular cyclorama or tower, but after five years of inconclusive debates between the various committees, in 1960 the NTS stepped in and effectively took over the project, by guaranteeing the 'outstandingly large amount' of £10,000. The powerful NTS Secretary, James Stormonth-Darling, secured agreement for a far more ambitious and overtly modern project, which would form the pivot of a 'chain link' of 'history on the spot' interpretation centres to serve motor-borne tourists to the Highlands – and to carry it out, he became determined to secure the services of Matthew as consultant architect. Jackson and Kininmonth's old-fashioned monumental scheme was dropped, and Matthew was appointed architect for the entire project by NTS – to the fury of Kininmonth. With Stormonth-Darling's wholehearted support, Matthew argued against any 'hole in corner' treatment to the Bannockburn site, and prepared an open landscape arrangement focused on the Borestone. By January 1962 the project had expanded substantially, with a budget of £60,000, and, after the initial idea of a Geddes or Wallace Monument-like outlook tower had been discarded, Matthew settled on a structure that combined International Modernist and 'Scottish' connotations. Like Asplund's Woodland Cemetery at Stockholm, it comprised a formal processional way ascending to a focal open colonnade, here in the form of a broad, circular 'rotunda', originally intended by Matthew to be built in timber so as to evoke military defences or prehistoric henges, but eventually executed by Stevenson largely in precast concrete. The rotunda marked a change of alignment of the processional route, which headed off at an angle towards Pilkington Jackson's statue, which was set on a powerfully chamfered, almost Lorimerian base (a relic of the Kininmonth–Jackson scheme). In Matthew's original scheme the resemblance to Stockholm was accentuated by the inclusion of a visitor centre block directly abutting the rotunda, but this was later built near the entrance

Architect to the welfare state

road by another architect.[84]

In the mainstream work of RMJM the project that marked most closely the transition from 'hands-on' to 'hands-off' work was the Edinburgh University redevelopment – a multi-stage programme, which Matthew – so deeply involved at first, as we saw in Chapter 8 – gradually devolved by 1961–2 in its planning aspects to Percy Johnson-Marshall's new consultancy firm, and in its architectural aspects to John Richards. In his linked capacity as university Major Buildings Committee convener Matthew reserved a piece of the action for Alan Reiach by diverting to him the commission for a basic science building (the Appleton Tower) to the northeast of George Square. As the architectural climate was now on the cusp of the turn against tower blocks, Percy's 1962/3 proposal for the university CDA, although typical of the age in its vastly ambitious scale, conformed to the 1960s drift away from free-standing high blocks, and towards a more densely integrated, medium-rise decked formula. In a Geddesian vein, Percy recalled that his concept was inspired both by practical traffic requirements and by the historic precedent of the late 18th-century South Bridge, 'which had astonished me when I first came to Edinburgh – a structure almost akin to the Pont du Gard at Nîmes, with buildings all around it!'[85] This ambitious plan, with its network of upper-level decks, was in the event almost completely unrealised; but it did subtly influence what was actually built in the existing RMJM section of development to the southeast of George Square, while respecting the general lines of Spence's 1955 masterplan, by nudging its later phases down in height to a 'street' scale, unifying them with the use of York stone cladding, and threading a modest grouping of coffered-slab decks around them.[86]

In June 1962 superstructure construction of the 168 ft high Arts (David Hume) Tower and lecture theatres by Crudens got under way, with John Richards in charge (helped by assistant Euan Colam), and in March 1963, as the first contract

was going smoothly, Crudens were awarded the contract for the second stage of the project, with two four-storey teaching blocks and a 600-seat lecture theatre. The Arts Tower contract included a relatively conventional RC crosswall inner structure, but the cladding, in deference to the setting, included more unconventional use of natural materials: bands of polished slate and glass on the long elevations (which were recessed and set forward in a variegated way typical of Matthew), smooth stone slabs on the end walls, and rubble on the basement. This contextualism, appropriately to 18th-century Edinburgh, was of a different, subtly more 'classical' character than the rough 'vernacular' style of some of the 1950s projects.[87] By late 1963 and early 1964 extensive consultation was under way with a 'tower users committee' on furniture and fittings, and careful landscaping and artwork schemes were being prepared for the exterior and internal courtyards by William Gordon and others. With Arts and Crafts meticulousness, Matthew kept a close watch on the standards of finish and snagging, including matters such as gutter and manhole detailing, and in November 1967 Richards wrote to Colam that he had 'drawn my attention again' to the problems of seating detailing and noise insulation in the lecture hall: 'I must report back to Sir Robert shortly.'[88] The Arts Tower block and small lecture theatre were completed in 1963 at a final cost (£609,000) actually below the tender figure. All in all, the project seemed 'a win for Modernism over the city's powerful traditionalism. To many, it seemed an insolent, even cruel win.'[89] Following completion of the David Hume Tower, work proceeded apace on the remaining buildings of the Arts complex, including Spence's library, designed by Hardie Glover and built from 1967, and RMJM's Arts and Social Sciences Faculty Phase 2, including two- and four-storey teaching blocks and the 600-seat George Square Theatre, built by Crudens in 1964–7.[90]

At Edinburgh University Matthew allowed Percy to build up his vast decked concept in conjunction with his own, limited redevelopment, as the two of them were still on close terms: he emphasised in 1965 that all buildings on the campus must conform to Percy's plan.[91] Indeed, in a later version of Percy's redevelopment plan, a key axial position in the middle of Buccleuch Place was occupied by a building proposed for Matthew's own department – a massive, stepped, medium-rise structure. We shall return later to the parallel expansion and subdivision of the department in the 1960s, and the eventual swing away from redevelopment to conservation at the end of the decade.

RMJM's parallel modernisms: 'Cartesian' and 'empirical'

Following the successful work at George Square, John Richards was made a partner in 1964, and was immediately handed two important commissions to develop: for a new central swimming pool in Edinburgh, and a new university at Stirling. Such was Matthew's confidence in the quietly ambitious Richards that he allowed him almost complete autonomy in both, including design concept as well as execution. Richards's own architectural ethos of precision and restraint was given full rein at the Central (later Royal Commonwealth) Pool, an Olympic-length pool commissioned in June 1965 to serve both as city central baths and as main pool for the 1970 Commonwealth Games. Here Richards chose to sink the pool down into the rear of a falling site, with an ingenious section that allowed the front to be expressed as a self-effacing composition of severe horizontal planes: 'We felt that if the purpose of the building was good, all you needed to do was reveal it ... you actually had to strip away the architecture – we called it "noise".'[92] But the detailed execution of the pool was devolved largely, in turn, to others, such as Euan Colam, for in December 1965 Richards was presented with the even greater challenge of designing a new university at Stirling, the only Scottish site in the ambitious programme on which

9.9 March 1971 view of Stirling University, showing the multi-purpose Phase 1 (Pathfoot) Building. (Planair)

the Tory government had embarked (in Matthew's words) 'with a rush of blood to the head – without, I am certain, making any serious study of the economic implications'.[93]

RMJM were architects for three of the new universities – Stirling, York and Bath – in addition to a further university at Coleraine commissioned separately by the government of Northern Ireland (see Chapter 10). Initially, the contact for all the English and Scottish projects was through Stirrat and the London office, with its educational connections. Stirling – the first wholly new university built in Scotland since 1593, and the only wholly 'post-Robbins' new university – emerged as the chosen site for a new central Scottish university (in preference to Cumbernauld and Falkirk) only during 1965, and the first two briefing meetings were held in December 1965 at the new London office at Weymouth Street, with Richards representing Edinburgh, along with Stirrat, Newnham, Derbyshire, Morris and the newly appointed principal, Tom Cotterell. At these two meetings the main strategic decisions were taken – above all that, because of the extreme urgency of building, with first admission of students in 1967 and a gradual build-up in numbers from 150 in 1967–8 to 450

9.10 June 1966 aerial view of the SSHA Castle Street development, Dunbar, designed by RMJM with input in 1961–2 from fourth year students in Matthew's university department: the project comprised a mixture of low-rise cottages and three–four storey flats. Immediately behind is Basil Spence's influential Lamer Street fishermen's housing of 1949–52. (Planair)

in 1969–70, a preliminary general-purpose (Phase 1) building of around 130,000 sq ft should be constructed as soon as possible, suitable for 'recycling' thereafter. RMJM's appointment would include development plan preparation and design of Phase 1, and in the event the firm went on to design most of the permanent accommodation too.[94]

Although Matthew attended several key meetings in December 1965 and early 1966, it was Richards who mapped out a development plan that would exploit the sumptuously landscaped site – the grounds of Airthrey Castle, north of Stirling. Derbyshire recalled that

> we were all aghast at the magnificence of the site, and its breathtaking setting. How could anyone dare to sully its beauty with any more buildings?! The Edinburgh team, showing more aplomb than they probably felt, rose splendidly to the occasion and produced a solution which we all greatly admired.[95]

The Phase 1 building was located on its own at the north of the site and took the form of a simple, low, open, 'loosely structured shed' allowing maximum use flexibility, and externally resembling the Commonwealth Pool; it was built using a steel-framed prefabricated system devised by Richards's team. Derbyshire recalled

that, a year or so earlier, on a visit by Matthew and Richards to inspect the landscaped site of York University, 'it was obvious that our insistence on CLASP looked like the nanny state to them. Robert said nothing, but John said, "You know, I can build a good first-stage building as quickly and cheaply as you can with your consortium!"' Now, Richards's opportunity had arrived, and the multifunction Phase 1 building was erected successfully in only ten weeks.[96] For the permanent Stirling buildings, following the publication of the University Development Plan in 1968, a more traditional picturesque vista was set out, with a mixture of clustered social and teaching buildings and low residential slab blocks on the other side of a landscaped loch – 'white buildings against dark hillsides on a beautiful site'.

Graham's group developed a rather more diverse workload, with a succession of housing projects as its focus. In the process, his team steadily progressed from more romantic vernacular efforts of the 1950s to a more abstract approach. The building of Barshare at Cumnock, for example, continued throughout the mid 1960s, with Stage 4 including a four-storey block to 'give focal interest' at the centre of the scheme. By 1962 and 1963 Graham's team were having to deal with the first local criticisms, including claims of smoky chimneys in some of the single-storey houses, due to downdraughting from adjacent taller houses, which Graham countered by pointing out that the councillors themselves had insisted on these fires, and advocating exclusively central heating in future phases. In 1963 Matthew had the unusual experience of presenting, as RIBA President, a Saltire housing award to Graham for Phase 1 of Barshare.[97] Other small jobs were fed to Graham's group by the Cumnock Town Council, alongside the town planning commission, including a sports pavilion designed by job architect Andrzej Malczewski as a dramatic juxtaposition of rectangular brick blocks and triangular stair-tower, and with a highly complex structure of timber trusses. More sober was Andrew Gilmour's Senior Citizens Club in the town centre (1962–5), with its plain harled blocks lit by high-level strip windows. Other follow-on low-rise 'vernacular' housing projects for small burghs included a 200-dwelling scheme in 1962–6 at Ferguson Park, Blairgowrie, which juxtaposed a dramatic crescent of patio houses with higher blocks up a hill, all harled in white; and an SSHA commission for infill houses and flats in the historic harbour area at Castle Street, Dunbar, echoing Spence's adjacent development in its picturesque layout and harl-and-rubble construction. Exploiting Matthew's university connection, the latter project was dealt with as a 'live' fourth-year project for Tony Forward's students in 1961–2, and was built in 1963–5.

In these small-town projects there was of course a clear continuity with the picturesque and 'vernacular' ideas of the 1950s and earlier decades. But equally important, now, in the work of Graham's team and of some other contemporary practices, such as Wheeler & Sproson, was the influence of the pioneering low-rise, high-density housing that was then being built in large quantities at Cumbernauld New Town, more nervously and abstractly 'clustered', yet still evocative of earlier patterns of town building. In a 1966 speech to the Cumnock councillors Matthew forcibly emphasised this exemplary role, arguing that 'even that pace-setter, Cumbernauld, does not shout to the sky in an aggressive way, but it points clearly to the future.' Bobby Hunter's Cumnock, he argued, was like Cumbernauld in its 'enthusiasm and determination to turn hopes into actions – with an ideal constantly in mind'.[98] All this served only to accentuate Matthew's disillusionment with the turn of events in Glasgow, following the sacking of RMJM from the follow-on multi-storey contracts to Hutchesontown, and the constructional tribulations of Hutchesontown 'B' itself. Matthew had always had a somewhat jaundiced 'Edinburgh' view of Glasgow, and now, in the wake of these reverses, during the mid 1960s he for a

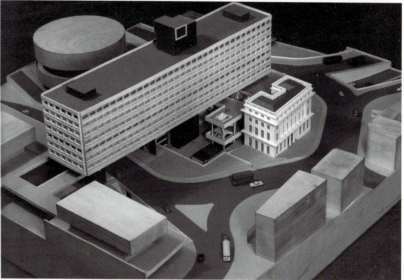

time virtually ceased having any interest in the city's regeneration problems: 'He said he'd come to the conclusion that the housing problem of Glasgow was, quite simply, insoluble!'[99]

Within the workload of partners such as Graham, Richards and Carter, Matthew now generally confined his direct involvement to points of crisis, where a decisive conceptual direction was needed. One of his boldest interventions, in August 1963, helped rescue the Pilgrim Street development in Newcastle – one of the ambitious multilevel redevelopments, combining public, traffic and infrastructure improvements and 'commercial' office developments, with which the reformist regime of the Council Leader, T Dan Smith, and the City Planning Officer, Wilfred Burns, hoped to make Newcastle's city centre a beacon of planned

(top) **9.11** Kenneth Graham (left) leads a site inspection of the Dunbar project under construction in 1965. (RMJM)

(bottom) **9.12** 1966 model of the Pilgrim Street development in Newcastle as finally approved, seen from northwest and showing the Royal Arcade facade (in the event, demolished). (RMJM)

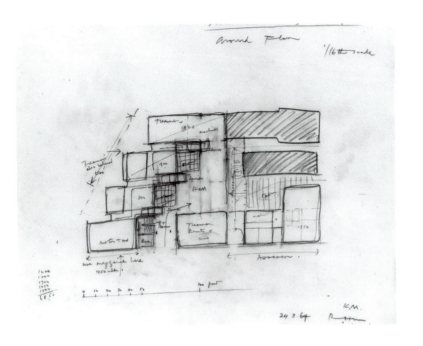

Modernity. First broached with RMJM in July 1962, this job was 'claimed' by Edinburgh owing to its closeness, and Graham's connections with the North-east of England. It comprised around 300,000 sq ft of offices, shops and ware-houses, and a multi-storey car park – all to be crammed onto a new roundabout above an inner ring road underpass, while preserving and incorporating a 19th-century classical covered arcade, designed by John Dobson. A scheme had already been drawn up by the City Engineer, and within RMJM a somewhat sceptical view was taken of the firm's involvement: it was 'generally felt that the name of Robert Matthew was wanted on the drawings for submission to the RFAC, with any improvements he could make'. Nearly a year of debates about the 'awful brief', with its warren of traffic routes and 'useless arcade', culminated in a somewhat acrimonious meeting in Newcastle in July 1963, when an initial scheme by Spaven and Graham for a 16-storey tower block on a podium was rejected by Burns and City Architect George Kenyon, on grounds including the 'intrusion' and 'isolation' of the tall block.[100] Matthew was brought in to resolve this impasse. At an August meeting at Regent Terrace, attended by Matthew, Graham, Spaven and job architect John Smith, and with Newcastle represented by Kenyon, Matthew

simply got out his felt pen and scored right across this jumble of roads and underpasses. With his instinctive eye for form, he saw that the way to cut through the problem was to get rid of the podium and put the tower on its side, as a huge seven-storey slab spanning the entire site, and going right above the 36 ft high arcade. He just slapped that on the table and said, 'That's it, George, that's the answer!' Kenyon used to suck up to Robert and so he said, 'Yes! Well done, Sir Robert!' The basis of the scheme, as built, was there in that sketch – but then I had to take it, and make it work!

There were innumerable problems of

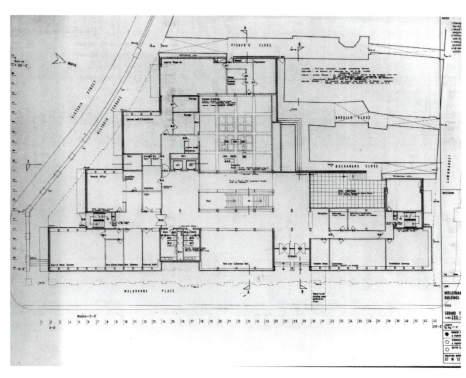

9.15 Detailed ground floor plan (1966) of Midlothian County Buildings Extension as eventually built. (RMJM)

implementation, especially over the preservation of the Royal Arcade, but the complex, as eventually completed in May 1970, with its 84 ft span, precast-clad slab block on a deck some 50 ft above the inner ring road, remained true to that impulsive sketch by Matthew.[101]

Of all the mid and late 1960s projects of the RMJM office in Scotland or England, in only one case did Matthew involve himself at a relatively detailed level in the design – the Midlothian County Buildings Extension in Edinburgh's Melbourne Place (1964–70). This was unsurprising, as this project was located in the heart of Geddesian 'Old Edinburgh', at the junction of the 'Royal Mile' and George IV Bridge, and the job was another of those cases of Matthew's overlapping 'identities'. The project was for a complex of offices, to serve the turn-of-the-century classical County Council headquarters immediately opposite. The project's history, spanning the full decade of the 1960s, was as protracted as that of Pilgrim Street, but for very different reasons; and, like Pilgrim Street, it was eventually executed in detail by Graham. It began with a competition of 1960, with a brief calling for two diagonally adjoining infill blocks occupying

part of the site. The winning entry, by old-fashioned classical Art Deco bank and school specialist Reid & Forbes, was of 'contextual' historicist character, with crowstepped facade to Lawnmarket and classical frontages to east and south, but such was the revolution in architectural opinion in Edinburgh since the 1950s that the RFACS rejected it 'very emphatically' in March 1961 on grounds of excessive conservatism. Matthew, as an RFACS member, was instrumental in this rejection, attacking the 'ludicrous juxtaposition of two entirely different architectural expressions in the same building', and advocating instead a 'design truly representative of the 20th century' – but eventually, in 1964, with the site now substantially enlarged, he himself was asked to take on the commission.[102]

His solution was an exemplary case of Geddes-style conservative surgery, and actually retained most of the plan features of the Reid & Forbes solution, including the position of the main entrance and an internal courtyard, but, as so often in Matthew's projects, the site had now been enlarged, by including a tenement block at its southeast corner: the completed building in 1970 was twice as large as Matthew's 1964 brief. The

(opposite top) **9.13** Midlothian County Buildings Extension, Edinburgh: 1964 sketch by Matthew for ground floor. (EULMC)

(opposite bottom) **9.14** 1963/4 sketches by Matthew for 'burgage-plot' facade expression of the Midlothian County Buildings Extension site: the lower sketch shows the south facade to Victoria Street, while the upper sketch shows the north facade to Lawnmarket. A more sober treatment was eventually adopted. (EULMC)

Architect to the welfare state

9.16 View of newly completed Midlothian County Buildings Extension from northeast in 1970.   (H Snoek: RIBA)

schizophrenic architectural character of the Reid & Forbes design also left its mark on Matthew's own design, whose evolution here followed a similar course to that of New Zealand House, with a more picturesquely variegated original arrangement being regularised and rectangularised in execution. First, he experimented with a variety of solutions, including a ten-storey New Zealand House-style slab on a podium. Eventually, however, he settled on something more directly evocative of Old Town 'tradition' – a single dense mass, cut into four north–south burgage-plot strips. In his first sketches of February 1964 the latter were shown expressed at the steeply falling south end through three gabled blocks interspersed by jutting towers, while the north facade to the medieval Lawnmarket was split into three rectangular-capped blocks echoing the adjacent Royal Mile facades. Eventually, as executed in detail by Kenneth Graham and Ian Samuel, this facade was unified and squared up, whereas the south frontage retained its stepped burgage-plot character, albeit in more rectangular form; the main east facade presented a far stronger contrast in its more overtly Modern long bands of windows. A hint of a podium was retained at ground and basement parking level, where it was expressed to Victoria Street as a plinth clad in Matthew's beloved rock-faced rubble

(here, Craigleith sandstone) – a material that shoots up at one point on the main east facade to form a mini-tower. Otherwise, the walling above was Portland stone cladding with bands of teak-framed windows. All in all, the project was almost a nostalgic throwback to the approaches and materials of Matthew's 1950s vernacular buildings, but all in a more compactly dense, regularised manner. After 40 years' use, however, it was eventually demolished in early 2007.

Hospital frustrations in Edinburgh and Dundee

Although in some ways bypassed by the emergence of Richards and Graham, Spaven continued to act as Matthew's main office manager, and to oversee other emergency programmes, such as the succession of thermal power stations awarded to RMJM by the SSEB and increasingly dealt with by Chris Carter (who subsequently became a partner). The series commenced with Cockenzie, where the firm was appointed in 1960 as consultant architects for the main station, with its paired 500 ft chimneys, and executive architects for the administrative and ancillary buildings – a substantial five-storey block linked to the station by a 175 ft bridge. Matthew initially involved himself in great detail at the negotiating stage, attending key site meetings and the RFACS presentation in November 1962, but once detailed design began, matters were dealt with largely by Carter, whose 'Cockenzie Section' moved in July 1962 to a separate office in the Cowgate.[103] Working from Hill Street, Dennis Ashmead supervised a number of university projects, notably the Joint Agricultural Building at Aberdeen University (completed 1968), a combination of a seven-storey teaching slab block and lower assembly and library buildings, whose location on the edge of Matthew's old town development plan area dictated 'traditional' stone walling at ground level.

Hospitals, owing to the complexity and political sensitivity of the Royal Infirmary of Edinburgh project, were kept largely at Regent Terrace under the supervision of Spaven and Gwent Forestier-Walker. The RIE negotiations spanned the entire period covered by this chapter, and at the end of it the actual start of any building work still seemed hardly any nearer. In 1961 RMJM and the hospital board finally agreed formally that the architects should prepare a detailed plan based on Matthew's and Llewelyn-Davies's initial proposals of January 1961 for a massive T-shaped block. A two-year period of complex investigations, including many dozens of working party meetings, was followed in December 1962 by an outline application to the Royal Fine Art Commission for Scotland. This was a purely advisory body, which nevertheless showed its teeth to some effect, as had its English equivalent in the case of New Zealand House. At a meeting on 19 December, from which Matthew tactfully absented himself, the proposal's townscape implications were comprehensively savaged. Commissioners criticised the potentially 'disastrous effect' on the skyline of the 'dominant' 52 m high block, and laid the blame firmly on the (in their view) perverse way in which the staged development procedure had necessitated building on the upper part of the site. Given these constraints, they conceded, 'it would be difficult to evolve any more sympathetic layout or massing' than that now proposed.[104]

In retrospect, this reversal proved to be a decisive turning point in the RIE project. In contrast to New Zealand House, or even George Square, this was not a commission in which Matthew had invested any great personal enthusiasm or commitment – indeed, he may perhaps have suspected all along that the problems and constraints would ultimately prove insoluble. Now, the £7m project began slowly but surely to unravel. Matthew swiftly came up with a new, lower-height proposal, by spreading the redevelopment more evenly over the site – including the cleared space that would have been left vacant under the previous, high-rise proposal. This then, of course,

immediately reintroduced the old dilemma of decanting and phasing. Predictably, when he submitted his first provisional sketches of his revised plan to the Regional Board in March 1963, the Board now began to express serious doubts at the loss of expansion space, and at the possibility that the Infirmary would become a 'building yard' for a decade: the possibility of building anew elsewhere was raised once more. Nevertheless, in August 1964 the SERHB authorised RMJM to proceed with preparation of a development plan – effectively conceding that all the previous debates and proposals, and Forestier-Walker's entire contribution to the project, had been mere 'feasibility work'. And in October 1964 a new model showed a six-phase development from west to east, including nine open quadrangles and 860 beds in total. To maximise the momentum of redevelopment, Phase 1 would be built on additional land at the extreme northwest corner of the site, including a boiler house and residential accommodation. By June 1967, with a new cost limit of £14.4m agreed, detailed design work for Phase 1 at last began, with an anticipated start of construction in 1970. Already, by the end of 1966, RMJM had carried out over £150,000 worth of work, and by November 1969 a further £50,000 of design work on Phase 1 was scheduled for completion – with more to come![105]

That these difficulties and delays at RIE did not stem solely from the phasing constraints of the city centre site is indicated by the troublesome history of the firm's other front-rank teaching hospital and medical school project – Ninewells,

9.17 RMJM partner Chris Carter seen in 1971, with a view of his major work, Cockenzie Power Station, in the background. (John Dewar Studios)

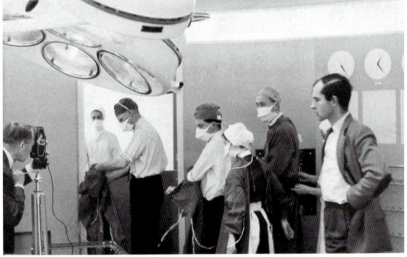

(top) **9.18** Ninewells Hospital: the 'mock-up shed' seen in 1964. (RMJM)

(bottom) **9.19** 'Operation' in progress in the full-scale mock-up suite at Ninewells, June 1964. (RMJM)

Dundee, for the Eastern Regional Hospital Board and the University of St Andrews. The trouble at Ninewells really began *after* its basic design had been finalised, in February 1962, at an estimated cost of £9m. As part of the early/mid 1960s ethos of 'systematised' building, it was decided to try to circumvent the long-winded system of preparing all working drawings before proceeding to construction – something that, it was hoped, would save three or four years in eventual completion, as with 'package deal' housing projects. Instead, detailed drawings would be done while construction, by a nominated contractor, was under way, based on approximate quantities only; 'packages of design' would be priced as they were produced.[106] In the early 1960s the practice of management contracting was only in its infancy: here,

the parallel streams of activity were to be controlled by a 'programme coordination group' with representation from the design team and contractor, and supported by a 'programme evaluation group' and research programme teams. In November 1963 the lowest tender, from Crudens, was accepted. But the polycentric system of responsibility was quite unlike the tight control of a package deal in housing – and differences between contractor, designers and clients began to surface almost immediately.[107]

It was also hoped to speed up work by an elaborate programme of full-scale mock-ups and work studies, for which £50,000 was allocated following negotiations between J K Johnston and the Scottish Office, who hoped to reuse the findings in other hospitals. A huge steel shed was built, well away from the hospital, and inside this a full-scale operating theatre suite was constructed. It was given a full-scale test in June 1964, with a 'mock operation' to test that lighting, clocks, etc., were to hand, and was then dismantled; a 48-bed mock-up ward was built in its place. Arguably, these mock-ups helped minimise the delays caused by the collaborative architect–contractor design process – a task whose 'immensity took most people by surprise'.[108] The fundamental problem, however, was a misunderstanding over contractor–designer–client relations, and especially over the timing of production of working drawings, which rapidly developed into an all-embracing crisis during 1964: essentially, Crudens claimed that working drawings were not being produced on time, but they themselves had failed to produce 'a strategic programme in network form' for the architects and engineers to work from.[109] With successive modifications to the brief, delays mounted. After Wightman turned down an offer to become a partner and take full charge of the project, the Edinburgh partners took the drastic step of closing the Dundee office and centralising all work in Edinburgh under Spaven's oversight, with Graham in charge of working drawings and John Richards the design work.[110] At the time,

Modern Architect

9.20 1966 plan of main deck level of Ninewells as built. (RMJM)

9.21 1980s aerial view of Ninewells from northwest. (Planair)

the move was represented purely in management terms, to allow better oversight of the project. But it also seems likely that the move, and the consequent sale of Hawkhill House, was also motivated by the mounting concern in the mid 1960s about the firm's estate duty liabilities.[111] At any rate, the move was reluctantly accepted by the Health Board and the university, but it very soon became clear that it had not improved the project's management at all, as Graham and Richards were not significantly available

to help, and there was insufficient space to accommodate the project team in Edinburgh; the Board and university protested that the move, and the break-up of the Dundee team, had been 'carried out under a false prospectus'.[112]

From around 1964 Matthew became less and less involved with Ninewells, and Spaven, Wightman and others were left to handle the constant progress meetings. As it happened, by the mid and late 1960s the reputation of Crudens as a contractor was beginning to attract ever stronger whiffs of controversy and scandal, both in wider UK dealings (especially with Newcastle's council leader, T Dan Smith) and in council housing matters in Dundee. As we shall see in Chapter 10 in the case of Northern Ireland, Matthew tended prudently to distance himself from controversy and acrimony, and it may be that he began now to see it as essential to move away from his once cordial relations with Harry Cruden and his firm, but as a result (in the words of project architect Jim Latimer) the Ninewells project rapidly 'went to pigs and whistles'.[113] In July 1967 the parliamentary Public Accounts Committee investigated the project's continuing difficulties and severely criticised the 'ineffective collaboration', and in October Wightman wrote confidentially to Matthew, complaining of a lack of back-up for effective on-site staff, such as Stewart Clark and Tony Johnson, from the Melville Street office in Edinburgh.[114] Eventually, as we shall see, it was only in the early 1970s, after a period of lengthy arbitration, that progress with this traumatic contract was decisively accelerated, with final completion in April 1974. All in all, the construction stage of Ninewells seemed to provide a comprehensive refutation of the claimed advantages of 1960s multi-disciplinary, cross-industry teamwork in the timely 'delivery' of large public sector building projects – especially those, as in this case, of highly innovative or complex design.[115]

Synthesis or fragmentation? Matthew's disengagement from academia

The atrophying of Matthew's commitment to his university department followed a different path from the experience in RMJM, with a gradual shift from breakneck growth to crisis and fragmentation, culminating in Matthew's own retirement from the Forbes Professorship and departmental headship in the summer of 1968. At first, however, the picture was one of victorious consolidation of Matthew's university-based education strategy. From 1963, all five years of the

Edinburgh BArch course were handled within the department, and in 1964 the intake was doubled from 15 to 30. By 1963 there were 124 students, eight staff and 20 researchers, with numbers expected to more than double in the following few years.[116] Interdisciplinary and specialist research sections proliferated: 1965 saw a new building science unit, and 1967 a course on housing and building, for students from developing countries.[117] In April 1968 the possibility of reabsorption by ECA was decisively removed, when the College finally threw in its lot with Heriot Watt University, which had offered chairs to both Cowan and Travis. During the mid and late 1960s the department, like a handful of others across the UK, established a 'twinning' arrangement with an African equivalent – located within the engineering faculty of Khartoum University. This department, founded in 1957, saw its first graduating architecture student in 1962, and thereafter Edinburgh supplied an external examiner, initially in the form of Matthew himself, and then, from the late 1960s, Percy Johnson-Marshall. The department also helped set up an architectural science laboratory in Khartoum, and the Ministry of Overseas Develop-ment helped finance a senior lecturership there in architectural science.

Gradually, as Matthew's department became larger and larger, and scattered in a range of houses around George Square, it became more and more unwieldy and impersonal. Even as early as 1962, Matthew no longer attended all the Wednesday departmental meetings as a matter of course, and as the years passed he gradually began easing himself out still further – a tendency radically accentuated during his RIBA presidency in 1962–4, which the university acquiesced in only on condition that Percy Johnson-Marshall should stand in as head of department, in addition to his acting headship of the ARU. In 1965 Matthew's secretarial support became more dispersed, when Elsa Inglis became the department's first administrative assistant and – after Dorothy Taylor (finding

9.22 Fifth-year graduation photograph at the Edinburgh University Architecture Department in George Square, 1966, showing Matthew at the back flanked by Percy Johnson-Marshall on the right and lecturer Peter Savage on the left. (EULMC)

the new arrangement difficult) had moved to another department – Margaret Shaw became his personal secretary within the department.[118]

Matthew attempted to pull together this increasingly disparate organisation through insistent promotion of interdisciplinary links, and also, unsurprisingly, by architectural means: by pressing for a monumental new department building, shared with Geography, to be designed by RMJM and built as part of Percy's University CDA plan.[119] Eleanor Morris recalled that 'he and Percy were definitely for tearing the whole area down, and we all lined up behind him' – and at the centre of the area was going to be Matthew's department, medium-rise but quite monumental, with a plan of overlapping hexagons and an area of no less than 200,000 sq ft, to house 152 students and 20 staff. The grandiose project actually got very close to being built, only failing at the last hurdle, owing to expenditure cuts during the 1966/7 devaluation crisis.

But even as Matthew's vision neared this monumental final realisation, hairline cracks within his original structure began to widen into chasms. The three key divisive factors were: first, the disastrous dissension of 1961–2 within the Housing Research Unit; second, the growing ambitions of Percy Johnson-Marshall to set up his own department; and, third, Matthew's conflicting commitments and diminishing interest. In 1975 Percy summed up the interaction of these factors:

When the ARU was threatened with imminent disaster in 1961, I agreed to become its Director and to find a successor. Fortunately, I found Charles Robertson, but I had to direct the Unit for four difficult years. When you, Robert, became simultaneously RIBA President and IUA President, I had to take on the task of Acting Head of the Department of Architecture for two years, or permission for such outside duties would not have been given by the university. During this period, I was slowly building up planning studies in the university, and this culminated in the setting up of the Department of Urban Design and Regional Planning in 1966.[120]

As we saw in Chapter 8, the polarisation of the HRU staff into two opposed camps was finally brought to an end in 1961, when Matthew finally agreed to orchestrate a sideways move, putting Percy in charge of the unit – as well as the administrative work previously dealt with by Nuttgens. Both Frank Clark and Percy had stayed on the sidelines of the HRU troubles, and both now benefited: Clark, despite his 'declining powers' and worsening disorganisation, was able for a time to 'luxuriate' in extensive postgraduate teaching, initially with ECA students but soon, in 1962, acquiring students of his own, with the establishment of a diploma course in civic design. A new and energetic young lecturer, Laurie Fricker, was appointed to supervise them. As an acquaintance of Buckminster Fuller – with whom Matthew was developing IUA-related links at the time – Fricker was also useful to Matthew in his extra-university life. Initially, he found Matthew an offputtingly 'Olympian' figure:

> I thought at first, in terms of Payne Knight's comparison, that he was like a cedar – evergreen, spreading widely, and choking growth at ground level. But I found out within two years that I was completely wrong, and that he was not a cedar, but an oak – deciduous, permitting both light and rain to fall between its leaves, and sustaining ground-level flora.

Fricker eventually left the department only in December 1967, having developed a close working relationship with Matthew. Although obviously still asymmetrical in character, this was an early example of a new, more informal and egalitarian type of 'network' friendship with much younger colleagues and professional collaborators that Matthew now began to develop during the 1960s and early 1970s as he moved towards old age – friendships free of the old tensions of rivalry or dominance, and focused instead on the issues and ideals that increasingly motivated Matthew in the last 15 years of his life.[121]

With Percy Johnson-Marshall, on the other hand, things were more complex and fraught, and Matthew continued to perpetuate more abrasive behaviour patterns, of the kind associated also with his dealings with Alan Reiach and, of course, Stirrat. One family member recalled that

> in general, Robert wasn't rude to people outside the family – he was usually very controlled – but there were people who were, for whatever reason, exceptions, people like Alan or Percy. Robert was really awful to Percy – it really was extraordinary – it was a standing joke – but then, in many ways, Percy *was* a joke!

Percy's outward image was that of a 'slightly woolly headed, delightful person, very sociable, who spoke in chromatic chords and got on terribly well with everybody'.[122] In contrast to the imperial and racial neuroses of Stirrat, Percy was an obsessive multi-culturalist:

> He and his wife were marvellously kind to overseas students – you'd go round to Bella Vista for lunch on Sunday, all these people from different countries would troop in, and April would say, 'Who are all these people, Percy?' He'd reply, 'They're postgrads – I asked them for tea' and she'd say, 'You might have asked *me*!'[123]

With Percy's admiration for Geddes and his growing love for Edinburgh and Scotland, there was the basis for a real friendship with Matthew: arguably, the two of them had far more in common than either had with Stirrat, and in January 1966, for example, Matthew lavishly praised Percy's newly published Geddesian synthesis of world planning innovation, *Rebuilding Cities*, as 'Percy's great work'.[124] But he was at the same time constantly drawn back to a more dominant behaviour pattern, which, in turn, would impel Percy inexorably to break away. However, Percy was no 'pushover' like Clark: 'Percy was quite tough in his own way, behind the charm, quite prepared to hound Robert, over things like money, and get what he wanted.'[125] All the time, Percy was steadily advancing his career as an academic, planning consultant and proselytiser, by flowing into gaps left open by Matthew:

Modern Architect

acting HRU head from 1961, acting head of department from 1962, and consultant planner for the EU redevelopment (succeeding Spence) also from 1961/2.

During the early 1960s, relations between Percy and Matthew became strained, as Matthew piled on the pressure for progress on the projects he had transferred to Percy as his 'dowry' from 1960. For example, as April Johnson-Marshall recalled,

in 1961 Percy went on holiday with me and the children, in the middle of the work on the Belfast Plan, and Robert, who thought he should've stayed behind, was very offended, and cross words were exchanged – he, unlike Percy, wasn't a chap who'd allow family to get in the way![126]

Percy's RMJM-related planning consultancy practice, with its concentration on multilevel decked complexes, existed in uneasy tandem with his growing planning research activity in the university, and his temporary headship of the HRU. When some HRU architects complained about his decision, as a planner, to involve the unit as a 'job architect' for five industrialised tower blocks as part of his Salford redevelopment scheme, 'I had to remind those chaps that both Robert Matthew and I were qualified architects, and also that it wasn't every day that you got five blocks handed to you to play around with!' With the initial five-year funding package coming to an end, the unit was increasingly short of money, despite its rent-free university accommodation, and had to look for work where it could.[127] But Percy had at least found a permanent director: Charles Robertson, a young architect who had worked with Spence on Hutchesontown 'C', and became HRU deputy director in 1962 and full director in 1963. Once back under unambiguously 'architectural' control – first by Robertson, then (from 1972) by former RMJM assistant architect Andrew Gilmour – the unit (renamed Architecture Research Unit in 1965) secured a succession of 'live' commissions, mostly low-rise and medium-rise

high-density housing projects, some in London.

Inspired by his temporary stewardship of the HRU, Percy began to think of setting up a unit dedicated specifically to planning, and in 1963, with Matthew's help, he set about this task in earnest, having begun his postgraduate diploma course in civic design the previous year. Already, from 1960, Matthew and Percy had begun a fresh round of proselytising in the US, to try to secure funding for a Planning Research Unit focusing on a mix of planning in Europe and educational advice for developing countries. In September 1963, en route to the IUA Congress in Cuba and Mexico, Matthew again laid siege to the Rockefeller and Ford Foundations, and by the end of that year, fortified by some £50,000 in research grants, the PRU was finally established. Its first task was to carry out a Geddes-style regional survey and plan of a 133 square mile zone around the newly designated West Lothian new town of Livingston. The Livingston survey, originally assigned personally in 1962 by the Scottish Office to Matthew, along with Donald Robertson, Professor of Applied Economics at Glasgow University, was passed on officially to Percy in February 1964; its survey focused on the growth potential not only of the new town but also of other new local investment, such as the new BMC Bathgate plant. The PRU had five architect-planner staff, two landscape architects and three researchers, and soon settled into the same hand-to-mouth existence as the ARU.[128]

But by 1965 Percy already had his sights fixed on a more fundamental split: the formation of his own department, breaking away from Matthew as Matthew himself had done from the ECA. With his book, *Rebuilding Cities*, almost completed, in 1965 Percy secured his own chair of Urban Design and Regional Planning, and began to offer a diploma course in regional planning from October 1966. Although he avoided any suggestion of overt self-aggrandisement, shyly protesting his reluctance to take on the administrative responsibilities, the situation proved awkward and hurtful for Matthew: 'Percy was wanting to be his own man, and Robert didn't want to separate from him!'[129] Percy's cause was helped by a wider shift in Matthew's status within the university in 1965, when Matthew's ally, Sir Edward Appleton, was succeeded as Principal by zoologist Professor Michael Swann. Almost immediately a chill wind began to ruffle Matthew's university 'empire'. The trouble was not so much over policy or over the university building programme, although Swann was somewhat more sympathetic to conservation than Appleton had been.[130] The main trouble, as in the case of Lyon at ECA a decade earlier, was a rapidly developing personality clash, and Swann began to niggle at Matthew's external commitments, especially his private practice, as justification to rein in his power. His first step was to exploit the tensions between Matthew and Percy: 'Swann said, "Percy can neither live with or without Robert Matthew!" – and he decided to bring matters to a head, by dividing the department. Percy wasn't entirely keen to split off – he was terrified of having to run a department – but Swann finally insisted!'[131] Percy's Department of Urban Design and Regional Planning was finally established in February 1967, with the civic design and regional planning diploma courses, and the PRU, as its main constituent activities. To crown his great year of emancipation, in the autumn Percy bought Bella Vista from RMJM for £5,020, taking advantage of the firm's drive to cut its estate duty liability, and lived there until his death in 1993.

Matthew's vulnerability to Swann's campaign stemmed especially from his own diminishing attention to the department. Usually, he was still the first person to arrive at the departmental meetings every Wednesdays, but his attendance was beginning to slip. Even then, matters could still be disguised effectively. For example, Fricker recalled one staff meeting at which unusually, Frank Clark was there on time and Matthew was late – the opposite of the usual pattern. Now, we landscape students and staff had promised to design a garden on the west side of 18 George Square, and so on this occasion, as Matthew comes in, late, he looks over to Frank and says, 'Frank – now, what are you doing about that garden?' And everyone turned to Frank, almost as if *he* had been late! Matthew had thrown the scent off, not intentionally, to hurt anyone, but by instinct, like the fox throws the scent when it's being hunted!

Another junior colleague recalled one 1960s staff meeting, when lecturer Tony Forward was called out to take a phone call from Pat Nuttgens: 'We were sitting there with Tony on the other side of the door, speaking very loudly in his slow, deliberate way. Matthew turned to Dick McCarron and said, "Go though and tell Tony to use the phone!"'[132]

Matthew was also beginning to relax his grip over the other activities and offshoots of his Edinburgh University department. During his RIBA presidency in 1962–4 it had been agreed that he would be only minimally present on some Wednesdays and Thursdays. After 1964 his attention never returned to its previous levels – with problems and misunderstandings the inevitable result. In mid 1966, for example, he was abroad when Percy Johnson-Marshall, Elsa Inglis and others decided to respond positively to an unsolicited letter from the American Modern architect Richard Neutra (1892–1970), offering to give a lecture in the department.[133] Matthew had already developed a strong antipathy to Neutra's brash, self-promoting ways, and,

when Robert came back, he said 'Oh no! Who got us into that?' I said, 'I did, in good faith and in consultation with our colleagues!' Robert replied, 'You'll also find you'll need to organise a tour of Scotland for him, and probably a concert for his wife too!'

In the event,

we ended up having a dinner at Keith Marischal, with Neutra and Matthew sitting diagonally opposite each other – Robert always liked to sit in the middle of the big rectangular table – with comments flying across the table between them, boastful on Neutra's part, caustic on Robert's![134]

As a sop to Neutra's musician wife, Dione, she was invited to play her cello to the assembled party prior to the dinner, but as so often with the Matthew family, matters then took a unexpected and bizarre turn:

They were running late, and poor Lorna was very worried about the food – especially about the beef getting overcooked. As Mrs Neutra played on and on, we were all sitting there, thinking about the beef down in the kitchen. Salvation eventually came from an unexpected quarter. Lorna and Robert had a parrot down at Keith at that stage, and suddenly, everyone became aware that this parrot had begun to 'accompany' Mrs Neutra – quietly at first, but then with increasing force. As the musical squawks rose to a crescendo in the background, it became virtually impossible to keep a straight face. Eventually, a bag was put over the musical bird, and it was removed – but it had done its job, and we all at last got our dinner![135]

Swann's next move, in 1967, was to persuade Matthew to go part time – with a number of new responsibilities, with which we shall deal shortly. He would retain the Forbes chair in a personal capacity – with a consequent cut in his own salary – while an additional full-time chair would be created for a new departmental head. Academic protocol dictated that Matthew should be formally excluded from discussion about his successor as head of department, but the way the process was managed was somewhat hurtful to him. Inglis recalled that 'they could easily have had an informal word with him, and even let him know who the candidates were, but Swann didn't get on with him, so I was told to

keep the list of candidates under lock and key in my room!' The successful candidate, announced in June 1968, was Guy Oddie.[136]

Matthew's new, part-time responsibilities from 1968 within Edinburgh University comprised chairmanship both of the Architecture Research Unit, and – his main focus of interest – of a new School of the Built Environment. The latter represented a new permutation of his incessant quest for interdisciplinarity in architecture – a search that reflected especially strongly, in a specifically 1960s way, the ideal of rationalised integration of the building process. In contrast to the 'system building' preoccupations of Stirrat Marshall, John Richards and others, focused on physical prefabrication, this attempted synthesis of disciplines was Matthew's own closest approach to the systems ethos. In the early 1960s, as shown in the Buccleuch Place building project, a link-up with Geography, with Planning as the go-between, seemed to be the most natural extension, with a grand synthesis over rational land use the Modernist goal. But gradually, sensitive to the atrophying of the special, integrated relationship of architecture and planning, Matthew instead began to pursue a link with engineering and the building sciences, not from mechanistic reasons but with a Modernist idea of a Bauhaus-style 'basic design' course at the back of his mind. Matthew was well aware of developments at Liverpool University, where a chair of building science had been established in the late 1950s, along with a building engineering degree whose first year was partly shared with the Architecture Department.[137] Initially, his ambitions were bound up with his continuing good relations with Harry Cruden, who had indicated he wished to sponsor a degree in building. Matthew tried to persuade Cruden to found, instead, a degree in architectural science, in collaboration with Arnold Hendry, appointed in early 1964 to the newly established chair of civil engineering. This, however, was the time when Matthew, prompted by the Ninewells

Architect to the welfare state

9.23 Matthew (as PRIBA) with the Glasgow Institute of Architects president, Jack Coia, at a reception at Glasgow School of Art during the May 1964 RIBA Conference, Glasgow. (Glasgow Herald and Evening Times)

difficulties, had begun to distance himself from Crudens, and when 'in mid 1964, Robert made a speech at the RIBA conference in Glasgow, condemning package deal builders, Cruden decided he would give nothing to the Department of Architecture!'[138]

Eventually, Matthew, with Appleton's support, successfully revived the idea of a chair of architectural science, located within the Architecture Department. At interviews in 1966 the front runner was Liverpool physicist C Barrie Wilson, who, after two years in the Civil Engineering Department, finally received his chair in 1968, at the same time as Oddie's appointment. And in October of the same year Hendry agreed to join Architecture, Planning and Building in founding a new School of the Built Environment, spearheaded by a joint first-year civil engineering–architecture course, based essentially on an architects' first-year studio course, with building science a common element.[139] Percy Johnson-Marshall and Matthew collaborated enthusiastically in this common cause, and Matthew gave an introductory lecture hailing the collaboration as a Fuller-style 'synergetic' response to the vast obsolescence of 'slum' areas – 'a new kind of grouping, cutting across the established pattern of faculties [dedicated to] understanding the behaviour of people in relation to physical environment'.[140] However, the course's start, in late 1968, coincided exactly with the time of maximum student unrest, and the joint course became

an easy target in the newspapers as a 'fiasco'.[141]

In addition to his evolving Edinburgh responsibilities, Matthew continued to involve himself in collaboration with, and advice to, other higher education institutions, especially in Scotland. The demands of loyalty to old allies were prominent in these activities: for example, the ultimately unsuccessful attempts by Arthur Ling, established in the town planning chair at Nottingham, to build up his department, were loyally supported by Matthew, and in January 1968 he successfully interceded with Lord James to secure a chair of architecture at York for Pat Nuttgens.[142]

'A grand reappraisal of the profession': Matthew's RIBA presidency, 1962–4

It was above all his two-year RIBA presidency, in 1962–4, coupled with his knighthood, that confirmed Matthew as a fully accepted establishment figure, and banished the residual taint of his supposed socialist associations. In the process, the now consensual acceptability of the new private/public architectural apparatus was underlined. The position carried with it considerable powers of patronage, including nomination of the Hon. Secretary, Hon. Treasurer, Vice-Presidents, members of standing committees, and the nomination of private architects for the several hundred competitions each year. Much of the workload consisted of routine representational events, including ceremonial visits and speeches to local architectural societies across England: in ten days in March 1963, for instance, he visited and addressed the Manchester Society of Architects, the Wiltshire and Dorset Society, and the Northamptonshire, Bedfordshire and Huntingdonshire Society, as well as giving a lecture at the AA on London local government reorganisation. Lorna felt that although 'he did go round all these towns and attend all the presidential dinners, as you have to, I don't think his heart was in it – he actually thought it was really boring, whereas he loved the overseas presidencies.' In his October 1962 inaugural address Matthew claimed that 'what the RIBA expects of its President is that he should be a super-man who, in addition to earning his bread and butter, should be available 25 hours a day, 8 days a week and 13 months in the year, to discharge all possible manner of functions.'[143]

Even with the engagement of Massey, and the other stand-in assistance, the job was still an onerous one, not least because, unprecedentedly, it was entirely overlapped by his IUA presidency (see Chapter 11). Yet Matthew turned out to be 'one of the few people who went through the RIBA presidency without becoming a wreck!'[144] To ease some of the burden, Holford had proposed, just before resigning from office, that a new position of 'president-elect' should be created. Two days after leaving the job, in July 1962 he posted the 'old gong' to Matthew, adding with some relief in his covering note that 'this is my second day of vacation!'[145] Matthew returned the compliment at Holford's portrait presentation the following year, hailing his presidency as 'the most statesmanlike term of office in our history', and one that had raised the 'influence and prestige' of the profession to new heights. Reminiscing, he recalled his friendship with Holford since student days: 'He came from the classical tradition in Liverpool, I from the last remnants of the Gothic in Edinburgh.' Echoing his and Lorna's own situation, Matthew urged that one should not be 'unmindful that there is a reverse side to the picture', as 'the wives of eminent men have much to put up with: in his devotion to the causes of architecture, planning and education, he has spent his energies to a degree few of us can appreciate. Lady Holford has had the brunt of it all.' In a more sceptical vein, Stirrat Marshall's protégé, Andrew Derbyshire, argued in 1997 in a letter to Lionel Esher that, after 1961, Matthew 'withdrew from architectural design and became a man of affairs, an architectural statesman devoted to national and international causes in

which his eloquent intelligence and ruthless pursuit of what he believed to be right were powerfully deployed.'[146] On the whole, this picture of withdrawal from active architectural design was an accurate one, although there were significant exceptions – including, as we shall see in the next chapter, Matthew's leading role in the design of an entire new university! Above all, although he himself was now in private practice, Matthew's RIBA presidency was associated with the social-democratic ideal of 'public architecture', and helped reinforce its brief ascendancy in the 1960s. In Bill Allen's opinion, Matthew, through

his energy and wide standing, and by the unique coincidence of his RIBA and IUA presidencies, brought the Institute to the apex of its influence. He was the last of the generation of the great post-war Presidents, following Spence and Holford, who 'made' the institution. The struggles of Stirrat Marshall and others of us – we were all in each others' pockets – had made the RIBA the correct place for young architects to head for, and to qualify at – and Robert's presidency crowned that achievement.[147]

Only days into his presidency, Matthew was already manoeuvring to try to ensure that a genuine 'official architect' would succeed him in 1964. Stirrat, despite his standing as a 'populist leader' of younger left-wing architects, was himself of course no longer in public employment, and in any case preferred to exert his influence behind the scenes. Matthew's attention therefore focused on Donald Gibson, then Honorary Secretary of the RIBA. Gibson modestly countered by suggesting private practitioner Leonard Howitt instead, but Ricketts wrote to Matthew, having 'intercepted' Gibson's note, that 'I can't think, can you, that this suggestion of Howitt as one to be groomed for President is one to be taken seriously': it was urgently desirable that the next President should be either 'Donald himself' or some other official architect.[148] By February 1964 Ricketts

Architect to the welfare state

and Matthew had focused on a sharp choice between Gibson and two other well-known figures: Hugh Wilson, the Cumbernauld Chief Architect; and Lewis Womersley, City Architect of Sheffield. Another front runner, Lionel Brett (4th Viscount Esher), although qualified as a quasi-public architect through his work as chief architect-planner for Hatfield New Town in 1949–59, was still shaking off the damage his reputation had suffered from a succession of building-defect causes célèbres. Against Gibson, Ricketts argued, there was the potential of his department to 'alarm the profession', but Stirrat had suggested the previous day what most 'privately feel': that 'Gibson, at present, looks a smaller man than he really is, Womersley a rather bigger one.' Wilson, while 'universally popular', seemed 'a later rather than immediate choice'. Possibly, a more formal 'progression system' was needed, including new posts of president-elect and senior vice-president, with the aim of securing a degree of order, midway between Tory Party-style secretive anarchy and the rigidity of some institutions, such as the chartered surveyors.[149]

In the event, it was decided instead to make Gibson President for only one year (1964–5), while Esher would serve a further year as vice-president before his full two-year presidency (1965–7): in November 1964 Matthew acclaimed his successor as 'above all, a development man, a man of action'.[150] But it was Matthew's own presidency that finalised the RIBA's transformation from a 'moribund learned society' into an influential, modern institution, which by the end of 1963 reached its maximum ever membership size, at around 14,000, with 110 staff. His 'public authority' ethos was expressed through a range of modernisation policies, mostly inherited from Holford's presidency, and, indeed, developed in close collaboration with Holford – including an insistence on representation by official architects on all RIBA committees, and the creation of a new, efficiency-orientated sub-profession of 'architectural technician'.[151]

The most fundamental of Matthew's reform efforts at the RIBA was concerned with the internal organisation of the Institute's staff, where he and Holford together remodelled the administration on civil service lines, with departments headed by under-secretaries replacing the old learned society pattern. In the autumn and winter of 1962, in the wake of publication of the Office Survey, there was a substantial recasting of the existing structure, with its deputy secretary, general office, five assistant secretaries and range of departments. The Board of Architectural Education, administratively headed by Elizabeth Layton, had been recently reconstituted in 1960 with a view to more exacting assessment of course teaching.[152] In 1962 the general office and old departments were replaced by four new departments headed by under-secretaries – Central Services, Professional Services, Membership Services and Information Services; these were matched in 1967 by new departmental boards. Other key officials included the Overseas Relations Secretary, a post held by Kathleen Hall from 1962 to 1971. The central policy committee provided liaison between the departments, and also between the RIBA and its allied societies (numbering 48 in 1939) – a regional organisation that was steadily elaborated during the 1960s.[153] This amounted, Matthew explained in 1962, to a 'grand re-appraisal of the profession … in which the first major step was taken at the Oxford Conference on Education in 1958 [and] has culminated in the report of the Office Survey team on *The Architect and His Office*.' This reappraisal was motivated by the belief 'that architecture today is more than an art, that it is a service to the client and to the community. Our task now is to do everything possible to ensure that this service achieves the highest possible levels in design, teaching and management.'[154]

So much for the internal organisation of the RIBA: but what were the tasks that this transformation was intended to address? To be sure, corporate efficiency was, indeed, central to Matthew's reforms: for example, in 1963, he bemoaned the fact that the British profession lacked any management handbook of architectural practice, whereas the US had had one since 1921.[155] But by 1963 reform of that deficiency was well in hand, following publication the previous year of the findings of the 'Office Survey': *The Architect and His Office*. This investigation of the organisation of architectural practices across Britain had been commissioned during Holford's presidency, and overseen by a committee including Andrew Derbyshire and J M (Mike) Austin-Smith as its architect members. The *AJ* hailed *The Architect and His Office* in January 1963 as 'the most revolutionary document in the history of the architectural profession'. Based on a sample of registered architects, of whom some 30 per cent were public and 70 per cent private, it concluded that many private practices were too small to be viable, and recommended multidisciplinary collaboration. The report set out a range of sweeping reforms in administration, architectural education and consulting, in a form that would be suitable for implementation during Matthew's term of office, and would support the coming era of mass prefabrication. Derbyshire recalled that:

the Office Survey was sparked off by an earnings survey which showed architects were the poorest-paid of professions, and Gordon Ricketts, with Bill Holford's endorsement, decided he wanted to find out what architects actually *did* for their money. With Leverhulme money, we produced a report which showed how diverse and chaotic architects' work practices actually were: even under the then mandatory fee scale, they got poor pay because they wasted so much time. The implementation of this report fell to Robert during his presidency. He restructured the RIBA around it, and the Institute began producing standard documents, including a *Handbook of Architectural Practice and Management*, to help architects organise their work more effectively and make more

money – with what long-term success I don't know!

In his inaugural address of October 1962, indeed, Matthew pointed to the Management Handbook as an 'all-important' initiative.[156]

But collective order was not to everyone's liking, and during the mid 1960s the tensions stirred up by this advance of the 'public sector' interest in the RIBA reached boiling point. The growing pressure, spearheaded by Stirrat Marshall, for 'integration' of the executive with the members became a 'resigning issue', with Secretary Gordon Ricketts sharply opposed.[157] Always, however, Matthew insisted that his reforms were not concerned merely with bureaucratic consolidation per se.[158] Within the RIBA, the previously dominant private practice grouping was still in retreat, with the traditional private practitioners feeling themselves ever more squeezed between public architecture and the speculative or package deal builder: the Office Survey had specially highlighted the problems of the small office. In early 1965 a group of small practitioners, led by Leslie K Watson, went so far as to propose setting up an 'Association of Private Architects', but with Matthew's support Ricketts was able to 'steadily whittle away' its 'initial grandiose aims of a full-blown Association' until it became 'an informal discussion group under the aegis of the RIBA'.[159] But the public–private conflict only worsened, and Ricketts eventually became overwhelmed by it: in January 1968 he committed suicide by jumping off a cliff in Kent. In the wake of this bombshell the council, with Stirrat Marshall acting as broker, appointed Scottish Office civil servant Patrick Harrison, a specialist in regional planning and new towns policy, to help defuse the conflicts and crises within the Institute.[160]

The office of RIBA President also carried with it an *ex officio* role on a variety of bodies and one-off events, some of which zigzagged across the professional fault lines of individualism versus corporatism. The most notable individual 'event' during Matthew's presidency was the competition for the new National Theatre on the South Bank, on which he acted (alongside Holford and three others) as assessor; in 1962 the government had agreed in principle to the building of a new opera house and theatre. From Matthew's point of view the chief concern was the rising pressure from the private architectural world for a two-stage designer competition, rather than a limited competition – a controversy that might be exacerbated by his dual role as assessor and PRIBA. Hugh Casson wrote to him in July 1962 that 'the resentment throughout the profession over the 1st XI chosen for Churchill [College, Cambridge] still smoulders', and warned against selecting a 'Golden Few'. In the event, however, the 'client body' – the South Bank Theatre Board – rejected an open competition, owing to the 'rapidly evolving' principles of theatre design – and a two-stage designer selection process was adopted. Eventually the assessors unanimously selected the most adventurous finalist, Denys Lasdun, with his markedly avant-garde metaphoric 'cluster' planning ideas. From that point – typical of his compartmentalised approach – Matthew rapidly lost interest in the project, and in May 1965 he decided not to attend a preview of Lasdun's concept model.[161]

The package-deal builder seemed to be a far greater and more real threat than the posturings of the private-architect defenders, with forests of system-built tower blocks, using contractors' 'closed' systems, springing up everywhere.[162] Everything about this issue was seen as a matter of great sensitivity within the RIBA. For example, in March 1964 a minor private architect based in Yeovil, Leslie H Kemp, wrote complaining of his lack of work since returning from Canada some years previously, and lamenting that architects had 'abdicated' work to the spec builder. Ricketts briefed Matthew that, although Kemp was an 'unsuccessful, chip on shoulder fellow ... for political reasons it is important that the President should offer to see him ...

we'll discuss fighting the spec builder and put his name on our list for work'. Kemp's grievance was completely defused at a 'cordial' meeting with Matthew in May 1964.[163] At a post-Office Survey RIBA conference on 'The Architect and Productivity' chaired by Matthew in July 1963 in Sheffield, he declared that the way for the architect to outstrip the package-deal builder, and keep leadership of the building process, was through 'top-level R&D'.[164] The advances of public architecture meant that, equally, there were internal battles to be fought within the state machine – always with the aim (as with the Valuer versus Architect battle in the LCC) of promoting research-led, quality 'design' as against simple, quantitative 'production' interests. Within central government, for example, 1963 saw a tremendous argument over the proper status of the post of Director-General of Research and Development in the Ministry of Public Building and Works, held since 1962 by Donald Gibson: should the post report directly to the Minister (thus assuming Permanent Secretary status) or not? After a compromise acceptable to Gibson had been suggested by the Minister, Geoffrey Rippon, and endorsed by Cabinet – that Gibson should report to him but be paid less than the Permanent Secretary – one council member recalled that

Rippon rang up Robert and said, 'I know you have a meeting of the RIBA tonight, and that the Institute is very concerned. The Cabinet has made this decision, and I'd be prepared to come to the Institute tonight if you'd give me a few minutes, to make the official announcement of the outcome.' As a result, this important announcement, which would normally have been made in the House, was made in Portland Place – and it was Robert's influence and standing with the Minister which made it possible![165]

Central government 'quangos' should also, Matthew believed, benefit from the same 'teamwork' formula of 'matching administrators and technical men at all levels' – although the escalating problems at Ninewells might have given him some cause to reconsider the assumed efficacy of public sector 'teamwork'.[166] At the local authority level the chief battle was over the status of architecture in the 1964–5 reorganisation of London local government. Matthew, along with other architect-planners of the first post-war generation, was torn between a desire to bolster the powers of the new Greater London Council, as an Abercrombie-style regional authority and successor to the LCC, and a concern to ensure that the new London boroughs would have powerful borough architects. On this issue, he developed a close working relationship with the new and design-minded Tory Minister of Housing, Sir Keith Joseph – in another striking demonstration of his insistence on the priority of issue-based and professional relationships over party politics. In January 1963 Joseph agreed to speak at a heated January 1963 meeting at the RIBA, chaired by Matthew, who hailed the Minister for his 'courage' in coming to debate the Bill 'face to face': 'we feel, whatever our politics, that he is fighting on our side'. Eventually, Joseph's circular on the reorganisation stipulated that all the new boroughs must appoint a borough architect at chief officer level: he explained to Matthew in August 1964 that the RIBA campaign had been decisive in giving him 'an opportunity to strike a blow for good architecture'.[167] Paradoxically, Matthew's post-presidency relations with the new Labour government were never as close as those with Joseph and Rippon.[168]

In the years after his presidency he continued the fight against the menace of any revived 19th-century-style liberalism. The particular bogeyman in these years seemed to be the Monopolies Commission, which in 1967 began a war of attrition against the 'senior professions': in 1967–71 Matthew chaired a defensive 'liaison group' of a group of professions on monopoly issues, and in 1970 wrote to *The Times* that the commission was 'clearly out of its depth' in its 'naïve and doctrinaire view (based on

9.24 Matthew seen leading an RIBA delegation to Sir Keith Joseph, Minister of Housing and Local Government, in March 1963, to press the case for enhanced research on urban renewal. The delegation, seen leaving the RIBA, comprised (from left), Arthur Ling, Matthew, Sir Hamilton Kerr MP, Dr Barnett Stross MP, Robert Gardner-Medwin and Gordon Ricketts. (*JRIBA*, April 1963, 134) (RIBA; photo by Sam Lambert)

19th century economic theory)'. 'To label [professional] self-discipline "restrictive practices against the public interest" was an inversion of the truth'; if restraints were lifted, 'all aspects of national life would inevitably and permanently suffer', and in architecture 'the jungle would begin at Portland Place'.[169] The defence of professionalism, in Matthew's view, depended above all on proper educational provision, focused especially on the work of the Board of Architectural Education in validating and overseeing courses. The aim, within Britain, was to bring as many schools as possible within universities, as he had done. The Robbins report was not only helping to cement the new universities building programme, with which RMJM was so intimately involved, but also gave a boost to the 'broad discipline of architecture', which 'fits very well the way that many universities are going'. During his presidency, the task of educational reform was largely the responsibility of Hugh Wilson: by 1967, in the UK, only 15 per cent of entrants to the profession did so under their own resources, while 85 per cent claimed exemption through study at schools of architecture.[170]

Increasingly, the work of educational coordination was moving onto an international plane. We shall examine in Chapter 11 how Matthew channelled the new (1965) Commonwealth Association

313

9.25 Meticulously signed and dated examples of Matthew's doodles from meetings of the mid and late 1960s. (EULMC)

of Architects above all into the issue of educational intercompatibility; by 1967 the RIBA had recognised 21 schools of architecture outside the UK, of which only one (in Switzerland) was outside the Commonwealth.[171] More contentiously – despite the opposition of many of the local societies to 'flooding the market' – during Holford's presidency he and Matthew also tried to expand the profession laterally, by evolving a new sub-profession of technicians, with the aim of 'unifying the industry' through 'an unified system of education for everyone in Building'.[172]

In his inaugural address as RIBA President in August 1962 Matthew reiterated that the leitmotif of his presidency would be education: the increase of student numbers, and the recognition and organisation of research and training of teachers. This enhancement of education

should, he argued, be aimed at one challenge in particular – the need to integrate architecture and planning, in the light of his own worries about the depredations of output-led massed housing, and Jane Jacobs's 'wholesale assault on contemporary planning'. More generally, Matthew began increasingly to move towards an agenda of 'environmentalism'; overall, the aim must be to design 'healthy, vital, living towns, not merely architectural monuments, profitable investments or exhibitions of the highway engineer's skill'.[173]

The politics of 1960s architecture in England and Scotland

Matthew's RIBA presidency unleashed the floodgates of architectural establishment opportunity for him – beginning of course with continuing responsibilities within the RIBA itself, where in 1967, for example, he took up – with some diffidence, fearing a loss of 'voluntary enthusiasm' – the chair of one of the four new departmental boards – Membership and Public Affairs, which included overseas relations. Although Park Square East ceased in 1964 to be a detached branch office of the RIBA, Matthew continued to be ready to offer it (and himself, if available) for Institute-related hospitality, especially for overseas visitors.[174]

The most palpable sign of Matthew's reinforced 'establishment' status in the wake of his knighthood and RIBA presidency – aside from his now regular consultations from ministers and senior politicians – was his elevation to the cadre of those deemed to be qualified to chair major public inquiries into matters of state policy on the built environment. This was something of central importance to town planning in particular, whose 40-year 'rise' in Britain from the 1930s had been driven forward by individual causes célèbres.[175] In a sense, Matthew was now reclaiming some of the elevated development-control territory that he had surrendered on giving up his LCC architecture-planning role a decade earlier. And, appropriately enough, his first major commission concerned a redevelopment scheme in Central London – for the 'Broad Sanctuary' site immediately to the west of Parliament Square. Ironically, the strategic context of the proposal betrayed somewhat the way in which Matthew's 1953 'retreat' back to Scotland, and his forthright public-architecture ideology, had slightly sidelined him in the London establishment world. The Broad Sanctuary site formed part of a wider area plan drawn up in 1964–5 by Leslie Martin for the redevelopment of Lower Whitehall and Parliament Square as an integrated government precinct – planned, with Martin's usual astringent impersonality, with a grid-like array of courtyards stretching north of a traffic-free Parliament Square, planned using complex mathematical modelling to keep building height to seven storeys. While the general redevelopment, to be carried out over as much as 50 years,

carefully respected the scale of Westminster Abbey and Palace through its medium-rise height, the proposal also envisaged more immediate construction of two new buildings of monumental scale, including a government conference centre of architecturally 'national or international significance' on the Broad Sanctuary site, originally proposed in the Westminster City plan of 1946.[176]

In retrospect, given the later upsurge in conservationist agitation, one commentator concluded that Martin's model 'was one of the least successful acts of communication ever'. And indeed, the Ministry began, in effect, to undermine it straight away, by deciding in November 1965 to proceed with it only in fragments, beginning with the Broad Sanctuary site. In February 1966 Matthew responded positively to an approach from Jim Jones, MHLG Deputy Secretary, asking him to chair a three-week inquiry to assess whether Martin's plan was the best solution for Broad Sanctuary. Assisted by Ministry official D R Lewis, Matthew's inquiry, carried out over six days in May 1966, was eventually published in spring 1967.[177] The contentious issue was Martin's concept of Parliament Square as a vast open space, with the new conference centre standing proudly on its own – a total redevelopment that would require demolition of the professional institutes of the civil engineers and chartered surveyors on Great George Street. The proposal faced two sets of opponents at once: the two influential institutions – with the ICE represented by the influential consultant planner and townscapist Thomas Sharp (1901–78) – and the growing conservation lobby, headed by the Victorian Society. One 'Vixoc' committee member, journalist Nicholas Taylor, blasted Martin's proposal as 'the original sin of town planners, a preference for the clean sweep'.[178] Within the restricted scope open to him, Matthew eventually fell back on his own preference for a compromise between conservation and redevelopment, recommending that the ICE building should be spared, while allowing a 'unified architectural entity of the highest quality' on the remainder of the site.

The publication of Matthew's Broad Sanctuary report was followed, more unexpectedly, by a year and a half of quasi-legal wrangling with the ICE's witnesses, Sharp and H C Delves, who threatened to sue him personally over the allegedly 'tendentious' way in which his text reported the precise nuances of their views. Delves, for example, claimed that his opposition to comprehensive redevelopment had been misrepresented as opposition to all comprehensive planning. Sharp was a veteran of numerous battles at planning inquiries, and had a temperamental weakness for disputes and controversies.[179] Ultimately, the wider Martin redevelopment concept was nullified by the economic traumas of the late 1960s and 1970s, and the further rise of the conservation lobby – with the Victorian Society's campaign of opposition seen in retrospect by Alan Powers as 'one of the significant turning-points in the conflict between modern architecture and conservation' – but a national conference centre was indeed built on the half-island site defined in Matthew's report (in the 1980s, by Powell & Moya). In 1970–2, as we shall see in Chapter 12, Matthew was also involved as competition assessor for another site in the area, the Bridge Street parliamentary office complex, whose winning design, by Robin Spence and Robin Webster, remained unbuilt.[180]

The modest level of financial remuneration for such inquiries was all the more pertinent as Matthew, unlike some establishment architects more closely integrated with the private enterprise ethos, had shown a general reluctance to become involved in the lucrative business of private consultancy to rich commercial development companies. The early 1960s had seen a brief dalliance with Harold Samuel's Land Securities Investment Trust Ltd: here, Matthew deployed New Zealand House-style arguments for 'landmark' towers in support of a planning application for a huge office redevelopment at Vauxhall, but was disconcerted

to find himself appearing against the LCC. In 1964, with the additional complication of his RIBA presidency in mind, he disengaged himself from a similar commitment to advise Samuel's architect, Fitzroy Robinson, on the redevelopment of the far more sensitive Queen Anne's Mansions site overlooking St James's Park, which was clearly destined to fall foul of the LCC policy against further new offices in central London. Eventually, in March 1964, Samuel's patience ran out and Matthew's consultancy was terminated; he was replaced, appropriately enough, by the more private-enterprise-orientated Basil Spence, whose eventual project for the site stirred up a hornet's nest of controversy.

Matthew's obvious worry about any open clash with his old department stemmed from a more general continuing feeling of loyalty to the LCC. In June 1965, for instance, just after the LCC had passed into history, he opened a photographic exhibition of the department's projects in the National Housing Center, Washington, DC. His speech hailed its work, whether under an LCC or GLC label, as 'representative of British urban architecture today – building mainly for social purposes', and recalled with rosy fondness that it had been 'about the perfect client for a large group of young, ambitious and skilled men and women. We were given our head ... it's not so much a department, as a way of life.'[181] In the rosy glow of hindsight, even old LCC adversaries became nostalgic chums: September 1967 saw a glowingly cordial exchange of letters with Matthew's former sparring partner, Cyril Walker, now a chartered surveyor in private practice. Matthew helped find an opening through the RMJM London office for Walker's student civil engineer son, Brian, and a cheerful lunch at the Reform Club to 'talk over old times' duly followed. On a 1965 visit to County Hall with Charles Robertson, 'it was like a family reunion – the secretaries were all the same ones he'd had, and were clearly delighted to see him!'[182]

In addition to the Broad Sanctuary

project, Matthew's RIBA presidency also led directly to a range of lower-key consultative applications extending beyond his presidency, including membership of the national consultative council of MPBW, and membership of the BBC General Advisory Council between 1963 and 1968. The GAC, although a prestigious-sounding appointment, was actually a large and unwieldy body of some 64 members, with the built environment interest represented by Matthew and Robert Grieve. In addition to making representations on specific programmes or issues – such as his growing hobby horse of the conservation of the Edinburgh New Town – Matthew tried to pursue a wider agenda of increasing the coverage of architecture and the built environment on television, closely advised by the RIBA's Malcolm MacEwen. He forcefully but unsuccessfully argued for a 'fundamental shift in values in the BBC towards a deeper appreciation of the importance of the environment in fostering human welfare and happiness'.[183]

Matthew was equally frustrated in his attempts to pursue essentially the same agenda of 'environmentalism' through the town planning establishment within the MHLG and TPI. His initiatives were in response to the combination of the new movement of 'urban renewal' and the increasingly optimistic climate of revival of regional planning in the 1960s. All in all, planning seemed to be rebounding from its 'slough of despond' the previous decade, with a nationwide proliferation of 'development and growth' programmes linking planning and economics, and an upsurge in the number of new planning courses recognised by the TPI for exemption from intermediate or final examinations: by the mid 1960s there were 13, including Percy's own at Edinburgh.[184]

The urban renewal movement of the late 1950s and early 1960s was partly an attempt by architects to reclaim some of the old ground of the 'architect-planner'. In late 1962 Matthew declared that the encouragement of research into urban renewal would be a priority for his presi-

dency, and to prepare the ground he turned to Keith Joseph, whose portfolio also included planning. At an October meeting he persuaded Joseph that MHLG should sponsor a programme of urban research, using as a first case study Percy Johnson-Marshall's impending planning consultancy for Salford, and perhaps including Liverpool too. Matthew thanked Joseph for having reorientated MHLG from a negative, restrictive outlook, focused solely on housing output, to a positive, creative force, as 'you are so well seized with the social value of our work'. After further meetings with Joseph aimed at 'crash action' in initiating research on urban renewal, MHLG's chief planner, J R James, a powerful ally of Matthew's, was authorised by the Minister to convene a 'brainstorming' meeting at LSE in July 1963, which expanded the aspiration to a fully fledged government-financed Urban Research Council, with cross-connections to social and economic studies: none of these initiatives had any substantial outcome.[185] The RIBA's push into the field of urban renewal was also prompted partly by motives of professional defensiveness, in the face of novel initiatives from new cross-disciplinary voluntaristic groupings such as the Civic Trust – originally set up in 1957 at the instigation of Duncan Sandys, to promote civic amenity improvement through coordination of local amenity societies, but which, in 1962–3, threatened for a time to set up a 'Town Planning Advisory Service', focused on central area redevelopment – including the organising of competitions to 'obtain designs from which the client could pick': Matthew had to step in to help block the proposal, ensuring that the advisory service would be confined to 'preliminary reconnaissance' of the problems of any particular town.[186]

The revival of Matthew's interest in regional planning came slightly later, in the mid 1960s, in collaboration with Robert Grieve. In January 1965, chairing the opening discussion at a TPI conference in Edinburgh, Matthew argued passionately for a Geddesian vision of interdisciplinary 'creative planning' in opposition to a static, bureaucratic development control, and explicitly evoked the international environmentalist movement of 'Ekistics' with which he was becoming increasingly involved (see Chapter 11). Matthew argued that 'Patrick Geddes was the father of Ekistics – and he was therefore and above all a creative man.'[187] Seven months later, Matthew again attempted to turn rhetoric into action at an MHLG-sponsored elite symposium on the subject of 'A Planning Research Institute' at Churchill College, Cambridge, opened by Crossman. The common concern of the symposium, which formed part of the modernisation agenda of the post-1964 Wilson government, was how to help government expand statutory planning in a 'creative', diverse way, without falling into the trap of becoming an 'esoteric ... clique'. In the end, however, the session became bogged down in arguments about the name of the proposed body: should it be a 'research council' (favoured by Matthew) or a less high-powered, academic 'institute' (favoured by Crossman and J D Jones); should it focus on 'urban planning' issues, or 'development studies'?[188] But in any case, as Matthew's cross-reference to Ekistics at the Edinburgh TPI conference showed, the focus of his environmentalism was rapidly reorientating itself towards more cosmopolitan, internationalist pattern of networks of association – as we shall see in Chapter 11.

Proselytising civic amenity in modern Scotland

Unlike the uneasy balance among the 'great men' of London architectural affairs, in Scottish architectural establishment matters Matthew was a largely unchallenged colossus, with especially pervasive influence in Edinburgh and 'East Coast' matters. It was here that he was more than compensated for his relative loss of influence in London after 1953. In this, Matthew contrasted interestingly with Spence, whose personal involvement in Scotland faded out after the high point of the Edinburgh

University and Glasgow Gorbals projects. That disparity of commitment was briefly glossed over in June 1965, in a programme of joint celebrations in their honour, culminating in an EAA-sponsored dinner in the ECA sculpture court, organised by Dunbar-Nasmith and hosted by EAA president Ian Carnegie; in his speech, Matthew claimed he and Spence were both 'Gothic' men.[189] While Spence still claimed Scottish roots, Matthew lost no opportunity to emphasise his more wholehearted commitment.[190] Matthew was kept plugged into Scottish affairs not only by the time he spent in Edinburgh and Keith, but also by his twice-weekly return sleeper trips to London, a journey on which numerous other Scottish elite figures were habitually to be encountered.[191] His ambassadorial role as host-in-chief to visiting English and overseas figures and delegations continued unabated: for example, in July 1968 John Summerson, after a successful lecture visit orchestrated by Matthew, wrote to him that although 'I fell in love with Edinburgh in 1929–31, I was also, for various reasons, very unhappy in those years and left with a sense of frustration and failure. To be received there in the circumstances of last week blotted out the discord and left only the harmony.'[192]

In contrast to his London role, it was unquestioned that, in Scotland, Matthew would be approached to act as assessor or panel member for virtually all top government architectural and planning posts, in his capacity as the country's 'grand old man of architecture'. In 1966, for example, no sooner had he served on the interview board for a Scottish Office chief architect, than the SDD Secretary, Alan Hume, wrote again that 'once again we are turning to you to help, because nobody can command the same experience and authority. We are losing Nicoll, whom you helped us choose as our Chief Planning Officer, to Strathclyde University.' And within eight weeks Hume was back in touch to report that the chosen candidate (Cotton) had resigned for 'domestic reasons' and transferred to MPBW: Cicely Naismith told Matthew, doubtless to his relief, that he was 'off the hook' this time, as 'you will be in Greece!'[193]

Hospital architecture was another area where Matthew played a leadership role in Scotland, especially in view of the strong links between SDD Architects and the South-Eastern Hospital Board architect John Holt, coupled with Matthew's own RMJM hospital design work. In June 1966, for example, he opened a 'morale boosting' exhibition of Scottish hospital design at the new Scottish Hospital Centre, a single-storey building at the Western Infirmary designed by Holt's office for use by multidisciplinary and user-study teams. His speech highlighted the problems of protracted hospital briefing, spanning many years, as 'a terrible trial of spirit' for an architect.[194]

Other establishment-cum-philanthropic duties within Scotland followed, again more straightforwardly than in London. In all such cases the task of the 'great man' was to praise Scottish progress and pride in public while, if necessary, working behind the scenes to ensure a 'fair deal' in future. In February 1968, for instance, John Paterson wrote to him to ask him to lobby the Secretary of State for the involvement of Scottish exhibition designers in Powell & Moya's British Pavilion at the Osaka Expo-1970, arguing that 'Scotland has made a contribution as a country to the UK as a whole out of all proportion to her size and population.' Matthew agreed that the Central Office of Information 'never employ Scottish designers', even when an exhibition was being held in Scotland.[195]

What was the specifically architectural focus of Matthew's personal proselytising in Scotland? Clearly, he had now completely given up his 1950s quest for a 'national Scottish modern architecture'.[196] What replaced it was a growing concern with the inspiration of heritage. His main emphasis was now on an explicitly Geddesian planning formula of creative interaction of new and old, inspired especially by his beloved Edinburgh. Margaret Richards recalled that

he knew and loved Edinburgh intimately, could name every building and every architect, and could shock you, especially, with his detailed knowledge of Victorian Edinburgh – another David Walker, but twenty years earlier! More than friends or most family members, the city of Edinburgh was truly one of the great loves of Matthew's life![197]

In a 1964 public lecture in Reading – significantly entitled 'Architecture Today, Yesterday and Tomorrow' – he juxtaposed futuristic slides of Cumbernauld's traffic-segregated network with illustrations of Priene, Oxford and Cambridge as examples of 'variety, compactness and integration', but hailed Geddes's Outlook Tower above all as a unique synthesising and condensing device. And two and a half years later, in his address to Social Science Faculty freshers, he again pointed to Geddes and his followers, inspired by Edinburgh's beauty, as pioneers of a new sensibility in the urban and rural built environment:

Here in Edinburgh is a combination of nature and the works of men – a townscape of superlative quality – the rocks and valleys, sudden views of gardens and brilliant greens – if you are lucky, Ben Lawers can be seen on the skyline, and maybe, with a glass, even the dark silhouette of Professor Grieve sitting on a rock contemplating the results of Highland development. Geddes built his tower at the highest point he could find, and the Outlook Tower [gives] a total vision of the town, live and inert – as good a textbook as any on the subject of man in relation to his environment.[198]

Within Scotland, indeed, Grieve, as SDD planner-in-chief (1961–4) and, from 1965, first chief executive of the newly created Highlands and Islands Development Board, was his most effective ally and advocate of creative Geddesian regional planning.[199]

In Matthew's 1960s Scottish vision of a regionally planned synthesis of new and

9.26 Early 1960s view of New Lanark
in decay, before start of rehabilitation
work. (A L Hunter)

old, within a framework of enlightened, state-controlled economic expansion, the highly politicised situation on Clydeside presented the least harmonious element. But his attitude to Glasgow, the epicentre of all this activity and controversy, remained as ambiguous as ever.[200] Publicly, he applauded the beginning of the planner-led CDA programme, arguing in 1964 that 'Glasgow today is at the beginning of the biggest job of city rebuilding ever undertaken in the British Isles.' But privately he was depressed and alienated by the advance of package-deal mass housing: citing the greater architect control allowed by the old separate-trades contracting system, he rebuffed overtones (brokered by Cleeve Barr) for a Clydeside consortium led by contractor George Lawrence and Paisley Burgh Engineer MacGregor: Matthew argued that, while he favoured 'maximum rationalisation of normal methods', he was not prepared to get involved in 'the "system" business'.[201] Increasingly, as we shall see in Chapter 12, Matthew's interest in Glasgow began to shift towards conservation issues: immediately prior to the 1964 RIBA conference there, for example, he was in close consultation with Nikolaus Pevsner to see whether pressure could be brought to bear on the Corporation over the threatened Ingram Street (Mackintosh)

tearooms: Pevsner promised to 'try and stir up more feeling about this'.[202]

In the 1970s and 1980s the emphasis in Glasgow housing would shift to local housing associations. In the early 1960s the time was not yet ripe for that – but a harbinger of this future was emerging in Glasgow's rural hinterland, when Matthew played a key role in the launching of a conservation drive to 'save' the pioneering Dale/Owen industrial-utopian planned village of New Lanark and bring 'the whole township back to life'. The village had been left to decay in the early 1960s by its last owners, the Gourock Ropework Company, and in 1962 Lanark Town Council had declined an offer by the company to sell them all the housing in the village (175 tenement houses) for £250. Matthew, working with the Scottish Office and the Adam Housing Society, successfully pressed in 1963 for a housing association, the New Lanark Association Ltd, to be set up, and begin rehabilitation of the tenements, helped by an SDD housing subsidy and Pilgrim Trust grant, and a substantial Historic Buildings Council for Scotland grant. In a September 1963 letter to Lanark County Council he hailed New Lanark as 'a unique example of community planning ... bold and thoroughly Scottish in feeling ... [in a] magnificent and unspoiled landscape'. 1964 saw the appointment of Ian Lindsay & Partners to modernise Caithness Row as a pilot project – carried through in 1965–7, as the first phase of a long restoration programme that was ultimately, after many crises, to lead to the 1973 designation of New Lanark as a Conservation Area, and the 1974 foundation of the New Lanark Conservation Trust. In 1967 Matthew confidently predicted that 'I have no doubt at all that the whole township will come back to life, as a remarkable piece of the Scottish and Welsh heritage.'[203]

The inaugural meeting of the New Lanark Association in late 1963 provided a typical example of one of Matthew's favourite ways of expressing his status as patriarch of Scottish architecture: namely, to turn up at a meeting and sit impressively throughout it, without saying a word. Laurie Fricker recalled that he himself, representing Edinburgh University along with Norman Dunhill, arrived at the meeting, which was to be addressed by Kenneth Dale Owen – a Texan businessman who was Robert Owen's great-great grandson, and had come to Scotland especially for the event. Fricker was surprised to find Matthew already sitting there quietly at the back:

He recognised me with a pleasant smile. Then Owen began his speech, which was a lot of absolute nonsense, about how much his great grandfather would have approved of this initiative, stemming as it did from enlightened private enterprise self-interest, not from any 'socialist' government bureaucracy, and so forth. An administrator from SDD sitting next to me leaned back and whispered to Matthew, 'Why don't you speak up and contradict him, Robert? – after all, it's because of your influence in the Scottish Office that this has got anywhere at all!' But he simply chuckled ruefully, shrugged his shoulders and said nothing! He wasn't going to get involved arguing with somebody who was obviously an utter fool! He just came in, sat there, said nothing, and then at the end, just got up and left. Keeping his powder dry – that was typical of him![204]

Far more easily assimilable within Matthew's Geddesian regional planning strategy was the urban built environment of the 'historic' east coast: ironically, the zone covered by Mears's South-East Plan rather than Abercrombie and Matthew's Clyde Plan.[205] From 1963, Matthew acquired a convenient vehicle to pursue this strategy, in effect stepping into the footsteps of Mears, after he carried out a skilful *coup d'état* within the Saltire Society Housing Design Award Panel, following the sudden death of his friend Robert Hurd. Reacting to the growing award-winning success of RMJM projects from Barshare onwards, Hurd had just invited Matthew to join the panel, but following his death unsuccessful attempts were made in October 1963 by an 'anti-architectural' faction led by the society's Honorary Secretary, R M Gorrie, to block Matthew's appointment. The latter, as so often, was able to turn this to advantage, and after an urgent exchange of correspondence between the RMJM secretariat and the society, Matthew found himself appointed not just a member but the convener of the panel, with Grieve co-opted as an additional member to deputise in Matthew's absence; within months, Gorrie had been replaced as Honorary Secretary altogether.

During his tenure, until 1968, Matthew skilfully combined a deferential respect for the conservation legacy of Hurd with exploitation of the awards presentation as an opportunity for generalised attacks on 'indiscriminate' building of tower blocks and the 'constantly lowering' design standards of private housebuilders; he lavishly praised contextual Modernist architects such as Wheeler & Sproson, designers of numerous sensitive interventions in Fife coastal burghs.[206] Matthew also spread his 'patronage' by encouraging the careers of other up-and-coming modern architects, such as the flamboyantly 'sculptural' Peter Womersley, a Yorkshireman who had moved to the Borders after designing a pioneering split-level house at Farnley

Hey, near Leeds. Ironically, Womersley's biggest career break – a competition win (in 1961) for a new Roxburgh County Buildings (headquarters) at St Boswells – was awarded by Kininmonth, as assessor, but Matthew soon began to help him behind the scenes. He was impressed by Womersley's energy as consultant architect for an abortive street improvement 'facelift' scheme of 1961–3 for the Royal Mile, modelled on the Civic Trust-sponsored Magdalen Street project in Norwich (1957), overseen by a steering panel including himself, but ultimately stymied by insistence on 'petty individual rights'.[207] Despite this debacle, Matthew took steps to encourage Womersley's continued advancement. In March 1963, for example, Professor Michael Woodruff of Edinburgh University's Department of Surgical Science wrote to Matthew asking for his advice on the selection of an architect for a proposed transplantation surgery unit, funded by a £200,000 Nuffield grant. Apologising that 'I know how fantastically busy you are', Woodruff explained that although Holt had done the indicative plan submitted to the Nuffield, he was too busy to draw up detailed plans and had instead suggested 'a young architect, Peter Wormsley [sic]'. As Womersley had no experience in operating theatre design, Woodruff asked Matthew to adjudicate on his suitability: 'If you know Wormsley, and feel he could do the job satisfactorily, I will at once agree to his appointment.' Matthew scrawled laconically on the note, 'Dealt with by telephone, 13 March 1963'. And cordial relations with Womersley continued throughout the 1960s, with an increasingly conservationist slant.[208]

More generally, as the 1960s progressed, Matthew's Geddesian strategy in Scotland began steadily to tilt towards a conservationist and environmentalist outlook – a harbinger, on his home territory, of his more general shift in ethos from the end of the decade. His work on the RFACS – on which he served for an unprecedented 22 years – echoed this shift. At the beginning of the decade, his position on the Commission was more or less that of a thrusting Modernist, with Kininmonth and Pilkington Jackson as conservative opponents.[209] Yet, as early as 1962, he made an unfashionable defence of the Victorian heritage, warning that a paper by the RFACS Secretary on urban renewal should avoid any general condemnation of 19th-century tenements. Here, as always, Edinburgh was the focus, and having himself retreated from further skyline interventions following completion of the Arts Tower in 1963, Matthew was now able, chameleon-like, to begin merging his ambiguous position on Edinburgh high building with his more uncompromising opposition to massed tower blocks in Glasgow, joining a movement of opposition that was fuelled in 1963 by a proposed hotel tower in George Street and in November 1964 by an unprecedented proposal for a 250 ft high office tower above Haymarket Station, on the western fringe of the New Town – controversies that persuaded the City Council to appoint Holford to draw up a 'High Buildings Policy' for the city.[210] Accordingly, Matthew himself now began to take a new and hard line on the issue. In mid 1964, perhaps tongue-in-cheek, in view of its location only 100 yards away from his own recently abandoned 19-storey RIE slab proposal, he promised to 'thunder a bit' against a proposed extension to George Heriot's School, stressing with 'all the force at my command' that it would have a 'disastrous' effect on the skyline profile of 'one of our National architectural treasures'.[211] As the 1960s wore on, the focus of these efforts shifted to outright conservation. For this the RFACS was not an ideal vehicle, although its remit had been extended in 1964 to include developments affecting listed buildings: as Bannatyne put it in 1965, 'this Commission is not a preservationist body; we are concerned, rather, with the seemly development of the urban environment and with the conservation of the countryside.'[212] Matthew's admiration for the Victorian heritage was not confined to works in 'austere' or 'modern' styles, but equally embraced highly decorated historicist eclecticism. In 1965, for instance, he fought unsuccessfully for preservation of two next-door Princes Street buildings of highly contrasting character: William Burn's chaste New Club palazzo (1834) and David Rhind's overpoweringly ornate Venetian Renaissance Life Association of Scotland (1855–8). In this fight, Matthew, who helped enlist the backing of Nikolaus Pevsner in London, found himself pitted against the 'philistine' Labour Secretary of State, William Ross, along with some novel allies, such as McWilliam of the Scottish Georgian Society.[213]

But, as we shall trace in Chapter 12, it was not these piecemeal cases that would finally harness Matthew's attention and commitment to the conservation of Edinburgh, but, rather, the 'big idea' of 'saving the New Town'. A decisive role in that process would be played, from 1967, by the newly founded Scottish Civic Trust, with Matthew as one of its dominant members. The foundation of the SCT, as a spin-off from the successful, London-based Civic Trust, originally stemmed from a suggestion by Duncan Sandys to Lord Muirshiel, the modernising Tory Secretary of State for Scotland, shortly after Sandys's own establishment of the Civic Trust in 1957. However, this suggestion took several years to bring to fruition – an outcome that, like the founding of the London organisation itself, owed much to discontent at the Town Planning Institute's increasingly reactive and ossified stance on the historic environment. During the early 1960s Matthew was at first concerned to ensure that the expansion of the Civic Trust did not go too far, to the point where it began to impinge on the freedom of architects in 'creative planning'. But after that principle was secured, he turned his attention to the establishment of 'regional' Civic Trusts, beginning with Scotland, and followed perhaps by Wales and Northwest England. During 1965 Matthew began to canvass Scottish opinion about the organisation of the putative SCT: the RFACS's Bannatyne, for instance, advocated

'a fully independent unit linked to, but not controlled by, the Civic Trust in England', which would follow CT policies for its first years; technical services would be centralised in London. By July 1965 Leslie Lane had reached provisional agreement that Muirshiel would organise the fund-raising and serve as chairman of the trustees; from 1966 Matthew and others joined Muirshiel in the preliminary meetings of the SCT trustees. The SCT's first director, Border TV head of programming Maurice Lindsay, was initially appointed in mid 1966 and, after a delay caused by illness, he took up his post in April 1967, with the task of consolidating the work of the 28 local civic societies in Scotland, and if possible expanding their numbers.[214]

In general, given his aversion to 'county' landed life, and the potential conflict of interest with his Historic Buildings Council for Scotland membership, Matthew's conservationist interests did not extend to the world of the country house and estate – other than in very selective and personal cases, concerned mainly with 'castles' rather than classical mansions.[215] The one outstanding exception, stemming from his continuing close relations with the Forbes-Sempills, was that of Craigievar, where Matthew, in negotiations of 1962–3, used his new influence with the NTS to ensure that the Trust would take on the house without an endowment. With advancing age, Willie (nearly 70 years old) and Cecilia Sempill had found the upkeep of the castle an increasing burden, and Matthew hatched a plan that they should move to a smaller house nearby, with the castle taken over either by the government Ministry of Public Building and Works or by NTS – in both cases using the argument that it was the most important Renaissance-era tower house in Scotland. A trust was set up to negotiate a solution, headed by NTS's Stormonth-Darling. Initially preferring the first option, with strong HBCS support (from Lord Cawdor), Matthew strongly pressed the cause of Craigievar in correspondence and a confidential meeting with MPBW staff – but ultimately, by November 1962, the Ministry's officials refused to recommend purchase without endowment to the Treasury, and the other state control option, that of 'ancient monument scheduling', was also ruled out, as being unsuited to a building whose importance stemmed partly from the furnishings and contents accumulated by Cecilia over the previous two decades. In the end, in October 1963, with the help of pressure from Ian Lindsay and a locally led appeal to raise £90,000, the fall-back solution of direct purchase of house and contents by NTS was finally agreed.[216]

Over the ensuing two-year transition period Matthew then had the stressful and somewhat thankless task of acting as an intermediary between NTS and the family, drawing up a landscaping and traffic scheme, and mediating in a series of increasingly acrimonious disputes between the family and the Trust, centring on the location of new toilets and on the design of a new curator's house. The tense relations with NTS were handled exclusively by Robert and Cecilia, who explained to him that 'I haven't told Willie about the [curator's] House

because it would upset him too much!'[217] The matter was unexpectedly resolved in 1965 by William Sempill's death, following which the emphasis shifted to the design of his memorial, in the isolated, upland kirkyard of Leochel-Cushnie. As with his earlier, 1920s Swedish-style memorial for Mercia in 1934, and his '17th-century classical' Dunblane plaque in the 1950s, memorials gave Matthew the chance to more openly revisit old themes – in this case the rubble 'vernacular' of the 1950s. Out of a large diversity of sketch designs, in consultation with the sculptor Maxwell Allan, Matthew eventually decided on a solution that comprised a massive battered rounded slab formed of thick rubble slabs, on which could be set a plain ashlar inscription and a cross slab above. After first considering a position against the cemetery wall, Matthew eventually decided on a free-standing arrangement, strikingly contrasting with everything else in the small churchyard. Lady Sempill continued, during her remaining 20 years of life, to act as 'Godmother' to the castle, always 'alert for any attempt by the Trust to make it a showpiece'.[218]

Chapter 10

The 'Matthewing' of Ulster: regional planning and university building, 1960–9

It was all-consuming – the biggest thing we'd done. 'Matthew' passed into the language – towns were 'Matthew towns' and you said of housing schemes, 'Have they been Matthewed?'

J A Oliver, 1987[1]

The name of Sir Robert Matthew needs no introduction to the people of Northern Ireland.

Rt Hon W K Fitzsimmons, 1968[2]

I have felt from the beginning that the New City was pure propaganda.

Edward Richardson MP (Stormont), 1964 [3]

10.1 The reformist Unionist government of Captain Terence O'Neill, pictured at Unionist headquarters before the 1965 elections. From left (front): H V Kirk, Prime Minister Terence O'Neill, Brian Faulkner, Harry West; (back) Brian McConnell, W J Morgan, William Craig, William Fitzsimmons, Maj. J D Chichester-Clark. (photographer/source unknown)

Planning and parity

The only place where Matthew exercised as pervasive an influence as in Scotland was 'across the water', in Northern Ireland. Here, he masterminded, from 1960 to the early 1970s, a bold and far-reaching strategy of regional planning and reconstruction. Ironically, however, because of the somewhat introverted and (after 1969) strife-ridden political and social situation in Northern Ireland, this achievement was scarcely known or publicised in the wider world.

Over the half century that separated the setting up of a post-partition home rule government at Stormont in 1921 and the beginning of civil unrest in 1968–9 – a period during which the Ulster Unionist Party exercised unbroken political power – the most important tensions within Northern Ireland on social policy matters (including the built environment) were not between unionists and nationalists but within the unionist camp, between conservatives and reformists. To the conservatives, the very survival of Northern Ireland depended above all on maintaining the demographic and political status quo, not just on political-religious lines but also including the strong polarisation between the 45 per cent of the 1.4 million population who lived in the Belfast urban area and the largely rural remainder; anything smacking of socialism was feared chiefly for its destabilising potential, as much for its incompatibility with traditional Ulster Protestant values of thrifty self-reliance. To the reformists, participation in the Union required Northern Ireland, as by far the smaller partner, to follow a policy of 'parity' with the social and eco-

325

The 'Matthewing' of Ulster

nomic reforms stemming from the class politics of the 'mainland', now including the emergence of the welfare state with its taxation and service implications. After 1945, the idea of parity saw a growing consensual support among the unionist middle classes, to be embraced in its own right as a mark of civilised progressiveness.[4]

Up to the early 1960s, generally speaking, these reformist social policies were driven forward not by Northern Ireland's local or national politicians, but by a growing cadre of civil-servant administrators who were able, because of the very continuity of unionist rule, to develop long-term departmental policies that were both 'progressive' and 'undemocratic' at the same time.[5] From 1963 to 1969, as we shall see later, that situation changed, when Prime Minister Terence O'Neill took personal charge of this reform programme and pushed through a succession of increasingly controversial reforms, including the planning initiatives that form the focus of this chapter. These, arguably, helped destabilise the unionist community and fuel the outbreak of civil unrest. Prior to O'Neill, the Prime Minister for 20 years had been Basil Brooke (Lord Brookeborough), whose 'most notorious pet aversion was to planning, which he regarded as a socialist menace'. But the strength of the Stormont administrative elite was shown by its ability to gradually advance the cause of reform, even under the 'iron grip' of this 'reactionary' political environment.[6]

Prior to World War II, unionist fears of demographic destabilisation and socialist contagion had prevented the emergence either of a concerted public housing policy or of statutory planning powers in the British sense. Not until 1944 did an Interim Development Act oblige all urban and rural authorities to prepare schemes.[7] In the interwar years, subsidised private housing had been dominant, both north and south of the border, to the point where, in Northern Ireland, there was no tradition of urban council housing. But in 1946, under a new and populist

working class minister, William Grant, and a clutch of innovative younger administrators, notably Ronald Green, the newly established Ministry of Health and Local Government (including housing and planning) was able to secure rapid acceptance of the British conception of housing as a state-directed social service.[8] Significantly, the centrepiece of the 1946 reforms – the setting up of a new province-wide, exchequer-funded housing body modelled on the Scottish Special Housing Association, the Northern Ireland Housing Trust, with the aim of building 25 per cent of an expanded housing drive – looked not to England but to the Scottish 'kith and kin' for inspiration, beginning a process that would culminate 14 years later in Matthew's appointment as a planning 'czar'. But ironically, Scotland, with its by now extreme passion for public housing, stood at the opposite extreme of the UK housing scene from Northern Ireland, setting up a tension that was to continue into the Matthew era, and the largest authority in the province, Belfast Corporation, was the most hostile of all towards public housing – the complete opposite to Glasgow in Scotland. Yet Belfast Corporation, like Glasgow, was also fixated on extending its boundaries – a policy vehemently opposed, needless to say, by other local authorities and in Parliament. The potential for instability grew further after 1954, when a fresh and unwelcome consequence of parity began to emerge – the demand to reflect the British government shift from general needs housebuilding to slum clearance, something that pointed a dagger at the heartlands of religious-political identity.[9]

Breaking the deadlock: the commissioning of the Matthew Plan

Even by the end of the 1950s, then, the demands of parity and the visceral fears of the unionist community were beginning to grate ominously against one another, and Green and his colleagues, especially the outstandingly able John A Oliver, Senior Assistant Secretary in charge of housing and planning policy since the late 1950s, were looking urgently for a way to cut through the tangle of conflicts and obstacles. The negative, procrastinating attitudes of Belfast left the Corporation in a potentially rather weak position, when confronted with reformist arguments for parity.[10]

In November 1959 the Ministry, now under a more progressive-minded minister, John Andrews, decided to force a showdown, by finally ruling out any boundary extension and piling on the pressure with a devastating memo, by Green, which urged a sevenfold increase in Belfast's housing drive, and accused the Corporation of being 'determined – for private reasons – that they will not build houses if they can possibly avoid it. The nub of the matter is the failure of the Corporation to carry out their statutory duties.'[11] Two decades later, Oliver still recalled with relish the moment of the Corporation's fatal slip, which allowed the floodgates to be opened. At a meeting on 29 February 1960 the leader of the 'opposition', Alderman Sir Cecil McKee, unguardedly let slip a suggestion that the Corporation

> might be agreeable to build a few houses outside the boundary, provided the Ministry appointed an independent adviser to select the sites and advise upon them. We seized on their suggestion immediately. We appointed Robert Matthew of Edinburgh, a leading national and international figure in architecture and planning.

Oliver and the Department's (Scottish-born) chief architect and planning officer, James Aitken, 'travelled at once to Edinburgh, in March 1960, in order to settle the arrangement. Matthew, unwilling to step into a situation of controversy and act simply as a referee, preferred to make a proper study of the whole situation, analyse all the relevant factors and give us the benefit of a development plan.'[12]

Oliver and Green had realised that town and country planning offered them the means to cut through the tangle of opposing arguments, and that Belfast Corporation, weakened by its own self-contradictory position on output and land, was in a far less powerful position than Glasgow to mount any effective resistance. The polarisation here was not of 'planners versus housers', but of 'planners versus reactionaries'. The stage was therefore set for a far more effective intervention than any regional plan in Britain, the Clyde Valley included. To signal the change in emphasis, Aitken began to focus solely on planning, and was redesignated Chief Planning Officer in the early 1960s. Partly because of his Clyde and London experience, and partly because of the political advantages of a 'Presbyterian Scot' in winning over potential unionist opponents, Matthew was a uniquely suitable choice. In general, Stormont administrators found relations difficult with their counterparts in London, who were 'very reluctant to come over' and inclined to adopt patronising airs when they did; but 'we got on well with the Scots – they always liked coming over!' From 1962, the involvement of Massey, an Irish-born military man, as Matthew's personal assistant helped cement relations.[13]

From the moment of his first arrival in Northern Ireland for an initial, Geddes-style reconnaissance visit in May 1960, Matthew made it clear that the Clyde Plan experience would condition his response here – although Belfast was not so complex as the Clyde Valley,

Belfast's planner is Man in the news

by MARTIN WALLACE

"I'M GOING TO COMMANDEER an umbrella," said Professor Robert Matthew after his first day in Belfast. He had seen housing developments on the fringe of the city, talked to Mr. John Andrews and his officials at the Ministry of Health and Local Government, and watched rush-hour traffic crawling across the Queen's and Albert Bridges in a downpour.

This is an introductory visit for the 53-year-old Edinburgh architect, who is to prepare a survey of Belfast and the surrounding region with regard to housing development. It will be the first of many brief visits.

Briefing Professor Matthew on his first viewing of the Belfast problem is Mr. James Aitken, chief architect of the Ministry of Health and Local Government (right).

"I intend to set up a team, which will be here all the time, with an office in Belfast," he added. His other commitments — among them the chair of architecture at Edinburgh University and a redevelopment scheme in the Gorbals—necessarily limit the time he can spend in Ulster.

How long will the survey take? A similar venture in the Clyde valley took two or three years, he pointed out, but Belfast is not so complex an area. "We'll do it in less than that here."

"You have the same basic problem," Professor Matthew continued. "Belfast is a busy industrial city, built up almost to its boundaries, with little surplus ground. As far as I can see, population and employment are going to increase."

He talked about some of the problems—whether building on the periphery of Belfast should be allowed to continue, whether there should be a jump to towns farther out, how to persuade industry to go where you want it to go, whether to build new towns.

"There are two basic viewpoints in planning. The negative one is to protect good agricultural land, lines of communication, the coastline. The positive side is finding the best places for development. One thing planning must not do is slow up housing. One of my jobs, as I see it, will be an examination of all the small towns that are within the regional influence of Belfast. There's no point in starting from scratch if you've something to start on.

Mixed development

"But there's no blueprint for a regional plan. In Glasgow, we drew the line of green belt in as close as we could—but it's maintained in the form of public parks, an urban green belt rather than a rural one."

Professor Matthew's experience is wide. He was with the Scottish Department of Health from 1936 till 1946, and consultant with the late Sir Patrick Abercrombie to the revolutionary Clyde Valley Regional Planning Advisory Committee.

As chief architect to London County Council, he pioneered "mixed development" in the post-war years. Roehampton, with its blend of low houses and tall blocks of flats amid fine gardens, is a classic example of this trend in planning.

In the Gorbals, 17-storey towers of maisonettes will sit beside 2-storey and 3-storey buildings. At Edinburgh, he is establishing a new course which will make the university a centre for regional planning.

The Abercrombie report was presented in 1946, incidentally, but only in recent years have its proposals begun to be accepted and implemented. A new town at East Kilbride was begun some years ago, for example, but Glasgow's "Operation Overspill" is a much newer drive to transfer industry and people to less congested areas.

Will Northern Ireland, its government and local authorities, be equally slow to adopt a realistic plan for the Belfast region?

New planning laws?

The interesting thing is that the Government has promised new planning legislation, and will obviously consult Professor Matthew on general issues before his actual report appears. And the report itself could recommend legislative changes.

"I'm going to look at the problem on its merits," Professor Matthew explained. "If I felt that existing legislation was inadequate in some essentials, I would feel justified in making some suggestions.

"You know, regional planning has taken a step backwards in the past 10 years in Britain, primarily due to the lack of enthusiasm among local authorities which are preoccupied with their little problems. Regional planning cuts across borders, across preconceptions.

"There's nowhere, except the Clyde valley, in Britain that's doing regional planning—and precious few places in the world. You can take a big jump ahead here."

10.2 Newspaper report on Matthew's first visit to Northern Ireland in May 1960. (*Belfast Telegraph*, 13 May 1960)

allowing the report preparation to be compressed into only two or three years.[14] He told the liberal, pro-reform *Belfast Telegraph* that 'You have the same basic problem' of a big city built up 'with little surplus land', and the same general solution should apply, exploiting the ability of regional planning to cut 'across boundaries, across preconceptions, both by restricting any further development of the city ... while encouraging growth points elsewhere'. Sensing the possibilities offered by the much greater relative power of the Ministry in Stormont, Matthew boldly predicted that, whereas regional planning had 'taken a step backwards in the past ten years in Britain', in the face of resurgent municipal particularism, 'you could take a big jump ahead here.'[15] The rhetorical conception of Northern Ireland as a *tabula rasa* – suitable, unlike Britain, for radical regional planning solutions – was to stay with Matthew throughout his involvement with the province – which spanned, as with all his later enthusiasms, almost exactly a decade. Yet very soon it became clear to his team that the situation was in practice far from being a *tabula rasa*, and that any attempt to intervene too deeply in the wider 'complexities of political, economic and social policy in Northern Ireland ... would not be welcomed'.[16] One young architect who had just entered practice in Belfast in 1960 summed up the constrained, yet nonetheless real, space for reformist activity and idealism that greeted Matthew in 1960:

> As people who lived there, who'd been brought up there, who were in it for the long run, we knew not to be carried away by false dawns, and not to hope that anything really radical could happen. And the same applied in a different way to Robert Matthew: there was no clean sheet for him, either, and people's reactions to anything he proposed would have been easy to predict – yet he was a big enough person to make his own mark on the situation, despite all the obstacles![17]

Cleverly, Matthew tried to defuse the passions of the 'Belfast problem' by diverting attention away from religio-political housing questions, and towards a London-style rhetoric against 'sprawl' and encroachment on the countryside. Exploiting the consensual support, from both unionists and nationalists, for the sanctity of the 'rural essence' of the territory, Oliver and Matthew set out to dress up an essentially anti-Belfast policy as a pro-countryside one, disguised in Geddesian rhetoric of a 'greenscape' around the city.[18] But Oliver and Green could nevertheless foresee trouble ahead, in the raising of conflicting expectations and fears – for example in the restriction of the plan area to the Belfast Urban Area (BUA), inevitable in the political context of the day, where

> we foresaw that there would be trouble over this, and that, once the benefits of this type of planning came to be generally appreciated, the parts of the Province that had been left out would inevitably complain. We managed to have concluded in Matthew's terms of reference a phrase setting the study in the context of Northern Ireland as a whole, but that was not enough.

As we shall see later, this limited reform would ultimately please no one: both unionist and nationalist opinion in the west would regard it as an undesirable 'consolidation' of the east, while traditional unionist elements in the east, in Belfast or around Portadown/Lurgan, would feel threatened by even the limited demographic disturbance that Matthew proposed.[19]

On the whole, Matthew tried to base the organisation of his Belfast plan, where possible, on Clyde Plan precedents. He opened up a local office at 93 Holywood Road, run by a seconded member of the government planning staff, while maintaining general oversight himself from outside, and produced the report in two stages, an interim report identifying housing sites, followed the next year by the full report; Matthew's overall fee was to be £23,500. To head the Belfast office, Aitken seconded a 'meticulous and careful' planner from the Department, the tall, laconically spoken Cecil Newman. The commission was a clear candidate for application of the 1959 planning liaison arrangement with Percy Johnson-Marshall. Accordingly, Edinburgh input was handled not through RMJM but through Percy's office at Bella Vista, with Richard Bigwood as deputy in charge of the team, and day-to-day oversight by P D McGovern, an Ulster-born architect-planner newly arrived back in Edinburgh.

In his interim report on housing sites, submitted in January 1961, Matthew closely followed the Clyde Plan formula of 'containment', drawing a green belt around the city, within which only 'rounding-off and infilling' should be permitted, including designation of six sites for building some 5,000 Corporation overspill houses. In January 1962 the new and somewhat more reform-minded Minister of Health, furniture remover William Morgan, wrote to Matthew congratulating him on his knighthood as 'lending still further weight to your Plan work', and asking whether he would be prepared to meet planning authorities to let them see 'how your mind is working' and prepare them for 'some radical thinking and decisive action'.[20] At the same time, work was busily under way on the full report, with a target of 1 September 1962 for publication and the sections parcelled out Clyde Valley style: overspill to Bigwood, planning and legislative context to Newman, location of industry to McGovern; a committee of outdoor recreational societies surveyed the rural hinterland. An explicitly Geddesian framework of survey, analysis and proposal was adopted, looking openly to contemporary Scottish attempts to fuse economic growth policy and physical planning, epitomised by the Toothill Report of 1961.[21] By comparison with Glasgow, with its focus on the material deficiencies of the 'slums', here a more overtly poetic, Geddesian language could be used, calling for an overall 'greenscape', and stressing the harmful effect of Ulster's 'uncoordinated' planning on the

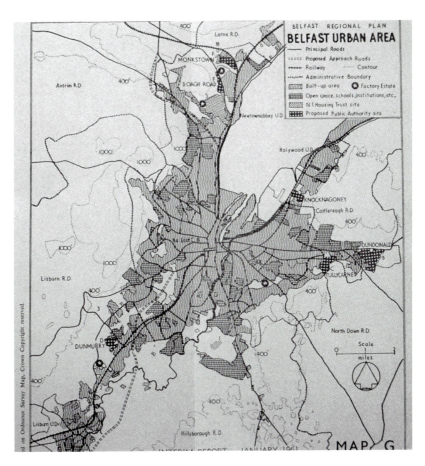

'quality of environment, the most powerful aid to prosperity in the modern world'. Especially valuable and worthy of protection, in Matthew's mind, was the 'vigorous vernacular' of rural Ulster buildings.[22]

During late 1961 and early 1962 Matthew's team beavered away, but by the end of the period the stresses of the two-centre approach were beginning to tell, as the tired, overworked and reticent Newman increasingly began to resent what he saw as the high-handed interventions of Percy Johnson-Marshall and McGovern from Edinburgh; here, as in Matthew's other dealings with Northern Ireland, we witness a more dramatic variant of his usual rapidly rising and falling pattern of engagement with any project. With only two and a half months to go before presentation of the report, Matthew could not afford to let the threads of the job unravel at this crucial stage, and so from late July 1962, following warnings about Newman from Oliver, he threw himself into the job almost

10.3 1961 map of Belfast Urban Area showing housing sites proposed by Matthew on 'rounding off and infilling' principle. (Belfast Regional Survey and Plan, Interim Report on Housing Sites in the Belfast Area, Belfast, 1961, Map G) (Government of Northern Ireland, Ministry of Health and Local Government)

uninterruptedly for a month, visiting Belfast as well as working from Humbie and Edinburgh, and forcibly pressing on Oliver the claims of Newman to promotion. The aim was to have ready six copies of the full report, with restricted colours and dyeline reproduction, ready for government use by 1 September. By early August the report had reached the stage of a mass of typescript notes and half-written chapters, with Matthew expressing some exasperation at the 'haphazard collection of notes ... almost impossible to read' on legal and administrative matters, assembled by Newman. Matthew had to redraft and pull together the entire report, and wrote a new introduction (paragraphs 1–7) and conclusion (128 onwards). On 31 August, with relief, he wrote to Oliver that the report was complete and had been delivered to his office – eventually, 20 preliminary copies were made – and, with even more relief, he and Lorna headed off for three weeks' holiday in the south of France.[23]

The thorniest strategic issue to be faced was whether or not to recommend, on the British pattern, the building of a new town as a keystone of the plan. Pressures *within* Northern Ireland for strategic population dispersal were relatively weak; the Chief Civil Defence Officer's plea for all new development to be at least 15 miles from Belfast city centre on grounds of the city's vulnerability to nuclear attack was an isolated one. Stronger were the voices of those worried about the political uncertainties of any large-scale population movement, and about the sheer cost of a new town.[24] The final report was built up on the foundation of the housing land restrictions proposed in the interim housing report, now dramatised, slogan-like, as the 'Matthew Stop-Line'. The imposition of the Stop-Line, which predictably enraged Belfast Corporation, was matched, in the Abercrombie tradition, by proposals to 'de-magnetise the centre'.[25] Matthew advocated 18 per cent overspill from the BUA and 12 per cent from the city itself, and – most radical of all – the establishment of not just a new town but

a 'new city', 22 miles southwest of Belfast, around an existing double core comprising the towns of Lurgan and Portadown and their rural hinterlands – expanding the existing population of 35,000 to 100,000 by 1981. Originally, Matthew had been informally asked to consider recommending one new town site north and one south of Belfast, possibly to allow the strategy to be defended politically against unionist criticisms as one of 'consolidating' heartland areas, but in his report his penchant for theatrical gestures pushed its way to the fore. The only new settlement was to be Portadown/Lurgan, plus town expansion schemes including Ballymena and Antrim, to the north of Belfast.[26] To counteract any political restriction of his plan to the east of the province, Matthew also boldly foregrounded the problematic relation of the survey area to Northern Ireland as a whole, by calling for the extension of survey to the whole province, and – even – for the creation of a new Ministry of Planning and Development, modelled on the Scottish Development Department.[27]

For Oliver, Aitken and their allies the completion and release of the Belfast Regional Plan was *the* watershed in the strategy of planned modernisation of Northern Ireland. 'It represented the undisputed origin of a huge programme of government involvement and of the assumption by government of responsibility for the physical development of the country ... it placed our feet on a path from which we were never to turn back ... an activist role,' which was to endure, under whatever disguise, into and through the era of civil unrest from the late 1960s. Within Ireland, of course, it also formed part of a succession of reformist unionist initiatives in the built environment, stretching back through the planning proposals of Geddes, Unwin and others to the pioneering public housing programme of the late 19th and early 20th centuries.[28] But more immediately, in late 1962, there was the question of whether the Belfast Region report should be publicly issued and, if so, in what form. This was, after all, a time when the NI government was still headed by the ageing Lord Brookeborough, a politician unlikely to favour such proposals as a central planning ministry able to over-rule local control over land use – something that was unproblematic for Scotland's SDD, but potentially explosive in Northern Ireland, where 'he and his more dyed-in-the-wool chaps would want to sit on the stile, and stay sitting on it!'[29] Eventually, the preamble and proposals (paras 1–214) were released as a command paper in late February 1963.[30]

Towards a 'New Ulster': following through the Belfast Regional Plan

Leaving Percy Johnson-Marshall and Newman to squabble in undignified fashion over the acknowledgements page of the report (with Newman attacking Marshall's 'disagreeable' attempts to portray himself as 'overall leader of the team'), Matthew now rapidly switched his attention to the presentation of and follow-up to the report.[31] Already, he had discussed with Green and Oliver the idea of giving a public lecture at the Stormont parliament to present his plan – as a way of confronting and disarming potential opposition. Oliver excitedly wrote on 19 February that 'the idea of an Address by yourself has caught fire and is spreading rapidly ... it went down so well at Cabinet last week that the Prime Minster offered there and then to take the chair.' The March lecture promised to be 'one of the most influential lecture audiences I can remember assembled under Government auspices here', the nearly 300 invitees including all senators and MPs, local authority representatives, professional bodies, trade unions, universities and statutory bodies.[32]

On 26 February 1963, presented to Matthew by Oliver as 'our D-Day', publication of the report recommendations was accompanied by a blizzard of publicity and enforcement initiatives masterminded by Oliver, including a House of Commons statement by Morgan, and a circular letter by Oliver (and planning circulars 49–51) to local planning authorities compelling the adoption of the stop-line with immediate effect. And in press releases the same day the department boldly highlighted Matthew's call for the extension of regional planning to the whole province, through the creation of an SDD-style Ministry of Development, which could over-ride the 37 local planning authorities. And the radicalism of Matthew's 'dramatic' concept of a new regional city, concentrating overspill rather than scattering it, Mears-style, between lots of small towns, was presented as a revolutionary transformation of parity: a 'psychological lift ... a replacement of a general attitude that the best thing that can be done is not to go too far behind the rest of Britain, by a determination to go straight ahead'.[33]

Public reaction from the increasingly confident unionist reformist grouping was warm: Oliver reported to Matthew that 'D Day' 'went off with a bang', that a follow-on meeting with the local authorities for the new city location had been a 'whizz-bang success', free from 'any silly parochial jealousy'. Support was especially concentrated among groups with a technical or architectural stake in the proposals. For example, John E Sayers, editor of the pro-planning *Belfast Telegraph* and advocate of 'constructive unionism', wrote to Matthew, hailing 'the great vision of your work ... Northern Ireland has needed a call to planning for a long time'; and Hugh McIlveen, a former Matthew student at Edinburgh and newly

SIR ROBERT EXPLAINS

Sir Robert Matthew, speaking on his planning report for the Belfast area to Senators, M.P.s, local and planning authorities and representatives of the professions, at a meeting at Parliament Buildings to-day.

New city can be world-known asset

10.4 Newspaper report (from Stormont cuttings file) on Matthew's March 1963 address at Stormont on his Belfast Regional Plan proposals. Terence O'Neill is visible sitting to Matthew's right. (*Belfast Telegraph*, 4 March 1963)

STORMONT DIARY

Planning becomes respectable

Planning, once a dirty word in the Tory vocabulary, has become as respectable as free enterprise, even though it may represent a challenge to the laissez faire attitude, once regarded as the hallmark of Conservatism.

T°O paraphrase an English Conservative politician, we are all planners nowadays. The Ulster Government, which might be loosely described, as it is constituted to-day, as "progressive Conservative," thus finds no difficulty in accepting the Matthew plan for the Belfast region.

Mr. W. J. Morgan (centre)—"the time is ripe for regional planning in Ulster." Mrs. Dinah M'Nabb (right) suggested Elizabethville for the name of the new town. Mr. Simpson (left) thought the Chandos Council was redundant.

10.5 Extract from the Belfast *Newsletter*, May 1963, reporting parliamentary debate on the Matthew Plan. (*Newsletter*, 10 May 1963, 6)

appointed partner in one of Northern Ireland's most progressive private practices, wrote that 'as an Edinburgh man, Sir Robert undoubtedly combined with his shrewd and penetrating approach an inherent appreciation of the natural environmental qualities with which the country is endowed'; McIlveen and a number of other practitioners had formed an urban renewal pressure organisation, the Architectural Group, to campaign for some of these aims. Behind closed doors within the Ministry, too, the planning cause seemed to surge forward, with Newman now also promoted to deputy chief planner status, and tasked with working on an extension of the Belfast Regional Plan formula to the remainder of the Province, while Aitken concentrated on developing a plan for the 'new city'. Oliver explained to Matthew that 'We want to strike the note that this is to be a local job, and he [Aitken] is therefore to gather around him a design team of youngish local architects and planners.'[34]

Matthew's 'Stormont Address', in March 1963, was a masterpiece of carefully crafted reason and passion: in such set pieces, he was sometimes able to express a degree of emotion that he found difficult in conventional 'personal' or family contexts. He set out a balanced mixture of prudence and visionary boldness, calculated to appeal to an audience dominated by reformist unionists. On the one hand, he stressed that his plan was grounded in solid fact, and cautioned

against architectural 'flights of fancy of a "new Jerusalem"'; what was mainly needed was for people on the ground to fight for a better 'character of Environment', for a general 'lift-up' across Ulster's towns and villages. But this was balanced with an impassioned evocation of 'human endeavour at its highest', arguing that, with the lack of any coordinated regional planning in England, Northern Ireland had the chance to leap beyond her inferiority complex of leeway and parity: 'I have taken a cool look at this situation in relation to Northern Ireland, and I do so with a Scottish background that in some respects in similar.' This more exalted aspect of Matthew's address focused above all on the utopian vision of the 100,000-inhabitant New City. Matthew declared that

> Here, above all, is your opportunity to 'make up leeway', but to build up something, to get your teeth into it and really let go. Make it a modern city in the very best sense of the word – with space for all kinds of amenities and full advantage taken of the new thinking on traffic planning. Let every child run to school, every mother walk to the shops, without hazard to life from intervening traffic. Let it be a pleasure to go to the city centre in safety.

If the city could be planned with imagination, then 'it could become an asset to be talked about in the industrial boardrooms of London, Paris and New York.'[35]

Although the parliamentary debates on the report were not polarised on unionist-nationalist lines, nationalist opinion still tended to be preoccupied with the rural 'essence' of Ireland, and thus to be suspicious of planned urbanism on principle: nationalist senators attacked the government's insistence on 'going across the water' to Matthew rather than engaging 'an Irishman', and lambasted his strategy as an attempt to 'de-ruralise Northern Ireland and make it a compound of industrial towns and cities', including the 'monstrosity' of the new city; the aim should instead be 'how to keep people on the land'. Gerry Fitt MP suggested that the new city should be called 'Disneyland' because 'the whole idea is crazy and impractical'.[36] More serious, at this stage, were divisions within unionism: for example, Brian Faulkner, potential populist rival to O'Neill, and currently Minister of Commerce, argued that one could not 'dragoon' growth industries into the new city.[37] In general, throughout his career, Matthew was usually able to use his many-faceted institutional personae to avoid becoming the target of personal attacks, but in Northern Ireland, uniquely, the situation was almost reversed: he himself became a high-profile target of criticism, behind whom the entire reformist technical grouping could hide: 'He took all the flak for it!'

Within the Ministry, Green's team were now pressing hard for the follow-on steps recommended by Matthew, and more generally seeking to give 'planning its due'. He wrote to Matthew in early April 1963 that the Minister had agreed to Oliver's promotion to Second Secretary, with direct access to the Minister – a step that might in turn 'lead to the setting up of a separate Ministry of Planning'. Oliver was now working on legislation intended to allow the Ministry 'to take effective control of high-level, long-term planning' from the local authorities; Matthew had 'framed the statutory picture' and now the community's task was to 'take a firm grip on land and on physical development'.[38]

Looking to the future, Aitken had from August 1963 been busy recruiting a 16-strong, Stormont-based Ministry design team for the new city, which was now targeted to expand from its 35,000 existing population to 120,000 by 1981 and 180,000 by 2000. For the key post of Head of New City Design he had settled on Geoffrey Copcutt, a mercurial architect who had in 1960–3 masterminded the pioneering high-density megastructural design of the town centre at Cumbernauld New Town. Copcutt was a 'flamboyant but highly unstable' designer and propagandist – large, bearded in Morris style, and tartan-suited, who found it difficult to work within the bureaucratic structures of public authority architecture. By 1963 even the tolerant Cumbernauld chief architect Hugh Wilson had reached the end of his patience, and had had to reassign the town centre project to someone else, and 'when, one day, he bumped into Aitken and learnt he was looking for a chief architect for the new city, he said, "We've got a first-rate chap in our department, who's just what you need!" – and off went Copcutt to Northern Ireland with the most glowing references!' Initially, he made a highly positive impression on progressive architectural opinion, giving briefing seminars, for example, to McIlveen's Architectural Group, with Cumbernauld never far from his thoughts: 'He'd always carry a portable model of Cumbernauld Town Centre in the back of his Beetle car!'[39] And by the end of 1963 Copcutt's team had produced a preliminary report on the new city.

'O'Neillism' and the acceleration of planning reform

Over the late autumn and winter months of 1963/4 Matthew concerned himself with the fine-tuning of the formal hardback version of the report in the lead-up to its March 1964 publication. There was no intention on his part, or that of his Stormont colleagues, that he should now fade gracefully from the scene. Within Matthew's habitual concept of decade-long commitments to particular 'causes', he was only a quarter or third of the way through his commitment to Ulster. And now, significantly, the Stormont administrative team were able to actually accelerate their reforms – with the direct backing of the new, reformist Prime Minister, Captain Terence O'Neill. In June 1964 Matthew spoke of O'Neill's support and 'warm understanding' of the architectural and town planning problems of Northern Ireland, even in his previous post of Minister of Finance.[40] But the fact

STOP-LINE NOT DEATH BLOW TO BELFAST

THE Minister of Health and Local Government, Mr. William Morgan, has commented that without a stop-line around Belfast the whole of Sir Robert Matthew's regional plan would be rendered useless, and the economic future of Ulster could be jeopardized.

says Corporation report

MATTHEW PLAN ATTACKED

'Belfast must get new industry first'

UNTIL BELFAST'S NEED for new industry is satisfied any attempts to disperse industry from the city should be resisted, members of the Corporation were told to-day.

The advice is given by the town planning section of the city surveyor's department in a report which marks a new stage in the controversy over the stop-line.

The report says that if the Matthew proposals were adopted, 12,000-17,000 of the houses needed within the period ending in 1981 to meet the needs of the population now residing within the Belfast area—including Carrickfergus, Bangor and Newtownards—would have to be built outside the area.

The town planners' report also declares that a

10.6 January 1964 extracts from the *Belfast Telegraph*, from the Stormont press cuttings file, reporting the fierce political controversy over the Matthew Plan. (*Belfast Telegraph*, 3 January and 18 January 1964)

that the furious progress of regional planning in Northern Ireland was, despite O'Neill's backing, progress without solid political foundation, would, as we shall see, only gradually become obvious.

By the end of 1963 the division of the Ministry of Health between Green and Oliver had been followed by the formation of a Belfast Town Planning Committee (in August), the establishment of a chair of architecture at Queens University Belfast, and a course in town planning at Belfast College of Technology.[41] It seemed especially important to win over local opinion around Portadown and Lurgan, and so Matthew agreed to make another lightning trip in December 1963, this time to proselytise for the new city in a TV interview and a BBC-arranged public meeting, 'Target New City', at a Portadown secondary school on 13 December – along with

various local dignitaries, industrialists and farmers. He was armed with briefing notes by Newman, including prompts for potential questions from farmers and other aggrieved local residents, and warning that 'the unasked question in everyone's minds is: will the new citizens from Belfast be Nationalist (RC) moving into unionist Portadown and Lurgan?'[42] The meeting itself went off without controversy, but – significantly for his own future involvement in Northern Ireland – Matthew pointedly inserted a plea that there could be 'nothing more valuable for the future of the new city than to build a new university there'.[43] In the wake of this trip, a lively debate began about the plan report, with Belfast Corporation beginning to rally opposition to this 'death blow to Belfast', but others rallying to its defence, such as Major R T Bunting of the Northern Ireland Ratepayers Association, who attacked Belfast's 'narrow parochialism' and launched a 'Save the Matthew Report' campaign; the *Belfast Telegraph* called for an end to 'this Cold War'.[44]

On 13 April 1964 Oliver proudly sent Matthew the 'final volumes' of the Survey and Plan (one volume with text, one with boxed maps), published on that day, and Matthew's reply not only contrasted Stormont's energy with the lack of similar activity in Britain, but also, with a typical self-confident eye for posterity, predicted that 'they will now form part of the documentation of Regional planning education – and there is all too little substantial material available in this field.'[45] But now, there was no question of pausing for breath. Instead, throwing caution to the winds, Oliver and O'Neill pressed the accelerator pedal down further, with the publication of a command paper in March 1964 on the administration of town and country planning in the province, which argued for rapid progress towards establishment of an SDD-style Ministry of Development on 1 January 1965. Oliver confided to Matthew that 'you will see how much we have leaned on the advice which you give in your survey; in fact the Paper might be said to be another chapter of Matthew!'[46]

In 1965 the New Towns Act (Northern Ireland) set in train this centralised planning process, which would apply not only to the new city but also to existing growth centres, beginning, within Matthew's framework, with Antrim (which was now to expand to 30,000 in association with the huge, development-assisted British Enkalon factory) and Ballymena.[47] There was strong opposition within O'Neill's cabinet to the establishment of the Ministry of Development, and he carried it through only by a coup while other ministers were on holiday, appointing a heavyweight ally, the Unionist Chief Whip, William Craig, to head it in summer 1964.[48] Equally important was the growing closeness to the Ministry of Commerce, with the aim of working out a fully planned economy to match the physical planning strategy charted by Matthew. Again, a Scottish

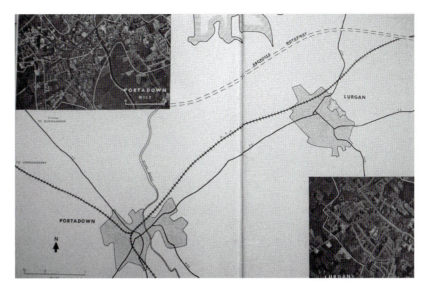

link was the key here: in February 1965 Professor Tom Wilson, an Ulster-born political economist at Glasgow University (and a prominent advocate of Jack Sayers's 'Constructive unionism') prepared, with Matthew's backing, an economic plan for the province, which also stressed the need for economic development outwith the BUA, but, controversially, proposed four development centres within a 30-mile radius of Belfast.[49] All in all, by 1968 the O'Neill government had carried into effect the entire development strategy mapped out by Matthew in 1962–4, including one new town/city and two expanded towns, and a centrally directed strategic development system orchestrated by a new planning ministry.

(top) **10.7** 1964 map of the 'new city' site at Portadown-Lurgan. (*Belfast Regional Survey and Plan 1962*, Belfast, 1964, inside back cover). (Government of Northern Ireland, Ministry of Health and Local Government)

(bottom) **10.8** Section of the Geddes-style fold-out panoramas of Belfast from the published Belfast Regional Plan (*Belfast Regional Survey and Plan 1962*, Belfast, 1964). (Government of Northern Ireland, Ministry of Health and Local Government)

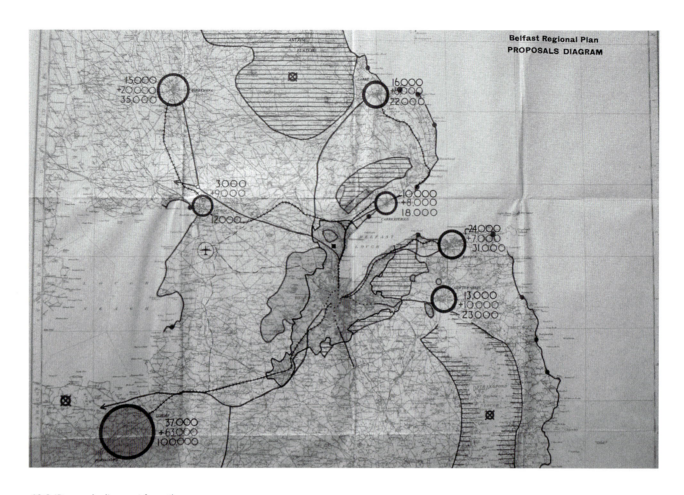

10.9 'Proposals diagram' from the published Belfast Regional Plan, showing the 'Matthew stop-line' and the proposed 'new city' and enlarged towns. (*Belfast Regional Survey and Plan 1962*, Belfast,1964, Map 4) (Government of Northern Ireland, Ministry of Health and Local Government)

New City to ghost town: the Craigavon debacle

That sequence of innovation constituted a remarkable achievement, in its (in hindsight) noble technocratic isolation; but by 1965 the politically exposed situation of that strategy, and the excessive responsibility piled up on the Matthew report, were already beginning to become clear.[50] This emerged first in the storm of controversy stirred up by the attempts to realise Matthew's 'new city', not least when Craig in January 1965 announced that it was to be called 'Craigavon' – commemorating the first prime minister of unionist Northern Ireland. Craig's aim in this was to cement unionist support for the project, not least through the nationalist protests it inevitably provoked: MP Austin Currie, for example, branded it an 'odious sectarian name'.[51] Likewise, the Development Commission, announced in October 1965 and headed by prominent unionist oil executive S J McMahon, contained no Catholic members: the

development area itself, covering no less than 100 square miles, was officially designated by parliamentary order in July 1965 – with the existing boroughs of Portadown and Lurgan embedded intact within it – and 8,000 acres were 'vested' (compulsorily purchased) at one single swoop in December, in one of the most striking demonstrations of the technocratic power of the new Stormont planning system. But already, a year before any of this, the underlying tensions of the new city project had been thrust into full public view – and by none other than Geoffrey Copcutt, whose penchant for maverick contentiousness burst out into the wider realms of politics, and inflicted a major public embarrassment, which in retrospect possibly delivered a mortal psychological blow to the entire 'Matthew project' in Northern Ireland.[52]

During 1964, Copcutt's team had completed a preliminary report on the new city, which, when eventually published, proposed a basic structure like a more dispersed Cumbernauld, with a 'linear urban core', strongly set apart from the countryside around by a ring distribution road, and individual zones containing fairly dense 'clusters' of compact residential 'sections' – each with its communal facilities (such as schools) grouped at the centre, implicitly intended to encourage Catholic–Protestant integration. These would be interspersed by three commercial centres: Lurgan, Portadown and a new regional high-grade shopping and office centre in between. As late as June 1964 Copcutt was still fulsome in his praise of Matthew's new city concept as 'a stroke of genius'.[53] But, by then, he was in fact becoming steadily more 'disenchanted with the Stormont scene', not only for its dominance by administrators, but because of the many unspoken politico-religious constraints that hemmed in his freedom of action as a city designer; he later claimed that, on arriving, he had been told by senior civil servants that the government 'would not countenance any scheme that might upset the voting balance between Catholics and Protestants'. Now, shooting from the hip, 'Geoffrey began to say that nothing could be achieved until Ireland was one country!'[54] In August 1964 Copcutt abruptly resigned in a blaze of publicity, sending the government, and the main Belfast newspapers, a memo setting out his comprehensive objections to the new city project – arguments that, although stemming from his own very individual viewpoint, anticipated many of the later objections both to the Matthew planning strategy and to 'O'Neillism' in general.[55]

Copcutt's memo argued that the project combined an undesirable degree of centralised *dirigisme* with an excessive politicisation of the rightful dominion of the architect-planner: 'Religious and political considerations are dominant in the new city decision. [Stormont] has asked us to engineer propaganda rather than design a city.' O'Neill's 'unswerving pursuit' of all aspects of the Matthew plan had, he claimed, dictated the choice of Lurgan and Portadown as a site, even

though they would be impossible to integrate within a single plan. He suggested that the new city should be abandoned altogether in favour of Londonderry, which was 'the obvious candidate for injection and expansion' and should, at the very least, become the site for any new university. Privately, Oliver and his colleagues were severely rattled by Copcutt's typically confrontational gesture, but publicly the damage-limitation reaction was one of calmly 'allowing the whole thing to die down'. James Latimer recalled that 'I had phone calls from people in Stormont – for example from Jimmy Aitken, who was practically in tears! I said, 'Jimmy, don't blame yourself – we had to work with him in Cumbernauld!' Matthew weighed in the next day in the *Belfast Telegraph,* betraying in his exasperation a perhaps slightly patronising attitude towards Ulster affairs: 'I am not alarmed by anything that [Copcutt] said ... it is symptomatic of this small area that [his criticisms] should be regarded as so important. The thing is out of proportion. Copcutt never expressed his anxieties about the project, and had ample opportunity to discuss them.'[56] But, in the reactions of others, the seeds of the political undermining of his strategy were becoming visible, as different groups tried to appropriate Copcutt's criticisms for their own ends. In Derry and the west, both unionist and nationalist opinion hailed Copcutt as a standard-bearer of their cause, while, less plausibly, the *Irish Times* went on to claim that he had resigned in protest against anti-Catholic discrimination. More significantly, traditional unionist opinion in Belfast and the east, represented especially in the Belfast *Newsletter*, saw the scandal as a humiliation for O'Neill's 'so-called "brave new Ulster and its new image"', and highlighted the growing unease among local (Protestant) farmers about the new city.[57]

What Copcutt brought into the open was the potential of the controversies surrounding regional planning to spread beyond the strictly technical arena, and to do damage to O'Neill's wider agenda of

The 'Matthewing' of Ulster

'reform, reconciliation, economic and social equality', especially in the context of the growing split between O'Neill and Brian Faulkner, skilful exploiter of the fears of 'traditional unionism'. In general, O'Neill had set out to construct a moderate constituency, with a strong intellectual-elite bias, relying heavily on media presentation.[58] But the Eton-educated, aristocratic former Guards officer fatally neglected the vital need to reassure and reinforce his wider political and public position within unionism – something that even his closest allies, such as John Oliver, fully recognised:

> He'd go out of his way, he'd invite us to dinner, he'd pick our brains – yet he had this weakness at the same time, that he was essentially a snob and a cad, who made no attempt to prepare the ground for his reforms – he'd make a big speech, 'We must have a new Ulster, a liberal Ulster!', and so forth – without having told his colleagues, whereas he should have gone into a smoke-filled room and sat about with them, and said, 'If you support me on this, I'll support you on that.' He never did that – when the Commons finished, he'd go straight off, leaving others thinking, 'Where do we come into this?'[59]

Ultimately, like Gorbachev's *perestroika* in the 1980s, his reforms proved to be a Pandora's box, which hastened the collapse, rather than regeneration, of the Stormont system.

Especially following the headline-grabbing exchange visit of O'Neill and Irish Taoiseach Sean Lemass in January/February 1965, a range of elements within unionist opinion became increasingly alienated, and susceptible to the arguments of Faulkner and more extreme figures. Belfast Corporation's immediate reaction to the Copcutt affair was to denounce O'Neill's 'dictatorial style of governing'. And in the west, criticisms came not just from nationalists, who attacked Craigavon as 'a unionist city', but also from unionists.[60] All shades of opinion in counties Tyrone, Fermanagh and Derry argued that they had been deliberately omitted by Matthew: 'Fuel had been unwittingly added to the fire of the "west of the Bann" grievance that was then beginning to burn.'[61] The 1964/5 centralisation of planning seemed set to undermine the decentralised unionist powers of local patronage – the chief remaining support for the Orange system after the economic failures of the inter-war years. It was only after the huge Craigavon vesting order had been issued in December 1965 that the opposition seriously began to gather force, when it became obvious that the farmers of the Craigavon hinterland would fiercely resist displacement: a 'Residents Protection Association' began to mount vigorous national protests against 'government authority' in early 1966, and by late 1966 the more militant agitations of the Revd Ian Paisley were in full flow, with O'Neill the chief bête noire: his paper, the *Protestant Telegraph*, did not mince its words, and branded the Ministry of Development 'jackbooted thugs' who were employing 'Nazi methods' to swamp the loyalist yeomanry of North Armagh with an alien horde.

Although, in 1966, O'Neill replaced Craig by the more emollient Fitzsimmons, and as late as 1967 piously claimed that Craigavon could become an 'integrated and vital community', O'Neill's opponents had now 'belled the cat'. When, in early 1967, the initial residents began to move into Craigavon's first housing area, Brownlow, they separated out spontaneously by denomination, with Catholics largely on the east side and Protestants in the west. Only 2,000, rather than the planned 3,000, new jobs had been provided by then. Whatever was said publicly about the 'west of the Bann' issue, people were reluctant to move out of Belfast, and by 1969 Craigavon could still be branded a 'ghost town'.[62]

An 'advanced education factory': the New University of Ulster

All that, however, was jumping ahead of the sequence of events in which Matthew was involved. For in early 1966, just as the Craigavon story was beginning to unravel, far from disengaging from the replanning of Northern Ireland, Matthew opened up a vigorous second front in his strategy, when he was appointed architect for the province's first and only completely new university, at Coleraine – a commission that also included the replanning of its hinterland region, of Coleraine–Portrush–Portstewart. By this stage Matthew well understood the distinctive position of Northern Ireland within his own career, bringing as it did a combination of unparalleled authority with vulnerability to political controversy and public criticism: replying to a March 1966 letter of congratulations on his appointment from engineer Sir Frederick Snow, he quipped that 'Northern Ireland problems are not new to me – they have a quality all of their own!' But he was less than two-thirds of the way through his decade of commitment to the province, and so he ploughed vigorously on.[63] And as it turned out, this new university project was indeed to turn out to be yet another controversial enterprise, cut short well before completion. In this instance, Matthew was not directly involved in the pre-history and initial shaping of the project. This lay in an unsuccessful attempt by the Stormont government in 1961 to piggyback the province onto Britain's Robbins committee on higher education expansion, followed by the appointment in 1963 of a Committee on Higher Education in Northern Ireland, under the chairmanship of Sir John Lockwood of London University; it recommended the building of a New University of Ulster (NUU), as well as of an 'Ulster College', to be built at Jordanstown, just north of Belfast.[64] Thus, from the beginning, just as in the case of 'council housing', Northern Ireland's new university was established as a centrally driven project – in strong contrast to the British experience of fervent local civic advocacy of the new universities.[65]

By May 1964, despite Matthew's preference to site any new university in the 'new city', and despite the countervailing pressure to base the new institution around Magee College, Londonderry (a Presbyterian church training college), it had instead been decided, after protracted wrangling, to locate it at Coleraine, a small, historic, largely Protestant town located in the northwest – but just east of the symbolic river Bann. This site essentially represented a compromise between the various unionist factions, appeasing somewhat the 'west of the Bann' lobby although not, as we shall see, the defenders of Derry itself. With the aim of catching up 'leeway' with Robbins in Britain, the committee's report in February 1965 recommended an initial development programme faster than any of the British new universities. Just as at Stirling, a multi-purpose Phase 1 building, to house elements of all five main schools (Biological Sciences, Physical Sciences, Social Sciences, Humanities and 'Education Centre') would be completed within two years and would house an initial intake of 400, with permanent buildings following at a slower pace. In 1965 an academic planning board was set up, under Sir James Cook, vice-chancellor of Exeter University, which began work in January 1966. The aim was to admit the first 400 students in 1968 and build up to 2,000–3,000 in 1973 and 6,000 in 1980. There would be a close grouping of schools, including the novel 'Education Centre' dedicated to integration of teacher training and education research, and providing for a three-year diploma or four-year degree course.[66]

Despite its very different governmental origins, NUU nevertheless conformed quite closely in its chosen location to the standard British 'new university' formula laid down by the UGC – namely, two to four miles from the centre of a (usually) historic town, with a 200-acre minimum site for 3,000 students. We shall return later in this chapter to the linked issue of the ways in which its specific planning and design concept related to the wider architectural concepts and debates of the new university programme. Its 300-acre site lay two miles northwest of Coleraine, on a prominent ridge-top site overlooking the Bann. Coleraine itself was a compact plantation town of 13,600 inhabitants, adjoined by the somewhat stodgy seaside resorts of Portrush and Portstewart; in a significant difference from the British norm, there was no immediate intention to build large halls of residence, as many students would board in these two towns. The Ministry decided that the whole area should be planned together, with all three towns and the university treated as a single planning unit. Oliver and Aitken then had the brainwave of making the replanned three towns and university one of the units in a new area-planning mosaic of the province, adumbrated initially in a 1964 White Paper on planning administration. Even if the university would not now, as Matthew had proposed, help prop up the Craigavon project, it could instead do equally useful work, from the planning perspective, in supporting the extension of regional planning to north and northwest Ulster – while being justified to unionist politicians as a way of 'consolidating' the Coleraine area. To steer through this potentially controversial project, within the very tight deadline involved, Oliver and his colleagues turned again to Matthew. At the end of 1965, and again in January 1966, he wrote to Matthew to propose a fourfold commission: first, 'the overall planning and construction of a modern university, as a matter of urgency'; second, to ensure all supporting services; third, to plan the wider setting so that university and hinterland 'could develop in a manner worthy of one another'; and fourth, to enable the area to 'take its place in the regional planning of Ulster'.[67]

Because of the sensitivities of the job, it was seen very much at this stage as a personal commission, rather than a corporate RMJM job. In fact, as we shall see below, Matthew moved immediately to involve John Richards and the full apparatus of the Edinburgh office. What was never even raised was the possibility of any involvement by Stirrat Marshall in London; instead, the 'Johnson-Marshall' involvement was that of Percy, working as planning consultant to Matthew. At Oliver's suggestion, he began work immediately by meeting Cook for a working lunch at the Athenaeum on 24 February 1966.[68] As Matthew was now a 'known quantity' in Ulster, and associated with controversial matters, the personal attribution to him of both the architectural and planning elements of the project caused some awkwardness when his appointment was announced by Craig in parliament in March 1966; when Craig emphasised that 'Sir Robert's quality as a regional and area planner is already well known to us', nationalist MP O'Reilly quipped, 'Too well known!'[69] The expected pleas were made for 'Irish' or 'Ulster' architects to be involved, for the university to be based around Magee College and for extension of the district plan area to embrace Derry, 'in view of the fact that it was left out of the Regional Plan for the remainder of the Province'; eventually, in 1966, it was decided to merge Magee and the NUU with effect from 1968.[70] The coastal location of the project, too, caused nationalist MPs to speculate mischievously whether it was a defeatist gesture that portended 'a second flight of the Earls'.[71] At the same time, the new vice-chancellor, Professor Alan Norman Burges, a 55-year-old Australian, currently professor of botany at Liverpool University, was announced. Unlike Cotterill at Stirling and many of the other British new university vice-chancellors, Burges was actively 'not interested in the design or building process', and any architectural views that he did have were of a most traditional, Oxbridge-cloistered kind.[72]

An initial familiarisation visit, including the 'essential business meeting' that would settle the lines of the university's architectural development, was fixed for late April 1966. Matthew initially involved John Richards, whose work at Stirling was running slightly ahead of the

Coleraine project. On 20 April they were met at Aldergrove by Oliver and taken to meet the Academic Planning Board and the Minister of Education, W K Fitzsimmons, who stressed the department's aspiration for 'buildings of architectural merit – the sky's the limit!' They then motored over to Coleraine, with Matthew's first impressions being that the site was 'good, without being dramatic', that Coleraine itself was a 'tight little burgh', but that the Coleraine–Portrush–Portpatrick area was, on the whole, architecturally 'a hotch-potch'.[73] The twenty-first of April 1966 was the decisive day for the project as a whole, with a succession of almost continuous meetings with the eight-strong Academic Planning Board, chaired by Cook, and with Ministry/local officers, at which the main lines of the development phasing were set. In an indication of the reliance now placed on Richards by Matthew in matters of strategic project planning, he allowed him to take the lead here in developing and presenting different phasing options. The key issue was the relative timing and phasing of the three main elements of the project – the Development Plan, the initial general-purpose phase (system-built for speed), and the main permanent buildings – so as to maintain the overriding schedule set by the 1968 opening target. Matthew began the discussion by emphasising that the development plan preparation would have to parallel at least the planning of the initial phase of buildings. How, then, should these buildings be phased, bearing in mind the limited capacity of the Northern Ireland building industry? Over lunch, Matthew and Richards privately worked out two alternative options for the Academic Planning Board. On the one hand, the first phase could take the form of a giant building of 300,000 sq ft, designed by RMJM, to house two years' intake – in which case one-third of the university would be system-built. On the other hand, the initial multi-purpose building (Phase 1) could be more modest in size, but the planning of the main complex would also have to start straight-

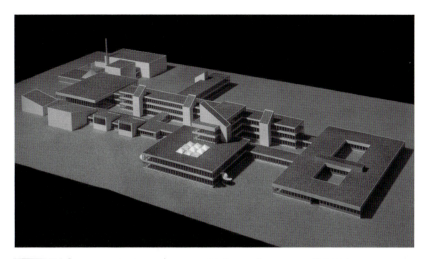

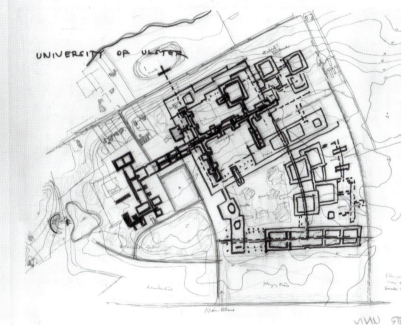

away, and the first group of permanent main buildings (Phase 2) would also have to be designed by RMJM – something that might spread the load contractually and reduce the amount of system-building needed, but might cause political embarrassment, given the mounting pressure to use Northern Irish architects on the project.[74]

In the afternoon of 21 April, after Matthew had explained the two options, the Board decisively voted for the second option, citing the need to 'set standards' for the whole programme as justification for committing, effectively, the bulk of the project to his firm. Under the phasing of the approved second option, starts would still be very concentrated, requir-

(top) **10.10** 1967 model of Phase 1 of the New University of Ulster: general teaching and administration took up 88,000 sq ft, science teaching/research 25,000 sq ft, unions and refectories 35,000 sq ft. (John Dewar Studios)

(bottom) **10.11** New University of Ulster, May 1967 sketch layout of Development Plan by Matthew. (EULMC)

341

The 'Matthewing' of Ulster

the finalised development plan and the laying of the foundation stone by the Governor of Northern Ireland in June 1967, saw a high-pressure succession of meetings and correspondence between Matthew's colleagues and the university and Ministry authorities. On the university side, the chief actor was the Registrar, W T Ewing – initially, along with the Librarian (F J E Hurst), the only academic staff members, but soon joined, during 1966, by the Buildings and Estate Officer, John Y Noble (a surveyor by profession). For his part, Matthew initially maintained a tight control over the RMJM involvement, seeing this as a suitable opportunity to become involved once again, however fleetingly, as a 'project partner' on a building of national importance; indeed, he remained the official project partner until his death, aided by a succession of partners and associates-in-charge. Matthew acted, in effect, as the project architect until at least January 1967, helped in negotiations and programming matters by John Richards. In August 1966 a job architect, Chris Butler-Cole, was transferred from the RMJM London office to help Matthew, and a full-time project administrator, Angus Robin, was appointed to deal with the mounting bureaucratic workload; and in late January 1967 Dennis Ashmead, one of the most experienced university specialists in the Edinburgh office, was transferred to work full time on Coleraine (with Butler-Cole becoming his deputy), acting as, in effect, deputy project architect to Matthew himself. An RMJM branch office, staffed initially by Dan Bain, was set up in summer 1966 in a nearby villa, 'Fortview'.[76]

Alongside all this ran the largely autonomous work of Percy Johnson-Marshall's team on the Coleraine–Portrush–Portstewart Area Plan. This was the time when, at Edinburgh University, Percy was in the process of breaking away from Matthew's hegemony, and in April 1967, to avoid giving any cause for offence, Matthew tactfully deferred giving a lecture on the subject to Coleraine Rotary Club until Percy could make a

10.12 Front cover of the Coleraine-Portrush-Portstewart Area Plan prepared by Percy Marshall's staff with RMJM in 1968: the perspective shows the focal position of the new university between Coleraine (foreground) and the two seaside towns (in distance). (RMJM)

ing spending of £900,000 (Phase 1) in 1967, and no less than £3m (for Phase 2) in 1968 – a pace faster than anything achieved in the British new universities. The university was also presented with a further choice by Matthew in relation to the visual, townscape aspects of the project: given its gently sloping ridge-top situation, should it be 'buried from view in the centre of the site', or should it be 'outward looking'? Burges forcefully advocated the latter, and Matthew agreed to 'knock up' the student numbers into a draft schedule of accommodation for Phase 1, and to begin sketch layout work as soon as possible.[75]

The ensuing year, until submission of

formal presentation to the Steering Committee. But the plan followed the precedent set by Matthew's Belfast area growth towns in calling for rapid population expansion within the 90 square mile study area, from 32,000 in 1966 to 58,000 by 1981. Typically of the late 1960s, this expansion was to be ordered in a relatively concentrated manner, in this case linear in form – with seven new urban residential 'community groups', along with four rural village centres.[77]

During the whole of this period, despite the ad hoc way in which the project organisation was allowed to mushroom, Matthew held everything together through the force of his own *auctoritas*. Robin recalled ten years later that Matthew's 'instructions were that one should try to know the client well enough to know what he was thinking' – and as a result, at Coleraine 'early relations with the client were first class'. Within the firm, Matthew's exacting attention to detail ensured high standards and dedication. By September 1966 it was also established that RMJM would also provide QS and engineering services for Phase 1, in order to bring the 'whole team under one roof'.[78] As the pace of work accelerated, in addition to normal trips by ferry or airline plane to Aldergrove with hired car at the other end the firm also laid on a fortnightly chartered flight, using a wartime Dove light aircraft, from Strathallan aerodrome to Ballykelly. Ashmead recalled the enjoyable *esprit de corps* during the first couple of years of the project:

Anyone could book a seat on the plane – engineers, landscape people, or whoever. It was quite fun, and there was the added peculiarity that the Ballykelly airstrip had a railway crossing it: if a train was coming, you had to circle for a bit! Then at Coleraine, there was the socialising among the team, usually in Sir Robert's absence – although at one particularly long job meeting in a local hotel, with the discussion going on and on, we decided to slip off down to this nice little mod-

ern bar designed by a local architect. No sooner had we fled out of the back door and along a back street to the bar, and set up the drinks, when Sir Robert walked straight in through the front door – he was very intuitive![79]

Significantly, Vice-Chancellor Burges, although present at many key meetings, showed a very patchy grasp of all these building-related discussions: at a June 1966 meeting, for example, he was still unclear about the difference between Phase 1 and the first part of the main complex (i.e., Phase 2), and mistakenly called for the latter to be completed in 1968 rather than 1969.[80] More ominously, some significant differences of organisational approach emerged between the architects and client. Ewing demanded that RMJM should work from UGC cost limits towards an estimate of what could be afforded, while at the same time insisting on faster and faster progress towards the fixed 'building targets which you now have before you': as early as July 1966, John Richards noted the 'somewhat worrying' conflict between the two objectives, and that either overspending or delay would inevitably result.[81] Ashmead recalled the university's important place in O'Neill's dash for reform:

There was a very highly charged atmosphere over there – you couldn't pin it down precisely, but it seemed to be terribly important for Ulster to get its new university built and to get the money spent. It would be too much to say that you could feel the troubles looming ahead, but there was a very political atmosphere in the air.[82]

Before Matthew and Butler-Cole could get to work, from November 1966 onwards, on the sketch design for Phase 1, it was decided to confirm the feasibility of using system building – seen by the architects as vital, given the construction period of only one year. Rapidly, it was conceded by the UGC that time was far too short for any competitive tendering, and the choice was reduced to a negotiated contract with Laing or Gilbert-Ash from England, with the large Belfast contractor F B McKee, using Bison Preferred Dimension Frame, or with a local Coleraine consortium (included in the list for cosmetic reasons only). McKee emerged the clear and logical winner, and the contract was agreed on 28 November, with start of work scheduled for May 1967.[83]

Spine and Diamond: Matthew's development plan for Coleraine University

Now the way was clear for Matthew, assisted initially by Butler-Cole, to produce his sketch design for Phase 1 and, almost in tandem, his development plan for the whole university. This was, arguably, the largest and most complex 'design' he ever prepared himself – although, from early 1967, the weight of work on detailed realisation of the concept gradually shifted from him to Ashmead (in both cases working with the help of Butler-Cole and his team). Ashmead recalled that 'as a budding job architect, he gave you a lot of responsibility – but he was also very demanding, and you had to be sensitive to what he wanted!'[84]

How did Matthew's overall design solution fit into the wider context of the 'new universities' movement in Britain and elsewhere?[85] As part of the expansion of mass higher education during the '*trente glorieuses*' of 1945–75, many completely new 'campus' complexes were commissioned, especially in the US and other English-speaking countries; one of the set pieces of the latter was the British 'New University' programme of *c*.1958–70. Internationally, the new universities movement closely followed the general trajectory of planning within modern architecture, from highly dispersed layouts of separate blocks in open space in the 1940s and early 1950s to densely mixed-together 'clusters' in the 1960s. Within it, educational and architectural reformism ran in tandem, but never precisely in step; what everyone was agreed on was that the new universities must above all break decisively from the old

academic traditions of pomp and splendour. Educationally, the emphasis was on the breakdown of distinctions and barriers between subjects and departments, and the creation of novel relationships between subjects, but the great pioneer in this area, Sussex (planned from 1959), combined a highly innovative structure of large, multidisciplinary 'schools' with Spence's rather more stately, romantic architectural vision. Architectural innovation in the early and mid 1960s focused on different ways of mixing together the university's different functions, to encourage this interdisciplinarity, while pursuing the flexibility for later expansion in all directions. The important thing was that the whole complex – in contrast to the supposedly homogeneous muddle of the old civic universities – should be a single, distinctive, individual design concept, integrating the educational philosophy of the institution within a wider utopian vision of 'community'. Highly stacked, centralised solutions were rare – for example at Essex (ACP, from 1963). More popular was the solution that focused on a linear 'spine' with functions clustered on each side, sometimes in a rhetorically bold manner, as with Lasdun's UEA (from 1963), and sometimes more quietly and homogeneously mixed together, as at Gabriel Epstein's Lancaster (1963–8), which even integrated the library (elsewhere usually a free-standing building) into the overall 'fruit salad' mixture.[86]

RMJM's own new university work, which expanded to take in no less than three separate projects – York, Stirling and Coleraine – along with the nearly new Bath university, sprang from within this experimental English movement. But it added to it, largely at Stirrat Marshall's instigation, a new emphasis on rationalist efficiency and system building. At first, the tone was set by Stirrat's preference for dispersed, muted layouts, avoiding flamboyant gestures: for example at the CLASP-built York, 1962–70, where the development plan spread out all functions into mixed-function 'colleges' in landscaping. Later, under the influence of Hugh Morris, the linear platform principle of the abortive 1961/2 LCC Hook New Town plan was imported to Bath University (from 1963), where the schools were attached to the spine, in turn traversed by massive slabs at right angles. At Richards's Stirling, the last RMJM university in Britain itself, although the teaching accommodation was designed on an extensible 'spine and rib' principle, overall there was a return to a more traditional, even stately pattern of clearly segregated functions – teaching, social, residences – within the lavishly landscaped setting. The prefabricated, multifunction first phase, of course, was planned in a completely mixed-together way, but was set far away from the main grouping.

In his plan for Coleraine, Matthew took his cue from the Vice-Chancellor's call for an outward-looking design fully exploiting the hilltop site. Ashmead recalled the somewhat theatrical occasion, in early February 1967, at which Matthew released this overall landscape concept to the media:

This was the first time I had visited the site with Sir Robert, and we stopped on the road to Portstewart, and climbed the slope to the crest – my immediate reaction being how windswept and bleak it was, with even the trees being rather bent over by the gales coming straight in off the sea! But when we got to the top of the slope, we found a big Ulster TV van sitting up there, with some people waiting to interview Sir Robert. They asked him, 'What's your overall vision for the site?' Without a moment's hesitation, he said, 'It's going to be here on the crest – everyone's going to have views!' Now even up to that stage, there had still been some debate on that point, and one of the feasibility studies back in 1966 had looked at putting the main complex in the bowl at the back of the site. But once he said, so firmly and in public, 'That's where it's going to be!' – that inevitably became what happened![87]

In educational terms, Coleraine was organised into broad 'schools' like Sussex, although the Education Centre introduced an element of vocational training that was generally kept out of the more elitist British new universities.

In Matthew's own previous university work, notably at Crombie Hall, there had persisted strong elements of the now old-fashioned idea of 'added' forms or colour. Matthew now decisively jettisoned this legacy, and joined in with the early 1960s tendency of a more integrated, intensified planning – but in his own idiosyncratic way. Matthew decided that the basic pattern of the university should be a linear spine running northwest–southeast along the crest of the hill overlooking the Bann. In this, he was perhaps influenced by Morris's concept at Bath, or by Cumbernauld Town Centre; in general, 'Cumbernauld was in the bloodstream' of many new university designers at the time.[88] But this Coleraine spine would be of completely different character from any of the other British new universities, as it would be dominated by the university library. Almost all the others had followed the traditional pattern of setting apart a massive, rectangular university library, often in a dominant position like the chapel of an Oxbridge college. At the suggestion and urging of F J E Hurst, the librarian, who vigorously championed the advances in modern conveyor belt and book retrieval systems, Matthew devised the concept of a 'library spine' or 'library concourse', which would act as 'the heart of the university, from which all subsequent phases will grow'.[89] This was, in effect, a Cumbernauld-style linear megastructure, four storeys in height, with open vehicular ground floor, two pedestrian concourse levels above interpenetrating the adjacent flanking schools, and the top floor occupied by the linear library; the library would always stretch the full length of the site, expanding as the university expanded. Several universities, such as Essex and UEA, raised up the main pedestrian spine or platform, but only Matthew, at Coleraine, encased it megastructurally, above and below. The library would thus both be abolished, and made into the dominant element of the whole complex. The strong linearity of the spine would be powerfully offset, again just as at Cumbernauld, by a pedestrian cross-axis providing the main route between communal and teaching buildings. It would be superimposed across the undulating section of the site, with its prominent dip in the centre.

The southwestern arm of this cross-axis would be largely taken up by the covered-in principal social concourse of the university, named the 'Diamond' to echo traditional plantation towns; the northeast end of the concourse would be crowned by the university's only vertical punctuation – a tower block, housing administration offices, built largely to encase the main boiler flue (as at Lancaster), and rising from an elevated podium ascended by a ceremonial flight of steps. The main entrance hall of the university would be at the intersection of the spine and concourse. Low-rise teaching buildings arranged round courtyards would sprout from the spine in 'additive' fashion. Overall, then, the plan had a strongly cruciform character.[90] Although there was no direct precedent in Britain for the dominant motif of the 'library spine', it was parallelled in West Germany, at Konstanz and at Universität Bielefeld (1970–5). Matthew settled on the principle of the 'rolling development of the university and a central library spine' as early as the beginning of February 1967, envisaging a peak building rate of £2m of building a year.[91] The complex would be extensible both lengthways and laterally; 200 acres, over and above the main 300 acre site, were reserved for expansion. In September 1967 Matthew produced a romantic coloured painting of the university seen from the Bann. In dramatised form, it showed, as at Lancaster, a generally low-rise agglomeration with only one tall block, massed in a jaggedly stepped manner, like his original New Zealand House project.[92]

Coleraine, Phase 1: the initial multi-purpose building

While Matthew and Ashmead hammered out their multi-purpose, megastructural concept for Phase 2, the initial drive of designing and building was concentrated some distance away to the south, in the all-purpose, self-contained Phase 1 building. Its detached position, at the southern extreme of the site, was intended to cement the university as closely as possible into the existing town context – albeit at the cost of creating an awkward gulf in the middle of the university after the building of Phase 2. The design of Phase 1, commissioned in late November 1966, proceeded some three months in advance of the overall development plan, with the aim of receiving the first 450 students in October 1968. Like Richards at Stirling, Matthew decided to opt for a self-contained low-rise building, contrasting with the massive main buildings, and whose system-built construction would not prejudice construction decisions about the latter; it would bring together all facilities of the university for the first two years, including lecture theatres, laboratories, offices, union, refectory and games hall. But unlike Richards's single-storey, lightweight-looking block, Matthew decided that he wanted from the start a 'proper building' on several floors, despite the tight deadline of the 'crash programme', and he designed Phase 1 in his time-honoured manner, with a main block, and smaller objects added all around. In this instance, with the overriding demand for speed, this was for a very practical reason: with all the various appendages 'slung around the main teaching-concourse block, the contractor could build what was available and not be pinned in by a frozen design': all in all, the £900,000 Phase 1 building totalled 148,000 sq ft.[93]

At this point, the issue of the specific architectural form of Phase 1 had to be tackled, and here, on an early visit to the site in February 1967, Matthew set down for Ashmead some very firm guidelines that could apply not just to

Phase 1 but to the main complex as well:

> He was adamant, first and foremost, that it was not to be a 'beautiful English-style university'. I don't really know what was behind this – maybe he just wanted it to look different from the lush landscaping of Stirling, or maybe, being quite politically sensitive, he had the notion that Northern Ireland was not the right place to do something 'pretty'. But anyway, he said that on a bleak site like this – so different from the rolling parkland at Airthrey – you had to have bold skyline shapes, commending the vista out to the north-west. The buildings, in effect, would have to do the job of the landscape. He wanted bold detailing, he wanted the structure to 'read', he wanted a strong skyline with vertical and geometrical accents like the massive triangular skylights.

All this would really come into its own with Phase 2, where the artificial landscape concept would, in effect, chime in with the megastructural thinking of the 1960s. But even for Phase 1, despite the smaller scale, 'Sir Robert made it very clear he didn't want some mild, flat-roofed building that could be mistaken for Coleraine Secondary Modern!' For the detailing and materials of Phase 1, Matthew also firmly guided Ashmead and Butler-Cole away from anything suggestive of the picturesque, and towards a relatively precise, industrial finish. The only British new university of this kind was the grid-plan Warwick, by Yorke, Rosenberg & Mardall (from 1963). And, sure enough,

> Sir Robert suggested we all went down to Warwick and had a look – which we of course all did straight away – and were duly struck by the rather abstract shapes and the tiled cladding everywhere. That was typical of him: at no stage did he actually say: 'I want you to use white tiling!', but we were still left with the distinct impression that we were quite free to use any colour we wanted – just so long as it was white!

Afraid of tiles falling off, Matthew insisted that they should have thin concrete surrounds, a prudent measure unsuccessfully opposed by Butler-Cole's team: 'We thought it was an "impure" solution, but that was what he wanted, and what he wanted went!' [94]

For the lower scale of Phase 1, with its jutting triangular lecture theatre shapes, the pre-war work of Gropius, as at Impington Village College (1935–7), was still an important factor, and there were other, more indirect overseas influences.[95] As the design developed, 'it was a question of constantly taking ideas back to Sir Robert, gauging his reaction as to how well his demand for structural expression and bold shapes was being met, and making any changes he wanted.' In the planning of Phase 1, the annexes, including the games hall and lecture theatre, were linked simply by corridors, and unified by insistent horizontal window banding; skyline punctuation was provided by the triangular projections of the staircases and lecture theatres, and a slender boiler chimney. It was a mark of the distant relations between client and architect, and, in particular, of Burges's lack of interest in the buildings, that the 'industrial' finished appearance of Phase 1 came as a

10.13 1968 drawing by Maxwell Allan for stone to commemorate the opening of Phase 1 by Prime Minister Terence O'Neill. (Allan & Sons Ltd, Edinburgh)

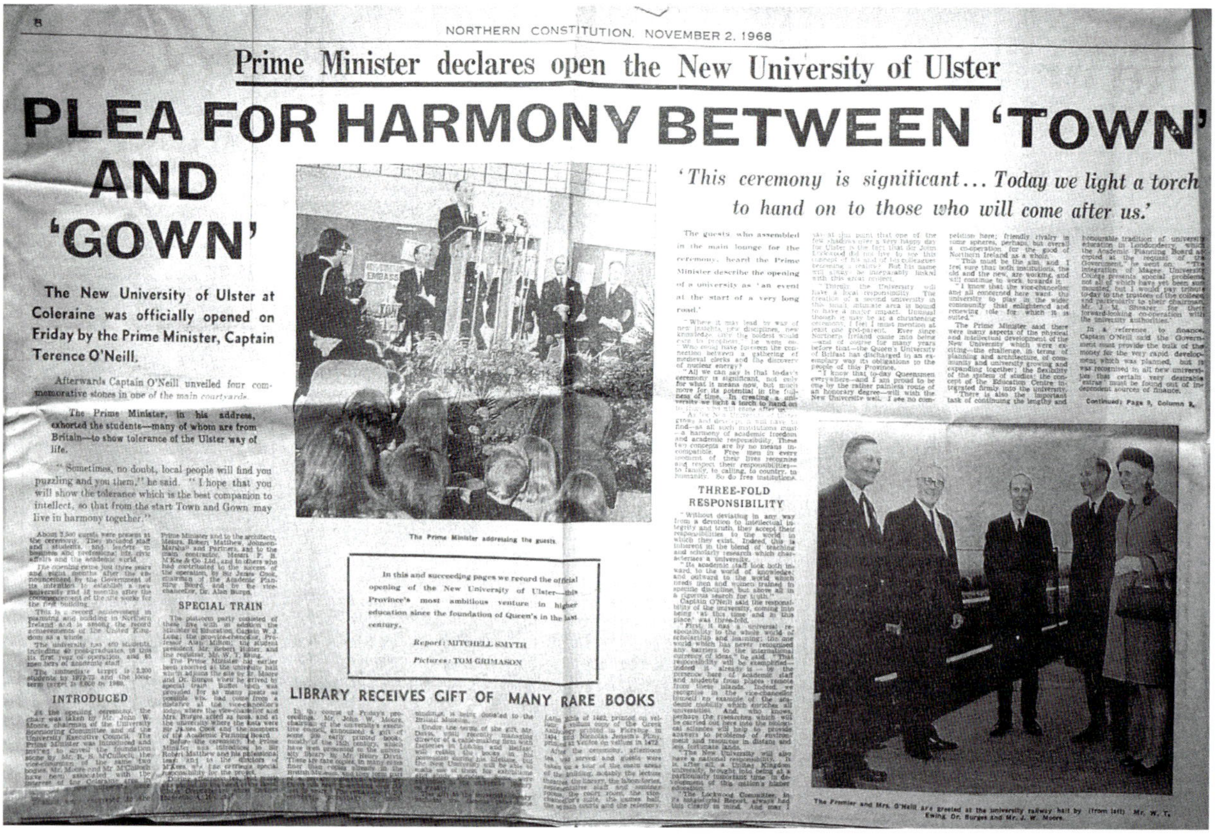

NORTHERN CONSTITUTION, NOVEMBER 2, 1968

Prime Minister declares open the New University of Ulster

PLEA FOR HARMONY BETWEEN 'TOWN' AND 'GOWN'

The New University of Ulster at Coleraine was officially opened on Friday by the Prime Minister, Captain Terence O'Neill.

Afterwards Captain O'Neill unveiled four commemorative stones in one of the main courtyards.

The Prime Minister, in his address, exhorted the students—many of whom are from Britain—to show tolerance of the Ulster way of life.

"Sometimes, no doubt, local people will find you puzzling and you them," he said. "I hope that you will show the tolerance which is the best companion to intellect, so that from the start Town and Gown may live in harmony together."

SPECIAL TRAIN

INTRODUCED

The Prime Minister addressing the guests.

In this and succeeding pages we record the official opening of the New University of Ulster—this Province's most ambitious venture in higher education since the foundation of Queen's in the last century.

Report: MITCHELL SMYTH

Pictures: TOM GRIMASON

LIBRARY RECEIVES GIFT OF MANY RARE BOOKS

'This ceremony is significant... Today we light a torch to hand on to those who will come after us.'

THREE-FOLD RESPONSIBILITY

Continued: Page 9, Column 2.

The Premier and Mrs. O'Neill are greeted at the university railway halt by (from left) Mr. W. T. Ewing, Dr. Burges and Mr. J. W. Moore.

10.14 Newspaper report of the opening ceremony. (Northern Constitution, 2 November 1968, 8)

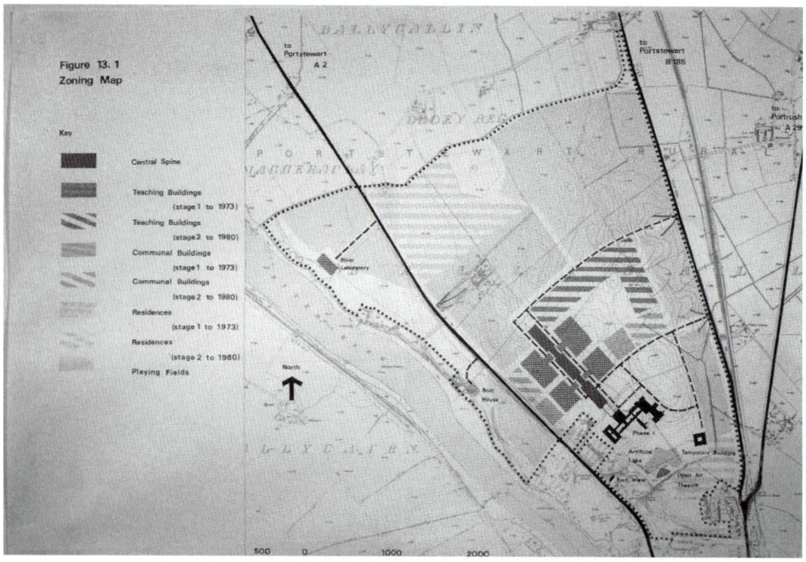

10.15 New University of Ulster Development Plan, 1968: development map of campus (Phase 1 at bottom right of map). (RMJM)

rude shock to him: 'The poor old Vice-Chancellor really didn't have a clue – he said he'd thought he was getting a university of Portland stone and ivy-clad walls, not a factory!'[96]

Originally, it was envisaged that the Phase 1 building would be converted eventually into self-contained offices on completion of the main complex. But as Matthew's development plan spine concept began to emerge during early/mid 1967, he instead decided to use it to house the Education Centre, extending the library spine southwards eventually to connect with it – although there would at first be a large gap between the two, and Cumbernauld Town Centre already showed how disjointed a half-built linear master-plan could look.[97] The library in Phase 1 was directly aligned with the library spine of the main complex. Despite the more intense density of the library spine, Matthew's vision for Coleraine was fairly consistent with his overall additive approach to institutional planning – far more so than, for example, Ninewells. Certainly, John Richards felt acutely the contrast between Phase 1 and his own more unified concept at Stirling:

> To me, Robert's approach seemed to be like that of a jackdaw, sticking things on to other things – and the New University of Ulster plan conformed to that approach. It was,

basically, a collage of objects and shapes joined together by corridors, and, as such, it was not much different from Crombie Hall a decade earlier. Arguably, all Robert's buildings, like his lamps and chairs, and the insides of his houses, were really the same design – assemblages of objects and forms, rather than abstractions or platonic forms – albeit varied in scale and arrangement!

Butler-Cole also agreed with that verdict: 'Matthew was very good at working out what had to go where, but not at bringing it together architecturally: Coleraine was a sprawl of different bits and pieces, a relationship diagram turned into a building, whereas the Pathfoot Building at Stirling was architecture.' Arguably, though, Matthew's somewhat anarchic concept was more in tune with advanced university planning trends of the 1960s than the more traditional, stand alone polished beauty of Stirling.[98]

At a press conference in June 1967 Matthew summarised overall progress at Coleraine. Site work had now begun for Phase 1, and an interim report on the Development Plan was about to be published. He summarised the Development Plan as an attempt to take full advantage of the material features of the site. The collective and recreational buildings, and the sites for future residences, would face southwest over the Bann, while the teaching buildings would stretch in 'introverted spits' northeast of the spine. And the area plan would aim to create in the three-towns triangle 'an overall environment worthy of a university town'.[99] As at Stirling, construction of Phase 1 proceeded quickly and smoothly, and on 3 October 1968 the first intake of nearly 400 students was admitted. Prime Minister O'Neill officially opened Phase 1 on 25 October, arriving from Belfast by special train. Matthew travelled by car to the opening ceremony with Ashmead, Robin and three other colleagues, and en route, perhaps just to keep them on their toes, sprang on them a disconcerting practical joke. Ashmead recalled that:

On the way, I said, just in casual conversation, 'Isn't it a shame that there aren't any semi-mature shrubs in the central courtyard!' That was where the great O'Neill was to speak. I wasn't quite sure if Sir Robert had heard this, but, as it happened, we were just going past a churchyard, and all of a sudden he said to Angus Robin, 'Angus, stop the car! Look at those fine Irish yews in there! There's five of you in the car – what are you waiting for?' Luckily I was able to say, 'But we don't have any spades with us!' But I still don't know whether he actually meant it seriously![100]

In his inaugural speech O'Neill hailed this 'record achievement in building for Northern Ireland', opened only three years and eight months after the first declared intention by government, and highlighted the flexibility of the studies system and the integration of the Education Centre into the university; hopefully, the controversies about 'location' would be replaced by a 'harmony between town and gown'. All in all, 'today we light a torch to hand to those who will come after us'. Ronald McCulloch, vice-chairman of the university executive council, explained that the architects 'fulfil the role of team leaders in an activity of this type, and without the dedication, devotion and real personal interest taken by each member of the team, and in particular, the personal involvement and leadership of Sir Robert Matthew, it would not be possible for us to be here today.'[101]

10.16 Front cover of the first issue of the NUU Student Newspaper. (*Phase 1*, 25 October 1968)

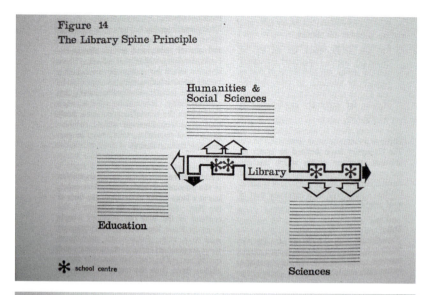

Figure 14
The Library Spine Principle

Humanities &
Social Sciences

Library

Education

Sciences

✳ school centre

(top) **10.17** New University of Ulster Development Plan, 1968: diagram of library spine. (RMJM, *The New University of Ulster, Report on the Development Plan,* Coleraine, 1968, 32) (RMJM)

(bottom) **10.18** New University of Ulster Development Plan, 1968: perspective of library spine (on left) and tower (right). (RMJM, *The New University of Ulster, Report on the Development Plan,* Coleraine, 1968, 53) (RMJM)

Arrested development: the truncation of the Coleraine Development Plan

With Phase 1 virtually complete, in mid 1968 the Northern Ireland government approved the negotiation of a £2m contract with McKee for Phase 2, as the first part of the main complex. This 250,000 sq ft building phase would comprise 'a spine of composite nature', with the first part of the main library on the top floor, and the transverse concourse stretching across from the vast glazed hall of the Diamond to the ten-storey humanities tower at the east.[102] In the detailed design of Phase 2, the most passionately debated issue had been the precise way in which the library would thread through the spine: should it be at ground, middle or upper level? The decision to go for the latter led, in turn, to adoption of a system of peaked, raking rooflights. Further skyline drama was provided by stair towers and by the main administration tower

block, clad in tiled precast concrete slabs, with a glazed stair tower and boiler flue at one end. The design of the Diamond – the main social circulation space, partly enclosed as a great hall, with a metal latticework roof expressed on the outside as a line of glazed 'diamonds' – was actually inspired by Stirling & Gowan's Leicester Engineering building (1959). Ashmead recalled that

> I discussed at length with Sir Robert how we could get the bold detailing he desired, and how we could make statements out of the structural elements. I drew his attention to the strong way in which the roof structure was expressed at Leicester – a very bold shape, with the lecture theatre, toplit roof, and the whole thing tiled – and he responded very positively![103]

From autumn 1968, however, everything associated with the project, and Matthew's Ulster work in general, began rapidly to unravel. As early as July 1968, with growing economic problems embroiling the UK economy in general, trouble loomed when the UGC intervened in the Phase 2 contract, insisting on splitting it into two stages. The Ministry of Education now accepted that development might for the time being have to be curbed at the 3,500 target originally envisaged for 1973, leaving the complex in a raggedly uncompleted form in which the spine principle of Phase 2 would be hardly visible, with the relatively short section of north–south spine massively counterbalanced by the transverse buildings. There was also a gradual breakdown of relations between RMJM and the client, as Matthew became steadily more disengaged, while the university insisted on incessant detail changes to the spine building, resulting in further and further departures from UGC procedures. By early 1969 Ashmead was 'on the verge of a nervous breakdown', and eventually resigned. He was replaced by Chris (J C) Carter, with David S Sturrock as project architect, and the total number of staff involved (including services consultants) rose to as many as 75.[104] All the

inherent difficulties of distance-working were exacerbated by the growing clashes with university officials, such as Buildings Officer John Noble, and Carter recalled with a shudder, a decade later, the constant stress of 'making visits and attending meetings often at great personal inconvenience, with difficult travelling in all weathers in chartered light aircraft'.[105]

During the early 1970s, following appeals from the university to intervene personally, Matthew himself was drawn into a succession of meetings to sort out the overspending on Phase 1, and the disorganisation of the Phase 2 'Spine' contract. By 1978 outstanding fees had reached £366,000, and expensive legal action and arbitration followed over the ensuing two years.[106] The symbolic final straw for the building of Coleraine, however, came in 1973, shortly after final occupation, when the boiler house chimney incorporated in the tower block accidentally caught fire. Wightman recalled that

Chris Carter reported the accident at a partners' meeting, and said that the

chimney itself had gone up in flames, like a kind of Roman candle. There was a pause, and then Matthew said slowly, 'Excuse me – maybe I'm being dumb – but surely if you design a chimney for a boiler, surely it must by definition be fireproof?' I don't remember Chris's answer![107]

Dash towards disintegration: the breakdown of Matthew's Ulster vision

By 1973, however, the Coleraine project had become submerged in what was fast turning into a general tide of civil unrest across Northern Ireland. Ironically, the development policies of Green's and Oliver's team, under the umbrella of O'Neillism, were at last bearing fruit, with a doubling of housing output, and in May 1968 Matthew was appointed, with Professors Tom Wilson and Jack Parkinson, to draw up a 1970–5 programme of economic, physical and social development, intended to 'roll forward the Matthew Plan of 1963 and the Wilson Economic Plan of 1963'. During the time around 1969–70, most of Matthew's

10.19 Aerial view from southwest of university complex following completion of building work in 1973, showing the library spine principle, the gap between the main complex and Phase 1 (in the near background) and the relation of the entire university to the town of Coleraine (in the distance). (RMJM)

10.20 New University of Ulster, early 1970s view of completed Diamond and steps to south-east (EULMC)

(opposite) **10.21** Diagram drawn up by Chris Carter in 1978 to illustrate the range of staff involved in the NUU project since 1966. (RMJM)

efforts on the Ulster front were devoted to meetings in Edinburgh on the preparation of this Northern Ireland Development Plan.[108] But time was now fast running out for O'Neillism, with the simultaneous rise of civil rights militancy on the nationalist side, and increasingly intransigent resistance amongst unionists. Following clashes surrounding a banned civil rights march in October 1968, and an attempt in November to use New Town legislation to circumvent local-authority 'gerrymandering' around Londonderry, eventually O'Neill resigned in April 1969, and the spiral into civil conflict gathered pace. At Craigavon, described as a 'ghost town' as late as 1969, the situation decisively worsened with the start of the 'troubles' in that year, when floods of Catholic refugees from Belfast only polarised the population further: by 1979 the total population was 57,500 (including 12,000 in new areas) rather than the 100,000–120,000 projected, and Craigavon subsided into a warring collection of public housing estates between Portadown and Lurgan.[109]

Unrest spread to the New University of Ulster itself, where in March 1969, for example, a planned civil rights march 'vigil' at the Diamond in Coleraine town centre was called off after threats by loyalist paramilitaries. Ironically, of course, some of the British new universities,

including Essex and East Anglia, were also the focus of militant protest from 1968 onwards, but these British protests, uncomplicated by national-political divisions, soon died away by the mid 1970s. Coleraine University stagnated, and by 1983, even including Magee, it had only just exceeded 2,500 students.[110] By the late 1970s the lack of maintenance had left the complex in growing disrepair and squalor: Derbyshire recalled that

we in London knew absolutely nothing about it during its construction – but when I eventually visited it several years later, I was shocked at the campus, and thought it was utterly dismal, and disregarded all the rules of university growth, by scattering itself across spaces that were to be infilled later – by buildings that never came![111]

More generally, the years around 1970 saw increasingly desperate attempts to use the Development Programme as a way of dampening the political unrest: as finalised in 1970, it pledged a 20 per cent boost in public spending, including the raising of industrial and housing subsidies, the acceleration of redevelopment in Belfast, and higher spending on roads, education and health. Following the abolition of Stormont and the imposition of direct rule in 1972, the centralisation of planning, housing, industry and roads at the province-wide, rather than local, level was finally completed.[112]

Well into the onset of conflict, Matthew had been proceeding on business-as-usual lines, as an, in effect, honorary member of the Northern Ireland reformist architectural and planning establishment, fit to be consulted on even minor issues, as he was in Scotland.[113] Perhaps most remarkable, in retrospect, in 1967 he strongly supported a new twist to the agenda of 'parity', by presiding over the founding of Northern Ireland's first preservation group, the Ulster Architectural Heritage Society. Matthew established himself, just as in Scotland, as an overarching, Geddesian figure able to reconcile the conflicting pressures of

Modern Architect

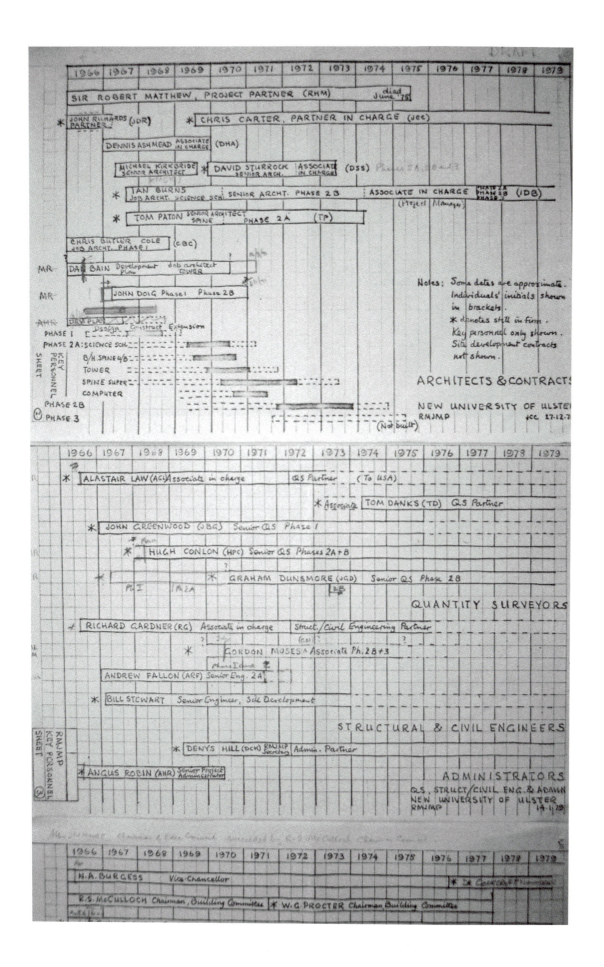

ARCHITECTS & CONTRACTS — NEW UNIVERSITY OF ULSTER

Years: 1966 1967 1968 1969 1970 1971 1972 1973 1974 1975 1976 1977 1978 1979

SIR ROBERT MATTHEW, PROJECT PARTNER (RHM) — died June 75

* JOHN RICHARDS (JDR) PARTNER | * CHRIS CARTER, PARTNER IN CHARGE (JCC)

DENNIS ASHMEAD ASSOCIATE IN CHARGE (DHA)

MICHAEL KIRKBRIDE SENIOR ARCHITECT | * DAVID STURROCK ASSOCIATE SENIOR ARCH. IN CHARGE (DSS) Phases 2A, 2B+3

* IAN BURNS JOB ARCHT. SCIENCE SCH. SENIOR ARCHT. PHASE 2B | ASSOCIATE IN CHARGE PHASE 2A PHASE 2B PHASE 3 (IDB) (Project Manager)

* TOM PATON SENIOR ARCHITECT SPINE PHASE 2A (TP)

CHRIS BUTLER COLE JOB ARCHT. PHASE 1 (CBC)

MR — DAN BAIN Development Plan job architect TOWER

MR — JOHN DOIG Phase 1 Phase 2B

AHR — DEV PLAN
PHASE 1: Design Construct Extension
PHASE 2A: SCIENCE SCH.
B/H SPINE 4/8
TOWER
SPINE SUPER
COMPUTER
PHASE 2B
PHASE 3 (Not built)

KEY PERSONNEL SHEET

Notes: Some dates are approximate. Individuals' initials shown in brackets. * denotes still in firm. Key personnel only shown. Site development contracts not shown.

RMJMP JCC 17-12-7

QUANTITY SURVEYORS / STRUCTURAL & CIVIL ENGINEERS / ADMINISTRATORS — NEW UNIVERSITY OF ULSTER

Years: 1966 1967 1968 1969 1970 1971 1972 1973 1974 1975 1976 1977 1978 1979

* ALASTAIR LAW (AGL) Associate in charge | QS Partner (To USA)

* Associate TOM DANKS (TD) QS Partner

* JOHN GREENWOOD (JBG) Senior QS Phase 1

* HUGH CONLON (HPC) Senior QS Phases 2A+B

* GRAHAM DUNSMORE (JGD) Senior QS Phase 2B

QUANTITY SURVEYORS

* RICHARD GARDNER (RG) Associate in charge | Struct./Civil Engineering Partner

* GORDON MOSES Associate Ph. 2B+3

ANDREW FALLON (ARF) Senior Eng. 2A

* BILL STEWART Senior Engineer, Site Development

STRUCTURAL & CIVIL ENGINEERS

* DENYS HILL (DCH) RMJMP Secretary Admin. Partner

* ANGUS ROBIN (AHR) Senior Project Administrator

ADMINISTRATORS

QS, STRUCT/CIVIL ENG. & ADMIN
NEW UNIVERSITY OF ULSTER
RMJMP 14-1-79

Years: 1966 1967 1968 1969 1970 1971 1972 1973 1974 1975 1976 1977 1978 1979

H.A. BURGESS Vice-Chancellor | * Dr. ...

R.S. McCULLOCH Chairman, Building Committee | * W.G. PROCTER Chairman Building Committee

development and conservation. Chaired by Charles Brett, a solicitor and NI Labour party activist who later headed the Housing Executive, the other committee members included Professor Alexander Potter of Queens University, Alistair Rowan and the young secretary, Desmond Hodges.[114] This was Matthew's first involvement in Northern Ireland with anything other than a central government department or sponsored organisation, although the membership was drawn from the same 'constructive unionist' circles as for the other branches of O'Neillism. At the inaugural meeting on 15 November 1967 in Belfast Harbour Office, he argued that he was 'certainly not 100 per cent preservationist, for while there is much to keep, there is much, especially in the larger towns, to clear away ... but I go the whole way with the stated object of the society.' The Belfast stop line had been 'just that ... ' It was a device intended to 'give a pause for reflection', in the heritage as in any other field. The essence of Matthew's approach was based on maintaining 'parity', especially with Scotland: while Northern Ireland had 'no County History, no local authority list of buildings, no Ancient Monuments Society, no Pevsner guide' ... 'the tide is already flowing, and can take much with it', as evinced in the newly founded Scottish Civic Trust, and 'Maurice Lindsay, its poetic, energetic director'. But the message was grounded in a wider romantic concept of the interplay of modernity with tradition and the rural vernacular – a concept that struck a specially strong chord in Ulster: 'That almost indefinitely old, unselfconscious tradition of building handed down through the centuries ... this ubiquitous vernacular – the common architectural world language – man's constant companion since building started, a vernacular that to my mind is the very heart of the cultural tradition'.

Over the following decades, the UAHS did 'staunch work' in pockets all over the province, saving and actively restoring things like housing or courthouses. But no one, Matthew included, could have foreseen even at the end of 1967 that the major 'conservation' issue in Northern Ireland would become, within a handful of years, not the building of new roads but the blowing up of buildings, and the disfigurement of the urban environment by the squalid trappings of armed counter-insurgency conflict. Just as with Scotland itself, Matthew had since 1960 bound himself up intimately with Northern Ireland, had come to exercise real power there, and had exposed his own personality and personal reputation to the admiration and censure of a relatively small community. This community, unlike Scotland but like his own family, was a divided one, and he must, by 1968–9 – if not much earlier – have begun to suspect that his own planning and authority might have been actually serving not only to arouse expectations of reform but also, indirectly, to deepen the insecurities and collective fears of both communities. Hugh McIlveen recalls that:

By 1969 or 1970, the shutters were dropping everywhere, and we had full-scale anarchy from then until 1973 or 1974. Those were very, very bad years, even for people like ourselves – architects, engineers, contractors – who were very easy to pick off: it happened to some of my friends! So in the liberalist sense, even to mention planning, social infrastructure, demographic theory and so on – not only would have been a waste of time, but would have been politically dynamite! And at that stage it became inevitable that Matthew would drop out of Ulster affairs. Quite apart from the very real danger, I would have thought that, having tortured his way through all he had done, coming across to present ideas to people who mostly didn't want to know – he'd have had enough of it![115]

In 1971 Matthew wrote to Arthur Brooke, Minister of Commerce, of the 'crazy situation in Ulster', stemming largely from a 'failure of education', and of the impossibility of realising the targets set out in the Development Plan: 'Yes, things are not working out as we all hoped when meeting in Stormont in 1968–70.'

National and regional planning was *intended* to be a dynamic process, and that dynamism – in a divided society in which the state's role was ultimately to protect ethnic dominance – inevitably had the effect of helping unravel the settlements of the two communities. When bolstered by the *dirigisme* of a central cadre of bureaucrats without effective local control, as exemplified in the setting up of the Ministry of Development, the dash towards disintegration became a headlong one, and far outstripped any positive impact of creating a new modern identity. The contrast with the Clyde Valley, Scotland's only source of real conflict over regional planning, was a stark one, as Glasgow – however much Abercrombie and Matthew disapproved – was allowed to contest the planners' ideology with its own counter-strategy of massed tower block construction. In Northern Ireland, by contrast, the Stormont elite kept the lid of the pressure cooker tightly screwed down, even as Matthew's plans notched up the heat inexorably – leaving a full-scale explosion as the only outlet. Most often, in Britain, the indictment against planning was that it was a paper tiger, promising sweeping reconciliation but achieving little. The problem with Matthew's Northern Ireland planning strategy, arguably, was the opposite: that it was all too effective!

Chapter 11

Commonwealth of Design:
Matthew's global vision, 1962–8

*a world mission, well beyond professional
pride and prestige.*

Robert Matthew, 1967[1]

*Through these international groups, we see
and feel at first hand some of the forces at
work in the world today, forces we should
understand something about if we are to
be effective, even at home. No country is an
island, not any more.*

Robert Matthew, 1970[2]

11.1 Polaroid picture of Matthew en
route from Pakistan back to the UK
on 30 January 1965. (EULMC)

During the mid and late 1960s the dominant element in Matthew's life was his
rapidly growing role as a global architectural statesman. In this, he focused on

the contribution architects could make to
the general course of international goodwill, especially in the critical areas of
'east–west' and 'north–south' relations:
the latter, especially, was reaching a decisive stage of transition at the time, with
the sudden rush towards the dismantling
of British imperial rule, and the consequent construction of new institutions of
voluntary cooperation. But Matthew's
new orientation towards international
'networking' equally reflected the evolution of his own career, with his scaling-
down of his RMJM and university
'domestic' commitments. Personally, his
growing circle of complex and often
colourful international acquaintances
represented a recreation of 'Kensington
Square' on a global scale, with Matthew
playing the same role of unruffled
intermediary-cum-host. Prior to the
1960s, Matthew's overseas commitments,
including the IUA, had been less than
that of 'tropical specialists' such as Max
Fry and Jane Drew.[3] It was only from
1961 onwards, when he became President
of the IUA for four years, followed immediately by the same term as founder-
president of a new 'Commonwealth
Association of Architects', and his RMJM
workload began to re-orientate itself overseas, especially to a large-scale masterplanning project in Islamabad, the new
capital of Pakistan, that he emerged as
one of the most influential internationalists in British architecture. The driving
force behind this development was personal: Matthew's passionate love of travel

and fresh experiences, and his boredom with his entrenched UK establishment activities. He no longer documented his travels in the loving detail of his early journals of the 1920s–1940s, but the underlying *Wanderlust* was the same.[4]

Matthew's IUA presidency, 1961–5: internal and external conciliation

The 1960s saw a gradual shift in Matthew's urge to travel, and experience other cultures, from the established institutional framework of the IUA to more informal and innovative networks such as the 'Ekistics' grouping. Within the IUA he became President in 1961 (in succession to Hector Mardones Restat of Chile), serving eventually for two two-year spells, a period that entirely overlapped his RIBA presidency. He envisaged the Union's role as a dual one: on the one hand, as a way in which architects could help in the wider promotion of international friendship, at a time of global tension; and, on the other, to provide a wider international reinforcement for specifically architectural concerns, such as the coordination of architectural education or of architectural competitions. Matthew's enthusiasm contrasted with the scepticism of some other internationalists, such as Bill Allen, who recalled

that 'I had no time for the IUA, which I thought was just a talking shop – whereas Robert got deeply involved with it.' Matthew unashamedly believed that international goodwill was a worthwhile goal in itself:

> The Congress is undoubtedly a 'junket' – a vast and deliberately planned piece of junketing arranged mainly for the purpose of promoting goodwill. Surely, when almost every other type of international meeting seems to promote quite the opposite, this is something we have usefully achieved.[5]

Aidan explained the complexities of this outlook:

> My father was always more of an internationalist than a nationalist, but eventually he began to expand his ideas to unrealistic proportions. The IUA was especially important to him, as he was very strong on the power and potential of the architectural profession, and jealously tried to preserve it. But more generally, too, he thought worldwide, and believed we should be working on a world rather than a national or even continental scale. He was violently opposed to the European Common Market for just this reason,

seeing it as the wrong sort of 'region-alism' – an exclusive power structure that was no different from negative nationalism. What he was always searching for was a regionalism based on cultural characteristics, a regionalism that would treat all the world's countries the same, and that could genuinely enrich the world.[6]

The IUA President's duties included overseeing the biennial Congress and Assembly, and the intervening executive committee meetings. The President also took the initiative on wider strategic issues affecting the internal organisation of the IUA itself and its external projection – the most important of the latter being the uniquely controversial Cuban Congress of 1963, and, of the former, the mounting crisis over the overstretched resources of the IUA. Equally important was the indefinable chemistry formed out of the interrelationships of individuals and of geopolitical attitudes. The role of individual personality was emphasised by the context of IUA activities, in which participants were torn from their everyday existence and thrown together with each other for short, intense periods: Matthew doubtless used the IUA's colourful stock of personalities as a therapeutic device, providing a circle of friends who, unlike his family, RMJM or university colleagues, never intruded too closely on his personal space.

Let us first review the *internal* challenges that faced Matthew during his presidency. Within the IUA's key personnel, the executive dominance of Pierre Vago as secretary continued unabated, and Matthew maintained an excellent working relationship with him. Vago's fiery and contentious temperament allowed Matthew to project himself as an unflappable bulwark figure, who could support and at the same time counterbalance Vago's emotionalism. The early 1960s saw a gradual trend away from European dominance: Matthew acknowledged it was a 'fair criticism that for too long the IUA was predominantly a European affair', but cautioned that

activities must not be spread too thinly. January 1962, for example, saw the death of the Swiss Jean Tschumi, President of the first Congress in London in 1948, and IUA President in 1952–8.[7] At the same time, non-Europeans began to rise gradually in influence – with Matthew's enthusiastic encouragement. One of his most ambitious protégés was Jai Bhalla, President (1961) of the Indian Institute of Architects and later President of the CAA (from 1969, following Matthew's presidency). Initially a Reiach-like helper-figure for Matthew at an international level, Bhalla, an administrator-architect rather than a highly active designer, 'modelled himself' on Matthew's statesman-like profile – to the point where his wife, just like Lorna, complained of neglect due to his peripatetic lifestyle. Matthew, initially, carefully managed Bhalla's rise, for example by restraining him during a dispute with a North Korean candidate over voting in the 1967 Executive Committee elections at Prague.[8]

Despite the gradual widening of membership to the developing world, the most problematic geopolitical relationship within IUA was still the Cold War east–west one. Here Matthew's obstinate even-handedness drove him, despite his own personal antipathy towards communism, to continue his special effort to cultivate friendships within the socialist bloc. There was, after all, a huge amount in common between the architectures of the two 'blocs', focused on providing their citizens with a 'constructed happiness' of material-cum-social betterment in both the collective and individual spheres. Most of their competition was merely over which was the more efficacious, and overt differences were concentrated in the macro and micro extremes, in the overriding political rhetoric and the details of planning.[9] Matthew's official PRIBA role underlay his more formal contacts with the socialist bloc. In a melancholy official vein, he sent condolences in July 1964 to the USSR Academy of Architects on the 'great blow' of the death of former IUA Vice-President Arkadi Mordvinov.[10] But the links, ever since the 1958 Moscow Congress, had also been personal and real: in December 1963 Nikolai Kolli sent Robert and Lorna his congratulations on the 'excellent achievement' of New Zealand House – 'I admire the layout, the architectonic conception, the interiors and all the details of this fine building' – and promising that, on Matthew's next trip to the USSR, he would show him round the 'new housing neighbourhoods of Moscow'.[11] In this context of even-handedness, tact was required in fending off the many overtures from communist-backed 'world peace' organisations. In May 1962 the President of the USSR Union of Architects wrote to Matthew, as PRIBA, inviting him to attend a 'World Congress for General Disarmament and Peace' in Moscow in July: Matthew asked Vago to send a 'polite refusal' to avoid 'all political implications', adding that it was 'best if I don't get involved'.[12] In 1966 Matthew reacted more sternly to an agit-prop 'peace' memo issued by the Foreign Ministry of North Vietnam, and an accompanying letter signed by the President of the Vietnam Union of Architects: he argued that 'we do not, of course, take any notice of these political handouts, but I do think that it might be useful, if you find a suitable opportunity, to let the Vietnam Architects know they should not send out this kind of document.'[13]

For the Paris-headquartered IUA, Matthew was especially important as a link to the anglophone architectural world – a world that, despite Abercrombie's central role in the re-formation of the IUA in 1946–7, had since then become semi-detached in its attitude towards the Union. With the nation-based structure of IUA, the crucial factor was the level of RIBA support. Matthew's key helper among RIBA officials was Kathleen Hall, secretary of the Foreign Relations Committee, and his chief ally among the office-bearing members was Gontran Goulden, long-standing head of the Building Centre (1947–74). In March 1962 Matthew unsuccessfully tried to exempt from cuts the RIBA commitment to pay ten per cent of all future IUA conferences, and tried to stop Goulden from cutting the order for the *UIA Revue* for the bookshop from 250 to 25: staffed by 15 French architects, the *Revue* was always staggering along on the edge of closure. In 1966 Matthew discussed with Robert Gardner-Medwin the difficulties in 'getting top men to IUA meetings recently', owing to UK public-sector travel and subsistence restrictions, and general unconcern with things abroad. Events neglected included a housing seminar in Bucharest and an industrialised building seminar in Beograd; in December 1967 he had to vigorously combat a financially motivated cancellation of the Executive Committee meeting scheduled in London for October 1968.[14] One of Matthew's most pressing 'anglophone' problem areas within IUA was the role of the British Commonwealth countries – a problem that Matthew tackled largely through the formation of the CAA, in close alliance with the IUA. More difficult was the question of the role of the United States, which, even more than Britain, regarded the IUA with suspicion as a 'European' organisation. We shall see later how Matthew succeeded in defusing the greatest crisis in IUA–US relations – the furore over the 1963 Congress in Cuba. More usually, the giant AIA hardly even noticed the IUA, whose budget was only two per cent of its own. US involvement focused on a succession of enthusiastic representatives on the Executive Council – Henry Churchill, James (Jim) Lawrence Jr, (from 1964) Henry Wright and (from 1968) Dan Schwartzman. All, however, proved ineffective, being either overburdened with work in their own practices, or, through excessive internationalism, unrepresentative of American architectural opinion. Lawrence resigned in 1964, after the AIA had forced through an isolationist line on Cuba, and by October 1965 Vago was complaining that despite the 'high hopes' invested in his successor, Wright, he had proved almost invisible, not replying to letters or attending meetings.[15] Matthew did his best to compensate, attending *ex officio* the 97th AIA and

11.3 Matthew speaking at IUA meeting in Paris in 1966. (EULMC)

Pan-American Architects' Convention in Washington in June 1965, where he passionately advocated greater AIA commitment to IUA.[16]

The IUA's internal organisation was always a carefully balanced mixture of national-geographical factors, reflecting the ongoing impulse for international goodwill, along with thematic factors, which were more self-contained in character and reflected its functional tasks.[17] We shall come later to its effectiveness in the tasks themselves – including the long and ultimately unproductive efforts to collaborate with the UN on housing reform. But internally, within the IUA itself, the early 1960s saw mounting unease about the match between activities and resources, and a growing consensus, encouraged by Matthew, that the organisation was overstretched, and should either cut back its activities or boost its personnel and finances. Following his presidency, from 1967 Matthew initiated a root-and-branch review of the Union's tasks and structure, impeccably rational in its aims, but which, ironically, contributed to the acrimony that engulfed the Union for several years in the early 1970s.

As early as 1962, Vago began to criticise the IUA's unwieldy structure of six permanent thematic '*commissions de travail*' (health, structure, research, education, planning and housing/'habitat'),

supplemented by ad hoc working groups (for instance on industrialised building and natural disasters), as ineffective through lack of funds and direction. In August he sent Matthew some 'holiday thoughts', arguing that as Mme Sonia de Peborgh, who had been engaged to help Tschumi oversee the commissions, had irritated everyone through her 'meddling and tactlessness', the number of commissions should now be halved by abolishing three (health, structure and research) and transferring Peborgh to work solely on Habitat, one of the three to be retained.[18] Eventually, in 1965, Jean-Pierre Vouga took over responsibility for the commissions, followed in 1967 by Professor Marc Saugey. Under the same heading of prevention of bureaucratic proliferation, Matthew and Vago also opposed the formation of a separate international society of women architects. And the constant growth in the numbers of national groups, which reached 70 in 1967, led to the recurrent demand for redistribution of the geographical division of the Executive Committee membership. The feeling of overstretch was matched by mounting financial crisis: despite increased UNESCO grants in the early 1960s, the IUA's reserves fell from $23,000 in 1965 to only $4,000 by 1968.[19] One consequence of the overstretch was a final schism in the old 1940s/1950s attempts to unify architecture and planning: in the early 1960s the newly founded (1962) International Society of City and Regional Planners (ISOCARP) was supported by dissident architect-planners within the IUA Town Planning Commission, who felt that it and the other commissions had become mere 'puppet bodies to be manipulated by the Secretariat on behalf of the Executive Committee'.[20] Despite efforts by Ling, within the TPC, and Matthew, as President, to paper over the split, the confrontational attitude of Vago, accusing the dissidents of 'spreading lies' and illicitly soliciting work in 'developing countries', provoked a corresponding separatist determination among a faction of Dutch architect-planners led by S J van

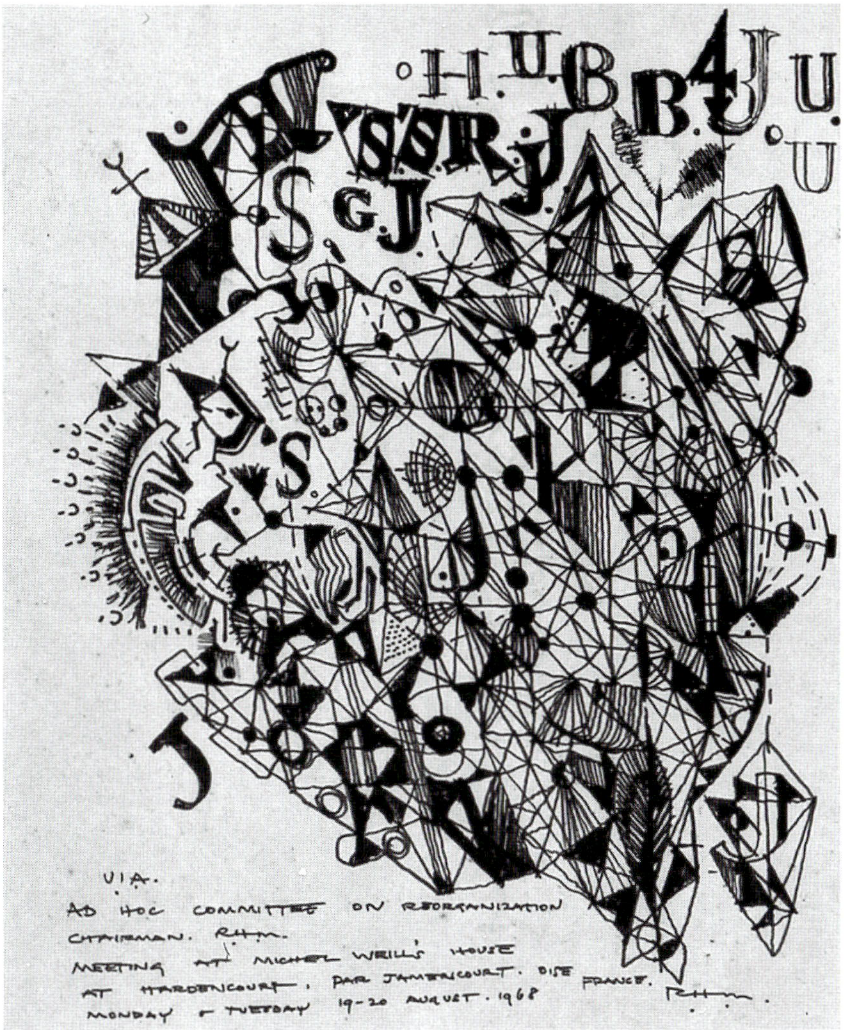

11.4 Doodle by Matthew at August 1968 meeting of his IUA ad-hoc reorganisation working group at Michel Weill's house. (EULMC)

Embden of Delft. But, as Matthew pointed out to Vago, ISOCARP was hardly a fitting target for his tirades: originally founded solely by planners, such as Robert Grieve of Scotland, it was organised purely on an individual basis. The episode well illustrated the damaging vein of paranoia and demarcation-squabbling within the IUA under Vago's secretaryship.[21]

At the July 1965 Paris Congress, when Matthew was succeeded by Beaudouin as President, he began immediately to set out an agenda for reform of the IUA, to make it fit to participate in the wider environmental reform agenda that he now favoured, under the influence of the sweeping utopianist doctrines of Buckminster Fuller and Doxiadis. Already, at Mexico in 1963, he had questioned whether the aspirations of IUA could be achieved within present resources. Now, he insisted that the IUA did not exist solely for the professional benefit of architects, but to help 'improve the whole physical environment of people throughout the world'. At a time when vast expense was being devoted to hoisting 'a tiny prefabricated mobile home into outer space', and most architectural schools still taught as if 'the entire population of the world is fit and healthy, and aged between 20 and 25 years', the world was 'crying out … for massive action in relation to basic needs – food, health, work, shelter'. Hitherto the IUA had been sustained largely by Vago's 'selfless effort', and had 'hung by a thread … a tough thread, no doubt'. But given the vast global need, 'goodwill is not by itself enough', and the IUA could not now continue on a 'shoestring'. In

361

Commonwealth of design

11.5 Meeting of the IUA Executive at St Moritz, February 1963: from left, Yang Tingbao, Matthew, Vago. (Foto Max, St Moritz)

late 1966 Vago asked Matthew to take on the role of freewheeling 'prophet', exploiting the 'prestige and moral authority' of a past president to undertake a general review of the working and organisation of the Union. After a special 'brainstorming' meeting in Geneva in February 1967, Matthew accepted the commission.[24]

At the Prague Assembly Matthew made a personal 'intervention', which set out his own evaluation of the IUA's impact after 19 years. As a result of all architects' common 'urge towards a constructive betterment of the human condition', 'this Union has a world mission well beyond professional pride and prestige'. But with the IUA's survival and growth also came a 'self-awareness' of its 'strength and weakness'. Thus the time was now ripe for a 'comprehensive reappraisal'. Too many activities and commissions had been added, and the secretariat must now correspondingly be strengthened, focusing on the two fields of professional relations and architectural education. In a later article for the *UIA Revue* he argued that, with the IUA's 'unparalleled' growth over 20 years, 'the world needs our contribution desperately': the Union, accordingly, would have to evolve from 'easy informality' to 'greater structure'.[25] In October/November 1967 the views of national sections were canvassed, predictably with wildly

contrasting results. The dominant theme was a call for a resources-dictated scaling-down of the three remaining commissions: some of their work should be transferred to the national groups to reduce international travel costs and embrace 'developing' countries, and some to Vago, working with additional assistants (beyond his existing secretary, Martine Favier) – although there were also calls for reduction in the size of the Executive Council.[26] Throughout 1968 there were frequent meetings of Matthew's working group, at the RIBA and in Paris. By May of that year Matthew was drawing up his report, which envisaged a new IUA set of statutes to replace the old 1948 one, aspiring 'to unite, on a democratic basis, the architects of the world with the aim of fostering friendship as well as intellectual, artistic, professional ties' and to 'develop progressive ideas ... for the welfare of the community, especially in developing countries'. After many meetings with Vago, Weill and Saugey, the new (from 1967) Delegate-General to Commissions and Work Programmes, Matthew finished his report by November 1968, to allow ample time for debate and decision at the next executive committee meeting, in Buenos Aires/Bariloche in 1969.[27]

But the gathering IUA crisis was also a personal one, centred around the role of Pierre Vago. After 20 years as Secretary-General, Vago had decided to retire in 1969, and hoped to prepare beforehand for an orderly 'succession'. Like any long-standing chief executive, he looked on the Union as partly his personal possession. Already in 1961, for example, Henry Churchill had complained that 'I find more and more people saying that Pierre Vago *is* the IUA, and this of course is so. The fact that it is so puts the IUA in jeopardy. Like De Gaulle ... people in AIA are asking, is it worth building up relations with the IUA if it's doomed?'[28] Vago, whose relations with the 'elected' council members were tempestuous at the best of times, now became increasingly fretful and paranoid as the time to stand down grew nearer. As the impending reform of the organisation became mixed up with the succession issue, Matthew inevitably had to juggle the roles of impartial advocate of structural reform and emollient chief intermediary between Vago and his adversaries. Vago was an example of the kind of acquaintance that Matthew could relate to easily – like Reiach in his emotional vulnerability, but, unlike Matthew's own family, not so close as to impinge on his private emotional space. Gradually, Matthew built up a distinctive relationship with Vago, for whom he acted as a reliable and dispassionate confidant.

Vago's own preferred successor as Secretary-General was Weill, and for a time, in early 1968, he looked with growing suspicion at the rise of Marc Saugey as head of the Commissions.[27] By late 1968 the 'threat' from Saugey had faded, only to be replaced by a new uncertainty: Vago wanted to retire with 'some official post', and Orlov of the Soviet section proposed that he should become the next president, after Beaudouin. But this posed the obvious objection against successive presidents from the same country. As the decisive reorganisation meeting at Buenos Aires approached, pressure for the reforms grew: Mahdi Elmandjara, the Moroccan UNESCO Assistant Director-General for Social and Human Sciences and Culture, told the January 1969 Executive Committee meeting in London that if IUA could change from a 'shoe-string' outfit to a functional organisation 'adapted to the post-industrial society', with proper administrative support, then UNESCO would entrust more work to it. In his eventual report Matthew accordingly proposed a substantial administrative reorganisation, with the executive committee becoming a council 'bureau' and many of the Secretary General's roles taken over by a 'coordinating group' or 'Board of Delegates of the Council'.[28]

Looking outwards: IUA–UN relations

As Elmandjara's intervention suggested, the IUA could best enhance its global impact by collaboration with other international organisations – above all, the UN and its various branches. Here,

unfortunately, the record was poor, and, despite Matthew's efforts as a mediator and facilitator, the position failed to improve during the 1960s. The amateurish and small-scale IUA contrasted starkly with the vast, multifaceted UN bureaucracy, which itself offered the IUA several potential avenues of approach. In relation to the educational and socio-cultural aspects of IUA work, UNESCO seemed a natural partner: we shall review this largely unproductive collaboration shortly. More important seemed the UN's direct interventions in the wider built environment. These were dealt with chiefly by the UN Housing, Building and Planning Branch, which, administratively, formed part of the UN's Bureau of Social Affairs, itself part of the UN Social and Economic Council, or 'ECOSOC'.[27] Since the late 1950s, the head of the branch, Ernest Weissmann – an émigré Yugoslav architect who had worked with CIAM and Le Corbusier in the 1930s and 1940s, and (in Vago's pejorative words) was 'one of the first architects to get into the morass of the UN' – had cleverly built up its activities, until in 1965 it became a fully fledged UN 'Centre', intended in turn as the kernel of a new institution like UNESCO.[28]

From around 1958 until the mid 1970s the IUA, and Matthew in particular, became embroiled in a protracted attempt to establish closer relations with the UN Housing, Building and Planning organisation – a strategy of UN collaboration on 'habitat' first adumbrated by Le Corbusier at CIAM 7 in Bergamo in 1948. Although these negotiations appeared, at the time, frustrating and unproductive, especially as the most prominent specific initiative – a collaboration on international documentation of low-cost housing – came ultimately to nothing, they would eventually have a more intangible long-term outcome after Matthew's death when an ambitious long-term programme of global housing reformism, named simply 'Habitat', began to take root. By now, the involvement of Modernist architects with international housing issues was a well-established pattern, driven by polymath planner-researchers such as Jaqueline Tyrwhitt, who organised in 1954 the first UN Seminar on Housing and Community Planning, in New Delhi, and subsequently completed several reports on urban expansion and housing in developing countries – all characterised by a continuing logic of rationalist mass production, despite the anti-Functionalist overtones of the Habitat movement.[29] The protracted IUA–UN collaboration on this issue was initiated in 1958 by Vago, who asked the IUA permanent representative at the UN, Henry Churchill, to speak to Weissmann; a formal collaboration proposal followed. In March 1959, ECOSOC prepared a feasibility study on a 'Long Range Programme of Concerted International Action' [on housing], and at the 1959 Lisbon Executive meeting Matthew was asked to form an ad hoc committee, which proposed in early 1960 a long-term collaborative study of low-cost housing. After this had been bandied around the Ford Foundation, ECOSOC and the Secretary General's department, Churchill conceded there was 'little or no confidence' in collaboration with the 'long-winded, verbose' UN. After his death in 1962 Churchill was replaced as IUA UN representative by Frederick G Frost Jr of New York, who established 'excellent' lines of communication with the Bureau of Social Affairs.[30]

The IUA–UN housing debate was seemingly re-energised when, in December 1961, the General Assembly promulgated a 'UN Development Decade', including scope for low-cost housing demonstration projects, and Matthew used his RIBA presidency to try to make progress, canvassing Cleeve Barr in December 1962 on the possibility of a UN-sponsored international conference on low-cost housing, hosting a conference on IUA/UN relations in February 1963 at Portland Place, and arguing that the IUA could help in international liaison at professional, rather than ministerial, level.[31] He argued in his October 1962 presidential address that 'there can be no stable basis for peace' until skills and resources in housing production were placed 'unreservedly at the disposal of the technologically backward countries'. 'A great deal has been heard about the problems of world food. But we cannot conquer hunger, poverty, illiteracy and ill-health without the provision of buildings on an unprecedented scale ... The world building problem is as serious as the world food problem, and it is hard to see that one can be solved without the other.' George Atkinson pertinently suggested to him that the IUA 'might be more acceptable than the UK' in ex-colonial circles. But, the following month, there was fresh despondency, when Doxiadis reported to Vago on a two-week seminar of 21 'experts' convened by Weissmann to discuss a three-year housing/planning collaboration: 'It was awful. Nothing was said during this committee of bureaucrats. I was scandalised.'[32]

In September 1963, en route to the IUA Cuba Congress, Matthew intervened personally by visiting Henderson, Weissmann and colleagues in New York, and Doxiadis, as Greek delegate to the UN Housing Building and Planning Committee, endorsed the expansion of the 'Branch' into a 'Centre' (eventually implemented in 1965). Matthew acknowledged the new status of Weissmann's Centre, following his retirement from the IUA Presidency, by attending the yearly sessions of the Housing Building and Planning Committee, as a representative of the IUA and the IFHTP: these sessions included New York in 1965, Geneva in 1966 and 1967, and New York in 1969. By February 1966, prior to Weissmann's retirement, Vago was expressing himself 'terribly sceptical and pessimistic about relations with UN and Weissmann', whose 'empire grew into a Centre, while we in UIA stay poor'.[33] With the imminent retirement of Weissmann in early 1966, Matthew was briefly canvassed by the Ministry of Overseas Development as a possible successor, at a tax-free salary of $21,000 per annum, but he was put off by the stipulation that he would have to give up his interest in RMJM, and might also be ruled out owing to age; eventually,

Caribbean UN insider Joe Crooks was appointed.[34]

From late 1966 fresh attempts began to revitalise the low-cost housing project, including the setting up of a UN housing research centre in New Delhi, headed by a young and ambitious Romanian architect, Dr Alexandru Budisteanu. That year also saw the establishment of a housing documentation centre in New Delhi, along with a working group on which Matthew would head a group of IUA architects; in December 1966, with the beginnings of disillusionment in the West about industrialised building, the push towards more low-technology solutions became marked.[35] Following an IUA international seminar on development policies and urbanisation at Pittsburgh in October 1966, a succession of projects was drawn up, including a UN demonstration housing competition in Peru, and a UN project, 'Trend in House Design', headed by Eric Carlson (chief of the UNHBP Housing Section). In April 1967 an Inter-Regional Seminar on Rural Housing, held in Venezuela, yielded (in Matthew's opinion) a 'rich treasure trove' of papers on rural housing conditions. But by early 1967 the balance was swinging back from hope to disillusionment, with Frost confessing to Matthew that he felt 'discouraged' and 'pessimistic' about the project: the Housing, Building and Planning Division was 'well intentioned', but had 'succumbed to the bureaucratic disease of paper production'. Ringing the changes, he suggested that another American, Dan Schwartzman, should take over as UN representative.[36]

Representing IUA at the fifth session of the UN Housing, Building and Planning Committee in Geneva in October 1967, Matthew attempted to push things forward, exploiting his close relations with Romanian architects. He offered the help of the IUA Housing Commission, chaired by Horia Maicu of the Romanian Union of Architects – 'one of Romania's outstanding architects' – and which had held, in July 1966, a housing colloquium in Bucharest organised by Alexandru Budisteanu. In March 1968 Joe Crooks suggested the IUA might organise a low-cost housing data project, with Maicu soliciting national sections and Housing Commission members to send in examples of 'interesting achievements' within a year. In May, with the climate swinging yet again towards optimism, the ECOSOC committee endorsed a proposal to establish an Institute for Documentation on Housing, Building and Planning at New Delhi.[37]

The other main strand of IUA–UN collaboration was concerned with UNESCO – a somewhat more entrenched and formidable body, in its monumental Modernist Paris headquarters (built 1956–8), than the New York-based ECOSOC. UNESCO, founded in 1945 in London, as the successor to an earlier League of Nations-sponsored institute, had expanded to 120 member nations by 1966. Its geopolitical aims of building 'the defences of peace … in the minds of men' by international collaboration in economic, social and cultural matters were partly pursued by distributing a substantial budget (rising from $8m in 1950 to $170 million in 1975) to dependent organisations categorised in various grades of relevance. During the 1950s IUA had secured designation by UNESCO as a Category B ('advisory and informative') organisation, carrying an annual subsidy of only $5,000; Vago thereafter argued vainly for promotion to Category A.[38]

IUA attempts at collaboration with UNESCO focused on the field of education, and pointed in two almost opposite directions, both driven by a concern to attract subsidies from UNESCO: the design of educational buildings, and the education of the architect. The record in the latter case was uncontentious, if ineffective. In 1962 the IUA's committee for Education of the Architect, chaired by Robert Gardner-Medwin, initiated attempts at collaboration at its Prague meeting; over the ensuing four years, through a small working group set up by the Executive Committee in 1965 and chaired by Matthew, proposals were drawn up for an 'International Board of Architectural Education'. Although

Matthew enthusiastically supported it, Vago doggedly argued for a European rather than global scope, and by 1966 Matthew had shifted his efforts to the newly formed (1965) Commonwealth Association of Architects (CAA). This had proceeded, as its first priority, to establish a Commonwealth Board of Architectural Education (CBAE), financed by an £8,000 annual grant from the Commonwealth Foundation, to harmonise educational qualifications and promote indigenous architectural education in developing countries.[39] Matthew argued that IUA should look to CBAE as 'mutually reinforcing each other' in this field. For IUA, he estimated, an equivalent operation to CBAE would require two staff (with travelling expenses) and would cost between $20,000 and $33,000 p.a. – which would require substantial UNESCO support of the working group. Slightly despairingly, Matthew suggested that people should pressurise their own national UNESCO branches.[40]

In the field of promotion of educational architecture, IUA–UNESCO relations took an acrimonious and destructive turn, when UNESCO moved to deploy its massive resources to suppress an active IUA initiative – despite frantic efforts by Matthew to keep the two sides together. In 1960, at an Executive Committee meeting in Copenhagen, the IUA, at the instigation of its working commission on schools, took one of the boldest decisions of its early history: to establish at Lausanne an International Centre for School Buildings, funded by the Swiss regional government, against opposition from the RIBA, which wanted the centre to be in London. Opened in December 1961, it was headed by Jean Piaget of Switzerland, with the help of architect-librarian Pierre Bussat, and flourished for three years, building up a large library and documentation.[41] At first, UNESCO's attitude was supportive, and it provided a modest subsidy, but in 1962 that position changed. In July a UNESCO International Education Building Conference was held in London – partly stimulated by the impact of the English (CLASP) and

Mexican school pavilions at the Milan Triennale in 1960 – with representatives from 59 countries, paid for 75 per cent by UNESCO, and 25 per cent by the British government.[42] The conference concluded that global cooperation in education building know-how was essential, and that three regional centres of research should be established. Matthew, as the head of the UK delegation to the conference, gave the proposal his full support; however, by December 1962, it was clear that it would be incompatible with the continued existence of the Lausanne centre, and UNESCO duly withdrew its support from the latter – to the outrage of Vago, who thundered against its 'scandalously inadequate, bureaucratised' output. Vago was especially incensed by the role of UNESCO's School Construction Section, and its research architect, a 'cocksure' young newly graduated American named Beynon, in 'poaching' director Pierre Bussat from Lausanne to head one of five new research centres – the Latin American Center for School Construction, in Mexico – and in trying to 'get rid of' Lausanne's documentation.[43] Eventually, despite the ineffective attempts of IUA education representative Ernest A Grunsfeld at mediation, including holding a cocktail party for Beynon's staff to 'break the ice', the withdrawal of UNESCO support was inevitably followed by closure of the Lausanne centre in September 1965, and local dispersal of its resources. During 1965 Vago's tirades against UNESCO rose to a climax. He lamented to Matthew that

these gentlemen at UNESCO have no other calls on their time, and like to call us to visit them at their offices where we are kept for hours. [In Lausanne,] we created an instrument of work ... it has been destroyed – one day this abscess will have to burst.[44]

Outside the education field IUA collaborations with UNESCO were episodic, but more productive. Around the time of the 1963 Skopje earthquake Matthew initiated a brief flurry of exchanges, involving pioneering Modernist and disaster relief specialist Edward D Mills, on the possibility of an IUA contribution to the setting up of international disaster relief mechanisms.[45] More promising seemed a UNESCO-brokered meeting of experts in September 1967 in Rome to discuss the problems of architectural education for preservation. Responding to an overture by Mahdi Elmandjara (transmitted via Donald Gibson at MPBW), Matthew recommended Donald Insall as the best British conservation architect.[46]

Cold War mediation at the 1963 IUA Congress, Havana

If the IUA's external relations were sometimes problematic, the Union's own congresses threw up more passionate confrontations, at both a personal and a geopolitical level – conflicts that Matthew, as President, saw it as his personal duty to resolve. Occasionally, problems stemmed from simple inefficiency, most notoriously in the 'Second Seminar on Industrialised Building', held in Brazil in November 1962 – whose chaotic outcome emphasised the strong degree of mutual trust on which ambitious international meetings rested. This conference, to be chaired by Beaudouin, had been convened by 'a young irresponsible group in São Paolo, whose impressive programme had no basis to it'. Matters began placidly enough: Lorna recalled that, en route to Brazil, 'we flew through a large electric storm, and Robert, typically, remained sound asleep the whole time!' But on arrival, he found that 'absolutely nothing had been done – no hotels, conference venues, nothing was ready!' Senior officials in the Brazilian Institute were 'astonished' to find important architects materialising from all over the world, but were 'unable to overcome their internal political differences and put up a united front to protect the name of the Brazilian Institute of Architects'. So Matthew, working with Vago and several British architects (including Reiach) and with the help of the local British Council office, 'set to work personally to organise the confer-

ence on the spot, and really stirred up a hornet's nest! I expect he offended a great number of Brazilians, but he got it done – and was absolutely exhausted by it!'[47]

External political controversy was clustered around the biennial congresses, with their somewhat formal, repetitive character, focused on the international goodwill aspect of IUA activity. Most congresses were in fact uncontentious, but a minority attracted bitter geopolitical conflict – above all, the Seventh Congress, held in Havana, Cuba, on 28 September–3 October 1963, in a curious tandem arrangement with the Eighth Assembly, held in Mexico City on 7–12 October. By the 1960s the roles of the various IUA representative bodies were as follows. While the 'prime minister' and 'head of state' of IUA were Vago and the President of the day, the 'cabinet' was the Executive Committee, comprising representatives from the four geographical groups. The 'parliament' was the biennial Assembly, whose role was largely that of ratifying decisions formulated by the Executive Committee. In uneasy parallel with each Assembly was the Congress, 'the great catch-all gathering', always until 1963 held in the same city and at the same time.[48]

Although the twin-site arrangement for the 1963 Congress and Assembly came to be dominated by issues stem-

11.6 Matthew and Reiach in Brasilia, November 1962. (EULMC)

ming from the 1959 Revolution, the double arrangement was originally approved well before that – in fact, at the 1959 Lisbon Executive Committee – and for a reason internal to IUA: the intense competition between pre-revolutionary Cuba and Mexico to host the first IUA Congress in the Americas. It was decided to hold the Congress in Havana, and the Assembly and meetings of working commissions in Mexico City, with Executive Committee meetings in both countries. At the time, Havana seemed an uncontentious location, but following the Revolution, and the 'Bay of Pigs' invasion of 17–19 April 1961, the position changed radically, and the 1961 London Assembly had to formally re-confirm the arrangement. Architecturally, the revolutionary government's embrace of populist nationalism provoked the departure from Cuba of most prominent Modernist architects.[49] By early 1962, with abortive US preparations under way for an invasion of Cuba (Operation Mongoose), and then during and after the missile crisis of 16–28 October, it had become obvious, first, that the IUA was staring in the face its worst ever 'diplomatic crisis', and also, second, that the dual-site formula offered a potentially face-saving scope for compromises. The crisis saw a gradual rise, then fall, in bellicosity on the part of the US government, which initially tried to force the cancellation of the Havana event, but then, faced with a blunt refusal by Matthew and Vago to give way, eventually backed down itself and restricted its aims to securing a US boycott of the event. Throughout, as we shall see, Matthew and Vago fought together to uphold the principle of a strong, apolitical stance, as justification for resisting the pressure against Havana – but here they faced the inconsistency of the agreed one-year postponement of Moscow following the 1956 Hungary crisis.

Initially, in spring 1962, the US State Department attempted to impose, through the compliant medium of the AIA and its IUA representative Ernest Grunsfeld, a militantly intransigent opposition to the Havana Congress, and used

Ramón Corona Martin, the Mexican Vice-President of the IUA, to manipulate the Executive Committee to shift the Congress to Mexico. In March 1962 Harlan Cleveland, State Department Assistant Secretary with responsibility for International Organisations, warned the AIA that

> Cuba is impossible for these reasons: one, no American will be permitted to go; two, those delegates who come from even friendly foreign countries might have unpleasant experiences if they went through the US either way; three, the other American countries who also have embargoes will probably put hurdles in the way of their delegates ... and finally, I believe most of the good architects have left Cuba.

The State Department argued forcefully that the Congress should be moved to Mexico, and began to pressure potential US delegates and organisations: overseas architects were threatened with a refusal of future US visas.

Vago immediately put up a fierce resistance to this pressure – although, behind the scenes, he and Matthew also prepared for a possible compromise, for example by sounding out Soviet architects about their attitude to a change of venue to Mexico.[50] Matthew's own exasperation mounted inexorably with each successive US intervention and – the obstinate streak in his character once fully aroused – solidified into a granite determination to resist. A typical vignette of these pressures took place in December 1962, when Buckminster Fuller, who had hoped to present his influential 'World Design Decade' student-research proposal to the IUA at Havana, passed Matthew and Vago copies of correspondence with Dr George Bundy, Assistant for National Security to President Kennedy. Perhaps unsurprisingly – only two months after the Cuban missile crisis – Bundy's letter was subtly menacing in tone. He warned Fuller that, while his proposal was unlikely to receive 'serious consideration at a meeting organised by the present Communist regime in Cuba', he had heard that, most fortunately, 'the Executive Committee of the IUA has seen fit to provide for the possibility of an alternative conference session in Mexico City. You may wish to work toward the realisation of the alternative in order that the conference may be carried out in a climate more conducive to achievement of its professional objectives than that of Havana.' Crushed, Fuller limply bleated that 'I do agree that a trip by me to Cuba would not at the present time be desirable', promised to 'work towards the realisation of the alternative IUA world Congress in Mexico City', and concluded by hailing Bundy's 'extraordinary service to our country and to our President'. In a covering letter to Vago, Fuller explained that he did not want to 'jeopardise my passport or antagonise the US government'. Eventually, like all US citizens, he was banned outright from travelling to Havana, and found that at Mexico City, no provision had been made for presentation of his 'World Students' initiative.[51]

In January 1963, despite an 'unsympathetic' attitude at the Foreign Office, Matthew decided to throw his weight uncompromisingly behind Havana. He would, however, work not to aggressively confront but to limit and moderate US opposition. He repeatedly offered to visit the USA and intercede with the State Department, and at the last Executive Council meeting before the conference, at St Moritz in February 1963, brokered adjustments to the Havana and Mexico programmes, designed to avoid the impression that there would be 'two congresses'.[52] In doing so, he was aware that the Cubans had, during spring 1962, significantly complicated his task by a further provocative gesture: the setting up, under IUA auspices, of an international competition for a 'Monument to the Victory of Playa Girón in the Bahia de Cochinos' (Bay of Pigs) – to take place during the week preceding the 1963 Congress, with Matthew, as IUA President, nominated as chair of the assessors! The jury was balanced evenly between communists and non-communists, the former including Yang Tingbao of China (vice chair) and Niemeyer of Brazil alongside three others.[53] Matthew eventually accepted the competition framework as it stood, but distanced himself from it by arriving three days late; MacEwen worked strenuously at the RIBA to dampen any British press interest in the story, and in the end only the *People* published it.[54]

Countered by Matthew's and Vago's balance of emollience and toughness, by the time of the February 1963 St Moritz Executive Committee the 'opposing camp' was in some disarray, with a growing split within the AIA between 'internationalists' and 'anti-communists' over the issue. For example, following a mix-up within the AIA over the Havana boycott decision, the AIA representative on the IUA Executive Committee, Jim Lawrence, wrote furiously to AIA President Henry Wright that 'I've never been so humiliated and angry as I was today', and condemned the US's 'shameful ... damnable ... insulting refusal to attend a world cultural congress – if we stay away we only harm ourselves, not Castro'. He protested that, whatever the arguments against offending the State Department – chiefly, that funds for a forthcoming Pan-American Architects' Conference might be jeopardised – the AIA should not be 'for sale'. Wright sheepishly wrote to Matthew to emphasise the political *force majeure* character of the decision, and advised him not to fly to Washington to try to 'help with this situation'. Some other countries followed the US boycott: for example, the official architect to the King of Morocco, on sending his apologies, cited US threats to deny him a visa as the cause. But because of the bipolar geopolitical situation, there was always an alternative view: for example, whereas the West German delegation decided to attend only as individuals, the DDR section lambasted the Mexican Assembly as a pseudo-event, organised by 'those interested in spoiling the cordial atmosphere of the Havana Congress'.[55]

As the Congress approached, the fervid atmosphere heightened further. The Cuban ambassador in Paris wrote of 'forces conspiring' against the Congress,

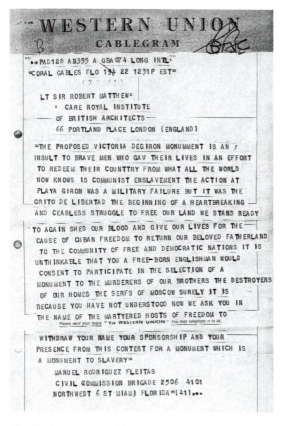

WESTERN UNION
CABLEGRAM

PAD126 AB355 A GBA 074 LONG INTL
CORAL GABLES FLO 19 22 1231P EST

LT SIR ROBERT MATTHEW
: CARE ROYAL INSTITUTE
OF BRITISH ARCHITECTS
66 PORTLAND PLACE LONDON (ENGLAND)

=THE PROPOSED VICTORIA DEGIRON MONUMMENT IS AN
INSULT TO BRAVE MEN WHO GAV THEIR LIVES IN AN EFFORT
TO REDEEM THEIR COUNTTRY FROM WHAT ALL THE WORLD
NOW KNOWS IS COMMUNIST ENSLAVEMENT THE ACTION AT
PLAYA GIRON WAS A MILITARY FAILURE BUT IT WAS THE
GRITO DE LIBERTAD THE BEGINNING OF A HEARTBREAKING
AND CEASLESS STRUGGLE TO FREE OUR LAND WE STAND READY
TO AGAIN SHED OUR BLOOD AND GIVE OUR LIVES FOR THE
CAUSE OF CUBAN FREEDOM TO RETURN OUR BELOVED FATHERLAND
TO THE COMMUNITY OF FREE AND DEMOCRATIC NATIONS IT IS
UNTHINKABLE THAT YOU A FREE-BORN ENGLISHMAN WOULD
CONSENT TO PARTICIPATE IN THE SELECTION OF A
MONUMENT TO THE MURDERERS OF OUR BROTHERS THE DESTROYERS
OF OUR HOMES THE SERFS OF MOSCOW SURELY IT IS
BECAUSE YOU HAVE NOT UNDERSTOOD NOW WE ASK YOU IN
THE NAME OF THE MARTYERED HOSTS OF FREEDOM TO

WITHDRAW YOUR NAME YOUR SPONSORSHIP AND YOUR
PRESENCE FROM THIS CONTEST FOR A MONUMENT WHICH IS
A MONUMENT TO SLAVERY=
   MANUEL RODRIGUEZ FLEITAS
   CIVIL COMMISSION BRIGADE 2506 4101
   NORTHWEST 6 ST MIAMI FLORIDA=[411...

11.7 Anti-communist cablegram to Matthew from Manuel Rodriguez Fleitas, 22 August 1963, protesting at the IUA's decision to proceed with the Playa Giron Competition. (EULMC)

(opposite) **11.8** 1963 IUA Congress, Havana: 'First Meeting of Professors and Students of Architecture'. (*Arquitectura Cuba*, 1963, 10) (Colegio Nacional de Arquitectos Cuba)

and Matthew wrote sternly to Franco warning that the event 'must emerge free from any sort of political implication – in or out of session', and that 'the IUA is concerned only architecturally' with the Playa Girón competition.[56] On the other side, Matthew began, from July onwards, to find himself the target of a mounting bombardment of cables, letters and telegrams from Americans and Miami-based anti-communist émigré groups, such as 'Brigade 2506, Association of Bay of Pigs Veterans', protesting against the Congress and the Playa Girón competition. At first, the letters were mainly reasoned in tone, as in the case of that from AIA President J Roy Carroll, which criticised Matthew for lending his 'professional support to an objective which appears to be based wholly on partisan politics'. But rapidly the onslaught became more heated. One émigré architect, for instance, pleaded that 'it is intolerable that you, a free-born Englishman, would consent to participate in the selection of a monument to the murderers of our brothers, the destroyers of our homes, the serfs of Moscow'; and a 1 September press release from the 'Agencia de Informaciones Periodisticas' labelled the Congress a 'Subversion Meeting', held in a 'concentration camp' by the 'pro-communist international association of architects'; largely attended by Russian military agents posing as architects, it would 'smuggle Red agents' back into the 'free world', evading the 'watchful eye' of the United States by exploiting less vigilant countries such as Canada. The invective continued after the Congress, too. In late October, Thomas

Lismore, an American teacher exiled from Cuba by the revolution, penned Matthew a stream of nationalist vitriol:

You must be an imbecile to imagine that any convention held in a communistic state is non-political. I cannot imagine what induced you to attend such a farce unless it was the traditional greed of certain inhabitants of Great Britain who are unable to travel on their miserable salaries ... I consider you the most perect [sic] example of an '*hijo de puta*' [son of a whore] that has disgraced Britain for a long time.[57]

The ideological fault lines opened up by Havana stretched all the way back home to Britain and, even, Edinburgh. Communist-inclined architects saw the Havana Congress as a major propaganda focus: for example, in addition to the 29 'mainstream' British delegates who travelled by air – including establishment figures such as Gontran Goulden and Cumbernauld chief architect L Hugh Wilson – a group of eight communists travelled on a Soviet ship, the *Maria Yulianova*, for a subsidised fare of £56, organised by the Architects' Sub-committee of the 'Britain–Cuba Committee'. Conversely, Matthew's Edinburgh University planning assistant, Eleanor Morris, found the situation

very difficult, being myself an American. All of Matthew's left wing friends, like the Tindalls, were passing round a petition from the intelligentsia to the British Government to ask Kennedy to lift the blockade. They said, 'Better Red than dead – will you sign this petition?' I said, 'No, I can't and I won't!' I was horrified that Matthew was going to Havana, and he knew I was horrified! As far as I was concerned, they were simply a communist regime that was doing damage to the US. Personally, I believe that Matthew himself was 'pro' the communists. Certainly I knew that some of my other colleagues were, like Percy or Richard Bigwood – though some

1er. Encuentro Internacional
de Profesores y Estudiantes de Arquitectura
Première Rencontre Internationale de Professeurs et d'étudiants en Architecture
lst International Meeting of Professors and Students of Architecture

1) *Recepción a los delegados del Encuentro de Profesores y Estudiantes en el Círculo Social de la Universidad de La Habana.*
Réception offerte aux délégués à la Rencontre de Professeurs et d'Etudiants, Cercle Social de l'Université de La Havane.
Reception for delegates of the Meeting of Professors and Students, in the Social Centre of the University of Havana.

2) *Sesión de Trabajo del Primer Encuentro Internacional de Profesores y Estudiantes de Arquitectura.*
Séance de Travail à la Première Rencontre Internationale de Professeurs et d'Etudiants en Architecture.
Working Session of the 1st. International Meeting of Professors and Students of Architecture.

El Comité Ejecutivo de la U.I.A. acordó en su reunión de Charleroi (Bélgica) en Abril de 1962, patrocinar la celebración en La Habana del Primer Encuentro Internacional de Profesores y Estudiantes de Arquitectura, coincidiendo con la celebración del VII Congreso de la U.I.A.

El Comité Organizador del Evento se constituyó en Cuba con profesores y estudiantes de la Escuela de Arquitectura de la Universidad de La Habana, trabajando en coordinación con la Sección Cubana de la UIA. El Comité Organizador del Encuentro envió invitaciones a todas las instituciones docentes de Arquitectura del Mundo.

El Primer Encuentro Internacional de Profesores y Estudiantes de Arquitectura sesionó del 27 al 29 de septiembre con una concurrencia muy nutrida. Se inscribieron 430 extranjeros (de los cuales 395 eran estudiantes) y 432 cubanos (388 estudian-

tes). Se hicieron representar por delegados oficiales 57 Escuelas de Arquitectura y otras 17 escuelas enviaron delegados en calidad de observadores, representando un total de 43 países. Además asistieron como observadores distintos profesores que se inscribieron sólo en el Congreso, pero la dominante proporción estudiantil hizo común llamar al evento "El Encuentro de Estudiantes".

Se contó con la asistencia de destacados profesores como los decanos de la Facultad de Arquitectura de la Universidad Católica de Chile; de Córdoba, Argentina; de Montevideo; y de la Facultad de Arquitectura de Caracas, y distinguidos profesores de China, Japón, Yugoslavia, España, Checoslovaquia, Nueva Zelandia, Italia, Israel, Hungría, Viet Nam, Perú, México, Brasil y Colombia. Junto a la proporción dominante de los estudiantes se destacó la numerosa representación latinoamericana. La participación decisiva de los estudiantes de países subdesarrollados económicamente, sensibilizados p o r las causas que frenan el desarrollo de sus países, hizo situar el tema socio-económico como base para la discusión del temario del Encuentro que cubría: I.—**Organización de la Enseñanza Superior; II.—La Enseñanza de la Arquitectura y III.—El Ejercicio de la Profesión.** En forma directa y franca los estudiantes trataron temas vitales que afectan a los países subdesarrollados y no liberados, apoyados por la gran mayoría de las delegaciones. Las resoluciones finales fueron ratificadas en la plenaria de clausura por 40 Escuelas a favor, 5 en contra y 2 abstenciones, estando 10 delegaciones ausentes. El Ejecutivo de la UIA asistió al acto de clausura del Encuentro cerrado brillantemente con el discurso del Dr. Ernesto Guevara, Ministro de Industrias del gobierno revolucionario de Cuba.

El debate suscitado con el Encuentro fue encauzado en forma serena por el Presidente de la UIA y profesor de Arquitectura, Sir Robert Matthew, y por la precisión de conceptos en los pronunciamientos del Presidente de la República en la apertura del Congreso y del Primer Ministro Fidel Castro en la clausura, que tuvieron la aceptación unánime de los congresistas.

El eco internacional del Encuentro se refleja en el Seminario que celebraron en el Instituto de Arquitectos de Roma los delegados italianos al Congreso y al Encuentro, donde el estudiante Renato Nicolini manifestó: **"En la historia de las investigaciones arquitectónicas modernas muy frecuentemente se recurre por parte de fuentes autorizadas a la exhortación para distinguir netamente ideología, economía y sociedad, por un lado, y el "puro y desinteresado" ejercicio de la profesión por el otro. Tal exhortación lleva obviamente a evitar el análisis de la relación entre ciencia, investigación científica y sociedad. Este análisis ha sido afrontado en el último Congreso Internacional de los Estudiantes y de los Profesores de Arquitectura en particular en lo que respecta al nexo entre educación (preparación de técnicos, formación cultural, etc.) y estructura social."**

2

1

CLAUSURA DEL CONGRESO
CLÔTURE DU CONGRÈS
CLOSING OF THE CONGRES

1) Arq. Fernando Salinas,
   Relator General.
   Rapporteur Général
   General Spokesman.
2) Presidencia.
   La présidence
3) Dr. Fidel Castro y Arq. Sir Robert
   Matthews.
4) Congresistas e invitados.
   Congressistes et invités.
   Delegates and guests.

4   3

had resigned from the party after Hungary. In fact, it wasn't until after I left the department that I realised that I'd been working, in effect, in a communist cell. Richard Bigwood actually told me: 'You are a front!'[58]

In fact, as we have repeatedly seen, Matthew himself vehemently opposed communism and all other extreme political doctrines; but he sought to harness the energies of a wide range of highly committed people – including political zealots – and passionately protected them, where necessary, from attack.

In the event, after all the prior acrimony, the Havana Congress passed off largely without controversy. Matthew liaised with Cuban leader Fidel Castro through the medium of Osmani Cienfuegos, Minister of Construction – an architect who, although 'always clad in uniform with bulging guns and ammunition pouches', proved 'a very kind and nice person', and joined Matthew each breakfast at his hotel to brief him on any potential problem . En route to Cuba – travelling indirectly (as necessitated by the US visa restrictions) via the USA, West Indies and Mexico – Matthew called on the AIA headquarters in Washington on 17 September, and stayed that night at Carroll's home to try and begin the process of repairing relations with IUA, as well as to develop closer US links on RMJM's account. He recalled later that 'with the Cuban Congress at Havana drawing near, I had urgent telegrams for the AIA President, warning of the possible effects of continuing. I went to his home to persuade him to take no action – and he did not. The Americans then came in force to Mexico, and now they are taking a wide part in the affairs of the IUA, particularly in the Americas.' Arriving in Havana on 27 September, with Vago, the first task was the three sessions of the Playa Girón competition, held at the University Dental Building on 27 and 30 September and 1 October. Matthew's notes explained that, of the 274 entries, there was a wide variation between those emphasising massive monumentality, and light-structural concepts

in which 'even an idea could be considered as the monument'. In the end, the first prizewinner, envisaging an abstract outcrop of jabbing forms on the shore, was Polish (by Grazyna Boczewaka and four others).[59]

At the same time as this, on 26–8 September, the other potentially explosive event of the Congress was taking place at the 'Habana Libre' (formerly Hilton) Hotel, where most delegates were accommodated. This was the 'First International Meeting of Professors and Students of Architecture', organised by the Cuban architects under IUA auspices and opened by Cienfuegos. It was openly envisaged by the Cubans as an agit-prop counterpoint to the main convention, and was the chief destination of the contingent on the *Maria Yulianova*. Of the 430 overseas delegates (in addition to 432 Cubans) only a minority were also delegates to the IUA Congress. Matthew attended to monitor events, and later drily reported to the Executive Committee at Acapulco on 8 October that it had been an 'impassioned and over-elated assembly … with orators who were in no way architectural students'. Typical was the closing speech, by Dr Ernesto (Che) Guevara, Minister of Industry. To extended roars of acclamation from the audience, Guevara gave an 'uncompromising' exposition of the 'responsibilities of architectural education based on the realities of the social, political and economic problems created by imperialism', argued that 'we have to be scientists and revolutionaries at the same time', and rejected any reactionary attempt to 'apply narrow professional ideas while others are wearing themselves out in the struggle'. The concluding resolution of the session called for architectural teaching to be thoroughly integrated into the 'anti-imperialist revolution'.[60] Matthew stood up at the end of the meeting and emphatically dissociated the IUA and the Congress from what had just transpired, but the damage had been done, and American opponents, such as Joseph Watterson FAIA, had been supplied with the fuel that would allow them to claim

(opposite) **11.9** 1963 IUA Congress, Havana: report on closing ceremony in *Arquitectura Cuba*, including Matthew, Fidel Castro and USSR cosmonaut Valentina Tereshkova. (*Arquitectura Cuba*, 1963, 25) (Colegio Nacional de Arquitectos Cuba)

that 'the Congress was marred by too much political polemics and not enough discussion of architecture', and to argue disingenuously that this, rather than any action by the US government, 'may have been the reason Bucky Fuller was not able to lead a discussion as planned'. Matthew and Cienfuegos also managed to defuse another potentially politicised event, a working group on building industrialisation.

The Cuban government had thrown open the resources of the city of Havana to the 1,200 Congress delegates, who came from 69 countries, with heavy concentrations from communist and South American countries, and also France (70 delegates). One-third of Havana's taxi fleet was allocated to the delegates as a gesture of hospitality, and at the opening session, held in a vast stadium, the Coliseum of the Sports City, and inaugurated by the President of Cuba, delegates were greeted by a flamboyant performance of 500 dancers depicting 'the entire history of Cuba', and a 'Cuban national exhibition', held in a prefabricated concrete complex designed by a team of architects led by Juan Campo. The young English architect J M Austin-Smith recalled that

> everywhere in the town, young uniform-clad soldiers could be seen, presumably keeping order. There was one particularly attractive young girl sitting on an old kitchen chair outside a bank with a bandolier of bullets and a rifle across her lap. 'What are you doing here?' questioned Sir Robert Matthew. 'I am guarding the bank,' she replied. 'What would you do if the enemy came?' said Sir Robert Matthew. 'I would S-C-RR-EAM!' she replied.

During the conference, Austin-Smith acted as Matthew's personal assistant, helping liaise with Cienfuegos and sort out problems. For instance,

> one day we were shown round a new music school which had just been completed in parkland on the outskirts of Havana. 'Robert,' said Lady

Matthew, 'you know that you are meant to meet the British Ambassador in twenty minutes' time?' 'Mike,' said Sir Robert Matthew, 'get me a taxi, will you?' With little hope of finding a taxi in the middle of what seemed like the countryside, I set out across the grass. Lo and behold, I could scarcely believe my eyes when a taxi rolled along a nearby pathway. I hailed it and led it to Sir Robert Matthew, who calmly got in and drove off.[61]

In his welcoming address, Cienfuegos judiciously tempered hospitality with militancy, proclaiming that 'the Cuban people, who are valiantly carrying on the real struggle, the Cuban people, who know how to receive their guests, the Cuban people, who know how to destroy their enemies, welcome you!' But he was politely rebuked by Matthew, who insisted that 'we meet here as *architects*, uniting our common interest in promoting architecture in the service of man, and refusing to be divorced by our disagreements on other matters. That is the rock on which our progress has been built, and it would be foolish to destroy it.' Firmly, Matthew nudged the Congress away from the well-worn left–right polarisation, towards his own growing preoccupation with global environmental reformism, an issue 'very close to my own heart'.[62] This was, for him, the Congress's key unifying element, and Matthew spoke in passionate Geddesian terms of the 'world building crisis' of chaos and misdeployed resources, a 'poverty, material and aesthetic' more serious than disease or food shortages; it should be tackled by a 'combined attack, by the mobilising of world resources', in which architects and the IUA could help by promoting low-cost housing and schools, and helping train more architects. In response to his pressure, the conference itself focused substantially on this theme, with a consensual emphasis on the need for state coordination (rather than outright ownership) and lectures concentrating on technical argumentation. For example, Wilson expounded the Cumbernauld planning formula in

Monumento Playa Girón

Resultado del Concurso Internacional

Concours International pour le Monument á la Victoire de Playa Giron
International Competition for a Monument to the Victory of Playa Giron

Arq. Augusto Pérez Beato

Para conmemorar a perpetuidad la victoria de la Revolución cubana sobre las fuerzas de la regresión y recordar el sacrificio heroico de los combatientes y de los civiles inmolados, se realizó entre el pueblo de Cuba una colecta pública para la construcción del Monumento. Dicha colecta alcanzó la suma de $2,200,000.00.

Primeramente se hizo una convocatoria para un concurso en el cual participarían arquitectos, pintores y escultores latinoamericanos, la que posteriormente fue anulada por no ajustarse a las reglamentaciones de la Unión Internacional de Arquitectos en concursos internacionales de arquitectura. El Colegio Nacional de Arquitectos de Cuba, como Sección Nacional de la UIA obtuvo la responsabilidad de organizar una nueva convocatoria de carácter mundial en la cual participarían arquitectos, en colaboración con escultores y pintores u otros técnicos. Dicha convocatoria y las bases correspondientes se hicieron de acuerdo con las reglas para concursos de la UIA a quien sometieron para su aprobación las bases y la composición del Jurado del Concurso.

El plazo de admisión fue cerrado (de acuerdo con las bases) el día 31 de Julio de 1963 y en total se recibieron 274 proyectos procedentes de arquitectos de 35 países distribuidos en la forma siguiente:

Inglaterra	11
Suiza	6
URSS	35
Hungria	4
Francia	4
China	21
Brasil	16
Indonesia	1
Suecia	5
Polonia	27
Rumania	13
México	7
Mongolia	1
India	12
Alemania	22
Australia	2
Checoslovaquia	21
Grecia	2
Chile	1
Irlanda	1
Ecuador	1
Canadá	3
Viet Nam	1
Bulgaria	10
Portugal	1
Uruguay	1
Bélgica	1
Noruega	1
Italia	4
Estados Unidos	2
Cuba	13
Yugoslavia	7
Japón	11
Bolivia	1
Argentina	1
Sin identificar	3

El Jurado previamente seleccionado, estuvo compuesto por:

Arq. Sir Robert Matthews (Inglaterra)
Arq. Yang Ting Pao (China)
Arq. Pierre Vago (Francia)
Arq. Icaro de Castro Mello (Brasil)
Arq. Vittoriano Vigano (Italia)
Arq. Guillermo Jones Odriozola
(Uruguay)
Escultor Berto Lardera (Italia)
Arq. Oscar Niemeyer (Brasil)
Arq. Jan Zachwatowicz (Polonia)

Suplentes: (cubanos)

Arq. Antonio Quintana Simonetti
Arq. Hugo Consuegra
Arq. Román García Rodriguez

En sustitución del Arq. Niemeyer que no asistió, actuó el Arq. Quintana. Para la exhibición de los proyectos se utilizaron nueve plantas del edificio "Retiro Odontológico", habiéndose realizado el montaje de modo que sirviera al Jurado para su estudio y a la vez para el disfrute del público. La exposición comprendió más de 6 kilómetros lineales de proyectos y permaneció abierta durante 60 días.

El Jurado, de acuerdo con las facultades que le confería el art. 13 de las bases, acordó modificar la distribución de los premios en la forma siguiente:

Un primer premio de
15,000 dólares
Dos segundos premios de
3,000 dólares c/u.
Un tercer premio de
1,000 dólares

También se acordó otorgar diez menciones honoríficas.

Después de amplias deliberaciones el otorgamiento de los premios y las menciones se dio a conocer el 4 de octubre de 1963, en la forma siguiente:

detail, arguing that neighbourhood units had little social significance compared with small/mid sized towns. This consensual emphasis was sustained at the final session, at the Theatre of the Cuban Workers' Centre, hailed by the 'British-Cuban' delegation as a 'charged occasion', with no less than cosmonaut Valentina Tereshkova on the platform.[63] The climax of the conference was the 'profoundly human and moving' (according to the Cuban published proceedings) closing address by Fidel Castro, who surprised Western delegates such as Goulden by his informality and accessibility: 'one could walk to within ten feet of Fidel when he was speaking'. True to his ability as a consummate actor, Castro, unlike Cienfuegos and Guevara, confined himself strictly to the conference theme. Austin-Smith recalled that 'towards the end of his speech, he gave a mischievous glance towards Sir Robert Matthew, who was sitting next to him on the platform. "I promised Sir Robert Matthew," he said, "that I would keep well away from political matters such as the fallacy of American capitalistic reliance on per-capita analyses of consumption."' Instead, Castro argued more obliquely against doctrinaire importation of 'industrialised' techniques to the 'developing' countries. Partly, the reason was economic and social. Contrary to the Chinese indignation at the 'imperialist' use of the term 'developing countries', there could be no building industrialisation in 'a country of illiterates', and Cuba had had to scale back aspirations from the 'luxury' of early post-revolutionary housing. But equally, he contested, there were environmental motives: cities must not become covered in 'a mass of steel and cement', denuded of trees.[64]

With the largely trouble-free conclusion of proceedings at Havana, the main danger had passed, and attention now shifted to the 7–12 October Assembly in Mexico. Smaller in size, it had 963 registrant architects from 29 countries and nearly 300 'wives', but the final session of the conference, with ad hoc Mexican additions, achieved an audience of over 2,000. Of the 102-strong US delegation, some 70 per cent were Texans, but there were as many as 57 delegates from communist countries, including China's Yang in his vice-presidential capacity; the French delegation of 73 transferred from Havana largely en bloc. Sylvia and Aidan had already arrived in Mexico, travelling direct from Jamaica, and hiring a car in Yucatan for touring. With the start of Keith Ingram looming, their leisure time there and in Oaxaca was occupied with shopping for vernacular craft items – rugs, pottery, etc. In the end much of this effort was wasted, however, as in Mexico City Corona Martin's son 'said he'd take charge of packing things up to send to Edinburgh – and just shoved everything in any old how – so that when we opened the boxes back home, most of the objects were smashed to bits'.[65]

In a show of pomp intended to outdo Havana, the 'inaugural Congress of the Symposium', in the Palace of Fine Arts in Mexico City, was attended by the President of Mexico, and the entire diplomatic corps and members of the Cabinet were invited. The assembled delegates were serenaded by the Mexico City Symphonic Orchestra, and participants were subsequently invited to an 'official banquet' on the terraces of Chapultapec Castle, a *ballet folklorico* at the Palacio de Bellas Artes, and an evening of individual hospitality at the homes of Mexican architects. The main Assembly sessions, and the working commissions, were held in the newly completed auditorium of the Instituto Politécnico Nacional at Zacatenco, on the city outskirts. With the admission of South Korea the IUA now embraced 60 member countries, and in a vote Prague defeated Buenos Aires and Sofia as the venue for the 1967 Congress.[66] The disconnection between the work at Havana and Mexico City at times caused confusion. For example, Neil A Connor of the US Federal Housing Administration had the 'somewhat embarrassing' experience of boasting that the US led the world in output of new housing under construction, only to find that the Soviet delegate had already reported, in Havana, a building programme twice as large.[67]

Arguably, for all the acrimony and inconvenience of the accompanying ideological conflict, the dual-site event ultimately redounded to the benefit of the IUA, with different government and ideological systems vying for its favour and attention. Another unintended positive outcome stemmed from the AIA's embarrassment at its supine attitude to US government manipulation; thereafter, it assumed a far more internationally involved stance. As early as November 1963 Jim Lawrence was firmly driving home the message to Robert Cutler (chairman of the AIA International Relations Committee) that the AIA 'had been wrong ... to boycott Havana', given that the Congress had turned out to be 'remarkably free from [political] coloration'. He continued that although the AIA should not expect to be 'king-makers' within IUA, and should participate like any other nation, it was essential that a full US delegation was sent to future congresses and assemblies: 'Nothing else will do ... this is a most important moment to project the image of our national organisation before the world.'[68]

Post-colonial diplomacy: founding the Commonwealth Association of Architects

Although Matthew carved out a distinctive role for himself within the IUA, as a mediator and 'listener' figure, and as a champion of collaboration on low-cost housing and educational harmonisation, inevitably his influence was circumscribed by the rambling and multi-polar character of the organisation, and by the clash of world ideologies, stemming from the Cold War, which overshadowed its work. It was the other geopolitical 'grand theme' of the mid 20th century, that of decolonisation, that allowed Matthew to play a far more decisive and dominant role as an architectural diplomat. As far back as his 1954 New Zealand House appointment and his 1957 role as UK assessor in the Jinnah Memorial Competition he had begun to engage with

the issues of decolonisation, but only in the early 1960s did it become a central focus of his thinking, when he became the first president and chief father figure of the Commonwealth Association of Architects (CAA): a body intended to replace the old imperial role of the RIBA, as 'the fountain of all wisdom, residing at Portland Place', with something modelled on the ethos and constitution of the IUA, but combining internationalism with greater cultural coherence and a single working language (English).[80]

Hindsight now suggests that the main significance of the Commonwealth was as a cushioning device during the transition between dependence and autonomy – a phase that climaxed in the late 1950s and early 1960s, when the trickle of states seeking independence turned into a raging flood.[81] But apart from its geopolitical significance, the Commonwealth also provided an effective vehicle for international collaboration in tackling real problems – including that of the built environment, where Western 1950s interest in 'regional' and 'national' modernisms was displaced to the developing countries, and the old colonial planning techniques were modified by Modernism's more complex concepts and language. In developing countries, expatriates played a key role in training the rising professions and imposing images of dominant culture, some arguably embodying inappropriately high standards of technology. Any remaining dependence became more indirect, and mediated via embryonic 'emancipatory' organisations such as George Atkinson's BRS Tropical Building Section. The degree of dependence varied radically between countries, with India, for instance, boasting an extensive architectural profession and a range of 'colonial' and 'vernacular' building trends. Gradually, though, a shift towards new kinds of regional Modernism became felt.[71]

The roots of the CAA lay in the late 1950s, when pressure began to grow from the sovereign 'Dominion' countries (India, Australia, Canada, New Zealand,

Commonwealth of design

11.11 Group photograph of Commonwealth Conference at RIBA, 25 July 1963. (JRIBA, September 1963, 345) (RIBA)

Group of Members of the Commonwealth Conference at 66 Portland Place, 25 July

Back row: A. MacDonald, G. R. Ricketts, W. O. McCutcheon, A. Chitty, S. C. Lock, M. MacEwen, R. S. Greig, G. C. Dovey, W. J. Cantwell

Fifth Row: A. C. Lewis, G. C. Hodges, N. M. Fraser, J. B. Aga, Prof. G. Quine Lay, P. L. Oldfield, Dr T. Howarth, A. A. Geeraerts, Prof. N. L. Hanson

Fourth row: F. N. Mbanefo, L. Hugh Wilson, Miss K. Hall, G. Venne, Mrs E. Layton, Miss J. Milne, M. D. Ringrose, E. Maxwell Fry, D. Nears-Crouch

Third row: The late A. S. Patil, S. Molligoda, R. Ireland, Zahir-ud Deen, Eu Jin Seow, Prof. W. G. Gregory

Second row: D. B. Mills, David Benton, Prof. R. Gardner-Medwin, P. E. A. Johnson-Marshall, P. N. K. Turkson, Lim Chong Keat, O. Olumuyiwa, H. E. Gonsal

First row: R. de Giorgio, L. de Syllas, Max E. Collard, J. Lovatt Davies, G. Laurenson, (a photographer), Sir Robert Matthew

RIBA JOURNAL SEPTEMBER 1963

South Africa) for a shift from coordination by the RIBA towards a more decentralised organisation: the prime movers were architects based in London, such as the Canadian Bill Allen, or Leo de Syllas, an early post-war partner in Architects' Co-Partnership, and head of its Lagos branch office. Max Fry, who, with Jane Drew, had carried out a vast range of colonial projects in the early post-war years – including their pioneering Modernist design for Ibadan University College (from 1951) – was also involved in a supporting role.[72] In the late 1950s 16 per cent of the RIBA membership lived and practised overseas, including many Australian, New Zealand and South African architects, who enjoyed membership via a 'devolution' scheme established in 1930, but only the five 'dom-inions' were represented formally; modest subsidies to the allied societies were paid by the RIBA. There was a widespread desire to strengthen links, especially in mutual recognition of educational qualifications, an area where the RIBA would have to take the initiative. Yet there was a clear acknowledgement that these links, to be credible and sustainable, would have to have a built-in emancipatory, devolutionary character.

In the late 1950s De Syllas, then teaching at the AA, formed with Anthony Chitty a 'Commonwealth Plan Committee' under RIBA auspices. In December 1958 Allen wrote to Spence, as RIBA President, warning that this committee's work had 'come off the boil', and urging accelerated progress with plans for a 'Commonwealth organisation' to facilitate homogenisation of architectural qualifications, encourage mobility of architects, and provide mutual educational support; the RIBA's dominance in these matters was anomalous, and 'if it is to be a Commonwealth in truth it should operate so, and share the load.' Allen proposed a division of teaching subjects between 'uniform' ones (deriving from scientific laws) and locally adaptable ones (culturally based). The initiation of the new organisation must, he insisted, come from the RIBA.[73] As a gesture to this mounting climate of opinion, presidents Kenneth Cross (1956–8) and Basil Spence (1958–60) undertook lengthy overseas tours – in 1957 to North America and Australia (Cross) and in March/April 1959 to Africa (by Spence, with Spragg). Both tours focused on professional institutions and architectural schools, but they had a very different character: Cross's focused on professionally organised 'white' countries, but Spence's was concerned largely with countries that were still British colonies dominated by white European colonial elites – and also included, as an uncontentious matter, a lengthy visit to South Africa.[74] In the 'dominion' countries the architectural profession was generally highly organised: for example, in Australia an architects' association (the Victorian Architects ' Association) had been founded as long ago as 1851, and the Royal Australian Institute of Architects in 1929.[75]

In 1959, with Iain Macleod's appointment as Colonial Secretary, the pace of decolonisation was speeded up dramatically, and South Africa was forced out of the Commonwealth in 1961. Within the RIBA, 1962 saw the appointment of Kathleen Hall as the new, reformist Overseas Relations Secretary.[76] Within architecture it was the demands of education that forced the pace, and propelled Matthew, with his IUA/RIBA educational involvements, to the fore. In 1959 the overseas examining panel of the RIBA issued a paper advocating a uniform examination system throughout the Commonwealth, in the interests of 'freedom of movement', and proposing a 'Commonwealth organisation' of architects to administer it: while 'the responsibility for initiative in the collective forward movement is ... ours, at least for the time being', soon the Commonwealth countries would have to be weaned off the Institute and the 'mother country'. To jolt this programme forward, in collaboration with a committee of RIBA and Commonwealth colleagues Matthew helped organise a four-day RIBA Conference of Architectural Schools in the Commonwealth, in September 1960, chaired by Max Fry and inaugurated by Holford in his capacity as President. Holford, of course, still retained a strong personal and consultancy interest in the country of his birth, South Africa.

The September 1960 conference brought together 14 Commonwealth countries, with papers focusing on collaboration between schools and societies, and on the likely functions of any new, pan-Commonwealth body – including education and registration, and building research.[77] In 1962, under Matthew's presidency, the RIBA decided to organise a conference of Commonwealth architectural societies in London from 21 to 25 July 1963 – for which purpose the Institute set up a Commonwealth Conference Committee, chaired by de Syllas. The conference was attended by 38 delegates and observers from 21 societies, with Matthew as chairman; the vice chairmen, carefully balancing 'old' and 'new' decolonisers, were Max Collard (President of the Australian Institute) and Oluwole Olumuyiwa, General Secretary of the Nigerian Institute of Architects. Olumuyiwa, despite his English training

11.12 Tom Colchester and his CAA personal Secretary seen in 1969. (*JRIBA*, October 1969, 435) (RIBA)

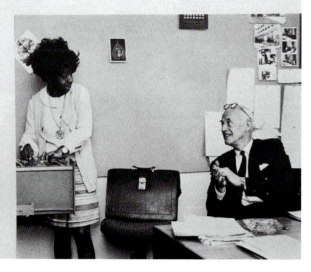

The Commonwealth Association of Architects

The Commonwealth Association of Architects is not part of the RIBA, but an independent body, for which the RIBA provides an office. This enables the CAA Secretary, Thomas Colchester, seen here with his secretary, Marylin Jones, to keep in the closest touch with the RIBA, and to make use of its information, library and other services. He also helps deal with RIBA overseas affairs. A continuous stream of enquiries and visitors from the Commonwealth comes to Mr Colchester, who was largely responsible for persuading the RIBA and the Architects' Registration Council to liberalise the ARCUK regulations for the admission of overseas architects to the UK register.

and his initial work for ACP in London, was a flamboyant advocate of African cultural and architectural autonomy. In his 1962 RIBA presidential address Matthew described this conference in a semi-emancipatory, semi-paternalistic way, arguing that 'architecture overrides national boundaries, and we in this country have in any case a special responsibility for leadership and special relations in some of the developing countries.'[78]

The 1963 Commonwealth conference was held at the RIBA, with Gordon Ricketts heading the conference secretariat. Matthew's dominance of proceedings was underlined by the inclusion in the programme of visits to RMJM buildings, including a tour of the newly completed New Zealand House, and a government reception at the Commonwealth Institute. Eight out of the 38 delegates were of Asian or African ethnic origin – a minority position, but a vast increase over the likely equivalent even five years earlier. Although Matthew knew some already, others, such as Collard or Olumuyiwa, would become very familiar collaborators after the conference. The conference's main decision was to establish the CAA as soon as possible, 'without distinction of politics, race or religion', modelled expressly on the scope of the IUA, and embracing all Commonwealth countries with nationally organised societies of architects.[79] At the concluding

press conference Matthew set out the strictly limited and interlocking set of initial aims of the CAA. First came architectural education, with efforts towards inter-recognition of qualifications, and pragmatic initial acceptance of RIBA entrance requirements as an 'initial yardstick'. Second was a demand for government pressure to build up the 'strength' of the profession, by encouraging their training and employment, especially in countries with almost no architects, such as Pakistan. Finally, there was 'technical aid' for developing countries – which could include, of course, the training of more architects. Matthew ended, in proper decolonising style, by quoting a Maori proverb, translated as: 'By grouping together, the object will be attained.'[95]

In practice, the process of decolonisation in architecture was at first largely symbolic, as the RIBA continued to exercise, during 1964–5, an overwhelming influence on the nascent CAA. That influence was channelled mainly through Matthew, as immediate past president – especially following the death of Leo de Syllas in a car crash early in 1964.[96] In setting up the CAA as an active organisation, Matthew followed his standard formula of staged build-up of support. Research and lobbying led to the establishment of a secretariat (from January 1964) and a steering committee, which met formally in Singapore in

September 1964. June 1964 saw appointment of a permanent salaried Secretary: Trevor Charles (Tom) Colchester, a 55-year old ex-African colonial civil servant, who had specialised in Kenyan housing and planning matters. Although steeped in the colonial engineering/administrative tradition, he had made the mental adjustment to a post-colonial outlook, and was hailed by Matthew as 'a true Commonwealth man, uncommitted ... nationally'. Colchester, for his part, recognised that 'Robert was not really a Commonwealth man as the word might then be used', but saw the CAA as part of a wider tapestry of international networks and initiatives.[81]

The first concern was the financing of the new body. At first, a guaranteed annual income of £5,500 (mostly RIBA grant) was secured, and by 1968 the CAA's independent income had gradually risen to £6,000, partly supported by a levy on the overseas societies. Dwarfing all that, however, was an £8,000 annual grant (soon raised to £10,000) approved by the newly founded Commonwealth Foundation, to allow the creation in October 1966 of a new and ambitious initiative, the Commonwealth Board of Architectural Education, which would place educational harmonisation at the centre of the CAA's work: Matthew argued that education was 'the key service' that the CAA could give to the profession and to society. The CBAE grant absorbed half of the Foundation's sponsorship budget.[82] To carry through this agenda effectively, the establishment of an autonomous, non-British body was a vital prerequisite. That much was demonstrated by the uncertain outcome of several pre-CBAE initiatives involving direct liaison or 'aid' from Britain – in some cases through financial grants from the Ministry of Overseas Development. For example, since 1962 a scheme of 'twinning' of UK and overseas architectural schools had been attempted, with Ministry aid, inspired by the successful link between the AA and Kumasi College of Technology in Ghana. In 1963–6, under the headship of AA tutor John

Lloyd, who drew extensively on the Africanist ideology of Kwame Nkrumah, the school developed a short-lived international reputation for new, expressive approaches to Modernist teaching in Africa; O H Koenigsberger, head of the Tropical Studies department at the AA, had previously considered a twinning relationship with Zaria. Five such links had been established by UK universities by 1969, but Bill Allen, then principal of the AA, stressed the suspicion of any formal arrangements as 'a form of academic imperialism', and the need to 'Africanise' schools as soon as possible.[83] Difficulties grew after around 1966, with the gradual spread of military dictatorships in leading African countries such as Ghana or Nigeria. The lack of a consistent policy prompted Matthew in March 1965 to host an evening 'working supper' party at Park Square East, including Colchester, Sir Andrew Cohen (Director of Overseas Development), Layton, Bill Allen, Koenigsberger, Gardner-Medwin (representing Liverpool) and representatives of other schools. Colchester tabled a paper that warned that British qualifications were potentially unpopular, and that any twinning should use international staff 'from UK schools of progressive ideas', in order 'to counter the tendency to call a twinning scheme a neo-colonialist manoeuvre'.[84] In September 1965 Colchester also criticised an Edinburgh University conference on African development, co-organised by Matthew, on the grounds that 'some of the faculties rather showed a disposition to welcome African links as a sort of academic VSO expiating the sins of the slave trade.'[85]

Matthew's own most significant initiative of educational collaboration in the lead-up to the foundation of the CBAE was a campaign of two high-profile visits to India, in September 1964 and March 1965. India had seen a relatively strong build-up of architectural education, with six schools of architecture founded since independence, and the growth of even stronger expectations. The September 1964 visit, focused on the School of

Planning and Architecture at New Delhi (under Professor D V R Rao), was also facilitated by Matthew's strong links with Jai Bhalla, IUA Vice-President, who became increasingly dominant in the IIA following the death of ex-President A A S Patil. The relationship between Matthew and the much younger Bhalla was similar to that with other 'helpers' such as Reiach or Percy Marshall, but also showed evidence of the growing standing of India, and its special ability to exert 'reverse influence' within the Commonwealth. Bhalla's own special agenda was the status of the architectural profession within India, especially in relation to the entrenched power of the engineer-domi-

nated government Public Works Department.[86] Here, Bhalla had hit on a key architectural issue of decolonisation, right across the former British empire. The 'PWD' was a generic, archetypally colonial system that had originated in the 19th-century Indian Army Corps of Engineers. Post-war PWDs became more specialised, and some were reorganised to give the architects more power, as in Hong Kong, Nigeria or Kenya, where Tom Colchester himself had broken up the PWD to allow more autonomy for architecture. But the architects would always be headed by an engineer. Following this Indian visit, Matthew responded to Bhalla's concerns by asking Colchester's secretariat to compile an international comparative report on the 'PWD problem' across the Commonwealth, to help 'enable us to carry further the fight for our rights' – following which Matthew himself would visit India to focus on the issue.[87] Colchester's eventual report on the 'PWD problem', delivered to Matthew in early February 1965, gave a balanced overview of the legacy, of which he himself, of course, had extensive personal experience. The implication of this system for India, Colchester recognised, was potentially a vicious circle. To disrupt the 'invaluable all-purpose organisations of District Engineers' by hiving off architects at local level would cause chaos, yet to have, as Bhalla advocated, 'a separate group of architects in national and state governments', divorced from fieldwork, would risk impotence – unless they had the same pay as engineers and enjoyed direct accountability to Ministers. Having battled so hard over the pay comparability issue within DHS in the 1940s, Matthew himself was, naturally, warmly disposed towards the latter argument.[88]

On his March 1965 visit to Delhi, rather as we saw in the case of his 'Stormont address' on Belfast regional planning two years earlier, Matthew was received as an authority figure, with special meetings convened for key 'heads of institutions in the country to benefit from your advice'.[89] That advice led inexorably away from engineer domination of

Indian architecture. In April, Bhalla could report that the visit had secured a government commitment to appoint a commission, headed by Professor Thacker, to reorganise the architects' wing of the PWD, and that the government had agreed a formal invitation to the CAA to hold its 1967 conference in India. By November 1965 a draft Regulation Bill had already been prepared by the IIA.[90]

First President: CAA conferences and educational work

The venue of the CAA's inaugural June 1965 conference was, of course, already long settled: in 'a master-stroke of diplomacy', Matthew had suggested that it be held in Malta, one of the Commonwealth's smallest states, and neutral in the Commonwealth's geopolitical disputes over decolonisation. Reflecting the recent concerns about the PWD issue, the conference theme was 'The Architect in Public Service', but the dominant single initiative was the formal approval of the establishment of the CBAE. This chimed in with the views of some progressive-minded younger architects working in Commonwealth countries. In the May 1965 AR, for example, a young British lecturer at Zaria, Charles Cockburn, warned against caution in the CAA's mission, and urged that it should actively proselytise a broader, anti-elitist approach to the built environment, avoiding large prestige buildings in favour of cheap mass programmes. It could act as a 'grand external examiner' to the Commonwealth, and stimulate debate and research, especially through the role of the Secretary.[91] The cause of international goodwill became especially pertinent with the outbreak of war between India and Pakistan during the conference: Zahir and Bhalla, both Nairobi-born and Bombay-trained, and long-standing friends, attempted to set an example by breakfasting publicly together.[92]

Pursuing his time-honoured policy of appealing direct 'to the top', Matthew sent a CAA handbook and final report and recommendations from Malta to all Commonwealth Prime Ministers.[93] There were only three acknowledgements. Keith Holyoake of New Zealand sent a positive reply, and the UK's Harold Wilson praised CAA as 'a most promising example of practical cooperation within the Commonwealth'. But Matthew's geopolitical 'masterstroke' at Malta had not convinced everyone, as was suggested by the acknowledgement from Joan E Wicken, personal assistant to the Tanzanian president, Mwalimu Julius Nyerere: her letter expressed surprise that South Africa, as a non-Commonwealth country, should be a member of the CAA and a participant at Malta, arguing that this had 'no legal basis'.[94] Matthew was always ready, on representational trips, to divert opportunistically to advise on local problems, and in Malta he was lobbied by Professor Edwin J Borg Costanzi of the Royal University of Malta to help in a fight to preserve architectural education from a threatened move of the engineering and architecture department to a polytechnic. Matthew visited Malta twice in August and September 1965, and lobbied Sir John Fulton, who had recently completed a report on the organisation of the university, but met with procrastination on the part of the university authorities and ultimately inconclusive results.[95]

During late 1965 the follow-up negotiations for CBAE focused on potential financial assistance from the new Commonwealth Foundation, a member-government-supported institution established in December 1965, with John Chadwick as director, and a £250,000 annual income. Its task was to support conferences of Commonwealth bodies, facilitate other exchanges, and help set up new institutions – especially professional associations in culture and the arts – 'in order to reduce the present centralisation in Britain'.[115] With the fruitless exchanges between IUA and UNESCO in mind, Matthew sensed that the CAA, and especially the CBAE, was an initiative tailor-made for support by the Foundation, and he encouraged Colchester to keep the CBAE proposal at the 'head of the queue' for support: a draft applica-

11.15 Matthew seen with Jai Bhalla and the renowned politician, Pandit Vijaya Lakshmi (Congress leader and sister of Nehru) at the CAA New Delhi conference in March 1967. (Punjab Photo Service)

tion was already sitting in waiting by November 1965. On 4 March 1966 Matthew moved in for the kill, hosting a lunch at the Reform Club for Chadwick, along with Colchester and Roger Greig, Secretary of the Australian Institute of Architects – who, Colchester briefed Matthew beforehand, was 'probably the best manager of [architectural] institute affairs after Ricketts'. He added that 'Chadwick is quite happy to have a look between now and Friday at our application for funding which I have had set up and waiting'. One obstacle – the presence of any non-Commonwealth institutions as members – was quickly swept aside, when the Royal Irish Institute agreed to change its membership to associate status, opening the way to a similar solution over South Africa. Although a £15,000 annual subsidy for CBAE was sought, the grant that was eventually approved was £10,000 for two years, extensible to three. It was settled by mid 1966 that the Board should have 7–10 members, including one representing each of the five regions of the Commonwealth, plus 'additional' specialist members; it would communicate with the CAA through the Association's Executive Committee, and would focus especially on the equivalence of architectural qualifications.[116] The CBAE met for the first time in October 1966 at

the RIBA, and its initial membership comprised Hugh Wilson (chair), Matthew, Collard, Medwin, Howarth, Koenigsberger, M Onfowuka (Nigeria), Zahir-ud-Din (Pakistan), J C Parkin (Canada) and Colchester as secretary. In his speech, Matthew welcomed the CBAE as 'probably the first example of a body organised to promote professional education on an international Commonwealth-wide basis', and announced that 50 school exams had already been 'adopted' as equivalent to the RIBA standard. He eventually retired from the board in 1969.[96]

Central to the devolutionary ethos of the CAA was the IUA-inspired principle of regional activity, to reflect local conditions by collaborative or exhortatory work. In November 1966 Colchester and Olumuyiwa embarked on a whistle-stop tour of Ghana and East Africa to try to convert 'ministers and the public to the importance of the profession'. In Africa the problem, unlike India, was not one of small numbers and domination by engineers, but of polarisation between white expatriate and ethnic African architects.[97g] Within Nigeria, for example, in 1967 the issue was exploited by the Nigerian Institute of Architects, led by Olumuyiwa, as a 'psychological argument' to dramatise their demand that the Federal military government should establish architectural registration. The Institute argued that only registration could 'arrest the situation in which expatriate architects are able to practice in Nigeria whereas Nigerian architects are denied reciprocal facilities in foreign countries.' Bemused, Colchester reminded Olumuyiwa that full reciprocity was available abroad to all Nigerian architects, whereas the NIA practised an actively exclusionary policy (against expatriates).[98] A slightly different issue, involving conflict *within* the 'colonial' grouping, and not just confined to Africa, was the ever-rumbling tension between resident expatriates and overseas (usually British or American) 'intruders'. Fuel was periodically added to this smouldering resentment by trade promotion and 'consultancy aid' efforts, such as a 1968 initiative of the Board of Trade to sponsor work by British architects in Commonwealth countries in hospital design, suggesting that the RIBA might help with liaison. Matthew knew nothing of the plan, and was caught unawares by the furore: one expatriate, in Trinidad, wrote angrily to him, 'If you want a free trip to get a suntan, OK, but while you are on the beach, we want to remain on the drawing board!' Angered by the way in which the initiative cut crudely across his own diplomatic strategies, Matthew weighed in immediately within the RIBA, and 'blocked any idea of RIBA resources' being used to support it.[99]

The second CAA conference, in New Delhi in March 1967, with a substantial focus on Chandigarh, was both a celebratory event, after two years of full existence, and – typically of Matthew – the cornerstone of a blizzard of CAA and CBAE initiatives in and around the Indian subcontinent. At the conference itself, delegates from 20 countries (including, still, Ireland and South Africa) were welcomed by Vijaya Lakshmi Pandit – the former National Congress leader, ambassador to the USA, UK and USSR, and the first woman to preside over the UN.[100] At the closing session Matthew declared that, at this second gathering, 'we have become fully alive', and promised an annual programme of £3,000–4,000 for promoting regional activities. To the Indian Institute, he urged that 'you must press your Government and other clients to accept your fee scale and give up tendering and fee cutting'. After the conference, CBAE members fanned out to architecture schools across the subcontinent.[101] Matthew and Zahir acted as external examiners at the Delhi School of Architecture; of this visit, Colchester later recalled that 'I shall not forget [Matthew's] scrutinising hundreds of old exam papers over past years at the University of Delhi, obtained incidentally in the face of outraged officialdom, on the personal fiat of a vice-chancellor.' For his part, Zahir recalled that 'this must be one of the rare occasions that a Pakistan external examiner was accepted for the

School of Architecture in Delhi – albeit in company with the distinguished Sir Robert Matthew!'[102] With Hugh Wilson and the RIBA's Layton, Matthew went on to Pakistan on 22 March – partly to bolster the morale of the 'pitifully weak' Institute – spent three days visiting two schools of architecture at Lahore and meeting Ministry of Education officials, and pressed for the government School of Architecture to be made a full-time institution. In a report Layton wrote that India, with all its difficulties, 'in retrospect ... looked quite rosy compared to the situation in Pakistan', and asked that Pakistan should be given 'first priority' in aid.[103] Originally, Pakistan had been left with no architectural schools at partition. During the mid 1960s Matthew had been negotiating with the West Pakistan University of Engineering and Technology at Lahore, but proposals to establish a formal association with his Edinburgh department, linked to a branch office of RMJM to oversee the firm's work at Islamabad, came to nothing.[104]

Spurred on by the main conference and Matthew's call for regional activity, Bhalla initiated the first of a series of Asian regional conferences, based at Singapore and Kuala Lumpur in December 1967, which resolved to establish a regional centre at postgraduate level to train architectural teachers and research workers. Bhalla argued that 'we must sell architecture; aggressively, not as a service, but as a basic fact ... [as] an architect in society has usually a double role – as a professional and as a citizen.' The second Asian conference, at Colombo a year later, set up 'ARCASIA' (Architects' Regional Conference for Asia) – a Singapore-based, independent regional postgraduate research institute, intended to interact with proposed CAA final-level schools in India, Malaysia, Singapore, Hong Kong, Ceylon and Pakistan; and in 1969, moves began to establish a CAA Asian Documentation Centre in New Delhi.[105]

During the two years that followed New Delhi – the last of his double presi-

385

11.16 CBAE visit to the West Indies, 1968. From left: Max Collard, Mr and Mrs Lovatt Davies, Hugh Wilson, Matthew, and Tom Colchester and his wife. (EULMC)

dency – Matthew concentrated on consolidation work.[106] His own remaining academic activities were often bound up with these links. Building on the Khartoum links with Alexander Potter, Matthew continued to act as external examiner there in 1966–7, and in 1967 attracted a large group of Sudanese PhD postgraduate students to study in Edinburgh.[128] But Matthew also began to find these external academic commitments increasingly tiring, and on his 1966 and 1967 trips to Khartoum along with Arnold Hendry, at 60 years of age, became exhausted by the heat and the disorganisation in Khartoum:

> Nothing worked effectively, and he didn't have a lot of patience for it. One day, they took us on an excursion to a gorge of the Nile, involving several hours' driving through the desert. By mid morning, it was desperately hot, and then they got stuck in the sand. People had to get out and push, but Robert was getting so tired and short-tempered by then, that he simply wouldn't get out of the car – and just wanted to know when we were getting back. The following year's trip to Khartoum wasn't much more successful, as he had a bad tummy upset![107]

At his RIBA Gold Medal presentation in 1970 Matthew spoke fulsomely of the CAA and his successor, Bhalla: the CAA, he declared,

> expresses both a protest and a hope: a protest at the prolongation of an

established institutional idea, in the shape of the RIBA, into a new situation, beyond its usefulness; a hope that these common factors existing in the Commonwealth countries – greatly aided by a common language – could usefully be brought together, to focus on the new problems now acutely arising in many parts of the world. The CAA lies midway between the national institutions like the RIBA, and the world coverage of the IUA. Jai Bhalla, now president, is also a Vice-President of the IUA. He has great energy, and although a young man, has already been through a considerable baptism of fire in the field of international cooperation. I handed over the presidency to him last year in great confidence. Through these international groups, we see and feel at first hand some of the forces at work in the world today, forces we should understand something about if we are to be effective, even at home. No country is an island, not any more.[108]

Of the global 'forces' that Matthew came to understand better through his CAA role, by far the most contentious was the decolonisation-related issue of the membership of South Africa. Indeed, it was largely as an indirect response to this problem that, by the time of Matthew's 1970 speech, the qualifications for membership of CAA had been reconstructed, through alterations to the 1965 Articles of Association: a new class of 'associated Institutes' had been created, and full

C27. August 1963 view of the south side of George Square, Edinburgh, showing the Arts Tower nearly completed, but demolition of the remaining houses not yet begun. (M Glendinning)

C28. Mid 1970s view of the newly completed Ninewells complex, Dundee, from east. (Planair)

Modern Architect

C29. Robert Matthew (on left) seen with undergraduate students from his Edinburgh University department in 1961 at the opening of the Pinkie Braes housing scheme in Galt Crescent, Musselburgh. This 30-unit development, built by the Scottish Special Housing Association, was the first of a number of student 'live' projects within the department (with student work commencing in 1958), and was inspired by earlier projects in Birmingham. A post-completion user-study was subsequently carried out by the department's Housing Research Unit. In this view, on Matthew's immediate right are staff members Reg Gray (taller) and Pat Nuttgens (with red tie). (RMJM)

C30. 1968 photograph by Matthew of William Sempill's tombstone, Leochel-Cushnie kirkyard, Aberdeenshire. (EULMC)

SIR ROBERT H. MATTHEW

BELFAST
Regional Survey
and Plan 1962

C31. Dust-jacket front cover of the two-volume published version of Matthew's Belfast Regional Plan. (*Belfast Regional Survey and Plan 1962*, Belfast, 1964) (Government of Northern Ireland, Ministry of Health and Local Government)

C32. 1967 colour concept sketch by Matthew of the New University of Ulster, as seen from the River Bann. (EULMC)

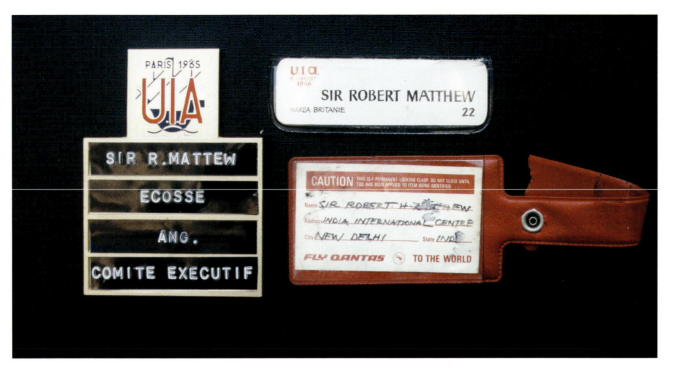

C33. Matthew's own badges from 1960s meetings: IUA Paris 1965, IUA Romania 1966, CAA Delhi 1967. (M Glendinning)

C34. Aerial photograph by Matthew of the skyline of Rio de Janeiro, taken during IUA conference trip to Brazil in November 1962. (EULMC)

C35. Robert and Sylvia Matthew shopping for 'vernacular' souvenirs in Taxco Market, Mexico, October 1963. (EULMC)

Modern Architect

C36. Still from Aidan Matthew's 8 mm film of the September 1964 China tour, showing Liang Sicheng escorting Sylvia, Robert and Janet Matthew round the Imperial Palace, Beijing. (Aidan Matthew)

C37. Still from 1964 China film, showing Robert Matthew and interpreter talking to children in back streets of Beijing. (Aidan Matthew)

C38. Still from 1964 China film, showing Arthur Ling relaxing on a river cruise on 21 September in Hanchow. (Aidan Matthew)

C39. Spring 1963 view at Lahore airport, taken by Matthew: from left, Mrs Ferraris, Gio Ponti, Alberto Rosselli, Maurice Lee. (EULMC)

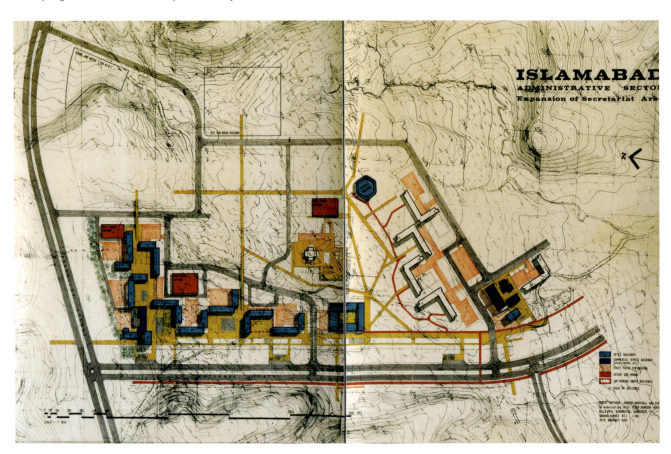

C40. November 1968 final plan of Islamabad Administrative Sector extension, including location of National Archives. (RMJM)

C41. The design team for the Castle Terrace Theatre project, Edinburgh, seen in discussion in 1974 in the East Fettes Avenue project office. Staff members visible include John Richards (light blue shirt), Kenneth Graham (with pipe) and Ian Samuel (kneeling at left). (RMJM)

C42. 1995 view of the remodelled kitchen at Keith Marischal, including tiles by William Gordon. (RCAHMS)

C43. 1972 painting of Jessie Matthew by Harry More Gordon, hanging at Keith Marischal until 2003. (Harry More Gordon)

C44. Official RIBA notice of Matthew's Gold Medal presentation on 16 June 1970. (RIBA)

RIBA

Royal Institute of British Architects 66 Portland Place London W1N 4AD

Royal Gold Medal

Presentation to

Sir Robert Matthew

CBE, PPRIBA, MTPI, FRIAS, ARSA, MA, LLD

Jean-Jacques Mayoux, Professor of English Literature and Language, l'Académie de Paris à la Sorbonne

Patrick Nuttgens, PhD, MA, DA (Edin), ARIBA

Clough Williams-Ellis, CBE, MC, JP, FRIBA, MTPI, FILA

will also speak

Tuesday 16 June 1970 at 6pm

Admission free, visitors welcome

45. Poster prepared by Robert Matthew for 'open day' at Keith Marischal, May 1974. (EULMC)

Feb 2, 1970 Dear Robert –

You will be so overwhelmed with plaudits that I don't expect you will even see this yelp of delight of mine at your golden glory – so grandly won. If a rusty old Welsh penny-farthing bicycle can properly say "well done" to such a majestic vehicle as the "Flying Scotsman" – so say I, and with affectionate admiration.

Bless you – Clough.

PORTMEIRION—THE VILLAGE LOOKING EAST

C46. Congratulatory note from Clough Williams-Ellis to Matthew on his Gold Medal, February 1970. (EULMC)

C47. 1970 Assembly Rooms conference poster and 'vernacular' bric-a-brac in the staircase hall at Keith Marischal, seen in 1999. (EULMC)

C48. 1981 view of completed IBP flats, Tripoli, Libya. (RMJM)

C49. Matthew seen in Perugia during the city-extension competition in autumn 1971. (EULMC)

Modern Architect

C50. The first floor 'television room' in Keith Marischal, 1995, with bric-a-brac and Keith Ingram table in corner: latterly, Lorna sat during the day at the table on the left. (RCAHMS)

C51. Aerial photograph taken by Robert Matthew in 1962, captioned simply 'Air – Clouds'. (EULMC)

membership had been restricted to institutes within Commonwealth countries. The early 1960s, in precise step with the lightning progress of decolonisation through Africa, saw a sharp transformation in attitudes towards South Africa – and this was an issue where Matthew, partly through stubborn dislike of 'political agitation', was somewhat behind the march of liberal opinion, participating along with many others in contacts at an official level until at least 1960.[109] But by 1963 the climate of opinion concerning South Africa had completely changed, and when, in July of that year, Matthew proposed to make a visit there in his official RIBA presidential capacity, and to combine that visit with an IUA executive committee meeting there, a chorus of conflicting internal debate and dissension broke out within RIBA, articulately orchestrated by the communist Malcolm MacEwen. He argued that the CAA was 'bound initially to be rather a tender plant', and that the mounting 'political pressures' on Nigeria, Ghana and others would completely undermine the Association if nothing was done. To visit South Africa in 1964 would be to 'put one's hand into the lion's mouth', especially as holding a IUA meeting there might expose non-white delegates to 'humiliation'. He advised Matthew to begin distancing the RIBA and CAA from the Institute of South African Architects (ISAA) by the indirect means of shifting responsibility towards ISAA. The ISAA should be asked to adopt as policy 'the Declaration rejecting discrimination on grounds of race, politics and religion that was contained in the [1963 Commonwealth] conference report', allowing any visit to South Africa to be presented as 'support to an institute' trying to uphold CAA/IUA principles. Gordon Ricketts, by contrast, argued trenchantly for retention of the South African link, citing the recent Cuban furore as a precedent for a militantly 'apolitical' stance – an argument that ignored the growing 'taboo' status of South African apartheid:

I don't believe it is consistent or our duty to proclaim against barriers of colour, race and creed, and then in fact tacitly to take sides by offending the South Africans while fostering the coloured element. Either our organisations are apolitical or they are not ... If Cuba, why not South Africa?[110]

Although Matthew firmly agreed that it was wrong, in principle, to 'politicise' architectural diplomacy, his inherent pragmatism soon got the upper hand in the obviously special case of South Africa, which combined colonialism and racial extremism in a way that clearly evoked uncomfortable memories of 1930s and 1940s fascism in Europe. He recognised that MacEwen, despite his reputation for trenchantly flamboyant opinions, was the one offering the more sensible advice in this case, and he followed it in full – while taking care to disguise the inexorable logic of separation. First the IUA meeting, and then the RIBA visit, was cancelled, citing conflicting diary commitments. In December, for the moment, ISAA was accepted as a full member of the CAA, albeit protesting at its exclusion from the main committees and executive. By 1965 it started to become obvious that even that position could not long be tenable. In January, for example, Alexander Potter reported to Colchester on a recent pan-African economic conference, arguing that although 'the Pan-African scene is full of dissension, confused allegiance,' nonetheless conferences in Africa about Africa would only work if South Africa, Rhodesia and Portugal were absent, 'whether by exclusion, abstention or connivance'.[111] And feelings only became stronger after the 'UDI' that year of the secessionist government in Southern Rhodesia. Although Matthew was, on principle, against active exclusion of South Africa from the CAA, he now began pragmatically to consider how to get the same objective through indirect means. Rapidly, as we shall see in the next chapter, thoughts began to turn to an overall restructuring of the membership, which would take in South Africa as well as Ireland, and adjust similarly the

11.17 Model of final design for International Labour Office, Geneva, 1966. (EULMC)

CBAE eligibility requirements. By late 1968 the possibility of a compromise deal between the Wilson government and Rhodesia was casting a long shadow over Commonwealth institutions: any settlement, Colchester speculated to Matthew in November, might fracture the Commonwealth and leave the CAA as 'a species of Commonwealth Old Boys' Club'. In a doomsday warning he advised that contingency plans should be set up for the CAA's 'reversion to a juvenile or embryonic form', such as a 'coordinating council of RIBA Allied Societies Overseas', confined to countries interested in keeping the Commonwealth links alive.[112]

North, south, east, west: private international interventions in the 1960s

Owing to the overwhelming predominance of the IUA and CAA within Matthew's international work, his other international activities took on a somewhat fragmented character for the time being – albeit with a gradual, inexorable tendency towards consolidation around issues of global architectural ethics. To the Jamaica Society of Architects, in September 1963, he argued in a Vaumarcus-like tone that architectural internationalism could become a microcosm of 'the true fellowship of man, which is at the heart of the poetry of our national Scottish poet, Robert Burns, and is ... more alive in the hands of architects than it is in many others ... a common love of architecture as an art and as a service to man.'[113] Throughout the 1960s

Matthew accumulated the usual variety of international honours and private consultancy work. In 1965, for instance, in the wake of his IUA presidency, he was awarded the Medal of Honour (the equivalent of the RIBA Gold Medal) by the Federation of Danish Architects. At the award ceremony at the Danish Embassy in November 1965, Hans Henning Larsen, head of the Federation, argued that Matthew's 'open mind in planning, in technique, and in human intercourse' had helped bring greater 'freedom' to over-doctrinaire Functionalism.[114]

Throughout the period, where his time allowed, Matthew continued to serve on international competition juries and consultative committees – spanning a full range of different political and ideological contexts. In 1963, for example, an eminent Israeli IUA executive colleague (1963–7), fellow 'Delian' and former director of the National Planning Agency, Arieh Sharon (1902–84), secured Matthew a place on a committee tasked with arbitrating on plans for a new engineering building at the 'Technion' of the Israel Institute of Technology, Haifa. Here, he had to arbitrate in a dispute within the IIT over the small-windowed design proposed, which was seen by some faculty members as 'prison-like' and 'psychologically unfortunate, in view of the history of the Jewish people (Ghettoes, etc.)'.[115] More straightforward in design, but convoluted in organisation, was a 1966 commission to advise on the design of a new headquarters for the International Labour Office (a UN agency) in Geneva, on a suburban site adjoining the former League of Nations complex and the Red Cross headquarters. This was the latest in a succession of Modernist projects for international organisations, of which the most recent IUA-sponsored competition for the World Health Organisation headquarters in 1959 had been won by Jean Tschumi with a tall slab block.[116] Typically of such a UN-sponsored project, the arrangements were of great complexity: Matthew was appointed, along with W K Harrison of New York (chair), F Peyrot of Switzerland,

C Villanueva of Venezuela and M
Sulikowski of Poland, to advise on plans
being drawn up by another team of
designers, including Nervi and
Beaudouin. The cumbersome parallel
arrangement of designers and advisers
resulted in an austerely geometrical 12-
storey slab block of conventional CIAM
type, here offset by the abstract device of
concave sides. Matthew and the other
advisers approved the plans, despite
reservations that the tall block 'perhaps
had a certain rigidity of design', and the
project was duly constructed from 1969
onwards.[117]

The 1960s also saw Matthew's involvement as juror in two major architectural
competitions, all on Vago's recommendation, and with the usual, often inconclusive results, as the projects were part-
executed or deferred. The first stemmed
from Matthew's lengthy connection with
University College Dublin, and Professor
M Hogan, for whom since 1954 he had
been evolving a general development
plan for a new site south of the city centre at Belfield. In February 1961 Hogan
reported to Matthew that the government had decided to hold an international competition for the layout of the
whole group; eventually, the competition
was held in July 1964, with a seven-strong
jury, including Matthew, a Swiss and a
Dane, and four Irish judges. Of the 105
entries, the winner was a young Gdansk-
based Polish architect, Andrzej Wejchert,
whose plan, not unlike Gabriel Epstein's
contemporary concept for Lancaster,
envisaged a covered, kinked pedestrian
spine mall with courtyard blocks clustered at right angles on either side: Phase
1 comprised the administration block,
hall and theatre. Eventually Wejchert
established an associateship with Dublin
architect Andrew Devine to build the
project.[118]

Far more problematic, as was typical
of large redevelopment programmes by
the late 1960s and early 1970s, was a
competition for a multi-purpose city hall
and opera complex to be built on the
bank of the Binnen Amstel at Waterloop-
lein, at the southeastern edge of the city

centre of Amsterdam. First contacted by
Amsterdam's City Architect, through IUA,
in February 1966, Matthew formed part
of a multinational jury drawn from
across northwestern Europe.[119] During
1967 he discovered with mounting dismay the complex and time-consuming
character of the competition, beginning
in January 1968 with an initial two-stage
deliberation to cut the initial 845 entries
to 20, and then to seven, and ending in a
five-day marathon session to select the
eventual winner and distribute a 'bewildering, indiscriminate' variety of also-ran
premiums. In this session Matthew
amused himself, characteristically, by
drawing an intricate diagram of the way
in which the winner emerged from the
complex discussions. The selection
process was made yet more difficult by
the way in which, typically of the diversity of 1960s urbanism, the seven finalists
varied radically in their approaches: there
were stadium-section cantilevered-out
blocks, low-rise dense grids around courtyards, irregular, mound-like agglomera-
tions, and more conventional
tower-and-podium solutions. Despite his
own liking for the latter, Matthew fully
supported the eventual consensus to
reject the (in his words) many 'dominat-
ing' and 'ostentatious' entries, and award
first prize to the 'sober, almost austere'
design by the 38-year-old Viennese architect W Holzbauer – a relatively low-rise,
street-scaled stadium-section solution

11.18 Matthew seen during the
February 1968 jury meeting for Amsterdam City Hall: the hatted figure in
the right background is jury chairman
Huig Aart Maaskant. (EULMC)

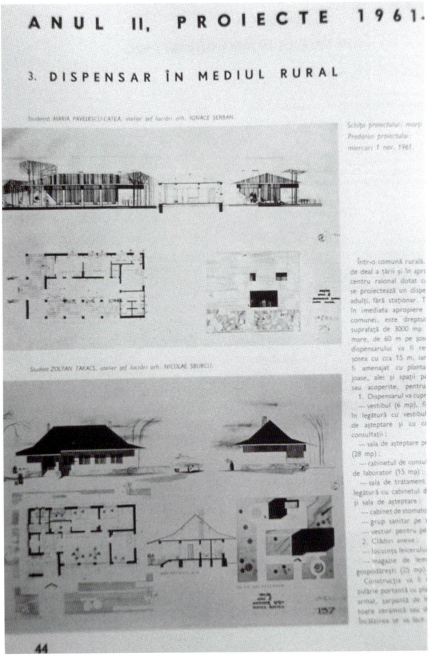

11.19 Projects for rural dispensary by students at the Institutul de Arhitectura Ion Mincu, published in *Studii si Proiecte*, 1964, showing the eclectic range of stylistic solutions. (Institutul de Arhitectura Ion Mincu)

with offices above and two council chambers projected outwards.[120] Eventually, this project, despite its relative modesty of scale, became a particular target of the upsurge in environmental militancy in Amsterdam in the 1970s, and, following incessant delays and disruption, was nicknamed the 'Stopera'. It was finally built in the 1980s in a somewhat more clustered, brick Post-Modern style.[121]

Reflecting his complex patterns of engagement with the geopolitical relationships of the day, Matthew's foreign travel during those years balanced a wide range of different aims and ideological positions, often at the same time. For example, his autumn 1963 trip to the IUA Congress and Assembly, in Cuba and Mexico, was prefaced by an intensive visit to the USA, largely in his private-practice capacity, to investigate the possibilities of RMJM involvement in 'urban renewal' work, and by a whistle-stop tour of the West Indies as RIBA President. The West Indies trip originated in an August 1962 invitation from the Jamaica Society of

406

Modern Architect

Architects for a presidential visit, to rein-force 'our young society', and by July 1963 it had been decided that Aidan, Sylvia and Lorna would join Robert and Lorna for this stage of his trip, as part of an extended round-the-world trip, linked chiefly with Robert's urban-renewal investigations in the USA. The visit to the newly independent (1962) Trinidad, organised by Anthony C Lewis, ASTT President and the foremost 1960s 'mod-ern regionalist' architect of the West Indies, began on 22 September when Matthew's party arrived by boat in Port of Spain from Barbados (Matthew himself having flown there direct from New York on the twentieth).[122] Following an inten-sive tour conducted by Lewis, and a cock-tail barbecue party in overpowering heat hosted by the Governor-General, Sir Solomon Hackey, and featuring a local steel band and dancing, Matthew opened an ASTT-hosted British Council exhibition of 'Tropical Architecture in the Common-wealth' – comprising, slightly controver-sially, buildings largely by British firms such as Maxwell Fry or Norman & Dawbarn. Then the party left for Kingston, Jamaica, curtailing their stay there because of a 'terrible hurricane' and proceeding straight to the IUA Mexico Assembly. Although only a small part of Matthew's complex schedule, for the Trinidad archi-tects the visit was of overwhelming sym-bolic importance: Lewis exultantly wrote immediately afterwards to Massey that

> Sir Robert's visit here was a historical one, as it was the first time that a president of the RIBA and IUA ever vis-ited our shores. To the Architects' Society of Trinidad and Tobago, this was the most important event that has taken place since the founding of the Society.[123]

On a visit such as this, Matthew was in effect acting as a quasi-official agent of decolonisation. But he was careful to bal-ance this activity with equivalent efforts on the Cold War front, through a con-stant stream of visits and contacts in the socialist bloc. Of all his Soviet friends, Georgi Orlov, later IUA Vice-President and President, ultimately became the closest: they were not only strong allies during the trying years of the secretary-generalship of Henri Eddé (see Chapter 13) but collab-orated occasionally on other projects, such as an Arts Council of Great Britain project in 1967 to host an exhibition of Constructivist art. By contrast, Matthew's Czech contacts, stemming largely from the 1967 IUA Congress at Prague, caused him growing worry as the Soviet invasion of August 1968 unfolded. In April he was gaily corresponding with Vaclav Gekan, an engineer at the Czech embassy in Iraq, on multi-storey building construction, but by September there was anxious cor-respondence with Stanislav Trubacek, a young architect just returned home from visiting London and Edinburgh.[124]

'The oval ball': Matthew in Romania

Matthew made great efforts to ensure that he was not tied in his east–west con-tacts to the 'Soviet bloc', by pursuing a wider, more diverse pattern of détente. In 1965, for example, he began, initially under IUA auspices, a prolonged and mutually constructive engagement with the architectural profession in Romania, whose government, newly led from that year by Nicolae Ceaucescu, had set out the promise of a more liberal attitude to art and culture, and a more autonomous foreign policy line. Initially, Matthew's invitation to Romania was a straightfor-ward cultural-exchange matter, promoted by the Romanian Institute for Cultural Relations with Foreign Countries, who twice wrote to him in 1964 and 1965 inviting him, in his capacity as IUA President, for a 15-day all-expenses-paid visit to inspect the Romanian system of architectural education.[125] Pleading pres-sure of IUA work, Matthew cut the visit to one week and deferred it to March 1966, by which time he could draw on the experience of a similar visit by *AR* editor J M Richards: his tour had focused both on modern housing and planning, and on rural medieval churches and conserva-tion, and many of his hosts, and the same general subject matter, also featured in Matthew's trip.[126]

На трибуне докладчик Конгресса Лян Сы-чэн
(Китайская Народная Республика)

11.20 Liang Sicheng speaking at the 1958 IUA Moscow congress. (USSR IUA Section/Gosstroiizdat 1960)

Sandwiching his Romanian expedition incongruously (but typically) between two far-flung extremes – external examining in Khartoum, and his regular early April trip to Islamabad – Matthew arrived in Bucharest laden with boxes of lecture slides of GLC housing to show the Romanians. A prior briefing from the British Embassy had alerted him to attacks by Ceaucescu against 'architectonic monotony' in housing, at a recent nationwide 'Building Workers' Confer-ence'.[127] Met by President Moiescu and Vice-President Livizeanu of the Romanian architects' institute, he was treated to a well-coordinated mixture of visits to modern housing – generally following CIAM open-plan *Zeilenbau* layouts – and to architectural-professional and educational subjects. A young Romanian architect/planner representative on the UN Committee on Housing, Building and Planning, Alexandru Budisteanu, acted as his personal guide throughout, and more senior figures, such as Professor Ascanio Damian (rector of the Bucharest University School of Architecture) and Nicolae Badescu (head of the State Committee for Building, Architecture and Planning) made appearances as appropriate. The modern tour subjects were combined with a more 'traditional' architectural element. Here, his hosts had also done their homework thoroughly, as the subjects were not medieval churches but Matthew's beloved vernacular build-

ings.[128] Matthew was carried away by enthusiasm for the high value given in Romania to this 'cultural asset' – including 'magnificent drawings' prepared by vernacular expert Professor Ionescu, and for the way in which government regional architectural offices were striving to foster 'strong regional characteristics' in rural building, and 'carry on the feeling of tradition, but using the most modern of techniques and materials'. The work of Nicolae Porumbescu, for example, at Suceava and Baia Mare, combined a concrete Brutalist-style plasticity with carved wood and abstract peasant motifs blown up to a large scale, in a manner reminiscent of some of Wright's 'regionalist' works; Porumbescu was a vocal advocate of greater 'specificity' and 'particularisation' within Modernism.[129] On his return, Matthew acclaimed Romania as 'likely to make a great contribution in the immediate future of international architecture': in Romania, perhaps, his old 1950s ideal of a 'national' or 'local' Modernism, now unfashionable in Britain, could still be realised. He admitted, too, that his feelings of warmth towards his hosts had been especially stirred by the discovery of the strong tradition of rugby football in Romania, with Professor Damian being an ex-international: 'Somehow, devotion to the oval ball makes a cultural link of an unexpected kind!'[130]

Immediately, Matthew sought to give practical direction to this enthusiasm by vigorously developing the already strong Romanian input into the IUA housing efforts.[131] In early July, between meetings of the ILO Assessors in Geneva, Matthew paid a flying visit back to Bucharest at Damian's invitation, to attend an IUA housing colloquium organised by Budisteanu, who by then had become a particular protégé in international housing matters. After staying with Robert and Lorna at Keith during a spell researching a Glasgow University report on Euro-pean housing, Budisteanu was successfully nominated by Matthew to a newly created post of head of research in the Training and Information Section of

Crooks's UNCHBP in New York – an appointment that, in effect, allowed Matthew to make a direct and personal contribution to the diversification of international goodwill in one of his most favourite fields of work.[132] In late 1967 Budisteanu wrote to update Matthew on developments since the beginning of his 'completely new life in the US'. After getting his UN job and marrying a young chemical engineering graduate, he had moved first to Israel, to monitor a regional development project, and then to the New York office, where he had to chair experts' meetings in housing and town planning, and visited Expo 67 to study Habitat.[133] Apart from this specific follow-up, Matthew's visits left him with an enduring network of Romanian architect friends, and led ultimately to a further visit in 1971.

Exploring Maoist China

September 1964 witnessed an even more daring attempt by Matthew at creative east–west engagement, when, again *ex officio* as IUA President, he led a small delegation to visit the People's Republic of China: the party consisted of himself and Arthur Ling, accompanied by Aidan, Janet and Sylvia. The invitation stemmed from the Chinese Society of Architects; the prime mover, naturally, was Matthew's close IUA ally, Vice-President Yang Tingbao. Aidan and Sylvia joined the trip from Japan (as part of their round-the-world study tour) while Ling came from New Zealand. For Matthew, the trip, from 7 to 23 September, formed the first half of a more extended schedule, flying initially from London to Hong Kong, and continuing at the end of the expedition to a CAA meeting in Singapore (on 25 September), followed by an assessment meeting to the New Delhi School of Architecture on 4–6 October and Islamabad on 7–10 October – arriving back in London at 9.30 a.m. on 13 October and travelling straight to a late morning RIBA policy meeting!

Matthew's two chief hosts in the PRC were Yang himself and Liang Sicheng, head of the architecture school at Tsinghua University. Yang (1901–82) was one of a group of around 15 Chinese architects trained in the US Beaux Arts system in the early 20th century. He established China's first university architectural course at Nanjing in 1927; after the 1949 revolution, which paradoxically fossilised rather than overthrew the Beaux Arts influence, he devoted himself mainly to teaching. Liang, a contemporary of Yang's at the University of Pennsylvania, established China's second university architecture course at Shenyang in 1928, followed in 1947 by a department at Tsinghua, and although (unlike Yang) he was later targeted in the Cultural Revolution purges, he continued to hold his chair until his death in the early 1970s; a distinguished historian as well as architect, he devoted special efforts to unearthing a 'classical language' of traditional Chinese architecture.[134]

The trip had two main components: a week based in Beijing, hosted by Liang, and five days around Shanghai, hosted by Yang. With the relatively closed character of China, even before the Cultural Revolution, the party made a considerable impression wherever it went. Sylvia recalled it as 'a most extraordinary trip: everywhere we went, there were three cars full of people, with a great crowd of hangers on. Aidan, Janet and I were always in the last car, and so were always covered in dust!'[135] As recorded in his frank and detailed diary notes on the trip – the last time in his life that he would resurrect his old schooldays passion for detailed chronicling – Matthew's reaction to both of his main hosts was characterised by conflicting elements: on the one hand, a positive combination of personal admiration and public diplomatic goodwill; on the other, a marked lack of empathy for the likely psychological pressures on influential professional people within an authoritarian system, or on the populace as a whole within a country that had recently undergone the devastating experience of the government-organised 'Great Famine' (1958–61), in which 38 million people had died. The same subtle gap between intentions and prejudices characterised the entire trip: Matthew's determination to use the visit to 'promote peaceful collaboration' and his unquenchable curiosity about other cultures and hankering for 'vernacular' authenticity conflicted, as we shall see, with his visceral revulsion against 'Third World' physical squalor, and his slightly dehumanised view of citizens of totalitarian states.[136] Most mid-20th-century social reformists brought up in the last decades of British imperialism lived out similar tensions, whether articulated consciously or not. This conflict in no way vitiated their high ideals, but rather threw them into sharper relief.

Passing into China at Guangzhou (7–10 September), where they were hosted by 'the elderly Professor Lin', the party experienced its first full-scale official visit, to a porcelain factory – where they were received with

great ceremony, with tea, and interminable speeches about how much everything had improved under communism. Soon we would get very used to these, but on this first occasion eventually Robert couldn't resist mischievously interjecting, 'You've been making the best porcelain in the world for several thousand years – I can't imagine Chairman Mao has made any difference to that!' The poor interpreter nearly choked!

On arriving at Beijing airport on the tenth, Matthew's initial impression of Liang was highly favourable: 'Highly intelligent and not at all bigoted – speaking perfect English – a wonderfully active man of 64, not strong physically, thin as a sheet and tiny, walking with a stick, but alive as a squirrel!'[137] With Liang as guide, the party toured a mixture of ancient and new buildings, but unlike the Romanian situation, where new housing and planning seemed both 'modern' and related to 'vernacular regional' culture, the built environment in China was too polarised for Matthew to be able to arrive at any overall synthesising appreciation. Inspired by Liang's enthusiasm,

Matthew instead focused his admiration on the landscaping and picturesque grouping of elite palaces, whose landscaping chimed in with his own agglomerative approach. Humbler 'vernacular' buildings, owing to their association with a poverty and squalor unknown in Europe, posed a more awkward dilemma, as he recorded in visiting an old village of courtyard houses on 13 September near the Great Wall: 'If these had been clean and well-kept, they would have been charming ... as it is, they are rather revolting ... with messy, disordered and dirty rooms.'[138]

In contrast to Romania, all modern Chinese architectural production and design, including the work of Liang's department, still remained wedded to the Beaux Arts approach, whose products (despite their resemblance to his own monumental student projects) now met with Matthew's almost undiluted scorn. Modern Beijing, he claimed, had 'no buildings of distinction': of the ten ' prestige buildings' constructed in the late 1950s, Matthew recorded sceptically the claim that their erection took only ten months, and noted of the People's Congress Hall that the 'detail was of a mixed variety ... Chinese and classical in an unhappy blend'. Inspecting the projects of the municipal 'Beijing Building Design Institute', Matthew commented in his diary that their 'architectural character varied enormously from Chinese, Russian, heavy Modern and nondescript ... out-of-date European models, flats based on pre-war English models.' Sylvia Matthew recalled that

Robert looked at these plans, and spotted immediately that they were lifted straight from the LCC, before his time: the only difference was that in London, the whole flat was for one family, whereas in China, there was one family in each *room*!

Touring a furniture exhibition at a joinery works, Matthew noted 'a deplorable standard of design ... based on the worst of European models ... but outdoing some of our most vulgar lines!' Undeterred,

Matthew and Sylvia pressed on (in spare moments) with the usual search for 'folk' artefacts, noting on 16 September that he had 'at last' picked up a worthwhile collection of baskets – 'an unwieldy package to carry around'.[139]

Matthew's tours were interspersed with official engagements, including a dinner with a government minister at which a letter of greetings from Vago was handed over, and a session on planning, chaired by Ling, in which preservation of old buildings was a key topic. The evening of 14 September included an outing to a 'revolutionary opera', which, he recorded, was 'a real pantomime – typical propaganda – clapping is only at a few stirring sentiments on the party line'. Liang seemed 'obviously greatly impressed – it is unimaginable in England, but one can see that where most of the people are childlike in outlook a pantomime with a moral is bound to be successful.' Strenuously trying to balance this liberal Western prejudice, however, Matthew noted that contemporary British drama, with its more cynical outlook, 'to a keen Communist foreigner, must reflect a sad and sometimes hopeless state of society'. More generally, Matthew found difficulty in suppressing a mounting impatience at the excesses of totalitarian propaganda: 'Forced labour is said to be unknown, except in prison, but it is not clear who goes to prison, and why,' and 'there are said to be no flies now in China!' Slightly baffled, Matthew noted that Liang

> defended Stalin stoutly – convinced world revolution inevitable for all countries – even highly intelligent people like Liang cannot picture the British situation with a stable government representing the bulk of the people through Parliament – the picture of the capitalist countries is still a standard one of exploitation of the rich, oppression and domination by the upper classes, and inevitable exploitation of colonial people.[140]

At Shanghai the party was met by Yang, who, Matthew noted with dismay, was as susceptible as Liang to the 'belief, common even among the most intelligent and experienced architects, that there is a natural law affecting the development of societies, and that this will inevitably lead to universal Communism'. Sylvia recalled Yang as 'slightly brasher' than the 'delightful, elderly' Liang. Again, there was the mixture of traditional elite architecture, such as the temples and landscape architecture of Soochow, with modern architectural and industrial efforts, and revolutionary operas and dinners in the evening. Matthew argued that some traditional architecture 'seems to give the basis of a development of modern architecture – if they would not concentrate so much on European precedent'. Exploring the 'teeming' back streets of Shanghai with Aidan, followed by an 'army of children', Matthew recorded that the total British population of Shanghai was now 35 – a 'pathetic ghost of imperial days!'[141]

Returning eventually to Hong Kong, Matthew recorded his surprise at the 'sudden change from the Communist situation to luxury capitalist [society] – most marked in the appearance of the women – no pigtails and school clothes here'. And once back in Britain and composing notes on the tour, Matthew began to edit and reinterpret these raw experiences, with his instinctive hankering for 'fairness' and balance.[142] He mounted, jointly with Ling, an RIBA lecture on the tour in January 1965 (and a subsequent *AJ* special article), accompanied by several hundred slides and an 8 mm film taken by Aidan. In this lecture he carefully concealed his own relatively sceptical personal views behind a more diplomatic and relativistic front. For example, he argued that what might seem 'intolerable ... propaganda' in one culture could seem 'natural, even desirable' in another. He spoke of the 'overwhelming sense of commitment to the National Cause', the 'new morality', the well-nourished children and lack of beggars, and the unequalled participation of women in 'National Affairs'. Whatever Matthew's private reactions, here in public he politely argued that the 'group-decision' political formula involved 'no coercion', but, rather, indicated general 'acceptance of a regime that is strong enough to hold together an immense and diversified country and pull it up by its own bootstraps'. But in a later article, while praising the Chinese 'will to get things done, and the knowledge of what had to be done', he insisted that his deepest impression had been an architectural one – that of the Chinese 'vernacular', which he hailed as being 'at least as beautiful as that of Greece and Rome, and far more lasting' – although one might incidentally remark that, if the 'vernacular' could embrace even Graeco-Roman classicism, it could include almost anything![143]

RMJM International: Islamabad and US urban renewal

Occasionally, Matthew's international network of contacts spawned a potential project of such a scale as to demand its transformation into an RMJM project – with all the usual consequent problems and challenges of long-distance coordination with local collaborators and officialdom.[168] The early and mid 1960s saw the beginnings of two widely contrasting initiatives of this type: a commission to participate in the planning and design of the new capital of Pakistan, Islamabad; and the beginnings of a campaign, which ultimately proved abortive in the early 1970s, to capitalise on the intense, but short-lived, US interest in planned urban renewal.

Although neither of these two projects fully developed in the way Matthew hoped, it was the Islamabad initiative that bore the more substantial fruit. The designation and early development of Islamabad was largely the result of decisions taken by Pakistan's dominant leader during the late 1950s and 1960s, Field Marshal Mohammad Ayub Khan. First commander-in-chief of the Pakistan army, he seized power in 1958 and, after several years of martial law, introduced a presidential democracy in June 1962, sweeping the polls in the 1965 elections. To emphasise the reformist dynamism and military efficiency of his rule, Ayub

initiated a whirlwind-like period of building and development activity, including a five-year plan for architecture and a massive, US-sponsored refugee housing project at Korangi Township, Karachi. Here, alongside government architect Zahir-ud-Din, design responsibility for the masterplan had been allocated by the government to Constantinos Doxiadis (1913–75), the prominent Greek architect-planner, who had first come to its attention as a speaker at Tyrwhitt's 1954 low-cost housing conference at New Delhi, and as the mastermind of a vast 1955–6 proposal for a comprehensive housing programme for all of Iraq. The building of 14,000 basic 'nucleus' houses on a rigid grid layout at Korangi in six months (1959–60) was a remarkable achievement, but Doxiadis's success in establishing himself in Pakistan also owed much to a late 1950s commission to build part of Lahore University, which he allegedly gained by undercutting the fees of another consultant, Raglan Squire of London.[144] Thus ensconced in Ayub's favour, Doxiadis then moved quickly to secure the planning consultancy for the next, and grandest, project of Ayub's rule – the building of Pakistan's new capital. Up to 1958, Raglan Squire, in association with chief government architect M A Mirza, had been engaged in inconclusive planning studies for sites in or near the post-1947 capital, Karachi.[145] In early 1959, however, a commission under Major-General Yahya Khan decided that the new capital should be built not in Karachi, with its poor climate and (in Ayub's view) corrupt moral culture, but on the Potwar plateau near Rawalpindi. In September 1959 the government established a Federal Capital Commission to prepare a Master Plan for the new city, which was officially named Islamabad in February 1960. Islamabad was strikingly located, some nine miles northeast of the city of Rawalpindi, at the edge of the mountains, its 25 square miles lying within a wider planned capital zone of 350 square miles, at an elevation of 1,500–2,000 feet and occupied by natural terraces.[146]

At first, after Squire's associate, William Whitfield, had spent some effort doing drawings for a parliament building for a Karachi site, Squire was approached by the Pakistan government to undertake the Islamabad masterplan, but he turned down the commission in disillusionment at working in Pakistan. In late 1959, with Doxiadis hard at work on Korangi, he was introduced to Yahya Khan, and 'was quick to offer his services to the Federal Capital Commission free of cost as the chief coordinator'.[147] As we shall see later in this chapter, Doxiadis set out, Geddes style, to classify all possible permutations of urban development within a 'scientific' framework using a bewildering range of Greek-derived jargon names, while insisting on the need to acknowledge local cultural preferences. Doxiadis Associates' Master Plan and Master Programme, presented to the newly appointed site development authority, the Capital Development Authority (CDA), in May 1960, and in refined form in October 1960, envisaged Islamabad as the first practical application of Ekistics on a city scale. The particular ekistic model on which it would be based was that of the 'Dynapolis', by which was meant a city optimised for movement through a basically linear plan – in the case of Islamabad, spreading out in a southwesterly wedge parallel to the hills, from the fixed focus of a triangular area of national public buildings at the northeast – and through provision of a modular, ever-extensible grid of fast highways totally segregated from all pedestrian traffic; the existing city of Rawalpindi would be contained within a square extension zone to the south. The 'Dynapolis' concept reflected the strong emphasis among many post-CIAM urbanists – such as the 'Team 10' group, Kenzo Tange (in his 1965 rebuilding plan for earthquake-devastated Skopje), or the planners of Cumbernauld New Town – on fast road transport axes as a key element in a more dynamic, less diagrammatic city. Doxiadis's descriptions of Islamabad echoed some of the rhetoric of the American writer Melvin Webber, and

argued that the Dynapolis model would 'avoid the mistakes of the traditional static settlement and would allow unimpeded growth in the future.'[148] But despite the novelty of the rhetoric of dynamism and movement and Doxiadis's insistence on a mobile, low-rise configuration rather than any kind of high-rise monumentality, the 'Dynapolis' grid was still basically a CIAM concept, related to Le Corbusier's more static grand plan at Chandigarh: the relentless, unitary, southwestward march of 2,200 yard wide 'Class 5 Community' sectors, each with hierarchical subdivision of roads and functions and communal central area, was linked to a strict segregation of uses into eight zones or sectors, including administrative, diplomatic, institutional, industrial, services, commercial, university, public housing, green belt and national park.[149]

But in Ayub's mind the overriding aim was for speed, to make Islamabad 'the fastest built capital in the world'; and by mid 1961 the CDA was beginning to focus on the need to begin design of individual sections of Doxiadis's plan. Already, Doxiadis himself, 'with his extreme enthusiasm for the project', was busy preparing plans for some of the key public buildings, as well as designing the low-income single-storey housing in the first residential area. But it was clear that here he was overreaching himself, and Zahir-ud-Din, newly appointed as Director of Planning for Islamabad, pressured the 'young and energetic' Secretary to the CDA, Akhtar Mahmood, to widen the field. The initial preference was to approach 'a single architect of great eminence' to design the detailed layout and major buildings. But Le Corbusier was ruled out for obvious political reasons (as architect of Chandigarh), Gropius and Tange could only promise the involvement of junior colleagues, and so, instead, Zahir and Mahmood decided to try to form 'a group of like-minded architects' of second-rank international standing. Letters were sent to Gio Ponti, Marcel Breuer, Arne Jacobsen, Sven Markelius – and Robert Matthew. All were figures

Commonwealth of design

11.21 Matthew inspects the future site of Islamabad on 28 September 1961 in the company of the CDA Secretary, Akhtar Mahmood (on right) and Zahir-ud-Din (in his role as Chief Architect and Planning Officer; at centre). (EULMC)

admired by Zahir for their sensitivity and restraint, and Matthew was known to him through his 1957 Jinnah Memorial jury work. Architecturally, the hope was to offset the universal Modernism of the highway grid with an 'Islamic' character, oblique and allusive rather than literal and overt: in early 1964 Ayub Khan himself demanded that the character of the capital city must be 'the sum total of the aspirations, the life and the contributions of the people of the whole of Pakistan'.[150]

The first and most urgent need was for an elite 'hostel', 'Pakistan House', to house the advance guard of the civil service elite, and for this the CDA in 1962 appointed the Italian architect Gio Ponti, who worked in Islamabad mainly through his partner, Alberto Rosselli: the use of explicit 'Islamic' motifs on Pakistan House was a disappointment to Zahir, although it pleased the CDA leadership.[151] For the further design of the residential sections from 1962 to 1966 the CDA turned to a team of expatriate architects, planners and engineers headed by chief architect Gerald Brigden, whose designs moved away from Doxiadis's rigid terraced layouts towards a more 'regional' planning in courtyard layouts, influenced by contemporary British low-rise high-density practice.[152] Derek Lovejoy & Associates were appoint-

ed landscape architects, with lavish funds for afforestation of the 'great cyclorama' of the city's setting, hillside consolidation, hard urban landscaping, and water gardens. The overall zonal planning of the city would be the responsibility of Zahir's own staff, but for the symbolically all-important Administrative Sector, containing all the city's main national institutions, the CDA approached Matthew to act in conjunction with Doxiadis as architect-planner, or 'Chief Coordinator of the Administrative Sector' – with the intention that the individual buildings in the area would be divided up between Ponti, Matthew and Marcel Breuer.

Doxiadis's plan had allocated the Administrative Sector a hilly site in the form of a mile and a half long rectilinear strip fronting the northeast side of the main northwest–southeast urban boulevard, National Avenue, opposite the point where Capital Avenue met it at right angles. On this strip would have to be fitted the President's Palace (axially located at the northeast end of the Capital Avenue vista), Supreme Court, National Mosque, Secretariat (ministry) group, Amphitheatre, and a range of national cultural institutions – National Library, National Museum, National Archives, Armed Forces Museum – as well as processional routes and grand areas for public assembly. To coordinate a group of diverse, eminent architects to design these buildings would require 'superlative diplomacy', to tax even Matthew's skills. In Lovejoy's opinion, Matthew 'had a difficult task, welding the prima donnas of the Administrative Sector into a team'. At first, the main tension was with Doxiadis, who 'resented the intervention of Sir Robert as principal coordinating architect', but Matthew managed very soon to turn a negative into a positive relationship. Zahir recalled that, from this point, Doxiadis was 'allowed only to remain as principal master planner', while Matthew became 'coordinating architect ... the central team leader of architects working on various projects'. The grouping of the President's House and flanking parliamentary and secretariat blocks, 'as it finally emerged, is largely due to Sir Robert's efforts'. Aidan recalled that 'We didn't have to work directly together with Doxiadis at Islamabad. He was largely dealing with the roads and the housing, while we were liaising mainly with people like Gio Ponti.'[153]

On 28 September 1961, two weeks after Ponti's first visit to discuss the design of Pakistan House, Matthew arrived for a familiarisation visit to Rawalpindi, and was shown the site and introduced by Zahir to the CDA hierarchy. Perhaps naturally contrasting this scenic, *tabula rasa* setting with the more intractable challenge that currently faced him in Belfast, Matthew exclaimed that, 'architecturally, it is a wonderful problem'. He was also offered the first opportunity to design individual public buildings within the zone, and, characteristically, replied that he was 'not particularly interested' in designing the capital's most monumental set pieces, and would prefer to undertake 'buildings within the cultural complex, which could be designed on a human scale: the National Museum, National Archives and National Armed Forces Museum'.[154] By early November Wazir Ali Shaikh, newly appointed CDA Chairman, wrote to Matthew formally offering him the commission to design the 100,000 sq ft National Library and the 180,000 sq ft National Museum – as well as plan the sector as a whole. In a significant indication of the personal nature of the commission, the letter was addressed to him at the University of Edinburgh. Two months after his initial reconnaissance, Matthew returned in November to Rawalpindi, this time with Breuer, for meetings and site inspections with Doxiadis and Shaikh, at which Matthew stressed the need to control interim development; but by January 1962 Breuer had withdrawn, saying he could not reach a 'satisfactory working arrangement' with the CDA.

On his return, Matthew began to make arrangements to delegate the day-to-day execution of the project. It would

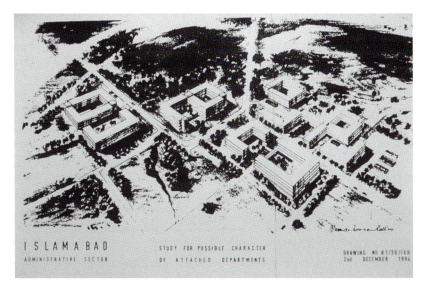

11.22 December 1964 RMJM study for layout of 'Attached Departments' in Secretariat extension zone. (RMJM)

be handled by a combination of Percy Johnson-Marshall's team in Edinburgh for strict planning matters, and Maurice Lee in the London RMJM office to oversee direct negotiations with the CDA and other architects. Lee was a natural choice, as he had been based on the Northwest Frontier in 1945, spoke fluent Urdu, and was always eager to work on projects in the East. Following his first, extended visit to Rawalpindi in late January 1962, Lee wrote a substantial report on the prospects of the project, which now included additionally the design of the 750,000 sq ft National Archives and the 90,000 sq ft Armed Forces Museum – with the aim of creating a unified cultural centre that could, in Zahir's words, 'serve as a show window for the contemporary national arts'. Potentially disruptive local constraints, Lee argued, included the possibility of a coup and repudiation of the contract – against which the best precaution was to ration the time spent on the project, with fees paid in advance; as it was, arguably, 'Commonwealth aid', it might also be possible to get a government guarantee.[156]

But, for the moment, the tightness of the schedule allowed no time for caution, as Ponti's partner and son-in-law, Rosselli, was already at work designing his secretariat buildings (eight low but massive L-shaped blocks); to allow work on the first four of them to begin in early 1963,

415

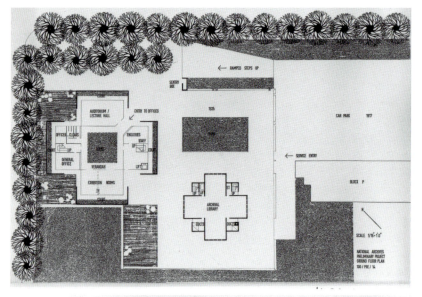

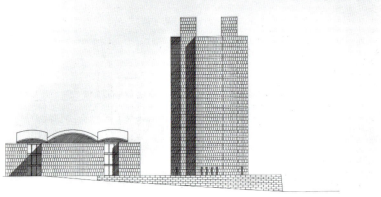

11.23 National Archives, Islamabad: 1969 ground floor plan and elevation. (RMJM)

northwest would be formed out of Rosselli's L-shaped blocks.[158] All public buildings would be accessible by a pedestrian network, including a high-level esplanade paralleling the north-west–southeast National Avenue on either side of the central square. Immediately facing the Administrative Sector on the other side of National Avenue was a relatively densely zoned strip of building areas for lesser public institutions, commercial and residential buildings, with low-density housing sectors stretching to the southwest.

By July 1963 it had been decided to commission Louis Kahn to design the President's House and, later, by early 1964, Arne Jacobsen for the National Assembly. By July 1964, with Matthew's section plan now fully entrenched, some of the secretariat blocks were reaching seven storeys, over 3,000 dwellings had been completed, and vital infrastructure – including a huge sewage plant – had been put in place. In a reflective article following two visits of inspection by President Ayub, Zahir mused that despite the CDA's attempt at a synthesis of modernity and 'Islamic tradition', 'reflecting the spirit rather than the substance' through 'bold engineering' and abstract 'surface treatment and decoration', Rosselli's Secretariat buildings were still 'fiercely criticised' by many government administrators and politicians as 'too Western in style', with their massive stair towers imparting an abstract rhythm and their facades composed of precast modular units within an *in situ* frame.[159]

By August 1964, with Doxiadis taking something of a back seat, Jacobsen, too, had decided on withdrawal, owing to the impossibility of building his 'sleek and serene' design without intrusive modifications by the CDA.[160] Matthew was now facing the likelihood that the National Assembly building, too, would be passed to Kahn: he warned Doxiadis that Kahn was 'a difficult man to "coordinate" – he was in London a few days ago and again went well outside the terms of his reference – one must expect this!' But

Matthew's section plan would have to be agreed by Doxiadis and approved by the CDA in September 1962. Correspondence with Ponti, Doxiadis and Shaikh became virtually continuous, and by March 1962 Matthew had already produced an initial sketch layout, and Lee was busy getting a contour model made for consideration by CDA and the President himself.[157] The focus of Matthew's spaciously disposed sector – in Doxiadis's words, the 'brain centre and pulsating heart' of the city – was an L-plan group comprising the President's House (Aiwan-e-Sadr) terminating the Capital Avenue vista on its hill above Parliament Square, and cultural buildings on the southeast side, planned mostly in loosely rectangular form with central courtyards. The secretariat to the

Matthew persevered in his attempts at oversight, and in January 1965, for example, attended a high-level government meeting in Rawalpindi to examine Kahn's preliminary plans for the President's House and estate, and to fine-tune the Central Area of the Administrative Sector. Kahn had revised his plans for the central area by generally increasing the buildings' scale, while incorporating a broad ramped approach from National Avenue to Central Square, freeing the pedestrian esplanade from any processional function. And in March 1965 he prepared an addendum to the Administrative Sector Development Plan, earmarking roughly 150 acres for expansion of the Secretariat Area. The same report proposed detailed design controls over street furniture and traffic signs, and set out schematic plans for Matthew's own 'cultural buildings group', including the four-storey, slab-like National Museum and Library, a three-storey stepped slab for the Armed Forces Museum, and a four-storey, more expressionistic, fan-shaped Arts Council. The furthest advanced of all his cultural projects was the National Archives, located overlooking the Esplanade in the middle of a line of L-shaped secretariat blocks. Following intensive discussions with the Director of Archives in October 1964, plans were finalised for a one- and two-storey T-shaped administrative and public reception block with central courtyard, adjoined at the rear by a multi-storey archival library stack block, with eleven floors above and four below ground level. The stack block comprised four vertical elements of slightly different height, to maintain the building's presence among the massive secretariat blocks. Subsequently, both the public and stack block were slightly heightened – the latter to 14 storeys.[161]

By this stage, Maurice Lee accompanied Matthew on almost all his Islamabad trips, and recalled the difficulties, as well as Matthew's incidental activities:

Percy did much of the planning from Edinburgh, while on the cultural buildings we were supposed to design, we were so badly briefed, I often woke up sweating! The trips always included boring periods when nothing was happening, and typically, Robert always wanted to keep going at times like those, and keep touring round looking everywhere for the 'vernacular': in his rather Arts and Crafts way, he was always terribly interested in the way people built. We'd go into villages, and I could chat up the locals in Urdu, while Robert took photos or bought

417

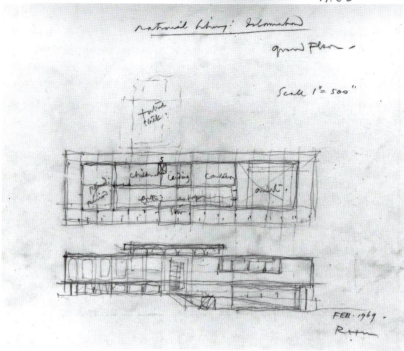

national library: Islamabad

ground Plan —

Scale 1" = 500"

FEB. 1969.
R.M.

11.25 Sketch for National Library by Matthew, February 1969. (EULMC)

baskets – he was a great collector of vernacular craft techniques. People often thought we were daft! And sometimes he got us into difficulty. Once, for instance, we took a plane to Peshawar, and I took him up the Khyber Pass in a hissing, boiling, broken-down taxi we picked up in Peshawar. Half way along the route he persuaded the very reluctant driver to stop so that we could photograph a village. Normally, Robert and his camera had a magnetism for the children, and they just followed him around like the Pied Piper, but on this occasion we were mobbed and stoned by them, and I believe it was only my few remembered words of Pushtu for greeting which surprised them long enough for a lull which allowed our escape. I doubt, though, if Robert actually noticed what was going on – certainly he got his pictures, as always![162]

Islamabad eventually became the formal capital of Pakistan in 1967. Throughout the later 1960s Matthew stayed in fairly close touch with affairs there, with Zahir as his main contact.[163] From the sidelines he observed the fluctuating fortunes of the architects of the chief public

buildings, with Kahn rapidly falling from favour owing to his argumentative and abrasive manner.[164] In November 1966 Kahn was replaced as architect for the Presidential Palace by Edward D Stone, then working for the Pakistan government to design the Pakistan Institute for Nuclear Science and Technology, and who had been lobbying since 1959 for a share of the Islamabad project. His monumentalising approach evoked Islamic motifs far more literally, including vast arched canopies, and ultimately proved more attuned to the client's needs; he was eventually also assigned the commissions for the National Museum, Foreign Office and Supreme Court.[165]

We shall see in Chapter 13 how Matthew's involvement with Islamabad ultimately petered out, in frustrating circumstances, in the early 1970s. Similar high hopes and eventual frustrations, within a sharply contrasting economic and political context, also applied to the Edinburgh office's other major overseas initiative of the 1960s – the beginnings of a protracted attempt to develop links between Matthew's university and RMJM activities, and institutions in the United States, with the aim of exploiting the growing US interest in 'urban renewal'. In general, the early 1960s were a time of close US–British relations in general, with Britain still suspicious of the Continent. That closeness was fully reflected in architectural and planning debates, where a critical lubricant was provided by the financial support for British research programmes offered by US charitable institutions.[166]

Although, even at the height of President Johnson's 'Great Society' drive of the mid 1960s, the US never attempted to construct a comprehensive welfare state on the European model, the three post-war decades nevertheless saw some vigorous governmental attempts to promote planning of the built environment. Following pioneering interwar initiatives such as the efforts of Clarence Stein in New York State, and the regeneration strategies of the Tennessee Valley Authority, and moves towards integrated urban renewal in 1930s and 1940s housing legislation, a fully fledged urban renewal strategy was set out in the 1965 Housing and Urban Development Act, which established a federal Department of Housing and Urban Development (HUD) as a Cabinet-level agency. At first, however, the role of HUD was largely a hortatory one of setting standards, and it seemed to many to be a 'benevolent, but apparently toothless' research and development organisation, not unlike the Building Research Station.[1667] Mostly, US urban renewal efforts were privately led, and focused on the radical regeneration of decayed areas with prestige civic, cultural and commercial development, such as the multilevel Penn Center, whose 'traffic architecture' helped inspire the British work of Colin Buchanan (especially the 1963 report *Traffic and Towns*); public housing, in contrast to Britain, was seen in utilitarian and strictly circumscribed terms. From a European social-democratic perspective the urban challenges of capitalist America seemed of an extreme, polarised character: indeed, in mid 1970 Matthew provocatively compared them to the urban problems of Africa.[168]

Ever since his 1949 building delegation trip Matthew had maintained close links with individual key American architects and planners, such as Stein, Mumford and Wurster. From early 1963 he began a new and more systematic programme of fostering ties, prompted perhaps, paradoxically, by the close negotiations necessitated by the IUA Cuba dispute, and also by a broader feeling that, with Britain's final emergence from wartime austerity into a more affluent society, the capitalist mechanisms of the United States might have something to teach Britain. Matthew's overtures to the USA exploited his authority as PRIBA and PIUA as a way of opening a range of doors. During the period covered by this chapter the emphasis was on learning *from*, and seeking financial support from, America; only after 1969, as we shall see in Chapter 13, did the relationship intensify for a few years into a more active

two-way collaboration. Initially, Matthew's efforts followed two parallel strands: first, a pursuit of academic research and funding ties that could benefit the Edinburgh university department; and, second, a research programme undertaken by Aidan into the efficient organisation of architectural practice and building production – areas in which, as Matthew first discovered on his 1949 trip, the Americans had established a substantial 'lead' over Britain and Europe.

Matthew's interest in the subject was first seriously ignited when he accepted in February 1963 an invitation to lecture on 'American Cities' in the geographical/sociological session of the British Association for American Studies annual conference, to be held in Edinburgh in April. Although he modestly stressed to the organisers that he was 'no expert on American cities', in fact he had maintained over the years a close interest in the subject, and was already well aware, for example, of the revolutionary impact of Jane Jacobs's critiques. But he proceeded initially by extensive consultation and discussion, both with Eleanor Morris in his own department and with Allan Temko, a San Francisco architectural critic and geographer (now London-based) who had recently blazed a trail of criticism of orthodox Modernism in the US. In his lecture Matthew began by dismissing any idea that American urbanism was a purely laissez-faire matter: communal utopianism and collective planning had been central from the beginning, and there was much to learn from the US emphasis on efficiency and adequate investment in city renewal. But Matthew largely echoed Mumford (and Geddes) in his diagnosis of the chief built-environment problem of the American city – not slums or bad housing, but uncontrolled sprawl. With the emergence of the metropolitan region, with its anonymous 'slurbs', 'the city, as we have known it historically, no longer exists. It has become part of a larger urban pattern – a nodal point – one of many – in a vast suburban tract.' During mid 1963 Matthew pursued

11.26 Matthew seen with Hayden B Johnson, Deputy Director of Port Development, at the rooftop helipad of the New York Port Authority headquarters (111 8th Avenue, Manhattan) prior to his helicopter trip to La Guardia Airport on 19 September 1963. (Port of New York Authority)

a range of initial US 'networking' opportunities within Britain and Europe, at a range of events including an Edinburgh University conference on 'Transportation and the Regional City' and discussions brokered by Ministry chief planner J R James on possible US-sponsored planning research (both in June 1963) and Doxiadis's first 'Delos Symposium' on world built- environment problems in July, heavily dominated by American participants.[169]

But Matthew's systematic cultivation of US contacts really got into its stride during his September 1963 transatlantic trip, the focus of which, ironically, was the IUA Havana Congress. Matthew arranged to stay in the north-eastern US for four days en route, packing in an incredible variety of diplomatic and path-breaking activities, in a textbook demonstration of his bulldozer-like energy when on an important overseas tour. Arriving

in New York on the afternoon of 16 September, he travelled straight to Amenia, NY, for dinner with Lewis and Sophie Mumford, and the Steins. Over dinner they discussed planning education and a possible strategy for pursuing grant support for Percy's planning research unit in Edinburgh; although Matthew fully acknowledged the force of Jacobs's 'attack on current city planning and rebuilding', he still felt more naturally at home with regional planners such as Mumford and Stein, who were seen by Jacobs as 'anti-city'.[170] The next day the emphasis shifted to architectural diplomacy, with an official visit to the AIA in Washington, in his RIBA presidential capacity, combined with a brief urban renewal meeting with William Slayton, Federal Commissioner for Urban Renewal, and a lunch in Matthew's honour, hosted by Gutheim, at the Washington Center for Metropolitan Studies, followed by an overnight stay with AIA President J Roy Carroll in Philadelphia for pre-Cuban IUA fence-rebuilding purposes. The next day (the eighteenth) was devoted to a whirlwind tour of architects and planners in Philadelphia, focused especially on the Penn Center as a paradigmatic urban renewal scheme, and including a meeting with its mastermind, Edmund N Bacon, Executive Director of the Philadelphia City Planning Commission. Matthew also squeezed in a short chat with Lou Kahn about Islamabad over lunch.[171] The morning of the ninteenth was spent covering his RIBA and Edinburgh interests, in a protracted but ultimately abortive meeting at the Rockefeller Foundation seeking funding for J R James's urban renewal research strategy. And from lunchtime onwards Matthew became IUA President once again, spending that afternoon and the following morning in inconclusive meetings at the UN Department of Social Affairs discussing how the IUA could help the UN. To round off the trip, and leave him conveniently at La Guardia Airport, Hayden B Johnson, deputy director of the New York Port Authority – a contact made at the June Edinburgh conference – arranged lunch for Matthew at the Port Authority HQ at 111, 8th Avenue, repairing afterwards to the roof for a short but 'very exciting' helicopter ride over the city, flying finally out over the World's Fair site in Queens to the airport, in time to catch his Barbados flight at 3.30 p.m.[172]

Matthew's September 1963 visit left him bubbling with a new enthusiasm for US efficiency, especially in urban reconstruction, but equally enthusiastic about Jacobs's iconoclastic contribution to the debates about urban renewal.[173] In a December 1963 lecture in Yorkshire he acclaimed the Penn Center as 'a pioneering piece' of redevelopment – a 'collaboration on a great scale' between the private and public sectors.[174] Frequent correspondence with Mumford continued, and a visit to Scotland was promised, spurred by Mumford's 'sentimental attachment to Edinburgh, through old Geddes'.[175] But in the immediate after-math of the September trip the initiative for US research passed from Robert to Aidan. Straight after the family's stay in Mexico he and Sylvia were sent by RMJM on a ten-month study tour of the US, working from east to west, with the aim of looking at how American architectural offices operated, sending monthly reports back as well as tactfully putting out feelers for possible collaboration or work for RMJM. In a sense, this was a follow-up of Robert's 1949 productivity tour, channelled through his private practice, and Aidan's involvement in it – and in RMJM in general – was chiefly at Robert's instigation. But although Sylvia opposed Aidan's decision to join the firm, foreseeing the possibility that he might suffer 'reverse discrimination', this initial project went very successfully: Ken Feakes, for instance, recalled that

> Aidan brought back an extremely good study of how to run working drawing programmes: he had systematically studied the working practices of architects such as Yamasaki, SOM, Saarinen, and worked out how much time they spent on design, site supervision, working drawings. He had found that there was a wide difference between the 'design' practices and other more humdrum ones – but that they all had in common a really efficient working drawings system, which could produce full working drawings for any project, however big, in three months![176]

Aidan and Sylvia were also charged with finding vernacular crafts acquisitions for Keith Ingram, especially en route between America and the China trip: in Japan, for example, they found 'lots of lacquer work, baskets and other nice things for the shop'.[177]

The year 1965 saw a fresh flurry of transatlantic diplomacy, focused especially on an invitation to Matthew, still IUA President, to visit the AIA's 97th Convention on 14–18 June. This was held in Washington DC jointly with the 11th Pan-American Congress of Architects, a large gathering of around 1,800 AIA members and 800 from Latin America, on the theme of 'Cities of the New World'. Tipped off by IUA contacts such as Henry Wright that the Pan-American organising association was inefficient and unpopular among both Latin-American and US architects, Matthew put in a powerful pitch for the IUA, as a unique global forum for debating the built environment as a totality; but Vago enviously noted to him that the AIA's budget was 50 times that of the IUA.[178] To coincide with the AIA convention, Matthew took the opportunity to flag up the British social-democratic architectural tradition for a US audience, when he opened an official British photographic exhibition of the work of the LCC. His lecture unabashedly trumpeted the achievements of his old department, arguing that LCC architecture 'might well, in total, be said to be representative of British Urban Architecture today – building mainly for social purposes – with a strong eye to the quality of environment.'[179]

From then on, Matthew maintained a highly variegated range of US contacts – a subtle element of 'Americanisation' in his career that was refreshed annually, as we shall see shortly, by his participation in Doxiadis's 'Delos' symposia, attended by a high proportion of Americans.[180] Matthew's contacts within US landscape architecture were enhanced by his friendship with Ian McHarg, a former DHS architect who, since 1954, had been professor and head of the Landscape Architecture and Regional Planning Department of the University of Pennsylvania; McHarg was a pioneer in expanding the scope of landscape architecture to take in the wider 'planning' aspects of land use.[181] August 1965 even brought a US job offer, from Bernard F Sliger, dean of Louisiana State University, asking whether Matthew would be interested in becoming head of a new school of environmental design at LSU.[182] And even after Matthew was no longer PRIBA or IUA President, he was still used by both organisations in negotiations with the USA – for example in February 1967,

at an NCARB/ARCUK/RIBA meeting to discuss wider inter-recognition between the UK and the USA, he represented both RIBA and IUA. And by 1968 Matthew was focusing ever more closely on contacts at HUD: for example, in August 1968 James A More of the department wrote to him (under his IUA aegis) on behalf of the Kaiser Commission on the rebuilding of depressed urban housing, asking him to organise a visit to Cumbernauld for Howard Moskof, executive director of the Commission, on a forthcoming visit to Scotland.[183]

'The architect as world planner': Robert and Bucky

The 1960s, as a time of loosening up for Matthew in the wake of his earlier, highly focused rise, saw a growing tendency on his part to echo and revisit Geddes's attempted synthesis of the rational and the spiritual. In the last few years of his life this role fully matured, in the form of an enthusiastic espousal of the causes of conservation and environmental activism; but already, in the early 1960s, he was beginning to address environmental issues in an indirect way, by pursuing a supporting, enabling role in relation to two more flamboyant, Geddes-like polymath figures – the American engineer Richard Buckminster Fuller, and the Greek architect Constantinos Doxiadis, leader of the 'Ekistics' movement. In both these cases it is unclear how seriously Matthew took the relationship, or whether he saw Fuller and Doxiadis merely as intriguing mavericks. And in both cases, too, a subtext of the relationship was the further promotion of links with American or Anglophone thinkers and innovators – a tendency that complemented Matthew's energetic east–west and Commonwealth 'post- colonial' diplomacy.

Running throughout the Modern Movement – even 'high' CIAM International Modernism – was a persistent thread of attempts to unite the 'scientific' and the 'artistic' under a banner of multidisciplinary reformism.[184] The contribution of Buckminster Fuller, as a non-architect anchored chiefly in the 'scientific' side of the balance, was a distinctive one, developing utopian speculations based on scientific concepts of innovation and efficiency in a far more bold and specific way than polymaths from the 'artistic' side could have done. There is no space here for a general account of Fuller's life and work, which are dealt with in countless publications. It developed through a succession of overlapping enthusiasms or campaigns, of which the most obvious and salient were the built 'designs' that dominated his activities up to around 1960, from the Dymaxion House of 1927 – a living machine hung from a mast – to the geodesic dome of the 1940s, and, finally, culminating in his US Pavilion at Expo 67.[185] But paradoxically it was not these, but Fuller's more abstract metaphysical proselytising, that forced the pace in his relationship with architecture. These efforts were concerned with ethical as well as natural/scientific issues: the more efficient use of resources, he argued, could help redistribute global inequalities and thus avoid wars, while the resulting rational order, based on advanced communication networks, would echo, and reinforce, the 'sublime regularity' of the universe's wider 'interconnected and unitary' spiritual and even divine order.[186] Fuller combined two trends that were often seen in opposition: a focus on 'third world' redistribution, and a high-technology ethos. In 1964, for example, he predicted that by 1990, to solve the world housing problem, 'we will float large colonies of homes round the world in tensegrity geodesic cloud island spheres taxi-served by helicopters'.[187] Thus, although in many ways he foreshadowed the ecological movement of the 1970s onwards, and wrote explicitly of his World Science Decade (see below) as a 'world human ecology program' in 1963, his technological optimism set him apart from many of the later environmentalists, and instead pointed forward to the electronic communication discourses of the 'Internet age'.

How was all this relevant to Robert Matthew? Chiefly because, by 1961, Fuller was about to launch himself into a new 'network' mission of global coordination, which would require the significant involvement of the architectural profession. He had become convinced that architects (especially idealistic students), being 'professional comprehensivists', were ideal allies in researching and promoting his latest grand initiative – a 'World Science [Design] Decade' (WSD) for the years 1965–75, which would systematically catalogue all the world's natural resources, as a prelude to a radical global upgrading of productivity. Although he had already enlisted the help of the 'radical' journal *Architectural Design* and its editor, Monica Pidgeon, Fuller also identified the IUA as an ideal international gateway to allow him to communicate his ideas to architects worldwide – and, just at that very moment, Matthew was about to assume the presidency of the IUA, at the London conference he himself had helped organise.[188] Although Fuller, typically of people of his generation, emphasised his lack of sympathy for traditional politics, he was also an astute self-publicist who constantly sought out sympathetic people of influence. Thus, from 1961 onwards, Fuller relentlessly set about 'wooing' Matthew.

At the 1961 IUA Congress itself Pidgeon, as a member of the organising committee, invited Fuller to speak, and he turned up at the plenary session with a fully worked-up proposal for WSD, as a 'world re-tooling design programme' under which students would catalogue the 'prime tool network' of total available energy resources. Appealing to architects' grandiosity and utopian zeal, and echoing the technological theme of the 1961 Congress, he pointed forward to 'The Architect as World Planner': 'The architectural profession is not only altruistic enough but it is also prone to take the responsibility of comprehensive design critic,' and was 'able to think regarding such world planning in a manner transcendent of any political bias'. It was *design* reform, not political reform, that must harness young people's zeal, and the next Congress 'should then be almost completely preoccupied with reviewing all such inventories and plans'; this would be 'world news of the first order': from now on, 'the trend of world students will ... be toward becoming architects – that is, comprehensive and cooperative design science artists.'[189]

To Matthew, steeped in the Geddes tradition, with its combination of polymath ethos and fertile jargon, the four-hour discourses of Fuller, the 'mid century polymath, the *uomo universale* of the age', would have seemed familiar territory, and its restless questing for new stimuli would have struck a special chord with him. He was both amused and impressed by Fuller. Later, speaking at the award, to Fuller, of the 1968 RIBA Royal Gold Medal, he interpreted his work in the light of his own growing conversion to environmentalism: Fuller was

> a philosopher in the sense of possessing an inexhaustible concern with the nature of people and things – Citizen of the World, USA Region – his interpretation of the power of design, in a comprehensive sense, in this age, to steer our global space-ship out of its collision course, is a flame to the inspiration of young people.[190]

With the blessing of Matthew as IUA President, and the final approval of the 1961 Congress and 1962 Executive Committee, Fuller persuaded Southern Illinois University at Carbondale to underwrite a research programme for WSD under the executive direction of British sociologist John McHale, and the establishment of a 'World Resources Inventory Office' at the university; some $70,000 of subsidy had been provided by late 1965. Between 1963 and 1967 the office published six volumes.[191]

A key role in Fuller's wooing of Matthew was played by Frank Clark's landscape assistant lecturer at Edinburgh, Laurie Fricker. He had, around 1960, under Fuller's influence, shifted the focus of his considerable idealism from CND to the cause of ecologically oriented environmental design – feeling it

had many potential affinities with landscape architecture. Fuller's proposed alternative term for 'architect' was 'comprehensive (no one problem to be solved by any one discipline) anticipatory design (putting things together) science (taking things apart)'. 'I thought: "That suits me a lot better than "architecture"!' In 1962, he arranged for Fuller to stay at Keith, where his friendship with Matthew developed further: 'Matthew had to carry the baggage of being an architect, yet he could sup with the devil – Fuller! Although he was sceptical intellectually, emotionally he was fascinated by geodesic domes and Fuller's word skeins.' The visits to Keith became a virtually annual event, and Aidan recalled that 'my father and Bucky got on like a house on fire, and Bucky came and stayed with us several times. He and my father would sit outside chewing the fat, and he was delighted with my mother – gave her poems and so on.' In August 1965 Fuller wrote to Matthew that 'I miss you very much. You and Lorna are my youngest grown up friends.' Lorna herself, though, was more sardonic in her judgement, recalling Fuller as 'a dotty fellow who lived in a dome himself, wrote poems, and all that sort of thing!'[192]

But in reality, despite the furious productivity of report writing at Fuller's Carbondale office, the collaboration was very far from smooth. First, from the very beginning, the link with IUA contained the seeds of trouble, as the Paris-led Union, and Vago in particular, were strongly influenced by an essentially Beaux Arts concept of collective dignity, and alarmed not only by Fuller's redefinition of 'design' in ecological rather than material architectural terms, but also by what they saw as his 'American' or 'Anglo-Saxon' individualism and self-promotion: already at the April 1962 Charleroi Executive Committee, a majority of the committee expressed opposition to collaboration with him.[193] Fuller and McHale worked flat out to prepare Volume 1 of the WSD report series for presentation to the 1963 IUA Congress, but the momentum was interrupted by the Havana debacle, where Fuller, having acquiesced meekly in the US government's attempts to undermine the Congress and build up the rival Mexico meeting, found that the latter made no reference to his WSD initiative – which would have been showcased in Cuba – and once again had to proselytise it in a more informal manner.

The emphasis then shifted to the Paris 1965 conference, whose theme was to be 'Education', with Matthew brokering, through the RIBA and IUA, contact with a group of academics in schools of architecture and planning to whip up support for Fuller's initiative. Gardner-Medwin, who chaired the group, was torn between admiration for Fuller's loquacity and caution: 'Nobody at our meeting could be described as enthusiastic about this – there was apprehension that one man, and one country, could try to dominate the Congress.'[194] Others were more sceptical still: following a lengthy discussion with Percy Johnson-Marshall and Fuller, Robert Grieve concluded that 'after four hours, Fuller had said nothing of vital importance that Geddes had not said many years ago', and complained that his report was 'extremely unclear' as to how architectural students could contribute meaningfully to his agenda: their first task, Grieve chided, should be 'to be able to build well, build for the 20th century and master their own discipline.'[195]

By 1965 it had become clear that Fuller's proposed participation in the Paris Congress, with a multimedia exhibition of the findings of the student 'world inventory', had stirred up a hornet's nest of resentment in France, with clashes initially focusing on the specific issue of the amount of space reserved for his display, but with more general francophone/anglophone cultural resentments swirling in the background. On the one hand, the IUA French section, as organisers of the Congress, expressed growing frustration at the fact that Fuller, by March 1965, was seeking an area equal to that for the whole of the reminder of the Congress; they complained to Matthew that there was a danger that 'our Conference and its theme will be entirely submerged and suffocated by this affair which, I must confess, is very unpleasant', and Vago added that 'our friend [Fuller] is certainly becoming somewhat overwhelming!' The issue of payment then became increasingly prominent: Matthew had assured Fuller in February 1964 that the exhibition space would be free of charge, but as his space requirements mushroomed, he was shifted to other potential venues: the Gare d'Orsay, the Hotel Palais d'Orsay, and finally the outdoor spaces of the Tuileries Orangerie. The August 1965 issue of *Architectural Design* complained that Fuller's 'lively' Orangerie display, with its plastic/bamboo structures and displays (contributed largely by English, American and Australian students, from institutions including Nottingham, Reading, the AA, Colorado and Sydney), had been ignored by 'the Beaux Arts organisers' of the Congress.[196]

The hostility between Fuller and the French organisers reached its climax only after the Congress, when Fuller was sent a bill for $836 for rental of a hall at the Hotel Palais d'Orsay for the lecture; he acknowledged that Colin Fournier of the AA had booked the hall for him, but insisted he had been told there would be no charge, and he wrote to Matthew that he was 'shocked and disgusted'. Matthew came down clearly on Fuller's side, and organised, under IUA-UK auspices, a 'whip-round' to raise £300 towards the bill.[197] Ironically, of course, had Fuller been allowed to travel to Havana in 1963, none of this would have happened, as the Cubans would almost certainly have made strenuous efforts to assist Fuller's agit-prop events. At any rate, by early 1966, the IUA presidency having passed from Matthew to Beaudouin, the affair seemed beyond remedy, and Fuller began to use it as a pretext to justify his own growing boredom with the WSD initiative, and his inevitable disillusionment with the architectural profession as a vehicle for his views. In March 1966 he was writing to Matthew in terms very different from his former fulsome praise of architects

Knowing that by the right of succession they were coming into control of the IUA after the 8th Congress, the French architects blocked those who sought to extend the IUA's spirit ... the question now is whether the world architectural profession, which now functions as a slave activity, is to become obsolete as all slave functions are progressively taken over by automata ... the young world will not wait among the architects ... because of the whole episode of the French architects and the irresponsible hands into which the IUA has fallen, I am no longer hopeful that the practising professional architects will comprehend and realise the new potential emancipation of world society from its frustrated past.[198]

After 1967, growing disillusioned with the architectural profession and keen for new forms of global networking, Fuller transferred his attention to his 'World Game' – a form of participatory conference/workshop to synthesise his ideas, first held at New York in 1969, and soon afterwards he (with McHale) left Carbondale for a post at Philadelphia. He still visited Keith regularly, however, and Matthew continued to act as a link between Fuller's utopianism and the architectural profession in later years of student unrest and eco-extremism. He also backed Fuller's efforts from the early 1960s to proselytise his geodesic domes and other high-technology solutions in countries such as Ghana, Nigeria and India: by the 1980s over 300,000 geodesic domes had been built worldwide. Aidan recalled that

he remained interested in Bucky's ecological work, for example, in shelter from earthquakes, and in developing countries in general: people could be given the kit of parts, but could be prepared to build in indigenous materials – applying energy saving design, and alternative technologies, to the developing world, rather than just aping us, which he thought was inappropriate.[199]

Bob the Delian: Matthew, Doxiadis and the Ekistics movement

But the trend in architectural utopianism was now beginning to flow away from integrated social and high-tech visions of planned salvation, and towards more humanist, environmentalist, conservationist approaches – something that Matthew, with his fondness for the 'vernacular' and for 'heritage', was better positioned to exploit than Fuller, who rapidly became a 'seer concerned about the future, for a world no one any longer believes in'. For Matthew, the monodirectional character of the relationship with Fuller had become somewhat stifling, especially as a more 'humanistic' and collaborative participatory alternative had in the meantime become available, in the form of the Ekistics movement led by Islamabad masterplanner Constantinos Doxiadis – a movement of which Fuller was an enthusiastic participant. The prestigious, multidisciplinary company brought together by Ekistics provided, for Matthew, the decisive intellectual bridge between the 1940s/1950s world of modern architecture-planning and his 1970s world of environmental activism.

Although the Ekistics movement still exists today, Doxiadis, its dominant polymath-figure, is nowadays less well known among historians than Fuller, and so it is worth providing a little background on his past – especially as his character, as a dominant 'man of action', was somewhat closer to Matthew's own. Born in 1913 to Greek émigrés in Bulgaria, and trained in architecture and engineering, Doxiadis became chief city planner of Athens at the age of 23, and first post-1945 Minister for Reconstruction, supervising the rebuilding of bridges, railways, 3,000 villages, and 200,000 new or modernised 'basic' dwellings. In 1948 he was also elected chairman of a UN working group on housing policy, and became coordinator of Marshall Plan aid to Greece – international contacts that brought him an invaluable familiarity with the international apparatus of built-environment reformism and with US capitalistic ways of promoting the 'business' of architecture. Greece not being a country trammelled by the western European social-democratic apparatus of collective state action, Doxiadis always relied heavily on his personal charisma, and from the 1940s his personality became increasingly channelled into an English-speaking path, to get his various initiatives the maximum exposure. In 1948 he became elected chairman of a UN working group on housing policy; from 1954 he was fed a stream of UN commissions for technical assistance to national housing programmes in seven countries; and in the late 1950s he won an influential urban-renewal competition for a 10,000-dwelling project at New Eastwick, Philadelphia, with a layout of mainly two-storey row-houses. In 1959 he opened a Washington office (having developed close links with the Ford Foundation).

The watershed between Doxiadis the Greek architect-planner and Doxiadis the internationalist came in the early 1950s, as he gradually refocused on the task of devising a 'total', synthesising solution to the world's built-environment problems – a strategy underpinned, in the traditional Modern Movement way, by an unapologetic rhetoric of crisis and salvation. From then on he ceaselessly pursued this international 'mission', and after 1953 took up a similarly peripatetic lifestyle to Matthew's, spending much of his time in aeroplanes while, at the same time, developing a similar domestic status as 'uncrowned king' of architecture in his own country.[200] By the time Doxiadis was 49, in 1962, he had become arguably the world's most prominent internationally active masterplanner. Working with a range of talented collaborators, including Jaqueline Tyrwhitt – the polymath CIAM Secretary, planning academic at SPRND and Harvard, and former amanuensis of Sigfried Giedion – he developed his Athens base to serve both his own engineering–planning–architecture practice, Doxiadis Associates, and his academic work, with the establishment of an 'Athens Technological Institute' (1958) and graduate research school, the Athens

Center of Ekistics (1960). Looking sceptically from the sidelines, Zahir-ud-Din recalled that Doxiadis 'was a visionary, and his team, which he carefully selected, believed firmly in his views and opinions [to the point where] each member had almost been indoctrinated to believe in the ideas of Doxiadis, and that there was no room for dissidence or divergence of opinion with the great master.'[201]

Doxiadis's ultimate, unrealised aspiration was to found a fully fledged 'university of Ekistics'. By 'Ekistics', Doxadis meant a spatially informed science of human settlement, intended, like all planning movements since Geddes, to combat a fundamental social and economic crisis of disintegration or uncontrolled growth, and perpetuating the turn-of-century fascination for classificatory Greek names for all possible sizes and types of settlement, from the individual person (*anthropos*) to the entire world (*ecumenopolis*), with an implied universal privileging of the traditional Greek *polis* and Greek cultural experience in general. However, all this was fused with a Modernist element of futuristic emphasis on movement and change through a range of physical or communication devices as simple as a linear city plan, or 'Dynapolis'.[202] Like Geddes with his 'thinking machines', ekistic research was structured through a highly complex hierarchy and pattern of concepts, including, from 1965, the so-called 'ekistic grid', whose 120 cells (or 'pigeon-holes') measured scale of settlement against a range of classificatory criteria, including chronological period and geographical location, as well as five 'ekistic elements': nature, man, society, shells (i.e. buildings) and networks. All this echoed some of the classificatory prescriptions of the last years of CIAM in the 1940s and 1950s, such as the 'CIAM Grille', devised by Corbusier/ASCORAL in 1947–9 for analysing development according to scale, function, time and typology – a framework so complicated that it had proved almost impossible to use. But all Doxiadis's initiatives freely mixed these theoretical or abstract elements with an element of American-style self-promotion: his aim, like Geddes's, was not to abolish capitalism but to channel it rationally.[203]

Forming, storming, norming: launching the 'Delos Decade'

The decisive, final stage in the internationalisation of Doxiadis – his transformation, and that of Ekistics, into a 'network' of global scope – came in July 1963, in a typical Doxiadis *coup de théâtre* fashion, when he organised a floating eight-day symposium of 35 'thinkers', including Matthew, on board the cruise ship *New Hellas*, travelling around various scenically spectacular calling points in the Aegean, and concluding with the issuing of a 'Declaration of Delos'. At first glance the effort seemed a somewhat derivative one, modelled on the cruise of the 4th CIAM Conference by the SS *Patras* from Marseille to Athens and back in July–August 1933, which led to the 'Charter of Athens', key manifesto of orthodox Modernist urbanism. In both cases the meeting was one of international reformism, seeking to embed itself in, and legitimise itself through, the universal Western prestige of Greece; and in both cases the overall aspiration was the rational reform of an allegedly chaos-ridden built environment. But where the 1933 event had been a loosely organised – at times chaotic – effort by an architect-dominated group of over a hundred 'rebels', three decades later Doxiadis's was arranged prescriptively, yet with a far more diverse 'network' of participants, mostly people of some establishment authority, drawn together largely through the connections and organising ability of Tyrwhitt, the effective heir to the heritage of CIAM. Matthew argued beforehand that 'this kind of multidisciplinary meeting, focusing very different and authoritative viewpoints, is significant and useful.' Tyrwhitt, as editor of *Ekistics* journal since its beginnings in 1955, a permanent resident in Greece, and co-organiser of most key 'Athens' initiatives, including the Delos cruises, brought ready-made the full CIAM/MIT

array of conferences, teaching programmes, meetings and books, helping to nudge Doxiadis's activity away from physical infrastructure planning towards intangible communication networks.[204] The Delos courses were facilitated by subsidies from the Ford Foundation, and so, appropriately, over half the participants were anglophone, with US representatives (other than, of course, Fuller) including anthropologist Margaret Mead, literary and cultural critic Marshall McLuhan, Ed Bacon of Philadelphia, Charles Abrams of MIT and Britons including Tyrwhitt, the *Economist* editor, Barbara Ward, the Edinburgh University animal geneticist Professor Conrad Hal Waddington, and (representing architects), Llewelyn-Davies – and Matthew. The presence of Giedion gave the symposium a symbolic link with Athens 1933. Matthew was involved initially in his capacity as IUA President, but his energetic contribution in his own right, and his incessant intellectual curiosity, won him a permanent place in what turned out to be an open-ended series of symposia: he attended ten in all. Aidan recalled that 'my father thought Doxiadis was a rogue, but thoroughly enjoyed the symposia!'[205]

Many of the participants, on assembling at the first Delos symposium in 1963, were baffled and annoyed by the apparently ad hoc, makeshift informality of the event, but from the beginning Doxiadis set out to exploit both the instinctive respect for Greek culture and the drama of the settings visited by the ship. The cruise started under a full moon, and the sun rose next morning with the boat anchored off the dazzlingly white houses of Hydra. Although most symposium sessions were held inside the ship in the mornings (followed by afternoon cultural visits), some evening meetings were held in classical theatres. His plan was to use the beauty and emotional-cultural symbolism of Greece, and the enforced waterborne isolation, to create the emotional heat that could weld the disparate group into a 'community', and bring it into line behind his own intellectual agenda. That specific agenda, for this initial symposium, was little more than to gain acceptance of the idea that there was a general crisis of human settlement, which demanded a multidisciplinary and dynamic response. The aim of the first session was to gain acceptance of the paradoxical idea that economic advance might actually lead to a deterioration in the fabric of settlement and the spatial life of cities, and that this deterioration might constitute an international menace as serious as war or disease. Behind the overt agenda of reform of degraded settlements was another aspiration: to foster, just like CIAM, a global network of experts – now, of course, multidisciplinary rather than exclusively architectural. More speculative are claims that Doxiadis's activities had further, covert links, for example with US anti-communist interests or even with the CIA.[206]

All this was a high-risk strategy with a strong possibility of disintegration. And, indeed, the rebellious and fragmentary discussions of the initial phase, with speakers such as Fuller criticising the jargon-ridden rhetoric of Ekistics, and arguing that it was not legitimate to talk of a discrete crisis of settlements and the built environment, was soon followed, under the influence of the 'magic of Greece', by a phase of growing acceptance of the legitimacy of Ekistics as a basis at least for debate, and a willingness to work together in drafting a joint 'declaration of Delos' and setting up an international organisation for ekistic study. Now the debate could flow freely back and forward. Waddington, for example, lambasted the obsession of planners with 'static architecture', and insisted on the evolutionary necessity of electronic communication systems as a kind of prosthetic, biotechnical force that would mingle human and machine, while Mead talked of the need to balance scientific research with the creation of a more sensitive 'landscape of the spirit' for children. Matthew played a key role in helping to bring the discussions, as Doxiadis wanted, from these sorts of ringing slogan to the reaching of practical agreement. In

11.27 Delos 2, 1964, view of the sixth discussion session, held off the island of Patmos. From left: Buckminster Fuller, Tyrwhitt, Mead, Doxiadis, Llewelyn Davies, Matthew, and Mohamed Makiya (Iraq). (EULMC)

this sort of high-powered company, as in IUA, his preferred image was not of dominance but of the reasonable conciliator: 'He tried to play the same role he played in IUA and CAA, in securing mutually agreed statements at the end.' Matthew focused on three issues in the discussions: first, how professional institutions, with their apparent 'vast power' but their 'powerlessness' in reality, could be properly linked into the Ekistics movement; second, the need for a firm distinction between 'academic' debate and practical 'operative' planning; and, third, whether the CIAM 1933 ideas – neighbourhood planning, density reduction, zoning, traffic separation – were any longer relevant as a practical part of any physical element of reform.[207]

Eventually, in the final session in the theatre at Delos, Giedion favourably compared the complexity of Ekistics with the simple rhetoric of CIAM Modernism, and concluded that 'Greece has done it again!' More immodestly, Doxiadis exulted that the symposium would help the 'creation of a universal city for man'.[208]

11.28 A page from *Ekistics* magazine reporting the Delos 2 symposium: at bottom right, Lorna Matthew and Margaret Mead are pictured dancing a reel at Aghios Ioannis, near Sparta, on 16 July 1964. (*Ekistics,* 18, 107, October 1964, 186) (Doxiadis Associates, Athens)

cipitous ridges, hundreds of feet above the deep, dark-blue sea of the Aegean islands. From Piraeus they went to Itea and then to Delphi; then to Katakolon and Olympia; to Gytheion and Sparta and Mystra; to Sifnos, Santorini and Patmos; and then back to the mainland, to Nafplion, Tiryns, Mycenae and Epidaurus; finally, to Mykonos and Delos and back to Piraeus. But of course, they were not interested only in places. They wanted to get in contact with the spirit of Ancient Greece, and they wanted to see how a modern Greek looks at it, how he interprets it; they also wanted to get to know how the people living on this land act and react, how they sing and dance, how they laugh and meditate. And their host gave them the opportunity to fulfil this desire too.

Climbing by torch-light up the steep hills where the ancient theatre of Delphi stands, they were happily surprised, on the night of Tuesday, July 14, to find there the troop of the Greek Art Thearte Company directed by Karolos Koun, who had come to Delphi specially to give them a performance of that rich and gay fantasy, «The

Disembarking from the «Philippos» off the island of Patmos

Mr. Fitch's mule picks its way slowly up the 400 steps leading to the village of Santorini

Mr. Koestler reciting his Ode to Ekistics at Antoninis' taverna, Mykonos

Lady Matthew and Dr. Margaret Mead dance a reel together at Aghios Ioannis, near Sparta

186

Doxiadis's gamble that he could cajole this disparate group into endorsing his own strategy of aggrandisement had succeeded. In the 'Declaration of Delos' drafted by Barbara Ward (Lady Jackson) the language of crisis was ratcheted up, in a way that anticipated the environmentalist rhetoric of the 1970s: the declaration argued that 'the failure to adapt human settlements to dynamic change may soon outstrip even disease and starvation as the greatest risk, short of war, facing the human spirit'; the remedy was both 'scientific', through the need for intensive research, and spiritual, by reaffirming that 'we are citizens of a worldwide city, threatened by its own torrential expansion'. Arguably, many of these ideas were platitudes of the 'more flexible' Modernism of the Team 10 era, mixed with a dose of Geddesian charisma and Fuller-like technological rhetoric.[209]

What was Matthew's own verdict on the first Delos symposium? In a follow-up interview in August Matthew admitted that he had at first been sceptical, but echoed the declaration's apocalyptic talk of the 'pull towards chaos' as a 'threat to the future of civilisation', and forcefully endorsed the Ekistics movement's attempt to reform, rather than reject, the Modernist concept of scientific, rational reform directed by 'experts'. The CIAM Charter of Athens, he argued, had done a great service in

> bringing directly into the field of architecture the ideas of pioneers like Patrick Geddes. It might be said that CIAM first promulgated the concept of architecture as a social service – but now, due to the all-embracing nature of the crisis ... the original concept of CIAM is now extended [by Doxiadis] to embrace all kinds of social and scientific discussions.

Aidan was rather more sceptical:

> Ekistics was a jumble of woolly ideas, couched in dense and impenetrable language – a pseudo-scientific approach, argued densely and exhaustively, but ending up with something you could have put on the back of an envelope in the first place![210]

In practical terms Matthew's usefulness to Doxiadis stemmed largely from his IUA presidency: and indeed, at the September 1963 Cuban IUA Congress, Matthew arranged for the closing meeting to award Doxiadis the newly instituted Patrick Abercrombie award for planning, arguing that the Delos symposium had highlighted the 'world building crisis' as something more serious than worries of disease or food – a 'poverty, material and aesthetic' that demanded a 'combined attack, by the mobilising of world resources'. Doxiadis's speech of thanks emphasised that only two per cent of

human activity was influenced by architecture – a proportion that must now be increased.

By the time of the second symposium in 1964 it had become clear that the 'Delos' cruises, and other linked research events in Athens, were to be an annual event, combining cultural tourism with the typical Modernist ideal of a cumulative, methodical team effort, managed by Tyrwhitt, and with a hard core of regular attendees, including Robert and Lorna Matthew. Tyrwhitt's *Ekistics* journal reported that the cultural component of the tour included Aristophanes comedies in the theatres at Delphi and Epidauros, and evening dances, including one at Mystra led by the 'fragile and always charming' Barbara Ward, and one on the island of Patmos where 'Lady Matthew took the initiative and danced with extreme brio with a local dancer.' The 1964 course had 31 participants, 19 being anglophone, including one US congressman; two, for the first time, came from the USSR. It concentrated on three follow-up tasks: to develop the ekistic 'discipline of settlements'; to train people in it; and to remove political and economic obstacles. In practical terms, there would now be an annual Delos symposium; a World Association of individuals concerned with human settlement would be set up; and pressure would be exerted on the UN to recognise human settlement as 'a separate section of activity', and to hold a UN 'Year of Human Settlements'.[211] Matthew's 1964 contribution was focused in two areas: helping draw up a proposal for UN action on settlements; and working with Llewelyn-Davies on an educational reform programme that would move away from 'rule-based' training towards a conception of 'design as an exercise in solving open-ended problems'.[212] His contribution to the final 1964 Delos statement emphasised the need for international action and flexibility, arguing that 'the world is greatly unsettled, as Bucky Fuller has so rightly reminded us. It is no time for any of us to become fossils.'[213] Following the 1964 symposium, Doxiad is moved to set up his international supporting society, the World Society for Ekistics (WSE; formally inaugurated in July 1965), and asked Matthew to join its executive committee. In his reply, Matthew wrote with warmth, and even a degree of deference, that at Delos 2

I felt we had moved on. On this occasion there was a great measure of understanding, but still a wide gap between the 'practical' men and the theorists. This is a great work you are doing, and I'm tremendously grateful to have been in at the start. Lorna sends warmest greetings ... we have enjoyed getting to know your family – I hope we will keep this up, especially with your daughter coming to London. Be sure to let us know when she arrives.

In May 1965 Doxiadis visited Edinburgh to lecture and discuss the setting up of WSE, and Matthew hosted a lavish party for him at Prestonfield House.[214]

At the third Delos symposium in July 1965 the anglophone dominance of Delos reached its height, with 26 out of 32 delegates. Seventeen were from the USA, including Mead, Fuller, Joseph Watterson of the AIA and MIT urban studies director Charles M Haar; the UK contingent included Matthew, Llewelyn-Davies, J M Richards, Percy Johnson-Marshall, Waddington and historian Arnold Toynbee, 'nearly eighty but on our excursions ashore ... nearly always first up the hill paths, agile as a mountain goat'.[215] The symposium had become essentially an Anglo-American forum, even an indirect vehicle of Americanisation, coincidentally hosted in Greece, and drawing a universal cultural prestige from that fact. Although Doxiadis, in fulsome Geddesian mode, called for a century of Delos symposia, following which one would be 'in the happy position to state that humanity has entered into the phase of the universal city, or "ecumenopolis", developing man and the surface of the earth in an Apollonian harmony' – the more immediate aim was to complete an initial ten-year cycle of meetings. And in 1965 the practical focus was now on two issues only – how to tackle the effects of greater

density stemming from population growth, and the need for institutions to encourage *regional development* – with Matthew arguing simply for the scope of urban design to be expanded more widely to the scale of the individual town – to prevent the risk of 19th-century-style mistakes being repeated on a larger scale. In the final meeting on 18 July in the Delos amphitheatre Fuller summarised the first three symposia in suitably hellenophile manner:

At the first [symposium], we were a little like the chorus in Aeschylus's *The Persians*, weaving in and out in a rich, chaotic pattern. At the second, things became more systematised. Here at the third, we have seen human intellect come into high focus upon the task at hand. What has come into being here is one of humanity's most hopeful undertakings.[216]

Matthew was unable to attend the 1966 symposium, which saw a slight diminution of US–British dominance (23 out of 36), and a two-strand focus on transport systems for 'choice and mobility' and the protection of 'beauty' in the natural and urban environment. The attendance for the first time of the Japanese architect Kenzo Tange ensured a further nudge of the Ekistics movement towards the Metabolist and Archigram ideas of electronic communication networks.[217] 1967 was the year that, in April, saw the overthrow of the Greek government by a military regime. This posed some organisational challenges for Doxiadis, who had largely withdrawn from any political role in Greece: the symposium went ahead, but without communist representatives and with a revived US–UK dominance (24 and 5 out of 36). By now, the event had mushroomed into an annual 'Athens Ekistics Month', from 10 July to 4 August, including a 12-day International Seminar on Ekistics, a one-day educational meeting, the symposium itself, followed by the general assembly of WSE and five days of ekistic research discussions.[218] Tyrwhitt's journal *Ekistics* was, meantime, busy propagating all

these initiatives in a more systematic worldwide form. All of this was held together largely by the force of Doxiadis's charisma, something that Matthew was able to tolerate, but which appealed less to others: Bill Holford, for example, wrote to Matthew that he would stay away from Delos 6 (in 1968) partly because of 'the "inflation" [of Doxiadis] of the last few years'.[219] The 1967 symposium, at any rate, tried to draw together the lessons of the previous four events into a coherent 'strategy for human settlements'. The language of apocalyptic threat – evoking a 'downward spiral of disintegration' – stayed the same. But, possibly under the increased influence of US capitalism, there was a shift away from Western European-style statist solutions towards a libertarian strategy aiming 'to give citizens, within a context of recognisable social and physical order, access to the widest possible range of free choice'. The redistributive impulse should instead be focused on an appeal, devised by Barbara Ward, for rich countries to contribute one per cent of GNP to alleviating development problems of poor members.[220] Writing later to thank Doxiadis, Matthew put a positive interpretation on the

post-coup difficulties, declaring that

of course, the symposium was clearly dominated by our American friends, but I am sure that those who criticised will realise that it was remarkable to have had a meeting at all this year ... and a great advantage to have an injection of new interests – bankers, insurance, the 'systems' men. If any of your [family] are likely to come to London, our house is always at your disposal, as we have a house-keeper there.

To maintain momentum between symposia, Matthew set up a British group of 'Delians' on the IUA national-committee principle, with Nottingham University geographer Gerald Dix as secretary.[221]

The conclusion of the first five-year Delos 'cycle' was marked at the 1968 symposium, which saw a slight retrenchment in the US–UK numbers (32 out of 43, including McGeorge Bundy, now Ford Foundation Vice-President, and Richard Meier, professor of environmental design at Berkeley); there were six from France but, again, none from the Eastern bloc. This symposium culminated in another formal Declaration of Delos, which opportunistically and somewhat disin-

433

Commonwealth of design

genuously tried to co-opt the 1968 upsurge in student protests as evidence of growth in concern about the 'ekistic crisis'. The declaration also acknowledged the consequent need, alongside a continuing rigorous scientific element of research, to move towards more participatory methods of education and planning: 'for planning *for*, we must substitute planning *with*'.[222] With this Declaration, it was now becoming obvious that the Ekistics movement was a significant international bridge between the old style of reformist planning, targeted at expunging the 'Palaeotechnic' legacy of the 19th century, and the new environmentalist movement of the late 20th century, equally impassioned in its arguments but far more sweeping in its definition of threat.

This bridging effect was evident not least in the development of Matthew's own views, which were now starting to shift away from the 1950s/1960s acceptance of expert-directed technocratic reform and architecture-planning interventionism towards a new and more implicitly spiritual world outlook, focused on the dual concerns of conservationist national-cultural identity 'at home', and a global environmentalism abroad. The two overlapped, of course, and as early as September 1968 Matthew was writing to the Préfet de Paris against the proposed demolition of Les Halles, emphasising that he was 'on the side of preservation'.[223] This 'network', extending outwards from Ekistics to the nascent ecological movement, was immediate and obvious in character. But a second, subtler, different network of endeavour and idealism also stretched out from the Ekistics movement and the work of Fuller and Marshall McLuhan towards the next phase of technocratic confidence –

towards the post-1990s era of dematerialised, digital space and communication networks, including above all the Internet itself. To realise this new utopia, however, the specific built-environment concerns of people like Doxiadis, with his concern with establishing vast physical nets, would need to be left far behind: in letters of 1972, McLuhan complained that the other Delos participants were 'earnest men, rather all 19th-century types, still preoccupied with bricks and mortar' and ignorant of the 'new kind of (electronic) world city, far outside the keen of Doxiadis'.[224]

Matthew would have had little interest in this kind of dematerialised, depersonalised vision of impermanence. It was, rather, his conservationist and environmentalist impulses that grew stronger and stronger throughout the late 1960s and early 1970s – a process that ultimately amounted to a virtually complete renewal of his personal world outlook. But it was arguably because of Matthew's similarity of character with Doxiadis – as another, albeit far more flamboyant, leader figure – that he was able to shift so easily into this process of renewal, which completely eluded many younger Modernist colleagues, even Lasdun or the Smithsons, still trapped within the confines of 'conventional architecture'. This ethical re-evaluation and purification was never explicitly articulated in words by Matthew himself, but it was clear in his repeated attempts to ground Ekistics in the Geddesian ethos of neotechnic scientific-spiritual renewal: in 1965, indeed, he argued that Geddes was 'the father of Ekistics'.[225] In the next two chapters, we shall trace in greater detail the two strands of this renewal, which occupied and energised Matthew for the last six years of his life.

Crisis and Regeneration

Chapter 12

The journey home, 1969–75

I am never on the side of the status quo – change always has to go on.

Robert Matthew, 1970

Our voice is still a quiet one, but, like Dr Schumacher, I have a hunch that, more often than not, the small is the more beautiful in the end.

Robert Matthew, 1973

Robert liked big ideas, and he saw the Edinburgh New Town as a big idea, worth preserving for its grand consistency as much as for the specifics of its architecture. He hadn't much time for fiddling with the problem, and if an individual building wasn't worth saving he wouldn't go to the wall for it. But keeping the whole New Town intact – he'd put his heart and soul into that!

John Richards, 2003[1]

In June 1970 Matthew's Establishment career was crowned by the award of the RIBA Royal Gold Medal for Architecture: little did he suspect, at that point, that he only had five more years to live. Indeed, far from there being any slackening of pace, the last few years of his life were arguably the most restlessly innovative of all. It was now that the sharpest divergences began to open up between him and many of his contemporaries – including some who had at times outstripped his achievements, but had now slid into relative inactivity or incapacitation. By the early/mid 1970s Bill Holford, for example, was worn out by years of caring for his terminally ill wife, and

Basil Spence, disillusioned by controversies about some key projects, such as Hyde Park Cavalry Barracks, had slipped into semi-retirement in Malta. Robert Matthew, by contrast, not only maintained his furious pace of activity and global travel, but threw himself into yet another of his periodic world view revolutions, largely giving up the conventional orthodoxies of the Modern Movement for a heady lifestyle of environmental activism. Of course, given the large investments involved in building projects, architects by nature have to be sensitive to shifts in the wider social, economic and cultural context of their work, responding with idealism, professionalism or pragmatism as they see fit. Sometimes these shifts are driven by changes in personal circumstance, such as Matthew's move to London in 1946 (which led him to downplay his Scottish concerns for a while); or a combination of personal and external circumstance may be at work.

The post-1968 revolution in Matthew's thinking fell partly into the latter category, responding to the wider revulsion

12.1 'Family Scenes': August 1973 cartoon sketch by Matthew. (EULMC)

against technocratic Modernism, but also developing long-standing trends in his own thinking. Matthew's new world view, in effect, neatly replaced the two-strand vernacular/Scottish and international/progressive pattern of his old Modernist affiliation, putting in place, instead, two complementary groups of values and aims – a 'journey home', which combined architectural conservationism and Scottish nationalism, and an increasingly insistent drive to 'far horizons', which built on his old internationalist wanderlust and his growing enthusiasm for international networks, and replaced his old concern for town planning with a noisy passion for global environmental activism, especially after the UN Stockholm Conference on the environment of 1972. This chapter, and the next, deal with these two strands of work in his final years, tracing a crescendo of proselytising and agitating activity that was cut off, with shocking suddenness, in 1975. Matthew's was not a career that subsided to an anticlimactic and undignified end, but one that ended, as it had begun, in compulsive, restless struggle.

End of the drive: the breakdown of Modernist 'Progress'

The external element in Matthew's shifting world outlook was dramatised, above all, by the explosion of anti-establishment protests in 1968. In a St Andrew's Night lecture on BBC TV Scotland in November 1968 he argued that during the past two years a 'shock of violence' had hit many big urban centres around the world 'like a bomb'.[2] Then, with the 1970s, came the more insidious economic malaise of 'stagflation' in Britain, and the idea that the country was suffering from a general 'systems failure' and 'becoming ungovernable'; he wrote to an overseas friend in April 1975 that 'we here are in extreme doubt about the future ... galloping inflation can lead anywhere'.[3] There had been a sea change, too, in the public reception of architecture, an individualising trend that dissolved the old post-war avant-garde reformism and encouraged a decline in respect for architects'

professional judgement. The architectural profession, Matthew stressed, had been the target of 'fierce criticism', and, despite the Modern Movement's own origins in idealistic protest against Victorian urban degradation, things had been turned almost upside down, with *architects* now 'often seen to be the agents of disorder and congestion, rather than the reverse'. Doxiadis had recently described architects, including himself, as 'criminals', concerned with 'building high monuments to themselves' and making towns 'more uncomfortable, more inhuman and altogether less fit for people to enjoy life in'.[4] This dramatic reversal in public opinion regarding modern architecture and planning posed Matthew, for virtually the only time in his career, with a clear challenge to his innate confidence in his own beliefs and abilities, and he conceded publicly that 'some of my best achievements have received great criticism, which leaves us very puzzled ... the "public" is the individual family, and [a house and garden] is all they want – they don't look forward to the future.' As Noel Annan later argued:

it was a strange epitaph for professionals who had prided themselves on discovering how human beings lived ... A new generation of planners criticised Our Age for imposing grand solutions and monuments to architects' vanity instead of asking the public what it wanted: a worthy sentiment, but the public always wants many things – and they conflict.[5]

Characteristically, Matthew treated this challenge not as a source of disillusionment and defeatism but as a stimulus to change and reform. First, he believed, one needed to understand the causes of the crisis. Partly, he felt, the public revulsion had been due to the application of 'uncontrolled urbanisation' and 'unrestrained technology – high buildings, massive road systems', 'clean sweep' planning and 'root and branch surgical treatment' to towns, without adequate collaboration with other social professions, who 'might have given us insight into the human problems we had to cater for', and the 'social damage' that mass redevelopment would cause.[6] As Matthew had always been sceptical about the wildest excesses of 'systems' thinking, he could here indulge in a little self-satisfaction: despite the post-war ferment of ideas and new materials, today's 'housing is not very revolutionary'... 'none of it [the experimentation] seems to have come to any fruition'. Matthew cited as his favourite current London housing project Darbourne & Darke's Lillington Street – a resolutely low-tech, brick and *in situ* concrete, 'traditional image' project. Some other Modernist architects were coming to the same chastened conclusion: for example, Max Fry wrote to Matthew in 1972 that 'a great deal of what we architects did in the 30s ... by way of incorporating industrialised models [has] led to high maintenance costs and ... premature obsolescence.'[7] The most egregious example of the corruption of Modern Movement idealism, in Matthew's opinion, was the tower block, which he had done so much to promote, but whose 'utterly destructive' use for mass housing output, 'plucking acres out of the sky' at the hands of David Gibson and others, had led Corbusier's ideas to 'boomerang on the heads of all of us'. What was 'old and familiar' had 'disappeared almost overnight ... replaced by what often seemed brash and uncongenial ... even menacing blocks'.[8] In university building, too, the ongoing experience of the New University of Ulster had highlighted the dangers of haste: 'There's a frenzy to get these new universities developed as soon as possible, which forces the architect to produce comprehensive plans far too fast.' With hospital projects, the problem was arguably the opposite, and Matthew in 1974 bemoaned the confusion and frustration stemming from 'the interminable and inordinate length of time taken to brief, design and build'. The outcome was arguably a *reductio ad absurdum* of Modernist 'progress': after 'nearly a quarter of a century of development, will the result, if there ever is an end result – will it not be obsolete?'[9] All

in all, architects, for all their grandiose utopianist rhetoric, had been shown to be 'by themselves, a feeble instrument for betterment'. At the 1973 RIBA Conference at Stirling University Matthew noted that whereas the last RIBA conference devoted to housing, in 1967, at Brighton, had seen a mood of 'impatience to get on with the job', and a dismissal of the warnings of Mumford and others as 'jeremiahs', now, things were 'a great deal more humble' – a mood amounting even to 'defeatism'.[10] Where, then, could architects look for any hope of a way forward? Modern Movement idealism, he insisted, was still a valid aim, but now had to be grounded in the 'humility' of the present. Architects must shift from 'the heady heights of creating monuments for posterity (and also for the architects themselves) to less spectacular, but much more realistic problems of providing good physical environments for real people'.[11] Rather than 'systems' and 'machines', it was 'creative design' and 'human judgement' that gave the vital spark, and helped create 'the element that lifts the human spirit ... the indefinable quality that gives life to us all'. Although scientific advice could not be denied, and 'the grand solidarity of traditional building has melted away, probably for ever', the important thing was to invest more in good materials and quality construction: asked in 1970 where his favourite Modern architecture could be found, he pointed to countries of overall consistency rather than flamboyant highlights: Switzerland, Denmark and, above all, West Germany.[12] 'This is not an age of monumental building,' Matthew argued, although 'when the occasion arises, we can produce a Canberra, an Islamabad, a Chandigarh – with qualities we need not be ashamed of.'[13]

Within the social organisation of architecture, Matthew now acknowledged, mass building had created a 'great gap between the planners and those for whose benefit planning is done'. Now, in reaction, architecture must involve 'people themselves, individually, by families, or by groups ... now it is everyone's business'. This drive for 'participation' was given official blessing by the 1969 Skeffington Report, *People and Planning*. Yet the means were still largely lacking, despite Max Lock's earlier efforts at community mobilisation in his 1940s plan for Middlesbrough. There were 'almost non-existent' means for involving individuals, and 'the essential feedback is painfully slow', as 'town building, unlike scientific experiment in the lab, is slow and not subject to quick or precise approval.'[14] Internationally, the late 1960s had seen the rapid expansion of grass-roots urban activism, with writers such as the American Paul Davidoff arguing for an anarchistic community-based 'advocacy planning', anticipating the 1968 student uprisings, in which the May 1968 occupation of the Ecole des Beaux Arts played a key role. From this perspective, *all* post-war planning seemed insufferable 'paternalism'.[15]

The new emphasis on conservation not only extended the framework of 'community' back into the past, to co-opt the layered messages of past generations, but also, more pragmatically, with its campaigning immediacy, offered a compelling way of engaging the public. In 1974 Matthew argued that amenity societies were 'now the mouthpiece of public opinion', and that 'every child should be made aware of the philosophy of conservation as an integral part of his education'.[16] In parallel with conservation, the new housing association movement also offered great hope as a 'third force' against 'the dehumanising effects of the massive scale of much modern development'. Here, 'participation must extend to much fuller tenant involvement in expressing real human needs (not just in saying what they think of what they are given) and also in the management of housing'.[17]

As the high tide of Modernist confidence receded, with it ebbed some of the old moral force of the public professional ethos. That process of stripping away highlighted, in even sharper perspective, Matthew's bitter opposition to the laissez-faire ethos – still associated in his mind

above all with the bad old 19th century, but with signs of a growing awareness of a potential revival in economic liberalism: he showed some disappointment at the election of the Tory (Heath) government in 1970 – Dunbar-Nasmith recalled that the news was broken to him on a visit to the Sorlins in Paris, and 'he was out of sorts and grumpy for the rest of the day.'[18] The fate of professionalism, positive or negative, was not an abstract matter, but one that directly shaped the built environment, through its effects on architecture and planning. At a 1974 conference, for example, Matthew pointed to the challenge of finding an equivalent of the old 'estate development' of the 19th century, since, 'if desperate, the public will take anything' from speculative builders. In 1972, goaded by a pro-laissez-faire project at the Conference of the Architectural Association of Ireland, Matthew responded with an outburst hinting at the passion with which he regarded this issue. He thundered that planning was a direct expression of the 'social responsibility' involved in property ownership:

No town, indeed no tolerable human situation, can exist on a free-for-all basis ... It is a fantasy, in the minds of those who imagine that their property exists in a vacuum. It doesn't seem to have occurred to that kind of mind that, if it did exist in a vacuum, maybe on the moon, there would be little or no demand for their expensive lettable floor space, and the total value would probably be nil.[19]

In a 1971 speech Matthew criticised both sides of the party political divide: 'To the present government, the commercial ethos, the ethic of the market, maximum competition in all its forms, is all-important ... the free-for-all men!' But the attitude of the Labour government had also been damagingly naive, challenging the professions from a viewpoint of misplaced egalitarian opposition to a 'privileged elite'. Rather, a professional person 'has a moral obligation to employ his skills increasingly in solving the problems of the community through the agency of the person who pays him'.[20] But even this position became increasingly untenable with the unfolding in 1973–4 of the Poulson corruption scandal, which exposed the inability of both the RIBA and ARCUK to deal with the most flagrant transgressions of their codes from within the heart of the professional environment – a breach of architecture's social contract that, as Malcolm MacEwen candidly argued in December 1974, had left 'a cancer eating at the heart of professionalism'. Already, Ivan Illich had comprehensively attacked the professions as a conspiracy against society.[21] Accordingly, Matthew began to shift his defence of professionalism from the national to the international and global level. If, as he now fervently believed, architects had a duty to take up the fight against global environmental chaos, then it was all the more essential to maintain their 'hippocratic' position that 'the human environment should take priority over all other interests', and emerging countries had a duty to foster professional bodies and a supporting bourgeois infrastructure: in most countries, professionals were 'middle class and of the bourgeoisie – right – and likely to remain so'. The Commonwealth, Matthew argued in 1971, was especially valuable in being 'able to maintain its professional integrity and not get mixed up in competitive industry and commerce'.[22]

RMJM crises in the years of inflation

The last years of Matthew's life were years of runaway inflation, not just in the economic situation but in the size of RMJM itself, whose staffing had doubled eight times in under 20 years. Around 1970 the whole partnership had a total of 350 personnel and in 1973, 512, including 24 partners; by 1975 Edinburgh alone had reached nearly 300 staff, and London had for the first time slightly overtaken it; it seemed possible that the firm might grow to nearly 1,500. Aidan recalled that 'it grew exponentially, never stopped growing, never turned down anything.'

The growth curve began to flatten only in the mid 1970s oil crisis, with staff being laid off for the first time. Managing this unwieldy organisation effectively became difficult, if not impossible: attempts at reform initially concentrated on tinkering with details, while persevering with the overall partnership framework – governed by a single deed of co-partnership, with all ultimate power residing with the partners, hierarchically headed by the 'senior partner' in Edinburgh (Matthew). In the early 1970s this absolute power started to become diluted, as all partners became full members of a single 'firm', with 'local offices' in Edinburgh and London; a joint committee supposedly ensured coordination, with annual partners' and associates' conferences to discuss strategic direction of the firm's management. The first conference, in Stirling, had as its theme the problems of controlling the firm's 'growth', and John Richards warned against both mushrooming bureaucracy and 'obsessive individualism'.[23] Aidan's career in the Edinburgh office progressed steadily, and he became an associate in April 1972, working on overseas projects on Islamabad and Libya, but also on domestic work somewhat in the 'vernacular' tradition.

Within Edinburgh, the efforts at coordination had been spearheaded by a new chief coordinator, Denys Hill, who joined in 1969, and by 1973 was designated 'partner in charge of central administration'. Based in 15 Hill Street, this former African colonial administrator greatly accentuated the firm's existing trend towards multidisciplinary working. Spaven recalled that

all this discontent at the way we'd got so big, and hadn't got the right organisation for it, came to a head in the 1970s, with endless debates and partners' meetings, concerned with just about anything except architecture and buildings! Denys Hill tried to bring the organisation together, but he didn't succeed, as the loyalties remained with the groups.

441

Hill's attempts at reform were not universally welcomed by the existing administrative staff. Flora Isserlis, for example, recalled how

the climate changed very much for the worse with the coming of this dreadful ex-colonial type. The firm seemed to be going up like a whoosh, with projects being built like mad, but what was actually happening was even more fragmentation, with the firm breaking up into little units all over Edinburgh, and a little van that spent its time buzzing round between them.

Inevitably, the firm focused on an architectural answer to this problem, in the form of its new, central office development at Bell's Brae, to be created out of a group of old industrial buildings in the historic heart of Edinburgh's Dean Village, on ground already owned by the partners. When Jim Latimer's integrated redevelopment proposals of 1969 for the two halves of the site proved unaffordable, a scaled-down development, comprising conversion of the bottle store only, was approved.[24] A further centrifugal factor in the early 1970s was a move by Alan Wightman to set up an autonomous branch of the partnership in Stirling, theoretically equal in status to Edinburgh and London. Wightman had never taken full-heartedly to the enforced move from Dundee to Edinburgh, and the arrival of Denys Hill was the last straw: 'He was a pushy type, very "English" in his ways, who came from industry, and neither Tom Spaven nor I liked his way of working.'[25]

Matthew's response to this confusing mosaic of fragmentation and corporate intervention was one of ever-increasing detachment, as observed by a range of colleagues and associates. In Spaven's opinion:

By the 1970s, he had very little contact with the rest of the office, or with buildings. His concern with detail had gone: he was either worn out, with trying to influence something that was beyond his control, or recognised he'd just have to leave it, with the

broadening of his whole life. But he was still determined to keep prime position – remembering, I suppose, how his father had been Lorimer's 'kick-me-around' – and insisted on keeping a higher share of profits than the other partners.

Stuart Matthew argued that Robert had

lost touch with the practice; he was no longer able to do what he enjoyed in the firm, so he detached himself, and took himself off to his top flat in Regent Terrace, so he could get out of the way. He was fed up with the office, as so many things were going wrong. Yet at the same time he couldn't properly delegate, and so he wouldn't let go, and had to be kept informed of everything.[26]

It was largely through his attendance at partners' meetings that Matthew tried to keep his finger on the firm's pulse, and numerous meetings had to be rearranged around his other commitments. At these meetings he still attempted, if he felt inclined, to manipulate matters. Spaven recalled that

the way Robert's mind worked emerged, for example, when we had a difficult letter to write. He'd deal with it by saying, 'We'll all jot things down!' – getting peace and quiet for his own view. Then – 'How would this do?' – he'd read out his own letter – and we'd usually leave it unaltered. Stuart once told me that when Robert played rugby, he never liked passing the ball – a Burmese gentleman: Ma Baw!

There was also still the occasional opportunity to keep everyone on their toes. Matthew used his RIBA Gold Medal award in 1970 as the occasion to treat the Edinburgh partners to a dinner at Prestonfield House, but after dinner things took an unexpected turn, as 'out of nowhere, Robert sprang a sharp one on us, by suddenly asking each of us our views on religion – and then summing up our views himself! But, of course, he didn't tell *us* what *his* own beliefs were!'[27]

As we shall see later, these years saw a tremendous outpouring of idealistic endeavour on Matthew's part, in the areas that drew his attention and enthusiasm. His private practice work was not, now, one of those areas, and inevitably discontent began to bubble up among the other partners. Derbyshire argued that

> as Robert had always used the firm to support his lifestyle and his wider architectural standing, in a way there was no change now. But the Edinburgh partners – John Richards especially – were becoming more and more fed up about how much of the profits were going to Robert, while he was at the same time switching himself off the practice.

In 1969 Spaven and Hill blocked a proposal that he should offset his loss of university salary (£2,400 p.a.) by increasing his level of drawings from the firm or transferring a lump sum. Yet 'there was an equal and opposite argument, as no one could ignore the fact that it was Robert's connections that got us all the work overseas.' At a September 1970 partners' meeting Matthew bluntly asked the other partners, 'If I stayed on, can you afford me?' He made clear his desire to avoid curbing his standard of living, including above all his overseas travel, and stressed that at his age, if he was to build up an alternative practice, he could not afford to delay. In a conversation with Alan Wightman shortly afterwards, he cited, as reasons for a possible severance from RMJM, his lack of personal input into specific projects, and his impatience with 'abstract management', as opposed to design work in small teams.[28] In 1971 Richards, who was now fully financially self-sufficient within the practice, prepared a more comprehensive overview of Matthew's position, and of possible retirement scenarios. Acknowledging Matthew's increasing 'discontent' with the mushrooming of 'management' bureaucracy in the firm and, at the same time, his desire to maintain his standard of living, including his international

diplomacy work, Richards argued that while Matthew's annual profit-share drawings (currently, around £23,000 p.a.) were well in proportion to his overall 30 per cent stake in the Edinburgh firm, the real difficulty stemmed from his expenses, which were running at around £12,600 annually – 12 per cent of total office overheads. Of these expenses, which included 60–85 per cent of the utility costs of Keith Marischal, Regent Terrace and Park Square East, it could be argued that around £8,600 were for non-office activities – yet, Richards equally acknowledged, 'Could we do without his reputation?'

In all this, Matthew's estate duty liability problem also had to be borne in mind, as he still had a share in four of the Edinburgh properties, and was continuing to take on additional partnership-related liabilities, including overdraft guarantees, that could undermine any attempt to reduce his overall share in the firm's assets.[29] Arising out of his mid-1960s estate duty researches, Matthew took some action to reduce his liability, especially by conveying Keith and Regent Terrace to trustees for his children (in practice, to Lorna). A further round of discussions began in 1971, with a report by chartered accountant D S Anderson, discussing ways of offsetting potential estate duty liability by withdrawing his own capital from the firm: the danger, as before, was that the firm would otherwise have to sell properties on his death. By 1974 Anderson reported that by adjustments to life assurance policies, and the sale of selected properties, beginning with 8 Melville Street, it might be possible to create surpluses for the partners, amounting to £113,500 for Matthew, £64,000 for Spaven, and £19,500 each for Richards and Graham. As part of the process of scaling back the firm's contribution to Matthew's wider activities, and building up a cash 'war-chest' for estate duty purposes, it was also possible finally to dispose of the Keith Ingram business, following Sylvia's eventual decision not to continue with the management of the firm. The shop had moved to more prominent premises at 39 Frederick Street in March 1969, but despite Sylvia's efforts its financial position had not improved. Eventually, in early 1974, the firm was disposed of and the Frederick Street shop was sold, allowing the start-up loan of nearly £11,000 from Matthew to be repaid, and a substantial additional sum (£28,000) to be realised in 1975 from the liquidation itself. This helped offset the firm's bank overdraft, which by 1973 had reached over £11,000.

With the broadening of the partnership and, especially, the radical expansion of the London office, the tension between Robert and Stirrat Marshall became less marked – although some of the younger London partners, such as Hugh Morris, became correspondingly 'irritated by Matthew's grandeur'.[30] Stirrat and Robert found much common ground in dealing with the intractable tension with Percy over competition for planning consultancy work, and Percy's fears that Stirrat was encouraging confusion over the Johnson-Marshall name in order to siphon off his clients. Stirrat sent Derbyshire and Lee up to Edinburgh, in two unsuccessful attempts to pacify Percy, but the tension came to a head in early 1975, during Matthew's final illness, when Percy wrote him and Stirrat a lengthy and impassioned memo, emphasising the lasting bitterness caused by the Central Lancashire debacle. The fires of conflict, he argued, had once again been stoked by Stirrat's announcement in 1974 of his own impending retirement at age 65, and the Edinburgh decision to set up a planning arm, which meant that 'I could be faced with a large rival firm carrying my own name.' The now terminally ill Robert replied to Percy's diatribe with dignity, contending that although he had personally disbanded RMJM Edinburgh's planning team at the time of Percy's initial move to Scotland, matters had now inevitably changed with the firm's vast expansion, and it was 'increasingly difficult to convince incoming partners of the equity of what seemed to them to be a one-sided arrangement'. Acerbically,

Robert noted that since 'there will shortly come a time when the senior partners leave the scene, and the direction of the firm, to others' ... 'the scope for any change would be limited'. It may have been that Percy was hoping, on the back of these arguments, to be able finally to join the RMJM partnership, but any move in this direction was firmly rebuffed by John Richards and the other Edinburgh partners.[31]

Most of the workload of RMJM was now completely divorced from Matthew's oversight, and large projects were routinely carried through without any reference to him at all, even in Scotland. Increasingly, the economic and social troubles of those years cast a pall over even the firm's proudest achievements – as in the case of Stirling University, whose completion was marred by student rioting in 1972 during a visit by the Queen, followed a year later by the untimely death of Principal Tom Cottrell. Elsewhere, crises in implementation of some complex projects required Matthew's intermittent attention, as at Coleraine University, with the growing disorganisation in the contract. At Ninewells, too, the 'steaming cauldron of claim and counterclaim' resulting from the mounting overspending and delays forced Matthew to become involved more than he would have liked, although much of the negotiation work was devolved to Spaven. By the late 1960s the dispute between Crudens and the Eastern Regional Hospital Board over payments had gone to arbitration. Spaven reported that

at that stage, the *Scotsman*'s George Hume got his teeth into it, and when I was on holiday in Ireland, in pouring rain, Bruce Moncrieff of our office phoned up: 'Robert has been on to me, and says you're to come back to Edinburgh to deal with the Scotsman article.' I said, 'I'm so fed up, I don't care if you send a helicopter back to fetch me, I'm not coming.' Bruce said, 'That's what I hoped you'd say.' [At the arbitration] I was cross examined for eight consecutive days by Lord Ross – not a nice experience. And eventually, the arbitrator, perhaps because he was a QS, made a £2m award in favour of the contractor, arguing that the contractor had lost money as a result of not receiving information on time – which reflected badly on us. But Robert's concern, it seemed to me, was to avoid becoming too much embroiled himself – which was a bit selfish, I felt.

The arbitration award, made in two stages in 1973–4, coincided with the eventual completion of the Ninewells complex, five years late and nearly a decade after the first sod was cut, with the final cost now expected to reach £22.5m.[32] In the final two years of construction of Ninewells, press and political comment focused on the difficulties, with the *Daily Record* writing of 'The Monster of Ninewells', and West Fife MP Willie Hamilton comparing it to Concorde.[33] On its completion, though, opinion began to change, as the sophistication of the plan and the services, and the magnificence of the setting and Frank Clark's landscaping, became appreciated. The building was acclaimed as 'Britain's first custom-built teaching hospital this century', and in 1973 *Sunday Mail* journalist Innes Irvine wrote lyrically of 'Ninewells, the £22.5m bargain ... Dundee is getting the very last word in luxury hospitals.'[34]

At the Royal Infirmary of Edinburgh the problems facing Matthew and RMJM were of a different and less publicly controversial character, owing to the failure, after a decade and a half of planning and debate, to embark on any construction at all. Only in February 1972, after two years of successive postponements during the 1967–9 economic crisis, were detailed proposals for the first block of Matthew's step-by-step medium-rise courtyard development concept agreed. Phase 1 was to be a medium-rise rectangular block with central courtyard, at the northwest corner of the steeply sloping site, containing five storeys at the north and seven at the

12.2 1977 progress photograph of the construction of RIE Phase 1. (John Dewar Studio)

south, and housing mainly outpatient clinics and upper-floor nurses' accommodation, all unified externally by dominant horizontally banded windows; at the rear, a central boilerhouse with chimney would serve the entire hospital. The overall RIE development plan now called for replacement of the 1,100 existing beds by 860; decanting following completion of Phase 1 would allow a west-to-east wave of construction to begin, with a total estimated cost of £25m.[35] Eventually, after several more years of postponements, building work on Phase 1 began only in April 1975, two months before Matthew's death.[36] Matthew had long ceased to have any close connection with the project, which was overseen by associate Percy Murray until eventual completion in 1981. At that point, with all further work abandoned, one could reasonably have concluded that, for RMJM, the RIE project had been a profoundly negative experience, amounting to little more than a succession of frustrating and abortive schemes. Equally, however, one could argue that a protracted hospital project with very little eventual construction was actually quite a lucrative affair, so long as constant pressure was applied to maintain the flow of income: by 1966 some £200,000 in design

12.3 1974 cartoon from the RMJM practice newsletter about the evolution of the practice's architecture. (*Roundabout RMJMP*, November 1974, 6) (RMJM)

fees had already been paid. By 1969 a further £89,000 of design work had been done, and Vernon Lee of RMJM wrote to the SERHB to accept *ex gratia* payment of £60,000; further substantial fees accrued by the 1980s following completion of Phase 1.[37]

In all this there was almost no opportunity for Matthew to actually design buildings any more. It was only in two unrealised projects – for the Burrell Collection, Glasgow, and the Edinburgh Opera House – that he was able to give rein to his design imagination on a significant scale for the last time; he was also involved in an unsuccessful competition entry in 1971 for a city-centre redevelopment in Karlsruhe. The Burrell Collection competition of 1970–1 stemmed from the donation to Glasgow Corporation of the art collection of Sir William Burrell, turn-of-the-century industrialist, art collector and patron of Robert Lorimer. After obstacles stemming from location restrictions in Burrell's will

had been overcome, a landscaped location in Glasgow's Pollok Park was secured, gently sloping with woodland on one side and open parkland on the other. The conditions of the competition, judged by assessors including architects Jack Coia, Theo Crosby and Bill Howell, stipulated that the collection should be shown 'as it would be in a private house', bizarrely incorporating three complete room interiors transplanted from Hutton. Matthew initially dealt with the RMJM competition entry himself, producing, as usual, vast numbers of alternative sketches, before finalising one sketch solution and passing it over to other staff to produce the detailed drawings. His layout envisaged an informally grouped low-rise building, nearly all on one level for disabled-access purposes, and with emphatic horizontally banded exterior offset by vertical projections, somewhat in the manner of his own Coleraine Phase 1, with outer walls of light grey Irish granite, and Brathay blue-black sloping slate roof. On plan, Matthew proposed a circuit of rooms roughly in chronological order, with focal groupings around tapestries, stained glass and Hutton Rooms. The landscaping strategy envisaged a transition from the 'formality' of the building to the 'pastoral park', using 'broad terracing in the Scottish manner', with evergreens. In the event, Matthew's design was not shortlisted, and the prize was awarded in 1971 to a somewhat more avant-garde perimeter-plan concept by three young Cambridge graduates, Barry Gasson, Brit Andreson and John Meunier (completed 1983).[38]

An apparently more promising outlet for Matthew's design efforts began to emerge the following year, in the form of an ambitious project for a cultural centre in the Festival Hall tradition in the centre of Edinburgh, on a site in Castle Terrace directly facing the Castle. An ominous element, however, was the fact that this scheme already had a long stop–go history of machinations and changes of plan, and came complete with William Kininmonth in his customary aggrieved position as displaced former architect.

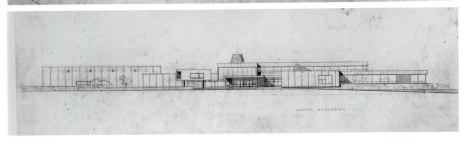

The first abortive plan for the site, envisaging a theatre, hotel, conference hall and office complex, was proposed to the Corporation in 1960 as a joint scheme by Edinburgh property developer Meyer Oppenheim. Then, in 1964, the Corporation engaged Oppenheim's consultant architect, Kininmonth, to produce a scaled-down proposal, including two theatres (seating 2,400 overall), hotel block and conference hall, possibly in partnership with Scottish and Newcastle Breweries. After a tour of European theatres and opera houses, Kininmonth submitted an outline plan in 1965, but after the Arts Council of Great Britain exp-ressed severe doubts about the viability of the (then) £4m project, it was shelved again, and Kininmonth had to produce a further scaled-down plan for a £4m maximum cost, including one large theatre suitable for staging grand opera. In 1971 the government offered a grant of £2.25m for this scheme – half the estimated cost.[39]

In March 1972, however, with the appointment of a new city architect, Brian Annable, the project was scaled up again, with support from Scottish Office chief architect Bruce Beckett, to a £9m scheme, including reconstruction of the adjacent Lyceum Theatre. The expanded scheme, officially known as the Castle Terrace Theatre Development (CTTD), was more popularly known as the 'Opera House'. Now the council began to pile pressure on Kininmonth, owing to the 'inadequate' resources of his firm, to collaborate with Renton Howard Wood, a large, London-based commercial offshoot from Basil Spence's practice.[40] During the convoluted negotiations other possible alternatives were suggested by both sides, including RMJM, but Matthew, anxious to avoid any suggestion of once more 'poaching' a job from Kininmonth, swiftly turned down the suggestion – perhaps scenting the possibility of subsequently securing the job by legitimate means. Eventually, in September 1972, the

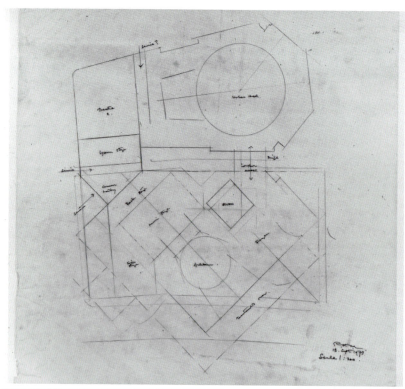

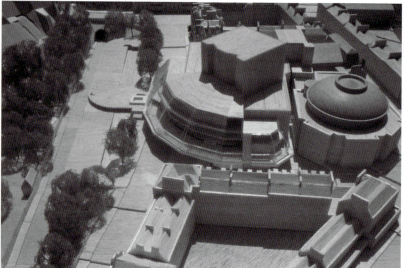

(top) **12.6** Castle Terrace Theatre Development, Edinburgh: September 1973 sketch layout by Matthew. (EULMC)

(bottom) **12.7** July 1974 model of initial CTTD proposal, showing the overhang across Castle Terrace and the massive fly-tower; the existing Usher Hall is on the right. (RMJM)

council formally terminated Kininmonth's appointment. He denounced bitterly the 'clever and unscrupulous scheme' hatched allegedly by public sector architects in the Scottish Office and City Council to remove him, and obtained backing from an RIAS investigation into the episode.[41] By mid 1973 Annable had shortlisted seven private firms, with Renton and Matthew's practices the front runners. Already, Bruce Beckett had been in informal discussion with Matthew in February 1973,

ostensibly in his RFACS capacity, and despite Annable's strong backing for Renton's firm, as 'brilliant designers', councillors eventually backed RMJM in a 36 to 25 vote – a result reported by *Building Design* as 'a favourite son vote'.[42] In a somewhat undignified last-ditch effort to salvage something from the debacle, Kininmonth pleaded at a meeting with Matthew at Regent Terrace that the two firms should work together, but 'in the end it was John Richards who said, "It won't work – we can't work in harness with someone who has such different ideas!"'[43]

When putting RMJM's case to the council, Matthew had promised not only to supervise the project personally but also to set up a dedicated design unit, including Graham and Richards. And indeed, a special office, headed by Graham in close collaboration with Richards, was immediately established in a separate office block near Fettes College – a 'kind of hotbed, or think-tank, for the development'. The complex would comprise a new 1,400-seat theatre, a 250-seat studio theatre, and the refurbishment of the Lyceum – all in all, a project as big as the National Theatre in London, and which would form part of a new circuit of large stages across Britain.[44] But, from the beginning of the CTTD project, optimism was tempered with caution: journalists pointed out the potential conflict with Matthew's role in RFACS, which had already criticised the 'bulk and dominance' of a volumetric mock-up prepared by Annable's staff. Matthew responded that 'what we said in the Commission was that the site was a fine one. But the bulk of the building seemed to be too large.' He acknowledged that 'the building has to express its function as a modern theatre complex, and pay great respect to the site. We have got to get a lot of things on the site, and this will be one of the problems.' Could it be that Matthew, mindful of the RIE experience, foresaw that the ambitious scheme might never be carried through to completion, and instead saw it chiefly as a source of income for the practice in economically troubled times? Certainly, by July 1974, £500,000 had already been spent on preliminary design work, including Kininmonth's schemes.[45] Whatever Matthew's inner feelings, he set to work on the project with furious energy, revisiting his favourite Festival Hall themes in an extensive literature survey and a one-week tour of opera houses in Germany in January 1974.[46]

In July 1974, after evaluating 'dozens of alternative plans' sketched out by Matthew in collaboration with Richards, the team unveiled its 'striking, futuristic' outline proposals, which fitted the required accommodation into the cramped site by the ingenious device of setting the 1,400-seat Theatre 1 diagonally, sweeping out over Castle Terrace at first-floor level with a 'great curving foyer and restaurant'. Overall, with its sandstone cladding and copper roofs, the building presented a monumental but highly compact mass, with one egregious exception – the 120 ft high fly-tower at the back, a square block that would tower 30 ft over the Usher Hall. Although all too aware of the previous RFACS criticisms, Matthew insisted obstinately, using Modernist arguments of 'honesty', that he had made no effort to 'hide' the tower, as 'what is functional is not necessarily ugly, and we shall ensure that it is not'. But Matthew cannot have been surprised that, within a month, the scheme was flatly turned down by his fellow RFACS commissioners, claiming that the Corporation's 'too ambitious' plans had 'severely overloaded' the site.[47] Many years earlier, Matthew had succeeded in reversing similar rebuffs over New Zealand House and George Square, but now he was older and the Edinburgh conservation lobby was far more organised – with Matthew himself, as we shall see shortly, now one of its most trenchant upholders. Immediately, work began on a height-reduction exercise, cutting 13 ft from the fly-tower, but now costs were escalating wildly: the estimated final cost was now £20m, and the Corporation estimated that over £1m would be spent on design work by the beginning of 1975. By

12.8 Model of Matthew's entry for 1971 Karlsruhe redevelopment project: decked courtyards and towers in the Barbican manner. (John Dewar Studios)

that time, and the onset of Matthew's final illness, the fortunes of the scheme were firmly set on a downward spiral, with local authority reorganisation and Scottish Office cost-cutting pointing towards far cheaper alternatives for conversion of existing theatres.[48]

Gold Medallist and elder statesman

By 1969, as he moved deeper into his sixties, Matthew remained determined not to fall into the stereotypical traps of old age, either by slowing up his pace of work, or by giving up his lifelong addiction to travel and change, and his insistence on turning his career upside down every decade or so. When asked by RMJM colleagues, 'Aren't you thinking of retiring?', he would say, 'I can't think of anything I'd rather do than what I'm doing now.' He simply 'planned to carry on working until I burst!'[49] Matthew maintained his reputation as a peripatetic enigma, by keeping up his punishing pace of foreign travel: where in mid 1969 he spent 35 per cent of his time abroad, and divided the remainder evenly between Edinburgh and London, during the whole of 1974, the last full year of his life, no less than 96 days (30 per cent) were devoted to foreign trips. Matthew emphasised his nomadic image by always travelling light: in a 1975 obituary, J J Mayoux asked 'who has not seen Robert arriving from afar with a small case, carrying his all in as little space and bulk as

12.9 Matthew seen in 1971 preparing a lecture in Park Square East. (RMJM)

449

The journey home

12.10 Matthew seen in September 1971 at 31 Regent Terrace: the tensegrity structure in the background was made by Matthew himself, and the standard lamp with punched holes was originally designed by him in 1963 for Keith Ingram. (RMJM; photograph by the late John Paterson)

a Greek philosopher?' In a 1970 interview to mark his Royal Gold Medal award, he even claimed rhetorically that 'There's nowhere I prefer living: all I ask is that it should be near an airfield since I'm always travelling.' Lorna added exasperatedly that 'since he never goes out of doors, this is the reason he doesn't mind where he lives!'[50]

With advancing years, and the reassurance of Cicely Naismith's reliable back-up at all times, this unrelenting asceticism could also now be overlaid by a restrained eccentricity – already present in latent form in Matthew's established informality of dress and manner. In 1972, for example, the secretary of the CAA wrote to Cicely that she had 'noticed today that Sir Robert's glasses were tied together with elastic bands ... he had been round to the place where he thought an optician's was located, only to find a bank sitting in its place. He had gone to the wrong corner.' Accordingly, she had ordered a new frame for him, and had 'cleaned his glasses'.[51] Even Matthew's photographic memory was no longer completely reliable: in the early 1970s, Sylvia reported with alarm, 'You know that room in his house with all the old *RIBA Journals* stacked in it, where he used to be able to say, "That article of 1937, yes, I remember," and go and find it straight away – well, he can't do that any more!' Overall, the decline in Matthew's relatively small university income continued (falling from £75 to £10 a month during 1973, with a substantial superannuation of £28,000 on his final retirement in October 1974).[52] But the

consultancy work more than compensated for that, with fees including £925 in 1971 for assessing the Parliament office competition in London, £525 p.a. for his three-year stint as conservation adviser to the Scottish Secretary in 1970–3, and £2,000 for assessing the two-stage River Clyde 'Ideas Competition' and study in September 1973. In 1972 he withdrew most of the funds from the Swiss bank account he had used for income from international competition assessor work; other smaller accounts in Yugoslavia and Czechoslovakia were more difficult to access, and were left undisturbed.[53]

Although all three of Matthew's houses remained in full use right up to 1975, by then it was becoming clear that the days of Park Square East were numbered. While the round of RIBA- or CAA-related parties and hospitality continued, often hosted by Lorna on her own, Margaret Hemslie's health posed a growing difficulty. Lorna reported to Robert Scott Morton in June 1973 that she herself was having to stay with Robert in London for three continuous weeks: 'since our London housekeeper's had a coronary, she can't cope with Robert, so I have to be in London with him.' From around 1970 Janet's doctor husband, Desmond, used the first-floor back drawing room as his consulting room.[54] More seriously still, Matthew's lease on the house, which he had occupied at a modest rate of £410 p.a. since 1956, was inexorably coming to an end, with the original terminating date of April 1973 extended twice for a year by the Crown Estates Commissioners, in exchange for a higher rent (£1,600 p.a.). In late 1973 Matthew was further dismayed to discover that Hugh Casson's practice was working on a CEC-sponsored scheme for a developer, Albany Development Ltd, for the reconditioning of the entire island site of which Park Square East formed the west face, including conversion of the Park Square East houses into flats: a move soon seemed inescapable.

Increasingly, Matthew began to spend longer chunks of his time in Scotland: in November 1968 Cicely reported to the UK

Committee of Delians that 'he is always in Scotland at the weekend'. At Keith, accordingly, there was a growing consolidation of involvement, with over £10,000 paid out on repairs and maintenance between 1967 and 1974.[55] Nearly a third of the £10,000 was accounted for by the installation of space (central) heating in 1970, a project that Matthew had been hesitating over for six years. By 1974, with mounting inflation, the annual household bills were exceeding £1,500 and the heating bill was nearly £1,000. Two years earlier Matthew had finally got down to the long-deferred business of designing a rationally planned kitchen for Keith, at the west end of the first floor, adjacent to what was now called the 'television room': two C-shaped arrangements of complex, timber-framed cupboards and open shelves, one for storage and one for food preparation, were installed. In September 1973 auctioneers Lyon & Turnbull valued the contents of Keith at a total of £20,284, including (in Matthew's study) 12,000 architectural transparencies valued at £2,000.[56] With the growing concentration on Keith went a new focus on the amenity of the surrounding area. In March 1972, for example, Matthew wrote to East Lothian chief planner Frank Tindall reporting that he had 'noted today, ominously, a surveyor with a theodolite on the Haddington–Dalkeith road' and expressing fears that this might herald a spate of straightening and widening that could damage its 'informality' and 'character'.[57]

Supported by this attention, Keith's role as the focus of family activities was progressively consolidated, whether Robert was at home or away. In the latter case, Lorna's letters would keep him posted about family and social events, highlighting sardonically anything slightly out of the ordinary, and Jessie and Aidan kept in touch as well. In a typical letter of July 1968 Jessie, on holiday from Oxenfoord, wrote to Robert at Delos, sending him a drawing of a flower and reporting that William Gordon had finished constructing a badminton court near the house. She, Lorna and William had gone

to an exhibition opening in Edinburgh (only to find 'the usual set' there), and she herself had also gone, at the end of term, on a school visit to the John Knox House in the Royal Mile, but had found its museum-like interior 'deadly boring'. On leaving Oxenfoord shortly afterwards, Jessie spent two years in Edinburgh doing A-levels, and then moved in the early 1970s to the Central School of Art in London. Her relationship with Robert had matured into a more equal, adult friendship: in 1972 he commissioned a painting of her at Keith by H More Gordon, and in June 1973 sent her a cheerful 21st birthday card (accompanied by a £100 cheque from Lorna).[58] In general, William Gordon was now fully established at Keith, spending much of the time there in his own studio and living space, and Janet and her family were also frequent visitors. But anyone could find themselves drawn into a supporting role, even on a casual visit. For instance, Dennis Ashmead, calling briefly on Matthew at Keith in the early 1970s some time after leaving RMJM, recalled that

> Lady Matthew came in with tea, looked at the fireplace and said, 'That fire's smoking,' to which Sir Robert said, 'I can see that!' – and then added, without warning, turning to me, 'What are you going to do about it?' Before I knew where I was, instead of sitting down having tea and cakes, I found myself kneeling down with a screwed up copy of the *Scotsman*, getting a fire going.

Robert's domestic dependence on Lorna continued unabated: Patrick Harrison recalled one occasion at Keith in the early 1970s, when 'Robert said to Lorna, "I'll get the coal," and went off. He

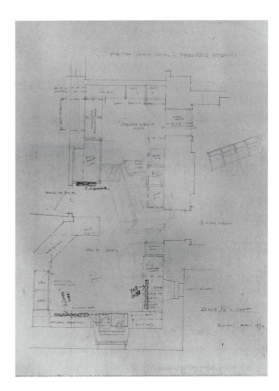

12.11 April 1972 design by Matthew for reconstruction of the kitchen on the first floor (west end) of Keith Marischal. (EULMC)

12.12 Front and back of 21st birthday card from Robert and Lorna to Jessie: 'featured' buildings include, from left to right, Keith Marischal, Oxenfoord Castle School and Park Square East. (EULMC)

came back a quarter of an hour later, still holding the shovel, saying, "Now where *do* we keep the coal?"'[59]

With Matthew beginning, for the first time, to withdraw selectively from key activities, especially his university chair, his public persona was now approaching a symbolic point, at which the outside world might start to interpret him, despite all his efforts, as being partly 'in retirement'. In April 1974, for example, historian and fellow 'Delian' Arnold Toynbee wrote to him that 'The erasures of the two addresses at your letterhead are sad, but are prudent, no doubt. As you can see, my wife and I have done the same.'[60] The risk of such a perception

growing was, if anything, heightened by the award to Matthew in June 1970 of the RIBA Royal Gold Medal for Architecture, with accompanying tributes that had something of an equivalent professional character to an academic *Festschrift* – providing a revealing glimpse of a generation now beginning to move gradually away from centre stage.[61]

The announcement of the RIBA Gold Medal award in February 1970 provoked a torrent of letters and congratulations. Among British modern architectural contemporaries, Hugh Casson sent a quirky sketch of dancing kilted figures, and Gibberd wrote that although some recent Gold Medal awards had been controversial

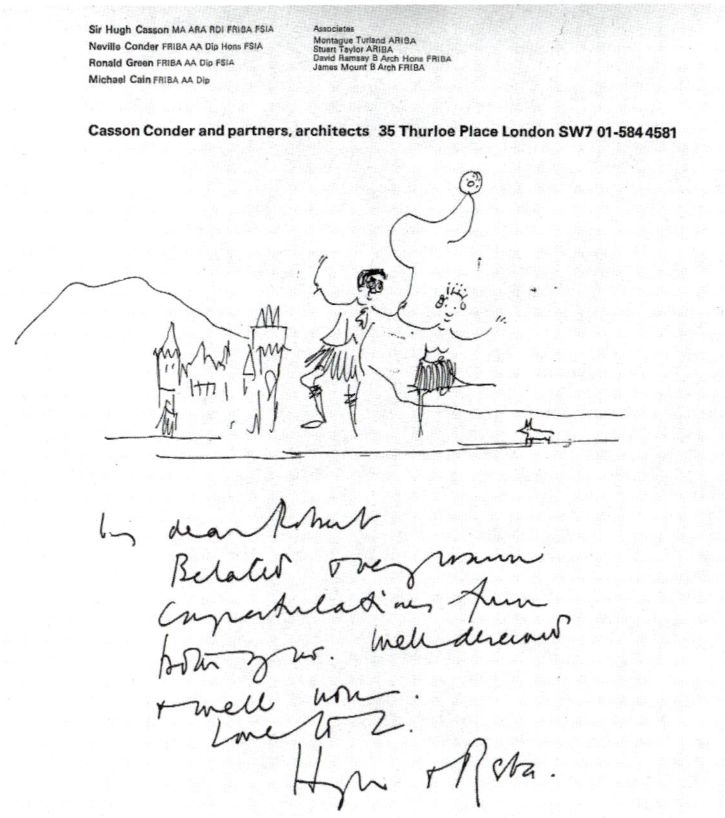

Sir Hugh Casson MA ARA RDI FRIBA FSIA
Neville Conder FRIBA AA Dip Hons FSIA
Ronald Green FRIBA AA Dip FSIA
Michael Cain FRIBA AA Dip
Associates
Montague Turland ARIBA
Stuart Taylor ARIBA
David Ramsay B Arch Hons FRIBA
James Mount B Arch FRIBA
Casson Conder and partners, architects 35 Thurloe Place London SW7 01-584 4581

12.13 Congratulatory note from Hugh Casson to Matthew on the initial announcement of his RIBA Gold Medal, February 1970. (EULMC)

among 'many of us', in Matthew's case 'there can be no doubts, as you have given the profession unstintingly of your vast ability, energy and enthusiasm'. Max Fry highlighted Matthew's 'continuous fight to raise the prestige of architecture itself in the world', adding that Jane [Drew] 'loves you very much'. Overseas tributes varied from more formal institutional congratulations to an effusive personal tribute from Jai Bhalla, writing as both Commonwealth and Indian president.[62] Other correspondents, facing the ravages of illness and advancing years, took a more melancholy line. Bill Wurster, for instance, wrote from San Francisco that although 'plagued now by Parkinson's disease' ... 'I think often of our trip round the world when you gave us those wonderful hours in Edinburgh.' And E A A Rowse, newly moved back to Sussex from Addis Ababa consultancy work following a series of strokes, sent congratulations 'from one who early on knew of your high merit', and insisted that he intended to return to Africa or Asia to work on regional development, where 'my last chance of usefulness may or may not lie'. Even more afflicted now was Bill Holford, whose letter to Matthew moved briskly from congratulations to a lengthy update on his wife's condition, following her severe cerebral stroke: as early as April 1965 Crossman had found Holford 'a tired man, and a bit of a spent force', and in 1969 he had given up his London planning chair to devote himself to the distressing business of caring for Marjorie.[63] Matthew, of course, had had an all too lengthy experience, in his youth, of mental incapacity on the part of close relatives. Now, on the cusp of old age, the exhaustion or disintegration of some others only highlighted the unabated force of his own driving nervous energy: 'He lived at high tension all through his life – right up to the very end.'[64]

Matthew's formal Gold Medal investiture ceremony, in June 1970, featured speeches by Clough Williams-Ellis and by Jean-Jacques Mayoux, professor of English Literature at the Sorbonne. Ellis hailed Matthew as 'that rare thing ... a good man and a good thing – that is, both a

12.14 Portrait of Robert and Lorna (looking at an Islamabad plan), taken in 1970 by Henk Snoek to coincide with the Gold Medal award. (Henk Snoek; RIBA)

humane and civilized person and a BENIFICENT and creative citizen and public figure' ... 'If a rusty old Welsh penny farthing may impudently tinkle its little bell in greeting to the thundering Flying Scotsman, then, "Ting-a-Ling!"'[65] There were 73 guests and partners, stretching right back into Matthew's student days. On top of the ceremony itself, large parties were arranged: at Humbie, with 125 present, and at Park Square East, with 80 of Matthew's southern acquaintances. In his own award speech Matthew candidly observed that he could boast of neither a governing 'philosophy' nor a colourful, drama-packed life:

I have not even had the advantage of being wheeled in an infant pram from London or anywhere else to Edin-burgh. As for philosophies, I have found myself, from an early age, a sceptic and maybe a true agnostic – a weak position for action, were it not for a small streak of pragmatism – taking situations 'as found' – somewhat in sympathy with the Geddesian [preference for] 'short views' – when entirely rational far-sightedness might well have obliterated the possibility of any action at all. On the contrary, I have never consistently nor even conveniently planned [something that is] certainly not very convenient for my wife and family, who have had to endure much in the interests of what I hopefully thought of as 'good works'.[66]

Despite Matthew's own visceral aversion to any suggestion of 'retirement', his tendency of loyalty to his closest old acquaintances became more pronounced at this point.[67] Clough Williams-Ellis remained a close friend, and wrote in August 1973 thanking Matthew for sending 'such a long and warming letter to such an old, T model relic as myself ... I felt it a great triumph luring you down to the Portmeirion festivities – brilliantly recorded by your daughter's photography – she is a flyer!' He hailed Matthew as a soul-mate in 'my lifelong crusade against a creeping aridity, an effort to increase enjoyment ... my leaning towards colour and gaiety ... my visceral urge for insobriety'. The regional-planning activist F J Osborn was also valued as an old ally. In June 1969 Matthew wrote to Percy Marshall asking whether his planning research unit could get some information for Osborn's journal, *Town and Country Planning*: 'I feel FJ needs some support – he is still lively.'[68] A special sentimental place was reserved for old Scottish and LCC connections. In 1969, for example, Bob Grieve, after five years at the Highlands and Islands Development Board, wrote to Matthew suggesting meeting for a drink to reminisce over 'the difficulty of achieving anything in planning', quoting Burns: 'That I, for puir auld Scotland's sake/Some usefu' plan or buik could make/Or sing a song at least!'[69] In his dealings with old LCC colleagues, Matthew meticulously upheld the collective attribution of his department's achievements: in April 1972, for example, he and Martin wrote to the Festival Hall general manager in support of Edwin Williams, who had complained about postcards of the hall attributing its design to Matthew and Martin, and argued that his and Moro's involvement should be acknowledged as 'not a mistake, hoax or fraud'.[70] Old adversaries, too, continued occasionally to re-surface, as for example when his old sparring-partner, Sidney Loweth of Eastbourne, penned him a characteristic tirade in September 1973, spurred by debate on the persecution of Soviet Jewish architects:

May I draw your attention, as one of our leading communist architects ...

and ask you what you and your fellow 'reds' are doing about it. I would suggest that instead of [appeasing] the communists that you might suggest that we might give them Karl Marx from Highgate Cemetary [sic] together with his monumental tombstone.[71]

Within the UK, Matthew's post-1968 public life was more narrowly focused than before, and especially in three main areas: advice on higher education matters, especially in Edinburgh; an elder statesman role within the RIBA, especially as the spearhead of a drive to expand members' services; and work as an adviser and juror in key government-sponsored projects.

Even within the higher education world, Matthew found himself increasingly involved with retirements and leave-takings of one kind or another. The most important of these, naturally, was his own slow but inexorable withdrawal from active involvement in the Edinburgh University architecture department, offset by his headship of the new School of the Built Environment. Following the controversial inauguration of its first-year joint course in the midst of the student unrest of 1968, this course staggered along for a number of years, along with a succession of other SBE activities, such as a 1974 conference on listing and conservation of historic gardens, and intermittent efforts to promote research on Geddes and his planning legacy – including the work of Abercrombie – and secure the archival material in the Outlook Tower.[72] Arguably, had Matthew remained more focused on university affairs, not only might the SBE have stood a better chance of survival, but there might also have been a different and more positive outcome to the repeated proposals in the early 1970s for closer university–ECA relations, including a December 1972 proposal by Cowan that the college should move into the university, and collaboration of mid-1974 over appointment of a joint ECA/University chair of town and country planning.[73] But by the early 1970s, although he was legally allowed to retain

his personal chair until age 70 (effectively, until September 1977), Matthew had begun to contemplate still further disengagement, by giving up the Forbes chair altogether – which would help, in a small way, to counter the university's mounting financial crisis during the years of inflation. After reassurances that he could keep an emeritus professorship and retain oversight of the ARU, he agreed to retire from the chair at the end of September 1974: his ARU chair would now be his sole anchor in the university.[74]

Others were in the same position as himself. In July 1973, for example, he travelled to Liverpool to preside over Robert Gardner-Medwin's valedictory at Bluecoat Chambers, organised by the Liverpool Architectural Society; and seven months later he acted as referee for Medwin's application to work for the UN as consultant. In 1969 Matthew supported Arthur Ling in a more dramatic crisis of enforced retirement, which culminated in Ling's withdrawal from the architecture and planning chair at Nottingham University, following a critical report by an RIBA visiting board, and a radical reorganisation that hived off planning into the social science department.[75] Matthew was also involved as a mediator in abortive negotiations of 1967–70 for the merger of the AA with Imperial College – a proposal that foundered over the AA's insistence on retaining its student participation system, and its power to sack unsatisfactory lecturers and technical staff – and as an intermediary in the 1969 search for a successor to Llewelyn-Davies at the Bartlett, following the latter's move into the chair vacated by Holford: he and vice-chancellor Noel Annan vainly attempted to entice Nuttgens away from the headship of Leeds Polytechnic.[76]

Matthew's educational and overseas/Commonwealth involvements also overlapped substantially – with many universities in newly independent countries temporarily employing large numbers of European staff while indigenous staff numbers were being built up.

12.15 1969 meeting of RIBA Membership and Public Affairs Board. Seen clockwise: Matthew, Gordon Mattey, Max Fry, Christopher Ratcliff, Barry Newton (student), Ivor Smith, Patrick Harrison. (*JRIBA*, October 1969, 423) (RIBA)

Matthew took care to keep track of the careers of protégés, especially if involved in overseas development work. After former Edinburgh lecturer Tony Forward, for example, was appointed head of the Addis Ababa architecture department for two years in May 1969, Matthew helped him find temporary lecturers to build up the department, and then assisted his return to England in 1971.[77] And Matthew's continuing RIBA involvement still included much hosting of parties and visiting architects in London or Edinburgh, as well as other linked goodwill work, such as his membership, until 1974, of the council of the Architects' Benevolent Society.[78] All this continued even after his final retirement from the RIBA Council in July 1971; many of his allies, of course, remained on the Council, such as Kenneth Campbell, who remained a member for 22 years, chaired the Board of Architectural Education, and became vice-president in 1975–7.[79]

Far more crucially, however, Matthew continued to play an active behind-the-scenes role in the Institute's mounting financial and credibility crises of the early 1970s, helping to support unpopular membership fee rises and service cuts – and helping steer the RIBA towards a slightly more market-responsive role. An editorial in the October 1973 *JRIBA* talked of the 'monumental crisis' confronting the Institute and the profession:

> No member of this Institute can fail to have noticed that the profession is under attack from the left, the right, and the middle ... the popular image of 'architecture' and 'the architect' is now tinged with resentment bordering on disgust (it is not so long since the *Daily Mail* referred to the RIBA as the 'Repulsive Institute of British Architects').[80]

But the RIBA was under attack not only by the wider public but from within. As at 1969, the Institute's central organisational structure was still essentially that implemented in 1963 in the wake of the 1961–2 Office Survey – namely, a modernised civil service formula, with over 100 staff, and parallel structures of elected members, headed by the President, and officials, headed by the Secretary. The process by which the name of the President simply 'emerged', and was confirmed unanimously by Council, had been modified to allow for contested election of a 'senior vice-president', on probation to become president the next year. Below the Council, and the Policy and Finance Committee, the main business of the RIBA was carried out by four departments, each with a parent board: Professional Services; Education; Membership and Public Affairs; and Library. What was new, however, was an ambitious programme of regionalisation, begun in Esher's presidency, involving opening of branch offices in provincial cities – an unsustainably ambitious programme of growth that began to succumb to inflation and economic crisis in 1971. Those years also saw a growing crisis of confidence in the succession of corporatist presidents, and a 'design-first' faction headed by Eric Lyons had secured the defeat, in the 1968 vice-presidential election, of Mike Austin-Smith, the candidate favoured by Matthew and his allies, and the election instead of the distinguished architect-landscapist Peter Shepheard: he took up his two-year presidency in 1969–71.[81] Under the impetus of the following presidents, Alex Gordon (1971–3) and Fred Pooley (1973–5), the regionalisation programme was slashed and a more modest fee-rise proposal was passed. Further economies followed as the economic crisis reached its climax in 1973–4.[82]

As a Council and committee member, Matthew was also involved in the first post-1968 moves to introduce participatory involvement within the RIBA, notably by inclusion of a student representative, Barry Newton, on the Membership and Public Affairs Board. At first, this caused little more than a ripple in the established pool of gentlemanly power. Charles McKean, later secretary of the RIAS, but then a junior RIBA staff member recalled one meeting in 1969 when

> the board were all sitting round the table, including grand people like Max Fry, Jane Drew, and Robert Matthew himself, who was in the chair. Discussion was proceeding, when the student rep – someone from Leicester or Nottingham, I think – nervously put up his hand. After several minutes Matthew said, 'I think the student representative wishes to make a contribution.' Then there was silence, and the student haltingly said his piece. Then silence again, broken eventually by Matthew, who said, 'Well, we must thank the student representative for his contribution. Now, what were we saying?' And the discussion continued as before.[83]

Increasingly, Matthew's RIBA involvement became focused on one specific area of innovation – the creation of a new, professionally organised infrastructure of members' services, ultimately stemming from the Office Survey recommendations but also responding, more immediately, to modernisation pressures from a building industry subcommittee of NEDO (the National Economic Development Organisation), chaired by Anthony Laing. Despite Matthew's strong reservations about any radical shift to free-market models of organising architecture, the

12.16 1969 photo of NBS staff. From left, Frank Day (architect), Tony Allott (NBS Technical Director) and Aylwyn Lewis. (*JRIBA*, October 1969, 423) (RIBA)

new initiatives were shaped in a hybrid private-public manner, rather than the modernised civil service pattern of the 1963 reforms – with the aim of raising income that could be recycled into the wider RIBA, under charity tax provisions. In 1969 the RIBA set up two wholly owned subsidiary companies, RIBA Services Ltd (RIBAS) and National Building Specifications Ltd (NBS), both chaired by Matthew from their creation in 1969 until August 1974; the managing director was Aylwyn M Lewis. RIBAS and NBS functioned in tandem, with RIBAS as an umbrella company, and NBS pursuing the specific task of establishing and marketing a specifications database. The intention of NBS, Matthew explained in March 1973, was to help boost building efficiency and productivity by enhancing the industry's 'communications system' with a library of 'data sheets' and standard specification clauses for adoption in project documents. After some two years of initial negotiation, a two-stage approach was agreed on – first, to publish the data in book form, in a series of four volumes (the first three launched by Matthew in 1973) in collaboration with the *Liverpool Daily Post and Echo*, and then to 'computerise' the data in collaboration with Oldacres Computers Ltd.[84] From the beginning, however, the bold project was beset by organisational and financial difficulties, requiring a substantial bail-out by RIBAS in December 1972, and by 1974 it was still not clear that the project had been properly targeted, as key clients such as the GLC and DoE were still 'puzzling out' how to use the NBS data, despite having subsidised their preparation. In August 1974, following renewed alarm over significant losses at both companies, and a report by Lewis to Matthew that the budget was 'in shreds', Matthew resigned from the boards of both RIBAS and NBS – doubtless tired of the ceaseless financial wrangling, and anxious to prioritise his activities.[85]

During his last six years Matthew also reined in fairly radically his London-based representational activity. Being temperamentally opposed (despite his brief dalliance with Cruden) to potentially compromising links with developers and commercial firms, he steered clear of the potentially lucrative field of private consultancy work – except on rare occasions when there was the justification of a generally 'public' context. In 1969–70 he became briefly involved with an initiative of Grosvenor Estates to formulate a management and planning strategy for Mayfair and Belgravia in the post-leasehold enfranchisement era. And in the same years he joined Esher, Holford, Llewelyn-Davies and Keith Joseph as a trustee of a developer-financed, charitable national housing trust, the World of Property Housing Trust. RMJM itself made some substantial financial contributions, and by 1971 the trust had in hand development programmes totalling £8m.[86]

Architectural competition jury service provided another hybrid public-private outlet, but Matthew became involved in only two significant London competitions during this period, both in 1968–9. The first, and more controversial, was for a central London mosque in Regent's Park, on a site provided by the Crown Lands Commissioners in 1944, and for which an earlier, massive design had been rejected by the RFAC. Doubtless Matthew's appointment stemmed from his close Pakistani connections – and, in the event, the competition followed a similar course to the Qaid-e-Azam monument

competition a decade earlier, with attempts by the commissioning agency – the London Central Mosque Trust (LCMT) – to overturn the verdict in favour of a more conventionally 'Islamic' design. The brief specified a congregational hall for nearly 1,000 worshippers, with women's gallery for 500, plus an Islamic cultural centre and flats. From the very beginning there were suggestions of controversy, with a complaint by Philip Powell to the RIBA about a 'cloak and dagger' atmosphere. Eventually, Matthew and his colleagues (one Spanish and one Pakistani) chose a relatively traditional design by Gibberd, with minaret and great golden anodised dome, and Moghul arched windows round the outside to evoke 'pan-Islamic symbolism'. The joint third prize went to the highly decorated, conventionally Islamic-historicist designs of the Cairo-based Arab Bureau for Designs and Technical Consultations. Matthew congratulated Gibberd on his 'beautifully simple' design, which had 'managed (as few could) to bridge the mysterious gap between the Moslem world and ours!' Persevering in the face of attempts by the LCMT to depose him in favour of the Cairo group and pay him off with the £3,000 prize, Gibberd agreed to modify his design to make it more 'traditional' still, by raising the dome higher on a drum, making it more pointed, and moving the minaret to integrate it with the main building. The mosque was eventually built in 1974–7, and in 1980 Gibberd admitted that 'I have a capacity for revising my designs (I swallow my pride and do not resign).'

Ultimately less productive was the all-Commonwealth competition of 1968–72, chaired by Matthew, for a parliamentary office building facing the Palace of Westminster, on a pivotal corner site laid down in Martin's 1965 Whitehall plan, and in conformity to Martin's concept of an array of dense, stepped courtyards – a formula familiar in general terms to Matthew from his own proposal for Edinburgh Royal Infirmary. Lionel Esher, in his formal letter of invitation to Matthew in June 1966, predicted ambiguously that this 'could be one of the outstanding competitions of our time', and admitted that Lasdun had originally been considered as chairman, but had been ruled out on the grounds that he was a possible architect for the new Foreign Office building. The eventual jury comprised Matthew, Lasdun, Eric Bedford (MPBW Chief Architect), Robin Boyd (of Australia) and J C Parkin (Canada) – the latter two both CAA allies of Matthew. During 1968–9 a series of preliminary assessors' meetings warned that the brief, combined with Martin's dense, medium-rise formula, might seriously 'overload' the site. After a lengthy two-stage judging process of the 246 entries, in March 1972, an entry by Robin Spence (nephew of Basil) and Robin Webster was selected as first prizewinner. It envisaged a dark, glazed, somewhat palazzo-like block, raised up a floor, with a big central courtyard boldly roofed with a space frame. Eventually, the scheme fell foul of the mounting economic crisis that engulfed the Heath government, and was postponed – in the event, for good – in May 1973. In parallel with this competition, there was also a limited amount of follow-on to Matthew's 1966 Broad Sanctuary report, which had recommended that, to allow retention of the ICE/RICS buildings in Great George Street, only part of the site should be developed – ultimately by a government conference centre, for which Lasdun did a feasibility study in April 1970. In December 1970 Lasdun wrote confidentially to Matthew that

> if by chance you have occasion to see Peter Walker [Minister], it would be a great help to remind him of your findings at the Inquiry on Broad Sanctuary. Perhaps you might suggest to him the importance of making public what his intentions are for the future of this area?

Eventually, despite the conservationist defeat of Martin's wider Whitehall plan, the proposed conference complex was indeed built on this site – in the inverted-ziggurat, megastructural six-storey form of the Queen Elizabeth II Conference Centre, designed by Sir Philip Powell of Powell & Moya and opened in 1986.[87]

The most significant consultative London 'establishment' commission of Matthew's last years was concerned not with any individual building, but, characteristically, with more nebulous matters of design quality and organisation in government building projects: the Matthew/Skillington Inquiry on the Promotion of High Standards of Architectural Design, commissioned in December 1972 by Rippon's DoE and carried out in 1973–4 by Matthew with civil service administrator W P D (Pat) Skillington. This was perhaps the most extreme London-based example during Matthew's career of the devotion of effort to a purely organisational, bureaucratic task – indeed, it might have been a challenge more naturally suited to Stirrat Marshall – and, as so often with these kinds of efforts, there was no decisive, quantifiable outcome. Nor was it a lucrative exercise for Matthew himself, as he was paid, after tax, only £616 for 46 days' work (£13 per day, in contrast to the £70 daily minimum charged by RMJM for partner consultancy work). The initial stimulus for the inquiry was to work out a job specification for a new chief architect post at DoE at deputy secretary level, recently secured by Deputy Secretary J D Jones, with the aim of correcting several years of weakness and fragmentation at chief architect level. But more generally in the background was a climate of unease within the English public-architectural community about the encroachment of management bureaucracy at the expense of design values, both within the design of the government's own projects (for which the Property Services Agency, or PSA, had been responsible since its formation in 1972) and in the DoE's work in vetting or approving others' proposals and giving design and R&D guidance for new buildings and conservation: the post of Chief Housing Architect had been vacant since Whitfield Lewis had left some years before.

Matthew and Skillington began work

with an extensive programme of inter-views around the DoE and PSA regional offices, where they found much discontent at the subordination of designers to bureaucrats.[88] The chief tension was between the desire of Jones (a planner) and Skillington (an administrator) to appoint just one post, focused on PSA's work, and Matthew's determination, as ever, to expand the brief and press for *two* chief architects, one covering PSA and the other – a 'Chief Environmental Architect' – within 'Central DoE' to take the lead in 'environmental planning, including conservation'.

By January 1974, when the first part of the report was passed to DoE, it had become clear that Matthew had overcome Skillington's reservations and had secured the line he wanted: Bruce Beckett wrote admiringly that 'knowing Pat as I do, I can only marvel at your powers of persuasion'.[89] The jubilation was, however, premature, as, despite pressure by Pooley and Harrison, Jones remained 'very uneasy' about the idea of two chief architects, and the report was summarised in a grossly misleading memo by an administrator within DoE, and then simply shelved by the new Labour Environment Secretary, Anthony Crossland, for a year. When eventually published in March 1975, following ingenious behind-the-scenes machinations by Matthew, Harrison and Colin Boyne of the *AJ*, the Chief Environmental Architect post had vanished – to be replaced by a toothless 'Environmental Board' within DoE – but it was agreed that Dan Lacey (then head of the Department of Education architects) would be immediately appointed Director General of Design Services in PSA. Matthew speculated that 'the "planners" have resisted the whole idea of an environmental division and would be at one here with the administrators.' Although this retreat was met with fury from the PSA/DoE regional architects, who wrote to Matthew of their 'anger and despair' at the 'cynical and deliberate misinterpretation by other disciplines and administrators', Matthew, now terminally ill, replied

sanguinely that 'I do not myself take a pessimistic view of the outcome', and insisted that Lacey would be up to his 'tough and strenuous task'; Patrick Harrison argued: 'How lovely we were able to achieve anything at all – as the forces of inertia were colossal!'[90]

The 'uncrowned king' of conservation in Scotland

As we shall see later, Matthew's new burst of idealistic zeal from the late 1960s expressed itself most passionately through a commitment to global environmentalism. But it was intrinsic to the small-is-beautiful ethos of the ecological movement that the universal should be firmly grounded in the particular and local, and so these last years of Matthew's life also saw a radically enhanced commitment to conservation, especially at home in Scotland – an ever more intense focus on Scottish roots that reverted in some ways to his childhood upbringing within Lorimerian Arts and Crafts traditionalism. It might seem a little odd that Robert Matthew became one of Scotland's most important conservationists, in view of his reputation in some of Edinburgh's introverted heritage circles even today as 'the destroyer of George Square'.[91] But such a reversal, with all its uncomfortable contradictions, was only in keeping with his restless and complex character, insistent on the need for critical openness to change.

To some extent, Matthew's renewed passion for Scotland was shaped by the wider political and economic instability of early 1970s Britain. In response to that climate, Scottish nationalism had made rapid strides, and now Matthew began privately to talk with increasing enthusiasm of his support for Scottish independence: such a stance would have allowed him to reconcile his alienation from Labour, owing to the tax burden, with a continuing commitment to 'socialism' in a general sense. Sylvia wrote to him after a dinner at Prestonfield House in November 1974 that 'I don't think I am a converted Scottish Nationalist, but it was very interesting to talk about it.'[92] As always, Matthew strenuously avoided any undignified public political declarations of affinity, and channelled his views into the strictly cultural domain. He argued with vigour, for instance, in his 1974 presidential address to the Saltire Society, that 'in these days, when many individuals and groups seem determined to play down the reality of a Scottish culture and indeed to argue that the very idea is somehow anti-English, or anti-European, or anti-global', it was vital 'to reaffirm, for all to hear, our belief that this country has a cultural identity of its own'. Yet, at the same time, Matthew still took pains to steer clear of any suggestion of parochialism, and was always ready to set the Scottish position more dispassionately in a wider international perspective.[93]

Matthew's turn to conservation was also, naturally, firmly rooted in international developments, above all the sudden shock of the 1968 unrest across Europe and North America, and the moral challenge it posed to the post-war ethos of materialist corporatism and admiration of the New. In 1969 he conceded that 'in the last few years, and I speak from long and bitter experience, public opinion on the quality of environment has visibly moved from almost total indifference to one of concern, if not alarm.' One obvious by-product was the equally sudden public shift towards conservation. In 1972 Matthew argued that 'this whole conservation business has come more or less out of the blue, to the planning process – a process steeped in official pronouncements and prestige – as a kind of emergency operation'; 'lay opinion' was now rapidly engaging itself on the side of conservation, and 'has suddenly and sharply exposed wide areas for the operation of value judgements'.[94] Matthew juggled with the need to reconcile his innate self-confidence with the contradictions in his own previous world outlook:

I am frequently charged with being, on the one hand, a dyed in the wool preservationist, and on the other a callous destroyer. I plead guilty to both, for choices have to be made. The world cannot become a vast museum, with the living populations relegated to marginal and temporary shanty towns. Values have to be set and acknowledged, but once made, these should be as permanent as we are capable of making them. The limited stock of high quality buildings we are now fortunate to possess is quite literally irreplaceable.

The aim of conservation must be to 'maintain a high level of environment' rather than pursue 'inflexible preservation'; yet he claimed that, in RMJM, 'I have a rule in my office about listed buildings – that they must not be demolished'. During the mid 1960s, certainly, he had made efforts to persuade British Home Stores to move the site of their redevelopment in Edinburgh's Princes Street so as to spare the florid Victorian facade of the Life Association of Scotland building.[95] And by 1974 he was echoing full-blown green rhetoric, claiming that the architectural heritage was an 'irreplaceable resource'. Yet Matthew was still privately able to recognise, as with Alois Riegl's concept of *Alterswert*, the essential transience of the heritage. William Gordon recalled that 'just before he died, when he was planning to build a new house here at Keith, I asked him, "What will you do with the old one?" He said, "Leave it to fall down!"'[96]

This conflict of values went back, among other things, to Geddes, whose very catchphrase 'conservative surgery' was an oxymoron. By the late 1960s there was a growing tendency among activists to oppose the words 'preservation' and 'conservation' to one another – the latter being attributed conservative-surgery overtones of progressive change. But Matthew's turn to conservation was no unexpected volte-face: ever since 1953, and even at the height of his thrusting modern period, he had been a faithful member of a whole range of heritage organisations in Scotland – the Historic Buildings Council for Scotland (HBCS), Saltire Society, Royal Fine Art Commission for Scotland (RFACS) and Scottish National Buildings Record Council – as well as more specific bodies such as the [Calton] Terraces Association, which he chaired for its first seven years from 1966. For the National Trust for Scotland he had already masterminded the flagship Bannockburn project, which formed the centrepiece of James Stormonth-Darling's tourism-orientated modernisation drive.[97] He also continued a lesser involvement in other heritage-related organisations, such as the Royal Commission on the Ancient and Historical Monuments of Scotland. All of these organisations were 'hats' that Matthew could put on or off at will in relation to specific causes.

Heritage and Modernity: the Scottish Civic Trust and the 'Saltire'

We shall come to the biggest of those causes – the 'saving' of the Edinburgh New Town – in a moment. First, however, we need to trace the parallel story of Matthew's more general contribution to the growth and victory of conservation in Scotland. Throughout his early and mid 1960s phase of Modernist confidence, with its continuing emphasis on Newness and Bigness, Matthew's preferred vehicle for environmental intervention in Scotland had been the RFACS, and during this period Matthew's contributions to RFACS casework had shown a general bias towards change rather than preservation. In 1967, for example, he had commented to the RFACS that 32–5 St Andrew Square was 'not of great architectural quality' and could readily be demolished if the replacement were of 'high architectural quality'. But during the mid and late 1960s a more overtly conservationist undertone became perceptible in Matthew's Scottish activities: for example, media appearances of 1968–70 included a 1968 St Andrew's Day radio lecture on general built-environment problems, and three television appearances in 1970, one on new university planning and the other two on the conservation of the Edinburgh New Town.

The first of Matthew's new conservation initiatives in Scotland was his pressure for extension to Scotland of the area improvement policies of the London-based Civic Trust, through the moves of 1965–7 to set up a separate Scottish Civic Trust (SCT), under the chairmanship of Lord Muirshiel; Matthew inevitably was appointed one of the SCT's seven trustees.[98] Although Matthew remained a member of the RFACS (and, indeed, was twice reappointed 'for the last time', finally in 1971, because of his 'unique value' as a deal-broker and a general authority on new and historic architecture), the SCT immediately became the main vehicle for his environmental interventions in Scotland, its rise coinciding exactly with his turn to conservation. Importantly, he and Maurice Lindsay immediately hit it off, and Lindsay, well accustomed from his television work to dealing boldly and cordially on first name terms with 'VIPs', became a prototype for a new, more informal and less subservient kind of ally in Matthew's mellower 'retirement' years: in November 1967, for example, Matthew hailed the 'poetic, energetic director of the Civic Trust'.[99]

What the Glasgow-based SCT link also brought was a growing focus on the regeneration of Glasgow, including both the city centre and the West End terraces. Much of this was routine casework, as with an application for office infill in 1968 in 12–13 Woodside Terrace, where Lindsay asked Matthew to formulate an SCT response, promising that the Corporation was 'willing to impose the views you expressed', or complicated negotiations of mid 1974, with Hugh Casson as intermediary, to try to ensure that two major bank developments opposite Queen Street Station would not be built in the form of high towers.[100] Especially important, though, was the help of Lionel Esher, who developed (partly against his own Modernist instincts) an influential conservation plan for the city in 1971. Matthew, Coia and Ninian Johnston, as RFACS commissioners, attended Esher's presentation meeting in the City Chambers in September 1971. This inaugurated a three-year, SCT-orchestrated and Glasgow-Corporation-financed 'Facelift in Glasgow' campaign of cleaning and improvements, involving 10,000 Glaswegians, with the aim of establishing a 'climate of environmental optimism', especially through stone cleaning; the project's director was Peter Draper. David Walker recalled that pressure from Esher and the Glasgow planners for de-listing of some Glasgow buildings came to nothing: 'Somebody, probably Robert, was looking after me, as I heard no more about it.'[101]

Matthew's SCT work was also complementary to his continuing collaboration with RFACS, not only in Glasgow but also in casework all over Scotland – for example at Ballachulish, where he and Bannatyne clashed with Arup in 1973 over a 'heavy and intrusive' bridge design. And it also complemented his deepening links with the Saltire Society, with its established 'conservationist' record of progressive Geddesian environmentalism. Having chaired the housing awards panel since the death of Hurd in 1963, in the early 1970s he became the society's president.[102] The 1969 and 1970 award ceremonies saw Matthew shift his focus of attention away from his old mid-1960s bête noire of package-deal public housing towards the likely 'disastrous' effects of any increased reliance on 'free enterprise' spec building; he stressed that 'public authorities, bless them', had shown that high-quality, coordinated design and landscaping was possible within tight cost limits; and he sardonically commented that although it was sometimes said that spec housing individualism was spurred by desire to avoid being 'confused with public housing – Alas! there is little chance of this confusion. Today, the least attractive elements of the environment, architecturally speaking, are nearly always the creation of the private builder.' Increasingly, Matthew began to interpret the housing awards through a heritage filter, arguing in 1974 that the award-winning schemes of the past 40 years 'are now, in fact, part of our heritage'.[103]

More generally, Matthew's Saltire speeches sought to provide a Scottish context for his growing environmentalism, arguing that the small size of Scotland made it a potential exemplar of the small-is-beautiful ethos: in 1973, he told the AGM quite explicitly that the Saltire must uphold 'the continuity of our national culture', as 'our voice is still a quiet one, but, like Dr Schumacher, I have a hunch that, more often than not, the small is the more beautiful in the end.' But what was even more remarkable than these activities at the interface of modernity and conservation was the way in which Matthew also came to dominate the Edinburgh-based world of straightforward conservation and preservation, steering the capital's established culture of Geddesian architectural pride into the 1970s era of environmental activism through a multitude of initiatives, apparently unconnected but in fact, as one key participant later recalled, all fitting in effect into a 'single grand plan'.[104] In Edinburgh there were a number of tensions, arising chiefly from the George Square controversy, that did not apply to his relations with the Glasgow-based SCT. Conflict and debate were endemic in this new and more 'participatory' world, as Matthew found in early/mid 1974, when a bitter row erupted over proposals supported by himself, Muirshiel and Lindsay to merge the SCT with the SGS, Saltire and two other small groups, to create a new 'Scottish Saltire Trust' with joint membership and single executive, with the aim of securing fundraising economies of scale, and overcoming what was felt to be the stagnation of the Saltire. Despite efforts to avoid 'the impression of a takeover' by SCT, the proposal collapsed in acrimony, with the SGS fearing that the 'enthusiasm of voluntary effort' would be undermined, and the Saltire insisting on a confederative structure with parallel executives.[105]

Matthew doubtless felt a little uncomfortable in this new activist setting, and thus when he began to frame his work in increasingly conservationist terms from the late 1960s, he understandably decided to direct his own interventions mainly through official channels. But even this would have to be on the right terms. At

463

12.17 Robert Matthew seen in November 1970 in the Edinburgh New Town immediately following the announcement of his appointment as Conservation Adviser to the Secretary of State for Scotland. (*Glasgow Herald*)

first, in the mid 1960s, the governmental context seemed unfavourable to any general pro-conservation initiative, with Sir Douglas Haddow (Secretary of the Scottish Development Department, or SDD) opposing any confrontations with local authorities, and his successor Alan Hume (1965–73) more sympathetic to conservation but still inclined to defer to municipal power: 'They held that the local authorities should be left to answer for their indifference to conservation at the polls.'[106]

How, then, was any pro-conservation intervention by Matthew in Scottish government affairs to be structured? After Ian Lindsay's death in 1966, Matthew had turned down an offer of Lindsay's post of chief investigator; he had no intention of

ever again becoming a salaried official, even part time![107] Matthew would exercise his influence, it was clear, indirectly – by pressure on, and advice to, others. The obvious candidate to succeed Lindsay was David Walker, a young SDD inspector whose encyclopedic knowledge of 18th- and, especially, 19th-century Scottish architecture had already attracted the attention of both Matthew and the eminent St Andrews historian and pioneering conservationist Dr Ronald Cant. With the growth of the Victorian Society in England in the early 1960s, 19th-century architecture was increasingly coming into fashion. But Walker was still, in 1966, only 33 years old, administratively inexperienced, and, being 'over-committed to the cause', inclined to weigh in on the conservationist side in controversial cases. The matter became more urgent with the passing of the 1969 Town & Country Planning (Scotland) Act, which provided for a system of statutory listed-building consent (LBC) administered by SDD and the local authorities: soon, the SDD would need to decide or adjudicate on large numbers of controversial demolition cases. The 1969 Act also introduced the principle of public consultation on planning cases through advertisement; previously, applications were treated as confidential, and thus pro-conservation officials such as Walker 'had to learn the black arts of being a subversive, to get controversial information into the public domain without being found out'.[108]

In 1970 a compromise over the succession to Lindsay was eventually decided on by Matthew and Cant, in consultation with David, 26th Earl of Crawford, former head of the (English) National Trust and one of the most influential figures in heritage circles in Britain as a whole. Their compromise solution, endorsed by Alan Hume and the Tory junior Scottish Office minister, George Younger, was that, to tide matters over until Walker was sufficiently experienced to allow Lindsay's post to be revived for him, full time, Matthew would take on a parallel appointment from 1 December 1970. Alongside his renewed HBCS membership, he would be appointed, initially for three years, as special 'consultant adviser' to the Secretary of State on the 'conservation of buildings and areas of architectural and historic importance'. His appointment was on the strict understanding that he would deal with policy issues only, not routine HBCS or listing casework. To provide him with background information, SDD deluged Matthew with boxloads of technical memos and circulars. Meanwhile, Walker and two colleagues would deal with everyday casework, with advice from Lord Stratheden, the HBCS Chairman since 1969, and from Anthony Dale, MHLG chief inspector in England. In all these areas, a powerful precedent was provided by the strong advances of conservation in England during the ministerial regimes of Crossman and Anthony Greenwood at MHLG, and (especially) Lord Kennet as junior minister in the Department from 1966 onwards. Until Scotland could 'catch up', Dale provided 'a marvellous source of advice and wisdom on what one could get away with!' Hailed in the press as 'Scotland's first conservation supremo', Matthew argued that conservation must take account of change, 'using imagination to link the best of the past with the things of the present'.[109]

'Conservation supremo': opportunities and limitations

Matthew recognised from the start that his role as 'supremo' could be only a hortatory one, given the limited amount of time that he himself was prepared to devote to this activity. He therefore concentrated his efforts almost entirely on setting strategic goals and pressuring for the organisational frameworks that could give them effect. He aimed to build up the historic buildings branch of SDD on a long-term basis, through a range of arguments, including pressure for more resources, more sympathetic administrative staff, and establishment of specialised conservation sections within local authorities. As with his orchestration of the famous campaign of 1949 against control of London County

Council housing design by the Valuer's department, concerted 'external pressure' on civil servants considered dilatory by Matthew and his allies was a key factor. At first, the immediate administration of historic-building matters was in the vacillating hands of the HBCS Secretary, Tom Rarity. The secrecy of the pre-1969 Act system encouraged a 'terrible divide' between administrators and inspectors: 'the files were hidden from us as far as possible!' But from 1970 Matthew and his helpers ratcheted up the pressure rapidly. Maurice Lindsay, for example, criticised Rarity for his 'footering around behind a barrage of pedantic verbiage' and his 'words to avoid action' in cases such as the proposed restoration of Grosvenor Terrace, Glasgow, and Rarity was duly replaced in 1972 by the more dynamic Harry Graham, with Ronnie Cramond as administrative Assistant Secretary and Murray Bell as Under-Secretary. Walker recalled that 'things changed literally overnight after Harry Graham came, with administrators and professionals working as a team for the first time. That was probably Graham's and Cramond's influence, but Robert Matthew clearly gave it his full backing as part of his "grand plan".'[110]

The reforms that followed began with reorganisation of the HBCS, with £50,000 extra grant being made available for conservation areas outside Edinburgh. In April 1972 the HBCS set up a new subcommittee, chaired by Lord Stratheden, to oversee the SDD listing programme. At

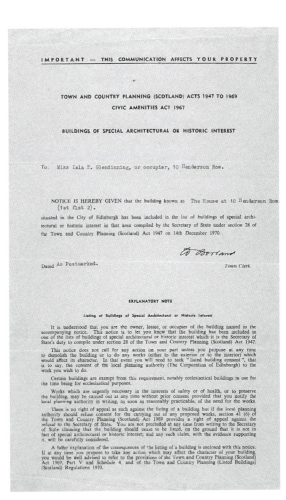

12.18 An example (dated 28 June 1971) of an owner's notification of the 'listing' of an Edinburgh New Town tenement flat. (Miss Isla Glendinning)

12.19 1970 views of Rossend Castle as a gutted ruin, and 1977 view after restoration. (Ian Begg, Architect)

Matthew and Cant's suggestion, and in response to a 1969 initiative by Nikolaus Pevsner on an equivalent English committee (chaired by Holford), it recommended a 25-year rolling cut-off date to deal with the issue of 20th-century architecture. In late 1972 Matthew met Anthony Dale, to make sure that these reforms were properly coordinated with the English experience.[111] In a follow-up Act of 1972 listed building consent for demolition was made a fully statutory procedure, with obligatory notification of the SCT, SGS and local societies. In its first five years the SCT had already commented on 66 major demolition cases, but now this number increased exponentially, and in 1973 Cramond secured it a £6,000 grant, to allow it to undertake 'environmental coordination' of the work of local civic societies, while avoiding 'narrow, "preservationist"' confrontations with local authorities. With Matthew's encouragement, it had already (in 1972) boldly intervened in the long-running New Lanark saga, by convening a public meeting in Lanark Town Hall, to start a

joint subsidy scheme similar to that in the Edinburgh New Town.[112] In the wake of the 1967 Civic Amenities Act Matthew tried to develop the potential of the conservation area concept that it had introduced, and in March 1973 he chaired an Edinburgh conference, organised by the SCT, NTS and Cockburn Association, on how to help 'lay conservationists' present their case to public inquiries.[113]

However, there were limits to Matthew's input into policy: in July 1972, for example, the NTS's Stormonth-Darling wrote to him, after a meeting, that he had been 'surprised to realise how little St Andrew's House was keeping you in touch', and offered to 'keep you in touch privily' with potential controversies, on the principle that the Secretary of State must have intended Matthew to 'do your own scouting and come to your own conclusions in giving your advice to Government'.[114] And in individual cases Matthew was able to give only a selective and occasional input, relying largely on Walker for advice on Victorian architecture. Like Maurice Lindsay, Walker was being gradually built up into a privileged helper-figure, and his relationship with Matthew would have almost certainly become somewhat closer had the latter survived beyond 1975. In 1973, for example, he endorsed a proposal (eventually unsuccessful) to award Walker an RIBA honorary fellowship, highlighting his 'extraordinary knowledge and judgement ... I do not know of anyone else in Scotland with more claim to an honorary fellowship.'[115]

In general, during his three years as official government adviser, Matthew felt constrained to avoid any open interventions in individual controversies. In 1970–1, for example, revival of a longstanding proposal by Burntisland town councillors to demolish the dilapidated Rossend Castle was met by a storm of conservation protest, and the Fife-based modern architect Anthony Wheeler put forward an SCT-backed counter-suggestion for restoration, strongly supported behind the scenes by Matthew. The town council was split on party lines, with the Labour Dean of Guild backing demolition and the Tory Provost opposing it. After the start of demolition was narrowly averted on 14 August, and the castle 'spotlisted' in December, a public inquiry was held the following year, with Ian Begg (supported by Stuart Matthew) leading opposition to demolition, and Robert Matthew exerting behind-the-scenes pressure while insisting that he could not give evidence at the inquiry himself.[116] The same restraint applied over a proposed tall office tower at Edinburgh's Haymarket, where Matthew had to turn down a suggestion by Maurice Lindsay that he represent the SCT at a public protest meeting in September 1972.[117]

In his few open casework contributions in the early 1970s Matthew's earlier, more ambiguous attitudes to preservation still resurfaced occasionally. For example, in December 1971, the former Tory Junior Minister Tam Galbraith, Lord Strathclyde, asked for the recent listing of his Ayrshire house, Barskimming (by Walker's colleague, Michael Gibb), to be rescinded, as much of it was neoclassical

revival of the late 19th century, built by Wardrop and Reid following the destruction of the 1771/1816 main block in a fire of 1882. Walker recalled that 'Galbraith had been a sympathetic Minister, so this was a surprise to us! This was pretty soon after Matthew's appointment, so Ronnie Cramond thought he would try him out on a specific listing case.' After visiting the house, armed with a copy of Ian Lindsay's 1948 listing guidelines, Matthew reluctantly agreed to the de-listing. But at an HBCS meeting a couple of weeks later, at which he was sitting opposite Walker, 'Matthew said to me, "Was I right about Barskimming?" I said "No – the 1880s-revival work there is just as interesting as the original!" He said ruefully, "It's too late now, but I did wonder if I'd done the right thing!"'[118] Matthew also used the consultancy to lay down markers for other initiatives: in 1972 he campaigned for a Pevsner-style 'Buildings of Scotland' series, and supported James Stormonth Darling's NTS proposal to convert 7 Charlotte Square into a showpiece 'Georgian House'.[119]

In 1973, what was intended to be an initial three-year term as Secretary of State's adviser came to an end. By now, concentrating his energies on his international 'mission' of reform of human settlement (see Chapter 13), Matthew was increasingly pruning back his other commitments. He thus decided to keep on his HBCS membership, but to relinquish his adviser post. Part of the underlying agenda of this move was to allow Matthew to align himself even more closely with the conservation cause, by commenting on individual cases. Now, he could begin to weigh in openly against controversial developments – as in June 1974, when he and Cant persuaded the Scottish Office to sanction the transfer of Rossend Castle to a restoring purchaser – with the result that Robert Hurd and Partners bought it in 1975 and restored it as offices for their own use.[120] In February 1974 Matthew wrote to the Secretary of State, Gordon Campbell, to help block Glasgow Corporation's planned demolition of C R Mackintosh's Martyrs School, arguing that 'I wish to add my own personal plea in the strongest terms ... the name Charles Rennie Mackintosh is much revered abroad, if not in Glasgow. We are surely past the stage when a unique part of this country's architectural heritage has to disappear on account of urban road works', and 'it would be especially ironic if in European Architectural Heritage Year, Scotland were to add to the long and shameful record of demolition.' It is not quite clear whether Matthew saw that 'shameful record' as including his own earlier work at George Square in Edinburgh or in Glasgow's Gorbals, but in the event he lived only another year, and did not even survive the whole of EAHY.[121] In September 1976, just over a year after Matthew's death, David Walker was finally appointed as a full-time successor to Ian Lindsay as SDD chief inspector.

Robert Matthew, saviour of the Edinburgh New Town

The £50,000 SDD grant negotiated by Matthew in 1972 for the SCT to disburse in conservation areas across the country was matched by another grant of equal size for a purpose even dearer to his heart: the conservation of the Edinburgh New Town. Throughout the 1960s and early 1970s he had been pursuing a relentless campaign to save the New Town from long-term decay, a campaign that ran constantly in parallel with his general conservation proselytising work, forming a more specific and urgent counterpart to it. We now have to focus in more detail on this literally monumental achievement, which stands as Matthew's major contribution to both Scottish and world conservation. Initially, this requires us to retrace our steps to the early 1960s. At that time – as is difficult to grasp now, with the huge values of most houses in the area – the entire New Town, after two wars and an intervening depression, had been overtaken by a general, insidious decay and lack of stonework and roof maintenance, and certain parts – the so-called 'tattered fringes', places like Stockbridge – had undergone

a sharp social as well as physical decline, becoming essentially dilapidated slums not unlike the Gorbals, albeit on a pocket-sized scale, as for example in Jamaica Street. Paradoxically, although Matthew was busily pursuing his own campaign of surgery in the 18th-century South Side in the same years, he was probably at that stage the only individual with both a concerned awareness of the New Town conservation problem *and* a sufficiently national standing to do something about it. As early as his 1937 polemical town-planning exhibition for the Edinburgh Architectural Association he had grasped that the New Town was under subtle erosion, and that 'with the usual unbounded enthusiasm of students, the dire consequences of what would certainly happen if nothing was done were pointed out'.[122]

Initially, around 1962, Matthew's strategy was to use Bannatyne and the RFACS as his immediate vehicle for agitation, as well as trying to pressure Malcolm MacEwen in London to orchestrate a BBC debate. In 1963 efforts to stir up the Cockburn Association and the SGS to draft a proposal to submit to the Secretary of State came to nothing, and in August 1965 he first put to an RFACS meeting the suggestion that the Commission 'should put forward the idea of a top level conference concerned with the protection of our "architectural heritage"', especially the 'large-scale preservation' of the New Town.[123] Nothing happened for another year – until an unexpected boost came from England. Under the dynamic influence of Lord Kennet, the Ministry of Housing in 1966 established the so-called 'Blueprint' programme, a series of four conservation studies of historic cities – York, Bath, Chester, Chichester – which were published as substantial paperback books, and helped prepare for Duncan Sandys's 1967 Civic Amenities Act and the establishment of the conservation area concept. Matthew immediately latched onto the Blueprint scheme, and began to agitate for Edinburgh to be piggybacked onto the series as a fifth area project. His first tactic, in LCC Valuer style, was a head-on attack, at a government-sponsored conference on building maintenance in 1966, on neglect of the New Town, with doom-laden warnings of vast and escalating costs. And in September 1966 he persuaded Lord Johnston, the RFACS chairman, to ask Secretary of State William Ross to ask MHLG to include the New Town in the Blueprint series, and be designated a 'national conservation area'.

But at this point Matthew's first, shock-tactic approach began to backfire a little. Ross, a wily and somewhat philistine character, conceded in principle the feasibility of a joint Corporation/HBCS rehabilitation committee on the New Town, knowing that he could rely on the Tory majority on Edinburgh Corporation, obsessed always with keeping local taxation levels down, to scupper any costly proposal. In early 1967 the SDD Secretary, Alan Hume, always mindful of local municipal autonomy, informally told Matthew to 'go away ... and form a sufficiently strong public opinion' to change things within the Corporation.[124] There was no help to be expected from Kennet, who saw Scotland as rather 'backward' in conservation matters, and any Edinburgh involvement as likely to confuse his initiative. And Scottish ministers, for nationalistic reasons, were disinclined to take on any initiatives openly inspired by English advances.[125] As it turned out, however, the exclusion of Edinburgh from the Blueprint programme was a blessing in disguise, as it compelled Matthew to scale up his ambitions, putting the earlier initiatives behind him, as mere 'flowers in the spring', and forcing him to build up a case for Edinburgh not just as a leading British historic Georgian city, but as a place of world significance.[126] From now on Matthew employed only the most elevated international rhetoric about the New Town, arguing in 1969 that 'what was done there in seventy years stands today as one of the outstanding pieces of town planning on the heroic scale in this or any other country.'[127] These high claims, alongside the Walter Scott/R L Stevenson/

Geddes 'Old Edinburgh' ideology, have mutated eventually into the justifications for today's World Heritage Site status.

For this enhanced level of proselytising, Matthew was well aware that the RFACS was a grossly unsuitable vehicle, not least as its very terms of reference seemed to discourage proactive activity. As early as 1965, in response to a circular inviting RFACS to extend its remit to comment on proposals affecting listed buildings, Bannatyne drafted a letter, in conjunction with Matthew, which argued that 'this Commission is not a preservationist body; we are concerned, rather, with the seemly development of the urban environment and with the conservation of the countryside.'[128] But, as luck would have it, it was just at this very point that the formation of the SCT allowed Matthew to change, almost overnight, to a brand-new racehorse. His plan was to strike at the very first meeting of the Trust, at the Bute Hall in Glasgow on 23 May 1967, but as so often, he prepared his ground meticulously beforehand, so that the actual intervention would be largely a formality. Exploiting his connections with the London Civic Trust, he got Leslie Lane to soften up Muirshiel informally on the New Town issue in January 1967, and to broach the idea of an opinion-forming public meeting.[129] By the time of the inaugural SCT meeting it was already accepted by all the Trustees that the New Town was 'at the top of the list', and that Maurice Lindsay should immediately move to set up a special meeting of trustees the next month. Lindsay later recalled that

> as I stepped down from the platform of the Bute Hall ... after our official launching ceremony under the chairmanship of the then Principal, Sir Charles Wilson, Sir Robert Matthew murmured in my ear, 'We'll have to do something about the Edinburgh New Town, Maurice.' 'Yes, we will,' said I, wondering what on earth he was talking about. I soon found out.

In his speech to that inaugural SCT meeting

Matthew had argued more generally that 'we are now in one of the great ages of construction', but that the work of 'creating new communities' could be enhanced by 'keeping the best from the past' – a role complementary to that of the Saltire Society.[130]

Closely advised by the Civic Trust in London, by early September 1967 Lindsay was able to report to Lane that he and Matthew had decided to aim at a high-profile public meeting in May 1968 at the Edinburgh Assembly Rooms, to 'publicly declare the importance and value of the New Town of Edinburgh', with an Anglo-American list of celebrity speakers, including Summerson, Mumford and Casson, to emphasise the fact that 'Edinburgh is a European heritage'. To solidify domestic support, every household in the New Town would receive an invitation through their letter box.[131] In February 1967 David Walker and Stewart Cruden (MPBW Inspector of Ancient Monuments for Scotland) had already provided behind-the-scenes fuel for this campaign through an assessment for the HBCS of New Town houses urgently in need of attention, arguing that the problem was not one of serious structural disrepair but of preventable neglect and unsightly minor alterations and repairs: the background streets were just as important as the set pieces, and no individual cases could be isolated. And in August 1967 the cause of the New Town had been given a further popular airing in John Paterson's ambitious 'Two

Hundred Summers in a City' exhibition, held in Waverley Market during the Festival – although one should remember that the following month the consultative 'Princes Street Panel', including Reiach and Kininmonth, had recommended the phased redevelopment of all Princes Street and the lanes behind.[132]

The Assembly Rooms conference, June 1970

By November 1967, in discussion with Lane, Lindsay and Muirshiel at Boodles in London, the Assembly Rooms 'public meeting' had become a major conference. Matthew had been giving thought to Edinburgh Corporation's cost objections. His response was typically Geddesian in character: to organise a rapid condition survey of the entire New Town, in order to get approximate costings for restoration. To circumvent the obstacle of the cost of this survey itself, he hit on the idea of using a volunteer army, and turned to James Dunbar-Nasmith, now head of the EAA, to stir up the Association's member practices to carry out, free of charge, a collaborative survey. But almost immediately it became crystal clear that the one-year timetable was wildly ambitious, and so the date of the New Town conference was put back first to late 1969, and finally to 6 June 1970.

By February 1969 the two parallel initiatives – the survey, and the conference organisation – had both swung into action. The 18-month survey was officially announced in May 1968 by Maurice

12.21 1970 EAA Survey of New Town: composite photograph of Regent Terrace, including no. 31 at centre. (Edinburgh Architectural Association)

Lindsay, who noted that the costs of restoration in Bath had been £4,000 per house: for any initiative to make much impact on the vast New Town area that figure would have to be substantially improved on in Edinburgh. After Matthew and Nasmith set up a steering committee chaired by John Reid (the heir to Ian Lindsay's practice), from February to November 1969 the team of over 120 architects, engineers, quantity surveyors and photographers beavered away on the basic condition survey – aided by grants of £500 from the HBCS and £200 from the NTS. The New Town was divided into eight areas, each surveyed by a ten- or twelve-strong team, who passed the findings to quantity surveyors for analysis. Meanwhile, from September 1968 the conference organising committee, chaired by Matthew himself, had been working in parallel, meeting mainly at 31 Regent Terrace. In December 1969, for example, there was debate about whether to co-opt leading Edinburgh conservationist Colin McWilliam to the committee, to represent the SGS. Matthew, although on good personal terms with McWilliam, saw him as too independent minded, but he was admitted, and in February 1970 his wife Christine was also taken on as secretary to the committee. As Matthew had predicted, within three months of his admission McWilliam began to enliven the tidily orchestrated structure, by suggesting that local residents should be included on the working party. Matthew sidelined this proposal, fearing that it might fall foul of the law of unintended consequences. Indeed, many of the

residents' letters that the committee did receive were concerned not with classical architecture but with the likely burden on the rates or the bogeyman of socialist intervention: for example, a letter to Matthew in May 1970 from a Mrs Isobel Harries of 76 Great King Street thundered that 'I view with grave suspicion anyone who wishes to interfere in any way whatsoever in my private property.'[133]

Where Matthew excelled, as he had shown in countless major projects of the past, from the Royal Festival Hall onwards, was in delegating a multi-strand project and then calmly and gradually gathering in the threads as the deadline neared. Now, with only four months to go, the analysed data of the survey were passed to an appraisal group chaired by Matthew and supported by the SCT – all, again, carefully squared with the 'touchy' officials of Edinburgh Corporation. Matthew himself set about synthesising the findings and writing the keynote speech for the conference, focusing on the headline-grabbing figure of £8.35 m for restoration of the whole New Town – a sum accounted for mostly by stone repair. Matthew had not, however, proceeded with a more sensationalist suggestion from Michael Middleton of the London Civic Trust, to also work out a figure for the total *demolition* and rebuilding of the New Town![134]

Since mid 1969 Matthew and the committee had also begun finalising the conference schedule and order of speakers. This threw up the usual last-minute problems. None of the three originally suggested keynote speakers could come,

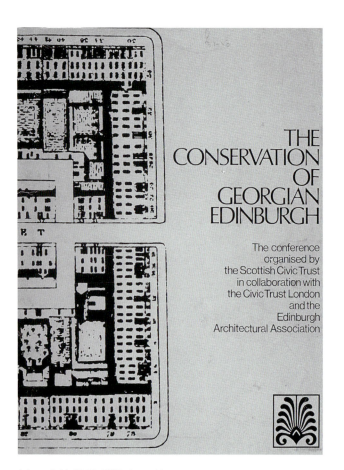

(above left) **12.22** 1970 Assembly Rooms conference, cover of delegate pack. (Scottish Civic Trust)

(above right) **12.23** 1970 Assembly Rooms Conference, insert flyer in delegate pack. (Scottish Civic Trust)

and a hope that Prince Philip could be induced to open the conference was not realised.[135] Instead, a rather larger group was put together, mostly from outwith Scotland in order to project dramatically the New Town's international standing. Most were from London – Holford, Sandys, Buchanan, Spence and Betjeman – but there were also, 'to give a foreign touch', Count Sforza, deputy Secretary General of the Council of Europe, and Francois Sorlin, General Inspector of Historic Monuments in Paris, as well as New Town historian Youngson from Edinburgh, and Matthew's former Edinburgh University assistant, (Professor) Pat Nuttgens, to round things off. Matthew, typically, briefed everyone on the 'home team' what to say: Nuttgens, for instance, was to stress the cultural significance of the New Town, and the importance of the Blueprint studies in England.[136] Matthew himself would deliver the most substantial speech, summarising the findings of the survey. In late July 1969 Spence reluctantly dropped

out of the event, owing to the conflicting demand of the official opening of his Rome embassy, but he stressed his continuing support for the cause of the New Town, which was 'a very personal one for me'. Owing to the calling of a general election, Secretary of State Ross also withdrew, delegating the ministerial opening role to junior minister Lord Hughes.[137]

Only at the last minute, in late May 1970, did all the costings for Matthew and Dunbar-Nasmith's appraisal group come together, with its £8.35m estimated total. Dunbar-Nasmith wrote that these costs were 'very much less than anyone had supposed', especially in comparison with Bath or the Continent, which 'might appeal to the canny Scots'. The total cost of the conference itself, including survey and committees, was listed at £4,591, and there were over 1,000 attendees. Excluded from reckoning was a vast amount of unpaid work by survey volunteers and committee members. Nuttgens recalled that 'on the day, each of us had

12.24 June 1970 view of Matthew outside 31 Regent Terrace, at that time being stone-cleaned; a conference poster is in the window. (Scottish Civic Trust)

been briefed to speak for an exact number of minutes. We all did, as we were so frightened of Matthew. Everyone got a packed lunch, with a small bottle of wine – it was all done very well, as one would expect.' A conference bus tour was laid on, with Matthew, Walker and Lindsay among the guides. Each attendee got a stylish conference pack, complete with anthemion-based logo.

With this supporting international and London cast, Matthew was at last able to steamroller finally and definitively across Edinburgh's municipal cautiousness, and, in his conference address, to trumpet his post-Blueprint argument of the unique and exceptional status of the New Town. It was now not just a 'national treasure' but something that, 'by the severest architectural and environmental standards, stood in the highest class of worldwide examples'. Thus it richly merited 'special exception as far as finance is concerned – the conference will make the case for that special exception'. He argued for a tripartite split in funding responsibility of 2:1:1 between the HBCS, local authority and the owners, which would imply a £375,000 annual contribution by the HBCS alone, compared with its existing national budget of £80,000. Lord Hughes nevertheless publicly accepted the tripartite funding principle, and

pledged to look at ways of exploiting section V of the 1969 Town & Country Planning (Scotland) Act. The concluding resolution called on the SCT to begin setting up a permanent advisory committee.[138]

Towards the Edinburgh New Town Conservation Committee

No sooner was the June 1970 Assembly Rooms conference over, and the publication of the proceedings by Edinburgh University Press under way, than Matthew began pressing home his advantage in his time-honoured manner, through a series of inner-circle steering committee meetings, mostly at 31 Regent Terrace. The most crucial decisions were taken at a small meeting on 28 July, seven weeks after the conference, held in Dunbar-Nasmith's office, with Muirshiel, Matthew and Lindsay also present. They discussed how to pressure SDD, still under its 'pre-enlightened' administrators, into pledging finance, and whether the recent change of government from Labour to Tory could be exploited – especially as the Queen Mother had been induced to write to Muirshiel pressing for the 'recently elected government … to carry out the recommendations which have been made'. Muirshiel, it was agreed, would now write to the new Tory

1, Melville Street, looking west

When the Scottish Civic Trust was founded in May 1967 one of its trustees, Sir Robert Matthew, urged that it should make the fabric of the *New Town* of Edinburgh one of its most urgent concerns.

The *New Town*, dating from 1767, remains a unique example of Georgian town planning and distinguished architecture, and over the years it has grown in international fame. Yet, though it has remained remarkably intact, its external condition is now deteriorating rapidly, and is subject to heavy pressures of various kinds. Even before the passing of the Civic Amenities Act (1967)—and through it the creation of the Conservation Area concept—it had become clear that a cooperation of interests similar to that which originally produced the New Town would be needed if its fabric were to be conserved and its vitality maintained, while continuing to serve the modern needs of those who use it.

The moment seemed ripe. The Melville Street/Melville Crescent pilot project instituted by the Historic Buildings Council for Scotland and Edinburgh Corporation had been launched as the first preservation project in the joint operation by the HBC and Corporation. During the 1968 Edinburgh International Festival the exhibition '200 Summers in a City' had greatly aroused public interest in the history and architectural merit of the New Town.

12.25 *The Conservation of Georgian Edinburgh*, 1972 (1970 conference proceedings): extract from introduction. (Edinburgh University Press)

Secretary of State, pressing home this letter and the conference resolutions. The group noted approvingly that SDD had now approved in principle the setting up of an 'executive' rather than merely 'advisory' body.[139]

What was crucial was the internal composition of the new committee. Matthew and Lindsay had shown the limits of their tolerance of local residents' participation, and the 28 July meeting went for an 11-member executive weighted 6:5 in favour of government. Following the winding-up of the conference organising committee in December 1970, the initiative thereafter passed to a succession of meetings between Matthew, Muirshiel, Dunbar-Nasmith and Maurice Lindsay with civil servants and ministers.[140] At these steering meetings, the proposed New Town committee was successively expanded to 18 members, including six Corporation representatives, five from central government, six from the SCT and other societies, as well as Matthew himself, in his capacity as Secretary of State's conservation adviser. The final meeting, on 22 December, with junior minister George Younger, approved an annual HBC grant of £50,000, to be matched by £25,000 from Edinburgh Corporation – less than the amount demanded in Matthew's conference speech, but still a useful start.[141]

During 1971 and early 1972 the new permanent committee acquired a name – the Edinburgh New Town Conservation Committee (ENTCC) – and concentrated on organising its affairs, still largely under Matthew's influence. Hurd's partner, Ian Begg, became interim director, bringing his Canongate experience to bear on the task of helping Matthew accentuate the social-regeneration orientation of the ENTCC on the 'tattered fringes' of the New Town, especially around Fettes Row and Stockbridge, and civil servant Bob Walker was seconded to become interim secretary. Attempts by City Architect Alex Steele to restrict the 'social' aspect of the ENTCC's work, by excluding the northern edge of the New Town, were firmly suppressed: David Walker recalled that

> Robert Matthew, with the vociferous support of George Hay, the government architect who dealt with Edinburgh HBC matters, held out firmly for holding the line at Fettes Row, and eventually managed to get his views accepted; the west end of Fettes Row was completely refaced, in one of the first and biggest jobs the ENTCC ever tackled.

A friend of Nuttgens reported to him at this stage that Matthew 'controls a majority of the committee' and that the Edinburgh councillors were 'stupefied by Sir Robert's prestige'.[142]

To supplement the government support for the ENTCC, it was decided to launch an appeal for £500,000, and to strengthen the executive committee Matthew pressed strongly for appointment of a full-time director, at a starting salary of £8,000, and successfully secured the appointment of Desmond Hodges, the young secretary of the Belfast-based Ulster Architectural Heritage Society since its foundation in 1967: we saw in Chapter 10 that Matthew had played the role of founding father to the UAHS in 1967.[143] Having been poached by Matthew for Edinburgh, Hodges set about his new task with gusto. Within four months he had come up with a draft policy programme, launched the £500,000 appeal and begun an energetic search for premises: the ENTCC was settled in 13A Dundas Street by September 1973.

12.26 *The Conservation of Georgian Edinburgh,* 1972 *(*1970 conference proceedings): illustrations accompanying Matthew's speech. (Edinburgh University Press)

12.27 1980s ENTCC map of New Town. (Edinburgh World Heritage)

Supported by Matthew in meetings with councillors and Ronnie Cramond of SDD, Hodges pressed for a 'broad interpretation of the word "conservation"' in the ENTCC's activity, and for generous Corporation and HBC grants. However, SDD stepped in to discourage an attempt by Hodges, with Matthew's encouragement, to involve the ENTCC in lobbying against the Edinburgh Corp-oration Tory administration's ambitious urban road-building proposals, including an inner-ring motorway:

Matthew had chaired a May 1972 'teach-in' on Edinburgh transport chaired by Archibald Hendry, at which the public transport cause was strongly champi-oned, and he had also tried to persuade the ENTCC to lobby against the 'extreme environmental damage' threatened by the long-proposed Haymarket office tower.[144]

In a 1972 foreword to a local history of Great King Street, Matthew summarised the great strides made on the New Town since 'the now historic meeting called at the Assembly Rooms in June 1970 to focus public attention'. He reminded readers that 'It has not always been so. Thirty years ago (or less) few voices could be heard raised, either in praise of these great city streets and squares, or in anger and protest when part of the fabric became threatened.' But that all had changed in the 1960s, above all because the 'menace' of motor traffic had underlined the need that 'cities must be tended and cherished, or they deteriorate and perish under a tangle of deplorable overgrowth.' Perhaps a little contritely, in view of his own exploitation of precisely the opposite argument a decade earlier over George Square, he conceded that 'we have learned one lesson – buildings are infinitely more adaptable than we have hitherto been persuaded to believe ... there are many ways of using these solid structures today, or any other day.'

In December 1973, after the end of Matthew's three-year stint as government conservation adviser, he was asked to stay on as an ENTCC member.[145] Arguably, of course, that government advisory appointment may itself have been facilitated partly by the prestige of Matthew's New Town achievement; its commencement, after all, had almost immediately followed the Assembly Rooms conference, which expunged most of the anti-conservation stigma attached to Matthew in Edinburgh in the wake of George Square. We should also bear in mind that, by that date, the George Square and university redevelopment itself was almost dead, and Percy Johnson-Marshall was representing himself as a conservationist, organising a heritage-orientated ideas study. After Matthew's death in 1975 others continued to implement his New Town strategy, including publication in 1978 of a comprehensive maintenance manual.[146]

But by the end of 1973, in any case, Matthew's attention was already passing beyond the New Town to the more natural focus – for a Geddesian 'Goth' such as himself – of the Old Town. Indeed, Aidan argued that his father, despite all his New Town organisational work, in reality 'didn't have a natural feel for the New Town or Georgian architecture, and had more of a natural affinity with medieval towns' – as became clear when he reluctantly had to organise repairs to his own house at 31 Regent Terrace in the early 1970s.[147] At an October 1974 'think-tank seminar' at Prestonfield House preparing for European Architectural Heritage Year (1975), Matthew pleaded with the council and societies to argue for a 'major exercise [in the Old Town], as in the New Town, and concentrate their efforts to raise public opinion' about its reputation. As always for Matthew, conservation itself was not enough – the old had to be balanced by the new, to make sure the city stayed a 'living entity' – but he now began to foresee an increasing role for private developers rather than the state in carrying this agenda forward. Here again, it was the experience of the New Town and later planned suburbs that seemed to provide the lessons, in regulating private development: Matthew called for a 'charter in estate planning and management'.

Typically, Matthew exploited, in turn, the multiplier effect of his New Town initiative to make an *international* impact in the world of conservation – applying the lessons to other urban regeneration challenges in the UK, such as in London's Covent Garden. Previously, Matthew's attempts to put the heritage in an international context had been filtered through the lens of the vernacular. He referred in 1967, for example, to 'the ubiquitous vernacular – the common architectural world language'; and on his second visit to Bucharest in 1971, to receive his honorary doctorate, he hailed Romania's strong vernacular tradition, and bemoaned Modernism's neglect of the 'age old [vernacular] experience of building'. But by 1970, in correspondence with senior US heritage officials, he was also beginning to argue for a bipolar interpretation of the British architectural heritage in international terms. On the one hand, there were local traditions and materials; on the other, the classical 'town building on a heroic scale' exemplified by the Edinburgh New Town.[148]

The chief stimulus to Matthew's growing conservation internationalism was European Architectural Heritage Year (EAHY), declared by the Council of Europe Committee on Monuments and Sites for 1975. The three-year preparation period began in 1972 with the setting up of various national committees to coordinate individual national initiatives, including a UK council chaired by the Duke of Edinburgh, and a Scottish committee organised by the SCT and chaired under its aegis by Muirshiel, and with Dunbar-Nasmith as its secretary. In 1972, in the wake of the New Town success, Muirshiel invited Matthew to become a member of the EAHY Scottish committee, and at its first meeting in 1973 it was decided that Scottish efforts should focus on restoration of one complete New Town terrace in Edinburgh, the same in Glasgow, as well as a scheme in a historic small burgh and in the Highlands. Scotland would also contribute to the wider UK build-up to EAHY, for example by hosting in Edinburgh, in June 1974, a four-day international conference on the economic and social implications of conservation, organised largely by SCT. Matthew, in his concluding speech, argued for a holistic view of the urban environment as 'indivisible', and hailed conservation, rather than redevelopment, as 'more likely to succeed in keeping existing communities and social institutions together'. He pointed to the ENTCC as evidence of the importance of attuning fiscal practice to conservation needs, and to the need for powers of compulsion to override individuals who might not wish to participate, although voluntary effort and education must be the cornerstone. Amenity societies were now the true 'mouthpiece of public opinion': 'every child should be made aware of the philosophy of conservation as an integral part of his education.' We shall see in the next chapter how Matthew also intervened significantly in preparation for EAHY at an international level.[149]

━━━━━

Chapter 13

Towards far horizons, 1969–75

Noah built an Ark to save mankind from the rising waters. Today, and through the next generations, a thousand million arks must be planned and built, to meet the menace not of nature but of man's inhumanity to man.

Robert Matthew, 1975[1]

In the last chapter we saw the volte-face from modernity to conservation in Matthew's domestic activities from the late 1960s – something that was typical of the cut-and-thrust fluctuations in architectural debate of the time, even if few other architects of his generation made such a dramatic jump from one extreme to another. In this chapter we trace a strikingly different pattern, more typical of the evolution of town and country planning in its cumulative character. The international planning movement, from the beginning, was driven forward not by fluctuating fashion and debate but by a succession of broad-minded, liberal Great Men, such as Geddes, Unwin and Abercrombie, each of whom stood on the shoulders of the last and sought through international prose-lytising to enhance the strategic scope and practical effectiveness of the movement. For Matthew, the task was a similar one of consolidation and further broadening, shifting the emphasis from the built environment to broader environmentalism.

Overseas challenges of RMJM

During the late 1960s and early 1970s the part of Matthew's private-practice work that chiefly interested and motivated him was his portfolio of multidisciplinary overseas projects, often attempting to exploit the opportunities available in oil-rich countries, in contrast to the crisis-ridden UK.[2]

Of all these overseas development involvements, arguably the most successful was, ironically, focused on a country threatened at the time with war and disintegration: a multifaceted educational building and planning programme in Nigeria. Its federal government had fallen under military rule in 1966, followed in May 1967 by the secession (as the Republic of Biafra) of the eastern states of the federation, and two-and-a-half years of destructive civil war from July 1967 to January 1970. Within Nigeria the Geddesian architect-planner Max Lock had already, since 1964, blazed a trail of post-colonial development enabling work. Commissioned by the UK Overseas Development Ministry and the government of Northern Nigeria, as consultant planner of Kaduna, capital of the region, he had set out to exploit indigenous professional skills.[3] But when it came to large, nationwide building programmes, different skills were required. And so Matthew was approached personally by the International Development Association to act as executive architect for an ambitious IDA-financed programme of well over 100 standard secondary schools and colleges across Nigeria, designed largely locally and totalling some $20m in value; RMJM had already been engaged in 1962 to undertake a building costs study for the government of Northern Nigeria.[4] The Washington-based IDA, a UN agency working for the International Bank for Reconstruction and Development (IBRD) and popularly known as the 'World Bank', specialised in the granting of low-interest loans, interest-free credit, and grants to the world's poorest countries, including sub-Saharan Africa. The educational building programme, initially approved by the IDA in March 1965 to a level of some $20m (for 'Education Project 01') but subsequently extended over two decades, was initially focused on grant-aided building of secondary schools, technical and teacher training colleges throughout the federation, but later phases also took in primary schools and education research establishments, embracing many tens of thousands of pupils and students.

Matthew recognised immediately that, whatever the old tensions with Stirrat, this was a consultancy job demanding immediate and decisive delegation to the London office, so as to exploit its long-standing school-design expertise. Working through Peter Newnham as partner-in-charge, Matthew set up a 20-strong multidisciplinary RMJM office in Lagos,

and after that kept in touch through correspondence and visits, including a lengthy stay in the country at the time of the 1969 CAA conference, and during the Biafran war. For the first few years of the project Matthew acted as the external contact with the IDA, negotiating to secure additional credit for the programme of (eventually) 180 building sites.[5] By the mid 1970s, with the sudden increase in Nigerian government work following discovery of the country's rich oil reserves, progress had been rapid, and hundreds of standardised secondary and primary schools were under way, using simple, low-tech plans, along with eight universities, all organised by London, but secured by Matthew. In the words of Ken Feakes, 'We all knew through the grapevine that this very good programme had come to us as a "Robert thing", as the World Bank wanted to find someone who could actually implement such a big programme, and looked to him.' During these years, the London partner in charge of the programme was Frances Baden-Powell, but Aidan also spent 18 months in Kaduna in 1976–7, setting up an 'anchor team' to establish planning and design standards for the seven new universities. Another programme involving close collaboration with London proposed the regeneration of the decayed harbour heritage of Geelong, near

479

Melbourne: brokered by Charles Robertson in 1972, it eventually came to nothing when Gough Whitlam's Labor government was deposed in 1975.[6]

The record of implementation was more patchy in the firm's other two major overseas programmes of the period: the continuing capital-city planning and architectural consultancy for Islamabad, and a new commission to design a suburban residential zone outside Tripoli, the capital of the North African state of Libya.

At Islamabad (declared capital of Pakistan officially in 1967), the collaboration with Percy over the planning elements continued formally in force, but the years 1968–71, a time of growing political instability within civilian-ruled Pakistan, culminating in the secession of Bangladesh and Pakistan's resounding military defeat by India, witnessed a steady lessening in impetus in the Islamabad project as a whole, and a corresponding petering-out of RMJM's involvement. Architecturally, these years saw at an international level the disintegration or non-fulfilment of a number of wildly ambitious new city-planning projects across the world, at the end of the high Utopian period of Modernism, especially those, such as Tange's Skopje plan, that emphasised a high-technology, high-speed car-based formula.[7] And in Pakistan, as the country returned gradually to civilian rule, the iron efficiency of the military gradually relaxed, with inevitable disruptive effects on the project. The mounting political instability within Pakistan meant that the CDA felt itself beleaguered on all sides, threatened financially with a cut-off of funding at the end of the initial Five-Year Plan period in June 1970, and politically by demands from East Pakistan for transfer of institutions to Dacca. The knock-on result was a constant changing of plan, insufficient supply of briefing information, and payment of fee accounts very late (or never).[8]

By early 1969, with just over a year left before RMJM's contract was scheduled to expire at the end of the Five-Year Plan,

the pace of design work at Islamabad had sharply increased, with the CDA, under director Anwar Said, anxious to get the Museum and Archives under construction within the following year, and fearing that otherwise the funds would be reappropriated and reallocated to school building by a hostile Ministry of Education. The principal architects still working on the Administrative Sector were Stone and Rosselli, with Matthew still involved in direct negotiations with the CDA Design Committee and numerous meetings in the Edinburgh office, and Aidan acting as chief Edinburgh-based project architect for the Archives building (in collaboration with Zahir).[9] But, increasingly, the firm was running into difficulties in finalising any of these schemes. While Doxiadis's 'Dynapolis' formula of open-ended grid planning was well established, implementation at the level of individual areas was becoming confused, as emerged in Matthew's own last negotiating trip to Pakistan in July 1968, and a lengthy follow-up visit by Aidan in March/April 1969. They found that individual sections of the original Administrative Area were being developed autonomously without reference to RMJM, including Stone's ceremonial buildings and presidential complex around the central square, and landscaping and building work authorised elsewhere by CDA in conflict with the Master Plan. But although over £7,000 of planning fees were still outstanding, the CDA had still asked Matthew in 1968 to masterplan a large northerly extension to the Secretariat area. The outline plan eventually approved for the extension, envisaging the same kind of open layout, low-rise blocks and tower punctuations as before, was critically received in March 1969 by the CDA with grumbles about its 'monotonous' character, but RMJM were urged to proceed as soon as possible with a complete revised masterplan for the entire extended Administrative Area, including a model, with the caveat that nothing would be built for ten years. Aidan reported back to Robert in April that the firm's plan for the original area

Modern Architect

had been substantially spoiled, especially by Stone's landscaping interventions at the junction of National and Capital Avenues. More generally, although Stone's Supreme Court design had been approved, 'massive cuts are expected in government spending', especially on 'prestige buildings'.[10]

Matthew's own individual projects within the Administrative Sector – the National Museum, National Archives and National Library – were also increasingly threatened by delays and changes of plan, and consequent arguments over cost increases. Zahir recalled later that 'unfortunately, Sir Robert had been denied a substantial part of his fees by CDA's grossly underestimating the initial cost of the projects and fixing the fees on this figure, to which Sir Robert agreed like a gentleman!'[11] The Archives and Museum plans were formally approved by the CDA in 1968. For their execution, to save on foreign exchange, Matthew proposed to emulate Rosselli and Stone by appointing an associate local architect, in this case Zahir's firm, Zahir-ud-Din Khwaja & Associates. Their draughtsmen would be supervised, from 1969, by an associate-level RMJM employee, Sandy Gracie, at a cost of some £300 per month, a task that, Aidan commented, required 'great tact and stamina in tiring, hot and difficult surroundings'. Design work, Robert later recalled, was also complicated by the impact of a government committee, including cabinet members, set up to control architectural standards: their 'insistence that the architectural character of Islamabad should combine Islamic elements with modern techniques caused some architects, including myself, some difficulty at times'.

Work on the National Archives design proceeded relatively uncontentiously on this basis, despite the earlier change of site by the CDA. Full documents and drawings were issued by Gracie's team in November 1970, only ten weeks late, and eventually the building was completed in 1973, under Zahir's oversight and with 'Islamic' touches, but essentially as designed by RMJM. The National Museum

and Library, both to adjoin the main 'cultural square', were less fortunate. The former was bracketed with the Archives as part of the instalment of work being expedited by the CDA before the end of the Five-Year Plan, but the difficulty, Aidan reported to Robert in April 1969, was that while the CDA wanted to retain RMJM 'for prestige reasons', unlike the Secretariat and Presidential complex, they were not paying directly for the buildings, and the Ministry of Education 'want to drop us'.[12] At the Museum, RMJM had to cope with a demanding chief curator, M Naqvi, who constantly pressed for a 'more impressive entrance', and by late 1970 preparation of drawings had been delayed by five months, protracting Gracie's stay in Lahore at ZDK's expense. Eventually, the National Museum commission fell foul of the 1971 crisis, and RMJM's design was never built.[13]

The National Library project, although stemming directly from the CDA, proved an even more intractable problem, owing largely to the mounting tension between East and West Pakistan. Matthew reported to Richards in July 1968 that the previous chief librarian, who had moved to East Pakistan, had been replaced at the existing Karachi library by a more forceful figure, A Qazi, who 'wants to start again, but I think will be restrained by the CDA'. In a sign of the administrative frustrations of the project, he added that 'To settle the account to date CDA require copies of all schemes done so far! They have lost their copies.'[14] A virtually new scheme was indeed the outcome, planned on a sloping site, with entrance from the Cultural Square down a broad and imposing staircase, with integral auditorium and terracing all around, and with an overall area of 118,000 sq ft. Qazi also succeeded in imposing a new departmental layout based on the United Nations library in New York. By early 1969 the antagonisms with East Pakistan were beginning to tell, with demands that a Dacca equivalent library should be built at exactly the same time; in the meanwhile, Qazi had come up with a fresh set of design demands, including that the facade 'should be an "open book",whatever that means!' and that there should be an 'imposing' entrance: 'Qazi has fixed ideas of what he wants and is very difficult to persuade. He is persistent to the point of irritation.'[15]

Eventually, by November 1970, a further drastic change of mind by the CDA, including the cutting-out of air conditioning from the Library building, pointed to the need for a further complete redesign, for which an £8,800 fee was offered by CDA; and so, the following month, Matthew finally resigned the commission, observing that RMJM had 'met severe difficulties in the past in connection with our appointments for the National Museum and National Archives Building, owing to CDA's delays in supply of essential information and in payment of outstanding fee accounts.' Matthew also wrote dissociating RMJM from any further involvement in 'the CDA's planning decisions taken without our advice or knowledge', and the outstanding £7,120 planning fees for the Administrative Area were written off.[16]

By 1998 Islamabad's population would climb to over 500,000, but the architectural tensions of the attempt to balance Islamic tradition and modernity in its buildings were never resolved. Writing in retrospect, in 1974, to a researcher, Matthew defended the CDA, and Pakistan architects, from any suggestion of a crudely iconic approach:

> My recollection is that well-known architects were chosen for the various projects in Islamabad for a combination of reasons. Certainly, it was a matter of national pride that the architects should be internationally famous. But it would be wrong to suppose that the client was naïve. President Ayub took a personal interest and the CDA was guided both by Doxiadis and myself, especially in the early days.

In the opinion of eminent Pakistani architect Kamil Khan Mumtaz, however, the architecture of the new capital was split by an unbridgeable gulf between 'the desire of the lay public for an architectural expression of its Islamic culture and traditions' and the 'professional architects' compulsion to project an image of modernity'.[17]

Matthew and Gadafi: building for revolutionary Libya

Matthew's other major involvement with the Islamic world had an even more controversy-ridden outcome – trouble that it fell largely to Tom Spaven to sort out. In this case, Matthew was first the beneficiary, and then the victim, of revolutionary political developments in the host country, the Libyan Arab Republic. This North African state, which became independent from Italian colonial rule in 1951/2 under King Mohammed Idris al-Sanusi, was enriched by substantial oil discoveries from 1959 onwards, and in September 1969 Idris was overthrown by a military coup led by the 27-year-old Colonel Muammar Gadafi. Gadafi's increasingly idiosyncratic personal rule combined Nasserite ideals of pan-Arab nationalism with socialist elements. An initial four-year phase of European-style state socialism and economic nationalisation (including the oil industry) was followed, in 1973, by the declaration of a Mao-style cultural revolution that jettisoned conventional government structures in favour of Islamic socialist 'people's committees' controlled directly by Gadafi. This was followed, in 1977, by the more extreme step of the declaration of a 'people's revolution' and a change in the name of the state itself, from the Libyan Arab Republic to the Socialist People's Libyan Arab Jamahiriya (SPLAJ).[18]

RMJM became initially involved in Libya in the wake of the 1969 revolution, which at first seemed to endorse the welfare state corporatism with which the firm was so familiar. In the wake of the 1973 revolution, however, things became far more difficult. The ultimate origins of the Tripoli IBP project lay in an energetic attempt by the Idris regime in the 1960s to begin modernising the country on planned welfare state lines, exploiting the oil boom of 1961 onwards. This drive included the commissioning of advisory plans from Western architects, and the building of a new University of Libya, split between Benghazi and Tripoli, with preliminary designs prepared in 1965 by James Cubitt & Partners. Housing, to be built by private industry from 1965 under the £400m 'Idris Scheme', was the centrepiece of the Idris regime's development programme, but following the revolution the new government instead set up a 'National Housing Corporation', chaired by Ahmed Ali Mahmoud Misirati and with a Mr Sifaou as director-general.[19] Matthew's initial contact with this initiative came through Doxiadis, who had prepared a consultative report in 1964 on the possibility of mass housing in Libya.[20] Immediately following the revolution, the new NHC took steps to develop the first of these townships, Gargaresh/West Gurgi, a 230 hectare flat site some four miles southwest of the centre, with 5,000 dwellings, bisected by the Old Gurgi Road. Following the initial successful experience with Cubitts, a number of British architectural firms with multidisciplinary and overseas experience were approached by Misirati, with Matthew, through his contacts with Doxiadis, as the unofficial front-runner; another key intermediary was a Libya-based Hungarian architect, Imre Radnoti, who had previously worked in RMJM. In early November 1970 Misirati wrote to the consultants calling for proposals that would contribute 'to the formulation of the new Libyan environmental character, reflecting the speedily developing modern way of life'. Matthew, as the favoured candidate, was interviewed first, followed by a fall-back group. By an embarrassing coincidence, the paths of the two delegations crossed at Heathrow Airport, on 23 November. David Rock, then of BDP, recalled that 'we were all gathering at Heathrow, when Grenfell Baines said, "Hey ho! Here comes Robert Matthew!" And indeed it was him, having already gone, and come back, and got the job.'[21]

Typically, Matthew's success was as much a surprise to his partners as to the other firms. Spaven recalled: 'The client wanted Robert specifically, not the firm: he must have got it through his IUA or international contacts. Robert agreed to take it, before consulting any of the partners; he was like that! He had said, in typical Robert style, "I can do it, of course!"' Spaven readily offered to organise the project for him – partly for sentimental reasons, having been stationed in the Western Desert during the war.[22] But he might not have been so eager had he known the political and organisational pitfalls that lay in wait for the Tripoli job over the coming decade, not least because Matthew, to secure it, had (as at Islamabad) accepted a low commission, here of only 1.5 per cent. What attracted Matthew to this project was not the prospect of profit, but a vision of the 'vernacular' in modern housing, and the opportunity to develop a mass housing and planning programme rooted in the social, cultural and architectural conditions of a non-Western country. As at Cumnock, the key factor was the presence of a client, Misirati, who shared this Geddesian vision of rooted Modernity. In Spaven's opinion,

> Robert was very interested, and involved, in planning the project in a way that was close to the native environment, and in ensuring at the briefing stage that we really understood the Libyan way of life – for example, the need for privacy in individual houses.[23]

During the negotiations of early 1971 Robert brought Aidan in to help Spaven and himself. By April of that year, following a personal visit by Robert in March, a formal contract was signed between RMJM and the NHC, covering the initial planning of the scheme, including roads, public utilities and social institutions. But what was needed first, in authentic Geddesian fashion, was a survey, in the form of a sociological user-study investigation (with the help of Edinburgh University sociologists and Barrie Wilson's building scientists), of the 'traditional' Libyan way of life and the attitudes of

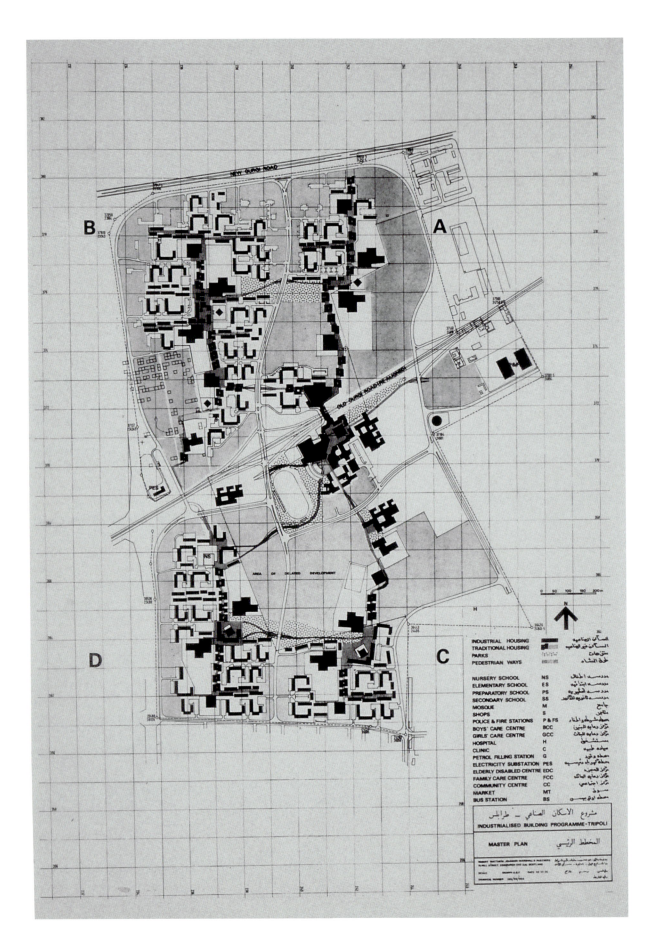

B

A

D

C

INDUSTRIAL HOUSING
TRADITIONAL HOUSING
PARKS
PEDESTRIAN WAYS

NURSERY SCHOOL	NS
ELEMENTARY SCHOOL	ES
PREPARATORY SCHOOL	PS
SECONDARY SCHOOL	SS
MOSQUE	M
SHOPS	S
POLICE & FIRE STATIONS	P & FS
BOYS' CARE CENTRE	BCC
GIRLS' CARE CENTRE	GCC
HOSPITAL	H
CLINIC	C
PETROL FILLING STATION	G
ELECTRICITY SUBSTATION	PES
ELDERLY DISABLED CENTRE	EDC
FAMILY CARE CENTRE	FCC
COMMUNITY CENTRE	CC
MARKET	MT
BUS STATION	BS

مشروع الاسكان الصناعي – طرابلس
INDUSTRIALISED BUILDING PROGRAMME-TRIPOLI

MASTER PLAN   المخطط الرئيسي

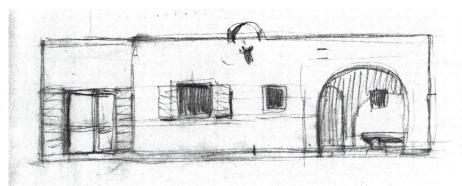

(opposite) **13.2** Early 1970s layout of Tripoli IBP residential area plan. (RMJM)

(left) **13.3** Early 1970s sketch by Matthew for low-rise house-type, Tripoli. (EULMC)

(below) **13.4** Perspective of zone of three-storey industrialised flats, Tripoli. (*Roundabout RMJMP*, November 1974, 3) (RMJM)

potential inhabitants, as well as of more modern aspects such as car parking and children's play facilities. Jim Latimer, with his Cumbernauld experience, was brought in to design the housing. A Tripoli branch office of RMJM was eventually set up and, from November 1973, was staffed by Henry Sherbrooke, as resident project director, with his wife Maggie as secretary. But the first need was for a feasibility report to synthesise the initial survey findings. Produced in October 1971, this concluded that, despite the modernity of features such as high car ownership, there was still a need for emphasis on inward-looking private open space, and inclusion of a guest room within the dwelling; shared spatial structures were seen as threatening of privacy.[24] A programme of 5,000 dwellings, ten schools, three mosques and 203 shops should be completed in 1973–7, and the industrialised-building procedure was set out, involving selection of a contractor, who would build an NHC-owned factory.[25]

In June 1972, following another week-long visit by Matthew to Tripoli in December 1971, a detailed Design Report was presented to the NHC. It divided the site into four 'environmental areas', with potential pedestrian/vehicle separation via a pedestrian spine, and a layout of interlocking courtyards structured by the Libyan stress on family privacy. A fairly high density of two dwellings per hectare was to be obtained, despite a high proportion of one- and two-storey houses; only 21 per cent of houses were to be in two-storey flats. Partly, of course, the low-rise, high-density concept of the IBP was dictated by earthquake conditions.

VIEW ALONG A MAIN PEDESTRIAN ROUTE SHOWING THE USE OF 'B' TYPE BRIDGE FLATS TO DEFINE THE ROUTE AND TO SHADE THE PATHWAY.

Spaven recalled that 'the plan was entirely Robert's idea, as was the attempt to express it in a "traditional Libyan" way'. While generally leaving detailed design to Latimer, Sherbrooke and others, Matthew took a close interest in the 'traditional' house types, and numerous sketch drawings survive in his collection. These concepts of traditional low-rise, high-density housing were partly influenced by earlier European-led efforts at a vernacular North African housing style, especially by Italian architects such as Giovanni Pellegrini in the 1930s.[26] Gradually, however, pressure for output pushed up the percentage of flats, and by

485

the time that initial cabinet approval was obtained, an initial contract composed entirely of 3,000 flats was demanded, and revised plans were accordingly produced by June 1973, envisaging the flats as a central 'spine', with traditional low-rise houses around the periphery.

But by June 1973 the political context of the development had begun to shift radically, in ways that would increasingly confuse and impair progress. Following Gadafi's declaration of a cultural revolution in that month, and the takeover of government administration by People's Committees, Misirati was sacked as NHC chairman and replaced by a Mr Muntasser, a lorry driver who already chaired the People's Committee in charge of the NHC, although Sifaou stayed on as Director-General. Site work was increasingly impeded by the oppressive attentions of the security agencies. Spaven recalled that

> from our perspective, Muntasser was very different from Misirati, who was a lovely chap. Muntasser had no interest in, or idea of, housing; he was simply an ideological member of the revolution, and, as Gadafi's excesses got worse, things became more and more difficult.

Ironically, Gadafi's new drive to expunge foreign influence actually encouraged, in housing, the building of repetitive, massed ranks of flats more directly reminiscent of European patterns. In Spaven's words, 'As you might expect, Robert held up his hands in horror at all that, and after the removal of Misirati, he completely lost interest in the project, which left it largely up to me to hold things together.' Matthew had made no less than eight personal visits of up to a week's duration, between November 1970 and October 1972, but following Gadafi's cultural revolution, he never returned.

From this point, Matthew devolved all negotiations involving visits to the SPLAJ to a combination of Aidan, Spaven, Tom Danks (QS) and Jim Latimer. The two tasks were to arrive at an agreed phased programme of construction, and to organise some form of multinational contractual joint venture to do the industrialised building work. Spaven and the others toured Europe before settling eventually on a combination of an Italian main contractor, Ing. Recchi SpA of Turin, and the Danish firm of Højgård & Schultz A/S of Copenhagen for the precast concrete. Here the Danish reputation for the highest quality in concrete industrialised building, established in Britain by systems such as Jespersen, was decisive, and Spaven recalled that 'to our astonishment, Højgård & Schultz produced exactly the same quality in Tripoli as at home in Denmark!' In mid 1974, by which time the RMJM Tripoli office, under senior architect Raymond Brownell, was eight strong, the first contracts for RMJM-designed housing started being let. June 1974 saw the placing of a £3.3m, 400-dwelling contract with Egyptian firm SPICO for one- and two-storey traditional housing. The following month saw the signing of a LD30 million contract with the Italian-Danish joint consortium for the first, far more significant industrialised contract, for 3,008 dwellings in 188 identical three- and four-storey blocks of flats, and construction of a precasting factory. Aidan recalled that

> by this stage, the conditions in Libya were almost the opposite of Islamabad under the military. We were supposedly working with the government, but actually there wasn't any 'government' to work with – there was no civil service infrastructure, no committee meetings, and the minister in charge was one of Gadafi's side-men, a man in his twenties who knew nothing about building at all! We were just left to get on with it.[27]

By November 1974 *Roundabout RMJMP* summarised progress in Tripoli, arguing that while the latest master-plan envisaged 60 per cent flats, the essential planning aims of the 1972 Design Report had been preserved, including division of the township into four local environment areas, each of around 1,200 dwellings, in the centre, and low-density traditional

Modern Architect

dwellings around, planned with a 'framework of sheltered play spaces and walkways' providing safe and pleasant routes to school and shops, especially for children. The flats would be arranged in U-shaped groups of three and four storeys, around the pedestrian spine, with gardens for all ground-floor flats, and all dwellings featuring the 'Libyan arrangement' of independent guest-room with WC, plus terrace and balcony.[28] In mid 1976 the IB factory started production of the precast concrete for the flats, and with the first two completed houses 'received with enthusiasm' in Libya, the firm had been commissioned to design the public buildings of the development – 11 schools and a district centre. Completion of the initial IB flats followed in February 1977. By then, the political radicalism of the SPLAJ regime had begun to spiral into a growing confrontation with the West, yet RMJM, echoing Matthew's trenchantly apolitical ethos even after his death, continued unobtrusively to maintain links, culminating in their commission for the $72m Jamahiriya Museum (opened 1988), a UNESCO-supported national antiquities museum housed within the walls of the Sarayya al Hamra citadel, and planned in exemplary Geddesian conservative-surgery manner, with dense courtyards and arched facades: the contents ranged from prehistoric and classical Roman remains to heroic paintings of Gadafi, and a VW Beetle that he had driven during the 1969 revolution.[29]

Matthew, Metcalf and 'Operation Breakthrough'

The other major overseas RMJM concern of Matthew's last years also became a victim of cultural differences, of a contrasting kind: an almost completely abortive drive to exploit the United States's transient enthusiasm in the 1960s for large-scale urban renewal, led by the federal Department of Housing and Urban Development (HUD). In the late 1960s the envisaged role of HUD had begun to change from a hortatory to an executive character. Following the Johnson

13.5 1988 interior detail of Jamahiriya Museum, Tripoli. Sited within a historic Ottoman citadel; the four-storey complex, planned in low-rise high-density form, was entirely hidden from the outside world, and a model of Geddesian conservative surgery. (RMJM)

administration's New Communities Act of 1968 and the National Housing Act of the same year, which committed the federal government to devise ways of eliminating all substandard housing during the 1970s, and claimed that 26 million dwellings would need to be built or rehabilitated to make this possible, HUD began to scale up its aspirations dramatically, and in 1969 launched Operation Breakthrough, an initiative to galvanise private industry into providing affordable housing through aggregated production techniques akin to car manufacture. President Richard Nixon's Housing and Urban Development Act of 1970 presaged a wide-ranging programme of housing and community development assistance: in his 1970 State of the Union Address Nixon identified violent and decayed cities as the 'most conspicuous area of failure in American life'.[30]

In April 1969, at the invitation of the cultural affairs office of the US Embassy, Matthew attended a talk at the embassy by his old friend Frederick Gutheim on the opportunities and challenges of the new policy, especially in relation to Washington DC planning issues. In personal discussion, Gutheim suggested to Matthew that the situation was ripe for exploitation by British multidisciplinary architectural firms skilled in the ways of social-democratic urban renewal and overspill. In a background report commissioned from the RIBA, Malcolm

MacEwen reported that the AIA was also now moving towards a more 'disinterested' and 'environmental' stance, and that its new Executive Vice-President, William Slayton, was pressing for a more radical, political interventionism.[31] During 1969 Matthew moved rapidly to follow up this lead. In August he organised for HUD chief George Romney a tour of new public housing in London and Central Scotland. And in September, en route to the IUA Congress in Argentina, he visited the IDA (World Bank), the New Communities Division of HUD, and the UN Centre for Housing, Building and Planning; Spaven later recalled that 'we took lots of slides of Barshare and other housing schemes to show them, but it didn't really make a real connection with their concerns.' On the same trip Gutheim treated Matthew to a tour of the rapidly developing Washington/Baltimore/Annapolis triangle. On his return, Matthew wrote to thank Gutheim for his hospitality, suggesting that RMJM should possibly link up with 'an outstanding US firm', and asking, 'Is there any merit in thinking about some sort of collaboration? – maybe I'm getting too old, but Aidan is keen to look abroad and is now around the Red Sea, not a very peaceful part of the world!'[32]

In 1970, after a further visit to London by Gutheim, and exploratory visits to the USA by Aidan, Matthew chose the firm of Bill Metcalf & Associates, hospital specialists, as best suited to provide the necessary local technical and cultural back-up: Aidan recalled that 'after we'd discussed several firms, Fritz eventually said, "Let's go and see Bill Metcalf!" – and he introduced us.' During 1971 and early 1972 the preparatory work got under way for setting up the collaboration. This was formalised as a new, Washington-based joint partnership, Sir Robert Matthew, Metcalf & Partners (MMP), confirmed formally in spring 1972. The alliance was celebrated at two parties hosted by Frank Corner, now the newly appointed New Zealand ambassador to the US.[33] Already, however, there were signs that the impetus of Nixon's urban renewal programme, and

thus of MMP, was ebbing; 1973 saw Nixon's declaration of a moratorium in housing and community-development assistance, with further cuts from 1974. In this more austere climate, it was agreed that cost planning, not architectural design or planning, should now be the focus of MMP's work. Matthew sent as partner-in-charge (from 1975, managing partner) Alastair Law, previously chief quantity surveyor in the New University of Ulster project. From that point, although MMP did do the structural engineering design for a large hospital at Wilmington, Delaware, the great majority of its US work was based on cost, specification and contract planning, rather than any kind of design, and the work of MMP soon gravitated towards the Middle East, opening a Cairo office in 1974, and providing design and cost guidelines for an Egyptian government programme of health centres.[34] Matthew continued to cultivate productive relationships both within the US, and with visiting US architects.[35]

Along with Metcalf, Meller and one other US partner (Phil Tobey), all the Edinburgh partners were also automatically partners of MMP. But among the Edinburgh staff the collaboration was seen as, at best, a money-wasting distraction: 'The rest of us became very worried about Matthew Metcalf, with all that money pouring into it; we were bemused by it, and as to why Robert should have been so keen on it.' 'It never really came to anything at all.'[36] Possibly, one driving force might have been personal: Matthew's own gradually falling income and moves towards partial retirement from the late 1960s, and a consequent hope that this association might support his own continuing travel to and from North America: he wrote to Corner in 1972 that he expected to be in Washington 'from time to time' now that 'we have an American association'.[37] From the American side, however, there was also a relative lack of enthusiasm behind the collaboration: in Spaven's view, 'we were always facing an "America for the Americans" attitude.'[38]

Modern Architect

Ambassador emeritus for social architecture and conservation

During the years from the late 1960s, Matthew's own overseas work gradually shifted from a commitment to organisations towards a commitment to issues. In particular, it began to reflect his new passion for conservation, a movement that combined strong local roots, in countries such as Scotland, with internationalist exchanges, led by the UNESCO offshoot ICOMOS, set up in 1965, the year after the passing of the 'Venice Charter', foundation of the modern international conservation movement. In 1972, following the energising of the environmental conservationist cause by the UN's Stockholm conference, ICOMOS embarked on a more concerted initiative in the European heartland of conservation, establishing in 1972–3 an international committee under the chairmanship of Lord Sandys, charged with organisation of a 'European Architectural Heritage Year' (EAHY) in 1975. Launched at a conference in Zurich in June 1973, EAHY was a typical cultural umbrella event, with associated publications, case studies and conferences drawn from a variety of countries; it culminated in 1975 in a grand conference in Amsterdam.[39]

Matthew was involved in EAHY from the start, at the invitation of Count Sforza, both as a British representative and as a spokesman for the architectural profession; the British delegation was largely organised by the Civic Trust and the RIBA. Confidently, he hailed the EAHY initiative as exemplifying a great advance from the natural resources conservation approach dominant at Stockholm, to 'include, not only stones and mortar, but as well the more unquantifiable elements of aesthetic and cultural value'.[40] But when it came to the June 1973 Zurich conference, attended by 300 delegates from 31 countries, Matthew was in for something of a shock, as the architect-dominated British delegation found itself in a minority of one, the event otherwise being monopolised by preservation zealots, who violently attacked any kind of modern architecture: he recalled later that one German delegate said that 'architects are not our friends'. Organisationally, too, there was a sharp split at Zurich, between the government conservation bureaux that represented most countries, and the voluntaristic approach of the UK and Switzerland; the UK was represented directly by its national civic trusts. At the CAA assembly in Ottawa in November 1973 Matthew reported the general distaste for, even 'acute hostility' towards, the architectural profession at Zurich, and warned that in Britain, too, conservation zealotry was now so strong that 'major changes of any kind' were almost impossible; there was a real risk of an explosion of public anger that could push the architectural cause 'back to square one, or even further back'. The profession's credibility was slipping badly, and if architects did not 'move fast', they would lose out not only in helping guide the conservation movement, but also 'on the whole wider front of the environmental battle'.[41]

The Civic Trust/Scottish Civic Trust-based preparations for EAHY in Britain ensured a wide geographical spread, with a strong Scottish representation, in the pilot conservation projects that formed a prominent component: Chester, Poole, NTS Little Houses and Edinburgh's New Town. But Matthew's concern was with the wider international picture, especially in resolving the growing architecture/conservation split, and his ideal opportunity to intervene in both fields together came in October 1973 when Sandys suggested the holding of a symposium in Poland, under joint ICOMOS–IUA sponsorship and focusing on the problems of integrating modern architecture into historic towns, partly in order 'to involve "Communist countries" in our campaign'. He asked Matthew, 'Could you give the lead on the architects' side?' Eventually, the event was fixed for 4–20 October 1974 at Kazimierz, the historic Jewish quarter of Kraków, and it was decided that Matthew would expand his trip into a more general ambassadorial trip to Poland, hosted by the Polish Society of Architects. His fare would be paid by the British Council, and he would be guest of honour at the conference itself, which he would address on the subjects of the ENTCC and vernacular architecture, in both cases on the basis that 'the present age can and must make its own positive contribution to the ancient towns and villages of Europe.'

As the Kazimierz conference approached, however, events took an unexpected turn. At the end of September Matthew began to get indications that he might now be not just guest of honour but also president of the conference, responsible among other things for framing of conclusions and resolutions. Added to that, and to his growing ill-health, the British industrial relations crisis of 1973–4 turned his travel arrangements into a 'horrible ordeal'. On arriving at Heathrow Airport, a baggage strike meant that he had to fly instead to Prague and take the train from there. Once arrived at Kazimierz, Matthew found that he would indeed be chairing the seminar, which was dominated by delegates from Poland, the USSR, Scandinavia and the Netherlands. In his own lectures at the conference Matthew himself 'showed lots of slides' on the current situation of conservation in Scotland, while in his main lecture, on world vernacular architecture, he argued that there remained 'a thread of simple building' based on local materials and 'sadly ignored since the Industrial Revolution'; this vernacular was both intensely local in character, but also universal, and therefore universally under threat of extinction by modernity. In the evenings Matthew was able to relax in the company of Polish friends, including Helena Syrkus, who recalled after his death in 1975 how she had hosted him 'only a year ago in my house, enjoying friendship and also food and drink, nattering until midnight'. On his return from Kraków Matthew wrote to his chief hosts, Henryk Buszko of the Society of Polish Architects, and Adolf Ciborowski, to express his hope that the meeting had

helped to bring together IUA and ICOMOS in a 'friendly way', and had shown how to 'resolve any difficulties between "conservationists" on the one hand, and architects and planners on the other'.[42] EAHY arguably represented a conclusion of the early 'revolutionary' phase of the conservation movement, at any rate in Western Europe, although radical innovations were still under way, such as the founding of the militant campaigning group 'SAVE Britain's Heritage' in the same year. Owing to the onset of his final illness at the beginning of 1975, Matthew was not able to take part in this new phase of triumph and consolidation, although he did doggedly try to continue the agenda of involving the design professions in the conservation movement.

In Matthew's wider overseas architectural links old friendships continued to play a strong role, although often now threaded more tenuously around Matthew's many overseas trips and activities, and the gradual retrenchments and growing forgetfulness of advancing years. Cicely Naismith and family members were often pressed into hospitality duties at short notice: in 1969, for instance, Anders Tengbom wrote to report that both his parents had died and that a colleague hoped to call on him in London, but Cicely replied that this could be difficult, as 'Sir Robert doesn't have a secretary in London now' and would be away on those dates. And in the same year Gontran Goulden warned him that a proposal to elect him to the French Académie d'Architecture (in recognition of his IUA work) had come to nothing because he had forgotten to reply to a succession of letters, and the Académie were 'a little upset'.[43] Most of Matthew's overseas friendships continued to be linked to, or mediated through, the IUA, CAA or RIBA, with new generation groups coming to the fore as older contacts faded away. Among his Soviet acquaintances, for example, following the illness and death of his old friend Nikolai Kolli, the gap was increasingly filled by Matthew's friendship with Georgi Orlov: he and Robert stayed several times in

Modern Architect

each other's houses, in London and Moscow, on IUA and housing-related business, and Matthew arranged for him to be elected an honorary corresponding member of the RIBA.

Matthew's sense of even-handedness ensured that, as in his contacts with Czechoslovakia, he maintained links with both official and 'opposition' elements, and drew the line only when called on to openly support dissidents.[44] In 1972–3, for example, he politely rebuffed attempts by architect-MP Sydney Chapman to persuade him to become a patron of the Committee for the Release of Soviet Jewry, while offering financial help behind the scenes, and offering to help lobby privately the case of any architect suffering persecution: 'Though I fully sympathise with the aims of your committee, and wish you every success, I feel that if I were to become publicly involved it might cause great embarrassment as past president of the IUA.' In 1973 the issue of Soviet Jewish architects drew another tirade from Matthew's old adversary, Sydney Loweth. In an unsolicited personal letter to Matthew Loweth attacked his support for continuing RIBA links with its Soviet counterpart, blasting him as 'one of our leading Communist architects', and demanding that 'you and you [sic] fellow "reds", instead of paying that large sum of money to the Communists, might suggest that we give them Karl Marx from Highgate Cemetary [sic] together with his monumental tombstone.'[45] Just as in the 1960s, Matthew firmly resisted all attempts by Communist 'front' organisations to infiltrate international architectural affairs.[46]

Of the two non-Soviet communist countries Matthew had visited in the 1960s, Romania and China, the latter now disappeared from his field of vision.[47] His Romanian connection, however, went from strength to strength, at a time when the Ceaucescu regime was enjoying a considerable vogue in Western Europe as a non-Soviet model of communism, and in October 1971 he was awarded the degree of Honoris Causa at Bucharest University, the first time such an award had been made to a non-Romanian. Robert and Lorna flew out to Bucharest on 12 October, and were feted for over a week as guests of the Architects' Union of Romania (of which Ascanio Damian was now vice-president). At the award ceremony on 14 October, conferred in the huge assembly hall of the Ion Mincu Institute of Architecture, and reported in the party newspaper *Scinteia*, Dr Octavio Doicescu, chairman of the Architects' Union, lauded the 'renowned British architect' not only for his 'architectural creativity' but for his higher education and IUA work. In his reply, Matthew argued that Geddes's vision of 'Folk, Work and Place' had been resoundingly achieved in Romania's decentralised regional planning policy and its support for vernacular-inspired new architecture: 'I greatly hope that in your country, with so much to give to others, you will bring the younger generations into the work of the IUA, to the benefit of us all.' Matthew's trip was followed up by an open-house policy towards Romanian architectural visitors to Britain.[48]

During Matthew's last years the accelerating pace of his environmental involvements, added to his other socially orientated commitments, increasingly crowded out his more conventional international-establishment activities.[49] In these years Matthew was also involved as assessor for a handful of international architectural competitions. The aftermath of the 1968 Amsterdam city hall competition, for example, stretched over several years.[50] Less well known, but equally conditioned by the demands for contextual solutions in old city fabric, was a two-stage competition in September/ November 1971 for planning a new business district in the historic Italian

13.6 Certificate of Matthew's honorary Romanian doctorate, awarded in September 1971. (Institutul de Arhitectura Ion Mincu, Bucharest)

Sir Robert Matthew, CBE, MA, LLD,
    PPRIBA, ARSA, MTPI
Johnson-Marshall and Partners
15 Hill Street
Edinburgh

With the compliments of

J.F.H. Villiers
Cultural Attaché

BRITISH EMBASSY
BUCHAREST

FLACĂRA
23 October 1971

la institutul de arhitectură

Săptămîna trecută, în cadrul unei solemnități care a avu
loc în marele amfiteatru al Institutului de arhitectură «Io
Mincu» din București, profesorului Robert Matthew di
Marea Britanie i-a fost conferit titlul de Doctor Honori
Causa al institutului bucureștean de arhitectură.

13.7 Newspaper report of Matthew's degree award ceremony in Bucharest. (*Flacara*, 23 October 1971)

town of Perugia, to be located in a redeveloped former industrial zone. Nominated, again, by the IUA, Matthew chaired the meeting, which eventually selected a bold entry by Tokyo architect Tsuto Kimura and colleagues, featuring a spine with slabs branching off at right angles. In Matthew's view, Kimura's scheme showed a 'very strong architectural form' and 'a well balanced synthesis between the demands of the programme and the construction of rich and imaginative space'. Other competition jury commissions via IUA included one in 1970 for a masterplan for the Free University of Brussels, and one in 1975 for a national cultural centre for Bahrain, won by Basil Spence but never built.[51]

Mediation and crisis management in the IUA

Matthew's IUA work from 1969 onwards was strongly polarised in character, between a period of intense internal crisis in 1969–71 and a time of more outward-looking stability from 1972 onwards. The crisis phase followed the fundamental reappraisal of IUA finance and reorganisation that Matthew himself

had instigated, but it was dramatically worsened by the unexpected and divisive outcome of the long-planned retirement of Vago from the Secretary-General post at the Buenos Aires Congress of 1969. Vago's growing sensitivity about the succession, and Matthew's role as mediator, had been presaged already at the Prague 1967 assembly, when, in the vote for the Secretary-General post, Vago received only 80 per cent of the votes cast, and, complaining that one-fifth of the IUA were against him, threatened to resign on the spot. Uproar broke out, and Matthew immediately took the floor and asked everyone present to demonstrate support for Vago by a show of hands. Everyone did so, and the crisis was avoided – or, rather, deferred.[52]

Matthew's diplomatic skills, and his tendency towards compartmentalisation of his life, were ideally suited to acting as a mediator of the tensions within IUA, which combined personality clashes with geopolitical conflict at one remove. Even now, in his 60s, at any one time he was able to switch easily between personal friendships and a more detached attitude to more formal, overtly political initiatives from the same people. For example, Georgi Orlov, although also a close personal friend, wrote to Matthew in June 1972 in his capacity as President of the USSR Architects, inviting him to an assembly of 'workers of culture' convened by the 'Belgian Association for Security and Cooperation in Europe'; Orlov's letter argued that as architects were 'the most humanitarian profession of creators', they were especially obliged to participate in 'peace' initiatives. Matthew decided to ignore the letter, after discussing it with Gontran Goulden, who agreed with him that

> the trouble with these Soviet things is that you never know what may come next, but I do not need to tell you! The aims of the group seem to be perfectly straightforward, but is the Soviet group following the party line? I guess so, but then, how is one to know?'[53]

During 1968 and 1969 Matthew's IUA reorganisation commission moved towards its conclusion, its work accelerated by a rapid deterioration in the IUA's finances: in November 1968 Vago reported that only 7,000 francs were left in its account – 'a very serious business!' And by June 1969, despite Matthew's attempts at fundraising among British architects, only $4,000 had been raised, and Vago warned that so long as 'everything is based on an unpaid secretary general and five girls, we may as well cease activities'. Disaster was staved off only by Goulden's efforts, as treasurer, in collecting subscriptions arrears.[54] Matters gradually built up to a head at the 1969 Congress at Buenos Aires, when Matthew's report was due to be presented. Immediately beforehand, Vago exploded to Matthew that

> if a democratic organisation like UIA is not capable of assuming its responsibilities, either the architectural profession will cease to play a role on the international plane or it will be replaced by an active minority replacing the extinct organisation. I think that you are the most authorised and respected person to give the warning.

Apart from that, I do not know how things will go off at Buenos Aires. In spite of all our efforts, the Congress remains a large question mark.'[55]

In his notes for the October 1969 General Assembly and Council in the exclusive Patagonian alpine resort of Bariloche, and the Congress in Buenos Aires that followed it, Matthew prepared to set out a new, confident agenda for the future, based on a new structure and statutes, with an expanded budget and a more professional approach: there would be triennial congresses and a new central coordinating group, or 'Bureau', formed of the Secretariat and the four vice-presidents charged with regional action. The vice-presidents proposed for 1969–72 were Orlov (continued from 1967–9), Dan Schwartzman (USA), Luis Arizmendi (Spain) and Jai Bhalla (India). Matthew wrote confidently that the enhanced IUA could become 'a positive force for peace in a decisive world situation', but warned that to expand it from a 'contact' to a 'service provider' role would require more money to fill in gaps in its 'loose net'. And Bhalla demanded more rhetorically that the IUA should assert 'leadership' and create a sense of 'destiny' in pursuit of the 'better society', especially in developing countries. But ironically, following these fine sentiments, the 1969 General Assembly and Congress turned out to be the most destructive in the history of the IUA, not least because this time, unlike Cuba in 1963, it was the internal, personal tensions within the organisation, rather than any external threat, that were at work.

First, on 14–16 October, came the General Assembly, at the Llao-Llao Hotel at Bariloche, reached by the 114 delegates on a two-hour chartered flight from Buenos Aires, and described by SPAN architect Eric Lyons (part of the UK group) as 'a monstrous Swiss chalet-style edifice, superbly sited in the prettiest scenery you could imagine'. In the main session, in a converted ballroom, a sour note began almost immediately, in the discussions on Matthew's reform

package. These, without decisive direction from chairman Beaudouin, became bogged down in an acrimoniously confused debate. RIBA Overseas Relations Assistant Secretary Kathleen Hall recalled that 'the meeting was soon out of control', and here, as at Prague, Matthew intervened, to suggest that Vago's proposals should be taken as the basis for discussion:

When things appeared to be completely out of hand, Sir Robert mounted the platform and started to speak slowly and clearly in English. The babble of foreign voices stopped, people began to look happier, and eventually left the hall under the impression they had got what they wanted. The character of the man had come through, clear-sighted, wise and humane.[56]

Far worse was to come, however, in the elections for office holders, 'the climax of the Assembly, which loomed ahead throughout the previous items and caused lots of subtle (and some crude) electioneering in the chamber and in the corridors outside'. Vago had given up the Secretaryship on the assumption that he could move smoothly into the Presidency for a three-year transitional period to 'tide over' the IUA under its new structure; his candidacy was proposed by the Soviet section. But by the summer of 1969 it was becoming clear that there were strong fears that Vago might continue to hold the reins if elected President. In a strong movement to broaden the control of the IUA beyond Europe, Ramón Corona Martin began to emerge as a serious Latin-American competitor, writing in August to 'open his heart' to Matthew. He argued that 'Pierre is a lovely chap but he seems to own the place and this does away with giving an opportunity to others'; furthermore, giving the presidency to two Frenchmen in a row 'gives the impression (which we want to destroy) that the UIA is exclusively a European institution'.[57]

In the event, at the Assembly, Vago – to his bitter astonishment – was defeated by Corona Martin, by only two votes (80:78). In the afternoon the elections for the Secretary-Generalship seemed almost an afterthought, and – Michel Weill of France having withdrawn 'at the last moment' in response to the anti-French feeling – the eventual contest was between a fairly obscure Swiss delegate, Francois Peyrot, and a 46-year-old

(opposite) **13.8** Full-page sheet of doodles by Matthew at UIA executive meeting, Llao-Llao Hotel, Bariloche, October 1969. (EULMC)

Lebanese, Henri Eddé, a former chair of the UN Housing, Building and Planning Committee and a 'proud member of a great Beirut political family'.[58] Supported by Matthew and many others, Eddé won by 98 to 64 votes, and hailed his election as 'a mission designed to aid architects in developing countries'. The effective over-throw of Vago led to pandemonium, with delegates passionately at odds. In an attempt to salvage the situation, Matthew immediately persuaded Corona Martin to suggest that Vago should be designated honorary life president and permanent consultant, and cooled tempers with a soothing encomium, charged with more emotion than he would normally have betrayed in a mainstream policy speech: he declared that Vago had earned 'our abiding esteem and love', and that, hav-ing 'given his life to the UIA unselfishly and without reserve, his monument is the UIA itself'. In his memoirs, 30 years later, Vago still recalled the episode with some passion. Before the Assembly, 'I thought my election would pose no prob-lems, but I noticed that Orlov was pale.' Afterwards, he found that 'the intention was only to put a shot across my bows [against] France's too important role. No one expected this result.'[59] Now the dele-gates duly moved back to Buenos Aires for the congress, on 20–25 October, with over 3,000 delegates from 33 countries – by far the largest total in IUA history. The atmosphere of the Congress was not enhanced by the fact that Argentina was in a state of civil unrest, with the dele-gates protected by the police and army, and 'heady talk of revolution' among the local architectural students.[60]

In the immediate aftermath of Bariloche–Buenos Aires there were attempts to acclaim the outcome as an optimistic vindication of the IUA's inter-nationalism: for example, the *Architects' Journal* reported it as 'the start of a new era'. But within a month it became clear that the IUA's brave new start was doomed to collapse at the first hurdle, and that power would effectively revert within a year to the IUA's old 'French' oligarchy, not because of Matthew's reorganisation plan, nor because of the victory of Corona Martin, but because of the abrasive personality of Henri Eddé.[61] Initially, Matthew and others thought that the trouble was merely a personality clash with Vago, although the Beirut-based Eddé's unwillingness to spend more than three or four days a week in Paris raised eyebrows almost immediate-ly. Vago complained bitterly that Eddé was determined to exclude him from any further IUA involvement, and wrote to Matthew in November that 'this gentle-man' had prohibited IUA staff from speaking to him. By January 1970 the lan-guage had sharpened, with Vago speak-ing of 'cette petite ordure qui s'est installée au Secrétaire-Général'. Eddé had also quarrelled with long-standing secre-tary Martine Favier, who resigned in protest, leaving the staff rudderless; her eventual successor as 'Miss UIA', Francine Troupillon, would stay for 30 years.[62] Increasingly, all the key figures within IUA were forced either to follow a 'tightrope walk' between the two, or to take sides. Matthew valiantly attempted to mediate, for example by flying from London to Paris for a day trip on 13 March 1970, having lunch with Marc Saugey and Swiss executive member C E Geisendorf, and separate afternoon meet-ings with Eddé and Vago.[63] By April 1970 Matthew began increasingly to side open-ly with Vago, arguing that the schism, by isolating the Secretariat, was beginning to choke off the IUA's most vital external contacts, such as that with UNESCO, and that Eddé was neglecting external corre-spondence.[64] There were also ominous signs that rival organisations were exp-loiting the conflict: the Mexican presi-dent of the Federation of Pan American Architects, for example, was said to be trying to build up his organisation at the IUA's expense.[65]

October 1970 brought a sudden and unexpected development offering hope of a break in the impasse, when Eddé revealed that he had been appointed Minister of Works in the Lebanese govern-ment, which would require him to stay in Beirut on an almost full-time basis:

Matthew now argued that 'I find it hard to picture a Minister of Public Works and Agriculture (even in a tiny country) finding time to continue as Secretary-General.' Writing to the protesting Vago, Matthew argued that 'I have been very much divided, in my mind, ever since the sad South American occasion, as to whether I should pull out of the IUA or not.' On the one hand, there was 'loyalty to you – what happened at Bariloche was a great shock to me – I foresaw immediately what was likely to happen.' But, on the other hand, there was the continuing task of trying to keep going the UN Low-Cost Housing Documentation project, where 'I am now more or less a spectator.' He wrote in similar terms to Georgi Orlov, arguing that, in Eddé's absence, the President should call together a Bureau meeting, to review the 'unusual situation'.[66] Others were less restrained than Matthew in their councils, and the normally mild-mannered Geisendorf wrote to him in late November that Eddé should retire in an 'honourable' way or be sacked, owing to his 'autocratic, destructive' behaviour: 'The very fact that he has accepted the position of Minister of Public Works and Agriculture in the government of a country involved in the Arab-Israeli conflict' was incompatible with IUA internationalism. By November Eddé had effectively conceded defeat, and Weill was appointed interim Secretary-General (an appointment made permanent in July 1971).

By July 1971, although Eddé was still resentfully threatening to stand as President in 1972, things had begun to return gradually to a generally French-dominated normality, and Goulden wrote to Matthew to report on a 'successful' council meeting in East Berlin: although Corona Martin had been weak in the chair, Weill had 'carried him along', and it had been 'pleasant' to have a whole week of meetings without tension, and a relief to be able to return to the old, time-honoured ideological tensions, as for example when the North Koreans 'trotted out the old story about the wicked Japanese and South Koreans trying to

form an Asiatic Society of Architects'.[67] And at the 1972 Congress and Assembly in Bulgaria, on the theme of 'Architecture and Leisure', matters had returned to normal, with Orlov and Bhalla the new president and vice-president, and a triennial balanced budget of $246,500 duly agreed. The chief tension now stemmed from the current Sino-Soviet hostility, and when Orlov's candidacy was approved (Vago recalled), 'only the five Chinese delegates remained seated, but after a pause I smiled at Yang Ting Pao and he got up, followed by the others.' To Vago's delight, Eddé, who had put himself forward as a council member, received only a handful of votes and 'stormed out in a fury'.[68]

Only in the last months of his life, in early 1975, was Matthew's IUA work disturbed by another serious conflict over politicisation of the Union, when Bhalla and Orlov emerged at the Venice meeting as rival candidates for the presidency. Orlov put himself forward for an unprecedented second term, as candidate of a 'bloc' of Eastern and Western European nations, while Bhalla presented himself as a developing-world champion. Matthew, from his sickbed, weighed in powerfully on Bhalla's behalf, lobbying Mike Austin-Smith of the RIBA that if the Institute supported a second term for Orlov,

I would, I think, feel constrained to withdraw from the [RIBA] delegation to Venice, as I would certainly vote against the Orlov proposition, which, as you know, I think sets a deplorable precedent and would be an unfortunate expression of politics, quite apart from the question of who Orlov's successor should be.

At Venice, in the event, Bhalla was elected as president for 1975–8 by 119 votes to Orlov's 89, with Weill continuing as Secretary-General and Geisendorf succeeding Goulden as Treasurer.[69] Bhalla stepped up the proselytising of IUA in developing countries, touring Africa to whip up enthusiasm for it (while securing the postponement of South Africa's expulsion until 1987), and managing to get China to accept Hong Kong as a member.

Frustrations of the 'Basic Housing Project'

Alongside all these often tempestuous, personality-related differences, Matthew attempted to continue his methodical pursuit of the IUA–UN Low-Cost Housing initiative. Ever since 1959, as we saw earlier, there had been repeated attempts by Matthew to establish collaboration with the UN Centre on Housing, Building and Planning, most recently in a 1967 Geneva meeting, when the committee decided to start a 'Basic Housing' documentation programme, focusing on case studies: R J (Joe) Crooks, the Caribbean director of UNCHBP, wrote formally to Matthew in March 1968 suggesting the project should take the form of comparative examples of good practice selected by a panel of assessors, including both built form and user feedback, all for the use of 'the man in the field, especially in the developing countries'. Initially, on Matthew's recommendation, IUA Housing Commission chairman Horia Maicu of Romania took charge, soliciting national sections to send in 'interesting achievements', but by September 1969 only one-third of sections had replied, and Vago suggested that the outlook was generally 'hopeless'.[70]

In the chaotic aftermath of the Bariloche debacle Matthew finally took personal control of the initiative, with the organisational help of the Frankfurt (Main)-based Dipl. Ing. R von Steinbuechel-Rheinwall of the West German section, in close collaboration with Crooks's Polish deputy, Adolf Ciborowski. During 1970 Matthew and Steinbuechel set about organising the case studies, helped by Orlov with Soviet examples.[71] By January 1971 finance of $8,500 from the UN was secured, and a succession of day trips by air to Frankfurt began, to discuss progress with Steinbuechel. Matthew himself, helped by the Edinburgh University ARU, prepared a number of the case studies,

including detailed project description sheets for Commonwealth countries, including not only the UK but also the high-rise public housing of Hong Kong and Singapore, and the early stages of Islamabad.[72] Eventually, publication of the results was stalled in early 1972 by the UN, which was then in the throes of a financial crisis, and the complete case study material was finally sent by Steinbuechel to New York only in November 1972. By late 1973 and early 1974 the impetus had slipped away once more, with Crooks requesting more information and circulating fresh questionnaires, and Steinbuechel once more collecting information. Eventually, with Matthew's illness and death in 1975, the project lapsed – but, as we shall see, its spirit lived on and found new life in the diverse UN initiatives in the wake of the 1976 Habitat conference in Vancouver.[73]

Growing pains of the CAA

We saw in Chapter 11 how Matthew's own attitudes had shifted in response to the rapid disintegration of the remnants of the British Empire, embracing the dynamic of decolonisation with increasing enthusiasm. In 1971, speaking at a Commonwealth Society meeting in Edinburgh, he frankly acknowledged the personal disorientation of the 'traumatic experience of passing rapidly from one era to another', and the 'change from dependence to independence': 'I need not point out – you have only to take a look! – that I was brought up in an Empire-based education.' Admittedly, to him, the empire had been 'a series of second-hand impressions' – 'Kim and his gun', his father's South African war service, and New Delhi – 'the most monumental expression of imperialism'. But change was inevitable, in 'the Darwinian sense that the fittest, by definition, has the capacity to adapt to the changing needs of the times': the CAA had emerged as a 'concrete expression' of that 'change from imperialism to Commonwealth'.[74] Matthew was also sensitive to subsidiary tensions within the Commonwealth, such as between francophone and anglophone Canada, recalling that in 1968, when the CBAE visited Laval architecture school in Montreal – a visit timed so as to make possible simultaneous CBAE recognition of both it and the 'English' (McGill) university school – the freshers had laid on a comprehensive boycott, including rolls of toilet paper suspended from the ceiling, inscribed with 'various sentiments about the oppressive nature of the British – the boycott was laid on thick'. Zahir was also part of the deputation, and he recalled that 'we were astounded to find only one student in the class, who had a fifty-year-old plan pinned on his drawing board. To top everything, a tattered Union Jack was helplessly hanging from the ceiling.'[75]

But the more sensitive Matthew became to the political forces of change and division, the more convinced he became, correspondingly, of the unifying potential of the ideal of professionalism, with its implicit encouragement – in 'developing' countries – of the emergence of a bourgeoisie: professional people were 'middle-class and of the bourgeoisie – right – and are likely to remain so', but their ranks were not closed. And the professions helped allow the Commonwealth to 'maintain its professional integrity and not get mixed up in competitive industry and commerce': in contrast to political divisions, '*professional* bonds are not easy to break'. In 1975 Tom Colchester recalled that Matthew saw in 1963 that, unlike the IUA,

> more could probably be done on a world front in a positive and congenial way by drawing together the best of the RIBA's imperial past, the contemporary wish of rich peoples to help the third world, and the claims of newly emergent nations to express their identity in their own professional culture.

Now he was no longer president of the RIBA, IUA or CAA – but he still continued to exert a dominant role within the latter. In Colchester's opinion it was Matthew's passionate sincerity in this core belief that so often helped overcome opposition: 'When Robert expounded his concepts of the architect's contribution to society, it was no shibboleth made tawdry by repetition, but a view conscientiously held and executed.'[76]

During the last five years of his life Matthew's CAA concerns became sharply polarised between the general, positive confidence that the Association was firmly established, and the very negative specific issue of the ever more controversial membership of South Africa. In 1969, on Matthew's departure from the presidency, the CAA's finances stood at a very healthy £18,000, following a £10,000 renewal of the Commonwealth Foundation grant, and a further £3,000 windfall grant due to devaluation. In the early 1970s finances became more straitened for a while, owing to Commonwealth Foundation grant reductions and RIBA cutbacks.[77] Between 1969 and 1974 Matthew continued to rely on the work of Colchester, who still worked part-time from a small room in 66 Portland Place, concentrating especially on the educational field.[78] However, towards the end of his tenure there were some rumblings of discontent, for example in 1970 from Bhalla, who complained to Matthew of Colchester's 'undue influence' in the selection of elected officers. When Colchester retired in 1974, he was replaced by another ex-East African expatriate, Tom Watson, a Scot who had left his practice in Uganda during the Amin expulsions, and was seen by Matthew as 'a tough character – very different from Tom Colchester but probably good for the job nowadays, with younger, thrusting men in the councils of the CAA'.[79] Watson's energy, and persuasive powers with the Commonwealth Foundation (which secured a £10,000 grant), allowed the development of a number of new policies, including the development of slide lecture packages and low-cost textbooks on a shoestring budget. These new initiatives were overseen by Kathleen Hall (previously RIBA overseas head for a decade), who joined the secretariat as projects director.

For Matthew, the CAA and IUA were of

13.10 Group photo of CAA conference, Nigerian Institute for International Studies, Lagos, March 1969. In centre of front row: A E Egbor, President of the Nigerian Institute of Architects; Matthew; Oluwole Olumuyiwa, NIA Vice-President; Tom Colchester. Visible in back row: Alan Vaughan Richards (with beard, above Egbor); Jai Bhalla (above Colchester); Hugh Wilson (right of Bhalla); Arthur Ling (front, two from right). (VC10 Photo Services, Lagos)

a more personal significance than the RIBA: for example, in 1974 he suggested to the editor of the Indian Institute of Architects' newsletter that he would prefer to be referred to as past president of the IUA or CAA rather than of the RIBA, in view of the 'international reputations and global outlooks' of the two former organisations. In the 1965 *Handbook of Commonwealth Architects* he had emphasised that there was 'plenty of room' for both CAA and IUA, especially with the CAA specialising in educational matters. As between IUA and CAA, Matthew's own personal preference was undoubtedly for the latter – he held that there was 'much more similarity of view' between Commonwealth countries than European ones.[80]

Aside from the constant running sore of South Africa (see below), the greatest single challenge of Matthew's CAA presidency came at the end: the March 1969 biennial conference at Lagos, Nigeria. As in the case of Cuba, unexpected political developments in the host country had radically changed the context of the conference since Lagos was chosen, with civil war raging between 1968 and 1970.[81] The Nigerian CAA conference presented Matthew with three problems: the unpopularity of Nigeria itself in many countries, owing to charges of genocide against the Ibos; the ongoing militant stance taken by Nigeria on South Africa

(fully reflected by the Nigerian Institute of Architects, which excluded South Africa from the conference); and Matthew's own concern, on behalf of RMJM, to keep alive his World Bank schools programme in Nigeria, under negotiation since 1965. Although CAA conferences were normally far smaller and more intimate than the IUA's, with dozens rather than hundreds of participants, many people were deterred from travelling to Lagos owing to the war; 19 countries (including Ireland but excluding South Africa) were represented. Matthew's response drew, typically, on his time-honoured vernacular concepts. At the opening ceremony, from which the President, Major-General Yakubu Gowon, was 'unavoidably absent', Matthew argued that the conference could powerfully help develop 'an African capacity to answer African problems in African materials, and a national vernacular of style and feeling'. Nigeria, he argued, could boast not only an 'ancient town tradition' and an outstanding sculptural vernacular, but a resilient society within which 'women count for a great deal'; what was lacking was 'middle grade skills' such as architecture.

The concrete efforts of the conference were concerned, as always within CAA, with education and registration, especially focusing on Nigeria as the potential leader of the new Africa. On educational standards the conference advocated a move away from RIBA to CAA standards – which, Matthew stressed, would mean '*not* standardisation' nor any kind of imposition of 'some outmoded British pattern of education'. But it was in the linked area of registration that the conference secured its most significant and unexpected success. A Nigerian architects' registration bill had been languishing for several years, but that situation changed on the penultimate day of the conference, when the entire delegation was received by General Gowon at his headquarters at Dodan Barracks. At Matthew's suggestion Bhalla, the new president, asked bluntly whether Gowon would be prepared to sign the much-delayed Architects' Registration Bill:

> The General looked around, a little taken aback, but there were many countries represented around the table and he was a young and buoyant man, and he made up his mind there and then, 'Yes, I will sign!' – and he did! A decree was promulgated immediately by the Federal government.'[82]

The unexpected success of Lagos, at a total cost to CAA of £5,137, was followed up in July 1970 by an executive committee meeting at the RIAS in Edinburgh and a grand dinner party at Keith.[83] And in May 1971 the CAA conference was dovetailed into the Royal Australian Institute of Architects Centenary Meeting in Sydney, with Matthew staying on afterwards as RAIA's guest for the whole of the convention. At this CAA meeting Matthew's main organisational task was to avert a potential slight to Australia if Max Collard (one of two candidates for the presidency) was defeated in a contest: he persuaded both to stand down, and prevailed on Bhalla to continue for a second term. Bhalla's acceptance speech, in terms more fulsome than Matthew's normal rhetoric, struck a Gandhi-like tone of high principle: 'Let us, therefore, send out of this conference a message to this groping, uncertain and disorientated world, that love and not hatred, that

freedom and not fear, faith and not doubt, have in them the healing of the nations.'[84] During his presidency, as in the IUA, Bhalla devoted special attempts to proselytising the CAA cause in Asia, and successfully secured the passage of an Indian Architects' Registration Act in 1972. At Canberra Bhalla was faced with the potential embarrassment of the outbreak of war between India and Pakistan, but as the main delegation of the IAP failed to materialise (owing to internal dissension), leaving Pakistan represented solely by Bhalla's old friend Zahir, the potential for conflict was averted.[85]

At the RAIA Canberra conference

(top) **13.11** Matthew outside the Lagos CAA conference, in discussion with Egbor and Captain Nelson Soroh (attending in lieu of General Gowon, head of the Nigerian military government). (VC10 Photo Services)

(bottom) **13.12** Matthew and Bhalla seen at the CAA Lagos conference exhibition, examining a model of Alan Vaughan Williams's striking, organic-form Akerele House. (VC10 Photo Services)

Matthew warmly acclaimed the urban conception of the Australian capital, but he also felt the need for frankness, and, in a speech drafted with Harrison, turned a more critical eye on the Australian built environment, dominated by privatised forces. For him, professional organisation, as always, was the key: citing as an example the position in Britain, where 50 per cent of architects worked in public organisations, Matthew declared trenchantly that 'a country where the public service is held in low regard is in no shape to tackle in any effective way the problems of the environment.'[86] During the early 1970s the dwindling funding from the Commonwealth Foundation led to a slight scaling-back in CAA operations, with a decision to make the conferences triennial, but a full schedule of CBAE activities continued, with Matthew retiring at the fourth meeting, in Nairobi in March 1969. Between then and 1973 he set about fostering a systematic Commonwealth collaboration of university architectural research units, beginning with contacts with Professor A C Light of Auckland University and John Chadwick of the Commonwealth Foundation, and ultimately leading in January 1972 to a formal Seminar on Architectural Research in Commonwealth and UK Universities, held in Edinburgh University.[87]

South Africa: to split or not to split?

The issue of South African membership was far more explosive for the CAA, as an explicitly decolonising organisation, than for the IUA. It was also increasingly uncomfortable for the architectural upholders of Cold War apolitical balance, including even non-Europeans such as Jai Bhalla – as the external political climate began to change, with the development of a consensus between the Western intelligentsia and the newly independent African states that South African racial apartheid was something that, uniquely, fell outside the old, respectful demarcation of professional and political spheres. For someone like Matthew, who had been so confident in resisting the powerful AIA in a matter of extreme contentiousness

such as the Playa Giron competition, the amorphous but ever-advancing anti-apartheid coalition posed a far more disorientating challenge. In response, he and his CAA and RIBA colleagues found themselves constantly in reactive mode, oscillating adventitiously between resistance to, and complicity with, the anti-apartheid agenda – their main counter-argument being that it was wrong to transfer to professional groups or individuals, by association, the guilt of an oppressive political regime. But Matthew's overriding aim was to prevent the CAA itself from splitting over the issue, and in this he was resoundingly successful.

We saw in Chapter 11 that Matthew's attitudes to the issue were in a state of flux during the early 1960s; in late 1963 he cancelled an official IUA visit to South Africa, while at the same time expressing 'delight' that South Africa intended to join CAA as a full member.[88] After 1969, with the anti-apartheid movement in full flood, Matthew, as past president, remained at the centre of discussion on the issue. He and Colchester became 'increasingly worried at the potential disruption to the CAA by South African membership', and began to distance themselves from the old, strict separation of professional and political. Colchester argued in 1970 that although the profession within South Africa, dominated largely by 'English' rather than Afrikaners, did not show 'the nasty side of apartheid' through any formal 'race bar', and that architects were 'a decidedly liberal influence' in South Africa, nonetheless South African (and Rhodesian) membership was no longer 'politically sustainable'. In October 1970 he suggested to Matthew and Bhalla the 'ignominious' and 'pusillanimous line of trying to get the Commonwealth Foundation to coerce us to exclude South Africa and Rhodesia, so as to save us making our mind up'. Only two months later pressure mounted further, as UNESCO suspended all relations with the IUA and other NGOs for maintaining links with South Africa. A choice loomed between humiliating retreat and fruitless resistance, until Bhalla, as president, had the face-saving brainwave of creating a new class of associate membership, which would also have to apply to Ireland. Once the Commonwealth Foundation had duly made its formal request, Bhalla, Matthew and Colchester rapidly worked out an amendment to the CAA Articles of Association, to be approved at the 11 May Canberra assembly. Colchester reported to Bhalla that he had wanted to ask South Africa and Rhodesia to stay away from Canberra altogether 'so as to keep the temperature down, but Robert thought this went too far, and thinks we should merely hint'. In the end, the change was managed bloodlessly; the constitutional amendment was passed, and South Africa and Ireland were consigned to the new associate status.[89]

During 1971 this compromise seemed to have successfully eased any direct pressure on Matthew, Bhalla and Colchester, and in May 1971 Matthew felt confident enough to arrange extensive hospitality for R A Pistorius, the town and regional planning director of Natal province, on an October study tour to Edinburgh and Cumbernauld. But the following month the heat once more began to be felt indirectly, with the beginnings of a two-pronged attack elsewhere: on the one hand, within the RIBA, with anti-apartheid architects within the Institute arguing to sever its formal alliance with ISAA; and on the other, against IUA by UNESCO, which, as part of its policy of excommunication of South Africa, began pressing for further information on possible racial discrimination within South African architecture. Matthew and Colchester both agreed that it was essential for CAA to keep out of this new crisis, in view of its 'satisfactory settlement' in Canberra, but the Association gave IUA all the information it could. Colchester advised Weill that a direct IUA approach might place ISAA 'on the horns of a dilemma' of potentially 'repudiating its own government's policy', but suggested that a planned joint RIBA–CAA commission to inspect South African schools in March 1972 might uncover sufficient evidence

of indirect discrimination as to justify further IUA and RIBA sanctions.[90] Inexorably, the ratcheting-up of pressure on the IUA and RIBA continued, with radical younger RIBA members such as Kate Macintosh lobbying Matthew and president Alex Gordon in late 1972 and 1973. At this point Matthew and some others began to feel that enough, for the moment, had been conceded: in a memo Gordon complained of the 'pseudo-liberal ... gesture' beliefs of the anti-apartheid organisations, and Matthew noted in the margin their 'holier-than-thou' attitude: 'South African architects are not necessarily moral enemies.' On a January 1973 paper by the Anti-Apartheid Movement arguing for the RIBA's guilt by association with ISAA, he scrawled 'Would the next move be to expel those RIBA members on political grounds?'[91]

Matters within the RIBA came to a head in February 1973, in a special Council meeting on the future of the formal alliance with ISAA – an occasion that Matthew used as a platform for a powerful defence of his cherished apolitical stance. In a passionate speech to the Council he argued strongly against severance of links. This was partly on practical grounds – in that to press ISAA to repudiate its own government's policy was a 'self-defeating and barren' gesture based on 'a tragic misreading of the totalitarian situation'. But, more fundamentally, his opposition was based on the conviction that the RIBA was not 'set up to deal with fundamental political issues, such as freedom, justice and civil liberties ... we, in this Institute, are not set up to fight apartheid, or any other unpopular form of national policy'; at an international level, it was vital to avoid overt politicisation, as this could lead in unpredictable directions, for example towards an anti-American position over Vietnam. The demand to extend political condemnation of South Africa to architecture, on the grounds that South African architects are 'part and parcel of the government machinery and of apartheid policy', and that the RIBA 'become likewise part of the apartheid apparatus, and so stand condemned', was 'nonsense', stemming as it did from 'condemnation by association, [which] is, to my mind, the most useless and despicable of arguments'. Tackling head-on the issue of the unique pariah status of South Africa by citing an even more extreme example, Matthew noted that

> in the architectural press recently, [someone asked] could Robert Matthew have kept links with Nazi Germany? The answer is not only could I have done so, but I did, constantly, through the thirties, with students, teachers and practising architects, and I would defy anyone to say that it was not the right thing to do. I have never, on that account, heard anyone say that, by these arguments of association, I was a Nazi – any more than I have been accused, through the years, of supporting many oppressive governments whose architects I have supported through various international organisations.[92]

Swayed partly by this impassioned argument, the council decided not to cut the ISAA alliance but to form a study group, chaired by James Dunbar-Nasmith and with Matthew as a member, to investigate the reform potential of continued contact – for example, in encouraging ISAA in its opposition to the National Party government proposal to set up a separate 'Bantu School of Architecture'. By April 1974, despite continuing pressure from an 'Architects' Discussion Group' led by Macintosh, it had been agreed to set up a fund of £2,000 to help finance mainstream architectural training for black students; Matthew himself helped underwrite the first three students.[93] But Matthew consistently preferred pragmatic compromise to principled confrontation. By the time of his death matters in CAA, IUA and RIBA were clearly moving slowly and inexorably towards more radical steps: within IUA, Bhalla managed to defer expulsion (until, eventually, 1987), while the CAA's Canberra compromise allowed for the easier solution of simply abolishing associate membership –

agreed at the 1976 conference at York University.[94]

'The True Wealth of Nations': world ecological campaigner

Overall, the 1960s and 1970s, as part of the broad movement of decentralisation, as well as of fragmentation of any kind of unified 'Modern Movement', saw a marked tendency of contextualisation and even politicisation of what had once been called 'tropical architecture': in the late 1960s, for example, the Architectural Association's Department of Tropical Studies, under director Otto Koenigs-berger, was transferred to University College London, becoming eventually the Development Planning Unit.[95] Increasingly, the architectural specifics of Modernist design and city planning were generalised into the broader architectural context. But in the process, paradoxically, they lost some of their distinctive essence and practical power: the broader the global sweep, the shallower the potential reformist impact and the distinctiveness of the architect's or planner's contribution.

Matthew's own career trajectory fully reflected the excitement and the contradictions of this broad movement. Where once his work had been almost entirely contained within disciplined, highly structured programmes of building or planning, now it became both more individualised and more generalised: he became one activist participant in the broad environmental movement alongside many others – a dissolution of hard professional boundaries that to some extent conflicted with his intransigent defence of the professional sphere elsewhere. Among some of those left behind by Matthew's unceasing, restless self-development, his new phase of global activist striving was uncharitably interpreted as a kind of airy hubris, divorced from the architect's traditional task of design. Stuart Matthew, for example, argued that

> with Robert, the 1970s saw a kind of

megalomania, where he went far beyond himself and his capacity to achieve results, and there was no one to express doubts – they were all there to do his bidding! Yet Robert, although he was the big boss in the office, had lost his real power, and had got beyond his capacity to achieve – he had got himself into a state of mind rather than of fact.'[96]

Matthew's emergence as an environmental campaigner sprang, logically, from the planning, rather than architectural, side of his career – from the concern of a succession of reformists, from Geddes, Unwin and Clough Williams-Ellis through to Doxiadis, to fight for a spatial and spiritual regeneration of a built environment fragmented by some apocalyptic menace of materialistic chaos. Always, these reformists had emphasised the need for ever-broader, internationally cooperative formulas of renewal; all that was needed now, Matthew argued, was to scale up this rhetoric to a global scale.[97] At the RAIA convention in Sydney in May 1971 he evoked Clough Williams-Ellis's polemical text *England and the Octopus*, arguing that the architectural profession still had to fight 'the Octopus, [which was] now a worldwide menace, that terrifies us all'. This was 'a race against time' that 'takes us straight into politics', by contesting 'the fetish that growth was the only way open'. All in all, 'the quality of environment, like peace, is, I believe, indivisible in this small and finite planet.'[98]

   This new 'political' language began to sit rather oddly alongside his intransigent resistance to traditional politicisation of international architectural affairs: the interests of global peace and cooperation seemed to require militancy in the one, but self-restraint in the other. Here, Matthew was reflecting the shift from the specific language of built-environment reformists towards a more generalised, mainstream 'ecological' rhetoric. Yet the local and specific also played a role in the new 'small is beautiful' ethos, and Matthew's old Arts and Crafts fascination with the vernacular came strongly into play,

alongside the global: Aidan recalled that

he believed we should be working on a world, rather than continental scale, and so was very much against the European Community. But while he was opposed to nationalism as such, he was very much for the role of regional identities to enrich the world, in Scotland and everywhere else. He was very keen, for example, to encourage the Nigerians to conserve their indigenous architecture, rather than knocking it down and building 'Western' buildings. This led, in turn, to the idea of alternative technologies for the Third World – not just copying us! – so that you could give people a kit of parts, and they would build in indigenous materials.

In October 1971, in his honorary degree acceptance speech at Bucharest, Matthew made his most comprehensive attempt to integrate the specific ethos and potential of architecture with the new demands of world ecology. He spoke now not of the 'octopus' but of the menace posed to 'this space-ship, earth', by 'indiscriminate industrial growth' and squandering of 'finite resources'. It was because these problems 'know no academic or national boundaries' that architects were so well suited to tackle them: 'We are, above all, concerned with relationships, relations of people to their physical environment; of buildings and cities to their setting in nature and to the sources of energy.' Architecture could both encompass and transcend the material world of resource crisis, by creating 'that element that lifts the human spirit, that transforms the bricks and stones and solid concrete – that element that is more than the sum of the parts – the indefinable quality that gives life to us all'.[99]

   Within the burgeoning environmental movement, despite the headline-grabbing prominence of counter-culture activist groups, the organisational landscape was dominated in practical terms not by long-haired anarchists but by the United Nations and national/international NGOs

– a new, polycentric environmental establishment within which Matthew, with his multifaceted organisational experience and diversity of contacts, could feel quite at home. The UN itself played a dominant role, not only through existing programmes such as Crooks's Housing, Building and Planning bureau, but also, far more importantly, through its ability to organise major international congresses to galvanise global interest and attract the involvement of key NGOs.

The initial bridge to allow Matthew to cross from planning to environmental activism was provided by Doxiadis's Ekistics organisation. By now, the day-to-day running of the organisation was in the hands of the vice-president of the Athens Center of Ekistics, Panayotis Psomopoulos, who became a close collaborator of Matthew's. Matthew was well aware of the problems faced by Doxiadis in trying to point both ways: in 1971 he argued that Ekistics had a weak academic base, and was difficult to extend to 'bigger sets of problems of the ecological type', given that its 'rather detailed theory' was so firmly based on 'the morphology of cities'. Other key 'Delians', and Doxadis himself, were also aware of the need to keep in touch with the issues thrown up by the international ferment of 1968: at Delos 7, 1969, for instance, Margaret Mead pondered how to relate Ekistics to the new citizen-participation and environmentalist movements, and argued for research to be extended to a Fuller-style global process of 'planetary simulation'. One easy response, energetically followed by Doxiadis, was to step up the temperature of the rhetoric of crisis. At Delos 9, 1971, he proposed a 'Declaration on the State of Emergency in Human Settlements', identifying the mushrooming of unplanned 'anti-human constructions' as 'the largest single cause of misery, insecurity and communal upheaval ever experienced by the human species'. Doxiadis reeled off a list of 'Architectural Crimes', including high-rise building, sprawl, 'unconnected buildings' and 'false monumentality' – for all of which 'Repentance and Action' were needed.[100]

It was Doxiadis's achievement to have made the annual Delos symposium a sufficiently attractive experience, mingling intellectual and aesthetic stimulation, to induce a wide range of independent-minded people to participate year after year. Matthew, for example, wrote to Doxiadis on the latter's 60th birthday in April 1974, hailing 'the unique experience of the Delos Decade … a period of probing and questioning … a kind of anvil on which to hammer out your own thoughts as they developed … an exchange of ideas on a world scale'. Not only did the trips generate a constant flow of entertaining correspondence with stimulating and intellectual people, but they also, in themselves, became an annual family treat for Lorna, and, eventually, for Jessie: in 1972 Matthew wrote to Psomopoulos that '[Jessie] would love to come to Greece again'.[101] In return, Matthew steadily increased his time commitment each summer, attending many of the Athens seminars of 'Ekistics Month'. He also played a linchpin role in founding a 'UK Committee of Delians', following Delos 5 in 1968, to keep up the momentum of discussion. But the UK meetings were often inconclusive, and repeatedly witnessed criticisms of the grid-like rigidity of Doxiadis's system and its '54 Laws' of development, and the repetitiousness of the resulting debates.[102] In November 1974 a British Delians follow-up to Delos 11 provoked debate on whether Ekistics was truly a new discipline or simply a reformulation of Geddes's multidisciplinary planning ethos: Matthew argued that Ekistics represented a significant, systematic development of Geddes's theories into a 'cross-disciplinary science'.[103]

Throughout the early 1970s Matthew provided Psomopoulos and Doxiadis with recommendations for UK invitees to Delos, and by 1973 was a member of the full WSE nominating committee. But from around 1972 the Doxiadis 'machine' was increasingly disrupted when the leader himself fell victim to a debilitating, degenerative illness: amyotrophic lateral sclerosis, a progressive motor-neurone disease that gradually led to complete paralysis, until Doxiadis's eventual death in June 1975. In the light of this illness, in February 1974, with preparations for a major Ekistics contribution to the Vancouver 1976 Habitat conference well under way, Matthew agreed to step in the following year as WSE acting president – little suspecting that he himself would not survive to take up the position.

From around 1970 Matthew also began to break out from Ekistics into a more autonomous environmentalist role, stimulated by the approach of the 1972 Stockholm conference into a frenzy of juggling between different NGOs – an exercise that was to shade almost imperceptibly into a more concerted process of preparing for the Vancouver 1976 conference. The Commonwealth, in particular, seemed to Matthew to be an ideal vehicle, in its combination of global influence and anglophone cultural links. But rather than attempting to galvanise the CAA, with its limited remit of educational and professional liaison, for this wider task, he rapidly focused on a smaller Commonwealth organisation specifically orientated towards the environmentalist issue: the Commonwealth Human Ecology Council (CHEC), offering himself as a representative of CAA in its activities. CHEC was a remarkable example of the potential effectiveness of a small organisation led by a single, determined individual, if it focused on a single issue: the effect of 'the interaction of society and the environment' on 'the development of resources'. It was set up between 1966 and 1969 by New Zealand-born London physiotherapist Zena Daysh, a figure of single-minded 'idealism and tenacity', as the ultimate outcome of a succession of advisory committees she had organised since 1942, focusing on nutrition and preventive medicine, and bridging Britain's transition from wartime mobilisation to peacetime decolonisation. Daysh, with her flamboyant egalitarianism, and her fervent belief in the Commonwealth as a global mission – 'a world possession, or spirit' – was tireless in lobbying officials and organisations for assistance. In 1969–70 she negotiated an invitation by the Royal Commonwealth Society to base CHEC in its London headquarters, with substantial grant aid from the Commonwealth Foundation and UNESCO.

The aims of CHEC were now, almost by accident, tailor-made for the new 1970s era of social environmentalism, but Daysh also had an acute sensitivity to the potential of co-opting enlightened establishment figures such as Matthew: she felt by 1970 that 'in some ways, the most interesting thing about the Commonwealth is its scope for *professional* collaboration.' Matthew first became involved in CHEC through the intermediary of CAA, and by March 1971 he had already agreed to join the CHEC governing council.[104] Interestingly, whereas in the world of architecture Matthew seemed to many above all a politician or a diplomat, in the CHEC context he projected himself above all as an architect. In Daysh's opinion,

By comparison with a heavyweight representative of social government infrastructure, such as our chairman, Sir Hugh Springer, Matthew seemed to me above all to be someone who was both professional and artistically inspired, a highly cultivated chap, a big-time, gracious architect who brought us style and experience. Matthew played a big role in our work in the early 1970s, and he was thoroughly 'Commonwealth' in his thinking, but his ideals always related, at heart, to architecture.[105]

In 1972, leaping further into involvement with CHEC, Matthew agreed to chair its second international conference in Singapore, in late April – only to receive a rude shock when the event was cancelled at the last moment by the Lee Kwan Yew government, for fear of political controversy. Eventually, with Matthew playing his usual crisis-management role, the conference was shifted to Hong Kong University, with 59 delegates, including Percy Johnson-Marshall as part of the UK delegation – but the debacle prompted

Colchester to articulate to Matthew his more general worry about CHEC, and the way in which it had 'jumped straight into being a full-scale Commonwealth body' without any 'proper UK nucleus'. Colchester agreed with Matthew that, not least because of Springer's status, CAA must not defect from CHEC: 'We cannot let it sink, even if it is a rather curious crew.' Matthew shared Colchester's misgivings about the amorphous character of CHEC, but, as we shall see later, he also saw it as one potentially useful strand in his own personal strategy leading up to the Stockholm 1972 and Vancouver 1976 conventions.

The sudden growth of CHEC, and the wider frenzy of NGO and UN activity in the years around 1970, formed part of two overlapping phenomena: the explosion of counter-culture efforts in many areas of society, especially in the wake of the post-1968 unrest; and the beginning of environmentalism in all its forms, including the concerns for the strictly natural environment, as well as for human ecology matters such as architecture and the wider built environment. In Chapter 12 we touched on the relationship between counter-culture and environmentalism, and on Matthew's sharp awareness of the heritage in relation to Scotland and the UK. But the same relationship applied even more powerfully in an international, global context, given the strong arguments for global interdependence of environmental factors. In the founding of organisations such as Friends of the Earth (1970) the language of millenarian crisis familiar from generations of architectural and planning debate was expanded into one of global 'eco-doom' – a style of rhetoric also familiar from a quarter-century of the menace of the 'nuclear holocaust' – and mingled with the activist, iconoclastic style of student protest. In architectural/built-environment events and publications of the early 1970s, such as the 1972 RIBA conference, 'Designing for Survival', or Theo Crosby's *How to Play the Environment Game* (1973) at the Hayward Gallery, the overlap between architecture and

environmentalism was further accentuated.

Internationally, all these conflicting elements and expectations found their first point of convergence in June 1972, in the First UN Conference on the Human Environment at Stockholm – a vast, 12-day gathering of representatives of 113 countries and 400 NGOs, and 1,500 journalists. Initially authorised by the General Assembly in 1968, the conference was headed by a Secretary-General, the 'ebullient Canadian' UN Deputy Secretary, Maurice F Strong.[106] Strong's strategy for the conference, hailed by Matthew for its vigour and boldness, was typical of the new and less hierarchically structured approach, allowing for several strands of parallel activity, including an official proselytising effort headed by the renowned economist/journalist and cultural establishment figure, Barbara Ward (Lady Jackson). She co-authored with bacteriologist Rene Dubos a hortatory text to provide a 'conceptual framework' for Stockholm: *Only One Earth: The Care and Maintenance of a Small Planet*, published by Andre Deutsch (London) in early 1972. Ward had since 1968 been Professor of International Economic Development at Columbia University, assistant editor of *The Economist* since 1939, and author of *The Rich Nations and the Poor Nations*, 1962; as a regular 'Delian', she was steeped in the Ekistics philosophy and well known to Matthew. In her book, and in a parallel outpouring of special issues by other writers, the enthusiasms as well as the internal conflicts of this vast new coalition were set out – between nature and society, pessimists and optimists, lovers and haters of science, and so forth. All were unified by an almost religious demand for 'planetary order', arguing that all the groups of experts had 'combined in a single witness of advanced science' to outline 'a vision of unity'.[107] A more apocalyptic tone was struck by a special January 1972 issue of the *The Ecologist*, 'A Blueprint for Survival', which stressed the 'unsustainable' character of 'the industrial way of life, with its ethos of expansion' – which would inevitably lead to social breakdown, then to nuclear war.[108] The counter-cultural rhetoric of opposition to large-scale economic development reached a climax in the 1973 book *Small is Beautiful*, by economist E F Schumacher, originator of the concept of intermediate transfer of technology to developing countries.[109]

Matthew himself realised from the beginning the potential importance for architecture of the movement led by Stockholm, in an age that had resoundingly rejected modern Progress; but he also fully recognised that his own contribution could best be channelled through organisational work rather than individual activism or creative innovation. In the preparation for Stockholm a new range of relationships and commitments could be tested out for the first time, for possible subsequent reuse. It was clear that the governmental role would be a central one, as the UK delegation would be led by the Secretary of State for the Environment, supported by four working parties; Matthew's own correspondence on Stockholm was generally carried on through the CAA and Edinburgh University. All his international institutional connections were initially tried out in relation to Stockholm: Ekistics, for example, was involved from the outset, and in March 1972 Matthew pressed Mike Austen-Smith to ensure IUA contributed a statement to the NGO meeting at Stockholm.[110] Matthew soon concluded that the CAA, in alliance with CHEC, was ideally placed both to contribute to, and to learn from, Stockholm: by January 1972 he had secured the holding of a CAA conference in Canada in November 1972 on the theme of 'Environmental Problems', and had promised to present there a paper on what Stockholm should mean for architects and planners.[111]

In the event, the Stockholm conference itself, as so often with large and diverse international gatherings, disappointed many of the high expectations, especially within the built-environment grouping, as issues of pollution and resources grabbed the headlines – in addition to the inevitable political problems, including a boycott by most Eastern bloc countries. At the first plenary session Strong warned of the risk of war from conflicts over pollution, and there followed debates about 'eco-doom' and a resolution to set up 'Earthwatch' – a global monitoring system of pollution and climate change, and to institute a World Environment Day (5 June).[112] The conference culminated in the agreement of a formal Declaration on the Human Environment, whose list of principles tried to balance social and political factors by setting out two main groups of recommendations. First, more perfunctorily, there came the management of human settlements, including the state-coordinated setting-up of development assistance and research agencies, and planning of experimental settlements. Then came management of natural resources, including UN-supported agencies on food, pollution and educational proselytising: as a first step, the UN should move to establish a coordinating council for environmental programmes.[113]

In the wake of Stockholm, the first step actually taken was the setting-up of the UN Environment Programme (UNEP), located in Nairobi and financed by a special environmental fund under Strong. Meanwhile, NGO activists such as Matthew busied themselves evaluating and digesting the lessons of the conference. For Matthew, the worst aspect of 'the traumatic experience' of Stockholm was, he felt, the neglect of human settlements and practical reforms in favour of theoretical debate about pollution and of the 'total resources of the earth' issue – although he freely acknowledged the ground-breaking importance of the event, as the first occasion on which the UN had 'brought the subject of the human environment into the limelight of world politics'.[114] At the October 1972 CAA executive meeting in Cyprus Matthew reported that 'this remarkable conference', and Strong's personal energy in carrying forward its agenda, had helped coalesce the wider realisation that 'the resources of this planet are finite, and that many human activities are harmful' – even if architects and town planners had been all too familiar with 'these great issues – all through my own life-time'. Matthew pressed the CAA to continue to 'act as a spur' to the IUA to keep up its contacts with Strong and UNEP, in order to ensure a continuing architectural participation in the 'global attack' on environmental problems.[115]

'A thousand million arks': preparing for Habitat 1976, Vancouver

Even before the Stockholm conference, however, a more appropriate focus for architectural contributions to the 'global attack' – something 'right on our plate', as Matthew put it – had begun to emerge: a follow-up conference in Vancouver, Canada, in 1976, focusing solely on the specific issue of human settlement. Already, in January 1972, Colchester had reported to Matthew that he had found out that Canada was hoping to host a 'human environment follow-up confer- ence' in 1975.[116] Following a formal pro- posal by Canada at Stockholm, a UN General Assembly resolution of 15 December 1972 instructed UNEP to mount a second conference in Vancouver, between 31 May and 10 June 1976, with themes including 'human needs in the environment of human settlements; set- tlements and national development plan- ning; planning and managing housing, settlements; international resources; global situation of housing; eco systems'. All these sorts of subjects were, of course, long familiar from the Ekistics world, but UNEP insisted that the conference would be *solution*-orientated, focusing on specific planning, design and infrastructure poli- cies. In parallel, a UN housing agency, also based in Nairobi, would be estab- lished under UNEP auspices.[117]

During early 1974 the organisation of Vancouver – now to be called 'Habitat 76', perhaps partly on the precedent of Moshe Safdie's daring housing project at Expo 67 – was sketched out. In April the 44- year-old Colombian banker and econo- mist Enrique Peñalosa Camargo was appointed Secretary General, with Professor Duccio Turin of the Bartlett School as his deputy – hailed by Matthew

as a 'good contact'. From the start, an extensive audio-visual element – films, slides, even videotape – was envisaged, instead of huge exhibitions: a consider- able departure from UN tradition. Ward had been already commissioned in September 1973 to write the accompany- ing book, as in Stockholm, but this time with extensive research help from the Canadian government. This time, too, Matthew was involved in commenting on drafts of the book: Ward complained to him that writing 'an outline of "Settle- ments" is like trying to untangle the rele- vant threads in a Shetland jersey: everything fits in with everything else!' Ward was also charged with convening a seminar of experts who would draft guidelines for the conference, its findings published in 1973 as *Housing Settlements – Crisis and Opportunity*.[118] As with Stock- holm, Habitat 76 was organised on paral- lel government/NGO lines: in the former area, Peñalosa's UN Habitat Secretariat would be supported directly by Canada's Department of External Affairs, while the latter would be coordinated by an NGO working group on Human Settlements, chaired by J G Han van Putten, the Dutch head of the International Council of Local Author-ities. His job was, in Daysh's words, to act as 'a bridge between all the myriad NGOs and Peñalosa – a heavy- weight, very effective former local- government administrator'.[119]

For Matthew, during what would prove to be his last year-and-a-half of life, the world of NGO preparation for Vancouver, with the van Putten commit- tee at its centre, became the focal point of all his efforts.[200] In sharp contrast to orderly organisations such as the LCC or even RMJM, this was a confused, ever- shifting landscape, and his first task was to focus and prioritise his effort, and decide which organisations to channel it through, so as to make best use of his particular expertise. Although the focus of Habitat 76 was narrower than that of Stockholm, it was still a wide-ranging conference, and well peopled with confi- dent generalists such as Ward, and so Matthew decided to work from the particular to the general, taking as his anchor and starting point one of his most cherished themes – the potential contribution of the architectural profession.[121]

That was the positive aspect; but there was also the more negative fact that architects, with the growing hostility towards them in Western countries affected by the conservation movement, were 'in danger of losing out on the whole wide front of the environmental battle'. One of the first and most obviously suitable vehicles for action was WSE.[122] By the time of Delos 11, 1974, the focus was firmly on a major Ekistics contribution to Vancouver, through the definition of global objectives for inclusion in a Charter of Human Settlements to be declared there. Matthew argued that Vancouver was more worthy of support than Stockholm, as it was more 'practical' in aims, and 'focuses on a narrower front'.[123] The Delos 11 symposium's final statement, 'Action for Human Settlements', laid out a range of demands, some reminiscent of old-style sanitary standards (persons per room, etc.), others more sweepingly moralistic: 'the right to dignity [and protection of] human scale ... heritage ... ethnic values'. The final 'call to action' thundered, in familiar Ekistic style, that

Humanity, for the agony of isolated rural areas and the suffering of exploding cities, calls out for action. Humanity, from the misery of the favelas and the mental anguish of the suburbs, demands solutions. This is the challenge that confronts each and every one of us: to turn banners into tools; to turn theories into solutions; to turn words into action. Let us begin tonight![124]

Following Delos 11, WSE confirmed Matthew as its chief representative on the van Putten committee and for Vancouver 1976 in general.

But WSE could not directly represent Matthew's central concern – the contribution of the architectural profession. For that, the involvement of IUA,

RIBA and CAA was needed. The role of IUA was seen chiefly as that of advising on architectural organisation and building technology, working in tandem with CAA. The contribution of the RIBA was chiefly that of feeding specifically British experience into the debates – and it was in this context that, in mid 1974, the first mention was made, with Matthew's enthusiastic support, of the possibility of producing a film for submission to the conference, about the problems of new towns, rural housing, or central redevelopment. At a meeting in late July at the RIBA on Vancouver, £30,000 was promised for the film, and Theo Crosby produced an outline – but Matthew criticised it as downplaying redevelopment problems. By late 1974 the IUA had largely delegated to Matthew the authority to pursue its interest through the vehicle of CAA and the Commonwealth grouping.[125] The decisive step came in September 1974, when Matthew was appointed chairman of an ad hoc Habitat Committee of the Joint Standing Committee of Commonwealth Associations, with the specific aim of preparing for Vancouver: his official role on the van Putten committee was as representative of this Commonwealth ad hoc committee, with Percy Johnson-Marshall acting as a deputy (and, in the event, succeeding him after his death). For its first meeting on 24 September in Marlborough House, Matthew prepared a dossier, 'Approach to Vancouver', which explained progress so far for the benefit of the non-architectural NGOs involved (surveyors, pharmacists, etc.), and set out the roles of IUA, RIBA, WSE, CIA (Canada) and CAA, emphasising the advantages of the Commonwealth's 'common heritage' of administrative and cultural background as a basis for action. And at the November 1974 CAA meeting in Kingston, Jamaica, Matthew argued that the 1976 CAA conference at York should focus on the implications of Habitat 76 for the Commonwealth; he forcefully counselled the CAA not to overreach itself, and to delegate Vancouver-related work to CHEC.[126]

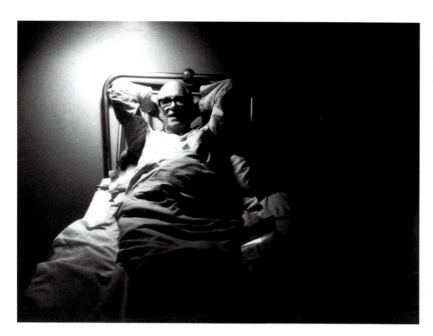

13.13 Matthew seen in the Western General Hospital, Edinburgh, following his February 1975 operation. (EULMC)

By October 1974 the Habitat preparations were beginning to gather a tremendous momentum, with Matthew acting as the 'linking agent' between CAA, IUA, CHEC and WSE activities.[127] A decisive development was a meeting that month between Matthew and Adolf Ciborowski of UNCHBP. Ciborowski had suggested that the architectural profession, under whatever organisational heading, should make three major contributions at Vancouver, all preferably of an audio-visual character: first, to compile a draft 'Charter for Housing' – an initiative of a kind rooted both in UN traditions and in the specifically architectural MoMo rhetorical heritage of Le Corbusier and CIAM; second, to compile a statement on architectural educational needs in relation to housing; and, third, to make a film on the world housing crisis. The latter, of course, was essentially an internationalisation of the earlier RIBA film proposal (and of a parallel proposal for a film prepared by Australian architects), but the other two were completely new. For simplicity, Matthew undertook to organise and, if necessary, write all three himself, working in the first instance through CAA, but fully coordinating it with the van Putten and ad hoc Commonwealth committees.

A mission cut short: Matthew's last illness

During early 1974 events in this and other fields had seemed to be moving smoothly towards another of Matthew's 'combined operations' initiatives, with a range of helpers and allies working in the direction of goals defined partly by Matthew himself. But in the middle of that year this tidy pattern irrevocably fell apart, after Matthew began to feel seriously unwell. The first signal of trouble was a growing feeling of lethargy – something previously unknown to him. In response, Matthew arranged for a BUPA health check in July, and when the blood test showed the possibility of jaundice, he was then referred to a liver specialist in London. After waiting in London for weeks, during August he was eventually admitted to a hospital in Euston Road for tests. The results suggested the likelihood of a cancer of the stomach, which had also spread to the liver. Lorna broke the news to their children, but – doubtless out of respect for Robert's private and compartmented character – the diagnosis was never explicitly revealed to him, and it was always discussed with him as an illness of the liver, or as a problem of recurrent jaundice: Aidan recalled that 'he never really knew what was wrong with him – it just wasn't one of those things to be discussed openly.' Throughout these increasingly distressing developments Matthew determinedly maintained his punishing schedule of trips, including the Kazimierz meeting and the CAA Jamaica meeting. But in early December he suddenly fell ill with severe abdominal pains, during a brief visit to St Quentin, north of Paris, to advise on a town extension plan – with Aidan accompanying to help with translation in meetings with the mayor and officials. On his return, in January 1975, he was admitted to the Western General Hospital for an operation, carried out at the beginning of February.[128] The operation revealed inoperable cancer of the bowel, which had spread widely; nothing further could be done. Again, the results were not discussed openly with him, but it seems unlikely that someone as perceptive as Robert would not have progressively sensed the true state of affairs, and the possibility, even the likelihood, that he had only months – in the event, less than five – to live.

At any rate, Matthew's life, for its remaining short span, now took on a fevered and almost schizophrenic character. On the one hand, there was the over-riding concern with the progression or relief of the illness. On the other, there was the concern to conceal this from public view, and to maintain control over affairs and continue with business-as-usual activity, even as his remaining months contracted into weeks. In hospital, Matthew was bombarded with concerned private letters from family and friends, and books to satisfy his restless desire for continued activity: for example from Janet, passing on reassurances from husband Desmond about the 'international reputation' of the surgeon, and 'sending another Maigret', together with 'Sian's drawing of Grandpa in hospital'; from Jessie, after the operation, updating her father with progress on her photography course at the Central School of Art; or from Jai Bhalla, sending 'our prayers for a speedy recovery'. Matthew resigned from a raft of committees, including the ad hoc Commonwealth Habitat committee, and his planned WSE presidency; at Daysh's insistence he agreed to stay on the van Putten NGO committee, to keep a foothold in his new world of international environmentalism.[129]

But at the same time Matthew's lifelong abhorrence of overtly emotional displays, in the style of his father, dictated the keeping-up of a defiant facade of normality, maintained especially by Naismith. Her letters to bodies such as WSE or CHEC regarding Matthew's illness – mostly resigning committee memberships – were peppered with breezy references to 'taking things quietly for three months'. In early February, just after Matthew's operation, Naismith wrote to Spaven and Hill that, in view of his relatively light appointments diary until April, 'as I said to him before he went into hospital, he could not have chosen a better time to be ill from this point of view'. Patrick Harrison, who had phoned frequently, wrote in early February that he was glad to hear the operation had been a 'success'.[130] Stuart Matthew, visiting Robert in the Western General, recalled that

> although he was lying ill in pain, there was no chat about 'how was he'. His illness was never an object of discussion. Alan Reiach was there, Aidan had just come out of the room, and Robert was lying discussing affairs of the day in architecture and planning – he carried on as if the hospital was another 'office' – he just couldn't, and wouldn't, give up.[131]

If Matthew knew of the gravity of his situation, he betrayed this only through the most subtle nuances: Andrew Derbyshire recalled that

> when he came out of hospital after his operation, and we were having a conversation about the firm, I said, 'Robert, you're looking a lot better.' He gave me a completely withering look, as if to say, 'Can't you see I'm dying, you bloody fool!' I realised I'd probably dropped a huge clanger.[132]

During early February Matthew attempted to convalesce at Humbie, despite a further severe attack of jaundice that increasingly confined him to bed. Stuart recalled that, even at this stage,

> he would say nothing at all about his illness, although once at a meal at Humbie, I was sitting at the end of the table, and could see he was suffering dreadfully, but he stayed at the table until he couldn't keep back the sound of pain, and then just went out without a word.

Progressively, he was put on a higher and higher dose of morphine, especially at night, with eventually 24-hour nursing cover: during the day he stayed awake, working on his Vancouver commitments, for as long as he could endure, and then

Towards far horizons

13.14 Copy of letter written by Robert to Aidan Matthew from Fez, 16 May 1975. (EULMC)

'he'd have another shot of morphine, and down he went'.

Behind the scenes, energetic attempts were now under way to consolidate Matthew's financial position further against death-duty liability, and collect together all his property insurance policies (totalling £120,000), life insurance policies (£30,000), and valuation papers in the office of his solicitor, Maurice Kidd. Following the sale of redundant offices, RMJM paid him a first instalment of £20,000, and he in turn disbursed gifts to Janet (£1,000), Aidan, Jessie and Sylvia (£700 each), and Margaret Hemslie (£500, partly in anticipation of redundancy); the idea that RMJM should also pay Aidan a 'special bonus' of £5,000 was turned down, as a case of 'too obvious tax avoidance'.[133] The further concentration of household expenditure and general attention on Keith Marischal was accelerated; HBC Secretary Graham, advised by David Walker and SDD architect Neil Hynd, expedited a grant application for substantial repairs, including roof and chimney repairs and woodworm fumigation.[134] Walker recalled his last visit to Keith in March:

> Towards the end, when he was in a bad colour, Robert asked me out to Keith Marischal to talk things over. It was an orientation exercise to ensure that I would still be going in the right direction beyond his lifetime. It was quite a long talk and, at the end of it, he asked his son to show me round the buildings at Keith. All in all, it was a somewhat silent and sombre visit.[135]

Some suggestions went further: his accountant, Norman Lessels, advised him to make preparations for the subdivision of Keith into three houses, on the grounds that it was better to buy Lorna a house in London than invest the money in Keith; in mid May, the welcome news of a further year's lease at Park Square East arrived, but a London move for Lorna now seemed unavoidable. Finally, on 6 June, by now confined to bed at Keith, Matthew signed a new, consolidated will.[136]

In the public domain, Matthew now embarked on a fevered last-minute burst of activity, for as long as his declining health could hold. Most of his remaining work effort was now focused on Vancouver, although now doubtless with an increasing suspicion that he himself might not live to participate in the conference, and that, indeed, any arrangements or appointments more than a few weeks away might never be realised. In other areas, such as RMJM, Matthew simply drifted away altogether from everyday matters: Derbyshire recalled that, at partners' meetings, Robert 'seemed far more detached, and showed us models of tensegrity structures he'd designed at Humbie, and abstract paintings he'd done.' At this stage he wrote to WSE finally declining the presidency. During periods of pain and loss of concentration in bed at Keith Marischal, he fell back on the consolation of these activities, alongside a last, defiant, never-to-be-realised architectural project, for a new house at Keith, down in the meadow to the northeast of the existing house. Matthew's sketches – jotted down largely on scrap paper or hotel notepaper – showed a complex grouped somewhat in the manner of Boyd Anderson's house at Gogarbank, with terracing, changes of level and interplay of volumes – but contained a curved plan to maximise shelter for a terraced kitchen garden, ornamental pond and putting green to the rear, and outlook to the north. The house itself was envisaged as an irregular, linear one- and two-storey agglomeration, with an entrance wing and garage at the centre, leading on the left to the main house (planned on split level lines), loggia, Matthew's work-room and patio, and on the right to a separate workshop for William Gordon, and walled garden and kitchen garden. Aidan recalled that 'he thought about it very carefully, consulted William about his workshop and so on – but it was all just fanciful, and my mother was just humouring him.'[137] Had Matthew been facing a long retirement, then this new Keith would have been an ideal 'retirement home', complete with window seat at the best outlook point, all on a radically smaller and more practical scale than the old house – although, with its north outlook, it would not have got any direct sunshine.

But Matthew was not, it was now clear, destined for any kind of quiescent retirement – as he made clear in January 1975, as he began, in a race against time, to try to carry through to completion his Vancouver commitments, with the help of a range of friends and allies who fully understood his position, and were determined to give him all the support he needed. His immediate, Habitat-related tasks, all linked to the CAA and the van Putten NGO committee, were the drafting of the 'Charter for Housing' and statement on architectural education, and making as much progress as possible on preparation of the CAA film. If his health could hold up for long enough, Matthew was determined to attend the IUA General Assembly and Congress at the beginning of May, to present the two papers formally, and meet all his old international contacts, probably for the last time – although, awkwardly, for the first time since 1963 the event was split between two cities: the General Assembly in Venice, followed by the 12th Congress in Madrid. In mid January Matthew began intensive discussions with Ron Gilling, who advised that the film should be tied to the Charter for Housing, but that if it could not be completed by August it should be dropped altogether, and effort should be diverted to helping IUA produce an audio-visual document. Matthew was also strongly pressing the Commonwealth Foundation to support

the film, and eventually a grant of £10,000 was authorised by the foundation, to be spent before April 2006 on slide lectures and low-cost housing studies.[138]

By late January 1975 Tom Watson confirmed to Peñalosa that the CAA intended to submit (via IUA) three AV presentations at Vancouver: first, the Charter on Housing and Educational Statement, written by Matthew and illustrated by a short film; second, a film on the rehabilitation of a community in South Africa; and, third, a film on 'good' and 'bad' housing in southern Africa. And in mid February he wrote to Matthew thanking him for providing a 'captive audience' during a visit in hospital, and asking whether he could now proceed to draft the Charter for Housing and the Educational Statement, as a basis for the film or AV presentation, which could fill the IUA's 25-minute AV slot at Vancouver. If finance could be secured, John Byrom of Edinburgh University would help prepare the film, which could focus on the double subject of Edinburgh and Kenya.[139] By March 1975 Matthew was working on the draft Charter from his Humbie sick-bed. Following his February operation, he gradually increased his rate of work to roughly half of each day by late April, allowing him to contemplate the exhausting enterprise of Venice and Madrid; as always, he drew on contributions by allies and helpers – for example, in a list of ten 'principles of Habitat' drawn up by Arthur Ling.

Matthew's initial notes, intended for use both in the Charter and by CHEC and by Delos 12, pointed out that the UN had not, up to now, provided any housing bill of rights; the nearest equivalent had been the 1961 International Labour Conference's statement that each family should be entitled to a separate, self-contained dwelling. Housing, he argued, was a 'common basic human need', bound up with both spiritual dignity and national progress. The responsibility for organising and, even, paying for these programmes was still, in Matthew's view, that of national government. But as

Margaret Mead had already observed at a meeting of the van Putten committee in New York, most of these needs were profoundly shaped by cultural, social and geographical relativism, and were focused on highly subjective areas such as 'territoriality, privacy, dignity, morality'.[140] In April, conference deputy-secretary Duccio Turin wrote to ACE vice-president Panayotis Psomopoulos that the aim of Vancouver was not to reach some 'superficially universal consensus'; rather, it would aim at programmes with immediate local applicability, unified only by basic concepts of 'minimum needs' of shelter and equitable resource distribution.[141]

In late April, after attending the opening of a photographic exhibition by Jessie in London, and a final pre-conference CAA executive meeting with Ron Gilling, Olumuyiwa and Watson on 24 April (held at his bedside in Park Square), Matthew set off for the first stage of the IUA marathon – the General Assembly in Venice – accompanied by Lorna and Janet, and joined soon by Jessie. Jessie now threw herself full time into the role of facilitator and organiser of what now seemed certain to be her father's last foreign trip, having arranged at short notice a suspension of her course at the Central School. Sylvia Matthew recalled that

> Lorna simply couldn't cope with it all at this stage, and it was Jessie who now took charge. She was devoted to Robert, and simply dropped everything, so that she could drive him around when they were abroad, and help look after him for the remaining short time after they got back.[142]

On arriving at Venice, Matthew was at first too exhausted to participate, but he recovered sufficiently to intervene in the assembly, helping, in his last act of architectural politics, to coordinate Bhalla's successful fight to wrest the presidency from Orlov. The occasion also allowed Matthew to 'network' with key Vancouver personalities, including new allies such as Richard Hughes of the UNEP Nairobi centre, vice-chairman of the Environment Liaison Board on NGOs.[143] He also made a final and unscheduled appearance at the assembly podium, pleading that the profession must redouble its efforts to address the great problems of global inequality: Bhalla wrote to him that 'your presence at the Congress despite poor health was a source of great inspiration – your stirring call to the Assembly ... would ever inspire the architects of the future.' Energised by this success, Matthew travelled on to Madrid, stopping in Marseille to receive a batch of correspondence from Cicely Naismith, who was holding the fort back in Edinburgh. She reported that Duccio Turin was firming up an invitation to WSE to attend Habitat as an accredited NGO, that the 24 Park Square East lease had finally been extended for a further year, and that the £11,800 final settlement for the winding-up of Keith Ingram had been received.[144] In Madrid – the first IUA Congress attended by over 4,000 delegates – Matthew, suspecting doubtless that this might be the last Congress he himself attended, continued at a frantic pace his work on the statement and charter guidelines, coordinating distribution of paperwork with Duccio Turin, and debating with Hughes whether the definition of the right to shelter should mention both individuals and families, as in the Universal Declaration of Human Rights; the twelfth resolution adopted by the congress eventually acknowledged the importance of 'imaginative and responsible action by architects in the social and political field for the improvement of human settlements and the environment generally'.[145]

Matthew's Statement text grappled with two key issues: first, how to bring out the specific contribution that architects could make; and, second, how to avoid being drawn towards inappropriately elaborate solutions devised in the developed world. In the first area Matthew relied on the now time-honoured post-1968 device of architectural self-castigation, pointing to the damaging consequences of the 'anti-social' post-war architectural and planning maldistributions – in particular, the 'imposition on bewildered

Modern Architect

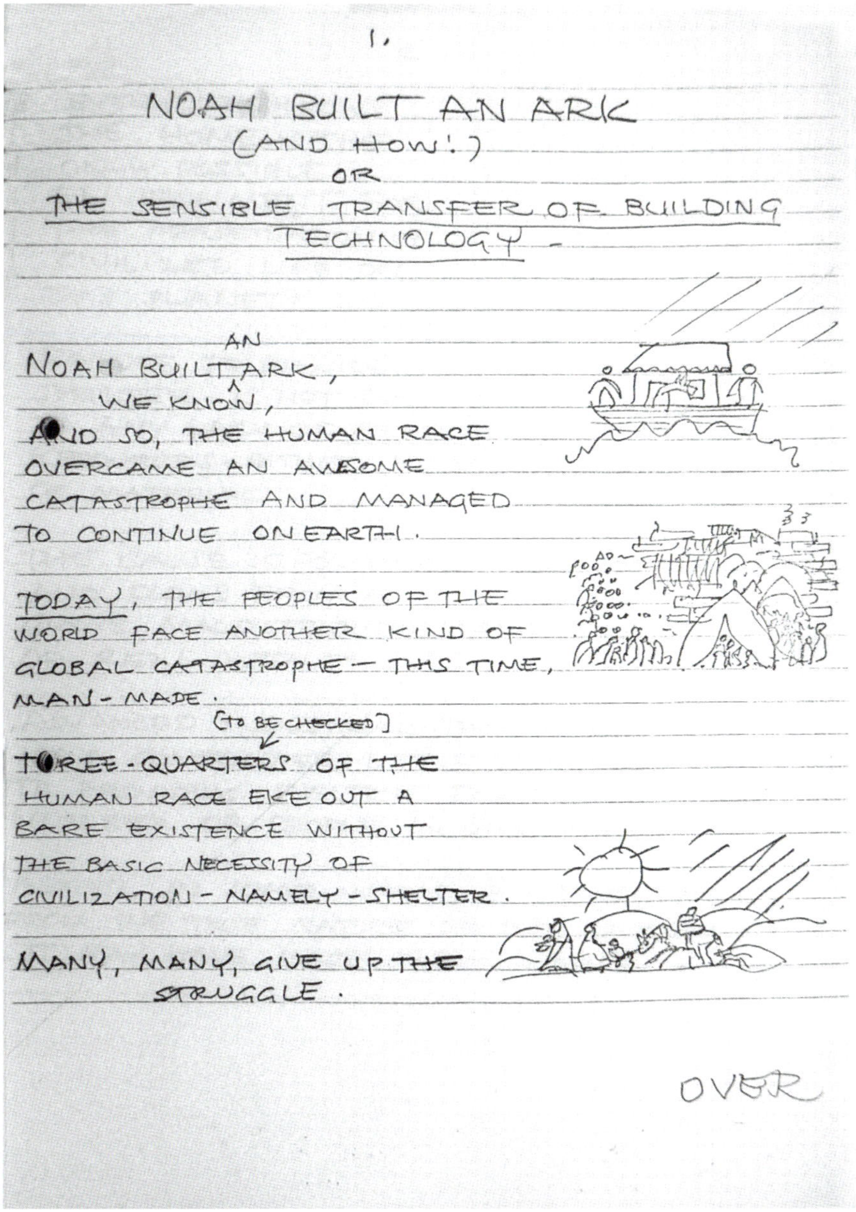

1.

NOAH BUILT AN ARK
(AND HOW!)
OR
THE SENSIBLE TRANSFER OF BUILDING TECHNOLOGY -

NOAH BUILT AN ARK,
WE KNOW,
AND SO, THE HUMAN RACE
OVERCAME AN AWESOME
CATASTROPHE AND MANAGED
TO CONTINUE ON EARTH.

TODAY, THE PEOPLES OF THE
WORLD FACE ANOTHER KIND OF
GLOBAL CATASTROPHE – THIS TIME,
MAN-MADE.

[TO BE CHECKED]
THREE-QUARTERS OF THE
HUMAN RACE EKE OUT A
BARE EXISTENCE WITHOUT
THE BASIC NECESSITY OF
CIVILIZATION – NAMELY – SHELTER.

MANY, MANY, GIVE UP THE
STRUGGLE.

OVER

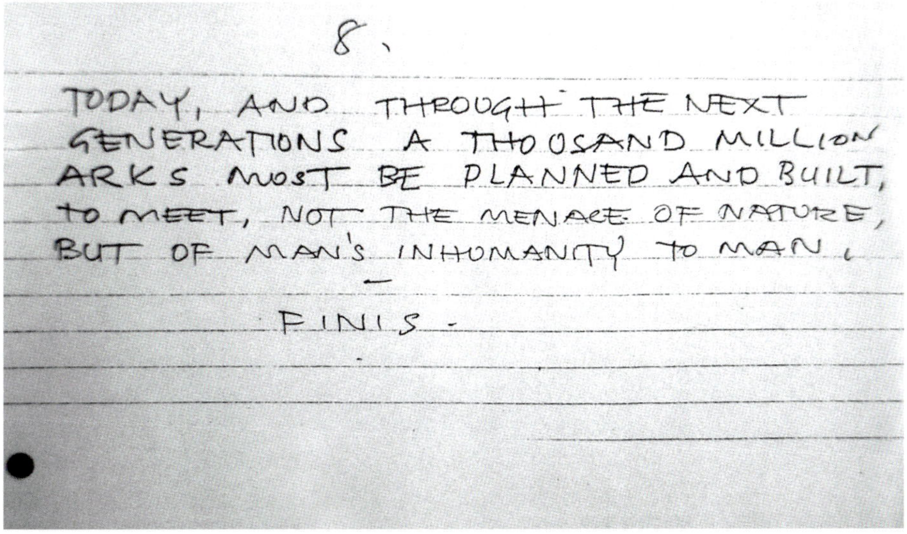

8.

TODAY, AND THROUGH THE NEXT
GENERATIONS A THOUSAND MILLION
ARKS MUST BE PLANNED AND BUILT,
TO MEET, NOT THE MENACE OF NATURE,
BUT OF MAN'S INHUMANITY TO MAN.

FINIS.

13.15 First and last pages of Robert Matthew's draft film script on the global housing crisis, May 1975. (EULMC)

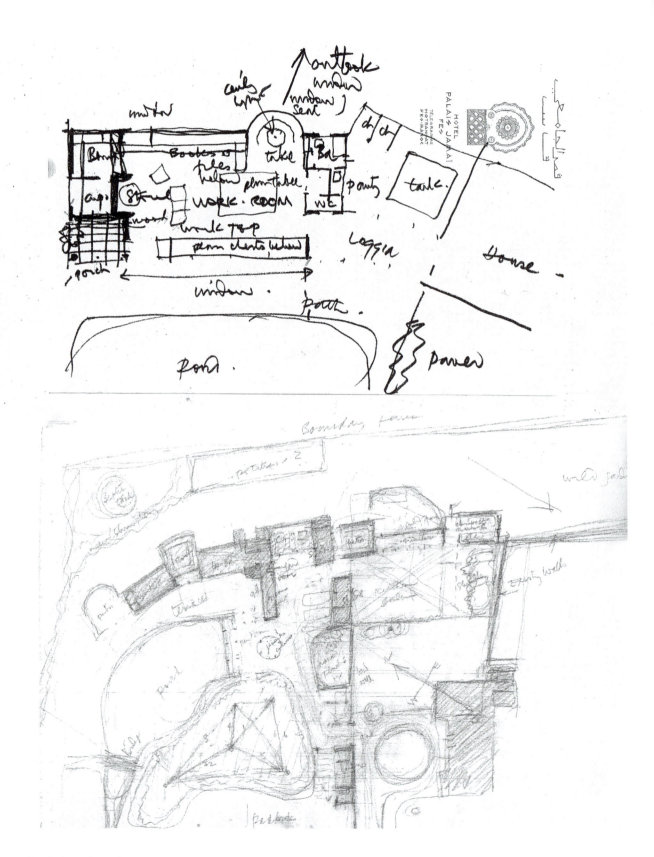

13.16 Sketch plans of new house at
Keith Marischal, drawn by Robert
Matthew at Fez, May 1975. (EULMC)

and helpless peoples of superhuman scale in the built environment'. He apologised for architects' role in this movement, but urged that 'now enough of the consequences are available to see, we pledge ourselves to its eradication', by backing programmes capable of 'injecting a life-giving quality to human settlements'. Of course, one could argue that this entire debate over 'concentration' was very much a preoccupation of the developed world, but Matthew then went on to denounce any imposition of inappropriately costly standards of housing on underdeveloped countries (a principle already emphasised at Stockholm in 1972), and, in particular, to insist on the right to 'participation by the people themselves', and that housing 'is not a consumer product, whose value disappears almost as soon as it is created, but part of creative production'.

Madrid was Matthew's last opportunity to meet most of his international friends – an experience that was clearly traumatic for many of them. Helena Syrkus wrote to Lorna after his death that 'although I have seen it in his face in Madrid, it was a terrible blow to me!' At the end of the Congress, having secured approval from Bhalla and the IUA Executive for his texts (leaving Mike Austin-Smith to get them edited and sent off to Paris on Matthew's behalf), Robert, Lorna and Jessie set off for a recuperative holiday in Morocco, with Jessie taking organisational charge and acting as hire-car driver and coordinator: with her help, he was able to indulge for the last time his passion for vernacular collecting, buying six carpets from the Maison Moulay Rachid at Fez.[146] While staying at the Hotel Palais Jamais at Fez he was delighted to receive a letter from Barbara Ward, inviting him to be a consultant on her official Habitat report on human settlements, and mentioning almost in passing that she had had three operations during the winter. In his reply, Matthew professed himself 'totally amazed at your powers of recuperation ... use me as you wish'. Modestly, he downplayed his own predicament, emphasising that he had had 'one fewer operation [than Ward], albeit set back by that particularly debilitating yellow menace – jaundice'. Writing with unusual passion, combined with a degree of detachment spurred by his own predicament, he exclaimed to Ward, 'What a year it is – great forces boiling up, and yet so much ignorance and concentration on such local matters as (in UK) possible national bankruptcy!'[147]

'Noah Built an Ark (and How!)': the final weeks

Matthew's film script, although composed hastily, written out unsteadily by hand and illustrated with small vignette sketches, was the last significant 'work' of his career: if he suspected that he had only months or weeks to live, then it was his only way to 'send a message to Vancouver'. As suggested by its very title – *Noah Built an Ark (and How!)* – *The Sensible Transfer of Building Technology* – the rhetorical conventions of the cinema, and the knowledge, or suspicion, of his own short remaining time left, allowed him to revisit his favourite theme of housing reform with a hitherto unprecedented emotional immediacy. In his script he fused the old Arts and Crafts moral-architectural veneration for 'the home' with a Fuller-like rhetoric of technological 'appropriateness'. Matthew argued that 'advanced industrial technology has contributed little or nothing to providing shelter for the vast number of people in dire need', but had instead concentrated on serving a 'minute, privileged few' – a 'remote and inaccessible' formula that gave no help to the 'unsheltered, the unhoused, the great underprivileged'. What was wanted was not, of course, the 'mud and thatch' of 'the Bad old Days', but 'sensible transfer' of technology, combining on the one hand regional, national and local characteristics – a last hint of Matthew's 'vernacular' enthusiasm – with the 'true needs of Man in Society on the other'. Arguing that 'the ingenuity and imagination of Man is unlimited and immeasurable – this is the true Wealth of Nations', Matthew insisted that the United Nations must set up an agency for housing like

WHO or WFO, to 'lead the application of technology'. In his peroration, he proclaimed that 'Noah built an Ark to save mankind from the rising waters. Today, and through the next generations, a thousand million arks must be planned and built, to meet not the menace of nature, but of Man's inhumanity to Man.' Andrew Derbyshire commented that

That film script was almost the last thing he did, and it epitomised his lifelong philosophy of socialism with a small 'S'. The challenge was not in putting up fancy buildings but in building for the people. For Robert, housing for the masses, in whatever form, was the key problem for the whole world. As a memorial to his life, that film script summed up what he stood for.[148]

To try to carry the film forward, Robert had alerted Aidan to be ready to coordinate a range of possible Edinburgh helpers, and on 16 May he wrote to Aidan to report progress, again expressing himself in unusually free and emotional language. He wrote that if Aidan had been in Venice and Madrid, 'you would have seen me in action (unexpectedly)', and that now 'Jessie is doing well, driving and photographing' both the scenery and the 'vernacular building'. He listed the various texts and guidelines he had drafted: although 'Cicely seems quite bemused by the papers', luckily Turin had been at both Venice and Madrid. The text of the film, drafted in Tangier in 'very rough' form ... 'written straight out without amendments – aimed at the main political meeting [at Vancouver]' would now need to be taken forward quickly, and Robert asked whether Norman Raitt of the ARU and the Edinburgh University film unit could produce the film (including examples of, e.g., Brazilian favelas), and whether Les Brown might do cartoons for an accompanying pamphlet – whose costs Matthew would pay himself; funds might also come from his 'great ally' Richard Hughes of UNEP. After signing the letter, 'Love, Daddy', Robert added a postscript, again perhaps betraying a sense of apocalyptic exhilaration:

Am still only going half days, but much stimulated by Venice and Madrid – spoke twice from the podium but most work done behind the scenes – many old friends – the Commonwealth now taking a powerful part. Bhalla delighted to be the new President, and Austin-Smith and Ron Gilling both firm characters. Jaundice now reached mildly irritating stage, and still tiresome, still not eating well, but letter from Barbara Ward ... says three operations last winter and still going! Puts me in the shade! Her summing up of the UNCVTAFD conference at Copquoc, Mexico, last autumn, is extraordinary! She was chairman, Cicely will get it for you if you are interested – I guess firing a shot across the bows of the special meeting of the UN Assembly in September in a New Economic Order![149]

On May 22 Aidan wrote in reply that the letter and film script had arrived, and that he would phone him in London to discuss it: more generally, he was 'Delighted you're OK!' In fact, Matthew was very far from all right, as he had become considerably weaker while in Morocco. He had fired off his last, vigorous shot, and was now exhausted and severely ill. Although still promising to attend events later in the year, such as a CHEC conference in Auckland in November, or an 'Architects' Week' in Ghana, for which Tom Watson had recommended him, in fact only a few, final dates remained – beginning with one of the 'sudden meetings' habitually called by van Putten, who had been visiting Vancouver to inspect venues for the anticipated large meetings of the Habitat 'Forum' for NGOs, including many thousands of students.[150] The six-hour marathon meeting, to discuss the venues and programme, at the Royal Commonwealth Society on 2 June, was attended by van Putten, Ward, Daysh and others. It left Matthew drained of any further energy: Daysh later recalled that 'I feel relieved that I had the last glimpse of him on June 2nd when he came to the van Putten meeting in London, though then one could not escape the fact that he was probably a dying man.'[151]

One final act of self-disciplined idealism remained. Matthew was determined to cast his vote in the 6 June referendum on British membership of the EEC, this being a matter on which he held strong views. Lorna recalled that 'he opposed the Common Market, as he felt it was setting up a European elite, whereas he himself was committed to *world* citizenship.' But his vote was registered at Humbie, and so he set out north on the train, and an ambulance was hired to drive him from Edinburgh to Keith, on the 4th. After a day's rest from the afflictions of his jaundice, he was then driven down to Humbie Primary School to cast his vote in the referendum – which resulted, in the event, in a 2:1 majority in favour of membership – and returned to Keith – never, in the event, to emerge again. Although the stream of concerned visitors continued, Matthew's condition had now deteriorated beyond the point where he could maintain a social front – a situation of passivity that was quite alien to one of his disposition. Tom Spaven recalled:

I remember feeling a hell of a sense of shock, seeing Robert in bed in the weeks before his death. The change in him was incredible – he seemed so completely different, he seemed really to have given up. Probably, up to then, he hadn't accepted his illness was going to be fatal, and if by now he'd finally realised that it was, then he maybe still felt someone, somewhere, had made a mistake. Stirrat had always said that Robert thought he'd live to a hundred. But now, he just seemed unnaturally quiet – not serene or anything like that, but silently disappointed and even angry that it had come to this, that he had no control over things any more, and could no longer even make a contribution to things.[152]

During his last days in bed at home,

Aidan and Lorna largely oversaw care arrangements: 'We had decided by then to put him on the maximum dose of morphine.' Jessie recalled 'driving up and down from London in my little yellow Mini: I called on Pat at Wetherby and said "You'd better come now if you want to see him at all" – and he did!' Nuttgens recalled that 'Throughout his career, Robert had never praised people to their face, but at the end all that changed, and he was able to express his real appreciation of others.' Cicely Naismith fended off business correspondence with euphemistic replies, and a stream of clearly valedictory letters arrived. A book was sent by Clough Williams-Ellis, who would eventually survive Matthew by three years; the RIBA sent a message that he would at last be elected a Fellow; a similar message arrived about membership of the Athenaeum Club in London; and a more emotionally worded letter arrived from Jai Bhalla, hailing Matthew as 'my guru, mentor and guide', and declaring that all he had achieved was 'primarily due to your guidance and blessings ... I take this opportunity to assure you that I would continue to serve the profession to the best of ability.' Bhalla emphasised that

I am writing to Michel [Weill] to see that the IUA Statement and Charter on Housing, as drafted by you, is sent to Mr Turin urgently. Please look after yourself. Your health and welfare is more important and the profession in all parts of the world needs your continued guidance for many long years to come.[153]

But there were to be no 'long years to come', only a few remaining days, and Matthew eventually died in bed on 21 June. Immediately, in a last echo of his own passion for exhaustively orchestrated events, arrangements began for his funeral, at 3.30 p.m. on the 25th – an event largely pre-planned by Robert himself, and coordinated by Aidan and Jessie. Whereas, when alive, he himself had been able to keep separate and under control all the different 'compartments' and conflicting elements in his life, at Robert's funeral, for once, they all overlapped and even collided together, with results that were disorientating to some participants, and poignantly memorable to others.

To begin with, there was the question of how far the funeral should be religious in character: Laurie Fricker recalled that Matthew had pronounced himself 'adamantly opposed to a funeral service for himself', yet there were the conventional expectations concerning a major public figure to satisfy, as well as the 'strong moral commitment to humanity left in a person such as Matthew if you skim off the Christian religion – that commitment to service to your fellow men that underlies, for example, the Sermon on the Mount'.[154]

The result was a compromise: there would be a public funeral service and interment at Humbie parish church, organised largely by RMJM, and a family wake at Keith – in both cases, with prominent elements of non-Christian religious symbolism. This led to unconventional and unsettling juxtapositions between the institutional and the spiritual. Mourners arriving at Humbie for the funeral – on a hot, cloudless summer's day – were directed by policemen to a huge field nearby, and made their way on foot down a narrow, tree-shaded lane to the kirkyard, where they were greeted by a friend of Bridget Sempill's, playing the pipes. In the church, which was profusely decked with wild flowers (organised by Jessie), the Christian ceremony was augmented by more secular eulogies, including an extract, read by Aidan, from Nehru's 1947 speech at Gandhi's funeral, lamenting that 'the light has gone out of our lives and there is darkness everywhere – our beloved leader, Bapu as we called him, is no more.' The coffin was carried to the interment site, in a corner of the kirkyard, by a mixture of partners from the firm and other eminent Scottish friends, such as the painter Robin Philipson.

Subsequently, in 1977, a large memorial stone was set on the kirkyard wall, carved in a dignified, somewhat classical manner by Matthew's old collaborator, Maxwell Allan; Allan did the commission free of charge 'as a token of the respect I had for him and in appreciation of all he did for me during the years I knew him'.[155] After the public funeral, the wake struck a note of quasi-pagan celebration, strongly influenced – in a significant echo of Matthew's younger life – by elements of Steiner-Waldorf ritual. Mourners were greeted in the front courtyard by the same piper, by a huge spread of food and drink in the house, and, on the main (south) lawn, by a great bonfire set in a great circle cut in the turf, with dancing around it. Aidan had devised this idea, in an indirect echo of the Steiner midsummer's day ceremony (which always took place on 24 June): 'We already had a tradition at Keith of having midsummer bonfires.' This wake-cum-festivity continued well into the night, although some had to leave early, such as the daughter of Constantinos Doxiadis, who had to be rushed to the airport by Cicely to return to London: Doxiadis himself died on 28 June, feverishly writing to the last, like Matthew.[156]

Appropriately, given Matthew's own multifaceted personality and career, those attending the funeral came away with a wide range of impressions. Sylvia Matthew, with her own Steiner upbringing, was able to appreciate fully the spiritual eclecticism of the event, including the

quite magical atmosphere of the approach to the church, with people from all over the world walking quietly along the lane through the trees, beneath the cloudless, hot sky, with the sound of the pipes in the distance.

Others found the experience somewhat disorientating or alienating, and assumed that the occasion was in some way controlled by another group. Stuart Matthew, for example, felt that the funeral 'was an office affair, not a family affair – a big office "do" with police at street junctions, and so forth – all quite theatrical – I was appalled.' But Flora Isserlis, from RMJM, found the event equally bewildering:

> I went out with Walker, our company accountant, who I could see was flabbergasted by it all. Lady Matthew rushed up and kissed me, and Walker said, 'Who's she?' Then we went back to Sir Robert's house for tea, with vast numbers of people milling around, and some dancing around a huge bonfire at the back. I asked Tom Spaven if Sir Robert's drawing board had been ceremonially burned and he said that I should know by now it was completely non-flammable.

And Elsa and Arnold Hendry, from Matthew's university department, were similarly confused:

> Arriving at the house, we found a huge pile of wood on the lawn. Not realising this was for a bonfire, when I heard Lady Matthew say, 'What about lighting the fire?' I thought, 'How can she be thinking of a fire in this boiling heat?' But eventually the bonfire was lit, and the girls started dancing around it, with the people from abroad saying in wonder, 'This must be a Scottish tradition.'

On the margins of the gathering, too, old antagonisms flared fitfully into life, in the fevered atmosphere. Margaret Richards, for instance, recalled that 'inside the house at Keith, after the funeral, there was Stirrat sitting drinking whisky, and saying what an awful man Robert had been. I just said to him, 'You're sitting there, drinking his whisky, while he's in his box – yet he's ten times the man you are!'[157] The following day, with all the exotic visitors either gone or departing, Cicely Naismith began writing to those who had sent their apologies. To Zena Daysh, for example, she wrote that 'the church was decked with wild flowers and the coffin was carried by some of his partners and associates. We are now left with a horrid feeling of emptiness.'[158]

The empty chair

Initially, the 'emptiness' was concealed by a short-term burst of memorialising activity, as in the case of the death of any major public figure. Naturally, there was a flow of obituaries, spread out over the second half of 1975, with the UK obituaries being followed, after an interval, by the overseas ones.[159] Most of them emphasised Matthew's special skill as an organiser and inspirer, rather than as an active designer, but some particularly close protégés went further in their eulogies: Nuttgens wrote that his influence on the environment was 'probably greater than that of any other architect of his time. ... He left scarcely any kind of architecture untouched, and touched nothing that he did not transform.' Letters of tribute to Lorna were generally more fulsome, and, in their often very specific way, highlighted once again the compartmented character of Matthew's life: for example, Andrew Kerr of the ENTCC wrote in December 1975 that the Committee had been 'his conception, and it was his flair that ensured success'.[160]

Formal overseas letters of condolence from national architectural organisations, Eastern as much as Western, were on the whole sent to the RIBA, where Austin-Smith dealt with them – for example, from Nguyen Khanh, president of the Union of Architects of (newly re-unified) Vietnam, or the Board of the USSR Union of Architects. Some added a personal touch, such as Professor Edmund Collein of the DDR [East German] Union of Architects, recalling Matthew as 'a true friend' to himself and his wife. Commonwealth countries tended to direct their condolences via the CAA – for example, the Trinidad and Tobago Society of Architects, or the Indian Institute of Architects, whose president, A P Kanvinde, wrote personally to Ron Gilling, as CAA President, recalling Matthew's participation at Venice and Madrid, and vowing that his achievements and his 'warm and affectionate nature' would 'remain a perpetual source of inspiration'.[161] Some personal

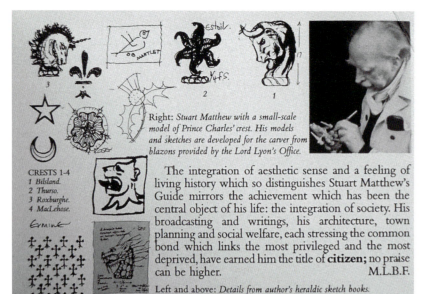

CRESTS 1–4
1 Bilsland.
2 Thurso.
3 Roxburghe.
4 MacLehose.

Right: *Stuart Matthew with a small-scale model of Prince Charles' crest. His models and sketches are developed for the carver from blazons provided by the Lord Lyon's Office.*

The integration of aesthetic sense and a feeling of living history which so distinguishes Stuart Matthew's Guide mirrors the achievement which has been the central object of his life: the integration of society. His broadcasting and writings, his architecture, town planning and social welfare, each stressing the common bond which links the most privileged and the most deprived, have earned him the title of **citizen;** no praise can be higher.

M.L.B.F.

Left and above: Details from author's heraldic sketch books. Original photography by Hamish R. Stille.

13.17 Stuart Matthew's work in the 1970s and 1980s as overseer of heraldic carvings for new knights at the Thistle Chapel (St Giles's Cathedral, Edinburgh) maintained the family tradition of love of heraldry: this inside back cover page of his 1988 guidebook to the chapel shows some examples of his drawings.
(S Matthew, *The Knights and Chapel of the Thistle, Edinburgh*, Edinburgh, 1988, 130)

13.18 Tensegrity structures made by Robert Matthew in 1975 from file hangers and string, latterly mounted on a first floor wall in Keith: 1995 view. (RCAHMS)

condolences sent to Lorna suggested a more heartfelt, rather than formulaic, grief: for example, Helena Syrkus lamented that 'Yesterday I got a message [in the post] from him – his so clever and deeply human statement for Vancouver – he was in such a haste to finish it at Madrid.'[162]

But, all too soon, the emptiness began to become more pervasive, as the melancholy business of settling Robert's affairs proceeded. Cicely was kept on until the end of 1975, working at Regent Terrace with the task of helping in all aspects of the winding-up. For Lorna, the prospect was, overnight, one of curtailment of the

lifestyle of round-the-world, first-class travel: by September Cicely was busy arranging an OAP card to secure her reduced-fare bus and rail travel.[163] Following settlement of death duties, the RMJM company accountant helped review Lorna's finances, and the office also paid her rent at Park Square East up to the end of the lease on 4 April 1976, along with Margaret Hemslie's £500 redundancy some four months before that. It was decided that Lorna should keep a presence in London, and a smaller house, 6 Barnsbury Square, was purchased within months. In Robert's absence, she found little to occupy her, but eventually became closer to William Gordon. The two of them sold their London properties and bought a small joint flat, spending most time at Keith; Gordon eventually died there in 1996.

With the concentration of all Edinburgh RMJM activity at Bell's Brae, Regent Terrace now became largely surplus, too, and by December 1975 Cicely was already exploring whether it could be let to the university as student accommodation – concluding, however, that the risk of 'whoopee parties' was too great. Alongside all these negotiations she was also busy with the 'rather bleak and gloomy' task of sorting out Matthew's personal papers into cardboard file cases, and in early November an initial consignment of over 40 cases was deposited in Edinburgh University Library.[164] She finished working for Lorna and RMJM in January 1976, leaving a large amount of miscellaneous unsorted personal papers, drawings, architectural books and other material still at Keith.[165] Around 1985, plans for Lorna to sell Keith altogether and spend all her time in London were thrown into reverse, and instead she decided to prioritise staying near Aidan: Keith became the main Scottish base for both Lorna and Aidan, and by 1989 Aidan had organised the partition of the house, converting the towerhouse east section (previously his father's 'territory') for his own occupation and ownership, while Lorna and William Gordon continued to occupy the western section. The divided arrangement continued until Lorna's death in 2003, when the entire house was reunited and sold to a new owner.

With the disappearance of Robert, tensions began to emerge among some of those left, over disposal of the family assets. As with the acquisition of Keith Marischal and Keith Ingram, Stuart, despite his many-faceted health problems (now including severe agoraphobia), began once again to act as intermediary in dealing with the Edinburgh properties – this time, on Lorna's behalf. In late 1976 she wrote to him that she was 'very anxious to have the house at Regent Terrace sold, and off my mind, in the shortest possible time', and that he should try to get as near to £50,000 as possible for it. By March 1977, with Regent Terrace sold, and Stuart investigating ways of disposing of the furniture, relations had deteriorated, and Stuart and Lorna were squabbling about Stuart's old office table, then at Keith, which Lorna wished to buy from him at an (in his view) unreasonably low valuation. Fretting that his help over the properties was being overlooked or belittled, Stuart solemnly typed out, on Lorimer & Matthew headed notepaper, a 'Note Regarding Irrelevant Points and Misleading Statements Made by Lorna on Telephone'.[166] But, in a more positive vein, Stuart was also turning his mind to the idea of commemorating Robert in some way, possibly through an 'Early Years' book emphasising his connection with the Lorimer & Matthew crafts heritage. After the Scottish Arts Council turned down an application for grant support, Stuart sent a circular letter to relatives and friends asking them for 'fair and unfair recollections' to help in 'piecing together the jig-saw'. Already, in 1976, other commemorative ideas were being pooled by the EAA, including that of a 'Scottish Conservation Centre' with Scottish, UK and international support; or, alternatively, a travelling scholarship 'associated with the developing countries'. All in all, the memory of Matthew and sense of loss seemed uniquely strong

in Scotland: David Walker, for example, recalled that 'when he died it hit me as hard as Ian's [Lindsay] death nine years earlier ... on the professional as against the administrative side, suddenly I was aware of being very much on my own, with no one to lead me or set out what I had to do. It was an eerie feeling.'[167]

A divided legacy

Overall, Matthew's legacy – the extent and manner in which his memory was respected or preserved at all – was sharply polarised. On the one hand, as we shall see later, there was a highly positive international legacy. On the other, there was a somewhat neglected, or negative, evaluation within the UK – with the exception, of course, of Scotland. This divided legacy was not something specific to Matthew, but formed part of the broader breakdown of organised, welfare state modernity that had been ongoing since the late 1960s – a movement that only gathered in force in Britain during 1975 and 1976, with the mounting economic instability since the 1973 oil price rise now reaching a climax.[168]

Although the post-1968 counterculture radicalism soon faded, the crumbling of deference to the old corporatist authority systems – including big

(top) **13.19** Robert Matthew's medal cabinet in the first floor corridor, Keith Marischal, 1995. (RCAHMS)

(middle) **13.20** The staircase hall at Keith, 1995. (RCAHMS)

(bottom) **13.21** The staircase hall at Keith laid out with candles during Lorna's funeral wake, 5 November 2003. (M Glendinning)

government and the organised professions – continued in different forms. In the libertarian, free-market reaction that followed, especially in England, the values that Matthew represented were comprehensively rejected.[169] Architecturally, too, the almost universal acceptance in the 1970s of the modest, anti-authoritarian neo-vernacular proved to be short-lived. But, already, the entire debate was being drowned out by a new cacophony, led by 'New Right' critics stridently opposed to the entire ethos of 'social' Modernism, and advocating a fundamentalist return to classic 'beauty' and 'tradition'. From 1984 onwards this movement was most publicly led by Prince Charles.[170] However, its most forcible attacks stemmed from philosopher-journalist Roger Scruton, who appropriated and modified the post-1968 attacks on supposed Modernist corruption and megalomania, generically including Matthew as part of a general anti-professional diatribe. In 1984, for example, he wrote of 'one of the greatest catastrophes that the world has ever known in peacetime: the rise of modern architecture', arguing that it had first developed as a secret conspiracy and that 'when, at last, its members emerged into the open, seized control of our cities, and shook them free of human significance, the public merely gazed on their work in mute astonishment ... [as by then] the culprits had gained fortunes and titles, and were able to get their way in most matters that could be settled by the offer of a trip to Bermuda or a case of Lafite'. The *AJ*'s 'Astragal', in turn, bitterly denounced Scruton's 'ridiculous attack [against knighted architects] ... a regrettable libel on sincere and honourable men'.[171]

In this climate it was unsurprising, therefore, that Matthew's reputation in England rapidly slid towards oblivion – even as some of his collective government initiatives continued to proceed steadily towards implementation. The development of the Broad Sanctuary site culminated in the construction of the new Queen Elizabeth II Conference Centre, designed by Powell & Moya, while the uncertain outcome of the Skillington Report had spurred, by 1977, the creation of a Croydon-based 'Design Office' within the PSA Directorate of Design Services, intended to act as a quasi-R&D guarantor of quality within government-designed buildings.[172] In February 1980 Lorna deposited a selection of drawings with the RIBA Drawings Collection; but by November of the same year, in sharp contrast to the implied comparison with Gandhi in Aidan's funeral oration five years before, Matthew was omitted altogether from a new compendium of Modern architects, and *Building* magazine could pose the rhetorical question, 'Whatever happened to Sir Robert Matthew?' Increasingly, the disciples of Leslie Martin in the Cambridge School of Architecture attributed the design of the Royal Festival Hall personally to him, and the draft of a 1992 Phaedon monograph on the hall by John McKean credited it exclusively to Martin; following protests by Stuart Matthew, the attribution was changed to a more neutral formula.[173]

In Scotland, on the other hand – at any rate, in Edinburgh – Matthew's memory was still treated with a degree of veneration, in a range of commemorative events and institutions spanning the modernity/conservation divide. In June 1984, for instance, John Richards delivered a public lecture in Edinburgh, 'Robert Matthew and his work', meticulously prepared beforehand in correspondence with a range of Matthew's colleagues and acquaintances throughout the UK. And in 1992 the Edinburgh University Architecture Department opened a 'Matthew Gallery' for temporary exhibitions. However, efforts in 1976–7 by Stuart to canvass support for a Scottish Arts Council-supported short illustrated biography, aimed at 'piecing together the jigsaw' with 'favourable and unfavourable recollections', came to nothing.[174]

All these conflicting responses could be seen playing themselves out within the multinational, microcosmic world of RMJM. Here, it was a mark of how far his disengagement had gone that Matthew's death left sporadic gaps, rather than a yawning void. In general, matters seemed to go on much as before – although there were strong underlying tensions over status, as Spaven recalled:

I was quite surprised at the way that nothing momentous seemed to happen after his death. At the annual partners' meeting in Aberdeen the following month, everyone else was there, including Stirrat, and it was almost as if nothing had happened. The groups continued to function, as mini-private practices, although we did have to have a limited reorganisation within the Edinburgh partnership, as there wasn't any longer a senior partner. Of course, there was no question of anyone stepping into Robert's shoes, as there was only one Robert! I would have liked an element of succession, but John and the others wouldn't accept me as senior partner, so we moved to a different organisation. After my retiral, though, John became chairman. But as to the wider structure of the firm, we basically did nothing – a touch of Micawber.

Overall, Spaven felt that 'when Robert died, quite simply, something went out of my life. I must have enjoyed it all – otherwise I wouldn't have felt so sorry at his demise. After that – what was there ahead of me? My personal satisfaction had more or less disappeared, with all the endless meetings.'[175]

For both Spaven and Aidan, the Edinburgh office, without Robert's background presence, became a steadily less congenial setting; both eventually left in the late 1970s. In the London office, Matthew's memory soon started to fade, especially after Stirrat, in 1977, retired to the country, to a converted mill near Stroud, at his wife's urging, but against his own inclination. In Saint's words, 'Without the constant ringing of the telephone, he felt purposeless, and he drank too much' – so that, despite the opening of a small branch office for him in Bristol, his health steadily declined and he died of a heart attack in 1981 – at

13.22 Clearance of the last contents of Keith on 'removal day', November 2003. (M Glendinning)

almost exactly the same age as Matthew.[176] Within RMJM, it was above all overseas that Matthew was missed: Ken Feakes recalled that 'RMJM meant Robert Matthew to most people overseas. People would say years after he died, "Is Robert Matthew still in the firm?" Then, when you said, "No," they'd look disappointed, as if the essence of the firm had gone when he died.'[177]

Within the Edinburgh office, the increasing focus was on the continuing development of the Bell's Brae site, with the second stage (the Miller Row block) fully realised in the 1980s as a semi-

13.23 The CTTD team seen following cancellation of the first project in 1975. Kenneth Graham and John Richards are seated behind the model. (*Evening News*, 31 October 1975)

OPERA HOUSE TEAM'S LAST LOOK AT TWO YEARS' WORK

Picture of dejection

Report by JIM McGHEE
Picture by BILL STOUT

The back-room professionals were in sombre mood as they gathered round the wooden model of the Opera House—the nearest they will probably ever get to the real thing.

"As that one finally fell on the grand concept which was the biggest job of their careers, the only tangible evidence the architectural team of 14 had to show for two years' hard work was a sheaf of drawings and a few models.

"We are naturally all very disappointed, said Mr Kenneth Graham (fourth left), a 40-year-old partner with Robert, Matthew, Johnson - Marshall & Partners.

Most of the team had been at the Edinburgh District Council meeting which killed the project and a short phone call to their base in East Fettes Avenue told colleagues they could all down enquire.

"We had just been carrying on as normal up till then," added Mr Graham. "We had a good brief and we tried to answer it. We think we succeeded. It was the job of a lifetime."

For him, the two years' work had produced more than the mere tangible results. They had also brought valuable experience on the making of an opera house.

tore, said architects obviously kept a professional attitude to all projects, but a local team creating an opera house in their own city also got emotionally involved.

The team of two partners, four senior architects, one architect, three architectural assistants, one architectural student and three model-makers would now be deployed, wherever possible, to other projects.

The drawings and models are to be handed over to the district board.

Before the fruits of their labours were handed over, the architectural team took a last look at what would have been the high spot of their careers. With faces that sum up their disappointment, Michael Duncan (left), Robert Hislop, Ian Douglas, Kenneth Graham, Allan Swan, (the Bect), John Richards, Andrew Davis and Ian Hall linger over the model it took them too long to build from the drawing board.

GREGORY PHILIP reports on the alternatives ...

Now let's make some cash for city

With the death of the Castle Terrace theatre project, appeals went out to Edinburgh today for the site to be alternatively developed as soon as possible.

Two leading councillors said that this was essential. And Lord Provost John Millar said he hoped that something of benefit to the capital would finally occupy the site — which has been derelict for more than 12 years — although he still felt the project should have at least considered to the state of tender.

Councillor James Kerr, leader of the Labour group on the district council, who successfully led the campaign to scrap the scheme said enough time had been spent debating its future.

commercial package-deal development styled in a more 'vernacular' and less 'modernist' form. In a 1984 issue of the office magazine, John Richards enthused about the project as 'a small college ... a place where highly mobile professional people come together to meet and cooperate ... in a richly varied pattern of internal spaces [clad in] a very simple and conservative architectural style'.[178] Until 1984 the Edinburgh office continued to be intermittently much preoccupied with the Castle Terrace Theatre (Opera House) project. The initial proposal, prepared by Matthew, Graham and others, with the 14-strong RMJM team at East Fettes Avenue, staggered on through mid 1975, until in late September the Scottish Office, facing Treasury cutbacks due to the economic crisis, withdrew its support, and the scheme collapsed. In an *Evening News* article of 31 October the RMJM team were pictured sitting despondently around the model, mourning the disappearance of (in Graham's words) 'the job of a lifetime'.[179] In 1983 a newly elected Tory municipal administration revived the proposal, reduced to a 1,500-seat, £11.5m theatre-only brief. A team under John Richards drew up a simple, no-frills scheme with less than half the area of the 1975 design, externally expressed in a spindly Post-Modern classi-

cal style; but this scheme, too, was scrapped in 1984 when Labour regained control, and it was only a decade later that the Castle Terrace 'hole in the ground' was finally filled, by a mixed commercial development in a postmodern classical style (designed by ex-RMJM architects Campbell & Arnott) and an embedded new home for the Traverse Theatre (by Nicholas Groves-Raines, with, ironically, Aidan Matthew acting as project manager).[180]

Organisationally, following Spaven's retirement, John Richards became chairman of the Edinburgh office between 1977 and 1986, and of the Scotland–London joint committee in 1983–6. These were years in which the economic crises had created a growing climate of uncertainty within the Edinburgh office, with Denys Hill reporting in mid 1977 a likely loss of over £160,000, owing to lack of work and inflation, during the current year, and calling for radical cost-cutting. By the mid 1980s the overseas offices in Hong Kong, Bangkok, Dubai, Libya, Egypt and Saudi Arabia were largely supporting the finances of the firm. Now, as Richards subsequently argued,

the organisational diagram of the firm, the joint committee and its sub-committees, the loosely associated partnerships in Saudi Arabia and the USA, the Edinburgh, Stirling and London local offices in the UK, and their group, committees and subcommittees, began to look like one of those complicated little dolls with arms and legs which jerk up when you pull the bit of string at its bottom.

Eventually, in 1986, with a total of no less than 12 London and 13 Edinburgh partners and 31 associates, the entire structure of partnership was abandoned, and the firm was re-formed on a commercial basis, as a holding company (RMJM Ltd) and subsidiaries, including an Edinburgh company (RMJM Scotland).[181] This adjustment to the capitalist temper of the times (in combination with overseas expansion during British recessions) appeared to suffice, and ten years later RMJM, with 450 staff and 40 per cent of its workload outside the UK, wrested the top place from BDP in the *AJ*'s table of the 100 largest UK practices; it was the fourteenth largest firm in the world. And in 2001, with the Edinburgh office heavily committed to the 'iconic' Scottish Parliament project, the firm took a further step away from the staid, anti-commercial conventions of the mid 20th century, in a £500,000 'management buy-in', with the aim of projecting the firm as an all-in design-and-build developer.[182] Yet the legacy of Matthew was still, on occasion, cited as an inspiration within the firm: in 2002 Edinburgh design director Paul Stallan told an Architectural Heritage Society of Scotland conference on 20th-century architecture of the 'value that we place on the last century's architectural legacy, bequeathed to us by Robert Matthew and his colleagues'.[183]

The embrace of Matthew's legacy by the world of architectural heritage in the 1990s – the decade of triumph of revived global capitalism and of the final collapse of 'public authority architecture' – was also slow and hesitant. Throughout the history of the Modern Movement an influential element, epitomised by the work of Frank Lloyd Wright, had emphasised 'heroic' self-promoting

13.24 John Richards receiving the Queen's Award for Export Achievement in 1983 from the Lord Provost of Edinburgh, outside the Bells Brae office. (*Scotsman*)

individualism as against collectivism.[184] The same happened within the world of heritage, which moved selectively to embrace Modernism from the 1980s. At first, the focus was on architects who had been distant from the dominant MoMo ethos of collectivism: 1983 saw publication of a book on the work of Erno Goldfinger, even as collective elements of the Modern Movement, such as public housing, and local-authority architects' departments, were still neglected or even attacked.[185] At this stage there was no place for the memory or legacy of a Robert Matthew. That changed, however, when historians began to advance and argue the less popular cause of social modernism – led by Andrew Saint of the Survey of London, and Martin Cherry, head of listing at English Heritage. Precociously, in 1987, Saint had published *Towards a Social Architecture* – a combined biography of Stirrat Johnson-Marshall and history of the English prefabricated schools movement. Here, the tension between Robert and Stirrat was hinted at in a contrast between 'the Scottish cavalier and the English roundhead, the increasingly pleasure-loving monarch versus the stubbornly puritan cooperator'. Paradoxically, of course, Matthew, with his Presbyterian family background, was in some ways a more authentic 'roundhead' leader than

Stirrat![186] Matthew also made an indirect appearance at the 'chaotic but inspirational' LCC Day organised at the AA for the 20th Century Society by Saint and Elain Harwood in 2002, with more than 70 ex-LCC architects in the audience. And, from 1994 onwards, English Heritage's listing teams had been attempting to uncover precisely those values in a painstaking research exercise prior to embarking on systematic post-war listing.[107]

Among the first post-war buildings selected for listing in this English Heritage programme were two of the most prestigious projects Matthew had been involved in – the Royal Festival Hall (listed Grade 1 in 1988) and New Zealand House (listed Grade 2 in 1995). On the whole, the Festival Hall listing was the more popular of the two – albeit tempered by growing claims of acoustical deficiencies. Ever since its construction, the Festival Hall, as a British nationalist symbol, had enjoyed a wide spread of political and public support: even in February 1998 Tony Blair chose to deliver a speech on 'Why the [Millennium] Dome is Good for Britain' at 'The People's Palace, Royal Festival Hall'. At an October 1992 twentieth Century Society conference, 'Refashioning the Fifties', Gavin Stamp strongly contrasted the two: 'I now recognise the Festival Hall as one of *the* great British buildings of the 20th century, [but] revisionist as I am, I can't bring myself to like New Zealand House. We must recognise certain buildings as brutes.'[188] The listing of New Zealand House, with its less immediately accessible character, was almost immediately criticised. In 1996, for example, Scruton argued that English Heritage, as a government bureaucracy not dissimilar to the post-war welfare state organisations, had violated the anti-Modernist essence of conservation by listing this 'macabre steel and glass structure', thus making 'a building which has no other meaning than its impermanent function into a permanent feature of the landscape'. Reviving his old crusade to ferret out supposed Modernist establishment

corruption, he called for the eventual 'demolishing [of] these monuments to human folly', followed by a 're-assessment of ... awards, accolades and knighthoods' bestowed on their designers.[189]

Worldwide afterglow: Vancouver and all that

By contrast with the virtual submergence of his memory in the shifting sands of British architectural and conservation debate, within his beloved world of international architectural and environmental fellowship Matthew's legacy seemed far more secure. Within the IUA, for example, the 1978 Congress in Mexico saw the inauguration of a 'Sir Robert Matthew Prize' – the fourth instituted by the Union, and this time focusing on 'improvement in the quality of human settlements': early recipients included a housing-rehabilitation programme in Mexico City (1987) and the vast public housing drive of the Singapore government (1990). Bhalla, as president at the 1978 Congress, sent a telegram to Lorna stressing how much the IUA was 'missing Sir Robert's advice'. Over the following 20 years the IUA Congresses grew exponentially in size, reaching a maximum of over 10,000 delegates and 22 speakers in the chaotic Barcelona congress of 1996.[190] Within the CAA Matthew's reputation was even more firmly entrenched. As early as 1979 Olumuyiwa (by now President) invited Lorna to a lunch of thanks at Portland Place in recognition of Robert's CAA work, and in 1983 the Association followed IUA in instituting a Robert Matthew Award – in this case bestowed biennially, on 'the most innovative contribution' by an architect to their country of origin: its first recipients were Philip Cox of Australia (1983) and Arup Associates (1985). The CAA continued its activities on a relatively modest scale, compared with the vast inflation of the IUA; it was still supported mainly by the RIBA and the Commonwealth Foundation – with the inevitable hiccups during UK recessions. With the ending of apartheid in South Africa, the CAA's most divisive domestic issue completely disappeared, in favour of the more diffuse concerns about globalisation, which echoed many of the debates of Matthew's time. There were the general political questions of the extent to which Western aid and continuing involvement in the developing world merely represented a repackaged colonialism; and there were more specifically architectural concerns about 'the continuing Western grip' on architectural practice.[191] Within CHEC, and on the van Putten NGO committee, Matthew was replaced immediately by Percy Johnson-Marshall, who continued his overall approach, both in the preparation of papers for Vancouver and afterwards, becoming 'CHEC's No. 1 professional' until the final decline of his health around 1989. CHEC, even more than CAA, remained a small, specialist organisation, with Springer being followed as chairman in 1997 by L M Singhvi, a former Indian High Commissioner to the UK, but Zena Daysh still effectively running the organisation under various titles. In WSE, on the other hand, Matthew had no such direct heir, although Lorna was invited to become an honorary member in July 1975 by president Eiichi Isomura. Psomopoulos continued as Secretary-General, and (after 1983) succeeded Tyrwhitt as editor of *Ekistics* magazine – which continued to be sent to Lorna at Keith until at least the late 1990s. Overall, whatever their specific work programmes, all these bodies were ultimately useful mainly as vehicles for networking and international goodwill.[192]

But what of the 1976 Vancouver Habitat conference itself – the focus of Matthew's urgent last efforts? Rather like Matthew's own career, Habitat was one of those phenomena of a diffuse, rather than concentrated, character, whose significance was as much in its density of connections to others as in its unitary impact – a complex pattern of links over time, and at any one time, which can only be properly grasped in retrospect. Making connections across time, many ecological activists now identify Habitat 1976 as the beginning of the general acceptance of ecological issues as a

13.25 Hellman cartoon about the impending refurbishment of the Royal Festival Hall by architects Allies Morrison, 2004. (*AJ*, 12 February 2004, 14)

mainstream political agenda – a trend leading to the Rio 'Earth Summit' of 1992 and the Habitat 2 convention at Istanbul of 1996. In this perspective, Vancouver occupies a central place in a century-long movement of environmental internationalism that began with turn-of-century figures such as Geddes. That *longue-durée* narrative was not, of course, clear in 1976. What seemed most important then was the 'synchronic' rather than 'diachronic' connections: the density of links between NGOs, in an ever-shifting mosaic of organisations and individuals coalescing around the Habitat issue, many already familiar from our story. Take, for example, Jaqueline Tyrwhitt, veteran of many influential episodes of built-environment research and proselytising. In 1976 she retired from teaching at Harvard and became a leading delegate to Habitat, leading the Ekistics input to the conference, and opening a permanent channel of influence through which many WSE figures would flow, to occupy key positions in the UN-led international development movement. But for Tyrwhitt herself Vancouver was, in many ways, the culmination of her career, and had Matthew and Doxiadis survived in full vigour to May 1976, they would doubtless have played a similarly prominent role.

Paradoxically, as with many events seen as significant in hindsight, the

13.26 Article by Zena Daysh in
Human Ecology, May 2003.

A WINDOW ON THE JOURNAL

Truth Identified, Extrapolated, Implemented

By ZENA DAYSH, CNZM

Behind the above title is the truism that truth is the first victim of confusion and fear. All articles in this 20th edition of the journal reflect faith and dedication and mirror the aims, purpose and activities of the Commonwealth Human Ecology Council

Indian writer and editor Sima Sharma, who in the mid-1990s grounded CHEC's philosophy editorially in this journal, offers many wise perspectives in the new publication, *Faith*, she has edited. We quote from her as a background to the turbulent and changing world of today that is dealt with in this volume:

Religion, with faith as its premise, has played a major role historically and contemporarily, providing the basis and principles for ethics and moral philosophy. This was contested by the rise of scientific humanism and the secular West. These issues are today

Congratulations to Zena Daysh (left) on her 88th birthday from Anna Tibaijuka, Executive Director, UN-Habitat, in Nairobi, May 2002

a 'community health/agro-economic/social ecological' group at the London School of Hygiene and Tropical Medicine. This widened academic/development group, embracing 37 disciplines, laid down the principles and formulated a framework for a Commonwealth-wide human ecology pilot project. The Committee on Nutrition in the Commonwealth was chaired by the Dean of the School, Dr Andrew Topping, and I was once again the convener – having extended my nutritional and sociological interests to widen the agenda of the committee. This committee formed philosophical and scientific bases and

actual experience of the Habitat 76 conference itself for the participants at the time was somewhat disjointed and incomplete – beginning with the posthumous outcome of Matthew's own urgent last efforts. Immediately after his death, Aidan began working closely with CAA to help realise the 'action-orientated programme' of slide lectures and textbooks proposed by Robert for Vancouver, together with an architectural-education supplement focusing on the issue of architecture school inter-recognition. During the remainder of 1975 Aidan also tried, without success, to carry forward Robert's plan for a documentary film. One film-maker he contacted, Michael Radford, proposed a 25 minute documentary with a full crew filming for three weeks in Europe and Central America at a total cost of over £12,000, and with three alternative theme approaches: a Geddes-style polemical exposition, contrasting Western 'super-slum' luxury with third-world shanty towns and pollution; a 'two countries treatment'; or an exclusively third-world subject. All three alternatives would argue for establishment of an international agency concerned with human settlement, but, in the event, nothing came of the project.[193] To accom-

modate the Habitat conference, which was held in Vancouver's Queen Elizabeth Theatre between 31 May and 11 June 1976, a special pavilion was designed by architect Arthur Erickson, including papier mâché self-built modules of hyperbolic paraboloids. By January of that year an advance draft declaration of principles had been prepared by the conference secretariat, focusing on the threat to the quality of human life in settlements by such pressures as population growth, underdevelopment, and urbanisation. The final drafts of Barbara Ward's accompanying book, *The Home and Man*, were meantime grappling with the difficulty of getting a 'coherent grip' on the entire 'habitat', owing to its all-inclusiveness, and instead fell back on more general declarations of the comprehensiveness and long roots of its crisis, which stemmed from the 'great accelerations' of the past 500 years.[194]

The fragmentary and frustrating experience of Vancouver for many of the participants was summed up in the account of one British NGO member, David Hall, director of the Town and Country Planning Association. This organisation, typically of the Osborn tradition, sent its own highly motivated, independent delegation, contrasting strongly in its assertiveness with the Foreign Office-mandated unobtrusiveness of the British official delegation. Hall identified two major, specific deficiencies of Habitat, aside from the usual, more general conference problems of venue or schedule changes or loss of materials, which at times made the conference seem like 'punching a mattress'. The first specific difficulty was the continuing post-Stockholm hegemony of natural-environment concerns, and the resulting

intellectual frustration arising from the dominance of ... North Americans whose preoccupations were not with human settlements but with the saving of whales, the control of nuclear power, and conservation generally ('*Human* settlements this way', said a sign pointing towards the TCPA stand and away from a display about bee-keeping).

As a result, the 'gigantic settlement slums' of the third world were, paradoxically, 'given little of the attention of the Forum', lending a hollow ring to Secretary-General Peñelosa's resounding declaration that the conference would 'show people how they can recapture control of their environments through direct action'. Second, Hall pointed to 'the ultimate frustration: the failure of government delegates to agree on the declaration of principles', stemming from the success of 'the Arabs and their allies' in including a statement that 'Zionism was a form of racialism' inimical to human rights in habitation – with the result that the UK, US, Canada and several other countries abstained from the declaration.[195] Despite this failure of rhetoric, though, the recommendations for national and international action were unanimously agreed, providing a comprehensive framework for future possible lines of work – including, even, the direct activism advocated by Peñelosa. As Barbara Ward put it in a press conference, 'As long as you stay within the boundaries of good behaviour, you are not going to get very far in persuading

governments to act. We must boldly fight and harass governments to get these recommendations adopted.'[196]

The immediate outcomes of Vancouver, however, continued to emphasise the UN- or government-led top-down approach. The UN set up in 1978 a permanent UN Commission on Human Settlements (and secretariat), and a UN Centre for Human Settlements (UNCHS-Habitat) in Nairobi. Over the next two decades UNCHS-Habitat took the lead in gradually shifting the emphasis of action to NGO initiative, and in formulating a 'Habitat Agenda for a Global Plan of Action for Sustainable Urban Development, and Adequate Shelter for All'. Efforts gradually built up to the holding of a Second UN Conference on Human Settlements (Habitat II) in Istanbul in June 1996. Attended by 15,000 people, this convention was organised in a far more openly polycentric fashion than Vancouver, with a main conference (focusing on two main themes, 'Adequate shelter for all', and 'Development of sustainable settlements in an urbanising world') and thematic dialogues. The two dominant problems of Vancouver – intrusion by natural-environmentalists and by extraneous geopolitical issues – had disappeared, although there was a concluding declaration signed by 171 governments. The focus was purely on settlement, and the pivotal organising role was played by a network of 190 NGOs, together with 500 civic leaders and mayors.[197] The years after Istanbul saw purposeful follow-up work to implement the Habitat Agenda/Plan of Action, focused overwhelmingly on 'bottom-up' local and community initiatives in developing countries.

Perhaps the single most novel aspect of all these initiatives from Istanbul onwards, and something that marked them off from all previous efforts, was their optimism, and their general conviction that overwhelming crises could be overcome – for example, in South Africa, Habitat II was told that 7 million dwellings had been constructed since 1994. Although about 50 per cent of the world's population was now urban, with some 180,000 being added to that total every day, and some 650 million of these urban dwellers lived in health-threatening poverty – a total that would probably more than double by 2025 – the old thread of doom-laden chaos polemic about the built environment that had stretched from Geddes and Clough Williams-Ellis to the environmental activist age seemed finally to have been broken – a situation of which Matthew, with his overriding ethos of purposeful application, would surely have approved![198]

Modern Architect

Conclusion

For us, a man is a hero and deserves special interest only if his nature and his education have rendered him able to let his individuality be almost perfectly absorbed in its hierarchic function, without at the same time forfeiting the vigorous, fresh, admirable impetus which make for the savour and worth of the individual.

Hermann Hesse, *Das Glasperlenspiel*, 1943[1]

In the Introduction, I hinted briefly at the likely difficulty of tracing in any coherent way the interaction between Matthew's own multifaceted personality and the equally complex, fluctuating context in which he lived. Now, several hundred pages of dense narrative later, we have to confront the task of whether it is possible to draw together any of these threads. Doubtless to Matthew himself, at the fevered end of his career in spring 1975, the only important feeling would have been a sense of incompleteness and frustration, with the vision of Vancouver cruelly cut off from him. But, for us, a calmer process of evaluation is hopefully possible.

How, then, were the general themes we identified at the beginning of the book refracted through Matthew's own character, and vice versa? Throughout this story we have repeatedly witnessed a pattern of dominant and subordinate cultural and architectural themes working in parallel with one another, such as public collectivism and private individualism, modernity and tradition, Britishness and Scottishness – in each case, allowing the individual person a degree of freedom and flexibility of emphasis. Unlike some more doctrinaire figures wedded to a single ideology or viewpoint throughout, such as Stirrat Johnson-Marshall, with his unremitting pursuit of systems anonymity, or Basil Spence, with his loyalty to traditional ideals of beauty and art, Matthew proved able to exploit these fluctuations and, every so often (as in the late 1940s era of the LCC's rise and the early 1970s era of conservation) actually to help steer the wider course of events, while remaining always within the general conventional outer limits of the Modern Movement. The fact that Matthew was at no stage an avant-garde figure may make him appear less accessible to today's individualistic architectural culture than, for example, Lubetkin or the Smithsons. But that kind of judgement is essentially anachronistic, running counter to the cooperative temper of the mid 20th century. Even of a figure of the stature of J M Keynes, it could be said by his biographer, Robert Skidelsky, that

> the pantheon of great thinkers remains almost unknown to the general public. This class of historical actor does its work silently: they are the back-room boys of our civilization. Their ideas permeate the atmosphere from which practical persons draw such intellectual nourishment as they do. But the source of this nourishment remains obscure to them.[2]

Matthew's career fluctuated between

Skidelsky's categories of backroom boy and practical person, drawing on a range of innovators, such as Rowse, Fuller, Abercrombie or Jane Jacobs, synthesising their ideas and then, in turn, stimulating activity in a wide range of built-environment fields. Because of his insistence on multi-disciplinary flux, Matthew always remained something of a 'metic', never wholly and exclusively belonging to, and accepted by, any single grouping. We saw earlier that whereas to a non-architect such as Daysh, Matthew appeared above all as 'someone who was both professional and artistically inspired, a highly cultivated chap, a big-time, gracious architect who brought us style and experience', to even an administratively inclined architect such as Derbyshire, he was 'an able, possibly gifted (but not passionate) designer whose political commitments and social genius seduced him from the drawing board to the heady world of power'. Many of today's architects also occupy a position midway between design and context – but a context that Matthew would have found incomprehensible, dominated as it is by market competition. We saw repeatedly during our story how Matthew's hybrid, multi-strand existence was powerfully reinforced by his character, with its strong tendency to controlled compartmentalisation, and its tension between a restless addiction to periodic career change and his intense sense of roots in Edinburgh and Scotland. Matthew's restlessness and constantly self-renewing sense of mission also ensured that, unlike almost all of his contemporaries, such as Holford, Spence, Gibson or Stirrat Marshall, his reaction to the ageing process would be, essentially, to ignore or defy it, and, finally, to go down fighting. In 1990 the (then) 73-year-old Noel Annan could say of his contemporaries of 'Our Age' that 'for us the owl of Minerva had folded its wings. All we could do was comfort ourselves with Shakespeare's reflection that a few of us had "writ the style of gods and made a push at chance and sufferance".'[3] To Matthew, pushing onwards to the very end, to indulge in such reflective melancholy would have seemed an alien luxury.

What, then, of the specific relationship between Matthew's own personality and the context within which he lived? Analysed in the terms of a Jungian-based personality definition, Matthew can perhaps best be understood under the category of the 'field-marshal' – a rare category of pragmatic organiser-leaders, pursuing a personal 'mission' with open-minded force.[4] How did this personality interact with the great narratives and dominant ethical positions of the day? First, his position in relation to the tension between collectivism and individualism was powerfully structured by the prominence, and interaction, of Scottish Presbyterian personal ethical values, and Arts and Crafts architectural-ethical values, within his upbringing. In combination, they helped shape his own approach to leadership and negotiation, combining the self-assurance of the Presbyterian 'elect' with a stubborn, almost perverse non-conformity and individuality, and a love of vernacular, rather than grandly monumental, architecture. Even to such a self-effacing character as Stirrat Johnson-Marshall it would have been unthinkable to arrive at an important interview in a battered, elderly car and wearing an old duffle coat – as did Matthew at his initial 1955 interview for Ninewells Hospital. Another way in which Matthew's career arguably reflected the Presbyterian evangelical-missonary ethos, as well as the more general Victorian ethos of gentlemanly restraint, was his preference for issue-based or professional friendships over purely personal ones: these relationships at one remove allowed him to pursue his 'causes' in a more intense manner, while preserving a space of immediate individual privacy. Likewise, with underprivileged people requiring his help, he could show unfailing generosity and encouragement, in a mixture of the Presbyterian Scottish democratic approach with the *noblesse oblige* courtesy of the gentleman. With some of his family and close colleagues, conversely, he could at times show a negative,

uncommunicative streak, denying himself and others the benefits of a positive approach of 'appreciative enquiry'. But whereas some other leading men of affairs, such as 19th-century architect Sir George Gilbert Scott, expressed pangs of conscience at their neglect of their families, there is no evidence that Matthew's personality was significantly troubled by this potential conflict.

Also arguably stemming from his Arts and Crafts and Scottish East Coast roots, as well as the more general architectural ethos of Modernist collectivism, and the earlier conventions of gentlemanly self-

restraint and courtesy, was his visceral aversion to anything smacking of commercialism or aggressive self-promotion – an aversion that, for instance, largely accounted for his intense dislike of Richard Neutra, schooled in the Frank Lloyd Wright ethos of constant self-trumpeting. Any latent tendency of dominant behaviour towards others was strictly restrained, and emerged only rarely – in contrast to other forceful leader-figures of the time, such as government minister Richard Crossman, whose diaries record a constant series of clashes with his civil servants, or architect Erno

Goldfinger, whose most recent biography attributes to him the most grotesquely exaggerated tendencies of bullying, hectoring and sexual exploitation of staff and subordinates.[5] Such behaviour traits would have been regarded by the mature Matthew as not only crassly objectionable but also self-defeating.

Ultimately, at the core of Matthew's career, there lay the sense of mission, typical of his 'field-marshal' personality in general, but shaped also by the social and cultural conventions of Presbyterian Scotland, and of the international Modern Movement. The search for *arête* (virtuous achievement) in preference to worldly wealth and success has been a repeated preoccupation of elite groups within Western societies, and under Protestant Christianity became almost indistinguishable from the search for individual salvation. We saw in Chapter 1 the scorn with which, in his clash with Revd Bellhouse, Matthew rejected the now widely discredited orthodoxies of Presbyterian Christianity itself. But during the Modern Movement years the appropriation of the salvation language of Christianity by the prevailing community utopias of the age provided Matthew with a powerful alternative collective framework, within which he could pursue and subsume his powerful but ever-mutating sense of mission, as one of a new, secular caste of the elect. The considered evaluations of those who knew Matthew well hint at the latent tensions between ends and means, and individual and collective ambition, that necessarily accompanied a lifetime of mission. In a 1997 exchange of recollections between Lionel Esher and Andrew Derbyshire, for example, the latter wrote of Matthew's 'eloquent intelligence and ruthless pursuit of what he believed to be right', while Esher argued that 'behind his distinguished looks, his charm of manner, and his soft lowland voice lay an iron determination to get his way – the way he thought right for a liberal and caring society'. Pat Nuttgens's obituary judgement could serve as an epitaph for Matthew's eclectic career: 'He left scarcely any kind of architecture untouched, and touched nothing that he did not transform.'[6]

The careers of almost all 'great men' throughout the ages have had to balance the high ideals of public achievement with the private pressures and costs that lay behind. Arguably, Matthew himself was partly a victim of his own driving forcefulness if, as seems possible, his stressful existence contributed to his early death. But as someone who would have found retirement intolerable, to be cut short in his prime was for him the best outcome, not least because he was spared having to sit on the sidelines as the tide of Thatcherite neo-liberalism and architectural Post-Modernism drowned his legacy from view. Only now, perhaps, in an age dominated by a new, globally homogenised type of 'modern architecture', are we in a position fully to appreciate the richness of the legacy of Matthew's life and achievement, combining as it did the social idealism of modernity with the contextual power of place.

Patrick Harrison

Obituary of Robert Matthew

RMJM staff newsletter, 1976

There is a children's story by John Buchan about a magic walking stick which at a twirl and a wish transports its possessor anywhere in the world. In a characteristically Scottish way, Buchan makes his stick one of a pair, Beauty and Bands: Beauty can be used only for pleasure, Bands for duty, and misuse incurs loss. Which one does the schoolboy hero possess? Alas, too late he discovers he possesses Bands and loses it by having too much fun. This long forgotten tale was brought to mind when Robert Matthew once remarked, quite uncensoriously, of a gifted and admired contemporary: 'A pleasure-lover!' Pleasure might be a proper part of life, and a legitimate pursuit for some; but for Robert Matthew there was never the slightest doubt that his formidable endowments were committed, like Bands, to duty. And, like Bands, they took him far and wide.

His career fell into three phases. First the spell with the Department of Health for Scotland as a housing architect, ultimately as Chief Architect and Planner; then the years at the LCC: in both he created highly effective organisations, the shape of which long remained. From 1953 he was a freer agent with a wider canvas, having a chair in Edinburgh University, a large practice and leadership of his profession nationally and internationally as President of the RIBA, the International Union of Architects and the Commonwealth Architects Association. His purely architectural abilities and achievement were considerable and

have probably been under-rated; but it was as a public servant in the cause of architecture that he will be remembered.

Architecture is a social, public art; and for Robert Matthew, commitment to his calling meant commitment also to ensuring its public and social relevance. This led him to redefine and re-establish the role of architecture and architects in a modern industrial world. By the Thirties vernacular architecture had gone, and 'fine building' – the former province of architects – was going. Building had become a mass operation having fewer and fewer contacts with local labour, local materials, styles or needs and was falling increasingly under the remote control of political and commercial forces which were brutalising it. Robert Matthew believed architects must re-invest it with humanity, seemliness and fitness for purpose, by designing a wider range and greater quantity of building than before and by winning acceptance with the public and with local and central government as the proper people to do the job. The shortcomings of postwar British architecture – although they lie more in the commercial field than in the public sector – too often blind us to its many qualities and to the scope and opportunity architects have gained in this country, uniquely in world terms, to influence the quality of the environment for the better. This owes more to Robert Matthew's vision and example than to anything else, and much of his later life was spent attempting to do for architecture internationally, and especially in the developing world, what he had done for it at home.

Unlike others who saw and understood the problem he was undoctrinaire about solutions and stood back from the dogmas and cliques that have often beset the profession, recognising that excellence comes in many forms and that the future will require diverse approaches to the exercise of the art. But he held strongly a few simple principles which gave force to his actions. For example, he believed architecture serves a basic and universal human need which transcends politics, and that in their shared skill and knowledge architects are themselves a force for good in the world. Thus, whether Cuba, South Africa or his staff at the LCC were under consideration, he believed that for architects, as architects, commitment to their profession was quite separate from their personal political commitments as men. He believed in the importance of a strong public architecture in which professionals could act both (as he had done) as architectural administrators and also as practising architects, holding that the 'mixed economy' of public and private offices was mutually reinforcing and enlarged the total skill and experience of the profession. He believed also that architects should be independent of the commercial interest and political expediency that he saw as inimical to architectural quality. None of this implied isolationism: architects must be better informed about developing technology and social needs, and his innovations at Edinburgh University, where he associated building science and a housing research unit with the architectural school, testify to this conviction. Likewise his decision to leave the drawing board to become an architect-at-large put him in touch with life at many points. Although uncompromising in his vindication of architectural values he understood and respected the necessary complexity of the world and the right of others to hold and defend hostile views. To win one must be good and be wanted. The respect he himself won

enhanced architects and architecture everywhere.

Critics of Robert Matthew's later years might say that his determination to be at full stretch led him to be stretched too thin, and that after leaving the LCC he lacked the power base to be fully effective. There may be some truth in this. However, he saw the move to the chair at Edinburgh as a development, fulfilling both the traditionally high Scottish estimation of teaching and also his conviction that architectural education should be influenced by people experienced in large-scale social building. But university life was insufficient to engage his full energies, and it may be questioned whether the relatively narrow view of the world given by even a large private practice, or the authority going with Presidency of the RIBA, gave adequate scope to his unusual aptitude for administration and public life. Many people noticed that the bigger, more hazardous, more difficult the situation, the better he was. His handling of Castro at the UIA Congress in Cuba, to mention only one example of very many, displayed judgement and statesmanship of a high order which could have carried him far in diplomacy or even national politics. It is likely that had he held a really senior post in the Civil Service or office in Government, he could have done more and, from within, achieved the fundamental reordering of values on which he could only advise in the Matthew/Skillington report to the Secretary of State for the Environment on standards of architectural design in public architecture. Had he reached the House of Lords, he could not have failed to make a strong impression and would have had the opportunity to speak influentially for architecture and environmental issues. However, it would be wrong to stop short at such judgement of his personal success. He gave himself unstintingly and enlarged the scope and opportunity for architecture everywhere: now it's up to others.

If he was best in the big situation, he could occasionally be trying in the small one. He was blessed in an exceptionally resilient wife, whose resourcefulness was essential to the fulfilment of his exacting operational requirements. He also made heavy demands on those around him in practice, university or at the RIBA – demands that were willingly met because he never spared himself and had the rare gift for drawing out energies and qualities in others they had not realised they possessed.

To some who did not know him well he may have seemed, with town houses in London and Edinburgh, a place in the country, and incessant globe-trotting, just another big-shot private practitioner, a high-liver. This was far from the truth. These seeming fruits of success were simply the logistics to keep a quite exceptional piece of weaponry active in a grand cause. Personally, few people can have been less self-indulgent. While he was an observant traveller and could be marvellously convivial in the line of duty, he was in many ways sedentary and reclusive, liking nothing better than to work alone in his study at Humbie, puffing a cheroot and being brought occasional trays of tea. A tot of whisky, a glass of Scottish beer, a plate of mince – and delight in the bizarre combination of cheese and banana – these were the extent of gastronomic pleasure. He was widely read: music, sculpture and painting he enjoyed and practised all of them. But like travel, conversation, people, they were a necessary sustenance, not ends in themselves. He was a fine speaker and possessed a distinguished appearance which he owed to a handsome and vigorous alertness and not at all to dress.

Pleasure-lover, then, he certainly was not, but work was his pleasure and for that he had a robust appetite, zest, and unlimited stamina. Though a lifelong socialist and agnostic those labels tell one little. His real hatred was of dogma; and he is best seen as a particularly rich member of that great tradition of large-minded, cultivated and disinterested Scots who have given so much to Britain and the world by their unaffected devotion to serious ends.

Notes

Many of the following references derive from two batches of personal papers deposited with Edinburgh University Library (Special Collections): an initial batch deposited in November 1975, and subsequently catalogued; and the remainder, deposited following Lorna's death in November 2003, and still unsorted and uncatalogued as at 2006. 'EULMC' (Edinburgh University Library Matthew Collection) citations with 'MS' references refer to files in the original, catalogued deposit; 'EULMC' citations without 'MS' references refer to the later, uncatalogued material.

Introduction

1   Thucydides, *History*, II.43 (Pericles' Funeral Oration).
2   Robert Skidelsky, *John Maynard Keynes 1883–1946*, London, 2003.
3   Critique of historically distorting effects of 'iconic' Modernism: M Glendinning, *The Last Icons: Architecture Beyond Modernism* (The Lighthouse Scottish Architecture and Design Series, Issue 1), Glasgow, 2004.
4   B Dennis and D Skilton, *Reform and Intellectual Debate in Victorian England*, Lndon 1987, 18; N Annan, *Our Age*, London, 1990; H Perkin, *The Rise of Professional Society in England since 1880*, London, 1990, 83–4, 121, 368.
5   Annan, *Our Age*, 9, 299.
6   Annan, *Our Age*, 13.
7   J R Seeley, *The Expansion of England*, London, 1883.
8   K E Foote et al., *Re-Reading Cultural Geography*, Austin, Texas, 1994.
9   M Glendinning, R MacInnes, A MacKechnie, *A History of Scottish Architecture* (hereafter *HSA*), Edinburgh, 1996, 334; R H Matthew (hereafter RHM), foreword to A W Cleeve Barr, *Public Authority Housing*, London, 1958.
10 G Stephens, 'The historical demography of architects', *Journal of the Society of Architectural Historians (JSAH)*, December 1996, 435–7.
11 M Glendinning and S Muthesius, 'Reinvigorating the English tradition of architectural polemic', in I Abley and J Heartfield (eds), *Sustaining Architecture in the Anti-Machine*

Age, Chichester, 2001, 134–41; I Boyd Whyte (ed.), *Man-Made Future: Planning, Education and Design in Mid-Twentieth-Century Britain*, London, 2007; T J Clark, *Farewell to an Idea, Episodes from the History of Modernism*, New Haven, 1999; H J Cowan, *A Historical Outline of Architectural Science*, Amsterdam, 1986; F M Lea, *Science and Building, A History of the Building Research Station*, London, 1971.
12 Lea, *Science and Building*, 101; A Saint, *Towards a Social Architecture*, London, 1987, 249; R Crossman, *The Diaries of a Cabinet Minister*, vol. 1, London, 1975.
13 F Toennies, *Gemeinschaft und Gesellschaft*, 1887; R Williams, *Keywords*, London, 1976, 65–6; T A Markus, *Visions of Perfection*, Glasgow, 1985.
14 P Wagner, *Sociology of Modernity*, London, 1994,17–18.
15 Glendinning and Muthesius, 'Reinvigorating the English tradition'.
16 Crossman, *Diaries of a Cabinet Minister*, vol. 1, 24 and 263.

Chapter 1

1   E Cumming and W Kaplan, *The Arts and Crafts Movement*, London, 1991; S McKinstry, *Rowand Anderson*, Edinburgh, 1991; *Transactions of the National Association for the Advancement of Art, Edinburgh Meeting 1889*, London, 1890; P Savage, *Lorimer and the Edinburgh Craft Designers*, Edinburgh, 1980.
2   Information from Stuart Matthew (hereafter SRM) and June Douglas-Hamilton.
3   McKinstry, *Anderson*, 139–44.
4   Savage, *Lorimer*; *HSA*, 334.
5   Savage, *Lorimer*, 39.
6   Information from SRM and June Douglas-Hamilton.
7   *Diary of Services of the First Battalion of the Royal Scots during the Boer War*, London, 1904; *The Royal Scots in South Africa during the War, 1899–1902*, London, 1904; D Judd and K Surridge, *The Boer War*, London, 2002.
8   Savage, *Lorimer*, 27 and 53.
9   S McKinstry and J Plenderleith, 'Thomson and Schleiermacher', in G Stamp and S McKinstry, eds, *'Greek'*

Thomson, Edinburgh, 1994, 73–9.

10 Interview with SRM, 1995.

11 Interview with Lorna Matthew (hereafter LLM), 1995.

12 Interview with SRM, 1995.

13 Interview with SRM, 1995.

14 Interview with SRM, 1995.

15 Interviews with SRM and P Nuttgens, 1995; S Platt, 2003; J A Matthew, 2007.

16 Interview with SRM, 1995; G Newman, 'Zeppelins Above!', *History Scotland,* March/April 2004, 49–51; Annan, *Our Age,* 71; *Evening News,* 1 February 2007, 28–9.

17 Interview with SRM, 1995; Edinburgh University Library Matthew Collection (hereafter EULMC), RHM lecture text for British Architects' Conference, Newcastle, May 1958 and for 14 May 1964 lecture at Edinburgh University.

18 Interview with SRM, 1995.

19 Savage, *Lorimer.*

20 Interview with SRM, 1995.

21 Interview with SRM, 1995.

22 Interview with SRM, 1995.

23 Interview with SRM, 1995.

24 B Russell, *Why I am not a Christian*, London, 1957, 59.

25 John Calvin, *Instituites of the Christian Religion*, 1537; E W Smith, *The Creed of Presbyterians*, 180–1; L Boettner, *The Reformed Doctrine of Presbyterianism*, 1932, Chapter 1; see also A Lownie, *John Buchan, the Presbyterian Cavalier*, London, 1995; J Buchan, *Collected Writings*, London, 1946.

26 Collection of SRM.

27 Interviews with SRM and LLM, 1995, and Aidan Matthew (hereafter RAM), 2005: T R S Young, ed., *The Edinburgh Institution, 1832–1932*, Edinburgh, 1933, 355.

28 Interview with SRM, 1995.

29 In Britain, the interwar era saw a growing trend away from uniformed activities, such as the Boy Scouts, towards 'civilian' activities such as youth-hostelling or the YMCA: H Lorimer, *Scottish Geographical Magazine*, vol. 113, 1, 1997, 42–9; interview with SRM, 1995.

30 *The World's Youth*, vol. 1, 7, October 1925.

31 S Pedersen and P Mandler, eds, *After the Victorians*, London, 1994.

Chapter 2

1 Matthew's marks, course details, etc: Edinburgh College of Art archival files, student records, courtesy of Professor B Edwards, 2003.

2 EULMC, transcript of lecture of 6 March 1965 to Sheffield Branch of Edinburgh Graduates.

3 'The Palace of Nations', *Country Life*, 5 February 1938, 133 ff.; *The Architectural Work of Sir John Burnet & Partners,* Geneva, 1930; D Walker, *St Andrew's House: An Edinburgh Controversy*, Edinburgh, 1989; F Borsi, *The Monumental Era*, London, 1987.

4 D D Egbert, *The Beaux Arts Tradition in French Architecture*, Princeton, 1980; R Middleton (ed.), *The Beaux Arts and 19th-*

century French Architecture, London, 1982; A Drexler (ed.), *The Architecture of the Ecole des Beaux Arts*, London, 1977; L Campbell, 'A call to order: the Rome Prize and early 20th century architecture', *Architectural History*, 1989, 136.

5 A Saint, *The Image of the Architect*, London, 1983, 68; R N Shaw and T G Jackson (eds), *Architecture, a Profession or an Art?* London, 1892; Saint, *Towards a Social Architecture*, London, 1987; H B Creswell, *The Honeywood File*, London, 1929; L Budden (ed.), *The Book of the Liverpool School of Architecture*, Liverpool, 1932; C H Reilly, *Architectural Problems*, Liverpool, 1924; L Budden, 'Charles Reilly, an appreciation', *RIBA Journal (JRIBA)*, March 1948, 212–3; P Richmond, *Marketing Modernisms, The Architecture and Influence of Charles Reilly*, Liverpool, 2001; C H Reilly, *Scaffolding in the Sky*, London, 1938; A Powers, *Architectural Education in Britain, 1880–1914*, PhD thesis, Cambridge 1982; A Mace, *The RIBA*, London, 1986.

6 E Mumford (ed.), *The CIAM Discourse on Urbanism*, Cambridge, MA, 2000; A Jackson, *The Politics of Architecture*, London, 1970.

7 Information from Brian Edwards; EULMC, text of 1954 lecture by RHM, 'The influence of environment'.

8 P Geddes, 'Life and its science', in *The Evergreen*, Spring 1895; C H Meller, *Patrick Geddes*, London, 1990; P Geddes, *Cities in Evolution*, London, 1915, 1968 edition, 92–3; *Collecting Cites: Images from Patrick Geddes's Cities and Town Planning Exhibition*, catalogue of exhibition in Collins Gallery (Glasgow), 1999; P Geddes, *City Development: A Report to the Carnegie Dunfermline Trust*, Edinburgh, 2004 (copy in RHM book collection, RCAHMS); P Geddes, 'Civics, as applied sociology', in H Meller (ed.), *The Ideal City*, Leicester, 1979; A Picon, *Les Saint-Simonians*, Paris, 2002; P Geddes and Colleagues, *The Masque of Ancient Learning*, Edinburgh, 1913; P Geddes, *Dramatisations of History*, London, 1923; *Edinburgh Review*, 88, Summer 1992; V Welter and J Lawson (eds) *The City after Patrick Geddes*, Bern, 2000; V Welter, *Biopolis, Patrick Geddes and the City of Life*, Cambridge, MA, 2002; V Welter, 'Biopolis', *Architectural Heritage*, 6, 1996, 61ff.; *Edinburgh Architectural Research*, 1994, 98–118; *Edinburgh Architectural Research*, 1995, 11–30.

9 P Geddes, *Cities in Evolution*, London, 1915, 359; R L Stevenson, *Edinburgh Picturesque Notes*, Edinburgh, 1903, 77; Sir J H A Macdonald, *Incongruity and Disfigurement in Edinburgh and Elsewhere*, Edinburgh, 1907 (text of address to Edinburgh Architectural Association, 4 November 1907); G Bruce, *To Foster and Enrich*, Edinburgh, 1986, 55–6.

10 Interview with Alan Wightman, 2004.

11 P Abercrombie, *Planning in Town and Country*, Liverpool, 1937, 16; G Dix, 'Patrick Abercrombie', in G Cherry, *Pioneers in British Planning*, London, 1981, 103–30.

12 *RIBA Journal*, July–August 1975, 5; interview with SRM, 1995.

13 Edinburgh College of Art archival files, student records,

courtesy of Professor B Edwards, 2003; interview with SRM, 1995.

14 EULMC, RHM travel notebooks for 1926.

15 *RIAS Quarterly*, 26, Summer 1928.

16 Savage, Lorimer; EULMC, unpublished autobiographical notes by SRM (hereafter 'SRM notes').

17 Interview with SRM, 1995.

18 Interview with SRM, 1995; D M Walker, letter of July 2006 to M Glendinning.

19 S Blackden (ed.), *Hew Lorimer, an Appreciation*, Edinburgh, 1987, 5.

20 Letter from Professor D Walker, 2005; *Hew Lorimer, Sculptor*, catalogue of exhibition, Talbot Rice Gallery, Edinburgh, 1988.

21 Interview with SRM, 1995; D Walker, letter of July 2006 to M Glendinning.

22 Interview with SRM, 1995.

23 *RIAS Quarterly*, 17, September 1926.

24 Interview with Robert Scott Morton, 1995.

25 EULMC, unsorted notes from RHM RIBA lecture in 1950s, during Robertson term as PRIBA.

26 Notes on EAA dinner, 2 June 1965, *Yearbook of the EAA*, 1966.

27 R S Morton, *Alan Reiach, a Memoir*, Edinburgh, 1989, 3–5.

28 Interviews with SRM and RAM, 1995.

29 Interview with SRM, 1995; interview with Christine Somerville, 1997.

30 Annan, *Our Age*, 77.

31 Christopher Reed, *Bloomsbury Rooms*, New Haven, 2004, 232–3; Skidelsky, *Keynes*, 140–149, 257–60, 456–7; Wyndham Lewis, *Apes of God*, 1930.

32 Interview with SRM, 1995; EULMC, file MS2534, note of January 1962.

33 Interview with SRM, 1995.

34 Interview with SRM, 1995; SRM notes; A J Mullay, 'Off the Rails', *History Scotland,* November/December 2003, 32.

35 EULMC, RHM travel notebooks for 1929.

36 'Students' notes', *RIAS Quarterly*, Spring 1929; J A Arnott, *EAA Transactions*, 1933, 134–47; interview with LLM, 1997.

37 G E Cherry and L Penny, *Holford*, London, 1986; Richmond, *Marketing Modernisms.*

38 L Campbell, 'A call to order', 131; *RIBA Kalendar*, 1962–3; Building Centre, *The Classical Tradition in British Architecture*, London, 1982.

39 Interview with SRM, 1995.

40 Interview with SRM, 1995.

41 *Edinburgh Evening News*, 16 October 1933, 13; interview with SRM, 1995.

42 Interview with SRM, 1995.

43 Interview with SRM, 1995.

44 Interviews with SRM and LLM, 1995, and with RAM, 2006.

45 Interviews with LLM and RAM, 1995.

46 Interview with Elspeth Hardie, 2003.

47 G E Cherry, *The Evolution of British Town Planning*, Leighton

Buzzard, 1974, 107; M Green, *Children of the Sun*, London, 1977; *Architectural Review*, 78, 1935, 216; T H Eriksen, *Small Places, Large Issues*, London, 2001, 15; Fascist sympathies: S Games (ed.), *Pevsner, Art & Architecture, The Radio Talks*, London, 2002, xxiii.

48 C W Ellis, *Britain and the Beast*, London, 1937, 1–7.

49 S Pedersen, P Mandler (eds), *After the Victorians*, London, 1994, 234.

50 Public Works Administration, *Public Buildings: Architecture under the Public Works Administration 1933–9*, Washington DC, 1939; D Lilienthal, *TVA: Democracy on the March*, London, 1944.

51 R Östberg, *The Stockholm Town Hall*, Stockholm, 1929; C Caldenby, J Lindvall, W Wang, *20th Century Architecture: Sweden*, Muenchen, 1998.

52 The growing conflation of architecture and social science: R Ellis and D Cuff, *Architects' People*, New York, 1989, 26. Cult of scientific research: see e.g. H G Wells, *The Shape of Things to Come*, London, 1935; Saint, *Towards a Social Architecture*; D Bernal, *The Social Function of Science*, London, 1939; S Collini, *Absent Minds*, Oxford, 2006.

53 Saint, *Towards a Social Architecture*, 5.

54 A Jackson, *The Politics of Architecture*, London, 1970, 63.

55 Saint, *Towards a Social Architecture*, Chapter 1.

56 Architectural Association, *School of Planning and Research for National Development*, 1936 (prospectus); Architectural Association, *Exhibition of School of Planning and Research for National Development*, July 1935 (catalogue).

57 P Shepheard, obituary of Lionel Budden, *JRIBA*, September 1956, 478; University of Liverpool, *Prospectus of the Liverpool School of Architecture, Session 1941–2*, Liverpool, 1941.

58 Richmond, *Marketing Modernisms*; C Craven, *Design Culture in Liverpool*, Liverpool, 2002; Cherry and Penny, *Holford*, 48–57.

59 See also *Tower Block*, 110.

60 Low cartoon: *Guardian*, 31 May 1934. On Germany, numerous copies of *Moderne Bauformen* from 1931–3 survive in his collection.

61 *The Swedish Match Company's Head Office, Stockholm*, Stockholm, 1931.

62 'Slum clearance', *JRIBA*, 22 February 1936.

63 'Slum clearance', *JRIBA*, 22 February 1936. Livett: EULMC, letter from R A H Livett to RHM, 20 November 1935.

64 *Architects' Journal* (hereafter *AJ*), 17 May 1934, 712; see also P Jones, *Ove Arup*, London, 2006, 88–96.

65 Bergpolder and Highpoint: *AJ*, 2 May 1935, 660; *AJ*, 17 January 1935, 113; R Pommer, 'More a necropolis than a metropolis. Ludwig Hilberseimer's high rise city and modern city planning', in R Pommer, D Spaeth, K Harrington, *In the Shadow of Mies*, Chicago, 1988, 16–42.

66 *AJ*, 26 April 1934, 5, and 9 August 1935, 195. *Slum Clearance and Rehousing: the First Report of the Council for Research on Housing Standards*, London, 1934; *AJ*, 28 June 1934, 937–43; '*AJ* Housing Supplement', *AJ*, 28 June 1934, 1937; also *AJ*,

19 September 1935, 422–3, for scheme of Y-plan towers and five-storey *Zeilenbau* redevelopment. Lubetkin and Tecton with Arup/Cement Marketing Company Ltd, *Working-Class Residential Flats in Reinforced Concrete, Report on a Competition*, London, 1935; *AJ*, 21 March 1935, 439–41; Jones, *Arup*, 125. E Darling, 'Kensal House', *Twentieth Century Architecture*, 8, 2007, 105–16.

67 Information from A Reiach, December 1984..

68 See also RHM general statement of own *Weltanschauung*: *Outlook*, vol. 1, 3, June 1936, 68–73; courtesy of Clive Fenton.

Chapter 3

1 Skidelsky, *Keynes*, 264.

2 Gibson, *The Thistle and the Crown*, Edinburgh, 1985; Sir D Milne, *The Scottish Office*, London, 1957.

3 Royal Commission on Housing in Scotland (Ballantyne Commission), evidence volume, 202 (evidence of 29 April 1913 session); Royal Commission on Housing in Scotland, *Special Report with Relative Specifications and Plans prepared by John Wilson, Arch Inspector to the Local Government Board for Scotland*, Edinburgh, 1917; letter from D Walker to M Glendinning, July 2006.

4 John Wilson, *Scotsman*, 14 March 1935, 6; Department of Health for Scotland, *Working-Class Housing on the Continent*, Edinburgh, 1935; see also J Frew, 'Ebenezer MacRae and reformed tenement design', *St Andrews Studies*, II, 1991, 80–7; J Frew, 'Towards a municipal housing blueprint', *Architectural Heritage*, 11, 2000, 43–54; J Frew, 'Homes fit for heroes', *Journal of the Architectural Heritage Society of Scotland*, 16, 1989, 26–33.

5 Draft of 12 August 1997 for new entry by Lord Esher on RHM in *Dictionary of National Biography*, courtesy of Sir Andrew Derbyshire, 2004; RCAHMS Spence archive file.

6 Interview with W Allen, 1997.

7 S Pedersen and P Mandler (eds), *After the Victorians*, London, 1994.

8 See e.g. R Steiner, *The Spiritual Guidance of Mankind*, London, 1925 edition; A Beard (ed.), *Rudolf Steiner, Architecture: an Introductory Reader*, London, 2003; *Scotsman*, 31 August 1996, 13. Interviews with LLM and SRM, 1995. Interview with C Somerville, 1997.

9 Interview with SRM, 1995.

10 EULMC MS2541, note of 19 August 1964 by RHM; EULMC text of 15 November 1967 to Ulster Architectural Heritage Society inaugural meeting; S Blackden (ed.), *Hew Lorimer: an Appreciation*, Edinburgh, 1987, 5; J R Allan, *Scotland 1938*, Edinburgh, 1938, 113–30.

11 Cf. W Benjamin, *Charles Baudelaire, a Lyric Poet*, London edition, 1989, 74; M Briggs, *The Architect in History*, London 1927; Spiro Kostof, *The Architect*, 1977; A Saint, *The Image of the Architect*, London, 1983.

12 Interviews with Elspeth Hardie, 2003, and Robert Scott Morton, 1995.

13 One of Robert's poetic concoctions from Hamilton House days, dated May 1940, is reproduced at the head of this chapter.

14 EULMC, text of RHM lecture to Institute of Public Administration, London, 27 March 1961, 'The architect and the administrator'.

15 Interview with Robert Scott Morton, 1995.

16 EULMC, text of RHM lecture to EAA, 13 March 1952, 'Local authority architecture in the profession'.

17 Glendinning et al., *History of Scottish Architecture*, 428; information from F Tindall, 1995.

18 Glendinning et al., *History of Scottish Architecture*, 1996, 421. National Archives of Scotland (NAS), file DD6–1083; EULMC correspondence files, 1937–8.

19 NAS DD1–21, 1938 paper.

20 Interview with Robert Scott Morton, 1995.

21 Patrick Abercrombie, *Planning in Town and Country, Difficulties and Possibilities*, Liverpool, 1937 (text of inaugural lecture in UCL planning chair), 11, 13–14, 16, 32–47, 56–7.

22 K D Lilley, 'On display; planning exhibitions as civic propaganda or public consultation', *Planning History*, vol. 25, 3, 2003, 3ff.; Adrian Marshed, *JSAH*, March 2004, 75 (on Bel Geddes Futurama).

23 EULMC, notes by RHM for 1937 exhibition.

24 *Scottish Architect and Builders' Journal*, April 1939.

25 Cf. J Leavis, 'Penguin special', *Telegraph Arts*, 7 May 2005, 1–2.

26 Interview with RAM, 1997.

27 Interviews with RAM, 2005, and Janet O'Neill, 2007.

28 Interview with RAM, 2004.

29 EULMC, letter from Budden to RHM, 1 June 1942.

30 G E Cherry, *The Evolution of British Town Planning*, Leighton Buzzard, 1974, 134–5.

31 Interview with W Allen, 1997.

32 Tait: *Everybody's Weekly*, 25 January 1941; H J Cowan, *A Historical Outline of Architectural Science*, Amsterdam, 1966. Reith: D Le Mahieu, 'John Reith', in S Pedersen and P Mandler (eds), *After the Victorians*, London, 1994, 193–213; S Collini, *Absent Minds*, 437.

33 Alker Tripp, *Road Traffic and its Control*, London, 1938.

34 See e.g. 1940 Council, *Ground Plan of Britain*.

35 RIBA letters: *JRIBA*, March 1941, 75; *JRIBA*, 1942, 165; F E Towndrow (ed.), *Replanning Britain* (report of Town and Country Planning Association Spring 1941 meeting), London, 1941; RIBA, *Towards a New Britain*, London, 1943; A d'Egville, *Brass Tacks for Britain*, London, 1945; *Builder*, 18 August 1947, 57; *Builder*, 7 August 1942, 107; G E Cherry and L Penny, *Holford*, London, 1976, 88–95.

36 Cherry and Penny, *Holford*, 94–134; E U Marmaras, *Planning History*, vol. 25, 3, 2003, 9ff.

37 Gibson, *Thistle and Crown*, 106–7, 114–5; R Galbraith, *Without Quarter*, Edinburgh, 1995, 243–7.

38 Galbraith, *Without Quarter*, 243–7.

39 NAS, file DD1–65, 9 September 1941.

40 D Chapman, *Wartime Social Survey, The Location of Dwellings in Towns*, London, 1943.

41 NAS file DD1–46; interview with LLM, 1997.

42 NAS file DD1–46.

43 NAS file DD1–46.

44 Interview with Robert Scott Morton, 1995; A Reiach and R Hurd, *Building Scotland*, 1941 (2nd edn, 1944).

45 Cherry and Penny, *Holford*, London, 1986.

46 J Allan, *Lubetkin*, London, 1992, 462; interview with M Tindall, 1997.

47 T Johnston, *Memories*, London, 1953, 166.

48 Cf. R Lyle and G Payne, *The Tay Valley Plan*, Dundee, 1950.

49 Cd 6153, *Report of the Royal Commission on the Distribution of the Industrial Population*, London, 1940.

50 NAS files DD12–34, 92, 94, 95; I Levitt, 'New towns, new Scotland', *Scottish Historical Review*, October 1997, 225–30.

51 Abercrombie, *Planning in Town and Country*, 11, 14, 50, 56; Abercrombie general bibliography: Antonio Manno, *Patrick Abercrombie, A Chronological Bibliography*, Leeds, 1980; G Dix, 'Patrick Abercrombie', in G E Cherry (ed.), *Pioneers in British Planning*, London, 1981, 103–30.

52 *Scottish Field*, December 1967, 20.

53 NAS files DD12–34, 92, 94, 95, RHM meetings book of Central and S E Scotland Planning Advisory Committee.

54 Interview of 2004 with A C Wolffe by G Stell and V Steele.

55 NAS files DD12–34, 92, 94, 95, letter of 21 January 1945 from T A Jeffryes to RHM.

56 Interviews with P Harrison, 2007, and M Tindall, 1997. The approach of the Tay planners was similar to that of Mears. (*Tay Valley Plan*, 289–91).

57 *Scotsman*, 7 January 1944; NAS file DD12–95; I Levitt, 'New towns, new Scotland'.

58 Interview with Sir R Grieve, 1995; R Grieve, *Grieve on Geddes*, Edinburgh, 1990.

59 *Scottish Field*, December 1967, 20; interview with RAM, 1995.

60 Tacitus, *Histories*, Book 1, 49.

61 Interview with Sir R Grieve, 1995.

62 Interview with Sir R Grieve, 1995; RHM, *Scottish Field*, December 1967, 20.

63 EULMC, letter of mid 1945 from Abercrombie to RHM.

64 EULMC, letter from T F Lyon to DHS, 19 July 1947.

65 EULMC, Gold Medal papers, letter of 16 February 1970 from Hugh T McCalman to RHM.

66 NAS file DD6–61, note of 1 February 1945 from C Mitchell to Hogan; NAS file DD2–1634.

67 Nuffield conferences: EULMC, correspondence of 26 May and 8 July 1945.

68 Greater London Record Office/London Metropolitan Archives (LMA) file LCC/GP/2/92.

69 Interview with E Hardie, 2003.

70 EULMC, diary by RHM of Sweden trip, March–May 1945 (and *passim* for Sweden trip).

71 Leuchars flight: EULMC, letter of 16 June 1945 from RHM to Lorna; Tengbom senior was the de facto court architect (A L Morgan and C Naylor, eds, *Contemporary Architects*, Chicago, 1987, 895).

72 EULMC, Sweden diaries.

73 See e.g. M Quantrill, *Aalto, A Critical Study*, New York, 1983.

74 EULMC, Swedish Timber files, letter of 25 April 1945 from Goodall to E F Muir, Ministry of Works.

75 EULMC, Sweden diary. See also Stevenson and M Brown, *The Planning of East Kilbride 1946–1951*, c.1995, 6.

76 In RHM collection: Nordiska Museen and Erik Andrén, *Skansenboken*, Stockholm, 1943; *Friluftsmuseet på Fölisön*, Helsinki, 1937; interview with M Tindall, 1997.

77 EULMC file; *Builder*, 12 July 1945 and 19 October 1945.

78 EULMC, letter of 15 February 1946 Munthe to RHM; Glendinning and Watters (eds), *Home Builders*, 232.

79 *The Thistle Foundation*, Edinburgh, 1946.

80 See scheme for Lunt Hamlet, Lincolnshire, by P Chetwynd Stapylton, in Liverpool University School of Architecture, *Prospectus for 1941–2*, Liverpool, 1941.

81 The Thistle Foundation, 'Response to Proposed Listing under the Planning (Scotland) Act', December 2001, 9–13.

82 C Fenton, 'A century of change in George Square', *Book of the Old Edinburgh Club*, new series, vol. 5, 2002, 49.

83 Brown, *Planning of East Kilbride*, 6; *Builder*, 7 November 1952, 657–67; J Lindsay, *Elizabeth B Mitchell, The Happy Town Planner*, Bishop Auckland, 1993.

84 A Marwick, *British Society since 1945*, London, 1987, 55; A Jackson, *The Politics of Architecture*, London, 1970, 165. *B*, 11 May 1945; P Hennessy, *Never Again, Britain 1945–1951*, London, 1992; W Crofts, *Coercion or Persuasion? Propaganda in Britain after 1945*, London, 1989.

85 Annan, *Our Age*, 35.

Chapter 4

1 J M Richards, *Memoirs of an Unjust Fella*, London, 1980, 195.

2 'State within a state': lecture by Andrew Saint at Twentieth Century Society conference on post-war architecture, November 1992; M Laughlin, M Gelfand, K Young, *Half a Century of Municipal Decline*, London, 1985; K Young and N Rao, *Local Government since 1945*, Oxford, 1997; A Saint, *Politics and the People of London, The LCC 1889–1965*, London, 1989; W E Jackson, *Achievement: A Short History of the LCC*, London, 1965, 33–71.

3 *JRIBA*, August 1970, 344.

4 *Builder*, 16 December 1949; interviews with A Ling, 1987, and J Whitfield Lewis, 1987.

5 *Builder*, 16 December 1949; interview with J Whitfield Lewis, 1987; *JRIBA*, January 1946, 89; *JRIBA*, December 1945, 53; Glendinning and Muthesius, *Tower Block*, 104.

6 *Illustrated Carpenter and Builder*, 12 January 1945; *Architectural Review*, May 1948, 180–3.

7 *JRIBA*, December 1945, 601; *JRIBA*, June 1946.

8 LMA, file LCC/Min/6483; interview with RAM, 2003; RHM,

Britansky Suyuznik, 21 March 1947.

9   LMA, file LCC/Min/6483; *Builder*, 4 January 1946; *Builder*, 17 May 1946.

10 EULMC, letter 18 May 1946 from Abercrombie to RHM, and undated May 1946 letter from E Morton; LCC, *Minutes*, 28 May 1946.

11 EULMC file MS2536, transcript of May 1970 RIBA Gold Medal speech by Clough Williams-Ellis. Publications by Ellis: *The Pleasures of Architecture*, London, 1924; *England and the Octopus*, London, 1928, 66; *Architecture Here and Now*, London, 1934; 'The new architecture', *Britain Today*, August 1954, 6–10; *Portmeirion, the Place and its Meaning*, London, 1963; (with Amabel Williams-Ellis) *Architect Errant*, London, 1971. A Powers, *Serge Chermayeff*, London, 2001.

12 EULMC, letter of 2 August 1946 from Cyril Walker to RHM; EULMC, letter of 14 October 1946 from W Braxton Sinclair & Barton to RHM.

13 EULMC, correspondence with Edwin Williams, April 1947.

14 Interview with Sylvia Platt, 2004.

15 Interviews with RAM and Sylvia Platt, 2003, and with J O'Neill, 2007.

16 Adrian Ashton, *An Architect Abroad*, Sydney, 1950, 90–2; P Goad, 'Modernism, colonials and the lesson of travel', lecture to DOCOMOMO Conference, Ankara, 2006.

17 Letter from J O'Neill, December 2006. *Scotland on Sunday*, 21 February 1999, 3; *Glasgow Herald*, 3 January 1962, 3; I R Gow, *Craigievar Castle* (NTS guidebook), Edinburgh, 2004; Jones, *Arup*, 133, 146–9, 153; interview with LLM, 1997.

18 EULMC, texts of RHM lectures to Manchester Luncheon Club, 18 February 1955 and Institute of Public Administration, London, 27 March 1961.

19 EULMC, file MS2540.

20 LMA files LCC/Min/11620, 11701, 11674, 11680, 11675.

21 *JRIBA*, August 1970, 344–5.

22 EULMC, letter of 27 November 1946 from C S Mardall to Matthew.

23 Country Life, *Recent English Architecture 1920–1940*, London, 1947; see also J M Richards, *An Introduction to Modern Architecture*, London, 1940; A Trystan Edwards, *Good and Bad Manners in Architecture*, London, 1945.

24 EULMC, letter of 17 May 1946 from Ling to Matthew.

25 Lecture by Louise Campbell at 'The Man-Made Future' conference (Percy Johnson-Marshall project), Edinburgh University, 2003.

26 EULMC, letter of 27 November 1946 from C S Mardall to Matthew; *Builder*, 24 May 1946; *AJ*, 15 May 2003, 18; J Summerson, *Architecture in England*, London, 1946, 38. Pimlico: *AJ*, 30 May 1946, 2 December 1950, 481–92, 12 August 1954, 189–94.

27 EULMC, letter from Abercrombie to RHM, 15 July 1946; EULMC, letter from Grieve to RHM, 5 November 1946; NAS, file DD1-21, September 1946 paper; EULMC, letter of 16 December 1946 from Reiach (on DHS headed paper) to RHM.

28 EULMC, letter from Reiach to RHM, 5 March 1947; *Builder*, 26 August 1949, 254–6; *Builder*, 16 September 1949, 359.

29 Interview with R Scott Morton, 1995; H Myles Wright and R G Medwin, *The Design of Nursery and Elementary Schools*, London, 1938; EULMC, letters of 3 January 1947 from Medwin to RHM; EULMC, letter of 2 March 1947 from Connell to RHM.

30 EULMC/LMA LCC records, Cabinet Office meetings files, notes of 13 March 1947 meeting; E V Marmaras, 'Central London in the 1950s', *Planning History*, vol. 19, 2, 1997, 12.

31 L Campbell (ed.), *To Build a Cathedral*, Coventry, 1987; L Campbell, *Coventry Cathedral*, Oxford, 1996; A Saint, *Towards a Social Architecture*, New Haven, 1987; LMA, file CL/GP/2/93, General Purposes South Bank Subcommittee, 24 July 1950, report by Clerk, 16 August 1950.

32 'Modern monumentality' debates: L Campbell, *Coventry Cathedral*, 273–4; J Ockman, *Architecture Culture 1943–1968*, New York, 1993, 27–30, 47–54; L Mumford, *City Development, Studies in Disintegration and Renewal*, London, 1946; L Campbell, lecture at 'Man-Made Future' conference, Edinburgh University, 2003; *Architectural Review*, September 1948, 117–28.

33 Ockman, *Architecture Culture*, 82.

34 Neo-Romantic movement: M Yorke, *The Spirit of Place*, London, 1988, 14; D Mellor, *A Paradise Lost*, London, 1987; M Garlake, *New Art, New World*, New Haven, 1998; J Piper, *British Romantic Artists*, London, 1942; B Appleyard, *The Pleasures of Peace*, London, 1989.

35 Volker Welter, *Biopolis*, Cambridge, MA, 2002; EULMC file MS2536, notes for May 1970 talk at RIBA by Williams-Ellis.

36 S E Rasmussen, *London, the Unique City* (English translation), London, 1937.

37 Planetarium: EULMC/LMA, LCC records, Cabinet Office meetings files, notes of 13 March 1947 meeting; Centre for musical activities: EULMC, text of RHM lecture to Devon and Cornwall Society of Architects, 27 March 1953.

38 *Builder*, 5 July 1946, 5–6; lecture by R Hewison at Twentieth Century Society conference, October 1992, 'Refashioning the Fifties'.

39 EULMC, notes by RHM of meeting with Nicholson, 27 January 1947; EULMC file MS2536, notes for May 1970 talk at RIBA by C Williams-Ellis. Brief by council: LMA, file CL/GP/2/96, General Purposes Committee papers, 16 June 1947. Festival of Britain (general): *The Story of the Festival of Britain*, London, 1951; E Harwood and A Powers, *Twentieth Century Architecture 5, The Festival of Britain*, London, 2001; M Banham and B Hiller (eds), *A Tonic to the Nation*, London, 1976; I Cox, *The South Bank Exhibition, Festival of Britain Guide*, London, 1951.

40 'Bare list': EULMC, text of RHM lecture to Liverpool University Architectural Society, 23 November 1951. Budden: EULMC, letter of 5 July 1947 from Matthew to Budden.

41 EULMC, July 1947 letters to Council Leader and Chair of

General Purposes Committee; *Göteborgs Konserthus*, Göteborg, 1939.

42 City Building Committee, Göteborgs Konserthus, October 1935; see also hall at Malmö, *Builder*, 25 October 1946, 420–2. EULMC, Festival Hall cuttings file, 1946, roneoed drawings of proposed Radiohuset. See also M Forsyth, *Buildings for Music*, Cambridge, 1985, 272–5, 329–35.

43 EULMC, letter of 29 August 1947 from Matthew to Allen; EULMC, text of RHM lecture to Liverpool University Architectural Society, 23 November 1951.

44 'Not a difficult decision': EULMC, text of RHM lecture to Liverpool University Architectural Society, 23 November 1951. LMA, file LCC/Min/6490, papers of General Purposes Committee, May–July 1948. 'Lying flat': interview with SRM, 1995.

45 Interview with SRM, 1995.

46 'Dudok' manner: interview with P Moro, 1995.

47 Interviews with A Ling and Percy Johnson-Marshall, 1987.

48 Reiach discussions: LMA, minutes and presented papers of General Purposes Committee, 12 July 1948, 7 October 1948, and 4 December 1948 report by Matthew to South Bank Subcommittee. R Scott Morton, *Alan Reiach: A Memoir*, Edinburgh, 1989.

49 Saint, *Towards a Social Architecture*; J L Martin, B Nicholson, N Gabo (eds), *Circle*, London, 1937; J L Martin and S Speight, *The Flat Book*, London, 1939; P Carolin and T Dannatt, *Architecture, Education and Research*, London, 1996, 19; A Powers, *Serge Chermayeff*, London, 2001, 97–103.

50 *Builder*, 8 February 1946, 137; F J Osborn (ed.), *Making Plans*, London, 1942, 13.

51 Interview with W Allen, 1996; LMA, papers of General Purposes Committee, 12 July 1948; *Builder*, 28 May 1948; T Dannatt, 'Towards a new order', in Carolin and Dannatt, *Architecture, Education and Research*, 13–25; Martin and Speight, *The Flat Book*; LMA, papers of General Purposes Committee, 12 July 1948; *Builder*, 28 May 1948; A Powers, 'Sir Leslie Martin', *Twentieth Century Society Newsletter*, September 2000; interview with W Allen, 1996.

52 LMA, file LCC/Min/6491; EULMC, file MS2537, draft of RHM lecture at Heriot-Watt University Symposium on Aesthetics, 1 August 1974.

53 'One of the historical buildings': LMA, LCC General Purposes Committee presented papers, report of 23 August 1948 by Architect for meeting of 4 October 1948. Approvals: LMA, file LCC/Min/6491. Acoustic advisers: EULMC file MS2537, draft of RHM lecture for Heriot-Watt University Symposium on Aesthetics, 1 August 1974; 'The South Bank concert hall', *Builder*, 17 December 1948, 713; 'Reverberation', *Builder*, 8 April 1949, 434.

54 *JRIBA*, December 1948, 72; *JRIBA*, August 1949, 436 (acoustics article by W Allen).

55 M Glendinning, 'Teamwork or masterwork? The design and reception of the Royal Festival Hall', *Architectural History*, 2003, 299; M Glendinning, 'The Royal Festival Hall: a postscript', *Architectural History*, 2005, 323–6.

56 Glendinning, 'Teamwork or masterwork?', 295, 299.

57 LMA file CL/GP/2; Glendinning, 'Teamwork or masterwork?', 294.

58 EULMC, text of RHM lecture to Liverpool University Architectural Society, 23 November 1951; LMA file AR/BR/16/LA/0348/C/TP, memorandum of 24 August 1948 from A G Ling; W Allen, *JRIBA*, August 1949; interviews with W Allen and L Martin, 1995; LMA file LCC/Min/6491; P Parkin, W Allen, H Purkis, W Scholes, 'The acoustics of the Royal Festival Hall, London', October 1952 (DSIR paper); H Bagenal, 'Concert halls', *JRIBA*, January 1950; N Bullock, *Building the Post-War World*, London, 2002, 62–3. Four alternative arrangements of the required accommodation were evaluated; on the opposition of Parkin and others to the fan shape, see also P H Parkin et al., *JRIBA*, December 1948, 70–6; *JRIBA*, January 1949, 126–9.

59 EULMC, text of RHM lecture to Liverpool University Architectural Society, 23 November 1951; interviews with W Allen, and P Moro, 1995.

60 LMA, reports dated 7 October 1948, 4 December 1948 in presented papers for General Purposes (South Bank) Subcommittee; *AJ*, 9 February 1950; interviews with Percy Johnson-Marshall, 1987, and with L Martin and W Allen, 1995.

61 *AJ*, 9 February 1950; interview with P Moro, 1995.

62 LMA, report dated 1 December 1948 in presented papers for General Purposes (South Bank) Subcommittee of 7 December 1948; interview with W Allen, 1995.

63 LMA file LCC/Min/6491.

64 Letter from Sir A Derbyshire to Lord Esher, 13 November 1997. November 1949 scheme: interview with W Allen, 1995; LMA file LCC/Min/6491, 1 December 1948 report to General Purposes (South Bank) Subcommittee meeting of 7 December 1948.

65 LMA file CL/GP/2/96, joint report 9 February 1949 to General Purposes (South Bank) Subcommittee and papers of subcommittee meetings, 6 and 7 December 1948 and 14 February 1949; interview with W Allen, 1995; *Evening News*, 29 April 1949 (news cutting, EULMC); 'Design of Thames concert hall', *The Times*, 30 April 1949 (news cutting, EULMC).

66 *Evening Standard*, 29 April 1949; *The Times*, 30 April 1949; 'The South Bank concert hall', *Builder*, 6 May 1949, 547–52.

67 Interviews with P Moro and L Martin, 1995.

68 *AJ*, June 1951, 170–1; interviews with P Moro and L Martin, 1995.

69 Interviews with P Moro and L Martin.

70 'Frenzy of energy': EULMC, text of RHM lecture to Liverpool University Architectural Society, 23 November 1951.

71 EULMC, manuscript diary of 1949 US trip. The trip served the function of an 'escape mechanism'.

72 EULMC, letter of 9 August 1949 from C E Nicholson to Matthew in Chicago.

73 EULMC, letter of 6 August 1949 from Martin to Matthew.

74 'All my energies': EULMC, letter of 30 December 1949 from Matthew to Wyndham Gooden. Attlee speech: *The Times*, 13 October 1949 (news cutting, EULMC); *JRIBA*, August 1970, 345.

75 LPO condemned as 'Communist controlled organisation': LMA, file CL/GP/2/93, Conference on Concert Hall Musical Policy and Management, 7 July 1949. Naming fiasco LMA file CL/GP/2/92, letter of 6 October 1949, Matthew to Roberts; 30 January 1950 papers for South Bank Subcommittee; 2 February 1950, letter from LCC Clerk to Sir Alan Lascelles, Private Secretary to the King and 20 February 1950 reply; report to General Purposes Committee, 6 March 1950; South Bank Subcommittee, 13 March 1950.

76 J Eastwick-Field and J Stillman, *AJ*, 24 August 1950 (news cutting, EULMC).

77 Personal communication to author from Jules Lubbock, 2003.

78 Corbusier: Harwood and Powers, *Festival of Britain*, 8–10. Wright: interviews with LLM and L Martin, 1995; A Ashton, *An Architect Abroad*, Sydney, 1950, 81, 90–2.

79 Acoustic crisis: interview with W Allen, 1995; Parkin, Allen, Purkis and Scholes, 'The acoustics of the Royal Festival Hall' (DSIR October 1952 paper).

80 Checking: EULMC, text of RHM lecture to Liverpool University Architectural Society, 23 November 1951; interview with P Moro, 1995. Puppet theatre: letter from J O'Neill, 2006.

81 Shove appointment and difficulties: LMA, council meeting papers, 26 July 1949. Shove controversies: LMA, file CL/GP/2/93, papers for South Bank Subcommittee, 24 July 1950; report by Clerk, 16 August 1950; *Daily Express*, 4 May 1951 (news cutting, EULMC); LMA, file CL/GP/2/100, letter of 13 June 1951, 14 June 1951 Report by Clerk to General Purposes (Staff) Subcommittee; 2 July 1951 General Purposes Committee report; 30 July 1951 interview papers for General Manager; 10 February 1954, report by Clerk.

82 C Williams-Ellis note, EULMC, file MS2536, May 1970 text for talk at RIBA; EULMC, letter of 11 May 1951 from R Gardner-Medwin to RHM; *Daily Mirror*, 4 May 1951.

83 *JRIBA*, August 1949; H Morrison, 'The meaning of this year', *The Times Festival of Britain Supplement*, May 1951, 18; *Observer*, 6 May 1951; 'The Festival Hall: musical centre of London', *The Times*, 4 May 1951, 5; *News Chronicle*, 16 May 1951 and 9 May 1951; *Daily Dispatch*, 4 May 1951; Australian Broadcasting Corporation weekly digest, 9 June 1951; *The Times*, 4 May 1951; *News Chronicle*, 16 May 1951; 'Our London correspondence', *Manchester Guardian*, 16 May 1951; *Daily Worker*, 4 May 1951. All of above in news cuttings, EULMC.

84 *The Times*, 4 May 1951; *News Chronicle*, 16 May 1951.

85 C Williams-Ellis, 'The new architecture', *Britain Today*, August 1954, 6–10; C Williams-Ellis, 'Idea and realization', in LCC, *Royal Festival Hall*, 1951, 13; Harwood and Powers (eds), *Festival of Britain*; J Drew, 'Introduction', *Architects' Yearbook 4*, London, 1951; R Lutyens, 'London's new concert hall', *Country Life*, 28 July 1950, 292; R Lutyens, 'Buildings on the South Bank', *Guardian*, 5 May 1951, 6; London County Council, *Royal Festival Hall*, London, 1951, 10; *The Times*, 4 May 1951 (news cutting, EULMC).

86 EULMC, letter from Moro to RHM, 1 April 1952; LMA, files LCC/GP/2/108, LCC/GP/2/99.

87 For hagiographic rhetoric see e.g. J McKean, *Royal Festival Hall*, London, 1992.

88 *JRIBA*, August 1970, 345.

89 General references to Royal Festival Hall: LCC, *Royal Festival Hall*, London, 1951; Festival Council, *The Story of the Festival of Britain 1951*, London, 1952; Michael Forsyth, *Buildings for Music*, Cambridge, 1985, 272–5, 349, 331; J Symons, *Royal Festival Hall, Concert Hall Notebook*, London, 2000; Royal Festival Hall, *Royal Festival Hall 1951–2001, Past, Present, Future*, London, 2001. Articles: *AJ*, 12 May 1949, 431–8, and 10 May 1951, 590–614; *JRIBA*, August 1949, 436 (acoustics), and April 1952, 196–204; *Architectural Design*, December 1949, 289–94, and January 1957, 25 (J L Martin); *Architectural Review*, June 1951, 336–94; 'The Royal Festival Hall', *Builder*, 25 May 1951, 730–53, and 19 May 1954, 500–1 (on the organ). *AJ* contract progress reports: 9 and 23 February 1950, 16 March 1950, 27 April 1950, 22 June 1950, 20 July 1950, 24 August 1950, 14 December 1950, 1 February 1951, 22 March 1951 (offprint news cuttings, EULMC). M Glendinning, 'Teamwork or masterwork? The design and reception of the Royal Festival Hall', *Architectural History*, 2003, 277–319; M Glendinning, 'The Royal Festival Hall: a postscript', *Architectural History*, 2005, 323–6.

Chapter 5

1 R Furneaux Jordan, *Architectural Review*, November 1956, 324; Lord Esher, manuscript draft for *Dictionary of National Biography* entry, 1986 (per Sir A Derbyshire).

2 K Campbell obituary, *The Times*, 30 July 2002, 30; LMA, file LCC/Min/6492; EULMC, letter of 6 August 1949 from Martin to RHM.

3 EULMC, 1949 plans and papers for Woodberry Down and Poplar Health Centre, and pamphlet, Stadt Wien, *Stadtrandschule Leopoldau*, Vienna, 1949.

4 P Abercrombie, 'Twenty years after', *JRIBA*, March 1952, 157; A Saint, lecture to 1992 'Refashioning the Fifties' conference.

5 LMA file LCC/Min/11620, LCC/Min/6491; presented papers of Town Planning Committee, 23 May 1949; presented papers for General Purposes Committee, 29 November 1948; J Forshaw and P Abercrombie, *The County of London Plan*, London, 1943, 21; E J Carter and E Goldfinger, *The*

County of London Plan Explained, London, 1945; L Mumford, *The Plan of London County, Rebuilding Britain Series*, 12, London, 1945.

6   A Downs (ed.), *Peter Shepheard*, London, 2004, 60–1; Glendinning and Muthesius, *Tower Block*, 97–100; D Schubert, 'Origins of the neighbourhood units idea in Great Britain and Germany', *Planning History*, vol. 17, 3, 1995, 32; RHM, 'Regional planning and founding of new towns', *Der Aufbau* (Vienna), March 1948.

7   RHM appreciation of F Mears, *Glasgow Herald*, 27 January 1953.

8   EULMC, text of RHM lecture at Oxford, 21 January 1947; P Abercrombie, 'Where does planning stand today?', text of 1955 lecture, *Journal of the Town Planning Institute*, January 1956.

9   EULMC, text of RHM lecture of 26 June 1947 to Batti-Wallah Society.

10 EULMC, RHM lecture to Batti-Wallah Society.

11 Glendinning and Muthesius, *Tower Block*, 27, 39, 46, 66, 373.

12 EULMC, text of RHM lecture at Oxford, 21 January 1947; *Builder*, 28 March 1947; LMA file LCC/Min/11620, presented papers for Town Planning Committee, 23 May 1949, Report on Draft Development Plan and new Planning Standards.

13 S W Goldhagen and P Legault, *Anxious Modernisms*, Montreal, 2000, 13; LMA, file LCC/Min/6491, presented papers for General Purposes Committee, 29 November 1948; LMA, file LCC/Min/11621, report of 6 June 1949; *Architectural Review*, November 1956, 317.

14 A Ling, 'Peasant architecture in the northern provinces of Spain', *JRIBA*, 27 June 1936, 845. Interview with Sir P Powell, 1987; Percy Johnson-Marshall, *The Listener*, 24 November 1949.

15 W A Storrer, *Marcel Breuer*, London, 1956; *Archis*, May 1996, 21; Francesco Passanti, 'The vernacular, Modernism and Le Corbusier', *JSAH*, December 1997, 438 ff.; I Hyman, *Marcel Breuer, The Career and the Buildings*, 2001; M Macleod, 'Urbanism and Utopia', PhD thesis, Princeton, 1985. 'Organic' MoMo variations in Brazil etc: H Segawa, 'The reception of the Brazilian tradition', lecture to DOCOMOMO 2002 conference, Paris; H R Hitchcock, *Latin American Architecture since 1945*, New York, 1955; J M Rovira, *Jose Luis Sert*, Electa, Milan, 2003.

16 *AJ*, 31 October 1966, 36; *Journal of Design History*, vol. 11, 1, 1998. Bergamo and Syrkus: Ockman, *Architecture Culture 1943–1978*, 1993.

17 Post-war English Picturesque/Townscape: J M Richards, *The Castles on the Ground*, London, 1945 (and review by C Williams-Ellis, *Town and Country Planning*, Spring 1947); J M Richards, *Memoirs of an Unjust Fella*, London, 1980; K Stansfield, 'Thomas Sharp', in G E Cherry (ed.), *Pioneers in British Planning*, London, 1981; A Powers, 'Brave New Britain', lecture in 'Refashioning the Fifties' conference,

1992.

18 LMA, file LCC/Min/11679, report of 22 November 1951 by Architect for Town Planning Committee meeting of 26 November 1951.

19 EULMC, RHM texts of lecture of 21 January 1947 at Oxford and of 'Replanning Britain' lecture of October 1947 in Vienna; EULMC, Joint report of 10 April 1946 by Architect, Director of Housing and Valuer, Chief Engineer; LCC, *Stepney and Poplar Reconstruction Area, Report*, c.1948.

20 EULMC, joint press notice, 6 June 1950.

21 Glendinning and Muthesius, *Tower Block*, 116–7.

22 LMA, minutes of General Purposes Committee, 7 January 1949; Festival Council, *The Story of the Festival of Britain 1951*, London, 1952, 9.

23 Chrisp Street: LMA, file LCC/Min/11621, Joint Report of 6 June 1950, and report of 18 June 1949 for Town Planning Committee by Architect, Engineer, Director of Housing on Chrisp St Market; file LCC/Min/11620, memo of June 1951 by Architect, Director of Housing and Health Officer on Health Centre, East India Dock Road; *The Sphere*, 18 November 1950; HM Dunnett, *Guide to the Exhibition of Town Planning and Building Research*, London, 1951.

24 EULMC, text of RHM broadcast to schools, 1 June 1951; EULMC, text of RHM lecture, 'Housing in redevelopment areas', to Housing Centre conference, 6 June 1951; EULMC, text of RHM lecture to September 1952 IFHTP congress.

25 Glendinning and Muthesius, *Tower Block*, 104.

26 EULMC, file LCC/Min/6490, report of 9 July 1948 by Clerk; EULMC, RHM report of 26 June 1948 on Sweden visit, letter of 21 June 1948 from H Manzoni to RHM and reply; Glendinning and Muthesius, *Tower Block*, 25; EULMC, file LCC/Min/6490, report of 2 October 1948 to Housing and Public Health Committee, on organisation of Walker's staff.

27 J M Richards, *Memoirs of an Unjust Fella*, 126–7. Boyne: *The Times*, 18 October 2006, 72.

28 *AJ*, 10 March 1949, 17 March 1949, 19 May 1949 (Mills and Richardson), 9 June 1949 (Gardner-Medwin); see also *Builder*, 13 May 1949 and 27 May 1949.

29 Glendinning and Muthesius, *Tower Block*, 106.

30 Interview with Whitfield Lewis, 1987.

31 Interview with E Denington, 1987.

32 EULMC, letter from Martin to RHM, late July 1949.

33 EULMC, text of RHM lecture on research and development at Architectural Association, 3 January 1951.

34 *ABN*, 2 June 1950, 561 for picture of 'Mr Whitfield Lewis's team'; *Architectural Review*, November 1956.

35 Glendinning and Muthesius, *Tower Block*, 104–5.

36 EULMC, text of RHM lecture on R&D at Architectural Association, 3 January 1951.

37 E Hollamby and D Gregory Jones, 'The structure and personality of the LCC Architect's Department', *Architecture and Building*, May 1957, 171–82.

38 Architecture and Planning Group of the Society for Cultural Relations between the British Commonwealth and the USSR, *Architecture of the USSR*, March 1948, foreword by A Ling.

39 Interviews with E Hollamby and A Ling, 1987; lecture by A Saint at 'Refashioning the Fifties' conference, 1992.

40 C Penn, *Builder*, 26 March 1948, 357–69.

41 Loweth: *Builder*, 23 May 1947, 489; *Builder*, 26 August 1949, 265; *Builder*, 16 September 1949, 360; *Builder*, 23 September 1949, 391; *Builder*, 9 October 1949, 455; Yale University Press, *Endpapers*, Winter 1999, 1–3.

42 *Builder*, 2 December 1949, 727–8.

43 P Hennessy, *The Secret State, Whitehall and the Cold War*, London, 2002; EULMC, letter of 7 July 1950 from Abercrombie to RHM; Saint, lecture to 'Refashioning the Fifties' 1992 conference.

44 *Building Design*, 27 June 1965 (obituary).

45 R Schneider, R Stregers, *Glück Stadt Raum in Europa 1945 bis 2000*, Basel, 2002; RIBA, *Exhibition of Danish Architecture Today*, 1950; RIBA, *Switzerland Planning and Building Exhibition*, London, 1946; Svenska Arkitekters Riksförbund, *Ny Arkitektur i Sverige*, Stockholm, 1961; S Silow (ed.), *Kooperativa Förbundets Arkitektkontor, 1935–49, Part 1*, and *1925–1949, Part 2*, both Stockholm, 1949; 'Contemporary architecture in Sweden', *Builder*, 22 January 1946; Swedish Design Association and Göteborg City Building Authority, *Utställningen Bo Bättre*, Guldheden, Göteborg, August-September 1945; 'The new empiricism', *Architectural Review*, 1947, 199ff.; G E Kidder Smith, *Sweden Builds*, Stockholm, 1950; H Ibelings, *De moderne Jaren Vijftig en Zestig*, Rotterdam, 1995; J P Mieras, *Na-oorlogse Bouwkunst in Nederland*, Amsterdam, 1954; Bouwcentrum Rotterdam, *Building in the Netherlands*, Rotterdam, 1953; RIBA/Bund deutscher Architekten, *German Architecture Today*, 1955.

46 EULMC, letter of 26 March 1953 from Abercrombie to Matthew; interviews with Whitfield Lewis, 1987, and J Partridge, 1988.

47 Interview with J Partridge, 1988.

48 *Builder*, 25 March 1949; EULMC, letter from E A Sharp to LCC Clerk, 28 December 1949.

49 LMA, file LCC/Min/11620, report of 6 June 1949 to Town Planning Committee by RHM; interview with R Stjernstedt, 1988.

50 Interview with E Denington, 1988.

51 EULMC, text of lecture by RHM at September 1952 IFHTP congress; LMA, LCC council minutes, meeting of 21 November 1950 and report by RHM, 25 October 1950.

52 LMA, LCC Housing committee presented papers, 11 April 1951 note by RHM, and 7 March 1951 report by RHM on new type plans; Glendinning and Muthesius, *Tower Block*, 53.

53 LMA, LCC Housing Committee minutes, presented papers, 14 January 1953 memo by RHM.

54 Trinity Road, Roehampton: Glendinning and Muthesius, *Tower Block*, 55–63 and 374; LMA, LCC Housing and Planning (Joint Development) Subcommittee, 25 June 1952; cf. Le Corbusier, *The Marseilles Block*, London, 1953.

55 EULMC, letter of 22 January 1952 from Whitfield Lewis to RHM.

56 LMA file LCC/Min/11670, presented papers to 18 June 1951 Town Planning (Development Plan) Subcommittee, and presented papers for the Housing Committee of 24 January 1951 and 5 March 1952.

57 J M Richards on Matthew's LCC as 'one of the most powerful forces in English architecture: a great empire in which the concrete never set': Richards, *Memoirs of an Unjust Fella*, 195; *Architectural Review*, November 1956.

58 EULMC, letter of 5 May 1952 from RHM to Elspeth Fraser; EULMC, RHM notes of meeting of 10 June 1952 with Kent County Council; LMA, file LCC/Min/11700, paper to Development Plan Subcommittee of 16 February 1953 on proposed cut in zoned density.

59 LCC, *First Day of Public Local Inquiry on the County of London Development Plan 1951, 29 September 1952, Central Hall, Westminster, before K S Dodd, Chief Inspector of Special Inquiries*; LMA, file LCC/Min/11700, papers of Town Planning (Development Plan) Subcommittee, 26 January 1953, and file AR/TP/4/46.

60 P Vago, *Une vie intense*, Bruxelles, 2000.

61 *B*, 4 October 1946, 339–40.

62 Syrkus: Morgan and Naylor, *Contemporary Architects*, 880–2; J Roguska, *Helena i Szymon Syrkusowie*, Warszawa, 2000, 114.

63 EULMC, letter of 27 July 1950 from Abercrombie to B Blackshaw, *A Comparative Study of The Utilisation of Space in Current Types of Dwellings in Fourteen European Countries, 1946–9* (report to UN Economic Commission for Europe, Industry and Materials Subcommittee, Housing Subcommittee), Geneva, 1951.

64 EULMC, RHM manuscript diary of 1949 US trip.

65 Waterhouse inaugural address as PRIBA: *JRIBA*, December 1948, 55–8; UNO headquarters, *Builder*, 15 August 1947, 176–7.

66 EULMC, text of 9 June 1950 RHM lecture at Kingsway Hall, and of 28 November 1950 lecture at RIBA; EULMC, November 1949 correspondence with J C Weston of DSIR; *Builder*, 19 August 1949 and 16 September 1949, 361–2.

67 EULMC, letter of 23 September 1949 from Matthew to Dennis Winston, University of Sydney.

68 EULMC, letter from Clarence Stein to RHM, 14 September 1952.

69 Saint, *Towards a Social Architecture*, 245–6.

70 Richards, *Memoirs of an Unjust Fella*; L Esher, *A Broken Wave*, London, 1981; interview with Maurice Brown, 1995.

71 Esher, *Broken Wave*, 1981.

72 EULMC, undated letter from Harold Macmillan to RHM on CBE, 1952.

73 RHM article in *Quarterly of the Royal Incorporation of Architects in Scotland*, August 1952.

74 EULMC, text of RHM lecture to Essex Chapter, January 1952; to Edinburgh Architectural Association, 13 March 1952; at Architecture Club Supper Debate, 18 March 1953; to Ministry of Education Conference on 'Problems of the Local Authority Architect', 1 October 1953; to Manchester Luncheon Club, 18 February 1955; to Oxford students about public architecture, 15 January 1953; to Institute of Public Administration, London, 27 March 1961.

75 Saint, *Towards a Social Architecture*, 245–6.

76 EULMC, C Stein to RHM, 14 September 1952.

77 References on public–private debate: EULMC, letter from J M Richards to D E E Gibson, 4 December 1951; J M Richards to Percy Marshall, 14 December 1951; *AJ*, 31 January 1952; letter of 12 March 1952 from John Wellborn Root to RHM on organisation of Holabird and Root; notes of *AJ* guest editors' meeting of 31 March 1952; *AJ*, 15 May 1952; *AJ*, 14 August 1952; notes of 1 September 1952 editors' meeting; *AJ*, 23 October 1952; letter of 19 December 1952 from Cleeve Barr to RHM; E E Hollamby and D Gregory Jones, 'The structure and personality of the LCC Architect's Department', *Architecture and Building*, May 1957, 171–82.

78 *Builder*, 2 December 1949, 728.

79 EULMC, notes on 29 October 1952 discussion on planning, prior to 18 December 1952 *Architects' Journal*.

80 EULMC, notes on 29 October 1952 discussion on planning.

81 EULMC, text of RHM lecture of 22 May 1959 to RIBA Symposium on Urban Renewal.

82 EULMC, text of RHM lecture of 14 December 1962 to Edinburgh Master Builders. Interviews with RAM, December 2005, and with J O'Neill, 2007.

83 Interview with RAM, December 2005.

84 *Weekly Scotsman*, 13 October 1949 ('A Scot plans the new London').

85 Interview with SRM, 1995.

86 Thistle Foundation, *Response to Proposed Listing under the Planning (Scotland) Act 1997*, Edinburgh, 2002, 9–13.

87 Interview with SRM, 1995.

88 EULMC, minutes of SPAR group meeting of 9 May 1951; letter of 18 October 1951 from Abercrombie to RHM; letter of 6 January 1952 from Gardner Medwin to RHM.

89 EULMC, letter from Abercrombie to RHM, 20 April 1952; RHM letter to McCalman, 24 February 1953; manuscript commentary of March 1953 by RHM; letter of 20 April 1953 from Jeffryes to RHM.

90 EULMC, text of RHM lecture of 18 February 1949, 'Building design in Scotland', to Saltire Society London branch, and 1949 review of Reiach and Hurd's *Building Scotland*.

91 EULMC, letter of 30 October 1949 from RHM to Medwin.

92 EULMC, letter of 14 September 1950 from RHM to Medwin; EULMC, letter of 26 May 1951 from Medwin to RHM.

93 EULMC, text of RHM valedictory speech of April 1953 at County Hall, and letter of 16 December 1951 from L Budden to RHM.

94 Richards, *Memoirs of an Unjust Fella*, 275; *Builder*, 15 October 1948, 449; interview with Ralph Cowan, February 2006; EULMC, letter of 11 September 1947 from E A A Rowse to RHM, letter of 26 September 1947 from Medwin to RHM, 23 July 1948 copy of Prospectus for Joint Appointment of Professor of Architecture, Edinburgh University, and Head of the School of Architecture at ECA, sent by Edinburgh University to RHM; *JRIBA*, February 1949, 162–7 (lecture by Professor R Gordon Brown).

95 EULMC, letter of 10 October 1951 from G Douglas Matthew to RHM; letter of 22 May 1952 from Sir E Appleton to RHM, and reply by RHM, about committee meeting of 26 June 1952; letter of 14 June 1952 from David Talbot Rice to RHM; ECA prospectus for 1952–3.

96 EULMC, letter of 17 June 1952 from Kininmonth to RHM; letter of 9 July 1952 from T Stewart to RHM about income tax calculations.

97 EULMC, letter of 10 September 1952 to RHM from Charles Stewart, Secretary of Edinburgh University, formally offering him the chair of architecture.

98 EULMC, letter of 19 September 1952 from C H James to RHM.

99 EULMC, letter of 8 December 1952 from RHM to Edinburgh University Assistant Secretary; letter of 18 March 1953 from Kininmonth to RHM – marked 'Confidential'.

100 EULMC, letter from H Fenwick to RHM, 6 January 1953, and reply, 12 January 1953.

101 EULMC, letters of 6 January and 25 January 1953 from Melville to RHM, and reply of 12 January 1953; letter of 17 March 1953 from T Spaven to RHM.

102 Visit by Tito: *The Times*, 18 March 1953, 14. EULMC, letter of 9 January 1953 from RHM to Roberts.

103 LMA, General Purposes Committee minutes, report of 30 March 1953 by Mishcon; April 1953 valedictory speech by RHM in County Hall; Council minutes, 21 April 1953, speeches by Mishcon and N Kenyon; EULMC, letter of 1 May 1953 by T G Randall to RHM; *London Town*, May 1953.

104 EULMC, letter of 13 January 1953 from Medwin to RHM.

105 Catherine Croft, report on 'LCC Day' at AA, *Building Design*, 22 March 2002, 20.

106 Interview with Martin Richardson, 1989. 'Ultimate finishing school': Catherine Croft, report on 'LCC Day', *Building Design*, 22 March 2002, 20.

107 Glendinning and Muthesius, *Tower Block*, 187 and 266.

108 Congratulations on appointment: for instance EULMC, letter of 13 January 1953 from Medwin to RHM.

109 'Scottish cavalier': Saint, *Towards a Social Architecture*, 1987, 247. See for instance RHM in 1958, Glendinning and Muthesius, *Tower Block*, 110.

Chapter 6

1   *JRIBA*, August 1970, 344.
2   Interviews with W Allen, 1997; SRM, 1995; Mary Tindall, 1997; Janet O'Neill, 2007.
3   Interview with J O'Neill, 2007.
4   Interview with SRM, 1995; EULMC, letter of 2 March 1977 from Stuart to LLM, and attached note by Stuart, 'Notes regarding irrelevant points & misleading statements made by Lorna on telephone'.
5   Interviews with J O'Neill, 2007, and Mary Tindall, 1997.
6   Interviews with LLM, 1997, and RAM, 2005.
7   Interview with SRM, 1995.
8   EULMC, letter from RHM to J Patterson, 15 May 1953.
9   AHRC Sir Basil Spence Project, Report by Clive Fenton, February 2005; meetings with Lorna included 6 July 1954 and 4 January 1955.
10 EULMC, text of RHM lecture, 'Design appreciation', to Council of Industrial Design Scottish Committee, at Moray House, Edinburgh, 14 November 1953.
11 Interview with RAM, 2005.
12 Interview with LLM, 1995.
13 EULMC files and interview with RAM, 2005.
14 A Slaven and S Checkland (eds), *Dictionary of Scottish Business Biography*, vol. 2, 1990.
15 Interview with J O'Neill, 2007.
16 Draft of 12 August 1997 for *Dictionary of National Biography* entry on RHM by Lord Esher (courtesy of Sir A Derbyshire).
17 *JSAH*, December 1997; *Builder*, 15 December 1948, 448–50, address by R Neutra to AA.
18 Interview with P Nuttgens, 1995; *AJ*, 9 October, 1952.
19 J Dunbar-Nasmith, 'Memories of Edinburgh College of Art', *Decades 6*, 2006. G Brown troubles: interview with P Nuttgens, 1995.
20 Interview with P Nuttgens, 1995; EULMC, text of 14 October 1975 lecture at RIBA by P Nuttgens; P Nuttgens, *The Art of Learning*, Lewes, 2000, 56.
21 EULMC, text of RHM lecture to Aberdeen Society of Architects, 9 March 1954; *Guardian*, 5 April 1954, 7; EULMC, text of RHM lecture at Reform Club, 13 October 1953.
22 EULMC, text of RHM lecture to students, Edinburgh University Architecture Department, 25 April 1968.
23 Interview with P Nuttgens, 1997.
24 Interviews with P Nuttgens, 1995, R Cowan, 2006, H McIlveen, 2004.
25 Interviews with Cowan, 2006, and W Campbell, 2003; EULMC, letter of 15 May 1953 from RHM to J Patterson.
26 EULMC, letter of 25 May 1953 from RHM to Stirrat Johnson-Marshall (hereafter SJM); EULMC, letter from RHM to D E E Gibson, 17 March 1954; EULMC, text of RHM lecture at RIBA, 3 November 1964, 'Introducing Sir Donald Gibson'.
27 EULMC, letters of 2 September 1954 from RHM to ECA Chairman of Governors, 3 August 1954 from RHM to Holford, 2 December 1954 from RHM to Appleton, and 16 March 1955 from Appleton to RHM.
28 Interviews with R Cowan, 2006, and P Nuttgens, 1995; EULMC, text of RHM lecture of 25 April 1968 to Edinburgh University Architecture Department students.
29 Interview with H McIlveen, 2004.
30 Interview with LLM, 1998. Slightly different version of story: *JRIBA*, August 1970, 345. EULMC, text of RHM lecture of 25 April 1968 to Edinburgh University Architecture Department students.
31 EULMC, letters from L Budden to RHM, 28 January 1954, 20 February 1954; letters from Matthew to Budden, 1 February 1954, 4 March 1954.
32 'The New Adam – unoriginal sin?', *The Student*, 27 January 1955, 10–11; P Nuttgens, 'The architecture of compromise', *The Student*, 10 February 1955, 30–4.
33 See also Nuttgens, *The Art of Learning*.
34 EULMC, letter of 9 March 1955 from Kininmonth and reply of 14 March 1955.
35 EULMC, text of RHM 26 November 1956 lecture at Galashiels, 'Architecture and the present day'. Cf. the slightly later, London-based 'Anti-ugly action': G Stamp, 'The Anti-Uglies', lecture to Twentieth Century Society Annual General Meeting, Kensington Library, 2 June 2006.
36 EULMC, letter of 19 September from Leeds Polytechnic Registrar to RHM.
37 New ECA School of Architecture building, 1961: interview of January 2006 with R Cowan.
38 EULMC, letter of December 1953 from Ministry of Education to RHM.
39 Interview with P Nuttgens, 1995: the thesis was entitled 'Planning and architecture of the settlements of the North-East of Scotland'.
40 Interview with P Nuttgens, 1995.
41 EULMC, letters of 22 November 1955 from RHM to W Wurster and of 9 December 1955 from RHM to E A Sharp.
42 Interview with P Nuttgens, 1995.
43 Interviews with Sir J Dunbar-Nasmith and Hugh McIlveen, 2004.
44 Interview with Hugh McIlveen, 2004.
45 Interview with P Nuttgens, 1995; interview with W Allen, 1997.
46 EULMC, notes for 24 May 1955 lecture to EAA.
47 EULMC, letter of 17 March 1954 from RHM to L G MacDougall; EULMC, letter of March 1954 from RHM to A B Gardner.
48 EULMC, letters of 4 August 1954 from RA Bannerman to RHM, 16 August 1954 from Bill Spragg to RHM, and replies; interview with K Feakes, 2004.
49 Interview with T Spaven, 2004.
50 Interview with T Spaven, 2004.
51 *Scotsman*, 3 January 2000, 10; interview with J Dunbar-Nasmith, 2004.
52 Interview with Sir James Dunbar-Nasmith, 2004.

53 Interview with M Richards, 2003.

54 Letter of 1984 from J Dunbar-Nasmith to John Richards, courtesy of John Richards.

55 A Ravetz, *The Government of Space*, London, 1986; G Cherry (ed.), *Pioneers in British Planning*; *Architect and Building News*, 29 November 1955, 855–8; *AJ*, 12 January 1956, 41–7; see also Ministry of Housing and Local Government, *Design in Town and Village*, London, 1953.

56 P Oliver (ed.), *Encyclopaedia of Vernacular Architecture of the World*, Cambridge, 1997; P Nuttgens, 'Regional planning in the 18th century', *Prospect*, 17, 1960, 20–6.

57 M Casciato, 'Neo-Realism in Italian architecture', in Goldhagen and Legault, *Anxious Modernisms*, 25–54; E Rogers, editorial in *Casabella-Continuita*, April–May 1957; M Tafuri, *History of Italian Architecture, 1944–1985*, Cambridge, MA, 1989. English neo-Romantics: N Pevsner, *The Englishness of English Art*, London, 1955, 5–25; J Gloag, *The English Tradition in Design*, London, 1959; M Yorke, *The Spirit of Place*, London, 1988.

58 *Builder*, 3 November 1953; EULMC, text of RHM lecture of 18 February 1955 to Manchester Luncheon Club; Simon Houfe, A Powers, J Wilton-Ely, *Sir Albert Richardson*, London, 1999.

59 EULMC, text of lecture of 14 March 1956 to Institution of Civil Engineers, Edinburgh; EULMC, text of lecture, 'The influences of environment', to COID conference, Edinburgh, 14 November 1953.

60 Interview with P Nuttgens, 1995; *Sunday Herald*, 19 May 2002, 3; interview with LLM, 1997.

61 EULMC, text of lecture to COID conference, 14 November 1953; *Builder*, 4 December 1953 and 26 November 1956, 'Architecture and the present day', February 1960, 'Scotland and the Modern Movement in architecture'; EULMC, text of 18 February 1949 lecture to Saltire Society.

62 EULMC, text of RHM Burns Night 'Immortal memory' toast, 1954.

63 EULMC, letter of 1954 from RHM to Vasilides.

64 EULMC, letter of 5 June 1953 to NTS; letter of 4 September 1953 from RHM to D L Macintyre, Ministry of Works.

65 *Imperial Calendars*, 1950s/1960s; EULMC, letter of 10 August 1954 from RHM to Abercrombie).

66 EULMC, letter of 29 July 1953 from RHM to J Shearer; EULMC, file MS2533, letter of 12 March 19 from Angus Acworth to Matthew and reply of 28 March 1956.

67 EULMC, letter of 7 November 1954 from C Sempill to RHM; Ian Gow, Report of NTS Craigievar Subcommittee, 5 November 1993.

68 EULMC, text of RHM Burns Night 'Immortal memory' toast, 1954, and of RHM lecture of 29 October 1953, 'Architecture in evolution'.

69 EULMC, text of RHM lecture of 25 April 1968 to students, Edinburgh University Department of Architecture.

70 J D Richards, article in Wiley *Encyclopaedia of Architecture*, 353.

71 *JRIBA*, August 1970, 346.

72 Interview with Spaven, 2004; EULMC, text of RHM lecture of 25 April 1968 to students, Edinburgh University Department of Architecture.

73 EULMC, text of RHM lecture of 25 April 1968 to students at Edinburgh University Department of Architecture; *Scotsman*, 12 April 1956, 10.

74 Interview with Sir James Dunbar-Nasmith, 2004.

75 Interview with Sir James Dunbar-Nasmith, 2003.

76 *Builder*, 1 June 1956; *Scotsman*, 12 April 1956, 10; interviews with A Derbyshire and K Feakes, 2004; letter from A Derbyshire to L Esher, 13 September 1997 (courtesy of Sir A Derbyshire).

77 Interview with W Campbell, 2003; see also *AJ*, 5 July 1956, 221; *Prospect*, 104, Summer 1956, 12 ff.; *Builder*, 3 May 1957; *Scotsman*, 12 April 1956, 10. Summerson: *Scotsman*, 11 May 1957; letter of 1984 from J Dunbar-Nasmith to John Richards, courtesy of John Richards.

78 Peter Inch Catalogue 144, 2004, 27. Matthew's loan repayments to Cruden included, for example, £1,058 repaid in mid 1958.

79 RMJM Sighthill store (RMJMSS), Turnhouse job file, letters of 10 September 1953 and 26 May 1956. Allan also often worked in collaboration with Hew Lorimer, for example on the 27-ft-high Our Lady of the Isles statue, South Uist (Talbot Rice Gallery, Hew Lorimer, *Sculptor*, Edinburgh 1988). Matthew's detached house designs for Cruden included one of three bedrooms, one and two storeys, with flat terrace-roofed living/dining projection and integral garage (EULMC drawings).

80 RMJMSS job file; interview with Sir James Dunbar-Nasmith.

81 Letter of 1984 from J Dunbar-Nasmith to John Richards, courtesy of John Richards; interview with J Richards, 2003.

82 The project got under way in spring 1954 with a flurry of correspondence and meetings between Anderson, Matthew, Dunbar-Nasmith, Bill Allen of BRS, the British Electric Development Association, and a friend of Dunbar-Nasmith's at Ferranti (to advise on the gadgets).

83 RMJMSS, job file, minute of 16 March 1954 meeting, letter of 24 April 1954 from Anderson to RHM, letter of 8 June 1954; interview with Sir James Dunbar-Nasmith, 2004.

84 Interview with T Spaven, 2004; interview with Sir J Dunbar-Nasmith, 2004.

85 Interview with Sir James Dunbar-Nasmith, 2004; RMJMSS, Gogarbank file, letter from RHM to Anderson, 18 November 1954, and of 19 September 1955 from Moray County Council to Anderson.

86 Interview with Sir James Dunbar-Nasmith, 2004.

87 RMJMSS, Gogarbank file. Postwar heating: Glendinning and Muthesius, *Tower Block*, 14–21.

88 RMJMSS, Gogarbank file, early 1957 note by Dunbar-Nasmith, and note of 6 December 1958 from Anderson to Spaven.

Notes

89 Interviews with K Graham, 2003, and with T Spaven, 1995.

90 Interview with M Richards, 2003.

91 RMJMSS, Hawick file, letters of 1 April 1955 and 9 May 1955 from Burtons to RHM, and of 22 July 1955 from RHM to N Martin of Burtons in Leeds; interviews with T Spaven, 1995, and Sir J Dunbar-Nasmith, 2006.

92 RMJMSS, Hawick file, letter of 27 July 1955 from RHM to Burtons.

93 Interview with P Nuttgens, 1995.

94 RMJMSS, Hydro files, letters of 19 January 1952, 13 February 1953, and 11 March 1953 from Johnston to RHM.

95 RMJMSS, Hydro files, letters from Lawrie to RHM, 16 December 1954, and RHM to J Williamson, 5 April 1955.

96 Interview with T Spaven, 1995; RMJMSS, Hydro files, letter of 4 October 1954 from Fulton to RHM.

97 RMJMSS, Hydro Files, letter of 23 February 1955 from Lawrie to RHM.

98 Interview with T Spaven, 1995.

99 RMJMSS, Hydro Files, discussion with RHM, 6 August 1956; RHM letter to NSHEB 2 October 1956.

100 Letter of 13 September 1997 from A Derbyshire to Lord Esher; courtesy of Sir Andrew Derbyshire.

101 EULMC, text of RHM lecture of 14 March 1956 to the Institution of Civil Engineers, Edinburgh and East of Scotland branch. Marchwood: interview with Alan Wightman, 2004.

102 EULMC, 14 March 1957 paper to Ministry of Works, 'Design of a thermal power station'.

103 The initial Kincardine cost target in 1952 was £40m: EULMC, letter of 5 May 1953 from G F Kennedy to V Pask, British Electricity Authority, and reply of 7 May 1953.

104 EULMC, paper of 14 March 1957 to Ministry of Works.

105 Interview with T Spaven, 1995.

106 EULMC, paper of 14 March 1957; RMJMSS, Kincardine file, paper of 26 March 1954 to ICI Research Department; RMJMSS, letters of February 1955 from RHM to W Allen.

107 Letter from Derbyshire to L Esher, 13 September 1997, courtesy of A Derbyshire.

108 Interview with J Dunbar-Nasmith, 2004.

109 Mid 1955 advice on distillery buildings at Glenlivet: RMJMSS, Glenlivet file, 1955.

110 RMJMSS, Aberdeen University file, 1953-5.

111 RMJMSS, Aberdeen University file, note of 15 September 1955 by W Angus; RMJMSS, letter of 8 March 1956 from RHM to W S Angus, and drawings by M Brown for 23 August 1956 University Court meeting; interview with P Nuttgens, 1995.

112 C Fenton, 'A century of change in George Square', *Book of the Old Edinburgh Club*, new series, vol. 5, 2002; R D Anderson, A Lynch, N Phillipson, *The University of Edinburgh: An Illustrated History*, Edinburgh, 2003; B Edwards, *Basil Spence 1907-1976*, Edinburgh, 1995; *Marketing Modernisms*, 109.

113 EULMC files.

114 RCAHMS, Spence diaries, courtesy of Clive Fenton; EULMC, Development Committee minutes, 29 November 1954, 78.

115 *Builder*, 29 July 1955, 172-3.

116 RMJMSS files; EULMC, drawings of Edinburgh University alterations; letter of 1994 from Dunbar-Nasmith to J Richards (courtesy of J D Richards).

117 EULMC, letter of 24 February 1955 from Patrick Cumming to RHM; RCAHMS Spence files, letter of 24 February 1955 to Spence, 10 January 1955 from A R Dow to Spence. Spence's interview was at 3 p.m., and Matthew's at 3.15. Nuttgens, Reginald Fairlie, Edinburgh, 1959.

118 Interview with J Dunbar-Nasmith.

119 RMJMSS, Dundee file, letter of 4 March 1955 from Knox to RHM and reply.

120 RMJMSS, Dundee file, letter of 24 March 1955 from Knox to RHM.

121 Interviews with J D Richards, 1995, and J Latimer, 2007.

122 He started in June 1956: RMJMSS, Dundee University file, note of 26 January 1956, minute of Library Committee, 12 April 1956; note of 15 November 1956 from RHM to Cumming; 24 January 1957 correspondence with UGC; notes of site meeting of 20 May 1960.

123 Interviews with A Wightman and T Spaven, 2004; Nuffield Provincial Hospitals Trust, *Studies in the Functions and Design of Hospitals*, London, 1955.

124 E F Catford, *The Royal Infirmary of Edinburgh, 1929-1979*, Edinburgh, 1984, 119-22.

125 EULMC, notes of preliminary meeting with Board, 1 September 1955, and note from RHM to University, 8 September 1955; note of 6 December 1955 from RHM to Medical Superintendent.

126 RHM, Preliminary report, March 1956.

127 Interview with W Campbell, 2003.

128 EULMC, letter from J Dannatt to RHM, 13 June 1953.

129 EULMC, 1952-3 Salaried Committee papers; letters of 20 March 1955, October 1953 and February 1954 from PJM to 'Prof' (RHM). 1954 had seen the first election of a respectably Modernist public architect – C H Aslin of Herts – to the RIBA presidency, in succession to the now old-fashioned Howard Robertson (1952-4).

130 EULMC, RIBA Salaried Committee papers for 1952/3: letters of October 1953, February 1954, 20 March 1955 from PJM to 'Prof' (RHM).

131 EULMC file MS 2533, letter of P Abercrombie to RHM, 28 November 1953, and reply, 3 December 1953.

132 EULMC, file MS2533, May 1954 report and 17 May 1954 letter by Vago to UNESCO Director-General, Education Committee reports 1955.

133 EULMC, file MS2555, notes of executive committee meeting of 20-30 May 1954.

134 EULMC file MS2533, letter of 12 August 1955 from R G Medwin to RHM; note by P Abercrombie to RHM, July 1955.

135 *ABN*, 21 July 1955, quoted in P Vago, *L'UIA*, 93–5; EULMC file MS2533, letter of 29 June 1955 from Professor Dr Wolfgang Rauda to RHM; file MS2538, letter of 3 June 1955 from Vago to RHM and reply of 7 June 1955; file MS2552, notes of executive council meeting, April 1956.

136 A M Foyle (ed.), *Conference on Tropical Architecture 1953: A Report of the Proceedings of the Conference held at University College*, London, March, 1953; London, 1954. EULMC, file MS2538, note of 13 September 1954 from Ellis to Vago, and 4 October from Ellis to RHM.

137 EULMC, file MS2538, letters of 5 June 1956 from Winterson to RHM, 27 June 1956 from Allen to RHM.

138 Interview with W Campbell, 2003.

139 Interview with M Lee, 1997. Interview with Spaven, 1995.

140 Interviews with Dunbar-Nasmith, 2004, Bill Campbell, 2004. 'Ruthlessness': cf. Jones, *Arup*, 126.

141 Interview with D Taylor, 1995.

142 Interviews with Nuttgens, Somerville and Taylor, 1995.

143 Interviews with Biddy Nuttgens, 1995, J O'Neill and J A Matthew, 2007.

144 Interview with Spaven, 1995.

Chapter 7

1 November memo: see RMJMSS, New Zealand House files.

2 RMJMSS, New Zealand House files, 23 April 1956 H Robertson, E Gillett and A Minoprio report to Commisioners of Crown Lands.

3 M Glendinning, 'Una lezione di civiltà', *Fabrications*, vol. 14, 1 and 2, December 2004, 85ff.

4 R Bruegmann (ed.), *Modernism at Mid Century*, Chicago, 1994; L Campbell, *Coventry Cathedral*, Oxford, 1996; I Gournay and J Loeffler, 'Washington and Ottawa', *JSAH*, December 2002, 481–507; J Loeffler, *The Architecture of Diplomacy*, New York, 1998; L J Vale, *Architectural Power and National Identity*, New Haven, 1992; A J Wharton, *Building the Cold War: Hilton Hotels and Modern Architecture*, Chicago, 2001.

5 J Clark and P Walker, *Looking for the Local: Architecture and the New Zealand Modern*, Wellington, 2000, 38–41; P Walker, 'Modern architecture in New Zealand', *Docomomo Journal*, September 2003, 43–7; J A Lee, *Socialism in New Zealand*, London, 1938; L Lipson, *The Politics of Equality*, Chicago, 1948; J Wilson (ed.), *Zeal and Crusade, The Modern Movement in Wellington*, Christchurch, 1996. RHM collection includes: RIBA, *Architecture in Australia*, London, 1956; S Brittan, *The Treasury under the Tories*, London, 1964; R W Winks, *Those New Zealanders*, Christchurch, 1954.

6 www.primeminister.govt.nz.

7 Interview with K Feakes, 2004.

8 S Bradley and N Pevsner, *London 6, Westminster*, New Haven, 2003, 414–6.

9 RMJMSS, New Zealand House files.

10 Typescript memorandum by R M Campbell, 'The Battle', 28 March 1961; courtesy of RAM and June Douglas-Hamilton, 2005.

11 'The Battle'.

12 Bullock, *Building the Postwar World*, 252–5.

13 *JRIBA*, August 1970, 346.

14 S Petersen and P Mandler (eds), *After the Victorians*, London, 1994, 240; J Summerson, introduction to *Ten Years of British Architecture*, Arts Council, 1958, 6–7, and introduction to T Dannatt, *Modern Architecture in Britain*, London, 1959, 15.

15 J Melvin, *F R S Yorke and the Evolution of English Modernism*, London, 2003.

16 EULMC, letter of 25 May 1953 to SJM.

17 RMJMSS, New Zealand House files, note of 30 July 1954 from RHM.

18 RMJMSS, New Zealand House files, 11 April 1956 note.

19 Historic Scotland, List for Calton Ward 3, Part 2, item 72, listed 1968.

20 Interview with April Johnson-Marshall, 1997.

21 Interview with M Lee, 1995. Cherry, *Pioneers in British Planning*, 65; Saint, *Towards a Social Architecture*, 239–49.

22 Saint, *Towards a Social Architecture*, 239–49.

23 A Derbyshire, 'The story of a contradiction' in *RMJM 40*, Edinburgh, 1996; Saint, *Towards a Social Architecture*, 246; interview with A Derbyshire, 2004.

24 EULMC, letter from SJM to RHM, 19 May 1953; letter from PJM to RHM, 20 March 1955.

25 Interview with Sir A Derbyshire, 2004.

26 Saint, *Towards a Social Architecture*, 246; T H Eriksen, *Small Places, Large Issues: An Introduction to Social and Cultural Anthropology*, London, 2001, 53.

27 Interview with Sir A Derbyshire, 2004.

28 Interview with April Johnson-Marshall, 2004.

29 Saint, *Towards a Social Architecture*, 249. The general suggestion of autocratic leanings is nonetheless confirmed by Aidan. (Interview with RAM, 2005.)

30 Interview with Alan Wightman, 2004.

31 Interviews with M Lee and J D Richards, 1995.

32 A Ravetz, *The Government of Space*, London, 1986.

33 RMJMSS, New Zealand House files.

34 EULMC, note of 15 March 1984 from P Nuttgens to J Richards. 'Horrified': interview with J Latimer, 2007. Rudolph, Neo-Liberty: T Rohan, 'The dangers of eclecticism', in Goldhagen and Legault, *Anxious Modernisms*, 204–6.

35 New Zealand Governor-General Willoughby Norrie dismissed by Campbell as 'worse than useless': 'The Battle', 13; RMJMSS, New Zealand House files, letter from R Campbell to RHM, 27 March 1956.

36 'The Battle', 11; EULMC files.

37 'The Battle'.

38 EULMC, letter of 28 August 1997 from L Esher to A Derbyshire, courtesy of Sir A Derbyshire; Richards, *Unjust Fella*, 244.

39 'The Battle', 13.

40 RMJMSS, New Zealand House files, note of 9 April 1956

lunch Corner–Bedford.

41 RMJMSS, New Zealand House files, note of 9 April 1956 by Corner; report by Robertson, Gillett and Minoprio to CCL; 2 May 1956 note by Campbell to High Commissioner.

42 RMJMSS, New Zealand House files, RHM defence paper of 15 June 1956; note of meeting of 29 June 1956, and note of 2 July 1956 by RHM.

43 RMJMSS, New Zealand House files, note of 5 April 1961 from Campbell to RHM; 22 June 1956 notes of meeting between RHM, Prime Minister Holland, High Commissioner, A M Mackintosh; note of 1 August 1956 from R Campbell to Holland; note of 17 October 1956 by R Campbell.

44 RMJMSS, New Zealand House files, RHM note of 15 October 1956 to R Campbell; notes of 18 October 1956 of Royal Fine Art Commission; RMJMSS, New Zealand House files, R Campbell note to RHM, 4 October 1956.

45 RMJMSS, New Zealand House files, notes of 17 October and 8 November 1956 from R Campbell to High Commissioner; note by R Campbell, 25 October 1956; note of 16 October 1956 from RHM to Campbell.

46 RMJMSS, New Zealand House files, 25 October 1956 Campbell note; interview with M Lee, 1995, and information from Robin Skinner, 2006.

47 RMJMSS, New Zealand House files, note of 30 October 1956 from Prime Minister Holland to High Commissioner; note from RHM to High Commissioner with fee statement, 26 October 1956.

48 RMJMSS, New Zealand House files, note of 8 November 1956 from R Campbell to High Commissioner.

49 RMJMSS, New Zealand House files, telegram of 27 November 1956 from Prime Minister Holland; November memo by RHM; note of 29 November 1956 talk between Edwards and High Commissioner.

50 'The Battle', 12; RMJMSS, New Zealand House files, note of 1 December 1956 statement by CCL; *Architect and Building News*, 6 December 1956, 743; *Builder*, 7 December 1956, 966–8.

51 'The Battle'; note of 5 December 1956.

52 RMJMSS, New Zealand House files, 26 February 1957 statement by Prime Minister Holland.

53 EULMC, file MS2533, 31 January 1957 note by Alister McIntosh, Department of External Affairs; RMJMSS, New Zealand House files, 31 January 1957 note from Eve to High Commissioner, Sir C Webb.

54 RMJMSS, New Zealand House files.

55 Interview with K Feakes, 2004. 'Midway Gardens': interview with Sir A Derbyshire, 2004.

56 Interview with K Feakes, 2004.

57 Interview with K Feakes, 2004.

58 Glazing: interview with K Feakes, 2004. RMJMSS, New Zealand House files, press release of 11 June 1959. Letter from Sir A Derbyshire to L Esher, 1 September 1997, courtesy of Sir A Derbyshire.

59 RMJMSS, New Zealand House files, note from SJM to RHM, 26 July 1957, and note to RHM, 13 August 1957.

60 RMJMSS, New Zealand House files, note of 26 August 1957 from RHM to Wilson; interview with M Lee, 1995.

61 Interview with M Lee, 1995.

62 Interview with K Feakes, 2004.

63 RMJMSS, New Zealand House files, correspondence of 3 February 1959 with LCC; interview with K Feakes, 2004.

64 RMJMSS, New Zealand House files, 11 June 1959 press release.

65 Interviews with M Lee, 1995, and K Feakes, 2004.

66 Letters from J O'Neill and S Platt to M Glendinning, 2006.

67 H R Hitchcock, 'English art in the early 1960s', *Zodiac*, 12, 1964, 31.

68 Cf. the example discussed in Rohan, 'Dangers of eclecticism', 207–211.

Chapter 8

1 RHM, 'Regional planning in action', *Glasgow Herald*, 21 January 1959, supplement, iii.

2 Interview with K Graham, 2003.

3 Interviews with C Somerville and D Taylor, 1996.

4 EULMC, file MS2533, note of 2 February 1961 from W Musonda to RHM. Support of student activist group ('Subtopia Attack'): EULMC, note of 27 November 1960 from C Macintosh to RHM.

5 EULMC, RIBA letter of 22 March 1958; PJM, obituary of RHM, Royal Society of Edinburgh *Yearbook*, 1976; L Martin, 'Conference on architectural education', *JRIBA*, June 1958, 279–82.

6 *JRIBA*, 65, 1958, 266–7; M Crinson, lecture at Society of Architectural Historians of Great Britain Education Conference, 20 March 1993, 'Education for change, 1930–60'.

7 Annan, *Our Age*, 291.

8 Crinson, 'Education for change' lecture.

9 *Building Design*, 25 January 2002, 24.

10 *AJ*, 15 January 1959, 91; interview with E Morris, 1997; P Willis (ed.), *Furor Hortensis*, Edinburgh, 1974, 13.

11 *Builder*, 1 June 1960.

12 Status of ARU/HRU directorship post in mid 1960s: information from Jessica Taylor, 2006; interview with Charles Robertson, 2007; EULMC, letter from RHM to Liverpool University, 9 February 1954. 'Brilliant': interview with W Campbell, 2003; Nuttgens, see also obituary, *The Times*, 29 March 2004.

13 EULMC, PJM letters to RHM, October 1953 and February 1954; EULMC file MS2533, letter from H Casson to RHM, 8 January 1961.

14 Interview with E Morris, 1997.

15 Interviews with S Platt and A Wightman, 2003.

16 EULMC, letter of 30 May 1957 from PJM to RHM.

17 RCAHMS, Sir Basil Spence archive, personal correspondence files, letter of 11 January 1959 from PJM to Spence,

pleading for new professional and educational arrangements suitable to train 'a new kind of architect' who 'could tackle the city as a collective work of art'.

18 'Three-legged': interview with Sir A Derbyshire, 2004; EULMC, letter of 23 March 1975 from PJM to RHM.

19 Interview with P Nuttgens, 1995.

20 Interview with Dorothy Taylor, 1996.

21 Collection of Eleanor Morris, Minutes of Architecture Department Staff Meeting, 30 November 1960; *Builder*, 5 August 1960.

22 Interview with E Morris, 1997.

23 Interview with April Johnson-Marshall, 1997.

24 Ian McHarg/Morris & Steedman link: EULMC, letter of 9 January 1958 from McHarg to RHM; S A F Macintosh, 'The private houses of Morris & Steedman', M Arch Honours dissertation, Glasgow School of Art, 1995; M Glendinning (ed.), *Rebuilding Scotland*, East Linton, 1997 (chapters by D Page and R Steedman); *Scotsman*, 23 August 2006, 33 (Morris obituary).

25 Willis, *Furor Hortensis*.

26 Willis, *Furor Hortensis*, 17.

27 R Ellis and D Cuff, *Architects' People*, New York, 1989, 267–9.

28 Interview with W Campbell, 2003.

29 Interviews with P Nuttgens, 1995, April Johnson-Marshall, 1997, and W Campbell, 2003.

30 Interview with P Nuttgens, 1995.

31 EULMC, file MS2544, 25 October 1959 RHM submission to Gulbenkian for abortive 'Project Vernacular', April 1960 resubmission, and 26 February 1960 letter from Edinburgh University Press to RHM.

32 Cleeve Barr: interview with C Robertson, 1988; EULMC, letter to RHM by Colin Boyne, 20 November 1958.

33 Interview with C Robertson, 1988; *Builder*, 28 October 1960; *JRIBA*, August 1970, 346.

34 Interview with C Robertson, 1988.

35 Interview with P Nuttgens, 1995. See also F McLachlan and R Wedgwood, 'Inside Out: Social Housing at Southfield', *ARQ*, vol. 7, 1, 2003, 33–4.

36 Interview with C Robertson, 2007; EULMC, PJM letter of 17 March 1975 to RHM and SJM, Glendinning and Muthesius, *Tower Block*, Chapter 26.

37 EULMC, letter from RHM to F Gutheim, 21 January 1957.

38 Interview with P Nuttgens, 1995.

39 EULMC, note of 9 February 1961 meeting between ECA and Edinburgh University architecture department; interview with E Morris, 1997.

40 EULMC, letter of 26 October 1961 to RHM from Everard Haynes, RIBA.

41 EULMC, copy of Queen's College Dundee Development Plan, May 1959; interview with A Wightman, February 2005.

42 EULMC, copy of Royal College of Science and Technology development plan revision, early 1962; interview with A Wightman, 2004.

43 C Fenton, 'A Century of Change in George Square', *Book of the Old Edinburgh Club*, new series, vol. 5, 2002, 80.

44 Interviews with S Platt, 2006, and J O'Neill, 2007; EULMC, 1960 correspondence, and interview with SRM, 1995.

45 Interview with K Graham, 2003.

46 Interview with T Spaven, 1995.

47 Interview with K Feakes, 2004.

48 Interview with RAM, 2005.

49 Interviews with K Feakes, 2004, and J Latimer, 2007.

50 RMJMSS, Firhill file, letters of 13 February 1957 from T Spaven to P Newnham and from RHM to SJM; note of 20 February 1957 by P Newnham.

51 RMJMSS, Firhill file, T Spaven to P Newnham, 30 November 1957.

52 RMJMSS, Firhill file, Cunliffe to RHM, 20 November 1957; interview with K E Graham, 2003.

53 Interviews with F Isserlis, 1997, and K Feakes, 2004.

54 Interview with K Feakes, 2004.)

55 Interviews with John Richards and Kenneth Graham, 2003.

56 Interview with M Richards, 2004..

57 Interview with K Feakes, 2004.

58 G Alex Bremner, 'Some Imperial institute', *JSAH*, vol. 62, 1, March 2003, 50–74; Survey of London, vol. 45, *Knightsbridge*, London, 2000, 207–9.

59 U Kultermann, *Zeitgenoessische Architektur in Osteuropa*, Cologne, 1985; interviews with A Derbyshire, 2004, and K Feakes, 2004.

60 Interview with M Lee, 1995. Singapore: *Architectural Review*, January 1962.

61 Interview with K Feakes, 2004.

62 Interview with Sir A Derbyshire, 2004.

63 Interview with M Lee, 1995.

64 Interview with K Feakes, 2004.

65 Standard Life Montreal project, 1959: EULMC, pencil drawings collection.

66 Informality: interview with C Somerville, 1996.

67 Graham Law: *King's College Cambridge Annual Report*, October 1997, 6–7.

68 Interview with M and J Richards, 2003.

69 Interview with M and J Richards, 2003.

70 'Hot Dog' Paterson and Linda Westwater: interview with Margaret Richards, 2003.

71 Interview with W Campbell, 2003.

72 Interview with K Graham, 2003.

73 Interview with Eleanor Morris, 1997.

74 Interview with C Somerville, 1996.

75 *Builder*, 14 June 1957, 1085; interview with April Johnson-Marshall, 1997.

76 EULMC, file MS2551, letters of 31 July 1959 to RHM from S Tutuchenko and P Abrosimov, and of 22 July 1959 to RHM from D Taylor, RIBA; EULMC, text of RHM lecture of 14 December 1962 to Edinburgh Master Builders.

77 EULMC, letter of 16 April 1957 from RHM to Scott-

Moncrieff. Interview with Sir J Dunbar-Nasmith, 2004. Percival: M Glendinning and S Muthesius, *Provincial Mixed Development*, Norwich, 1986.

78   Interviews with W Campbell, 2003, and T Spaven, 2004; RMJMSS, Aberdeen residences file, letter from W S Angus to RHM, 16 May 1958.

79   Interview with W Campbell, 2003.

80   Interview with W Campbell, 2003; EULMC, letter of 10 January 1960 from W S Angus to RHM, and letter of thanks of 26 January 1959 from Derrick Heathcoat Amory.

81   RMJMSS, Aberdeen file, letter of 14 July 1958 from D J Matthews to RHM; 17 March 1960, August 1960 and 9 December 1960 from W Angus to RHM; 31 July 1961 from Spaven to W Angus; 7 July 1964 from Deputy Secretary of university to RHM.

82   RMJMSS, Hydro files, letter of 11 March 1957 from Thurgarland to Spaven, and of 25 March 1957 from Spaven to Thurgarland; interview with Spaven, 1995.

83   RMJMSS, Hydro files, letter of 11 April 1957 from Thurgarland to Spaven.

84   RMJMSS, Hydro files, letter of 13 November 1957 from Fulton to RHM, and ensuing correspondence.

85   RMJMSS, Hydro files, letter of 18 December 1957 from A Funton to RHM, and 2 January 1958 reply.

86   RMJMSS, Hydro files, letters of 8 January 1958 and 20 March 1958 from Fulton to RHM.

87   Graham: interview with W Campbell, 2003.

88   Interview with K E Graham, 2003.

89   RMJMSS, Cumnock files, letters from R Hunter to RHM of 8 November, 4 December, 18 December 1956.

90   RMJMSS, Cumnock files, notes of 11 September 1957 meeting.

91   Interview with K E Graham, 2003; RMJMSS, Cumnock files.

92   RMJMSS, Cumnock files, letters from 4 July 1961 from Hunter to Spaven. RMJMSS, Cumnock files, letter of 27 June 1959 from Hunter to Graham, 6 December from Rosie to Graham.

93   *Glasgow Herald*, 30 December 1959.

94   Harold Macmillan's famous 1957 pronouncement that 'most of our people have never had it so good': D Sandbrook, *Never Had It So Good: a History of Britain from Suez to the Beatles*, London, 2005; Annan, *Our Age*, 330.

95   1950s/early 1960s rejection of CIAM Functionalism: K Lynch, *The Image of the City*, Cambridge, MA, 1960; *Architectural Design*, January 1955; *Architectural Review*, December 1955 on Brutalism; *Architectural Design*, April 1957, 113; Bullock, *Building the Postwar World*; *Zodiac* 1, 1957; B Appleyard, *The Pleasures of Peace*, London, 1989, 123; Ockman, *Architecture Culture*; J Jacobs, *The Death and Life of Great American Cities*, New York, 1961.

96   Cf. the 1956–60 building of Brasilia, or Renaat Braem's 'Cité Modèle' housing project at the 1958 Brussels World's Fair.

97   EULMC, letter from MARS to RHM, 12 July 1957, 30 August 1956 from M Laird to RHM.

98   EULMC, papers from May 1958 British Architects' Conference, Newcastle-upon-Tyne; EULMC, text of RHM lecture to Civil Engineers, Glasgow, 17 March 1961.

99   EULMC, text of RHM talk at RIBA symposium, 22 May 1959.

100   EULMC, file MS2577, text of RHM lecture at September 1961 'Symposium on Tall Buildings' at Hong Kong University. Coventry: text of RHM lecture at RIBA Conference, Coventry, 11 July 1962; EULMC, text of RHM lectures at May 1958 RIBA conference and RIBA Symposium on the Living Town, 22 May 1959.

101   'Uneconomic, disastrous': EULMC, text of RHM paper at 1 February RICS conference; EULMC file MS2577, text of September 1961 RHM Hong Kong paper on tall buildings; *AJ*, 18 February 1960, 783–4; *Builder*, 19 February 1960, 371–4; *Architecture and Building*, March 1960 94ff.

102   *Builder*, 8 July 1960, 47ff.

103   *AJ*, 10 July 1958; *AJ*, 25 June 1958. Berlin proposal: EULMC, Hauptstadt Berlin drawings and papers.

104   EULMC, text of *c*.1959 RHM lecture, 'Regional planning in Scotland'.

105   RHM, 'Regional planning in action: Scotland takes the lead', *Glasgow Herald*, 21 January 1959, iii.

106   EULMC, 14 May 1953 letter from J M Richards to RHM.

107   'Scenographic': interview with J Richards, 1995.

108   Interview with I Arnott, 1988; EULMC, text of RHM Dundee lecture, 'Buildings of Scotland', 20 February 1960, and *c*.1959 lecture on Hutchesontown B.

109   Piling: RMJMSS, Hutchesontown file, note of 23 July 1957 from Fairhurst, and 19 August 1957 from F A Macdonald to RHM. 'Rhapsodising': interview with Spaven, 2005.

110   Hansaviertel Interbau: *Interbau Berlin*, Berlin, 1957. G Dolff-Bonekaemper, *Das Hansaviertel*, Berlin, 1999, 66–8; J K Geist and K Kuervers, *Das Berliner Mietshaus*, vol. 3 (1945–89), München, 1989. Block 21 was by Dutch designers J H van den Broek and J B Bakema.

111   Interview with W Campbell, 2003; Leith Fort competition report, *Builder*, 31 January 1958, 214; Edinburgh Central Library, Housing Committee minutes of 28 January 1958, 315–20.

112   RHM, 'Regional planning in action', *Glasgow Herald*, 21 January 1959.

113   RMJMSS, Hutchesontown file, report of 4 February 1958 and RHM 1958–9 lecture.

114   Bathrooms dispute: RMJMSS, Hutchesontown files, letter of 31 January 1958 from W Horne to Town Clerk.

115   Visits by Arnott and the others to LCC Roehampton and Brandon: interview with I Arnott, 1988.

116   Interview with J L Paterson, 1987.

117   Interview with J L Paterson, 1987; *AJ*, 5 April 1964; RMJMSS, Hutchesontown files, note of 17 July 1958

Modern Architect

Housing and Works meeting at Regent Terrace; 1 October 1960 report by Paterson; note of 1 November 1960 from Resident Engineer to Spaven; 16 January 1961 discussion report. 'Sharp claws' and 'multifaceted, hydra headed' character: EULMC, text of 1958–9 RHM lecture; Glendinning and Muthesius, *Tower Block*, Chapter 25.

118 Interview with I Arnott, 1988.

119 Springburn, Royston: interview with I Arnott, 1988.

120 Hotel project: *Builder*, 20 November 1959; RMJMSS, College of Nautical Studies and Hutchesontown Nursery School files.

121 George Square: EULMC, text of RHM Town and Gown lecture of 5 November 1960, and Merchant's Hall, Edinburgh, lecture of 28 April 1960.

122 Fenton, 'Century of change', 75; C Fenton, 'Appleton's architects, building the University of Edinburgh, 1949–65', PhD thesis, University of Edinburgh, 2002; *Builder*, 29 July 1955, 172–3; R Anderson, M Lynch, N Phillipson, *The University of Edinburgh: An Illustrated History*, Edinburgh, 2003. Spence against mediocrity: *Scotsman*, 26 February 1959, Building and Civil Engineering section, 7.

123 EULMC, file MS2533, letter of 28 March 1956 from RHM to A Acworth.

124 EULMC, file MS2555, letter from Abercrombie to RHM, 16 December 1956.

125 EULMC, University file.

126 Fenton, 'Century of change', 79.

127 RMJMSS, Arts Tower file, RHM memo of 13 October 1956.

128 EULMC, text of reply by RHM to Principal of Edinburgh University at dinner of 21 October 1963.

129 EULMC, 17 June 1958 letter of appointment from C Stewart to RHM: 'You have, of course, been working on this project for a considerable time.'

130 RCAHMS Sir Basil Spence archive, file SBS 185, letter of 5 January 1959 from Spence to Glover and of 10 November 1959 from Spence to Glover.

131 EULMC, letter from R Sillitto to Dean of Arts Faculty, 26 June 1959; R Steedman, 'Morris & Steedman', in M Glendinning (ed.), *Rebuilding Scotland*, East Linton, 1997, 123–4.

132 Eleanor Robertson, lecture to Architectural Heritage Society of Scotland, 21 October 1997; Eleanor Robertson, *AHSS Magazine*, 6, 1997, 14–16; *Architectural Heritage*, xvii, 2006, 1–14 and 139–56.

133 Letter from D Walker to M Glendinning, July 2006; University of Edinburgh, *University Development and George Square*, Edinburgh, 1960, 28.

134 Fenton, 'Century of change', 63. Opposition letters to *Scotsman*: see e.g. 8 May 1959.

135 Fenton, 'Century of change', 61–2. Hurd and the 'Anti-Ugly' opposition to his 1957–9 building for Emmanuel College, Cambridge: N Pevsner, *Cambridgeshire*, 1970, 74; G Stamp, 'The Anti-Uglies', lecture to Twentieth Century Society AGM, Kensington Library, 2 June 2006.

136 Listing: EULMC, file MS2538, 20 July 1957, RHM note to K Macrae, RIAS Secretary; D Walker, 'Listing in Scotland', *Transactions of the Ancient Monuments Society*, 58, 1994. 'Fatal': EULMC, text of 20 February 1960 RHM lecture in Dundee. EULMC, text of 10 February 1961 RHM broadcast; interview with P Nuttgens, 1995.

137 EULMC, notes of 4 February 1960 Working Group meeting, and other meetings in series.

138 Fenton, 'Century of change', 62–3.

139 Interview with L Fricker, 1997.

140 EULMC, minutes of Arts Faculty Building Committee, 11 July 1960. Contract: RMJMSS, Arts Faculty files, letter of 18 December 1961 from J D Richards to Crudens, and of 16 August 1960 from Richards to assistant secretary of university.

141 EULMC, text of 21 October 1963 RHM speech.

142 Saint, *Towards a Social Architecture*, 246.

143 EULMC, notes from RHM speech to Royal Society of Medicine, 18 October 1965; *The Lancet*, 28 October 1961.

144 E F Catford, *The Royal Infirmary of Edinburgh*, Edinburgh, 1984, 122. Overview of MoMo hospital architecture: *Architectural Review*, July 1965, 447–53.

145 RMJMSS, ERI file, letter from Secretary to Regional Hospital Board to RHM, 8 December 1959, and of 18 March 1958 from Scottish Office to RHM.

146 RMJMSS, ERI file, 1961 correspondence; Catford, *Royal Infirmary*, 125.

147 J F A Hughes, 'The brutal hospital', PhD thesis, Courtauld Institute, 1996; *Architectural Review*, June 1965, special issue: 'Health and Hospitals'.

148 Hawkhill House: interview with A Wightman, 2004; RMJMSS, Ninewells files.

149 *Architectural Review*, June 1965, 456; A Wightman, 'Ninewells Hospital, Dundee, memorandum on factors influencing the height and bulk of the hospital buildings', unpublished paper of 24 April 1959, courtesy of A Wightman.

150 Interview with A Wightman, 2004.

151 Interview with A Wightman, 2004.

152 Tom Sommerville, *Ninewells Revisited*, unpublished paper of 1986.

153 Interview with A Wightman, 2004.

154 Sommerville, *Ninewells Revisited*; see also G H Bell (ed.), *Hospital and Medical School Design*, Dundee, 1961.

155 Interview with A Wightman, 2004.

156 Interview with A Wightman, 2004.

157 Glendinning and Muthesius, *Tower Block*, 132–147. See also RMJM, *The Design of Ninewells Teaching Hospital and Medical School, A Symposium*, Edinburgh, 1973; interview with J Latimer, 2007.

158 Interview with A Wightman, 2004.

159 *AJ*, 15 January 1959, 91; interview with April Johnson-Marshall, 1997.

160 Interviews with RAM, 2005, and J O'Neill, 2007.

161 Interview with Sylvia Platt, 2003. Jehovah's Witnesses: interview with RAM, 2005.

162 Reiach: interview with John Richards, 1997.

163 Matthew pressure on Russell Trust to grant-aid Reiach on an architectural photography trip to America: EULMC, file MS2533, letter of 30 January 1957 from RHM to Russell Trust, and of 13 February 1957 to Reiach.

164 EULMC, file MS2533, letter of 8 March 1957 from RHM to M H Kenchington, and letter of 3 June 1957 from R H Cuthbertson to RHM seeking support in application to build controversial Modernist house in Barnton.

165 Interview with RAM, December 2005.

166 Interview with Charles Robertson, 1988; *JRIBA*, 65, 1958, 266; *JRIBA*, 67, 1960, 319–25.

167 *JRIBA*, March 1960, 150; interview with P Harrison, 2007.

168 RIBA *Kalendars*: 1957–8, 7; 1959–60, 4–5; 1960–1, 6–7; 1961–2, 4–5; 1962–3, 6–7.

169 EULMC, file MS2555, letter of 15 November 1956 from Bill Ellis to RHM.

170 EULMC, file MS2555, letter of 16 December 1956 from Abercrombie to RHM, 22 November 1956 from RHM to Tschumi, 27 November 1956 from Bill Ellis to RHM. Tension with IFHTP: EULMC, letter of 1 November 1956 from R Gardner-Medwin to RHM, and of 12 December 1956 from RHM to Abercrombie.

171 EULMC, file MS2551, minutes of IUA Executive Committee, Berlin, August 1957.

172 P Abercrombie, *The Master Plan of Addis Ababa*, 1956. Obituaries: *Town and Country Planning*, 56, 567–72; *The Times*, 25 March 957, 14 (by Forshaw); *JRIBA*, May 1957, 292; *Town Planning Review*, July 1957, 81–4 (by Holford); *The Listener*, 8 August 1957 (by Clough Williams-Ellis).

173 EULMC, file MS2555, letter from RHM to Vago, 18 September 1956, and reply of 25 September 1956.

174 EULMC, letter from RHM to Nears, 9 January 1958. Ling travelled to the congress via a convention of 'World Architectural Students' in Leningrad.

175 Interview with S Platt, 2003.

176 State Building Architecture and Design Literature Press (edited by V O Vinograd and others), *5th Congress of the UIA*, Moscow, 1960; EULMC, file MS2533, report by A A Bellamy. 'Crude and curious': EULMC, file MS2551, RHM report on the IUA congress, 1958.

177 State Building Architecture and Design Literature Press (edited by V O Vinograd and others), *5th Congress of the UIA*, Moscow, 1960.

178 EULMC, file MS2551, RHM report on the IUA congress, 1958; EULMC, file MS2533, letter of 28 August 1958 from RHM to T Brimelow, Foreign Office; *Les Nouvelles de Moscou*, 23 and 27 July 1958; L Tonev, 'Moscou 1958', *L'UIA*, 99.

179 Influence of 1958 UIA congress in legitimising mikroray-on planning: Triin Ojari, 'Floor space: the Modernist residential housing ideology and Mustamäe', *Studies in Art and Architecture*, Tallinn, 2004/2, 66–70.

180 EULMC, file MS2555, text of RHM lecture at Mexico City, 21 September 1970; *L'UIA*, 211.

181 EULMC, file MS2553, note of 27 November 1958 from Taylor (RIBA) to RHM; RCAHMS, Spence collection, file SBS 182, letter of 29 January 1959 from Spence to A E Mould. 'Moskwa days': EULMC, letter of 24 September 1958 from PJM to RHM. 'Schemes': interview with A Wightman, 2004.

182 EULMC, file MS2552, note of executive committee meeting, 9 September 1959. EULMC, file MS2552, note of 11 May 1961 from RHM to A Sharov, and of 12 October 1961 from RHM to M Bryer.

183 *JRIBA*, August 1970, 347.

184 EULMC, file MS2551, general correspondence for 1961 Congress.

185 EULMC, file MS2551, letter of 12 July 1957 from Vago to RHM, and RHM paper of 25 September 1958.

186 EULMC, file MS2551, 18 January 1960 draft of proposal.

187 EULMC, file MS2551, 18 January 1960 draft of exhibition proposal; letter from RHM to Vago, 6 January 1960; letter from Crosby to PJM, 6 January 1960; T Crosby, *Architecture – City Sense*, London, 1965; D Sharp, 'London 1961', in *L'UIA*, 110.

188 R P Andrew and A E Brooks (eds), *Final Report of the 6th Congress of the International Union of Architects, London*, 3–7 July 1961, London, October 1962.

189 EULMC, letter of 5 January 1961 from G Ricketts to RHM. Hryniewiecki: lecture by K Murawska at Edinburgh University, 9 February 2007.

190 EULMC, file MS2551, letter of 27 July 1959 from J M Richards to RHM, 24 March 1960 from G Ricketts to RHM. EULMC, letter of 24 January 1957 from W Ellis to RHM.

191 Andrew and Brooks (eds), *Final Report of the 6th Congress*, 1962, 175; J M Richards, *Unjust Fella*, 205–6.

192 Andrew and Brooks (eds), *Final Report of the 6th Congress*, 1962, 61–95.

193 Andrew and Brooks (eds), *Final Report of the 6th Congress*, 1962, 175; Richards, *Unjust Fella*, 205–6.

194 Andrew and Brooks (eds), *Final Report of the 6th Congress*, 1962.)

195 *Builder*, 7 July 1961, 3–4; Andrew and Brooks (eds), *Final Report of the 6th Congress*, 1962; *UIA Revue*, 10, October 1961; *JRIBA*, June 1961, 286–293.

196 EULMC, file MS2533, note of 24 June 1959 from W Cleeve Barr.

197 EULMC, file MS2533, general correspondence of 1959–60.

198 EULMC, file MS2553, IUA December 1959 document on low-cost housing; note of 19 May 1960 from E Weissman to H Churchill; Churchill to Vago, 24 October 1961, and Vago to RHM, 7 November 1961.

199 EULMC, file MS2551, mid 1957 paper by RHM.

200 F Lea, *Science and Building: A History of the Building Research Station*, London, 1971; *AJ*, 2 April 1953, 418.

201 Max Fry and Jane Drew's contemporary University

College, Ibadan: H Le Roux, 'Modern architecture in post-colonial Ghana and Nigeria', *Architectural History*, 47, 2004, 361ff.

202 EULMC, file MS2577, correspondence of March–April 1961. EULMC, file MS2533, note of 13 March 1959 from RHM to Professor R T Kennedy; EULMC, correspondence of March–August 1959 on trip.

203 EULMC, 20 December 1960, report of jury; letter of 15 March 1960 from Department of Education to RHM; letter of 7 March 1960 from Ecochard to RHM; letter of 5 June 1961 from Assistant Civil Engineer, Public Works Department to RHM. Ecochard (general): M Eleb, 'An alternative to Functionalist universalism', in Goldhagen and Legault, *Anxious Modernisms*, 55–74; M Ecochard, *L'Architecture d'Aujourd'hui*, June 1955, 36–40.

204 Zahir-ud-Din Khwaja, *Memoirs of an Architect*, Lahore, 1998, 63–7; *The Times*, 9 June 2004, 65; R Squire, *Portrait of an Architect*, Gerrards Cross, 1984, 188–97.

205 See e.g. file MS2533, letter of 9 February 1961 from A Stephenson to RHM.

Chapter 9

1 RHM RIBA Presidential inauguration speech: *JRIBA*, November 1962, 405ff.

2 Interview with Sylvia Platt, 2003.

3 EULMC, file MS2534, correspondence of 1–15 January 1962; file MS 2533, letter of 1 January 1962 from Home Office to RHM; *Builder,* 23 February 1962; 'A salute to that quartet of knights', *AJ*, 16 January 1963; *Sunday Times*, 21 December 2003, 5.

4 Interview with RAM, 2005.

5 EULMC, letter of 12 December 1968 from RHM to Watterson.

6 EULMC, preliminary correspondence for lecture to Institution of Civil Engineers, Glasgow, and Edinburgh University dinner.

7 'Amazingly efficient': interview with M Higgs, 1997; interviews with J O'Neill, 2007, Elsa Hendry, 1997, and Christine Somerville, 1996.

8 *Architectural Review*, July 1975 (obituary by Oddie).

9 Interview with C Somerville, 1996; EULMC, text of RHM lecture of 15 March 1963 to Wiltshire and Dorset architects.

10 Interviews with RAM, 2005, and Jessie Matthew, 2007.

11 Interview with RAM, 2005.

12 Interviews with S Platt, 2003, SRM, 1995, K Feakes, 2004, RAM, 2005.

13 EULMC, letter from Miss Margaret Harris to RHM, 24 October 1968.

14 EULMC, inventory of contents of 24 Park Square East, prepared in March 1975 by Phillips Ltd.

15 Interview with S Platt, 2003.

16 Interview with S Platt, 2003.

17 Interview with M Tindall, 1997.

18 Interview with SRM, 1995. Matthew's Canadian relatives: EULMC, file MS2533, letter of 12 June 1968 from 'Aunt Mabel' to RHM.

19 EULMC, file MS2533, letter of 26 May 1962 from C W Ellis to RHM, 21 and 27 October 1965 from RHM to R Crossman, 6 February 1967 from Lionel Brett to RHM, and 22 February 1967 from RHM to A Greenwood.

20 Interview with SRM, 1995.

21 Interviews with SRM, 1995, and RAM, 2005.

22 Interview with SRM, 1995.

23 'I went out to Keith': interviews with SRM, 1995, and M Richards, 2004.

24 Habitat-style: interview with LLM, 1997; EULMC, undated KI leaflet.

25 Interviews with A Wightman, 2004; EULMC, sketch drawings by RHM for KI.

26 Interviews with S Platt, 2003, and J Richards, 1997.

27 J Berry, *Herman Miller*, London, 2004.

28 Interview with S Platt, 2003; EULMC, RMJM correspondence file, letter from Bank of Scotland to Sylvia Matthew, 3 July 1973.

29 EULMC, estimate letter of 1 May 1965 by J B Moncrieff, RMJM accountant. Graham and Richards goodwill payments to Matthew of nearly £8,000 by early 1965, and overdraft guarantees: EULMC, 1971 paper by John Richards; file MS2533, letter of 4 September 1969 from British Linen Bank to RHM.

30 EULMC, letter of 2 June 1966 from Casson to RHM; estimate letter of 1 May 1965 by J B Moncrieff.

31 EULMC, estimate of February 1965 by J B Moncrieff.

32 EULMC, RMJM Edinburgh Financial Statement from 1 April to 5 May 1967; Second Report by D S Anderson, 18 July 1966; letter of 13 August 1969 from Cicely Naismith to RHM; J B Moncrieff estimates of 3 February 1965 and 19 May 1965; letter of 26 August 1965 from D S Anderson to M Kidd; letter of 6 September 1965 from D S Anderson to RHM; letter of 2 June 1966 from H Casson to RHM, and of 21 June 1966 from J B Moncrieff to RHM.

33 EULMC, letter of 25 January 1967 from J B Moncrieff to K Buffery, RMJM London office.

34 EULMC, texts of RHM lectures to East Anglian Society of Architects, 2 May 1963, and Southeastern Society of Architects, 10 May 1963; EULMC, text of RHM lecture of 9 and 11 May 1964 to RIBA Conference, Glasgow.

35 EULMC, text of RHM lecture to July 1965 IUA congress.

36 RHM foreword to A W Cleeve Barr, *Public Authority Housing*, London, 1958; A E Sloman, *A University in the Making*, London, 1964; S Muthesius, *The Postwar University*, New Haven, 2000; P Dormer and S Muthesius, *Concrete and Open Skies*, London, 2001.

37 EULMC, letter of 25 November 1965 from RHM to BBC; EULMC, text of RHM lecture, 'Architecture today, yesterday and tomorrow', Reading, 13 January 1964, and RHM lecture to Edinburgh University, 14 May 1964; EULMC, text of

RHM lecture of 17 June 1964 to assembly of Canadian architects.

38　R Crossman, *The Diaries of a Cabinet Minister*, vol. 1, London, 1975 (1976 edition), 24, 623; L Esher, *JRIBA*, November 1965; Sir W Holford, 'The built environment', lecture to University College London, 24 November 1964, 17; Holford, *Architectural Technology and South Kensington* (address to Imperial College, London), 1962, 7.

39　EULMC, 'A fortnight in China', diary and summary of China trip, edited by RHM and RAM, 1964.

40　Skidelsky, *Keynes*; EULMC, text of RHM lectures of 2 May 1963 to East Anglian Society of Architects, 19 September 1965 to the RIBA, 1 May 1965 to the EAA Shopping Symposium. RHM, 'Fortnight in China', entry for 12 September 1964.

41　Argument with Crossman over public versus private housing standards: EULMC, file MS2548, letter of 21 October 1965 from RHM to Crossman and reply of 3 November 1965; text of RHM lecture at Saltire awards ceremony, 8 November 1963.

42　A Saint, *Towards a Social Architecture*, 193–4; *JRIBA*, January 1995, 139–45; O Marriott, *The Property Boom*, London, 1967; D Senior, *Your Architect*, London, 1964, 223.

43　*JRIBA*, November 1962, 408; EULMC, text of RHM lectures to East Anglian Society of Architects, 2 May 1963, to Edinburgh University, 14 May 1964, and to the Northants, Bedfordshire and Huntingdonshire Architects, 21 March 1963.

44　*Scottish Field*, September 1962, 67; EULMC, file MS 2538, letter of 6 December 1965 from M MacEwen to G Ricketts, and reply of 9 December 1965.

45　Interviews with RAM, 2005, Charles Robertson, 1988, and SRM, 1995.

46　'Grumbled': interview with S Platt, 2003. Interview with RAM, December 2005.

47　EULMC, letter of 25 November 1965 from RHM to BBC General Advisory Council; interview with RAM, 2005; EULMC, text of 18 October 1963 lecture to Royal Society of Medicine.

48　EULMC, RIBA correspondence of 2 October 1962, and text of RHM lecture of 6 July 1961 on 'Women's Organisation' programme.

49　On Ian Nairn, see obituaries in *The Times*, 18 August 1983, and *Architectural Review*, September 1983. I Nairn, *Your England Revisited*, London, 1964; I Nairn, *Britain's Changing Towns*, London, 1967. Polemical debate between Nairn and M MacEwen: *JRIBA*, June 1966, 259, and July 1966, 298; see also R Martin, *The Organizational Complex*, Cambridge, MA, 2003. Matthew support for Eric Lyons appeal against SPAN planning refusal in 1961–2: EULMC, file MS2543, correspondence of 7–17 February 1961 and 1962 between Lyons and RHM.

50　*JRIBA*, November 1962, 406–7.

51　EULMC, text of RHM lectures, 'Impact of change', 29 November 1968; to Edinburgh University, 14 May 1964; at Reading, 13 January 1964; and to the assembly of Canadian architects, 17 June 1964: Crossman, *Diaries*, vol. 1, 158–9.

52　M Bruton, 'Colin Buchanan', in G Cherry (ed.), *Pioneers in British Planning*, London, 1987, 263ff. C Buchanan, *Mixed Blessing*, London, 1958; C Buchanan, *State of Britain*, London, 1972; C Buchanan, *Traffic in Towns*, London, 1960–3; British Road Federation, *Urban Motorways*, London, 1958. Cf. the Barbican project for over 2,000 flats in interlocking squares, punctuated by towers (initial concept by Chamberlin, Powell & Bon, 1956): *Barbican, This Was Tomorrow*, catalogue of 2002 exhibition, Museum of London.

53　EULMC, text of RHM lecture to Fifth International Congress of the World Precast Concrete Society, 23 May 1966; RHM lecture to Annual Dinner of the Institute of Heating and Ventilation Engineers Scottish Branch, Glasgow 15 November 1966; G Cherry, *The Evolution of British Town Planning*, Leighton Buzzard, 1974.

54　*JRIBA*, November 1962, 407; *Building*, 17 February 1967, 79. On the shift from CIAM rationalism to more complex 'urban design', especially in the US: *Harvard Design Magazine*, Spring/Summer 2006.

55　Wilfred Burns, *New Towns from Old*, London, 1963, xi.

56　EULMC, text of RHM lecture of 13 January 1964 at Reading; *Harvard Design Magazine*, Spring/Summer 2006.

57　EULMC, text of RHM lecture to Cairo University Faculty of Engineering, 1 April 1964, and to AIA/Pan American Convention, Washington DC, 14 June 1965. On 'vernacularism' in the traditional sense of anonymous, informal building: B Rudofsky, *Architecture without Architects*, New York, 1965.

58　*Illustrated London News, Supplement*, 28 October 1967, 25–77.

59　RHM interview in *Illustrated London News, Supplement*, 28 October 1967.

60　*Architectural Design*, December 1962; A Smithson (ed.), *Team Ten Primer*, London, 1962, 559–60; R Banham, *Theory and Design in the First Machine Age*, London, 1960, 160; R Landau, *New Directions in British Architecture*, London, 1968.

61　Henry-Russell Hitchcock on Spence as England's 'leading architect' in 1964: H R Hitchcock, 'English Architecture in the early 1960s', *Zodiac*, 1, 1964, 47; see also RCAHMS, Spence archive, personal correspondence files, letter from S Loweth to Spence, 20 July 1969.

62　See e.g. *AJ*, 6 June 1966, 276; *Builder*, 15 January 1965, 107; *Architect and Building News*, 29 January 1969, 27 (Casson); *Architectural Review*, May 1969 (Lasdun); *JRIBA*, May 1967, 191–200 (Martin); *Architectural Design*, September 1965, 429.

63　Interview with RAM, 2005; Sir A Derbyshire, 'The story of a contradiction', *RMJM 40*, unedited version, c.1996.

64　Neglect: interview with M Lee, 1995; see also A Derbyshire, *AJ*, 12 June 1997; P Willis, *New Architecture in*

Scotland, London, 1977, 46, 52, 76, 92.

65   Interview with A Wightman, 2004.

66   On Morris, see J and M Richards, *JRIBA*, April 1966, 155–63. Interview with Sir A Derbyshire, 2004.

67   Interview with J Richards, 2003.

68   Interview with A Wightman, 2004.

69   Interviews with A Gilmour, 1987, and J Latimer, 2007.

70   Interview with M Richards, 2003.

71   Interview with M Richards, 2003.

72   'Rule of iron': interview with RAM, 2005; interview with F Isserlis, 1997.

73   Interview with K E Graham, 2003.

74   EULMC, file MS2569, report by J D Richards on industrialised building, 7 February 1964.

75   'Fragmentation' and 'unhappy' character of Edinburgh practice: interview with C Butler-Cole, 2007.

76   RMJMSS, Pilgrim Street file, minutes of May 1962 meeting.

77   *Builder*, 31 July 1964; Glendinning and Muthesius, *Tower Block*, Chapter 26; interview with C Robertson, 1987.

78   Interview with John Richards, 2003, and Derbyshire, 2004.

79   Abortive RHM–PJM proposal of 1963 for a 'NATO Institute of Science and Technology': EULMC, file MS2540, April 1963 correspondence with Midlothian County Council.

80   EULMC, letter of 6 October 1966 from RHM to SRM.

81   RMJMSS Loretto Chapel file, letters of 18 August 1952 from Mungo Campbell to RHM, and replies of 22 September 1962 and 30 March 1963.

82   RMJMSS Loretto file, letters of 17 May 1963 to SRM, 15 August 1963 from M Campbell to 'Willie', 20 August 1963 from RHM toW Mackinlay; minutes of meeting at Loretto on 19 October 1963; letter of 25 October 1963 from K Graham to M Campbell.

83   RMJMSS Loretto file; *AJ*, 13 October 1965; *Scotsman*, 16 July 1965.

84   National Trust for Scotland archive (per S Loftus and J Hanraets, NTS), minute of 10 January 1962 Executive Committee meeting; EULMC, file MS2534, letter from Wemyss to RHM, 6 January 1962. 1955 sketch with hall, RHM timber proposal, and visit to Waterloo: information from J Hanraets. Gettysburg: *Docomomo US National News*, Autumn 2004, 2.

85   Interview with PJM, 1987.

86   PJM, *University of Edinburgh, George Square Redevelopment*, 1963; memorandum by PJM to University, 25 November 1963; Fenton, 'Century of change', 65–6.

87   Construction difficulties of Arts Tower: RMJMSS, Arts Tower file, letter of 29 August 1962 from J Richards to Crudens; 6 April 1967 from J D Richards to Factoral Secretary; J Richards letter of 28 September 1967.

88   RMJMSS, Arts Tower file, letter of 24 November 1967 from J D Richards to E Colam.

89   Note by R Scott Morton, 1984.

90   *Architectural Review*, June 1968; RMJM, Faculties of Arts and Social Sciences, Development Plan 1964–70, January 1964.

91   EULMC, text of RHM lecture to Sheffield Branch of Edinburgh University Graduates' Association, 6 March 1965.

92   Commonwealth Pool: Royal Fine Art Commission for Scotland, 'Minds Meeting' lecture series, 1993: 'The Architecture of Precision', by J Richards. *Architectural Design*, January 1967; Glendinning, *Rebuilding Scotland*; *JRIBA*, August 1970; *AJ*, 16 September 1970; *Swimming Pool Record*, December 1969.

93   EULMC, text of RHM lecture to students of Edinburgh University Architecture Department, 25 April 1968; Muthesius, *Postwar University*.

94   RMJMSS, Stirling University first file, minutes of meetings of 10 December 1965, 23 December 1965, 20 March 1966.

95   Derbyshire, in *RMJM 40*.

96   *AJ*, 5 June 1968, 1203–98; *Scotsman*, 1 January 1995; J Richards obituary, *Scotsman*, 13 November 2003, 20; Docomomo Scottish National Group, *Report* 7, May 2004, Stirling University.

97   *Architectural Design*, January 1962; *AJ*, 27 February 1962, *Municipal Journal*, 8 December 1961; RMJMSS, Barshare files, Spaven note of 15 December 1962, note for 13 May 1963 Cumnock Town Council meeting; *RMJM Roundabout*, October 1973, 2–4. Saltire award: *Evening Dispatch*, November 1963, 6.

98   EULMC, text of RHM speech at Cumnock Centenary Dinner, 7 December 1966, and at RIBA Symposium on Manchester Central Area Redevelopment, 17 April 1964.

99   Interview with J D Richards, 2003.

100 RMJMSS, Pilgrim Street file, note of meetings on 30 January 1963 and 1 July 1963.

101 August meeting: interview with K E Graham, 2003. Preservation of arcade: Charlewood & Curry, 28 July 1970, 'News Release, Pilgrim Street Development'.

102 EULMC, letter from RHM to I Finlay, 1 March 1961; *Builder*, 3 June 1960, 1049–50.

103 RMJMSS Cockenzie files, including landscaping file of May 1961 to October 1963, and main station file from October 1962 to 1965.

104 RMJMSS, ERI files letter of 7 January 1963 from RFACS to SERHB.

105 RMJMSS, ERI files, letters of 17 June 1969 and 21 November 1969 from RMJM to SERHB; Catford, *The Royal Infirmary of Edinburgh*, 128.

106 Interview with A Wightman, 2004.

107 RMJMSS, Ninewells files, minutes of preliminary meeting at 31 Regent Terrace on 3 December 1963 with Crudens; letter from I R Munro of Crudens to RMJM, 21 July 1964.

108 Interview with A Wightman, 2004. 'Immensity': Sommerville, *Ninewells Revisited*.

109 Sommerville, *Ninewells Revisited*.

110 Interview with A Wightman, 2004.

111 Interview with RAM, 2005.

112 Letter from A Wightman to M Glendinning, 23 February 2005; Sommerville, *Ninewells Revisited*.

113 Glendinning and Muthesius, *Tower Block*, 240. Interview with T Spaven, 1995; 'Pigs and whistles': interview with J Latimer, 2007.

114 House of Commons, Fifth Report of Committee of Public Accounts, session of 27 April 1967; RMJMSS, Ninewells files, letter from RHM to Lewis Robertson, Eastern Regional Hospital Board, 8 September 1967, and letter of 21 October 1967 from A Wightman to RHM; *Scotsman*, 18 October 1967, 18.

115 *Daily Record*, 19 July 1972, 9; *Scotsman*, 10 January 1973; *Sunday Mail*, 10 June 1973; *Scotsman*, 11 January 1974, 11; EULMC, text of lecture by RHM at British Council Hospital Planning Course, London, February 1974.

116 Edinburgh University Architecture Department files, per Mrs E Morris.

117 Zahir, *Memoirs of an Architect*, 57.

118 Interview with E Hendry, 1997.

119 EULMC, file MS2535, 2 March 1965 draft of letter by Matthew backing £1.5m fundraising appeal. *Builder*, 6 December 1961, 1092; interview with J D Richards, 2003.

120 EULMC, letter from PJM to RHM and SJM, 17 March 1975.

121 Interview with L Fricker, 1997.

122 Interviews with S Platt, 2003, and E Hendry, 1997.

123 Interview with A Hendry, 1997.

124 EULMC, file MS2533, letter of 29 January 1966 from RHM to Edinburgh University Press.

125 Interview with E Morris, 1997.

126 Interview with April Johnson-Marshall, 1997.

127 Interview with PJM, 1987; Glendinning and Muthesius, *Tower Block*, Chapter 26; MPBW and Edinburgh University Architecture Research Unit, *Decisions Affecting Design of Five Point Blocks*, Edinburgh, 1968; interviews with N Raitt, 1987, C Robertson, 1987 and 2007.

128 *AJ*, 16 January 1963; *Builder*, 10 August 1962, 308. 'Mini practices': interview with A Hendry, 1997. Interview with April Johnson-Marshall, 1997.

129 *Builder*, 4 March 1966, 152, review by John Rae; interview with April Johnson-Marshall, 1997.

130 Fenton, 'Century of change', 72.

131 Interviews with E and A Hendry, L Fricker, and E Morris, 1997.

132 Interview with L Fricker, 1997. Interview with C Butler-Cole, 2007.

133 B Lamprecht, *Richard Neutra*, Köln, 2004; R Neutra, *Life and Shape*, New York, 1962; T S Hines, *Richard Neutra and the Search for Modern Architecture*, Berkeley, 1982; *JSAH*, June 2002, 235.

134 Interview with E Hendry, 1997.

135 Interview with S Platt, 2003.

136 EULMC, file MS2533, letter of 6 June 1968 from Oddie to RHM; interviews with E Hendry and E Morris, 1997.

137 EULMC, file MS2539, letter of 9 January 1964 from Ling to A Goss, Leeds School of Art.

138 Interview with A Hendry, 1997. EULMC, text of RHM talk of 8 November 1963 at Saltire Awards.

139 SBE inspired partly by recommendations of the Banwell Committee for collaboration between architects and engineers: interview with A Hendry, 1997.

140 EULMC, text of October 1968 lecture.

141 Typescript paper of 19 May 1997 on SBE by Prof A W Hendry: courtesy of Professor Hendry.

142 EULMC, letter of 10 February 1968 from Nuttgens to Matthew and 12 January 1967 from Matthew to Ling.

143 *JRIBA*, November 1962, 405ff. EULMC, text of RHM lecture at 18 April 1964 to symposium organised by Northern Allied Societies, and of 20 April 1964 to EASA.

144 Interview with T Spaven, 1995.

145 EULMC, file MS2538, letter of 2 July 1962 from Holford to RHM.

146 EULMC, text of RHM speech at 26 November 1963 presentation of portrait to Holford; Letter from A Derbyshire to L Esher, 13 November 1997 (per Sir A Derbyshire).

147 Interview with W Allen, 1997; Saint, *Towards a Social Architecture*, 246.

148 Stirrat as 'populist': interview with W Allen, 1997; EULMC, file MS2538, letter of 4 July 1962 from G Ricketts to RHM.

149 EULMC, file MS2538, letters of 18 and 28 February 1964 from G Ricketts to RHM.

150 EULMC, text of RHM speech of 3 November 1964, 'Introducing Sir Donald Gibson', and 2 March 1965 reply to Gibson's speech at RIBA portrait ceremony.

151 D Sharp, *Country Life*, 25 June 1970, 1242−4.

152 *AJ*, 19 December 1962, 134 (on the Office Survey); EULMC, file MS2539, letter from D C Hall to Holford, 5 April 1962; G Ricketts to Matthew, 13 June 1962; EULMC, text of RHM lecture of 15 March 1963 to Wiltshire and Dorset architects.

153 A Mace, *The RIBA, a Guide to its Archive and History*, London, 1986; *JRIBA*, October 1969, 412−3.

154 *JRIBA*, November 1962, 405ff.

155 EULMC, text of RHM lecture to Northants architects, 21 March 1963; Brunton Baden Hellyard, *Management Applied to Architectural Practice*, 1964; *AJ*, 16 January 1963, 125.

156 Interview with Sir A Derbyshire, 2004. Management Handbook: *JRIBA*, November 1962, 405ff; *AJ*, 13 November 1963, 1040−1.

157 Interview with Sir A Derbyshire, 2004.

158 EULMC, text of lecture to Cambridge etc. architects, 29 September 1962.

159 EULMC, text of RHM lecture to RIBA General Meeting, 4 February 1964; file MS2538, letter of 2 April 1965 from L K Watson to RHM, and 18 May 1965 from G Ricketts to RHM.

160 Suspected suicide of G Ricketts, jumping off a Kent cliff, *AJ*, 17 January 1968, 202−3, and 14 August 1968, 271.

161 EULMC, file MS2543, letters from Cottesloe to Matthew, 3 August 1962, 18 September 1962, 25 October 1962, 12 December 1962; L Brett to RHM, 14 February 1963; 22 November 1963 Press Statement by South Bank Theatre Board; file MS2535, letter of 20 May 1965 from Board to RHM.

162 Organisation for European Economic Cooperation, *Prefabricated Building, A Survey of Some European Systems*, Paris, 1958.

163 EULMC, file MS2536, letter of 24 March 1964 from Kemp to RHM, 9 April 1964 Ricketts RIBA memo to P Massey; meeting of 4 May 1964 and follow-up correspondence. EULMC, text of RHM lecture to Architecture Club, 20 March 1963.

164 EULMC, text of RHM lecture to RIBA conference, July 1963; file MS2539, letter of 19 November 1962 from R Harrison to RHM. EULMC, file MS2538, RIBA evidence to Committee on Social Studies; RIBA General Meeting, paper of 28 January 1964; RHM lecture to Joint Building Group, 9 December 1964.

165 Interview with W Allen, 1997. Matthew, Rippon, Prince Philip and chaotic indistrialised building conference in November 1963: EULMC, file MS2538, correspondence of 13 November 1963. Matthew canvassed by Rippon November 1963 over designer for possible Foreign and Home Office redevelopment: EULMC, file MS2538, letter of 6 November 1963 from Rippon to RHM and 22 November 1963 reply.

166 EULMC, file MS2539, memo by RHM to Select Committee, 10 May 1965.

167 EULMC, file MS2538, 2 October 1962 note by RHM on 1 October meeting with Minister; 5 October 1962 note from Ricketts to MacEwen; 2 January 1964 letter from Corfield to RHM; 21 July 1964 note from RHM to K Joseph and reply of 12 August 1964.

168 Matthew attack on George Brown: EULMC, text of RHM speech to RIBA Regional Meeting, Birmingham, 11 April 1964.

169 EULMC, file MS2539, letter of 6 February 1967 from R Sheppard to RHM, RHM to A Crosland, 25 March 1969, RHM to *The Times*, 30 October 1970.

170 Robbins: EULMC, text of RHM lecture to RIBA General Meeting, 18 February 1964, 'The education of architects'. EULMC, file MS2539, letter of 2 July 1964 from E Layton to RHM, text of 19 February 1964 RHM reply to Leicester University Vice-Chancellor; EULMC, file MS2538, letter of 10 May 1968 from RHM to *New Statesman*.

171 EULMC, file MS2539, notes on NCARB/ARCUK/RIBA meeting of 6–8 February 1967.

172 EULMC, file MS2538 (on Committee on Training of Technicians, 1960–2), letter of 2 June 1961 from Harper to RHM, 9 June 1961 from Allen to RHM, 5 June 1962 from Baines to RHM.

173 Sempill: EULMC, file MS2538, 27 June 1962, Sempill to RHM. Matthew's qualified endorsement of Jacobs's condemnation of planning and praise of 'unplanned' vitality: *JRIBA*, November 1962, 405ff. 1962 Matthew attacks on urban motorway building in London and Beeching rail closures: EULMC, note of 11 June 1962 from C Buchanan to M MacEwen.

174 Boards: EULMC, file MS2538, letter of 29 August 1968 from P Shepheard to RHM.

175 A Ravetz, *The Government of Space*, London, 1986, 9.

175 *Architect and Building News*, 28 July 1965; *The Times*, 20 July 1965; Ian Rice, 'Ziggurats for bureaucrats', *Twentieth Century Society Newsletter*, 2003/4, 12; C Buchanan and L Martin, *Whitehall – a Plan for the National and Government Centre*, London, 1965.

177 S Games, 'Whitehall farce', *JRIBA*, April 1980, 55. See also EULMC, RHM note on 3 February 1966 meeting with J D Jones, note of 18 February from Jones to RHM; *AJ*, 8 June 1966, 1398–1400.

178 *AJ*, 8 June 1966, 1398–1400.

179 RHM/MHLG, *Report of a Public Inquiry into the Future Use of the Broad Sanctuary Site*, London, 1967. Greenwood, Times, 22 March 1967. Sharp: Cherry, *Pioneers in British Planning*, 171. EULMC, letter of 12 December 1967 from Sharp to MHLG, letter of 29 April 1968 from Sheriff Johnston to RHM, letter of 20 December 1967 from H C Delves to MHLG, letter of 4 August 1968 from Angus Robin to Maurice Kidd. The fee for conducting the inquiry was a modest £505 plus travelling expenses.

180 A Powers, obituary of Martin, *Twentieth Century Society Newsletter*, September 2000, 30; *JRIBA*, April 1980, 49–58.

181 EULMC, text of RHM lecture of 17 June 1965; letter of 18 June 1968 from Whitfield Lewis to RHM.

182 EULMC, letters from Cyril Walker to RHM, 29 August 1967, 9 September 1967, 19 September 1967; interview with C Robertson, 2007.

183 EULMC, letter of 21 January 1966 from RHM to M MacEwen; EULMC, letter of 28 May 1963 from RHM to Director-General of BBC; letter of 13 December from MHLG to RHM; letter of 6 May 1964 from BBC Chairman to RHM; letter of 16 June 1966 from H Evans, Editor, *Sunday Times*, to RHM; file MS2535, text of RHM talk of January 1966 and letter from Director of TV, 14 January 1966.

184 Cherry, *Evolution of British Town Planning*; A Ravetz, *The Government of Space*, London, 1986; *Town and Country Planning*, January/February 1968.

185 EULMC, text of RHM lecture of 7 February 1964 in Cardiff. Matthew-led deputation to Joseph in April 1963 to present the paper: *JRIBA*, April 1963, 134; EULMC, file MS2538, note of 2 October 1962 by RHM; note of 13 December 1962 from Massey to Ricketts; notes of 13 June and 18 November 1963 from J R James to RHM.

186 Initial Civic Trust gentlemanly focus on exemplar schemes such as 1959 'facelift' in Magdalen Street,

Norwich: *Builder,* 8 April 1960, 707; *Builder*, 2 December 1960, 1025. Pressure by post-1962 CT Secretary, Leslie Lane, with Matthew's backing, for more proactive stance: EULMC, file MS2541, note of 18 October 1962 from L Lane to RHM, 29 March 1963 from RHM to Ricketts, 2 May 1963 meeting of Lane, Spence, RHM; 19 August 1963 memo by RHM; letter of 18 July 1963 from L Lane to RHM; Civic Trust, *The First Three Years*, London, 1960; *AJ*, 23 April 1986, 28–33, Civic Trust, *Heritage Outlook*, November–December 1986, 110–1.

187 EULMC, file MS2535, note of 13 January 1965 and reply; text of RHM talk of April 1965.

188 EULMC, file MS2548, proceedings of 10 December 1965; Crossman, *Diaries*, vol. 1, 312.

189 *Edinburgh Architectural Association Yearbook*, 1966; EULMC, MS2535 papers of 2–4 June 1965.

190 EULMC, text of RHM talk of 14 December 1962.

191 EULMC, file MS2538, correspondence of July–November 1963 RHM – M Nicholson of Nature Conservancy Council, following 'conversation on the Night Scotsman recently'; EULMC, undated note of 1963 from Lord Thomson to RHM.

192 EULMC, letter of 2 July 1968 from J Summerson to RHM.

193 EULMC file MS2540, note of 26 April 1966 from Smith to RHM, and correspondence of April 1966 to June 1967.

194 EULMC, paper of 23 June 1966, and file MS2535; EULMC, text of 30 January 1967 'Keith Lecture' by RHM.

195 EULMC, letter of 19 February 1968 from J L Paterson to RHM; EULMC, text of 28 October 1964 RHM lecture to BBC. RHM as Salvation Army Scottish convener of property 1968–75: EULMC, file MS2540, correspondence of July 1967 to May 1968.

196 RHM on Scottish architectural 'ruggedness': EULMC, text of 29 November 1968 BBC TV lecture.

197 Interview with Margaret Richards, 2004.

198 EULMC, text of Reading lecture by RHM, 12 January 1964. RHM on Geddes as inspiration for 'creative' planning: EULMC, file MS2535, lecture of 10 October 1966 to Social Science Faculty.

199 EULMC, letter of 23 August 1965 from Grieve to RHM.

200 EULMC, text of 29 November 1968 BBC TV lecture; *Building Design*, 5 June 1970, 7. Stirrat criticism of Cumbernauld Centre as 'a flawed concept': interview with A Wightman, October 2004. RHM praise for HLM's megastructural Paisley municipal buildings as 'not only an outstanding group of buildings, but at the same time a piece of town planning, in the creative sense of the word': EULMC, text of RHM lecture of 27 February 1964.

201 *GIA Yearbook*, 1964; EULMC, letter from RHM to Cleeve Barr, 21 June 1965.

202 EULMC, file MS2540, letter of 17 October 1964 from Pevsner to RHM.

203 EULMC, file MS2533, text of RHM address to first meeting of UAHS, 15 November 1967.)

204 Interview with L Fricker. N Dunhill, 'An experiment in preservation: New Lanark 1825–1964', reproduced from *Ontario Housing*, 1964.

205 RHM praise in 1968 TV programe for Fife, and its regeneration, as a Geddesian paradigm: EULMC, file MS2536, note of 29 November 1968.

206 EULMC, file MS2541, correspondence of 1 October 1963 to 24 September 1968. Wheeler as Matthew's main protégé within the 'Saltire' scheme: interview with Sir A Wheeler, 1997.

207 1961–3 pilot scheme for High Street 'facelift': street furniture, paving, signage and lighting coordination (from St Mary's Street to Bridges) and Matthew lament of 1965 at failure of project owing to 'self-centred' shopkeepers: EULMC, text of 4 April 1963 RHM lecture to Institute of Builders; EULMC, file MS2535, text of RHM May 1965 lecture to EAA.

208 EULMC, file MS2533, letter of 8 March 1963 from M Woodruff to RHM. June 1967 Womersley telephone plea to RHM to intervene to save Selkirkshire trees from road widening scheme: EULMC, June 1967.

209 EULMC, file MS2540, note of 27 June 1962. March 1962 RHM RFACS memo condemning Roxburgh County Council road improvement plans as threat to 'the sturdy lowland Border character of the small country towns': EULMC, file MS2540, draft paper of March 1962.

210 Tenements: EULMC, file MS2540, correspondence of 16 March 1962; *Builder*, 27 November 1964.

211 EULMC, file MS2540, note of May 1964 by RHM.

212 RHM/Bannatyne refusal to back local preservation campaign, masterminded by activist 'warrior', Mrs M Needham, against a 'sensitive' Kininmonth redevelopment scheme for historic burgh of Linlithgow: EULMC, file MS 2540, C Nasmith to Mrs Needham, 24 September 1964; J Bannatyne to Nasmith, 30 September 1964. November 1967 RHM note on threatened 18th-century town houses at 32–5 St Andrew Square as 'not of great architectural value': EULMC, file MS2540, note of November 1967 by RHM.

213 EULMC, file MS2541, letter of 14 November 1965 from C McWilliam to RHM.

214 EULMC, file MS2542, letters of 14 April 1964 from L Lane to RHM; 27 August 1965 from J Bannatyne to RHM, 13 July 1965 from L Lane to RHM, 27 September 1966 from Muirshiel to M, 28 December 1966 from the SCT Hon. Secretary to RHM; *SCT Newsletter*, 13, Spring 1997, 8.

215 RHM 1966 advice to restoring owner of 17th-century Methven Castle: referred him to Lindsay, then to the 'very trustworthy' Wheeler & Sproson: EULMC, file MS2541, correspondence of March–May 1966).

216 EULMC, file MS2541, letters from Cawdor to RHM, 29 August and 18 November 1962l 18 December 1962 from Rippon to Matthew; *Glasgow Herald*, 11 October 1963.

217 'Battle of the lavatories' at Craigievar settled when

Matthew and Cecilia both paid half the added cost of toilets located away from the house: EULMC, file MS2541, letters from Cecilia to RHM, 25 November 1963, 17 February 1964, 25 February 1964, 30 April 1964, 12 August 1964; letter from Stormonth-Darling to RHM, 25 October 1963.

218 EULMC, letter of 18 July 1967 from Maxwell Allan to M; I R Gow, *Report of the Craigievar Subcommittee*, 5 November 1993, 8. (Manuscript; for NTS.)

Chapter 10

1 Interview with J A Oliver, 1987.

2 Rt Hon W K Fitzsimmons, Foreword to *Coleraine, Portrush, Portstewart Area Plan*, Belfast, 1968.

3 Edward Richardson MP (Stormont), quotation in *Belfast Newsletter*, 15 August 1964.

4 Parity: interview with J A Oliver, 1987; P Buckland, *A History of Northern Ireland*, Dublin, 1981; T Wilson (ed.), *Ulster under Home Rule*, Oxford, 1955.

5 Interview with J A Oliver, 1987.

6 T O'Neill, *Autobiography*, Dublin, 1972, 47; interview with H McIlveen, 2004.

7 Early Irish state housing: M Fraser, *John Bull's Other Homes*, Liverpool, 1996.

8 'You could see it all from the windows of Stormont!' J A Oliver, *Working at Stormont*, Dublin, 1978; Buckland, *History of Northern Ireland*; Wilson, *Ulster under Home Rule*.

9 Parsimony of NIHT: interview with J A Oliver, 1987.

10 Oliver, *Working at Stormont*, 80–1.

11 Glendinning and Muthesius, *Tower Block*, 287 and 403.

12 Glendinning and Muthesius, *Tower Block*, 403 (notes 8, 9); Oliver, *Working at Stormont*, 80–81. Civil servants on 'pathetic' efforts by 'discredited' Belfast Corporation to 'pick holes in the agreement': Department of the Environment for Northern Ireland (DOENI) file 4150/1959, note from Hoey to Secretary, 9 May 1960.

13 Interview with J A Oliver, 1987.

14 RHM visit: *Belfast Telegraph*, 13 May 1960.

15 *Belfast Telegraph*, 13 May 1960.

16 EULMC, Belfast Regional Plan files, notes of 7 July 1960 by P D McGovern.

17 Interview with H McIlveen, 2004.

18 EULMC, Belfast Regional Plan files, handwritten notes of August 1962 by RHM.

19 Oliver, *Working at Stormont*, 82–3. Consolidation: interview with H McIlveen, 2004.

20 R H Matthew and Ministry of Health and Local Government, *Belfast Regional Survey and Plan, Interim Report on Housing Sites*, Belfast, 1961; EULMC, Belfast Regional Plan files, letter from W Morgan to RHM, 2 January 1962.

21 EULMC, Belfast Regional Plan files, questions of 20 August 1962 arising out of Toothill Report manuscript.

22 EULMC, Belfast Regional Plan files, letter of 26 February 1963 from J A Oliver to planning authorities. RHM Stormont stress on example of Geddes: EULMC, Belfast Regional Plan files, text of 4 March 1963 RHM lecture.

23 Newman depression following failure to win superintending-grade planning post in 1962: EULMC, Belfast Regional Plan files, letters of 13 June 1962 and 27 February 1963 from Oliver to RHM. Matthew's holiday was at the Villa Pelet, Bormes les Mimosas, Var, followed by a IUA trip to Brazil. EULMC, Belfast Regional Plan files, KM, minutes of meeting at Belfast on 19 and 20 July 1962; note from Newman to RHM, 14 August 1962; letter of 20 August 1962 from P McGovern to C Naismith; RHM draft text of 28 August 1962 and comments of 11 August 1962; letter of 31 August 1962 from RHM to J A Oliver.

24 EULMC, Belfast Regional Plan files, letter of 27 September 1961 from Chief Civil Defence Officer to RHM; note of 5 May 1961 by P McGovern.

25 Glendinning and Muthesius, *Tower Block*, 403 (note 10).

26 Interview with H McIlveen, 2004.

27 EULMC, Belfast Regional Plan files, NI Government Information Service press release, 26 February 1963.

28 Fraser, *John Bull's Other Homes*.

29 Interview with H McIlveen, 2004.

30 Machinations within NI government over publication of plan (initially for limited circulation): EULMC, Belfast Regional Plan files, letter of 7 November 1962 from Newman to Massey; *The Times*, 24 October 1962; Cd 451, Government of Northern Ireland, Belfast Regional Survey and Plan, Recommendations and Conclusions, presented to Parliament by Command of His Excellency the Governor, February 1963; EULMC, Belfast Regional Plan files, letter from Newman ('Cecil') to Massey ('Paddy'), 17 January 1963.

31 EULMC, Belfast Regional Plan files, letters of 26 November 1962 and 6 March 1963 from 'Cecil' to 'Paddy'.

32 Intrigue against Brookeborough's leadership by O'Neill reform faction: EULMC, Belfast Regional Plan files, letter of 27 February 1963 from J A Oliver to RHM.

33 Morgan speech: EULMC, Belfast Regional Plan files, 26 February 1963 press release.

34 EULMC, Belfast Regional Plan files, letter of 27 February 1963 from J A Oliver to RHM; letters of 27 February 1963 from Royal Society of Ulster Architects and from J E Sayers, and from H McIlveen to Belfast Telegraph; H McIlveen, *Perspectives of a Partnership*, Banbury, 1996.

35 Polarised press and parliamentary debates between 'progressives' and 'reactionaries': EULMC, Belfast Regional Plan files, cutting from *Belfast Telegraph*, 3 March 1963; Parliament of Northern Ireland, House of Commons Debates, 5 March 1963; RSUA policy release, May 1963.

36 *Belfast Newsletter*, 10 May 1963, 6.

37 *Belfast Newsletter*, 10 May 1963, 6; Parliament of Northern Ireland, Senate Debates, 12 November 1963, interventions by Senators Lennon, Donaghy, Bonhill; EULMC, Belfast Regional Plan files, letter of 24 October 1963 from J A Oliver to RHM.

38 Oliver, *Working at Stormont*, 83–4. Stresses between Green, Oliver, Newman, etc: EULMC, Belfast Regional Plan files, letter from R Green to RHM, 4 April 1963; *Belfast Newsletter*, 10 May 1963, 6, 'Planning becomes respectable'; letter of 23 May 1963 from C Naismith to C Newman.

39 Interview with D Whitham, 1994, and H McIlveen, 2004.

40 EULMC, Belfast Regional Plan files, text of RHM RIBA lecture, January 1964.

41 EULMC, Belfast Regional Plan files, 3 December 1963 briefing information by Ministry.

42 Stern RHM backing for stop-line, condemnation of high flats, meeting with Copcutt and colleagues: *Belfast Telegraph*, 13 December 1963; EULMC, Belfast Regional Plan files, 6 December 1963 from McGovern to Copcutt, and briefing notes for 13 December 1963 meeting.

43 *Belfast Telegraph*, 14 December 1963.

44 EULMC, Belfast Regional Plan files, *Belfast Telegraph*, cuttings of 30 January 1964 (Bunting), 18 January 1964 (Morgan), 28 February 1964, 3 March 1964; letter of 10 January 1964 from C Newman to RHM; *Newsletter*, 4 March 1964 (Boyd).

45 EULMC, Belfast Regional Plan files, letter from J A Oliver to RHM, 13 April 1964, and reply of 3 May 1964; Sir RH Matthew, *Belfast Regional Survey and Plan 1962*, Belfast, 1964, 2 volumes.

46 EULMC, Belfast Regional Plan files, letter of 25 March 1964 from J A Oliver to RHM; Cd 465, *The Administration of Town and Country Planning in Northern Ireland*, March 1964, paragraphs 16–18; Parliament of Northern Ireland, House of Commons Debates, 4 November 1964, col. 351.

47 Reluctant beginnings of slum redevelopment and urban motorway building in Belfast: Glendinning and Muthesius, *Tower Block*, 403, notes 22–4.

48 L Allen, 'New towns and the Troubles', *Town and Country Planning*, November/December 1981, 284.

49 Oliver, *Working at Stormont*, 88; Northern Ireland Government, *Economic Development, Northern Ireland*, Belfast (HMSO), 1965.

50 A Murie, 'Planning in Northern Ireland: a survey', *Town Planning Review*, October 1973, 337–58.

51 *Belfast Telegraph*, 18 January 1965.

52 1962 row over Copcutt anarchic tendencies at RIBA Coventry conference: EULMC, letter of 31 May 1962 from MacEwen to RHM.

53 *Belfast Telegraph*, 18 June 1969.

54 *Irish Times*, 24 April 1967; interview with D Whitham, 1997.

55 Copcutt and 'new city': Maureen Moriarty-Lempke, *Planning in Divided Societies*, unpublished MS, University of Massachusetts, n.d. (*c*.2000).

56 EULMC, Belfast Regional Plan files, letter of August 1964 from Newman to P McGovern; *Belfast Telegraph*, 15 August 1964; interview with J Latimer, 2007.

57 *Irish Times*, 14 August 1964; *Belfast Newsletter*, 18 August 1964.

58 Wichert, *Northern Ireland Since 1945*, 87.

59 Interview with J A Oliver, 1987.

60 *Belfast Telegraph*, 14 August 1964; *Derry Journal*, 25 October 1965.

61 Glendinning and Muthesius, *Tower Block*, 402, note 1.

62 Moriarty-Lempke, *Planning in Divided Societies*; Craigavon Development Corporation, *Craigavon City*; Blackman, 'Craigavon', in *Capital and Class*, 117–42; Bannerman, 'Craigavon', 118–19.

63 EULMC, Belfast Regional Plan files, RHM to Snow, 11 March 1966.

64 Public Record Office for Northern Ireland website, entry by Grace McGrath, 'Lockwood Committee, November 1963', reference proni.nics.gov.uk/Education/Ed39.htm.

65 Muthesius, *The Postwar University*; M Brawne, *University Planning and Design*, London, 1967. UGC controls slightly weaker in Northern Ireland. York: *AJ*, April 1970, 259–62; Bath: *AJ*, 17 November 1965, 1120–4.

66 Internet reference: en.wikipedia.org/wiki/University_of_Ulster_at_Coleraine.

67 RMJMSS, letter of 14 January 1966 from J A Oliver to RHM.

68 RMJMSS, New University of Ulster files, letters from Oliver to RHM, 1 and 28 February 1966.

69 Government of Northern Ireland, Commons Debates, 9 March 1966, columns 196–8.

70 Government of Northern Ireland, Commons Debates, 9 March 1966. Unionist pressure on Matthew against 'north-east bastion' policy and consequent 'extirpation' of Magee: RMJMSS, New University of Ulster files, letter of 9 May 1966 from W M Stewart to RHM.

71 Government of Northern Ireland, House of Commons Debates, 9 March 1966, columns 196–8.

72 RMJMSS, New University of Ulster files, note of 25 January 1979 by Chris Carter.

73 RMJMSS, New University of Ulster files, meeting of 20 April 1966, notes by RHM.

74 RMJMSS, New University of Ulster files, minutes of 21 April 1966 meeting; RMJMSS, New University of Ulster files, minutes of 21 April 1966 meeting, and paper of 3 May 1966, 'University development', by Burges.

75 RMJMSS, New University of Ulster files, minutes of 21 April 1966 meeting; RMJMSS, New University of Ulster files, minutes of 21 April 1966 meeting, and paper of 3 May 1966, 'University development', by Burges.

76 New University of Ulster (general): *Sunday Times Magazine*, 9 November 1969, 84; *Architectural Review*, April 1970, 285; *AJ*, 9 November 1977, 905.

77 RMJMSS, New University of Ulster files, letters of 28 April 1967 from A Robin to Rotary Club, 23 June 1967 from PJM to Standing Committee, 23 June 1967 and 25 September 1968; RMJM with Percy Johnson-Marshall and Associates, *Coleraine, Portrush, Portstewart Area Plan*, Belfast, 1968.

78 RMJMSS, New University of Ulster files, letter of 8

September 1966 from RMJM to University.

79   Interview with D Ashmead, 2004.

80   RMJMSS, New University of Ulster files, note of 9 June 1966 with Vice-Chancellor.

81   UGC pressure rebuffed over £30,500 architects' fees as at early 1967 – double the York, Stirling and Bath fees of £15,000. RMJMSS, New University of Ulster files, letter of 1 July 1966 from W T Ewing to J D Richards and 15 July 1966 reply; letters of 29 March and 28 August 1967 from A Robin to RHM.

82   Interview with D Ashmead, 2004.

83   RMJMSS, New University of Ulster files, letter of 16 September 1966 from A Robin to UGC; notes by RHM for press conference, 9 June 1967; letter of 21 October 1966 from Doherty to A Robin; letter of 15 November 1966 from W Ewing to A Robin; notes of 17 November 1966 meeting with Bain; construction comprised Bison Preferred Dimension.

84   Interview with D Ashmead, 2004.

85   S Muthesius, *The Postwar University*, London, 2000.

86   Expansion of existing universities and 'utopianist' debates: Muthesius, *Postwar University*, 164–8, 242–5.

87   Interview with D Ashmead, 2004.

88   Interview with Peter Winchester (job architect for Spence's Falmer House, University of Sussex), 2004.

89   RMJMSS, New University of Ulster files, notes of 7 April 1967 meeting.

90   RMJM, *The New University of Ulster, Report on the Development Plan*, 52–3.

91   RMJMSS, New University of Ulster files, notes of 3 February 1967 meeting.

92   RMJMSS, New University of Ulster files, letter of May 1967 from RHM to Vice-Chancellor.

93   Interview with D Ashmead, 2004.

94   Interview with D Ashmead, 2004; T Birks, *Building the New Universities*, Newton Abbot, 1972, 105–114; Muthesius, *Postwar University*.

95   Tile fixings: interview with C. Butler-Cole, 2007.

96   Interview with D Ashmead, 2004; Rowan, *North-West Ulster*, 211–2.

97   RMJMSS, New University of Ulster files, meeting of 5 May 1967; Birks, *New Universities*, 105–14; Cherry and Penny, *Holford*, 107.

98   Interviews with J D Richards, 2003, and C Butler-Cole, 2007. Stirling as 'older' pattern: Muthesius, *Postwar University*, 173.

99   RMJMSS, New University of Ulster files, notes of 9 June 1967 press conference. Interim report on the Development Plan was presented in August 1967, and finalised report published a year later: RMJM, *The New University of Ulster, Report on the Development Plan*.

100   Interview with D Ashmead, 2004.

101   *Northern Constitution*, 2 November 1968. New University of Ulster (general): *Sunday Times Magazine*, 9 November 1969,

84; *Architectural Review*, April 1970, 285; *AJ*, 9 November 1977, 905.

102   RMJM, *The New University of Ulster, Report on the Development Plan*, 53.

103   Leicester University (Stirling) the main inspiration for 'diamond' roofline of the Diamond: interview with D Ashmead, 2004.

104   Interview with D Ashmead, 2004.

105   1969 personality clash between RMJM on-site supervisor Michael Kirkbride and university Buildings and Estate Officer John Y Noble and university appeal to Matthew to intervene in June 1969: RMJMSS, New University of Ulster files, RMJM versus New University of Ulster, Statements of Evidence, January 1979, including 25 January 1979 note by J C Carter, 19 December 1978 by Angus Robin, and October 1970 letter from W T Ewing to RHM.

106   RMJMSS, New University of Ulster files, RMJM versus New University of Ulster, Statements of Evidence, January 1979 October 1970 letter from W T Ewing to RHM; by 1970, Phase 1 costs still in contention, with some £40,000 overspent.

107   Interview with A Wightman, 2004.

108   EULMC, RHM diaries for 1969 and 1970; Government of Northern Ireland, *Northern Ireland Development Programme 1970–75: Government Statement* (Cd 547), Belfast, 1970, 3.

109   Moriarty-Lempke, 'Planning in divided societies'; O'Neill, *Autobiography*; J A Oliver, *Working at Stormont*; Buckland, *History of Northern Ireland*; Wilson, *Ulster under Home Rule*.

110   Expansion of BDP's Ulster College at Jordanstown: Muthesius, *Postwar University*, 178. 1975–7 building by Peter Moro of the theatre envisaged in Matthew's development plan: *AJ*, 9 November 1977, 65. *Chronicle*, 1 March 1969.

111   Interview with A Derbyshire, 2004.

112   *Northern Ireland Development Programme 1970–75*, 29–30.

113   See e.g. EULMC, Belfast Regional Plan files, note of 27 May 1969 on stop-line; file MS2533, note of 1 July 1968 from Vick to RHM.

114   EULMC, letter of 24 July 1967 from Potter to RHM; interview with J A Oliver, 1987.

115   Interview with H McIlveen, 200.

Chapter 11

1   EULMC, June 1967 text of RHM lecture for IUA congress, Prague, 1967.

2   *JRIBA*, August 1970, 347.

3   Other 'internationalist' architects: H Le Roux, 'Modern architecture in post-colonial Ghana and Nigeria', *Architectural History*, 47, 2004, 361ff.; *JRIBA*, May 1964, 187–90; O Uduku, *Habitat International*, 30, 2006, 396–411; R Windsor-Liscombe, *JSAH*, June 2006, 188–213.

4   Interviews with C Somerville, 1996, and Sir J Dunbar-Nasmith, 2004.

5   RHM defence of international goodwill agenda against

'junketing' criticisms: *JRIBA*, August 1970, 347; interview with W Allen, 1997.

6   RHM in 1966: 'We are now a peripatetic lot ... not only the city, but the world is our textbook.' *JRIBA*, July 1975, 5; EULMC, text of RHM Freshers' Address, Social Sciences Faculty, 10 October 1966.

7   IUA French Section, *L'UIA, 1848–1998*, Paris, 1998; P Vago, *Pierre Vago, Une Vie Intense*, Bruxelles, 2000.

8   Bhalla mollified by RHM in 1961 clash with North Korean candidate: EULMC, file MS2555, circular from Vago to Sections, 18 July 1961; letter from G Goulden to RHM, 11 August 1961; RHM to Bhalla, 23 August 1961.

9   See for instance *Constructed Happiness: The Domestic Environment in the Cold War Era*, Estonian Academy of Arts, May 2004; R Stegers (ed.), *Glueck Stadt Raum in Europa 1945 bis 2002*, Basel, 2002.

10 EULMC, file MS2538, letter from K Hall to RHM, 15 June 1962; file MS2555, letter of 30 July 1964.

11 EULMC, letter of 15 December 1963 from Kolli to RHM; EULMC, file MS2533, letter of 25 February 1965 from RHM to Kolli.

12 EULMC, file MS2552, correspondence of May–July 1962.

13 EULMC, file MS2555, letter of 20 April 1966 from RHM to Vago. Post-1968 Czechoslovakia interventions: EULMC, file MS2549, August 1968 correspondence.

14 EULMC, file MS2538, letter of 27 May 1966 from R G Medwin to RHM, and 12 December 1967 from RHM to Gordon. RHM intercession in UIA row over attempts by 'discourteous' Ernö Goldfinger at 'advertising himself': EULMC, file MS2554, letter of 22 July 1964 from Vago to RHM; see also N Warburton, *Erno Goldfinger*, London, 2004, 61–3.

15 EULMC, file MS2555, letters of 3 February 1964 and 23 March 1964 from Lawrence to RHM.

16 EULMC, text of RHM speech of 14 June 1965. Abortive 1968 US attempt to form 'English-speaking' axis within IUA: EULMC, file MS2555, letter of 8 January 1968 from R Durham to RHM and reply. RHM–Vago negotiations on proposed 'east–west colloquium' on housing in India, shifted to Beirut in 1966: EULMC, file MS2557, 21 August 1963 from Vago to RHM, and list of potential speakers of 9 March 1965 by RHM.

17 See for instance Vago, *L'UIA*.

18 EULMC, file MS2554, Vago letter of 7 August 1962. Vago complaints to RHM on 'scandalous' anglophone lack of support for *IUA Revue*: EULMC, file MS2552, 15 November 1963, letter from J Lawrence to RHM, and Vago to RHM, 22 January 1964. Rows over proposed cuts in IUA commissions: EULMC, file MS2554, 8 April 1964, letter from Atkinson to RHM, and letter from R G Medwin.

19 EULMC, minutes of Executive Council of 27 May 1964. Kathleen Hall 1964 RIBA comments to Vago on need for ethnic balance in IUA regional groupings (e.g. to avoid giving 'the impression of grouping the coloured races togeth-

er'): EULMC, file MS2557, undated letter of 1964 from Hall to Vago. Crisis over Paris accommodation, RIBA help in furnishing HQ at 4 Impasse d'Antin: EULMC, file MS2556, letters of 17 May 1967 and 21 November 1967 from M Favier to RHM. Financial crisis, see EULMC, file MS2554, minutes of London Executive Committee, January 1969.

20 EULMC, file MS2555, letters of 16 July 1963 from Ling to RHM, 19 March 1964 from Vago to RHM, 15 April 1964 from Ling to Matthew, 4 May 1964 from Embden to Vago, 17 December 1964 from Vago to van den Broek, 7 January 1965 from Ling to Matthew, 19 February 1965 from Massey to Vago, 2 March 1965 from Vago to RHM, 11 March 1965 from Grieve to Massey, 31 March 1965 from Vago to RHM.

21 EULMC, text of October 1963 RHM speech to IUA, Mexico City. Paris congress: A G Heaume, 'Paris 1965', *L'UIA*, 120.

22 EULMC, June 1967 text of RHM report to September 1967 IUA Prague congress; EULMC, file MS2555, letter of 23 November 1966 from Vago to RHM, and minutes of 5 February 1967 Geneva brainstorming meeting.

23 EULMC, file MS2557, Red Book commentary, notes of 25–26 June 1968 Paris meeting and 19–20 August 1968 meeting.

24 EULMC, file MS2553, letter of 20 October 1961 from H Churchill to RHM.

25 Saugey 1950s hotels: C D d'Ayot, 'Saugey's Gamble', poster at DOCOMOMO International conference, Ankara, 2006. Matthew intercession in bitter 1965 row between Vago and Bruno Zevi over the Madrid Opera House competition (organised by a foundation with close ties with Franco extremism): Vago, *Pierre Vago – Une Vie Intense*; EULMC, file MS2556, letter of 15 February 1965 from Vago to RHM and 22 February 1965 from RHM to J M Richards. Vago's 1968 lobbying of RHM against 'domineering' Saugey: EULMC, file MS2557, letter of 4 April 1968 from Vago to RHM.

26 EULMC, file MS2555, letter of 8 November 1968 from P Vago to RHM; file MS2554, minutes of London Executive Committee meeting, 20–25 January 1969.

27 L Fasolo, *An Insider's Guide to the UN*, New Haven, 2002.

28 E Mumford, *The CIAM Discourse on Urbanism*, Cambridge, MA, 200, 128; EULMC, file MS2533, letter of 1 February 1966 from Vago to RHM.

29 See e.g. Jan van Ettinger (Bouwcentrum director), *Towards a Habitable World*, Amsterdam, 1960.

30 EULMC, file MS2553, letter of 31 October 1961 from Churchill to RHM. Attacks on 'anti-UN' Churchill by other New York architects: EULMC, file MS2554, letter of 19 February 1964 from C Aschner to Vago; file MS2553, 1965 report by RHM and letter of 12 August 1965 from Frost to Vago.

31 EULMC, file MS2554, letter of 5 December 1962 from Cleeve Barr to RHM.

32 EULMC, file MS2555, UN General Assembly resolution 17-0-xvi of 19 December 1961, letter of 17 July 1962 from

Churchill to RHM; letter of 11 March 1963 from Vago to RHM; *JRIBA*, November 1962, 407–8; EULMC, text of RHM address to 19 February 1963 RIBA conference.

33 Vago attacks on Weissmann's lack of support for IUA and lack of IUA–UN coordination: EULMC, file MS2533, letter of 1 February 1966 from Vago to RHM.

34 EULMC, file MS2533, letter of 12 January 1966 from W Woodhouse to RHM.

35 Frost opposition to 'industrialised production' approach 'involving complex technology' for developing countries as opposed to 'self-help': EULMC, file MS2533, letter of 21 December 1966 from Frost to Eric Carlson, Chief of the Housing Section of UN Housing, Building and Planning, and W Woodhouse report of 5–16 September 1966.

36 EULMC, file MS2533, letters of 3 May 1967 and 26 May 1967 from Frost to RHM.

37 EULMC, file MS2553, letter of 6 October 1967 from Vago to RHM; file MS2555, letter from Bhalla to Vago, 21 May 1968.

38 EULMC, file MS2553, letter from Vago to RHM, 5 November 1968; note of 1 June 1967 by UNESCO National Committee for the UK; P Valderrama, *A History of Unesco*, Paris, 1995.

39 EULMC, file MS2552, minutes of March–April 1962 Executive Committee meeting at Charleroi.

40 EULMC, file MS2553, notes of 17 December 1967 meeting in Paris; and report of 5–9 September 1966 Education of the Architect meeting in Paris.

41 Discontent at 'petrification' of its work: EULMC, file MS2553, letter of 14 September 1964 from BDA (West Germany) president to RHM.

42 *JRIBA*, November 1962, 401.

43 EULMC, file MS2555, correspondence of 1962.

44 EULMC, file MS2553, letters of 15 May 1965 from Vago to RHM, 20 May 1965 from Grunsfeld to RHM; 27 October 1967 memo by Vago; minutes of 9 July 1962 meeting of UK delegation to UNESCO; *Observer*, 12 August 1962; letters from Vago to RHM, 17 December 1962 and 14 August 1964.

45 RHM and 'Technological Red Cross': EULMC, file MS2554, letters of 30 December 1963 from RHM to Vago, 7 July 1966 from E D Mills to RHM; file MS2538, memo by RHM at RIBA council of 22 October 1963. IUA 1965 post-earthquake Skopje rebuilding competition won by Kenzo Tange: EULMC, file MS2553, letter of 12 August 1965 from F Frost to Vago; DOCOMOMO International conference, New York, 2004, lecture on Tange and Skopje; EULMC, file MS2553 1968, note by Fabio Penteado for Beirut meeting, and RHM notes.

46 EULMC, file MS2555, letter of 2 November 1967 from RHM to Gibson; see also Fasolo, *Insider's Guide to the UN*.

47 Interview with April Johnson-Marshall, 1997; EULMC, file MS2538, 18 December 1962 report by Sir Paul Slater, Director-General of the British Council. (EULMC, file

MS2552, 8 November meeting; cf. Richards, *Unjust Fella*, 209, on 1958 UNESCO planning conference in Brazil.)

48 *AIA Journal*, March 1964, 28.

49 E Rodriguez, 'Theory and practice of modern regionalism in Cuba', *Docomomo Journal*, September 2005, 33.

50 Vago debates with Matthew on how best to resist US pressure on IUA 'to enforce the mighty's will': EULMC, file MS2551, letter of 26 March 1962 from R Walker to E Grunsfeld, 16 April 1962 from Vago to RHM, and 8 October 1962 from M MacEwen to RHM.

51 EULMC, file MS2551, letter of 28 October 1962 from Fuller to Vago, 20 December 1962 from Bundy to Fuller, and 4 January 1963 from Fuller to Bundy.

52 EULMC, file MS2551, letter of 11 January 1963 from RHM to Vago, 16 January 1963 from Vago to RHM (with RHM MSS note on it), 3 August 1963 from Fuller to RHM, and 13 August 1963 from Vago to Massey.

53 EULMC, file MS2551, cable of 5 December 1962 from RM Franco to RHM; letters of 20 September 1962 from Massey to Vago, 25 September 1962 from Vago to RHM, 6 February 1963 from Massey to Vago, and guidance notes of early 1963 by M MacEwen.

54 EULMC, file MS2551, letter of 29 April 1963 from M MacEwen to Massey.

55 EULMC, file MS2551, letters of 7 March 1963 from J Lawrence to RHM, 28 February 1963 from Lawrence to H Wright; 2 April 1963 from Wright to RHM, 17 April 1963 from Vago to RHM, 26 April 1963 from R M Franco to Vago, 3 May 1963 from Vago to RHM, 26 July 1963 from K Hall to RHM, 8 August 1963 from Vago to Franco, 17 August 1963 from Dipl. Ing. Gericke (DDR) to RHM.

56 EULMC, file MS2551, letter of 12 August 1963 from Cuban Ambassador to Vago, and 23 August 1963 from RHM to Franco.

57 EULMC, file MS2551, letter of 31 July 1963 from Carroll to RHM and reply of 23 August 1963, 20 August 1963 from Vago to RHM, and 22 August 1963 cables to RHM from exiles; letter of 28 August 1963 from Jaime Varela Canosa to RHM; 1 September 1963 AIP press release; letter of 25 October 1963 from T Lismore to RHM.

58 Interview with E Morris, 1997; *New Cuba*, Summer 1964.

59 J M Austin-Smith, 'Havana 1963', *L'UIA*, 115.

60 Leycester Coltman, *The Real Fidel Castro*, New Haven, 2002; *Arquitectura Cuba*, January–March 1964; *New Cuba*, Summer 64; *AD*, September 1963; *AJ*, 9 October 1963 and 23 October 1963; *Builder*, November 1963; *AJ*, 6 November 1963; *Guardian*, 7 November 1963; *AJ*, 11 December 1963; *ABN*, 25 December 1963; *JRIBA*, December 1963, February 1964, March 1964; *Architectural Review*, October 1963; *AA Journal*, March 1964.

61 *AIA Journal*, March 1964, 30; Austin-Smith, *L'UIA*, 115.

62 *New Cuba*, Summer 1964; EULMC, file MS2551, letter of 15 August 1963 from Vago to RHM.

63 EULMC, file MS2551.

64 *Arquitetura Cuba*, January–November 1964; *New Cuba*, Summer 1964; *Architectural Review*, January 2000, on National Arts Schools by Ricardo Porro and others.

65 Interview with S Platt, 2003. Arrival in Mexico: Austin-Smith, *L'UIA*, 118.

66 EULMC, file MS2551, letter of 6 September 1963 from Corona Martin to RHM.

67 *AIA Journal*, March 1964, 39.

68 EULMC, file MS2552, letter of 15 January 1963 from J Lawrence to Cutler. Post-Cuba stabilisation: EULMC, papers of IUA Executive Council, Budapest, 27 May 1964. Prague conference: EULMC, file MS2549; *Architektura CSSR*, September/October 1966, 677–85.

69 RHM in 1968 on CAA as reaction against 'the image of the RIBA, the fountain of all wisdom, residing at Portland Place'; collaboration requiring a 'British-orientated system of alliance': EULMC, text of RHM CAA Jamaica speech, March 1968, and RHM speech to RICS Commonwealth conference, London, 28 August 1968; CAA, *CAA Handbook*, London, 1987; CAA, *Handbook of Commonwealth Architects*, 1965; CAA, *25 Years of Achievement, 1965–1990*, London, 1989.

70 General Commonwealth, British late-imperial and decolonisation books: K Nkrumah, *I Speak of Freedom*, London, 1961; Annan, *Our Age*, 356–7; J D B Miller, *The Commonwealth in the World*, London, 1958; J Springhall, *Decolonisation since 1945*, Basingstoke, 2000; D Judd and P Slinn, *The Evolution of the Modern Commonwealth*, London, 1982. M Beloff, 'The world as history', *Journal of Imperial and Commonwealth Studies*, 1, 1972, 111.

71 J Lang, Madhavi Desai, Miki Desai, *Architecture and Independence, The Search for Identity. India 1880 to 1980*, Delhi, 1997. N Pevsner, in J M Richards, ed., *New Buildings in the Commonwealth*, London, 1961, 14–17; I S Kaye, 'Architecture, history and the debate on identity', *JSAH*, September 2002.

72 M Fry and J Drew, *Tropical Architecture in the Humid Zones*, London, 1956; H Le Roux, 'Modern architecture in post-colonial Ghana and Nigeria', *Architectural History*, 47, 2004, 361ff.; U Kultermann, *Neues Bauen in Afrika*, Tuebingen, 1963; O Uduku, *Habitat International*, 30, 2006, 396–411.

73 RCAHMS, Spence Collection, RIBA files, letter of 16 December 1958 from W Allen to Spence.

74 RCAHMS, Spence Collection, MSS Diary of Tour of Africa, and letter of 12 June 1959 from Spence to G D Walford; *JRIBA*, August/September 1957.

75 Commonwealth-orientated RAIA presidents of the 1960s and 1970s included Max Collard (1963–4) and Ron Gilling (1970–1). (J M Freeland, *The Making of a Profession: A History of the Growth and Work of the Architectural Institutes in Australia*, Sydney, 1971, 78 and 158.)

76 D Austin, *West Africa and the Commonwealth*, London, 1957; A Mace, *The RIBA: A Guide to Its Archive and History*, London, 1986.

77 EULMC, text of RIBA paper for conference of 19–23

78 Matthew on coming 'Commonwealth Architects' Conference': *JRIBA*, November 1962, 408.

79 *JRIBA*, September 1963, 344ff.

80 RIBA, *Commonwealth and Overseas Allied Societies Conference*, London, 1963; T Colchester, *JRIBA*, November 1965, 492; T Colchester, 'The CAA', *JRIBA*, December 1964, 518–9. CBAE: *JRIBA*, August 1965, 74; *JRIBA*, July 1970, 262; *JRIBA*, September 1963, 344–354; EULMC, text of RHM CAA Jamaica speech, March 1968; EULMC, text of RHM lecture to RICS Commonwealth conference, London, 28 August 1968; CAA, *CAA Handbook*, London, 1987; CAA, *Handbook of Commonwealth Architects*, London, 1965; CAA, *25 Years of Achievement 1965–1990*, London, 1989.

81 *JRIBA*, September 1963, 344–54; Zahir, *Memoirs of an Architect*, 157.

82 *JRIBA*, September 1963, 344; EULMC, report on CAA Malta Conference, June 1965.

83 Difficulties of attracting high-quality teaching staff, and post-independence shifts to large social programmes: 'Modern architecture in post-colonial Ghana and Nigeria', *Architectural History*, 47, 2004, 361–92; J Lloyd, *Arena*, July–August 1966, 39–62; 'The AA in Africa', exhibition at AA, 2003, curated by O Uduku and H le Roux; M Fry and J Drew, *Tropical Architecture in the Humid Zones*, London, 1956; *AJ*, 15 October 1969, 976–7.

84 EULMC, file MS2559, January 1965 paper by T Colchester, letter of 25 February 1965 from Colchester to Matthew; Colchester note of 24 July 1964; letter of 30 November 1964 from V N Prasad to RHM.

85 1965 conference on collaboration with African universities at Edinburgh University: EULMC, file MS2559, letter from T Colchester to RHM, 23 September 1965.

86 EULMC, file MS2558, letter of 16 October 1964 from Rao to RHM.

87 Colchester–Bhalla debate on need for government architect in India, 1964–5: EULMC, file MS2558, letters of 2 November 1964 from Bhalla to RHM, and 7 January 1965 from Colchester to RHM.

88 EULMC, file MS2558, letter of 3 February 1965 from Colchester to RHM.

89 Special meeting in late March 1965 with the Minister of Works and Housing and civil servants: EULMC, file MS2558, letter from Joint Secretary of Ministry of Education to RHM.

90 EULMC, file MS2558, letter from Bhalla to RHM, 15 April 1965, and letter of 24 November 1965.

91 C Cockburn, 'Pattern of change', *Architectural Review*, May 1965, 333–5.

92 Informality at Malta: Zahir, *Memoirs*, 157–8.

93 EULMC, file MS2559, letter of 23 August 1965 from RHM to Nkrumah.

94 EULMC, file MS2559, letters of 13 September 1965 from

September 1960, and report of RIBA overseas examination panel, 10 February 1959.

Modern Architect

Holyoake to RHM, 7 October 1965 from H Wilson to RHM; file MS2558, letter from J E Wicken to Colchester, 17 September 1965.

95 EULMC, file MS2559, letters from Costanzi to RHM, 1 June 1965 and 28 August 1965; letter of 15 September 1965 from Sir Maurice Dorman (Governor-General) to RHM, and minutes of 6 December 1965 meeting of Matthew, Colchester and Costanzi at Park Square East.

96 EULMC, papers of 1966 IUA Executive Committee, Moscow. Tom Howarth's role: EULMC, file MS2558, letters of 27 May 1966 from Colchester to RHM, and of 26 May 1966 from T Howarth to RHM.

97 EULMC, file MS2558, letter of 29 November 1966 from Colchester to RHM.

98 EULMC, file MS2538, letter of 21 November 1967 from J Godwin to RHM. NIA: *Lagos Times*, 16 November 1967; letter of 28 November 1967 from Colchester to Olumuyiwa; 29 November 1967 from RHM to Godwin; 28 November 1967 from T Colchester to RHM; file MS2538, letter of 13 March 1968 from R Kirby, Zambian Institute of Architects, to RHM.

99 1968 Matthew exchanges with Charles Cockburn over overseas work: EULMC, file MS2558, letters of 18 September 1968 from P Newnham to RHM, 29 October 1968 from C Cockburn to RHM, and 12 November 1968 lunch meeting RHM–Cockburn.

100 EULMC, New Delhi conference report, March 1967.

101 Post-Delhi visits by Medwin, Howarth: EULMC, file MS2538, letter of 5 April 1967 from R G Medwin to RHM.

102 *CAA Newsletter*, 1975/2, 2; Zahir, *Memoirs*, 164.

103 EULMC, RHM notes of 22–28 March visit to Pakistan.

104 Interview with P Winchester, 2004; EULMC, file MS2538, letter of thanks from R S Rustomji, 29 March 1967; letters of 27 April 1967 from S A Rahim to RHM, 24 April 1967 from RHM to Sir Andrew Cohen, 18 May 1967 from Haworth to RHM and reply of 29 May 1967.

105 Bhalla, *Memoirs*, 67 and 159; EULMC, report of ARCASIA December 1968 conference; EULMC, file MS2558, letter of 27 June 1969 from Foreign Office to Colchester.

106 Interview with A Hendry, 1997.

107 EULMC, letter of January 1966 from Professor J R Lloyd to RHM; interviews with A Hendry, 1977.

108 *JRIBA*, August 1970, 347.

109 1959–60 involvement by array of welfare-state-connected British architects, including Matthew, Spence and Martin, in abortive project for a new Cape Town civic centre: RCAHMS, Spence Collection, SBS personal files, letters of 1 December 1959 from Morris to RHM and to Leslie Martin, 14 December 1959 from RHM to Spence, 2 March 1960 from Hal Kent to Spence, and 7 March 1960 from Spence to Hal Kent.

110 EULMC, file MS2559, letters of 29 July 1963 from M MacEwen to RHM, and 31 July 1963 from G Ricketts to RHM.

111 1963 cancellation of proposed IUA and RIBA visits to South Africa, and beginning of process of exclusion of South Africa: EULMC, file MS2559, letters of 27 August 1963 from Ringrose to RHM, 19 December 1963 from Matthew to Ringrose, 12 January 1965 from T Colchester to RHM; EULMC, file MS2558, letter of 17 September 1965 from J E Wicken to Colchester; H Floyd, *Building Shapes in Central Areas*, Cape Town 1963; R T Welch, *Urban Bantu Townships*, National Building Research Institute, South Africa, December 1963 (in RHM book collection).

112 EULMC, file MS2558, letter of 26 November 1968 from Colchester to RHM.

113 EULMC, file MS2548, September 1963; *JRIBA*, Novemebr 1962, 405ff.

114 EULMC, file MS2538, text of 8 November 1965 speech by M H Larsen.

115 EULMC, file MS2540, correspondence of May and June 1963.

116 A Nicolas, lecture to 7th Docomomo Conference, Paris, 2002.

117 EULMC, file MS2549 (ILO file), correspondence of January 1966 to June 1968.

118 EULMC, letter of 7 February 1961 from Hogan to Matthew, 16 March 1961 from UCD Secretary to RHM; file MS2549, correspondence about 1964 Site Layout and Arts Building Competition and 1966/7 library competition.

119 Negotiations with Vago over jury make-up, and criticism by jury member J Pedersen (Copenhagen City Architect) of the complexity of the judging system and its range of prizes, arguing that the number of entries approached the 'borderline that a competent committee can be expected to discuss': EULMC, MS2549, Amsterdam correspondence, February 1966 to March 1969.

120 EULMC, MS2549, Amsterdam correspondence, February 1966 to March 1969.

121 B Lootsma, *Superdutch: New Architecture in the Netherlands*, London, 2000, 12.

122 M Raymond, 'Modern Trinidad', *Docomomo Journal*, September 2005, 64–71; J M Richards (ed.), *New Buildings in the Commonwealth*, London, 1961.

123 EULMC, letter of 28 August 1962 from Jamaica Society of Architects to RIBA; letter of 27 September 1963 from A C Lewis to Massey; Trinidad press cuttings, October 1963; interview with S Platt, 2003.

124 EULMC, file MS2539, letters of 5 September 1967 from RHM to H Buszko, 16 September 1967 from W Gracja-Kawalex to RHM; file MS2533, letters of 4 December 1967 from RHM to Orlov, 17 January 1968 from C Naismith to G White, 5 June 1967 from Jiri Kroha to RHM, 4 April 1968 from V Gekan to RHM, 29 September 1968 from S Trubacek to RHM.

125 EULMC, letters of 15 September 1964 and 20 January 1965 from Livizeanu to RHM.

126 See e.g. M Liffe and G Sebastyen, *Die Entwicklung der*

Bautaetigkeit in Romaenien, Bucharest, 1964; J M Richards, 'Report on a visit to Romania', 18–27 March 1965 (unpublished typescript); Institutul de Arhitectura Ion Mincu, *Studii si Proiecte*, Bucharest, 1964, foreword by Professor Ascanio Damian; Professor arch. Gustav Gusti, *Architectura in Romania*, Bucharest, 1965.

127 EULMC, letter of 11 October 1965 from C Nasmith to Livizeanu; British Embassy briefing report to RHM, March 1966.

128 Bernard Rudofsky, *Architecture Without Architects: A Short Introduction to Non-Pedigreed Architecture*, New York, 1965.

129 *SAH News*, December 2004, 3. Late 1960s architectural 'particularism' as parallel to Ceaucescu's post-1967 socialist nationalism: C Popescu, 'Criticising Modernism', lecture to DOCOMOMO Conference, Ankara, September 2006.

130 EULMC, letter from RHM to Budisteanu, 23 May 1966, and reply of 28 May 1966; RHM, 'Report on visit to Romania, March–April 1966' (unpublished typescript).

131 EULMC, text of 23 May 1966 RHM lecture to World Precast Concrete Society.

132 EULMC, letters of 23 May 1966 from RHM to Badescu, 28 May 1966 from Budisteanu to RHM. Budidteanu's later career as official architect under Ceaucescu regime: D.C. Giurescu, *The Razing of Romania's Past*, London, 1990,61.

133 EULMC, file MS2533, letters of 5 November 1966 from Petrascu to RHM, 23 December 1967 and 24 June 1968 from Budisteanu to RHM. Budisteanu's later career as official architect under Ceaucescu regime: D.C. Giurescu, *The Razing of Romanaia's Past*, London, 1990, 61.

134 Ying Ruan, 'Accidental affinities: American Beaux Arts in Chinese architectural education and practice', *JSAH*, 61/1, March 2002, 30–47; J W Cody, *Building in China: Henry K Murphy's Adaptive Architecture*, Hong Kong, 2001; D Lai, 'Searching for a Modern Chinese Movement', *JSAH*, 64/1, March 2005, 22–55.

135 EULMC, RHM and RAM, *A Fortnight in China*, 1964, typescript diary. Cars: interview with S Platt, 2003.

136 EULMC, letters of thanks, 24–5 September 1964.

137 Porcelain factory, interview with S Platt, 2003; Liang: EULMC, diary for 10 September 1964.

138 EULMC, diary for 13 September 1964.

139 EULMC, diary for 16 September 1964. LCC designs: interview with S Platt, 2003.

140 Interview with S Platt, 2003; EUMLC diary for 14 September 1964.

141 EULMC, diary for 15 September 1964.

142 Interview with S Platt, 2003; EULMC, diary for September 1964.

143 *Scottish Field*, December 1967, 22; RHM and RAM, 'A fortnight in China'; EULMC, letters of 6 May 1964 from RHM to Yang, 12 August 1964 from Massey to Gregory; EULMC, file MS2535, text of RHM RIBA talk, 1 May 1965, letters of 26 December 1964 from RHM to A Ling and 12 October 1965 from J Tyrwhitt to RHM.

144 Pasir Penjang school at Singapore by M Lee: *Architectural Review*, January 1962.

145 Doxiadis's US-financed, 14,000-house Korangi development of 1959-60: Zahir, *Memoirs*, 68ff; J Hosagahar, 'South Asia', *JSAH*, September 2002, 356; R Squire, *Portrait of an Architect*, Gerrards Cross, 1984, 195–7. Doxiadis in Iraq: P Pyla, 'Rebuilding Iraq, 1955-8', *Docomomo Journal*, 35, September 2006, 71–7.

146 Zahir, *Memoirs*, 59.

147 Squire, *Portrait of an Architect*, 195–7. Doxiadis offered his services to Yahya: Zahir, *Memoirs*, 88. Doxiadis self-promotion: R Bromley, 'Towards Global Human Settlements', in J Nasr and M Volait, eds, *Urbanism: Imported or Exported?*, Chichester, 2003, 316–40.

148 *Interbuild,* March 1961. Links to ideas of Melvin Webber on mobility: Mark Clapson, paper at May 2000 conference in Luton on Americanisation. Kenzo Tange's bold proposals for vast megastructures and highway networks, and (1965) rebuilding plan for Skopje: U Kultermann (ed.), *Kenzo Tange, Architecture and Urban Design, 1946–1969*, London, 1970, 262–81, on Skopje; *JRIBA*, February 1965, 78–80 on Royal Gold Medal; G Kunihiro, lecture on Tange and Skopje, Docomomo conference, New York, September 2004; Zahir, *Memoirs*, 115.

149 *Journal of the Institute of Landscape Architects*, November 1969.

150 Zahir, *Memoirs*, 93–4; EULMC, text of lecture by RHM to Aberdeen Society of Architects, 27 February 1964; *Civil and Military Gazette*, 23 November 1961; *Islamabad Reporting Progress*, May–June 1964; Ahmed Zaib K Mahsud, 'Representing the state: symbolism and ideology in Doxiadis's plan for Islamabad', lecture to Third Annual Architectural Humanities Research Association Conference, Oxford, 17 November 2006.

151 Alberto Rosselli handled most of Ponti's Islamabad work from early 1962: L Doumato, *Gio Ponti*, Monticello, Illinois, 1987; N H Shapira, *The Expression of Gio Ponti*, Minneapolis, 1967; Zahir, *Memoirs*, 99.

152 *Architectural Review*, March 1967, 314–5.

153 *AJ*, 8 June 1966, 1401; *Architectural Review*, March 1967, 211; Zahir, *Memoirs*, 111; interview with RAM, December 2005.

154 Zahir, *Memoirs*, 109–110.

155 RMJMSS, Islamabad files, 28 September 1961 notes of visit; letters of 21 October 1961 from Zahir to RHM, 14 November 1961 from A Mahmood to RHM, 18 November 1961 from P Jamieson to RHM, 19 November 1961 telegrams to Shaikh, and January 1962 correspondence about Breuer.

156 RMJMSS, Islamabad files, report of January 1962 by Maurice Lee, 'General report on visit to Pakistan'; letter from Zahir to RHM, 24 April 1962.

157 RMJMSS, Islamabad files, letter of 12 July 1962 from Zahir to Ponti.

158 RMJMSS, Islamabad files, letter of 26 July 1963 from M Rauf to RHM, and of 29 February 1964 from B Jamieson to

RHM.

159 Rosselli's attempted synthesis between Islam and Modernism: Zahir, *Islamabad, Reporting Progress*, July–September 1964; Zahir, *Memoirs*, 109; N Taylor, *Architectural Review*, March 1967, 212–4.

160 EULMC, file MS2535, letter of 30 November 1965 from Jacobsen to RHM.

161 EULMC, file MS2560, letter from RHM to Doxiadis, 20 August 1964; *Pakistan Times*, 27 January 1965; *Architectural Review*, March 1967, 212; CDA, *Islamabad*, 65/1, March 1965.

162 Interview with M Lee, 1997; EULMC, letter from M Lee to J D Richards, 28 March 1984.

163 EULMC, file MS2533, letters of 22 May 1967 from A R Qazi, 13 June 1967 from T D M Bhamani, 11 May 1968 from Shaikh, and 2 September 1968 from S Khan.

164 Zahir, *Memoirs*, 109.

165 Zahir 'shocked' at the final design, which was cruder than an effort by 'a raw student of architecture' (Zahir, *Memoirs*, 119). General bibliography of Islamabad: CDA, *Islamabad, Our City*, 1961. Doxiadis Associates, *Islamabad, Progress and Plan*, 2 vols, 30 September 1960. *Ekistics*, vol. 14, October 1962, 148–61; November 1964, 320–5 and 346–64; May 1968, 329–33. *Town Planning Review*, vol. 38, 1, 1967, 35–42; Government of Pakistan, *Capital Territory Local Government Ordinance*, 1979; M Lee, *Architectural Design*, vol. 37, 1, 1967, 47–50; *Building*, vol. 210, 1966, 77–8; *Housing Review*, vol. 13, no. 3, 49–52; *Town Planning Review*, vol. 41, 317–332; N Taylor, 'Islamabad', *Architectural Review*, vol. 141, 1967, 212–6; 'New dimensions in architecture', broadcast talk by CDA, Radio Pakistan, 9 April 1963, and Zahir, *Memoirs*, 264; EULMC, file MS2554, IUA–UN basic housing project, Islamabad; *AJ*, 8 June 1966, 401.

166 Llewelyn-Davies establishment of 'Centre for Environmental Studies' at UCL in the early 1960s, and planning of several private new towns in the US: Mark Clapson, paper on 'Americanisation' at 6 May 2000 conference in Luton.

167 History of urban design movement, c.1956: *Harvard Design Magazine*, Spring/Summer 2006.

168 *Building Design*, 5 June 1970, 6–7.

169 EULMC, text of 'American cities' RHM lecture and correspondence, February–April 1963; also file MS2548; EULMC, letter of 15 June 1963 from J R James to RHM and others.

170 EULMC, correspondence of early 1963; Jacobs, *American Cities*, Pelican edition, 1964, 14 and 51; cf. L Mumford, *City Development*, New York, 1946; L Mumford, *The Highway and the City*, New York, 1953.

171 Obituary of Bacon (1910–2005): *SAH News*, February 2006, 7.

172 EULMC, August–September 1963 correspondence, especially with Johnson; letter of 12 July 1963 from Mumford to RHM.

173 EULMC, letter of 27 September 1963 from Gutheim to RHM.

174 EULMC, text of 6 December 1963 lecture to West Yorkshire Society of Architects; EULMC, text of 13 January 1964 Reading Museum lecture (on Philadephia success).

175 EULMC, letters of 26 December 1964 and June 1967 from L Mumford to RHM.

176 Sylvia on role of taking slides: interview with S Platt, 2003; interview with K Feakes, 2004.

177 Interview with S Platt, 2003.

178 EULMC, letters of 13 May 1965 from Vago to RHM and 19 May 1965 from H Wright to RHM.

179 EULMC, file MS2535, text of 17 June 1965 RHM lecture.

180 EULMC, file MS2544, correspondence of August 1965.

181 I McHarg, *Design with Nature*, New York, 1969.

182 EULMC, file MS2544, letter of 23 August 1965 from B F Sliger to RHM.

183 EULMC, file MS2539, notes of February 1967 meeting. US visitors hosted: EULMC, letter of 18 February 1966 from C W Barr to RHM; file MS2533, letter of 12 August 1965 from J A More to RHM; EULMC, letter of 16 August 1968 from Watterson to Matthew, and file MS2548.

184 R Neutra, *Survival Through Design*, New York, 1954, ix and 17.

185 General literature on Fuller: R W Markus, *The Dymaxion World of Buckminster Fuller*, Carbondale, 1960; *AD*, August 61; Fuller, *Operating Manual for Spaceship Earth*, New York, 1963; Fuller and John McHale, *World Science Design Decade*, Documents 1–6, Word Resources Inventory, Southern Illinois University, Carbondale, Illinois, 1963–7 (in RHM book collection; Volumes 1 and 2 with handwritten dedication to RHM by Fuller): *Phase 1 Document 1, Inventory of World Resources, Human Trends and Needs*, 1963; *Phase 1 Document 2, The Design Initiative*, 1964; *Phase 1, Document 3, Comprehensive Thinking*, 1965; *Phase 1 Document 4, The Ten Year Programme*, 1965; *Phase 1 Document 5, Comprehensive Design Strategy*, 1967; *Phase 2, Document 6, The Ecological Context: Energy and Materials*, 1967; *Washington Post*, 2 October 1966, 1; *Saturday Review*, 12 November 1966; *JRIBA*, August 1968, 341ff; J Meller (ed.), *The Buckminster Fuller Reader*, London, 1970; *Architectural Forum*, Special Issue 1, February 1972; Fuller, *Intuition*, Garden City, New York, 1972; L S Sieden, *Buckminster Fuller's Universe: His Life and Work*, Cambridge, MA, 1989; D Sharp, *AJ*, 14 December 1995; J Krausse, C Lichtenstein (eds), *Your Private Sky: R Buckminster Fuller Discourse*, Zurich, 2001.

186 Fuller, 'The prospect for humanity', *Saturday Review*, August 1964.

187 *Saturday Review*, August 1964; *AJ*, 13 May 1964.

188 Previous student-assisted geodesic dome: Sieden, *Universe*, 335.

189 Fuller, *Saturday Review*, August 1964.

190 Sharp, *AJ*, 14 December 1995; EULMC, text of 18 June 1968 RHM speech at RIBA.

191 Fuller and McHale, *World Science Design Decade*; *AD*,

192 Interview with RAM, December 2005. 'Youngest grown up friends': EULMC, letter from Fuller of 8 August 1965; interview with LLM, 1995; interview with L Fricker, 1997.

193 EULMC, file MS2551, letter of 6 June 1962 from M Pidgeon to RHM.

194 AA and student help for Fuller's Paris display: EULMC, file MS2552, letter of 11 October 1965 from Fuller to RHM.

195 EULMC, file MS2552, PJM notes of late 1963 on WSD; Richards, *Unjust Fella*, 211.

196 EULMC, file MS2552, letters of 5 March 1965 from Barge to RHM, 25 March 1965 from Vago to RHM, 11 October 1965 from Fuller to RHM; *AD*, August 1965.

197 EULMC, file MS2552, letter of 1 March 1966 from Fuller to Palais d'Orsay, and 13 April 1966 from Vago to RHM.

198 *AD*, December 1972; Sieden, *Universe*, 377; *JRIBA*, August 1968, 341ff.; *JRIBA*, June 1968, 269–71.

199 EULMC, file MS2575, correspondence of January 1966 with Fuller about November 1965 visit to Kumasi; KNUST, Kumasi, Occasional Report, 3, 1964, 'Buckminster Fuller at KNUST'; interview with RAM, 2005; interview with E Morris, 1997.

200 Publications by Doxiadis and ACE: C Doxiadis, *Raumordnung im Griechischen Staedtebau*, Heidelberg, 1937 (English translation, edited by J Tyrwhitt, *Doxiadis – Architectural Space in Ancient Greece*, Cambridge, MA, 1972); Doxiadis, *Dynapolis, the City of the Future*, text of lecture at Oslo Arkitektforening, 3 March 1960, Athens, 1960; Athens Center of Ekistics, 'Concept of City of Future', 1960 (the first internal document published by the ACE); Doxiadis Associates, 'Ecumenopolis, the settlement of the future', June 1961; C Doxiadis, *Architecture in Transition*, London, 1963; C Doxiadis, *Ekistics: An Introduction to the Science of Human Settlements*, New York, 1968. General literature: P Deane, *Constantinos Doxiadis*, Dobbs Ferry, New York, 1965; cf. V Welter and J Lawson, eds, *The City after Patrick Geddes*, Bern, 2000. Obituary (died 28 June 1975), *Building*, 4 July 1975; Doxiadis 'gospel': *Builder*, 29 November 1963, 1112.

201 Zahir on 'vast empire' of Doxiadis: Zahir, *Memoirs*, 111–2.

202 See for instance Doxiadis, *Between Dystopia and Utopia*.

203 Similarities to some postwar CIAM offshoots: e.g. the attempts at CIAM 9 in 1953 (at Aix) to agree a 'Charter of Habitation'.

204 EULMC, file MS2548, and text of lecture by RHM at Liverpool, 4 January 1963; see also N Warburton, *Erno Goldfinger*, London, 2004, 61–3 (on CIAM 4), and J Gold, *The Experience of Modernism*, London, 1997; M Wigley, 'Network fever', *Grey Room*, 4, 2001, 96–7.

205 Interview with RAM, 2005.

206 Wigley, 'Network fever', 89. Claimed CIA links: R Bromley, 'Towards Global Human Settlements'.

207 EULMC, file MS2561.

208 Deane, *Doxiadis*, 115, 117, 123; EULMC, file MS2561, note of

209 EULMC, file MS2561, July 1963 draft of 'Delos Declaration'.

210 EULMC, file MS2551; interview with RAM, 2005.

211 Comedies, dances: EULMC file MS2560, papers of 20 July 1964; *Ekistics*, October 1964, 187 (EULMC file MS2561).

212 EULMC, file MS2561, paper of 18 July 1964 by RHM and R Llewellyn Davies.

213 EULMC, file MS2560, papers of 20 July 1964.

214 EULMC, file MS2560, letter of 20 August 1964 from RHM to Doxiadis ('Dinos').

215 Richards, *Unjust Fella*, 210.

216 Fuller: EULMC, file MS2561. *AR*, December 1965, 399–401; Richards, *Unjust Fella*, 210.

217 EULMC, file MS2562, report D4.

218 *Ekistics*, July 1967.

219 EULMC, file MS2533, letter of 3 January 1968 from Holford to RHM.

220 EULMC, file MS2562.

221 EULMC, file MS2560, letter of 4 September 1967 from RHM to Doxiadis.

222 EULMC, files MS2560–2562.

223 EULMC, file MS2533, letter of 23 September 1968 from RHM to M Doublet.

224 Wigley, 'Network fever', 113.

225 EULMC, file MS2533, ref. BG9.

Chapter 12

1 *Building Design*, 5 June 1970, 7; EULMC, RHM lecture to Saltire AGM, 14 July 1973; interview with John Richards, 2003.

2 EULMC, RHM St Andrew's Night lecture, 'Impact of change', BBC TV Scotland, 29 November 1968.

3 EULMC, letter from RHM to J Gillespie, 7 April 1975; Skidelsky, *Keynes*, 846.

4 EULMC, text of RHM lecture of 27 October 1972 to Stirling University, 'The architect and the environment', and 19 December 1972 to the AA of Ireland.

5 EULMC, text of RHM lecture of 25 October 1974 at Prestonfield House Hotel; Annan, *Our Age*, 345.

6 Pioneer against highways: L Mumford, *The Highway and the City*, New York, 1953, preface to 1963 edition.

7 *ABN*, 5 February 1970, 36; *B*, 6 June 1970, 7. Planners initially insulated from worst attacks: Cherry, *British Town Planning*, 258–9.

8 EULMC, text of RHM lecture at Saltire Awards, 1970, AA of Ireland, 19 December 1972, and BBC TV programme, 29 November 1968.

9 *Architect and Building News*, 5 February 1970, 34; Glendinning and Muthesius, *Tower Block*, 310. Hospital delays: EULMC, RHM text of lecture for British Council Hospital Planning Course, 14 February 1974.

10 EULMC, text of December 1973 talk to Geriatrics Society, and of talk to RIBA, Stirling, 20–23 June 1973. Matthew

on sacrosanct public status of music: EULMC, text of RHM lecture at Saltire dinner of 13 January 1972 in honour of Alexander Gibson.

11   EULMC, text of 19 December 1972 to Architectural Association of Ireland, Dublin. RHM on architecture as inherently utopian: EULMC, text of RHM lecture at 14 October 1971 presentation of degree Honoris Causa, Bucharest.

12   Matthew praise of post-war West German social architecture: *ABN*, 5 February 1970, 35; EULMC, text of RHM lecture of 25 September 1969 to British Acoustical Society.

13   EULMC, text of RHM lecture of 27 May 1971 to RAIA Centenary Meeting, Sydney.

14   EULMC, text of RHM BBC Scotland St Andrew's Night lecture, 29 November 1968. EULMC, text of RHM lecture of 27 May 1971 to RAIA Centenary Meeting, Sydney; *Planning History*, vol. 26, 1 and 2, 2004, 17ff.

15   Ockman, *Architecture Culture*; A Ravetz, *The Government of Space*, London, 1986; R Goodman, *After the Planners*, London, 1972; D Eversley, *The Planner in Society*, London, 1973. Giancarlo de Carlo, *An Architecture of Participation*, Melbourne, 1972; R Montgomery, 'Architecture invents new people', in R Ellis and D Cuff (eds), *Architects' People*, New York, 1989, 269.

16   EULMC, papers of Council of Europe, Committee on Monuments, Edinburgh seminar, 22–5 January 1974.

17   EULMC, text of RHM summing-up lecture at June 1973 RIBA Conference.

18   Matthew attacks against beginnings of neo-laissez-faire movement in 1960s: EULMC, letter of 6 December 1965 from M MacEwen to G Ricketts; EULMC, Liaison Group file (opposition to Monopolies Commission investigation), letters of March 1969 from RHM to Crosland, 30 October 1970 from Matthew to *The Times*, 29 April 1971 from P Shepheard, PRIBA, to Secretary for Environment, and 22 November 1973 note by RHM.

19   EULMC, text of RHM talk at Prestonfield House, 25 October 1974, and at Dublin, 19 December 1972.

20   EULMC, text of RHM talk to Inverness architects, February 1971.

21   *RIBA Journal*, December 1974, 4.

22   EULMC, text of RHM talk to Commonwealth Society, Edinburgh, 17 March 1971; EULMC, text of RHM lecture of 27 May 1971 to RAIA Centenary Meeting, Sydney; *ABN*, 5 February 1970, 34–6.

23   Early 1970s reforms: establishment of joint committee, with Edinburgh, London and Stirling able to open 'local branches'. (*RMJM Roundabout*, July 1973; interviews with T Spaven, 1995, and A Wightman, 2004; RMJM, papers of June 1977.)

24   Bells Brae: interview with J Latimer, 2006.

25   Interview with A Wightman, 2004.

26   Interviews with F Isserlis, 1997, and T Spaven, 2004.

27   Interview with T Spaven, 1995; EULMC, letter of 20 July

1970 from RHM to Spaven.

28   Letter from A Wightman, 1995.

29   EULMC, letter of 7 January 1974 signed by RHM as financial guarantee for 'Westplan 2' Saudi work.

30   EULMC, note of 5 January 1971 from Stirrat to RHM; interview with A Wightman, October 2004. Interviews with A Derbyshire, 2004, and J Richards, 2003.

31   Rebuff of Percy bid to become partner: interview with A Wightman, 2004.

32   Interview with T Spaven, 1995.

33   RMJMSS, Ninewells files, 18 July note on cost increases by Spaven.

34   Praise for 'luxury' complex by Professor J P Duguid, Dean of the Faculty of Medicine at Dundee University: *Daily Record*, 19 July 1972, 9; *Scotsman*, 11 January 1974, 11; I Irvine, *Sunday Mail*, 10 June 1973.

35   RMJMSS, Ninewells files, letters of 4 February 1972 from RFACS to SERHB, and of 22 July 1977 from RMJM to RFACS.

36   Catford, *The Royal Infirmary of Edinburgh*, 128–30.

37   RMJMSS, RIE files, letters of 8 December 1959 and 27 March 1969 from SERHB to RHM, 21 November 1969 from Vernon Lee to SERHB.

38   1970 information pack for Burrell competition, and May 1971 report accompanying RHM design; R Marks, R Scott, B Gasson , J Thomson, P Vainker, *The Burrell Collection*, Glasgow, 1983.

39   *Evening News*, 2 January 1999, 7.

40   *Festival News*, August–September 1975, 3; *AJ*, 1 November 1972, 991; *Evening News*, 2 January 1999.

41   *AJ*, 1 November 1972, 991; *Building*, 13 July 1973.

42   *Scotsman*, 27 July 1973; *Building Design*, August 1973.

43   Interview with A Wightman, 2004.

44   *RMJM Roundabout*, August 1973; RMJMSS, CTTD file, 2 July 1973 Edinburgh Corporation job advertisement for project programmer, and letter of 13 September 1973 from J Richards to B Annable.

45   RFACS, *Report*, January 1970–December 1972; *Evening News*, 31 July 1973, 26 April 1974, 5 July 1974; *Scotsman*, 27 April 1974.

46   EULMC, letter from C Naismith to F Gutheim, 8 January 1974; *Scotsman*, 23 October 1974.

47   *Evening News*, 5 July 1974; *Scotsman*, 14 August 1974, letter by O Barratt.

48   *Scotsman*, 9 August 1974, 19 September 1974, 2 November 1974, 5 November 1974, 21 February 1975, 20 February 1975, 4 March 1975.

49   Interview with J Richards, 1995.

50   *RMJMP Roundabout*, Summer 1975. *Architect and Building News*, 5 February 1970, 34–6.

51   EULMC, letter of 17 January 1972 from CAA to C Naismith; financial arrangements file, 1965.

52   Interview with J Latimer, 2007.

53   EULMC, letters of 27 May 1971 from MPBW to RHM, 8

June 1973 from St Andrew's House to RHM, 4 September 1973 from Glasgow Corporation to RHM; 8 October 1973 note by C Naismith; note from Brown Campbell to C Naismith, 21 August 1975, and note of 1 June 1975 meeting.

54 EULMC, letters of 27 June 1973 from Patrick Harrison to LLM, and 17 June 1973 from LLM to R Scott Morton.

55 EULMC, file MS2560, correspondence of November 1968; EULMC, household financial file, 1974.

56 Interview with SRM, 1995; Lyon & Turnbull, inventory of Keith Marischal, 13 September 1973.

57 Tree-felling and road-alignment rows: EULMC, correspondence between RHM and Tindall, 9–17 March 1972; EULMC, letters of 24 September 1973 from G Waterston to RHM, and 28 September 1973 from Tindall to RHM. Survey of Keith by McWilliam for Lothian volume of the Buildings of Scotland series. (EULMC, letter of 23 June 1974 from C McWilliam to RHM.)

58 EULMC, letter of 10 July 1968 from Jessie to RHM.

59 Interviews with D Ashmead, 2004, and P Harrison, 2007. Interviews with P Harrison, 2007, P Nuttgens, 1995; letter of August 2006 from S Platt.

60 EULMC, letter of 18 April 1974 from A Toynbee to RHM.

61 JRIBA, August 1970, 343–7.

62 On previous awards: JRIBA, July 1969, 281–2 on Coia; JRIBA, June 1968, 269–71 and August 1968, 341–2, on Fuller; EULMC, Royal Gold Medal congratulatory letters of 1 February 1970 from Casson and Gibberd to RHM, 3 February 1970 from M Fry to RHM, 5 February 1970 from J Bhalla to RHM; EULMC, letter from W Wurster to RHM, 8 June 1970. Casson: see Manser, Casson.

63 Crossman, Diaries, vol. 1, 1975. Marjorie Holford traumas: EULMC, letter of 3 February 1970 from Holford to RHM; see also Cherry and Penny, Holford, 244–6; EULMC, letter of 16 February 1970 from McCalman.

64 'High tension to the end': interview with Nuttgens, 1995.

65 JRIBA, August 1970, 343–7; Morgan and Naylor, Contemporary Architects, 986–7.

66 EULMC, file MS2536, May 1970 MS copy; Building Design, 5 June 1970, 6–7.

67 Intermittent contacts with Elspeth Hardie and her husband Bob at Ganavan, near Oban (until Bob fell seriously ill in 1973 and later died): EULMC, letter of 27 May 1969 from E Hardie to RHM; interview with E Hardie, 2003.

68 Matthew avoidance of involvement in Osborn's 'British Committee for World Town Planning Day', a goodwill initiative under which telegrams were sent to a 'focus country': e.g. EULMC, letter of 10 June 1969 from RHM to PJM, and 24 February 1969 letter from F J Osborn to RHM.

69 EULMC, letter of 19 June 1969 from R Grieve to RHM.

70 EULMC, letters of 6 April 1972 from E Williams to RHM, 10 April 1972 from RHM and L Martin to Festival Hall Manager. EULMC, letters of 7 June 1972 from C Lucas to RHM, February 1972 from W Morris to Douglas Matthew, February 1974 from RHM to R Gardner-Medwin, and 1 November 1972 from S Kadleigh to RHM; correspondence of June 1969 RHM–N Pevsner.

71 EULMC, letter of 22 September 1973 from S Loweth to RHM; see also Sidney Gabriel letter, JRIBA, September 1973, 458.

72 EULMC, letters of 27 September 1974 from J Byrom to RHM, 11 July 1971 from P Willis to RHM, 2 November 1973 from J Byrom to RHM, June 1970 from the School of Built Environment to C Naismith, 13 May 1970 from G Dix to RHM; EULMC, file MS2533, letter of 3 October 1972 from P Savage to RHM, 10 October 1972 from RHM to D McAra.

73 A W Hendry, typescript recollections dated May 1979; EULMC, letters of 20 December 1972 from R Cowan to RHM and Oddie, and 16 July 1974 from Secretary of Heriot Watt University to RHM.

74 EULMC, letters of 26 February 1973 from RHM to C Stewart, and 6 May 1974 from Professor B Saul (Faculty of Social Sciences) to RHM.

75 EULMC, letters from R G Medwin to RHM, 25 July 1973 and 25 February 1974, 13 July 1969 from Ling to RHM, 14 July 1969 from Ling to P K Harrison, Ling to RHM, 30 July 1969, Douglas Jones to RHM, 31 July 1969, notes of 17 December 1969 meeting with Ling.

76 Negotiations about Bartlett and abortive AA–Imperial College merger: EULMC, letters of 28 May 1969, 25 June 1969 (and 2 September 1969) from N Annan to RHM and reply of 21 August 1969: EULMC, file MS2560, AA correspondence, October 1967 to July 1970.

77 EULMC, letter for Forward to RHM, 28 May 1969, April 1971, November 1973. .

78 EULMC, file MS2539 (1971–4).

79 Matthew as RIBA host and conference chair: EULMC, letter of 8 September 1971 from P K Harrison to RHM; EULMC, correspondence of October 1974; EULMC, letters from J Dunbar-Nasmith to RHM, 20 and 25 June 1973, and 20–3 June 73 summing up of RIBA Stirling conference.

80 The automatic identification of 'architects' with 'bureaucrats': JRIBA, October 1973, 466; see also A Powers, Twentieth Century Society Newsletter, September 2000, 30 (on L Martin as ally of bureaucracy).

81 Downs, Shepheard, 86–8.

82 EULMC, circular letter of 1 November 1971 by RHM, 8 August 1972 from Alex Gordon to RHM about fee rises of up to 50 per cent.

83 Interview with C McKean, 2003.

84 EULMC, file MS2539, memos of 28 January 1972 and April 1972 to RHM, and text of RHM speech, 14 March 1973.

85 AJ, 17 April 1974; EULMC, file MS2539, letter of 20 June 1974 from A Lewis to RHM.

86 EULMC, file MS2540, World of Property Housing Trust, correspondence of March 1968 to April 1971.

87 EULMC, file MS2543, letter of 14 December 1970.

Modern Architect

88 EULMC, file MS2547, inquiry papers; file MS2546, letters of 5 May 1973 from Jack Whittle to RHM, and of 16 April 1973 to Pearce by R H Ouzman.

89 EULMC, file MS2550, letter of 30 January 1974 from B Beckett to RHM; memo of 6 February 1974 from J D Jones; *AJ*, 27 March 1974.

90 EULMC, file MS2538, letters of 21 August 1974 from Pooley to RHM, 14 February 1975 from J D Jones to RHM, 4 March 1975 from A Crossland to RHM, 11 March 1975 from P Harrison to RHM, 14 March 1975 from RHM to Skillington; 12 March 1975 to RHM from 12 regional PSA Bristol architects, and reply of 14 April 1975; interview with P Harrison, 2007.

91 *Architectural Heritage*, 12, 2006; *AHSS Magazine*, 6, 1997, 14–16; Eleanor Robertson, lecture of 21 October 1997 to AHSS, Edinburgh.

92 EULMC, letter of 12 November 1974 from Sylvia Matthew to RHM.

93 EULMC, text of RHM Saltire speech, 31 October 1974.

94 EULMC, text of RHM 27 October 1972 Stirling public lecture, and BBC TV Scotland St Andrew's Night lecture, 29 November 1968; Jacobs: *Death and Life of Great American Cities*.

95 Interview with K E Graham, 2004.

96 EULMC, text of February 1971 RHM lecture to Inverness architects; EULMC, transactions of Council of Europe, Committee on Monuments and Sites, seminar in Edinburgh, 22–5 June 1974.

97 Calton: EULMC, file MS2541, minutes of Terraces Association, 1966–1973, letter of 20 November 1971 from RHM to Sir J Miller, and minutes of AGM, 24 January 1973 (Matthew's last AGM). Bannockburn: miscellaneous NTS files on the site, per S Loftus, Jan Haenraets of NTS.

98 EULMC, file MS2542, letters of 27 September 1966 from Muirshiel to RHM, and 15 January 1967 from Bannatyne to RHM 27-9-66 (along with Grieve, Bill Taylor, and Lord Weir).

99 EULMC, file MS2540, letter from D Johnston to RHM, 15 September 1971, correspondence of 20 February 1967, and 19 January 1967 from L Lane to RHM; 'poetic', text of RHM speech of 15 November 1967 to Ulster Architectural Heritage Society; interview with J Gerrard, 2004. Lindsay remained SCT Director until 1983.

100 EULMC, file MS2544, letter of 16 October 1968 from M Lindsay to RHM; file MS2540, letter of 17 July 1974 from H Casson to RHM.

101 EULMC, file MS2541, 14 September 1971 note; Scottish Civic Trust, *The First Five Years*, Glasgow, 1972.

102 On Ballachulish, see e.g. file MS2540, correspondence of January 1973.)

103 EULMC, papers of 16 September 1969 and 13 November 1970 for Saltire awards, and letter of 22 September 1969 from the Council of the Scottish Association of Registered House Builders to RHM; also file MS 2540, letter of 6

September 1971 from J Bannatyne to RHM.

104 Letter from D Walker to MG, January 2005.

105 EULMC, file MS2542, letters of 19 February 1974 from M Lindsay to RHM, 18 March 1974 from M Lindsay to M Gilfillan, 7 April 1974 from Muirshiel to RHM, 7 July 1974 from M Lindsay to RHM, and minutes of 1 May 1974, 3 June 1974 and 2 July 1974 meetings chaired by RHM at Gladstone's Land.

106 Letter from D Walker to MG, January.

107 Interview with D Walker, 2005.

108 Letter from D Walker to MG, January 2005.

109 D Walker, 'Listing in Scotland', *Transactions of the Ancient Monuments Society*, vol. 58, 1994, 178; *Scotsman*, 28 November 1970, 11.

110 EULMC, file MS2542, letter of 5 July 1971 from M Lindsay to RHM.

111 For all this, see Walker, 'Listing in Scotland', 178, and Walker, 'The Historic Buildings Council for Scotland', in L Borley (ed.), *Dear Maurice*, East Linton, 1998, 176–92.

112 SCT, *The First Five Years*.

113 EULMC, file MS2544, reports of *c*.1969; Civic Trust, *Conservation Areas: A Survey*, fascimile reprint from *AJ*, 18 January 1967, 125ff; Department of the Environment/SDD/Welsh Office, *Aspects of Conservation*, 2, *New Life for Historic Areas*, London, 1972; Civic Trust, Conservation in Action, A Civic Trust Conference, Royal Festival Hall, 8 and 9 July 1971, delegate brochure; EULMC, file MS2542, 24 March 1973, notes of 'lay conservationists' conference.

114 EULMC, file MS2540, letter of 4 July 1972 from J Stormonth-Darling to RHM.

115 EULMC, letter of 30 January 1973 from RHM to Judith Strong, RIBA.

116 I Begg, *Rossend Castle: A Recent Story of Reconstruction after 25 Years of Struggle*, Edinburgh, 1977; EULMC, file MS2542, press cuttings collection of 1970–1; letter of 7 April 1971 from M Lindsay to RHM; file MS2541, letters of 12 February 1970 from P S Davison to RHM, and 18 November 1970 from M Lindsay to Fife County Planning Officer; (press debate) letter of 23 November 1970 from SRM to *Scotsman*, 16 November 1970 from R M Livingstone, Labour Party, 24 November 1970 from George Younger to RHM, 4 August 1971 from C Naismith to P S Davison. See also RHM advice about Castle Menzies caravan development 1974: EULMC, file MS2541, correspondence of May and June 1974.

117 EULMC, file MS2540, 13 September 1972 note by C Naismith.

118 EULMC, file MS2544, correspondence of 29 and 30 December 1971.

119 EULMC, file MS2540, letter from J S Darling to RHM, 4 July 1972, and correspondence of January and July 1972.

120 Historic Buildings Council for Scotland, *Report for 1974–5*, Edinburgh, 1975, 5.

Notes

121 EULMC, file MS2554, October 1974 correspondence on heritage conference in Poland. Martyrs School: see EULMC, file MS2544, letter of 14 February 1974 from RHM to Gordon Campbell.

122 COID Scottish Committee, *Design Appreciation*, Edinburgh, 1953 (transcript of lecture by Matthew); EULMC, text of lecture by RHM to Architectural Association of Ireland, Dublin, 19 December 1972.

123 EULMC, file MS2540, letters of 18 January 1963, 17 January 1965 and 20 August 1965 from J Bannatyne to RHM.

124 EULMC, file MS2540, letters of 18 January 1963, 20 August 1965, 8 September 1966 from Bannatyne to RHM, 29 June 1966 from Lord Johnston to W Ross; January/February 1967 papers for New Town Subcommittee; text of February 1971 RHM lecture to Inverness Architects.

125 Interview with Lord Kennet, 1991.

126 EULMC, text of RHM lecture to EAA dinner, 20 November 1969.

127 EULMC, text of RHM lecture to EAA dinner, 20 November 1969.

128 EULMC, letter of 20 August 1965 from J Bannatyne to RHM.

129 EULMC, lecture to Architectural Association of Ireland, Dublin, 19 December 1972; file MS2542, letter of 19 January 1967 from L Lane to Muirshiel.

130 EULMC, file 2540; file MS2542, letter from M Lindsay to RHM, 18 May 1967; *SCT Newsletter,* Spring 1997, 9.

131 EULMC, file MS2540, letter of 1 September 1967 from M Lindsay to Leslie Lane.

132 Princes Street Panel: D Whitham, 'Princes Street', 2006 leaflet; Princes Street Panel, *Principles and Standards for the Application of Building Controls in the Central Area of Edinburgh,* Edinburgh, 1967.

133 EULMC, file MS2542, letter of 7 May 1970 from Harries to RHM; file MS2541, correspondence of 13 February 1969.

134 EULMC, file MS2542, minutes of first meeting, 20 January 1970; letter of 24 November 1969 from M Lindsay about the setting up of the appraisal group; letter of 10 November 1969 from J Reid to Reiach & Hall. £8.35m cost: *Weekend Scotsman*, 28 February 1970. 'Demolition costing for entire New Town': EULMC, file MS2541, letter of 5 January 1970 from M Middleton to M Lindsay.

135 EULMC, file MS2542, minutes of 22 May 1969 conference committee.

136 Briefing of home team: EULMC, April 1970 letter from RHM to Nuttgens.

137 EULMC, file MS2542, letter of 15 July 1969 from Spence to RHM.

138 *Weekend Scotsman*, 28 February 1970; R Matthew, J Reid, M Lindsay (eds), *The Conservation of Georgian Edinburgh,* Edinburgh, 1972, xiii. Anna G Dunlop, 'The conservation of Georgian Edinburgh', *The Accountant's Magazine*, July 1970, 312–15.

139 EULMC, file MS2542, notes of executive meetings of 28 July 1970 and 11 August 1970.

140 EULMC, file MS2542, committee meeting notes of 28 July 1970, 11 August 1970, 27 October 1970, 8 December 1970; letters from Queen Mother's secretary to Muirshiel, 30 June 1970, 11 August 1970 from Muirshiel to Secretary of State for Scotland, 15 December 1970 from R F Butler to Edinburgh Deputy Town Clerk.

141 Borley, *Dear Maurice*, 193–201.

142 R Walker was a higher executive officer in the HBCS Secretariat. Information from J Knight, 2003; EULMC, letter of 9 December 1971 from Nuttgens to RHM. Letter from D Walker to MG, January 2005.

143 EULMC, file MS2542, letter of 2 July 1971 from R Walker to RHM.

144 EULMC, file MS2542, letter to *Scotsman*, 20 March 1972, by RHM, Oddie, Bigwood, PJM; minutes of 'teach-in', 18 May 1972; letters of 5 April 1973 from ENTCC to RHM 'for your approval', 3 August 1971 from RHM to Sir G Greig Dunbar, 31 January 1972 from R Walker to D Hodges, 11 October 1972 from R Cramond to D Hodges, 8 December 1972 meeting with R Cramond and Councillor Smith; notes of committee meeting, 19 May 1972.

145 EULMC, file MS2542, letter from D Hodges to RHM, 11 June 1974.

146 A Davey, B Heath, D Hodges, R Milne, M Palmer, *The Care and Conservation of Georgian Houses*, Edinburgh, 1978.

147 'Affinity': interview with Aidan Matthew, 2005.

148 EULMC, file MS2533, correspondence of 7 May 1970; text of 14 October 1971 RHM lecture at Bucharest, 15 November 1967 lecture to Ulster Architectural Heritage Society, and 18 January 1970 broadcast, 'A future for the past', BBC Scotland *Life and Letters* programme, 18 January 1970.

149 EULMC, text of RHM lecture at October 1973 CAA conference, Ottawa, and of June 1974 Edinburgh conference on conservation.

Chapter 13

1   Robert Matthew, *Noah Built an Ark (And How!) – The Sensitive Transfer of Building Technology*, film script, 1975.

2   Increasing numbers of commercial RMJM projects in the Middle East in 1970s to compensate for decline of UK social workload: *Roundabout RMJMP* 1975, 'The world'.

3   A H Kirk-Greene (ed.), *Crisis and Civil War in Nigeria*, Oxford, 1971; J de St Jorre, *The Nigerian Civil War*, London, 1972; D A Low, *Eclipse of Empire*, Cambridge, 1991; J Okpaku (ed.), *Nigeria, Dilemma of Nationhood*, 1972; Max Lock Exhibition Memorial Group, *Max Lock 1909–1958*, exhibition catalogue, *c*.1999.

4   EULMC, file MS2558, letter of 20 December 1965 from RHM to O Olumuyiwa.

5   Schools in Nigeria: see O Uduku, 'Educational design and modernism in West Africa', *DOCOMOMO Journal* 28, March

2003, 76–82.

6   Interview with RAM, December 2005.

7   Fragmentary fulfilment of Tange's Skopje plan: G Kunihiro, lecture on Skopje to DOCOMOMO conference, New York, 27 September 2004.

8   RMJMSS, Islamabad files, letter of 15 December 1970 from RHM to CDA Director of Architecture, and note of 14 April 1969 by RAM.

9   RMJM, Islamabad, *National Library, Preliminary Project, Interim Stage*, March 1969. RMJMSS, Islamabad files, letter from RHM to Said, 15 December 1970, and RAM report to RHM and J Richards, 5 November 1970.

10 RMJMSS, Islamabad files, RAM note to RHM of 14 April 1969.

11 Zahir, *Memoirs*.

12 RMJMSS, Islamabad files, RAM note to RHM of 14 April 1969.

13 RMJMSS, Islamabad files, RAM note to RHM of 14 April 1969, and RAM note of 5 November 1970 to RHM and J Richards.

14 RMJMSS, Islamabad files, letter from RHM to JDR, 26 July 1968.

15 RMJMSS, Islamabad files, National Library papers of March 1969; and RAM note to RHM of 14 April 1969.

16 RMJMSS, Islamabad files, 5 November 1970 note of 5 November 1970 from RAM to RHM, and 15 December 1970 from RHM to A Said: EULMC, 1 November 1973 letter from Gio Ponti to RHM; file MS2533, correspondence of 18 January 1971, and 7 December 1972 from RHM to W Siddiqi.

17 RMJMSS, Islamabad files, 1974 RHM letter to S Nilsson; K K Mumtaz, *Modernity and Tradition: Contemporary Architecture in Pakistan*, Karachi, 1999, plate 86 and page 111.

18 en.wikipedia.org/wiki/ muammar_al_Qaddafi; D Vandewalle, *A History of Modern Libya*, Cambridge, 2006.

19 Italian pre-war: V Capresi, poster at Docomomo 2006 conference, Ankara.

20 Doxiadis Associates, *Housing in Libya*, 1964; *Interbuild*, March 1966, 9.

21 RMJM, *IBP Tripoli, Stage 1, Feasibility*, October 1971 (RHM interviewed on a flying two-day visit to Tripoli, on 21–3 November). Radnoti: interview with J Latimer, 2006.

22 Interview with T Spaven, 2004.

23 Interview with T Spaven, 2004.

24 RMJM, *IBP Feasibility Report*, October 1971.

25 RMJM and National Housing Corporation, Libyan Arab Republic, *The IBP, Tripoli*, 1975; RMJM, *IBP Tripoli, Seminar on Housing in the Middle East*, September 1975; RMJM, *IBP Feasibility Report*, October 1971; RMJM, *IBP, Design Report*, June 1972. Interviews with T Spaven, 1995 and 2004, and J Latimer, 2007; *Roundabout RMJM*, April 1973, November 1974, March 1976, October 1977, December 1977.

26 G Pellegrini, 'Manifesto of colonial architecture', *Rassegna di Architettura*, 1936.

27 Interview with Aidan Matthew, December 2005.

28 *Roundabout RMJMP*, November 1974, March 1976, October 1977, December 1977; RMJM, *IBP Tripoli, Seminar on Housing in the Middle East*, September 1975; interview with T Spaven, 1995.

29   Interview with T Spaven, 1995.

30 R Nixon, State of the Union Address, 22 January 1970.

31 EULMC, 1969 manuscript report by M MacEwen.

32 EULMC, file MS2560, 22 August 1969, letter from Matthew to Romney.

33 EULMC, letter of 25 July 1974 from R Campbell to RHM.

34 EULMC, notes of 29 April 1969 talk by Frank Corner, letters of 9 October 1969 and 5 October 1970 from RHM to Corner, and 22 January 1971 from D Brodeur to RHM, 27 March 1972 from RHM to Corner; *Roundabout RMJM*, 'The world', 1975.

35 EULMC, letter of April 1972 from DoE to RHM; EULMC, letter of 31 January 1974 from R D Katz to RHM.

36 Interviews with A Wightman and T Spaven, 2004.

37 EULMC, letter of 27 March 1972 from RHM to F Corner.

38 Interview with T Spaven, 2004.

39 See e.g. J Delafons, *Politics and Preservation*, London, 1997, 110–15.

40 EULMC, text of RHM lecture of 29 October 1974 at Bond Club Dinner on EAHY

41 EULMC, file MS2558, RHM draft for 29 September 1973 Ottawa conference speech, 'UN action on the environment, Stockholm and after'.

42 EULMC, letter of 31 December 1975 from H Syrkus to RHM; EULMC, file MS2554, correspondence of October 1974, and letter of 21 October 1974 from RHM to Buszko and Barucki.

43 EULMC, letter of April 1969 from G Goulden to RHM; EULMC, letters of 10 June 1969 from L Uhlin to RHM, 19 September 1969 from B Tschumi to RHM, 16 November 1969 from H S Laessig to RHM; file MS2544, letters of 10 June 1969 from RHM to PJM, June 1969 from F J Osborn to RHM, December 1969 from della Paola to RHM.

44 Other friendships in the 'Eastern Bloc': EULMC, letter of 22 August 1973 from RHM to Anna Opochinskaya, and January 1969 correspondence with S Trubacek.

45 EULMC, letter of 21 December 1972 from RHM to S Chapman, 14 June 1973 reply, and 22 September 1973 from S Loweth to RHM.

46 EULMC, letter of 3 April 1974 from C Naismith to M Weill, and reply; contrast with EULMC, file MS2555, letter of 1 May 1971 from International Organisation for Justice and Development.

47 EULMC, file MS2538, correspondence of 8 October 1974.

48 EULMC, cutting from *Scinteia*, 5 October 1971; file MS2537, letters of 22 July 1971 from Damian to RHM, 5 October 1971 from Petrascu to M, 5 October 1971 from E Popescu to RHM; EULMC, letter of 7 March 1974 from L Stadecker to RHM.

Notes

49 EULMC, correspondence of December 1969 declining invitation to Isfahan conference.

50 EULMC, files MS2549, 2550.

51 EULMC, file MS2550, correspondence of February 1969 to December 1972.

52 Vago, *Une vie intense*; Vago (ed.), *L'UIA*, 153.

53 EULMC, file MS2555, letters of 19 January 1972 from G Orlov to RHM, and 11 February 1972 from G Goulden to RHM.

54 EULMC, file MS2555, papers of 6 February 1968 executive committee, letters of 28 November 1965 from Vago to G Goulden, 2 May 1969 from RHM, and 30 June 1969 from Vago to G Goulden.

55 EULMC, file MS2554, letter of 26 September 1969 from P Vago to RHM.

56 *Roundabout RMJMP*, Summer 1975, 2; *JRIBA*, December 1969, 508–10.

57 *JRIBA*, December 1969, 508–10; EULMC, file MS2555, letter of 7 August 1969 from R C Martin to RHM.

58 H Eddé, *Le Liban d'ou je viens*, Paris, 1977, 68–9.

59 EULMC, file MS2552, Bariloche papers; Vago, *Une vie intense*, 460.

60 EULMC, file MS2552, letter of 10 November 1969 from L E Shore to RHM and reply; E Lyons, *JRIBA*, December 1969, 510.

61 Vago, *Une vie intense*, 460.

62 EULMC, file MS2552, letters of 27 November 1969 from P Vago to RHM, January 1970 from P Vago to E Goldfinger, 30 March 1970 from Corona Martin to RHM, and 10 February 1970 from Dan Schwartzman to Corona Martin.

63 EULMC, RHM diary for 1970.

64 EULMC, file MS2552, letters of 7 April 1970 from Eddé to RHM, 20 April 1970 from RHM to Geisendorf, 22 April 1970 from RHM to Corona Martin, 18 August 1970 from Geisendorf to G Goulden; file MS2553, August 1970 correspondence.

65 EULMC, file MS2552, letters of 12 June 1970 from Geisendorf to RHM, 10 February 1971 from Schwartzman to RHM.

66 EULMC, file MS2554, letter of 20 November 1970 from RHM to G Orlov; file MS 2552, letter of 21 November 1970 from Eddé to RHM.

67 EULMC, letter of 27 July 1971 from G Goulden to RHM, and letter of July 1971 from Schwartzman to RHM.

68 Vago, *Une vie intense*, 460; EULMC, file MS2552, 1972–3 correspondence.

69 EULMC, file MS2538, correspondence of March 1975.

70 EULMC, file MS2553; MS2554, letters of 6 March 1968 from R J Crooks to RHM, RHM to Vago, 16 September 1969, and reply 26 September 1969.

71 EULMC, notes of September 1970 IUA meeting; EULMC, file MS2534, letter of 8 October 1970 from RHM, and 20 November 1970 from RHM to G Orlov.

72 EULMC, file MS2554, sample sheets by RHM – e.g. for Wah Fu multi-storey public housing, Hong Kong – and letter of 1 February 1972 from RHM to Steinbuechel.

73 EULMC, file MS2554, note of 12 March 1974 meeting at UNCHBP, letter of 12 May 1972 from Steinbuechel to RHM, 1 November 1973 from A Ciborowski to RHM, 12 January 1974 from M Piche to ARU Edinburgh, 12 December 1975 from C Naismith to Mrs Steinbuechel.

74 EULMC, papers of Commonwealth Society Edinburgh meeting of 17 March 1971.

75 Zahir, *Memoirs*, 164–5.

76 Colchester, *CAA Newsletter*, 1975.

77 EULMC, file MS2558, notes of council meeting, Edinburgh, July 1970.

78 EULMC, file MS2558, RHM circular letter 1 November 1971; EULMC, letter of 23 January 1970 from T Colchester to Kathleen Hall on parochial government architecture in small island territories.

79 EULMC, file MS2558, letter from J Bhalla to RHM, 5 October 1970; MS2559, letter of 25 February 1974, letter from RHM to R G Medwin; *CAA, 25 Years of Achievement*, London, 1990, 46.

80 EULMC, text of RHM speech to CAA, Canberra, May 1971; file MS2558, letter of 29 August 1974 from RHM to A P Kanvinde; CAA, *Handbook of Commonwealth Architects*, London, June 1965; MS2556, letter of 1 March 1971 from Weill to RHM.

81 1967–70 secession of eastern provinces as 'Biafra' : J de St Jorre, *The Nigerian Civil War*, London, 1972; A H M Kirk-Greene (ed.), *Crisis and Civil War*, Oxford, 1971.

82 EULMC, papers of 21 September 1970 IUA meeting, Mexico City.

83 EULMC, correspondence about 1970 Edinburgh meeting.

84 *CAA, 25 Years of Achievement* (article by R Gilling); EULMC, notes of CAA Canberra meeting.

85 EULMC, file MS2558; Zahir, *Memoirs*, 165.

86 EULMC, text of RHM 27 May 1971 lecture to CAA, Canberra.

87 EULMC, file MS2548; letter of 7 July 1969 from RHM to A C Light, and 23 March 1969 from T Colchester to RHM.

88 EULMC, file MS2559, 19 December 1965 letter from RHM to A Ringrose, ISAA.

89 EULMC, file MS2559, letters of 21 October 1970, 25 November 1970, 7 January 1971, 16 June 1971 from T Colchester to J Bhalla, 18 November 1970 from Commonwealth Foundation to T Colchester; file MS2558, letter of 8 November 1970 from T Colchester to Weill; file MS2538, letter of 18 November 1971 from Rhodesian Institute of Architects to CAA; minutes of Executive Committee, Sydney, 13–14 May 1971.

90 No formal ISAA race bar: EULMC, file MS2558, letters of 4 January 1971 and 6 November 1971 from T Colchester to Weill, 18 October 1971 from Weill to RHM, 4 January 1971 from T Colchester to J Bhalla.

91 EULMC, file MS2559, letters of 5 April 1972 from RHM to

Corona Martin, December 1972 from Kate Macintosh to RHM, 8 January 1973 from A Gordon to RHM, 2 February 1973 from R Cunliffe to RHM, and 15 January 1973 from Anti-Apartheid Movement to RHM.

92 EULMC, file MS2559, 7 February 1973 papers of special council.

93 EULMC, file MS2559, 13 November 1973 and 18 April 1974 meetings of Ad hoc South Africa Committee; letters of 18 July 1973 from F Burn RIBA to RHM, 5 June 1974 from Hans Hallen to RHM and reply of 5 July 1974, 6 January 1975 from J Dunbar-Nasmith to RHM, 4 February 1975 from Dick Gardner RIBA to RHM; file MS2558, letter of 7 June 1974 from J Bhalla to RHM.

94 CAA, 25 Years of Achievement, 46 (article by R Gilling).

95 H le Roux and O Uduku, 'The AA in Africa', Poster, Docomomo Conference, New York, 2004.

96 Interview with SRM, 1995.

97 EULMC, notes of CAA Lagos conference, 21 March 1969, and IUA General Assembly, Buenos Aires, October 1969.

98 EULMC, papers of 27 May 1971 meeting, Sydney.

99 EULMC, text of speech at 14 October 1971 conferral of degree at Bucharest.

100 EULMC, file MS2562, papers of Delos 9, 1971.

101 See e.g. EULMC, file MS2560, letter of 22 March 1972 from RHM to Psomopoulos, and August 1972 correspondence with Arieh Sharon.

102 Criticisms of symposia by 'British Delians', EULMC, file MS2560.

103 EULMC, file MS2560, correspondence of November 1968, November 1971, May 1973, 28 January 1974, February 1974.

104 Commonwealth Foundation, Higher Education in the Commonwealth.

105 Interview with Z Daysh, 2004.

106 EULMC, note by RHM on CAA October 1973 conference.

107 Only One Earth, 5–7, 27–8, cover.

108 Ecologist, January 1972, 1–2; Nature, 14 January 1973, 64–5.

109 E F Schumacher, Small is Beautiful: A Study of Economics as if People Mattered, London, 1973; Department of the Environment, How do you Want to Live? A Report on the Human Habitat, London, 1972. Cf. also RIBA 1972 conference report, 'Designing for Survival': papers on growth, architecture.

110 EULMC, file MS2565, letter of 23 March 1971 from RHM to Secretary of State for Scotland; MS2554, letter of 23 March 1972 from RHM to M Austen-Smith.

111 EULMC, file MS2558, letter of 25 January 1972 from T Colchester to RHM.

112 The Times, 8 June 1972; Scotsman, 6 June 1972 and 15 June 1972.

113 Call by Strong for 'global unity', 'interdependence', and 'peaceful and just world community' (Only One Earth).

114 EULMC, file MS2533, text of RHM lecture to International Centre for Social Gerontology, Washington, DC, December 1973, and to Stirling University ('The architect in the environment'); CHEC News, no. 1, January 1974.

115 EULMC, file MS2538, letter of 1 November 1972. RHM CAA paper on Stockholm follow-up: EULMC, papers for October 1973 Ottawa conference, note on Stockholm 1972.

116 EULMC, file MS2558, letter of 26 January 1972 from T Colchester to RHM.

117 UN General Assembly Resolution 3001-xxvii, 15 December 1972. (EULMC, file MS2558, letter of 29 September 1973 from T Colchester to RHM; draft for RHM report of November 1973 on CAA Assembly, Ottawa.)

118 EULMC, files MS2567 and MS2560, letter of 11 July 1973 from B Ward to RHM; file MS2558, letter of 14 June 1974 from RHM to R Gilling.

119 Interview with Z Daysh, 2004.

120 EULMC, file MS2567.

121 EULMC, file MS2558, letter of 29 August 1974 from RHM to A P Kanunde.

122 CHEC News, January 1974, no. 1. EULMC, file MS2563.

123 EULMC, file MS2537, text of RHM lecture of December 1973 at Washington, DC.

124 EULMC, text of closing declaration of Delos 11, 12 July 1974.

125 EULMC, file MS2558, letters of 5 April and 14 June 1974 from RHM to Gilling Film: file MS2567, note of 23 June 1974; MS2558, letter of 29 August 1974 from RHM to A P Kanunde.

126 EULMC, file MS2558, note of November 1974 meeting, CHEC: file MS2565.

127 EULMC, file MS2560, letter of 3 February 1965 from C Naismith to T Spaven.

128 1974 illness: interviews with Janet O'Neill and Jessie Matthew, 2007.

129 EULMC, miscellaneous illness letters of 1975; file MS2565, letter of 21 January 1975 from C Naismith to Z Daysh, and 3 February 1975 from C Naismith to T Spaven.

130 EULMC, file MS2565, letters of 21 January 1965 from C Naismith to Z Daysh, and of 3 February 1975 from P Harrison to RHM.

131 Interviews with SRM, 1995, and W Campbell, 2003.

132 Interview with Sir A Derbyshire, 2004.

133 EULMC, financial papers of 6 March and 19 March 1975, letters of 18 March and 23 May 1975 from N Lessels to RHM, note of 17 April 1975 meeting with Kidd, letter of 18 August 1975 from C Naismith to Kidd.

134 EULMC, letter and quotation of 5 March 1975 from Maxwell Bros., Haddington, letters of 22 October 1974 from D Douglas to RHM; 16 March 1975 from RHM to H Graham; and 2, 7 April 1975 from H Graham to RHM.

135 Letter of January 2005 from D Walker to M Glendinning.

136 EULMC, letter of 12 May 1975 from P Balshaw to RHM, 22 April 1975 from N Lessels to RHM, and 5 June 1975 note from Kidd.

137 Interview of December 2005 with RAM.

138 EULMC, letters of 13 January 1975 from Gilling to RHM, and 4 January 1975 from RHM to Commonwealth Foundation; *CAA Newsletter*, 2, 1976, 3.

139 EULMC, file MS2558, letters of 27 January and 14 February 1975 from T Watson to Penalosa.

140 EULMC, RHM notes of March 1975 for Charter, and International NGO Committee notes 1975; letter from Psomopoulos, 17 April 1975.

141 EULMC, file MS2560, letter of April 1975 from D Turin to P Psomopoulos.

142 Interview with S Platt, 2003.

143 EULMC, letter from RHM to RAM, 16 May 1975.

144 EULMC, letter of 28 May 1975 from J Bhalla to RHM; file MS2565, letter of 12 May 1975 from C Naismith to RHM.

145 Universal Declaration of Human Rights: UN 48, 25(1). IUA, *XII Congreso Mundial de la UIA*, Madrid, May 1975.

146 EULMC, letter of 31 December 1975 from H Syrkus to LLM.

147 EULMC, letter of May 1975 from RHM to B Ward.

148 Interview with Sir A Derbyshire, 2004.

149 EULMC, letter of 16 May 1975 from RHM to RAM.

150 EULMC, letter of 22 May 1975 from RAM to RHM; file MS2558, letter of 27 May 1975 from T Watson to RHM.

151 EULMC, file MS2565, note of 27 June 1975 from Z Daysh to C Naismith; 24 April 1975 paper by van Putten; letters of May 1975 from van Putten to RHM; minutes of meeting, 2 June 1975.

152 Interviews with T Spaven, 1995, 2004.

153 Morphine: interview with RAM, 2005. EULMC, letter of 6 June 1975 from Nasmith to Psomopoulos; Clough Williams-Ellis obituaries, *JRIBA*, June 1978 (by M Fry), *BD*, 14 April 1978 (by Gibberd), *Guardian*, 16 April 1978. EULMC, letters of 6 June 1975 to RHM from C W Ellis, Edwin Johnston and the Royal Scottish Academy's secretary; letter of 28 May 1975 from J Bhalla to RHM.

154 Interview with L Fricker, 1997.

155 EULMC, letter from M Allan to LLM, 4 September 1978.

156 EULMC, file MS2560, letter of 26 June 1975 from C Naismith to Psomopoulos.

157 Interviews with S Platt, 2003, SRM, 1995, F Isserlis, 1997, E and A Hendry, 1997.

158 EULMC, file MS2565, letter of 26 June 1975 from C Naismith to Z Daysh.

159 Obituaries: *AD*, September 1975, 576; *AIA Journal*, August 1975, 66; *AJ*, 2 July 1975, 13; *AR*, July 1975, 54; *Architectural Record*, September 1975, 33–7; *B*, 27 July 1975, 39; *BD*, 27 June 1975; *Design*, December 1975, 66; *Evening News*, 23 June 1975; *Glasgow Herald*, 23 June 1975; *IIA Journal*, October 1975, 27; *JRIBA*, Jul–Aug 1975, 5; *New York Times*, 22-6-75; *Saltire News*, Dec 1975; *Town and Country Planning*, September 1975, 385; *The Times*, 23 June 1975; *IUA Informations*, July 1975.

160 Nuttgens, *AJ*, 2 July 1975; *Roundabout RMJMP*, Summer 1975; EULMC, letter from Kerr to LLM, 11 December 1975.

161 EULMC, letters of 9 August 1975 from N Khanh to RIBA,

26 June 1975 from USSR Architects to RIBA, 12 August 1975 from Collein to Austen-Smith and reply, 20 August 1975 from SATT to CAA, 7 July 1975 from IIA to CAA, 15 July 1975 from A P Kanvinde to T N Watson.

162 EULMC, letters of 31 December 1975 from H Syrkus to LLM, 5 February 1976 from E Hardie to SRM.

163 EULMC, letter of 9 September 1975 from C Naismith.

164 EULMC, letter of 6 November from EU Depute Librarian to LLM.

165 Taken together, the sorted EUL and unsorted Keith material (now also deposited in EUL Special Collections following Lorna's death in November 2003) provided the backbone of the archival material used for the present book. 'EULMC' citations with 'MS' references refer to files in the original, catalogued deposit; 'EULMC' citations without 'MS' references refer to the later, uncatalogued material. (EULMC, letters of 14 November, 16 November, 3 December 1975 from C Naismith to LLM, and of 1 December 1975 from Bank of Scotland to LLM.)

166 EULMC, letter from SRM to LLM, 2 March 1977, and 18 April 1977 notes by SRM.

167 EULMC, letters from E Hardie to SRM, 5 February 1976; September 1977 circular letter from SRM, January 2005 from D Walker to MG.

168 1976 'IMF crisis': K Burk and A Cairncross, *'Goodbye Great Britain': The 1976 IMF Crisis*, New Haven, 2002; also K Robbins, *The Eclipse of a Great Power*, Harlow 1983; G Jones and M Baines, *Britain on Borrowed Time*, London, 1967.

169 Annan, *Our Age*, 425; *London Review of Books*, 7 April 1994, 30–1; C Barnett, *The Verdict of Peace*, London, 2001.

170 *AD*, 101, 1993, 'Architecture and the environment: HRH the Prince of Wales and the Earth in balance'; C Jencks, *The Prince, the Architects and New Wave Monarchy*, London, 1988; M Hutchinson, *The Prince of Wales, Right or Wrong? An Architect Replies*, London, 1989; Prince of Wales, *A Vision of Britain*, London, 1989; *Perspectives in Architecture*, Issue 1, April 1994; D Watkin, *Morality and Architecture*, London, 1977; Annan, *Our Age*, 449.

171 *The Times*, 1 May 1984; R Scruton, *The Aesthetics of Architecture*, London, 1979; *AJ*, 9 May 1984, 31.

172 *DoE Construction*, June 1977, 21–37.

173 Interview with SRM, 1995; SRM correspondence files.

174 EULMC, text of 15 June 1984 lecture in Edinburgh by J D Richards; interview with PJM, 1987.

175 Interviews with T Spaven, 1995 and 2004.

176 Saint, *Towards a Social Architecture*, 248.

177 Interviews with RAM, 2005, and K Feakes, 2004; RMJMSS, Libya Museum file, project report of 22 December 1983, and report of 26 January 1982 by T Brian Stewart, resident manager, containing claim for LD 20,000 for Area 22 Public Utilities project at Gurgi.

178 J D Richards, 'Miller row: the brief', *Roundabout RMJMP*, December 1984.

179 *Scotsman*, 11 September 1975, 17 June 1975, and 18

September 1975; *Evening News*, 25 September 1975 and 31 October 1975.

180 *Evening News*, 1 March 1984 and 31 August 1974.

181 John Richards, 'Themes and variations', *RMJM 40*, 1996.

182 *AJ*, 16 May 1996, 55; *AJ*, 12 June 1997 (A Derbyshire); *BD*, 12 April 2001.

183 Lecture by P Stallan at Architectural Heritage Society of Scotland conference on postwar heritage, Pollock Halls, Edinburgh, 5 October 2002.

184 *AJ*, 11 February 2003, 16; J Richards and N Pevsner, *The Anti-Rationalists*, London, 1973; K Powell, *BD*, 24 May 2002, 8; *Archis*, May 1998. Collapse in infrastructure of 'public architecture': *BD*, 24 May 2002, 8–9.

185 J Dunnett and G Stamp, *Ernö Goldfinger Works*, 1, AA, London, 1983.

186 Saint, *Towards a Social Architecture*, 247; A Saint, *AJ*, 8 April 1987, 34–42..

187 English Heritage, *Something Worth Keeping?* London, 1996; *AJ*, 5 September 1996, 14. 'LCC Day': *BD*, 22 March 2002, 20.

188 Listing of New Zealand House: *Scotsman,* 25 November 1995, 6; P Carolin and T Dannatt (eds), *Architecture, Education and Research; the Works of Leslie Martin*, London, 1996; *AJ*, 16 January 1997, 52. Stamp: lecture at Twentieth Century Society conference, 'Refashioning the Fifties', at AA, October 1992. Rare call for demolition of Festival Hall, as an 'ugly, charmless, inefficient and indefensible relic of cheapjack postwar shoddiness, a ghastly period piece of no aesthetic merit': B Sewell, *Evening Standard*, 26 February 2002.

189 *AJ*, 26 October 1995, 54; R Scruton, *Perspectives*, February–March 1996, 89.

190 EULMC, J Bhalla telegram to LLM, October 1978. IUA congresses were reined back to a three- rather than two-year cycle: attendances included 5,000 at Berlin in 2002, and 7,000 in Istanbul in 2005. *AJ*, 11 September 1996, 14, 24; *BD*, 12 July 1996, 6; *BD*, 3 May 1996, 3; *AJ*, 1 August 2002, 12; *BD*, 23 August 2002, 1; *BD*, 13 August 1999.

191 EULMC, letter of 15 March 1979 from CAA Secretary to LLM; *BD*, 16 May 1997, 1; *Newsweek*, 11 January 2002, 37–41. *BD*, 9 August 2002.

192 *Human Ecology*, May 2003; EULMC, letter of 16 July 1975 from Eiichi Isomura to LLM.

193 EULMC, letter from Radford to RAM, 31 August 1975.

194 *Habitat Forum News*, January 1976.

195 *Town and Country Planning*, September 1976, 372–3.

196 *Town and Country Planning*, September 1976, 376 and 393.

197 UNCHS, *An Urbanising World: Global Report on Human Settlements*, Oxford 1996; *AJ*, 4 July 1996, 24; J Antoniou (ed.), *Implementing the Habitat Agenda, In Search of Urban Sustainability*, UCL, London, 2001).

198 Antoniou, *Implementing the Habitat Agenda*.

Conclusion

1 Hermann Hesse, *Das Glasperlenspiel*, Zurich, 1943 (English translation, New York, 1969), 13.

2 R Skidelsky, *J M Keynes*, London, 2003, xxx; Collini, *Absent Minds*.

3 Interview with Z Daysh, 2004. Letter from A Derbyshire to L Esher, 13 September 1997 (courtesy of Sir A Derbyshire). W Bridges, *Organisational Transitions*, London, 1986. Annan, *Our Age*, 451.

4 'Field-Marshal' (ENTJ): see e.g. D Keirsey, M Bates, *Please Understand Me*, Del Mar, California, 1984.

5 H Morton, 'Frank Lloyd Wright', *AD*, November 2001, 90–5; N Warburton, *Ernö Goldfinger*, London, 2004.

6 Letter from A Derbyshire to L Esher, 13 September 1997, and reply (courtesy of Sir A Derbyshire); P Nuttgens, *AJ*, 2 July 1975, 13.

587

Notes

Chronology

Owing to unavoidable variations in the degree of precision of dating, the entries for each year include a mixture of precise and general dates, beginning with events dated to the year as a whole. Any activities not attributed specifically to anyone else refer to RHM. For acronyms/initials etc., see Abbreviations list.

1875

Birth of J F Matthew.

1878

Birth of Annie Broadfoot Hogg.

1893

Establishment of R S Lorimer's practice, with J F Matthew as assistant.

1899–1901

J F Matthew's service in S Africa War (1st Battalion Royal Scots).

1902

April 3: Marriage of John and Annie Matthew.

1903

Birth and death of John Matthew (junior).

1906

December 12: Birth of Robert Hogg Matthew at 8 West Mayfield, Edinburgh.

1909

July 27: Birth of (George) Douglas Matthew at 22 Glenorchy Terrace.

1910

October: Birth of Lorna Pilcher.

1912

June 27: Birth of Stuart Russell Matthew at 30 Mayfield Terrace.

1914

RHM began school, at Edinburgh Institution Junior Dept.

1915

March 31: Birth of Margaret (Nannie) Matthew at 31 Dick Place.

1916

April 2: Zeppelin air raid on Edinburgh.

1920

Matthew family moved to 43 Minto Street.

1923

Became dux and head prefect of Edinburgh Institution; won Club Prize.
Participated in SSC trip to Chateau de Mouchac, Gironde.
Took part-time course at Geology Department, EU.

1924

Captain of Rugby 1st XV, Edinburgh Institution.
June: Gained Higher Leaving Certificate, left Edinburgh Institution.
October: Began Day School Stage I, School of Architecture, ECA.

1925

March: Awarded sessional prize.
August: YMCA First International Older Boys' Conference, Vaumarcus, Switzerland.
October: Began Day School Stages II and IIIa, ECA; Basil Spence began Stage I.

1926

Easter: Tour of castles in northeast Scotland.
October: Began Day School Stages IIIb and IIIc, ECA.
Late 1926: JFM partnership with Lorimer and nervous break-
down.

1927

Spring: Sketching tour to Italy.
June: Examination prize and RIBA Intermediate exemption.
Summer: Tour of East Anglia on Matchless motorcycle.
September: Emergency trip to East Anglia to fetch J F Matthew.
October: Began Day School Stage IV, ECA.

1928

Summer: Tour of English cathedrals on Matchless.
October: Began Day School Stage V, ECA; arrival of E A A Rowse
and J Summerson at ECA.

1929

January: Won RIBA Pugin Travelling Studentship.
July 10–16: Tour of Yorkshire and East Anglia on Matchless.
September: Death of R S Lorimer.

1930

First attempt at Rome Prize.
Summer: Joined Lorimer & Matthew on token pay.

1931

Second attempt at Rome Prize.
June: Elected ARIBA.
October: Became part-time instructor at ECA.
December 25: Marriage of RHM and LLM at Fountainhall Road
Church.

1932

Won RIBA Soane Medallion.
Won RIBA Arthur Cates Prize for Promotion of Architecture in
Relation to Town Planning (jointly with Basil Spence).
Moved to Lodge at Lamancha.

1933

Did drawings for Loretto School Hall.
Early 1933: Trip with LLM to Germany, Netherlands,
Scandinavia.
April: Competition entry for Prestwick Burgh Chambers.
Summer: Town Planning Summer School in Liverpool: met L
Budden and P Abercrombie.
October: Did drawings for Lorimer & Matthew Port Hopetoun
scheme.
Late 1933: Did drawings of Wheatsheaf Inn, Balgreen Road.

1934

Did drawings for T Campbell shop, 8 Picardy Place.
Rented flat at 12 Darnaway Street.
July: Trip with LLM to Germany, Denmark.
July: Won Andrew Grant Bequest Scholarship (ECA).
November: Death of Mercia Pilcher.

1935

Research for Bossom Prize entry.

1936

Won Alfred Bossom Travelling Studentship.
May: Took up post as Assistant Architect, DHS.
July: Birth of (Robert) Aidan Matthew.

1937

EAA Civic Survey and Town Planning exhibition at Royal
Scottish Academy, organised by Bossom students.

1938

Official government adviser to town planning exhibition in
Scottish Pavilion, Glasgow Empire Exhibition.
December: Won competition for Ilkeston Community Centre
(unbuilt) with Alan Reiach.

1939

Establishment of Edinburgh Rudolf Steiner School.
Early 1939: Moved to Hamilton House, Prestonpans.
March: Birth of Janet Frances Catriona Matthew.

Late 1939 to 1942

Design/conversion of emergency wartime hospitals; Home
Guard service at Prestonpans.

1940

Lorna and children evacuated to Rothiemurchus for several
months.

1941

Lorna and children moved to 'Briar Corner', Alderley Edge.
Began part-time town and country planning work within DHS
(full time from 1942).

1943

Appointed DHS Deputy Chief Architect with sole responsibility
for planning.
Clyde Valley Regional Planning Advisory Committee reconstituted by T Johnston.
September: P Abercrombie appointed consultant, with RHM as
deputy; formation of Clyde Plan team.

1944

January: Beginning of work on the Clyde Valley Regional Plan.
December 20: Acting Chief Architect, DHS (confirmed in post from 1 January 1945).

1945

March 4: Flight from Leuchars to Stockholm Bromma.
Late March: Excursion from Stockholm to Finland.
Early May: Return from Stockholm to Edinburgh.
Mid 1945: Lorna, Aidan, Janet returned to Hamilton House; Aidan, Janet joined Edinburgh Steiner School.
November: SRM won Thistle Foundation project.
December: Resignation of Forshaw from LCC.

1946

DHS planning work of Architect to LCC.
June: Publication of draft Clyde Valley Regional Plan.
September 2: Took up post as Architect to LCC.
September: First post-war meeting of RIA (later to become IUA) at RIBA.

1947

January: LCC 'Cultural Centre' on South Bank approved in principle by government.
March: Charles Holden appointed to coordinate South Bank Plan.
June: LCC General Purposes Committee issued accommodation brief for Cultural Centre.
July: Matthew family moved from Hamilton House to 36 Kensington Square.
August: Tour of concert halls in Sweden and Denmark.

1948

July: At work on Cultural Centre/Concert Hall designs in bed (with lumbago).
August: Cabinet approval of Cultural Centre/Concert Hall proposal.
October 11: Leslie Martin took up post as Deputy Architect.
November: Detailed plans of Concert Hall approved by LCC.

1949

First draft of LCC Development Plan submitted to Council.
Gained RIBA Distinction in Town Planning.
March: Media campaign began against LCC Valuer's housing.
May: Construction work commenced on Concert Hall.
May 6: Interview for post voted to return housing design responsibility to Architect.
July–August: Eight-week visit to USA (in UK building delegation).
August 20: Publication of full Clyde Valley Regional Plan.
October: Foundation stone of Concert Hall laid by Prime Minister Attlee.
December: Council commenced on East Kilbride and Glenrothes New Towns.

1950

March: Approval of name 'Royal Festival Hall'.
May: King and Queen visited Royal Festival Hall construction site.
May: Appointment of Whitfield Lewis as Principal Housing Architect.
Autumn: Design (by G Powell) of new point block type and first layout of Roehampton.
November: King and Queen visited Lansbury.

1951

Early 1951: Visits to County Hall by Le Corbusier and Frank Lloyd Wright.
March: Type plans for 11-storey point block, and Portsmouth Road mixed development, designed by Housing Division.
May 3: Opening of Royal Festival Hall.

1952

Guest Editor of AJ (with D Gibson, R G Medwin, SJM)
January: Death of Stuart Pilcher; RHM awarded CBE.
Early 1952: Move from Kensington Square to Holfords' house, 5 Cambridge Terrace.
June 1: Birth of Jessie Ann Matthew.
June: Appointed Forbes Professor of Architecture, EU (with effect from 30 April 1953).
Late 1952: Kincardine Power Station project informally broached with RHM.
September: Local inquiry into LCC Development Plan, Central Hall, Westminster.
November: Accepted commission to design Turnhouse Airport, Edinburgh.
December: Tom Spaven began working part-time for RHM.

1953

February: Purchase of Keith Marischal.
March: Informally sounded out about Perthshire hydro projects.
April: Resigned from LCC.
May: Family moved to Keith Marischal; RHM began work as Head of School at ECA.
May: Co-opted on to Scottish National Buildings Record Council.
June: Spaven began full-time work with RHM.
September: First reconnaissance of Old Aberdeen (re university student accommodation).
September: Commission for Dunblane commemorative panel passed from JFM (completed 1956).
September: Detailed design discussions on Kincardine with BEA and engineers.
October 29: Inaugural lecture at EU.
November: Nominated as UK representative on IUA Executive Committee (served until 1967).
December: Margaret Little joined RHM's new practice.

Modern Architect

1954

March: Appointed to advise on new site of University College Dublin.

April: New Zealand House project informally broached with RHM by telephone.

April: James Dunbar-Nasmith joined practice.

April 29: Departed Prestwick on round-the-world trip (to USA, Australia, New Zealand).

May 20–7: Returned home via IUA Executive Committee meeting in Athens/Mykonos.

Mid 1954: beginning of design work on Perthshire hydro projects.

June 8: Formally commissioned to design New Zealand House.

June: Beginning of design work on Boyd Anderson house.

August: Tour of embassies in Scandinavia.

Early September: Resigned as Head of School, ECA.

September: Start of construction of Turnhouse; Ron Thurgarland began work with RHM.

October: Co-organised Geddes Centenary celebrations (including conference), Edinburgh.

October: Appointed a Corresponding Member of the League of Philippine Architects.

October: Margaret Brown and Zena Little joined practice.

November: Graham Law joined practice.

1955

Produced outline plan for new campus, University College Dublin.

Spring: Basil Spence plan for EU George Square redevelopment.

January–March: 'Adam House' dispute with W Kininmonth.

February: Death of JFM.

March 3: Interviews for Queen's College Dundee extension.

April: Authorisation of Hawick project.

May: Appointed to UGC.

Mid 1955: Interviews for Ninewells project.

May: Formal agreement to separation of Forbes professorship and ECA school headship.

July: Death of Annie Matthew.

July: Headed UK delegation to IUA congress and Executive Committee, The Hague.

August: Began work on first design for New Zealand House.

August: Began work on conversion of 24 Park Square East to office.

September: Awarded commission for Royal Infirmary of Edinburgh development plan.

October 11: Elected FRIBA.

November: First discussions with SJM on forming partnership.

1956

January: Made first sketches for Queen's College Dundee extension.

January: Took on 17-year lease of 24 Park Square East, London.

January 1: R Cowan became ECA Head of School and Professor.

February: Completion of design for Gogarbank house.

March: Bought 31 Regent Terrace, Edinburgh.

March: Submitted initial report on Royal Infirmary of Edinburgh.

March: Submitted drawings for Crombie Hall, Aberdeen.

March: Completed initial design for New Zealand House.

March 29: Departure for New Zealand (via USA)

April 4: Meeting with New Zealand Prime Minister (with model).

April 12: Official opening of Turnhouse Airport.

April 16–21: Attended IUA Executive Committee meeting at Capri.

May 25: Partnership heads of agreement signed with SJM.

Late June/early July: Visit by New Zealand Prime Minister to London.

July: Appointed to UK organising committee for IUA congress in London.

July 1: Commencement of partnership with SJM.

October: Establishment of EU Department of Architecture.

November: Informal UK government approval of New Zealand House design.

November: Initial letter from Cumnock Town Clerk about Barshare.

1957

Leslie Martin became first external examiner of RHM's EU department.

Start of construction of Crombie Hall, Aberdeen, and Stage 1 of Dundee University Library.

Law and Dunbar-Nasmith left RMJM to set up their own practice.

January: Bill Campbell joined practice.

January: Start of construction of Lochay hydro station.

March: Final agreement between CEC and New Zealand government on New Zealand House.

March: Linda Westwater joined practice.

March: Death of Abercrombie.

April: Formally engaged by Glasgow Corporation (with Spence) for Gorbals redevelopment.

May: Awarded first EAA Centenary Medal for Turnhouse Airport.

August 19–22: Attended IUA Executive Committee meeting in West Berlin.

September 5–7: Attended IUA Executive Committee meeting in Paris; appointed IUA Vice-President.

October: John Paterson joined practice.

October 1957–June 1958: Prepared 'Hauptstadt Berlin' competition entry.

November: John Richards joined practice.

1958

Gordon Ricketts appointed RIBA Secretary.

EU Major Buildings Committee (chaired by RHM) set up.

January: RMJM awarded second place in Leith Fort competition.

February: Design for Hutchesontown 'B' accepted by Glasgow Corporation.

February: Served on jury for Qaid-e-Azam monument competition, Karachi (first place awarded to Raglan Squire).

May: Kenneth Graham joined practice; marriage of John Richards and Margaret Brown.

July 16: Aidan and Sylvia Cassidy married.

July 21: Formal inaugural session of IUA Moscow congress.

July 23: RHM's speech to IUA Moscow congress; meeting of executive committee with Khrushchev.

August: Formally appointed architect for EU Arts redevelopment.

September: Organising committee for 1961 IUA congress (chaired by RHM) set up.

1959

RIBA recognition of EU Architecture course to Intermediate level.

Engaged to prepare development plan for Cumnock.

Founding member of new RIBA Policy Committee.

Three new senior posts appointed in university department.

Purchased Bella Vista for PJM's occupation.

Prepared entry for Churchill College Cambridge competition, and abortive commercial projects in Montreal and Gorbals, Glasgow.

January: Named 'Man of the Year' by *AJ*.

April: Paper by Alan Wightman proposed low-rise solution for Ninewells Hospital.

April: Establishment of EU Housing Research Unit.

May: Commencement of foundation work on New Zealand House.

June: Received approval in principle for Arts redevelopment from EU.

July: Hosted official visit to Edinburgh by delegation of Soviet architects.

August: Visit to New Zealand (consulting architect to Auckland University)

September 21-2: Attended Lisbon IUA Executive Committee meeting (with Lorna and Lessie).

October: Commencement of construction of Barshare Stage 1.

December: Formally appointed architect for ERI redevelopment.

1960

Appointed architect for Cockenzie Power Station.

Appointed consultant architect for Bannockburn site by NTS.

January–March: Meetings of George Square working group.

January: Commencement of building work at Hutchesontown 'B'.

February 1: 'High buildings' paper to RICS conference.

March: Sounded out regarding Belfast regional planning, by J Oliver and J Aitken.

May 12: Made initial reconnaissance visit to Northern Ireland.

May 16: Laying of foundation stone for New Zealand House.

June: Assessor in Dumbarton redevelopment competition (won by Rae, Preston, Gardner, Strebel).

Summer 1960: Prepared abortive Army and Navy Club scheme (with Stuart).

September 5-11: Attended IUA Executive Committee meeting in Copenhagen.

September 19-23: Helped organise RIBA Conference of Commonwealth Architectural Schools, London.

October: Start of PJM's planning diploma course.

November: Start of foundation work on David Hume Tower.

December: Jury member for National Museum of Kuwait competition (winner: M Ecochard).

1961

RIBA recognition of EU course to Final level.

Designed landscaped garden and gazebo at Gogarbank.

Elected Honorary Fellow of the AIA.

Radical reorganisation of HRU – taken over by PJM.

January: PJM appointed planning consultant to EU.

January: Submitted interim report on housing sites around Belfast to NI Government.

March: Hosted 40 visiting Soviet architects.

April: Spaven, Lee and Newnham taken into RMJM partnership.

May: Presented detailed design report for Ninewells.

May: Chaired the last of 17 organising committee meetings for 1961 IUA congress.

June: Presented ERI feasibility model.

June 28-July 2: IUA Executive Committee and General Assembly held at RIBA.

July 3-7: 6th IUA Congress, South Bank, London (including 6 July 'informal visit' by Prince Philip and RIBA closing party, 7 July); RHM became IUA President (serving for two terms, until 1965).

September: Lecture on tall buildings at Golden Jubilee conference, Hong Kong University.

September 28: Made initial reconnaissance visit to site of Islamabad.

November 27: Return visit to Rawalpindi; meetings with Doxiadis, Breuer and CDA staff.

December: Accepted invitation by CDA to prepare plans for Islamabad governmental zone.

1962

Establishment of EU Planning Research Unit.

Appointed Honorary Fellow, League of Philippine Architects.

Completion of Commonwealth Institute, London (designed by Peter Newnham).

Initiation of Ellor Street redevelopment plan, Salford (by PJM and EU HRU/ARU).

York University Development Plan prepared by SJM and A Derbyshire.

Submitted abortive entry (with Stuart) for St Paul's Choir School, London.

Late January 1962: Made extended visit to Rawalpindi.

February 13: Knighted at Buckingham Palace.

February: Invited by Ricketts to become PRIBA.

March: Prepared initial sketch layout for Islamabad Administrative Sector.

March 30–April 1: Attended IUA Executive Committee, Charleroi.

July: Commenced of two-year term as PRIBA (with PJM standing in as head of department at Edinburgh).

July: Appointed Chairman of IUA Committee for Education of the Architect (until 1966).

July 11: Inaugural speech to RIBA conference, Coventry.

July: Patrick Massey appointed London personal assistant to RHM.

August: Commissioned to design enlargement of Loretto School Chapel.

Late 1962: Pushed through post-Office Survey reorganisation of RIBA.

October: RIBA Presidential Address.

November: Participated in IUA 'Second Seminar on Industrialised Building', Brazil, and in subsequent IUA council meeting in Rio.

1963

Appointed to BBC General Advisory Council (served until 1968).

Helped establish New Lanark Housing Association.

Stuart Matthew hospitalised with nervous breakdown.

Appointed Doctor of Law, Sheffield University.

January: Hosted RIBA meeting on London government (attended by Sir K Joseph).

January: Last Hutchesontown 'B' tower block completed.

February 25–March 1: Attended IUA Executive Committee in St Moritz, followed by trip to Pakistan.

February: Hosted RIBA conference on UN–IUA relations.

February: Publication of preamble and proposals of Belfast Regional Plan.

March 3: Delivered formal address to both houses of Stormont Parliament.

March–May: Presidential visits and lectures to five regional societies.

April: Lecture on 'American Cities' at British Association for American Studies conference, Edinburgh.

Late April: Buckminster Fuller stayed at Keith.

May 8: Official opening of New Zealand House by the Queen.

June: Juror in competition to select architect for National Theatre (D Lasdun).

June: Establishment of Keith Ingram Ltd (initially based at 124–6 Rose Street).

June 16–21: Visited Israel to advise on design of Haifa 'Technion', Israel Institute of Technology.

July: Chaired RIBA conference on 'The Architect and Productivity'.

July 6–13: Delos 1 Symposium, Greece.

July 21–5: Conference of Commonwealth Architectural Societies, RIBA.

August 29: Devised design concept for Pilgrim Street, Newcastle, at Regent Terrace meeting.

September 16: Beginning of US and Cuba trip: dinner with the Mumfords and Steins, Amelia, NY.

September 17: AIA meetings and lunch in his honour at Washington Center for Metropolitan Studies.

September 18: Philadelphia meetings (including Bacon, Kahn).

September 19: Ford, Rockefeller, UNCHBP meetings in New York.

September 20–5: Toured West Indies (representing IUA and RIBA).

September 26–October 3: IUA Havana, chairing both the main congress and Playa Giron competition.

October 7–12: 8th IUA General Assembly, Mexico City (followed by touring in Mexico).

October: Speech at opening ceremony of David Hume Tower.

October: Brokered NTS acquisition of Craigievar Castle.

October: Became Convener of Saltire Society Housing Design Award Panel (until 1968).

November: Crudens tender for Ninewells accepted.

December: Hosted RIBA meeting in support of Fuller's World Science Decade project.

1964

Kenneth Graham and John Richards became partners.

Cicely Naismith appointed Edinburgh personal assistant.

Closure of Dundee office; Ninewells project moved to Edinburgh.

January: Commissioned to design Midlothian County Buildings Extension, Edinburgh.

January 13: Lecture at Reading, 'Architecture today, yesterday and tomorrow'.

April 1: Lecture at Cairo University.

April 13: Belfast Regional Survey and Plan published in full.

April 17–18: Chaired RIBA regional symposium in Manchester on urban regeneration.

May: Chaired RIBA conference, Glasgow (speeches on May 9 and 11).

May 27–June 1: Attended IUA Executive Committee, Budapest.

June 17: Speech to annual conference of Royal Architectural Institute of Canada.

July 5–10: Member of competition assessors' panel for University College Dublin masterplan.

July 14–21: Attended Delos 2 symposium, Greece (including paper on 18 July by RHM and R Llewellyn-Davies).

September: Jessie began at Oxenford Castle school.

September 3: Flight to Rome and Hong Kong.

September 7–23: Tour of People's Republic of China (based in Beijing , 10–17 September, and Shanghai, 17–22 September) and return to Hong Kong.

September 24–5: CAA preparatory meeting, Singapore.

October 1: Visit to Angkor Wat, Cambodia.

October 4–6: In New Delhi.

October 7–10: In Rawalpindi/Islamabad.

October 13: Arrived back in London: straight to RIBA policy meeting.

October: Presented new RIE model (envisaging six-phase, all medium-rise plan)

1965

January: Chaired opening session at TPI conference, Edinburgh.

January 8–13: Attended IUA Executive Committee meeting at Torremolinos.

Late January: Examined Kahn plans for Islamabad at Rawalpindi meeting.

February: Visit by Buckminster Fuller to Keith.

March: RIBA portrait ceremony for RHM.

March: Negotiated World Bank approval of Nigerian school-building programme.

March: Hosted working supper at Park Square East on international architectural education.

March 18–19: Flying visit to Moscow to discuss urban landscaping with N Kolli.

March 21–3: Visit to New Delhi about architectural education.

May 1: Hosted 'China evening' (films, slides) with A Ling, at RIBA.

May: Hosted Edinburgh visit by Doxiadis (including party at Prestonfield House).

May: Attended Ove Arup's 70th birthday party in London (down by day, return overnight).

June: EAA dinner for RHM and Basil Spence at ECA.

June 14–18: Attended/lectured to AIA/Pan American Convention, Washington DC (June 17: opened LCC exhibition at National Housing Centre).

June 22–7: Chaired inaugural CAA Conference, Malta.

June 30–July 11: Attended IUA Congress and Executive Committee, Paris.

July 12–19: Attended Delos 3 symposium.

August 5: Arrived in Pakistan.

August: Attended Churchill College 'brainstorming' conference on planning research.

August: Chaired IUA General Assembly and Congress, Paris.

August–September: Two visits to Malta (advising on architectural education).

September: Co-organised EU course on African educational links.

September: Visit to UNCHBP, New York.

November: Awarded Danish Federation of Architects' Medal of Honour (ceremony at Danish Embassy, London).

December: Attended initial briefing meetings on Stirling University project.

1966

Formation of PJM's EU Planning department.

External examiner at Khartoum University.

January: Informally offered commission to masterplan New University of Ulster and hinterland zone (appointment confirmed March 1966).

February: London office asked to undertake Central Lancashire New Town study.

March 4: Hosted lunch at Reform Club on Commonwealth Foundation funding.

March 7–8: Member of panel of advisers for International Labour Office HQ, Geneva: first stage.

March 15–21: Attended IUA Executive Committee, Moscow.

March 28: Began one-week visit to Romania.

April 4–6: Member of panel of advisers for International Labour Office HQ, Geneva: second stage.

April 20–1: Familiarisation visit to Coleraine by RHM and J Richards.

May 9–24: Chaired Broad Sanctuary Inquiry, Westminster.

May 23: Lecture to World Precast Concrete Society, Royal Festival Hall.

June: Opened exhibition of Scottish hospital design at Western Infirmary, Glasgow.

June 30–July 4: Returned to Bucharest for IUA Housing Colloquium.

September: Appointed as a founder trustee of Scottish Civic Trust.

September 7: Attended UNCHBP committee at in Geneva.

September 26–8: Member of panel of advisers for International Labour Office HQ, Geneva: final stage.

October 27–8: Founder member of CBAE: met for first time at RIBA.

November 15: Address to Institution of Heating and Ventilation Engineers, Glasgow.

November 27–December 4: Nigeria visit (leading RMJM IDA Education Project negotiations).

December: Chaired IUA Committee on the Education of the Architect, Paris.

December 7: Address to Cumnock Centenary Dinner.

1967:

Formation of new RIBA departmental board on Membership (chaired by RHM).

Sale of Bella Vista to PJM.

External examiner at Khartoum University.

January 9: Elected Hon. Corresponding Member of *Bund deutscher Architekten*.

February: Devised plan for library spine and rolling development at NUU.

February 5: Attended brainstorming meeting in Geneva on future of IUA.

February 26–March 4: Nigeria.

March 11–18: Attended CAA Conference, New Delhi, and gave President's speech.

March 20: New Delhi, chaired meeting of CBAE.

March 22: Educational visit to Pakistan.

March 29: Budapest.

March 29–31: On jury for first stage of Prague concert hall competition.

May: Start of building work on NUU Phase I by contractor F B McKee.

May 23: Attended inaugural meeting of Scottish Civic Trust, Bute Hall, Glasgow.

June 27–July 1: Attended IUA General Assembly, Congress and Executive Committee, Prague.

July 22–9: Attended Delos 5 symposium and Athens Ekistics Month.

August: Presented interim report on NUU Development Plan, Stormont.

September 28–9: Attended meeting on IUA reorganisation, Prague.

September: Attended UNCHBP committee at Geneva.

November 15: Presided over inaugural meeting of Ulster Architectural Heritage Society, Belfast Harbour Office.

December 17: Chaired IUA Education of the Architect committee meeting, Paris.

1968

Appointed with Professor Tom Wilson to prepare 1970–5 Development Plan for Northern Ireland.

Appointed Scottish Convener of Property, Salvation Army (until 1975).

January: Death of Gordon Ricketts; succeeded by Patrick Harrison.

January 5–8, 12: Juror in Amsterdam City Hall competition first stage.

January 9–11: Attended IUA meeting, Lausanne.

February 6–10: Attended IUA Executive Committee, Lausanne.

February 27–March 4: Attended CBAE/CAA meetings, Montreal and Toronto.

March: Appointed trustee of World of Property Housing Trust.

March 15–17: Attended Ditchley Park Foundation conference on 'Big Cities': chaired session.

June: Guy Oddie appointed head of EU Architecture Department.

June 8: Delivered speech at Buckminster Fuller's RIBA Gold Medal presentation.

June and July: Two trips to Prague (about concert hall).

July 6–13: Delos 6 symposium.

July: Extended visit to Islamabad, Delhi, Thailand.

August 19–20: Chaired meeting of his ad hoc committee on UIA reorganisation in Paris.

August 28: Addressed RICS Commonwealth Conference.

September: Moved to part-time post at EU (with ARU and SBE chair); start of first-year joint SBE course.

September: Establishment of Edinburgh New Town Conference organising committee, meeting at Regent Terrace.

October 25: Official opening of New University of Ulster by Prime Minister O'Neill.

November: Finalised report on reorganisation of IUA.

November: Chaired first meeting of UK Committee of Delians

(Ekistics) at Park Square East.

November (five days): Juror in second stage of Amsterdam City Hall competition final stage (winner: W Holzbauer).

November 15–17: Attended Ditchley Park Foundation Anglo-American Conference on New Towns.

November 29: BBC TV St Andrew's Night programme, *The Impact of Change*.

December: extended Extended visit to Nigeria (on RMJM and CAA business).

1969

Withdrew from chair of RIBA Board of Membership.

Appointed chair of two new RIBA companies, National Building Specifications Ltd and RIBA Services Ltd.

January 20–5: Attended IUA executive Executive committeeCommittee, London.

February: EAA began nine-month survey of Edinburgh New Town.

March: Start of building work on NUU Phase 2 (Spine, etc.).

March: CDA approved his masterplan for the extension of the Islamabad administrative sector.

Early March: Visit to Ethiopia, followed by 4th CBAE meeting at Nairobi (RHM retired from CBAE).

March: CAA conference, Lagos, including meeting with Gen. Gowon at Dodan Barracks (RHM closing speech on 21 March), followed by visit to Ivory Coast.

July 12–19: Delos 7 symposium.

Early September: Attended sessions of UNCHBP, New York

September 29–October 3: Jury member in competition for London Central Mosque (winner: F Gibberd).

Early October: Visited New York and HUD/IDA in Washington, en route to Argentina.

October 12: Arrived in Argentina.

October 13–16: IUA Council meetings and General Assembly at Llao-Llao Hotel, Bariloche.

October 20–5: IUA Congress, Teatro San Martin, Buenos Aires.

October 26–9: Visit to Brazil.

November: Visit to Sierra Leone.

1970

January: Radio lecture on conservation, 'A future for the past'.

March: Visit to Uganda.

March 13: London–Paris day trip to mediate in Eddé–Vago IUA feud.

April 6–10: Competition jury member for masterplan for Brussels Free University.

June: Radio broadcast on new universities.

June 1–3: Attended IUA Council meeting in Paris.

June 6: Organised SCT Assembly Rooms Conference on Edinburgh New Town.

June 16: Awarded RIBA Royal Gold Medal (at RIBA ceremony); parties at Humbie June 11 June, Regent's Park 15 June 15.

July 13–15: CAA Executive meeting at RIAS (with party at Keith Marischal, July 11).

September 1–9: Meeting in New Delhi.

September 21: Attended IUA executive meeting, Mexico City.

October: RHM and R von Steinbuechel-Rheinwall began preparing 'basic housing' fiches for IUA–UN 'Basic Housing project' (project abandoned in 1974).

October 20–4: Attended congress of USSR Union of Architects, Moscow.

October–November: M Weill succeeded H Eddé as Interim IUA Secretary.

November: Completed the design of the Pakistan National Archives (completed by Zahir in 1973; National Museum and Library eventually cancelled).

November 21–3: RHM's first flying visit to Libya.

December 1: Appointed Consultant Adviser on Conservation, for three years, by the Scottish Secretary.

December: Post-Assembly Rooms conference steering group established ENTCC.

1971

Joined Consultative Architectural Committee of the International Organisation for Justice and Development.

Keith Marischal 'listed' by SDD.

March: Joined CHEC Governing Council.

Late March, late April: Visit Visits to Libya (IBP).

May: Burrell Collection competition entry submitted.

May: CAA conference, Australia (including May 11 Assembly at Canberra: S Africa and Ireland demoted to associate status).

May 27: Spoke at Centenary Meeting of Royal Australian Institute of Architects, Sydney.

Early June: Travel to Colombia, Peru.

July: Attended Delos 9 symposium.

July: End of term on RIBA Council.

August: SDD approved establishment of ENTCC.

September and November: Chaired two-stage competition for Perugia town extension.

Early October: Visit to Libya (IBP).

October 14: Conferral of degree *honoris causa*, Bucharest.

November 11–14: Bulgaria visit.

December: Libya: two IBP visits, followed by preparation of Design Report for Gargaresh/West Gurgi.

December: Authorised 'de-listing' of Barskimming House.

1972

January: Co-organised seminar on Commonwealth Architectural Research at EU.

February: Detailed proposals approved for RIE Phase 1.

March: Chaired jury for new parliamentary offices (the end of a four-year process: Robin Spence and Robin Webster awarded first prize).

Spring: Founding of MMP Ltd confirmed.

April: RAM became associate within RMJM.

April: Included on new listing committee established by HBCS.

April 12–14: IUA Council meeting, Munich.

Late April: Chaired CHEC 2nd International Conference,

University of Hong Kong.

May 2–9: Delhi.

May 9–10: Karachi.

May: Malaysia.

June/July: Visit to Libya (IBP).

July: Attended Delos 10 symposium.

September 17–30: Bulgaria (Sofia/Varna), attended IUA Congress, Assembly, Executive Committee.

October: Last of eight visits to Libya (IBP).

October: Attended CAA Executive meeting, Nicosia.

October 27: Stirling University lecture, 'The architect and the environment'.

November: Lectured on Stockholm 1972 environment conference to CAA meeting, Canada.

December: Matthew/Skillington Inquiry (on design standards in government architecture) commissioned (sat in 1973–4).

December 15: UN General Assembly Resolution charged UNEP to organise 1976 Vancouver HABITAT conference.

December 19: Lecture to University of Ireland, Dublin.

1973

Joined WSE nominating committee.

January: Buffet supper in London for Michel Weill.

February: Spoke at special RIBA Council meeting on links with ISAA.

March: Chaired Edinburgh conference on public participation in conservation.

March: Launch of first three volumes of NBS.

April: Original end of Park Square East lease (twice extended).

May 29–June 2: Helsinki.

June 4–11: Attended IUA council meeting and 25th anniversary party, Moscow.

June: presided Presided at R Gardner-Medwin valedictory banquet, Liverpool.

June: Zurich conference to launch EAHY.

June 20–3: Summing-up speech at RIBA annual conference, Stirling.

July: RMJM appointed architects for CTTD.

July 11: Royal luncheon party at Holyroodhouse.

August: On jury for Glasgow 'Ideas Competition'.

October/November: CAA conference, assembly and committees, Ottawa/Montreal: speech on 'UN Action in the Environment'.

1974

January: Chaired RSA conference on future of Covent Garden.

January 9–16: Toured German theatres (research for CTTD).

January 22–5: Lectured to Council of Europe conservation seminar, Edinburgh.

February: Retirement of Thomas Colchester from CAA Secretaryship; replaced by Tom Watson.

February 7–8: Attended IUA meeting, Paris.

February 15–25: CAA visit to New Delhi, combined with IUA Executive Committee meeting.

February 25–March 7: CAA visit to Australia.

March 7–20: Visit to New Delhi and Pakistan.

March: Joined new 'Van Putten committee' of NGOs preparing for Vancouver Habitat.

April: Ninewells Hospital finally completed.

April 21–6: Visit to Cairo, Karachi and Lahore.

May: Finally disposed of Keith Ingram.

June: Helped organise four-day EU conference on conservation.

July: First signs of illness (feelings of lethargy).

July: CTTD proposal turned down by RFACS.

July: Start of building work on Libyan IBP.

July 6–14: Attended Delos 11 symposium; appointed chief WSE representative for Habitat.

September: Appointed chairman of JSCCA (intended to prepare for Habitat).

September 30: Retired from EU Forbes Chair of Architecture; became emeritus Emeritus professorProfessor.

October 12–13: Czechoslovakia (en route to Poland).

October 13–21: Chaired conservation conference at Kazimierz, Kraków, Poland.

November 3–9: Visit to Jamaica (for CAA meeting, Kingston) and Barbados.

November 30–December 7: Paris and St Quentin (fell seriously ill en route).

December 14–18: IUA/CAA visit to Moscow, Karachi.

1975

January 21: Admitted to Ward D1 of Western General Hospital, Edinburgh.

January 30: Operation, followed by resignation from various committees.

March: Initiation of HBC-supported repair programme at Keith Marischal.

March: Worked from sickbed on Charter of Housing.

April: Start of work on RIE Phase 1.

April: Attended ISOCARP conference, Edinburgh: 'Planning for Our Inheritance'.

April 24: CAA Executive Committee meeting at his bedside, Park Square East.

April 30–early May: IUA Council and General Assembly, Venice: RHM's last public speech.

May 5–11: IUA Congress, Madrid: finished draft of Charter of Housing.

May 11–23: Toured Morocco by car with Jessie; drafted film script at Fez.

Mid May: Extension of Park Square East lease by a further year.

June 2: Attended meeting of Van Putten committee at Royal Commonwealth Society.

June 4: Driven by ambulance from London to Humbie to vote in EEC referendum.

June 21: Died in bed at Keith Marischal.

June 25: Funeral at Humbie Church (3.30 p.m.) followed by wake at Keith Marischal.

June 28: Death of C. Doxiadis.

July: LLM appointed honorary life member of WSE.

November: First consignment of personal papers passed to EULSC.

1976

LLM moved out of Park Square East.

January: Cicely Naismith finished working for LLM/RMJM.

May 31–June 11: Habitat conference, Vancouver.

1977

John Richards appointed chairman of RMJM (continued until 1986); Tom Spaven retired from RMJM.

LLM sold 31 Regent Terrace.

SJM retired from RMJM (died 1981).

Maxwell Allan carved RHM memorial stone for Humbie kirk-yard.

1978

UN established UN Centre for Human Settlements, Nairobi.

IUA established 'Sir Robert Matthew Prize' for design of human settlements.

1983

CAA instituted a Robert Matthew Award (first awarded 1983 to Philip Cox of Australia).

1984

Public lecture on RHM by John Richards in Edinburgh.

Edinburgh CTTD project finally abandoned.

1986

RMJM re-formed as a limited holding company and subsidiaries.

1988

April: Royal Festival Hall 'listed' Grade I.

1995

New Zealand House 'listed' Grade II.

1996

May 30–June 14: Habitat II conference, Istanbul.

2005 to 2007

Refurbishment of Royal Festival Hall by Allies & Morrison, architects.

Abbreviations

AA	The Architectural Association	*CQ*	*Concrete Quarterly*
AASTA	Association of Architects, Surveyors and Technical Assistants	CT	Civic Trust
		CTTD	Castle Terrace Theatre Development
ABN	*Architect and Building News*	CVRPAC	Clyde Valley Regional Planning Advisory Committee
ABT	Association of Building Technicians		
ACP	Architects' Co-Partnership	DHS	Department of Health for Scotland
AD	*Architectural Design*	DoE	Department of the Environment
AF	*Architectural Forum*	DSIR	Department of Scientific and Industrial Research
AGM	annual general meeting	EAA	Edinburgh Architectural Association
AJ	*The Architects' Journal*	EAHY	European Architectural Heritage Year 1975
AR	*The Architectural Review*	ECA	Edinburgh College of Art
ARCUK	Architects' Registration Council of the United Kingdom	ECOSOC	United Nations Social and Economic Council
		ENTCC	Edinburgh New Town Conservation Committee
ARIBA	Associate of the Royal Institute of British Architects	EU	University of Edinburgh
		EULMC	Edinburgh University Library Matthew Collection
ARU	Architecture Research Unit (University of Edinburgh)	FRIBA	Fellow of the Royal Institute of British Architects
		GAC	General Advisory Council (BBC)
ASTT	Architects' Society of Trinidad and Tobago	GLC	Greater London Council
B	*The Builder/Building*	*H*	*Housing*
BBPR	Banfi, Belgiojoso, Peressutti, Rogers	HBC	Historic Buildings Council
BDA	Bund deutscher Architekten	HBCS	Historic Buildings Council for Scotland
BEA	British Electricity Authority	*HR*	*Housing Review*
BRS	Building Research Station	h.r.p.a.	habitable rooms per acre
CAA	Commonwealth Association of Architects	HRU	Housing Research Unit (University of Edinburgh)
CBAE	Commonwealth Board of Architectural Education	HUD	Department of Housing and Urban Development
CBE	Commander of the British Empire	IBP	Industrialised Building Project (Libya)
CCL	Commissioners of Crown Lands	ICE	Institution of Civil Engineers
CDA	Comprehensive Development Area/Capital Development Authority (Islamabad)	ICOMOS	International Council on Monuments and Sites
		IDA	'World Bank'
CEC	Crown Estates Commissioners	IFHTP	International Federation for Housing and Town Planning
CHEC	Commonwealth Human Ecology Council		
CIAM	Congrès Internationaux d'Architecture Moderne	IIA	Indian Association of Architects
CLASP	Consortium of Local Authorities' Special Programme	ISAA	Institute of South African Architects
		ISOCARP	International Society of City and Regional Planners
CLP	J H Forshaw, P Abercrombie, *County of London Plan*, London, 1943	IUA	International Union of Architects (see UIA)
COID	Council of Industrial Design	JFM	John F Matthew
CPSU	Communist Party of the Soviet Union	*JRIBA*	*Journal of the Royal Institute of British Architects*

JSAH	*Journal of the Society of Architectural Historians*	RFAC	Royal Fine Art Commission
JSCCA	Joint Standing Committee of Commonwealth Associations	RFACS	Royal Fine Art Commission for Scotland
		RHM	Robert Hogg Matthew
LCC	London County Council	RIA	Réunion Internationale des Architectes
LCMT	London Central Mosque Trust	RIAS	Royal Incorporation of Architects in Scotland
LLM	Lorna Matthew	RIBA	Royal Institute of British Architects
LMA	London Metropolitan Archives	RIBAS	RIBA Services Ltd
LMS	London, Midland and Scottish Railway	RICS	Royal Institution of Chartered Surveyors
MARS	Modern Architecture Research Group	RIE	Royal Infirmary of Edinburgh
MHLG	Ministry of Housing and Local Government	RMJM	Robert Matthew, Johnson-Marshall (& Partners)
MIT	Massachusetts Institute of Technology	RMJMSS	RMJM Sighthill Store
MJ	*Municipal Journal*	RNZN	Royal New Zealand Navy
MMP	Sir Robert Matthew, Metcalf & Partners	RSUA	Royal Society of Ulster Architects
MoE	Ministry of Education	RTPI	Royal Town Planning Institute (see also TPI)
MoH	Ministry of Health/Medical Officer of Health	SAA	School of Applied Art
MoW	Ministry of Works	SAH	Society of Architectural Historians
MPBW	Ministry of Public Building and Works	SBE	School of the Built Environment, University of Edinburgh
MTCP	Ministry of Town and Country Planning		
MW	megawatt	SCPP	Scottish Council on Postwar Problems
NAS	National Archives of Scotland	SCT	Scottish Civic Trust
NBA	National Building Agency	SDD	Scottish Development Department
NBS	National Building Specifications Ltd	SERHB	South-Eastern Regional Hospital Board
NCB	National Coal Board	SGS	Scottish Georgian Society
NEDO	National Economic Development Organisation	SJM	Stirrat Johnson-Marshall
NGO	non-governmental organisation	SPCC	Society for Prevention of Cruelty to Children
NHC	National Housing Corporation	SPLAJ	Socialist People's Libyan Arab Jamahiriya
NIA	Nigerian Institute of Architects	SPRND	School of Planning and Research for National Development
NIHT	Northern Ireland Housing Trust		
NSHEB	North of Scotland Hydro-Electric Board	SRM	Stuart Russell Matthew
NTDC	New Town Development Corporation	SSC	Scottish Schoolboys' Club
NTS	National Trust for Scotland	SSEB	South of Scotland Electricity Board
NUU	New University of Ulster	SSHA	Scottish Special Housing Association
OAP	*Official Architecture and Planning*	TCPA	Town and Country Planning Association
PJM	Percy Johnson-Marshall	TPI	Town Planning Institute (see also RTPI)
p.p.a.	persons per acre	UAHS	Ulster Architectural Heritage Society
PPRIBA	Past President of the Royal Institute of British Architects	UEA	University of East Anglia
		UGC	University Grants Committee
PRIBA	President of the Royal Institute of British Architects	UIA	Union Internationale des Architectes (see also IUA)
		UNCHBP	United Nations Centre for Housing, Building and Planning
PRO	Public Record Office		
PSA	Property Services Agency	UNCHS-HABITAT	United Nations Centre for Human Settlements
PWA	Public Works Administration		
PWD	public works department	UNEP	United Nations Environment Programme
QS	quantity surveyor	UNESCO	United Nations Educational, Scientific and Cultural Organisation
RAIA	Royal Australian Institute of Architects		
RAIC	Royal Architectural Institute of Canada	UN-HABITAT	United Nations Human Settlements Programme
RAM	(Robert) Aidan Matthew		
RCAHMS	Royal Commission on the Ancient and Historical Monuments of Scotland	WSD	World Science (Design) Decade
		WSE	World Society for Ekistics
R&D	research and development	YMCA	Young Men's Christian Association

Bibliography

Owing to the dearth of books or other significant publications specifically about Robert Matthew, this bibliography largely contains references to 'contextual' works, concerning the architectural, cultural and political milieux of the various stages of his career. Accordingly, these works are here arranged in thematic groups, set in roughly chronological order.

Priority is given to any aspects of each headed theme that relate directly to Matthew's work (for example, within 'international' themes, to particular countries with which he was connected)

MODERN SOCIAL AND POLITICAL HISTORY

N Annan, *Our Age*, London, 1990

C Barnett, *The Verdict of Peace*, London, 2001

D Bernal, *The Social Function of Science*, London, 1939

W Bridges, *Organisational Transitions*, London, 1986

S Brittan, *The Treasury under the Tories*, London, 1964

K Burk and A Cairncross, *'Goodbye Great Britain': The 1976 IMF Crisis*, New Haven, 2002

S Collini, *Absent Minds*, Oxford, 2006

W Crofts, *Coercion or Persuasion? Propaganda in Britain after 1945*, London, 1989

R Crossman, *The Diaries of a Cabinet Minister*, vol. 1, London, 1975.

P Hennessy, *Never Again, Britain 1945-1951*, London, 1992

P Hennessy, *The Secret State, Whitehall and the Cold War*, London, 2002

J Huxley, *TVA*, London, 1943

G Jones and M Baines, *Britain on Borrowed Time*, London, 1967

D Lilienthal, *TVA: Democracy on the March*, London, 1944 (Penguin Special)

A Marwick, *British Society since 1945*, London, 1987

S Pedersen, P Mandler (eds), *After the Victorians*, London, 1994

H Perkin, *The Rise of Professional Society in England since 1880*, London, 1990

Christopher Reed, *Bloomsbury Rooms*, New Haven, 2004

K Robbins, *The Eclipse of a Great Power*, Harlow, 1983

D Sandbrook, *Never Had It So Good: a History of Britain from Suez to the Beatles,* London, 2005.

Robert Skidelsky, *John Maynard Keynes 1883-1946*, London, 2003.

C P Snow, *Science and Government* (The Godkin Lectures at Harvard University), 1960

F Toennies, *Gemeinschaft und Gesellschaft*, 1887

ARCHITECTURAL ORGANISATION

W Bridges, *Organisational Transitions*, London, 1986.

Brunton Baden Hellyard, *Management Applied to Architectural Practice*, 1964

H J Cowan, *A Historical Outline of Architectural Science*, Amsterdam, 1986;

A Drexler (ed), *The Architecture of the Ecole des Beaux-Arts*, London, 1977

A Jackson, *The Politics of Architecture*, London, 1970

H-W Kruft, *A History of Architectural Theory*, London, 1994

F M Lea, *Science and Building, A History of the Building Research Station*, London, 1971.

A Mace, *The RIBA*, London, 1986

O Marriott, *The Property Boom*, London, 1967

Organisation for European Economic Cooperation, *Prefabricated Building, A Survey of Some European Systems*, Paris, 1958

A Powers, *Architectural Education in Britain, 1880–1914*, PhD thesis, Cambridge 1982

A Ravetz, *The Government of Space*, London, 1986

A Saint, *The Image of the Architect*, London, 1983, 68

A Saint, *Architect and Engineer: a Study in Sibling Rivalry*, New Haven, 2007

A Saint, *Towards a Social Architecture*, London, 1987

D Senior, *Your Architect*, London, 1964

M E Taylor, *Private Architectural Practice*, London, 1956

P Thompson, *Architecture: an Art or a Social Service*, Young Fabian Group, London, 1963

HISTORY OF TOWN AND REGIONAL PLANNING

Patrick Abercrombie, *Planning in Town and Country, Difficulties and Possibilities*, Liverpool, 1937

Patrick Abercrombie, *Town and Country Planning*, London, 1933

P Abercrombie, *The Master Plan of Addis Ababa*, 1956
British Road Federation, *Urban Motorways*, London, 1958
M Brown, *The Planning of East Kilbride 1946-1951*, c. 1995
C Buchanan, *State of Britain*, London, 1972
C Buchanan, *Traffic in Towns*, London, 1960–3
Wilfred Burns, *New Towns from Old*, London, 1963
D Chapman, *Wartime Social Survey, The Location of Dwellings in Towns*, London, 1943
G E Cherry, *The Evolution of British Town Planning*, Leighton Buzzard, 1974
G Cherry, *Pioneers in British Planning*, London, 1981
G E Cherry and L Penny, *Holford*, London, 1986
E Darling, *Re-Forming Britain: Narratives of Modernity before Reconstruction*, London, 2007
A d'Egville, *Brass Tacks for Britain*, London, 1945
P Geddes, *Cities in Evolution*, London, 1915, 1968 edition
P Geddes, *City Development...A Report to the Carnegie Dunfermline Trust*, Edinburgh, 2004
P Geddes and Colleagues, *The Masque of Ancient Learning*, Edinburgh, 1913
P Geddes, *Dramatisations of History*, London, 1923
J Lindsay, *Elizabeth B Mitchell, The Happy Town Planner*, Bishop Auckland, 1993
R Lyle and G Payne, *The Tay Valley Plan*, Dundee, 1950
Antonio Manno, *Patrick Abercrombie, A Chronological Bibliography*, Leeds, 1980
Max Lock Exhibition Memorial Group, *Max Lock 1909–1958*, exhibition catalogue, c.1999
C H Meller, *Patrick Geddes*, London, 1990
L Mumford, *The Highway and the City*, New York, 1953
L Mumford, *City Development, Studies in Disintegration and Renewal*, London, 1946
F J Osborn (ed), *Making Plans*, London, 1942
Cd 6153, *Report of the Royal Commission on the Distribution of the Industrial Population*, London, 1940
Royal Institute of British Architects, *Towards a New Britain*, London, 1943
F E Towndrow (ed), *Replanning Britain* (report of Town and Country Planning Association Spring 1941 meeting), London, 1941
Alker Tripp, *Road Traffic and its Control*, London, 1938
V Welter and J Lawson (eds), *The City after Patrick Geddes*, Bern, 2000
V Welter, *Biopolis, Patrick Geddes and the City of Life*, Cambridge, MA, 2002

PRE-1939 SCOTTISH ARCHITECTURE

S Blackden (ed), *Hew Lorimer, an Appreciation*, Edinburgh, 1987.
E Cumming and W Kaplan, *The Arts and Crafts Movement*, London, 1991
M Glendinning, R MacInnes, A MacKechnie, *A History of Scottish Architecture* (hereafter *HSA*), Edinburgh, 1996
S McKinstry, *Rowand Anderson*, Edinburgh, 1991
Transactions of the National Association for the Advancement of Art,
Edinburgh Meeting 1889, London, 1890
R S Morton, *Alan Reiach, a Memoir*, Edinburgh, 1989
P Savage, *Lorimer and the Edinburgh Craft Designers*, Edinburgh, 1980
G Stamp and S McKinstry, eds, *'Greek' Thomson*, Edinburgh, 1994
R L Stevenson, *Edinburgh Picturesque Notes*, Edinburgh, 1903
D Walker, *St Andrew's House: An Edinburgh Controversy*, Edinburgh, 1989

INTERWAR BRITISH AND INTERNATIONAL ARCHITECTURE

J Allan, *Berthold Lubetkin*, London, 1992
The Architectural Work of Sir John Burnet & Partners, Geneva, 1930
Paul Bonatz und seine Schüler (ed. G Graubner, Stuttgart, c.1932)
L Budden (ed), *The Book of the Liverpool School of Architecture*, Liverpool, 1932
A Calverley Cotton, *The Planning of Modern Buildings, No. 1: Town Halls*, London, 1936
Cement Marketing Company Ltd, *Working-Class Residential Flats in Reinforced Concrete, Report on a Competition*, London, 1935
Country Life, *Recent English Architecture 1920–40*, London, 1947
Department of Health for Scotland, *Working-Class Housing on the Continent*, Edinburgh, 1935
S Games (ed), *Pevsner, Art & Architecture, The Radio Talks*, London, 2002
MARS Group, *New Architecture*, London, 1938
J L Martin, B Nicholson, N Gabo (eds), *Circle*, London, 1937
J L Martin and S Speight, *The Flat Book*, London, 1939
J Melvin, *F R S Yorke and the Evolution of English Modernism*, London, 2003
J Morris, A W Turner, M Eastment (Antique Collectors Club), *Portmeirion*, London, 2007
R Östberg, *The Stockholm Town Hall*, Stockholm, 1929
A Powers, *Modern: The Modern Movement in Britain*, London, 2005
A Powers, *Serge Chermayeff*, London, 2001
C H Reilly, *Architectural Problems*, Liverpool, 1924
C H Reilly, *Scaffolding in the Sky*, London, 1938
J M Richards, *An Introduction to Modern Architecture*, London, 1940
P Richmond, *Marketing Modernisms, The Architecture and Influence of Charles Reilly*, Liverpool, 2001
Eva Rudberg, *The Stockholm Exhibition 1930*, Stockholm, 1999
Slum Clearance and Rehousing: the First Report of the Council for Research on Housing Standards, London, 1934
The Swedish Match Company's Head Office, Stockholm, Stockholm, 1931
C Wilk (ed), *Modernism: Designing a New World, 1914–1939*, London, 2006
Clough Williams-Ellis, *The Pleasures of Architecture*, London, 1924
Clough Williams-Ellis, *Britain and the Beast*, London, 1937
Clough Williams-Ellis, *England and the Octopus*, London, 1928
Clough Williams-Ellis, *Architecture Here and Now*, London, 1934
Clough Williams-Ellis, *Architect Errant*, London, 1971
F R S Yorke and F Gibberd, *The Modern Flat*, London, 1937

POSTWAR LONDON ARCHITECTURE AND PLANNING

P Abercrombie, *The Greater London Plan 1944*, London, 1945

Architectural Review, June 1951, 336–94 (Festival Hall)

Architectural Review, November 2007, 58–66 (Festival Hall reconstruction)

M Banham and B Hillier (eds), *A Tonic to the Nation*, London, 1976

E J Carter and E Goldfinger, *The County of London Plan Explained*, London, 1945

I Cox, *The South Bank Exhibition, Festival of Britain Guide*, London, 1951

Festival Council, *The Story of the Festival of Britain*, London, 1951

J Forshaw and P Abercrombie, *The County of London Plan*, London, 1943

M Glendinning, 'Teamwork or Masterwork?', The Design and Reception of the Royal Festival Hall, *Architectural History*, 2003

M Glendinning, 'The Royal Festival Hall – A Postscript', *Architectural History*, 2005, 323–6

E Harwood and A Powers, *Twentieth Century Architecture 5, The Festival of Britain*, London, 2001

E Hollamby and D Gregory Jones, 'The Structure and Personality of the LCC Architect's Department', *Architecture and Building*, May 1957

W E Jackson, *Achievement: A Short History of the LCC*, London, 1965

M. Laughlin, M Gelfand, K Young, *Half a Century of Municipal Decline*, London, 1985

E J O Lloyd, J H Humphries, *A Survey of London Local Government*, London, 1944

London County Council, *Royal Festival Hall*, London, 1951

London County Council, *Administrative County of London Development Plan, Analysis*, 1951

London County Council, *First Day of Public Local Inquiry on the County of London Development Plan 1951, 29 September 1952, Central Hall, Westminster, before K S Dodd, Chief Inspector of Special Inquiries*

J McKean, *Royal Festival Hall*, London, 1992

L Mumford, *The Plan of London County, Rebuilding Britain Series*, 12, London, 1945

S E Rasmussen, *London, the Unique City* (English translation), London, 1937

Royal Festival Hall, *Royal Festival Hall 1951–2001, Past, Present, Future*, London, 2001

A Saint, *Politics and the People of London, The LCC 1889–1965*, London, 1989

J Symons, *Royal Festival Hall, Concert Hall Notebook*, London, 2000

The Times Festival of Britain Supplement, May 1951

POSTWAR SCOTTISH ARCHITECTURE

R D Anderson, A Lynch, N Phillipson, *The University of Edinburgh – an Illustrated History*, Edinburgh, 2003

E F Catford, *The Royal Infirmary of Edinburgh, 1929–1979*, Edinburgh, 1984

C Fenton, 'A Century of Change in George Square', *Book of the Old Edinburgh Club*, new series, vol. 5, 2002

R Galbraith, *Without Quarter*, Edinburgh, 1995

J S Gibson, *The Thistle and the Crown*, Edinburgh, 1985

M Glendinning (ed), *Rebuilding Scotland: The Postwar Vision 1945–1975*, East Linton, 1997

P Johnson-Marshall, *University of Edinburgh, George Square Redevelopment*, 1963

T Johnston, *Memories*, London, 1953

M Lindsay, *The Scottish Renaissance*, Edinburgh, 1948

R Marks, R Scott, B Gasson , J Thomson, P Vainker, *The Burrell Collection*, Glasgow, 1983

Sir D Milne, *The Scottish Office*, London, 1957

R S Morton, *Alan Reiach, OBE RSA RSW RIBA RIAS, A Memoir* (unpublished MSS), Edinburgh, 1989

P Nuttgens, *Reginald Fairlie*, Edinburgh, 1959

RMJM, *The Design of Ninewells Teaching Hospital and Medical School, A Symposium*, Edinburgh, 1973

South-Eastern Regional Hospital Board (SERHB), *Royal Infirmary of Edinburgh: Report on Reconstruction*, Edinburgh, July 1960

T Spaven, *The Early Years*, Edinburgh, 1975

Talbot Rice Gallery, *Hew Lorimer, Sculptor*, Edinburgh, 1988

University of Edinburgh, *University Development and George Square*, Edinburgh, 1960

D Watters and M Glendinning, *Little Houses*, Edinburgh, 2006

P Willis (ed), *Furor Hortensis*, Edinburgh, 1974

P Willis, *New Architecture in Scotland*, London, 1977

POSTWAR BRITISH ARCHITECTURE AND DESIGN

Barbican, This Was Tomorrow, catalogue of 2002 exhibition, Museum of London

A W Cleeve Barr, *Public Authority Housing*, London, 1958.

T Birks, *Building the New Universities*, Newton Abbot, 1972

N Bullock, *Building the Post-War World*, London, 2002

C Buchanan and L Martin, *Whitehall – a Plan for the National and Government Centre*, London, 1965

L Campbell (ed), *To Build a Cathedral*, Coventry, 1987

L. Campbell, *Coventry Cathedral*, Oxford, 1996

P Carolin and T Dannatt, *Architecture, Education and Research*, London, 1996

T Crosby, *Architecture – City Sense*, London, 1965

T Dannatt, *Modern Architecture in Britain*, London, 1959

A Downs (ed), *Peter Shepheard*, London, 2004

H M Dunnett, *Guide to the Exhibition of Town Planning and Building Research*, London, 1951

J Dunnett and G Stamp, *Ernö Goldfinger Works, 1, Architectural Association*, London, 1983.

B Edwards, *Basil Spence 1907–1976*, Edinburgh, 1995

L Esher, *Houses*, 1941

L Esher, *Landscape in Distress*, 1965.

L Esher, *A Broken Wave*, London, 1981

Festival Council, *The Story of the Festival of Britain 1951*, London, 1952

M Garlake, *New Art, New World*, New Haven and London, 1998

M Glendinning and S Muthesius, *Provincial Mixed Development*, Norwich, 1986.

M Glendinning and S Muthesius, *Tower Block: Modern Public Housing in England, Scotland, Wales and Northern Ireland*, New Haven/London, 1994

J Gold, *The Experience of Modernism: Modern Architects and the Future City, 1928–1953*, London, 1997

J Gold, *The Practice of Modernism: Modern Architects and Urban Transformation, 1954–1972*, London, 2007

E Harwood and A Powers, *Tayler & Green, Architects 1938–1973*, London, 1998

H R Hitchcock, 'English Art in the Early 1960s', *Zodiac*, 12, 1964, 31.

Simon Houfe, A Powers, J Wilton-Ely, *Sir Albert Richardson*, London, 1999

J F A Hughes, 'The Brutal Hospital: Efficiency, Identity and Form in the NHS', PhD thesis, Courtauld Institute, London, 1996

P Jones, *Ove Arup*, London, 2006

Arthur Korn, *History Builds the Town*, London, 1953

R Landau, *New Directions in British Architecture*, London, 1968

J Manser, *Hugh Casson*, London, 2000

R H Matthew, *Report of a Public Inquiry into .... the Broad Sanctuary Site, Westminster*, London, 1967

D Mellor, *A Paradise Lost*, London, 1987

Ministry of Housing and Local Government, *Design in Town and Village*, London, 1953

S Muthesius, *The Postwar University*, New Haven and London, 2000

I Nairn, *Your England Revisited*, London, 1964

Nuffield Provincial Hospitals Trust, *Studies in the Functions and Design of Hospitals*, London, 1955

P Nuttgens, *The Art of Learning*, Lewes, 2000

N Pevsner, 'The Picturesque', *AR*, April 1954, 227–9

N Pevsner, *The Englishness of English Art*, London, 1955

J Piper, *British Romantic Artists*, London, 1942

A Powers, J Dunnett, E Howard, *Elegant Variation: the Architecture of H T Cadbury Brown RA, Architectural Research Quarterly*, vol. 1, 10, supplement 10, Cambridge, 2006

A Powers, *Britain: Modern Architectures in History*, London, 2007

RIBA Journal, August 1970, 343–7 (RHM RIBA Gold Medal)

J M Richards, *The Castles on the Ground*, London, 1945

J M Richards, *Memoirs of an Unjust Fella*, London, 1980

RMJM, *RMJM 40*, 1996

A Saint, *Towards a Social Architecture*, London, 1987

A E Sloman, *A University in the Making*, London, 1964

A Smithson (ed), *Team Ten Primer*, London, 1962, 559–60

J Summerson, *Architecture in England*, London, 1946

J Summerson, introduction to *Ten Years of British Architecture*, Arts Council, 1958

A Trystan Edwards, *Good and Bad Manners in Architecture*, London, 1945.

N Warburton, *Erno Goldfinger*, London, 2004

I B Whyte (ed), *Man-Made Future*, London, 2006

M Yorke, *The Spirit of Place*, London, 1988

POSTWAR PLANNING IN NORTHERN IRELAND

J Bannon (ed), *Planning, the Irish Experience*, Dublin, 1969

P Buckland, *A History of Northern Ireland*, Dublin, 1981

Craigavon Development Corporation, *Craigavon City, Second Report of the Plan*, Belfast, 1967

Craigavon Development Corporation, *A New City in Northern Ireland, A First Report on the Plan*, Belfast, 1965

Cd 451, Government of Northern Ireland, *Belfast Regional Survey and Plan, Recommendations and Conclusions, presented to Parliament by Command of His Excellency the Governor*, February 1963;

Cd 465, Government of Northern Ireland, *The Administration of Town and Country Planning in Northern Ireland*, March 1964

Cd 547, Government of Northern Ireland, *Northern Ireland Development Programme 1970–75: Government Statement* (Cd 547), Belfast, 1970, 3

Government of Northern Ireland, *Economic Development, Northern Ireland*, Belfast (HMSO), R H Matthew and Ministry of Health and Local Government, *Belfast Regional Survey and Plan, Interim Report on Housing Sites*, Belfast, 1961

R H Matthew, *Belfast Regional Survey and Plan 1962*, Belfast, 1964, 2 volumes.

J A Oliver, *Working at Stormont*, Dublin, 1978

T O'Neill, *Autobiography*, Dublin, 1972

RMJM with Percy Johnson-Marshall and Associates, *Coleraine, Portrush, Portstewart Area Plan*, Belfast, 1968

RMJM, *The New University of Ulster, Report on the Development Plan*, Coleraine, 1968

S Wichert, *Northern Ireland Since 1945*, New York, 1999

R Wiener, *The Rape and Plunder of the Shankill*, Belfast, 1978

T Wilson (ed), *Ulster under Home Rule*, Oxford, 1955 1965

POSTWAR EUROPEAN AND WORLD ARCHITECTURE

'The New Empiricism: Sweden's Latest Style', *Architectural Review*, 1947, 199ff

Architecture and Planning Group of the Society for Cultural Relations between the British Commonwealth and the USSR, *Architecture of the USSR*, March 1948

R Banham, *Theory and Design in the First Machine Age*, London, 1960

Bouwcentrum Rotterdam, *Building in the Netherlands*, Rotterdam, 1953

R Bruegmann (ed), *Modernism at Mid Century*, Chicago, 1994

C Caldenby, J Lindvall, W Wang, *20th-Century Architecture: Sweden*, Muenchen, 1998

Capital Development Authority, *Islamabad, Our City*, 1961

J Clark and P Walker, *Looking for the Local: Architecture and the New Zealand Modern*, Wellington, 2000

T J Clark, *Farewell to an Idea, Episodes from the History of Modernism*, New Haven, 1999

P Collins, *Changing Ideals in Modern Architecture*, London, 1965

G Dolff-Bonekämper and H Kier, *Städtebau und Staatsbau im 20. Jahrhundert*, Munich, 1996

G Dolff-Bonekaemper, *Das Hansaviertel*, Berlin, 1999

L Doumato, *Gio Ponti*, Monticello, Illinois, 1987

C Engfors and E Rudberg (eds), *Femtiotalet (Arkitekturmuseet Årsbok)*, Stockholm, 1993

H Finsen, *Ung dansk arkitektur 1930–45*, København, 1947

A Forty, *Words and Buildings: a Vocabulary of Modern Architecture*, London, 2000

M Fry and J Drew, *Tropical Architecture in the Humid Zones*, London, 1956

S W Goldhagen and R Legault (eds), *Anxious Modernisms: Experimentation in Postwar Architectural Culture*, Cambridge, MA, 2000

W Gropius, *Scope of Total Architecture*, London, 1956

M Guccione, M M S Lagunes, R Vittorini, *Guida ai quartieri romani INA Casa*, Rome, 2002

Gustav Gusti, *Architectura in Romania*, Bucharest, 1965

Hansaviertel Interbau: *Interbau Berlin*, Berlin, 1957.

H R Hitchcock, *Latin American Architecture since 1945*, New York, 1955

Bertil Hulten, *Building Modern Sweden*, London, 1951

I Hyman, *Marcel Breuer, The Career and the Buildings*, 2001

H Ibelings, *De moderne Jaren Vijftig en Zestig*, Rotterdam, 1995

K Kaspar, *New German Architecture*, London, 1956

G E Kidder Smith, *Sweden Builds*, Stockholm, 1950

U Kultermann, ed, *Kenzo Tange, Architecture and Urban Design, 1946–1969*, London, 1970

U Kultermann, *Neues Bauen in Afrika*, Tuebingen, 1963

B Lamprecht, *Richard Neutra, Complete Works*, New York, 2000

J Lang, Madhavi Desai, Miki Desai, *Architecture and Independence, The Search for Identity. India 1880 to 1980*, Delhi, 1997

Le Corbusier, *The Marseilles Block*, London, 1953

H Le Roux, 'Modern Architecture in Post–Colonial Ghana and Nigeria', *Architectural History*, 47, 2004, 361ff

J Loeffler, *The Architecture of Diplomacy*, New York, 1998

K Lynch, *The Image of the City*, Cambridge, MA, 1960

I McHarg, *Design with Nature*, New York, 1969

J P Mieras, *Na-oorlogse Bouwkunst in Nederland*, Amsterdam, 1954

E Mumford (ed), *The CIAM Discourse on Urbanism*, Cambridge, MA, 2000

K K Mumtaz, *Modernity and Tradition – Contemporary Architecture in Pakistan*, Karachi, 1999

R Neutra, *Survival Through Design*, New York, 1954

R Neutra, *Life and Shape*, New York, 1962

J. Ockman, *Architecture Culture 1943-1968*, New York, 1993

J Pederson, *Architekten Arne Jacobsen*, København, 1957

M Quantrill, *Aalto, A Critical Study*, New York, 1983

RIBA, *Exhibition of Danish Architecture Today*, 1950

RIBA/Bund deutscher Architekten, *German Architecture Today*, 1955

J M Richards (ed), *New Buildings in the Commonwealth*, London, 1961

M Risselada and D van den Heuvel (eds), *Team 10, 1953–1981: In Search of a Utopia of the Present*, Rotterdam, 2005

J Roguska, *Helena i Szymon Syrkusowie*, Warszawa, 2000

A Rossi, *The Architecture of the City*, 1966

J M Rovira, *Jose Luis Sert*, Milan, 2003R Pommer, D Spaeth, K Harrington, *In the Shadow of Mies*, Chicago, 1988

R Schneider, R Stregers (for Akademie der Kunst, Berlin), *Glück Stadt Raum in Europa 1945 bis 2000*, Basel, 2002

N H Shapira, *The Expression of Gio Ponti*, Minneapolis, 1967

S Silow (ed), *Kooperativa Förbundets Arkitektkontor, 1935–49, Part 1*, and *1925–1949, Part 2*, both Stockholm, 1949

R Squire, *Portrait of an Architect*, Gerrards Cross, 1984

W A Storrer, *Marcel Breuer*, London, 1956

Svensk Byggnadstradition, Ferdinand Bobergs-Jubileums-Utställning, Stockholm, 1940

Svenska Arkitekters Riksförbund, *Ny Arkitektur i Sverige*, Stockholm, 1961

Swedish Design Association and Göteborg City Building Authority, *Utställningen Bo Bättre*, Guldheden, Göteborg, August-September 1945

Swedish Institute for Cultural Relations, *Modern Swedish Architecture*, Stockholm, 1952

M Tafuri, *History of Italian Architecture 1944–1985*, Cambridge, MA, 1989.

L J Vale, *Architectural Power and National Identity*, New Haven and London, 1992

R Venturi, *Complexity and Contradiction*, 1966.

A J Wharton, *Building the Cold War – Hilton Hotels and Modern Architecture*, Chicago, 2001

J Wilson (ed.), *Zeal and Crusade, The Modern Movement in Wellington*, Christchurch, 1996

INTERNATIONAL ARCHITECTURAL POLITICS

R P Andrew and A E Brooks (eds), *Final Report of the 6th Congress of the International Union of Architects, London, 3–7 July 1961*, London, October 1962

Arquitectura Cuba, January-March 1964

A Campbell, *It's Your Empire*, London, 1945

Leycester Coltman, *The Real Fidel Castro*, New Haven, 2002

Commonwealth Association of Architects, *CAA Handbook*, London, 1987

Commonwealth Association of Architects, *Handbook of Commonwealth Architects*, London, 1965

Commonwealth Association of Architects, *25 Years of Achievement, 1965–1990*, London, 1989

Commonwealth Foundation, Occasional Paper 14, *Higher Education in the Commonwealth*, London, 1972

M Crinson, *Modern Architecture and the End of Empire*, ////ashgate 2003

R Estevez Curbelo, ed, *Arquitectura Cuba*, special number, 1963

L Fasolo, *An Insider's Guide to the UN*, New Haven, 2002.

J M Freeland, *The Making of a Profession: A History of the Growth and Work of the Architectural Institutes in Australia*, Sydney, 1971, 78 and 158

D Judd and P Slinn, *The Evolution of the Modern Commonwealth*,

Modern Architect

London, 1982

A H Kirk-Greene (ed), *Crisis and Civil War in Nigeria*, Oxford, 1971

D Lai, 'Searching for a Modern Chinese Movement', *JSAH*, 64/1, March 2005, 22–55

D A Low, *Eclipse of Empire*, Cambridge, 1991

J D B Miller, *The Commonwealth in the World,* London, 1958

J Okpaku (ed), *Nigeria, Dilemma of Nationhood*, 1972

E Rodriguez, 'Theory and Practice of Modern Regionalism in Cuba', *Docomomo Journal*, September 2005

RIBA, *Commonwealth and Overseas Allied Societies Conference*, London, 1963

Ying Ruan, 'Accidental Affinities: American Beaux-Arts in Chinese Architectural Education and Practice', *JSAH*, 61/1, March 2002, 30–47 For Liang Sicheng's researches in the 1950s, and the Chinese embrace of 'Third World modernism' (including Cuban architecture) around 1962–3, just prior to Matthew's visit, see Duanfang Lu, 'Architecture and global imaginations in China', *Journal of Architecture*, vol. 12, no. 2, 2007, 127 and 136–7.

J Springhall, *Decolonisation since 1945*, Basingstoke, 2000

State Building Architecture and Design Literature Press (edited by V O Vinograd and others), *5th Congress of the UIA*, Moscow, 1960

Union Internationale des Architectes, *XII Congreso Mundial de la UIA* (proceedings) Madrid, May 1975

Union Internationale des Architectes, Cuban section, *Seventh Congress of the IUA, Architecture in Countries in the process of Development*, La Habana, Cuba, September 1963

Union Internationale des Architectes, French Section, *L'UIA, 1848–1998*, Paris, 1998

P Vago, *Pierre Vago, Une Vie Intense*, Bruxelles, 2000.

P Valderrama, *A History of Unesco*, Paris, 1995

D Vandewalle, *A History of Modern Libya*, Cambridge, 2006

Zahir-ud-Din Khwaja, *Memoirs of an Architect*, Lahore, 1998

BUCKMINSTER FULLER

R B Fuller, *Education Automation: Freeing the Scholar to Return to his Studies,* Carbondale, 1962

R B Fuller, *Operating Manual for Spaceship Earth*, New York, 1963

R B Fuller and John McHale, *World Science Design Decade*, Documents 1–6, Word Resources Inventory, Southern Illinois University, Carbondale, Illinois, 1963–7: *Phase 1 Document 1, Inventory of World Resources, Human Trends and Needs*, 1963; *Phase 1 Document 2, The Design Initiative*, 1964; *Phase 1, Document 3, Comprehensive Thinking*, 1965; *Phase 1 Document 4, The Ten Year Programme*, 1965; *Phase 1 Document 5, Comprehensive Design Strategy*, 1967; *Phase 2, Document 6, The Ecological Context: Energy and Materials*, 1967

R B Fuller, *Intuition*, Garden City, New York, 1972

M J Gorman, *Buckminster Fuller: Designing for Modernity*, Milan, 2005

J Krausse, C L Lichtenstein (eds), *Your Private Sky: R Buckminster Fuller Discourse*, Zurich, 2001

R W Markus, *The Dymaxion World of Buckminster Fuller,*

Carbondale, 1960

J Meller (ed), *The Buckminster Fuller Reader*, London, 1970

L S Sieden, *Buckminster Fuller's Universe – His Life and Work*, Cambridge Mass, 1989

DOXIADIS

P Deane, *Constantinos Doxiadis*, Dobbs Ferry, New York, 1965

C Doxiadis, *Raumordnung im Griechischen Staedtebau*, Heidelberg, 1937 (English translation, edited by J Tyrwhitt, *Doxiadis – Architectural Space in Ancient Greece*, Cambridge, Mass., 1972)

C Doxiadis, *Dynapolis, the City of the Future*, text of lecture at Oslo Arkitektforening, 3 March 1960, Athens, 1960

Doxiadis Associates, *Islamabad, Progress and Plan*, 2 vols, 30 September 1960

C Doxiadis, *Architecture in Transition*, London, 1963

C Doxiadis, *Between Utopia and Dystopia*, London, 1966

C Doxiadis, *Ekistics, an Introduction to the Science of Human Settlements*, New York, 1968

C Doxiadis and J G Papaioannou, *Ecumenopolis, the Inevitable City of the Future*, Athens Center of Ekistics, 1974

A A Kyrtsis (ed), *Constantinos A Doxiadis: Texts, Design Drawings, Settlements*, Athens, 2007.

M Wigley, 'Network Fever', *Grey Room*, 4, 2001, 96–7

1960s AND 1970s RADICALISM AND ENVIRONMENTAL ACTIVISM

Tony Aldous, *The Battle for the Environment,* London, 1972

J Antoniou (ed), *Implementing the Habitat Agenda, In Search of Urban Sustainability*, UCL, London, 2001

Department of the Environment, *How do you Want to Live? A Report on the Human Habitat*, London, 1972

R Dubos, *A God Within: A Positive View of Mankind's Nature*, London, 1972

R Ellis and D Cuff (eds), *Architects' People*, New York, 1989

D Eversley, *The Planner in Society*, London, 1973

Friends of the Earth, *The Stockholm Conference, Only One Earth: An Introduction to the Politics of Survival*, London, 1972

Giancarlo de Carlo, *An Architecture of Participation*, Melbourne, 1972

R Goodman, *After the Planners*, London, 1972

Jane Jacobs, *The Death and Life of Great American Cities*, New York, 1961; Pelican edition, London, 1964

M MacEwen, *Crisis in Architecture*, London, 1974

J G Mitchell and C L Stallings (eds), *Eco Tactics: the Sierra Club Handbook for Environment Activists*, New York, 1970

M Nicholson, *The Environment Revolution, a Guide for the New Masters of the Earth*, London, 1970

Bernard Rudofsky, *Architecture without Architects: A Short Introduction to Non-Pedigreed Architecture,* New York, 1965

E F Schumacher, *Small is Beautiful: A Study of Economics as if People Mattered*, London, 1973. United Nations (UNCHS), *An Urbanising World: Global Report on Human Settlements*, Oxford 1996

J van Ettinger, *Towards a Habitable World*, Amsterdam, 1960

Bibliography

J-L Violeau, *Les architectes et mai 68*, Paris, 2005

1960s AND 1970s CONSERVATION

I Begg, *Rossend Castle: a Recent Story of Reconstruction after 25 Years of Struggle*, Edinburgh, 1977

L Borley (ed), *Dear Maurice*, East Linton, 1998

Civic Trust, *The First Three Years*, London, 1960

Civic Trust, *Conservation Areas: A Survey*, fascicule reprint from *Architects Journal*, 18 January 1967, 125ff

Civic Trust, *Conservation in Action, A Civic Trust Conference*, Royal Festival Hall, 8 and 9 July 1971, delegate brochure

P Daniel, *Two Hundred Summers in a City, Souvenir Programme*, Edinburgh, 1967

A Davey, B Heath, D Hodges, R Milne, M Palmer, *The Care and Conservation of Georgian Houses*, Edinburgh, 1978

J Delafons, *Politics and Preservation*, London, 1997

Department of the Environment/SDD/Welsh Office, *Aspects of Conservation, 2, New Life for Historic Areas*, London, 1972

English Heritage, *Something Worth Keeping?* London, 1996

M Glendinning, 'The Grand Plan: Robert Matthew and the Triumph of Conservation in Scotland', *Architectural Heritage*, xvi, 2005, 72–102

R Hurd, *Scotland Under Trust*, London, 1939

Lanark County Council, *A Future for New Lanark*, 1973

R Matthew, J Reid, M Lindsay (eds), *The Conservation of Georgian Edinburgh*, Edinburgh, 1972, xiii

New Lanark Association, *New Lanark*, 1966

J Pendlebury, 'The Modern Historic City: Evolving Ideas in Mid-20th-Century Britain', *Journal of Urban Design*, vol. 10, 2, June 2005, 253–273

Scottish Civic Trust, *The First Five Years*, Glasgow, 1972

G Scott-Moncrieff, *Living Traditions of Scotland*, Edinburgh, 1951

Princes Street Panel, *Principles and Standards for the Application of Building Controls in the Central Area of Edinburgh*, Edinburgh, 1967

D Walker, 'Listing in Scotland', *Transactions of the Ancient Monuments Society*, vol. 58, 1994

A J Youngson, *The Making of Classical Edinburgh*, Edinburgh, 1966

ROBERT MATTHEW OBITUARIES

Architectural Design, September 1975, 576

AIA Journal, August 1975, 66

Architects Journal, 2 July 1975, 13

Architectural Review, July 1975, 54

Architectural Record, September 1975, 33–7

Building, 27 July 1975, 39

Building Design, 27 June 1975

Design, December 1975, 66

Evening News (Edinburgh), 23 June 1975

Glasgow Herald, 23 June 1975

IIA Journal, October 1975, 27

RIBA Journal, Jul-Aug 1975, 5

New York Times, 22 June 1975

Saltire News, December 75

Town and Country Planning, September 1975, 385

The Times, 23 June 1975

IUA Informations, July 1975

Roundabout RMJMP, Summer 1975

See also article in R J van Vynckt, *International Dictionary of Architects and Architecture*, Detroit, 1993, 556.

Index

Note: titles of books and journals are printed in *italics*; page numbers may include both text and illustrations, except for those in *italics* which refer only to illustrations

Modern Architect

Modern Architect